Thirteenth Edition
Antique Trader Books
ANTIQUES & COLLECTIBLES
PRICE GUIDE

# 1997 ANNUAL EDITION

## ANTIQUE TRADER BOOKS

# Antiques & Collectibles Price Guide

*Edited by*
*Kyle Husfloen*

An illustrated comprehensive price guide to the entire field of
antiques and collectibles for the 1997 market

Antique Trader Books
P.O. Box 1050
Dubuque, IA 52004

# STAFF

Assistant Editor . . . . . . . . . . . . . . . . . . . . . . . . . . . . . . . . . . Elizabeth Stephan

Editorial Assistant . . . . . . . . . . . . . . . . . . . . . . . . . . . . . . . . . . . Ruth Willis

Editorial Assistant . . . . . . . . . . . . . . . . . . . . . . . . . . . . . . . . Marti Hansel

Book Designer . . . . . . . . . . . . . . . . . . . . . . . . . . . . . . . . . Darryl Keck

Design Assistant . . . . . . . . . . . . . . . . . . . . . . . . . . . . . Lynn Bradshaw

Art Director . . . . . . . . . . . . . . . . . . . . . . . . . . . . . . . . . . . . . . . . Jaro Sebek

Customer Service/Order Fulfillment . . . . . . . . . . . . . . Bonnie Rojemann

ISBN: 0-930625-12-9
ISSN: 1083-8430

## Antique Trader Publications
### Publishers of:

*The Antique Trader Weekly*
*Toy Trader*
*Collector Magazine & Price Guide*
*Baby Boomer Collectibles*
*DISCoveries*
*The Big Reel*
*Postcard Collector*
*Military Trader*
Antique Trader Books

To order additional copies of this book or a
catalog please contact:

## Antique Trader Publications
### P.O. Box 1050
### Dubuque, Iowa 52004
### 1-800-334-7165

# A WORD TO THE READER

For over twenty-five years the Antique Trader has been publishing price guides to antiques and collectibles, and since 1984 we have produced the annual *Antiques & Collectibles Price Guide,* a comprehensive guide covering all facets of the world of collecting.

Each new edition contains all new, updated pricing information and, over the course of time, we have worked to accurately reflect current collecting trends. As new categories of collecting become established, we add representative listings to keep abreast of "hot" new markets, and continue to offer current information on well-established collecting specialties.

The staff and editors of *The Antique Trader Price Guide* pride ourselves on producing the most accurate and detailed descriptions of each item listed. For those who wish to really learn about and understand antiques and collectibles, this material is invaluable and helps define this work as a "reference" rather than just a "listing" of randomly gathered, briefly described items. A number of factors can determine what a particular item may sell for in a specific market, including color, condition, rarity, and local demand. We strive to give readers as much of this background detail as possible.

In this issue we have made one important change which we hope our readers will find helpful—we have increased the number and size of black and white photographs in all categories. Most collectors do find that a "picture is worth a thousand words," and with this new edition you'll see more photos reproduced in larger sizes. Now, in addition to *reading* a description of a certain item, you may well be able to see a good-sized photograph of it, highlighting important details which affect its market value.

Many of our categories are introduced by a brief paragraph explaining a bit of the history of the item and its place in the collecting world. In addition, in the Ceramics and Glass sections we often include sketches of markings used on specific categories included there. We also do a great deal of cross-referencing within the categories and note important reference books which will interest collectors. The comprehensive Index at the conclusion of our price listings, of course, is especially detailed and thoroughly cross-referenced for easy use.

Although we want all of our readers to find this an invaluable market guide, please keep in mind that it is *only* a guide to prices. It is not meant to set prices for items, but to help a collector or dealer determine what a proper price range is for a specific piece. As noted earlier, many factors will come into play when evaluating a proper market value for a specific piece. Please also keep in mind that although our descriptions and prices have been double-checked and every effort made to assure accuracy, neither the editor nor publisher can assume responsibility for any losses that might be incurred as a result of consulting this guide, or of errors, typographical or otherwise.

Our *Antiques &Collectibles Price Guide* follows a format which lists all categories alphabetically. However, we have organized the categories of Ceramics, Furniture and Glassware into their own sections with individual categories arranged alphabetically within each section. Therefore, all types of glass, including the major types such as Carnival, Custard, Depression and Pattern, are located within the Glass section. Our complete and expanded Index will help you locate specific categories you may be looking for.

A number of authorities help in the compilation of certain categories and we offer special thanks to Sandra Andacht, Little Neck, New York; Cecil Munsey, Poway, California and Edward Radcliff, Williamstown, West Virginia. In addition to the above mentioned experts, we were also most fortunate to draw upon the knowledge of a number of specialists whose contributions enabled us to expand several categories. I would like to thank them here and note their field of specialization: Tom Small, Frostburg, Maryland (Aladdin Lamps); Charles Reynolds, Falls Church, Virginia (Bottle Openers); Hickory Bend Antiques, Jasper, New York (Cash Registers); Doris Lechler, Columbus, Ohio (Children's Dishes and Doll Furniture & Accessories); Bob Brenner, Princeton, Wisconsin (Christmas Collectibles); Michael White, Fraser, Colorado (Coffee Grinders); Don Thornton, Sunnyvale, California (Eggbeaters); Jo Allers, Cedar Rapids, Iowa (Graniteware); Carol & Jimmie Walker, Waelder, Texas (Irons); Catherine Thuro-Gripton, Toronto, Canada (Kerosene Lamps); Carol Bohn, Mifflinburg, Pennsylvania and Bunny Upchurch, Boyce, Virginia (Kitchen Collectibles); Allan Hoover, Peru, Illinois (Salesman's Samples); Estelle Zalkin, Miami Beach, Florida and Wayne Muller, Pacific Palisades, California (Sewing Adjuncts); Clifford Boram, Monticello, Indiana (Stoves); Tony Hyman, Pismo Beach, California (Tobacciana); Ron Barlow, El Cajon,

California (Tools); Dave Cheadle, Englewood, Colorado (Trade Cards); Michael Cornish, Roslindale, Massachusetts (Tramp Art); and Richard S. Tucker, Argyle, Texas (Windmill Weights). In addition, in several categories of Ceramics we received invaluable help from: Stephen E. Stone. Aurora, Colorado (Blue & White Pottery); Susan N. Cox, El Cajon, California (Pennsbury Pottery); Charles W. Casad, Monticello, Illinois (Red Wing Pottery); and Dennis M. Thompson, Fairview Park, Ohio (Watt Pottery).

Photographers who have contributed to this issue include: E. A. Babka, East Dubuque, Illinois; Stanley L. Baker, Minneapolis, Minnesota; Dorothy Beckwith, Platteville, Wisconsin; Donna Bruun, Galena, Illinois; Herman C. Carter, Tulsa, Oklahoma; J. D. Dalessandro, Cincinnati, Ohio; Bill Freeman, Smyrna, Georgia; Jeff Grunewald, Chicago, Illinois; Louise Paradis, Sparta, Wisconsin; Joyce Roerig, Waltersboro, South Carolina; Ruth Eaves, Marmora, New Jersey; and Joe Hallahan, Dubuque, Iowa.

For other photographs, artwork, data or permission to photograph in their shops, we sincerely express appreciation to the following auctioneers, galleries, museums, individuals and shops: Adele Armbruster, Dearborn, Michigan; Brown Auctions, Mullinville, Kansas; Burmese Cruet, Montgomeryville, Pennsylvania; Burns Auction Service, Bath, New York; Butterfield & Butterfield, San Francisco, California; Fred & Jan Carlson, Hillsboro, Oregon; The Cedars - Antiques, Aurelia, Iowa; Norm & Diana Charles, Hagerstown, Indiana; Christie's, New York, New York; Cobb's Auctions, Columbus, Ohio; Collector's Auction Services, Oil City, Pennsylvania; Collector's Sales & Services, Middletown, Rhode Island; The Daguerreian Forum, Exeter, New Hampshire; S. Davis, Williamsburg, Ohio; DeFina Auctions, Austenburg, Ohio; Gail DePasquale, Leavenworth, Kansas; Marilyn Dragowick, Wilmington, North Carolina; William Doyle Galleries, New York, New York; DuMouchelle's, Detroit, Michigan; Dunning's Auction Service, Elgin, Illinois; Early Auction Co., Milford, Ohio; T. Ermert, Cincinnati, Ohio; Garth's Auctions, Inc., Delaware, Ohio; Glass-Works Auctions, East Greenville, Pennsylvania; Glick's Antiques, Galena, Illinois; Morton M. Goldberg Auction Galleries, New Orleans, Louisiana; Robert Gordon, San Antonio, Texas; Grunewald Antiques, Hillsborough, North Carolina; and Guyette and Schmidt, West Farmington, Maine.

Also to Harmer Rooke Galleries, New York, New York; Vicki Harmon, San Marcos, California; the Gene Harris Antique Auction Center, Marshalltown, Iowa; the late William Heacock, Marietta, Ohio; Leslie Hindman Auctioneers, Chicago, Illinois; Historic Americana Auction, Terrace Park, Ohio; International Carnival Glass Assoc., Mentone, Indiana; Jackson's Auctions, Cedar Falls, Iowa; Doris Johnson, Rockford, Illinois; Jewel Johnson, Tulsa, Oklahoma; James Julia, Fairfield, Maine; Agnes Koehn Antiques, Cedar Rapids, Iowa; Peter Kroll, Sun Prairie, Wisconsin; Bev Kubesheski, Dubuque, Iowa; Lang's Sporting Collectibles, Raymond, Maine; Jim Ludescher, Dubuque, Iowa; Joy Luke Gallery, Bloomington, Illinois; J. Martin, Mt. Orab, Ohio; Kevin McConnell, Pilot Point, Texas; Randall McKee, Kenosha, Wisconsin; McMasters Doll Auctions, Cambridge, Ohio; Dr. James Measell, Berkley, Michigan; Neal Auction Company, New Orleans, Louisiana; Nostalgia Publications, Inc., Hackensack, New Jersey; Pettigrew Auction Gallery, Colorado Springs, Colorado; Dave Rago Arts & Crafts, Lambertville, New Jersey; Darryl Rehr, Los Angeles, California; Jane Rosenow, Galva, Illinois; Tammy Roth, East Dubuque, Illinois; Shirley's Glasstiques, Brunswick, Ohio; Robert W. Skinner, Inc., Bolton, Massachusetts; Slawinski Auction Company, Felton, California; Sotheby's, New York, New York; Doris Spahn, East Dubuque, Illinois; George and Judy Swan, Dubuque, Iowa; Temples Antiques, Eden Prairie, Minnesota; Theriault's, Annapolis, Maryland; Town Crier Auction Service, Burlington, Wisconsin; Tradewinds Auctions, Manchester-by-the-Sea, Massachusetts; Treadway Gallery, Cincinnati, Ohio; Lee Vines, Hewlett, New York; Vintage Cameras and Imagery, Hardwick, Vermont; Bruce & Vicki Waasdorp, Clarence, New York; Chris Walker Auctions, Potosi, Wisconsin; Wolf's Auctioneers and Appraisers, Cleveland, Ohio; Woody Auctions, Douglass, Kansas; The Yankee Peddler Antiques, Denton, Texas; and Yesterday's Treasures, Galena, Illinois.

Today's antiques and collectibles market is certainly booming. And our Antiques & Collectibles Price Guide is positioned to support this huge and diverse market by offering the best, most well-rounded price guide available.

The staff of The Antique Trader Antiques & Collectibles Price Guide welcomes all letters from readers, especially those of constructive critique, and we make every effort to respond personally.

Kyle Husfloen, Editor

v

# ON THE COVERS:

**Front cover:** top left to right clockwise - Royal Doulton china figurine titled "Autumn Breezes," $175; Victorian cranberry glass vase with heavy gold floral decoration, 8¼" h., $225; a hand-painted Limoges porcelain game plate, one of a pair, 15⅝" d., the pair $695. The preceding photos courtesy of Temple's Antiques, Eden Prairie, Minnesota.

Bottom right - German carved wooden horse on a mechanized wheeled platform, labeled "GS - Made in Germany," 16" l., 14" h., $440.

Bottom left - pine storage bin with a paneled front decorated with hearts which slants out to open. 14 x 35¾", 33¼" h., on top are a Victorian kerosene table lamp with a glass front and cast-iron base beside a small, early grain-painted trunk, fully dovetailed, 9 x 17¾", 7½" h. Bottom photos courtesy of the Gene Harris Antique Auction Center, Inc., Marshalltown, Iowa.

**Back cover:** A marigold Carnival glass 'Peacocks on the Fence' pattern bowl, 8⅝" d., $235, photo courtesy of Temple's Antiques, Eden Prairie, Minnesota.

# ABC PLATES

*These children's plates were popular in the late 19th and early 20th centuries. An alphabet border was incorporated with nursery rhymes, maxims, scenes or figures in an apparent attempt to "spoon feed" a bit of knowledge at mealtime. They were made of ceramics, glass and metal. A boon to collectors is the fine book,* A Collector's Guide to ABC Plates, Mugs and Things *by Mildred L. and Joseph P. Chalala (Pridemark Press, Lancaster, Pennsylvania).*

## CERAMIC

**5⅛" d.,** puzzle scene, transfer-printed center scene of two blacks & the question "6. What Fruit Does Our Sketch Represent?," the reverse is marked "6. A Pear (Pair)," embossed alphabet border, overall glaze rot, plus small rim chip (ILLUS. front left) ...................................................... **$33.00**

**5¼" d.,** black transfer-printed center scene of woman & two girls, highlighted in green, red & blue, embossed alphabet border (ILLUS. back right) .......................................... **77.00**

**5¼" d.,** hunting scene, blue transfer-printed center scene of hunters riding elephants, band of green around rim, alphabet border, impressed "E G MEAKIN" on the back (tiny chip on foot rim) ................. **99.00**

**5⅞" d.,** children's activities, black transfer-printed center scene of children playing soldier, titled "L' Exercise," w/the translation "Drill"

below, embossed alphabet border, light spots of mellowing on the rim (ILLUS. front right) ............................. **55.00**

**6" d.,** black transfer-printed center scene of three people w/dog & puppies w/rhyme "There are no gains without pains" below, highlighted in brown, green, yellow & pink, alphabet border (large chip on rim) .................. **110.00**

**6" d.,** black transfer-printed center scene titled "The Blind Girl," highlighted in yellow, green, red & blue enamel, embossed alphabet border, unmarked (small rim chip)...................................................... **50.00**

**6" d.,** domestic animals, black transfer-printed scene of two large cats lolling in a cherry tree, two blue rim bands......................................... **120.00**

**6⅛" d.,** brown transfer-printed center scene of woman holding basket while young girl removes fruit, highlighted in green, red & ochre, embossed alphabet border (ILLUS. front center left) .................................. **77.00**

**6¼" d.,** black transfer-printed center scene of two boys w/whips, titled "Top-Whipping," highlighted in blue, red, yellow & green enamels, embossed alphabet border, reverse impressed "S&G Meakin" (ILLUS. front center right) ............................. **99.00**

**6¼" d.,** green transfer-printed center scene, two Dutch children being scared by a goose, surrounded by green transfer-printed alphabet in sign language, embossed alphabet border, reverse marked w/underglaze

*Grouping of ABC Plates*

registry mark of "426673" & "H. Aynsley & Co., Longton, England," early 20th century, rare ...................... **275.00**

6½" d., brown transfer-printed center scene titled "Leaving Home," embossed alphabet border (trace of mellowing) ......................................... **55.00**

6½" d., light blue transfer-printed center scene titled "Slope Arms - Our Defender," embossed alphabet borders, unmarked (1" hairline crack on reverse) ......................................... **50.00**

6⅝" d., hunting scene, brown transfer-printed center scene titled "The End of the Chase" (fox hunting), highlighted red & green enamel, embossed alphabet border, unmarked ................... **55.00**

6⅞" d., blue transfer-printed scene of "Iron Pier, Length 1000 Feet, West Brighton Beach," embossed alphabet border (light stain) ............. **110.00**

7" d., black transfer-printed center scene of "Canary Bullfinch and Goldfinch," highlighted in yellow, green & pink around outer rim, embossed alphabet border, impressed "Dawson" on back (short hairline crack off the rim) ................... **77.00**

7" d., blue transfer-printed center scene of two terrified children in wagon being pulled by a dog chasing a cat, the mother in background w/hands raised, embossed alphabet border (two hairlines off rim) ............................... **110.00**

7" d., brown transfer-printed center scene titled "Public Buildings at Philadelphia," highlighted in blue, red & green, embossed alphabet border, unmarked ............................ **105.00**

7" d., green transfer-printed center scene of Punch & Judy, green transfer-printed alphabet border, reverse underglaze mark "Allerton's - England" (ILLUS. back left, previous page) .................................... **99.00**

7" d., green transfer-printed center scene of "Man and Child on a Donkey," in red blue & green enamel, embossed alphabet border, unmarked ............................................ **77.00**

7¼" d., black transfer-printed center scene of "Peacock on a Banister," highlighted in red, green & blue enamel, embossed alphabet border, impressed "Elsmore - England" on reverse, after 1891 ........................... **99.00**

7¼" d., black transfer-printed center scene titled "Queen Victoria and Prince Albert of Saxe Coburg," black line border, embossed alphabet border ............................................... **385.00**

7¼" d., Franklin Maxim, "Three removes are as bad as a fire - A rolling stone gathers no moss," highlighted in green, blue, yellow & red enamel, embossed alphabet border (trace of large 'spider' crack on reverse) ...................................... **55.00**

7¼" d., purplish grey transfer-printed center scene of "Steeple Chase," embossed alphabet border, marked "England" on reverse, after 1891 ........ **55.00**

7⅜" d., brown transfer-printed center scene of "Chinonga Watching the Departure of the Cavalcade," embossed alphabet border, underglaze mark "CA & Sons - England," after 1891 ......................... **66.00**

7⅜" d., brown transfer-printed center scene titled "Iron Pier, Length 1000 Feet, West Brighton Beach" (NY?), highlighted in red, blue & brown enamel, embossed alphabet border, unmarked ............................................. **88.00**

7½" d., black transfer-printed center scene of "Stag and Hound," highlighted in yellow & green enamel, embossed alphabet border, unmarked (unseen chip & 1" hairline crack on reverse) ............................... **39.00**

7½" d., brown transfer-printed center scene of a couple on horses w/dogs, highlighted w/green, blue & pink ......... **99.00**

8" d., purple transfer-printed center scene of "February," highlighted in green, yellow, pink & blue (some stains) .............................................. **132.00**

# ADVERTISING ITEMS

*Thousands of objects made in various materials, some intended as gifts with purchases, others used for display or given away for publicity are now being collected. Also see: AUTOMOTIVE COLLECTIBLES, BLACK AMERICANA, BOTTLE OPENERS, BREWERIANA, BUSTER BROWN COLLECTIBLES, CANS & CONTAINERS, CARNIVAL GLASS, CHARACTER COLLECTIBLES, CHRISTMAS COLLECTIBLES, COCA-COLA COLLECTIBLES, COOKBOOKS,*

*DISNEY COLLECTIBLES, KITCHEN-
WARES, SALESMAN SAMPLES, SIGNS &
SIGNBOARDS, TOBACCIANA, TRADE
CARDS, and TRADE CATALOGS.*

*Chocolate Glass Advertising Bowl*

**Ashtray,** "Planters Peanuts," metal,
embossed lettering, bottom marked
"Made in U.S.A. by Diecasters Inc.
Ridgefield, N.J., 5¾" h., 6" d.
(minor rust pitting, nicks to back of
hat) ................................................. **$28.00**

**Backbar bottle,** "Alderney Whiskey,"
wheel-cut & gold-filled lettering, 6½" h. ... **65.00**

**Blotter,** "Bauman Florist," die-cut
Christmas floral decoration, ca. 1930 .... **18.00**

**Book ends,** "Baker's Chocolate," cast
iron, Amish woman, pr. ...................... **125.00**

**Bottle,** "Dr. Daniels Veterinary Colic
Cure," amber glass, ACL, 13½" h. ....... **55.00**

**Bowl,** "Phenix Nerve Beverage Co.,"
chocolate glass, large circular bowl
w/"Phenix 5" in shields on side,
interior of bowl embossed
"Property of Patent Applied For
Phenix Nerve Beverage Co.,"
probably Greentown, Indiana, ca.
1900, 6¼" h. (ILLUS. above) ...... **1,100.00**

*Wheaties Cereal Bowl*

**Bowl,** cov., 5" d., 2¼" h., "Wheaties
Cereal," milk glass, red silhouettes
of Joe DiMaggio & other athletes,
very minor scratches (ILLUS.) ............ **66.00**

**Box,** "Buster Brown Stocking," label
reads "Buster Brown's Stocking,"
above image of Buster Brown &
Tige, includes two pairs of stockings
(water stains, tears) ........................... **17.00**

**Box,** "Coleman's Mustard Oil," paper
graphics inside lid, 2 x 12 x 20" ........ **120.00**

**Box,** "Grandma's Borax Powdered
Soap," cardboard, red, black &
cream coloring, image of elderly
woman holding teapot, marked "The
Globe Soap Company, Cincinnati,
Ohio" near bottom, w/original
contents, 6" w., 8¼" h. (soiled
w/minor creases) ............................... **66.00**

*Quaker Rolled Oats Container*

**Box,** "Quaker Rolled Oats," cylindrical
cardboard w/paper label, red, yellow,
blue & creme, marked "The Quaker
Oats Company," rare, soiling, creases
& ink on top, 4½" d., 7" h. (ILLUS.) ....... **33.00**

**Bread box,** "Schepp's Coconut,"
1890s, 10 x 11" ................................. **85.00**

*Early Advertising Calendar*

**Calendar,** 1905, "J.E. Whittier & Co. Clothiers and Furnishers," black & white print of couple in early automobile w/gold border, reads "5639 The Up to Date Farmer Henniker, N.H.," full-pad, 10½" w., 13½" h. (ILLUS. bottom previous page) .................................................. **33.00**

**Calendar,** 1900, "Mutual Life Insurance Co. of New York," picture of building, full-year on one page ....... **75.00**

**Calendar,** 1904, "Hood's Sarsaparilla," die-cut cardboard, pictures a pretty woman, complete w/full pad & cover sheet ................... **222.00**

**Calendar,** 1909, "Dupont Perpetual" metal, 19 x 29" ................................. **400.00**

**Calendar,** 1913, "Ceresota Flour," w/picture of girl w/flour bag ............... **350.00**

*1914 Advertising Calendar*

**Calendar,** 1914, "Underselling Store Outfitters," posterboard, shows "Roughing It" by James Arthur, only December pad is left, 5¾" w., 9½" h. (ILLUS.) .............................................. **17.00**

**Calendar,** 1950, "Pepsi-Cola," full-pad.. **245.00**

**Calendar,** 1955, "Royal Crown Cola" ...... **55.00**

**Calendar holder,** "Crane & Co. Oil Merchants," aluminum, silver w/black graphic & lettering, Boston, Massachusetts (minor scratches) ....... **11.00**

**Can,** "Standar-Kaffe," tin, image of woman holding can & black gentleman in early car, ring at top pulled apart, paint chipping overall (ILLUS. top next column) .................. **358.00**

*Standar-Kaffe Tin*

*Indian Motorcycle Clock*

**Clock,** "Cat-tex Soles," electric light-up, die-cut numbers, red, yellow, black & blue, black cat in center of face surrounded by "Cat-Tex Soles," red reverse glass border reads "We Rebuild Soles like New - At Less Than New Cost" in white letters, 14" d. (minor scratches & soiling) ..... **468.00**

**Clock,** "Indian Motorcycles," electric wall-type, metal w/glass face, white face w/black roman numerals & black hands, red lettering, metal case has been repainted, 18½" d. (ILLUS. above) .............................. **1,870.00**

**Clock,** "Moxie," wall-type, round face w/Roman numerals, reads "Moxie - Compound For The Nervous System" around face, below face reads "Also A Delicious and Healthful Beverage - Only in Bottles - Never drawn from soda fountain," early 20th c. (ILLUS. top next page) ............................................. **7,700.00**

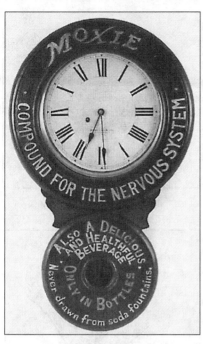

*Moxie Wall Clock*

**Corkscrew,** "Canadian Creme," wood & metal, in the shape of bottle, paper label reads "Canadian Brand Creme Ale," 4¼" h. (minor paint loss) ........... **17.00**

**Counter display,** "Aero Mayflower Transit Company," lighted, oak case w/colored glass front, reads "Exclusive Agent - Aero Mayflower Transit Company - Nation-wide Furniture Movers" above picture of moving truck & "Service to All 48 States and Canada," yellow, green & red, works, 17¼" w., 23" h. (ILLUS. bottom previous column) ................................. **660.00**

**Counter display,** "Calo Cat Food," die-cut, stand-up cat, "His Master's Choice!" ............................................. **50.00**

**Counter display,** "Cobbs Florida Coconut Patties," heavy pressed paper model of a large coconut, one end forms the lid, embossed lettering on the front, hand-painted letters, early 20th c., 9" l. ................. **165.00**

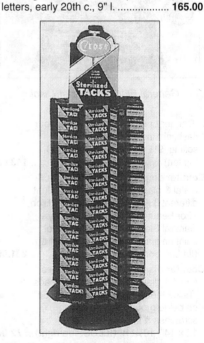

*Cross Sterilized Tacks Display*

*Aero Mayflower Counter Display*

**Cookbook,** "Esso," recipes on one page & Esso giveaway on other, marked "Aunt Julia's Cook Book," from "Lamb Bridge Service Station - Dean Myers, Prop., - South Fork, Pa. Telephone 9106 R4 South Fork," back features image of Esso man w/the words "Happy Motoring" (some light discoloration) ................... **44.00**

**Counter display,** "Cross Sterilized Tacks," rotating, metal, black, red & white, small sign at top, minor soiling, 21½" h. (ILLUS.) .................... **66.00**

**Counter display,** "Eveready," metal, orange, blue, green & creme, top reads "Eveready - Flashlights and Mazda Lamps," front reads "Let us reload your flashlight," side reads

*Eveready Counter Display*

*Minter's Candies Display*

*General Electric Counter Display*

*Morris' Supreme Bacon Display*

"Danger Lurks in Darkness - Is your flashlight in order?," scratches & soiling, 9½ x 11½", 16" h. (ILLUS. top left) .............................................. **143.00**

**Counter display,** "General Electric," metal & glass, electric, displays eight different bulbs, reads "Light Condition - For Beauty-Protection-Economy - General Electric Lamps," flaking of paint on glass overall, 27" w., 18" h. (ILLUS. bottom left) ......................... **231.00**

**Counter display,** "Minter's Candies," metal & glass, brown lettering reads "Tickle the Taste 1¢ each - 5 for 5¢" on beige ground, water stains, scratches & minor touch-up, 12 x 14", 10½" h. (ILLUS. top right)... **72.00**

**Counter display,** "Morris' Supreme Bacon," die-cut cardboard, blue orange, yellow, black & cream, in the shape of an old truck w/paper-wrapped bacon in the back, reads "Buy the Whole Piece! - Supreme Bacon," soiled & ragged edges, 14" w., 16" h. (ILLUS. bottom right) ................................................. **88.00**

**Counter display,** "Nemco Antenna," three antennas attached to metal base, black w/red & white lettering, reads "Nemco - the most advanced antennas in the world - The Rocket Line - Electronics Division-Van Norman Industries - Inc. Manchester, N.H.," 12" w., 24" h. (minor soiling & scratches) ................ **33.00**

**Counter display,** "Venus Pencils," tin, top of display is stepped, marked "Venus Pencils" at top, top of each step marked w/pencil quality, all above oval-shaped image of the Venus de Milo flanked by "Venus" & "Pencils" above "The Largest Selling Quality Pencils in the World," all done in green, yellow, blue & red, w/pencils, 20th c. .............................. **264.00**

**Counter display figure,** "General Electric Radio," jointed wood, figure of a standing soldier in red & white uniform, tall top hat w/G.E. logo, jointed at the legs & arms, 18½" h. ........................................... **850.00**

*RCA Nipper Counter Figure*

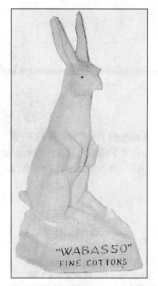

*Wabasso Fine Cottons Display*

**Counter display figure,** "Vernor's Ginger Ale," figure of an elf dressed in black pants, white shirt, blue vest, red suspenders & a green & gold hat, he holds a yellow & green sign reading "Drink Vernor's Ginger Ale," base 16" sq., figure 36" h. (ILLUS. bottom previous column) .............................. **4,950.00**

**Counter display figure,** "Wabasso Fine Cottons," papier-mâché, figure of white rabbit standing on its hind legs, raised gold letters, minor paint chips, 28" h. (ILLUS. above)............. **303.00**

**Counter display,** "Waterman's Fountain Pen," wood base & glass front w/wood display tray at top, white lettering on glass reads "Waterman's Ideal Fountain Pen," 16 x 16½", 17½" h. (minor wear) ...... **610.00**

**Counter display jar,** cov., "Planters Peanuts," clear glass slant-front 'streamline' jar & metal lid................ **100.00**

*Vernor's Ginger Ale Counter Figure*

**Counter display figure,** "RCA," model of Nipper the dog, papier-mâché, brown ears, black collar w/gold highlights, minor chips & crack, 13½" h. (ILLUS. top left)......... **413.00**

*Pepsi-Cola Crate*

*Caterpillar Fan*

**Crate,** "Pepsi-Cola," wood w/metal
bands, red & blue sides, water stains
& scratches, 12 x 18½", 27" h.
(ILLUS. bottom previous page)........... **55.00**

**Display rack,** "Amalie Motor Oil,"
metal, red, white & black sign reads
"Amalie Pennsylvania Motor Oil,"
38" h. (paint chips & rust) .................. **22.00**

**Doll,** "Jack Frost Sugar," cloth ............. **12.00**

**Doll,** "Kellogg's," Pop, lithographed
uncut cloth, 1948 .............................. **45.00**

**Doll,** "Sweetheart Soap," composition
& papier-mâché white baby,
mechanical, legs, arms & head move
when plugged in, w/pink wicker
bassinet, w/original signs & moving
crates, by Mechanical Man, 1932 ... **3,000.00**

**Doll,** "Sweetheart Soap," composition &
papier-mâché black baby, mechanical,
legs, arms & head move when
plugged in, w/pink wicker bassinet,
w/original signs & moving crates, by
Mechanical Man, 1932 .................... **4,000.00**

**Door push,** "Holsum Bread," painted
metal in the shape of a loaf of bread,
red, yellow & white, 41½" l. (very
minor scratches) .............................. **204.00**

**Door push,** "King Cole Tea & Coffee,"
porcelain, image of a king dressed in
red & white, yellow & white lettering,
rare, 3" w., 8" h. (faded overall,
minor chipping) ................................. **330.00**

**Door push,** "Majors Push," blue &
white, reads "Push - Majors Cement
- is Good for repairing China
Glassware Furniture," chip to bottom
edge, 3" w., 7½" h. (ILLUS. bottom) ... **43.00**

*Majors Door Push*

**Fan,** "American Maid Bread," die-cut
cardboard, in the shape of a
woman's head, wearing a pink, green
& blue hat, red lettering, 8½" w., 9" h.
(tear at thumb hole, creases)............... **33.00**

**Fan,** "Caterpillar Diesel," cardboard
w/wood handle, black cream &
yellow, front shows a man driving a
tractor below "This Farm is - Simple
and Easy to Operate - So is the
Caterpillar Diesel," reverse shows
four different farm scenes below
"Ask for a - Demonstration - On
Your Farm," marked "Form 3649 M
7:36 - Printed in U.S.A.," minor
soiling, 10" w., 14" h. (ILLUS. top).... **17.00**

**Fan,** "Tums," cardboard, orange, green, brown & red, marked "Crystal Drugstore Oroville, California phone 35," 6" w., 11" h. .................. **44.00**

**Fan,** "United States Tires," cardboard, yellow, blue, green & red, pictures old car flanked by tires, black lettering reads "United States Tires are <u>Good</u> Tires," car is separate & held on w/brass tack, 8" w., 9½" h. (creases, edge wear & soiling) .......... **99.00**

**Frame,** "The Brownie Boys," embossed oak, large photoengravure depicting five Scouts holding box camera, 20½ x 27½" .......................... **175.00**

**Glass,** "Pepsi," reads "Louisville's #1 Choice" below image of the Louisville Cardinal beside the Pepsi symbol (ILLUS. below left) .................. **31.00**

**Glass,** "Pepsi," reads "University of Arkansas" below picture of the Arkansas Razorback (ILLUS. below right) ...................................... **33.00**

*Two Pepsi Glasses*

*Whistle Soda Glass*

*Esso Santa Claus Mailbox*

**Glass,** "Whistle Soda," shows elf pushing bottle of Whistle Soda (ILLUS. bottom previous column) ....... **66.00**

**Hanging display,** "AC Spark Plugs," painted metal & wire, displays two AC Spark plugs w/yellow, red & white painted metal sign that reads "These Birds Were Caught Stealing Gas! - and Replaced with - Lively AC Spark Plugs," 7½" w., 6⅝" h. (rust in lower corner of sign) ........................ **204.00**

**Mailbox,** "Esso," metal, green w/white letters, reads "Be sure your letters are stamped" across top & "Santa Claus Mailbox" on front, sides read "Letters Will Be Postmarked With The Famous Santa Claus, Ind. Postmark" below postmark, minor soiling & rust, 12½" w., 17" h. (ILLUS. above) ................................ **231.00**

**Menu board,** "7-Up," hardboard, green, orange, black & cream, includes a bag of numbers, 26½" w., 16" h. (minor chipping to edges) ....... **110.00**

**Menu board,** "Nesbitt's," black, orange & cream, reads "a soft drink made from <u>real</u> oranges," marked "Copyright 1938 Nesbitts of California. Wiegand Mfg. Co. St. Louis 11-50/904.," 17½" w., 23½" h. (edge chips & scratches) ................... **33.00**

**Mirror,** "Skeezix Shoes," pocket-type, birthstones around rim ....................... **45.00**

**Mug,** "Planters Peanuts," pewter, 1983 ................................................... **35.00**

**Nut chopper,** "Planters Peanuts" ......... **35.00**

*Peanut Butter Pail*

**Order book,** "Cream of Wheat," salesman's, oval celluloid Rastus on leather cover ...................................... **85.00**

**Pail,** "Staple Brand Peanut Butter," yellow, blue, green & cream, label reads "Manufacturing & Guaranteed by Valley Preserving Co. Syracuse, N.Y.," wood handle, touch-up on yellow, 10¼" w., 9¼" h. (ILLUS. above) ............ **22.00**

**Paint book,** "Planters Peanuts," entitled "Mr. Peanut Happy Time Paint Book" ........................................ **25.00**

**Pencil,** "Poll Parrot Shoes," giant size.... **48.00**

**Pickle Jar,** "Acme Pickles," stoneware, barrel-shaped, marked "The J. Weller Company - Acme Pickles - Cincinnati, Ohio," late 19th c., 13¼" h. (fine hairline crack through "J") ............................................ **99.00**

**Playing cards,** "Life Savers," complete in box ...................................................... **35.00**

**Pocket knife,** "Goodyear" pearl on metal blue lettering & logo ................. **22.00**

**Poster,** "Western Cartridge Company," reads "The Elk Fight," ca. 1920, 15 x 20" ............................................ **675.00**

**Salt & pepper shakers,** "Esso," plastic, red, white & blue, decal reads "ESSO Extra," 2¾" h. (crazing of decals).......... **44.00**

**Salt & pepper shakers,** "Richfield," light brown plastic w/blue bottom, red, yellow & cream decals read "Richfield Ethyl" on salt & "Richfield Hi-Octane" on pepper, 2¾" h. (bottom of salt missing, crazing to decals) .............................................. **21.00**

**Salt & pepper shakers,** "Texaco," plastic, one red & the other silver, decal reads "Sky Chief Gasoline," crazing of decals, 2¾" h. (ILLUS. top next column) ...................................... **72.00**

*Texaco Salt & Pepper Shakers*

**Shoe horn,** "Shinola," iron, depicts two brushes & can of polish, marked "pat. 6/26/06," by Mayer & Levenson, 1½ x 4" ........................... **130.00**

**Sign,** "Birdseye Frosted Food," light-up-type, glass in metal frame, red, white & blue, image of Birdseye bird, 30" w., 15" h. (rust to hangers & metal frame, paint loss to reverse side) ................................................ **275.00**

**Sign,** "Bond Bread," porcelain, yellow w/white borders & black lettering, reads "The home-like loaf," 19" w., 14" h. (chipping).................................. **66.00**

**Sign,** "Chilton Paint," light-up-type, metal w/glass front, orange & black, made by Neon Products Inc. Lima, Ohio, 26½" w., 10½" h. (minor soiling) .............................................. **165.00**

**Sign,** "Feen-a-Mint," porcelain, red, blue & white, reads "The Chewing Laxative - Chew it Like Gum," marked "Reg. U.S. Pat. Off - Made in U.S.A.," scratches, chipping & fading, 6¼" w., 15" h......................... **314.00**

**Sign,** "Hires," painted metal, white & yellow stripes w/black block w/white lettering, sign reads "Drink Hires," 15½" w., 14½" h. (minor rust spotting & scratches) ......................... **28.00**

**Sign,** "Moxie," embossed tin, multi-colored scene of woman pouring a glass of Moxie, reads "Of Course You'll Have Some," in ornate wood frame, rare, 28¼" w., 36¼" h. (some in-painting)......................... **4,400.00**

*Robin Hood Flour Sign*

**Sign,** "Robin Hood Flour," porcelain, white ground w/blue & red lettering "La Farine Enrichie De Vitamines Robin Hood," overall chipping, 28" w., 15" h. (ILLUS.)......... **22.00**

**Sign,** "S&H Fro-Joy Ice Cream," curb-type, cast-iron stand w/painted tin sign, cream, orange & black, some rust & soiling, 20¼" w., 33¼" h. (ILLUS. below) ................................... **88.00**

*Ice Cream Curb Sign*

**Sign,** "Tippecanoe," paper, shows beige canoe marked "The Best For" in black letters above "Malaria, tired feeling," 25" w., 13" h.......................... **17.00**

**Spoon,** "Breyer's Ice Cream," tin, marked "Breyer's" .............................. **15.00**

**Spoon,** "Campbell's Soup," porcelain, yellow, black lettering on handle reads "Campbell's," Campbell kid dressed as a chef on spoon, 7" l. ....... **39.00**

**Spoon,** "Planter's Peanuts," serving-type, silver .......................................... **35.00**

*Rare Advertising String Holder*

**String holder,** "Swifts Syphilitic Specific," in the shape of kettle embossed "SSS - for the - Blood," traces of red & gold paint, Atlanta, Georgia, ca. 1880, rare (ILLUS.) ...... **550.00**

**String holder,** "Wingold Flour," flour bag-shaped....................................... **250.00**

**Tape Measure,** "Sunoco DX," yellow, blue & red logos, by Zippo, 1½" w., 1½" h. ................................................. **39.00**

**Tatting shuttle,** "Lydia E. Pinkhams' Vegetable Compound," bone, lithographed "Yours For Health," w/lithograph of stern-looking woman on reverse, 2¾" l. .............................. **88.00**

*Advertising Teaspoon*

**Teaspoon,** "Towle's Log Cabin Syrup," silver plate, figural cabin at top of handle (ILLUS.) ....................... **45.00**

**Teaspoon,** "Walter Baker Breakfast Cocoa," silver plated, figure of woman on handle, bowl marked "Walter Baker Breakfast Cocoa"......... **85.00**

**Thermometer,** "Apex," metal w/glass, round, white w/red & black, face reads "Apex - Hour Saving Appliances - The Peak of Quality - For More Than Forty Year," marked "Pam Clock Co. Rochelle N.Y. U.S.A.," 12" d. (soiling at bottom) ....... **28.00**

**Thermometer,** "Barq's," metal, painted black, red & creme orange, reads "Drink Barq's 'It's Good'" above bottle, 9½" w., 25" h. (minor scratches) ........................... **110.00**

**Thermometer,** "Carter Inx," porcelain, dated 1915 ................................. **215.00**

**Thermometer,** "Castor Oil," round, metal & plastic, red, white & green, dial made by Thermometer Corporation of America, 12" d. (rust on back) ........................................ **121.00**

**Thermometer,** "Land O' Lakes," round, metal & plastic, black, red, yellow, green & blue, reads "Amprotection" surrounded by chickens & eggs & "Copyright 1968 Merck & Co., Inc.," 10" d ................... **44.00**

**Thermometer,** "Occident," wood, cream w/black, blue & orange, reads "Russell Miller Milling Company - Makes Bread Better," 4" w., 15" h. (minor paint chips & soiling, red paint drips) ..................................... **160.00**

**Thermometer,** "Pepsi-Cola," metal, yellow, red, cream, blue & black, Reads "Say 'Pepsi, please'," marked "M-165 Made in U.S.A. AAW," 7½" w., 27" h. (minor rust & scratches) ........... **55.00**

**Thermometer,** "Quaker State Motor Oil," painted metal, cream colored, black & green lettering reads "It's a Lucky Day for your car—When You Change to Quaker State Motor Oil," w/four leaf clover at top, 8" w., 38½" h. (stained, small amount of rust at bottom) ................................. **132.00**

**Thermometer/Ashtray,** "Texaco," metal, paper advertisement thermometer reads "Crosby-Whipple Oil Corporation" w/Texaco logo in center, minor soiling, 3½" h. (ILLUS. top next column) ................. **72.00**

**Tin,** "Baldauf Drug Co. Healing Salve," pictures eagle, 1906 .......................... **35.00**

**Tin,** "Buffalo Brand Fancy Salted Peanuts," red to orange coloring ...... **145.00**

**Toothpick holder,** "Planters Peanuts," china, figure of Mr. Peanut standing on a half peanut shell, black letters read "Mr. Peanut," made in Japan, 4" h. (ILLUS. bottom next column) .................................... **110.00**

**Toy,** Cracker Jack prize, metal, horse & wagon, gold wash ........................ **300.00**

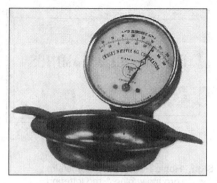

*Texaco Thermometer/Ashtray*

*Mr. Peanut Toothpick Holder*

**Toy race car,** "Junior Mints," die cast metal w/candy bar decal, mint on original display .................................... **20.00**

**Tray,** "Sparks' Perfect Heath," china, reads "Sparks' Perfect Health" above black & white image of Mrs. Cleveland & "Compliments of the Spark's Medicine Co. Camden, N.J.," all above "For Kidney and Liver Diseases.," marked "Robt. H. Payne Porcelain Show Cards, Camden N.J.," ca. 1880-1890, rare, 11¼ x 16¼" (ILLUS. top next page) .................... **2,200.00**

**Trolley car sign,** "Ivory Soap," cardboard, cream ground, blue & red lettering reads "No soap can make your skin as beautiful as a baby's, but if nature has given you a lovely complexion, Ivory will keep it lovely," next to picture of a baby, signed "Dorothy Hope Smith," framed, 22½" w., 12½" h. (nail holes along edges) ........ **33.00**

*Rare China Tray*

**Trolley car sign,** "Smith Brothers Cough Drops," cardboard, shows man waving cane running towards orange w/black & cream accents all above cough drop boxes, reads "And it's just as silly to ever be without a box of - Smith Brothers cough drops 5¢ ," framed, 20½" w., 10½" h. (#76 penciled on trolley car, nail holes & tears, bottom piece missing) ........................................... **121.00**

**Trolley car sign,** "Sunkist Lemons," cardboard, yellow, blue, green, orange & red, pictures teapot & cup w/lemons, reads "Sunkist California Lemons—in Hot Tea Aids Digestion Enhances Flavor! - Buy Lemons by the Dozen-For their many uses!," framed, 22½" w., 12½" h. (creases to one side) ...................................... **60.00**

**Trolley car sign,** "Sunkist Oranges," cardboard, red, orange, blue, white & yellow, reads "California's Gift to the Nation's Health - Sunkist Oranges" above three oranges, flanked by two adults & two children looking at oranges, all above "Richest Juice Finest Flavor," framed, 22" w., 11¾" h. (nail holes to edges) ............................................. **105.00**

**Trolley car sign,** "Victor Records," cardboard, shows young man & woman framed by a heart advertising the song "After I've Called You Sweetheart," 22½" w., 12½" h. (tear & holes in one side) .... **165.00**

**Weathervane,** "DeKalb," die-cut metal, painted like a corn cob w/wings, reads "DEKALB," 24" h., 18" w. (minor rust & scratches)......... **110.00**

# ALMANACS

*Almanacs have been published for decades. Commonplace ones are available at $4.00 to $12.00; those representing early printings or scarce ones are higher.*

**Ayer's American Almanac,** 1887 ........ **$7.00**

**Boston Almanac,** 1847, w/map ........... **95.00**

**No Nothing Almanac of 1855 (The)**.... **48.00**

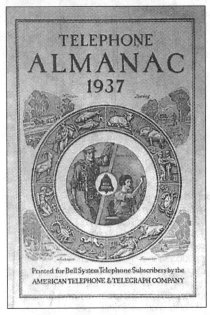

*Telephone Almanac*

**Telephone almanac,** 1937, "Printed for Bell System Telephone Subscribers by the American Telephone & Telegraph Company," 6¾" w., 10" h. (ILLUS.) ........................ **6.00**

# ARCHITECTURAL ITEMS

*In recent years the growing interest in and support for historic preservation has spawned a greater appreciation of the fine architectural elements which were an integral part of early buildings, both public and private. Where, in decades past, structures might be razed and doors, fireplace mantels, windows, etc., hauled to the dump, today all interior and exterior details from unrestorable buildings are salvaged to be offered to home restorers, museums and even builders who want to include a bit of history in a new construction project.*

*White Marble Fireplace Mantel*

**Fireplace mantels,** white marble, serpentine platform on pedestal base centered by carved shell cartouche above arched opening w/further carving, France, 19th c., pr (ILLUS. of one) .............................. **1,760.00**

**Gates,** wrought iron, four-section, composed of scrolls & panels, 10' l., 6' h., the pair ................................. **1,725.00**

*Walnut & Cypress Backbar*

*Italian Wrought-iron Gate*

**Backbar**, walnut & cypress, a long, wide rectangular top above a deep rounded cornice w/a dentil band above elaborate scroll-carved corners & a center boss above a pair of scrolling cornucopia over the wide arched opening w/two shelves flanked by heavy columns w/carved capitals over the counter top, the lower section w/a pair of long drawers over a pair of double-panel cupboard doors flanked by reeded pilasters, molded flat base, gilt trim, in three sections, New Orleans, Louisiana, ca. 1890 (ILLUS.) ............. **$1,870.00**

**Fireplace mantel,** black Tennessee marble, rectangular platform on pedestal base, each side w/green marble balls atop two columns, rectangular opening w/hearth w/center green marble ball, 19th c. .................. **1,208.00**

**Gates,** wrought iron, topped by lacy intertwining scrolls above rectangular frames surrounding further scrolls, Italian, late 19th c., the set (ILLUS.) ............................. **2,300.00**

*Griffin Face Ornament*

*Carved & Painted Bass Panel*

**Ornament,** painted cast iron, cast in the half-round in the shape of a griffin's face flanked by stylized scrolling leaf details, mounted on a black metal stand, American, late 19th c., repair to one leaf tip, 14½" w., 18½" h. (ILLUS. top) .......... **805.00**

**Panel,** carved & painted pine, depicting two large mouth bass amid swirls, enhanced w/paint decoration, L. A. Plummer, imperfections, 43½ x 56" (ILLUS. bottom)................................. **3,450.00**

**Panels,** painted pine, each panel relief-carved w/a large flower painted cream white over a red base, w/molded cornice above & below, some repairs to one, 30¾" l., 45½" h., the pair .................................................**6,325.00**

**Roof ornament,** zinc, figure of an owl, painted brown w/glass eyes, America, ca. 19th c., 27½" h. ........................... **1,064.00**

# AUTOGRAPHS

*Values of autographs and autographed letters depend on such factors as content, scarcity and the fame of the writer. Values of good autograph material continue to rise. A.L.S. stands for "autographed letter signed," L.S. for "letter signed," and S.P. for "signed photograph." Also see: MOVIE MEMORABILIA, POP CULTURE COLLECTIBLES and RECORD & RECORD JACKETS.*

**Cooke, Sam** (1935-1964), American musician, S.P., portrait from 1958 tourbook, signed to "Kathy, Luck, Sam Cook," matted & framed, 11 x 14".......................................... **$345.00**

**Dietrich, Marlene** (1901?-1992), German-American movie actress, S.P., black & white, shows Marlene Dietrich & Gary Cooper as they appeared in *Morocco*, inscribed in lower middle "M. Dietrich" in black ink, 1930, 8 x 10" .............................. **345.00**

**Disney, Walt** (1901-1966), American cartoonist, signed note paper stationery w/depiction of Mickey Mouse on bottom left corner & Walt Disney's name imprinted lower right, signed in middle "Walt Disney" in blue ink, autograph was given on opening day of Disneyland, in which Walt Disney was present giving out his autograph throughout the day, framed, 6 x 8" ..................................... **978.00**

**Garcia, Jerry** (1942-1995), American musician, S.P., color, signed in blue felt tip pen ...................................... **287.00**

**Hendrix, Jimi** (1942-1970), American musician, page from autograph book, blue ink on light blue paper reads "Love always to Christine, Jimi Hendrix" w/drawn heart, matted w/black & white photograph of Jimi Hendrix burning his guitar at Monterey Music Festival, ca. 1968, 14 x 18"............................................ **920.00**

**Hepburn, Katharine** (1909- ), American actress, S.P., photograph of Ms. Hepburn climbing up a ladder onto a boat, signed on bottom border "Katharine Hepburn" in black ink, 3½ x 6" (tears on right & left borders) ..**431.00**

**Joplin, Janis** (1943-1970), American musician, page from autograph book, dark blue ink on yellow paper reads "Love XXX Janis Joplin," matted w/black & white print, ca. 1969, framed, 16 x 20" .................... **805.00**

**Kelly, Gene** (1912-1996), American actor & dancer, black & white photograph of Kelly leaping through the air w/hands behind his back, signed on lower right "Gene Kelly" in blue ink, 8 x 10" ............................... **316.00**

**Kerr, Deborah** (1912- ), American actress, candid color photo of Kerr as she appeared in the film *The King and I* holding a bouquet of lilies, signed on lower right "Deborah Kerr" in black ink, 1956, 8 x 10" ................. **173.00**

**Lancaster, Burt** (1913-1994), American actor, S.P., color photo of a smiling Burt Lancaster, signed in lower left "To Ruth-Warmest Regards Burt Lancaster" in blue ink, 8 x 10" ................................................ **92.00**

**Leigh, Vivien** (1913-1967), British-American actress, signature on cream paper reads "Vivien Leigh" in black ink, framed in common mount w/a *Gone With the Wind* color photograph of her as Scarlett wearing the 'barbecue dress' ............ **460.00**

**McCartney, Paul** (1942- ), British musician, L.S. reads: "Dear Liz, - Hi—how are you, and how could I pass you on the street when we write so often? - I hope you don't mind this being a short letter but I'm awfully busy right now, and I hope you'll understand. - Keep smiling, see you again sometime, eh? - Lots of Love," signed in blue ball point pen, matted & framed w/color picture of McCartney, 16 x 20½" .............. **1,035.00**

**Minelli, Liza** (1946- ), American singer & actress, S.P., black & white photograph of Liza as a small child in a tutu at a bar, signed on lower right "Love, Liza Minelli" w/a heart in black ink, 8 x 10" ............................... **173.00**

**Nicholson, Jack,** (1937- ), American actor & director, S.P., black & white photo of Nicholson w/mustache & wearing dark sunglasses, signed on lower right "Best Jack Nicholson," 8 x 10" ................................................ **104.00**

**Nielsen, Leslie,** (1925- ), American actor, S.P., color photograph of movie poster for the 1956 MGM film *Forbidden Planet* depicting Robby The Robot holding a woman in his arms, signed on center "Leslie Nielsen" in silver metallic marker, 7⅞ x 9⅞" ........................................... **69.00**

**Presley, Elvis** (1935-1977), American singer & actor, S.P., black & white, shows a young Elvis leaning forward on his elbows, signed on left in blue ink "To Jo Ann From Elvis Presley," framed 8¾ x 11¼" (ILLUS.) ............. **173.00**

**Presley, Elvis** (1935-1977), American singer & actor, signature on pink paper, "Elvis Presley" in pencil, in common mount w/photograph of Elvis in concert & gold display 45 rpm record for "Blue Suede Shoes," matted in green & white w/a black lacquer frame, 17 x 21" .................... **403.00**

**Price, Vincent** (1911-1993), American actor, S.P., black & white photo of Vincent Price in white shirt & a tie, signed on lower right "Sincerely, Vincent Price" in blue ink, 8 x 10" ..... **115.00**

**Redford, Robert,** (1937- ),American actor & director, S.P., black & white photo of a bare-chested Redford sitting on the ground wearing sunglasses, signed on lower left "Robert Redford" in faded black ink, 7⅞ x 10⅛" .................................... **92.00**

**Taylor, Elizabeth** (1932- ), American actress, S.P., black & white dual image of Taylor as Martha from the movie *Who's Afraid of Virginia Wolf*, signed in center of photo "Elizabeth Taylor" in black ink, 1966, 6½ x 10¼" ... **316.00**

**Temple, Shirley** (1929- ), American actress, signed paper, inscribed "Love Shirley Temple" in pen & ink, matted & framed w/picture of Temple which appears to have been taken from a flyer or magazine, 14 x 19" ............................................. **345.00**

**Valentino, Rudolf** (1895-1926), movie idol, S.P., inscribed "Rudolf Valentino," matted w/plaque, 15½ x 21½" .................................... **1,150.00**

**Washington, George** (1732-1799), American President, cut-out on stationery, dated "20th day of January 1776," 3⅜ x 5" ................. **1,100.00**

# AUTOMOBILE LITERATURE

**Coreco Service Station Manual,** Continental Refining Company - Oil City, Pennsylvania" (minor soiling) ... **$39.00**

*Ford Model A*

**Ford V-8 operator's manual,** 1946...... **10.00**
**Packard Shop Manual,** cover reads
"Packard - Motor Car Company -
Service Department - Detroit,
Michigan - Constant Protection For
the Man Who Owns One," 1937 ......... **60.00**

# AUTOMOBILES

**Cadillac,** 1953 Eldorado ............ **$135,000.00**
**Duesenberg,** 1929 J-Murphy
   Roadster .................................. **650,000.00**
**Duesenberg,**1933 Rollston
   Convertible .............................. **850,000.00**
**Ford,** 1931, Model A 4-door sedan
   (ILLUS. above) .......................... **11,000.00**
**Ford,** 1963 Shelby Cobra............ **212,500.00**

# AUTOMOTIVE COLLECTIBLES

*Also see: ADVERTISING ITEMS,
AUTOMOBILE LITERATURE and CANS &
CONTAINERS*

**Antifreeze can,** "Thermo," red, black &
cream coloring, reads "One Gallon -
Thermo - Completely Denatured -
Alcohol - Formula No. 5-188 Proof -
Anti-Freeze - Publicker Commercial
Alcohol Co. Philadelphia, PA.," 9½" sq.
(denting, scratches, rust & soiling)...... **$22.00**

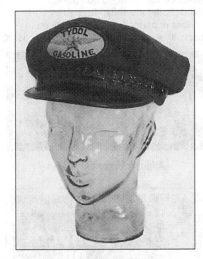

*Tydol Attendant's Hat*

**Ashtray,** "Goodrich," tire shaped,
   green glass embossed "Goodrich" ... **145.00**
**Ashtray,** "Sunco," metal, blue &
   yellow Sunco logo in center, 7¾" d.
   (soiling & scratches) ......................... **22.00**
**Ashtray,** "Texaco," china, green
   image of "Buffalo Division Office"
   above "Division Sales Meeting -
   January 9, 1968" on cream ground,
   made by The PJ McCarthy
   Company, Tonawanda, New York,
   6¾" d. (minor crazing) ...................... **49.00**
**Attendant's hat,** "Sunco," cloth w/vinyl
   bill, brass Sunco badge, size 7⅛
   (soiling) ............................................. **341.00**

**Attendant's hat,** "Tydol Flying A Gasoline," green w/black vinyl, w/Tydol patch, size 7¼, minor wear, band across front of hat broken (ILLUS. right column previous page) .. **176.00**

**Attendant's uniform,** "Texaco," green w/red & black Texaco patch, inside tag reads "Duro Prest No Ironing," size medium short ........................... **121.00**

**Badge,** "Esso Service," metal, blue & red logo, name tag reads "Bob Nolan," 1½" w., 2¼" h. (scratched) ... **121.00**

**Badge,** "Regal Oil Co.," metal, w/impressed red, black & white truck flanked by wings, impressed letters read "Regal Oil Co." above "87," 2¼" w., 2½" h. (minor scratches) ........ **38.00**

**Blotter,** "Atlantic Motor Oil," blue, orange, green, white & red coloring, reads "Special Offer - 5 gal. can- $4.00 - 1 gal. $1.05 - Atlantic N.C. - Motor Oil for Fords - Stops Brakes band chatter instantly," flanked by images of parrot & of oil cans, ink on back, 6" w., 3" h. (ILLUS. below) ........ **55.00**

*Atlantic Motor Oil Blotter*

*Sunoco Oil Blotter*

**Blotter,** "Sunoco Oil," image of Donald Duck wearing a suit of armor in Army jeep, reads "Reinforced for rationed driving - Sunoco Oil - Resists Motor-clogging Caused By Less Driving - Care for you Car - ...for your Country," World War II-era, bent corners, 6" w., 3¾" h. (ILLUS.) .......................................... **66.00**

**Calendar,** 1940, "Texaco," paper, colorful lithograph of Hal Roach's Our Gang w/pedal car in front of filling station w/sign that reads "Ask For - Texaco - Gas and Oil," reads "The Texas Company - F.E. Henderson - Phone 128W Grafton, N.D." flanked by two Texaco Logos, full pad, 20½" w., 29" h. (minor water stains) ..................................... **935.00**

**Chauffeur's badge,** 1933, Texas ....... **125.00**

**Chauffeur's badge,** 1938, Ohio .......... **18.00**

**Chauffeur's badge,** 1948, Ohio .......... **13.00**

*Champion Electric Clock*

**Clock,** "Champion Spark Plugs," metal & glass, light-up clock face w/Arabic numerals in semi-circle above rectangular light-up reading "America's Favorite - Champion - Spark Plugs," minor soiling & rust, 25" w., 16" h. (ILLUS.) ...................... **468.00**

**Clock,** "McCord Motor Gaskets," electric, metal & glass, square, face w/Arabic numerals & reads "Time To Buy - McCord Motor Gaskets," 14½" sq. (minor paint loss) ................. **77.00**

**Compact,** "Mobiloil," red w/red & silver Mobil winged horse in lower right hand corner, w/red velvet cloth case, 2¾" w., 2½" h. (mirror cracked) ... **88.00**

**Counter display case,** key rack, metal, black w/white, yellow, black, red & blue sign on top, reads "An Extra Key - is a time saver - Now- while you wait," soiled & scratched, 32" h. (ILLUS. top next page) ............ **28.00**

**Cup dispenser,** "Gulf," orange metal case w/paper cups inside, metal "Ajak Drinking Cups" plate above blue & green round Gulf logo, 3½" w., 15" h. (scratches & minor chips) ........... **77.00**

**Cutting board,** "Texaco," plastic, egg- shaped, yellow ground w/red & black lettering, reads "Slice n' Dice - Cut On Other Side - Content's - Texaco - Station" all above image of gas station, w/"504 Weat Main Street - Palmyra, New York - Phone 597.5551" below (touch-up to lettering) ............................ **35.00**

*Counter Key Rack*

*Dodge Fan*

**Fan,** "Dodge/Plymouth," cardboard w/wicker handle, round w/image of steering wheel, top two sections have outdoor scenes, bottom third has Dodge & Plymouth logos, outside reads "Be Alert-Play Safe - Keep Hands on Wheel - Watch Pedestrians," center of steering wheel reads "Use The Horn," handle broken at bottom, 8" w., 12" h. (ILLUS.) ............................... **50.00**

**Fan,** "Ford," cardboard, black & white lithograph of old car w/five smaller images on handle, green lettering on back, 8" w., 10½" h. (water stains & creases) ................................. **95.00**

**Floor display case,** "Pennzoil Lubrication," metal rack w/metal sign painted yellow w/black letters reading "Sound Your Z - 100% Pure Pennsylvania - Pennzoil - Safe Lubrication," 12½" d., 39" h. (minor rust & scratches).............................. **198.00**

**Gasoline pump globe,** "Atlantic Imperial," glass w/blue metal bands, white w/gold shield w/red & blue, reads "Atlantic Imperial," three-piece, 13½" d. ............................................. **440.00**

*Cities Service Pump Globe*

**Gasoline pump globe,** "Cities Service," glass, cloverleaf-shaped, white w/black rim & letters reading "Cities Service," three-piece, 13½" d. (ILLUS.) ............................................. **495.00**

**Gasoline pump globe,** "Flying A Gasoline," glass body w/red metal bands, white lettering reads "Flying A Gasoline," 'A' has wings, three-piece, 13½" d. (soiling & minor scratches to body & bands) ............. **825.00**

**Gasoline pump globe,** "Indian Gasoline," red metal frame w/milk glass lens, racing Indian figure in red & grey, blue lettering around edges reading "Indian Gasoline," 14½" d. (overall paint loss, missing piece on base)................................................. **770.00**

**Gasoline pump globe,** "Kanotex," clear glass w/metal band, fired on white ripple body, red, yellow & brown lens reads "Kanotex" atop star atop sunflower design, all above "Registered Trade Mark," 13½" d. .......................................... **1,430.00**

**Gasoline pump globe,** "Keystone," red keystone w/blue lettering, three-piece gill body, 13½" d. (minor scratches to lens) ............................ **187.00**

**Gasoline pump globe,** "Lion," glass body & lens, orange ground w/image of lion above "Lion," 13½" d. ............. **996.00**

**Gasoline pump globe,** "Los Angeles Refining Company (LARCO)," blue metal body w/glass lens, blue, grey & white lens w/shield reading "LARCO - Gasoline" surrounding stylized bird in flight, marked "Copyright 1935" at bottom, rare, 15" d. (minor holes in base, body repainted) ..................... **1,100.00**

**Gasoline pump globe,** "Mobiloil," metal base, oval, white w/red & black lettering reads "Gargoyle" above gorgoyle-type figure above "Mobiloil," 15½" w., 13" h. (ILLUS. below)....... **2,200.00**

**Gasoline pump globe,** "Red Hat Gas," black metal body w/black, white & red lens, black rim reads Motor Oil Gasoline, white center has image of red top hat w/blue band w/white stars flanked by "Red Hat,"15" d. (ILLUS. bottom previous column) ................. **2,310.00**

**Gasoline pump globe,** "Richfield Hi-Octane," glass, blue ground w/white & orange shield w/eagle above "Richfield Hi-Octane," one-piece, minor fading to lens edges, 15" d. (ILLUS. below) .................................... **414.00**

*Richfield Pump Globe*

*Mobiloil Pump Globe*

*Red Hat Gas Pump Globe*

*Texaco Gas Pump*

*Nash Hubcaps*

**Gasoline pump globe,** "Royal," glass, white, onion dome-shaped, red lettering around bottom reads "Royal," rare, 11" d., 13" h. (minor soiling) .......................................... **1,100.00**

**Gasoline pump globe,** "Vavoline Go-Mix," plastic body w/light blue lens w/red & white letters reading "Valvoline - Go-Mix - Outboard Fuel," w/silhouette of boat moving across center, 13½" d. (minor soiling to body) ............................................ **275.00**

**Gasoline pump,** "Texaco Fire Chief," glass plates at top read "Texaco Fire Chief Gasoline" to the right of Texaco symbol & red fire chief hat, glass encased number below, pump to side, National Dayton Ohio, Model A38, serial No. 13923296, restored, 74" h. (ILLUS. bottom right, previous page) ............................................ **1,100.00**

*Buick Goddess Hood Ornament*

**Hood ornament,** "Buick," zinc die-cast nickel plated goddess mascot, designed by William Schnell, marked "des. pat. 71217 November 5, 1926," manufactured by Ternstedt Mfg. Co., from 1927 Buick 12" wheelbase models & two open models, 5" l., 3" h. (ILLUS.) .................................... **105.00**

**Hood ornament,** metal, woman w/wings, minor wear, 10½" l. .............. **88.00**

**Hubcaps,** "Nash," painted metal w/Nash logo in center, soiling & minor paint chips, 3½" d., set of 4 (ILLUS.) .............................................. **61.00**

**Key holder,** "Mobiloil," diamond-shaped wood back w/white, red & blue Mobil symbol at top, metal hook below, 3¼" w., 6¾" h. (soiling)............ **55.00**

**Key ring,** "Texaco Ladies Room," painted metal, T-shaped, red & black on white, 3½" w., 5" h. (minor scratches) .............. **22.00**

**License plate,** 1912, Massachusetts, porcelain (minor edge chipping) ......... **22.00**

*Indiana License Plate*

**License plate,** 1913, Indiana, porcelain, rare (ILLUS.) ..................... **50.00**

**License plate,** 1915, New Hampshire, porcelain (minor scratches & chipping) ............................................. **72.00**

**License plates,** 1941, New York, pr..... **50.00**

**Lock,** "Sinclair," No. 622-WB, 3" h. (minor soiling, no key) ....................... **28.00**

**Lube sign,** "Texaco," porcelain, round, black "Texaco" above green 'T' outlined in black atop red five-pointed star, all above "Reg. T.M.," 8" d. (minor chipping to edges)......... **385.00**

**Map,** Standard Oil, "Kentucky-Tennessee," 1953.............................. **20.00**

**Match box holder,** "REO Speedwagon," brass, winged tire on front w/the letters "REO" in center, flanked by "Speed" & "Wagon," reverse reads "REO - Passenger Cars - Speed Wagons - Harrisburg Auto Co. - Harrisburg, PA.," 2¼" w., 1½" h. (tarnished) ................................................. **44.00**

*Conoco Oil Can*

**Motor oil can,** "Chesterfield," blue, yellow & cream coloring, w/silhouette profile of man in top hat above "The Aristocrat of - Super Motor Oils - 100% Pure - Pennsylvania Oil - Intercity Oil Company, Philadelphia, Pennsylvania," 9½" sq. (denting, scratches & fading) .............. **99.00**

**Motor oil can,** "Conoco," blue, yellow & white, shows image of Revolutionary-era soldier to the left of "One Half Gallon - Conoco - Reg. U.S. Pat. Off. - Motor Oil - Light - Continental Oil Company," original cap, minor scratches, fading & denting, 8" w., 7" h. (ILLUS. above).. **523.00**

**Motor oil can,** "Economy," red & green w/white lettering, has image of man pointing, reads "2 U.S. Gallons Net - Economy - Motor Oil - S.A.E. - United Oil Mfg. Co.," 8" w., 11½" h. (minor scratches & rust) ................... **61.00**

**Motor oil can,** "Olympia," black w/yellow & white, marked "Two U.S. Gallons - Olympia - Brand" above image of tipped oil can marked "Motor Oil" on the side & "100% Pure Parafine Base" on top, all above "2500 Mile Guarantee," United Oil Mfg. Co., 8" w., 11½" h. (minor scratches & denting).............. **110.00**

**Oil bottle,** "Standard," glass w/metal top & cap, embossed "Standard Oil Company" in circle surrounding "Service," 15" h. (replaced top) ........... **61.00**

**Oil bottle,** "Sunco," glass w/blue plastic top, fired on yellow & blue logo, 14" h......................................... **135.00**

**Pin back,** "Mobiloil Arctic," celluloid on metal, reads "Quick Starting Below Zero" below icicles, "Mobiloil - Arctic" below & "Full Protection at 400° F" above flames, 3½" d. (minor soiling & scratches)...................... **176.00**

**Pocket knife,** "Chevrolet," metal w/opalescent pearl sides, blue logo (opalescent pearl is loose, minor rust) .................... **22.00**

**Pocket knife,** "Cities Service," metal w/opalescent pearl sides, green lettering (one blade missing, one side loose) ..................... **28.00**

**Pocket knife,** "Esso," metal, in the shape of a gas pump, ½" w., 2½" h. (scratches)......................... **83.00**

**Pocket knife,** "Mercedes Benz," metal w/opalescent pearl sides w/silver Mercedes symbol on one side (minor soiling) ................. **18.00**

**Puzzle,** cardboard, lithographed image of old red roadster w/hills & trees in the background, printed in Germany, 10" w., 8" h. (creases & wear to edges)................. **22.00**

*Jenney Pump Sign*

**Pump sign,** "Jenney," porcelain, blue, black & tan coloring, silhouette of factory scene behind "Solvenized Hy-Power - Jenney - Manufacturing Co. - Boston," 12" d. (ILLUS.)........... **600.00**

**Pump sign,** "Royale Republic Regular," porcelain, rectangular, white ground w/red & blue trim, red, white & blue shield below "Royale" w/"Republic" across & "Regular" below, 10" w., 11" h. (chips to edges, loss of lustre) ...................... **275.00**

**Showroom car,** battery-operated, white molded fiberglass Thunderbird w/black white wall tires & red wheel, glass headlights & red glass tail lights, serial No. 4, 28" w., 64" l., 21" h. ............................................. **2,475.00**

**Tire gauge,** "Dodge," round, yellow
face w/orange & black lettering,
reads "Dodge" below numbers &
needle & "Made in U.S.A. U. Gauge
Co. New York" at bottom, 3" w., 2" h.
(minor soiling) ..................................... **72.00**

**Tire gauge,** "Model A Ford," round,
green face w/blue & red lettering,
reads "Recommended - Tire Pressure
- For Model A - Ford" below numbers
& needle, 3" w., 2" h............................ **132.00**

*Shrader Tire Gauge*

**Tire gauge,** "Shrader," cylindrical,
cream w/red & black letters read
"Schrader - Tire Gauge," w/various
illustrations, minor scratches & rust,
5½" d., 14¾" h. (ILLUS.)................... **264.00**

# BANKS

Original early mechanical and cast-iron still
banks are in great demand with collectors and
their scarcity has caused numerous reproductions
of both types and the novice collector is urged to
exercise caution. The early mechanical banks are
especially scarce and some versions are seldom
offered for sale but, rather, are traded with fellow
collectors attempting to upgrade an existing
collection. Numbers before mechanical banks refer
to those in John Meyer's Handbook of Old
Mechanical Banks. However, another book
Penny Lane—A History of Antique
Mechanical Toy Banks, by Al Davidson,
provides updated information and the number
from this new volume is indicated in parenthesis
at the end of each mechanical bank listing.

In past years, our standard reference for
cast-iron still banks was Hubert B. Whiting's
book Old Iron Still Banks, but because this
work is out of print and a beautiful book, The
Penny Lane Bank Book—Collecting Still
Banks by Andy and Susan Moore pictures and
describes numerous additional banks, we will
use the Moore numbers as a reference
preceding each listing and indicate the Whiting
reference in parenthesis at the end. The still
banks listed are old and in good original
condition with good paint and no repair unless
otherwise noted. An asterisk (*) indicates this
bank has been reproduced at some time.

**MECHANICAL**

*Always Did 'Spise A Mule*

*Boy Scout Bank*

5  **Always Did 'Spise a Mule,**
riding mule, PL 251 (ILLUS.
top) ............................. **$1,500.00 to 2,000.00**

21  **Boy Scout Camp,** PL 52
(ILLUS. bottom) ............................ **7,550.00**

39  **Cat & Mouse** - Cat Balancing
(PL 104)........................................ **2,530.00**

63  **Dog** - Bulldog bank - Coin on Nose
(PL 64) .............................................. **863.00**

69  **Dog** - Speaking, PL 447 (ILLUS.
top next column) ............................. **1,000.00**

71  **Dog** - Trick (PL 481)....................... **978.00**

*Speaking Dog Bank*

*Humpty Dumpty Bank*

*Eagle & Eaglettes Bank*

*Indian Shooting Bear*

*Small Jumbo Mechanical Bank*

*Mammy & Child Bank*

67 **Dog on Turntable,** PL 159
(hairline crack in base) ..................... **330.00**

75 **Eagle & Eaglettes,** PL 165 (ILLUS.
middle) ................................................ **1,200.00**

86 **Elephant -** Small Jumbo, PL 284
(ILLUS. bottom) ............................ **1,925.00**

127 **Humpty Dumpty,** PL 248, lacks
bottom to arm & bank (ILLUS. top
next column) ..................................... **288.00**

129 **Indian Shooting Bear,** PL 257,
repair to base & foot of Indian
(ILLUS. middle)................................. **920.00**

*Jonah and the Whale Bank*

138 **Jonah and the Whale,** PL 282
(ILLUS. above) .......... **2,000.00 to 2,500.00**

154 **Magician** (PL 315) ................... **2,530.00**

155 **Mammy and Child,** PL 318
(ILLUS. bottom previous
page) ........................ **8,000.00 to 10,000.00**

163 **Monkey and Coconut** (Pl 332) .. **3,600.00**

175 **North Pole** (PL 360) ................ **2,530.00**

7 **Octagonal Fort** (PL 363) ............. **3,450.00**

181 **Organ Grinder and Dancing
Bear** (PL 372) ............................... **7,800.00**

182 **Owl -** turns head (PL 375) ........... **430.00**

184 **Owl with Book -** slot in book
(PL 373) ........................... **450.00 to 500.00**

185 **Paddy & His Pig** (PL 376) ....... **2,500.00**

*Uncle Sam Mechanical Bank*

186 **Panorama Bank,** house-shaped,
PL 377 (shows rust & wear) ......... **3,220.00**

201 **Professor Pug Frog's Great
Bicycle Feat,** PL 400 (ILLUS. top
next page) ........................................ **7,800.00**

203 **Punch and Judy,** PL 404
(ILLUS. bottom previous column) .. **1,150.00**

222 **Stump Speaker**
(PL 453) ..................... **1,200.00 to 2,000.00**

230 **Uncle Remus** (PL 492) ............ **6,500.00**

231 **Uncle Sam -** with satchel &
umbrella, PL 493 (ILLUS. top this
column) ..................... **3,500.00 to 3,800.00**

*Punch & Judy*

*Professor Pug Frog's Great Bicycle Feat*

244 **World's Fair Bank -** with
Columbus & Indian (PL 573) ........... **805.00**

## STILL

*Camel & Biliken Still Banks*

74 **"Biliken," on base,** cast iron, A.C.
Williams Co., 1909-12, 2½" w., 4¼" h.,
W. 50 (ILLUS. above right) ................. **425.00**

597 **Bird (Owl) -** cast iron, Vindex, ca.
1930, 2½" w., 4¼" h. (W. 203) .......... **175.00**

598 **Bird (Owl) -** "Be Wise Owl," Be
Wise - Save Money" on stump, cast
iron, A.C. Williams, 1912-20s,
2½" w., 4⅞" h.................................... **145.00**

83 **Black Boy -** Two-Faced Black Boy
(Negro Toy Bank), cast iron, A.C.
Williams Co., Ohio, 1901-19, 4⅛" h.,
W. 43 (ILLUS. top next column) ......... **75.00**

*Black Boy Still Bank*

173 **Black Man -** Darkey
(Sharecropper), toes visible on one
foot, cast iron, A.C. Williams,
ca. 1901, 5½" h. (W. 18) .... **150.00 to 200.00**

1125 **Building -** Double Door, front of
building w/a door on each side of
central window w/"Bank" above, cast
iron, A.C. Williams, 1905-20s,
3 x 3⅞", 5⁷⁄₁₆" h. (W. 368) ................ **200.00**

1215 **Building** - High Rise, tiered, mesh sides & tiered roof, cast iron, Kenton Hardware Mfg. Co., 2¾" sq., 5¾" h. (W. 419)................................. **850.00**

767 **Camel** - Camel, large, cast iron, A.C. Williams, 1920s, 6¼" l., 7¼" h., W. 201 (ILLUS. left w/Billiken) ......... **275.00**

364 **Cat** - Cat with Bow, cast iron, Grey Iron Casting Co., Columbia, Pennsylvania, 1922, 2⅞" w., 4⅜" h.... **200.00**

349 **Cat** - Kitty Bank, kitten w/ribbon at neck, cast iron, Hubley, 1930-46, 4¾" h. (W. 335)................................. **145.00**

1546 **Clock** - "Time is Money" embossed on face, cast iron, A.C. Williams, 1909-31, 3⅝" h. (W. 225) .. **115.00**

357 **Dog** - Boxer (Bulldog), seated animal, cast iron, A.C. Williams, 1912-28 & Hubley (not date), 4½" h. (W. 105)............................................. **72.00**

414 **Dog** - "Cutie," puppy w/ribbon at neck, cast iron, Hubley, ca. 1914, 3⅞" h. (W. 334)................................. **44.00**

*St. Bernard with Pack*

437 **Dog** - St. Bernard with Pack (large), cast iron, A.C. Williams, 1901-30s, 7¾" l., 5½" h., W. 113 * (ILLUS.)............................ **100.00 to 125.00**

435 **Dog - Scottie,** Standing, cast iron, American-made, 3⁵⁄₁₆" h. (W. 108)............................................. **110.00**

499 **Donkey (small),** with saddle, cast iron, Arcade, 1913-32 & A.C. Williams, 1910-34, 4⅝" l., 4½" h......... **75.00**

180 **Dutch Boy on Barrel,** cast iron, Hubley, 1930s, 5⅝" h. (W. 36).......... **100.00**

**Egyptian tomb,** cast iron, 2⅛ x 5¾ x 6¼" ................................................. **450.00**

484 **Elephant** - Elephant on Tub, w/blanket, cast iron, A.C. Williams Co., 1920-34, 5⅜" h.......................... **99.00**

455 **Elephant** - Elephant, swivel trunk, cast iron, American-made, 3½" l., 2½" h. ................................................. **61.00**

*Prancing Horse Still Bank*

*Decker's Iowana Still Bank*

457 **Elephant** - Elephant with Howdah (tiny), cast iron, A.C. Williams, 1934, 3" l., 2¼" h. (W. 69)............................ **75.00**

520 **Horse** - Prancing Horse (large), rectangular base, cast iron, Arcade 1910 & A.C. Williams Co., 1910-34, 7³⁄₁₆" h., W. 78 (ILLUS. top) ............... **75.00**

535 **Horseshoe** - "Tally Ho," horseshoe framed by horseshoe w/fox hunt items, cast iron, Chamberlain & Hill, England, 4³⁄₁₆" w., 4½" h. (W. 168) .................................. **225.00**

228 **Indian** - Indian with Mohawk, cast iron, Hubley Mfg. Co., 1915-30s, 5⅞" h. (W. 39)................................... **225.00**

124 **Lindbergh, Charles** - "Lindy Bank," bust of Lindbergh, gold-finished aluminum, key-locked trap, Grannis & Tolton, 1928, 3⅞" w., 6½" h. ............................................... **295.00**

754 **Lion** - Lion, tail right, cast iron, A.C. Williams, 1905-31, 6¼" l., 5¼" h. .................................................. **72.00**

177 **Mulligan (Policeman),** cast iron, A.C. Williams Co., 1905-32 & Hubley, 1914, 5¾" h. (W. 8) ............. **225.00**

603 **Pig -** "Decker's Iowana," gold-painted cast iron, American-made, 4⅜" l., 2⁵⁄₁₆" h. W. 182 (ILLUS. bottom previous page) .................................. **95.00**

582 **Pig -** Seated Pig, cast iron, A.C. Willams Co., 1910-34, 3" h. ............... **75.00**

896 **Safe -** Jewel Safe, guard bars over keyhole, cast iron, J. & E. Stevens Co., ca. 1907, 3¼ x 3¾", 5⅜" h. .................................. **95.00**

50 **Sheridan -** Gen. Sheridan Base, officer astride rearing horse, cast iron, Arcade, 1910-25, 2⅜ x 4" base, 6" h. (W. 88).................................. **705.00**

587 **Turkey -** Small Turkey, cast iron, A.C. Williams, 1905-35..... **125.00 to 150.00**

*U.S. Mailbox Bank*

838 **U.S. Mailbox -** U.S. Mail, small, cast iron, Kenton Hardware Mfg. Co., 2904-10 & A.C. Williams Co., 1912-31, 1¹¹⁄₁₆" x 2¾", 3⅝" h., W. 127 (ILLUS.) .................................. **50.00**

# BARBERIANA

*A wide variety of antiques related to the tonsorial arts have been highly collectible for many years, especially 19th and early 20th century shaving mugs and barber bottles and, more recently, razors. We are now combining these closely related categories under one heading here for easier reference. A selection of other varied pieces relating to barbering will also be found below.*

## BARBER BOTTLES

**Amethyst,** ovoid bases tapering to bulbous necks, white enamel "Mary Gregory" style decorations of young boy & girl amongst flowers & leaves, ca. 1885-1925, 8" h. pr. ..................**$325.00**

*"Vegederma" Barber Bottle*

**Amethyst,** ovoid base tapering to lady's leg neck w/white enamel Art Nouveau profile of a woman w/long flowing hair above the word "Vegederma," ca. 1885-1925, 8¾" h. (ILLUS.) ........................................... **450.00**

**Clear,** angular body tapering to cylindrical neck w/two ridges & tooled mouth, white, black & gold label under glass reading "LeVarn's Rose Hair Tonic and Dandruff Cure Manufactured by The Mettowee Toilet Specialty Co. Granville, New York," ca. 1885-1925, 7⅝" h. ............. **70.00**

**Cobalt blue,** cylindrical body w/"Mary Gregory" style decoration of young woman amid tall grass & flowers, ca. 1885-1925, 8¼" h. ........................... **500.00**

**Cobalt blue,** cylindrical body decorated w/heavy multicolored enamel & gold floral decorations of flowers & leaves, reading "A.H. Seely Bay Rum" in white oval panel, ca. 1885-1925, w/original stopper, 10½" h. (ILLUS. top next column)..... **500.00**

**Jade,** frosted, spherical base tapering to slightly flaring neck w/heavy multicolored enamel Art Nouveau decoration, ca. 1885-1925, 8" h........ **525.00**

*"Bay Rum" Barber Bottle*

*Art Nouveau Barber Bottle*

**Milk glass,** bell-shaped w/multicolored floral decoration w/the head of a young girl in the center on green ground, ca. 1885-1925, 7⅝" h........... **825.00**

**Opalescent milk glass,** globular body tapering to thin cylindrical neck, body decorated w/red, yellow, green, black & gold sprigs of flowers & leaves above "Shampoo," ca. 1885-1925, 7" h. .............................. **170.00**

**Opalescent milk glass,** cylindrical body w/multicolored clover decoration surrounding "Toilet Water" in script, ca. 1885-1925, 8¾" .................................................. **150.00**

**Opalescent milk glass,** cylindrical body decorated w/multicolored enameled flowers w/the words "Sea Foam" in diagonal banner across flowers, ca. 1885-1925, 9" ................ **350.00**

**Opalescent milk glass,** cylindrical body w/multicolored enamel decoration of a deer jumping over a log w/the words "Witch Hazel" below, ca. 1885-1925, 9⅛" ............... **275.00**

**Ruby red,** bulbous base w/lady's leg neck decorated w/clear, white, blue & gold Art Nouveau decoration, ca. 1885-1925, 8" h. ........................... **1,650.00**

**Ruby red,** squatty ovoid bases w/thin cylindrical necks, bases read "Bay Rum" & "Toilet Water," ca. 1885-1925, w/original stoppers, 7" h., pr. .. **180.00**

**Turquoise,** Coin Spot patt., bulbous base w/thin cylindrical neck, ca. 1885-1925.................................. **150.00**

**Yellow green,** frosted, ovoid base tapering to lady's leg neck, decorated w/gilt Art Nouveau floral decoration, ca. 1885-1925, 7¾" h. (ILLUS.) ........ **350.00**

## RAZORS

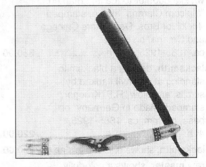

*W.H. Morley & Sons Straight Razor*

**Straight razor,** "W.H. Morely & Sons Corporate Mark," celluloid handle w/raised decoration of an eagle & American shields at both ends, marked "W.H. Morley & Sons Germany," ca. 1885-1935 (ILLUS.) .. **170.00**

**Straight razor,** etched w/Masonic symbols ............................................. **35.00**

## SHAVING MUGS

### FRATERNAL
**Benevolent & Protective Order of Elks,** decorated w/emblem below

"Henry M. Cody," stamped "T & V Limoges France 1917" on base, gilt trim, ca. 1885-1925, 3¾" h. (two shallow chips on base) ...................... **80.00**

**Brotherhood of Railroad Trainmen,** shows a caboose & attendant w/"B.R.R.T." & "Div. No. 534" on the side, all below "R.E. Jackson," stamped "V x D Austria" on base, gilt trim, ca. 1885-1925, 3⅝" h. .............. **350.00**

**Fraternal Order of Eagles,** decorated w/emblem below "Harry J. Mumma," marked "Ph. Eismann" in gilt on base, gilt trim, ca. 1885-1925, 3¾" h. (some paint loss) .................. **150.00**

**Knights of Columbus,** decorated w/emblem below "John McTindon," stamped "L & V Limoges France" on base, gilt trim, ca. 1885-1925, 3⅝" h. (some paint loss) ..................... **90.00**

**Sons of Veterans,** decorated w/emblem below "J.W.," gilt trim, ca. 1885-1925, 3¾" h. (some paint loss) .. **200.00**

## OCCUPATIONAL

**Bartender,** shows a bar room scene w/cigar counter to the left, marked "Malcom Clarens" above, stamped "Melchior Bros. Decorators Chicago and Omaha" on base, ca. 1885-1925, 3⅝" h. ...................... **350.00**

**Blacksmith,** depicts a blacksmith standing at an anvil flanked by scrolls, all below "R.F. Krueger," stamped "Made in Germany" on base, gilt trim, ca. 1885-1925, 4" h. ............................................... **220.00**

**Blacksmith,** shows blacksmith's anvil .. **250.00**

**Brew master,** shows a colorfully dressed king standing among beer kegs below "George Wolt," stamped & "T & V Limoges" on base, 1885-1925, 3⅞" h. ........................... **475.00**

**Brick mason,** shows a mason working on a wall next to an arch, flanked by colorful sprigs of flowers, reads "John Scheers" above, gilt trim, stamped "Welmar Germany" on base, ca. 1885-1925, 3⅝" h. (some paint loss) ....................................... **100.00**

**Butcher,** shows a butcher standing next to a very large prize steer, reads "William Collins" above, gilt trim, ca. 1885-1925, 3⅜" h. (some paint loss to trim) .................. **275.00**

**Furniture store,** shows salesman waiting on a female customer, reads "Kyman Barkoff" above & is stamped "T.P.C.D. Co. Semi-Vit" on base, ca. 1885-1925, 3⅝" h. (repaired crack) .. **385.00**

**Hatter,** shows a black bowler hat above "Hatter" all below "C.W. Cornell," stamped "T & V France" on base, gilt trim, 1885-1925, 3⅝" h. (some paint loss to trim) .................. **600.00**

**Jockey,** shows a nicely detailed jockey riding a horse below "Edd. Whelan," stamped "V x D Austria" stamped on base, gilt trim, ca. 1885-1925, 3⅝" h. ...................... **725.00**

**Painter,** shows a bench w/a can of paint & brush below an arched "Wm. E. Talbat," stamped "T & V Limoges France" on base, gilt trim, ca. 1885-1925, 3½" h. ...................... **275.00**

**Pharmacist,** shows a mortar & pestle below "Fred W. Wiedmayer" flanked by colorful sprigs of flowers, inside of rim marked "J.J. Wiedmayer Leetonia Toledo, Ohio, Feb. 20 1890," 3⅝" h. ................................... **110.00**

**Pharmacist,** shows a mortar & pestle flanked by colorful sprigs of flowers, all below "C.C. Bryan," gilt trim, ca. 1885-1925, 3¾" h. (glaze crack in base rim) ....................................... **60.00**

*Printer's Shaving Mug*

**Printer,** shows a printer working at his block flanked by sprigs of flowers, below "Joe Springer," gilt trim, ca. 1885-1925, 4" h. (ILLUS.) ................... **325.00**

**Railroad engineer,** photograph of locomotive & tender w/a passenger car, the locomotive marked "L.S. & M.S.," part of background may have been handpainted, marked "A.K. Leider" above, ca. 1885-1925, 3⅝" h. (ILLUS. top next column) .............. **4,700.00**

*Rare Railroad Shaving Mug*

**Railroad engineer,** shows highly detailed locomotive, marked "G. Fitch" above, stamped "T & V Limoges France" on base, ca. 1885-1925, 3⅝" h. (some paint loss)... **121.00**

**Railroad engineer,** depicts a detailed locomotive flanked by the dates "1862" & "1869" below "F.R. Sanford," gilt trim, 1885-1925, 3¾" h. ................. **190.00**

*Captain's Shaving Mug*

**Ship captain,** depicts a paddle wheel ship on rough waters w/two other ships off in the distance below a banner reading "Tommy Mathers," gilt trim, w/saucer, ca. 1885-1925, some paint loss to trim, 4⅛" h., 2 pcs. (ILLUS.)................................. **900.00**

**Shoemaker,** shows a high top shoe flanked by scrolls below "Wm. W. McFarlin," stamped "E. Berninghaus Clim(ax) Cincinnati, O." on base, gilt trim, 1885-1925, 3½" h. (paint loss to trim) ...................................... **230.00**

**Shoe salesman,** depicts a shoe salesman fitting a woman for a pair of shoes below "W.J. Pinkley," stamped "D & Co." on base, gilt trim, ca. 1885-1925, 3⅞" h. .............. **160.00**

**Store owner,** shows a colorful dry goods store scene w/a woman customer below "Wm. P. Parker," stamped "T & V France" on base, gilt trim, 1885-1925, 3⅝" h. ................... **400.00**

**Tinsmith,** shows a detailed tinsmith's furnace, sheerer & tools next to a sprig of flowers, all below "C.P. Bonell," marked "Geo. E. Wagner & Co. St. Joe, MO" in gilt on base, 1885-1925, 3⅞" h. ........................... **170.00**

**Trolley conductor,** shows an electric trolley car w/two conductors & five passengers, marked "Chas. W.T. Funston" above, gilt trim, stamped "GDA France" on base, ca. 1885-1925, 3½" h. (some paint loss) .. **468.00**

## GENERAL

**China,** the slightly ovoid mug shows a multicolored decoration of young girl reading a girl among morning glory bushes, gilt trim, ca. 1900-1935, 3¼" h. (some paint loss) .................... **65.00**

*Decorative Shaving Mug*

**China,** decorated w/Alpine scene w/cluster of grapes in gilt to the left w/"E.C.H. Norton" in diagonal banner, mug has full black wrap, marked "P. Eismann 1906 in gilt & stamped "T & V Limoges France" on base, gilt trim & base, ca. 1885-1925, 3⅝" h. (ILLUS.) ................................. **300.00**

## GENERAL ITEMS

**Barber pole,** turned & painted wood, spherical knob over baluster-shaped pole, painted red, blue, white & gold, ca. 1885-1925, 24¼" h. (old repaint)... **140.00**

*Oak Shaving Mug Rack*

**Display case,** "Shumate," wood w/heavy glass acid etched lid, bark green velvet backing w/slots for thirty razors, along w/twenty pinback buttons w/prices for various razors, compartment in back containing "Shumate Guarantee" forms, ca. 1890-1925, 6¾ x 36", 5½" h., the set .. **500.00**

**Shaving mug rack,** oak, raised acanthus leaves on upper left & right corners above forty-eight squares for mugs, ca. 1885-1925, 44¼ x 45½" (ILLUS. above) .............................. **625.00**

**Soap pot,** cov., opalescent milk glass marked "Chas. S. Roeberlein," ca. 1885-1925, 3¾" d., 2" h. ................... **210.00**

# BASEBALL MEMORABILIA

*Baseball was named by Abner Doubleday as he laid out a diamond-shaped field with four bases at Cooperstown, New York. A*

*popular game from its inception, by 1869 it was able to support its first all-professional team, the Cincinnati Red Stockings. The National League was first formed in 1900, it was not officially recognized until 1903. Today, the "national pastime" has millions of fans and collecting baseball memorabilia has become a major hobby with enthusiastic collectors seeking out items associated with players such as Babe Ruth, Lou Gehrig and others who became legends in their own lifetime. Though baseball cards, issued as advertising premiums for bubble gum and other products, seem to dominate the field there are numerous other items available.*

**Baseball card,** 1964, Topps Gum, Mickey Mantle, No. 50 ................... **$185.00**

**Baseball card,** 1968, Topps Gum, Mickey Mantle, No. 280 ................... **170.00**

**Book,** "Inside Baseball," (50 year history), Daley.................................. **12.00**

**Book,** "Lou Gehrig, Pride of the Yankees," Gallico .............................. **10.00**

**Book,** "My 66 Years in The Big Leagues," by Connie Mack, 1950, first edition, autographed ................. **200.00**

**Book,** "The Thrilling Story of Joe DiMaggio," Joe DiMaggio copyright, w/100 illustrations, 1950 ................... **75.00**

**Pen & Pencil set,** wood & metal, baseball-shaped, w/'signatures' of Bob Feller of the Cleveland Indians on pen & Mel Ott of the New York Giants pencil, includes original order form, 6" l. the set (ILLUS. below)........ **50.00**

**Pinback,** Dick Bartel New York Giants, w/original ribbon ................... **35.00**

**Tickets,** 1940 World Series, Cincinnati Reds vs Detroit Tigers, Briggs Stadium, Detroit, Michigan, ..... **55.00**

**Umbrella,** Baltimore Orioles, marked "Gulf Oil," mint in original sleeve....... **150.00**

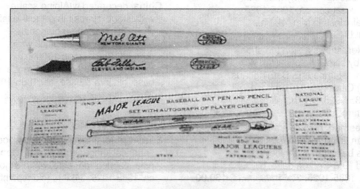

*Major League Baseball Pen & Pencil*

# BASKETS

The American Indians were the first basket weavers on this continent and, of necessity, the early Colonial settlers and their descendants pursued this artistic handicraft to provide essential containers for berries, eggs and endless other items to be carried or stored. Rye straw, split willow and reeds are but a few of the wide variety of materials used. The Nantucket baskets, plainly and sturdily constructed, along with those made by specialized groups, would seem to draw the greatest attention to this area of collecting.

**"Buttocks" basket,** ten-rib construction, woven splint, low bentwood handle, some age, 4¾ x 6", 3¼" h. plus handle ............................ **$138.00**

**"Buttocks" basket,** ten-rib construction, woven splint, coarse weaving, bentwood handle, 5¼" x 5½", 4" h. plus handle .............. **138.00**

**"Buttocks" basket,** sixteen-rib construction, woven splint, sharply tapering sides to wrapped rim & bentwood handle, old patina, 9½ x 11", 8" h. plus handle (some damage)..........**165.00**

**"Buttocks" basket,** twenty-eight-rib construction, woven splint,w/fine weaving, bentwood handle, old worn red paint, 11 x 12", 7" h. plus handle......**578.00**

**Cheese basket,** woven splint, low round form w/woven honeycomb design, wrapped rim & loom rim handles, good patina, 11¼" d., 5¾" h. ...............................................**688.00**

**Market basket,** woven splint, deep rounded sides & bottom w/round wrapped rim & bentwood handle, good age & color, 7" d., 5" h. plus handle (some damage, rim wrap incomplete ........................................**72.00**

**Market basket,** woven splint, deep round sides & base, narrow wrapped rim, high bentwood handle, old worn patina, 12" d., 7¼" h. plus handle, some minor base damage)...............**253.00**

**Nantucket basket,** label at base reads "Made by..Sylvard 97 Orange St. Nantucket," ca. 20th c., 8½" d. (label worn) ......................................**690.00**

**Nantucket baskets,** nesting-type, finely woven splint, wrapped rims above deep sides w/angular bentwood swing handles, paper labels on bottom read "David E. Ray," 19th c., 4¾" d., 5⅛" d., 6¼" d. & 8¼" d. (ILLUS. below) ...............**4,025.00**

**Storage basket,** cov., woven rice straw, deep rounded oval sides on an oval foot, flat double-hinged lids flanking high center wrapped handle,

*Nantucket Baskets*

small loop end rim handles, finely
woven, old varnish, Oriental Export,
7½ x 12¾", 7¾" h. plus handle
(some damage) ..................................**83.00**

**Storage basket,** cov., woven splint,
deep rectangular form w/wide splints
decorated w/potato print designs in
yellow, red & blue watercolor,
angled shoulder to a rectangular
domed lid, old varnish, 13" l...............**303.00**

**Utility basket,** woven splint, rectangular
base & oval sides w/wrapped rim &
small loop rim handles at sides, good
patina, 9½" l., 4½" h. ............................ **149.00**

*New England Utility Basket*

**Utility basket,** woven splint,
rectangular w/black painted X-form
handle, red, yellow & black painted,
New England, ca. 1860, 9½ x 11",
9" h. (ILLUS.) ................................. **1,600.00**

**Utility basket,** woven splint,
rectangular base w/oblong wrapped
rim w/bentwood end rim handles,
worn patina, 16½" l. ......................... **193.00**

---

# BIG LITTLE BOOKS

*The original "Big Little Books" and "Better
Little Books" small format series were
originated in the mid-30s by Whitman
Publishing Co., Racine, Wisconsin, and
covered a variety of subjects from adventure
stories to tales based on comic strips characters
and movie and radio stars. The publisher
originally assigned each book a serial number.*

*Most prices are now in the $25.00 to $50.00
range with scarce ones bringing more.*

**Billy the Kid,** No. 733, 1934 .............. **$30.00**

**Buck Rogers and the Doom Comet,**
No. 1175, 1936..................... **50.00 to 75.00**

**Dick Tracy and the Tiger Lily Gang,**
No. 1460, 1949 .................................. **55.00**

**Don Winslow of the Navy and the
Secret Enemy Base,** No. 1453, 1943 .. **20.00**

**Fighting Heroes Battle for Freedom,**
No. 1401, 1943 .................................. **24.00**

**Flash Gordon on the Planet Mongo,**
No. 1110, 1943 .................................. **24.00**

**G-Man and the Radio Bank
Robberies,** No. 1434, 1937 .............. **20.00**

**Lone Ranger and His Horse Silver,**
No. 1181, 1935 .................................. **45.00**

**Mandrake the Magician and the
Midnight Monster,** No. 1431, 1939 ... **65.00**

**Myra North Nurse and Foreign
Spies,** No. 1497, 1938 ...................... **14.00**

**Phantom,** The Return of, No. 1489,
1942.................................................... **65.00**

**Roy Rogers,** Robinhood of the
Range, No. 1460, 1942 ..................... **65.00**

**Sybil Jason in the Little Big Shot,**
No. 1149, 1935 .................................. **65.00**

**Tailspin Tommy in the Famous
Payroll Mystery,** No. 747, 1933 ........ **40.00**

**Tarzan of the Apes,** No. 744, 1933...... **65.00**

## RELATED BOOKS

**Donald Duck,** The Lost Jungle City, A
Big Little Book, movie flip pages,
No. 5773, 1975 .................................. **25.00**

**Mickey Mouse,** Mystery at
Disneyland, A Big Little Book,
No. 5770, 1977-78............................. **25.00**

**Tom & Jerry Meet Mr. Fingers,** 1975,
hard cover.......................................... **25.00**

---

# BLACK AMERICANA

*Over the past decade or so, this field of
collecting has rapidly grown and today almost
anything that relates to Black culture or
illustrates Black Americana in considered a
desirable collectible. Although many
representations of Blacks, especially on 19th
and early 20th century advertising pieces and*

*housewares, were cruel stereotypes, even these are collected as poignant reminders of how far American society has come since the dawning of the Civil Rights movement, and how far we still have to go. Other pieces related to this category will be found from time to time in such categories as Advertising Items, Banks, Character Collectibles, Kitchenwares, Cookie Jars, Signs and Signboards, Toys and several others.*

*Reference books dealing with Black Americana include: Black Collectibles by Lynn Morrow (1983); Collecting Black Americana by Dawn E. Reno (Crown Publishers, 1986); and Black Collectibles, Mammy and her Friends by Jackie Young (Schiffer Publishing Ltd., 1988). Also see: ADVERTISING, CANS & CONTAINERS, SIGNS & SIGNBOARDS and TOBACCIANA*

**Ashtray,** ceramic, "Coon Chicken Inn," w/black bellhop, 1940s, 4" d..... **$75.00**

**Book,** "Little Black Sambo," Platt & Munk, 1932...................................... **25.00**

**Creamer & cov. sugar bowl,** red & yellow plastic, figure of Aunt Jemima on front of sugar bowl & Uncle Mose on creamer, F. & F. Mold & Die Works, Dayton, Ohio, mint in original mailing carton, 2¼" h. & 2½" h., pr. .. **125.00**

**Figurines,** lavender bisque, gorilla couple doing the "Cakewalk," wearing period Southern dress, intricate design, unmarked, No. 1258, Schafer & Vater, 4" h. & 4½" h., pr. ....................................... **450.00**

**Firecrackers,** depicts black boy eating watermelon, marked "Dixie Boy," unopened package ................... **35.00**

**Make-up,** "Steins Black Face Minstrel Make up," in original box ................... **35.00**

**Match pack,** pictures black boy, from "Pickaninny" restaurant, ca. 1940s ..... **40.00**

**Menu,** "Coon Chicken Inn," cover depicts black person, ca. 1950, 12" h. .................................................. **23.00**

**Pail,** tin, pictures black child eating pan cakes, reads "Honey Dat's All!," w/bail handle..................................... **250.00**

**Pot holder hangers,** cast iron, chef chasing chicken & Mammy hanging clothes, pr. ....................................... **250.00**

**Print,** colored Mammy helping young white girl trim dessert w/strawberries w/package of Knox Gelatin in foreground, signed Harry Roseland, dated 1901, framed, 16 x 20" ............. **95.00**

**String holder,** Mammy in pink head wrap holding bouquet (crazing) ........ **245.00**

**Syrup pitcher,** red plastic, figural Aunt Jemima, F. & F. Mold & Die Works, ca. 1949, 5½" h. .................... **75.00**

**Tin,** cigar, "Negerites," photograph of black boys smoking ......................... **250.00**

**Tin,** coffee, "Machitz," pictures Golliwog-type black boys................. **185.00**

**Tin,** fruitcake, pictures Mammy serving Southern plantation family ..... **45.00**

**Tin,** molasses, "Aunt Dinah Molasses," picture of a Mammy, 1941................................................. **150.00**

**Toy,** jumping jack, lithographed tin, black man wearing hat, when top of hat pulled eyes, arms & legs move & mouth drops..................................... **300.00**

---

# BOOKS

## ANTIQUES RELATED

**Gardner, Paul V.,** "The Glass of Frederick Carder," 1971, Crown Publishers, New York, hard cover, 373 pp. ............................ **$50.00 to 100.00**

**Lagerberg, Ted & VI,** "Collectible Glass—Volume 2," art glass, Burmese glass illustrated on cover..... **33.00**

**Mebane, John,** "Bride's Baskets," 1976, 174 pp...................................... **34.00**

**Miller, Edgar,** "American Antique Furniture," 1937, two vols. ................. **39.00**

**Nutting, Wallace,** "Furniture Treasury," 1963, vols. 1 & 2 in one ...................... **17.00**

**Pearson, J. Micheal,** "Encyclopedia of American Cut and Engraved Glass—Volume II: Realistic Patterns," 1977, 172 pp., 9 x 11" ...... **100.00**

**Peterson, Arthur,** "400 Trademarks on Glass," 1968, patent information, 52 pp., hard cover ............................... **9.00**

**Revi, Albert C.,** "American Cut and Engraved Glass," 1973, 8½ x 11" ........................... **75.00 to 100.00**

**Thomas, John Carl,** "Connecticut Pewter and Pewterers," 1976, autographed ..................................... **105.00**

**Time-Life Books,** "Encyclopedia of Collectibles," illustrated, 16 volumes, the set................................................. **100.00**

**Weatherman, Hazel Marie,**
"Fostoria—First 50 Years," 320 pp. .... **65.00**

**Wiener, Herbert & Frieda Lipkowitz,**
"Rarities in American Cut Glass" ........ **55.00**

**Williams, Petra,** "Flow Blue China,"
1971, three volume set ..................... **100.00**

---

# BOTTLE OPENERS

*Corkscrews were actually the first bottle openers and these may date back to the mid-18th century, but bottle openers as we know them today, are strictly a 20th century item and came into use only after Michael J. Owens invented the automatic bottle machine in 1903. Avid collectors have spurred this relatively new area of collector interest. Our listing encompasses the four basic types sought by collectors: advertising openers, full figure openers which stand alone or hang on the wall; flat figural openers such as the lady's leg shape; and openers with embossed, engraved or chased handles.*

*The numbers used at the end of the entries refer to Figural Bottle Openers Identification Guide, a new book printed by the Figural Bottle Opener Collectors Club (F.B.O.C.).*

**Amish boy,** cast iron, figure of a boy
holding a black bag wearing black
hat, red shirt, black suspenders
w/black pants, 4" h., F-31
(ILLUS. below left).......... **$150.00 to 250.00**

**Barking at the moon,** aluminum,
figural group, a barking brown & white
dog sitting at the base of a crescent
moon, 2" h., N-529 ............. **75.00 to 150.00**

*Canvasback Duck*

**Bird's Birch Beer,** aluminum, model
of a grey bird perched atop a
branch, the bird marked "Birds," the
branch marked "Birch Beer," 3" h.,
N-574 ................................... **50.00 to 75.00**

**Buffalo,** aluminum, 2" h.,
N-595 ................................... **50.00 to 75.00**

**Cactus drunk,** cast iron, figure of a
man kneeling w/one leg outstretched,
wearing a cowboy hat, red scarf,
striped shirt, blue pants & black boots
clutching a cactus, 2" h., F-22
(ILLUS. below right) .......... **150.00 to 250.00**

**Canvasback duck,** cast iron, colorfully
painted duck w/red head & neck & a
yellowish white body, 1¹³⁄₁₆" h., F-107
(ILLUS. above) .................... **75.00 to 150.00**

**Cockatoo,** cast iron, colorfully
painted, 3" h., F-121 .......... **75.00 to 150.00**

**Cowboy w/chaps,** cast iron, figure of
cowboy wearing a cowboy hat, red
scarf, green shirt, black vest &

*Amish Boy & Cactus Drunk*

yellow chaps w/one hand on hip & the other holding a gun to the side of his hat, 4⅝" h., F-26 (ILLUS. below).............................. **350.00 to 550.00**

**Dinky Dan,** cast iron, figure of a young man standing w/his hands in his pockets wearing a yellow beanie-style cap, grey sweater w/the Greek letters Sigma, Delta & Theta & yellow pants, standing on a base marked "Cinderella Ball '52," 3⅞" h., F-42 (ILLUS. left, top next column............................. **150.00 to 250.00**

*Dinky Dan & Handy Hans*

*Cowboy Bottle Opener*

**Dolphin,** aluminum, model of stylized goldish green dolphin w/tail curled over its head, 4" h., N-616 .. **75.00 to 150.00**

**Donkey,** cast iron, 3¹⁄₁₆" h., F-61 (ILLUS. bottom right column).. **50.00 to 75.00**

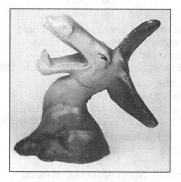

*Cast-iron Donkey Bottle Opener*

**Donkey,** cast iron, 3" h., F-60 ..................................... **50.00 to 75.00**

**Elephant,** cast iron, model of a rearing elephant w/raised trunk, rare, 2" h., F-45 (ILLUS. below right)..................................... **550.00 and up**

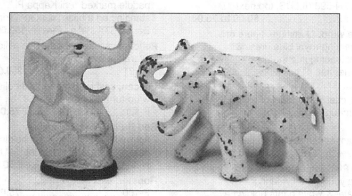

*Elephant Bottle Openers*

**Elephant (thin),** cast iron, model of
seated elephant w/raised trunk,
5" h., F-52 (ILLUS. left, bottom
previous page) ............... **350.00 to 550.00**

*Foundry Man*

**Foundry man,** cast iron, figure of bare
chested man wearing white pants
pouring hot metal, 3⅛" h., F-29
(ILLUS.) ............................... **75.00 to 150.00**

**Gobbler,** aluminum, model of gold-
painted turkey w/stern look on his
face, wearing suit w/arms crossed,
3" h., N-625 ........................... **75.00 to 150.00**

**Handy Hans,** cast iron, model of a
young man wearing a black sweater
& white pants, holding a paddle
marked "Sigma Alpha Mu," standing
on a base marked "Pledge Dance
'54," 3⅞" h., F-40 (ILLUS. right, top
previous page.................. **150.00 to 250.00**

**Hunting dogs,** aluminum, model of
two dogs, one chocolate brown &
one light brown, 2" h.,
N-587 ................................. **50.00 to 75.00**

**Indian chief,** aluminum, figure of
Chief wearing full headdress,
standing w/legs spread & hands on
hips, 5" h., N-598 (ILLUS. top next
column) ............................... **50.00 to 75.00**

**Lady in the wind,** aluminum, figure of
woman wearing royal blue dress &
hat, she is leaning into the wind
clutching her hat, 4" h.,
N-598 ................................. **50.00 to 75.00**

**Lion hoop,** cast iron, model of a lion
jumping through hoop, 3⅝" l.,
N-576 ............................. **250.00 to 350.00**

**Monkey,** cast iron, model of seated
monkey, 2⅝" h., F-89 ...... **150.00 to 250.00**

**Paddy the Pledgemaster,** cast iron,
figure of a young man wearing a
blue sweater & white pants holding a

*Indian Chief*

*Sea Horse*

paddle marked "Phi Kappa Pi,"
standing on a base marked "Dinner
Dance '57," 3⅞" h., F-41 ... **150.00 to 250.00**

**Pelican,** cast iron, model of a pelican
w/orange eyes, 3⅜" h.,
F-131 ................................. **250.00 to 350.00**

**Pelican,** cast iron, model of a pelican
w/up-turned orange beak, 4" h.,
F-130 ............................... **75.00 to 150.00**

**Red Riding Hood,** aluminum,
figure of Red Riding Hood holding a
basket w/the wolf at her feet, 4" h.,
N-568 .................................**50.00 to 75.00**

**Rooster,** cast iron, 4" h.,
F-100 ................................. **75.00 to 100.00**

**Sawfish,** cast iron, 5" l.,
F-157 .............................. **250.00 to 350.00**

**Sea gull,** cast iron, model of a sea gull
on a brown perch, 3" h.,
F-123 .............................. **50.00 to 75.00**

**Sea horse,** cast iron, 4" h., F-140
(ILLUS. bottom prevoius
page) ................................. **75.00 to 150.00**

**Skunk,** cast iron, 2" h.,
F-92c .............................. **150.00 to 250.00**

**Teen girl,** cast iron, figure of a teen-
aged girl lying on her stomach w/her
chin in her hands & her feet in the
air, wearing black pants, white shirt
& a red ribbon in her blond hair,
2" l., N-577 ...................... **250.00 to 350.00**

### WALL MOUNT

**Bear head,** cast iron, 3" h.,
F-426 .............................. **150.00 to 250.00**

**Black face,** cast iron, black face w/red
mouth & hole in the ears, marked
"Crowley," 4" h., F-404 .... **350.00 to 550.00**

**Four-eyes lady,** cast iron, four-eyed
woman w/red hair, red mouth &
gold earrings, 4" h., F-407
(ILLUS. below) .............. **150.00 to 250.00**

**Miner,** cast iron, a miner holding a
pick ax & beer mug, marked "Kaier's
Special Beer - Mahanoy City, PA,"
rare, 6⅞" h., F-405 (ILLUS. top next
column).................................. **550.00 and up**

**Monkey face,** cast iron, grey monkey
head w/red mouth, 6⅛" h., N-620
(ILLUS. bottom next
column) ........................... **250.00 to 350.00**

**Pirate,** bronze, pirate head wearing a
red scarf on his head, an eye patch
& holding a knife between his teeth,
5" h., N-512 ...................... **75.00 to 150.00**

*Cast-iron Miner*

*Cast-iron Monkey Face*

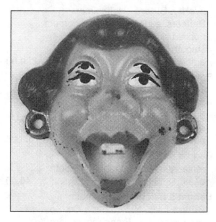

*Four-eyes Lady*

# BOTTLES & FLASKS

## BITTERS

*(Numbers with some listings below refer to those used in Carlyn Ring's For Bitters Only.)*

**American Celebrated Stomach Bitters,** square w/beveled corners, sloping collared mouth, smooth base, 1860-80, orangish amber, 8½" h. (unearthed, treated w/overall stain & scratches) ............................ **$77.00**

**Arabian Bitters -** Lawrence & Weichselbaum, Savannah, Ga., square w/beveled corners, applied sloping collared mouth w/ring, smooth base, 1860-80, yellowish amber, 9¾" h. (unearthed, heavy overall stain & iridescense) .............. **132.00**

**Argyle Bitters** Wheelock (E.B.) N.O., square w/beveled corners, applied sloping collared mouth, smooth base, 1860-80, olive-yellow, 9¾" h. (unearthed w/some haze, scratches & pick marks) .................................... **303.00**

**Aromatic Orange - Stomach Bitters -** Berry, Demoville & Co. Nashville, square, semi-cabin w/panel shoulders, applied mouth, smooth base, 1870-75, medium amber, 10" h. (about perfect) ....................... **675.00**

**Atwood's - Vegetable - Dyspeptic - Bitters,** w/paper labels, rectangular w/beveled corners, applied sloping collared mouth, smooth base, 1860-80, aqua, 6¾" h. (nearly complete original label on reverse) .................. **110.00**

**Atwood's Jaundice Bitters -** Free Sample, w/paper label, twelve-sided, machined mouth, smooth base, clear, 4" h. (90% original stained label) .................................................. **55.00**

**Atwood's Quinine Tonic Bitters,** w/label only, round, flared mouth, smooth base, 1860-80, dark puce, 6¾" h. (approximately 90% of front & back label) ..................................... **77.00**

**Ayallaa Mexican Bitters -** M. Rothenberg & Co. San Francisco, Cal., square, tooled lip, smooth base, 1910-11, reddish amber, hue, 9½" h. (perfect) ........................ **400.00**

**Baker's Orange Grove - Bitters,** square w/roped corners, sloping collared mouth, smooth base, 1840-60, apricot-puce, 9½" h. (⅛" flake top side of mouth) ............................ **468.00**

*Bakers Orange Grove Bitters*

**Bakers Orange Grove - Bitters,** square w/roped corners, light golden amber, mint, 9½" h. (ILLUS.) ............ **700.00**

**Baker's (E.) Premium Bitters,** Richmond, Va, oval, applied mouth, pontil scarred base, 1840-55, aqua, 6½" h. (very faint inside haze) ......... **625.00**

**Baker's (E.) Premium Bitters,** Richmond VA, oval, applied square collared mouth, pontil scar, 1840-60, aqua, 6¾" h. (unearthed, overall stain) ................................................. **121.00**

**Baker's (E.) Premium Bitters,** Richmond. Va., oval, tooled square collared mouth, smooth base, 1880-90, clear w/amethystine tint, 6¾" h. ................................................. **55.00**

**Bavarian Bitters -** Hoffheimer Brothers, square w/beveled corners, applied sloping collared mouth, smooth base, 1860-80, golden amber, 9¼" h. ................................. **220.00**

**Bavarian Bitters -** Hoffheimer Brothers, square, applied sloping collared mouth, smooth base, 1860-80, golden amber, 9¼" h. (spot of minor roughness on mold seam on neck) .................................................. **88.00**

**Begg's Dandelion Bitters,** rectangular, tooled mouth, smooth base, 1860-80, clear, 8" h. .................. **40.00**

**Bennet's Celebrated Stomach Bitters -** Jos. N. Souther & Co. Sole Proprietors San Francisco, square w/beveled corners, applied sloping collared mouth w/ring, smooth base, 1860-80, light yellowish amber, 9" h. (minor exterior residue) .................... **303.00**

**Bergmanns (Dr.) Magen Bitter,**
square w/rounded corners, rolled
mouth, smooth base, 1860-80, clear,
6¾" h. ................................. **66.00**

**Bischoff's Bitter's** Charleston, S.C.,
square, applied mouth, smooth
base, 1875-85, medium amber,
9⅜" h. (cleaned to original luster)... **1,450.00**

**Bismarck Bitters,** W.H. Muller, New-
York, USA - W.T.CO 3 U.S.A.,
square w/beveled corners, sloping
collared mouth, smooth base, 1860-
80, orangish amber, 7½" h.
(unearthed w/overall interior stain,
minor scratches & abrasions) ............. **66.00**

**Blue Mountain Bitters,** rectangular
w/beveled corners, tooled mouth,
smooth base, 1860-80, clear
w/amethystine tint, 7⅞" h. (light
interior haze)..................................... **66.00**

**Bodeker's Constitution Bitters**
Richmond, Va., w/motif of anchor,
strap-sided flask, tooled mouth,
smooth base, 1885-95, amber,
6½" h. ............................................. **1,050.00**

**Bodeker's Constitution Bitters,**
Richmond, Va., square, tooled
mouth, smooth base, 1880-90,
medium amber, 7⅞" h. .................... **850.00**

**Bonekamp (Mfr. & Prop. of),**
Stomach Bitters, John P. Fixmer,
Springfield Ills., square w/beveled
corners, tooled mouth, smooth base,
1880-1900, clear, 9" h. (some overall
stain, ⅛" chip on mouth) .................... **83.00**

**Botanic Stomach Bitters -** Botanic
Stomach Bitters, square, sloping
collared mouth, smooth base, 1860-
80, orangish amber, 9¼" h. (shallow
⅛" bubble burst on one corner) .......... **77.00**

**Brown (F.), Boston, Sarsaparilla &
Tomato Bitters,** oval, aqua, pontil,
9½" h. ................................. **300.00-400.00**

**Brown's Celebrated Indian Herb
Bitters -** Patented 1867, figural
Indian Queen, inward rolled mouth,
smooth base, 1860-80, amber,
12¼" h. ............................................. **468.00**

**Brown's Celebrated Indian Herb
Bitters -** Patented 1868, figural
Indian Queen, crude partially inward
rolled mouth, smooth base, 1860-80,
brilliant light yellowish green, 12¼"
h. (manufacturer's crude mouth
tooling, interior residue) ................ **6,050.00**

**Bryant's - Stomach - Bitters,**
eight-sided, lady's leg neck, applied
sloping collared mouth, pontil scar,

1840-60, deep yellowish olive,
12⅝" h. (light overall stain, ½" spider
crack in body) ................................ **1,650.00**

**Bryant's - Stomach - Bitters,**
eight-sided, lady's leg neck, applied
mouth, pontil base, ca.1860,
medium olive-green, 12⅝" h. (lightly
cleaned to original & about perfect
conditon) ..................................... **7,250.00**

**Buhrer's Gentian Bitters -** S. Buhrer
Proprietor, square w/beveled
corners, applied sloping collared
mouth, smooth base, 1860-80,
golden amber, 8⁹⁄₁₆" h. (pinhead
size bruise near base) ....................... **66.00**

**Burkart's Homestead Bitters,** square
w/beveled corners, sloping collared
mouth, smooth base, 1860-80,
golden amber, 9⅜" h. (unearthed
w/overall stain).................................. **143.00**

**Bull's (Dr. John) Compound Cedron
Bitters** Louisville, Ky., square
w/beveled corners, applied sloping
collared mouth, smooth base, 1860-
80, brilliant yellowish olive-green,
10" h. (some exterior scratches)....... **880.00**

*Professor Geo. Byrne Bitters*

**Byrne (Professor Geo. J.) New York
USA -** The Great Universal
Compound Stomach Bitters
Patented 1870, square w/pointed or
rounded shoulders & ropetwist
corner columns flanking shaped
panels, applied double collar,
smooth base, golden amber, 10¼" h.
(ILLUS.) ........................................ **4,290.00**

**Caldwell's (Dr.), Herb Bitters,** The Great Tonic (below) triangular, applied sloping collared mouth w/ring, smooth base, 1860-80, yellowish amber, 12¾" h. (minor exterior wear, ¹⁄₁₆" chip on base) ....... **154.00**

**California Fig Bitters -** California Extract of Fig Co., San Francisco, Cal, square, tooled sloping collared mouth w/ring, smooth base, 1870-90, golden amber, 9⅞" h. .......... **44.00**

**Carpathian Herb Bitters -** Hollander Drug Co, square w/beveled corners, applied sloping collared mouth, smooth base, 1860-80, yellowish amber, 9" h. (unearthed, overall haze, some pinhead size flakes on body) ..................................... **33.00**

**Catawba Wine Bitters** w/embossed grapes, applied mouth, iron pontil, 1860-66, bright bluish green, 9½" h. (lightly cleaned, appears about perfect) ......................... **6,300.00**

**Celebrated Berlin Stomach Bitters,** square w/beveled corners, tooled sloping collared mouth w/ring, smooth base, 1860-80, golden amber, 9⅛" h. ..................................... **99.00**

**Chandler's (Dr.) Jamaica Ginger Root Bitters -** Chas. Nichols Jr. & Co. Props. Lowell Mass., oval barrel-shaped, applied double collared mouth, smooth base, 1860-80, golden yellow shading to amber, 9⅝" h. ........................................... **6,050.00**

**Genl - Frank Cheatham's Bitters -** Nashville, Tenn., w/"W.McC. & Co." on smooth base, square, semi-cabin shaped, applied mouth, 1870-75, reddish amber, 10" h. .................... **5,750.00**

**Clarke's Compound Mandrake Bitters,** oval, flared-mouth, smooth base, 1860-80, aqua, 7⅝" h. ............. **44.00**

**Clarke's Sherry Wine Bitters -** only 25c, paper label w/"Dysentary & Diarrhea Sanative Cordial...," rectangular, open pontil, aqua, 8⅛" h. (70% label) ........................... **195.00**

**Clarke's Vegetable Sherry Wine Bitters,** Sharon, Mass., aqua, gal., 14" h. (ILLUS. top next column) ........ **468.00**

**Cocktail Bitters** Mobile Ala - Cribbs Davidson & Co, square w/beveled corners, applied sloping collared mouth, smooth base marked "L&W," 1860-80, yellowish amber, 9" h. (unearthed, overall stain & wear) ...... **660.00**

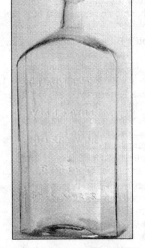

*Clarke's Vegetable Sherry Bitters*

**Commander's - Aromatic Bitters** A. Commander Sole Proprietor, New Orleans, Louisiana., round, tooled mouth, smooth base, 1890-1900, amber, 11" h. (exceptional) .............. **275.00**

**Congress Bitters** (on two side panels), rectangular w/beveled corners, modified cabin-shaped, applied sloping collared mouth w/ring, smooth base, 1860-80, light yellowish green, 10¼" h. (professionally cleaned, ¼" buffed chip on side of mouth) ........ **705.00**

**Copp's (Dr.) White Mountain (in shield) Bitters,** J. Copp & Co., Manchester, N.H., w/"JHC" monogram, oval, flared mouth, smooth base, 1880-1900, aqua, pt., 8¼" h. ............................................... **165.00**

**Crescent Bitters,** G.M. Bayly & Pond, New Orleans La, Trade Mark (motif of crescent moon) on two sides, square w/beveled corners, applied sloping collared mouth w/ring, smooth base w/"McC&CO," brilliant yellowish amber, 9¾" h. (¼" ground spot on base corner, minor exterior scratches & interior residue) .......... **3,300.00**

**Crooke's (H.M.) Stomach Bitters** (on shoulder), round bulbous neck, applied mouth, smooth base, 1870-75, olive-green, 10⅛" h. .......... **475.00**

**Cumberland Bitters,** Kinkade Handly & Co. - Nashville Tenn, square, applied mouth, smooth base, 1870-75, medium amber, 9⅞" h. ... **1,850.00**

**Curtis - Cordial - Calisaya - The Great - Stomach - Bitters,** round w/twelve-paneled shoulder, applied collared mouth w/ring, smooth base, 1860-80, yellowish olive, 11¾" h. (1" series of flat silver chips on top surface of mouth, ⅛" flake on ring of mouth)... **1,870.00**

**Dandelion and Wild Cherry Bitters,** round, applied sloping collared mouth, smooth base, 1860-80, aqua, 7⅜" h. ............................................. **176.00**

**Davis's Kidney and Liver Bitters -** Best Invigorator and Cathartic, square w/beveled corners, tooled sloping collared mouth, smooth base, 1860-80, golden amber, 10" h. ............................................... **154.00**

**De Andries (Dr.) - Sarsaparilla Bitters -** E.M. Rusha New Orleans, rectangular, corners beveled, applied mouth, smooth base, yellowish root beer amber, 10" h.............................................. **1,350.00**

**Deutenhoffs Swiss Bitters -** G.M. Heidt Savannah, Ga., square, applied mouth, smooth base, dark amber, 9¼" h. ................................ **825.00**

**Diamond's Blood Bitters** Buffalo N.Y., square w/beveled corners, applied sloping collared mouth, smooth base, 1860-80, golden amber, 7¾" h. ............................... **253.00**

**Dingens Napoleon Cocktail Bitters -** Dingens Brothers, Buffalo, N.Y., banjo shape w/lady's leg neck, applied sloping collared mouth, iron pontil, 1845-60, yellowish amber w/olive tone, 10½" h. (embossing appears weak) .............................. **4,400.00**

**Doyle's - Hop - Bitters - 1872** (on shoulders), square, amber, 9⅝" h. ..... **55.00**

**Doyles - Hop - Bitters - 1872,** modified cabin-shape, applied sloping collared mouth, smooth base, 1860-80, yellow w/hint of amber, 9½" h. (overall iridescent stain).............................................. **154.00**

**Drakes Plantation Bitters -** Patented 1862, cabin-shaped, five-log, golden yellowish amber, light inside haze, 10" h., D-109 (ILLUS. top next column)............................................ **308.00**

**Drake's (S T) 1860 Plantation Bitters -** Patented 1862, no "X," cabin-shaped, four-log, applied sloping collared mouth, smooth base, 1860-80, golden amber, 10¼" h. (D-110) ................................ **88.00**

*Drakes Plantation Bitters*

**Drake's (S T) 1860 Plantation Bitters -** Patented 1862, no "X," cabin-shaped, four-log, golden yellow, 10¼" h. (D-110) ................... **295.00**

**Drake's (S T) 1860 Plantation X Bitters -** Patented 1862, cabin-shaped, six-log, applied sloping collared mouth, smooth base, 1860-80, dense amber, minor spots of interior haze, 10" h. (D-108) .............. **66.00**

**Drake's (S T) 1860 Plantation X Bitters -** Patented 1862, cabin-shaped, six-log, applied sloping collared mouth, smooth base, 1860-80, light to medium pink, 10" h. (D-106) ......................................... **3,300.00**

**Drake's (S T) 1860 Plantation X Bitters -** Patented 1862, cabin-shaped, six-log, medium yellowish amber, 10" h. (D-105) ...... **350.00 to 400.00**

**Eagle Angostura - Bark Bitters,** round, sample size, tooled mouth, smooth base, 1870-90, deep amber, 4" h. (some manufacturer's annealing fissures in the neck) .......... **66.00**

**Eagle Aromatic Bitters -** Eagle Liqueur Distilleries, w/only paper labels, globular, tooled mouth, smooth base, 1870-90, golden amber, 8½" h. (full labels & shoulder embellishment) ................................ **330.00**

**English Female - Bitters -** Louisville, Ky - Dromgoole, rectangular w/beveled corners, applied sloping collared mouth, smooth base, 1860-80, aqua, 8½" h. (unearthed, overall haze, minor scratches) ..................... **94.00**

**'Electric' Brand Bitters -** H.E. Bucklen & Co., Chicago, Ill., square, original label, amber, 8⅞" h. ............... **39.00**

**Evans' (Gwilym) Quinine Bitters,** square, aqua, 8" h. ............................ **60.00**

**Ferro Quina Stomach Bitters,** Blood Maker, Mnfg. by D.P. Rossi, San Francisco, Cal, square w/lady's leg neck, tooled mouth, smooth base, 1880-1900, amber, 9¼" h. ................... **88.00**

**Fischs Bitters -** W.H. Ware, Patented 1866, figural fish, crude applied lip, light yellow w/tinge of amber in scales, 11¾" h. (pinhead flake on belly & patch of haze in base) .......... **795.00**

**Fischs (Doctor) Bitters -** W.H. Ware Patented 1866, figural fish, applied small round collared mouth, smooth base, 1860-80, yellow w/greenish tone, 11¾" h. (excellent condition)... **1,320.00**

**Fish (The) Bitters -** W.H. Ware Patented 1866, figural fish, tooled small square collared mouth, smooth base, 1860-80, clear, 11¼" h......... **1,210.00**

*The Fish Bitters*

**Fish (The) Bitters -** W.H. Ware, Patented 1866, figural fish w/paper label, applied round collared mouth, smooth base, 1866-80, dark golden amber (chocolate), weak lettering, 75% original label, 11⅜" h. (ILLUS.) ......................................... **523.00**

**Fish (The) Bitters -** W.H. Ware Patented 1866, figural fish applied round collared mouth, smooth base, 1866-80, golden amber, 11½" h. ...... **330.00**

**Franklin (Ben) Bitters -** Poor Richard's Tonic (paper label), barrel-shaped, ten rings above & below center band, applied small square collared mouth, pontil scar, 1840-60, golden amber in base shading to golden topaz in shoulder, 10" h. (½" crack in upper body ring, full labels are aged & difficult to read) .... **550.00**

**Fulton M. McRae, Yazoo Valley Bitters,** square w/beveled corners, applied sloping collared mouth, smooth base, 1860-80, golden amber, 8½" h. (some light interior haze)................................................. **110.00**

**Genuine Ango Stura Bitters -** O.B. Van Camp, round, tooled mouth, smooth base, 1860-80, golden amber, 8¼" h. .................................... **55.00**

**Genuine Bull Wild Cherry Bitters,** rectangular w/beveled corners, tooled wide collared mouth, smooth base, 1860-80, clear, 8¾" h. (⅛" flake on front panel edge) .......... **176.00**

**Globe Bitters,** Manufactured only by, Byrne Bros & Co., New York - Globe Bitters - Byrne Bros. & Co. New York, cylindrical w/light house neck form, applied square collared mouth, smooth base, 1860-80, 11" h........... **880.00**

**Golden Seal Bitters,** square w/beveled corners, applied sloping collared mouth, smooth base, 1860-80, golden yellow, 9" h. (some exterior high point wear especially at lower corner, minor interior haze) ..... **385.00**

**Greeley's Bourbon Bitters,** barrel-shaped, ten rings above & below center band, applied square collared mouth, smooth base, golden yellowish topaz, 9⅜" h. (buffed ⅝" mouth chip on underside of square collar, bubble burst on body) ............ **303.00**

**Greeley's Bourbon Bitters,** barrel-shaped, ten rings above & below center band, applied square collared mouth, smooth base, 1860-80, smokey topaz green, 9⅜" h. ............. **935.00**

**Greeley's Bourbon Bitters,** barrel-shaped, ten rings above & below center band, medium copper-puce, mint, 9⅜" h. (ILLUS. top next page) ... **475.00**

**Greeley's Bourbon Whiskey Bitters,** barrel-shaped, ten rings above & below center band, applied square collared mouth w/ring, smooth base, 1860-80, aqua, 9½" h. (light overall interior stain) ................................. **4,400.00**

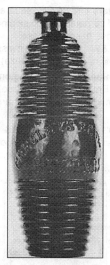

*Greeley's Bourbon Bitters*

**Greer's Eclipse Bitters** - Louisville, Ky., square w/beveled corners, applied sloping collared mouth, smooth base, 1860-80, brilliant golden amber, 9⅜" h. ...................... **198.00**

**Hall's Bitters,** barrel-shaped, applied flared collared mouth, smooth base, 1860-80, puce-amber, 9½" h. ........ **3,020.00**

**Hall's (Dr Thos.) California Pepsin Wine Bitters,** square, tooled lip, smooth base, 1875-80, amber, 9" h. .... **525.00**

**Hall's (Dr Thos) California Pepsin Wine Bitters,** square w/beveled corners, tooled sloping collared mouth, smooth base, 1870-90, yellowish amber, 9" h. (unusual neck flaw done during manufacture) ......... **176.00**

**Hardy's (Dr. Manly) - Boston - Jaundice Bitters -** Mass., rectangular w/beveled corners, applied sloping mouth, smooth base, 1860-80, aqua, 7⅜" h. ...................... **121.00**

**Harter's (Dr.) Wild Cherry Bitters** St. Louis, rectangular w/round corners, embossed cherry, applied sloping collared mouth, smooth base, golden amber, 7⅓" h. ......................... **88.00**

**Harter's (Dr.) Wild Cherry Bitters** St. Louis - Design Patented, rectangular, tooled sloping collared mouth, smooth base, 1860-80, yellow, 4½" h. (unearthed w/overall stain) .................................................. **99.00**

**Hart's Star Bitters,** motif circle enclosing "O.B.L.P.C." & five-pointed star enclosing "1868, Philadelphia PA," modified fish form, tooled square collared mouth, smooth base, 1870-90, 9¼" h. (professionally cleaned w/some remaining residue, ¼" buffed area on side of mouth) ............................ **330.00**

**Harvey's - Prairie - Bitters -** Patented, modified cabin-shaped w/columnar corners & patterned dome shoulder, sloping collared mouth, smooth base, 1860-80, golden amber (unearthed stained, ³⁄₁₆" hole & 5" crack on one columnar corner) ......................................... **1,760.00**

**Herb Bitters** (on paper label), E.A. Smith MD Brandon Vt. (embossed), oval tooled square collared mouth, smooth base, 1880-1900, aqua, 8½" h. (light interior stain) ................ **132.00**

*Hertrich's Gesundheits Bitters*

**Hertrich's Gesundheits Bitters,** Hans Hertrich Hof Erfinder Allein Destillateur, bulbous ovoid body on a cushion foot w/a tall slender tapering neck w/applied double collar, Europe, late 19th c., deep yellowish olive-green, 11⅞" h. (ILLUS.) ............................................. **550.00**

**Hibernia Bitters,** Braunschweiger & Bumsted., San Francisco, Cal., square, applied mouth, smooth base, 1883-84, medium amber w/reddish hue, 9⅞" h. ...................... **850.00**

**Hierapicra Bitters Extract of Figs -**
California - Botanical Society,
rectangular, deep aqua, 9⅝" h. ........ **350.00**

**Higby (J.T.) - Tonic Bitters -** Milford
Ct., square w/beveled corners,
applied sloping collared mouth,
smooth base, 1860-80, yellowish
amber, 9½" h. (some interior stain
near base) ........................................ **77.00**

*Highland Bitters and Scotch Tonic*

**Highland Bitters and Scotch Tonic,**
barrel-shaped, ten-rib, amber w/a
touch of apricot, one inch lip repair &
onion skin open bubble on back,
9⅝" h. (ILLUS.) ................................. **578.00**

**Holtzermans Patent Stomach
Bitters** (on shoulder), w/paper label,
cabin-shaped w/four roofs, 1870-90,
golden amber, 9⅝" h. ....... **250.00 to 325.00**

**Holtzermann's - Patent Stomach
Bitters,** cabin-shape, two-story,
stylized logs like hoops on barrels,
applied sloping collared mouth,
smooth base, 1860-80, light yellowish
amber, 9⅝" h. ............................... **2,090.00**

**Hopkins (A.S.) Union Stomach
Bitters,** square w/beveled corners,
applied sloping collared mouth,
smooth base, 1860-80, golden
amber, 9¾" h. .................................... **55.00**

**Hutchings - Syspepsia Bitters -**
New. York, rectangular w/beveled
corners, applied sloping collared
mouth, iron pontil mark, 1840-60,
aqua, 9½" h. (professionally
cleaned) ........................................... **176.00**

**Hygeia Bitters -** Fox & Co., square
w/beveled corners, applied sloping
collared mouth, smooth base
marked "L&W," 1860-80, yellowish
amber, 9⅛" h. (light interior haze) ...... **61.00**

**Iron & Quinine Bitters -** Burlington,
VT - N.K. Brown, rectangular, tooled
mouth, smooth base, 1860-80, aqua,
8½" h. .............................................. **165.00**

**Jewel Biters -** John S. Bowman & Co,
rectangular, applied mouth, smooth
base, ca. 1886, yellowish amber,
9¾" h. .............................................. **675.00**

*Dr. Jewett's Celebrated Bitters*

**Jewett's (Dr. Stephen) Celebrated
Health Restoring Bitters,** Rindge,
N.H., rectangular, minute no harm lip
edge roughage, medium yellowish
amber, 7½" h. (ILLUS.) ................. **1,595.00**

**Johnson's Calisaya Bitters -**
Burlington Vt. w/paper label, square
w/beveled corners, applied sloping
collared mouth, smooth base, 1860-
80, sunset pink puce, 10" h. .......... **3,850.00**

**Jones Universal Stomach Bitters -**
Manufactured by C.O. Jones & Co.
Williamsport, Penn, square
w/beveled corners, applied sloping
collared mouth, smooth base, 1860-
80, golden amber, 9⅛" h. (unearthed
w/overall stain & scratches) ................ **88.00**

**Kagy's Superior Stomach Bitters,**
rectangular w/beveled corners,
applied sloping collared mouth,
smooth base, 1860-80, golden
amber, 9½" h. (unearthed, light
overall stain) ...................................... **99.00**

*Kelly's Old Cabin Bitters*

**Kelly's Old Cabin Bitters -** Patented 1863, two story cabin-shape, applied sloping collared mouth, smooth base, dark olive-green, minor mouth roughness probably done during manufacture, ¼" shallow flake on base corner, 9⅝" h. (ILLUS.) ......... **6,050.00**

**Koch's (Dr. Med) Universal Magen Bitter,** square, applied sloping collared mouth, smooth base, 1880-1900, yellowish olive, 8¼" h. ............ **605.00**

**Lacour's Bitters -** Sarsapariphere, round, lettering in sunken side panels, applied mouth, smooth base, 1866-69, medium yellowish amber, 9⅜" h. (about perfect) ........ **1,150.00**

**Lacour's Bitters -** Sarsapariphere, round, lettering in sunken side panels, applied mouth, smooth base, 1870-73, pale yellowish green approaching clear color, 9⅛" h. (about perfect) ............................ **12,500.00**

**Landsberg's "Century" Bitters -** The Adler Company St. Louis, tall cylindrical neck, square w/panels around diamond shaped corners, one w/Eagle & one w/"1876" above diamond lattice border, applied sloping collared mouth, smooth base, 1860-80, golden amber, 11½" h. .......................................... **4,125.00**

**Langley's (Dr.) - Root & Herb Bitters -** J.O. Langley, proprietor, w/paper label, round, flared mouth, 8¾" h. (tubular pontil scar, retains 70% original reverse label) ........................ **77.00**

**Lawrence's Wild Cherry Bitters,** square w/beveled corners, applied sloping collared mouth, smooth base, 1860-80, yellowish amber, 9¼" h. (some exterior scratches) ........ **77.00**

**Lewis' Red Jacket Bitters -** New Haven, Conn., round, applied sloping collared mouth w/ring, smooth base, 1860-80, golden amber, 10⅞" h. ......... **72.00**

**Lippman's Great German Bitters -** Savannah Georgia, square, applied mouth, smooth base, 1875-85, yellowish amber, 10" h. (lightly cleaned to perfect condtion) ............. **575.00**

**Litthauer Stomach Bitters,** Invented 1864 by Josef Loewenthal, square tapered gin-shape, tooled sloping collared mouth, smooth base, 1860-80, clear, 7" h. ........................... **66.00**

**Loew's (Dr.) Celebrated Stomach Bitters & Nerve Tonic -** The Loew & Sons Co. Cleveland, O., square w/ribbed & swirled shoulder & neck, applied collared mouth w/ring, smooth base, 1870-90, brilliant yellowish green, 9¼" h. .................... **385.00**

**Loew's (Dr.) Celebrated Stomach Bitters and Nerve Tonic,** square w/beveled corners, tooled sloping collared mouth w/ring, smooth base, 1880-1900, golden amber, 3½" h. .... **209.00**

**Mackenzies (Dr.) Wild Cherry Bitters** Chicago, rectangular w/beveled fluted corners, tooled sloping collared mouth, smooth base, 1870-90, clear, 8¼" h. (minor interior stain) ..................................... **187.00**

**Magic Bitters** Prepared By Minetree & Jackson Petersburg, Va., round, tooled mouth, smooth base, 1880-90, amber, 7¾" h. (about perfect) ............ **575.00**

**Malakof Bitters,** N. Kieffer, N.O. - Patented Sept. 18th, 1866, cylindrical, sloping collared mouth w/ring, smooth base, 1840-60, deep golden amber, 11½" h. (unearthed, professionally cleaned, retains overall etching & roughness, ¼" buffed chip on base) ................... **468.00**

**Manly (Dr.) Hardy's - Boston - Jaundice Bitters,** rectangular w/beveled corners, tooled sloping collared mouth, smooth base, 1860-80, aqua, 7⅜" h. ....................... **44.00**

**Milburn's Kola Bitters** Made Only By Jas. A. Milburn & Co. Winchester, Va., rectangular, tooled mouth, smooth base, 1880-90, medium amber, 9½" h. .................................. **400.00**

*Jno. Moffat Phoenix Bitters*

*Old Sachem Bitters*

**Moffat (Jno.) - Price $1 - Phoenix Bitters -** New York, rectangular w/wide beveled corners, pontil scarred base, applied mouth, olive amber, 5½" h. (ILLUS.) .................... **688.00**

**Muller's Genuine Bismarck Bitters,** rectangular w/beveled corners, tooled mouth, smooth base, 1860-80, golden amber, 6¼" h. (unearthed, overall light stain & iridescence) ........................................ **55.00**

**National Bitters -** Patent 1867, figural ear of corn, applied sloping collared mouth w/ring, smooth base, 1860-80, brilliant aqua, 12⅝" h. ...... **3,575.00**

**New York Hop Bitters Company,** embossed flag, square, applied lip, aqua, 9½" h. ..................................... **325.00**

**Normandy Herb & Root Stomach Bitters,** w/paper label, square w/beveled corners, applied sloping collared mouth, smooth base, 1860-80, orangeish amber, 9⅛" h. (retains approximately 50% of original reverse label) ..................................... **88.00**

**Old Carolina Bitters -** Philip Wineman & Co, applied mouth, smooth base, 1875-85, yellowish amber, 9⅞" h. ............................... **1,150.00**

**Old Homestead Wild Cherry Bitters -** Patent (on shoulders), cabin-shape w/shingles, applied sloping collared mouth w/ring, fitted w/internal screw stopper of lighter green, smooth base, 1860-80, brilliant deep emerald green, 9⅞" h. ................. **33,000.00**

**Old Sachem Bitters and Wigwam Tonic,** barrel-shaped, ten-rib, light yellowish amber, 9½" h. (ILLUS.) .......................... **475.00 to 525.00**

**O'Leary's 20th Century Bitters,** square w/beveled corners, smooth base, tooled sloping collared mouth, golden amber, 8½" h. (some interior haze) ...................................................... **55.00**

**Oxygenated - For Dyspepsia** Asthma and General Debility - Bitters, rectangular w/beveled corners, applied sloping collared mouth, pontil scar, 1840-60, aqua, 6⅛" h. (unearthed w/light iridescent haze) .................................................. **60.50**

**Oxygenated - For Dyspepsia,** Asthma & General Debility - Bitters, w/paper label, rectangular w/beveled corners, applied sloping collared mouth, smooth base, 1860-80, aqua, ½ pt., 7⅝" h. (complete slightly soiled label on reverse) ..................... **55.00**

**Pendleton's - Pineapple Bitters -** Nashville, T., w/"L. & W." on smooth base, applied mouth, 1870-80, amber, 9" h. (about perfect) .......... **1,300.00**

**Pepsin Bitters -** Golden Gate Med. Co., rectangular w/beveled corners, tooled sloping collared mouth, smooth base, 1870-90, yellowish amber, 9⅛" h. (⅛" bruise on body near base, ¼" chip on body corner, two minor bubble bursts) ................... **94.00**

**Pepsin Calisaya Bitters -** Dr. Russell Med. Co., rectangular w/beveled corners, tooled sloping collared mouth, smooth base, 1870-90, amber, 4¼" h. (unearthed w/overall stain & etching) .................................... **66.00**

**Pepsin Calisaya Bitters -** Dr. Russell Med. Co., rectangular, three ribs on each bevel, green, pt., 7⅞" h. (faint spots inside cloud, pinhead flake on lip edge) ............................................. **95.00**

**Pepsin Calisya Bitters -** Dr. Russell Med. Co., rectangular, sloping collared mouth, smooth base, 1870-90, lime green, 7⅞" h. (light interior stain, some exterior scratches) .......... **22.00**

**Peruvian Bark Bitters -** New Orleans La - Dr. M. Perl & Co., square, applied mouth, smooth base, 1870-80, aqua, 8½" h. (light inside stain) .... **750.00**

**Peruvian Tonic - Bitters,** rectangular w/beveled roped corners, applied sloping collared mouth, smooth base, 1860-80, golden amber, 10" h. ......... **253.00**

**Petzold's (Dr.) Genuine German Bitters** Incept. 1862, oval log cabin-shape, tooled mouth w/ring, smooth base, golden amber 10⅝" h .............. **121.00**

**Peychaud's American Aromatic Cocktail Bitters,** paper label, cylindrical reddish amber, 6" h. (dug condition) ................................... **45.00**

**Prune Stomach and Liver Bitters -** The Best Cathartic and Blood Purifier, square w/rounded corners, sloping collared mouth, smooth base, 1860-80, golden amber, 9" h. ..................................................... **88.00**

**Quinine Tonic Bitters,** Manf. By Q.T.B. Chemical Co. Lexington, KY U.S.A. - Q.T.B., rectangular, tooled mouth, smooth base, 1860-80, clear, 8" h. (light interior stain) ...................... **61.00**

**Rattinger's (Dr.) Herb & Root Bitters,** St. Louis, Mo., square w/beveled corners, applied sloping collared mouth, smooth base, 1860-80, orangish amber, 9⅛" h. (some overall light wear, few pinhead flakes on edge of base) ................................ **66.00**

**Red Star Stomach Bitters,** Koehler & Hinrichs St. Paul. Minn. (in circle), round, tooled sloping collared mouth w/ring, smooth base, 1870-90, orangish amber, 11¼" h. (some faint areas of haze) ................................. **209.00**

**Renz's (Dr.) Herb Bitters,** square, applied mouth, smooth base, 1879-81, yellowish green w/hint of olive, 9⅞" h... **950.00**

**Ritmeier's (Wm.) - California Wine Bitters -** T.W. & Co., square w/beveled corners, applied sloping collared mouth, smooth base, 1860-80, golden amber, 9⅛" h. ................... **77.00**

**Roback's (Dr. C.W.) Stomach Bitters,** Cincinnati, O, barrel-shaped, iron pontil, whittling, 4" fold glass down inside left front, golden amber, 10" h. .................................... **450.00**

**Romany Wine Bitters,** rectangular w/beveled corners, tooled collared mouth, smooth base, 1860-90, aqua, 6½" h. ................................................. **44.00**

**Root's (John) Bitters -** Buffalo, N.Y. - 1834 (on two sides), rectangular w/beveled corners, modified cabin-shaped, applied sloping collared mouth w/ring, smooth base, 1860-80, medium bluish green, 10¼" h. (⅜" manufacturer's tooling mark on shoulder, ⅛" body bruise, ¼" potstone crack at base corner) ......... **770.00**

**Rosenbaum's Bitters -** San Francisco - N.B. Jacobs & Co., square, ampersand slants left, smooth base, 1860-69, peach color w/amber tone, 9⅞" h .................... **1,950.00**

**Royal Pepsin Stomach Bitters,** L & A Scharff Sole Agents St. Louis & Canada, rectangular, applied double collared mouth, smooth base, 1860-80, clear, 8¾" h ............... **83.00**

**Royal Pepsin Stomach Bitters,** L & A Scharff Sole Agents, St. Louis US & Canada, rectangular w/rounded corners, double collared mouth, smooth base, 1860-90, golden amber, 6⅜" h. ........................ **77.00**

*Russ' St. Domingo Bitters*

**Russ' St. Domingo Bitters -** New
York, square, indented panels, two
in-manufacture paper-thin open
bubbles, yellowish amber, 9⅞" h.
(ILLUS. bottom previous page) ......... **440.00**

**Salmon's Perfect Stomach Bitters,**
square w/beveled corners, tooled
sloping collared mouth, smooth
base, 1860-80, amber, 9½" h.
(unearthed, light overall stain) ............ **66.00**

**San Diego Wine Bitters,** round,
applied sloping collared mouth
w/ring, smooth base marked
"BFG&CO," 1860-80, shaded
yellowish amber, 10¼" h. (some
exterior stain & scratches) ............... **495.00**

**San Joaquin Wine Bitters,**
cylindrical, sloping collared mouth
w/ring, smooth base, 1860-80,
yellowish amber, 9¾" h. (unearthed
bottle, some scratches & light
stains) ............................................... **358.00**

**Schroeder's Bitter's** (below),
Established 1845 (above),
cylindrical, lady's leg neck, tooled
sloping collared mouth w/ring,
smooth base, 1860-80, amber, 9" h.
(unearthed, stained, etched, ⅛" flake
on side of mouth) ............................. **303.00**

**Schroeder's Bitters,** Louisville, KY -
KY G.W. Co., lady's leg neck,
amber, 9" h. ..................................... **300.00**

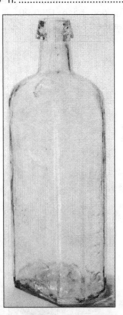

*Segur's Golden Seal Bitters*

**Segur's (G.C.) - Golden Seal Bitters**
- Springfield Mass., rectangular
w/beveled corners, open pontil, tiny lip
flake, ½" paper-thin open bubble,
aqua, 8¼" h. (ILLUS bottom previous
column.)............................................... **132.00**

**Severa (W.F.) - Stomach Bitters,**
square w/beveled corners, tooled
sloping collared mouth, smooth
base, 1860-80, golden amber,
9⅝" h. (some minor spots of interior
haze)................................................... **33.00**

**Simms (Dr.) Anti-Constipation
Bitters,** square w/beveled corners,
tooled sloping collared mouth,
smooth base, 1880-1900, reddish
amber, 9" h. (some exterior stain) .... **231.00**

*Simon's Centennial Bitters*

**Simon's Centennial Bitters -** Trade
Mark, figural bust of Washington on
pedestal, aqua, ¾ qt., 9¾" h.
(ILLUS.) ........................... **600.00 to 650.00**

**Sims' (Dr.) Anti-Constipation
Bitters,** square w/beveled corners,
tooled sloping collared mouth,
smooth base, 1880-1900, golden
amber, 7" h. ....................................... **77.00**

**Skinner's (Dr.) Celebrated 25 cents
Bitters,** So. Reading, Mass,
rectangular, rough pontil mark, aqua,
8½" h. ............................................... **275.00**

**Smyrna Stomach Bitters,** Prolongs
Life, Dayton, Ohio, square short
lady's leg neck, tooled mouth,
smooth base, 1860-80, golden
amber, 9" h. ..................................... **127.00**

**Solomon's Strengthening & Invigorating Bitters -** Savannah Georgia, square, applied mouth, smooth base, 1875-85, cobalt blue, 9¾" h. (professionally cleaned to original lustre, about perfect) ......... **1,250.00**

**Southern Aromatic Cock Tail Bitters,** J. Grossman New Orleans Sole Manufacturer, round, lady's leg neck, tooled mouth, smooth base, 1880-90, medium yellowish amber, 13" h. ............................... **350.00**

**Star Kidney and Liver Bitters,** square w/beveled corners, tooled sloping collared mouth, smooth base, 1860-80, golden amber, 8⅞" h. .................................. **55.00**

**Stewart's (Dr. H.C.) Tonic Bitters,** Columbus, O., rectangular, sheared mouth, smooth base, 1880-1900, orangish amber, 7¾" h. ..................... **55.00**

**Suffolk Bitters -** Philbrook & Tucker Boston, figural pig, double collared mouth, smooth base, yellow w/light olive tone, 10⅛" h. (⅛" very shallow bubble burst on nose) ....... **1,870.00**

**Sumter Bitters -** Dowie Moise & Davis Wholesale Druggists - Charlestown, S.C., square, applied mouth, smooth base, 1870-75, medium amber, 9⅞" h. (about perfect) ........................................... **575.00**

**Swiss Alpenkrauter Stomach Bitters,** w/paper label, "A.G.B. & S. Braem's Stomach Bitters and Tonic" embossed on base, round, lady's leg neck, applied mouth w/ring, smooth base, 1880-90, orangish amber, 11⅜" h. .............................................. **88.00**

**Swiss Stomach Bitters -** Arnold Koch, Birmingha, Pa., modified rectangular applied sloping collared mouth, smooth base, 1860-80, golden amber, 9⅜" h. (unearthed, light overall stain) ............................. **198.00**

**Tippecanoe XXX** Trade Mark Use No Nostrums Nor Preparations Called Bitters (on paper label), embossed Tippecanoe - H.H. Warner & Co., figural log form, applied mushroom mouth, smooth base, 1860-80, golden amber, 9" h. (ILLUS. top) ........ **72.00**

**Turner's Bitters,** oval, strapped sided, flared mouth, smooth base, 1860-80, clear, 8⅛" h. ...................... **66.00**

**Turner's Brazilian Bitters,** Philada, Pa., oval, strap-sided, flared mouth, smooth base, 1860-90, clear, 8" h. (overall interior haze) ......................... **66.00**

*Tippecanoe Bitters Bottle*

**Turner Brothers** New York, Buffalo, NY. San Francisco Cal., square, applied mouth, smooth base, 1861-68, shaded medium olive-green w/hint of yellow, shading darker in base & neck, 9½" h. .......................... **475.00**

**Tyree's (W.R.) - Chamomile - Bitters -** 1 - 8 - 8 - 0, square, semi-cabin shaped, applied mouth, smooth base, 1870-75, amber, 9½" h. .......... **425.00**

**Uncle Toms Bitters -** Thomas Foulds & Son - Trevorton Pa, square w/beveled corners, applied sloping collared mouth w/ring, smooth base, 1860-80, yellowish amber, 10" h. ..... **605.00**

**Utica - Hop - Bitters -** JKB & CO, square, applied sloping collared mouth, smooth base, Australia 1860-80, aqua, 9½" h. (unearthed, overall haze) ................................................. **77.00**

**Van Dyke Bitters Co.,** Proprietors St. Louis, U.S.A. - Dr. Van Dyke's Medicated Benedictus Gin Trade Mark Registered, square tapered gin shape, tooled sloping collared mouth w/ring, smooth base, 1880-1900, clear, 11" h. (light interior haze) .......... **88.00**

**Vigo Bitters,** square w/beveled corners, tooled sloping collared mouth, smooth base, 1860-80, golden amber, 9½" h. .......................... **60.50**

**Wakefield's Strengthening Bitters,** w/paper label, rectangular w/beveled corners, tooled sloping collared mouth, smooth base, 1860-80, aqua, 8" h. (full label on bottle reverse) ........ **77.00**

**Wallace's. Tonic Stomach Bitters -** L & W, square w/beveled corners, applied sloping collared mouth, smooth base, 1860-80, golden amber, 9⅛" h. .................................... **44.00**

**Wallace's Tonic Stomach Bitters -** Geo. Powell & Co, Chicago Ill, square w/beveled corners, applied sloping collared mouth, smooth base, 1860-80, orangish amber, 9" h.. **143.00**

**Wampoo Bitters -** Siegel & Bro, New York, rectangular w/beveled corners, applied sloping collared mouth, smooth base, 1860-80, golden amber, 9⅝" h. (unearthed, overall stain) ..................................................... **66.00**

**Warren's (Dr.) Universal Tonic Bitters** Steles & Devens Company Fond Du Lac Wis., square w/beveled corners, tooled sloping collared mouth, smooth base, 1870-90, light yellowish amber, 8¼" h. ...... **660.00**

**Warner's Safe Bitters** (above), safe w/"Trade Mark," Rochester. N.Y. (below) - A. & D.H.C., oval applied collared mouth, smooth base, 1860-80, golden amber, 7½" h. (pin point flake on mouth) ................................. **495.00**

**Warren's (Old Dr.) - Quaker Bitters -** Flint & Co. Prov. R.I., rectangular, aqua, 9¾" h. (some light haze & small base flake) ................................. **65.00**

**W.C. Bitters -** Brobst & Rentschler, Reading, PA., barrel-shaped, amber, 10⅝" h. (shallow lip flake) ................ **575.00**

**W.C. Bitters -** Brobst & Rentschler Reading, Pa., barrel-shape, tooled mouth w/ring, smooth base, 1860-80, yellowish amber, 10⅝" h. (⅛" flat flake on side of mouth) ............... **468.00**

**Weis' (Dr. Henry F.) Guard on the Rhine Stomach Bitters,** Dayton, Ohio - W.T. Co., U.S.A., square w/beveled corners, flared mouth, smooth base, 1860-80, golden amber, 9" h. .................................... **143.00**

**Wheeler's Genuine Bitters,** oval, applied sloping collared mouth w/ring, smooth base, 1860-80, light green, 8¾" h. .................................... **468.00**

**White's - Stomach - Bitters,** square w/beveled corners, applied mouth, smooth base, 1860-80, golden amber, 9½" h. .................................... **55.00**

**Wilson & Black's Best Stomach Bitters,** square w/beveled corners, applied sloping collared mouth, smooth base, 1860-80, orange-amber, 9⅛" h. (minor exterior stain) ................................................. **143.00**

**Woodcock Pepsin Bitters -** John H. Schroeder, rectangular w/beveled corners, sloping collared mouth, smooth base, 1870-90, 8" h. (light interior stain) ..................................... **66.00**

**Yerba Buena - Bitters,** S.F. Cal., flask-shaped, amber, 8½" h. (dug) ..... **75.00**

**Yerba Buena - Bitters,** S.F. Cal., flask-shaped, applied sloping collared mouth w/ring, smooth base, 1860-80, yellowish amber w/olive tone, pt. (pinhead body flake, minor interior stain spots, ⅛" shallow flake on base edge)................................. **110.00**

**Zingari Bitters -** F. Rahter (embossed on shoulders), cylindrical, lady's leg neck, amber, 12" h. . ........ **250.00 to 300.00**

## FIGURALS

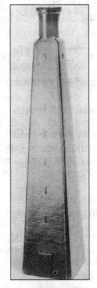

*Bunker Hill Monument Bottle*

**Bunker Hill Monument,** tooled lip, smooth base, ca. 1870, rich purple amethyst, 8" h. (ILLUS.) ............... **1,100.00**

**Cannon,** embossed "A.M. Bininger & Co. 19 Broad St. N.Y.," w/paper label, ca. 1870, medium amber glass, 12⅜" h. (ILLUS. top next page) ............................................. **3,850.00**

*Figural Cannon Bottle*

**Cherub** holding a medallion on his shoulder w/pressed wheel stopper in the short cylindrical neck, tooled lip, American made, ca. 1890-1910, medium purple-amethyst, 11" h. ............................... **180.00 to 200.00**

*Grant's Tomb Figural Bottle*

**Grant's Tomb,** figural monument base in milk white glass fitted w/pewter cap topped by a bust finial of U.S. Grant, 10" h. (ILLUS.) ........... **633.00**

## FLASKS

*Flasks are listed according to the numbers provided in* American Bottles & Flasks and Their Ancestry *by Helen McKearin and Kenneth M. Wilson.*

**GI-14 -** Washington bust below "General Washington" - American Eagle w/shield w/seven bars on breast, head turned to right, "E Pluribus Unum" in semi-circle above, vertically ribbed edges w/"Adams & Jefferson July 4, A.D. 1776" & "Kensington Glassworks Philadelphia," sheared mouth, pontil scar, 1820-38, aqua, pt. (faint interior haze, ¼" bruise on top of mouth) ......... **240.00**

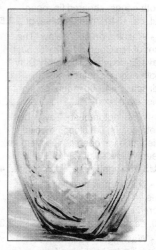

*Washington Fells Point Flask*

**GI-21 -** Washington bust (facing right) below "Fells," "Point" below bust - Washington Monument w/"Balto" below, sheared mouth, pontil scar, 1830-50, clear w/amethystine tint, qt., (ILLUS. bottom previous page)... **209.00**

**GI-32 -** "Washington" above bust, uniform without bars on lapel - "Jackson" above bust, sheared mouth, pontil scar, 1830-50, forest green, pt. (⅜" flat flake on side of mouth, embossed lettering weaker than usual) ...................................... **140.00**

**GI-33 -** "Washington" above bust, uniform without bars on lapel - "Jackson" above bust, sheared mouth, pontil scar, 1830-48, deep yellowish olive, pt. (exterior high point wear)............................................... **140.00**

**GI-38 -** Washington bust below "The Father of His Country" - Taylor bust, "Gen. Taylor Never Surrenders, Dyottville Glass Works, Philad.a." sheared lip, smooth base, ca. 1870, olive-yellow, pt. ............................... **880.00**

**GI-39 -** Washington bust below "The Father of His Country" - Taylor bust, "Gen. Taylor Never Surrenders," plain lip, smooth edges, pontil scar, 1840-60, brilliant rich medium yellow-green, qt. ......................................... **660.00**

**GI-42 -** Washington bust below "The Father of His Country" - Taylor bust, "A Little More Grape Captain Bragg, Dyottville Glass Works, Philad.a," smooth edges, sheared lip, open pontil, ca. 1840, medium blue, qt... **3,575.00**

**GI-44 -** Washington bust below "The Father of His Country" - Taylor bust, "I Have Endeavor'd To Do My Duty," smooth edges, sheared mouth, pontil scar, 1840-60, aqua, pt. (light interior stain ring) ............................... **40.00**

**GI-51 -** Washington bust - Taylor bust, smooth edges, flat slopping collar, applied blob lip, open pontil, medium to deep yellowish green, qt. (ILLUS. top right) ............................ **468.00**

**GI-54 -** Washington bust without queue - Taylor bust in uniform, sheared lip, open pontil, ca. 1840, deep wine amethyst, qt........ **2,310.00**

**GI-54 -** Washington bust without queue - Taylor bust in uniform, applied tapered collar, smooth base, ca. 1840, olive-yellow, qt. (mint w/little high-point wear) .................... **495.00**

*Washington-Taylor Flask*

**GI-54a -** Washington bust without queue - Taylor bust in uniform, sheared mouth, pontil scar, 1840-60, light yellowish green, qt. (minor exterior high point wear) .................. **210.00**

**GI-55c -** Washington bust w/short queue & plain toga - Dyottville Glass Works Philad.A, Taylor bust w/tie, applied sloping collared mouth, pontil scar, 1840-60, light green, pt. .... **187.00**

**GI-74 -** Taylor bust, facing right, w/"Zachary Taylor" above & "Rough & Ready" below - "Corn for the World" above cornstalk, vertically ribbed edges, sheared lip, open pontil, ca.1840, aqua, pt. (interior surface bubble burst, no harm)...... **1,375.00**

**GI-76 -** American Eagle w/shield w/five vertical bars, head turned right, above ten large five-pointed stars in semicircle above eagle standing on oval frame w/inner band of nineteen pearls - Taylor bust below "Rough and Ready.," ribbed sides, bluish aqua, pt. (ILLUS. top next page)...................................... **3,575.00**

**GI-80 -** "Lafayette" above & "T.S." & bar below - "DeWitt Clinton" above bust & "Coventry C-T" below, inward rolled mouth, pontil scar, 1824-25, light olive-yellow, pt. (exterior highpoint wear) ................................. **475.00**

**GI-81 -** "Lafayette" semicircle above bust & "S & C" below - "DeWitt Clinton" above bust & "C-T" below, sheared mouth, pontil scar, 1824-25, light yellow w/olive tone, ½ pt. (½" crack in corrugated sides near medial rib to left of Lafayette's head)............. **500.00**

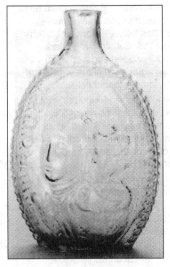

*Taylor - Eagle Flask*

**GI-86** - "Lafayette" above bust & "Coventry - C-T" below - French liberty cap on pole & semicircle of eleven five-pointed stars above, "S & S" below, fine vertical ribbing, two horizontal ribs at base, sheared mouth, pontil scar, 1824-25, yellowish olive, ½ pt. (¼" bruise on base ring) .......................................... **225.00**

**GI-86** - "Lafayette" above bust & "Coventry C-T" below - French liberty cap on pole & semicircle of eleven five-pointed stars above, "S&S" below, fine vertical ribbing, two horizontal ribs at base, sheared mouth, pontil scar, 1824-25, yellowish amber w/olive tone, ½ pt. ................. **468.00**

**GI-87** - "Lafayette" above bust & "Coventry C-T" below - French liberty cap on pole in oval frame w/"S&S" below, fine vertical ribbing, two horizontal ribs at base, sheared mouth, pontil scar, 1824-25, light yellowish olive, ½ pt. ...................... **4,400.00**

**GI-99** - "Jenny Lind" above bust - View of Glasshouse w/"Glass Works" above & "Huffsey" below, calabash, smooth sides, applied sloping collared mouth w/ring, pontil scar, emerald green, qt. ............................ **990.00**

**GI-99** - "Jenny Lind" above bust - View of Glasshouse w/"Glass Works" above & "Huffsey" below, calabash, smooth sides, applied sloping collared mouth, pontil scar, yellowish green, qt. (minor interior haze spots) .. **220.00**

**GI-104** - "Jeny (sic) Lind" above bust - View of glasshouse, calabash, vertically ribbed edges, applied collared mouth, pontil scar, 1845-60, root beer amber, qt. (two ⅛" manufacturer's annealing lines or stretch marks in one of vertical ribs) ............................................. **12,100.00**

**GI-107** - "Jenny Lind" above bust - View of Glasshouse w/"Fislerville Glass Works" above, calabash, vertically fluted edges, applied sloping collared mouth w/ring, pontil scar, 1845-60, aqua, qt. ..................... **33.00**

*American Eagle - Sunburst Flask*

**GII-7** - American Eagle w/head turned left, w/shield w/five vertical bars on breast, six small stars above eagle - large circular sunburst w/32 rays, beaded borders, open pontil, emerald green, pt. (ILLUS.) ........ **17,600.00**

**GII-22** - American Eagle above oval, ribbon & two semicircular rows of stars above, oval w/elongated eight-point star - large lyre w/two semi-circular rows of fourteen four-pointed stars above, sheared mouth, pontil scar, light green, pt. (manufacturer's pontil chip comes out to side of bottle) ............................................... **770.00**

**GII-26** - American Eagle above stellar motif obverse & reverse, horizontally corrugated edges, plain lip, tooled mouth, pontil scar, 1850-55, aqua, qt. ...................................................... **132.00**

**GII-26 -** American Eagle above stellar motif, obverse & reverse, horizontally corrugated edges, sheared lip, iron pontil base, ca. 1860, medium yellowish olive, qt. (mint, little high point wear)............ **2,090.00**

**GII-40 -** American Eagle on oval, obverse & reverse, heavy vertical ribbing, short, sheared neck, pontil, emerald green, pt. ........................... **660.00**

**GII-43 -** American Eagle w/head turned to right, large shield w/six bars on breast, sunrays above head, on oval frame w/pearls & "T.W.D." - Cornucopia w/produce, vertically ribbed edges w/"E Pluribus Unum - One of Many, Kesington Glass Works Philadelphia," plain lip, pontil mark, bright green, ½ pt. ................... **155.00**

**GII-45 -** American Eagle on oval w/"T.W.D." - Cornucopia filled w/produce, tip coiled to left & terminating in floral motif, vertically ribbed edges, sheared mouth, plain lip, pontil scar, 1830-60, aqua, ½ pt. .. **264.00**

**GII-49 -** American Eagle on oval - Stag w/antlers w/"Coffin & Hay" above in semicircle, "Hammonton" below in semicircle, sheared mouth, pontil scar, 1836-47, striated clambroth color, pt. ........................ **1,760.00**

*American Eagle - U.S. Flag Flask*

**GII-52 -** American Eagle w/shield & olive branches below - "For Our Country" below U.S. flag w/twenty stars, vertically ribbed edges, plain lip, open pontil, golden amber, pt. (ILLUS.) ........................................ **2,530.00**

**GII-53 -** American Eagle w/head erect & turned right, on shield w/olive branches below - "For Our Country" below U.S. flag w/twenty stars, vertically ribbed edge, plain lip, open pontil, aqua, pt. (light interior stain, minor mouth roughness)..................... **94.00**

**GII-54 -** American Eagle on Shield w/olive branches below - "For Our Country" below U.S. flag w/twenty stars, vertically ribbed edges, plain lip, open pontil, aqua, pt. (light interior haze)................................... **110.00**

**GII-61 -** American Eagle below "Liberty" - "Willington Glass, Co. West Willington Conn," smooth edges, sheared mouth, pontil scar, smooth base, 1840-72, green, pt. (½" shoulder bruise) ........................ **85.00**

**GII-61 -** American Eagle below "Liberty" - inscribed in four lines, "Willington - Glass, Co - West Willington - Conn," smooth edges, applied double collared mouth, smooth base, 1860-72, yellowish amber, qt. ....................................... **220.00**

**GII-61 -** American Eagle below "Liberty" - inscribed in four lines, "Willington - Glass, Co - West Willington - Conn," smooth edges, applied double collared mouth, smooth base, 1860-72, yellowish amber w/olive tone, qt. (½" fissures at medial rib near base)..................... **70.00**

**GII-62 -** American Eagle below "Liberty" - inscription in four lines "Willington - Glass, Co - West, Willington - Conn," smooth edges, applied round collared mouth, smooth base, 1860-72, deep yellowish olive, pt. (¼" bubble burst on collared mouth, weakened impression) ...................................... **99.00**

**GII-62 -** American Eagle below "Liberty" - inscription in four lines "Willington - Glass, Co - West, Willington - Conn," smooth edges, applied double collared mouth, smooth base, 1860-72, yellowish olive, pt. (interior residue that should wash out w/soap & water, embossing particularly strong).......... **154.00**

**GII-63 -** American Eagle below "Liberty" - inscription in five lines, "Willington - Glass - Co. - West Willington - Conn.," smooth edges, plain lip, deep olive-green, ½ pt. (ILLUS. top next page) ..................... **83.00**

*American Eagle & Liberty Flask*

**GII-63 -** American Eagle below "Liberty" - inscription in five lines "Willington - Glass - Co - West Willington - Conn," smooth edges, applied double collared mouth, smooth base, 1860-72, forest green, ½ pt. .................................. **130.00**

**GII-63 -** American Eagle below "Liberty" - inscription in five lines "Willington - Glass - Co - West Willington - Conn," smooth edges, applied double collared mouth, smooth base, 1860-72, olive-green, ½ pt. .................................. **187.00**

**GII-64 -** American Eagle below "Liberty" - inscription in four lines, "Willington - Glass, Co - West Willington - Conn," smooth edges, plain lip, pontil, golden amber, pt. .................................... **135.00 to 185.00**

**GII-64 -** American Eagle below "Liberty" - inscription in four lines, "Willington - Glass, Co - West Willington - Conn," smooth edges, applied sloping collared mouth, pontil scar, smooth base, 1840-72, green, qt. (¾" flat chips along top of mouth) ............................................ **85.00**

**GII-64 -** American Eagle below "Liberty" - inscription in four lines, "Willington - Glass, Co - West Willington - Conn," smooth edges, applied round collared mouth, smooth base, 1860-72, yellowish amber, pt. (some exterior high point wear) ................................................ **170.00**

**GII-64 -** American Eagle below "Liberty" inscription in four lines "Willington - Glass, Co - West Willington - Conn," smooth edges, plain lip, broad sloping collar, smooth base, 1860-72, yellowish olive, pt. (impression slightly weak) .. **165.00**

**GII-65 -** American Eagle below "Liberty" - inscription in five lines "Westford - Glass - Co - Westford - Conn," smooth edges, applied double collared mouth, smooth base, pontil scar, 1860-73, deep olive-amber, ½ pt. ............................. **165.00**

**GII-65 -** American Eagle below "Liberty" - inscription in five lines "Westford - Glass - Co - Westford - Conn," smooth edges, double collared mouth, smooth base, 1860-73, yellowish olive, ½ pt. .......... **120.00**

**GII-71 -** American Eagle lengthwise, obverse & reverse, plain lip, vertically ribbed, pontil, olive-amber, ½ pt. (very light scratches) ............... **253.00**

**GII-73 -** American Eagle w/head turned to the right & standing on rocks - Cornucopia w/produce & "X" on left, vertically ribbed edges, sheared mouth, pontil scar, light yellowish olive, pt. ............................. **143.00**

**GII-73 -** American Eagle w/head turned to the right & standing on rocks - Cornucopia w/produce & "X" on left, vertically ribbed edges, plain lip, pontil scar, 1830-50, yellowish olive, pt. ........................... **100.00 to 150.00**

**GII-79 -** American Eagle above oval obverse & reverse, edges w/single vertical rib, sheared mouth, pontil scar, 1846-1850, yellowish olive-amber, qt. (¼" bubble burst on base of flask) ................................... **130.00**

**GII-86 -** American Eagle above oval obverse & reverse, vertically ribbed edges, plain lip, pontil scar, 1850-60, yellowish amber w/olive tone, ½ pt. .... **99.00**

**GII-87 -** American Eagle above oval obverse & reverse, "X" in oval frame on obverse, plain lip, pontil scar, 1850-60, forest green, ½ pt. ............. **440.00**

**GII-106 -** American Eagle above oval obverse & reverse, w/"Pittsburgh, PA" in oval on obverse, narrow vertical rib on edges, applied mouth w/ring, smooth base, 1860-80, yellowish olive, pt. (faint interior residue) ............................................ **160.00**

**GII-107 -** American Eagle above oval obverse & reverse, w/"Pittsburgh, PA" in oval obverse, narrow vertical rib, applied string lip, smooth base, ca. 1870, dark olive-green, pt. .......... **187.00**

**GII-113 -** American Eagle above oval obverse & reverse, w/"Pittsburgh, PA, McC & Co" in oval obverse & reverse, smooth edges, applied mouth w/ring, smooth base, 1860-80, dark reddish amber, pt. (some interior haze).................................... **270.00**

**GII-128 -** American Eagle above oval w/head turned to left obverse & reverse, smooth edges, applied collared mouth, smooth base, probably Pittsburgh, Pennsylvania district, 1860-80, yellow w/light olive tone, ½ pt. (unearthed, overall stain & ⅛" bubble burst on eagle's body)... **660.00**

**GII-143 -** American Eagle w/plain shield in talons & pennant in beak, calabash, four vertical flutes on edges, applied double collared mouth, pontil scar, aqua, qt. ............. **149.00**

**GIII-4 -** Cornucopia with Produce - Urn with Produce, vertically ribbed edges, inward rolled mouth, pontil scar, 1830-48, deep yellowish olive, pt...................................................... **88.00**

**GIII-4 -** Cornucopia with Produce - Urn with Produce, vertically ribbed edges, plain lip, 1830-48, light yellowish olive, pt. .............................. **99.00**

*Cornucopia - Urn Flask*

**GIII-7 -** Cornucopia with Produce - Urn with Produce, vertically ribbed edges, sheared lip, pontil, deep yellowish olive-amber, ½ pt. (ILLUS.) .............................................. **99.00**

**GIII-7 -** Cornucopia with Produce - Urn with Produce, vertically ribbed edges, sheared lip, pontil, olive amber, ½ pt..................................... **110.00**

**GIII-7 -** Cornucopia with Produce - Urn with Produce, vertically ribbed edges, sheared mouth, pontil scar, New England, 1830-60, olive-amber painted w/black & gold paint, ½ pt. (some minor paint loss) .................... **110.00**

**GIII-7 -** Cornucopia with Produce - Urn with Produce, vertically ribbed edges, sheared lip, pontil, yellowish olive-green, ½ pt. .............................. **99.00**

**GIII-15 -** Cornucopia Produce - Urn with Produce, vertically ribbed edge, plain lip, pontil mark, light green, ½ pt. (minuscule inner lip chip) .......... **110.00**

**GIII-16 -** Cornucopia with Produce & curled to right - Urn with Produce & w/"Lancaster.Glass Works, N.Y" above, sheared mouth, vertically ribbed edges, iron pontil, bluish aqua, pt............................................. **308.00**

**GIII-17 -** Cornucopia with Produce & curled right - Urn with Produce, plain lip, double rounded collar, iron pontil, aqua, pt............................................. **130.00**

**GIII-17 -** Cornucopia with Produce & curled right - Urn with Produce, plain lip, double rounded collar, iron pontil, emerald green, pt. ........................... **715.00**

**GIII-18 -** Cornucopia with Produce and curled to right - Urn with Produce, vertically ribbed edges, sheared mouth, pontil scar, 1830-60, light bluish green, pt. (potstone w/¼" radiations in neck) ........................... **358.00**

**GIV-1 -** Masonic Emblems - American Eagle w/ribbon reading "E Pluribus Unum" above & "IP" (old fashioned "J") below in oval frame, tooled mouth, five vertical ribs, medium bluish green, pt. ............................... **260.00**

**GIV-1a -** Masonic Emblems - American Eagle w/ribbon reading "E Pluribus Unum" above & "IP" (old fashioned "J") below in oval frame, inward rolled mouth, vertically ribbed, pontil scar, 1820-30, bright bluish green, pt. .............................. **325.00**

**GIV-17 -** Masonic Arch, pillars & pavement w/Masonic emblems - American Eagle w/oval frame enclosing "KEENE" below, smooth edges w/single vertical rib, plain lip, pontil scar, 1820-30, yellowish amber w/olive tone, pt.................................. **187.00**

**GIV-18 -** Masonic Arch, pillars & pavement w/Masonic emblems - American Eagle without shield on breast, plain oval frame below w/"KCCNC" inside, smooth edges w/single vertical rib, sheared mouth, pontil scar, 1820-30, yellowish amber w/olive tone, pt. ................................. **176.00**

**GIV-19 -** Masonic Arch, pillars & pavement w/Masonic emblems - American Eagle without shield on breast, plain oval frame below w/"KCCNC" inside, smooth w/single vertical rib, sheared mouth, pontil scar, 1820-30, olive-amber, pt. (some exterior high point wear) ........ **132.00**

**GIV-24 -** Masonic Arch, pillars & pavement w/Masonic emblems - American Eagle grasping large balls in talons & without shield on breast, plain oval frame below, smooth edges w/single medial rib, sheared mouth, pontil scar, 1820-30, olive-amber, ½ pt. (1" fissure in neck) ........ **80.00**

**GIV-24 -** Masonic Arch, pillars & pavement w/Masonic emblems - American Eagle grasping large balls in talons & without shield on breast, plain oval frame below, smooth edges w/single medial rib, inward rolled mouth, pontil scar, 1820-30, yellowish olive, ½ pt. (impression slightly weak) ................................... **154.00**

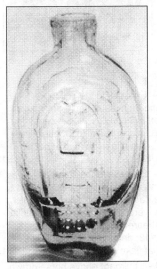

*Masonic Arch - Eagle Flask*

**GIV-26 -** Masonic Arch, pillars & pavement w/Masonic emblems - American Eagle grasping arrows & leaves in talons & without shield on breast, oval frame below w/"NEG," vertically ribbed edges, aqua, ½ pt. (ILLUS. bottom previous column) .. **1,100.00**

**GIV-28 -** Masonic Arch, pillars w/ribbing & pavement w/Masonic emblems obverse & reverse, plain lip, pontil, bluish green, ½ pt. (moldseam roughness, light interior stain) ................................................. **215.00**

*Masonic Arch Flask*

**GIV-28a -** Masonic Arch, pillars & pavement w/Masonic emblems obverse & reverse, arch & pillars without fluting, plain lip, pontil, light to medium bluish green, slight high-point wear, ½ pt. (ILLUS.) ................. **308.00**

**GIV-32 -** Masonic Arch w/"Farmer's Arms," sheaf of rye & farm implements within arch - American Eagle w/shield w/seven bars on breast, head turned to right, "Zanesville" above, eagle stands on oval frame w/"Ohio" inside & "J. Shepard & Co." beneath, vertically ribbed edge, open pontil, yellowish amber, pt. ...................... **500.00 to 1,000.00**

**GIV-37 -** Masonic Arch w/"Farmer's Arms" & sheaf of rye & farm implements within arch & "Kesington

Glass Works  Philadelphia" around edge - American Eagle w/shield w/seven bars on breast, head turned to right, on oval frame w/"T.W.D." inside, sheared lip, open pontil base, ca. 1850, aqua, pt............................ **330.00**

**GIV-40** - Clasped hands above square & compass all inside shield w/"Union" above shield - American Eagle carrying plain shield above "H&S" in oval frame, smooth edges, applied square collared mouth, pontil scar, 1860-80, aqua, pt.................... **154.00**

**GV-1b** - "Success to the Railroad" around embossed locomotive - similar reverse, sheared mouth, pontil scar, 1849-60, deep yellowish olive, pt. (1½" crack in each medial rib, ¾" spider crack on one panel above the T in "To") ........................ **500.00**

**GV-1b** - "Success to the Railroad" around embossed locomotive - similar reverse, sheared mouth, pontil scar, 1849-60, pale cornflower blue, pt. (¼" shallow chip on top of mouth, ½" crack in neck, other minor mouth roughness)............................ **140.00**

*Railroad Flask GV-3*

**GV-3** - "Success to the Railroad" around embossed horse pulling cart - similar reverse, sheared lip, pontil scar, 1830-50, light yellowish amber, pt. (ILLUS.) ..................................... **605.00**

**GV-3** - "Success to the Railroad" around embossed horse pulling cart - similar reverse, sheared lip, pontil scar, 1830-50, light yellowish olive, pt............................................................. **167.00**

**GV-5** - "Success to the Railroad" around embossed horse pulling cart - similar reverse, sheared mouth, pontil scar, vertically ribbed edges, Mount Vernon Glass Works, 1830-44, aqua, pt. ........................... **440.00**

**GV-5** - "Success to the Railroad" around embossed horse pulling cart - similar reverse, sheared mouth, pontil scar, vertically ribbed edges, 1830-44, forest green, pt. (⅛" flat flake on side of mouth) .................... **495.00**

**GV-5** - "Success to the Railroad" around embossed horse pulling cart - similar reverse, plain lip, pontil scar, 1830-48, yellowish olive, pt. (brilliant & crisp) ............................... **523.00**

*Railroad Flask GV-6*

**GV-6** - "Success to the Railroad" around embossed horse pulling cart obverse & reverse, w/"Success" above scene, plain lip, pontil, olive-amber, tiny flake on medial rib, pt. (ILLUS.) .......................................... **132.00**

**GV-9** - "Success to the Railroad" around embossed horse pulling cart - large eagle & seventeen five-pointed stars, vertically ribbed, heavy medial rib, sheared mouth, pontil scar, 1830-48, deep yellowish olive, pt. (⅛" flat flake on top of mouth)........... **150.00**

**GV-10** - "Railroad" above horse-drawn cart on rail & "Lowell" below - American Eagle lengthwise & thirteen five-pointed stars, vertically ribbed edges, sheared lip, pontil, yellowish olive, ½ pt. ....................... **200.00 to 250.00**

**GVI-4 -** "Baltimore" Monument - "Corn For The World" in semicircle above ear of corn, smooth edges, applied collared mouth, smooth base, 1860-80, brilliant medium bluish green, qt. (minor interior residue) .................. **1,980.00**

**GVI-6 -** "Baltimore" below monument - "Corn For the World" in semicircle above ear of corn, sheared mouth, pontil scar, 1840-60, aqua, pt. .......... **160.00**

**GVII-1 -** Log cabin w/hipped roof, rectangular, door at center w/window either side, "Tippecanoe" above door, cider barrel beneath right window - "Northbend" above door, applied short sloping collared mouth w/ring, pontil scar, ca. 1840, brilliant forest green, pt. (pin-sized hole in upper left hand corner above the "N" in North & ¼" spider crack on top log at roof level at one end of cabin) ......................................... **16,500.00**

**GVIII-2 -** Sunburst w/twenty-four triangular sectioned rays obverse & reverse, sheared lip, open pontil, New England, ca. 1815, grass green, pt. ......................................... **523.00**

**GVIII-5 -** Sunburst w/twenty-four rounded rays obverse & reverse, two dotted concentric rings enclosing medium size dot, horizontal corrugated edges, sheared lip, open pontil, possibly Pitkin Glassworks, ca. 1815, olive-amber shading to olive-green, pt. ................................ **825.00**

*Sunburst Flask*

**GVIII-7 -** Sunburst w/twenty-four rounded rays - similar but center circle fainter, horizontal corrugated edges, plain lip, pontil mark, olive-amber, pt. (ILLUS. bottom previous column) ............................................ **743.00**

**GVIII-26 -** Sunburst w/sixteen rays obverse & reverse, ray converging to a definite point at center & covering entire side of flask, horizontally corrugated edges, sheared mouth, pontil scar, 1820-30, brilliant yellow w/faint amber tone, pt. (faint ⅜" vertical hairline crack near medial rib) ................................................. **2,640.00**

**GIX-1 -** Scroll w/two six-point stars, both large, obverse & reverse, plain, tall neck, sheared mouth, pontil scar, aqua, qt. ............................................. **187.00**

**GIX-2 -** Scroll w/two six-point stars obverse & reverse, vertical medial rib, long neck w/sheared mouth, pontil scar, 1845-1860, light yellowish olive, pt. ............................ **880.00**

*Rare Blue Scroll Flask*

**GIX-2 -** Scroll w/two six-point stars obverse & reverse, vertical medial rib, long neck w/plain lip, sapphire blue, tiny mouth flake, qt., 9" h. (ILLUS.) ......................................... **2,310.00**

**GIX-6 -** Scroll w/two six-point stars obverse & reverse, one side w/"Louisville KY," the other w/"Glassworks," vertical medial rib, plain lip, pontil mark, light yellowish green, qt. ......................................... **270.00**

**GIX-10 -** Scroll w/two eight-point stars obverse & reverse, rolled lip, iron pontil, possibly Lancaster Glass Works, NY, ca. 1850, golden amber, pt......................................................... **523.00**

**GIX-48 -** Distorted octagon w/ "M'Carty & Torreyson" semicircle, five-pointed star within eight-pointed star, "Manufacturers," "Wellsburg, VA," in semi-circle below - large sunburst w/twenty-four rays from concentric rings at center, plain lip, ca. 1850 aqua, pt............................................. **990.00**

**GX-1 -** Stag standing above "Good Game" - weeping willow tree, vertically ribbed edges, sheared mouth, pontil scar, 1836-47, aqua, pt......................................................... **170.00**

**GX-8 -** Sailboat (sloop) w/pennant on waves - eight-point star w/three-pointed ornaments, vertically ribbed sides, sheared mouth, pontil scar, 1840-60, bluish green, ½ pt. (interior stain, exterior wear) ........................... **198.00**

**GX-15 -** "Summer" Tree - "Winter" Tree, smooth edges, applied double collared mouth, pontil scar, 1840-60, pale green, pt.................................... **187.00**

**GX-18 -** Spring Tree (leaves & buds) - Summer Tree, smooth edges, tooled mouth, smooth base, 1840-60, aqua, qt. (two ⅛" flat chips on mouth) .......... **65.00**

**GXI-7 -** "Pike's Peak" above prospector w/tools & cane walking left on oval frame - American Eagle w/pennant above large oval frame, applied collared mouth w/ring, smooth base, 1860-80, deep greenish aqua, qt. (faint interior haze spots)....................... **66.00**

**GXI-8 -** "For Pike's Peak" above prospector w/tools & cane standing on oblong frame w/"Old Rye" - American Eagle w/pennant above frame w/"Pittsburg PA.," applied lip, smooth base, ca. 1870, aqua, qt. ..... **165.00**

**GXI-16 -** Prospector w/tools & cane, large broad head, large eye, stocky body, walking left - American Eagle w/pennant & oval frame, inscribed "WMcC & Co." at top above space between "Glass" & "Works" over "Pitts.PA" at bottom, smooth base, aqua, pt. (ILLUS top next column) .... **264.00**

**GXI-22 -** "For Pike's Peak" above prospector w/short staff & pack standing on oblong frame - American Eagle w/long narrow pennant above oblong frame, aqua, pt........................ **99.00**

*Prospector with Tools Flask*

**GXI-22 -** "For Pike's Peak" above prospector w/short staff & pack standing on oblong frame - American Eagle w/long narrow pennant above oblong frame, applied collared mouth w/ring, smooth base, 1860-80., medium golden amber, pt. (minor interior stain)................................................. **825.00**

**GXI-27 -** "For Pike's Peak" above prospector w/tools & cane standing on oblong frame - American Eagle w/pennant above frame, applied collared mouth w/ring, 1860-80, aqua, pt. (weak embossing) .............. **90.00**

**GXI-30 -** "For Pike's Peak" above prospector w/tools & cane standing on oblong frame - American Eagle w/pennant above frame, applied collared mouth w/ring, smooth base, 1860-80, aqua, qt. ............................ **90.00**

**GXI-31 -** "For Pike's Peak" above prospector w/tools & cane standing on oblong frame - American Eagle w/pendant above frame, sheared mouth, pontil scar, 1850-60, deep aqua, pt. (two ⅛" chips inside sheared mouth, interior stain) .......... **198.00**

**GXI-36 -** "For Pike's Peak" above prospector w/tools & cane standing on oblong frame - American Eagle w/pennant above frame "Ceredo," applied lip, smooth base, ca. 1870, aqua, ½ pt. ..................................... **143.00**

**GXI-44** - Tall prospector w/derby, holding bottle to lips, cane left hand, walking right on irregular base - American Eagle w/olive branch above rectangular frame, applied collared mouth w/ring, iron pontil, 1845-60, aqua, qt. (¼" shallow buble burst below eagle) ........................ **1,650.00**

**GXI-50** - "For Pike's Peak" above prospector w/tools & cane - Hunter shooting stag, applied collared mouth w/ring, iron pontil mark, plain edges, aqua, pt. (2" teardrop amber slag on left shoulder near medial rib) .................................................. **275.00**

**GXI-50** - "For Pike's Peak" above prospector w/tools & cane - Hunter shooting stag, applied collared mouth w/ring, smooth base, 1860-70, brilliant deep yellowish olive, pt. ........ **660.00**

**GXI-50** - "For Pike's Peak" above prospector w/tools & cane - Hunter shooting stag, applied collared mouth w/ring, possibly Ravenna Glass Works, iron pontil, 1857-60, ice blue, pt. ..................................... **300.00**

*"For Pike's Peak" Flask*

**GXI-52** - "For Pike's Peak" above prospector w/staff w/two packs at end, bottle below right arm & cane in other hand, waling right - Hunter at left shooting stag at right, aqua, ½ pt. (ILLUS.) .................................. **399.00**

**GXII-13** - Clasped hands above oval w/"L.F. & Co" all inside shield w/"UNION" above - American Eagle above frame w/"Pittsburg PA," applied collared mouth w/ring, smooth base, 1860-80, aqua, qt. ...... **100.00**

**GXII 15** - Clasped hands above oval, all inside shield, w/"Union" above - American Eagle above frame w/"E. Wormser Co" ("o" of Co just outside frame), narrow beveled edge, rolled collared mouth, smooth base, 1860-80, bluish green, qt. (light interior stain in base, rolled mouth incomplete but not damaged) ............................. **605.00**

**GXII-15** - Clasped hands above oval, all inside shield, w/"Union" above - American Eagle above frame w/"E. Wormser Co ("o" of Co just outside frame), narrow beveled edge, rolled lip, smooth base, ca. 1870, yellowish green, qt. (bruise at base) ................ **495.00**

**GXII-19** - Clasped hands above oval w/"LF & CO" all inside shield below "Union" - American Eagle w/plain shield above oval frame inscribed PITTSBURGH.PA., applied collared mouth w/ring, smooth base, 1860-80, aqua, qt. ............................ **94.00**

**GXII-33** - Clasped hands above oval all inside shield w/"Union" above shield - American Eagle above shield-shaped frame, round collar just below plain lip, smooth base, 1860-80, golden amber, ½ pt. ........... **143.00**

**GXII-39** - Clasped hands above oval, all inside shield w/"Union" above - large cannon & American flag, applied mouth w/ring, smooth base, 1860-80, brilliant golden amber, pt. ....................................................... **600.00**

**GXII-43** - Clasped hands above square & compass above oval w/"Union" all inside shield - American Eagle, calabash, applied sloping collared mouth, smooth base, 1860-80, aqua, qt. ..................... **60.00**

**GXIII-4** - Hunter facing left wearing flat-top stovepipe hat, short coat & full trousers, game bag hanging at left side, firing gun at two birds flying upward at left, large puff of smoke from muzzle, two dogs running to left toward section of rail fence - Fisherman standing on shore near large rock, wearing round-top stovepipe hat, V-neck jacket, full trousers, fishing rod held in left hand w/end resting on ground, right hand holding large fish, Creel below left arm, mill w/bushes & tree in left background, calabash, edges w/wide flutes, applied sloping collared mouth, smooth base, iron pontil, 1860-70, light bluish green, qt. ..................................................... **253.00**

**GXIII-7** - Hunter facing front, legs wide spread, wearing wide-brimmed hat w/high peaked crown, long tight waisted coat, full trousers, hunting boots, holding gun by both hands, small game bag at right hip, grass at left, bow end of skiff & reeds at right - Two pointers running left over rough grassy ground, applied double collared mouth, pontil scar, 1860-66, aqua, pt. (some exterior stain on hunter side of flask, ⅛" chip on side of collar, ¼" flake on base) ................. **55.00**

**GXIII-8** - Sailor dancing a hornpipe on an eight-board hatch cover, above a long rectangular bar - Banjo player sitting on a long bench, smooth edges, plain lip, pontil mark, aqua, ½ pt. (unearthed, light overall stain & scratches) ..................................... **110.00**

**GXIII-11** - Soldier standing on patch of ground holding rifle & pointing to drum above bevel-edged narrow rectangular bar inscribed "BALT. MD." - Ballet dancer on patch of ground holding tambourine above bevel-edged narrow rectangular bar inscribed "CHAPMAN," applied mouth w/ring, smooth base, pontil, aqua, pt. .......................................... **187.00**

*Soldier - Ballet Dancer Flask*

**GXIII-12** - Soldier standing on patch of ground holding rifle & pointing to drum above bevel-edged narrow rectangular bar inscribed "BALT. MD." - Ballet dancer on patch of ground holding tambourine above bevel-edged narrow rectangular bar inscribed "CHAPMAN," plain lip, smooth edges, aqua, pt. (ILLUS. bottom previous column) ............................. **121.00**

**GXIII-16** - U.S. Army dragoon in full dress uniform, ca. 1851-58, mounted on steed, riding right, saber in left hand, blanket roll behind saddle - large hound walking right, applied collared mouth w/ring, smooth base, aqua, qt. (some minor exterior wear) ... **77.00**

**GXIII-17** - Horseman wearing cap & short jacket, riding a horse w/tail flying back - Hound walking right, applied mouth w/ring, smooth base, 1860-80, aqua, pt. (¼" flake on mouth, some very faint interior stain) ..................................... **50.00 to 100.00**

**GXIII-17** - Horseman wearing cap & short jacket, riding a horse w/tail flying back - Hound walking right, applied double collared mouth, smooth base, 1860-80, medium yellowish amber, pt. .......................... **350.00**

**GXIII-18** - Horseman wearing a short coat, hat blown off to the left, riding a horse w/tail flying back - Hound running right, applied double collared mouth, smooth base, 1860-80, aqua, ½ pt. .......................... **70.00**

**GXIII-23** - Flora Temple obverse, plain reverse, smooth edges w/beads at lower neck & shoulder, amber, pt. .... **225.00**

**GXIII-24** - Flora Temple obverse, plain reverse, smooth edges w/beads at lower neck & shoulder, applied mouth w/ring, handle, smooth base, 1860-80, probably Whitney Glass Works, brilliant light copper, pt. (¼" bruise on side of mouth) ............ **231.00**

**GXIII-35** - Sheaf of Grain w/rake & pitchfork crossed behind sheaf - "Westford Glass Co., Westford Conn," smooth sides, medium olive-amber, pt. ......................................... **132.00**

**GXIII-35** - Sheaf of Grain w/rake & pitchfork crossed behind sheaf - "Westford Glass Co, Westford Conn," smooth sides, applied double collared mouth, smooth base, 1860-72, reddish amber, pt. ............. **120.00**

**GXIII-35 -** Sheaf of Grain w/rake & pitchfork crossed behind sheaf - "Westford Glass Co., Westford Conn," applied double collared mouth, smooth base, 1860-73, yellowish olive, pt. ............................ **165.00**

**GXIII-36 -** Sheaf of Grain w/rake & pitchfork crossed behind sheaf & five-pointed star centered between rake & pitchfork handles - "Westford Glass Co, Westford Conn," applied double collared mouth, smooth base, 1860-73, dark yellowish olive, pt. (some minor exterior wear)......... **154.00**

**GXIII-37 -** Sheaf of Grain w/rake & pitchfork crossed behind sheaf - "Westford Glass Co., Westford Conn," smooth sides, applied double collared mouth, smooth base, 1860-73, dark olive, ½ pt. ................. **165.00**

**GXIII-37 -** Sheaf of Grain w/rake & pitchfork crossed behind sheaf - "Westford Glass Co., Westford Conn," smooth sides, applied double collared mouth, smooth base, 1860-73, olive-amber, ½ pt. .............. **110.00**

**GXIII-42 -** Sheaf of Grain w/rake & pitchfork crossed behind sheaf & two laurel branches curving down from small ring above grain - eight-petaled ornament, calabash, four wide vertical flutes, applied sloping collared mouth, pontil scar, 1845-60, aqua, qt. ............................ **50.00 to 100.00**

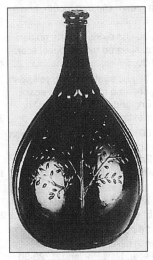

*Sheaf of Grain - Tree Flask*

**GXIII-46 -** Sheaf of Grain above crossed rake & pitchfork - tree & foliage, calabash, vertically ribbed, double round collar, open pontil, deep amethyst, qt. (ILLUS. bottom previous column) ............................ **495.00**

**GXIII-53 -** Anchor w/fork-ended pennants inscribed "Baltimore" & "Glass Works" on obverse - Phoenix rising from flames on rectangular panel inscribed "Resurgam" on reverse, rounded collar, smooth edges, applied collared mouth, smooth base, 1860-80, aqua, pt. (large bubble burst in upper banner of Baltimore) ..................................... **50.00**

*Anchor - Log Cabin Flask*

**GXIII-58 -** Anchor w/fork-ended pennants inscribed "Spring Garden" & "Glass Works" - three-quarter view of log cabin, smooth edges, round collar, apricot yellow, pt. (ILLUS.) ..................................... **286.00**

**GXIII-60 -** Anchor w/fork-ended pennants inscribed "Spring Garden" & "Glass Works," w/rectangular panel below - three quarter view of log cabin w/rectangular panel below, smooth edges, plain collar, applied collared mouth w/ring, smooth base, 1860-80, aqua, ½ pt............................ **88.00**

*"Traveler's Companion" Flask*

**GXIV-1 -** "Traveler's Companion" arched above & below star formed by a circle of eight small triangles - Sheaf of Grain w/rake & pitchfork crossed behind, applied flat collar, seamed base, honey amber, qt. (ILLUS.) ......................................... **550.00**

**GXIV-I -** "Traveler's Companion" arched above & below star formed by a circle of eight small triangles - Sheaf of Grain w/rake & pitchfork crossed behind, applied flat collar, seamed base, 1860-73, yellowish olive, qt. ......................................... **165.00**

**GXIV-7 -** "Traveler's Companion" arched above & below stylized duck - eight-pointed star, plain lip, smooth base, applied square collared mouth, iron pontil mark, 1845-60, brilliant yellowish amber, ½ pt. (lettering somewhat weak, ⅜" bruise on medial rib) ..................................... **220.00**

**GXV-27 -** Whitney Glass Wroks, Glassboro, New Jersey, base embossed, lettered, sloping collared mouth w/ring & internal screw stopper, smooth base, 1860-82, golden amber, pt. (stopper w/minor roughness)........................................ **88.00**

**Chestnut,** aqua, two piece mold patterned w/scrolls & four petaled flowers, sheared mouth, pontil scar, 5¾" h. ............................................... **275.00**

**Chestnut,** deep olive-green, free-blown, Ludlow-type, heavy rolled collared mouth, pontil scar, 1780-1830, 9⅛" h. ........................... **110.00**

**Chestnut,** 16 diamond, aqua, teardrop form, sheared mouth, pontil scar, 6¼" h. (¼" bruise near a bubble burst at base)......................... **97.00**

**Chestnut,** 24 ribs swirled to left, aqua, tooled mouth, pontil scar, 1820-40, 4⅞" h. (minor exterior high point wear)................................................. **154.00**

**Chestnut,** 24 vertical ribs, brilliant golden amber, sheared mouth, pontil scar, 1800-40, 4⅞" h. ...................... **132.00**

**Chestnut,** 24 ribs swirled slightly to left, golden amber, tooled mouth, pontil scar, 1820-40, 4½" h. .............. **209.00**

**Chestnut,** light sapphire blue, flared mouth, faint ogival pattern, pontil scar, Europe, 1840-60, 5¼" h. .......... **110.00**

**Pitkin,** 32 ribs swirled to the left, bluish green, sheared mouth, pontil scar, 1783-1830, 6¾" h. (minor exterior wear)................................... **358.00**

**Pitkin,** 32 ribs swirled to right, bluish green, sheared mouth, pontil scar, 1800-30, 6⅞" h. ............................... **523.00**

**Pitkin,** 35 ribs swirled to right, sheared mouth, pontil scar, 1800-30, light yellowish green, 6" h. ................ **550.00**

**Pitkin,** 36 ribs swirled to left, brilliant forest green, sheared mouth, pontil scar, 5¾" h....................................... **880.00**

**Pitkin,** 36 ribs swirled to left, golden amber, sheared mouth, pontil scar, 1800-30, 5¾" h. ............................... **440.00**

**Pitkin,** 36 ribs swirled to left, yellowish olive, sheared mouth, pontil scar, New England, 1783-1830, 6½" h. (minor exterior wear) ....................... **330.00**

**Pitkin,** 36 ribs swirled to right, yellowish olive, sheared mouth, pontil scar, New England, 1783-1830, 5¾" h. (a difficult to see ½" pot stone crack).... **198.00**

**Pitkin,** 36 ribs swirled to left, yellowish olive, sheared mouth, pontil scar, New England, 1783-1830, 4⅞" h...... **264.00**

**Pitkin,** 36 ribs swirled to right, yellowish olive, sheared mouth, pontil scar, New England, 1783-30, 5¼" h. ............................................... **275.00**

## INKS

**Cone-shaped,** aqua, vertical
embossing "J.J. Butler - Cinct. -
Ohio," inward rolled mouth, pontil
scar, 1840-60, 2½" h. (some light
interior haze).................................... **440.00**

**Cone-shaped,** yellowish olive,
sheared mouth, pontil scar, probably
from Stoddard Glasshouse, 2" h....... **303.00**

**Cylindrical,** master size, aqua glass,
embossed "American Standard Ink
Co Frederick Md.," pouring lip,
3⅝" d., 10" h. ..................................... **50.00**

**Cylindrical,** olive-amber, embossed
"Bertinguiot," slightly domed
shoulder, sheared mouth, pontil
scar, 2" h........................................... **209.00**

**Cylindrical,** master size, aqua,
embossed "S.O. Dunbar," applied
sloping collared mouth, iron pontil
mark, 1845-60, 8¾" h. (some interior
haze).................................................. **88.00**

**Cylindrical,** master size, aqua,
embossed "S.O. Dunbar Taunton
Mass," applied collared mouth
w/pour spout, pontil scar, 1840-60,
8½" h. (⅛" flake on top of mouth) ....... **39.00**

**Cylindrical,** cobalt blue, embossed
"Harrison's Columbian Ink," inward
rolled mouth, pontil scar, 1840-60,
2" h. (unearthed, overall stain,
probably treated) ............................. **385.00**

**Cylindrical,** small master size,
medium cobalt blue, embossed
"Harrison's Columbian Ink," applied
square collared mouth, pontil scar,
1840-60, 4" h. (shallow narrow
½" flake on side of flanged mouth) ... **440.00**

*Harrison's Columbian Ink Bottle*

**Cylindrical,** small master size,
medium sapphire blue, embossed
"Harrison's Columbian Ink," applied
flared round collar, open pontil,
4½" h. (ILLUS. bottom previous
column)......................................... **1,100.00**

**Cylindrical,** master size, deep cobalt
blue, embossed "Harrison's
Columbian Ink," applied square
collared mouth, pontil scar, 1840-60,
7" (mouth roughness w/three
pinpoint flakes on outer
circumference of flanged mouth,
some interior residue)...................... **435.00**

**Cylindrical,** master size, aqua,
vertically embossed "Hover Phila.,"
applied collared mouth w/pour spout,
smooth base, 1860-80, 9" h............. **143.00**

**Cylindrical,** master size, cobalt blue,
embossed "Underwood's Inks,"
tooled mouth w/pour spout, pontil
scar, 1870-90, 9¼" h. ...................... **133.00**

**Cylindrical** w/fluted shoulders, master
size, aqua, embossed "E. Waters
Troy. NY," applied square collared
mouth, pontil scar, 1840-60, 4¼" h.
(some interior stain, some exterior
stain on fluted shoulder) .................. **385.00**

**Domed w/offset neck,** light golden
amber, embossed "J & I E M,"
sheared mouth, smooth base, 1865-
80, 1½" h. (1/16" flake on mouth, ¼"
flake on side near base adjacent to
letter "J") ......................................... **132.00**

**Domed w/offset neck,** medium bluish
green, embossed "J & I E M,"
ground mouth, smooth base, 1865-
80, 1½" h. (unearthed, overall light
haze, ¼" ground spot on body below
neck)................................................ **121.00**

**Domed w/offset neck,** yellow w/hint
of green, embossed "J & I E M,"
sheared mouth, smooth base, 1865-
80, 1½" h. (light interior stain,
shallow ⅛" flake on top of mouth)..... **550.00**

**Domed w/offset mouth,** citron,
embossed "J & I E M," sheared
mouth, smooth base, 1865-80,
1⅝" h. (light overall haze, ⅛" flake
on body)........................................... **550.00**

**Figural lady's slipper,** fiery
opalescent, ground mouth, smooth
base, 1860-80, 3¼" h. (usual mouth
roughness)...................................... **468.00**

**Octagonal,** bright green, inward rolled
mouth, pontil scar, 1840-60, 2¼" h... **303.00**

**Octagonal** w/matching hinged lid, deep ice blue, ground mouth w/metal & glass closure, smooth base, 1870-80, probably Boston & Sandwich Glass Works, 2⅞" h. ........ **209.00**

**Pitkin-type inkwell,** thirty-six ribs swirled to right, conical form, yellowish olive, small tooled funnel mouth, pontil scar, 1½" d., 2¼" h. ...... **715.00**

**Rectangular,** bright green, embossed "T & M," inward rolled mouth, pontil scar, 1840-60, 2½" h. (unearthed, light overall stain) ............................ **110.00**

**Teakettle-type fountain inkwell** w/neck extending up at angle from base, amethyst cut to clear, polished diamond designs, ground mouth w/brass cap, smooth base, 1830-60, 2" h. .................................................... **605.00**

**Teakettle-type fountain inkwell** w/neck extending up at angle from base, five-lobed body form w/painted raised floral & leaf decor, fiery opalescent, ground mouth w/brass cap, smooth base, 1830-60, 2" h. (brass cap w/some minor damage).... **413.00**

**Teakettle-type fountain inkwell** w/neck extending up at angle from base, ten-sided w/painted raised floral & leaf decor, ground mouth w/brass cap, smooth base, fiery opalescent w/green, blue & amethyst painted decor, probably Boston & Sandwich Glass Works, 2½" h. (brass cap & collar damaged) .......... **385.00**

**Teakettle-type fountain inkwell** w/neck extending up at angle from base, light bluish green, ground mouth, smooth base, 1830-60, 2" h. (usual mouth roughness, brass cap missing) ......................................... **385.00**

**Teakettle-type fountain inkwell** w/neck extending up at angle from base, light greyish blue clambroth, generally rounded w/seven lobes at base & seven leaf flutes on dome, ground mouth, smooth base, 1830-60, 2¾" h. (brass cap missing) .. **935.00**

**Twelve-sided,** master size, aqua, embossed "Harrison's - Columbian - Ink," applied square collared mouth, pontil scar, 1840-60, 7" h. (two ¼" shallow chips on circumference of flanged mouth, ⅜" chip off one base panel)................................................ **110.00**

**Twelve-sided,** master size, aqua, embossed "Harrison's - Columbian - Ink," aqua, applied square collared mouth, pontil scar, 1840-60, 9" h. (overall light interior haze, 1" crack on shoulder in bubble burst open to inside, another ½" crack in another bubble)............................................. **523.00**

**Twelve-sided,** large master size, aqua, embossed "Harrison's - Columbian - Ink," applied square collared mouth, pontil scar, 1840-60, 1 gal., 11½" h. (overall interior stain spots, potstone in upper body on one panel, two ⅛" leg fissures)........ **770.00**

**Umbrella-type** (8-panel cone shape), aqua, embossed "S.O. Dunbar - Taunton," inward rolled mouth, pontil scar, 1840-60, 2⅜" h. (light interior stain) .................................................... **121.00**

**Umbrella-type** (8-panel cone shape), aqua, embossed "Waters - Ink - Troy, N.Y.," tooled mouth, smooth base, 1860-80, 2½" h. (light interior haze)................................................. **770.00**

**Umbrella-type** (8-panel cone shape), aqua, embossed "Waters - Ink - Troy NY," inward rolled mouth, pontil scar, 1840-60, 2½" h. ................... **1,100.00**

**Umbrella-type** (8-panel cone shape), bright green w/faint olive tones, sheared mouth, pontil scar, 1840-60, 2¼" h. ............................................... **495.00**

**Umbrella-type** (8-panel cone shape), bright light blue, inward rolled mouth, pontil scar, 1840-60, 2½" h. (some exterior wear particularly on each of the corners of the panels)................. **165.00**

**Umbrella-type** (8-panel cone shape), deep aqua, embossed "J.S. Dunham," inward rolled mouth, pontil scar, 1840-60, 2⅝" h. (light interior haze)................................................. **275.00**

**Umbrella-type** (8-panel cone shape), deep yellowish olive, sheared mouth, pontil scar, New England 1840-60, 2¼" h. ............................... **303.00**

**Umbrella-type** (8-panel cone shape), golden yellowish amber, inward rolled mouth, pontil scar, 2¼" h. (some exterior dullness & scratches on two panels)............................................. **132.00**

*Rare Umbrella Ink Bottle*

**Umbrella-type** (8-panel cone shape), light sapphire blue, sheared mouth, open pontil, dug w/overall light stain, 2³⁄₁₆" h. (ILLUS.)............................. **1,650.00**

**Umbrella-type** (8-panel cone shape), plum-puce, inward rolled mouth, pontil scar, 1840-60, 2½" h. (small spot of roughness where inward rolled mouth doesn't completely cover surface of lip)................................. **2,200.00**

**Umbrella-type** (8-panel cone shape), reddish amber, sheared mouth, pontil scar, 1840-60, 2½" h............... **154.00**

**Umbrella-type** (8-panel cone shape), reddish amber, sheared mouth, pontil scar, New England, 1840-60, 2½" h. (unusual mouth tooling)......... **303.00**

**Umbrella-type** (8-panel cone shape), rich golden amber, inward rolled mouth, pontil scar, New England, 1840-60, 2⅜" h. (small spot of roughness on one of base corners) ... **143.00**

*Sapphire Blue Umbrella Ink*

**Umbrella-type** (8-panel cone shape), rich medium sapphire blue, round collar, smooth base, 2½" w., 2¾" h. (ILLUS. bottom previous column) ..... **660.00**

**Umbrella-type** (8-panel cone shape), yellowish amber, inward rolled mouth, pontil scar, 1840-60, 2⅜" h.... **770.00**

## MEDICINES

**American Eagle Liniment,** hexagonal, tooled flared mouth, smooth base, 1860-80, deep aqua, 5¼" h. ................................................. **50.00**

**Berlin Series,** paper label w/"Unadulterated Paregoric Berlin," embossed bull's-eye, aqua, 8¾" h.... **110.00**

**Bonpland's Fever & Ague Remedy,** rectangular, pontil aqua, 5⅛" h. .......... **48.00**

**Boradent Co. Inc.,** San Francisco & New York - Creme De Camelia for the Complexion, paper label, rectangular, cobalt blue, 5" h. (some stain) .................................................. **25.00**

**Brant's Purifying Extract -** M.T. Wallace & Co., Proprietors - Brooklyn, N.Y., rectangular, light aqua, 10" h. .................................... **285.00**

**Brown (Wm). Druggist & Chemist,** 481 Washington St., Boston, indented panels, 8-sided, 8½" h. ......... **85.00**

*Carter's Spanish Mixture*

**Carter's Spanish Mixture,** cylindrical w/applied double collar, open pontil, yellowish olive-green, 8" h. (ILLUS.) ... **534.00**

**Chamberlain's Liniment -**
Chamberlain Medicine Co. - Des
Moines, Ia, w/paper label, aqua,
6¾" h. (99% front label) .................... **16.00**

**Christie's (Dr.) Magnetic Fluid,**
rectangular, open pontil aqua,
4⅞" h. ................................................ **25.00**

**Clark's California Cherry Cordial,**
amber, 8⅛" h. ..................................... **20.00**

**Clewley's Miraculous Cure for
Rheumatism -** Shaw Pharmacal Co.
- Office 66 Liberty St. New York,
embossed nun, rectangular, aqua,
6⅛" h. ............................................. **105.00**

**Dinsmore's (Mrs.) Cough & Croup
Balsam,** rectangular, clear, 6" h. ........ **15.00**

*L.P. Dodge Rheumatic Liniment*

*Ditchett's Remedy*

**Ditchett's Remedy for the Piles
N.Y.,** rectangular w/beveled wide
corners, double applied collar, open
pontil, olive-green, 8" h. (ILLUS.)... **4,400.00**

**Dodge (L.P.) -** Rheumatic Liniment -
Newburg, rectangular w/beveled
corners, applied tapered collar, open
pontil, ca. 1850, 1½ × 3", 6" h.
(ILLUS. top next column) ............... **1,650.00**

**Dunbars Rheumatic Remedy,**
Washington, D.C., clear ..................... **25.00**

**Dyer's Healing Embrocation,**
Providence, Rhode Island, pontil,
aqua, 6¼" h. ..................................... **55.00**

**Ellis (Charles) Son & Co.**
Philadelphia, rectangular, cobalt
blue, 4½" wide mouth ........................ **25.00**

*Fahrney & Son Preparation*

**Ewbanks Topaz Cinchona Cordial,**
rare square-shape, 1870, amber,
9¼" h. ................................................ **95.00**

**Fahrney (Drs. D.) & Son -**
Preparation For Cleansing The
Blood, Boonsboro, M.D., square
w/indented panels, applied double
collar, smooth base, medium apricot
amber, ca. 1870, 9¼" h. (ILLUS.
bottom) ........................................... **413.00**

*Farquar's Medicated Calif. Wine*

*Holman's Grand Restorative*

**Farquar's Medicated** - California - Wine & Brandy, square w/beveled corners, applied tapered collar, smooth base, ca. 1870, light stain, scratches, tiny open bubble on plain panel, puce, 9½" h. (ILLUS.) ............ **880.00**

**Farrell's (H.G.) Arabian Liniment,** Peoria, cylindrical, crude rolled lip, open pontil, aqua, 4" h. ....................... **48.00**

**Gargling Oil,** Lockport, N.Y., teal green, 5½" h. (dug, cleaned to near mint) ................................................. **25.00**

**Green's (Dr.) Nervura,** w/paper labels, rectangular, aqua, 9" h. (99% front label, 60% rear label) ........ **16.00**

**Harter's (Dr.) - Iron Tonic,** w/paper label, rectangular, amber, 9¼" h. (75% front label, 100% rear) .............. **22.00**

**Healy & Bigelow Kickapoo Indian Sagwa,** w/paper label on three sides, rectangular w/beveled corners, tooled double collared mouth, smooth base, 1890-1900, aqua, 8⅝" h. (label about 90% complete) ......................................... **154.00**

**Helmbold (H.T.) - Genuine Fluid Extracts** - Philadelphia, open pontil, aqua, 7¼" h. ..................................... **88.00**

**Holman's Natures Grand Restorative** - J.B. Holman Prop. - Boston, Mass., rectangular w/beveled corners, applied round collar, open pontil, ca. 1850, three minute lip flakes, olive-green w/hint of amber, 6¾" h. (ILLUS. top next column) ......................................... **2,530.00**

**Holman's Natures Grand Restorative** - J.B. Holman Prop. - Boston Mass., rectangular, aqua, 7¼" h. .............................................. **120.00**

**James (Dr. H.) No. 19 Grand St.,** Jersey City, NJ, and No. 14 Cecil St. Strand London, interior etching, oval, aqua, 8" h. ....................................... **100.00**

**Jayne's (Dr. D.) Alternative,** 84 Chest. St., Phila., flattened oval, open pontil, aqua, 7" h. (very light inside haze) ....................................... **42.00**

**Kennedy's (Dr. D.) Favorite Remedy,** Kingston, N.Y. U.S.A., w/paper label, rectangular, light amethyst, 7⅛" h. (99% front label) ..... **20.00**

**Kennedy's (Dr.) - Medical Discovery** - Roxbury, Mass., rectangular, aqua, 8½" h. ............................ **150.00 to 200.00**

**Kennedy's (Donald) Salt Rheum Ointment,** round, rolled lip, open pontil, 2" h. ....................................... **140.00**

**Kidder (Mrs. E.) Dysentery Cordial,** Boston, aqua, 7½" h. ......................... **95.00**

**Kilmers (Dr.) Cough Cure Consumption Oil.** Catarrh Specific - Dr. Kilmer & Co - Bighamton, NY, rectangular w/indented panels, applied double collar, smooth base, ca. 1870, aqua, 8¾" h. (ILLUS. top next page) ............................................... **715.00**

**Lactopeptine** - The Best Remedial Agent in ALL Digestive Disorders - The New York Pharmacal Association, square w/rounded shoulders, cobalt blue, 8" h. ............. **110.00**

*Dr. Kilmers Cough Cure*

*Dr. Miles' Heart Treatment*

**Langley's Red Bottle Elixer of Life,** cylindrical, applied square collared mouth, pontil scar, 1840-60, aqua, 4⅞" h. (some light interior haze)......... **88.00**

**Lyon's Powder -** B&P N.Y. (lettering on shoulder), cylindrical, lime green, 4" h. (exterior dullness)...................... **28.00**

**McEckron's A., Ring Bone Liniment,** N.Y., open pontil, aqua, 6⅞" h. ........... **78.00**

**McLane's (Doctor C.) - American Work Specific,** round, aqua, 4" h. .... **125.00**

**Merchant (G.W.)** Lockport, N.Y., round, iron pontil, forest green, 7" h. ................................................. **190.00**

**Mexican Mustang Liniment,** round, aqua, rare size, 7⅜" h...................... **155.00**

**Miles' (Dr.) Heart Treatment** (on paper label), rectangular w/one indented panel, double collar lip, smooth base, 100% label & contents, ca. 1910, aqua (ILLUS. top next column)............................................... **413.00**

**Morse's Celebrated Syrup,** Prov. R.I., large, oval-shaped, hugh iron pontil, deep aqua, 9½" h................... **175.00**

**Morse's (Dr. M.) Invigorating Cordial,** 7½" h. ................ **125.00 to 150.00**

**Munyon's Paw-Paw,** w/embossed tree, rectangular, amber, 10" h. .......... **28.00**

**Nichols Toilet Cream,** indented panel square, rectangular, green, 6⅜" h. ..... **75.00**

**Pages Vegetable Syrup for Females,** w/paper label, round, aqua, 8⅝" h. ..................................... **320.00**

**Peek's (Prof. W.H.), Remedy,** New York, square, plain base, amber, 8" h. ................................................. **135.00**

**Peruvian Syrup,** N.L. Clark & Co., Boston, round, aqua, 9⅞" h. ............. **175.00**

**Radway's Ready Relief (R.R.R. No. 1) -** Ent. Acord To - Act of Congress, pontil, rectangular, aqua, 6½" h. ................................................. **68.00**

**Risley's Extract Buchu -** New York, aqua, 7¾" h. ....................................... **90.00**

**River Swamp (The) Chill and (embossed alligator) Fever Cure** Augusta, Ga., rectangular w/beveled corners, tooled mouth, smooth base, 1880-90, amber, 6¼" h. (about perfect) ......................................... **1,550.00**

**Rogers (Dr. A.) Liverwort,** Tar & Canchalagua, rectangular w/rounded corners, applied sloping collared mouth, pontil scar, 1840-60, aqua, 8" h. ......................................... **66.00**

**Roger's (Dr. A.) Liverwort,** Tar and Canchalagua - A.L. Scovill - Cincinnati, rectangular, aqua, 8" h.... **110.00**

**Rossell's Concentrated Foam,** Mfg'd by Post Flavor Co. (in slugplate), round, cobalt blue, 7" h. (minor cloudy streaks & scuff) ...................... **50.00**

**Sanford's Extract of Hamaelis or Witch Hazel,** rectangular w/beveled corners, sapphire blue, 1⅝" × 2⅜", 7¼" h. (indented panel, two pinhead lip flakes) ......................................... **150.00**

*Seaver's Joint Liniment*

**Seaver's Joint & Nerve Liniment,**
cylindrical, flared lip, open pontil, ca.
1850, amber w/hint of olive, 4" h.
(ILLUS.) ....................................... **2,420.00**

**Swaim's - Panacea - Philada,** round
w/vertical indented panels, applied
sloping collared mouth w/ring, pontil
scar, 1840-60, deep yellowish olive,
8" h. ................................................. **413.00**

*Dr. Sweet's Panacea*

**Sweet's (Dr.) Panacea -** Exeter, N.H.,
rectangular w/wide beveled corners,
applied tapered collar, base pontil,
ca. 1860, yellowish amber, 2¼ × 3½",
8" h. (ILLUS.)................................. **3,190.00**

**Trask's (A.) Magnetic Ointment,**
square w/chamfered corners, pontil,
aqua, 3⅛" h. ...................................... **55.00**

**Warner's Safe Cure,** London, w/safe,
oval, emerald green, pt., 9½" h......... **120.00**

**Warner's Safe Cure Co.** Rochester,
N.Y., round, amber, 4½" h. (sample
size) ..................................................... **20.00**

**Warner's Safe Nervine,** Rochester,
N.Y., slug plate variant, blob top,
amber, 7⅜" h. (some inside &
outside staining) ................................. **45.00**

**Watkin's Worm Candy,** Newbern,
N.C., vial-form, tooled rim, smooth
base, 1880-90, aqua, 4¼" h. (dug
bottle w/minor but cleanable stain) ... **210.00**

**W.W.C. - Woodridge Wonderful
Cure Co.,** Columbus, CA - W.W.C.,
rectangular, applied mouth, smooth
base, 1880-85, amber, 8¼" h. .......... **190.00**

**Wheatley's (J.B.) Compound Syrup,**
Dallasburgh, Ky., iron pontil, bluish
aqua.................................................. **190.00**

**Wilson (B.O. & G.C.),** Botanic
Druggist, Boston, open pontil,
applied mouth, aqua,
9½" h. ............................. **225.00 to 250.00**

**Woods (Professor) Hair
Restorative,** aqua ............................. **58.00**

## MINERAL WATERS

**Ballston Spa.,** Lithia Mineral Water -
Artesian Spring Co. Ballston N.Y.,
cylindrical, applied sloping collared
mouth w/ring, smooth base, 1860-
80, aqua, pt. (deep ½" bubble burst
filled w/epoxy) ..................................... **80.00**

**Ballston Spa.,** Lithia Mineral Water -
Artesian Spring Co. Ballston N.Y.,
cylindrical, applied sloping collared
mouth w/ring, smooth base,
1860-80, emerald green, pt. ............... **80.00**

**Boardman (John) - New York -
Mineral Waters,** eight-sided, applied
blob top, iron pontil, ca. 1860, overall
light high point wear, medium
sapphire blue, 7½" h. (ILLUS. top,
next page)........................................ **176.00**

**Burgess - Mineral - Waters - N.,**
eight-sided, applied mouth, iron
pontil, 1845-55, cobalt blue, 7¼" h.
(cleaned to original luster, about
perfect) ......................................... **1,200.00**

**Caladonia Spring Wheelock Vt.,**
cylindrical, applied double collar
mouth, smooth base, ca. 1870,
honey amber, qt. (ILLUS. bottom
next page)........................................ **798.00**

*Boardman Mineral Waters*

*Caladonia Spring Bottle*

**Chemung Spring Water Trade Mark.**
This Bottle is Loaned and Never
Sold One Half Gallon (Indian at

spring), cylindrical, pontiled at base,
medium apricot, ¼" potstone crack
in side, 9" h. (ILLUS. below) ............. **578.00**

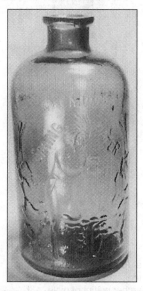

*Chemung Spring Water Bottle*

**Congress & Empire Spring Co,** "C"
(in frame), Saratoga. N.Y.,
cylindrical, applied sloping collared
mouth w/ring, smooth base, 1860-
80, deep emerald green, pt. (some
exterior body wear, scratches &
roughness on mouth ring) ................. **325.00**

**Congress & Empire Spring Co,**
Hotchkiss' Sons, "C" New-York,
Saratoga. N.Y. - Congress Water,
cylindrical, applied sloping collared
mouth w/ring, smooth base, forest
green, qt. ............................................. **90.00**

**Congress & Empire Spring Co,**
Hotchkiss' Sons, "C," New York,
Saratoga NY, embossed on obverse
only, cylindrical, applied sloping
collared mouth w/ring, smooth base,
1860-80, yellowish olive, pt. (light
interior stain) ...................................... **77.00**

**Congress & Empire Spring Co,**
Hotchkiss' Sons, "C," New York,
Saratoga. N.Y., cylindrical, applied
sloping collared mouth w/ring,
smooth base, 1860-80, yellowish
olive, pt. ............................................. **70.00**

*M.T. Crawford Bottle*

*Highrock Congress Spring Bottle*

**Crawford (M.T.) Hartford CT -**
Superior Mineral Water. Union Glass
Works Philad., cylindrical w/ten-
sided mug base, applied blob, iron
pontil, ca.1860, cobalt blue, 7¼" h.
(ILLUS.) ............................................. **325.00**

**Excelsior Spring,** Saratoga. N.Y.,
cylindrical, sloping collared mouth
w/ring, smooth base, 1860-80, bluish
green, qt. (bruise on top of mouth &
tiny chip on "i" in Excelsior) ................. **60.00**

**Excelsior Spring,** Saratoga. N.Y.,
cylindrical, tooled sloping collared
mouth w/ring, smooth base, 1860-
80, brilliant yellowish green, pt.
(numerous minor exterior "pick"
marks) ................................................ **49.00**

**Highrock Congress Spring -** motif of
rock - C & W Saratoga N.Y.,
cylindrical, smooth base, applied
double collared mouth, ca. 1870,
lightly cleaned, rich teal blue
(ILLUS. top next column) ................. **935.00**

**Highrock Congress Spring,** C & W,
Saratoga N.Y., cylindrical, applied
sloping collared mouth w/ring,
smooth base, 1860-80, yellowish
green, qt. (⅛" chip top of mouth,
fissures on interior of sloping
collared mouth) ............................... **100.00**

**Knowlton (D.A.) Saratoga. N.Y.,**
cylindrical, unusual applied sloping
collared mouth w/ring, smooth base,
1860-80, olive-green, pt. (¼" flake
on mouth, ¼" body bruise near
base) ................................................... **50.00**

**Middletown Healing Springs,** Grays
& Clark, Middletown, Vt., Saratoga-
type, amber, qt. (chip on collared
lip) ..................................................... **110.00**

**Middletown Healing Springs,** Grays
& Clark, Middletown, Vt., Saratoga-
type, yellowish amber, qt. (nicely
whittled) ............................................. **70.00**

**Missisquoi "A" Springs,** cylindrical,
applied sloping collared mouth
w/ring, smooth base, 1860-80,
yellowish olive, qt. ............................. **70.00**

**Oak Springs Orchard,** Acid -
Address, C.W. Merchant, Lockport.
N.Y., cylindrical, applied sloping
collared mouth w/ring, smooth base,
1860-80, Lockport bluish green, qt. .... **80.00**

**Pavilion & United States Spring Co**
(arch), "P." Saratoga, N.Y., - Pavilion
Water, cylindrical, applied sloping
collared mouth w/ring, smooth base,
1860-80, yellowish green, pt. (some
exterior wear & scratches, appears
to have been lightly professionally
cleaned) ........................................... **100.00**

**Rapp (A.W.) New York -** Mineral
Waters R This Bottle Is Never Sold
(embossed), cylindrical, applied
sloping mouth, iron pontil mark,
1845-60, sapphire blue, pt. (⅛"
bubble burst on the collar, some
exterior wear & scratches, ½" fissure
at iron pontil mark)............................ **154.00**

**Regis (St.) Water,** Massena Springs,
cylindrical, tooled sloping collared
mouth w/ring, smooth base,
1880-1900, colorless, pt. ................. **400.00**

**Saratoga (star) Spring,** Saratoga-
type, yellowish amber, qt. (¹⁄₁₆" spider
in rear)............................................... **145.00**

**Saratoga (star) Spring** (reverse "S"),
cylindrical, applied sloping collared
mouth w/ring, smooth base, 1860-
80, emerald green w/olive tone, qt.
(potstone bruise on applied mouth
ring) ..................................................... **60.00**

**Saratoga Vichy Water,** Saratoga,
N.Y. - "V," tall cylindrical form, tooled
heavy collared mouth, smooth base,
1880-1900, golden yellow, pt.
(appears to be professionally
cleaned, ¼" flake at base corner) ....... **90.00**

**Schmidtmann (H.) Mineral Water,**
New York, w/monogram, aqua, (few
scratches) ............................................ **15.00**

**Saratoga Red Spring,** cylindrical,
applied sloping collared mouth
w/ring, smooth base, 1860-80,
emerald green, qt. (potstone w/⅛"
radiating legs) ..................................... **70.00**

**Weston (G.W.) & Co.,** Saratoga-type,
rough pontil, olive-amber, qt.
(shallow lip chips) .............................. **95.00**

## PICKLE BOTTLES & JARS

**Aqua,** four-sided cathedral-type
w/Gothic arches on each panel,
round collared mouth, smooth base,
ca. 1870, ½ gal., 11½" h.
(ILLUS. top next column) .................. **132.00**

**Aqua,** cylindrical w/five-lobed vertical
panels, shoulder embossed "W.K.
Lewis & Co. Boston," tooled square
collared mouth, iron pontil mark,
1845-60, 10½" h. (some minor
interior base stain) ............................ **303.00**

**Greenish aqua,** six-sided w/Gothic
arches, small round collared mouth,
smooth base, 1860-80, 12¾" h. (⅛"
flake on one of base corners, some
minor interior stain rings) ................. **258.00**

*Cathedral Pickle Bottle*

**Deep greenish aqua,** four-sided
cathedral-type w/Gothic arches on
each panel, small round collared
mouth, smooth base, 1860-80,
11½" h. ............................................. **258.00**

**Light blue green,** four-sided,
cathedral-type w/Gothic arches,
small round collared mouth, smooth
base, 1860-80, 11½" h. .................... **605.00**

**Pale green aqua,** rare coffin-shape,
embossed "Warsaw Pickle Co.
Warsaw, Ill., w/magnified 4" h. Statue
of Liberty embossment. ................... **110.00**

## POISONS

**Aqua,** "Dead Stuck for Bugs," 7" h........ **35.00**

**Amber,** "J.T.M. - & Co.," tooled lip,
4¾" h. ............................................... **625.00**

**Amber,** "Poison" in large letters down
both sides, full label on front, large
diamonds down all four corners,
6½", pt. ............................................... **50.00**

**Cobalt blue,** "McCormick Bee Brand,"
3" h. ................................................... **45.00**

**Cobalt blue,** "Poison - Bowman's,
Drug Store - Poison," flattened
hexagonal form w/ridges on four
sides, w/"C.L.C. Co. Patent Applied
for 16" on smooth base, tooled lip,
1890-1910, 7½" h. ............................ **675.00**

**Cobalt blue,** "The J.F. Hartz Co.
Limited Toronto" embossed in large
heart, square, tooled square collared
mouth, smooth base, 1880-1900,
6⅛" h. ............................................... **605.00**

*Owl Drug Poison Bottle*

**Cobalt blue,** "The Owl Drug Co. - Poison" w/owl sitting on a mortar, triangular shape, tooled lip, smooth base, 1900-15, 9½" h. (ILLUS.) ........ **550.00**

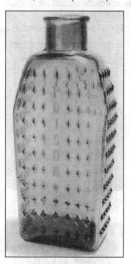

*Coffin-Shaped Poison Bottle*

**Cobalt blue,** "Poison - Poison, "Norwich" on base, coffin-shaped w/overall raised diamond design, embossed wording on two sides, short cylindrical neck, minor surface bruise on base, 7½" h. (ILLUS.) ....... **798.00**

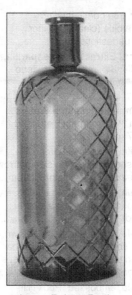

*Large Poison Bottle*

**Deep Cobalt blue,** master-size, cylindrical w/plain panel surrounded by overall lattice & diamond embossed design, short cylindrical neck, smooth base, ca. 1890, ½ gal. (ILLUS.) ............................................. **605.00**

**Green,** hexagonal, embossed skull & cross bones, 5¼" h. ......................... **125.00**

## SNUFF BOTTLES

**Golden amber,** square w/beveled corners, tooled mouth, pontil scar, 1840-60, 4¼" h. (retains half of original contents & paper cork) .......... **55.00**

**Light sea green,** free-blown, rectangular w/beveled corners, tooled flared mouth, pontil scar, 1830-60, 4⅜" h. (minor interior stain spots) ............................................... **176.00**

**Olive-amber,** "1st Quality Tobacco Scotch & Ruppert Snuff Made and Sold JB. Myers South 55th Street Baltimore" (paper label), free-blown square form w/chamfered corners, tooled mouth, pontil scar, 1830-60, 4¼" h. (perfect condition, stained label about 75% intact) .................... **110.00**

## SODAS & SARSAPARILLAS

**Andrae (G.) Port Huron,** Mich., soda, earlier slope shoulder, Hutchinson

stopper, iron pontil, medium
sapphire blue (cleaned, minor
ground perfections)............................ **135.00**

**Bull (John) Extract of Sarsaparilla,**
Louisville, Ky., rectangular, deep
aqua, 9" h. (some wear on rear
panel)................................................ **378.00**

**Cobbs Improved Mineral Waters**
**Boston "C,"** iron pontil, emerald
green, 7¼" h. ................................... **175.00**

**Coca-Cola,** embossed "Greenville,
Miss.," soda, straight on sides, arrow
case wear, amber (chip on bottom) .... **65.00**

**Coca-Cola,** embossed "Huntsville,
Ala.," soda, straight sides, amber
(cleaned)............................................. **65.00**

**Coca-Cola,** embossed "Morgantown,
W.Va.," soda, straight sides, amber
(cleaned to near mint, small bruises
on bottom) ......................................... **75.00**

**Coca-Cola,** embossed "Rock Hill,
S.C.," soda, straight sides, aqua
(cleaned to near mint)........................ **45.00**

**Coca-Cola,** San Francisco, tooled
crown top, smooth base, 1905-15,
very pale smokey yellowish green,
7⅞" h. ............................................... **400.00**

**Condarman Philada,** cylindrical,
applied heavy collared mouth, iron
pontil mark, 1845-60, light green,
½ pt. (professionally cleaned
w/some remaining etching &
scratches) ......................................... **40.00**

**Dearborn (J & A),** New York, iron
pontil, bluish green. ........................... **60.00**

**Dearborn & Co, Bottlers,** 83-3Av
(backwards N.) Y, embossed, soda,
cylindrical, applied heavy collared
mouth, iron pontil mark, 1845-60,
sapphire blue, ½ pt. (professionally
cleaned, weak lettering).................... **154.00**

**Dennis's (Dr. J.) -** Georgia
Sarsaparilla - Augusta, Ga, applied
mouth, iron pontil, 1845-55, aqua
w/dark olive-green striations,
10¼" h. (about perfect) .................. **1,300.00**

**Ebberwein (G.) Savannah Geo -**
Ginger Ale, cylindrical, soda, applied
heavy collared mouth, smooth base,
1860-80, olive-yellow, 7½" h. (overall
stain & scratches) ............................. **121.00**

**Engeman and Hubener,** New York,
embossed, blob top, aqua (light
case wear at base, nicely whittled) ..... **12.00**

**Gillett (T.W.) New Haven,** eight-sided,
applied blob top, iron pontil, ca. 1860,
sapphire blue, 7½" h. (ILLUS. top next
column)............................................... **385.00**

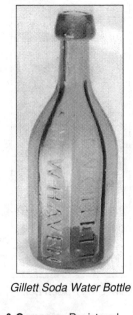

*Gillett Soda Water Bottle*

**Guyette & Company,** Registered,
Detroit, Mich.,This Bottle Is Never
Sold & "G" embossed on smooth
base, soda, Hutchinson stopper,
rolled lip, medium cobalt blue, ca.
1890-1910, 7" h. (ground
imperfections lower portion base)....... **95.00**

*Harris Soda Water Bottle*

**Harris (J.W.) - Soda Water - New
Haven -Conn.,** eight-sided,
embossed, applied blob top, smooth
base, ca. 1870, cobalt blue, 7½" h.
(ILLUS.) .............................................. **770.00**

*Harvey Soda Water Bottle*

*J. Harvey Soda Water Bottle*

**Harvey (IRA.) Prov. R.I. - H.** This Bottle is Never Sold, cylindrical, applied tapered collar mouth, iron pontil, ca. 1860, cobalt blue, 6¾" h. (ILLUS.) ........................................... **440.00**

**Harvey (J.) & Co. Providence R.I. - H.,** cylindrical, applied blob top, smooth base, ca. 1870, olive-amber, 7" h. (ILLUS. top next column)......... **163.00**

**Holland Rink Bottling Works,** Butte, Mont. in sunken panel, Hutchinson stopper, aqua, 6½" h. (dug) ............... **15.00**

**Keenan Mfg. Co.,** Butte, Mt.(in a circle), ten panels at base, Hutchinson stopper, aqua, 7¼" h. (dug) .................................................. **15.00**

**Kinsella & Hennessy,** Albany N.Y., soda, cylindrical, applied sloping collared mouth, smooth base, 1860-80, green, ½ pt. (heavy exterior wear, large bubble burst & large ½" chip from that bubble burst at base)................................................... **25.00**

**Kolb (J & F),** Erie, Pa, w/handwritten label, applied heavy collared mouth, smooth base, 1860-80, ½ pt. .............. **77.00**

**Ormsby (D.L.)** NY Union Glass Works, Phila., iron pontil, ice blue. ..... **75.00**

**Pepsi Cola** (in script) - Registered Con 6½ Fl. Oz., eight-sided, "Ideal Bott-Wks L.A. Calif. Pat Applied For" on smooth base, ABM lip, 1915-25, clear, 7⅞" h. (about perfect) ............. **750.00**

**Phillipsburg Bottle Work,** Phillipsburg, Mont., aqua, 6½" h. (near mint) ........................................ **35.00**

**Ryan (John) Savannah,** Ga, 1852, Excelsior Ginger Ale, round, applied heavy collared mouth, smooth base, 1860-80, olive-yellow, ½ pt. (professionally cleaned & buffed w/remaining scratches & stain)......... **132.00**

**Sand's Sarsaparilla -** Genuine - New York, rectangular, aqua, 10⅛" h. ........................................... **260.00**

**Schaum (F. & L.)** Baltimore Glass Works (embossed), soda, cylindrical, applied sloping collared mouth, iron pontil, 1845-60, dark yellowish olive, 7" h. (⅛" flake on neck just below the tapered collar, ¾" inside fissure on sloping collared mouth) .............. **303.00**

**Schoch (Geo.) Philada,** soda, squat cylindrical-form, applied sloping collared mouth w/ring, iron pontil mark, 1845-60, light bluish green, pt. (professionally cleaned w/some exterior scratches remaining) ............ **40.00**

**Smith (S.) Auburn, NY,** 1856 KR.S., ten-sided, heavy collared mouth, iron pontil mark, 1845-60, medium sapphire blue, ½ pt. (some interior residue)........................................... **385.00**

**Soda water bottle,** octangonal, unembossed, applied sloping collared mouth, smooth base, 1860-80, dense reddish amber, ½ pt. (oversized)...................................... **176.00**

*Southern Soda Bottle*

*Dr. Townsend's Sarsaparilla*

**Southern soda bottle,** embossed eagle on shield w/flags, cylindrical, applied tapered collar mouth, iron pontil, ca. 1860, medium sapphire blue, 7½" h. (ILLUS.) ...................... **550.00**

**Steinke & Kornahrens -** Soda Water - Return This Bottle - Charleston S.C.," eight-sided, applied mouth, iron pontil, 1845-55, cobalt blue, 8" h. (some area of outside haziness, about perfect) ..... **700.00**

**Thornton (R.) & Son, Hudson, NY. -** T & S 1867, cobalt blue. ................... **300.00**

**Townsend's (Dr.) Sarsaparilla** (embossed), square w/beveled corners, applied sloping collared mouth, smooth base, 1860-70, dark yellowish olive, 9" h. (some minor mouth roughness) ............................ **176.00**

**Townsend's (Dr.) Sarsaparilla** (embossed), square w/beveled corners, applied tapered collar, large ring open pontil, ca. 1850, medium emerald green, 9½" h. (ILLUS. top next column) ................................... **319.00**

**Vincent, Hathaway & Co.,** Boston, soda, round bottom, round, applied heavy collared mouth, smooth base, 1860-80, bright medium green, ½ pt. (light interior haze, minor exterior wear) .................................................. **77.00**

**Woodworth's (Dr.) Sarsaparilla -** Birmingham, Ct., rectangular, aqua, 10" h. ............................................ **150.00**

**Yager's Sarsaparilla,** rectangular, amber, 8½" h. .................................... **35.00**

## WHISKEY & OTHER SPIRITS

**Beer,** "Buckeye Bottling Works, Toledo O." embossed buck on front, golden yellow w/olive hue, qt. ............. **48.00**

**Beer,** "Bunker Hill Lager, Charleston, Mass.," ornate embossing, vertical fluting, bail & stopper, yellowish amber, pt. (¼" base ding) ................... **20.00**

**Beer,** "Feigenspan & Co. Newark, NJ," w/hand holding glass of beer embossed in a monogram, golden yellow, pt. ........................................... **60.00**

**Beer,** "Honolulu Brewing Co., Honolulu, T.H.," blob top, aqua, qt. ...... **45.00**

**Beer,** "Hoyt Brothers Lynn & Salem Mass. - Milwaukee Lager Beer," yellowish amber, pt. ........................... **50.00**

**Beer,** "Reymann Brewing Co., Wheeling, WV.," blob top, amber, qt... **25.00**

**Beer,** "Stone Beer, F. Sandkuhler's Superior Weiss Beer, Baltimore." (base chip) ....................................... **35.00**

**Beer,** "Twin City Bottling Co.," embossed pair of clasped shaking hands in slugplate, bail & stopper, golden amber, pt. ............................... **28.00**

**Bourbon,** "Bear (w/bear head in a triangle) Grass Bourbon S.F.

Braunschweiger & Co.," tooled lip, smooth base, 1895-1905, clear w/light sun colored tint, 11¾" h. ........ **675.00**

**Bourbon,** "Bear Grass Kentucky Bourbon (around triangle w/bear head in triangle), Braunschweiger & Bumstead Sole Agents, S.F.," large applied mouth, smooth base, 1881-85, amber shading slightly darker in top & base, 12" h. .......................... **4,800.00**

**Bourbon,** "Blake's (G.O.) Bourbon Ky. Whiskey Moore, Reynolds & Co Sole Agent's for Pacific Coast," applied mouth, smooth base, 1875-80, brilliant light to medium yellowish amber shading slightly darker in base & mouth, 12" h. ..................... **3,700.00**

**Bourbon,** "Cutter (J.F.) Extra Trade (star inside shield) Old Bourbon," applied mouth, smooth base, 1870-80, bright sparkling amber, 7⅜" h. (perfect) ........................................... **750.00**

**Bourbon,** "Cutter (J.F.) Extra Trade (star inside shield) Old Bourbon," applied mouth, smooth base, 1870-80, light to medium yellowish amber, 7⅜" h. (perfect) ........................... **1,900.00**

*J.H. Cutter Old Bourbon*

**Bourbon,** "Cutter (J.H.) Old Bourbon, A.P. Hotaling Sole Agents" w/embossed shoulder crown, applied mouth, smooth base, 1877-

80, shading slightly darker in mouth & base, light to medium yellowish amber w/faint hint of olive, 11⅞" h. (ILLUS.) ....................................... **1,200.00**

**Bourbon,** "Miller's Extra Trade (large shield) Mark, E. Martin & Co. Old Bourbon," applied mouth, smooth base, 1871-79, bright yellowish amber w/hint of olive, 7¼" h. .......... **475.00**

**Bourbon,** "Jesse-Moore & Co. Louisville Ky., G.H. Moore Old Bourbon & Rye, Moore Hunt & Co Sole Agents" (circular), antler motif w/"Trade Mark" (above), applied mouth, smooth base, 1878-82, light to medium yellowish amber w/hint of olive, 7⅜" h. ............................... **11,500.00**

**Bourbon,** "OPS (monogram) Bourbon Whiskey From A.P. Hotaling Old Private Stock San Francisco," applied mouth, smooth base, 1879-85, sparkling medium shaded amber w/hint of orange, 11⅞" h. .............. **4,100.00**

**Bourbon,** "Teakettle (picture of teakettle) Trade Mark Old Bourbon Shea, Bocqueraz & McKee Agents San Francisco," applied mouth, smooth base, 1871-87, rich amber shading to deep amber in neck & base, 12⅛" h. ................................... **575.00**

**Case gin,** free-blown, square tapered, applied mushroom mouth, pontil scar, 1780-1830, deep yellowish olive, 9¼" h. (minor exterior wear) .... **220.00**

**Case gin,** free-blown, tapered, applied collared mouth, pontil scar, 1780-1830, yellowish olive, 9½" h. (light interior stain) ..................................... **77.00**

**Case gin,** free-blown, tapered gin form, tooled mushroom mouth, pontil scar, 1800-30, yellowish olive, 9⅝" h. (very minor case wear on shoulders) .. **143.00**

**Gin,** "Carleton & Howards - Celebrated London Dock - Cordial Gin," tapered collar, smooth base, square, olive-amber, 10" h. ............... **500.00**

**Spirits,** free-blown, squatty cylindrical-form, sheared mouth w/string rim, pontil scar, England, 1750-1800, deep olive-green, 7" d., 4⅜" h. ......... **468.00**

**Spirits,** free-blown, globular, Wistarburg-type, sheared mouth, w/applied string rim, pontil scar, England, 1830-60, dark olive-amber, 7¾" d, 5⅛" h. (two ½" chips on string rim) ..................................... **77.00**

*Early Onion-form Seal Bottle*

**Spirits,** free-blown, squat onion shape, applied shoulder seal w/embossed date "1699" & a King's bust profile, applied ring lip, pontil scar, 1" & ½" lip chips, overall etching, deep olive-green, 6" d., 6" h. (ILLUS.)......................... **2,250.00**

**Spirits,** free-blown,cylindrical squat form, sheared mouth w/applied rim, pontil scar, Netherlands, 1710-30, deep yellowish olive, 7⅝" h. (almost entirely covered w/golden & cream colored iridescent stain).................... **143.00**

**Spirits,** free-blown, rectangular w/indented corners, sheared mouth w/applied pewter collar & cap, pontil scar, Europe, 1750-1850, amethyst w/white fernlike loopings, 7¾" h. (some light wear marks on one side)................................................. **3,300.00**

**Spirits,** free-blown, cylindrical, applied seal w/"Ino Walley Budleigh 1763," cylindrical, sheared mouth w/wide string rim, pontil scar, England, ca. 1763, deep olive-amber, 4½" d, 9" h. (some interior residue, a shallow ¼" flake on base, faint ½" spider crack on body to left of seal)......................................... **1,100.00**

**Spirits,** free-blown, cylindrical, applied seal w/"A. Kelly," applied sloping collared mouth w/ring, pontil scar, England, 1810-30, dark yellowish olive, 10½" h. (minor mouth roughness) .... **110.00**

**Spirits,** free-blown slender bulbous form, sheared mouth w/applied string rim, pontil scar, France, 1760-80, yellowish olive, 10½" h. (very faint interior haze spots, exterior high point wear) ................................. **88.00**

*W. Peters Early  Seal Bottle*

**Spirits,** free-blown "black glass," cylindrical, applied belly seal w/"W. Peters 1775," wide rounded shoulder, crudely applied double collared mouth, pontil, minor ³⁄₁₆" open bubble on rear w/overall scratches, deep olive-amber, 12½" h. (ILLUS.) ........................... **1,269.00**

**Spirits,** mold-blown, globular, eighteen ribs, swirled to left, flattened chest, tooled mouth, pontil scar, aqua, 6⅝" h. (minor exterior high point scratches) ......................... **77.00**

**Spirits,** mold-blown, early swirled, half-post, pinched at mid-body, sheared mouth w/applied pewter collar, pontil scar, Europe, 1775-1825, brilliant aqua, 7½" h. (faint interior haze, missing pewter cap).................................................... **715.00**

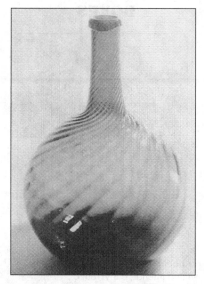

*Early Zanesville Spirits Bottle*

*Casper's Whiskey Bottle*

**Spirits,** mold-blown, globular w/24 ribs swirled to right, outwardly rolled lip, pontil scar, Zanesville, Ohio, ca. 1840, golden amber, 7½" h. (ILLUS.) ............................................. **385.00**

**Spirits,** pattern-molded, beehive-form, club bottle, ribbed & swirled to left, applied collared mouth, pontil scar, 1800-30, brilliant aqua, 8⅛" h. ......... **176.00**

**Whiskey,** "AAA, G MC M F (inside cross), Old Valley Whiskey," applied mouth, smooth base, shading darker in neck base & center, 1870-80, yellowish gold w/hint of olive, 7⅞" h. ................................................ **875.00**

**Whiskey,** "Ahrens-Bullwinkel Co., Trade (antlered deer standing) Mark, San Francisco, Cal.," cylindrical tooled lip, "5 38H" embossed on smooth base, 1900-10, medium yellowish amber, 11½" h. .................. **675.00**

**Whiskey,** "Altschul Distilling Co., Dayton," amber. .................................. **40.00**

**Whiskey,** "Casper's Whiskey Made By Honest North Carolina People," applied mouth, smooth base, 1880-90, cobalt blue, 11⅞" h. (ILLUS. above) ................................ **325.00**

**Whiskey,** "Casper's Whiskey Made by Honest North Carolina People," cylindrical w/fluted shoulder, tooled sloping collared mouth w/ring, smooth base, 1880-1900, cobalt blue, 11⅞" h. qt. (¼" shallow chip on top of mouth) .................................... **275.00**

**Whiskey,** "Casper's Whiskey Made by Honest North Carolina People," cylindrical w/fancy fluted shoulder, sloping collared mouth w/ring, smooth base, 1880-1900, cobalt blue, 11¾" h. (unearthed, ⅜" chip on side of mouth, light overall stain) ...... **253.00**

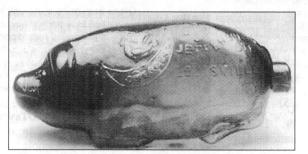

*Duffy Figural Pig Whiskey Bottle*

Whiskey, embossed "Duffy Crescent Salloon 204 Jefferson Street Louisville, KY" w/rooster perched on moon, pig-shaped, burst lip, smooth base, ca. 1870, golden amber, 7½" l. (ILLUS. bottom previous page)...... **1,155.00**

Whiskey, "Fire Copper Distilled, Sour Mash, Old Oaken Bucket, Pure Rye," figural wooden barrel-form, tooled sloping collared mouth w/ring, smooth base, 1860-80, clear, 7⅜" h. ............................................. **303.00**

Whiskey, "Good Old Bourbon in a Hog's-," figural pig, small tooled mouth, smooth base, 1870-90, yellow95amber darkening to deep amber at snout, 6⅝" h. ..................... **220.00**

Whiskey, "Hall (Edw. E.), New Haven, Ct.," paper label w/manufacturer's name & "Grocers and Wine Merchants, 381 State Street New Haven, Conn.," round, applied sloping collared mouth w/ring, smooth base, 1860-80, 11¼" h. (retains 70% label)............................ **154.00**

Whiskey, "Imported by R.F. Nichols & Co Camp St. New Orleans," sealed cylinder, applied mouth & seal, blown in three-piece mold, pontil scarred base, deep olive-amber, 11½" h. (perfect) .............................. **800.00**

Whiskey, "Jordan Giles & Co.," applied mouth "C & I" on smooth base, ca. 1873, cylindrical, medium yellowish old amber in embossed area, shading darker in neck & base, 12" h. (lightly cleaned restoring full luster)................................................ **800.00**

Whiskey, "Kane, O'Leary & Co, 221 & 223 Bush St. S.F." (in square slug plate), cylindrical, applied mouth, smooth base, 1879-891, light to medium amber w/orange hue, 12⅛" h. ...................................... **925.00**

Whiskey, "Krambambulia" w/paper label, jug-form, flattened chestnut form w/applied solid glass handle, applied mouth w/ring, pontil scar, 1840-60, golden amber, 8½" h. (label is 70% complete) ................... **149.00**

Whiskey, "Rothenberg (M.) & Co (large walking rooster) San Francisco, Cal." tooled lip, smooth base, 1900-10, shaded medium orangish amber, 11½" h. ................. **625.00**

# BOXES

*Sapphire Blue Glass Box*

Apothecary box, painted pine, green, w/fitted interior, early 19th c., 13½ × 19¾", 8¾" h. (imperfections) .. **$431.00**

Band box, wallpaper-covered, oval, covered in paper w/vermillion & black medallions on a blue ground, Pennsylvania, ca. 1837, 6 x 8⅝", 4¼" h............................................. **1,265.00**

Band box, wallpaper-covered, oval, covered in paper w/multicolored ground & stylized floral & foliate decoration, the interior bearing fragments of newspapers, the latest dating 1846, Pennsylvania, ca. 1846, 4½ x 7¾", 4¾" h. ................. **1,610.00**

Band box, wallpaper-covered, oval, covered in green paper w/persimmon polka dots, Pennsylvania, ca. 1840, 8½ x 13¼", 6" h. ...............................**1,265.00**

Band box, wallpaper-covered, oval, covered in blue paper w/orange & yellow stylized floral & foliate decoration, the interior lined w/newspaper *Hannover Gazette* dated March 11, 1841, Pennsylvania, ca. 1841, 11½ x 16", 9" h. .................**1,380.00**

Glass box, painted, squatty bulbous sapphire blue body w/hinged domed cover, decorated w/gold panels all over sides & cover w/blue hearts w/white enameled outlining, w/white scroll trim, w/three-footed base, 4½" d., 4" h. (ILLUS. above)............. **295.00**

Glass box, round off-white opalescent body w/hinged cover decorated w/appliqué purple branches & green leaves w/rose colored flowers, on three ormolu feet, 5½" d., 4⅜" h. ...... **595.00**

**Glass box,** round w/metal hinged cover & rim mounts, amber decorated w/gold flowers & leaves on top & sides, 6" d., 3⅛" h. ............. **195.00**

*Amber Glass Jewel Box*

**Jewel box,** amber glass, ovoid shape w/hinged cover, sanded gold panels w/white, blue & pink floral decorations, small blue flowers & leaves, three ormolu feet w/cupid heads, 4½" d., 5" h. (ILLUS.) ............ **325.00**

*Patriotic Painted Box*

**Painted box,** rectangular, hipped & hinged lid centering painted crossed American flags flanking a red, white & blue striped shield w/gold painted scroll surround opening to a conforming box w/red, white & blue chevrons, starred & C-scrolled painted decoration, 8⅞ × 12", 5¾" h. (ILLUS.) ................................ **460.00**

**Patch box,** round, emerald green glass w/hinged cover decorated w/heraldic emblem enameled in orange, white & gold, gold trim around sides, 1⅛" h., 2" d. (ILLUS. top next column) ................... **95.00**

**Patch box,** round, lime green glass covered w/lacy brass filigree, 1⅜" h., 2⅜" d. (ILLUS. below middle) .......... **110.00**

**Pine box,** carved & painted pine, pierced design w/mirrored backplates, possibly Connecticut, ca. 1800, 5½ × 8⅜", 4⅞" h. (imperfections) .............................. **2,300.00**

*Emerald Green Patch Box*

*Lime Green Patch Box*

*Pine Dome-top Box*

**Pine box,** rectangular dome-top, small grain painted w/original red & cream vinegar painting, New England, early 19th c., 13 × 24", 12" h. (ILLUS.) ....................................... **431.00**

**Trinket box,** cherry, carved pinwheel decoration, old finish, Connecticut, late 18th c., 7⅞" l. ............................. **863.00**

# BREWERIANA

*Beer is still popular in this country but the number of breweries has greatly diminished. More than 1,900 breweries were in operation in the 1870s but we find fewer than 40 major breweries supplying the demands of the country a century later. Although micro-breweries have recently sprung up across the country.*

*Advertising items were used to promote various breweries, especially those issued prior to prohibition, now attract an ever growing number of collectors. The breweriana items listed are a sampling of the many items available. Also see: BOTTLES & FLASKS, and SIGNS & SIGNBOARDS*

*Two Pre-Prohibition Beer Glasses*

*Two Enameled Beer Glasses*

**Beer can,** "Ebling," cone-top on slightly flaring foot, silver can w/red strip around middle w/"Ebling" in white above banner marked "Premium Beer," unopened, 12 oz. (some wear)..................................... **$35.00**

**Beer glass,** "Bull Frog," acid-etched, image of leaping frog flanked by "Bull Frog" above "North Western Brewery, - United Breweries Company, - Chicago.," pre-Prohibition.......................................... **90.00**

**Beer glass,** "Citizens Brewing Co.," acid-etched, image of factory surrounded by "Joliet Citizens Brewing Co., - Joliet Brewing Co. - Joliet, ILL.," pre-Prohibition................. **77.00**

**Beer glass,** "Dragon Ale," enameled, "Dragon Ale" atop yellow stylized dragon, Louisville, Kentucky (ILLUS. above left).......................................... **56.00**

**Beer glass,** "J. Steger," acid-etched, "J. Steger & Co." above image of Victorian man wearing top hat holding covered stein above "Mayville, Wis.," pre-Prohibition (ILLUS. right)..................................... **332.00**

**Beer glass,** "John Haas," acid-etched, "John" above rabbit flanked by stalks of grass & leaves above "Purity" all above "Ripon, Wis.," pre-Prohibition (ILLUS. left)..................................... **143.00**

**Beer glass,** "LaTropical Ale," enameled, "LaTropical" above "Taste Tells" atop outline of Florida, next to "Ale" all above "FLA Beer" (ILLUS. right, previous column).......... **56.00**

**Beer glass,** "Muhlhauser," acid-etched, round logo in upper left corner above "Muhlhauser - Hammond Brewing Co. - Hammond, Ind.," pre-Prohibition........................ **171.00**

**Beer glass,** "P. Binzel," acid-etched, "P. Binzel" above round logo w/a "B" atop barley & hops above "Trade Mark" flanked by more barley & hops above "Purity" all above "Oconomowoc, Wis.," pre-Prohibition.......................... **368.00**

**Calendar display,** "Hamm's Beer," woodgrained plastic, shingle roof protects unused 1969 calendar surrounded by "Born Before 1948," all above nature scene visible through gold-tone grill work centered by circle marked "Enjoy - Hamm's - Beer," 7 × 20" h. .............................. **20.00**

**Chair,** "Valley Forge Beer," painted oak, inverted baluster-shaped back w/carved profiles of two men above carved image of wood keg marked "Valley Forge" above "1933"............ **154.00**

*Grouping of Beer Mugs*

**Cork screw,** "Anheuser-Busch," metal, in the shape of a beer bottle w/impressed Anheuser-Busch logo, 2¾" h. (minor scratches & wear) ........ **83.00**

**Counter top display,** "Frankenmuth Beer & Ale," plaster, figure of seated Dachshund dog on base, base reads "Dog Gone Good Beer & Ale," 1940s, 5 × 6", 7" h. (some wear) ........ **26.00**

**Match pack,** "Atlantic Beer," pictures black man serving beer ...................... **30.00**

**Match safe,** "Schlitz Beer," brass case w/nickel silver details & black leather covered body, marked "Schlitz Milwaukee," has sticker on one end & cigar cutter on other, 5" h. ............... **38.00**

**Mug,** pottery, "Hagemeister" above diamond-shaped logo flanked by "Brewing" & "Company" above banner reading "Green Bay Wis.," pre-Prohibition (ILLUS. above left) .... **150.00**

**Mug,** pottery, commemorative, "Jax - Beer" above image of Sugar Bowl trophy above "Dec. 1972 Sugar Bowl - Oklahoma vs. Penn State" (ILLUS. above center) ...................................... **29.00**

**Mug,** pottery, "MIT - Club of New York" above image of steak & beer mug above "1949 - Steak-Stein Dinner - Ruppert Brewery of 22," New York City, New York (ILLUS. above center right) .............................. **33.00**

**Mug,** pottery w/salt glaze, impressed round logo flanked by "Schlitz" & "Beer" above "Milwaukee," impressed blue stripe at top of mug, all on slightly flared foot, pre-Prohibition (ILLUS. above far right) ...................................... **60.00**

**Pen holder,** "Inver House Whiskey," green plastic figure of whisky bottle w/paper label reading "Imported - Inver - House - Rare Scotch Whisky" w/pen & pen holder at shoulder, 8" h. ...................................... **99.00**

*Pair of Pilsner Glasses*

**Pilsner glass,** "Hoff-brau," enameled, "Hoff-brau" on banner above "Beer" atop shield w/stylized bird & crown, Fort Wayne, Indiana ........................... **40.00**

**Pilsner glass,** "Ritz," enameled "Perfection in Beer" above "Ritz," Chicago, Illinois (ILLUS. above left) ... **33.00**

**Pilsner glass,** "Sepp'l Brau," enameled "Sepp'l Brau - Beer - Star Union Products Co. - Peru, Ill." (ILLUS. above right) ........................... **40.00**

**Poster,** "Bock Beer," white, yellow, green & black on red ground, reads "The Original Old German" above a ram above a record w/label that reads "Best on Record" & "Bock Beer" on record 'vinyl,' all to the right of "The Origin of Bock Beer," Queen City Brewing Co., Cumberland, Maryland, poster by Game

*Grouping of Pub Pitchers*

*Bock Beer Poster*

**Pub pitcher,** square, silhouette of Napoleon below drawn curtain above "Courvoiser - The Brandy of Napoleon," lip & handle trimmed w/gold gilt (ILLUS. top center left) ........ **26.00**

**Salseman samples,** "Olympia Beer," three different sizes aluminum cans ranging from 7 oz. to 16 oz., in cardboard box, the set ........................ **20.00**

**Shot glasses,** "Jagermeister," glass, bell-shaped, marked w/"Jagermeister" w/head of a stag below cross, 4" h., set of four ............................................. **20.00**

*Tin Berger Sign*

Lithographing Co. Inc., Baltimore, Maryland, copyright 1948, 14" w., 18" h. (ILLUS.) .................................... **72.00**

**Pub pitcher,** figural, in the shape of suit of armor head piece, marked "Ballantine's Scotch Wiskey" (ILLUS. top left) ............................................. **23.00**

**Pub pitcher,** figural, in the shape of winking man's head wearing black top hat w/bottle as handle, bottle reads "Pickwick - Pure - Old - Pickwick - Whiskey" next to image of man holding his hat beside a bottle, marked "Pickwick Scotch Wiskey" around outside of base (ILLUS. top center right) ................................. **65.00**

**Pub pitcher,** figural, in the shape of a Royal Guardsman's head, marked "Windsor Supreme Canadian" around outside of base (ILLUS. top right) ............................................ **19.00**

**Sign,** "Berger," lithographed tin, die-cut, figure of young woman scantily dressed, she wears a hat reading "Berger" & holds a bottle w/label reading "Berger - Anisade," minor surface roughness & denting, 6" w., 19¼" h. (ILLUS.) ............................. **182.00**

**Sign,** "Bergoff Beer," tin over cardboard, shows colorful winter scene hunting dogs w/pink border, reads "Right-on every Point - Bergoff Beer" in border, 21" w., 13" h. (minor rust spots) .......................................... **50.00**

**Sign,** "Blatz," light-up-type, plastic, red & white, reads "Blatz - finest Beer," Blatz Brewing Co., Milwaukee, Wisconsin, 8" h., 9" w. (soiled) .......... **22.00**

**Sign,** "Old Dutch Beer," fiber, done in red, yellow, black & brown, reads "Drink - Carnegie - Pils'ner - 'The Beer Everyone Likes' - Duquesene Brewing Co. of Pittsburg-Chartiers Valley Brewery," 55½" w., 31½" h................................ **105.00**

**Sign,** "Pabst Blue Ribbon," light-up-type, plastic, red, white & blue, in the shape of the Pabst blue ribbon logo on white ground that read "What'll you have?," light made by Robertson Transformer Co. Blue Island, Ill., 7" h., 11" w........................................ **44.00**

*Rolling Rock Motion Sign*

**Sign,** "Rolling Rock," light-up motion-type, done in colors of brown, black, red, gold & black, depicts horse framed by horseshoe w/"Rolling Rock" above & "On Tap" below, Latrobe Brewing Co., Latrobe, Pennsylvannia, minor scratches & soiling, 15" d. (ILLUS.) .................... **220.00**

**Stein,** pottery w/flat hinged metal lid, Budweiser, color image of a buck above image of the state of Wisconsin above Budweiser logo, No. CS55713 (ILLUS. right, top next column) ............................................ **106.00**

*Two Budweiser Steins*

**Stein,** pottery w/flat hinged metal lid, Budweiser, color image of bald eagle above "Bald Eagle," No. CS106 (ILLUS. left) ..................................... **214.00**

**Tap knob,** "Molson," ceramic, three-sided ................................................. **50.00**

**Tavern sign,** painted & gilt decorated, molded frame enclosing the date & gilt eagle w/"1845" on each side, on black background, New England, ca. 1845, 44" w., 43" h........................ **5,750.00**

**Tray,** "Adolph Coors Golden Colorado Beer," painted metal, round, green & blue image of mountains in center, cream lettering reads "Adolf Coors - Golden, Colorado" all outlined in gold on red border, minor scratches, 13" d. (ILLUS. below)...................... **242.00**

**Tray,** Champlain Ales & Stouts, porcelain ......................................... **120.00**

*Adolph Coors Beer Tray*

**Tray,** "Genese Brewing Co.," painted metal, round, has image of gentleman wearing hat & long coat holding a pipe standing to the side of a pub table, border reads "Genese Brewing Co - Lagar Beer," done in yellow, red & green, Rochester, New York area, 12" d. (scratches & cracking) ........................................ **220.00**

**Tray,** "Bevo Beer," metal, rectangular, scene of brown, black & grey horses pulling a brown, cream & red wagon surrounded by wood grain border, early product of Anheuser-Busch Co., 13¼" w., 10½" h. (minor scratches) ........................................ **88.00**

# BUSTER BROWN

*Buster Brown was a comic strip created by Richard Outcault in the* New York Herald *in 1902. It was subsequently syndicated and numerous objects depicting Buster (and often his dog, Tige) were produced.*

**Comic strip,** shows Buster Brown & Tige teaching cannibals to play baseball, from *New York Herald,* 1909, 15 × 20" .................................**$83.00**

**Handkerchief,** early, signed, mint condition ............................................ **95.00**

**Lamp,** hanging-type, heavy plastic w/stained glass-look has Buster Brown in one panel & Tige in the next w/the number "5" between, done in red, blue, cream & green ....... **72.00**

**Music box,** paper lithograph on metal, round, hand-crank, plays "Three Blind Mice," top shows a skipping Buster Brown & Mary Jane, ca. 1910 ........... **170.00**

**Pull toy,** painted cast iron, figure of Buster Brown standing in a cart being pulled by Tige, Dent Mfg., early 1900s (cart has some paint loss) .................................................. **660.00**

**Rug,** depicts Buster Brown & Tige, Mohawk Carpet Co., 54" d............... **200.00**

**Seal,** cast iron, done in gold, brown & blue, three dimensional image of Buster Brown & Tige, from "Brown Shoe" plant in St. Louis, Missouri, ca. 1904-05, 17" d. ........................ **2,530.00**

**Sleigh,** wood w/steel runners.............. **500.00**

**Sparklers,** Undix brand counter display box w/red printing, display held one dozen individual boxes w/graphic of Buster Brown, only one box of sparklers remaining ............... **125.00**

**Wagon,** wooden w/wooden spoked wheels, all original ........................... **600.00**

# CANDLESTICKS & CANDLEHOLDERS

*King of Diamond Pattern Candlesticks*

**Candelabra,** cut glass, George III-Style, each w/a central tapered spike w/urn-form finial & scalloped cup supporting cascades of faceted drops, mounted at the center w/four scrolled candle arms alternating w/scrolls, the candle arms w/urn-form bobeches & star form drip-pans hung w/further faceted swags, raised on a baluster-form stem on a stepped square base, England, ca. 1900, 13" w., 29" h., pr. .............. **$4,600.00**

**Candlestick,** wrought iron, "hog scraper"-type, complete w/hook & thumb, 5" h. ........................................ **95.00**

**Candlesticks,** Arts & Crafts style, a wide disc foot supporting a very slender shaft slightly swelled at the bottom & tapering to a bulbous ovoid candle socket w/flared rim supporting a separate bobeche, marked "Jarvie," Robert Jarvie, early 20th c., 14" h., pr. ......................... **1,380.00**

**Candlesticks,** brass, cylindrical candle socket w/flattened rim above ringed & baluster-turned stem, on a squared & ringed base w/cut corners, stamped underneath "JOSEPH WOOD," American-made, 1730-34, 7⅜" h., pr. ...................... **4,380.00**

**Candlesticks,** brass, cylindrical socket above a swelled diamond pattern stem knob over the domed, ringed foot, w/pushups, marked "The Diamond Princess," late 19th c., 10¾" h., pr. ...................................... **193.00**

**Candlesticks,** brass, King of Diamonds patt., ring turned standard w/bulbous diamond cut center section on square feet w/cut corners, England, 12⅜" (ILLUS. previous page) ................................................ **595.00**

---

# CANES & WALKING STICKS

**Baleen & silver walking stick,** silver knob decorated w/swirls & scrolls marked "D.D.W.," shaft is highlighted w/dots of ivory w/brass ferrule, ca. 1840, 32¾" l................................... **$825.00**

**Bamboo & bone walking stick,** sword-type, bone handle is intricately carved w/leaves, fruit & a shield, the foil blade is fitted into a bamboo shaft w/white metal ferrule, ca. 1890, foil 22½" l., overall 37½" l................................................ **193.00**

**Coconut wood & whale ivory walking stick,** knob consists of four pieces of ivory & inlaid w/circle of mother-of-pearl, abalone & dark wood, shaft is of dark coconut wood w/copper ferrule, ca. 1850, 34¼" l. (age cracks in ivory) ........................ **330.00**

**Fraternity walking stick,** knob carved in the shape of a bull's head w/glass eyes above black painted band marked w/owners name "Jack Wing," the shaft is carved "1914 - Sigma Phi Epsilon" & the nicknames & initials of the fraternity brothers, white metal ferrule, 35½" (small chip in bull's horn) ................................... **165.00**

**Ivory & ebony walking stick,** turned knob & geometric ivory inlay, ca. 19th c.............................................. **632.00**

**Mahogany & ivory walking stick,** turned ivory knob, the octagonal mahogany shaft elaborately inlaid w/satinwood & mother-of-pearl diamonds & dots also has ivory eyelets & terminates in brass ferrule, possibly English, ca. 1830, 35¼" l. .... **385.00**

*Carved Pine Walking Stick*

**Pine walking stick,** long tapering shaft spirally carved w/figures of turtles, bull frogs, fish, hares & a long green snake terminating in a large alligator w/open jaws sprouting a red floral bud & leafage (ILLUS.).. **3,737.00**

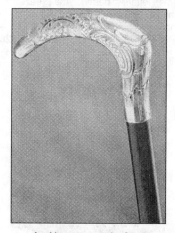

*Art Nouveau-style Cane*

**Rosewood cane,** crook handle w/gold end cap & an angled gold band w/presentation initials, horn ferrule, marked "Tiffany & Co, 18K," ca. 1915, 34⅜" l. ..................................... **523.00**

**Snakewood & sterling cane,** Art Nouveau-style sterling silver handle is decorated w/flowers & scrolls, the smooth shaft has brass ferrule, probably French, ca. 1890, 35" l. (ILLUS. bottom previous page)......... **358.00**

**Sterling cane,** "Sunday stick," handle is fashioned as a mallet-style putter, shaft is stepped partridge w/brass ferrule, London hallmarked 1907, 35¾" l. (ferrule is worn, putter has minor denting)................................... **825.00**

---

# CANS & CONTAINERS

*The collecting of tin containers has become quite popular within the past several years. Air-tight tins were first produced by hand to keep foods fresh and, after the invention of the tin-printing machine in the 1870s, containers were manufactured in a wide variety of shapes and sizes with colorful designs. Also see: ADVERTISING, COCA-COLA COLLECTIBLES and TOBACCIANA*

**Antifreeze,** Thermo 1 gal. can, has winter image of walking snowman holding thermometer over his shoulder & carrying a can of antifreeze w/snow covered car in the background, all above red ground w/white letters "Thermo - Anti-Freeze - Anti-Rust • Safe • Sure Protection," minor scratches & denting, 6½" d., 7¾" h. (ILLUS. below)........................ **$28.00**

*Thermo Antifreeze Can*

**Biscuits,** Loose Wiles Biscuit Co. 3 lb. tin, colorful stylized image of woman feeding an apple to two deer, marked "Loose Wiles Biscuit Company - Bakers of Sunshine Biscuits - Ne Weight 3 Lbs. Address: New York, N.Y. - Made in U.S.A.," 4" h., 10" d. (minor scratches) ........... **50.00**

**Cheese sticks,** Quinlan's Cheese Sticks 1 lb. can, yellow & cream on black background, marked "Readings-Original - Quinlan's - Cheese Sticks - Made By - Quinlan Pretzel Company - Reading, PA. - 'The Stick Is the Same - But the Taste is Delightful'," 3¾" d., 7" h......... **72.00**

**Cigars,** Class rectangular box, orange w/colorful peacock on the end, hinged cover, originally held fifty cheap cigars, made in Pennsylvania, ca. 1920s, 5" h. .................... **20.00 to 40.00**

**Cleanser,** Babbits Cleanser can, waxed cardboard w/tin top & bottom, Orange & cream ground w/blue lettering reads "Babbit's" above an image of uniformed man flanked by "At Your Service" all above "Cleanser," 3" d., 4¾" h. (minor soiling, scratches & rust) .................... **33.00**

**Coffee,** America Cup Coffee, key open-type............................................. **70.00**

**Coffee,** Monarch 1 lb. can, key-wind lid ....................................................... **37.00**

**Coffee,** Venizelos, 1 lb. can............... **450.00**

*Krispy Crackers Tin*

**Crackers,** Sunshine Krispy Crackers 1 lb. tin, blue cover & top part of tin w/arched 'windows' surrounding tin, image of cracker surrounded by "Sunshine - Krispy Crackers," all above a band of chefs carrying trays around bottom, soiling & scratches, 6" d., 7" h. (ILLUS.)............................. **39.00**

**Grease,** Mobilubricant 1 lb. can, cream ground w/red & black lettering "Mobilubricant - One Pound twenty-five cents - Vacuum Oil Company - Rochester U.S.A.," w/original contents, 2½" d., 8½" h. (scratches & soiling) ............................................. **88.00**

**Grease,** White Eagle 1 lb. can, red ground w/white rectangle w/red circle, reads "Dark - Graphite Axle - White Eagle - Grease" across circle & "Product of - Socony-Vacuum - White Eagle Oil Corporation," 3½" d., 4½" h. (scratches, soiling & denting) ......................................... **11.00**

*Dupont Gun Powder Can*

**Gun powder,** Dupont 1 lb. can, red w/black & white paper label w/graphics of American Indian & animals, reads "Dupont - Superfine - F - Gunpowder - Wilmington - Deleware" marked "E.I. Dupont De Nemours & Co. Inc. Wilmigton, Del. U.S.A. No. 23752 De 29 July 1924," soiling (ILLUS.) ................................... **83.00**

**Malt,** Bordens Double Malt 10 lb. can, white, blue & red ........................ **65.00**

**Marshmallow,** Angelus 5 lb. container, w/glass lid ....................... **135.00**

**Motor oil,** Amoco Permalube 5 qt. can, white ground w/blue lettering "Five U.S. Quarts - Permalube - Motor Oil" above red & blue stripes w/centered Amoco logo above "An American Oil Company Product," 6½" d., 9½" h. (minor fading, cover missing) ............................................. **44.00**

**Motor oil,** Penn Franklin 1 qt. can, green can w/image of Ben Franklin above white lettering "Penn Franklin" above black lettering "100% - Pure

Pennsylvania - Motor Oil," 4" d., 5½" h. (scratches, denting & rust on bottom) ............................................ **110.00**

**Motor oil,** Harley Davidson 1 qt. can, orange can w/black shield-like design w/cream letters reading "Genuine - Oil - Refinery Sealed - Harley-Davidson Motor Co. - Milwaukee - U.S.A" surrounding Harley-Davidson logo, w/original contents, 4" d., 5½" h. (scratches, denting & rust) ................................. **253.00**

**Nutmeg,** Zanzibar Nutmeg 6 lb. tin, done in yellow, black, green & blue, depicts village scene of working native women, reads "6 LBS. Net Weight - Zanzibar - Brand - Ground - Nutmeg," 6" w., 9¾" h. (soiling, water stains, paper label on lid is missing) ............................................. **44.00**

**Peanut butter,** Sultana 1 lb. pail, orange ground w/red & black lettering, seated children flank the central printing, pry-off lid, 4" h. .......... **95.00**

**Peanuts,** Planters Peanuts 10 lb. can, red, blue & black, reads "10 Pounds of Wholesome Whole Peanuts - The Planters - Pennant - Salted Peanuts," 8½" w., 9½" h. (minor dents, scratches & soiling)............................ **143.00**

**Rubber mend,** Magic Rubber Mend can, yellow ground w/red letters "Magic - Rubber Mend - Trade Mark Registered by - Eastern Rubber Co. - Philadelphia, Penna.," surrounding image of magician, 2¼" d., 4½" h. (denting, soiling & scratches) ............ **17.00**

**Syrup,** Towle's Log Syrup 1½ oz. (sample size) tin, label looks like log cabin, red side label reads "Towle's Log Cabin" above image of cabin & "Syrup" below (ILLUS. below).......... **375.00**

*Towle's Sample Size Tin*

*Blue Boar Tobacco Tin*

**Tobacco,** Blue Boar Rough Cut tin,
cylindrical w/small lift top, paper
label in color depicting boar hunt,
w/silver plated "humidor" which slips
over the can, ca. 1910-1916, product
of American Tobacco Company
(ILLUS.) .............................. **75.00 to 125.00**

**Tobacco,** Eve Cube Cut vertical
pocket tin, colorful lithograph
of semi-draped nude, Globe
Tobacco Co., Detroit,
1 × 3½ × 3⅓".................... **100.00 to 150.00**

**Tobacco,** Gold Dust vertical pocket
tin, colorful depiction of miners,
Houde Co., Quebec, Canada,
1 × 3 × 4½".................... **750.00 to 2,000.00**

**Tobacco,** Hi-Plane Smooth Cut
vertical pocket tin, lithographed in
white on a red background w/a
two-engine airplane, near
mint ..................................... **15.00 to 20.00**

**Tobacco,** Hi-Plane Smooth Cut
vertical pocket tin, lithographed in
white on a red background w/a four-
engine airplane, 1 × 3 × 4½". **100.00 to 750.00**

**Tobacco,** Lucky Strike Roll Cut
vertical tin, red circle on green
ground, American Tobacco
Company, ca. 1920s-30s,
1 × 3 × 4¼"........................... **20.00 to 50.00**

**Tobacco,** Lucky Strike Roll Cut
vertical pocket tin, red circle on
white background, American
Tobacco Company, ca. 1940s,
1 × 3 × 4½" ........................ **750.00 and up**

**Tobacco,** Mapacuba cube-shaped tin
w/slip top cover sealed w/original
revenue stamp & a paper slogan
sticker, attractive lithograph of

fanciful Havana harbor & ship scene,
non-embossed, w/all original stamps
& labels, made by Bayuk, factory
1600, Philadelphia, ca. 1930s,
5" sq. .................................... **30.00 to 45.00**

**Tobacco,** Old Rip Long Cut vertical
box, printed black on red, flip-top
cover, made by Ginna & Co. for
Allen & Ginters, late 19th c.,
3¼ × 4½ × 7¼"................. **100.00 to 300.00**

*Peachy Vertical Pocket Tin*

**Tobacco,** Peachy Double Cut vertical
pocket tin, yellow background
w/large peach & name in color,
made by Scotten, Dillon Company,
Detroit, factory number one,
ca. 1910-40, 1 × 2½ × 4"
(ILLUS.) ............................. **125.00 to 225.00**

**Tobacco,** Rex Pipe & Cigarette
vertical pocket tin, Spaulding &
Merrick, Chicago (division of Liggett
& Myers), 1 × 3 × 4½" ........ **75.00 to 125.00**

*Sweet Owen Can*

**Tobacco,** Sweet Owen round can, full-color fantasy tin loosely based on the late 19th c. tobacco tin of the same name, 1980s? (ILLUS. bottom previous page) ......................... **5.00 to 15.00**

**Tobacco,** Willoughby Taylor Aromatic Blend vertical pocket tin, printed predominantly in blue, Block Bros. Tobacco Co., Wheeling, West Virginia, 1 × 3 × 4½"............. **10.00 to 20.00**

**Transmission Fluid,** Cadillac, blue ground w/white lettering "Genuine Parts" below Caddilac logo, all above three red stripes marked "Automatic Transmission Fluid - for - Hydra-Matic Transmissions," w/original contents, 4" d., 5½" h. .......**143.00**

---

# CAROUSEL FIGURES

*The ever popular amusement park merry-go-round or carousel has ancient antecedents but evolved into its most colorful and complex form in the decades from 1880 to 1930. In America a number of pioneering firms, begun by men such as Gustav Dentzel, Charles Looff and Allan Herschell, produced these wonderful rides with beautifully hand-carved animals, the horse being the most popular. Some of the noted carvers included M.C. Illusions, Charles Carmel, Solomon Stein and Harry Goldstein.*

*Today many of the grand old carousels are gone and remaining ones are often broken up and the animals sold separately as collectors search for choice examples. A fine reference to this field is* Painted Ponies, American Carousel Art, *by William Mannas, Peggy Shank and Marianne Stevens (Zon International Publishing Company, Millwood, New York, 1986)*

**Horse,** bucking bronco in bucking pose w/head down, carved & painted pine w/relief-carved & incised saddle & blanket detail, inset w/faceted glass stones, w/leather straps & cast-iron stirrups & authentic horse shoes, very worn paint, Herschell-Spillman Company, North Tonawanda, New York, ca. 1910, 53" l., 4' 1½" h. (tail repaired) ...................................... **$4,312.00**

**Horse,** outer row stander, carved pine w/deeply carved mane & intricate saddle, one front leg lifted, Gustav &

*Carved Pine Horse's Head*

William Dentzel, Philadelphia, Pennsylvania, very worn paint, 60" l., 5' h. ............................................. **18,400.00**

**Horse's head,** carved pine, the horse's head w/flowing mane, elaborate strapwork & bronzed & gilded mane, attributed to Marcus Charles Illions, Coney Island, New York, ca. 1912, some abrasions & paint loss, 23" h. (ILLUS.) .............. **2,990.00**

---

# CASH REGISTERS

*James Ritty of Dayton, Ohio, is credited with inventing the first cash register. In 1882, he sold the business to a Cincinnati salesman, Jacob H. Eckert, who subsequently invited others into the business by selling stock. One of the purchasers of an early cash register, John J. Patterson, was so impressed with the savings his model brought to his company, he bought 25 shares of stock and became a director of the company in 1884, eventually buying a controlling interest in the National Manufacturing Company. Patterson thoroughly organized the company, conducted sales classes, prepared sales manuals, and established salesman's territories. The success of the National Cash Register Company is due as much to these well organized origins as to the efficiency of its machines. Early "National" cash registers, as well as other models, are deemed highly collectible today.*

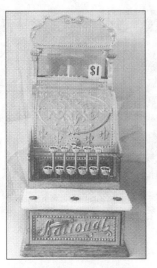

*National Model 5 with Sign*

**Brass,** "National," Model 2, wide scroll
case ............................................ **$1,200.00**
**Brass,** "National," Model 5, fleur-de-lis
case (ILLUS. above) ...................... **1,800.00**
**Brass,** "National," Model 7, fine scroll
case ............................................. **1,200.00**
**Brass,** "National," Model 12, fine scroll
case ............................................. **1,600.00**
**Brass,** "National," Model 30, fine scroll
case ............................................. **2,000.00**
**Brass,** "National," Model 52,
Renaissance case ........................ **2,500.00**
**Brass,** "National," Model 78, Empire
case ............................................... **700.00**

*National Model 216 with Sign*

**Brass,** "National," Model 82, scroll
case ............................................. **1,200.00**
**Brass,** "National," Models 215 or 216,
each (ILLUS. of one, bottom previous
column) ........................................ **1,200.00**
**Brass,** "National," Model 312 ............. **800.00**
**Brass,** "National," Model 374 ............. **800.00**

---

# CERAMICS

*Also see Antique Trader Books* American
& European Art Pottery Price Guide *and*
20th Century American Ceramics Price
Guide.

## ABINGDON

*From about 1934 until 1950, Abingdon
Pottery Company, Abingdon, Illinois
manufactured decorative pottery, mainly
cookie jars, flowerpots and vases. Decorated
with various glazes, these items are becoming
popular with collectors who are especially
attracted to Abingdon's novelty cookie jars.*

*Abingdon Mark*

**Bowl,** 12" d., shell-shaped, No. 533,
yellow glaze ..................................... **$25.00**
**Candleholder,** shell-shaped, double,
light green, 4" h................................ **27.00**
**Candleholders,** double w/ring divider,
ivory, 4" d., 4½" h., pr. ...................... **39.00**
**Cookie jar,** "Bo Peep"
(ILLUS. top next page) ..... **410.00 to 425.00**
**Cookie jar,** "Granny" .......... **175.00 to 225.00**
**Cookie jar,** "Jack-in-the-
Box" ................................. **390.00 to 400.00**
**Cookie jar,** "Pineapple" ...... **115.00 to 145.00**
**Cookie jar,** "Pumpkin" (Jack o'
Lantern) ........................... **550.00 to 575.00**
**Model of a conch shell,** pink, 9" h. ...... **25.00**

*Bo Peep Cookie Jar*

## AUSTRIAN

*Numerous potteries in Austria produced good-quality ceramic wares over many years. Some factories were established by American entrepreneurs, particularly in the Carlsbad area, and other factories made china under special brand names for American importers. Marks on various pieces are indicated in many listings*

*Austrian Marks*

**Butter pat,** fine green stripe on rim, ½" gold border w/engraving (O & EG Royal Austria) .................... **$40.00**

**Bowl,** fruit, fine green stripe on rim, ½" gold border w/engraving (O & EG Royal Austria) ..................... **35.00**

**Gravy boat & 10" l. undertray,** fine green stripe on rim, ½" gold border w/engraving, 2 pcs. (O & EG Royal Austria) ............................................. **30.00**

**Plate,** salad, 8" d. fine green stripe on rim, ½" gold border w/engraving (O & EG Royal Austria) ..................... **45.00**

**Plate,** dinner, fine green stripe on rim, ½" gold border w/engraving (O & EG Royal Austria) .......................... **45.00**

**Plates,** 10" d., each w/a different colorful floral bouquet in the center, delicate floral scrolls around the rim band, marked "Imperial Crown China Austria," late 19th - early 20th c., set of 6 .................................................. **110.00**

**Sardine box,** cov., full-figure fish on lid (Victoria Austria) ........................... **55.00**

**Soup plate w/flanged rim,** large, fine green stripe on rim, ½" gold border w/engraving (O & EG Royal Austria) .. **45.00**

**Soup tureen,** cover & 14" l. undertray, fine green stripe on rim, ½" gold border w/engraving, 13" d., 3 pcs. (O & EG Royal Austria) ..................... **75.00**

**Vegetable bowl,** open, fine green stripe on rim, ½" gold border w/engraving, 9" d. (O & EG Royal Austria) .............................................. **19.00**

**Vegetable bowl,** cov., fine green stripe on rim, ½" gold border w/engraving, 10" d. (O & EG Royal Austria) .............................................. **35.00**

**Vegetable bowl,** cov., fine green stripe on rim, ½" gold border w/engraving, 12" d. (O & EG Royal Austria) .............................................. **40.00**

## BAUER POTTERY

*The Bauer Pottery was moved to Los Angeles, California from Paducah, Kentucky, in 1909, in the hope that the climate would prove beneficial to the principal organizer, John Andrew Bauer, who suffered from severe asthma. Flowerpots, made of California adobe clay, were the first production at the new location, but soon they were able to resume production of stoneware crocks and jugs, the mainstay of the Kentucky operation. In the early 1930s, Bauer's colorfully glazed earthenware dinnerwares, especially the popular Ring-Ware pattern, became an immediate success. Sometimes confused with its imitator, Fiesta Ware (first registered by Homer Laughlin in 1937), Bauer pottery is collectible in its own right and is especially popular with West Coast collectors. Bauer Pottery ceased operation in 1962.*

*Bauer Mark*

**Ashtray,** La Linda patt., red, 4" sq. ..... **$25.00**

**Butter dish,** cov., Ring-Ware patt.,
yellow................................................. **125.00**

**Casserole,** cov., individual, Ring-
Ware patt., yellow .............................. **55.00**

**Creamer & cov. sugar bowl,** miniature,
Ring-Ware patt., yellow, pr. .................... **65.00**

**Mixing bowl,** Ring-Ware patt.,
chartreuse, No. 9, 10" d. ................... **125.00**

**Mixing bowl,** Ring-Ware patt., red,
No. 9, 10" d. ...................................... **125.00**

**Pitcher w/copper handle,** Ring-Ware
patt., turquoise ................................... **85.00**

**Pitcher,** Ring-Ware patt., green, 3 qt. ... **140.00**

**Plate,** 9" d., Ring-Ware patt., cobalt
blue ..................................................... **20.00**

**Plate,** dinner, Ring-Ware patt., yellow... **50.00**

**Plates,** decorated w/strawberries
w/motto, "Woman's work is never
done" & "Man's work is from sun to
sun," marked "Bauer USA, Los
Angeles," pr. .................................... **105.00**

**Teapot,** cov., Ring-Ware patt., red...... **125.00**

**Teapot,** cov., Ring-Ware patt., yellow... **95.00**

# BELLEEK

*Belleek china has been made in Ireland's County Fermanagh for many years. It is exceedingly thin porcelain. Several marks were used, including a hound and harp (1865-1880), and a hound, harp and castle (1863-1891). A printed hound, harp and castle with the words "Co. Fermanagh Ireland" constitutes the mark from 1891. Belleek-type china also was made in the United States last century by several firms, including Ceramic Art Company, Columbian Art Pottery, Lenox Inc., Ott & Brewer and Willets Manufacturing Co.*

## AMERICAN

**Pitcher,** tankard, 10⅝" h., h.p. scene
of three monks eating at a table,
natural colors w/gilt trim on rim &
long angled handle, marked
"Belleek" ......................................... **$413.00**

**Vase,** 8½" h., decorated w/h.p. daisies
(Ceramic Art Company)................... **475.00**

## IRISH

**Basket,** Henshall's Twig, ca. 1940s,
11 × 13".......................................... **1,700.00**

**Bowl,** 4½" d., Thistle Tea Ware "shell
plateux," w/molded shell sides, pink
& turquoise, first black mark ............. **190.00**

**Creamer & open sugar bowl,** Ivy
patt., third black mark, pr. ................. **135.00**

**Creamer & open sugar bowl,**
Shamrock-Basketweave patt., third
black mark, pr. .................................. **225.00**

**Cup & saucer,** Limpet patt., second
green mark ......................................... **30.00**

**Cup & saucer,** Limpet patt., third
black mark ............................. **90.00 to 95.00**

**Cup & saucer,** Shamrock-Basketweave
patt., third black mark .........................**110.00**

**Dessert set:** six cups & saucers, six
dessert plates; Tridacna patt., third
black mark, the set .......................... **395.00**

**Dish,** pot-shaped, swirl pattern
w/applied floral decoration, 3⅔" h..... **260.00**

**Inkstand,** Appleleaf, No. D269, first
black mark ...................................... **2,000.00**

**Marmalade jar,** cov., Shamrock-
Basketweave patt., third black mark .. **125.00**

**Marmalade jar,** cov., decorated
w/green flowers & avocado stems,
marked "Belleek - Ireland, Reg.
No. 0657," 2½" d. base, 4" h............. **154.00**

*Shamrock-Basketweave Tea Service*

**Plate,** 6¼" d., Limpet patt., first green mark.................................................... **30.00**

**Plate,** 7¼" d., Limpet patt., third black mark.................................................... **45.00**

**Salt dip,** shell-shaped, Limpet patt., second green mark............................ **25.00**

**Sugar bowl,** open, Lotus patt., third black mark .......................................... **60.00**

**Tea service:** large cov. teapot, creamer & open sugar bowl, twelve cups & saucers & twelve 8" plates; Shamrock-Basketweave patt., third black mark, the set (ILLUS. of part bottom previous page)..................... **1,500.00**

# BENNINGTON

*Bennington wares, which ranged from stoneware to parian and porcelain, were made in Bennington, Vermont, primarily in two potteries, one in which Captain John Norton and his descendants were principals, and the other in which Christopher Webber Fenton (also once associated with the Nortons) was a principal. Various marks are found on the wares made in the two major potteries, including J. & E. Norton, E. & L.P. Norton, L. Norton & Co., Norton & Fenton, Edward Norton, Lyman Fenton & Co., Fenton's Works, United States Pottery Co., U.S.P. and others.*

*The popular pottery with the mottled brown on yellowware glaze was also produced in Bennington, but such wares should be referred to as "Rockingham" or "Bennington-type" unless they can be specifically attributed to a Bennington, Vermont factory.*

*Bennington Mark*

**Book flask,** impressed "Ladies of Bennington, Ladies of Kossuth, Kossuth Own, Battle of Bennington" on the four sections of the spine, 5⅝" h. .......................................... **$4,125.00**

**Book flask,** spine impressed "Bennington Battle," mottled Flint Enamel glaze, 1849-58, 7¾" h. ........ **825.00**

**Book flask,** spine impressed "Ladies Companion," mottled Flint Enamel glaze, 1849-58, 8" h...................... **1,980.00**

**Book flask,** spine impressed "Bennington Battle," mottled Flint Enamel glaze, 1849-58, 10⅝" h. ... **3,575.00**

**Chamber set:** wash basin, pitcher & cov. soap dish; alternate rib pattern, impressed 1849 mark on basin & pitcher, mottled Flint Enamel glaze, basin 13½" d., dish 5" l., pitcher 11¾" h., 3 pcs. (ILLUS. of part, below) ............................................ **1,980.00**

**Flowerpot w/attached saucer,** molded cattails decoration, mottled brown Rockingham glaze, 10¼" h. ... **149.00**

**Jug,** stoneware, semi-ovoid, slip-quilled cobalt blue swirling leafy flower sprig on the front, impressed

*Bennington Washbowl & Pitcher*

mark "J. & E. Norton, Bennington, Vt. 1½," 1½ gal., 12½" h. (minor hairlines, small rim flakes) ............... **193.00**

**Lamp base,** olive green baluster-form standard on a brown stepped base, mottled Flint Enamel glaze, impressed 1849 mark, 8⅞" h. ........ **1,760.00**

**Model of a lion,** standing & facing left, one paw on a ball, "coleslaw" mane, tongue up, mottled Flint Enamel glaze, 1849-58, 10¾" l. (tail restored) ........................................ **4,400.00**

**Model of a poodle,** standing animal carrying a basket in its mouth, mottled olive green Flint Enamel glaze, 8⅜" h. ................................. **3,850.00**

**Picture frame,** rectangular, plain scalloped edge, mottled Flint Enamel glaze, 1849-58, 6 × 6½" ...... **825.00**

**Picture frame,** rectangular w/plain scalloped outer edge & beveled inner edge, mottled Flint Enamel glaze, 1849-58, 11¼" h. (upper left corner cracked)............................... **990.00**

**Pitcher,** 7⅝" h., graniteware, presentation-type, globular base, scalloped rim, high D-shaped handle, inscribed on side "To My Wife" embellished w/gold & blue vintage design, mid-19th c. ............... **880.00**

*Pond Lily Pitcher*

**Pitcher,** 8½" h., porcelain, Pond Lily patt., relief-molded white blossoms & leaves on a blue ground, USP ribbon mark (ILLUS.) .................................... **138.00**

**Pitcher,** 9½" h., porcelain, Paul & Virginia patt., relief-molded white figures & landscape on a blue ground, USP ribbon mark ................. **220.00**

**Toby bottle,** figural, depicting a man wearing a cloak & hat, w/mustache & tassels, holding a bottle, mottled Flint Enamel glaze, marked "L. Fenton & Co. Enamel 1849 Bennington, V. Pat.," 10¾" h. ........ **1,540.00**

**Vase,** 10¾" h., parian, decorated w/applied grapes & leaves on blue ground, unmarked ........................... **400.00**

**Vases,** 9⅞" h., tulip-shaped w/an octagonal flaring bowl raised on an octagonal flaring foot, mottled Flint Enamel glaze, 1849-58, pr. (glaze imperfections under bases, two tiny flakes on one rim) ......................... **2,420.00**

# BISQUE

*Bisque is biscuit china, fired a single time but not glazed. Some bisque is decorated with colors. Most abundant from the Victorian era are figures and groups, but other pieces from busts to vases were made by numerous potteries in the U.S. and abroad. Reproductions have been produced for many years so care must be taken when seeking antique originals.*

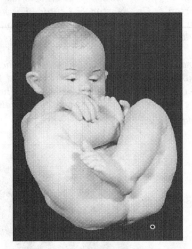

*Heubach Piano Baby*

**Basket,** miniature, quilted pastel blue, 1¾" h. ............................................... **$30.00**

**Figure of WW I nurse w/vase attached,** Heubach "sunburst" mark, 6½" h. .............................................. **250.00**

**Figures,** Dutch boy & girl seated, signed "Heubach," 5" h., pr.............. **395.00**

**Figures,** Dutch boy & girl seated, signed "Heubach," 6" h., pr.............. **495.00**

**Model of a dog** sitting & scratching his side, white w/grey spots, signed "Heubach," 7" l., 5½" h...................... 130.00

**Piano baby,** lying on back, reaching for toes, 10½" l. (ILLUS. previous page) ............................................... 665.00

**Plates,** 2¾" d., each decorated w/a different child's face, Heubach "sunburst" mark, set of 5................... 225.00

## BLUE & WHITE POTTERY

*The category of blue and white or blue and grey pottery includes a wide variety of pottery, earthenware and stoneware items widely produced in this country in the late 19th century right through the 1930s. Originally marketed as inexpensive wares, most pieces featured a white or grey body molded with a fruit, flower or geometric design and then trimmed with bands of splashes of blue to highlight the molded pattern. Pitchers, butter crocks and salt boxes are among the numerous items produced but other kitchenwares and chamber sets are also found. Values vary depending on the rarity of the embossed pattern and the depth of color of the blue trim; the darker the blue, the better. Some entries refer to several different books on Blue and White Pottery. These books are: Blue & White Stoneware, Pottery & Crockery by Edith Harbin (1977, Collector Books, Paducah, KY); Stoneware in the Blue and White by M.H. Alexander (1993 reprint, Image Graphics, Inc., Paducah, KY); and Blue & White Stoneware by Kathryn McNerney (1995, Collector Books, Paducah, KY).*

**Basin,** Apple Blossom patt., 7" d ...... $165.00

**Basin,** Apple Blossom patt., 14" d ...... 245.00

**Basin,** Bowtie (Our Lucile) patt., 15" d ................................................. 150.00

**Bowl,** berry, 4½" d., 2½" h., Plain ......... 45.00

**Bowl,** 9½" d., 5" h., Currents & Diamonds patt. .................................. 230.00

**Bowl,** Daisy and Lattice patt., milk-type, three sizes .............. 200.00 to 275.00

**Bowl,** 8" d., 4½" h., Heart patt ............. 300.00

**Bowl,** Incised Lines patt. ...................... 100.00

**Bowl,** miniature, 3½" d., w/bail handle.. 50.00

**Bowl,** 6" d., Peacock patt., nesting-type (ILLUS. right) ............................ 275.00

**Bowl,** 7" d., Peacock patt., nesting-type (ILLUS. center) ........................ 295.00

**Bowl,** 8" d., Peacock patt., nesting-type (ILLUS. left).............................. 325.00

**Bowl,** 6" d., Plain.................................... 70.00

**Bowl,** 9" d., Pyramid patt., part of nesting bowl set ................... 130.00 and up

**Bowl,** Zig-Zag patt., nesting-type ...................................... 150.00 and up

**Bowls,** Basketweave patt., nesting set, price depends on size, the set ... 220.00

**Bowls,** 6" d., 7" d, 8" d., Peacock patt., nesting-type, the set ................ 895.00

**Brush vase,** Morning Glory & Basketweave (Willow) patt ............... 175.00

**Butter crock,** cov., 7" d., 4" h ............. 245.00

**Butter crock,** cov., advertising-type, 6" d., 6" h ........................................ 100.00

**Butter crock,** cov., Apple Blossom, patt., 7" d., 5" h. ........................... 285.00

**Butter crock,** cov., Daisy & Waffle patt........................................................ 235.00

**Butter crock,** cov., Daisy and Trellis patt., 6" d., 4" h. ............................... 175.00

**Butter crock,** cov., Diffused Blue patt., 6" d., 5" h. ............................... 115.00

**Butter crock,** cov., Eagle patt., 6" d., 6" h. (ILLUS. right, top next page) .... 600.00

**Butter crock,** Indian patt., without cov., 2 lbs. ....................................... 600.00

**Butter crock,** cov., Indian patt., 3 lbs. .. 700.00

**Butter crock,** cov., Leaf Flemish patt., 8" d., 7" h. ...................................... 200.00

*Peacock Nesting Bowls*

*Eagle Pattern Salt & Butter Crocks*

**Butter crock,** cov., Peacock patt.,
w/bail handle, 3 lbs., 5" h. .................. **750.00**

**Butter crock,** cov., Plain, 4½" d., 4" h. .. **50.00**

**Butter crock,** cov., stenciled, 5 lbs..... **258.00**

**Butter crock,** cov., Swastika patt.
(Indian good luck sign), 6¼" d.,
5½" h. ................................................. **150.00**

*Willow Pattern Mug & Butter Crock*

**Butter pot,** cov., Willow patt., 3 lbs.
(ILLUS. right) .................................... **325.00**

**Canister,** cov., Basketweave &
Morning Glory (Willow) patt.,
"Cereal," average 5½" to 6½" h. ....... **475.00**

**Canister,** cov., Basketweave &
Morning Glory (Willow) patt.,
"Raisins," average 5½" to 6½" h. ...... **600.00**

**Canister,** cov., Basketweave &
Morning Glory (Willow) patt., "Rice,"
average 5½" to 6½" h. ...................... **475.00**

**Canister,** cov., Basketweave &
Morning Glory (Willow) patt.,
"Tobacco," average 5½" to 6½" h. ..... **600.00**

**Canister,** cov., Basketweave &
Morning Glory (Willow) patt.,
average 5½" to 6½" h. ...................... **475.00**

**Canisters,** cov., Diffused Blue patt.,
5¾" d., 6½" h., each (ILLUS. top
next column) .................................... **175.00**

**Casserole,** cov., Flying Bird patt.,
9½" d. ............................................... **500.00**

*Diffused Blue Pattern Canisters*

*Peacock Pattern Pitcher & Coffeepot*

**Cereal bowl,** Flying Bird patt., 4" d.,
2" h. ................................................. **250.00**

**Chamber pot,** cov., Bowtie (Our Lucile)
patt., 5⅜" h. (ILLUS. right, top next
page) .................................................**165.00**

**Chamber pot,** Open Rose and Spear
Point Panels patt., 9½" d., 6" h ......... **300.00**

**Coffeepot,** cov., Peacock patt.
(ILLUS. right, bottom) .................... **2,400.00**

**Cookie Jar,** cov., Brickers patt., 8" d.,
8" h. ................................................. **475.00**

**Cookie Jar,** cov., Diffused Blue patt.,
rounded body w/short cylindrical
neck & small handle, 8" d., 9" h. ....... **325.00**

**Cup,** Paneled Fir Tree patt., 3" d.,
3½" h. ............................................... **175.00**

**Cuspidor,** Peacock patt., 10" d., 9" h. ... **325.00**

**Cuspidor,** Poinsettia and Basketweave
patt., 9¾" d., 9" h. .............................. **180.00**

**Ewer & basin,** Floral Decal (Memphis
pattern), ewer 11¼" h., basin 15" d. . **365.00**

*Bowtie (Our Lucile) Pattern Waste Jar & Chamber Pot*

*Beaded Rose Pattern Toothbrush Holder, Ewer & Soap Dish*

**Ewer & basin,** Willow patt., ewer
9" d., 13" h., Basin 15" d., 4½" h....... **550.00**

**Ewer,** Banded Scroll patt., rare, 9" h... **750.00**

**Ewer,** small, Beaded Rose patt., 7" h.,
(ILLUS. center, bottom) ................... **245.00**

**Grease jar,** cov., Flying Bird patt.,
4" h. ................................................ **695.00**

**Hall boy,** Wildflower patt., 6¾"............ **300.00**

**Iced tea cooler,** cov., plain ovoid
body w/spigot, decorated w/thin blue
bands & printed "3" & "Iced Tea
Cooler," 13" d., 15" h. ...................... **310.00**

**Jardiniere & pedestal base,**
Cosmos/Open Rose patt., jardiniere
6" h. (ILLUS. next column)............... **950.00**

**Jardiniere,** Apple Blossom patt.,
6" h. .................................................. **425.00**

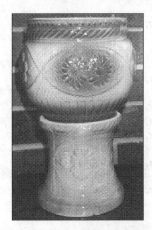

*Blue & White Jardiniere & Pedestal*

*Acorn, Cattail & Conifers Pattern Pitchers*

**Kettle,** cov., Peacock patt., w/bail
handle, 5 quart.............................. **1,000.00**

**Milk crock,** Apricot with Honeycomb
patt., 10" d., 5" h. ............................ **250.00**

**Mixing bowl,** Flying Bird patt., 6" d..... **225.00**

**Mixing bowl,** Flying Bird patt., 7" d..... **295.00**

**Mug,** Bands and Rivets patt................. **75.00**

**Mug,** Bowtie (Our Lucile) patt., 3¾" d... **100.00**

**Mug,** Grape Cluster in Shield patt.,
16 oz.................................................. **225.00**

**Mug,** Grape with Rickrack patt........... **150.00**

**Mug,** Willow patt., 3" d., 5" h.,
(ILLUS. left w/Willow butter pot) ....... **175.00**

**Pitcher,** 8½" h., decorated w/Dutch
scene ............................................... **275.00**

**Pitcher,** 8" h., Acorn patt., stenciled
design (ILLUS. top center) ............... **300.00**

**Pitcher,** Bands and Rivets patt.,
½ gal................................................. **285.00**

**Pitcher,** Bands and Rivets patt.,
¼ gal................................................. **285.00**

**Pitcher,** Bands and Rivets patt.,
⅝ gal................................................. **225.00**

**Pitcher,** 10" h., Beaded Rose
patt. .................................. **300.00 to 375.00**

**Pitcher,** 6½" h., Beaded Swirl patt...... **750.00**

**Pitcher,** 9" h., 7" d., Bluebird patt. ...... **425.00**

**Pitcher,** 4" h., Butterfly patt., (ILLUS.
left, top next column) ....................... **550.00**

**Pitcher,** 9" h., Butterfly patt., (ILLUS.
right, next column) ........................... **345.00**

**Pitcher,** 4½" h., Castle patt................. **225.00**

*Butterfly Pattern Pitchers*

**Pitcher,** 6" h., Castle patt................... **275.00**

**Pitcher,** 8" h., Castle patt.,................. **325.00**

**Pitcher,** 5" h., Conifers patt., stenciled
design (ILLUS. top right).................. **200.00**

**Pitcher,** Cattail patt., 1 gal. ................ **450.00**

**Pitcher,** Cattail patt., ½ gal. ............... **250.00**

**Pitcher,** Cattail patt., ¼ gal. ............... **195.00**

**Pitcher,** Cattail patt., ⅝ gal. ............... **325.00**

**Pitcher,** Cattail patt., straight sided..... **195.00**

**Pitcher,** 5⅞" h., Cattails patt.,
stenciled design (ILLUS. top left)...... **185.00**

**Pitcher,** Cherry Band patt.,
w/advertising, ................................... **300.00**

**Pitcher,** 7½" h., 6¼" d., Dainty Fruit
patt., (ILLUS. right, top next
page) ................................................ **550.00**

**Pitcher,** 7" h., 3½" d.,Diffused Blue
with Rose Decal patt........................ **125.00**

*Flying Bird & Dainty Fruit Pattern Pitchers*

**Pitcher,** 9" h., Dutch Boy & Girl
Kissing patt. ...................................... **250.00**
**Pitcher,** 9" h., 6" d., Flying Bird patt.
(ILLUS. above left)............................ **725.00**
**Pitcher,** Girl with Dog patt., 8¾" h. .. **1,200.00**
**Pitcher,** Grape Cluster in Shield patt.,
2 pt..................................................... **400.00**
**Pitcher,** Grape Cluster in Shield patt.,
3 pt..................................................... **425.00**
**Pitcher,** cov., 7" h., Grape Cluster on
Trellis patt., squat body, pg. 65 ........ **200.00**
**Pitcher,** sizes range from 5" to 9½" h.,
Grape Cluster on Trellis
patt. ................................ **165.00 to 245.00**
**Pitcher,** 7" h., Grape Leaf Band patt. . **165.00**
**Pitcher,** 9" h., 6½" d., Indian in War
Bonnet patt. ..................................... **300.00**

*Lincoln Head Pitchers*

**Pitcher,** Lincoln Head patt., large,
signed "UHL" (ILLUS. left) ............. **1,500.00**
**Pitcher,** Lincoln Head patt., small,
signed "UHL" (ILLUS. right) .............. **695.00**
**Pitcher,** 7" h., 7" d., Paul Revere patt... **475.00**
**Pitcher,** 7¾" h., 6½" d., Peacock patt.,
(ILLUS. left w/Peacock pattern
coffeepot) ........................................... **900.00**

*Rare Polar Pattern Pitcher*

**Pitcher,** 8½" h., 7¾" d., Poinsettia
with Square Woven Cane patt. ........ **350.00**
**Pitcher,** 10" h., 9¾" d., jug-form, Polar
patt. (ILLUS.) ................................... **650.00**
**Pitcher,** 8¾" h., Rose on Trellis patt... **375.00**

*Scroll & Leaf Pitcher*

**Pitcher,** 7" h., Scroll & Leaf patt.,
advertising-type, (ILLUS.) ................. **410.00**
**Pitcher,** 9" h., 6½" d., Stag patt. ......... **550.00**
**Pitcher,** 9" h., 7" d., Swastika (Indian
good luck sign) patt. ........................ **200.00**
**Pitcher,** 9" h., 7" d., Swirl patt............. **350.00**
**Pitcher,** 7½" h., Windmill patt. ............ **315.00**
**Pitcher,** 8½" h., Windy City patt.......... **300.00**
**Pitcher & mug set,** Flying Bird patt.,
includes pitcher & six mugs, rare... **1,800.00**
**Refrigerator jar,** cov., 7" d., 6½" h.,
3 lbs. ................................................ **325.00**
**Roaster,** cov., Wildflower patt., 12" d.,
8½" h. ............................................... **345.00**

**Salt,** cov., Apple Blossom patt., 6" d.,
4" h. .................................................. **375.00**

**Salt,** cov., Apricot patt., 5¾" d., 5" h..... **250.00**

**Salt,** cov., Blocks patt., 6½" d., 6¾" h. ... **175.00**

**Salt,** cov., Eagle patt., 6" d., 6" h. (ILLUS.
left w/Eagle patt. butter crock) ............. **500.00**

**Salt,** cov., Grape & Basketweave
patt., 6" d., 4" h. ............................... **235.00**

**Salt,** cov., Grape & Waffle patt., 6¾" d.,
6½" h. .............................................. **325.00**

**Salt,** cov., Grape & Waffle patt.,.......... **350.00**

**Salt,** cov., Peacock patt., 5" d., 5" h. .. **375.00**

**Salt,** cov., Swastika (Indian good
luck symbol), 6" d., 4" h. .................. **200.00**

**Salt,** cov., Waffle patt. ......................... **220.00**

**Sand jar,** Polar patt., 14½" d.,
12¼" h. .......................................... **1,250.00**

**Scuttle mug,** 4" d., 6" h. .................. **1,250.00**

**Soap dish,** Beaded Rose patt., 4¾" d.
(ILLUS. right w/Beaded Rose pattern
ewer)................................................ **150.00**

**Soap dish,** Bowtie (Our Lucile) patt.,
w/drainer insert, 5¼" d., 2⅛" h.,
3 pcs. .............................................. **165.00**

**Stein,** Windy City patt., 5½" h. ............ **165.00**

**Stewer,** cov., Wildflower patt., 2 qt. .... **345.00**

**Stewer,** cov., Willow patt., 2 qt........... **325.00**

**Toothbrush holder,** Beaded Rose
patt., 5" h. (ILLUS. left w/Beaded
Rose pattern ewer & soap dish) ....... **170.00**

**Umbrella Stand,** Two Stags patt.,
blue & white, 21" h........................ **1,750.00**

*Ovoid Diffused Blue Vase*

**Vase,** Diffused Blue, patt., wide ovoid
body tapering to a flaring short neck,
pointed shoulder handles
(ILLUS.) ............................... **300.00 and up**

**Vase,** Wicker Basket & Flower patt.,
waisted cylindrical form (ILLUS. left,
top next page) ..................... **350.00 and up**

**Waste jar,** cov., Apple Blossom patt.
(ILLUS. below right) ......................... **300.00**

**Waste jar,** cov., Bowtie (Our Lucile)
patt., 9½" h. (ILLUS. left w/Bowtie
chamber pot) .................................... **200.00**

**Waste jar,** cov., Rose & Fishscale
patt., 10" h. (ILLUS. below left)......... **325.00**

**Water bottle,** Diffused Blue patt., ovoid
body tapering to a small molded
mouth, lightly embossed w/scrolls

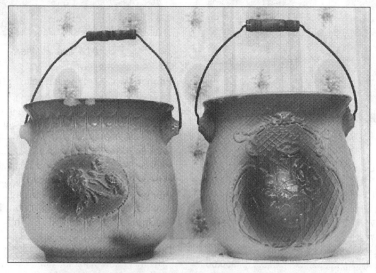

*Rose & Fishscale  and Apple Blossom Pattern Waste Jars*

*Wicker Basket & Flower Vase and Diffused
Blue Pattern Water Bottle*

around the shoulder & w/pointed
leaves around the base (ILLUS.
right)..................................... **245.00 and up**
**Water cooler,** cov., Cupid patt.,
w/spigot, 5 gal.................................. **675.00**
**Water cooler,** cov., Elk & Polar Bear
patt., w/spigot, 9½" d., 14" h. ............ **825.00**
**Water cooler,** cov., Polar patt.,
w/spigot, 2 gal.................................. **600.00**
**Water cooler,** cov., Polar patt.,
w/spigot, 4 gal.................................. **725.00**

## BLUE RIDGE DINNERWARES

*The small town of Erwin, Tennessee was
the home of the Southern Potteries, Inc.,
originally founded by E.J. Owen in 1917 and
first called the Clinchfield Pottery.*

*In the early 1920s Charles W. Foreman
purchased the plant and he revolutionized the
company's output, developing the popular line
of hand-painted wares sold as "Blue Ridge"
dinnerwares. Free-hand painted by women
from the surrounding hills, these colorful
dishes in many patterns, continued in
production until the plant's closing in 1957.*

**Baker,** divided, w/metal holder, Julie
patt.................................................... **$32.00**
**Baker,** rectangular w/slanted dividers,
Triplet patt., 8⅝ × 13" .......................... **18.00**
**Bonbon,** deep shell-shape, Nove Rose
patt...................................................... **40.00**
**Bonbon,** deep shell-shape, Tussie
Mussie patt. ....................................... **45.00**
**Bonbon,** flat shell-shape, Chintz patt. ... **45.00**
**Bonbon,** flat shell-shape, Nove Rose
patt...................................................... **45.00**

**Bowl,** cereal, 6" d., Poinsettia patt. ......... **9.00**
**Bowl,** salad, Mardi Gras patt. ............... **32.00**
**Cake plate,** flat, w/metal holder, Leaf
patt....................................................... **34.00**
**Casserole,** cov. Leaf & Bar patt........... **28.00**
**Casserole,** cov., Triplet patt................. **28.00**
**Celery dish,** leaf-shaped, Chintz patt. ... **35.00**
**Custard cups,** Leaf patt., set of 8........ **50.00**
**Pie baker,** Leaf & Bar patt., 9¾" d. ....... **20.00**
**Pitcher,** 6" h., vitreous china, figural
chick, white ......................................... **40.00**
**Pitcher,** 6¾" h., Sculptured Fruit patt.... **55.00**
**Pitcher,** 7½" h., Sculptured Fruit patt.... **50.00**
**Plate,** bread & butter, 6" d., Waltz
Time patt., Colonial shape ................... **9.00**
**Plate,** 9" d., Cock O' The Walk patt....... **15.00**
**Plate,** 10" d., Poinsettia patt................. **16.00**
**Plate,** 10½" d., divided, Leaf & Bar
patt....................................................... **28.00**
**Plate,** dinner, Waltz Time patt.,
Colonial shape .................................... **16.00**
**Plate,** divided, Petunia patt. ................. **18.00**
**Plate,** luncheon, Waltz Time patt.,
Colonial shape .................................... **14.00**
**Plate,** salad, Dutch Bouquet patt.,
Colonial shape .................................... **14.00**
**Plates,** dinner, Rustic Plaid patt.,
set of 6 ................................................ **30.00**
**Platter,** 11" l., Lyonnais patt. (fine
crazing) ............................................. **125.00**
**Platter,** Plume patt. ............................. **20.00**
**Salt & pepper shakers,** Spiderweb
patt., Skyline shape, pr. ...................... **15.00**
**Sugar bowl,** cov., Spiderweb patt.,
Skyline shape ...................................... **14.00**
**Teapot,** cov., vitreous china,
w/chevron handle, Castlewood patt.... **55.00**
**Teapot,** cov., Spiderweb patt., Skyline
shape.................................................... **70.00**
**Vase,** bud, 9¼" h., corset-shaped,
Flo patt................................................. **75.00**

## BOEHM PORCELAINS

*Although not antique, Boehm porcelain
sculptures have attracted much interest as
Edward Marshall Boehm excelled in hard
porcelain sculptures. His finest creations,
inspired by the beauties of nature, are in the
forms of birds and flowers. Since his death in
1969, his work has been carried on by his wife
at the Boehm Studios in Trenton, New Jersey.
In 1971, an additional studio was opened in*

*Malvern, England, where bone porcelain sculptures are produced. We list both limited and non-limited editions of Boehm.*

## BIRDS

**Green Jays w/Black Persimmon,**
No. 486, 1966-74, 18" h., pr. ....... **$1,900.00**

**Hummingbird,** Male on Cactus,
No. 440, 1958-75, 8½" h. .... **525.00 to 575.00**

**Kestrels,** Male & Female, No. 492,
1968-71, male 14" h., female
16½" h., pr. .................................. **2,150.00**

**Mallards,** in flight, No. 406, 1952-60s,
11½" from wing tip to wing tip,
11" h., pr. ...................................... **1,625.00**

**Northern Water Thrush w/Ferns &
Cladonia,** No. 490, 1967-73,
10½" h. ............................................ **850.00**

**Parula Warblers w/Morning Glories,**
No. 484, 1965-73, 9" w., 14½" h.... **1,900.00**

*Ptarmigans*

**Ptarmigans,** male & female on
individual bases, molded to
resemble snow-covered rocks,
No. 463, 1962-68, 14" h & 9½" h.,
pr. (ILLUS.) .................................. **1,800.00**

## BRAYTON LAGUNA POTTERY

*Durlin E. Brayton began his operation in Laguna Beach, California in 1927. After his marriage a short time later to Ellen Webster Grieve, who also became his business partner, the venture became a successful endeavor. One of the most popular lines was the Children's series which featured a rubber stamp-like mark, with the first name of the child followed underneath with a line which separates the words "Brayton Pottery." Both white clay and pink clay were used during Brayton's production. More than 150 people, including*

*approximately twenty designers, were employed by Brayton. Sometimes on items too small for a full mark, designers would incise their initials. It was not until after World War II and the mass importation of pottery products into the United States that Brayton's business declined. Operations ceased in 1968.*

$$Brayton$$
$$Laguna$$
$$Pottery$$

*Brayton Laguna Mark*

**Cookie jar,** "Matilda" ........................ **$495.00**
**Creamer,** figural calico cat ................... **45.00**
**Figure of a ballerina** .......................... **85.00**
**Figure,** Josephine Baker.................... **175.00**
**Figure,** old peasant woman .............. **125.00**
**Figurines,** Chinese children, pr. ......... **125.00**
**Figure group,** "Gay Nineties Singers
at Bar".............................................. **95.00**
**Figure group,** "Gay Nineties
Swimmers"........................................ **95.00**
**Figure group,** jazz singer, pianist &
piano, 3 pcs. .................................. **375.00**
**Model of a swan,** turquoise................. **85.00**
**Planter,** figural peasant woman ........... **50.00**
**Planter,** figural lady, mauve floral
decoration on cream ground,
10½" h. .............................................. **90.00**
**Salt & pepper shakers,** figural calico
dog & cat, green & yellow, pr............. **45.00**
**Vase,** corset-shaped, blue ................... **35.00**

## BUFFALO POTTERY

*Buffalo Pottery was established in 1902 in Buffalo, New York, to supply pottery for the Larkin Company. Most desirable today is Deldare Ware, introduced in 1908 in two patterns, "The Fallowfield Hunt" and "Ye Olden Days," which featured central English scenes and a continuous border. Emerald Deldare, introduced in 1911, was banded with stylized flowers and geometric designs and had varied central scenes, the most popular being from "The Tours of Dr. Syntax." Reorganized in 1940, the company now specializes in hotel china.*

*Buffalo Mark*

## DELDARE

**Candlesticks,** Ye Olden Days - Ye
Village Street, 9½" h., pr... **$845.00 to 875.00**

**Card tray,** The Fallowfield Hunt - The
Return, 7¾" d. ................. **400.00 to 410.00**

**Card tray,** Ye Olden Days - Ye Village
Street, 7¾" d. .................. **470.00 to 480.00**

**Dresser tray,** Dancing Ye Minuet,
1909, 9 × 12" .................................... **675.00**

**Hair receiver,** cov., Ye Village Street... **415.00**

*Deldare Humidor*

**Humidor,** cov., bulbous, There was
an Old Sailor, etc., 8" h. (ILLUS.) .. **1,075.00**

**Mug,** Ye Olden Days - Ye Lion Inn,
4½" h. .............................. **360.00 to 370.00**

**Pitcher,** 8" h., octagonal, To demand
my annual Rent - Welcome Me...,
1908................................................ **610.00**

**Plate,** 9½" d., The Fallowfield Hunt -
The Start, artist-signed, 1908 ........... **140.00**

**Plate,** chop, 14" d., An Evening at
Ye Lion Inn, artist-signed,
ca. 1980 .......................... **575.00 to 600.00**

**Saucer,** Ye Village Street...................... **50.00**

*Buffalo Soup Plate*

**Soup plate w/flanged rim,** The
Fallowfield Hunt - Breaking Cover,
9" d. (ILLUS.).................... **470.00 to 480.00**

**Soup plate w/flanged rim,** Ye Olden
Days - Ye Village Street, 9" d. .......... **450.00**

**Tea set:** cov. teapot, cov. sugar bowl
& creamer; Ye Olden Days, creamer
3" h., sugar bowl 4½" h., teapot
5¾" h., 3 pcs. .................................... **900.00**

## EMERALD DELDARE

**Card tray,** handled, Dr. Syntax
Robbed of his Property, 7" d............. **725.00**

**Plate,** 8½" d., Dr. Syntax - Misfortune
at Tulip Hall....................................... **550.00**

## MISCELLANEOUS

**Creamer,** Abino Ware ........................ **635.00**

**Cup & saucer,** Gaudy Willow patt. ..... **115.00**

**Pitcher,** jug-type, 7½" h., George
Washington, blue decoration, gold
trim, 1905 ......................... **545.00 to 575.00**

**Pitcher,** jug-type, 9½" h., John Paul
Jones decoration w/bust portrait
under the spout, 1907...................... **187.00**

**Pitcher,** tankard, 8¼" h., Robin Hood,
1906................................................ **275.00**

**Plate,** 9" d., scalloped rim, The
Gunner scene, deep bluish-green .... **125.00**

**Plate,** 9½" d., Dusky Grouse scene,
1908................................................... **60.00**

**Plate,** 9½" d., mallard duck scene, 1908.. **60.00**

**Plate,** 9½" d., wild turkey scene, 1907.. **60.00**

**Plate,** 10" d., Abino Ware, windmill
scene ................................................ **900.00**

**Plate,** 10¼" d., Roosevelt Bears series,
five single bear scenes & five action
scenes around border, one large
action scene in center of plate......... **1,075.00**

**Relish dish,** Vienna patt. ..................... **34.00**

## CAMARK POTTERY

*The name "Camark" originated from its location. The first three letters of two words, "Camden" and "Arkansas" produced the name Camark. The pottery was founded in late 1926 by Samuel (Jack) Carnes who had married Gressie Umpstead whose wealthy family helped Carnes in founding the Camark Art and Tile Pottery. About 1927, John and Jeanne Lessell, along with Jeanne's daughter, Billie, came to work at Camark. John Lessell, as Art Director for Camark, has been credited with creating iridescent and lustre ware using Arkansas clays. Even with Jack's pottery talents, being an astute businessman, and the hiring of well-known ceramic artists, art pottery was produced only a few years. There were too many economic hardships associated with the late 1920s. The business was sold but Carnes stayed on to help with the transition. As Camark moved into the 1930s, drip glazes became popular and creation of simple commercial cast ware and utilitarian items were manufactured. At that time, the pottery began producing assorted novelty pieces, some decorated artware and a variety of bowls, vases and planters. In 1962, the pottery was purchased by the Daniels family. After Mr. Daniels died in 1965, his wife, Mary, struggled to keep the pottery open. Mostly, the merchandise already produced was sold and not much new production occurred. In 1982, the pottery closed. However, in 1986, it was revived when the Ashcraft brothers, Mark and Gary, purchased the land, buildings, machinery, molds and inventory. As of this date, they have not produced any pieces and have stated that the old Camark molds will not be used. Also see:* 20th Century American Ceramics Price Guide *(Antique Trader Books, 1996)*

*Camark Marks*

Basket, yellow, 3 × 5" ........................... $6.00
Basket, two handled, flared, green,
    4½ × 5" ............................................... 6.00
Basket, double, center-handled, relief-
    molded cabbage leaf decoration,
    maroon, No. 138, 4½ × 5½" ................. 8.00

Bowl, 9½" d., 4" h., melon rib,
    scalloped edge, green, No. 624 .......... 10.00
Bowl, 9½ × 12", leaf-shaped, turned-
    up edge, yellow ................................... 10.00
Cornucopia-vase, horizontal rib,
    cream, 8" h., 9" d. ................................ 8.00
Flower arranger, curved holes for
    flowers, cream, 4" d., 2½" h. ................. 3.00
Pitcher, 3¼" h., relief-molded bead &
    scroll decoration, green, No. 139A ....... 4.00
Pitcher, 4¼ " h., relief-molded bead &
    scroll decoration, white, No. 139B ........ 5.00
Pitcher, 5¼" h., bulbous, relief-
    molded bead & scroll decoration,
    olive, No. 139C .................................... 8.00
Planter, two figural swans, white
    w/h.p. beak & eyes, 7 × 7" .................. 14.00
Planter, model of a rooster, pink .......... 25.00
Vase, 4¼" h., 4½" w., nautilus shell-
    shaped, dark green .............................. 8.00
Vase, 5" h., footed, flared, split top,
    leaf-shaped, green, No. 827 ................. 7.00
Vase, 5¾" h., 7" d., loving cup shape
    w/high handles, melon rib, scalloped
    edge, green, No. 505 ........................... 7.00

## CANTON PORCELAIN

*This ware has been decorated for nearly two centuries in factories near Canton, China. Intended for export sale, much of it was originally inexpensive blue-and-white hand-decorated ware. Late 18th and early 19th century pieces are superior to later ones and fetch higher prices.*

Bowl, 10"d., shallow scalloped rim ... $303.00
Dish, elongated oval w/shaped sided,
    10⅜" l. ............................................... 330.00
Dish, oblong, 12¼" l. .......................... 660.00
Fruit basket & undertray, oval
    w/reticulated sides & flaring rim,
    matching oval undertray, basket
    9¼ × 11", 5" h., 2 pcs. (minor
    imperfections) ................................... 633.00
Hot water dish, octagonal, 9⅜ ×
    10½" ................................................ 1,045.00
Jar, cov., square w/tin lid, 13½" h (chip
    on one top corner) .......................... 1,485.00
Pitcher, 6¾" h., ovoid body tapering
    to a flaring rim, arched strap handle
    (edge flakes) ..................................... 800.00
Pitcher, cov., 9" h., wide ovoid body
    w/intertwined handle & foo dog finial
    (chips) ............................................... 605.00

**Pitcher,** water, 13¼" h., tall pear-shaped body w/arched rim spout, long bamboo-form handle, decorated w/a continuous hill & stream landscape, 19th c. ............ **2,070.00**

**Planters,** oval w/deep gently rounded sides & a wide flattened rim, decorated w/continuous river landscapes, the rims decorated w/prunus blossoms & a 'crackle ice' pattern, 19th c., 10⅞" l., pr. ............. **920.00**

**Plate,** chop, 13½" d. ......................... **1,403.00**

**Platter,** 19" l., oblong octagon (old staple repair) ................................ **1,265.00**

**Platters,** 17" l., oblong w/cut corners, characteristic central landscape scenes, 19th c., pr. ...................... **1,265.00**

**Soup tureen,** cov., deep oblong sides, decorated w/continuous landscape scene, boar's head end handles, 19th c., 10¾" l. ................ **1,035.00**

**Soup tureen,** cov., deep oblong angled sides on a high flaring foot, molded end handles, low domed cover w/branch finial, the base decorated w/panels of landscape scenes, landscape on the cover, 19th c., 13" l. ................................. **1,495.00**

**Teapot,** cov., individual, cylindrical body slightly tapering to small opening w/a fitted cover w/knob finial, intertwined handle, 5¼" h. (mismatched lid) .............................. **688.00**

**Teapot,** cov., wide oval cylindrical body w/a rounded shoulder tapering to a small top opening w/a fitted cover w/knob finial, angled handle & nearly straight swan's neck spout, 19th c., 5¼" h. (worn gilding) ........... **550.00**

**Vegetable dish,** cov., almond-shaped, 9" l. ...................................... **105.00**

**Vegetable dish,** cov., almond-shaped, 11⅜" l. ................................. **440.00**

**Washbowl & pitcher set,** the pitcher w/a tall pear-shaped body w/a wide arched spout & plain arched handle, each decorated w/a hill & stream landscape, the bowl exterior w/bamboo boughs, late 19th - early 20th c., bowl 15½" d., pitcher 13⅛" h., the set ............................ **3,220.00**

## CERAMIC ARTS STUDIO OF MADISON

*Founded in Madison, Wisconsin in 1941 by two young men, Lawrence Rabbitt and Reuben Sand, this company began as a "studio" pottery. In early 1942 they met an amateur clay sculptor, Betty Harrington and, recognizing her talent for modeling in clay, they eventually hired her as their chief designer. Over the next few years Betty designed over 460 different pieces for their production. Charming figurines of children and animals were a main focus of their output in addition to models of adults in varied costumes and poses, wall plaques, vases and figural salt and pepper shakers.*

*Business boomed during the years of World War II when foreign imports were cut off and, at its peak, the company employed some 100 people to produce the carefully hand-decorated pieces.*

*After World War II many poor-quality copies of Ceramic Arts Studio figurines appeared and when, in the early 1950s, foreign imported figurines began flooding the market, the company found they could no longer compete. They finally closed their doors in 1955.*

*Since not all Ceramic Arts Studio pieces are marked, it takes careful study to determine which items are from their production.*

*Ceramic Arts Studio Marks*

**Bank,** figural, Mrs. Blankety Bank ....... **$90.00**

**Bell,** figural, Summer Belle (no clapper) ............................................... **60.00**

**Figurine,** Accordion Boy, 5" h. ... **50.00 to 60.00**

**Figurine,** Balinese Dancer, 9½" h. ........ **60.00**

**Figurine,** Bo Peep, 5¼" h. (ILLUS. top next page) ......... **25.00 to 35.00**

**Figurine,** Boy Blue .............................. **26.00**

**Figurine,** Colonial Man ........................ **30.00**

**Figurine,** Comedy, light green, 10⅜" h. ... **90.00**

**Figurine,** Cuban girl, shades of green .................................... **35.00 to 40.00**

**Figurine,** Drummer Girl, 4¼" h. ............ **70.00**

**Figurine,** Dutch Love Girl, blue or yellow, 4⅞" h., each ........................... **35.00**

**Figurine,** Gay 90s Man, second version (hat in right hand), 6½" h. ........ **50.00**

**Figurine,** Pensive ................................. **55.00**

*Bo Peep Figurine*

**Figurine,** Pioneer Susie, standing girl
w/broom, 5½" h. .................. **40.00 to 50.00**

**Figurine,** Rebakah, 10⅛" h.................. **87.00**

**Figurine,** Saxophone Boy, blue,
5½" h. .................................... **45.00 to 55.00**

**Figurine,** Southern Belle (Miss
Lucindy), yellow & green, 6⅞" h. ........ **50.00**

**Figurine,** Sultan on pillow, 4¾" h.......... **40.00**

**Figurine,** Summer Sally ........ **45.00 to 55.00**

**Figurine,** Water Woman, light green,
11½" h ............................................. **135.00**

**Figurine,** shelf-sitter, Kissing Girl,
blue, 4⅞" h.......................................... **35.00**

**Figurines,** Beth & Bruce, dancers,
5" & 6½" h., pr.................................... **65.00**

**Figurines,** Comedy & Tragedy, 10" h.,
pr. ..................................... **150.00 to 200.00**

**Figurines,** Gypsy Tambourine Girl &
Violin Boy, pr. .................................. **165.00**

**Figurines,** Hans & Katrinka, yellow,
6½ & 6¼" h., pr.............................. **120.00**

**Figurines,** Lu-Tang & Wing Sang,
6¼" h., pr............................. **75.00 to 85.00**

**Figurines,** Peter Pan & Wendy, on
bases w/tall leafy plants, pr. ... **95.00 to 125.00**

**Figurines,** shelf-sitters, Ballet En
Pose & Ballet En Repose, 5¼" h.,
pr. ..................................... **140.00 to 150.00**

**Figurines,** shelf-sitters, Cowboy &
Cowgirl, pr. ...................................... **125.00**

**Figurines,** shelf-sitters, Dutch Boy &
Girl, pr.................................................. **36.00**

**Figurines,** shelf-sitters, Nip & Tuck,
4¼" h., pr. .......................................... **40.00**

**Figure group,** Hansel & Gretel,
7" h...................................... **35.00 to 45.00**

**Model of a giraffe,** copper green
glaze, 6¼" h........................................ **75.00**

**Model of a skunk,** Daddy..................... **25.00**

**Models of Mother & Baby Gorilla,**
pr. ....................................................... **65.00**

**Planter,** model of a girl's head, Becky .. **75.00**

**Planter,** model of girl's head, Lotus,
beige w/black accents, 7⅞" h. ............ **75.00**

**Planter,** model of man's head,
Manchu, beige w/black accents,
7⅞" h. ................................................. **75.00**

**Plate,** 5⅜" d., relief-molded shape of
state of Wisconsin w/face of Paul
Bunyan in center, blue, marked on
reverse "The Ceramic Arts Studio,
Wisconsin Clays, Madison, Wis." ..... **165.00**

**Razor bank,** figural, barber's Head....... **95.00**

**Salt shaker,** figural frog, 2" h. .............. **29.00**

**Salt shaker,** figural Scottie dog, black .. **29.00**

**Salt & pepper shakers,** figural Calico
Cat & Gingham Dog, pr. ..................... **65.00**

**Salt & pepper shakers,** figural dog &
doghouse, pr....................................... **60.00**

**Salt & pepper shakers,** figural
elephants, pr....................................... **50.00**

**Salt & pepper shakers,** figural fish,
pr. ....................................................... **48.00**

**Salt & pepper shakers,** figural frog &
toadstool, pr....................................... **35.00**

**Salt & pepper shakers,** figural horse
head, grey, pr. ................................... **48.00**

**Salt & pepper shakers,** figural
monkeys, pr......................... **70.00 to 80.00**

**Salt & pepper shakers,** figural
Mother & Baby Cow, pr. ... **100.00 to 120.00**

**Salt & pepper shakers,** figural
Mother & Baby Kangaroo, pr. ............. **75.00**

**Salt & pepper shakers,** figural
Mother & Baby Monkey, pr. ............... **65.00**

**Salt & pepper shakers,** figural Native
Boy & Elephant, pr........................... **150.00**

**Salt & pepper shakers,** figural Native
Boy on Alligator, pr. ......................... **165.00**

**Salt & pepper shakers,** figural
parakeets, Chirp & Twirp, pr.............. **50.00**

**Salt & pepper shakers,** figural
Siamese Cat & Kitten, pr....... **55.00 to 65.00**

**Salt & pepper shakers,** figural Wee
Chinese couple, pr............................. **25.00**

**Salt & pepper shakers,** figural Wee
Eskimos, pr......................................... **46.00**

**Vase,** bud, 7" h., Chinese girl
Lu-Tang...............................**30.00 to 40.00**

**Vases,** triple-bud, figures of Lu-Tany & Wing-Sang standing in front of bamboo-form cylinders, white w/green trim, pr.................................. **70.00**

**Wall plaque,** pierced to hang, Chinese Lantern Man & Woman, light green, 8" h., pr. ......................... **75.00**

**Wall plaques,** pierced to hang, figural Comedy & Tragedy, 10⅜" h. & 10" h., pr. ........................................ **175.00**

## CHILDREN'S MUGS

*The small sized mugs used by children first attempting to drink from a cup appeal to many collectors. Because they were made of such diverse materials as china, glass, pottery, graniteware, plated silver and sterling silver, the collector can assemble a diversified collection or single out a particular type around which to base a collection. Also see: CHILDREN'S DISHES.*

**Staffordshire pottery,** cylindrical, black transfer-printed letter "K" (is for kitten...etc) & on reverse "L" (is for ladder...etc), 2½" h. ......................... **$99.00**

**Staffordshire pottery,** cylindrical, black transfer-printed design of the Bible surrounded by flowers, enamel trim in red, green, brown & yellow, titled "Search the Scriptures," 2½" h... **99.00**

**Staffordshire pottery,** cylindrical, black transfer-printed design of the Bible over the title "The Path of Truth is Plain & Safe," enamel trim in green, yellow & red, 2½" h................ **121.00**

**Staffordshire pottery,** cylindrical, black transfer-printed scene of boy on a hobby horse, enamel trim in yellow, red & green, titled "The Young Dragoon," 2½" h. ................... **121.00**

**Staffordshire pottery,** cylindrical, black transfer-printed poem concerning Christianity, pink lustre rim (1½" l. hairline off rim)................ **121.00**

**Staffordshire pottery,** cylindrical, black transfer-printed prayer "Grace After Meal....etc," highlighted in pink lustre, red, yellow & green enamels, 2½" h. (handle has been off & glued & there is an interior rim chip w/a 1½" l. hairline)................................. **72.00**

**Staffordshire pottery,** cylindrical, black transfer-printed scene of two people leading a two-wheeled cart w/chairs, clothing & a chest of drawers, highlighted in ochre, green & red, 2½" h..................... **99.00**

**Staffordshire pottery,** cylindrical, brown transfer-printed hunting scene titled "Partridge Shooting," enamel trim in red, yellow & green, 2½" h. (faint spider on bottom)...................... **55.00**

**Staffordshire pottery,** cylindrical, black transfer-printed scripture titled "Industry is Fortune's Handmaid," enamel trim in yellow, red, blue & green, 2⅜" h. .................................. **99.00**

**Staffordshire pottery,** cylindrical, black transfer-printed scriptural quotation "Speak not to deceive - Listen not to betray," surrounded by flowers & Bible trimmed in yellow, green, blue & red enamels, 2¾" h. (old rim restoration) ......................... **110.00**

**Staffordshire pottery,** cylindrical, brown transfer-printed scene titled "The Juggler," enamel trim in red, blue, yellow & green, 2¾" h. .............. **99.00**

**Staffordshire pottery,** cylindrical, black transfer-printed scene of two children playing w/tops titled "Whip Top," enamel trim in red, yellow & green, 2¾" h. .................................... **99.00**

**Staffordshire pottery,** cylindrical, black transfer-printed "Flowers that Never Fade...Charity," 2⅞" h. (½" l. hairline off rim).................................. **33.00**

**Staffordshire pottery,** cylindrical, dark green transfer-printed alphabet, flanked by scenic views of a cottage & a milkmaid w/cows, sparsely decorated w/red & blue enamel, 2⅞" h. ............................................. **121.00**

## CLEMINSON

*Betty Cleminson began her home-based business, named "Cleminson Clay" in 1941. Within two years it was necessary to move to larger facilities in El Monte, California and the name was changed to "The California Cleminsons." Originally, Mrs. Cleminson concentrated on creating butter dishes, canisters, cookie jars—mostly kitchen-related items. After the move, and with up to 150 employees, she was able to expand her lines with giftware such as vases, wall plaques, cups and saucers, cleanser shakers and a full line of tableware called Distlefink. The incised, stylistic "BC" mark was the first mark used; the California Cleminson mark can be found with or without the boy and girl on each side. The company went out of business in 1963.*

*Cleminson Mark*

**Lazy susan,** Gala Gray....................... **$50.00**
**Nesting platters,** set of 3 ..................... **30.00**
**Razor blade holder,** model of a
man's head........................................ **10.00**
**Soap dish,** model of a bathtub ............. **24.00**
**Wall plaque,** pierced to hang, heart-
shaped w/original ribbons................... **15.00**
**Wall pocket,** model of a coffeepot........ **24.00**

# COORS POTTERY

*In 1908 John J. Herold of Owens and Roseville moved to Golden, Colorado and together with the Adolph Coors family, opened Herold Pottery Company. He remained with the company for only two years but the name did not change until 1920 when it became the Coors Porcelain Company. Rosebud, a Coors product, is one of the most popular lines being collected today. There are several variations for the Rosebud and leaves but, generally, collectors are pleased to collect any variation. Glazes are green, orange, rose, white (ivory), yellow, or blue. Today the ivory glaze is a hard-to-find color.*

*Coors Ceramic Division is still operating today. They produce porcelain items used in chemical laboratories.*

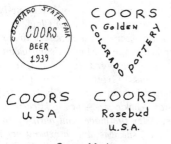

*Coors Marks*

**Apple baker,** cov., Rosebud patt., red .. **$38.00**
**Bean pot,** cov., Rosebud patt., rose,
10" d. ............................................... **65.00**

**Bean pot,** cov., Thermal Cooking
China line, green, 6" d. ...................... **65.00**
**Bowl,** 7" d., Thermal Cooking China
line, white w/floral decoration ............ **25.00**
**Cookie jar,** cov., w/large knob finial,
applied ear handles, Rosebud patt.,
maroon .............................................. **65.00**
**Dinner service:** six 7" d. bread &
butter plates, six 9¼" d. dinner
plates, six sauce dishes, four cups &
saucers, one meat platter & one
vegetable bowl; Rosebud patt.,
orange, 34 pcs. .............................. **545.00**
**French casserole w/tab ear handle,**
Rosebud patt., green, 8¾" d. .............. **65.00**
**Mixing bowl w/spout & handle,**
Rosebud patt., green, 7" d. ................. **55.00**
**Mixing bowl w/spout & handle,**
Rosebud patt., red, 11" d. ................... **45.00**
**Pie plate,** Rosebud patt., green,
11½" d. .............................................. **35.00**
**Plate,** bread & butter, Mello-Tone
patt., blue........................................... **10.00**
**Plate,** bread & butter, Mello-Tone
patt., yellow........................................ **10.00**
**Salt shaker,** tapered, Rosebud patt.,
rose, 4½" h. ....................................... **22.00**
**Salt & pepper shakers,** Rosebud
patt., small ......................................... **75.00**
**Teapot,** cov., Rosebud patt., orange,
large................................................... **95.00**
**Vase,** 5¾" h., 8½" d., body of vase
tapering to 3¾" d. mouth, square
shoulder handles, glossy turquoise &
pink .................................................... **45.00**

# DELFT

*In the early 17th century Italian potters settled in Holland and began producing tin-glazed earthenwares, often decorated with pseudo-Oriental designs based on Chinese porcelain wares. The city of Delft became the center of this pottery production and several firms produced the wares throughout the 17th and early 18th century. A majority of the pieces featured blue on white designs, but polychrome wares were also made. The Dutch Delftwares were also shipped to England and eventually the English copied them at potteries in such cities as Bristol, Lambeth and Liverpool. Although still produced today, Delft peaked in popularity by the mid-18th century.*

**Charger,** polychrome decoration w/a central large wheel designed w/floral trim & the wide edge w/clusters of small stylized florals, England, ca. 1760, 11¾" d. (rim glaze wear & chips) ............................................ **$518.00**

**Charger,** polychrome decoration w/an urn & a vase of flowers in the center & a border design of narrow panels alternating w/groups of long-stemmed flowers, Holland, 18th c., 12¼" d. (rim repair, glaze loss) ......... **403.00**

**Charger,** blue & white w/a central Chinese landscape scene w/hillside pagoda surrounded by an inner diaper & scroll-panel band & floral clusters on the outer rim, probably Bristol, England, mid-18th c., 13½" d. (glaze wear on rim) .............. **518.00**

**Charger,** decorated in blue & white w/an overall delicate leaf & flower decoration w/an orange enameled trim ring, Wincanton, England, ca. 1760, 13⅝" d. (rim glaze wear, small chips) ................................................ **633.00**

**Cruet,** cov., footed baluster-form body tapering to a flat rim fitted w/a flat cover, long D-form handle, a long swan's neck spout from the base & supported by a small S-scroll strut from the body rim to near the tip of the spout, decorated in blue & white w/overall florals, Holland, 18th c., 5½" h. (glaze chips) .......................... **920.00**

**Dish,** deep rounded sides w/a flanged rim, decorated in blue & white w/a central Chinese landscape w/buildings & a flowering tree, the border w/a repeating design of stylized leaves, Holland, mid-18th c., 12" d. (rim glaze loss) ...................... **546.00**

**Dish,** deep round sides w/a flanged rim, decorated in blue on white w/a central design of large florals & a border band of stylized florals & scrolls, Holland, 18th c., 12¼" d. (chips, glaze loss to rim) .................. **518.00**

**Mug,** tall slightly tapering cylindrical body w/a D-form handle, decorated in polychrome w/a central design of a peacock surrounded by an insect & flowers, Bristol, England, mid-18th c., 7⅛" h. (body restoration, glaze wear to rim) ................................................ **403.00**

**Plate,** 9" d., polychrome decoration of a large long-tailed peafowl w/sponged trees & ground in the background, England, mid-18th c. (rim repairs, glaze loss) ................. **1,495.00**

**Sack jug,** footed spherical body tapering to a short, slender cylindrical neck w/a molded rim & long handle, white decorated in blue w/"Sack - 1650," Lambeth, England, 17th c., 5½" h. (hairline crack, rim chips) .... **4,485.00**

**Tea canister,** cov., squared upright sides w/a flat shoulder to the short cylindrical neck fitted w/a domed cylindrical cover, the sides decorated in blue & white w/Chinese figural landscapes & birds & flowers, Holland, late 18th - early 19th c., 4⅛" h. (edge roughness) .................. **230.00**

**Vase,** 6⅜" h., ovoid body w/a short cylindrical neck & tapering to a flaring foot, decorated w/manganese large floral designs, Holland, mid-18th c. (rim glaze loss, foot rim chip).. **345.00**

# DERBY & ROYAL CROWN DERBY

*William Duesbury, in partnership with John and Christopher Heath, established the Derby Porcelain Works in Derby, England, about 1750. Duesbury soon bought out his partners and in 1770 purchased the Chelsea factory and six years later, the Bow works. Duesbury was succeeded by his son and grandson. Robert Bloor purchased the business about 1814 and managed successfully until illness in 1828 left him unable to exercise control. The "Bloor" Period, however, extends from 1814 until 1848, when the factory closed. Former Derby workmen then resumed porcelain manufacture in another factory and this nucleus eventually united with a new and distinct venture in 1878 which, after 1890, was known as Royal Crown Derby.*

*A variety of anchor and crown marks have been used since the 18th century.*

*Derby & Royal Crown Derby Marks*

**Cigarette lighter,** Imari patt. ............... **$95.00**
**Dinner service:** seven dinner plates, eight salad plates, eight bouillon cups, eight under plates, nine teacups, eight saucers, cov. teapot, cov. sugar bowl & creamer; Imari patt., Royal Crown Derby marks,

retailed by Tiffany & Co., New York, the set .......................................... **1,150.00**

**Figurine,** Dr. Syntax standing & reading a book, a tree stump behind him, shaped oblong base, white w/gilt trim, blue enamel base, ca. 1820, 3⅞" h. (wear) ......................... **259.00**

**Figurine,** Dr. Syntax tied to a tree, polychrome enamel decoration w/gilt trim, ca. 1820, 4" h. .......................... **518.00**

**Figurine,** Dr. Syntax debarking in Calais, the Doctor riding piggyback on a peasant woman, polychrome enamel decoration w/gilt trim, titled on the oval base "Debarquant á Calais," red painted mark, ca. 1860, 4½" h. (restorations) ........................ **431.00**

**Figurine,** Dr. Syntax walking, w/a walking stick in hand, round base, polychrome enamel decoration w/gilt trim, red painted mark, ca. 1860, 5¼" h. .............................................. **690.00**

**Mint dish,** leaf-shaped, decorated w/applied pink rose on mint green & white ground w/gold trim, 4¾" l ........... **40.00**

**Plate,** 9⅛" h., Imari decoration in blue, red, green & gilt ............................. **138.00**

**Vase,** 5¼" h., 'Repoussé Ware,' the bulbous lower body molded, enameled & gilded w/overall floral decoration, the slender neck w/a scalloped rim, printed mark & retailer's mark, ca. 1885 .................. **690.00**

# DOULTON & ROYAL DOULTON

*Doulton & Co., Ltd. was founded in Lambeth, London, about 1858. It was operated there till 1956 and often incorporated the words "Doulton" and "Lambeth" in its marks. Pinder Bourne & Co., Burslem was purchased by the Doultons in 1878 and in 1882 became Doulton & Co., Ltd. It added porcelain to its earthenware production in 1884. The "Royal Doulton" mark has been used since 1902 by this factory, which is still in production. Character jugs and figurines are commanding great attention from collectors at the present time.*

*Royal Doulton Mark*

## ANIMALS & BIRDS

**Cat,** character kitten, lying on back, brown & white, HN 2579, 1941-85, 1½" h. ............................................... **$75.00**

**Cat,** character kitten, licking hind paw, brown & white, HN 2580, 2¼" h. ......... **75.00**

**Cat,** character kitten, sleeping, brown & white, HN 2581, 1941-85, 1½" h. .... **75.00**

**Cat,** character kitten, sitting w/front paws raised, HN 2582, 1941-85, 2¾" h. ................................................. **40.00**

**Cat,** character kitten, looking up, tan & white, HN 2584, 2" h. ......................... **75.00**

**Cat,** Persian, seated, white, HN 2539A, 1940-68, 5" h. ..................... **250.00**

**Dog,** Airedale Terrier, Ch. "Cotsford Topsail," dark brown & black coat, light brown underbody, HN 1023, 1931-85, 5¼" h. ............................... **232.00**

**Dog,** Black Labrador Ch. "Bublikite of Mansergh," HN 2667, 1967-85, 5" h. . **120.00**

**Dog,** Boxer Champion "Warlord of Mazelaine," golden brown coat w/white bib, HN 2643, 1952-85, 6½" h. ............................................... **135.00**

**Dog,** Bulldog, seated, tan w/dark brown patches over eye & back, K1, 2½" h. ............................................... **125.00**

**Dog,** Bulldog, standing, white, brown collar w/tan studs, HN 1074, 1932-85, 3¼" h. ......................................... **175.00**

**Dog,** character dog, lying on back, white w/brown & black patches over ears & eyes, HN 1098, 1934-59, 2" h. ................................................. **150.00**

**Dog,** character dog, yawning, white w/brown patches over ears & eyes, black patches on back, HN 1099, 1934-85, 4" h. .................................... **40.00**

**Dog,** character dog w/ball, white w/light & dark brown patches, maroon ball, HN 1103, 1934-85, 2½" h. ................................................. **69.00**

**Dog,** character dog, lying, panting, white w/brown patches over ears & eyes, black patches on back, HN 1101, 1934-59, 2¼" h. ..................... **150.00**

**Dog,** Chow (Shibu Ino), golden brown, K15, 1940-77, 2½" h. ....... **125.00 to 135.00**

**Dog,** Cocker Spaniel, white w/light brown ears & eyes, brown patches on back, HN 1036, 5¼" h. (ILLUS. top next page) ..... **145.00 to 155.00**

**Dog,** Dalmatian, Fireside Models, DA 85, 1989, 13¾" h. ...................... **199.00**

**Dog,** Dachshund, standing, brown, HN 1139, 1937-55, 6" l. ................... **410.00**

*Royal Doulton Dog*

**Dog,** Dachshund, standing, HN 1140, 1937-68, medium............................. **185.00**

**Dog,** Dachshund, standing, brown, HN 1141, 1937-68, 2¾" h. ................ **175.00**

**Dog,** Doberman Pinscher Ch. "Rancho Dobe's Storm," black w/brown feet & chin, HN 2645, 1955-85, 6¼" h. ................ **130.00 to 140.00**

**Dog,** English Setter, Ch. "Maesydd Mustard," HN 1051, 1931-68, 4" h.... **175.00**

**Dog,** English Setter with Pheasant, grey w/black markings; reddish-brown pheasant; yellowish-brown leaves on base, HN 2529, 8" h. ........ **495.00**

**Dog,** Foxhound, sitting, white w/dark brown & black patches over ears, eyes & back, K7, 1931-77, 2½" h. ...... **60.00**

**Dog,** Fox Terrier, white w/light brown patches, HN 943, 1927-40, 5½" h. (repainted) ........................................ **250.00**

**Dog,** Gordon Setter, dark brown coat, light brown underbody, HN 1080, 1932-55, 5" h. .................................. **725.00**

**Dog,** Irish Setter, reddish-brown, HN 1056, 1931-68, 4" h. ......... **170.00 to 200.00**

**Dog,** Irish Setter, reddish-brown, HN 1055, 1931-85, 5" h. ........................ **120.00**

**Dog,** Pekinese Ch. "Biddee of Ifield," golden brown w/black highlights, HN 1011, 1931-55, 6½" h. ...................... **540.00**

**Dog,** Rough-haired Terrier, "Crackley Startler," white w/black & brown markings, HN 1014, 1931-85, 3¾" h..... **90.00**

**Dog,** Scottish Terrier Ch. "Albourne Arthur," black, HN 1016, 1931-85, 3½" h. ............................................ **225.00**

**Dog,** Scottish Terrier, seated, black w/grey highlights, K18, 1940-77, 2¼ × 2¾" ...................................... **120.00**

**Dog,** Springer Spaniel Ch. "Dry Toast," white coat w/dark brown markings, HN 2516, 1938-68, 5" h. .. **120.00**

**Dog,** Welsh Corgi, golden brown, K16, 1940-77, 2½" h. ................ **115.00 to 125.00**

**Dogs,** Terrier puppies in a basket, white w/light & dark brown markings, brown basket, HN 2588, 1941-85, 3" h. .................................. **100.00 to 125.00**

**Duck,** Mallard drake, standing, green, brown & white, HN 807, 1923-77, 2½" h. ............................................... **135.00**

**Duck,** Mallard drake, standing, green head, brown & white feathers, HN 2555, 1941-46, 5½" h. ...................... **250.00**

**Elephant,** trunk in salute, grey w/black markings, white tusks (china), HN 2644, 1952-85, 4¼" h. ...................... **125.00**

**Hare,** crouching, light brown w/white markings, HN 2592, 1941-68, 2¾" h... **120.00**

**Hare,** lying w/legs stretched behind, HN 2594, 1941-85, 1¾ × 5¼"............. **85.00**

**Penguin,** grey, white & black, green patches under eyes, K23, 1940-68, 11½" h. ................................................ **200.00**

**Penguin,** wings outstretched, K24, 1940-68, 2" h. ................................... **225.00**

**Tiger,** stalking, brown w/dark brown stripes, Rouge Flambe, HN 1086, 1931- by 1946, 5" h. ........................ **700.00**

## CHARACTER JUGS

*Cardinal Mug*

**Anne Boleyn,** miniature, 2½" h. ........... **44.00**

**Anne Boleyn,** large, 7¼" h. .................. **70.00**

**Annie Oakley,** Wild West series, 5¼" h. ................................................ **99.00**

**Antony & Cleopatra,** (two-faced), large, 7¼" h. ....................................... **70.00**

**Apothecary,** miniature, 2½" h.............. **44.00**

**Apothecary,** small, 4" h. ...................... **55.00**

**'Ard of 'Earing,** miniature, 2½" h........ **850.00**

**'Ard of 'Earing,** large, 7½" h. ............................. **900.00 to 950.00**

**Aramis,** miniature, 2½" h. ..................... **44.00**

'Arry, large, 6½" h............................ 165.00
Athos, small, 3¾" h............................. 28.00
Auld Mac, tiny, 1¼" h......................... 180.00
Auld Mac, large, 6¼" h. ....................... 70.00
Beefeater, tiny, 1½" h. ........................ 135.00
Benjamin Franklin, small, 4" h............. 53.00
Blacksmith, small, 3½" h...................... 55.00
Buffalo Bill, Wild West series, 5½" h. .. 99.00
Captain Hook, small, 4" h................... 346.00
Cardinal (The), tiny, 1½" h. ................ 225.00
Cardinal (The), small, 3½" h................ 41.00
Cardinal (The), "A" mark, large,
     6½" h. (ILLUS. bottom previous
     page) ................................................ 175.00
Catherine Howard, large, 7" h. .......... 115.00
Catherine of Aragon, 1975-89, large,
     7" h. ................................................. 115.00
Catherine Parr, 1981-89, large,
     6¾" h. ............................................... 115.00

*Clown Mug*

Clown without hat, red hair, large,
     7½" h. (ILLUS.) .............................. 2,700.00
Collector (The), large, 7" h., limited
     edition, 1988 ..................................... 120.00
Davy Crockett & Santa Anna, (two-
     faced), large, 7" h., limited edition,
     1985.................................................... 70.00
Dick Turpin, mask on face, horse
     handle, miniature, 2¼" h..................... 40.00
Doc Holliday, Wild West series, 5½" h.... 99.00
Don Quixote, miniature,
     2½" h. ................................. 40.00 to 50.00
Don Quixote, small, 3¼" h. .................. 45.00
Don Quixote, large, 7¼" h.................... 87.00

Falconer (The), miniature, 2¾" h.......... 42.00
Falconer (The), large, 7½" h. .............. 90.00
Falstaff, miniature, 2½" h..................... 42.00
Fireman (The), large, 7¼" h. ............... 85.00
Gaoler, miniature, 1¼" h...................... 44.00
Gardener (The), w/spade &
     vegetables handle, 1971, large,
     7¾" h. ................................................ 140.00
George Washington & George III,
     (two-faced), large, 7¼" h. .................. 80.00
Geronimo, Wild West series, 5½" h. .. 145.00
Gladiator, small, 3½" h. ....................... 525.00
Gondolier, miniature, 2½" h. .............. 300.00
Granny, small, 3½" h. .......................... 65.00
Granny, (toothless, early version),
     large, 6¼" h. ...................................... 900.00
Granny, "A" mark, large, 6¼" h............. 95.00
Gulliver, large, 7½" h........................... 495.00
Henry V, large, 7¼" h. (1st version).... 125.00
Henry VIII, two-handled (loving cup),
     limited edition, 1991, 7" h. ............... 795.00
Henry VIII, miniature, 2¾" h.................. 45.00
Jane Seymour, large, 7¼" h.............. 115.00
John Barleycorn, miniature, 2½" h. ..... 50.00
John Barleycorn, large, 6" h., limited
     edition,1978, signed by Michael
     Doulton ................................................ 78.00
John Doulton, small, 4¼" h., (time
     shown on Big Ben is eight o'clock) ... 105.00
John Peel, "A" mark, small, 3½" h. ........ 55.00
Lobster Man, miniature, 2¾" h............. 42.00
Lobster Man, small, 3¾" h. .................. 40.00
Lobster Man, large, 7½" h.................... 87.00
Long John Silver, miniature, 2½" h. ..... 42.00
Long John Silver, large, 7" h. limited
     edition, 1987, (D.H. Holmes) ........... 299.00
Mark Twain, large, 7½" h..................... 80.00

*Mephistopheles Mug*

**Mephistopheles,** large, 7" h.
(ILLUS. bottom previous page)...... **1,775.00**
**Mikado,** large 6½" h............................ **575.00**
**Mr. Micawber,** "A" mark, small, 3¼" h... **53.00**
**Mr. Micawber,** intermediate size,
5½" h. ................................................. **135.00**
**Mr. Pickwick,** miniature, 2¼" h............. **62.00**
**Neptune,** small, 3¾" h. .......................... **46.00**
**Neptune,** large, 6½" h. ........................... **75.00**
**Night Watchman,** miniature, 2¼" h. ...... **44.00**
**Night Watchman,** small, 3½" h. ............. **55.00**
**North American Indian,** small, 4¼" h.... **45.00**
**North American Indian,** Canadian
Centennial series, large, 7¾" h......... **140.00**
**Old Charley,** large, 5½" h.................... **125.00**
**Othello,** large, 7¼" h............................. **85.00**
**Owd Mac,** small, 3¼" h....................... **195.00**
**Owd Mac,** large, 6¼" h. ...................... **300.00**
**Paddy,** small, 3¼" h.............................. **40.00**
**Pied Piper,** large, 7" h........................... **80.00**
**Porthos,** large, 7¼" h.......................... **140.00**
**Red Queen,** small, 3" h.......................... **45.00**
**Regency Beau,** small, 4¼" h. ............. **455.00**
**Regency Beau,** large, 7¼" h. ............. **995.00**
**Robin Hood,** hat w/no feather, plain
handle, 1947-1960, large, 6¼" h. ..... **140.00**
**Robinson Crusoe,** small, 3½" h........... **60.00**
**Ronald Reagan,** large, 7¾" h., limited
edition, 1984 .................................... **375.00**
**Royal Canadian Mounted**
**Policeman,** bust, limited edition,
HN 2547, 1973, 8" h. ....................... **475.00**
**St. George,** small, 3¾" h.................... **120.00**
**Sam Johnson,** "A" mark, small,
3¼" h. .............................................. **175.00**
**Sam Johnson,** large, 6¼" h............... **210.00**
**Sam Weller,** miniature, 2¼" h. ........... **125.00**
**Sancho Panca,** miniature, 2¼" h......... **44.00**
**Santa Claus,** stocking handle, large,
7½" h. ............................................... **125.00**
**Simon the Cellarer,** "A" mark, small,
3½" h. ........................... **55.00 to 65.00**
**Simple Simon,** large, 7" h. ................. **490.00**
**Sleuth (The),** miniature, 2¾" h............. **45.00**
**Toby Philpots,** "A" mark, miniature,
2¼" h. ................................................ **29.00**
**Tony Weller,** "A" mark, extra large,
8½" h. .............................................. **250.00**
**Town Crier,** large, 7" h. ...................... **195.00**
**Ugly Duchess,** miniature,
2½" h. ........................ **245.00 to 300.00**
**Ugly Duchess,** small, 3½" h. ............. **300.00**

**Ugly Duchess,** large, 6¾" h. ............. **575.00**
**Viking,** miniature, 2½" h. .... **115.00 to 125.00**
**Viking,** small, 4" h. ............................. **100.00**
**Wild Bill Hickock,** Wild West series,
5½" h. ................................................. **99.00**
**Wyatt Earp,** Wild West series.............. **50.00**

## DICKENSWARE

**Ashpot,** figural bust, Sairey Gamp ....... **85.00**
**Figurine,** Alfred Jingle, 1st series,
brown & black, HN 541, 1922-32,
4" h. .................................................. **79.00**
**Figurine,** Oliver Twist, 2nd series,
black & tan, M 89, 1949-83, 4" h. ....... **79.00**
**Figurine,** Pecksniff, 1st series, brown,
HN 535, 1922-32, 4" h. ...................... **79.00**
**Pitcher,** 5½" h., jug-type, Pickwick
Papers - White Hart Inn ................... **200.00**
**Plate,** 10½" d., Sam Weller &
Mr. Pickwick in relief, 1938 ............... **90.00**
**Sugar bowl,** miniature, Sairey Gamp... **450.00**
**Sugar bowl,** Tony Weller.................... **345.00**
**Vase,** 4¼" h., Barkis.......................... **105.00**
**Vase,** 6" h., two-handled, Sairey
Gamp scene ..................................... **175.00**
**Vase,** 6½" h., two-handled,
Mr. Pickwick scene .......................... **175.00**
**Teapot,** cov., Tony Weller............... **1,550.00**
**Toothpick holder,** Sairey Gamp ........ **450.00**

## FIGURINES

**Abdullah,** HN 2104, multicolored
w/yellow chair, orange turban,
1953-62 ............................................ **430.00**
**A 'Courting,** HN 2004, red, black &
grey, 1947-53 .................. **475.00 to 500.00**
**Adrienne,** HN 2152, purple dress,
1964-76 ............................................ **148.00**
**Adrienne,** HN 2304, blue dress,
1964-91 ............................................ **160.00**
**Afternoon Tea,** HN 1747, pink & blue,
1935-82 ............................................ **350.00**
**Alice,** HN 2158, blue, 1960-81............ **136.00**
**Alison,** HN 2336, blue overdress,
1966-92 ............................................ **152.00**
**All Aboard,** HN 2940, blue shirt, tan
pants, black boots & cap, 1982-86 ... **180.00**
**Anna,** HN 2802, purple & white,
1976-82 ............................................ **125.00**
**Anthea,** HN 1527, purple dress, red
umbrella, 1932-49............................. **700.00**
**Antoinette,** HN 2326, white, 1967-79 .. **110.00**
**At Ease,** HN 2473, yellow, 1973-79.... **175.00**

**Babie,** HN 1679, green, 1935-92 .......... **90.00**

**Baby Bunting,** HN 2108, brown & cream, 1953-59 ............................... **250.00**

**Bachelor (The),** HN 2319, green & brown, 1964-75 ............................... **250.00**

**Ballad Seller,** HN 2266, pink dress, 1968-73 ........................................... **245.00**

**Bather (The),** HN 597, mottled grey robe, blue base, 1924-38 .............. **2,100.00**

**Balloon Boy,** HN 2934, 1984, 7½" h... **100.00**

**Balloon Girl,** HN 2818, 1982-present, 6½" h. .............................................. **100.00**

**Balloon Lady,** HN 2935, 1984-present, 8¼" h. .............................. **100.00**

**Beachcomber,** HN 2487, purple & grey, 1973-76 .................................. **225.00**

**Bess,** HN 2002, flowered cream dress & red cloak, 1947-69 ........ **265.00 to 300.00**

**Beth,** HN 2870, pink & white, 1979-83 .. **265.00**

**Belle,** HN 2340, green dress, 1968-88... **90.00**

**Bluebeard,** HN 2105, dark cloak, orange & green costume, 1953-92 ........................... **370.00 to 400.00**

**Boatman (The),** HN 2417, yellow, 1971-87 ........................................... **125.00**

**Bo Peep,** M 82, 1939-49, 4" h............. **875.00**

**Boy from Williamsburg,** HN 2183, purple jacket, red vest, 1969-83 ....... **150.00**

**Bride (The),** HN 1762, cream dress, 1936-49 ........................................... **995.00**

**Bridesmaid (The Little),** HN 1433, lavender & pink dress, 1930-51 ........ **200.00**

**Bridesmaid (The),** HN 2148, cream dress, 1955-59 ................................. **225.00**

**Bridget,** HN 2070, green, brown & lavender, 1951-73 ............ **235.00 to 250.00**

**Camille,** HN 1586, pink dress w/red bodice & overskirt, 1933-49 ............. **850.00**

**Captain Cook,** HN 2889, cream & black, 1980-84 ................................ **280.00**

**Carolyn,** HN 2112, white & green flowered dress, 1953-65 (ILLUS. top next column) ..................................... **300.00**

**Carrie,** HN 2800, turquoise, 1976-81 ........................... **160.00 to 170.00**

**Cavalier,** HN 2716, brown & green, 1976-82 ......................................... **200.00**

**Celeste,** HN 2237, pale blue, 1959-71 .. **198.00**

**Cellist (The),** HN 2226, black & brown, 1960-67 ............... **325.00 to 350.00**

**Charley's Aunt,** HN 35, black & white dress, 1913-38................................. **650.00**

**Charlotte,** HN 2421, purple, 1972-86... **200.00**

**Cherie,** HN 2341, bluish-grey dress, 1966-92 ......................................... **105.00**

*Carolyn*

**Chief (The),** HN 2892, gold, 1979-88 ........................... **175.00 to 200.00**

**China Repairer (The),** HN 2943, blue, white & tan, 1983-88...................... **175.00**

**Choir Boy,** HN 2141, white & red, 1943-75 ........................................... **145.00**

**Christmas Time,** HN 2110, red dress w/white frills, 1953-67 ...................... **370.00**

**Clarinda,** HN 2724, blue & white dress, 1975-81................................ **240.00**

**Clarissa,** HN 1525, green dress, red shawl, 1932-38 ................................ **650.00**

**Clockmaker (The),** HN 2279, green & brown, 1961-75................................. **235.00**

**Chloe,** M 9, pink dress, 1932-45......... **325.00**

**Clothilde,** HN 1599, purple dress, red & blue cape, 1933-49 ...................... **775.00**

**Coachman (The),** HN 2282, purple, grey & blue, 1963-71 ....................... **505.00**

**Cobbler (The),** HN 1706, green & blue striped shirt & hat w/yellow, 1935-69 ........................................... **255.00**

**Coppelia,** HN 2115, blue, red & white, 1953-59 ........................................... **500.00**

**Coralie,** HN 2307, yellow dress, 1964-88 ........................................... **155.00**

**Cradle Song,** HN 2246, green & brown, 1959-62 ............... **410.00 to 425.00**

**Daffy Down Dilly,** HN 1712, green dress & hat, 1935-75 ...................... **270.00**

**Dancing Years,** HN 2235, lavender, 1965-71 ........................................... **295.00**

**Daphne,** HN 2268, pink dress, 1963-75 ........................................... **130.00**

**Darby,** HN 2024, pink & blue, 1949-59 ... **150.00**

**Deauville,** HN 2344, yellow & white, limited edition, 1982 .......................... **250.00**

**Debbie,** HN 2385, blue & white, 1969-82 ............................................ **148.00**

**Delight,** HN 1773, turquoise, 1936-49 .. **725.00**

**Doctor (The),** HN 2858, grey pants & vest, black coat, 1979-92 .................. **215.00**

**Dorcas,** HN 1491, light greenish-blue dress, 1932-38 ................................ **595.00**

**Dreamweaver,** HN 2283, blue, grey & brown, 1972-76 ............................... **225.00**

**Drummer Boy,** HN 2679, multicolored, 1976-81 ............................................ **335.00**

**Easter Day,** HN 2039, multicolored dress, green hat, 1949-69 ... **365.00 to 400.00**

**Elegance,** HN 2264, green dress, 1961-85 ........................... **155.00 to 175.00**

**Elizabeth,** HN 2946, green & yellow dress, bonnet, 1982-86 .................... **215.00**

**Elsie Maynard,** HN 639, mauve & pink, 1924-49 .................................... **425.00**

**Emma,** HN 2834, pink & white, 1977-81 ............................................ **206.00**

**Ermine Coat (The),** HN 1981, red & white, 1945-67 ................. **215.00 to 225.00**

**Esmeralda,** HN 2168, yellow & red, 1956-59 ............................................ **260.00**

**Eventide,** HN 2814, blue, white, red, yellow & green, 1977-91.... **145.00 to 175.00**

**Fat Boy (The),** HN 2096, blue jacket, yellow scarf, 1952-67 ...................... **365.00**

**Favourite (The),** HN 2249, blue & white, 1960-90 ................. **150.00 to 160.00**

**Fiona,** HN 2694, red & white dress, 1974-81 ........................... **160.00 to 175.00**

**First Dance,** HN 2803, pale blue dress, 1977-92 ................ **190.00 to 225.00**

**First Waltz,** HN 2862, red dress, 1979-83 ............................................ **185.00**

**Flora,** HN 2349, brown & white, 1966-73 ............................................ **275.00**

**Flute,** HN 2483, red & white, limited edition, 1973 ...................................... **695.00**

**Foaming Quart (The),** HN 2162, orange & brown costume, 1955-92 .. **150.00**

**Forget-Me-Not,** HN 1813, red dress, blue hat, 1937-49 ............................ **455.00**

**Francine,** HN 2422, green & white, 1972-81 ................................ **80.00 to 85.00**

**Gay Morning,** HN 2135, pink dress, 1954-67 (ILLUS. top next column).... **250.00**

**Genevieve,** HN 1962, red dress, 1941-75 ............................................ **223.00**

**Gentleman from Williamsburg,** HN 2227, 1960-83, 6¼" h. ...................... **175.00**

**Georgina,** HN 2377, 1981-86, 5¾" h.... **119.00**

*Gay Morning*

*Giselle*

**Giselle,** HN 2139, blue & white, 1954-69 (ILLUS.) ............. **250.00 to 300.00**

**Golden Days,** HN 2274, yellow, white & blue, 1964-73 ................................ **175.00**

**Gollywog,** HN 1979, white overalls, 1945-59 ............................................ **465.00**

**Gollywog,** HN 2040, blue overalls, green hat, 1949-59 ........................ **168.00**

**Good Catch (A),** HN 2258, green & grey, 1966-86 .................................... **165.00**

**Good King Wenceslas,** HN 2118, brown & purple, 1953-76 .. **360.00 to 370.00**

**Goody Two Shoes,** HN 1905, pink skirt, red overdress, 1939-49 ............ **300.00**

**Goody Two Shoes,** HN 2037, red &
pink dress, 1949-89......... **110.00 to 125.00**

**Grandma,** HN 2053, red & cream
dress, blue shawl ............. **300.00 to 350.00**

**Gwynneth,** HN 1980, red dress,
1945-52 ............................................ **250.00**

**Gypsy Dance (A),** HN 2157, purple &
white dress, 1955-57 ........................ **575.00**

**Gypsy Dance (A),** HN 2230, purple &
white dress, 1959-71 ........ **225.00 to 275.00**

**Harlequin,** HN 2186, blue, 1957-69.... **225.00**

**Heart to Heart,** HN 2276, lavender,
green & yellow, 1961-71 ................... **495.00**

**Helmsman,** HN 2499, brown,
1974-86 ........................... **200.00 to 220.00**

**Henry Lytton as Jack Point,** HN 610,
6½" h. ............................................ **875.00**

**Her Majesty Queen Elizabeth II,** HN
2878, blue & crimson robes, white
gown, limited edition, 1983 .............. **425.00**

*Her Ladyship*

**Her Ladyship,** HN 1977, red & cream,
1945-59 (ILLUS.) ............................. **225.00**

**Hinged Parasol (The),** HN 1579, red
dress, purple ruffles, 1933-49 ........... **575.00**

**Hostess of Williamsburg,** HN 2209,
pink dress 1960-83 .......................... **225.00**

**Hurdy Gurdy,** HN 2796, blue
overdress, limited edition, 1975 ........ **750.00**

**In Grandma's Days HN 339,** green &
yellow dress, 1919-38...................... **875.00**

**Invitation,** HN 2170, pink dress,
1956-75 .......................................... **112.00**

**Isadora,** HN 2938, lavender, 1986-92.. **250.00**

**Janet,** M 75, white skirt, shaded rose
overdress, 1936-49........................... **525.00**

**Janet,** HN 1538, bluish-red dress,
1932-49 .......................................... **200.00**

**Janice,** HN 2165, pale blue w/black
overdress, 1955-65........................... **415.00**

**Jean,** HN 2032, 1949-59.................... **265.00**

**Jean,** HN 2710, white dress, 1983-86.. **180.00**

**Jennifer,** HN 2392, blue dress,
1982-92 .......................................... **145.00**

**Joan,** HN 1422, blue dress, 1930-49 .. **275.00**

**Joan,** HN 2023, blue dress,
1949-59 ......................... **260.00 to 265.00**

**Jolly Sailor,** HN 2172, black, brown,
blue & white, 1956-65 ...................... **650.00**

**Judith,** HN 2089, red & blue dress,
1952-59 .......................................... **310.00**

**June,** HN 2027, yellow & pink,
1949-52 .......................................... **575.00**

**Kate Hardcastle,** HN 2028, green &
red dress, 1949-52 .......................... **500.00**

**Lady Betty,** HN 1967, red dress,
1941-51 .......................................... **360.00**

**Lady Pamela,** HN 2718, purple
dress, 1974-81 ................. **170.00 to 175.00**

*La Sylphide*

**La Sylphide,** HN 2138, white dress,
1954-65 (ILLUS.).............. **395.00 to 400.00**

**Laurianne,** HN 2719, dark blue &
white, 1974-79.................. **180.00 to 200.00**

**Lavinia,** HN 1955, red dress, 1940-79 .. **108.00**

**Little Lady Make Believe,** HN 1870, red & blue, 1938-49 ........................ **500.00**

**Little Mistress (The),** HN 1449, green & blue, 1931-49 ............................... **450.00**

**Louise,** HN 2869, brown dress, white collar & cuffs, brown bonnet, 1979-86 ........................................... **190.00**

**Lucy Ann,** HN 1502, lavender gown, 1932-51 ............................................ **235.00**

**Magpie Ring (The),** HN 2978, cream, 1983-86 ............................................ **150.00**

**Make Believe,** HN 2225, blue, 1962-89 ............................................... **130.00**

**Marianne,** HN 2074, red dress, 1951-53 ............................................. **900.00**

**Marie,** HN 1370, shaded purple gown, 1930-88 .............................. **75.00 to 95.00**

**Marigold,** HN 1447, white & purple dress, 1931-49 ................. **500.00 to 525.00**

*Market Day*

**Market Day,** HN 1991, blue, pink & white, 1947-55 (ILLUS.) .................... **195.00**

**Mary Had a Little Lamb,** HN 2048, lavender, 1949-88 ............................. **86.00**

**Masque,** HN 2554, blue, 1973-75 ....... **200.00**

**Masquerade,** HN 2259, 1960-65, 8½" h. ................................................ **270.00**

**Master (The),** HN 2325, greyish-green jacket, 1967-92 ................................ **170.00**

**Maytime,** HN 2113, rose pink dress w/blue scarf, 1953-67 (ILLUS. top next column) .................................... **325.00**

*Maytime*

**Meditation,** HN 2330, peach & cream, 1971-83 ........................... **265.00 to 275.00**

**Memories,** HN 1856, blue & white, 1938-49 ............................................. **950.00**

**Mendicant (The),** HN 1365, brown, 1929-69 ............................................. **212.00**

**Mermaid (The),** HN 97, green seaweed in hair, beige base, 1918-26 ............... **600.00**

**Merry Christmas,** HN 3096, green & white, 1987-1992 ............................ **150.00**

**Midinette,** HN 2090, blue dress, 1952-65 ............................................. **275.00**

**Mirabel,** M 68, pink & green, 1936-49 ............................................. **500.00**

**Mirabel,** HN 1743, pale bluish-green dress, 1935-49 ........................... **1,450.00**

**Miss Demure,** HN 1402, lavender & pink, 1930-75 ................... **250.00 to 300.00**

**Miss Muffet,** HN 1937, green coat, 1940-52 ........................... **265.00 to 300.00**

**Mr. Micawber,** HN 2097, black jacket, beige trousers, 1952-67 ................... **350.00**

**Mr. Pickwick,** M 41, yellow & black, 1932-83 ............................................... **65.00**

**Monte Carlo,** HN 2332, green, limited edition, 1982 ..................................... **250.00**

**Mother's Help,** HN 2151, black & white, 1962-69 ................................. **190.00**

**Nana,** HN 1766, pink, 1936-49 ........... **435.00**

**Nanny,** HN 2221, blue & white, 1958-91 ............................................. **170.00**

**New Bonnet (The),** HN 1728, pink dress, green hat, 1935-49 ................ **775.00**

**Nicola,** HN 2804, red & lilac, 1987...... **200.00**

**Officer of the Line,** HN 2733, red & yellow, 1983-86 ................................. **215.00**

**Old Mother Hubbard,** HN 2314, green dress, polka dot apron, 1964-75 ....... **300.00**

**Olivia,** HN 1995, red & green, 1947-51 .......................................... **495.00**

**Orange Vendor (An),** HN 72, green coat, 1917-38.................................. **950.00**

**Organ Grinder (The),** HN 2173, green jacket, 1956-65 ...................... **800.00**

**Owd Willum,** HN 2042, brown jacket, 1949-73 ........................... **235.00 to 255.00**

**Pantalettes,** HN 1362, green skirt, red tie on hat, 1929-38............................ **395.00**

**Parisian,** HN 2445, 1972-75 ............... **230.00**

**Parson's Daughter,** HN 564, multicolored skirt, 1923-49 ............... **475.00**

**Past Glory,** HN 2484, red uniform, 1973-79 .......................................... **180.00**

**Patchwork Quilt (The),** HN 1984, green dress, 1945-59 ...................... **375.00**

**Paula,** HN 2906, yellow dress w/green trim, 1980-86 .................... **175.00 to 200.00**

**Pearly Girl,** HN 2036, red jacket, 1949-59 ........................... **230.00 to 240.00**

*Penelope*

**Penelope,** HN 1901, red dress, 1939-75 (ILLUS.) ............................. **305.00**

**Picnic,** HN 2308, yellow, 1965-88 ...... **104.00**

**Pillow Fight,** HN 2270, pink nightgown, 1965-69 .......................... **250.00**

**Piper (The),** HN 2907, green, 1980-92 ............................ **220.00 to 225.00**

**Poacher (The),** HN 2043, black & brown, 1949-59 ............... **195.00 to 200.00**

**Poke Bonnet (The),** HN 612, yellow skirt, green plaid shawl, 1924-38...... **975.00**

**Pollyanna,** HN 2965, white, grey & tan, 1982-85 ................................. **225.00**

**Premiere,** HN 2343, green cloak, 1969-79 .......................................... **140.00**

**Pretty Polly,** HN 2768, pink & white, 1984-86 .......................................... **150.00**

**Priscilla,** M 24, red gown w/green bonnet, 1932-45 ............................. **400.00**

**Priscilla,** HN 1340, red dress, purple collar, 1929-49................................. **400.00**

**Prized Possessions,** HN 2942, cream, purple & green, Collectors' Club edition........................................ **474.00**

**Professor (The),** HN 2281, brown & black, 1965-81 ................................. **155.00**

**Promenade,** HN 2076, blue overdress, peach skirt, 1951-53 .... **1,330.00 to 1,350.00**

**Punch & Judy Man,** HN 2765, green & yellow, 1981-90............. **365.00 to 375.00**

**Puppetmaker (The),** HN 2253, green vest, brown trousers, 1962-73 ......... **426.00**

**Rachel,** HN 2919, gold & green, 1981-84 .......................................... **240.00**

**Rag Doll,** HN 2142, white, blue & red, 1954-86 .......................................... **100.00**

**Rendezvous,** HN 2212, red & white dress, 1962-71................................. **400.00**

**Repose,** HN 2272, pink & green, 1972-79 ............................ **200.00 to 210.00**

**Rhapsody,** HN 2267, green dress, 1961-73 .......................................... **180.00**

**River Boy,** HN 2128, blue trousers, white shirt, 1962-75 ...................... **100.00**

**Robin,** M 39, blue shirt, green pants, 1933-45 .......................................... **550.00**

**Robin Hood,** HN 2773, green, 1985-90 .......................................... **180.00**

**Romance,** HN 2430, gold & green dress, 1972-81................................. **165.00**

**Rosalind,** HN 2393, blue dress, 1970-75 .......................................... **190.00**

**Rose,** HN 1416, bluish-purple dress, 1930-49 .......................................... **285.00**

**Rosebud,** HN 1983, pink dress, red shawl, 1945-52 ................. **390.00 to 400.00**

**Rosemary,** HN 2091, red & blue, 1952-59 .......................................... **550.00**

**Ruth,** HN 2799, green, 1976-81 ......................... **160.00 to 200.00**

*Sabbath Morn*

*The Shepherd*

**Sabbath Morn,** HN 1982, red dress, greenish-yellow shawl, 1945-59 (ILLUS.) ........................................... **250.00**

**Sam Weller,** M 48, orange vest, black hat & trousers, 1932-81 ...................... **89.00**

**Seafarer (The),** HN 2455, beige sweater, 1972-76 ............................ **140.00**

**Secret Thoughts,** HN 2382, green dress, 1971-88 ................................ **190.00**

**Sheikh,** HN 3083, white, 1987-89 ....... **100.00**

**She Loves Me Not,** HN 2045, 1949-62 ......................................... **300.00**

**Shepherd (The),** HN 1975, light brown smock, 1945-75 (ILLUS. top next column) ..................... **175.00 to 200.00**

**Shore Leave,** HN 2254, black uniform, 1967-79 ............. **190.00 to 200.00**

**Shy Anne,** HN 65, blue spotted dress, dark blue hem, 1916-38 ................ **3,250.00**

**Simone,** HN 2378, olive green dress, 1971-81 ........................... **140.00 to 150.00**

**Sleepy Darling,** HN 2953, blue & pink, Collector's Club edition, 1981 ............ **165.00**

**Sophie,** HN 2833, red & grey, 1977-87 ......................................... **168.00**

**Stop Press,** HN 2683, 1977-80 .......... **155.00**

**Sunday Best,** HN 2206, yellow gown w/large white & red floral design in skirt, yellow bonnet w/red ribbons & flowers, 1979-84 ............... **160.00 to 175.00**

**Sunday Morning,** HN 2184, rose-red dress, 1963-69 ................. **320.00 to 340.00**

**Susan,** HN 2952, 1982-present, 8½" h. ...................................... **225.00**

**Suzette,** HN 1487, pink dress, 1931-50 ...................................... **295.00**

**Suzette,** HN 1696, green dress & hat .................................. **770.00 to 795.00**

**Sweet & Twenty,** HN 1610, red dress, green sofa, 1933-38 ........................ **360.00**

**Sweet Anne,** M 5, cream to red skirt, shaded red & blue jacket, 1932-45 ... **298.00**

**Sweet Lavender,** HN 1373, green, red & black, 1930-49 ...................... **850.00**

**Taking Things Easy,** HN 2677, 1975-87 ........................... **170.00 to 180.00**

**Tall Story,** HN 2248, blue & grey, 1968-75 ........................... **195.00 to 200.00**

**Tess,** HN 2865, green dress, 1978-83 ........................... **195.00 to 200.00**

**Thanks Doc,** HN 2731, white & brown, 1975-90 ................................ **185.00**

**Thank You,** HN 2732, white, brown & blue, 1983-86 .................................. **155.00**

**Tinkle Bell,** HN 1677, pink dress .......... **89.00**

**Tiny Tim,** M 56, black jacket & red pants, 1932-83 ................................. **70.00**

**To Bed,** HN 1805, green shirt & shorts, 1937-59 ............... **165.00 to 175.00**

**Tom,** HN 2864, blue & yellow, 1978-81 ......................................... **310.00**

**Tootles,** HN 1680, pink dress, 1935-75 ........................... **100.00 to 110.00**

*Top O' The Hill*

*Uncle Ned*

**Top o' the Hill,** HN 1849, dark pink dress, 1938-75 (ILLUS.)... **200.00 to 225.00**

**Top o' the Hill,** HN 2126, green & mauve, Collectors' Club edition, 1988............................................................ **105.00**

**Top o' the Hill,** HN 2127, gold, Collectors' Club edition, 1986 ................................. **240.00 to 260.00**

**Toymaker (The),** HN 2250, brown & red, 1959-73..................... **300.00 to 325.00**

**Town Crier,** HN 2119, purple, green & yellow, 1953-76 ............... **235.00 to 240.00**

**Twilight,** HN 2256, green & black, 1971-76 ........................................... **195.00**

**T'zu-hsi,** Empress Dowager, HN 2391, red, white & blue, limited edition, 1983 ..................................... **995.00**

**Uncle Ned,** HN 2094, brown, 1952-65 (ILLUS. top next column)... **400.00 to 425.00**

**Vanity,** HN 2475, red dress, 1973-92 ... **95.00**

**Veneta,** HN 2722, white gown w/olive green overdress, 1974-81 ................ **140.00**

**Veronica,** HN 1517, red & cream, 1932-51 ........................................... **350.00**

**Victorian Lady (A),** M 25, red ruffled skirt, blue shawl, 1932-45.. **285.00 to 300.00**

**Victorian Lady (A),** HN 727, pink & green, 1925-38 ............................... **325.00**

**Viking (The),** HN 2375, blue & brown, 1973-76 ........................................... **285.00**

**Vivienne,** HN 2073, red dress, 1951-67 ........................... **230.00 to 240.00**

**Wayfarer (The),** HN 2362, green, grey & brown, 1970-76 ............................ **195.00**

**Wigmaker of Williamsburg,** HN 2239, beige jerkin, 1960-83 ......................... **175.00**

**Yeoman of the Guard,** HN 2122, red, gold & brown, 1954-59 .................... **850.00**

**Young Love,** HN 2735, cream, green, blue & brown, 1975-90 ..... **500.00 to 550.00**

**Young Master,** HN 2872, purple, grey & brown, 1980-89 ............................ **270.00**

## MISCELLANEOUS

**Bowl,** 7⅜" d., stoneware, low squatty rounded sides w/a wide mouth, incised & glazed w/a running band of enameled stylized flowers & leaves, modeled by Vera Huggins, titled "H. Gibbs 20th Jan. 1939," artist-signed, impressed marks .............................. **173.00**

**Bowl,** 7½" d., 'Chinese Jade' ware, mottled green glaze to a leaf- and fruit-molded body, signed "Noke" & w/monogram of Harry Nixon, painted mark & dated 1931, together w/a wooden Oriental-style stand, 2 pcs. . **805.00**

**Bowl,** 7½" d., collared based, Robin Hood series (Under the Greenwood Tree), scene of Robin Hood .............. **95.00**

**Charger,** the center incised w/large scattered leaves & a grape cluster & other fruits, the wide rim incised w/a vining band of grape clusters, hand-tinted, attributed to Frank Brangwyn, ca. 1930, printed mark, 12⅝" d......... **230.00**

**Charger,** Rustic England series, 13" d... **85.00**

**Cigarette lighter,** table model, Long John Silver..................................... **144.00**

**Cracker jar,** cov., Coaching Days series .................................................. **310.00**

**Cracker jar,** cov., decoration of stylized design w/animals, intaglio background & design on metal cover, artist-signed, Doulton - Lambeth.............................................. **295.00**

**Jar,** cov., stoneware, 'Toad Rock,' modeled in the form of an odd-shaped boulder on a low flaring foot, mottled yellowish green glazes, impressed title around base "The Toad Rock, Tunbridge Wells," impressed mark, ca. 1930, 5" h. ................................. **288.00**

**Jug,** miniature, Dutch-Harlem series .... **75.00**

**Loving cup,** 'Kingsware,' footed tall cylindrical body flanked by long pointed loop handles, decorated w/a half-length portrait of Dr. Johnson against a dark brown ground, a verse on the reverse, early 20th c., 10¾" h. ............................................ **460.00**

**Pitcher,** 4½" h., Coaching Days series.. **75.00**

**Pitcher,** 6¾" h., decorated w/scene of dancing ladies, long pinched spout, blue & white, marked "Morris D1016".. **175.00**

**Pitcher,** 8¾" h., wide ovoid body tapering to a swelled & incurved rim w/wide spout, molded plant stem handle, the sides w/a flow blue transfer-printed design w/a large horseshoe on each side framing a scene of deer in a landscape, overall floral background, ca. 1895 (rim chip) ........................................ **173.00**

**Pitcher,** jug-type, 10½" h., 'Regency Coach' patt., the ovoid body molded w/a colored stagecoach & inn landscape scene, No. 125 of a limited edition of 500, 20th c., printed marks .. **920.00**

**Plate,** 8½" d., Old Moreton series, Elizabethan court scene ..................... **45.00**

**Plate,** 9" d., Coaching Days series........ **55.00**

**Plate,** 10" d., Coaching Days series, coach outside inn.............................. **55.00**

**Plate,** 10" d., Fox-Hunt series, "Across the Moor" ............................................ **45.00**

**Plate,** 10" d., rack-type, "The Admiral".. **75.00**

**Plate,** 10" d., rack-type, "Robert Burns" ................................................. **70.00**

**Plate,** 10½" d., Motoring series, "Bloody Money" .............................. **150.00**

**Plate,** 10½" d., Motoring series, "Yokel & Motorist Outside Inn".......... **150.00**

**Plate,** 10½" d., Robin Hood series (Under the Greenwood Tree), scene of Robin Hood.................................... **59.00**

*Royal Doulton Spirit Barrels*

**Spirit barrels,** double, 'Kingsware,' two barrel-shaped dispensers w/metal spigots at the ends & raised on a double cross-form oak stand, the spigot ends decorated w/early tavern scenes, metal cap closures on the tops, ca. 1909, each 7" l., the set (ILLUS. of one) ....................... **1,035.00**

**Teapot,** cov., decorated w/flowers & green leaves w/raised gold veins, lavish gold trim, ca. late 19th c., Doulton - Burslem mark, 8½ × 12½" ... **200.00**

**Tobacco jar,** cov., figural, 'Kingsware,' modeled as an oversized pipe w/a silver edge ring on the bowl w/an inset cover, decorated w/a scene of 18th century gentlemen smoking against a dark brown ground, signed "Noke," ca. 1914, 12" h. ....................................... **863.00**

**Toothpick holder,** Dutch-Harlem series .................................................. **85.00**

**Vase,** 3¾" h., 5" d., pillow-shaped, flow blue, Babes in the Woods series, scene of girl comforting crying toddler .................................... **600.00**

**Vase,** 6½" h., slender ovoid body on a small footring, a short flaring two-lobed neck flanked by small leafy scroll loop handles, the paneled lobed body h.p. w/scrolled gilt stripes separating a pastoral landscape scene in color, early 20th c. (missing cover)................................................. **259.00**

**Vase,** 6¾" h., flambé glaze in mottled red & yellow glazes, signed by Harry Nixon, ca. 1930, printed marks........ **316.00**

**Vase,** 7½" h., decorated w/h.p. apple blossoms, artist-signed .................... **145.00**

**Vase,** 10" h., stoneware, footed slender baluster-shaped body, cylindrical neck w/flaring rim, incised scenes on the seashore w/green, blue & brown glossy glaze on a pale grey salt glaze ground, Doulton Lambeth mark .............................. **1,100.00**

**Vase,** 10¼" h., 'Sung Ware,' slender baluster-form body w/flaring neck, mottled blue & red glazes, printed marks, ca. 1935 .............................. **345.00**

**Whiskey flask w/original ball stopper,** 'Kingsware,' footed squatty teardrop-form body w/a short neck & arched spout, loop shoulder handle, decorated w/a bust portrait of Lord Nelson on a dark brown ground, "Dewars" on the reverse, ca. 1914, 7½" h ..................................... **546.00**

# DRESDEN

*Dresden-type porcelain evolved from wares made at the nearby Meissen Porcelain Works early in the 18th century. "Dresden" and "Meissen" are often used interchangeable for later wares. "Dresden" has become a generic name for the kind of porcelains produced in Dresden and certain other areas of Germany but perhaps should be confined to the wares made in the city of Dresden*

**Basket,** double, transfer-printed floral decoration, 10" h. (gold trim worn).... **$45.00**

**Bowl,** 9⅜" d., reticulated rim & polychrome enamel floral decoration w/gilt trim, marked "Dresden," Germany (minor wear) ...................... **137.00**

**Cups & saucers,** solid color & gilt w/polychrome scenes on cups, one set w/royal blue ground & crossed swords mark, other sets each w/a different ground color, monogrammed, marked "Dresden," six sets, 12 pcs. ... **1,023.00**

**Figure group,** man w/mandolin near brick wall w/reclining woman, applied florals, 6 × 7" ...................... **325.00**

**Figures of a man & a woman,** standing w/lambs at their feet, 7" h., pr. ....................................... **425.00**

**Ginger jar,** cov, rectangular, bird & tree decoration, 3½ × 7", 2" h ........... **250.00**

**Model of a dog,** male Pug, white w/brushed black spots, dark head w/touch of pink, curly tail, wearing gold collar w/gold porcelain balls, 9" l., 7" h. ...................................... **550.00**

**Plate,** 10¾" d., reticulated rim & polychrome enamel floral decoration w/gilt trim, marked "Dresden," Germany ............................................. **93.00**

# FIESTA

*Fiesta dinnerware was made by the Homer Laughlin China Company of Newell, West Virginia, from the 1930s until the early 1970s. The brilliant colors of this inexpensive pottery have attracted numerous collectors. On February 28, 1986, Laughlin reintroduced the popular Fiesta line with minor changes in the shapes of a few pieces and a contemporary color range. The effect of this new production on the Fiesta collecting market is yet to be determined.*

*Fiesta Mark*

**Ashtray**
|  |  |
|---|---|
| chartreuse | $65.00 |
| forest green | 72.00 |
| red | 48.00 |
| turquoise | 34.00 |
| yellow | 36.00 |

**Bowl,** individual fruit, 4¾" d.
|  |  |
|---|---|
| cobalt blue | 23.00 |
| forest green | 25.00 |
| grey | 26.00 |
| ivory | 21.00 |
| rose | 25.00 |
| yellow | 18.00 |

**Bowl,** individual fruit, 5½" d.
|  |  |
|---|---|
| chartreuse | 29.00 |
| forest green | 31.00 |
| light green (ILLUS. top next page) | 20.00 |
| medium green | 59.00 |
| red | 26.00 |
| turquoise | 20.00 |
| yellow | 18.00 |

**Bowl,** dessert, 6" d.
|  |  |
|---|---|
| chartreuse | 40.00 |
| cobalt blue | 35.00 |
| forest green | 41.00 |
| grey | 41.00 |
| ivory | 35.00 |
| red | 37.00 |

*Fiesta Individual Fruit Bowl*

**Bowl,** individual salad, 7½" d.
| | |
|---|---|
| turquoise | 70.00 |
| yellow | 67.00 |
| forest green | 40.00 |
| grey | 42.00 |
| medium green | 102.00 |
| red | 47.00 |
| yellow | 30.00 |

**Bowl,** nappy, 9½" d.
| | |
|---|---|
| cobalt blue | 50.00 |
| ivory | 44.00 |
| light green | 52.00 |
| grey | 58.00 |
| yellow | 36.00 |

**Bowl,** salad, 9½" d.
| | |
|---|---|
| ivory | 28.00 |
| turquoise | 30.00 |

**Bowl,** fruit, 11¾" d.
| | |
|---|---|
| cobalt blue | 154.00 |
| ivory | 161.00 |
| red | 154.00 |
| turquoise | 192.00 |

**Bowl,** cream soup
| | |
|---|---|
| cobalt blue | 50.00 |
| forest green | 53.00 |
| grey | 65.00 |
| red | 56.00 |
| rose | 61.00 |
| yellow | 35.00 |

**Bowl,** salad, large, footed
| | |
|---|---|
| ivory | 255.00 |
| yellow | 183.00 |

**Cake plate,** 10" d.
| | |
|---|---|
| turquoise | 605.00 |
| yellow | 491.00 |

**Candleholders,** bulb-type, pr.
| | |
|---|---|
| light green | 87.00 |
| red | 84.00 |

**Candleholders,** tripod-type, pr.
| | |
|---|---|
| cobalt blue | 396.00 |
| light green | 299.00 |
| yellow | 214.00 |

*Fiesta Carafe*

**Carafe,** cov.
| | |
|---|---|
| cobalt blue | 253.00 |
| red | 191.00 |
| turquoise | 211.00 |
| yellow (ILLUS.) | 186.00 |

**Casserole,** cov., two-handled, 10" d.
| | |
|---|---|
| chartreuse | 221.00 |
| forest green | 265.00 |
| medium green | 556.00 |
| red | 179.00 |
| turquoise | 108.00 |

*Fiesta Demitasse Coffeepot*

**Coffeepot,** cov., demitasse, stick handle
| | |
|---|---|
| ivory | 432.00 |
| light green (ILLUS.) | 275.00 |
| red | 358.00 |

**Coffeepot,** cov.
cobalt blue ...................................... 201.00
forest green.................................. 228.00
grey.............................................. 539.00
ivory.............................................. 133.00
yellow ........................................... 136.00
**Compote,** 12" d., low, footed
cobalt blue .................................... 116.00
red.................................................. 92.00
yellow ............................................. 49.00
**Creamer,** individual size
red................................................ 182.00
yellow ............................................. 52.00
**Creamer,** stick handle
ivory................................................ 35.00
rose................................................. 25.00
turquoise......................................... 51.00
yellow ............................................. 28.00
**Creamer**
cobalt blue ..................................... 18.00
forest green.................................... 27.00

*Fiesta Creamer*

grey (ILLUS.) ................................... 24.00
ivory................................................ 16.00
rose................................................. 28.00
turquoise......................................... 20.00
**Creamer & cov. sugar bowl,**
chartreuse, on chartreuse figure
8 tray, 3 pcs. ................................. 275.00
**Cup & saucer,** demitasse, stick handle
cobalt blue ..................................... 66.00

ivory.............................................. 59.00
light green...................................... 52.00
turquoise........................................ 61.00
yellow ............................................ 58.00
**Cup & saucer,** ring handle
chartreuse...................................... 34.00
medium green................................. 56.00
red................................................. 28.00
rose................................................ 34.00
yellow ............................................ 23.00
**Egg cup**
cobalt blue ..................................... 56.00
grey .............................................. 134.00
ivory................................................ 48.00
light green....................................... 42.00
rose............................................... 135.00
yellow ............................................. 43.00
**Fork** (Kitchen Kraft)
cobalt blue .................................... 145.00
light green....................................... 76.00
**French Casserole,** cov., stick handle
yellow (ILLUS. below).................... 212.00
**Gravy boat**
chartreuse...................................... 55.00
forest green.................................... 55.00
ivory................................................ 46.00
medium green................................ 144.00
red................................................. 57.00
turquoise........................................ 33.00
**Lid for mixing bowl,** size No. 1
cobalt blue .................................... 575.00
light green..................................... 795.00
yellow ........................................... 375.00
**Lid for mixing bowl,** size No. 3
ivory.............................................. 611.00
**Lid for mixing bowl,** size No. 4
red................................................ 850.00
**Marmalade jar,** cov.
cobalt blue .................................... 266.00
ivory.............................................. 178.00
red................................................ 235.00
turquoise....................................... 176.00

*Fiesta French Casserole*

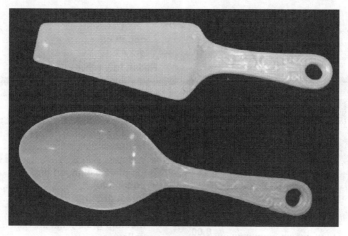

*Fiesta Pie Server and Spoon*

**Mixing bowl,** nest-type, size No. 1, 5" d.
   **cobalt blue** ..................................... 93.00
   **turquoise** ......................................... 69.00
**Mixing bowl,** nest-type, size No. 2, 6" d.
   **cobalt blue** ..................................... 75.00
   **ivory** ................................................. 95.00
   **red** ................................................... 74.00
   **yellow** ............................................. 61.00
**Mixing bowl,** nest-type, size No. 2, 6" d.
   **cobalt blue** ..................................... 75.00
   **ivory** ................................................. 95.00
   **red** ................................................... 74.00
**Mixing bowl,** nest-type, size No. 3, 7" d.
   **cobalt blue** ..................................... 118.00
   **light green** ....................................... 94.00
   **red** ................................................... 51.00
**Mixing bowl,** nest-type, size No. 4, 8" d.
   **cobalt blue** ..................................... 114.00
   **light green** ....................................... 71.00
**Mixing bowl,** nest-type, size No. 5, 9" d.
   **light green** ....................................... 112.00
   **red** ................................................... 112.00
   **yellow** ............................................. 100.00
**Mixing bowl,** nest-type, size No. 6, 10" d.
   **cobalt blue** ..................................... 212.00
   **red** ................................................... 146.00
**Mixing bowl,** nest-type, size No. 7, 11½" d.
   **light green** ....................................... 214.00
   **red** ................................................... 203.00
   **turquoise** ......................................... 196.00
**Mug**
   **chartreuse** ....................................... 71.00
   **cobalt blue** ..................................... 58.00
   **grey** ................................................. 78.00
   **medium green** ................................. 91.00
   **yellow** ............................................. 47.00

**Mug,** Tom & Jerry style
   **forest green** ..................................... 63.00
   **grey** ................................................. 78.00
   **turquoise** ......................................... 50.00
**Mustard jar,** cov.
   **cobalt blue** ..................................... 186.00
   **ivory** ................................................. 153.00
   **light green** ....................................... 148.00
**Onion soup bowl,** cov.
   **cobalt blue** ..................................... 437.00
   **ivory** ................................................. 510.00
   **red** ................................................... 688.00
**Pie server** (Kitchen Kraft)
   **light green** (ILLUS. top) ................. 118.00
   **red** ................................................... 135.00
   **grey** ................................................. 108.00
   **ivory** ................................................. 71.00
   **red** ................................................... 82.00
   **yellow** ............................................. 69.00
**Pitcher,** juice, disc-type, 30 oz.
   **cobalt blue** ..................................... 163.00
   **forest green** ..................................... 263.00
   **grey** ................................................. 145.00
   **red** ................................................... 410.00
   **yellow** ............................................. 47.00
**Pitcher,** water, disc-type
   **cobalt blue** ..................................... 150.00
   **grey** ................................................. 248.00
   **ivory** ................................................. 119.00
   **medium green** (ILLUS. top next
   page) ..................... 775.00 to 1,000.00
   **red** ................................................... 125.00
   **rose** ................................................. 194.00
**Pitcher,** w/ice lip, globular, 2 qt.
   **ivory** ......................... 100.00 to 125.00
   **turquoise** ......................................... 130.00
   **yellow** ............................................. 83.00

*Fiesta Disc-type Water Pitcher*

**Plate,** 6" d.
    chartreuse ......................................... 8.00
    light green ....................................... 4.00
    medium green ................................. 16.00
    yellow ................................................ 5.00
**Plate,** 7" d.
    ivory .................................................. 8.00
    medium green ................................. 28.00
    red ..................................................... 9.00
    rose .................................................. 13.00
**Plate,** 9" d.
    chartreuse ....................................... 18.00
    ivory ................................................. 13.00
    light green ....................................... 11.00
    rose .................................................. 22.00
    turquoise .......................................... 11.00
**Plate,** 10" d.
    chartreuse ....................................... 35.00
    ivory ................................................. 27.00
    light green ....................................... 25.00
    medium green ................................. 81.00
    yellow .............................................. 22.00
**Plate,** 10" d., calendar
    ivory (1954) ..................................... 40.00
    yellow .............................................. 28.00
**Plate,** grill, 10½" d.
    cobalt blue ...................................... 40.00
    light green ....................................... 28.00
    red ................................................... 48.00
    turquoise .......................................... 27.00
**Plate,** grill, 11½" d.
    cobalt blue ...................................... 63.00
    light green ....................................... 37.00
**Plate,** chop, 13" d.
    chartreuse ....................................... 55.00
    grey .................................................. 59.00
    ivory ................................................. 28.00
    yellow .............................................. 24.00
**Plate,** chop, 15" d.
    forest green ..................................... 75.00
    ivory ................................................. 47.00
    light green ....................................... 38.00
    yellow .............................................. 32.00

**Platter,** 12" oval
    chartreuse ....................................... 48.00
    cobalt blue ...................................... 28.00
    grey .................................................. 51.00
**Relish tray** w/five inserts
    multicolored ................................... 205.00
    yellow ............................................ 158.00
**Salt & pepper shakers,** pr.
    grey .................................................. 41.00
    medium green ............................... 109.00
    turquoise .......................................... 15.00
    yellow .............................................. 16.00
**Soup plate** w/flanged rim, 8" d.
    cobalt blue ...................................... 36.00
    forest green ..................................... 42.00
    light green ....................................... 29.00
    medium green ................................. 79.00
    yellow .............................................. 26.00
**Spoon,** (Kitchen Kraft)
    red (ILLUS. bottom, top previous
    page) .............................................. 106.00
**Sugar bowl,** cov.
    forest green ..................................... 32.00
    grey .................................................. 55.00
    light green ....................................... 28.00

*Fiesta Sugar Bowl*

    red (ILLUS.) ..................................... 37.00
    rose .................................................. 55.00
**Syrup pitcher** w/original lid
    cobalt blue .................... 275.00 to 300.00
    light green .................... 200.00 to 225.00
    red ................................................. 290.00
    turquoise ........................................ 267.00
**Teapot,** cov., medium size (6 cup)
    light green (ILLUS. top next page) .. 119.00
    red ................................................. 157.00
    turquoise ........................................ 107.00
**Teapot,** cov., large size (8 cup)
    red ................................................. 161.00
    turquoise ........................................ 138.00
**Tray,** Figure 8
    turquoise ........................................ 238.00
**Tumbler,** juice, 5 oz.
    cobalt blue ...................................... 34.00

*Fiesta Medium Size Teapot*

| | |
|---|---|
| grey | 300.00 |
| turquoise | 28.00 |
| yellow | 31.00 |
| **Tumbler,** water, 10 oz. | |
| cobalt blue | 52.00 |
| ivory | 46.00 |
| turquoise | 49.00 |
| **Utility tray** | |
| light green | 26.00 |
| red | 45.00 |
| yellow | 23.00 |
| **Vase,** bud, 6½" h. | |
| ivory | 61.00 |
| light green | 46.00 |
| yellow | 59.00 |
| **Vase,** 8" h. | |
| ivory | 425.00 to 450.00 |
| light green | 460.00 |
| yellow | 400.00 to 450.00 |
| **Vase,** 10" h. | |
| cobalt blue | 523.00 |
| light green | 450.00 to 500.00 |

## FLORENCE CERAMICS

*Florence Ward began her successful enterprise in 1939. By 1946 she had moved her home workshop into a small plant in Pasadena, California. About three years later it was again necessary to move to larger facilities in the area. Semi-porcelain figurines, some with actual lace dipped in slip, were made. Figurines, such as fictional characters and historical couples, were the backbone of her business. To date, almost two hundred figurines have been documented. For about two years, in the mid-1950s, Betty D. Ford created what the company called "stylized sculptures from the Florence wonderland of birds and animals." Included were about a half dozen assorted doves, several cats, foxes, dogs and rabbits. Several marks were used over the years with the most common being the circle*

*with 'semi-porcelain' outside the circle. The name of the figurine was almost always included with a mark. A "Floraline" mark was used on floral containers and related items. There was also a script mark and a block lettered mark as well as paper labels. The company was sold to Scripto Corporation in 1964 but only advertising pieces were made such as mugs for the Tournament of Roses in Pasadena, California. The company ceased all operations in 1977.*

*Florence Marks*

**Bust of Madame Du Barry,** low cut draped white bodice w/gold trim, large bow on left shoulder, upswept curls w/ribbon & flower, 8½" h. ....... $225.00

**Bust of elegant Oriental young man,** "Yulan," wearing cream uniform w/epaulettes, mandarin collar & cap, lavish gold, black trim, 5¾ × 7⅝" ............................................. 60.00

**Figure of an angel,** white robe w/gold trim, black & white tie at waist, hands together under chin, 7¾" h. ............................... 90.00 to 100.00

**Figure of a man,** "Blue Boy," standing on base, blue coat & knee pants, white stockings, collar & cuffs, right hand holding hat w/plume, 12" h. ............................... 230.00 to 250.00

**Figure of a man,** "Douglas," standing near post, wearing grey suit & vest w/violet tie & trim, right hand behind back & left hand on jacket lapel, 8½" h. ............................................... 150.00

**Figure of a man,** "Douglas," standing near post, wearing beige suit & vest w/green tie & trim, right hand behind back & left hand on jacket lapel, 8½" h. ............................................... 229.00

**Figure of a man,** "Edward," seated on teal arm chair, white hair, grey suit, spats & black tie w/black hat on right knee, 7" h. ............................................ 429.00

**Figure of a man,** "Gary," standing w/right hand in trouser pocket, left hand holding hat, white trousers & vest, rose jacket & hat w/black trim, 8½" h. ............................................... 259.00

**Figure of a man,** "Gary," standing w/right hand in trouser pocket, left hand holding hat, white trousers & vest, teal jacket & hat w/black trim 8½" h. ............................................. **229.00**

**Figure of a man,** "Jim," leaning against post, grey suit & vest, holding hat in left hand, 6" h... **75.00 to 80.00**

**Figure of a man,** "Louis XIV," knee britches, boots, shirt w/ruffled lace trim, knee-length coat, scroll-molded base, 22K gold trim, 10" h. ............... **245.00**

**Figure of a man,** "Mike," standing w/arms outstretched & raised, peach suit w/striped scarf at neck, 6¼" h. .... **120.00**

**Figure of a man,** "Rhett," standing by low stone wall, left hand in trouser pocket, white suit w/red trim, grey hat, 9" h. ............................................. **150.00**

**Figure of Madonna,** standing w/outstretched arms, white w/gold trim, 10½" h. ..................................... **189.00**

**Figure of a woman,** "Abigail," standing, wearing full-skirted dress, cape & bonnet, green, blue or tan, 8½" h., each..................................... **139.00**

**Figure of a woman,** "Abigail," standing, wearing full-skirted dress, cape & bonnet, pink or grey & burgundy, 8½" h., each..................... **150.00**

**Figure of a woman,** "Adeline," standing, wearing dress w/full shirt, low-cut bodice w/full sleeves & scarf wrapped over lower arms, rose & blue, 9" h........................................... **225.00**

**Figure of a woman,** "Amelia," standing, dark brown skirt w/tan bodice & overskirt gathered w/band of pink floral trim, right hand holding fan behind head, 8¼" h................... **159.00**

**Figure of a woman,** "Amelia," standing, burgundy skirt w/grey bodice & overskirt gathered w/band of pink floral trim, right hand holding fan behind head, 8¼" h.................... **175.00**

**Figure of a woman,** "Ann," standing, wearing beige dress, bonnet tied beneath chin, holding basket on left arm, 6" h............................. **90.00 to 100.00**

**Figure of a woman,** "Bea," standing, blue dress, holding white handbag in left hand, white bonnet tied under chin, 7¼" h......................................... **85.00**

**Figure of a woman,** "Betsy," standing, wearing green skirt & long full jacket w/tight bodice & long sleeves, hands in muff, ruffled floral trim on jacket, bonnet & muff, 7½" h. ........................ **125.00**

**Figure of a woman,** "Catherine," seated on white bench w/gold trim, wearing aqua dress w/white ruffled bodice & short sleeves, holding white hat w/gold trim in left hand, 6¾ × 7¾" ......................................... **525.00**

**Figure of a woman,** "Delia," standing, rose high-neck dress w/very wide cuffs, hands in muff w/gold trim, flat hat on top of head, ribbons under chin, 7¼" h ......................................... **175.00**

**Figure of a woman,** "Delia," standing, teal high neck dress w/very wide cuffs, hands in muff w/gold trim, flat hat on top of head, ribbons under chin, 7¼" h... **75.00**

**Figure of a woman,** "Elizabeth," seated on grey Victorian sofa, wearing teal dress w/white & gold trim & floral headpiece, 7 × 8½" ....... **429.00**

**Figure of a woman,** "Ellen," standing, violet skirt w/long, close-fitted jacket w/white & gold trim, hands in white muff, white & gold hat w/tie under chin, 7" h........................................... **150.00**

**Figure of a woman,** "Georgette," standing, wearing rose dress, white trim & large bonnet, holding package on left arm, 10¼" ............................ **275.00**

**Figure of a woman,** "Grace," standing, turned to right, teal dress, both hands holding white hat against skirt, 7¾" h........................................ **229.00**

**Figure of a woman,** "Irene," standing, violet dress w/gold trim, flower in upswept hair, right hand holding muff near face, 6" h. ........................... **80.00**

**Figure of a woman,** "Kay," standing, holding dress out at sides, large hat, white w/floral trim at bodice & lower skirt, gold trim, 7" h. ........................... **95.00**

**Figure of a woman,** "Lady Diana," standing, aqua & white dress w/gold trim, ruffled stand-up collar, flowers in hair, right hand outstretched, left arm bent toward body, 10" h............. **225.00**

**Figure of a woman,** "Marie Antoinette," ruffled bodice, hair ornamentations, roses & lace trim on gown, 22K gold trim, 10" h............... **250.00**

**Figure of a woman,** "Mary," seated on violet armchair, one foot on footstool, right hand resting on knee, left arm on chair, white dress w/floral trim, rose overskirt & bodice, large white hat, 7½" h. ............................. **429.00**

**Figure of a woman,** "Matilda," standing w/left hand near chin, left arm at side, holding muff, tan or blue dress, 10" h., each .......... **115.00 to 125.00**

**Figure of a woman,** "Melanie,"
standing w/arms down at sides, rose
dress & bonnet w/tie under chin,
7½" h. ............................... **120.00 to 125.00**

**Figure of a woman,** "Misha," Oriental
figure, Chinese red gown w/white &
gold trim, elaborate up-swept hairdo
w/ornaments, reading scroll, 11" h. .. **100.00**

**Figure of a woman,** "Pinkie," standing
on base, white dress w/pink trim,
pink hat w/loose ribbon, right arm
behind back, left arm held in front of
body, 12" h. ....................................... **295.00**

**Figure of a woman,** "Rebecca,"
seated in chair, green dress w/violet
trim, chin on left hand w/arm resting
on chair, 7" h. ................... **180.00 to 200.00**

**Figure of a woman,** "Sarah,"
standing, blue dress w/white & gold
trim, right hand at side, holding
handbag, left arm in front of body,
7½" h. .............................................. **127.00**

**Figure of a woman,** "Scarlett,"
standing, violet dress & bonnet, right
hand holding muff near face, left
hand holding handbag, 8¾" h. .......... **150.00**

**Figures,** "Blue Boy," figure of man
standing on base, blue pants & coat
w/white trim, white stockings,
holding plumed hat in right hand, &
"Pinkie," woman standing on base,
wearing white dress w/rose trim &
hat w/loose ribbon, right arm behind
back, left arm held in front of body,
12" h., pr. ......................................... **659.00**

**Figures,** "Louis XVI," standing, lace &
fur trim, white w/22K gold trim &
"Marie Antoinette," standing, ruffled
bodice, hair ornamentation, lace &
roses & 22K gold trim, 10" h., pr. ...... **350.00**

**Figures,** "Wynkin," standing, dressed
in blue sleeper, holding Teddy bear
in left arm, & "Blynkin," standing,
dressed in rose nightgown, holding
gown up in right hand & doll in left
hand, 5½" h., pr. .............. **170.00 to 200.00**

**Flower holder,** "Belle," standing,
white hat & dress w/ruffled green
bodice trim, green trim on skirt &
cuffs, flower on hat, right hand
holding skirt out & left hand on hip,
8" h. .................................................. **125.00**

**Lamp base,** figure of "Charles,"
standing, white suit & cape, ruffled
shirt, gold trim, right hand under chin
w/left hand behind back .................... **375.00**

**Model of a pouter pigeon,** tail
feathers fully spread, white & grey ... **450.00**

**Wall plaques,** rectangular, molded-in-
relief figure of girl w/brunette hair,
wearing long green dress w/mauve
accents & holding gold fan in hand,
the second is a molded-in-relief
figure of a girl w/blonde hair, wearing
long green dress w/mauve accents,
holding gold muff in her hand,
6½ × 9", pr. ...................................... **195.00**

## FLOW BLUE

*Flowing Blue wares, usually shortened to
Flow Blue, were made at numerous potteries
in Staffordshire, England and elsewhere. They
are decorated with a blue that smudged lightly
or ran in the firing. The same type of color
flow is also found in certain wares decorated in
green, purple and sepia. Patterns were given
specific names, which accompany the listing
here.*

**AMOY (Davenport, dated 1844)**
**Plate,** 8" d. ............................................ **$50.00**
**Plate,** 9½" d. ......................................... **150.00**
**Teapot,** cov. ...................... **670.00 to 690.00**
**Tea set:** cov. teapot, creamer & cov.
sugar bowl; 3 pcs. ................... **1,950.00**
**Vegetable bowl,** open, 8" d. ............... **350.00**

**EBOR (Ridgways, ca. 1910)**
**Butter dish,** cov., w/liner ................... **350.00**
**Creamer & cov. sugar bowl,** pr. ........ **300.00**
**Vegetable bowl,** cov., oval ................ **295.00**
**Vegetable bowl,** cov., round ............. **295.00**

**FLORAL (Thomas Hughes & Son, ca.
1895)**
**Cheese dish,** cov. .............................. **375.00**
**Jardiniere** ........................................... **395.00**
**Syrup pitcher,** cov. ............................. **295.00**
**Tea tile** ............................................... **110.00**
**Vase** ................................................... **595.00**

**LA BELLE (Wheeling Pottery, ca. 1900)**
**Bowl,** 7½" d. .......................................... **90.00**
**Plate,** 9½" d. .......................................... **85.00**
**Platter,** 12" l. ...................................... **165.00**
**Platter,** 14½" l. .................................... **325.00**
**Wash pitcher,** 11" h. ........................... **535.00**

**MONGOLIA (Johnson Bros., ca. 1900)**
**Bowl,** berry ........................................... **55.00**
**Cup,** tea ............................................... **25.00**

Cup & saucer ................................... 105.00
Plate, 6½" d............................... 60.00
Plate, 8" d................................. 80.00
Plate, 9" d................................. 95.00
Plate, 10" d............................... 105.00
Platter, 14" l. ............................. 320.00
Soup plate w/flanged rim.................. 110.00

**NON PAREIL (Burgess & Leigh, ca. 1891)**
Bone dish ................................... 75.00
Butter pat .................................. 40.00
Bouillon cup................................ 125.00
Cake plate, 11" d. ........................ 175.00
Creamer, 5" h.............................. 215.00
Cup ......................................... 120.00
Cup, demitasse ............................ 100.00
Plate, 6⅛" d............................... 50.00
Plate, 6¾" d............................... 65.00
Plate, 6⅝" d............................... 55.00
Plate, 7¾" d............................... 60.00
Plate, 8⅝" d............................... 80.00
Plate, 9¼" d............................... 100.00
Plate, 9¾" d............................... 110.00

*Non Pareil Plate*

Plate, dinner, 10" d. (ILLUS.) .............. 100.00
Platter, 10¾" l. ........................... 275.00
Platter, 13⅜" l. ........................... 350.00
Platter, 15½" l ........................... 400.00
Sauce tureen, cover & undertray, the
   set........................................ 635.00
Soup plate w/flanged rim.................. 100.00
Sugar bowl, cov. .......................... 140.00
Vegetable bowl, cov........................ 475.00
Vegetable bowl, open, 8¼" d............ 115.00
Vegetable bowl, open, 9½" d............ 135.00
Vegetable bowl, rectangular, 9½" l. ... 135.00

**OREGON (T. J. & J. Mayer, ca. 1845)**
Cup & saucer ................................ 275.00
Plate, 8½" d............................... 125.00
Plate, 9½" d............................... 150.00
Plate, dinner, 10½" d...................... 95.00

**SCINDE (J. & G. Alcock, ca. 1840 and Thomas Walker, ca. 1847)**
Cup & saucer ................................ 180.00
Plate, 7" d................................. 105.00
Plate, 9½" d............................... 135.00
Platter, 11 × 14".......................... 495.00
Razor box, cov. ........................... 650.00

**TOURAINE (Henry Alcock, ca. 1898 & Stanley Pottery, ca. 1898)**
Oyster bowl................................ 165.00
Pitcher, milk, large........................ 1,195.00
Plate, 9" d................................. 60.00
Soup plate w/flanged rim.................. 95.00
Tea set: cov. teapot, creamer & cov.
   sugar bowl; 3 pcs......................... 2,195.00
Vegetable bowl, open, oval, 8¾" ....... 100.00

**WARWICK (Podmore Walker & Co., ca. 1850)**
Pin tray .................................... 475.00
Pitcher, 2 qt. ............................. 425.00
Punch cup ................................. 175.00
Sauce tureen, cover & undertray,
   3 pcs..................................... 750.00
Wash bowl................................. 395.00

# FRANCISCAN WARE

*A product of Gladding, McBean & Company of Glendale and Los Angeles, California, Franciscan Ware was one of a number of lines produced by that firm over its long history. Introduced in 1934 as a pottery dinnerware, Franciscan Ware was produced in many patterns including "Desert Rose," introduced in 1941 and reportedly the most popular dinnerware pattern ever made in this country. Beginning in 1942 some vitrified china patterns were produced under the Franciscan name also.*

*After a merger in 1963 the company name was changed to Interpace Corporation and in 1979 Josiah Wedgwood & Sons purchased the*

*Gladding, McBean & Co. plant from Interpace. American production ceased in 1984.*

*Franciscan Ware Mark*

**Ashtray,** Apple patt., 4¾" sq. ............. **$95.00**

**Ashtray,** Apple patt., ca. 1940, 9" oval ...................................... **30.00 to 40.00**

**Ashtray,** individual, Desert Rose patt., 3½" d. ................................. **20.00 to 30.00**

**Baking dish,** Apple patt., 8¾ × 9½", 1 qt. .................................................. **200.00**

**Baking dish,** Apple patt., 9 × 14", 1½ qt. (small factory flaw) ................. **225.00**

**Baking dish,** October patt., 8" sq. ........ **65.00**

**Bowl,** soup, 5½" d., 2¼" h., footed, Desert Rose patt., ca. 1941 ............... **25.00**

**Bowl,** cereal or soup, 6" d., Apple patt. ..................................................... **14.00**

**Bowl,** cereal or soup, 6" d., Desert Rose patt., ca. 1941 ........................... **14.00**

**Bowl,** 8", divided, Starburst patt. ........... **30.00**

**Bowl,** salad, 10" d., 3¼" h., Desert Rose patt., ca. 1941 ........... **90.00 to 100.00**

**Butter dish,** cov., Apple patt., ca. 1940, ¼ lb. ...................................... **38.00**

**Butter dish,** cov., Desert Rose patt., ¼ lb. ................................................... **40.00**

**Butter dish,** cov., Ivy patt., ca. 1948, ¼ lb. ................................................... **65.00**

**Candleholders,** Desert Rose patt., ca. 1942, 3" h., pr. ................. **75.00 to 85.00**

**Candy dish,** Desert Rose patt., 6½" w., 7" l., 1" h. ............................ **125.00**

**Casserole,** cov., round, handled, Apple patt., ca. 1940, 1½ qt., 6¾" d., 3" h. ..................................................... **80.00**

**Casserole,** cov., round, handled, Ivy patt., ca. 1948, 1½ qt., 8" d., 4" h. .... **125.00**

**Casserole,** cov., Ivy patt., w/green band trim, 1½ qt. .............................. **150.00**

**Coaster,** Apple patt., 3¾" d., 1" h. ........ **30.00**

**Coffeepot,** cov., Desert Rose patt., ca. 1941 .............................................. **86.00**

**Coffeepot,** cov., Apple patt., ca. 1940, 7½" h. ................................................. **125.00**

**Coffee server,** cov., Apple patt. ........... **110.00**

**Coffee server,** cov., Desert Rose patt. .................................. **260.00 to 275.00**

**Cookie jar,** cov., Apple patt., ca. 1940, 9¼" h. ............................... **215.00**

**Cookie jar,** cov., Desert Rose patt., ca. 1942, 9¼" h. .............. **250.00 to 275.00**

**Creamer,** Tiempo patt. ........................... **10.00**

**Creamer & cov. sugar bowl,** individual, Apple patt., pr. .................. **55.00**

**Creamer & cov. sugar bowl,** Ivy patt., ca. 1948, pr. ..................................... **55.00**

**Cup,** child's, Meadow Rose patt. .......... **15.00**

**Cup & saucer,** demitasse, Coronado patt., grey glaze .................................. **45.00**

**Cup & saucer,** demitasse, Desert Rose patt., ca. 1941 ....................... **42.00**

**Cup & saucer,** Desert Rose patt., ca. 1941 ................................................ **10.00**

**Cup & saucer,** Desert Rose patt., jumbo, cup 4½" d., 3" h., saucer, 7" d. ....................................................... **49.00**

**Cup & saucer,** Ivy patt., jumbo, cup 4¼" d., 3¼" h., saucer, 7" d. .............. **65.00**

**Egg cup,** Apple patt., ca. 1940, 3¾" h. ... **25.00**

**Egg cup,** Desert Rose patt., ca. 1941, 3¾" h. ................................................. **26.00**

**Ginger jar,** cov., Desert Rose patt. ...... **250.00**

**Gravy boat w/attached undertray,** Desert Rose patt. ................. **45.00 to 55.00**

**Gravy boat w/attached undertray,** Apple patt., ca. 1940, 8¼" l., 3½" h. ... **37.00**

**Gravy boat w/attached undertray,** Ivy patt., ca. 1948, 9" l., 5" h. .............. **40.00**

**Jam jar,** cov., Desert Rose patt., 3½" h... **125.00**

**Lamp base,** hurricane-type, Desert Rose patt. ...................................... **225.00**

**Mixing bowl,** Apple patt., ca. 1940, 7½" d., 4¼" h. ................... **100.00 to 125.00**

**Mug,** cocoa, Apple patt., 10 oz. ........... **90.00**

**Mug,** Apple patt., ca. 1940, 12 oz, 4¼" h. ................................................. **40.00**

**Mug,** Desert Rose patt., ca. 1941, 12 oz. ...................................... **25.00 to 35.00**

**Napkin ring,** Desert Rose patt., ca. 1941, 1½" h. ....................................... **50.00**

**Napkin ring,** October patt., 1½" d., 1½" h. ................................................. **24.00**

**Pepper mill,** cylindrical, Desert Rose patt., 6" h. ......................................... **150.00**

**Pitcher,** milk, 6½" h., Meadow Rose patt., 1 qt. ..................................... **75.00**

**Pitcher,** water, 8¾" h., Desert Rose patt., ca. 1941, 2½ qt. ........ **95.00 to 125.00**

**Pitcher,** water, 8¾" h., Meadow Rose patt., 2½ qt. .................................... **145.00**

**Pitcher,** water, October patt., 1¾ qt...... **95.00**

**Plate,** side salad, 4½ × 8", crescent-
shaped, Apple patt., ca. 1940 ............. **32.00**

**Plate,** side salad, 4½ × 8", crescent-
shaped, Desert Rose patt.,
ca. 1941 ............................... **30.00 to 40.00**

**Plate,** bread & butter, 6½" d., Apple
patt., ca. 1940 ...................................... **5.00**

**Plate,** salad, 8½" d., Apple patt.,
ca. 1940 ................................................ **17.00**

**Plate,** luncheon, 9½" d., Apple patt.,
ca. 1940 ................................................ **17.00**

**Plate,** luncheon, 9½" d., Desert Rose
patt., ca. 1941 ..................................... **17.00**

**Plate,** luncheon, 9¼" d., Ivy patt.,
ca. 1948 ................................................ **20.00**

**Plate,** dinner, 10½" d., Apple patt.,
ca. 1940 ................................................ **16.00**

**Plate,** dinner, 10½" d., Desert Rose
patt., ca. 1941 ..................................... **13.00**

**Plate,** grill, 11" d., Apple patt.,
ca. 1940 ................................................ **80.00**

**Plate,** grill/buffet, 11" d., Ivy patt.,
ca. 1948 ................................................ **60.00**

**Plate,** chop, 12" d., Apple patt.,
ca. 1940 .............................. **60.00 to 70.00**

**Plate,** chop, 14" d., Apple patt.,
ca. 1940 .......................... **100.00 to 120.00**

**Platter,** 8½ × 12¾" oval, Desert Rose
patt., ca. 1941 ..................................... **32.00**

**Platter,** 10¼ × 14" oval, Apple patt.,
ca. 1940 .............................. **45.00 to 55.00**

**Platter,** 14", Meadow Rose patt., 1977... **45.00**

**Platter,** 13¼ × 19" oval, Apple
patt. .................................. **200.00 to 225.00**

**Relish dish,** Ivy patt., 10½" l................ **35.00**

**Relish dish,** Desert Rose patt., 11" l. ... **34.00**

**Relish dish,** oblong, three-part, Apple
patt., ca. 1940, 11¾" l......................... **70.00**

**Relish dish,** oval, three-part, Desert
Rose patt., ca. 1941, 12" l. ................. **80.00**

**Salt & pepper shakers,** Apple patt.,
ca. 1940, tall, 6¼" h., pr..................... **36.00**

**Salt & pepper shakers,** Desert Rose
patt., ca. 1941, tall, 6¼" h., pr............ **40.00**

**Salt & pepper shakers,** Ivy patt.,
2¾" h., pr. .......................................... **35.00**

**Salt shaker & pepper mill,** Desert
Rose patt., pr................... **170.00 to 190.00**

**Salt shaker & pepper mill,** Meadow
Rose patt., 6" h., pr........................... **195.00**

**Sherbet,** footed, Desert Rose patt.,
ca. 1941, 2½" h................................... **24.00**

**Soup plate w/flanged rim,** Desert
Rose patt., ca. 1941, 8¼" d. ... **20.00 to 30.00**

**Soup plate w/flanged rim,** Apple
patt., ca. 1940, 8½" d.......................... **20.00**

**Soup plate w/flanged rim,** Ivy patt.,
ca. 1948, 8½" d.................................... **28.00**

**Soup tureen,** cov., pedestal base,
Desert Rose patt.............................. **700.00**

**Soup tureen,** cov., three-footed, Apple
patt., ca. 1940, 7½" d., 5¼" h. ............. **488.00**

**Snack plate,** Apple patt., 8" sq. .......... **175.00**

**Sugar bowl,** cov., Apple patt., large ..... **35.00**

**Teapot,** cov., Apple patt., ca. 1940,
4¾" h. .................................................. **95.00**

**Teapot,** cov., Coronado Ware, coral
stain, ca. 1930s ................................. **55.00**

**Teapot,** cov., Desert Rose patt.,
ca. 1941 ............................................... **85.00**

**Thimble,** October patt...................... **45.00**

**Tidbit tray,** three-tier, Ivy patt.,
ca. 1948............................................... **75.00**

**Tidbit tray,** two-tier, Ivy patt., ca. 1948.. **78.00**

**Trivet,** Apple patt., round, 6" d............ **250.00**

**Tumbler,** juice, Desert Rose patt.......... **40.00**

**Tumbler,** juice, Meadow Rose patt.,
3¼" h. .................................................. **45.00**

**Tumbler,** water, Desert Rose patt.,
ca. 1941, 5" h. ..................... **30.00 to 35.00**

**Tumbler,** water, Apple patt., ca. 1940,
10 oz., 5¼" h....................................... **30.00**

**Vegetable bowl,** open, round, Apple
patt., ca. 1940, 7¾" d., 2" h. ............... **30.00**

**Vegetable bowl,** open, round, Desert
Rose patt., ca. 1941, 8" d.,
2¼" h. ................................. **25.00 to 35.00**

**Vegetable bowl,** open, Apple patt.,
9" d. .................................................... **45.00**

**Vegetable bowl,** open, round, Desert
Rose patt., ca. 1941, 9" d. .................. **32.00**

**Vegetable dish,** open, divided, Desert
Rose patt., 11" l. ................................. **30.00**

**Vegetable dish,** open, oval, divided,
Ivy patt., ca. 1948, 12" l. .................... **45.00**

**Vegetable bowl,** open, oval, Starburst
patt., ca. 1954..................................... **17.00**

# FRANKOMA

*John Frank began producing and selling
pottery on a part-time basis during the
summer of 1933 while he was still teaching art
and pottery classes at the University of
Oklahoma. In 1934, Frankoma Pottery became
an incorporated business that was successful
enough to allow him to leave his teaching
position in 1936 to devote full time to its
growth. The pottery was moved to Sapulpa,*

Oklahoma in 1938 and a full range of art pottery and dinnerwares were eventually offered. In 1953 Frankoma switched from Ada clay to clay found in Sapulpa. Since John Frank's death in 1973, the pottery has been directed by his daughter, Joniece. In early 1991 Richard Bernstein became owner and president of Frankoma Pottery which was renamed Frankoma Industries. Joniece Frank serves as vice president and general manager. The early wares and limited editions are becoming increasingly popular with collectors today.

*Frankoma Mark*

**Bottle-vase,** No. V-2, 1970, **turquoise** glaze, signed "John Frank," 12" h. .................................. **$35.00**

**Bottle-vase,** No. V-14, 1982, flame red glaze body on black base, signed "Joniece Frank," 11" h. .......... **65.00 to 75.00**

**Bottle-vase,** No. V-1, 1969, Prairie Green glaze w/black base, 15" h. ....... **75.00**

**Candleholders,** No. 300, jade green glaze, pr. (original sticker on one) ...... **70.00**

**Christmas card,** 1962 ......................... **35.00**

**Mug,** 1968, (Republican) elephant, white glaze ......................... **80.00 to 90.00**

*1969 Nixon-Agnew Mug*

**Mug,** 1969 (Republican) elephant, "Nixon-Agnew," flame-red glaze (ILLUS.) ........................................... **60.00**

**Mug,** 1972 elephant, green glaze ......... **65.00**

**Plate,** 8½" d., Christmas, 1965, "Good Will Towards Men," depicts Mary, Joseph & Jesus ............... **250.00 to 300.00**

**Plate,** 8½" d., Christmas, 1967, "Gifts For The Christ Child," depicts the three Wisemen ................................. **90.00**

## FULPER

The Fulper Pottery was founded in Flemington, New Jersey, in 1805 and operated until 1935, although operations were curtailed in 1929 when its main plant was destroyed by fire. The name was changed in 1929 to Stangl Pottery, which continued in operation until July of 1978, when Pfaltzgraff, a division of Susquehanna Broadcasting Company of York, Pennsylvania, purchased the assets of the Stangl Pottery, including the name.

*Fulper Marks*

**Center bowl,** embossed shield decoration at rim, caramel & green matte glaze, incised vertical mark, 9" d., 4" h. ...................................... **$220.00**

**Center bowl & frog,** wide flat rim w/embossed design, thick cream & mint green high glaze over an oatmeal olive matte glaze, seated cherub frog, pale green & white high glaze, both w/vertical marks, 9" d., 7" h. .................................................. **187.00**

**Vase,** 4" h., 6" d., squatty bulbous body w/flat neck flanked by angled handles, vivid violet & dark blue high glaze over rose matte glaze, vertical ink mark ............................................. **468.00**

**Vase,** 5" h., 6" d., bulbous body, pink matte glaze, incised mark ................. **143.00**

**Vase,** 7" h., ovoid body tapering to short neck w/flaring rim flanked by three small loop handles, green crystalline high glaze, vertical ink mark ................................................... **231.00**

**Vase,** 7½" h., waisted cylindrical body, thick butterscotch flambé glaze, impressed vertical mark .................... **440.00**

**Vase,** 9" h., tall ovoid body w/short, wide cylindrical neck flanked by small loop handles, matte rose glaze.......... **235.00**

**Vase,** 9" h., wide bulbous body w/a short wide cylindrical neck, flanked by arched loop handles, red & blue matte glaze, incised vertical mark .... **358.00**

**Vase,** 9½" h., footed trumpet-form w/narrow rounded body, three narrow stepped panels & double ring handles at top of one side & bottom of other side, rich caramel over blue high glaze, impressed "Fulper" ......... **440.00**

**Vase,** 11" h., tall slender footed baluster-form body w/short flaring neck, Chinese blue glaze ................. **350.00**

**Vase,** 11" h., wide squatty bulbous body tapering to a wide slightly flaring neck, shoulder handles, green drip glaze w/blue & white highlights, raised vertical mark ......... **413.00**

**Vase,** 12" h., wide bulbous ovoid footed body tapering to a short, wide cylindrical neck, angled shoulder handles, apple green glaze .............. **595.00**

**Vase,** 12" h., wide ovoid body on narrow foot, angled shoulder handles & short molded neck, medium blue, light blue & olive crystalline glaze, impressed vertical mark (base repair) ........................... **495.00**

*Fulper Vase*

**Vase,** 12" h., 7" d., wide ovoid body tapering to wide cylindrical neck w/flaring rim, green crystalline glaze w/olive & tan highlights, mark obscured by glaze (ILLUS.) ........... **1,430.00**

**Vase,** 13½" h., baluster-form body w/short flaring neck, cream high glaze over grey w/blue highlights, vertical ink mark ............................... **358.00**

# HALL

*Founded in 1903 in East Liverpool, Ohio, this still-operating company at first produced mostly utilitarian wares. It was in 1911 that Robert T. Hall, son of the company founder, developed a special single-fire, lead-free glaze which proved to be strong, hard and non-porous. In the 1920s the firm became well known for their extensive line of teapots (still a major product) and in 1932, they introduced kitchenwares followed by dinnerwares in 1936 and refrigerator wares in 1938.*

*The imaginative designs and wide range of glaze colors and decal decorations have led to the growing appeal of Hall wares with collectors, especially people who like Art Deco and Art Moderne design. One of the firm's most famous patterns was the "Autumn Leaf" line, produced as premiums for the Jewel Tea Company.*

*Helpful books on Hall include,* The Collector's Guide to Hall China *by Margaret & Kenn Whitmyer, and* Superior Quality Hall China—A Guide for Collectors *by Harvey Duke (An ELO Book, 1977).*

*Hall Marks*

**Baker,** French, fluted, Wildfire patt. .... **$25.00**

**Bowl,** 5¼" d., Cameo Rose patt.............. **4.00**

**Bowl,** 5½" d., Wildfire patt.................... **10.00**

**Bowl,** plum pudding, 6" d., Blue Willow patt. ........................................ **25.00**

**Bowl,** salad, 9" d., Rose Parade patt. ..................................... **40.00 to 50.00**

**Bowl,** 10½" oval, Cameo Rose patt. ...... **15.00**

**Casserole,** cov., Radiance shape, Stonewall patt., 7" d............................ **30.00**

**Casserole,** cov., Thick Rim shape, Springtime patt. .................................. **20.00**

**Casserole,** cov., Sundial shape, Chinese Red, No. 4, 8" d. ................... **30.00**

**Casserole,** cov., Thick Rim shape, Wildfire patt. w/cadet blue base.......... 40.00

**Coffeepot,** cov., dripolator-type, Kadota shape, Morning Flower patt., all-china ............................................... 85.00

**Coffeepot,** cov., dripolator-type, w/metal basket, Target shape ............ 35.00

**Coffeepot,** cov., dripolator-type, w/basket Trellis shape ........................ 45.00

**Coffeepot,** cov., Orb shape w/Bird of Paradise patt. ..................................... 30.00

**Coffeepot,** cov., Washington shape, plain green, fifteen-cup size................ 50.00

**Creamer,** Moderne shape, Wildfire patt.......................................................... 18.00

**Creamer & cov. sugar bowl,** Cameo Rose patt., pr...................................... 15.00

**Cup & saucer,** Cameo Rose patt. .......... 7.00

**Cup & saucer,** Wildfire patt .................. 19.00

**Custard cup,** Wildfire patt. .................. 12.00

**Gravy boat,** Wildfire patt...................... 30.00

**Pitcher,** ball-type, No. 3, Chinese Red... 40.00

**Pitcher,** ball-type, Royal Rose patt., No. 3 .................................................... 85.00

**Pitcher,** jug-type, 6½" h., Radiance shape, No. 5, No. 488 patt................. 25.00

**Plate,** 6" d., Wildfire patt......................... 7.00

**Plate,** 6½" d., Cameo Rose patt.............. 4.00

**Plate,** 7¼" d., Cameo Rose patt.............. 5.00

**Plate,** dinner, 10" d., Cameo Rose Patt. ... 8.00

**Platter,** 11 × 14" l., oval, Wildfire patt.... 28.00

**Salt & pepper shakers,** tab-handled, Pert shape, Rose White patt., pr. ....... 25.00

**Salt & pepper shakers,** handled, Springtime patt., pr. ........................... 25.00

**Salt & pepper shakers,** handled, Wildfire patt., pr. ................................. 38.00

**Salt & pepper shakers,** Pert shape, Rose Parade patt., pr. ....................... 40.00

**Salt & pepper shakers,** teardrop-shaped, Wildfire patt., pr.................... 32.00

**Sugar bowl,** cov., Moderne shape, Wildfire patt.......................................... 28.00

**Teapot,** cov., Airflow shape, Chinese Red, six-cup size ............................. 125.00

**Teapot,** cov., Aladdin shape, Wildfire patt., w/infuser ................................. 135.00

**Teapot,** cov., Boston shape, Chinese Red, six-cup size ............................. 150.00

**Teapot,** cov., Doughnut shape, Chinese Red, six-cup size ............... 350.00

**Teapot,** cov., French shape, Chinese Red, Lipton mark, six-cup size .......... 40.00

**Teapot,** cov., Hollywood shape, Chinese Red, six-cup size ............... 200.00

**Teapot,** cov., Medallion (Colonial) shape, Silhouette patt........................ 95.00

**Teapot,** cov., Melody shape, Chinese Red, six-cup size ............................. 250.00

**Teapot,** cov., Philadelphia shape, Chinese Red, six-cup size ............... 150.00

**Teapot,** cov., Streamline shape, Chinese Red, six-cup size .................. 95.00

**Teapot,** cov., Surfside shape, Chinese Red, six-cup size ............................. 475.00

**Teapot,** cov., Twinspout shape, forest green .............................................. 65.00

**Tea set:** cov. teapot, creamer & cov. sugar bowl, French shape, yellow, Lipton mark, 3 pcs ............................. 85.00

**Tidbit tray,** three-tier, Wildfire patt........ 80.00

**Water server,** w/stopper, Hot Point, delphinium ....................................... 100.00

## HARKER POTTERY COMPANY

The Harker Pottery was established in East Liverpool, Ohio, in 1840 by Benjamin Harker, Sr. In 1890 the pottery was incorporated as the Harker Pottery Company. By 1911 the company had acquired the former plant of the National China Company and in 1931 Harker purchased the closed pottery of Edwin M. Knowles in Chester, West Virginia.

Harker's earliest products were yellowware and Rockingham-glazed wares produced from local clay. After 1900 whiteware was made from imported materials. Perhaps their best-known line is Cameoware, decorated on solid glazes with white "cameos" in a silhouette fashion.

There were many other patterns and shapes created by Harker over the years. In 1972 the pottery was closed after it was purchased by the Jeanette Glass Company.

Harker Pottery Marks

**Bowl,** berry, 5⅔" d., Everglades patt.,
coral .................................................. **$5.00**

**Bowl,** soup, 7½" d., Everglades patt.,
coral .................................................. **8.00**

**Cake plate,** handled, Corinthian patt.,
teal w/cream gadroon border,
10½" d. ............................................. **8.00**

**Casserole,** cov., Everglades patt.,
coral ................................................. **35.00**

**Creamer & cov. sugar bowl,**
Corinthian patt., teal w/cream
gadroon border ................................. **12.00**

**Creamer & cov. sugar bowl,**
Everglades patt., coral ...................... **22.00**

**Cup & saucer,** demitasse, Rose patt.,
Cameoware line ................................ **12.00**

**Cup & saucer,** Everglades patt., coral ... **8.00**

**Custard cups w/original rack,** Dainty
Flower patt., Cameoware line, set
of 6 .................................................. **40.00**

**Dessert set,** plate & cup, Corinthian
patt., teal w/cream gadroon border,
2 pcs. ................................................ **8.00**

**Mixing bowls,** Apple patt., red, set of 3 .. **65.00**

**Mixing bowls,** Dainty Flower patt.,
Cameoware line, blue, set of 3 ........... **34.00**

**Pie server,** Lovelace patt. .................... **30.00**

**Plate,** dessert, Corinthian patt., teal
w/cream gadroon border ..................... **4.00**

**Plate,** salad, 7¼" d., Everglades patt.,
coral ................................................... **8.00**

**Plate,** dinner, 10" d., Everglades patt.,
coral ................................................. **12.00**

**Plate,** dinner, Provincial Wreath patt. ...... **5.00**

**Plate,** 10" d., 50th Anniversary, gold
rim (slight wear) ................................ **15.00**

**Platter,** 11¼" oval, Everglades patt.,
coral ................................................. **29.00**

**Porridge cup & saucer,** Dainty Flower
patt., Cameoware line, "Dad" .............. **20.00**

**Rolling pin,** floral & fruit basket decal,
gold trim, handle ring 14½" l. (wear
on inside from hanging) ...................... **95.00**

**Salt & pepper shakers,** Dainty
Flower patt., Cameoware line, range
size, pr. ............................................. **22.00**

**Scoop w/hole in handle** for hanging,
Amy patt. ........................................... **60.00**

**Serving fork,** Modern Tulip patt. ........... **22.00**

**Serving spoon,** Modern Tulip patt. ...... **22.00**

**Teapot,** cov., Dainty Flower patt.,
Cameoware line ................................. **35.00**

**Tidbit tray,** Provincial Tulip patt. ............ **8.00**

**Vegetable bowl,** open, Everglades
patt., coral, 8¾" d. ............................. **16.00**

# HARLEQUIN

*The Homer Laughlin China Company,
makers of the popular "Fiesta" pottery line,
also introduced in 1938 a less expensive and
thinner ware which was sold under the
"Harlequin" name. It did not carry the
maker's trade-mark and was marketed
exclusively through F. W. Woolworth
Company. It was produced in a wide range of
dinnerwares in assorted colors until 1964. Out
of production for a number of years, in 1979
Woolworth requested the line be reintroduced
using an ironstone body and with a limited
range of pieces and colors offered. Collectors
also seek out a series of miniature animal
figures produced in the Harlequin line in the
1930s and 1940s.*

**Baker,** oval, maroon, 9" l. .................... **$38.00**

**Baker,** oval, yellow, 9" l. ........................ **30.00**

**Bowl,** 36s, 4½" d., blue, light green or
medium green, each ........................... **38.00**

**Bowl,** 36s, 4½" d., forest green ............. **44.00**

**Bowl,** 36s, 4½" d., turquoise or
yellow, each ...................................... **28.00**

**Bowl,** fruit, 5½" d., blue, forest green
or yellow, each .................................... **9.00**

**Bowl,** oatmeal, 6½" d., blue, red or
rose, each .......................................... **26.00**

**Bowl,** oatmeal, 6½" d., turquoise .......... **18.00**

**Bowl,** individual salad, 7" d., chartreuse,
grey, red or rose, each ....................... **34.00**

**Bowl,** individual salad, 7" d., green ....... **30.00**

**Butter dish,** cov., ½ lb., maroon ......... **125.00**

**Butter dish,** cov., spruce green .......... **125.00**

**Butter dish,** cov., yellow ...................... **95.00**

**Casserole,** cov., blue or red, each ...... **125.00**

**Casserole,** cov., chartreuse ............... **160.00**

**Casserole,** cov., rose ......................... **110.00**

**Casserole,** cov., spruce green ............ **168.00**

**Creamer,** individual size, light green ..... **60.00**

**Creamer,** individual size, maroon ........ **30.00**

**Creamer,** individual size, yellow .......... **20.00**

**Creamer,** maroon ................................ **30.00**

**Creamer,** medium green ...................... **50.00**

**Creamer,** yellow .................................. **20.00**

**Creamer,** novelty, ball-shaped, rose ..... **48.00**

**Creamer,** novelty, ball-shaped,
turquoise ........................................... **38.00**

**Creamer,** novelty, ball-shaped, yellow .. **35.00**

**Cream soup,** handled, chartreuse,
maroon, or red, each ......................... **28.00**

**Cream soup,** handled, yellow .............. **22.00**

**Cup,** demitasse, maroon ...................... **95.00**

Cup, demitasse, spruce green .............. 98.00
Cup, demitasse, yellow ........................ 28.00
Cup & saucer, blue, chartreuse,
   maroon or red, each .......................... 20.00
Cup & saucer, turquoise ...................... 11.00
Egg cup, single, red or yellow, each..... 30.00
Egg cup, double, blue, chartreuse,
   red, turquoise or yellow, each............. 20.00
Egg cup, double, rose or spruce
   green, each........................................ 25.00
Gravy boat, chartreuse, turquoise or
   yellow, each....................................... 25.00
Gravy boat, grey, light green, or rose,
   each.................................................. 35.00
Nappy, 9" d., maroon, rose or spruce
   green, each........................................ 44.00
Nut dish, individual size, basketweave
   interior, blue, or maroon, each ............ 15.00
Nut dish, individual size, spruce
   green ................................................. 15.00
Pitcher, 9" h., ball-shaped w/ice lip,
   blue ..................................... 70.00 to 80.00
Pitcher, 9" h., ball-shaped w/ice lip,
   grey................................................... 140.00
Pitcher, 9" h., ball-shaped w/ice lip,
   light green.......................................... 90.00
Pitcher, 9" h., ball-shaped w/ice lip,
   maroon .............................. 90.00 to 100.00
Pitcher, 9" h., ball-shaped w/ice lip,
   red .................................................... 75.00
Pitcher, 9" h., ball-shaped w/ice lip,
   yellow................................................. 48.00
Pitcher, cylindrical, 22 oz., maroon ...... 75.00
Pitcher, cylindrical, 22 oz., turquoise
   or yellow, each................................... 48.00
Plate, 6" d., chartreuse, turquoise or
   yellow, each......................................... 6.00
Plate, 6" d., grey, light green, maroon,
   red, rose or spruce green, each .......... 8.00
Plate, 7" d., blue, light green, maroon,
   red or rose, each ............................... 12.00
Plate, 9" d., blue, chartreuse, forest
   green, maroon, red, rose or spruce
   green, each........................................ 15.00
Plate, 9" d., grey.................................. 12.00
Plate, 9" d., turquoise............................ 8.00
Plate, 10" d., red or rose, each ............. 35.00
Plate, 10" d., yellow.............................. 25.00
Platter, 11" l., oval, blue, grey, or
   rose, each.......................................... 25.00
Platter, 13" l., oval, blue, maroon, or
   rose, each.......................................... 45.00
Platter, 13" l., oval, yellow.................... 23.00
Salt & pepper shakers, blue,
   maroon, or red, pr., each ................... 18.00

Soup plate w/flange rim, blue,
   chartreuse, maroon or red, 8" d.,
   each.................................................. 30.00
Soup plate w/flange rim, grey,
   8" d................................... 30.00 to 35.00
Soup plate w/flange rim, medium
   green, 8" d. ....................................... 60.00
Soup plate w/flange rim, rose, 8" d..... 29.00
Soup plate w/flange rim, turquoise or
   yellow, 8" d., each.............................. 25.00
Sugar bowl, cov., grey, light green or
   red, each............................................ 32.00
Sugar bowl, cov., maroon .................... 34.00
Sugar bowl, cov., medium green ......... 50.00
Teapot, cov., light green ..................... 135.00
Teapot, cov., spruce green ................. 150.00
Teapot, cov., yellow............. 90.00 to 100.00
Tumbler, blue or red, each..... 40.00 to 45.00
Tumbler, maroon ................................. 40.00
Tumbler, spruce green ......................... 48.00
Tumbler, turquoise .............................. 35.00
Tumbler, yellow.................... 25.00 to 30.00

## HISTORICAL & COMMEMORATIVE WARES

*Numerous potteries, especially in England and the United States, made various porcelain and earthenware pieces to commemorate people, places and events. Scarce English historical wares with American views command highest prices. Objects are listed here alphabetically by title of view.*

*Most pieces listed here will date between about 1820 and 1850. The maker's name is noted in parenthesis at the end of each entry.*

*Almshouse New York Pitcher*

*Arms of Massachusetts Platter*

**Almshouse, New York platter,** flowers within medallions border, dark blue, 16½", Ridgway (network of wear, when tilted) ...................... **$523.00**

**Almshouse, New York - Deaf and Dumb Asylum, Hartford wash pitcher,** vine leaf border, dark blue, 8¾" h., rim chip & hairline on base, Ralph Stevenson & Williams (ILLUS. bottom previous page ...................... **935.00**

**Arms of Maryland soup tureen undertray,** w/pierced foot rim for hanging, flowers & vines border, spoked wheels equidistant around border, dark blue, 14¾", Mayer (mellowed & unseen chips on foot rim) ................................................ **3,520.00**

**Arms of Massachusetts platter,** flowers & vines border, spoked wheels equidistant around border, dark blue, ca. 1830, 9½" l., Mayer (ILLUS. above) ................................ **4,312.00**

**Arms of Rhode Island plate,** flowers & vines border w/spoked wheels equidistant around, dark blue, ca. 1830, 8½" d., Enoch Wood & Son (ILLUS. bottom previous column ............................................... **805.00**

**Bald Eagle sugar bowl,** w/matching cover, large leaves border, eagle w/wings spread, dark blue, 6¼" h. (handle & rim restored on base & cover has an extensive restoration) .. **1,100.00**

**Ballston Springs - Caldwell, Lake George - Northampton, Mass. compote,** footed, small flowers & moss border, brown, 10½" w., 5⅛" h., Meigh (some mottled mellowing on underside of base) ...... **303.00**

**Baltimore & Ohio Railroad (Inclined) plate,** shell border, dark blue, 9⅛" d., Enoch Wood & Sons (crack) ............ **345.00**

**Baltimore & Ohio Railroad (Level) plate,** shell border, circular center w/trailing vines around outer edge of center, dark blue, 10" d., Wood (restoration to several deep pits on back & a reglazing of the face) ........ **550.00**

**Belleville on the Passaic River soup tureen,** New York Bay & Highlands at West Point cov., shell border & circular center w/trailing vine around outer edge of center, dark blue, 15½" w., 11½" h., Wood (shallow flake on the finial & faint meandering internal hairline in base) ............... **8,800.00**

**Boston Athenaeum bowl,** flowers within medallions border, dark blue, 4⅜" d., 2" h., J. & W. Ridgway (rim chip) .................................................. **633.00**

*Arms of Rhode Island Plate*

*Boston Harbor Teapot*

**Boston Harbor tea service:** 8" h. cov. teapot, 7½" h. cov. teapot, 6½" h. sugar bowl, 5¾" h. creamer, 6⅛" d., 3½" h. waste bowl, six cups & saucers; flowers, foliage & scrolls border, spread eagle w/shield in foreground, city (Boston?) in far background, dark blue, Rogers, 8" h. teapot, unseen flake on cover; 7½" h. teapot, mis-match cover; sugar bowl, unseen flange chip on base; creamer, flake on lip; waste bowl, heavily crazed w/network of hairlines, 17 pcs. (ILLUS. of teapot)........................................... **4,675.00**

**Boston State House bowl,** footed, flowers & leaves border, dark blue, 10¼" d., 4¼" h., (invisible restoration to 3" section of rim that probably contained two faint hairlines) ............ **935.00**

**Boston State House creamer,** reverse - New York City Hall, fully opened roses w/leaves border, dark blue, 4¾" h., Stubbs (spout chips, cracks at handle) .............................. **431.00**

**Boston State House platter,** floral border, dark blue, 14⅝", Rogers (minute flake on inner rim & several short facial scratches)....................... **605.00**

**Boston State House platter,** floral border, dark blue, 18¾", Rogers (some short facial scratches & a few facial pock marks)......................... **880.00**

**Boston State House vegetable dish,** oval, floral border, dark blue, 11¼" l., Rogers (tiny restored chip on rim & unseen chip on foot/base) ............... **660.00**

**British America cup plate,** ferns on a background of moss border, pink, 4" d., Davenport (some glaze wear) .. **173.00**

**Buenos Ayres - Cities Series plate,** flowers & scrolls border, dark blue, 10" d., (Davenport) ........................... **159.00**

**Cadmus plate,** shell border, irregular opening to the center gives a "grotto" effect, dark blue 10" d. (Wood) ......... **303.00**

**Castle Garden, Battery, New York cup plate,** abbreviated border, dark blue, 3¾" d., Wood (small hairline base)................................................. **230.00**

**Cathedral at York (England) gravy tureen undertray,** embossed, Grapevine border series, dark blue, 7⅛" d. (Wood).................................. **209.00**

**Catskill Moss series, Hudson, New York urn,** handled, bunches of moss on a network of moss border, light blue, 13" d., 10" h. Ridgway (professional restoration to several large chips on base & to a 3" l. section that was missing on upper rim, internal faint "spider" crack on base, probably once had a cover) .... **660.00**

**Christ Church, Oxford (England) plate,** College series, dark blue, 10" d. (Ridgway) .............................. **148.00**

**Church in the City of New York (Dr. Mason's) plate,** spread eagle border, dark blue, 6 " d., Stubbs (light mellowing).......................................... **633.00**

**City Hall, New York - State House, Boston pitcher,** fully opened roses w/leaves border, dark blue, 6½" h., Stubbs (hairlines in base & restoration to spout & rim)..................................... **303.00**

**City of Albany - State of New York plate,** shell border, circular center w/trailing vine around outer edge of center, dark blue, 9½" d. (Enoch Wood) ................................................. **550.00**

**Columbian Star, Oct. 28th, 1840 - Log Cabin (side view) teapot,** cov., star border, light blue, 11½" w., 7" h. (Ridgway) ......................................... **550.00**

**Commodore MacDonnough's Victory plate,** shell border, dark blue, 9" d., Wood (overall slight dullness to face & short scratch that does not go through glaze).............. **248.00**

**Commodore MacDonnough's Victory saucer,** shell border, irregular center, dark blue (Wood).... **247.00**

**Cowes Harbor plate,** shell border, irregular center, dark blue, 6¼" d. (Enoch Wood & Sons) ..................... **345.00**

**The Dam and Water Works, Philadelphia (side wheel steamboat) plate,** fruits, flowers & leaves border, medium dark blue, 10" d. (Henshall) ... **396.00**

**The Dam and Water Works, Philadelphia (stern-wheel steamboat) plate,** fruits, flowers & leaves border, dark blue, 10" d., (Henshall) ....................................... **715.00**

**Dartmouth plate,** shells border, irregular center, dark blue, 9¼" d., Enoch Wood & Sons (a few knife scratches, glaze wear & very small hairline to underside) ........................ **230.00**

**Dorney Court, Buchinghamshire (England) openwork basket,** Grapevine border series, dark blue, (Wood) .............................................. **935.00**

**Entrance of the Erie Canal into the Hudson at Albany chamber pot,** cov., Aqueduct bridge at Rochester (twice on exterior), view of the Aqueduct Bridge at Little Falls (interior), floral border, irregular center, dark blue (Wood) .............. **2,475.00**

**Episcopal Theological Seminary - Lexington, Kentucky plate,** floral & leave border, purple, 10½" d. (two recorded, recently discovered) .........**358.00**

**Esplanade & Castle Garden - Almshouse, New York basket,** openwork, vine leaf border, dark blue, 10¼" w., 5¼" h., R. Steverson & Williams (border smeared & some interior wear, otherwise perfect) .... **2,640.00**

**Fall of Montmorenci Near Quebec plate,** shells border, circular center w/trailing vine around outer edge of center, dark blue, 9" d., Wood (three small camouflaged glaze flakes on inner rim) .......................................... **253.00**

**Florence (Italy) cov. soup tureen,** Acanthus handles & rose finial, Italian Scenery series, dark blue, 15" w., 12" h., Wood (some light mellowing, being cleaned, otherwise brilliant proof)................................... **4,125.00**

**Franklin wash bowl,** floral border, brown, 12½" d. (Davenport............... **605.00**

**Franklin (tomb) teapot,** cov., flowers, dark blue, Phillips (restored chips on cover & tip of spout restored) ........... **935.00**

**Franklin's Tomb coffeepot,** cov., high-domed, floral border, dark blue, 12" h., Wood Invisible restoration to rim & base (ILLUS. top next column).......................................... **4,950.00**

**Franklin's Tomb pitcher,** floral border, scalloped edge, dark blue, 7¾" h., .... **935.00**

**Franklin's Tomb sugar bowl,** cov., round, floral border, dark blue, 5¾" h., Wood (partially restored rim chip on cover, base is mellowed & four unseen short hairlines on foot rim) ................. **880.00**

**Gyrn, Flintshire Wales (England) platter,** fruits & flowers border, dark blue, 17⅛" l. (Ralph Hall)................. **920.00**

*Franklin's Tomb Coffeepot*

**Hallowell Bay of Quinte (Canada) platter,** Lake series, flowers & scrolls border, grey, 21¼" l., Morely (light mellowing which can be cleaned, otherwise perfect) ............. **495.00**

**Harbor Scene plate,** sea-plants & shells border, medium blue, 5¼" d., Rogers (rim chip) ............................ **230.00**

**Harvard College (four buildings) soup plate,** acorn & oak leaves border, dark blue, 10" d., R. Stevenson & Williams (minute glaze flake on rim) ......................... **330.00**

**Highbury College, London (England) platter,** College series, dark blue, 12½" l. (Adams) ............. **522.00**

**Hospital, Boston plate,** vine border, dark blue, 8¼" d. Stevenson & Williams (transfer a bit blurred, otherwise perfect) ........................... **110.00**

**Hudson, Hudson River plate,** birds, flowers & scrolls border, brown, 10½" d., Clews (unseen chip on foot rim, wear on inner rim & mellowed) .. **160.00**

**Insane Hospital, Boston plate,** flowers within medallions border, dark blue, 7¼" d. (Ridgway) ............. **193.00**

**Iron Works at Saugerties platter,** long stemmed roses border, brown, 12¼" l. (Jackson) ............................ **275.00**

**Lakes of Kilarney plate,** flowers & leaves border, medium blue, 9" d ...... **66.00**

**Lakes of Kilarney soup tureen,** scroll handles & finial, medium dark blue, 14" w., 8¼" h. (two small restored chips on cover & several unseen flakes on the flange of the base) ........ **825.00**

**Landing of General Lafayette at Castle Garden, New York,**

**16 August, 1824 cup plate,** floral &
vine border, view in oval medallion,
dark blue, 3½" d. (Clews) ................ **358.00**

**Landing of General Lafayette at
Castle Garden, New York, 16
August, 1824 luncheon plates,**
floral & vine border, dark blue, 8" d.,
(Clews), pr. ...................................... **518.00**

**Landing of General Lafayette at
Castle Garden, New York,
16 August, 1824 mustard pot,** cov.,
handled, cylindrical, floral & vine
border, dark blue, 3⅛" h., Clews
(minute base flake) ....................... **1,760.00**

*Landing of Lafayette Platter*

**Landing of General Lafayette at
Castle Garden, New York, 16
Ausust, 1824 platter,** floral & vine
border, dark blue, 17" l., Clews,
hairlines, repaired rim chips (ILLUS.).. **920.00**

**Landing of General Lafayette at
Castle Garden, New York, 16
August, 1824 cov. vegetable dish,**
floral & vine border, dark blue,
12½" d., 6" h., Clews (minor chips,
knife marks) ................................... **1,093.00**

**Landing of General Lafayette at
Castle Garden, New York,
16 August, 1824 wash pitcher,** floral
& vine border, dark blue, 9¾" h.,
Clews (crack around upper portion
of the handle)................................. **1,045.00**

**Landing of the Fathers at Plymouth,
Dec. 22, 1620 pitcher,** pairs of birds
& scrolls & four medallions w/ships &
inscriptions border, medium dark
blue, 5¾" h., Wood (invisible
restoration to tip of spout) ................ **770.00**

**Little Falls at Luzerne, Hudson
River platter,** birds, flowers & scrolls
border, black, 17¾" l. (Clews).......... **385.00**

**Louisville, Kentucky platter,** groups
of flowers & scrolls border, dark blue,
14½" l., Neff Wanton & Co. (very
minor glaze chips, knife marks) ......... **920.00**

**Melrose Abbey, Roxburyshire
(England) plate,** bluebell border,
dark blue, 6⅞" d. Adams (mismarked
as Branxholm Castle) ...................... **165.00**

**Nahant Hotel, Near Boston plate,**
spread eagles amid flowers & scrolls
border, dark blue, 8½" d., Stubbs
(minor chips, knife marks) ............... **403.00**

**Near Fort Miller, Hudson River -
Junction of Sacandaga and
Hudson River vegetable dish,**
open, birds, flowers & scrolls border,
red, 10¾" d. (Clews) ....................... **413.00**

**Near Hudson, Hudson River gravy
tureen, ladle & undertray,** birds,
flowers & scrolls border, light blue,
Clews (unseen flake on underside of
undertray & the base has mellowing).. **605.00**

**New York platter,** Select Sketches
series, light blue, 19½" l. (Jackson) .. **303.00**

**Octagon Church, Boston soup plate,**
flowers within medallions border,
dark blue, 10" d., Ridgway (small
area of glaze)................................... **230.00**

**Peace & Plenty cup plate,** wide band
of fruit & flowers full border, dark
blue, 3½" d. (Clews) ....................... **275.00**

**Peace & Plenty dish,** oval, lobed,
wide band of fruit & flowers border,
dark blue, 10¼" l., Clews (excellent
restoration to both the foot rim & a
small rim chip) ................................ **990.00**

*Peace & Plenty Plate*

**Peace & Plenty plate,** wide band of
fruit & flowers border, dark blue,
9" d., rim chip, glaze wear, Clews
(ILLUS.) .......................................... **201.00**

**Philadelphia - Cities Series plate,**
groups of flowers & scrolls border,
dark blue, 6¾" d. (Clews) ................ **413.00**

**Pine Orchard House, Catskill
Mountains soup plate,** shell border,
dark blue, 10¼" d., Wood (minor
chips, knife marks)........................... **460.00**

**Ship, Under Half Sail cup plate,** shell border, irregular opening to the center gives a "grotto" effect, dark blue, 3¾" d., Wood (light mellowing, otherwise brilliant proof) .................. **302.00**

**Skenectady on the Mohawk River - Newport, Rhode Island soup tureen,** w/matching cover, long-stemmed roses border, brown, 15½" w., 10¾" h., Jackson (invisible restoration to cover) ........................... **550.00**

**State House, Boston custard cup,** flowers within medallions border, dark blue, 2⅝" h., Wood (unseen flakes on foot rim) ............................. **165.00**

**States series cup plate,** three story mansion w/extension, fruit & floral border, dark blue 3¾" d., Clews (invisible restoration & reglazing of plate)................................................. **220.00**

**States series gravy tureen undertray,** two story building w/curved drive, fruit & floral border, dark blue, 8¼" w. (Clews) .............. **1,210.00**

**States series vegetable dish,** open, mansion, small boat w/flag in foreground, names of fifteen states in festoons on border, separated by five- or eight-point stars, dark blue, 12¼" (Clews) ................................ **1,050.00**

**Stratford on Avon, Warwickshire (England) plate,** bluebell border, dark blue, 8⅞" d., Clews (light scratching, when tilted, otherwise brilliant proof) .................................... **165.00**

**St. Paul's Church, Boston platter,** flowers within medallions border, dark blue, 9½" l., J. & W. Ridgway (cracks) .............................................. **316.00**

**Texian Campaign - Major General Taylor before Monterey, Sept 20th, 1846 platter,** symbols of war & a "goddess-type" seated border, green, 15½" l., Shaw (small glaze rub on inner shoulder, some on extreme edges of rim & a small discoloration near a stilt mark on the face)............................................... **1,430.00**

**Upper Ferry Bridge over River Schuylkill plate,** spread eagle amid flowers & scrolls border, medium dark blue, 8¾" d., Stubbs (minor discoloration) .................................... **144.00**

**Upper Ferry Bridge over River Schuylkill gravy tureen undertray,** spread eagles amid flowers & scrolls border, dark blue, 9" w. (Stubbs) ...... **248.00**

**Upper Ferry Bridge over River Schuylkill wash bowl,** spread eagle amid flowers & scrolls border, medium dark blue, 12½" d. (Stubbs) ................. **880.00**

**View Near Catskill on the River Hudson platter,** flowers between leafy scrolls border, dark blue, 12½" (A. Stevenson) ............................. **1,760.00**

**View of Newburgh relish dish,** Four Medallion Floral Border series, light blue, 6½" l., Wood (unseen flakes on foot rim) .......................................... **176.00**

**View of Trenton Falls plate,** shell border, circular center w/trailing vine around outer edge of center, dark blue, 6½" d., Enoch Wood & Sons (hairline to base, rim chip) ............... **173.00**

**Views of the Erie Canal...Aqueduct Bridge at Little Falls wash pitcher & Entrance of the Erie Canal wash bowl,** floral border, dark blue, Wood, 2 pcs. (ILLUS. below)......................................... **1,870.00**

**Wilkes Barre, Vale of Wyoming serving dish,** handled, American Scenery series, light blue w/applied grey handles & side decoration, 11½" w. ......................................... **165.00**

*Views of the Erie Canal Wash Bowl & Pitcher*

**Winter View of Pittsfield, Mass. (A)**
**cup plate,** scalloped edge, floral
border w/medallions of center view
border, dark blue 4½" d. (Clews) ...... **358.00**

**Winter View of Pittsfield, Mass. (A)**
**vegetable bowl,** open, floral
w/medallions of center view border,
dark blue, 12½" (Clews) ............... **1,100.00**

# HULL

*This pottery was made by the Hull Pottery
Company, Crooksville, Ohio, beginning in
1905. Art Pottery was made until 1950 when
the company was converted to utilitarian
wares. All production ceased in 1986*

*Reference books for collectors include*
Roberts' Ultimate Encyclopedia of Hull
Pottery *by Brenda Roberts (Walsworth
Publishing Company, 1992), and* Collector's
Guide to Hull Pottery—The Dinnerware
Lines *by Barbara Loveless Gick-Burke
(Collector Books, 1993).*

*Hull Marks*

**Ashtray,** heart-shaped, Butterfly patt.,
No. 83, 7" l. ...................................... **$50.00**

**Bank,** standing-type, Little Red
Riding Hood patt., 7" h. (ILLUS.
below) ............................. **575.00 to 585.00**

*Little Red Riding Hood Standing Bank*

**Bank,** wall-type, Little Red Riding
Hood patt., 9" h. ............................. **2,025.00**

**Basket,** Bow-Knot patt., blue to pink,
No. B-25-6¼", 6½" h. ...................... **260.00**

**Basket,** Bow-Knot patt., pink & blue,
No. B-12-10½", 10½" h. ................... **605.00**

**Basket,** Bow Knot patt., pink, No.
B-29-12", 12". ............................... **1,425.00**

**Basket,** Butterfly patt., cream &
turquoise, No. B13, 8 × 8".. **100.00 to 120.00**

**Basket,** Dogwood patt., center handles,
blue & pink, No. 501-7½", 7½"............. **231.00**

**Basket,** Ebb Tide patt., No. E-5,
6¼ × 9⅛" ......................................... **75.00**

**Basket,** Ebb Tide patt., model of a
large shell w/long fish handle,
No. E-11, 16½" l. ............................. **165.00**

**Basket,** Ebb Tide patt., 12", maroon..... **75.00**

**Basket,** Magnolia Matte patt.,
No. 10-10½", 10½" h. ....................... **173.00**

**Basket,** Mardi Gras patt., No. 65-8,
8" h. ............................................... **98.00**

**Basket,** Open Rose patt., pink &
green, No. 107-6", 6". ...................... **350.00**

**Basket,** hanging-type, Open Rose
patt., pink & blue, w/chains,
No. 132-7", 7" ................................. **295.00**

**Basket,** Parchment & Pine patt.,
brown, No. 8-16", 16" h....................... **90.00**

**Basket,** Rosella patt., No. R-12-7", 7".. **153.00**

**Basket,** Royal Woodland patt.,
turquoise, W22, 10½" l. ..................... **98.00**

**Basket,** Serenade patt., yellow,
No. S5, 6¾" ..................................... **70.00**

**Basket,** Tokay patt., round "Moon"
form, white, No. 11, 10½" h. .............. **78.00**

**Basket,** Water Lily patt., pink &
turquoise, No. L14-10½", 10½" h...... **350.00**

**Basket,** Windflower patt., pink,
No. W16-10½", 10½"......................... **375.00**

**Basket,** hanging-type, Woodland patt.,
rose, matte glaze, No. W31-5½,
5½" h................................................ **210.00**

**Batter pitcher,** side-pour, Little Red
Riding Hood patt., 7" h...................... **426.00**

**Bowl,** 7" oval, Dogwood patt., pink &
blue, No. 521-7" .............................. **120.00**

**Bowl,** 7" d., low, Orchid patt., blue,
No. 312-7"........................................ **170.00**

**Butter dish,** cov., Little Red Riding
Hood patt. (ILLUS. top next
page) ................................. **340.00 to 350.00**

**Candleholders,** Blossom Flite patt.,
No. T11-3", 3" h., pr. .......................... **70.00**

**Candleholders,** Woodland patt., rose
& green, No. W30, 3½" h., pr............. **100.00**

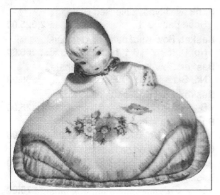

*Little Red Riding Hood Butter Dish*

*Bow-Knot Cornucopia-vase*

**Candleholders,** Iris patt., pink & blue,
No. 411-5", 5" h., pr. .......................... **175.00**

**Canister,** cov., "Flour," Little Red
Riding Hood patt. .............................. **600.00**

**Canister,** cov., "Salt," Little Red
Riding Hood patt. ........................... **1,025.00**

**Canister,** cov., "Tea," Little Red
Riding Hood patt. ............. **670.00 to 700.00**

**Casserole,** cov., figural hen on nest,
8" h., 2 pcs. ........................................ **55.00**

**Casserole,** cov., Serenade patt., blue... **100.00**

**Coffeepot,** cov., House 'n Garden
patt., Mirror Brown glaze ................... **40.00**

**Console bowl,** Bow-Knot patt.,
No. B-16-13½", 13½" l. ..................... **265.00**

**Console bowl,** cornucopia-shaped,
Dogwood patt., cream & turquoise,
No. 511-11½", 11½" d. ..................... **125.00**

**Console bowl,** Iris patt., pink & blue,
No. 409-12", 12" l............................. **295.00**

**Console bowl,** Magnolia Gloss patt.,
cream w/gold, No. H-23-13", 13" l. ..... **63.00**

**Console bowl,** Orchid patt.,
No. 314-13", 13" l............................. **375.00**

**Console bowl,** Water Lily patt.,
walnut & apricot, No. L-21-13½",
13½" l................................................ **110.00**

**Console bowl,** Woodland patt.,
No. W29-14", 14" l. ............................ **85.00**

**Cookie jar,** cov., Barefoot Boy, made
for Hull by Gen Refractories, 13" h. ... **435.00**

**Cornucopia-vase,** Bow-Knot patt.,
No. B-5-7½", 7½" h........................... **150.00**

**Cornucopia-vase,** double, Bow-Knot
patt., turquoise & blue, No. B-13-13",
13" h. (ILLUS. top next column)........ **295.00**

**Cornucopia-vase,** Open Rose patt.,
pink & blue, No. 101-8½", 8½" h....... **155.00**

**Cornucopia-vase,** Parchment & Pine
patt., No. S-2-R, 7¾" h. ...................... **45.00**

**Cornucopia-vase,** Rosella patt.,
No. R-13-8½"..................................... **55.00**

**Cornucopia-vase,** double, Water Lily
patt., pink & turquoise, No. L27-12",
12" l................................................... **195.00**

**Cornucopia-vase,** Wildflower patt.,
pink & blue, No. W7-7½", 7½" h. ........ **55.00**

**Cornucopia-vase,** Wildflower patt,
pink & blue, No. 58-6¼", 6¼" h......... **175.00**

**Cornucopia-vase,** Woodland Matte
patt., which w/gold, No. W5-6½",
6½" h. ................................................ **95.00**

*Woodland Gloss Cornucopia-Vase*

**Cornucopia-vase,** Woodland Gloss
patt., No. W10-11", 11" h. (ILLUS.)... **125.00**

**Cracker jar,** cov., Little Red Riding
Hood patt., 8½" h. ............ **665.00 to 700.00**

**Creamer,** side pour, Little Red Riding
Hood patt. ........................................ **140.00**

**Creamer,** Water Lily patt., No. L-19-5",
5" h.................................................... **45.00**

**Creamer,** Wildflower patt., peach,
No. 73-4¾", 4¾" h. ........................... **195.00**

**Creamer & cov. sugar bowl,** Butterfly
patt., Nos. B19 & B20, pr. .................. **50.00**

*Bow-Knot Ewer*

**Ewer,** Bow-Knot patt., No. B-1-5½",
5½" h. (ILLUS.)................. **155.00 to 175.00**

**Ewer,** Calla Lily patt., blue & cream,
No. 506-10", 10" h. ......................... **375.00**

**Ewer,** Calla Lily patt., turquoise,
No. 506-10", 10¾" h. ....................... **325.00**

**Ewer,** Continental patt., green, No. 56,
12½" h. ........................................... **65.00**

**Ewer,** Dogwood patt., cream & blue,
No. 520-4¾", 4¾" h. ....................... **145.00**

**Ewer,** Dogwood patt., peach,
No. 505-6½", 8½" h. ....................... **295.00**

**Ewer,** Iris patt., No. 401-8", 8" h......... **235.00**

**Ewer,** Iris patt., No. 401-13½", 13½" h... **475.00**

**Ewer,** Magnolia Matte patt., pink &
blue, No. 14-4¾", 4¾" h..................... **45.00**

**Ewer,** Magnolia Matte patt., No. 5-7",
7" h. ............................................... **105.00**

**Ewer,** Morning Glory patt., white,
No. 63-11", 11" h. ........................... **495.00**

**Ewer,** Open Rose patt., pink & blue,
No. 115-8½", 8½" h. ....................... **295.00**

**Ewer,** Parchment & Pine patt.,
No. S-7, 14½" h. ............................. **120.00**

**Ewer,** Poppy patt., cream & rose,
No. 610-13½", 13½" h. ..................... **850.00**

**Ewer,** Rosella patt., No. R-11-7",
7" h. ................................................. **55.00**

**Ewer,** Serenade patt., blue, No. S-13",
13¼" ............................................... **350.00**

**Ewer,** Sueno Tulip patt., blue, No. 109-8",
8" h.................................................. **245.00**

**Ewer,** Water Lily patt., walnut &
apricot, No. L-3-5½", 5½" h. ............... **85.00**

**Ewer,** Water Lily patt., No. 117-13½",
13½" h. ........................................... **375.00**

**Ewer,** Woodland Matte patt., W6-6½",
6½" h. ............................................... **84.00**

**Flowerpot w/attached saucer,** Sueno
Tulip patt., blue, No. 116-33-6", 6" h.... **120.00**

**Honey jug,** Blossom Flite patt.,
No. T1-6", 6" h. ................................. **37.00**

**Jar,** cov., figural wolf cover, yellow
base, Little Red Riding Hood patt..... **750.00**

**Jardiniere,** Bow-Knot patt., blue,
No. B-18-5¾", 5¾" h. ....... **155.00 to 175.00**

**Jardiniere,** Dogwood patt., turquoise
& peach, No. 514-4", 4" h. ............... **105.00**

**Jardiniere,** Iris patt., rose & blue,
No. 413-5½", 5½" h. ......................... **175.00**

**Jardiniere,** Open Rose patt., blue &
pink, No. 114-8¼", 8¼" h.................. **395.00**

**Jardiniere,** Orchid patt., pink & blue,
No. 310-4¾", 4¾" h. ......................... **155.00**

**Lamp base,** Rosella patt., ivory
(1946), 6¾" h. ................................. **175.00**

**Pitcher,** 4¾" h., Open Rose patt., blue
& pink, No. 128-4¾"........................... **95.00**

**Planter,** model of a poodle, Novelty
line, No. 114, 8" h. ............................. **25.00**

**Planter,** Woodland patt., glossy green
glaze, No. W19-10½", 10½" l............ **165.00**

**Rose bowl,** Iris patt., peach,
No. 412-4", 4" h. ............................... **95.00**

**Rose bowl,** Iris patt., pink & blue,
No. 412-7", 7" h. ............................. **195.00**

**Rose bowl,** Iris patt., rose & peach,
No. 412-7", 7" h. ............................... **95.00**

**Salt shaker,** Cinderella Kitchenware,
Bouquet patt., No. 25-3½", 3½" h. ........ **8.00**

**Salt & pepper shakers,** Little Red
Riding Hood patt., medium, 4½" h.,
pr. .................................... **915.00 to 950.00**

**Skillet serving tray,** handled, House
n' Garden patt., Mirror Brown, center
design of steer head, 2 × 7¾ × 11¼" .. **75.00**

**Spice jar,** cov., "Allspice," Little Red
Riding Hood patt............................. **850.00**

**Spice jar,** cov., "Cloves," Little Red
Riding Hood patt............................. **850.00**

**Spice jar,** cov., "Ginger," Little Red
Riding Hood patt............................. **850.00**

**Spice jar,** cov., "Nutmeg," Little Red
Riding Hood patt............................. **800.00**

**Spice jar,** cov., "Pepper," Little Red
Riding Hood patt............................. **850.00**

**String holder,** Little Red Riding Hood
patt., 9" h. .................................... **3,025.00**

**Teapot,** cov., Ebb Tide patt., No. E-14 .. **188.00**

**Teapot,** cov., Magnolia Gloss patt., pink or blue flowers w/gold trim, No. H-20-6½", each ........................... **60.00**

**Teapot,** cov., Magnolia Matte patt., No. 23-6½", 6½" h. ........................... **135.00**

**Tea set:** cov. teapot, creamer & cov. sugar bowl; Butterfly patt., 3 pcs. ..... **190.00**

**Tea set:** cov. teapot, creamer & cov. sugar bowl; Ebb Tide patt., Nos. E14, E15 & E16, 3 pcs. ............ **295.00**

**Tea set:** cov. teapot, creamer & cov. sugar bowl; Water Lily patt., gold trim, 3 pcs. ........................................ **165.00**

**Vase,** 4½" h., Wildflower patt., pink & blue, No. 56-4¾" ............................... **135.00**

**Vase,** 4¾" h., Bow-Knot patt., blue, No. B-2 5" ......................................... **175.00**

**Vase,** 4¾" h., Dogwood patt., pink & blue, No. 517-4¾" ............................... **80.00**

**Vase,** 4¾" h., Open Rose patt., pink & blue, No. 127-4¾" ............................... **53.00**

**Vase,** 4¾" h., Open Rose patt., No. 130-4¾" ........................................ **63.00**

**Vase,** 4¾" h., Open Rose patt., No. 131-4¾" ........................................ **63.00**

**Vase,** 5½" h., Water Lily patt., pink & green, No. L-1-5½" ............................. **38.00**

**Vase,** 5½" h., Water Lily patt., No. L-3-5½" ......................................... **40.00**

**Vase,** 5½" h., Woodland patt., dawn rose, No. W1-5½" ............................... **95.00**

**Vase,** 6" h., Orchid patt., No. 301-6" ... **155.00**

**Vase,** 6" h., Orchid patt., rose base, No. 304-6" ........................................ **165.00**

**Vase,** 6" h., Sueno Tulip patt., blue, No. 103-33-6" .................................. **250.00**

**Vase,** bud, 6" h., Sueno Tulip patt., blue & cream, No. 104-33-6" ............ **125.00**

**Vase,** 6" h., Sueno Tulip patt., pink & blue, No. 108-33-6" ........................... **125.00**

**Vase,** 6" h., Sueno Tulip patt., pink & blue, No. 110-33-6" ........................... **150.00**

**Vase,** 6¼" h., Open Rose patt., pink & blue, No. 120-6¼" ............................. **125.00**

**Vase,** 6¼" h., Open Rose patt., pink & blue, No. 122-6¼" ............................. **135.00**

**Vase,** 6¼" h., Open Rose patt., pink & blue glaze, No. 134-6¼" ..................... **90.00**

**Vase,** 6¼" h., Open Rose patt., pink & blue, No. 137-6¼" ............................. **125.00**

**Vase,** 6¼" h., Open Rose patt., No. 138-6¼" ........................................ **140.00**

**Vase,** 6¼" h., Magnolia Matte patt., No. 12-6¼" ......................................... **45.00**

**Vase,** 6½" h., Bow-Knot patt., No. B-4-6½" ..................................... **195.00**

**Vase,** 6½" h., model of a swan, Open Rose (Camelia) patt., white, No. 118-6½" ..................................... **135.00**

**Vase,** 6½" h., Open Rose patt., pink & blue, No. 123-6½" ............................. **110.00**

**Vase,** 6½" h., Open Rose patt., pink & blue, No. 133-6½" ............................. **125.00**

**Vase,** 6½" h., Pine Cone patt., pink, No. 55-6½" ..................................... **95.00**

**Vase,** 6½" h., Sueno Tulip patt., cream & blue, No. 100-33-6½" ........ **135.00**

**Vase,** 6½" h., Thistle patt., turquoise, No. 52-6½" ..................................... **120.00**

**Vase,** 6½" h., Water Lily patt., pink & turquoise, No. L-4-6½" ...................... **63.00**

**Vase,** 6½" h., Water Lily patt., walnut & apricot, No. L-5-6½" ...................... **50.00**

**Vase,** 6½" h., Wildflower patt., pink & green, No. W-5-6½" ......................... **125.00**

**Vase,** 6½" h., Woodland Matte patt., No. W-4-6½" ..................................... **65.00**

**Vase,** 7" h., Calla Lily patt., No. 530-33-7" .................................... **190.00**

**Vase,** 7" h., twin fish, Ebb Tide patt., green & pink, No. E-2-7" .................... **88.00**

**Vase,** 7" h., Iris patt., No. 402-7" ........................... **65.00 to 75.00**

**Vase,** 7" h., Iris patt., No. 403-7" ......... **135.00**

**Vase,** bud, 7" h., Open Rose patt., No. 129-7" ..................................... **155.00**

**Vase,** bud, 7½" h., Iris patt., pink & blue, No. 410-7½" ............................. **160.00**

**Vase,** 7½" h., Wildflower patt., pink & blue, No. W-6-7½" ............................. **95.00**

**Vase,** 7½" h., Wildflower patt., No. W-8-7½" ......................................... **80.00**

**Vase,** 7½" h., Woodland patt., rose, No. W17-7½" ..................................... **245.00**

**Vase,** 8" h., Calla Lily patt., No. 500-33-8" .................................... **165.00**

**Vase,** 8" h., Iris patt., No. 403-8" ......... **160.00**

**Vase,** 8" h., Sueno Tulip patt., pink & blue, No. 105-33-8" ........................... **235.00**

**Vase,** double bud, 8" h., Woodland Gloss patt., No. W15-8" .................... **170.00**

**Vase,** 8½" h., Bow-Knot patt., No. B-7-8½" ..................................... **195.00**

**Vase,** 8½" h., Bow-Knot patt., pink & blue, No. B-8-8½" ............. **170.00 to 190.00**

**Vase,** 8½" h., Bow-Knot patt., pink, No. B-9-8½" ..................................... **265.00**

**Vase,** 8½" h., Dogwood patt., pink & blue, No. 503-8½" ............................. **150.00**

**Vase,** 8½" h., Iris patt., cream & rose,
No. 402-8½"...................................... **125.00**

**Vase,** 8½" h., Iris patt., peach,
No. 403-8½"...................................... **160.00**

**Vase,** 8½" h., two-handled, Magnolia
Matte patt., pink & blue, No. 3-8½"..... **96.00**

**Vase,** 8½" h., handled, Open Rose
patt., No. 102-8½"............................... **133.00**

**Vase,** 8½" h., Open Rose patt., pink &
blue, No. 103-8½"............................. **165.00**

**Vase,** 8½" h., fan shape, Open Rose
patt., pink & blue, No. 108-8½"........ **195.00**

**Vase,** 8½" h., Open Rose patt., pink &
blue, No. 119-8½"............................. **168.00**

**Vase,** 8½" h., model of a hand holding
a fan-shaped vase, Open Rose
(Camelia) patt., No. 126-8½"........... **228.00**

**Vase,** 8½" h., Open Rose patt.,
No. 143-8½"...................................... **125.00**

**Vase,** 8½" h., Orchid patt., blue,
No. 302-8½"...................................... **205.00**

**Vase,** 8½" h., Water Lily patt.,
No. L-A-8½"...................................... **130.00**

**Vase,** 8½" h., Water Lily patt.,
No. L-8-8½"...................................... **128.00**

**Vase,** 8½" h., Woodland patt., glossy
finish, No. W-16-8½".......................... **65.00**

**Vase,** 9" h., Sueno Tulip patt., pink &
blue, No. 101-33-9"........................... **210.00**

**Vase,** 9½" h., Water Lily patt.,
No. L-10-9½"..................................... **163.00**

**Vase,** 9½" h., Wildflower patt., pink &
blue, No. W-13-9½".......................... **155.00**

**Vase,** 10" h., model of a unicorn,
Novelty Line, No. 98 .......................... **75.00**

**Vase,** 10" h., Orchid patt., blue,
No. 303-10"..................................... **335.00**

**Vase,** 10½" h., Bow-Knot patt., pink &
blue, No. 10-10½"............................ **375.00**

**Vase,** 10½" h., Bow-Knot patt., blue,
No. B-11-10½".................................. **225.00**

**Vase,** 10½" h., Dogwood patt., pink &
blue, No. 510-10½"........................... **265.00**

**Vase,** 10½" h., Iris patt., peach &
rose, No. 404-10½".......................... **225.00**

**Vase,** 10½" h., Water Lily patt., pink &
turquoise, No. L-12-10½"................. **195.00**

**Vase,** 10½" h., Wildflower patt., pink &
blue, No. W-15-10½" ....................... **195.00**

**Vase,** 12" h., Open Rose patt., pink &
blue, No. 124-12".............................. **350.00**

**Vase,** 12" h., Tokay patt., No. 12 ......... **61.00**

**Vase,** 12¼" h., Magnolia Matte patt.,
pink & blue, No. 17-12¼"................. **150.00**

**Vase,** 12½" h., Wildflower patt., pink &
blue, No. W-18-12½" ....................... **250.00**

**Vase,** 13" h., Sueno Tulip patt., pink &
blue, No. 109-33-13" (tight hairline
top) .................................................. **250.00**

**Wall pocket,** model of a sad iron,
Bow-Know patt., No. B-23-6¼",
6¼" h.............................. **225.00 to 250.00**

**Wall pocket,** Bow-Knot patt., model of
a whisk broom, blue, No. B-27-8",
8" h. ................................................. **162.00**

**Wall pocket,** Sunglow patt., model of
a pitcher, pink w/gold, No. 81, 5½" h. .. **65.00**

**Wall pocket,** shell-shaped w/twig
handle, Woodland patt., No. W-13-7½",
7½" h..................................................... **90.00**

**Window box,** Dogwood patt., pink &
blue, No. 508-10½" l. ....................... **225.00**

**Window box,** Woodland Gloss patt.,
pink & green, No. W-14-10", 10" l..... **150.00**

## HUMMEL FIGURINES & COLLECTIBLES

*The Goebel Company of Oeslau, Germany, first produced these porcelain figurines in 1934 having obtained the rights to adapt the beautiful pastel sketches of children by Sister Maria Innocentia (Berta) Hummel. Every design by the Goebel artisans was approved by the nun until her death in 1946. Though not antique, these figurines with the "M.I. Hummel" signature, especially those bearing the Goebel Company factory mark used from 1934 and into the early 1940s, are being sought by collectors though interest may have peaked some years ago.*

*Hummel Marks*

**Accordion Boy,** 1956-68, 5" h. ........ **$137.00**
**Adoration,** 1972-79, 6¼" h. ............... **171.00**
**Angel Lights candleholder,** 1972-79... **218.00**
**Angel with Birds font,** 1934-49,
3½" h. .............................................. **213.00**

**Apple Tree Boy,** 1956-68,
    4" h. ............................... **100.00 to 110.00**
**Apple Tree Boy,** 1972-79, 4" h............ **92.00**
**Apple Tree Boy,** 1940-57, 6" h.......... **250.00**
**Apple Tree Boy,** 1972-79, 6" h.......... **123.00**
**Apple Tree Girl,** 1934-49, 4" h. ......... **197.00**
**Apple Tree Girl,** 1940-57, 4" h. ......... **145.00**
**Apple Tree Girl,** 1940-57,
    6" h. ............................... **250.00 to 260.00**
**Apple Tree Girl,** 1956-68, 6" h. ......... **185.00**
**Apple Tree Boy & Girl book ends,**
    1956-68, 5¼" h., pr.......... **200.00 to 225.00**
**Artist (The),** 1963-71, 5½" h.............. **375.00**
**Artist (The),** 1972-79, 5½" h.............. **122.00**
**Auf Wiedersehen,** 1956-68, 5" h....... **172.00**
**Ba-Bee Ring plaque,** boy, 1934-49,
    5" d. ............................... **160.00 to 170.00**
**Baker,** 1956-68, 4¾" h...................... **154.00**
**Band Leader,** 1934-49, 5" h. ............. **355.00**
**Barnyard Hero,** 1940-57, 4" h. ........... **165.00**
**Barnyard Hero,** 1956-68, 4" h. ........... **110.00**
**Barnyard Hero,** 1956-68, 5½" h. ........ **240.00**
**Barnyard Hero,** 1963-71, 5½" h. ........ **160.00**
**Begging His Share,** 1940-57,
    5½" h. ............................... **250.00 to 300.00**
**Begging His Share,** w/candle hole,
    1956-68, 5½" h. ............................... **185.00**
**Begging His Share,** without candle
    hole, 1956-68, 5½" h. ....... **180.00 to 190.00**
**Be Patient,** 1940-57, 4¼" h. .............. **173.00**
**Be Patient,** 1956-68, 5¼" h. .............. **148.00**
**Be Patient,** 1963-71, 4¼" h. .............. **115.00**
**Be Patient,** 1940-57,
    6¼" h. ............................... **395.00 to 400.00**
**Be Patient,** 1956-68, 6¼" h. .............. **224.00**
**Be Patient,** 1963-71, 6¼" h. .............. **195.00**
**Bird Duet,** 1956-68, 4" h..................... **117.00**
**Birthday Serenade,** 1956-68, reverse
    mold, 4¼" h....................................... **385.00**
**Blessed Event,** 1963-71, 5½" h. ........ **232.00**
**Book Worm,** 1956-68, 4" h................. **160.00**
**Book Worm,** 1956-68, 5½" h.............. **185.00**
**Book Worm,** 1972-79, 8" h................. **650.00**
**Boots,** 1934-49, 5½" h........................ **395.00**
**Boots,** 1956-68, 5½" h........................ **123.00**
**Boots,** 1972-79, 6½" h........................ **153.00**
**Boy with Toothache,** 1963-71, 5½" h.
    (ILLUS. top next column) ..................... **115.00**
**Brother,** 1956-68, 5½" h..................... **135.00**
**Busy Student,** 1972-79, 4¼" h........... **111.00**
**Chef,** Hello, 1956-68, 6¼" h............... **148.00**
**Chick Girl,** 1934-49, 3½" h................. **349.00**
**Chimney Sweep,** 1956-68, 4" h. .......... **95.00**

*Boy with Toothache*

**Chimney Sweep,** 1956-68, 5½" h. ..... **143.00**
**Christ Child,** from Nativity set, 1940-
    57, 1½ × 3¾"........................ **80.00 to 90.00**
**Christ Child,** 1956-68, 2 × 6" .............. **76.00**
**Confidentially,** 1972-79,
    5½" h. ............................... **500.00 to 600.00**

*Congratulations*

**Congratulations (no socks),**
    1940-57, 6" h. (ILLUS.) .... **200.00 to 225.00**
**Congratulations (no socks),**
    1956-68, 6" h. ................................. **158.00**
**Culprits,** 1956-68, 6¼" h. .................. **198.00**
**Doctor,** 1940-57, 4¾" h. ..................... **167.00**

**Doctor,** 1956-68, 4¾" h. ..... **100.00 to 125.00**

**Doll Bath,** 1972-79, 5" h. .................... **145.00**

**Eventide,** 1940-57, 4¼ × 4¾" .................................. **325.00 to 350.00**

**Farewell,** 1956-68, 4¾" h. .. **200.00 to 250.00**

**Farewell,** 1972-79, 4¾" h. ............. **150.00**

**Favorite Pet,** 1956-68, 4¼" h. ......... **1,200.00**

**Feeding Time,** 1956-68, 4¼" h. .......... **129.00**

**Feeding Time,** 1956-68, 5½" h. .......... **225.00**

**Festival Harmony,** w/flute, 1972-79, 8" h. .................................................. **190.00**

**Flower Madonna,** white, 1956-68, 9½" h. .............................................. **135.00**

*Forest Shrine*

**Forest Shrine,** 1972-79, 9" h. (ILLUS.).. **315.00**

**For Father,** 1956-68, 5½" h. ............... **155.00**

**For Mother,** 1963-71, 5" h. ................. **118.00**

**Friends,** 1963-71, 5" h. ....................... **108.00**

**Globe Trotter,** 1940-57, 5" h. ............. **205.00**

**Going to Grandma's,** 1940-57, 4¾" h. ............................................... **300.00**

**Going to Grandma's,** 1934-49, 4¾" h. ............................................... **348.00**

**Going to Grandma's,** 1940-57, square base, 4¾" h. ......... **275.00 to 300.00**

**Going to Grandma's,** 1956-68, 4¾" h. ............................................... **220.00**

**Going to Grandma's,** 1972-79, 4¾" h. .............................. **160.00 to 170.00**

**Going to Grandma's,** 1934-49, 6" h. .. **775.00**

**Good Friends table lamp,** 1956-68, 7½" h. ................................ **270.00 to 275.00**

**Good Hunting,** 1963-71, 5¼" h. ............................... **155.00 to 175.00**

**Good Shepherd,** 1940-57, 6¼" h. ...... **270.00**

**Good Shepherd,** 1972-79, 6¼" h. ............................... **155.00 to 160.00**

**Goose Girl,** 1956-68, 4¾" h. ............... **153.00**

**Happy Birthday,** 1956-68, 5½" h. ...... **150.00**

**Happy Birthday,** 1972-79, 5½" h. ............................... **140.00 to 160.00**

**Happy Days,** 1934-49, 6" h. ............... **895.00**

**Hear Ye, Hear Ye,** 1934-49, 5" h. ....... **300.00**

**Hear Ye, Hear Ye,** 1972-79, 5" h. ............................... **100.00 to 125.00**

**Hear Ye, Hear Ye,** 1956-68, 7½" h. ............................... **295.00 to 325.00**

**Heavenly Angel,** 1972-79, 6¾" h. ...... **190.00**

**Herald Angels candleholder,** 1940-57, 2¼ × 4" ........................................... **205.00**

*Home From Market*

**Home From Market,** 1963-71, 5¾" h. (ILLUS.)............................................... **150.00**

**Joyful,** 1940-57, 4" h. ......... **130.00 to 135.00**

**Joyful,** 1972-79, 4" h. ........................... **68.00**

**Joyful ashtray,** 1956-68, 3½ × 6" ...... **104.00**

**Joyous News,** angel w/horn candleholder, 1956-68, 2¾" h. ................................ **120.00 to 150.00**

**Just Resting,** 1934-49, 5" h. ............................... **475.00 to 525.00**

**Just Resting,** 1940-57, 5" h. ............................... **225.00 to 250.00**

**Just Resting,** 1956-68, 5" h. ............................... **190.00 to 200.00**

**Just Resting,** 1963-71, 5" h. .............. **158.00**

**Kiss Me,** w/socks, 1956-68,
6" h. ................................. **600.00 to 700.00**

**Kiss Me,** 1963-71, 6" h. ..................... **230.00**

**Knitting Lesson,** 1972-79, 7½" h. ....... **274.00**

**Let's Sing,** 1956-68, 3¼" h. .................. **88.00**

**Let's Sing,** 1963-71, 3¼" h. .................. **76.00**

**Let's Sing ashtray,** 1956-68,
3½ × 6¾" ............................... **125.00**

**Little Band candleholder,** 1972-79,
3 × 4¾" ..................................... **140.00**

**Little Bookkeeper,** 1956-68, 4¾" h.... **849.00**

**Little Cellist,** 1972-79, 6" h. ............... **109.00**

**Little Fiddler,** 1972-79, 4¾" h. ........... **105.00**

**Little Fiddler,** 1972-79, 6" h. ............. **110.00**

**Little Fiddler,** 1956-68, 7½" h. ........... **385.00**

**Little Fiddler,** 1956-68, 11" h. ........... **800.00**

**Little Gabriel,** 1940-57, 5" h... **150.00 to 160.00**

**Little Gabriel,** 1956-68, 5" h. .............. **105.00**

**Little Gardener,** 1934-49,
4" h. ................................. **160.00 to 175.00**

**Little Goat Herder,** 1940-57, 4¾" h.... **215.00**

**Little Pharmacist,** 1972-79, 6" h. ....... **200.00**

**Little Scholar,** 1940-57,
5½" h. ............................. **165.00 to 175.00**

**Little Shopper,** 1956-68, 4¾" h............ **97.00**

**Little Shopper,** 1972-79, 4¾" h. ......... **115.00**

**Little Sweeper,** 1974-79,
4½" h. ................................. **75.00 to 80.00**

**Little Tooter,** 1956-68, 3¾" h. .............. **75.00**

**Little Tooter,** 1972-79, 3¾" h. .............. **75.00**

**Lost Sheep,** 1963-71, 4½" h................. **90.00**

**Lost Sheep,** 1956-68, 5½" h... **150.00 to 160.00**

**Madonna & Child,** from Nativity set,
1963-71, Madonna, 6¾" h., child,
3" h. ................................. **111.00**

**Madonna plaque,** 1934-49,
3 × 4" ............................... **160.00 to 165.00**

**March Winds,** 1940-57, 5" h............... **188.00**

**March Winds,** 1956-68, 5" h............... **125.00**

**Max & Moritz,** 1956-68, 5" h. ............. **150.00**

**Meditation,** 1972-79, 4¼" h. ................ **105.00**

**Meditation,** 1956-68, 5¼" h.. **145.00 to 165.00**

**Meditation,** 1934-49, 7" h. ............... **2,500.00**

**Merry Wanderer,** 1934-49, 4¾" h....... **340.00**

**Mischief Maker,** 1972-79, 5" h. .......... **113.00**

**Mother's Darling,** 1956-68, 5½" h...... **188.00**

**Mother's Helper,** 1940-57,
5" h. ................................. **210.00 to 225.00**

**Mountaineer,** 1963-71, 5" h............... **150.00**

**Mountaineer,** 1972-79, 5" h............... **113.00**

**On Secret Path,** last bee mark,
1972-79, 5½" h. ............................ **130.00**

**Out of Danger,** 1940-57,
6¾ h. ............................... **270.00 to 300.00**

**Out of Danger,** 1972-79, 6¼" h. ......... **263.00**

**Out of Danger table lamp,** 1940-57,
9½" h. ..................................... **395.00**

**Photographer,** 1963-71, 5½" h. ........... **174.00**

**Playmates,** 1934-49, 4" h. .................. **395.00**

**Postman,** 1972-79, 5" h..................... **106.00**

**Prayer Before Battle,** 1934-49,
4¼" h. ............................... **400.00 to 500.00**

*Puppy Love*

**Puppy Love,** 1934-39, 5" h.
(ILLUS.) ............................. **440.00 to 475.00**

**Puppy Love,** 1940-57, 5" h... **225.00 to 250.00**

**Quartet plaque,** 1940-57, 6 × 6" sq. ..... **295.00**

**Retreat to Safety,** 1956-68,
4" h. ................................. **100.00 to 125.00**

**Ride into Christmas,** 1972-79,
5¾" h. ............................... **245.00 to 250.00**

**Ring Around the Rosie,** 1972-79,
6¾" h. ........................... **1,600.00 to 1,700.00**

**School Boy,** 1934-49, 4" h. .. **235.00 to 250.00**

**School Boy,** 1956-68, 4" h. .................. **105.00**

**School Boy,** 1972-79, 4" h. .................. **105.00**

**School Boy,** 1934-49, 5½" h.. **300.00 to 350.00**

**School Boy,** 1972-79, 5½" h. ............... **102.00**

**School Boy,** 1956-68, 7½" h. ............. **435.00**

*School Boys*

**School Boys,** 1956-68, 10¼" h.
(ILLUS.) ........................................ **1,150.00**
**School Girl,** 1972-79,
5¼" h. .............................. **100.00 to 125.00**
**School Girls,** 1972-79, 7½" h............ **775.00**
**School Girls,** 1972-79, 9½" h.......... **1,025.00**
**Sensitive Hunter,** 1940-57, 4¾" h...... **186.00**
**Sensitive Hunter,** 1956-68, 4¾" h...... **118.00**
**Sensitive Hunter,** 1972-79, 4¾" h...... **110.00**
**Sensitive Hunter,** 1956-68, 5½" h...... **195.00**
**Sensitive Hunter,** 1972-79,
5½" h. .............................. **100.00 to 125.00**
**Serenade,** 1972-79, 4¾" h.................... **70.00**
**Serenade,** 1956-68, 7½" h................. **315.00**
**Serenade,** 1972-79, 7½" h................. **220.00**
**She Loves Me,** 1956-68,
4¼" h. .............................. **150.00 to 160.00**
**She Loves Me,** 1963-71,
4¼" h. .............................. **280.00 to 285.00**
**Shepherd's Boy,** 1940-57,
5½" h. .............................. **250.00 to 275.00**
**Shepherd's Boy,** 1956-68, 5½" h....... **140.00**
**Signs of Spring,** w/two shoes,
1940-57, 4" h. ................... **550.00 to 650.00**
**Signs of Spring,** 1956-68, 4" h. ......... **128.00**
**Signs of Spring,** 1963-71, 4" h. ......... **127.00**
**Signs of Spring,** 1972-79, 4" h. ......... **107.00**
**Signs of Spring,** w/two shoes,
1940-57, 5½ h. ................................. **330.00**
**Silent Night candelholder,** 1934-49,
5½" l., 4¾" h. .................... **600.00 to 625.00**
**Singing Lesson,** 1934-49,
2¾" h. .............................. **250.00 to 300.00**
**Singing Lesson,** 1956-68, 2¾" h. ........ **92.00**
**Singing Lesson,** 1972-79, 2¾" h. ...... **110.00**

*Sister*

**Sister,** 1934-49, 5½" h.
(ILLUS.) ........................... **350.00 to 450.00**
**Skier,** 1934-49, wooden poles, 5" h. .... **376.00**
**Smart Little Sister,** 1963-71, 4¾" h. ... **158.00**
**Smiling Through plaque,** 1972-79,
5¾" h. .............................. **135.00 to 140.00**
**Soloist,** 1934-49, 4¾" h. ..................... **288.00**
**Soloist,** 1940-57, 4¾" h...... **140.00 to 150.00**
**Soloist,** 1956-68, 4¾" h. ..................... **101.00**
**Spring Cheer,** 1934-49, 5" h. ............. **323.00**
**Spring Cheer,** 1940-57,
5" h. ................................. **200.00 to 225.00**
**Spring Cheer,** 1956-68, 5" h. ............. **209.00**
**Spring Dance,** 1963-71, 6½" h.......... **500.00**
**Standing Boy plaque,** 1940-57,
4⅛ × 5½".......................... **495.00 to 525.00**
**Star Gazer,** 1934-49,
4¾" h. .............................. **390.00 to 425.00**
**Star Gazer,** 1940-57, 4¾" h.
(ILLUS. top next page)......... **200.00 to 250.00**
**Stitch in Time,** 1963-71, 6¾" h. .......... **210.00**
**Stitch in Time,** 1972-79, 6¾" h. .......... **140.00**
**Stormy Weather,** 1934-49, 6¼" h. ..... **675.00**
**Stormy Weather,** 1940-57,
6¼" h. .............................. **440.00 to 550.00**
**Stormy Weather,** 1956-68, 6¼" h. ..... **300.00**
**Stormy Weather,** 1972-79,
6¼" h. .............................. **200.00 to 250.00**
**Street Singer,** 1940-57, 5" h.. **150.00 to 160.00**
**Street Singer,**1956-68, 5" h.. **100.00 to 125.00**
**Strolling Along,** 1940-57,
4¾" h. .............................. **235.00 to 250.00**
**Strolling Along,** 1972-79, 5¾" h. ....... **120.00**

*Star Gazer*

*Telling Her Secret*

**Surprise,** 1940-57, 4¼" h. ................. **153.00**
**Surprise,** 1956-68, 4¼" h... **100.00 to 125.00**
**Surprise,** 1934-49, 5½" h. .................. **350.00**
**Surprise,** 1956-68, 5½" h. ................. **160.00**
**Surprise,** 1963-71, 5½" h. ................. **150.00**
**Surprise,** 1972-79, 5½" h... **125.00 to 150.00**
**Sweet Music,** 1956-68,
    5¼" h. .............................. **100.00 to 120.00**
**Sweet Music,** 1974-79,
    5¼" h. .............................................. **100.00**
**Telling Her Secret,** 1956-68,
    5" h. ................................... **225.00 to 275.00**
**Telling Her Secret,** 1972-79, 5" h. ..... **165.00**
**Telling Her Secret,** 1940-57, 6½" h.
    (ILLUS. top next column) .................... **435.00**
**To Market,** 1940-57, 4" h. ...................... **130.00**
**To Market,** 1956-68, 4" h. ........................ **99.00**
**To Market,** 1934-49, 5½" h. .................. **400.00**
**To Market,** 1956-68, 5½" h. .. **200.00 to 225.00**
**To Market,** 1972-79, 6¼" h. ................. **255.00**
**Trumpet Boy,** 1940-57,
    4¾" h. .............................. **100.00 to 110.00**
**Trumpet Boy,** 1972-79, 4¾" h. ............. **86.00**
**Umbrella Boy,** 1963-71,
    4¾" h. .............................. **450.00 to 500.00**
**Umbrella Boy,** 1940-57,
    8" h. .............................. **975.00 to 1,000.00**
**Umbrella Girl,** 1956-68,
    4¾" h. .............................. **575.00 to 600.00**
**Umbrella Girl,** 1972-79, 4¾" h. .......... **348.00**
**Umbrella Girl,** 1940-57, 8" h. .......... **1,685.00**
**Umbrella Girl,** 1956-68,
    8" h. ................................. **850.00 to 900.00**

**Umbrella Girl,** 1963-71,
    8" h. .................................. **700.00 to 750.00**
**Village Boy,** 1956-68, 4" h. .. **75.00 to 100.00**
**Village Boy,** 1963-71, 5" h..................... **81.00**
**Village Boy,** 1940-57, 6" h.................. **200.00**
**Village Boy,** 1956-68, 6" h... **150.00 to 160.00**
**Village Boy,** 1972-79, 7¼" h............... **160.00**
**Visiting an Invalid,** 1972-79, 5" h. ..... **116.00**
**Volunteers,** 1956-68, 5" h. ............... **151.00**
**Volunteers,** 1934-49, 5½" h. .............. **775.00**
**Waiter,** 1956-68, 6" h. ......................... **140.00**
**Watchful Angel,** 1940-57, 6½" h........ **448.00**
**Wayside Devotion,** 1934-49,
    7½" h. .............................. **575.00 to 650.00**
**Wayside Devotion,** 1956-68, 7½" h... **244.00**
**Wayside Devotion,** 1956-68,
    8¾" h. .............................. **300.00 to 350.00**
**Wayside Harmony,** 1956-68, 3¾" h..... **96.00**
**Wayside Harmony,** 1972-79, 3¾" h..... **83.00**
**Wayside Harmony,** 1940-57, 5" h...... **215.00**
**Weary Wanderer,** 1940-57,
    6" h. .............................. **250.00 to 300.00**
**Weary Wanderer,** 1956-68, 6" h........ **165.00**
**Weary Wanderer,** 1963-71, 6" h........ **120.00**
**Weary Wanderer,** 1972-79, 6" h........ **120.00**
**We Congratulate,** 1940-57, 4" h. ....... **230.00**
**We Congratulate,** 1963-71, 4" h. ......... **92.00**
**Which Hand?,** 1972-79, 5½" h. ............. **92.00**
**Worship,** 1956-68, 5" h. ..... **120.00 to 150.00**

# IRONSTONE

*The first successful ironstone was patented in 1813 by C. J. Mason in England. The body contains iron slag incorporated with the clay. Other potters imitated Mason's ware and today much hard, thick ware is lumped under the term ironstone. Earlier it was called by various names, including graniteware. Both plain white and decorated wares were made throughout the 19th century. Tea Leaf Lustre ironstone was made by several firms.*

## GENERAL

**Butter dish,** cover & insert, Prize Bloom shape, all-white, T. J. & J. Mayer.............................................. **$145.00**

**Butter dish,** cover & insert, Wheat & Hops shape, all-white, J. & G. Meakin ............................................. **100.00**

**Chamberpot,** cov., Corn & Oats shape, all-white, Wedgewood............. **70.00**

**Cheese dish,** cover & underplate, Azalea patt., "gaudy," orange lustre florals, cobalt leaves, gold trim, underplate is white ground w/cobalt trim, Woods & Son, England, 2 pcs.. **275.00**

**Compote,** open, Boote's 1851, all-white, large, T & R. Boote................. **375.00**

**Compote,** New York shape, all-white, unmarked......................................... **200.00**

**Compote,** Prize Bloom shape, all-white, T. J. & J. Mayer ...................... **275.00**

**Compote,** Senate shape, all-white, T. & R. Boote .................................. **100.00**

**Creamer,** Fluted Round shape, all-white, Holland & Green (mended chips) ..................................................... **65.00**

**Creamer,** Portland shape, all-white, Elsmore & Forster............................. **80.00**

**Creamer,** Sharon Arch shape, all-white, Davenport (spout roughness) ............. **110.00**

**Creamer,** Washington shape, all-white, J. Meir ................................................. **65.00**

**Creamer,** Wheat & Clover shape, all-white, Tomkinson Bros. Co................. **95.00**

**Cups & saucers,** handleless, Laurel Wreath shape, all-white, Elsmore & Forster, set of 6 .............................. **190.00**

**Dinner service:** nine 10¼" d. plates (one restored, two w/hairlines), eight 8¾" d. plates (one w/hairlines, one restored), nine 7½" d. plates, five 10" d. soup plates, 12½" l. oval platter (restored), 15¼" l. oval platter & dome cover (finial chips), an additional dome cover (rim chip), a 10½" l. rectangular serving bowl (hairlines), two 7" h. hexagonal cov. sauce tureens & underplates & a 5¼" h. oval sauce tureen & cover (repairs); each w/a colorful central Oriental garden landscape, paneled dark blue border band w/floral reserves & gilt trim, ca. 1840, the set ................................... **1,610.00**

**Dinner service:** twelve 10" d. plates, six 10¾" d. plates, two platters, 14½" l & 16½" l., cov. vegetable dish, two cups & saucers, two oval serving dishes & seven small bowls; black transfer-printed ivy design w/copper lustre, the set (some stains & crazing......................................... **495.00**

**Dinner service:** twelve 9½" d. plates (one w/foot chip), twelve 10¼" d. coup plates (one w/rim chip), 12¾" l. cov. oval vegetable dish, 8¼" l. oval undertray, a 10¾", 13¼" & 21" l. oval platter (one w/restored hairline); transfer-printed Imari-style floral decoration in puce w/orange & black enamels & gilt trim, Ashworth & Bros., England, ca. 1870, printed & impressed marks, the set ................. **431.00**

**Dinner service:** a soup tureen w/a domed octagonal cover w/scrolled finial, the body w/ox-head handles & raised on a floral octagonal base, eleven dinner plates, thirteen salad plates, four bread & butter plates, seven soup plates, two small rectangular plates, two shaped plates, one square vegetable dish, one cov. square serving dish, one open square serving dish, one round platter, two large rectangular serving platters, two medium rectangular platters, one deep rectangular vegetable dish, one shallow rectangular vegetable dish & one small rectangular plate; all decorated in the Chinese Export Famille Rose style w/flower-filled urns, fruit & birds in green, rose, iron-red, yellow & gilt on a white ground, impressed mark "Mason's Patent Ironstone China," ca. 1870, tureen 14" l., 10" h., the set (ILLUS. of part, top next page) ................. **8,625.00**

**Egg cup,** Full Ribbed shape, all-white, Pankhurst ......................................... **105.00**

*Mason's Dinner Service*

**Gravy boat,** Laurel Wreath shape, all-white, Elsmore & Forster (some bull's eyes inside) ................................ **50.00**

**Gravy boat,** Royal (Lion's Head) shape, all-white, John Edwards .......... **30.00**

**Mug,** Bow & Tassel shape, all-white, Burgess & Goddard ............................ **45.00**

**Pancake server,** cov., Cable & Chain shape, all-white, John Maddock ......... **80.00**

**Pitcher,** 9¾" h., Ceres shape, all-white, Elsmore & Forster .................. **250.00**

**Pitcher,** 10¼" h., Ceres shape, all-white, Elsmore & Forster .................. **250.00**

**Plate,** 9½" d., transfer-printed Imari-style decoration w/cobalt blue & orange flowers & leaves, impressed "Mason's Patent Ironstone China," mid-19th c. ......................................... **40.00**

**Plates,** dinner, Athenia shape, all-white, Close & Co., pr. ........................ **50.00**

**Plates,** 9¾" d., Lily shape, all-white, H. Burgess, pr. .................................... **20.00**

**Plates,** 9¾" d., Virginia shape, all-white, Brougham & Mayer, set of 4 .. **110.00**

**Platter,** 14" l., octagonal, Double Sydenham shape, all-white, A. Shaw .. **40.00**

**Platter,** 16" l., Ceres shape, all-white, Elsmore & Forster............................. **50.00**

**Platter,** 16" l., Wheat shape, all-white, Turner Goddard & Co. ...................... **30.00**

**Platter,** 19" l., Nosegay shape, all-white, Cockson & Chetwynd.............. **95.00**

**Platter,** Morning Glory shape, all-white, Elsmore & Forster ................... **60.00**

**Pudding mold,** scalloped panel design on interior, all-white, 6" d., 3½" h. ............................................... **24.00**

**Punch bowl,** Quartered Rose shape, all-white, J. Furnival......................... **210.00**

**Punch cups,** Boote's 1851 shape, all-white, unmarked, set of 8 ................ **275.00**

**Relish dish,** Prairie Flowers shape, all-white, Powell & Bishop ................. **45.00**

**Relish dish,** Sydenham shape, all-white, T & R. Boots............................ **95.00**

**Sauce tureen,** cov., Bellflower shape, all-white, J. Edwards & Son............... **25.00**

**Sauce tureen,** cov., Sydenham shape, all-white, T. & R. Boote ......... **190.00**

**Sauce tureen,** cover, underplate & matching ladle, Sydenham shape, all-white, T. & R. Boote, 4 pcs. ......... **295.00**

**Sauce tureen underplate,** Fluted Pearl shape, all-white, J. Wedgwood (slight crazing at rim) ......................... **20.00**

**Shaving mug,** Baltic shape, all-white, J. Meir & Son ...................................... **75.00**

**Spooner,** Nautilus shell-shaped, all-white, impressed "21" ...................... **275.00**

**Stew tureen,** cov., w/matching ladle, Hyacinth shape, all-white, Wedgewood..................................... **200.00**

**Teapot,** cov., Hyacinth shape, all-white, H. Burgess ............................. **105.00**

**Teapot,** cov., Maltese shape, all-white, E. Corn .................................. **100.00**

**Teapot,** cov., Memnon shape, all-white, J. Meir & Son......................... **100.00**

**Teapot,** cov., Boote's 1851 shape, all-white, Red Cliffs, ca. 1960s ............... 60.00

**Teapot,** cov., Gothic shape, all-white, Holland & Green ............................. 200.00

**Teapot,** cov., Vintage shape, all-white, E. Challinor (excellent w/crazing) ....... 80.00

**Teapot,** cov., Wheat & Hops shape, all-white, J. & G. Meakin.................... 80.00

**Tea service:** cov. teapot, cov. sugar bowl, creamer, footed bowl, oval serving dish, twelve cups & saucers & fifteen 8" d. plates; Bryonia patt., black transfer-printed ivy design w/gilt trim, marked "U&C," 19th c., the set (some wear, stains & damages)......................................... 303.00

**Tea set:** cov. teapot, creamer & cov. sugar bowl; Block Optic shape, all-white, J.& G. Meakin, 3 pcs. ............. 110.00

**Tea set,** miniature: cov. teapot, creamer & cov. sugar bowl; Primary shape, all-white, unmarked, 3 pcs. (creamer w/spout nick, teapot w/underside lid chip) ....................... 200.00

**Toddy bowl,** cover & ladle, sixteen-sided, all-white, J. Furnival ............... 250.00

**Toothbrush holder,** vertical, Block Optic shape, all-white, J. & G. Meakin ................................................. 70.00

**Toothbrush holder,** cov., Wheat & Hops, all-white, J. & G. Meakin .......... 90.00

**Vegetable dish,** cov., oval, Ceres shape, all-white, Elsmore & Forster, medium size ..................................... 80.00

**Vegetable dish,** cov., Corn & Oats, all-white., Davenport........................... 80.00

**Vegetable dish,** cov., Oriental shape, all-white, W & E Corn (manufacturing flaw & stain) ........................................ 35.00

**Vegetable dish,** cov., Paris shape, all-white, J. Alcock (slight crazing)...... 60.00

**Vegetable dish,** cov., Prairie shape, all-white, Clementson ......................... 25.00

**Vegetable dish,** cov., Scalloped Decagon shape, all-white, Davenport ... 65.00

**Vegetable dish,** cov., St. Louis shape, all-white, J. Edwards ............... 65.00

**Vegetable dish,** cov., Wheat & Berry shape, all-white, Powell & Bishop....... 50.00

## TEA LEAF IRONSTONE

**Baker,** rectangular, Empress patt., Micratex by Adams, ca. 1960s, 7 × 9½" ............................................. 20.00

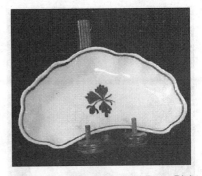

*Tea Leaf Crescent-shaped Bone Dish*

**Bone dish,** Scalloped Rim patt., Arthur Wilkinson, rim roughness (ILLUS.) ..... 23.00

**Bowl,** oatmeal, Alfred Meakin (rim roughness & crazing)........................... 55.00

**Bread tray,** oval, Cable patt., Anthony Shaw, 12" l....................................... 130.00

*Tea Leaf Bamboo Butter Dish*

**Butter dish,** cover & liner, Bamboo patt., Alfred Meakin (ILLUS.) ............. 80.00

**Butter dish,** cov., Fishhook patt., Alfred Meakin (some discoloration) .... 45.00

**Cake plate,** New York shape, J. Clementson (rim flake)................. 280.00

**Cake plates,** Bamboo patt., Alfred Meakin, pr....................................... 100.00

**Compote,** open, Plain Round shape, Arthur Wilkinson (three rim flakes) ... 130.00

**Cookie jar,** cov., Homer Laughlin "Kitcher Kraft" line, ca. 1930s ............. 75.00

**Creamer,** Bullet shape, Anthony Shaw (ILLUS. top next page) ..................... 210.00

**Creamer,** Chelsea patt., Alfred Meakin, 5½" h.................................. 180.00

**Creamer,** Fig Cousin patt., Davenport.. 600.00

**Creamer,** Fishhook patt., Alfred Meakin (medium base hairline) .......... 50.00

*Tea Leaf Bullet Shape Creamer*

*Tea Leaf Fish Hook Gravy Boat*

**Creamer & cov. sugar bowl,** Empress patt., Micratex by Adams, ca. 1960s, pr. ..................................... **90.00**

**Cup & saucer,** demitasse, Empress patt., Micratex by Adams, ca. 1960s .. **70.00**

**Doughnut stand,** Simple Square patt., Henry Burgess ........................ **250.00**

**Egg cup,** Boston shape, Alfred Meakin (slight rim discoloration) ....... **200.00**

**Egg cup,** Empress patt., Micratex by Adams, ca. 1960s ........................... **170.00**

**Ewer,** Daisy patt., Anthony Shaw, 12" h. ................................................. **150.00**

**Gravy boat,** Cable patt., Anthony Shaw.................................................... **80.00**

**Gravy boat,** Fish Hook patt., Alfred Meakin (ILLUS. top next column) ....... **35.00**

**Hot water pitcher,** Maidenhair Fern patt., Arthur Wilkinson ...................... **475.00**

**Ladle,** Staffordshire, England, 7" l. ..... **190.00**

**Mixing bowl,** Homer Laughlin "Kitchen Kraft" line, ca. 1930s, 10½" d. (slight lustre wear) ................ **15.00**

**Nappies,** Iona patt., Powell & Bishop, gold lustre, set of 6 (small chips) ........ **22.00**

**Oyster bowl,** footed, Arthur Wilkinson.. **75.00**

**Oyster bowl,** unmarked........................ **60.00**

**Pitcher,** 6" h., Empress patt., Micratex by Adams, ca. 1960s .......................... **60.00**

**Pitcher,** 6" h., Simple Square patt., Mayer.............................................. **140.00**

**Pitcher,** Cable patt., Anthony Shaw (medium base chip) ......................... **140.00**

**Pitcher,** milk, Gentle Square patt., Furnival (slight lip discoloration) ....... **120.00**

**Pitcher,** cov., Homer Laughlin "Kitchen Kraft" line (spout chip & medium base rim chip) ...................... **45.00**

**Plates,** 6" d., Empress patt., Micratex by Adams, ca. 1960s, set of 10 ......... **48.00**

**Platter,** 4 × 6", Powell & Bishop, gold lustre band........................................ **10.00**

**Platter,** 5½ × 7¼", Square Ridged patt., Red Cliff, ca. 1960s .................. **55.00**

**Platter,** 9 × 12½", Simple Square patt., Red Cliff, ca. 1960s .................. **15.00**

**Platter,** 12 × 16½", Lily-of-the-Valley patt., Anthony Shaw (rim flakes)......... **45.00**

**Posset cup,** Hanging Leaves patt., Anthony Shaw ................................. **400.00**

**Relish dish,** mitten-shaped, Chinese patt., Anthony Shaw ........................ **340.00**

**Relish dish,** oval, Cable patt., Anthony Shaw .................................... **35.00**

**Ring box,** cov., decorated by Ruth Sayers ................................................. **50.00**

**Sauce tureen,** cover & stand & ladle, Lion's Head shape, Mellor - Taylor, the set (small lid finial chip) ............. **400.00**

**Salt & pepper shakers,** Empress patt., Adams, pr. ............................. **150.00**

**Shaving mug,** Basketweave patt., Anthony Shaw ................................. **310.00**

**Shaving mug,** Chinese patt., Anthony Shaw................................................. **180.00**

**Shaving mug,** Hexagon patt., Anthony Shaw ................................. **150.00**

**Shaving mug,** Favorite patt., Grindley .. **300.00**

**Soap dish cov.,** w/liner, Daisy patt., Anthony Shaw ................................. **170.00**

**Soup ladle,** Empress patt., Micratex by Adams, ca. 1960s ...................... **250.00**

**Sugar bowl,** cov., Bamboo patt., Alfred Meakin (small inside rim chips) ................................................. **65.00**

**Sugar bowl,** cov., Simple Square patt., Mayeor................................... **150.00**

*Tea Leaf Vegetable Dish*

**Tea set:** demitasse, cov. teapot, creamer & cov. sugar bowl; Empress patt., Micratex by Adams, ca. 1960s, 3 pcs. .............................. **310.00**

**Tea set:** cov. teapot, cov. sugar bowl, creamer & waste bowl; Square Ridged patt., Powell & Bishop, gold lustre, 4 pcs. ...................... **135.00**

**Toothbrush box,** Cable patt., Henry Burgess ......................... **340.00**

**Toothbrush vase,** tapering cylinder, Anthony Shaw .................. **225.00**

**Toothpick holder,** decorated by Ruth Sayers, ca. 1980 ............... **65.00**

**Vegetable dish,** cov., Chelsea patt., J. Wedgwood (handle flakes) ......... **60.00**

**Vegetable dish,** cov., Square Ridged patt., Mellor - Taylor, 7 × 9" (ILLUS. above) ................................ **65.00**

**Waste bowl,** child's, Mellor - Taylor.... **175.00**

## TEA LEAF VARIANTS

**Baker,** oval, Teaberry patt., Clementson, 6½ × 9" (some discoloration) ..................... **50.00**

**Cake plates,** Morning Glory patt., Framed Leaf shape, unmarked, gold lustre, pr. (lustre wear)...................... **50.00**

**Cider mug,** Panelled Columbia patt., unmarked, copper lustre band (three flakes above foot ring) ..................... **100.00**

**Creamer,** Teaberry patt., Heavy Square shape, J. Clementson (faint spider near base)............................ **220.00**

**Creamer,** oval, Teaberry patt., J. Clementson (two base rim chips) ..... **275.00**

**Creamer,** Tobacco Leaf patt., Fanfare shape, Elsmore & Forster ................ **275.00**

**Cup,** child's, gold Pomegranate motif, unmarked............................... **40.00**

**Cup,** handleless, Wrapped Sydenham shape, unmarked, copper lustre scallops motif ..................... **45.00**

**Cup & saucer,** Laurel Wreath patt., copper lustre highlights, Elsmore & Forster ............................. **100.00**

**Cup & saucer,** Tulip patt., Elsmore & Forster, copper lustre trim (rim chip on saucer)......................... **70.00**

**Cup & saucer,** handleless, paneled, copper lustre band, Brougham & Mayer.................................. **25.00**

**Cup & saucer,** Ring O' Hearts patt., Livesley & Powell, copper lustre trim .. **40.00**

**Cups & saucers,** child's, Teaberry patt., Prairie shape, Clementson, 2 sets ............................. **1,000.00**

**Pitcher,** 9" h., Cinquefoil patt., unmarked.......................... **135.00**

**Pitcher,** 10" h., Gothic patt., Red Cliff, ca. 1960s, copper lustre band ........... **40.00**

**Pitcher,** Niagara shape, Edward Walley, copper lustre band (handle terminal crack) ................... **80.00**

**Place setting,** Tobacco Leaf patt., Fanfare shape, 9½" d., 8½" d., & 7½" d. plates, sauce dish, cup & saucer, Elsmore & Forster, 6 pcs. (saucer has rim chip) ................ **65.00**

**Platter,** oval, 10 × 14", Pepper Leaf patt., Crystal shape, Elsmore & Forster (crazing) .............................. **40.00**

**Platter,** 10 × 14", Teaberry patt., Heavy Square shape, Clementson (under rim flake) ...................... **100.00**

**Platter,** 13" l., Laurel Wreath patt., Elsmore & Forster, copper lustre highlights ........................ **150.00**

**Relish dish,** mitten-shaped, Morning Glory patt., Portland shape, Elsmore & Forster, copper lustre trim (broken sections have been glued together) ... **170.00**

**Sauce dish,** Morning Glory patt., Elsmore & Forster, copper lustre trim, 5½" d. ............................... **70.00**

**Sauce tureen,** cov. & stand, Laurel Wreath patt., Elsmore & Forster, copper lustre highlights.................... **525.00**

**Sugar bowl,** cov., Morning Glory patt., Portland shape, Elsmore & Forster (two inside rim chips)........................ **220.00**

**Sugar bowl,** cov., Prairie shape w/copper lustre band, Clementson ... **220.00**

**Teapot,** cov., Morning Glory patt., Portland shape, Elsmore & Forster .. **375.00**

**Teapot,** cov., Teaberry patt., Heavy Square shaped, Clementson (finial missing, spout chip repair)............... **260.00**

**Vegetable dish,** cov., Laurel Wreath patt., Elsmore & Forster, copper lustre trim ......................................... **220.00**

**Vegetable dish,** cov., Tobacco Leaf patt., Fanfare shape, Elsmore & Forster 8 × 10" oval (potting glaze defect under rim of lid) ..................... **200.00**

## LEEDS

*The Leeds Pottery in Yorkshire, England, began production about 1758. It made, among other things, creamware that was highly competitive with Wedgwood's. In the 1780s it began production of reticulated and punched wares. Little of its production was marked. Most readily available Leeds ware is that of the 19th century during which time the pottery was operated by several firms.*

**Plate,** 8⅛" d., pearlware, blue feather-edged design, eagle decoration, later polychrome glaze 19th c. ........ **$431.00**

**Platter,** 18½" l., pearlware, green feather-edged design, 19th c. ........... **144.00**

**Platter,** 19" l., pearlware, blue feather-edged design, 19th c. ...................... **144.00**

**Teapot,** cov., creamware, spherical body w/a flattened inset cover w/a trumpet flower finial, the serpentine spout molded w/leaves, a double-entwined loop handle, decorated in polychrome w/a large rose & small blossoms, ca. 1775, 4½" h. (small rim & spout chips) ............................. **747.00**

**Teapot,** cov., creamware, spherical body w/a beaded footring, a wide mouth fitted w/a low domed cover w/trumpet flower finial, leaf-molded swan's-neck spout & double-entwined loop handle, the body decorated in magenta w/a large floral bouquet, ca. 1770, 4¾" h. (restored cover rim chips, slight rim line, chips on rim & spout) ............... **575.00**

**Teapot,** cov., spherical body, reeded swan's-neck spout, entwined strap handle, black transfer-printed decoration, one side w/a half-length portrait titled "THE REV JOHN WESLEY - MA AGED 82 1785," the reverse w/the scroll-framed inscription "Let your conversation be as becometh the Gospel of Christ," late 18th c., 4¾" h. (professional restoration to spout, cover & handles) ......................................... **660.00**

**Teapot,** cov., creamware, oval cylindrical body w/a narrow angled shoulder to the short cylindrical neck w/a fitted, domed cover w/blossom finial, rib-molded swan's-neck spout & double-entwined loop handle, decorated in magenta w/narrow stripes alternating w/narrow leafy upright vines, ca. 1780, 5¼" h. (spout, rim & cover restoration, hairline in handle) ............................. **805.00**

**Teapot,** cov., creamware, bulbous ovoid body tapering to a flaring foot, a short cylindrical pierced gallery rim w/scalloped rim, the inset cover w/a large blossom finial, swan's-neck spout & D-form handle, decorated on polychrome w/a floral bouquet, ca. 1770, 5¼" h. (restored chips on gallery) ............................................. **747.00**

**Wall pocket,** creamware, cornucopia-form, decorated w/an allegorical figure of "Flora" in relief flanked by an eagle & ram's head corners, 19th c., impressed mark, 7¼" h. ....... **287.00**

## LIMOGES

*Numerous factories produced china in Limoges, France, with major production in the 19th century. Some pieces listed below are identified by the name of the maker or the mark of the factory.*

*An excellent reference is* The Collector's Encyclopedia of Limoges Porcelain, Second Edition, *by Mary Frank Gaston (Collector Books, 1992).*

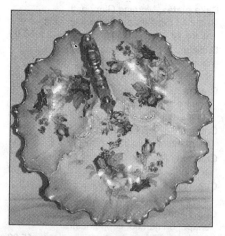

*Limoges Three-section Dish*

**Butter dish,** cover & insert, decorated w/soft pink roses on white ground .... **$75.00**

**Chocolate pot,** cov., ribbed mold, 5" scalloped base tapering to 3" neck, decorated w/delicate florals on white ground, gold trim around base, neck, handle & cover, signed "Haviland Limoges" ............................................ **165.00**

**Cup & saucer,** demitasse, jeweled, white & cream w/pastel pink & turquoise decoration, gold handle & trim ............. **48.00**

**Dish,** three-section w/ornate gold center handle, irregular shaded gold edge w/gold trim, each section decorated w/pink & peach roses, small lavender flowers & green foliage, unmarked, 11¼" d. (ILLUS. bottom previous page) ......................... **150.00**

**Ewer,** lavish raised gold decoration on cream ground, 6" h. .......................... **145.00**

**Game plate,** pierced to hang, h.p. colorful duck in flight against natural foliage & water background, heavy gold rococo edge, artist-signed, 11¼" d. ............................................ **225.00**

*Game Plate with Birds*

**Game plates,** pierced to hang, h.p. scene of pair of birds w/flowers & foliage, pastel background, heavy Roman gold rococo edge, 15⅝" d., pr. (ILLUS. of one) ........................... **695.00**

**Pitcher,** milk, grapes decoration ......... **245.00**

**Plaque,** pierced to hang, Art Nouveau portrait of woman w/long brown hair w/jewelling, deep charcoal grey background w/border of red, blues & green, 16" d. ................................... **550.00**

**Plate,** 6" d., decorated w/reddish-orange poppies, artist-signed, ca. 1898 ............................................ **75.00**

*Limoges Hanging Plate*

**Plate,** 9⅜" d., decorated w/h.p. fish, artist-signed, R.L.R. Limoges ............. **45.00**

**Plate,** 12⅞" d., pierced to hang, six h.p. peaches hanging from branches, green leaves, soft pastel background, leaves & branches highlighted w/gold, heavy gold rococo edge ..................................... **265.00**

**Plates,** 12½" d., pierced to hang, decorated w/detailed h.p. pastoral scene, lovely natural colors, one shows lady sitting by lake watching swan swimming, castle in background, heavy gold rococo edge, second plate shows similar scene w/lady in flowing gown standing amid greenery w/pink roses, castle in background, pr. (ILLUS. of one, above) ..................... **450.00**

**Punch bowl & stand,** interior & exterior decoration of h.p. red, white & pink roses on light green ground, artist-signed, 14" d., T & V, 2 pcs. .... **500.00**

**Ramekins w/underplates,** decorated w/deep pink roses, set of 6 ................ **95.00**

**Water set:** 12" h. tankard pitcher & five matching mugs; decorated w/green & purple raspberries, T & V - Limoges, France, 6 pcs. ....... **495.00**

# LIVERPOOL

*Liverpool is most often used as a generic term for fine earthenware products, usually of creamware or pearlware, produced at numerous potteries in this English city during the late 18th and early 19th centuries. Many examples, especially pitchers, were decorated with transfer-printed patriotic designs aimed specifically at the American buying public.*

**Bowl,** 9" d., 4¼" h., creamware, black printed transfers of various classical views & Masonic emblems w/"Seal of the United States" with a chain of fifteen states on interior base (some mellowing & wear to interior, restoration) ...................................... **$825.00**

**Pitcher,** jug-type, 5¼" h., creamware w/black transfer-printed w/Washington on one side, Lafayette on reverse, late 19th c., Richard Hall & Son .......................... **431.00**

**Pitcher,** jug-type, 5⅞" h., creamware w/black transfer-printed, Seal of the United States & "Peace, Plenty and Independence" on reverse (restoration which includes portions of the transfers) ............................ **1,045.00**

**Pitcher,** tankard, 5⅞" h., 4⅜" d., creamware, black transfer-printed scene of three-masted ship flying an American flag, highlighted in red, blue, green & yellow enamel (rim flakes) ........................................... **1,320.00**

**Pitcher,** tankard, 6⅛" h., 4¼" d., creamware, black transfer-printed of the Seal of the United States (restored rim & base chips) ........... **1,650.00**

**Pitcher,** jug-type, 6⅞" h., creamware w/black transfer-printed scene "The True Blooded Yankee" w/landscape scene on reverse, pink lustre decoration to rim & handle, h.p. anchor under spout (slight mellowing) ..................................... **1,100.00**

**Pitcher,** jug-type, 7¾" h., creamware w/black transfer-printed, "Arms of the United States - May Success Attend Our Agriculture, Trade and Manufactures" & "The True Blooded Yankee" on the reverse (restorations, which includes portions of the transfers).................. **990.00**

**Pitcher,** jug-type, creamware, black transfer-printed oval reserve, Washington w/chain of states, reverse, "O Liberty Thou Goddess" poem w/chain of states & Seal of the United States & "Herculaneum Pottery Liverpool" beneath spout (narrow shallow chip on side of spout & an invisible restored hairline off the base)..................................... **605.00**

**Pitcher,** jug-type, 9⅛" h., black transfer-printed scene of three-masted ship flying an American flag, reverse w/Seal of the United States & Washington monument w/chain of states (wear to gilt decoration) ...... **1,650.00**

**Pitcher,** jug-type, 9½" h., creamware, black transfer-printed "Britains Glory...Liberty to the Sons of Britain...The Spinning Machine...etc.," the reverse, "Fox Hunt...The Chase," both sides w/green, brown, yellow, red & pale blue polychrome, one transfer signed "T Baddesley... Hanley" (invisible restoration to a crack off the rim & two small chips)..... **412.00**

**Pitcher,** jug-type, 9¾" h., creamware, black transfer-printed scene of the three masted sailing ship "The Mercury" flying an American flag & trimmed in red, blue, green & yellow enamel, Seal of the United States - "Mary Clark" (within a wreath) under the spout & Washington w/chain of states on reverse (spout restoration)..................................... **1,320.00**

**Pitcher,** jug-type, 10" h., creamware, black transfer-printed scene of "The Tythe Pig" & reverse scene, "Sweet Maid An Emblem Of The Lamb," trimmed in red, yellow & green enamel w/"Heres God Bless the Plough..." poem beneath the spout within wreaths & scene of a shepherd w/sheep beneath the handle (several tiny flakes around the upper & lower rim & hairlines around the body which are restored on exterior) ................... **247.00**

*Liverpool Creamware Pitcher*

**Pitcher,** jug-type, 10¼" h., creamware, black transfer-printed scene entitled "The Gallant Defence of Stonington. August 9th 1814," the reverse w/"Washington in Glory" & "Seal of the United States" beneath the spout (ILLUS.) ...................... **17,600.00**

**Pitcher,** jug-type, 10½" h., creamware w/black transfer-printed oval reserve of Washington & Franklin & the map of the United States, Warren-Montgomery poem on reverse, "Jonathan and Mary Eldridge" - "Figure of Hope" under spout & Seal of the United States under handle, floral swag border at rim (small chip on base & mellowed)..... **1,650.00**

**Pitcher,** jug-type, 10½" h. creamware w/black transfer-printed oval reserve of bust of Washington crowned by figure of Liberty, w/chain of states, the reverse w/scene of American flag sailing vessel & map of the United States w/numbered key (heavy overall crazing & a poor restoration to entire base)............. **1,210.00**

**Pitcher,** jug-type, 11" h., creamware w/black transfer-printed scene of a three masted sailing ship flying an American flag, & trimmed in green, red, blue & yellow enamel, titled "Success to the Fortitude of Charlestown," English landscape scene on reverse, "E R - 1794" under spout (wear to gilt, restoration to rim, handle & base) .................. **1,540.00**

**Pitcher,** 11½" h., jug-type, creamware, black transfer-printed oval reserve, Apotheosis of Washington scene w/scene of three-masted "American flag vessel" on reverse, Seal of the United States under spout, worn gilt decoration, impressed "Herculaneum" on base (internal 1½" sq. crows-foot in side)............................................ **1,870.00**

**Plate,** 9⅝" d., creamware, black transfer-printed center scene of three-masted sailing ship flying an American flag & trimmed w/polychrome green, yellow, red & blue enamels (several tiny flakes on extreme edge of the rim).................... **330.00**

**Plate,** 10" d., creamware, black transfer-printed scene, round center design, "Sacred to the Memory of Washington" around scene w/allegorical figure of America & "Seal of the United States," so called "peanut" border on flanged rim, impressed "Herculaneum" on back. (restoration to an area on the shoulder)........................................... **660.00**

**Soup tureen undertray/platter,** oval, creamware creamware, black transfer-printed scene, round center design entitled "Sacred to the

Memory of Washington" around scene w/allegorical figure of America & Seal of the United States, so called "peanut" border on flanged rim, impressed "Herculaneum" on back, 14½" d.................................. **3,080.00**

# LLADRO

*Spain's famed Lladro porcelain manufactory creates both limited and non-limited edition figurines as well as other porcelains. The classic simple beauty of the figures and their subdued coloring makes them readily recognizable and they have an enthusiastic following of collectors.*

*Lladro Mark*

**All Aboard,** No. 7619, 5¼" h. ........... **$130.00**

**Angel Tree Topper,** No. 5719, blue, 1990, 7" h. ...................................... **220.00**

**Angels Ornaments,** miniature, No. 1604, 2" h., 1988, set of 3................. **375.00**

**Avoiding the Goose,** No. 5033, 9¾" h. ................................................. **295.00**

**Best Friend,** No. 7620, 1993 .............. **210.00**

**Beth,** No. 1358, 7½" h....................... **195.00**

**Bird Watcher,** No. 4730, 6¼" h. ......... **225.00**

**Blustery Day,** No. 5588, 6" h.............. **175.00**

**Boy Meets Girl,** No. 1188, 8½" h. ...... **323.00**

**Boy with Goat,** No. 4506, 10½" h. ..... **250.00**

**Boy with Smoking Jacket,** No. 4900, 7¾" h. ................................................. **195.00**

**Can I Play?,** No. 7610, 1990, 8¼" h. .. **360.00**

**Centaur Boy,** No. 1013, 8¼" h. .......... **325.00**

**Centaur Girl,** No. 1012, 9½" h............ **300.00**

**Claudette,** No. 5755, 14¼" h. ............. **285.00**

**Clown with Concertina,** No. 1027, 17¾" h. ................................................. **540.00**

**Debbie and Her Doll,** No. 1379, 10½" h. ............................................... **700.00**

**Demure Centaur Girl,** No. 5320, 5" h. ... **325.00**

**Dogs - Bust,** No. 2067, 7" h. .............. **700.00**

**Dressmaker,** No. 4700, 14¼" h. .......... **318.00**

**Dutch Girl,** No. 4860, 10¼" h. ............ **300.00**

**Dutch Girl with Braids,** No. 5063, 9¾" h. ................................................. **395.00**

**Exquisite Scent,** No. 1313, 11" h....... **400.00**

Flower Song, No. 7607, 1988,
7" h. ................................ **480.00 to 575.00**

Full Moon, No. 1438, 7½" h. ............... **610.00**

Garden Song, No. 7618, 1992, 8¾" h... **295.00**

Garden Treasure, No. 5591, 4¾" h.... **175.00**

Geisha, No. 4807, 12¼" h. ................. **260.00**

Girl with Doll, No. 1211, 8½" h. ......... **370.00**

Girl with Heart, No. 1028, 13" h. ........ **450.00**

Girl with Lantern, No. 4910, 8½" h. ... **275.00**

Horseman, No. 1037, 16" h. ............ **1,950.00**

In the Garden, No. 4978, 11" h. ......... **800.00**

La Tarentela, No. 1123, 16" h. ........ **2,100.00**

Lawyer, No. 1089, 11" h..... **380.00 to 400.00**

Lehua, No. 1532, 11" h. ...................... **345.00**

Little Boy Bullfighter, No. 5116,
10¼" h. .............................................. **400.00**

Little Boy Bullfighter, No. 5117,
9¾" h. ................................................ **400.00**

Little Gardener, No. 4726, 9¾" h. ...... **295.00**

Little Jester, No. 5203, 7¾" h. .......... **135.00**

Little Traveler, No. 7602, 1986,
8½" h. ............................................ **1,250.00**

Little Troubador, No. 1314, 13" h... **1,200.00**

Looking for Refuge, No. 4891,
11½" h. .......................................... **2,500.00**

Lovers in the Park, No. 1274,
11¾" h. .......................................... **1,050.00**

Maja Head, No. 4668, 12¼" h............. **675.00**

Midwife, No. 5431, 13" h. ................... **235.00**

Moon Glow, No. 1436, 7" h. ............... **550.00**

New Shepherdess, No. 4576, 9½" h.. **149.00**

Nostalgia, No. 5071, 6¼" h. ............... **310.00**

On the Farm, No. 1306, 9¾" h. .......... **240.00**

Oriental Music, No. 1491, 1986,
11¾" h. .......................................... **1,500.00**

Ox, No. 1390.30, white, 5¼" h. .......... **220.00**

Papillon Dog, No. 4857, 7½" h. .......... **500.00**

Penguin, No. 5248, 5½" h. ................. **175.00**

Penguin, No. 5249, 6" h. .................... **200.00**

Peter Pan, No. 7529, 1993, 9½" h... **1,050.00**

Poodle, No. 1259, 5½" h..................... **300.00**

Pretty Pose, No. 5589, 3½" h............. **175.00**

Rhino, No. 5437, 2" h. ......................... **99.00**

Roaring 20's, No. 5274, 13" h. ........... **195.00**

Saint Nicholas, No. 5427, 15½" h...... **600.00**

School Days, No. 7604, 1988, 8¼" h... **350.00**

Sea Captain, No. 4621, 14½" h. ......... **199.00**

Seal Family, miniature, No. 5318,
5½" h. ............................................... **225.00**

Seated Torero, No. 1162, 11¾" h. ..... **485.00**

Shepherd Sleeping, No. 1104, 14" h.. **1,625.00**

Shepherdess with Basket, No. 4591,
9¾" h. ............................................... **100.00**

Skye Terrier, No. 4643, 6" h.............. **350.00**

Soldier with Gun, No. 1164, 12¼" h.. **295.00**

Spring Bouquets, No. 7603, 1987,
8¼" h. ............................................... **585.00**

Spring Breeze, No. 5590, 7" h. ......... **175.00**

Spring Breeze, No. 1481, 8½" h. ................. **395.00**

Sunning, No. 1481, 8½" h. ................. **395.00**

Time to Rest, No. 5399, 4¾" h. .......... **295.00**

Tinker Bell, No. 7518, 1992, 7" h. .... **2,225.00**

Valencian Beauty, No. 5670, 6" h...... **138.00**

Wishing on a Star, No. 1475, 6½" h... **385.00**

Wistful Centaur Girl, No. 5319, 5½" h.. **325.00**

Young Madonna, No. 2149, 14½" h... **900.00**

Youth, No. 3538, 1983, 23½" h. ...... **1,500.00**

## LUSTRE WARES

*Lustred wares in imitation of copper, gold, silver and other colors were produced in England in the early 19th century and onward. Gold, copper or platinum oxides were painted on glazed objects which were then fired, giving them a lustred effect. Various forms of lustre wares include plain lustre—with the entire object coated to obtain a metallic effect, bands of lustre decoration and painted lustre designs. Particularly appealing is the pink or purple "splash lustre" sometimes referred to as "Sunderland" lustre in the mistaken belief it was confined to the production of Sunderland area potteries. Objects decorated in silver lustre by the "resist" process, wherein parts of the objects to be left free from lustre decoration were treated with wax, are referred to as "silver resist."*

*Wares formerly called "Canary Yellow Lustre" are now referred to as "Yellow-Glazed Earthenwares."*

### COPPER

Pitcher, 6¼" h., footed conical body
w/a narrow angled shoulder to the
tall cylindrical neck w/long arched
spout & angled handle, broad
canary band around the body
containing black transfer-printed
scenes, one a bust portrait of
"LaFayette" crowned, reverse of
Cornwallis resigning his sword at
Yorktown (handle restored)........... **$522.00**

Salt dip, footed, pink House patt.
band & pink interior, 2½" d., 2¼" h. .... **85.00**

### SILVER & SILVER RESIST

Pitcher, jug-type, 3⅝" h., brown
lustre ground decorated in silver
lustre relief scenes of cupids
shooting arrows & another w/cupids
in a wagon being drawn by two
greyhounds, mid-19th c. ................... **77.00**

**Pitcher,** jug-type, 5" h., angled handle, the ovoid body & tapering neck decorated in silver resist w/blue transfer-printed Cossack battle scene, blue floral border around rim ............... **181.00**

**Salt dip,** footed, round body w/molded vertical rib, overall silver lustre, 2¼" h. (unseen flake on foot rim) ...... **110.00**

## SUNDERLAND PINK & OTHERS

**Cups & saucers,** miniature, handled, decorated w/shaded pink lustre leaves, h.p. bright red & pink flowers w/tiny green berries, pink lustre rim, 2 pr. ................................................... **165.00**

**Pitcher,** 5½" h., bulbous ovoid body w/a short shouldered neck & angled handle, the sides decorated in purple lustre w/thin stripes between large round four-petal flowerheads around the sides, flowering vines around the neck, early 20th c. ............ **93.00**

**Pitcher,** jug-type, 7¼" h., the wide ovoid body decorated w/colored transfer-printed scenes of the "Sailor's Farewell" & the "Sailor's Return" & a prayer framed by a wreath, pink lustre banding around the rim, neck & base & pink lustre 'squiggles' around the body, early 19th c. ............................................... **275.00**

*Jug-type Pitcher*

**Pitcher,** jug-type, 7½" h., black transfer-printed Masonic devices, reverse w/Masonic poem w/floral border, splashed pink lustre ground (ILLUS.) ........................................... **357.00**

**Pitcher,** jug-type, 8¼" h., the wide ovoid body decorated on one side w/a large colored transfer-printed scene of the Farmer's Arms & "God Speed The Plow," the reverse w/a

view of the Sunderland Bridge, pink lustre band trim around the rim & base & h.p. colored blossoms around the neck, ca. 1840 (hairline cracks) ............................................... **247.00**

**Plate,** 8½" d., center oval reserve w/black transfer-print of the ships "Hornet" & "The Peacock," pink lustre border ................................... **412.00**

**Tray,** 7½" l., oval, pink lustre band border surround a pink lustre view of an English country church, unmarked ........................................ **255.00**

# MAJOLICA

*Majolica, a tin-enameled glazed pottery, has been produced for centuries. It originally took its name from the island of Majorca, a source of figurine (potter's clay). Subsequently it was widely produced in England, Europe and the United States. Etruscan majolica, now avidly sought was made by Griffen, Smith & Hill, Phoenixville, Pa., in the last quarter of the 19th century. Most majolica advertised today is 19th or 20th century. Once scorned by most collectors, interest in this colorful ware so popular during the Victorian era has now revived and prices have risen dramatically in the past few years.*

*Reference books which collectors will find useful include:* The Collector's Encyclopedia of Majolica, *by Mariann Katz-Marks (Collector Books, 1992);* American Majolica, 1850-1900, *by M. Charles Rebert (Wallace-Homestead Book Co., 1981);* Majolica, American & European Wares, *by Jeffrey B. Snyder & Leslie Bockol (Schiffer Publishing, Ltd., 1994); and* Majolica, British, Continental and American Wares, 1851-1915, *by Victoria Bergesen (Barrie & Jenkins, Ltd., London, England, 1989).*

## ETRUSCAN

*Etruscan Majolica Mark*

**Basket,** figural fish w/applied overhead handle, deep pink interior, ca. 1860, George Jones ................. **$950.00**

**Bowl,** figural chestnut leaf w/figural
bird handle, cobalt blue, 10 × 10".. **1,200.00**

**Bread tray,** Oak Leaf patt., Griffin,
Smith & Hill ........................................ **265.00**

**Cake stand,** Maple Leaf patt., tree-
trunk pedestal base, 9½" d., 5¾" h
(minor crazing) .................................. **193.00**

**Cup & saucer,** Shell & Seaweed patt.,
chips, saucer 8" d., cup 2¾" h.
(ILLUS. below) .................................. **445.00**

*Etruscan Cup & Saucer*

## GENERAL

**Compote,** footed, decorated w/leaf
design, artist-signed, 8½" l., Morley
& Co., Wellsville, Ohio ...................... **650.00**

**Dessert set:** large master cake plate
w/five small serving plates;
dandelion decoration on salmon
ground, "Zell," the set (some wear
on each plate) .................................... **175.00**

**Ice cream serving tray,** fan-shaped,
decorated w/birds & dragonfly, 16" d... **220.00**

**Inkwell,** France, 3 × 8" (small chip
under lip of ink container) ................. **450.00**

**Jardiniere,** rectangular, the sides
decorated in relief w/fish swimming
amid coral & shells on a green
ground, the edges applied w/scrolled
coral & seagrass, on four rocky feet,
19th c., 17" l. (minor chips & losses) ... **632.00**

**Match holder,** hat-shaped on leaf
base ................................................... **95.00**

**Plate,** 7¾" d., basketweave center
design, goldenrod, green & brown
(wear & glaze flakes) ........................ **72.00**

**Plate,** 10¼" d., pink berries &
blossoms on cream basketweave
ground ............................................... **75.00**

**Platter,** 9 × 12", handled, Begonia
Leaf patt. (ILLUS. top next column).. **175.00**

**Punch bowl,** figural lobster &
vegetables, Wedgwood, England,
19½" d. ............................................. **995.00**

**Smoking set,** figural hunter w/cigar
holder & match holder w/striker ....... **165.00**

*Begonia Leaf Pattern Platter*

**Toothpick holders,** figural monk, one
holding a book & one w/wine bottle,
each w/a basket on back for
matches or toothpicks, 5½" h., pr. .... **125.00**

**Tray,** decorated w/corner leaves &
floral center, polychrome 11⅛" l.
(wear & chips) ................................... **105.00**

**Tray,** decorated w/lavender flowers &
green leaves on deep yellow ground,
12¾" l. ............................................... **116.00**

## MC COY

*Collectors are now seeking the artwares of
two McCoy potteries. One was founded in
Roseville, Ohio, in the late 19th century as the
J.W. McCoy Pottery, subsequently becoming
Brush-McCoy Pottery Co., later Brush
Pottery. The other was founded also in
Roseville in 1910 as Nelson McCoy Sanitary
Stoneware Co., later becoming Nelson McCoy
Pottery. In 1967 the pottery was sold to D. T.
Chase of the Mount Clemens Pottery Co. who
sold his interest to the Lancaster Colony Corp.
in 1974. The pottery shop closed in 1985.
Cookie jars are especially collectible today.*

*A helpful reference book is the* Collector's
Encyclopedia of McCoy Pottery *by the
Huxfords (Collector Books), and* McCoy
Cookie Jars From the First to the Latest, *by
Harold Nichols (Nichols Publishing, 1987).*

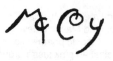

*McCoy Mark*

**Bank,** model of an owl, Woodsy
Owl ................................. **$90.00 to 100.00**

**Bank - cookie jar combination,**
Santa Claus ........................................ **95.00**

**Cookie jar,** Apples on Basketweave,
1957 .................................................... **55.00**

**Cookie jar,** Apollo, 1970-71 ............... **856.00**

**Cookie jar,** Astronaut, 1963 ............... **800.00**

**Cookie jar,** Barn, red, 1963 ............... **375.00**

**Cookie jar,** Basket of Eggs, 1977-79 .... **45.00**

**Cookie jar,** Basket of Potatoes,
1978-80 ............................................. **50.00**

**Cookie jar,** Bear (Cookie in Vest),
1943-45 ............................... **50.00 to 75.00**

**Cookie jar,** Bear (Hamm's Bear),
1972 ................................. **195.00 to 225.00**

**Cookie jar,** Bobby the Baker, 1974-79 .. **84.00**

**Cookie jar,** Boy on Baseball, 1978 ....... **250.00**

**Cookie jar,** Boy on Football,
1978 ............................... **210.00 to 250.00**

**Cookie jar,** Caboose, "Cookie
Special," 1961 .................................... **175.00**

**Cookie jar,** Cat on Basketweave,
1956-57 ............................................. **75.00**

**Cookie jar,** Chairman of the Board,
1985 ............................... **775.00 to 800.00**

**Cookie jar,** Christmas Tree, 1959 ... **1,177.00**

**Cookie jar,** Clown in Barrel, 1953-56 .. **125.00**

**Cookie jar,** Clyde Dog,
1974 ............................... **220.00 to 250.00**

**Cookie jar,** Coke Can, 1986 ............... **150.00**

**Cookie jar,** Cookie Cabin (log cabin),
1956-60 ............................................. **98.00**

**Cookie jar,** Cookie Safe, black,
1962-63 ............................................. **45.00**

**Cookie jar,** Crayola Kids cylinder ......... **60.00**

**Cookie jar,** Davy Crockett, 1957 ........ **525.00**

**Cookie jar,** Duck on Basketweave,
1956 (ILLUS. bottom previous
column) ............................................... **65.00**

**Cookie jar,** Dutch Treat Barn,
1968-73 ............................................. **45.00**

**Cookie jar,** Elephant, split trunk, 1945 .. **275.00**

**Cookie jar,** Engine, yellow, 1962-64 ... **215.00**

**Cookie jar,** Freddie the Gleep, yellow,
1974 .................................................. **750.00**

**Cookie jar,** Fruit in Basket (Bushel
Basket), 1961 ..................................... **51.00**

**Cookie jar,** Globe, 1960 .................... **280.00**

**Cookie jar,** Goody Goose, 1986-87 ...... **20.00**

**Cookie jar,** Indian Head, 1954-56 ...... **275.00**

**Cookie jar,** Kittens (Two) in a Low
**Basket,** 1950s ................................. **906.00**

**Cookie jar,** Little Boy Blue cylinder
w/decal, 1968-70 ................................ **75.00**

**Cookie jar,** Lunch Bucket, 1978-87 ...... **58.00**

**Cookie jar,** Mammy with Cauliflower,
1939 ................................................ **1,088.00**

**Cookie jar,** Mary, Mary, Quite
Contrary, 1970 .................................... **60.00**

**Cookie jar,** Mother Goose, brown,
1948-52 ............................................. **145.00**

**Cookie jar,** Oaken Bucket, 1961-71 ..... **45.00**

**Cookie jar,** Old Fashioned Auto
(Touring Car), 1962-64 ....... **90.00 to 125.00**

**Cookie jar,** Owl, brown, 1978-79 ......... **25.00**

**Cookie jar,** Owls, (Mr. & Mrs. Owl),
1953-55 ............................................. **95.00**

**Cookie jar,** Panda & Swirl,
undecorated ...................................... **195.00**

**Cookie jar,** Pineapple, natural colors,
1955-57 ............................. **90.00 to 100.00**

**Cookie jar,** Quaker Oats, 1970 .......... **385.00**

**Cookie jar,** Rocking Chair
(Dalmatians), 1961 (ILLUS. below) .. **375.00**

*Duck on Basketweave Cookie Jar*

*Rocking Chair (Dalmatians) Cookie Jar*

*Teepee Cookie Jar*

**Cookie jar,** Rooster, yellow & brown,
1956-58 ............................. **85.00 to 100.00**
**Cookie jar,** Sad Clown, 1968-70 .......... **75.00**
**Cookie jar,** Snoopy on Doghouse,
1970 ................................................. **195.00**
**Cookie jar,** Sad Clown, 1968-70 .......... **75.00**
**Cookie jar,** Spaceship (Friendship 7),
1962-63 ............................ **170.00 to 200.00**
**Cookie jar,** Teepee, 1956-59
(ILLUS.) ............................ **290.00 to 325.00**
**Cookie jar,** Turkey, brown, 1960 ........ **225.00**
**Cookie jar,** Turkey, green, 1960 ......... **350.00**
**Cookie jar,** Turkey, white, 1960 .......... **450.00**
**Cookie jar,** W. C. Fields,
1972-74 ............................ **185.00 to 200.00**
**Cookie jar,** Winking Pig, 1972 ............ **265.00**
**Cookie jar,** Wishing Well, 1961-70 ....... **42.00**
**Cookie jar,** Wren House w/brown bird
on top, 1958-60 ................ **125.00 to 150.00**

**Lamp base,** modeled as a pair of
cowboy boots, brown glaze, ca.
1956, small size .................................. **45.00**
**Planter,** model of a bird dog (ILLUS.
below) .................................................. **60.00**
**Planter,** model of a doe & fawn ........... **35.00**
**Planter,** model of a cart & dog ............. **26.00**
**Planter,** model of a spinning wheel
w/a Scottie dog & cat, ca. 1953 ......... **24.00**
**Vase,** 7" h., model of three white lilies
above green leaves on a brown
block base, ca. 1950 .......................... **48.00**
**Wall pocket,** leaf-shaped, pink & blue.. **30.00**
**Wall pocket,** model of an umbrella,
green & white ...................................... **45.00**

# MEISSEN

*The secret of true hard paste porcelain,
known long before to the Chinese, was
"discovered" accidentally in Meissen,
Germany, by J. F. Bottger, an alchemist
working with E. W. Tschirnhausen. The first
European true porcelain was made in the
Meissen Porcelain Works, organized about
1709. Meissen "crossed swords" marks have
been widely copied by other factories. Some
pieces listed here are recent.*

*Meissen Mark*

*McCoy Planter with Bird Dog*

**Chess set,** figural sea creature playing pieces & extra pawns & porcelain board, artist-signed & dated 1925, board & all pieces have crossed sword mark, board 20 × 20", complete set (many of the pieces have glued repair)........................ **$4,620.00**

**Figure of a female nude,** all-white, modeled seated on a drapery w/legs crossed & head turned to the right, designed by Weisz, underglaze-blue crossed swords mark & inscribed "ROBERT ULLMANN - 1940," 12½" h. (minor chip to one toenail & underside)..................................... **1,150.00**

**Figure of a maiden in Slavic costume,** standing wearing a gilt hat & floral wreath, a purple blouse over a light purple skirt, raised on a scroll-molded base, blue crossed swords mark, ca. 1900, 6½" h.................... **1,265.00**

**Figure of a woman,** seated in a Louis XV armchair, a Bible in one hand, wearing a lace veil & blue & white dress, seated beside a spinning wheel on a Rococo side table raised on a scroll-molded base, ca. 1900, blue crossed swords mark, incised "2685 43," 6" l., 6½" h. (repairs)..... **1,495.00**

**Figures of a Nubian & a maiden,** Art Deco style, both recumbent, she playing a flute, he holding a cockatoo, each raised on an oval base, blue crossed swords mark, 20th c., 8½" l., 8½" h., pr. .............. **4,600.00**

## METTLACH

*Ceramics with the name Mettlach were produced by Villeroy & Boch and other potteries in the Mettlach area of Germany. Villeroy and Boch's finest years of production are thought to be from about 1890 to 1910.*

*Mettlach Mark*

**Pitcher,** 8½" h., birch handle, green leaves in relief on grey, ca. 1890.... **$260.00**

**Plaque,** pierced to hang, polychrome scene of knight, impressed mark & "1384," 14½" d. (rim chips) .............. **385.00**

**Plaque,** pierced to hang, etched warrior scene, shows knight carrying weapon, blue background, artist-signed, ca. 1910, impressed castle mark, No. 1385 14½" d. (ILLUS. below) ....... **925.00**

*Warrior Scene Plaque*

*Cavalier with Barmaid Plaque*

**Plaque,** pierced to hang, etched scene of cavalier holding bar maid while cupid aims his bow & arrow at them, blue background, ca. 1900, impressed castle mark, No. 2322, 4½" d. (ILLUS.) ................................ **950.00**

**Plaque,** pierced to hang, painted underglazed scene of an old farmhouse scene, signed "Reils," No. 1044-1067, 17" d........................ **540.00**

**Plaque,** pierced to hang, etched scene of woman picking flowers, signed "Warth," No. 1473, 11 × 17".. **1,470.00**

**Plaque,** pierced to hang, phanolith,
white relief-molded classical scene
of Roman soldiers, teal blue ground,
impressed castle mark, 11" h.,
23½" w., framed 15¼" h., 27½" w. ... **990.00**

**Spirits barrel,** cov., tall cylindrical
body gently flaring at the top & base,
domed cover w/large knob finial, the
base decorated w/a wide center
band incised w/a band of large
swirled stylized green, yellow & blue
leafy blossoms on a pale cream
ground, button & lappet narrow
bands around the top & bottom rims,
a spiget hole w/metal spigot at the
base rim, matching floral decoration
on the cover, late 19th - early
20th c., 12" h. .................................... **495.00**

# MOCHA

*Mocha decorations found on basically
utilitarian creamware or yellowware articles
and is achieved by a simple chemical reaction.
A color pigment of brown, blue, green or black
is given an acid nature by infusion of tobacco
or hops. When this acid nature colorant is
applied in blobs to an alkaline ground color, it
reacts by spreading in feathery seaweed
designs. This type of decoration is usually
accompanied by horizontal bands of light color
slip. Produced in numerous Staffordshire
potteries from the late 19th centuries, its name
is derived from the similar markings found on
mocha quartz. In addition to the seaweed
decoration, mocha wares are also seen with
Earthworm and Cat's Eye patterns or a
marbleized effect.*

**Bowl,** 7½" d., 3½" h., green ribbed rim
w/marbleized band in black, blue,
white & tan (small chips & hairlines).. **$550.00**

**Mug,** cylindrical ironstone body
decorated w/blue wide center band
w/seaweed design, flanked by black
stripes, marked "Pint, G.R.," 5" h. ...... **193.00**

**Pitcher,** 7" h., white Earthworm patt.
between mocha brown bands,
19th c. (chip & cracked) .................... **460.00**

**Pitcher,** 7⅝" h., wide footed ovoid
body tapering slightly toward the
wide flat rim w/pointed spout, leaf
handle, decorated w/blue bands &
black stripes w/Earthworm patt.
design in black, white & blue (wear
hairlines, stains & rim chips) ............. **358.00**

# MOORCROFT

*William Moorcroft became a designer for
James Macintyre & Co. in 1897 and was put
in charge of their art pottery production.
Moorcroft developed a number of popular
designs, including Florian Ware while with
Macintyre and continued with that firm until
1913 when they discontinued the production
of art pottery.*

*After leaving Macintyre in 1913,
Moorcroft set up his own pottery in Burslem
and continued producing the artwares he had
designed earlier as well as introducing new
patterns. After William's death in 1945, the
pottery was operated by his son, Walter.*

## MOORCROFT

*Moorcroft Marks*

**Bottle w/original stopper,** squatty
bulbous body tapering to short wide
cylindrical neck w/flat flared rim,
orchid decoration in deep violet, rose,
chartreuse, blue, pink, yellow & white
against an ivory & pale blue ground,
impressed "Moorcroft Potter to H.M.
the Queen, Made in England," 6" h... **$413.00**

**Bowl,** 6" d., Pomegranate patt. ........... **575.00**

**Bowl,** 9¾" d., Hibiscus patt., coral
blossom on green ground ................. **310.00**

**Bowl,** 9¾" d., Hibiscus patt., red &
yellow blossoms on ivory ground ...... **310.00**

**Bowl,** 9¾" d., Hibiscus patt., red
blossoms on brown ground ............. **310.00**

**Creamer & sugar bowl,** Pansy patt.,
cobalt blue ground, Macintyre
period, ca. 1897-1913, creamer
3" h., sugar bowl 3¼" d., pr .............. **640.00**

**Cup & saucer,** Eighteenth Century
patt., Macintyre period, ca. 1897-
1913 ................................................. **380.00**

**Dish,** Pansy patt., 5¾" d. ................... **350.00**

**Egg cup,** round saucer-shaped base
dark blue crystals suspended in a
light blue background, impressed
mark, 2¼" h. ...................................... **55.00**

**Match striker,** wide conical form,
decorated w/forest scene in shades
of green, rust & ivory w/incised rings
at base, Macintyre mark, 3" h. .......... **550.00**

*Pitcher with Floral Decoration*

**Pitcher,** 6½" h. footed wide ovoid body, pinched spout, large C-form handle, deep blue floral decoration trimmed in white, green ground, impressed mark (ILLUS.).................. **413.00**

**Pitcher,** tankard, 11" h., Florian Ware, cylindrical body tapering to flat rim w/pinched spout, w/large squared handle at rim, h.p. floral & scrolling leaves in shades of blue, green & gold, trimmed in gold, khaki ground, impressed mark & painted signature....................................... **1,100.00**

**Vase,** 3¾" h., Pomegranate patt., marked "C. Burslem" ........................ **355.00**

**Vase,** 6" h., Flaminian Ware, baluster-form body w/a short rolled neck, red flambé, painted signature & date...... **825.00**

**Vase,** 6⅜" h., waisted cylindrical body w/polychrome lotus flower decoration, script signature..................................... **578.00**

**Vase,** 8" h., baluster-form body w/wide trumpet neck, floral transfer design decoration in shades of blue, gold & ivory, Macintyre mark ............ **440.00**

**Vase,** 9" h., baluster-form w/wide flaring neck w/rolled rim, Natural Ware, finger-formed rings & raised decoration at shoulders, celadon ground, impressed mark.................. **253.00**

**Vase,** 9½" h., inverted trumpet-form, Persian design, red, deep blue, green floral decoration on ivory panels, green ground, impressed mark & painted signature, ca. 1913-18.................................. **2,3100.00**

**Vase,** 9½" h., ovoid w/rolled rim, decorated w/poppies in rose, caramel, tan & teal on dark blue ground, script signature, impressed marks (ILLUS. top next column) .... **1,430.00**

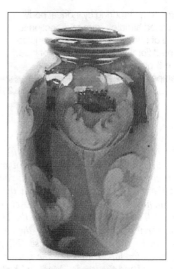

*Vase with Poppy Decoration*

*Florian Ware Vase*

**Vase,** 10" h., baluster-form, shoulder handles, Florian Ware, dark blue blossoms, green foliage against a cream ground, script signature, Macintyre period, ca. 1904-13 (ILLUS.) ......................................... **1,210.00**

**Vase,** 14½" h., 6" d., ovoid w/flat rim, Pomegranate patt., large red, deep blue, yellow & green fruit against khaki ground, impressed mark & painted signature (repaired top) ....... **805.00**

**Vases,** 8" h., tapering cylindrical body w/angled handles from mid-section to base of neck, Aurelian Ware, transfer-printed floral design in shades of blue, gold & orange, impressed mark & stamped "Made for C. Jenner & Co. Edinburgh," pr. .................................. **1,210.00**

# NIPPON

*"Nippon" is a term which is used to describe a wide range of porcelain wares produced in Japan from the late 19th century until about 1921. It was in 1891 that the U.S. implemented the McKinley Tariff Act which required that all wares exported to the United States carry a marking indicating the country of origin. The Japanese chose to use "Nippon," their name for Japan. In 1921 the import laws were revised and the words "Made in" had to be added to the markings. Japan was also required to replace the "Nippon" with the English name "Japan" on all wares sent to the U.S.*

*Many Japanese factories produced Nippon porcelains and much of it was hand-painted with ornate floral or landscape decoration and heavy gold decoration, applied beading and slip-trailed designs referred to as "moriage." We indicate the specific marking used on a piece, when known, at the end of each listing below. Be aware that a number of Nippon markings have been reproduced and used on new porcelain wares.*

*Important reference books on Nippon include:* The Collector's Encyclopedia of Nippon Porcelain, Series One through Three, *by Joan F. Van Patten (Collector Books, Paducah, Kentucky) and* The Wonderful World of Nippon Porcelain, 1891-1921 *by Kathy Wojciechowski (Schiffer Publishing, Ltd., Atglen, Pennsylvania)*

**Ashtray,** h.p. lake sunset scene, marked .............................................. **$60.00**

**Bowl,** 6½" d., 2½" h., octagonal, h.p. lake scene, marked ........................... **30.00**

**Bowl,** 8¼" d., decorated w/h.p. swan scene, heavy gold trim ........................ **35.00**

**Cake plate,** open-handled, decorated w/large pink flowers, scalloped edge w/pastel beading & heavy scrolling gold, 10" d., (Maple Leaf mark) ........ **450.00**

**Celery set:** 7¾" l. two-handled tray w/five 3½" l. salts; decorated w/outdoor scene of water, mountains, bridge & house, multicolored w/gold trim, 6 pcs. .......... **95.00**

**Chocolate set:** cov. chocolate pot & four cups; decorated w/pink & yellow Art Deco-style roses on white ground, heavy gold stipple overlay, 5 pcs. (Maple Leaf mark) .................. **350.00**

**Creamer & cov. sugar bowl,** decorated w/red roses on shaded green ground, pr. ............................. **135.00**

**Creamer & cov. sugar bowl,** h.p. scenic decoration w/lavender skies, jeweling (green "M" in wreath mark) ... **30.00**

**Ginger jar,** cov., heavily decorated phoenix bird, black, white & red, 7½" h. .............................................. **225.00**

**Hair receiver,** cov., pink & white w/gold beading, relief-molded leaves around base, lavish gold trim, 2¾" h. (green Maple Leaf mark) .................... **50.00**

**Humidor,** cov., footed, cylindrical body tapering slightly to cover w/knob finial, decorated w/scene of trees & water, 7½" h, (green "M" in Wreath mark) ................................. **350.00**

**Jam pot,** cov., & spoon, pink rosebud decoration on pot, jeweling on spoon, 2 pcs. ...................................... **30.00**

**Mayonnaise set:** 4⅞" d. bowl, 6⅜" d. underplate & matching ladle; decorated w/white, orange & purple flowers on light orange ground, lavish gold trim, 3 pcs. ...................... **55.00**

**Mustard pot,** cov., h.p. gold & pale orange Japanese scene .................... **55.00**

**Napkin holder,** h.p. extended hand-shape, (blue Maple Leaf mark) .......... **20.00**

**Nut set:** footed master bowl & five individual footed dishes; decorated w/lake scene, cherry tree & two geishas, Iron Red banding, 6 pcs. ...... **50.00**

**Pin box,** cov., pedestal base, pink & white w/gold trim & blue beading, 2⅞" h. .............................................. **45.00**

**Pitcher,** 7" h., decorated w/h.p. roses, gold trim, twig handle ........................ **45.00**

**Pitcher,** tankard, 13" h., floral decoration w/gold handle & gold beaded trim (Royal Nishiki Nippon mark) ................................................ **250.00**

**Plaque,** pierced to hang, decorated w/relief-molded deer near water, trees in background, 10½" d. (green "M" in Wreath mark) .......................... **850.00**

**Plaque,** pierced to hang, decorated w/relief-molded lion & lioness in mountain scene, green "M" in Wreath mark, 10½" d. (ILLUS. top next page) ........................................ **850.00**

*Plaque with Lions*

**Plaque,** pierced to hang, decorated w/relief-molded scene of Apollo w/dogs, 12" d. ............................... **1,200.00**

**Plaque,** bisque, pierced to hang, decorated w/beer stein, cigar, pipe, playing cards (green "M" in Wreath mark) ............................................. **250.00**

**Salt & pepper shakers,** palm tree decoration, jeweling, pr....................... **10.00**

*Nippon Sugar Shaker*

**Sugar shaker,** floral decoration w/gold jeweling, 5" h. (ILLUS.)............ **35.00**

**Syrup pitcher,** cov. & underplate, square, h.p. floral decoration w/ornate gold trim, 2 pcs. (blue Maple Leaf mark).............................. **130.00**

**Tea set:** cov. teapot, creamer & cov. sugar bowl; decorated w/white swans in flight on aqua ground, 3 pcs. (green "M" in Wreath mark).... **360.00**

**Vase,** 5½" h., bulbous melon-lobed body tapering to a short cylindrical neck, decorated w/a leafy branch & flowers, moriage trim (green Maple Leaf mark) ....................................... **125.00**

**Vase,** 9½" h., decorated w/colorful house scene (green "M" in Wreath mark) ................................................ **110.00**

**Vase,** 10" h., ovoid body w/slightly flared foot & short flared neck, scrolled & ribbed handles, decorated w/h.p. green flowers on ivory to lavender ground, relief-molded leaves & flowers 1½" h. on base, gold trim (green "M" in Wreath mark) ............... **295.00**

**Vases,** bulbous body, two-handled, floral decoration w/gold trim (Imperial Nippon mark), pr. .............. **225.00**

# NORITAKE

*Noritake china, still in production in Japan, has been exported in large quantities to this country since early in this century. Though the Noritake Company first registered in 1904, it did not use "Noritake" as part of its backstamp until 1918. Interest in Noritake has escalated as collectors now seek out pieces made between the "Nippon" era and World War II (1921-41). The Azalea pattern is also popular with collectors.*

*Noritake Mark*

**Basket,** "Dolly Varden," Tree in Meadow patt., No. 213, 2½ × 4⅜", overall 4" h. .................... **$100.00 to 150.00**

**Bowl,** 4½ × 8½", 11" h., decorated interior & exterior, h.p. nuts & leaves w/slipwork, jeweled handles ............. **150.00**

**Box,** cov., Art Deco scene of girl w/long hair, holding a doll in her hand, orange ground, black base, 6¼" d., 4½" h. ................................. **245.00**

**Casserole,** cov., Azalea patt., No. 16, 10¼" d. ............................................ **115.00**

**Cruet set w/original stoppers,** oil & vinegar, the two globular bottles at angles & joined at the base w/a curved handle joining them at the shoulder, Tree in Meadow patt., No. 319, tip to tip 6½" ...................... **185.00**

**Demitasse pot,** cov., Tree in Meadow patt. .................................................. **125.00**

**Dessert set:** 11" d. cake plate & four individual plates; floral decoration on white ground, tan border, 5 pcs. ....... **145.00**

**Dessert sets,** Art Deco-shaped large saucer/dish w/black, white & gold decor & cup w/gold handle, Art Deco woman's face molded in base, four sets .................................................. **300.00**

**Dinner service,** Nanette patt., No. 683, includes ten demitasse cups & saucers, 78 pcs. ............................. **495.00**

**Dish,** decorated w/scene of flapper & parrot, lustre ground, 5" d. .................. **33.00**

**Dish,** two-handled, decorated w/Art Deco poppies on lustre ground, 7" d. ... **55.00**

**Hair receiver,** cov., decorated w/cobalt floral design & gold trim, marked in gold, "EE" .......................... **45.00**

**Mustard jar,** cov., Tree in Meadow patt. .................................................. **60.00**

**Nut set:** 4" bowl & six matching 1" bowls; yellow interior w/h.p. relief-molded nuts, exterior brown, pink & blue, 7 pcs. ...................................... **185.00**

**Pancake server,** decorated w/large pink & red roses & lavish gold trim, scalloped base, 9" d., unmarked ...... **125.00**

**Plaque,** pierced to hang, decorated w/scene of Mitsui Line cargo ship, Mount Fuji in background (Nippon Toki Kaisha mark), 10½" d. .............. **175.00**

**Plate,** bread & butter, 6½" d., Azalea patt., No. 8 ......................................... **35.00**

**Plate,** 10½" d., Pattern No. 175, white & gold ................................................. **21.00**

**Relish,** two-compartment, Azalea patt., No. 171, 4¾ × 8¼" ..................... **55.00**

**Relish,** four-compartment, Azalea patt., No. 119, 10" l. ............................ **75.00**

**Spoon holder,** floral decoration, 8" l..... **50.00**

**Syrup pitcher,** cover & underplate, decorated w/Oriental woman holding fan, against a lustred orange ground, 3 pcs. ................................................. **85.00**

**Teapot,** cover, underplate, individual size, scenic decoration ...................... **60.00**

**Tea set,** child's: cov. teapot, creamer & cov. sugar bowl; decorated w/scene of children fishing, lustre ground, 3 pcs. (some wear) ............... **55.00**

**Tea tile,** Tree in Meadow patt. .............. **45.00**

**Urn,** cov., ornate shape w/cobalt floral decoration & gold trim, 9¼" h. to top of finial ............................................ **125.00**

**Vase,** 7" h., footed, h.p. parrot decoration against lustre ground ........ **65.00**

**Vases,** Art Deco style, decorated w/pink & white flowers on white shading to soft pink ground, pr. ........ **250.00**

# PENNSBURY POTTERY

*Inspired by the long tradition of Pennsylvania Dutch style pottery in Pennsylvania, Henry and Lee Below founded their pottery near Morrisville in 1950 and named it for the nearby Pennsbury Manor.*

*Specializing in Pennsylvania Dutch and country-style decoration, Pennsbury Pottery was hand-painted in a variety of colorful designs. Although tablewares were the major products, special commemorative items and a line of bird figures also originated at this pottery until its closure in 1970.*

*Amish Boy & Girl Ashtray*

**Ashtray,** Amish boy & girl w/umbrella, "It's making down," three cigarette rest, 5" d. (ILLUS.) ............................ **$22.00**

**Bowl,** 9" d, 3" h., Dutch Talk patt., various Dutch emblems & sayings scattered around the piece include: "Kissin Wares Out, Cooking Don't - My, You Look Good in the Face - Borrowing Makes for Sorrowing - Throw The Cow Over The Fence Some Hay - Go Pump Me A Drink" .... **125.00**

**Butter dish,** cov., Hex patt., 5" w., 4" w. .................................................... **85.00**

*Black Rooster Candleholder*

*Two Pennsbury Ducklings*

**Candleholder,** Black Rooster patt.,
w/finger hold, 5" d. (ILLUS.)............... **50.00**

**Canister,** cov., Black Rooster patt.,
w/black rooster finial, front reads
"Coffee," 8" h. ................................... **145.00**

*Amish Man Pennsbury Creamer*

*Boy & Girl Pattern Pie Plate*

**Creamer,** heart surrounding Amish
man, heart on reverse, 4" h. (ILLUS.
of front) ............................................. **45.00**

**Model of duckling,** lying down,
covered w/white high gloss, brown
stained beak & feet, black eyes,
marked Pennsbury Pottery on
unglazed bottom, 6½" l. (ILLUS.
left, top next column) ........................ **195.00**

**Model of duckling,** white high gloss,
standing on round green base,
marked Pennsbury Pottery on
unglazed bottom, 6½" h. (ILLUS.
right, top next column)...................... **185.00**

**Pie plate,** Boy and Girl patt., border
marked "Whispered words beneath
the bower, holding hands at some
late hour, usually lead as you well
know to raising young ones, crops
and dough," 9" d. (ILLUS. middle next
column)............................................. **100.00**

**Pitcher,** miniature, 2½" h., shows
Amish man standing in front of fence
(ILLUS. bottom next column) ............. **22.00**

*Miniature Pennsbury Pitcher*

**Pitcher,** 5" h., Delft Toleware patt.,
white body w/fruit & leaves outlined
in blue, blue inside ............................. **85.00**

**Pitcher,** 5" h., Blue Dowry patt., same
design as Folkart line, but in blue &
white .................................................. **72.00**

**Planter,** "Slick Chick on gourd," yellow
bird perched atop handle of dark &
light green gourd, unmarked 5½" h.
(ILLUS. top next page) ...................... **55.00**

*"Slick Chick on gourd" Planter*

**Plaque,** "Come in without knocking go out the same way," drilled for hanging, 4" d. (ILLUS. middle previous column) ............................................... **30.00**

**Plaque,** commemorative, reads "Pop's half et already," drilled for hanging, 4" d. (ILLUS. bottom previous column) ............................................... **30.00**

**Plaque,** Red Rooster patt., drilled for hanging, 4" d. ...................................... **35.00**

**Plaque,** Walking to Homestead patt., drilled for hanging, 4" d. (ILLUS. top this column) ................................. **43.00**

**Plaque,** "Hear Ye! If any Man insults Ye By offering Ye a Drink Swallow the Insult," drilled for hanging, 6" d. (ILLUS. bottom this column) .............. **35.00**

**Plaque,** Basket of Flowers patt., 6" d.... **47.00**

**Plate,** 8" d., Harvest patt. ..................... **65.00**

*Walking to Homestead Plaque*

*"Come in without knocking" Plaque*

*"Pop's half et already" Plaque*

*Pennsbury Pottery Plaque*

*Angel First Edition Plate*

*Large Black Rooster Pattern Plate*

*Red Barn Pattern Relish Tray*

**Plate,** 8½" d., shows profile of standing angel holding holly leaf atop base marked "Noel," flanked by red candles, border marked "1970" at top & "Angel" at bottom, reverse marked "Yuletide Plate Stumar First Edition, L.B. Original by Pennsbury Pottery hand-painted" (ILLUS. top)..... **65.00**

*Commemorative Pennsbury Tray*

*Pennsbury Warming Plate*

**Plate,** 10" d., Black Rooster patt. (ILLUS. middle previous column) ....... **55.00**

**Relish tray,** Red Barn patt., triangle shape w/handle, three-section each w/different scene, 14½" l., 11" w. (ILLUS. bottom previous column) ..... **215.00**

**Tile,** round, pictures a skunk, inscribed "Why be disagreeable when with a little effort you could be a REAL STINKER," 6" d. ................... **38.00**

**Tray,** commemorative for the Pennsylvania State Education Association, front shows the image of a ship flanked by "1857" & "1957" below "Greetings from P.S.E.A. - N.E.A., all above "Welcome," 7¼" l., 5" w. (ILLUS. of front, top) ................ **50.00**

**Warming plate,** electrified, Picking Apples patt., rare, 6" sq. (ILLUS. bottom) ............................................ **135.00**

# PICKARD

*Pickard, Inc., making fine hand-colored china today in Antioch, Illinois, was founded in Chicago in 1894 by Wilder A. Pickard. The company now makes its own blanks but once only decorated those bought from other potteries, primarily from the Havilands and others in Limoges, France.*

*Pickard Mark*

**Cake plate,** open-handled, creamy background w/swags of small roses around rim, large 5½" center medallion of large bouquet of roses, snowballs & buttercups, outlined in gold w/gold rim & handles, artist-signed, 12" d. ................................. **$235.00**

**Cake plate,** open-handled, iridescent background w/raised gold wheat stalks & pinecones, artist-signed, 12" d. .............................................. **295.00**

**Cake plate,** scenic decoration w/river through farmland, artist-signed ......... **300.00**

**Candy dish,** leaf-shaped, decorated w/violets & green lily pads, gold handle & rim, ca. 1910, artist-signed... **125.00**

**Coffeepot,** cov., pedestal base, marked w/gold circle, 9" h. ................ **295.00**

**Cracker plate,** decorated w/yellow irises & green leaves, scalloped gold rim, ca. 1905, artist-signed, 7¾" d. .... **135.00**

**Creamer & cov. sugar bowl,** floral etched allover gold, pr. ....................... **60.00**

**Creamer & cov. sugar bowl,** garden scene, matte finish, gold trim, artist-signed, pr. ........................................ **350.00**

**Creamer & cov. sugar bowl,** pedestal base, gold, rose & daisy pattern decoration, Bavarian blank, Shield & Lion mark, sugar 5" to top of finial, creamer 4" h., pr. ................. **295.00**

**Dresser tray,** decorated w/lavender violets, ivory & gold ground, artist-signed, 3 × 11". ................................ **225.00**

**Hair receiver,** cov., decorated w/pearlized purple flowers, artist-signed .............................................. **150.00**

**Mayonnaise dish,** handled, & matching underplate, decorated w/stylized blue cornflowers, lavish gold trim & heavy gold handles on bowl, artist-signed, ca. 1905-10, bowl 7¼" d., 2" h., plate 7¼" d., 2 pcs. (ILLUS. top next column) ....... **165.00**

*Mayonnaise Dish & Underplate*

**Mustard jar,** cov., enameled border ..... **55.00**

**Nappy,** two-handled, decorated w/red cherries & white cherry blossoms, scalloped gold rim & handles, artist-signed, ca. 1905, 5½ × 7¼" .............. **195.00**

**Nappy,** fruit decoration w/cobalt handle, artist-signed ......................... **225.00**

**Pitcher,** lemonade, stylized peacocks decoration, artist-signed ................... **350.00**

**Pitcher,** milk, 6¼" h., bulbous body decorated w/heavy gold gooseberries, leaves, ribbons on green satin background, heavy gold handle & band around base, artist-signed.......... **275.00**

**Plate,** 7½" d., decorated w/pastel poppies, artist-signed, ca. 1905........ **110.00**

**Plate,** 8½" d., decorated w/h.p. strawberries, gold border, artist-signed .............................................. **185.00**

**Plate,** 8½" d., decorated w/colorful long-tailed bird, scenic background, heavy gold border, artist-signed, Hutschenreuther blank ..................... **190.00**

**Plate,** 13½" d., handled, vellum apple blossoms in foreground, path between flowering trees is background, artist-signed ................. **110.00**

**Plate,** decorated w/almonds, artist-signed .............................................. **168.00**

**Platter,** ornate gold handles, turquoise & gold wide band around rim, artist-signed, ca. 1912, 9½ × 14¾"............ **135.00**

**Tea set:** cov. teapot, creamer & cov. sugar bowl; Dutch girls decoration, artist-signed, 3 pcs. .......................... **595.00**

**Tea set:** cov. teapot, creamer & cov.
sugar bowl; border design w/pink &
blue enameled flowers, artist-signed,
3 pcs. ................................................ **350.00**

**Vase,** 4½ × 11½", gold floral etch
decoration ........................................ **220.00**

**Vase,** 6½" h., bulbous body, violets &
green leaves decoration on cream
ground, gold neck & rim, artist-
signed, ca. 1910-12 ......................... **165.00**

**Vase,** 8" h., decorated w/scene of
castle & trees, yellow ground, artist-
signed .............................................. **350.00**

## PRATT WARES

*The earliest ware now classified as Pratt
ware was made by Felix Pratt at his pottery
in Fenton, England from about 1810. He
made earthenware with bright glazes, relief
sporting jugs, toby mugs and commercial
pots and jars whose lids bore multicolored
transfer prints. The F. & R. Pratt mark is
mid-19th century. The name Pratt ware is
also applied today to mid and late 19th
century English ware of the same general
type as that made by Felix Pratt.*

*Pratt Wares Mark*

**Pipe,** pearlware, figural coiled snake
w/bowl in the form of a woman's
face, rim of bowl & mouthpiece
decorated in yellow ochre & the
coiled body decorated w/dots of blue
& yellow, underside of coils
decorated in sponged blue, 9½" w.
(invisible restoration to base of the
bowl & to two small areas on the
underside of the bowl) ................... **$825.00**

**Pipe,** thin molded double ring snake-
form w/scaled body, petals & beads
adorn the handles in the body, a tiny
figure of a woman sits on the neck
and the serpent's head forms the
bowl, decorated w/brown, yellow
ochre, yellow & blue, 10¾" l.

(restoration to a small area of the
neck & a small chip on one of the
petals in the handle) ........................ **550.00**

**Pitcher,** jug-type, 5¼" h., molded
design of "The Miser" on both sides
w/a leaf border & acanthus leaves
under the spout & handle, decorated
in brown, green, yellow & blue
(highly professional restoration
around the handle) .......................... **385.00**

**Pitcher,** jug-type, 7½" h., pearlware,
decorated w/stylized scene of a tree
& an arched bridge w/a fence &
flying birds in the background, blue,
green, yellow ochre & brown
(professional restoration around
handle)............................................. **467.00**

## REDWARE

*Red earthenware pottery was made in the
American colonies from the late 1600s.
Bowls, crocks and all types of utilitarian
wares were turned out in great abundance to
supplement the pewter and handmade
treenware. The ready availability of the clay,
the same used in making bricks and roof tiles,
accounted for the vast production. The lead-
glazed redware retained its reddish color
though a variety of colors could be obtained
by adding various metals to the glaze.
Interesting effects occurred accidentally
through unsuspected impurities in the clay or
uneven temperatures in the firing kiln which
sometimes resulted in streaks or mottled
splotches.*

*Redware pottery was seldom marked by
the maker.*

**Basket,** divided w/overhead handle,
applied dark brown figures of
cherubs, impressed "Wedgwood Z,"
3¾" h. .............................................. **$187.00**

**Bowl,** cov., 6¼" h., baluster-form body
on cushion foot, molded rings at
neck, applied handles, decorated
w/incised vines issuing applied
flowers, flat lid w/full-figured bird
finial, 19th c., Adams County,
Pennsylvania ................................. **5,520.00**

**Box,** cov. w/applied relief in dark
brown of putti, classical scenes &
signs of the zodiac, glazed interior,
base impressed w/slightly curved
"Wedgwood T," 3½" d., 1⅝" h.
(multiple chips on rim of the cover &
the flange of the base).................... **110.00**

*Redware Charger*

**Charger,** sgraffitto decoration of an inscribed potted heart issuing stylized flowers & notched tulips w/a yellowish beige glaze highlighted w/red & daubs of brown glaze, coggle wheel rim, dated 1802, Conrad Mumbouer, Haycock Township, Bucks County, Pennsylvania, 11½" d. (ILLUS.)....................................... **21,850.00**

**Cheese mold,** cylindrical w/applied handle, molded rim & body, daubed w/manganese on a red body w/clear lead glaze, 4½" d., 3¾" h., 19th c., Pennsylvania ................................... **575.00**

**Coffeepot,** cov., cylindrical body w/applied molded spout & handle, domed lid w/flattened finial, fine manganese "tortoiseshell" decoration on red body w/clear lead glaze, 9" h., stamped John Bell, Waynesboro, Franklin County, Pennsylvania, ca. 1850-80 ........... **7,475.00**

**Creamer,** jug-form, ovoid body w/flat rim & small rim spout, loop handle, applied relief decoration of a Chinaman w/parasol & an East Indian w/parrot in a hoop, basketweave molded handle & spout, impressed pseudo-Chinese mark, Staffordshire, England, ca. 1755, 3" h. (spout chips)................... **747.00**

**Figural group,** dog resting on an alligator atop a turtle, label on underside "George S. McKerin Collection of American Potter No. 685," 19th ca., "Master Hobo Potter," Pennsylvania, 5" h. (ILLUS. below) .. **13,800.00**

**Flowerpot & saucer,** tapering cylindrical, the coggle rim above applied ovoid decorations w/light maganese speckled glaze, 19th c., Pennsylvania, 8¼" d., 8½" h............ **288.00**

**Flowerpot & saucer,** tapering cylindrical w/ruffled rim, glazed beige w/daubs of brown, Anthony Wise Baecher, Winchester, Virginia, ca. 1848-89, 7½" d., 7" h....................... **322.00**

*Redware Figural Group*

**hurn,** hand-decorated butterfly, salt glaze, sidewall stamped, 6 gal., signed (ILLUS. bottom previous page) ............................................. **1,250.00**

**hurn,** hand-decorated butterfly, salt glaze, unsigned, 6 gal...................... **450.00**

**ookie jar,** cov., cattail design, "Cookies," yellowish orange glaze (ILLUS. below).................................. **225.00**

**rock,** white-glazed stoneware, 4" wing & oval stamp, 2 gal.................... **250.00**

**rock,** white-glazed stoneware, small wing, 9½" d., 2 gal. ........................... **45.00**

**rock,** white-glazed stoneware, Nebraska advertising, 3 gal. (ILLUS. top next column) .................. **395.00**

**rock,** white-glazed stoneware, two birch leaves, Union oval stamp, 10¼" d., 3 gal...................................... **60.00**

**rock,** white-glazed stoneware, 4" wing, eared handles, Red Wing oval stamp, 13" d., 6 gal. ........................... **55.00**

**rock,** white-glazed stoneware, 4" wing, bailed handles, Red Wing oval stamp, 17" d., 12 gal. ....................... **110.00**

**rock,** white-glazed stoneware, bailed handles, 5" wing, Red Wing Oval stamp, 21" d., 30 gal. ........................ **185.00**

**uspidor,** "German"-style, white-glazed stoneware, w/incised design & blue bands, unsigned (ILLUS. middle next column) ......................... **475.00**

**ot water bottle,** leaf motif, brown, bottom signed Red Wing .................. **245.00**

**ot water bottle,** leaf motif, brown, unsigned ............................................. **85.00**

**ar,** cov., white-glazed stoneware, wire bailed handle, Hazel Pure Food Co., pure leafe lard stamp, 5 lbs....... **205.00**

**ug,** brown-glazed shoulder, advertising, "Red Wing Union Stoneware Co., Red Wing, Minn.," 3¼" h. (ILLUS. bottom next column) .. **575.00**

*Cattail Design Cookie Jar*

*Three Gallon Red Wing Crock*

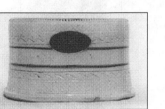

*German-style Cuspidor*

*Brown Glazed Red Wing Jug*

**Jug,** brown top, salt glaze bottom, North Star bottom marking, 1 gal. (ILLUS. top next page) ..................... **195.00**

**Jug,** syrup, white-glazed stoneware, cone-shaped shoulder, signed "Minnesota Stoneware, Red Wing, Minnesota," 1 gal. ............................... **75.00**

**Jug,** white shoulder, advertising "Creamery Package Mfg. Co. - Manufactures - Creamery & Dairy - Supplies - Minneapolis, Minn. - Poison-Acid," no wing, 1 gal. (ILLUS. middle next page) .................. **95.00**

---

Courtesy Christie's, New York, New York

*Various Redware Figurals*

**Jar,** cov., wide ovoid body w/narrow molded rim, eared shoulder handles, slip glaze w/dark splotches, early 19th c., New England, 9" h. (chips)... **2,990.00**

**Jar,** bulbous ovoid body tapering to flared rim, tooled lines & applied shoulder handles, rich amber glaze w/splotches of dark brown 8¼" h. (wear & chips).................................. **275.00**

**Jar,** tapering cylindrical body w/slightly protruding lip, tooled band, mottled amber glaze, old label on base "Bought at Farm Sale, Stony Creek, Edinburg, Va.," 8⅜" h. (small chips) .. **192.00**

**Jar,** bulbous ovoid body tapering to a wide, slightly flaring rim, tooled lines & applied eared handles, dark brown splotches on rich amber glaze, 8¾" h. (wear & chips & hairline around foot) ...................................... **275.00**

**Meat roaster,** scoop-shaped, w/applied finger crimped rim, strap handle & end spout, greenish amber glaze, 12" l. ..... **220.00**

**Model of a dog,** recumbent Boxer w/articulated claws & collar, glazed w/ivory slip sprinkled w/iron oxide, George A. Wagner Pottery, Weissport, Carbon County, Pennsylvania, ca. 1875-96 (ILLUS. No. 5)................................................ **1,840.00**

**Model of a squirrel,** seated & eating a nut, articulated tail, oval base w/floral stamp & punched border, "Master Hobo Potter," Pennsylvania, ca. 1830-50, 5" h. (ILLUS. No. 2) .. **3,220.00**

**Mug,** child's, enameled decoration of flowers shaded pink, black & shaded green w/black rim, 2¼" h. .................. **93.00**

**Pipe holder,** cov., three-footed, cylindrical w/perforated lid & four pipe stands, daubed w/manganese on red body w/clear lead glaze, ca. 1875-96, George A. Wagner Pottery, Weissport, Carbon County, Pennsylvania, 4" h.. **2,760.00**

**Planter,** hanging-type, tapering cylindrical w/everted brim above the body w/four large applied medallions, over an acorn drop finial speckled w/manganese powder on a red body w/clear lead glaze, ca. 1883, George S. Freshley, Lebanon, Pennsylvania, 9½" d................................................ **575.00**

**Plate,** 8½" d., center sgraffito design w/drummer & fife player, white slip stylized flowers on green & brown ground, coggled rim, probably by Jacob Medinger, Montgomery County, Pennsylvania, 1856-1932.... **990.00**

**Preserving jar,** domed cover, ovoid w/flared lip, dark tan glaze, impressed "M.C.25" on bottom, overall 11¼" h. (wear, chips & glued rim chip) ........... **275.00**

**Rattle,** model of a water spaniel, recumbent, articulated ears, haunches & tail, floral-stamped oval base, red body sprinkled w/manganese powder, w/clear glaze, "Master Hobo Potter," Pennsylvania, ca. 1830-1850, 4" h. (ILLUS. No. 4)................................ **4,025.00**

**Shaving mug,** baluster-form on circular foot, soap receptacle, applied strap handle, w/clear lead glaze, 19th c., Pennsylvania, 4¼" h. .............................................. **230.00**

**Teapot,** cov., Astbury-type, spherical body on three short feet, the molded rim w/a domed cover, an angled spout & D-form handle, decorated w/cream trim & florals & berries in relief, Staffordshire, England, ca. 1735, 3¾" h. (rim nicks on body, inner lid collar restored) .................... **920.00**

**Wall pocket,** punch-decorated rim & large applied medallions, arched back stamped "G.S. Freshley/Lebanon," unglazed, painted orange, ca. 1883, Lebanon, Pennsylvania, 10½" h. ........ **748.00**

**Wall pocket,** scalloped back centering an applied medallion flanked by applied foliate medallions above the pocket w/large applied medallion & embossed rim w/green & brown glaze daubs on an ochre glaze, ca. 1883, George S. Freshley, Lebanon, Pennsylvania, 14½" l. .......................... **518.00**

**Whistle,** figural Dachshund, barking, w/whistle in tail, applied eyes & ears red glaze w/manganese slip decoration, 4⅝" h., Jesiah Shorb, West Manheim Township, York County, Pennsylvania, 19th c. (ILLUS. No. 3, previous page) ....... **3,680.00**

**Whistle/rattle,** figural bird w/incised wings, red glaze w/daubs of green & brown, Bucks County, Pennsylvania, ca. 1800-15, 3⅛" h. (ILLUS. No. 1, previous page) ................................. **2,530.00**

# RED WING

*Various potteries operated in Red Wing, Minnesota from 1868, the most successful being the Red Wing Stoneware Company, organized in 1878. Merged with other local potteries through the years, it became known as Red Wing Union Stoneware Company in 1894, and was one of the largest producers of utilitarian stoneware items in the United States. After the decline in the popularity of stoneware products, an art pottery line was introduced to compensate for the loss and this was reflected in a new name for the company, Red Wing Potteries, Inc., in 1930. Stoneware production ceased entirely in 1947, but vases, planters, cookie jars and dinnerwares of art pottery quality continued in production until 1967 when the pottery ceased operation altogether.*

## Art Pottery

*Red Wing Ashtray*

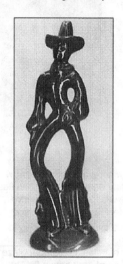

*Red Wing Cowboy*

*Art Deco Design Vase*

**Ashtray,** wing-shaped, marked "Red Wing Potteries 75th Anniversary 1878-1953", 7⅜" l. (ILLUS. top)........ **$65.00**

**Cookie Jar,** cov., yellow chef, marked w/Red Wing Pottery stamp ................. **95.00**

**Figure of a cowboy,** burnt sienna glaze, 11" h. (ILLUS. middle) .............. **65.00**

**Planter,** 'The Muse', green, figure of woman w/harp & deer, marked "Red Wing USA #B-2507," 13¾" l. ............ **105.00**

**Planter,** swan-shaped, green, marked "Red Wing USA #259," 5⅛" l. ............. **28.00**

**Vase,** Art Deco design, spherical body w/three swirled squared small openings around the sides, green matte, 6" h. (ILLUS. bottom previous page) ................................ **62.00**

*Red Wing Art Pottery Vase*

**Vase,** 7½" h., four embossed peacock on a green glaze, marked Union Stoneware Co. (ILLUS.) .................... **85.00**

**Vase,** 8⅞" h., bud, green, Old Red Winged Pottery stamped .................... **95.00**

## Stoneware

*Note: Beater jars had inside round bottoms for convenient household necessities & were issued by different stores for their advertising.*

*Stoneware Beater Jar*

**Beater Jar,** white-glazed stoneware w/blue bands, "Red Wing Beater Jar, Eggs-Cream, Salad Dressing (ILLUS.) ............................................. **125.00**

*Greek Key Bowl*

**Bowl,** 8" d., Greek Key motif, blue white glaze (ILLUS.) ..................

**Bowl,** 8" d., stoneware, paneled stoneware, Advertising Swanson Nelson, Chisago City ..................

**Bowl,** 9" d., spongeware, paneled stoneware ......................................

**Bowl,** 11" d., spongeware, paneled stoneware ......................................

**Butter crock,** low white-glazed stoneware, "10 lbs.," signed Minnesota Stoneware Co. ..........

*Saffron Casserole Dish*

**Casserole dish,** cov., Saffron ware (ILLUS.) .......................................

**Churn,** salt glaze, cobalt blue markings, no lid, 4 gal.................

**Churn,** white-glazed stoneware, la wing, red oval wing stamp below wing, 5 gal. ...............................

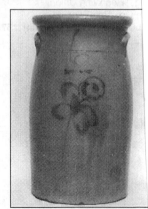

*Hand-decorated Churn*

*North Star Jug*

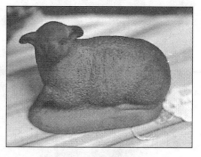

*Model of Sheep*

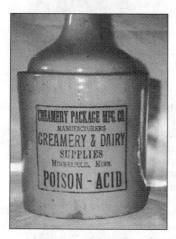

*Poison Advertising Jug*

*Cherry Band Design Pitcher*

**Jug,** white-glazed shoulder, 4" wing,
Red Wing oval stamp ........................ **90.00**

**Jug,** white-glazed stoneware,
beehive-shaped, 4" wing, Red Eing
oval stamp, 5 gal. ........................... **295.00**

**Koverware,** white-glazed stoneware,
stamped, placed inside of crock to
keep contents submerged in brine,
13¾" d., 15 gal. ............................... **190.00**

**Model of a sheep,** "lunch hour piece,"
rare (ILLUS. top) ............................. **325.00**

**Mug,** beer, blue bands, Red Wing
Stoneware ........................................ **42.00**

**Pitcher,** 9¼" h., Cherry Band design,
blue & white glaze (ILLUS. bottom) .. **100.00**

**Poultry feeder,** white-glazed
stoneware pottery drinking fount &
buttermilk feeder, bell-shaped, 1 qt.,
rare, 2 pcs. (ILLUS. right, top
next page) ....................................... **260.00**

**Poultry feeder,** white-glazed
stoneware fount & buttermilk feeder,
bell-shaped, ½ gal., 2 pcs. (ILLUS.
left, top next page) ........................... **125.00**

*Union Stoneware Jug*

**Jug,** white-glazed stoneware,
beehive-shaped, "wing" & oval Union
stamp, 3 gal. (ILLUS.) ...................... **285.00**

*Red Wing Poultry Feeders*

*Wall Salt Box with Sponge Band*

*Red Wing Water Cooler*

**Salt box,** cov., wall-type, sponge band design (ILLUS. middle previous column) ............................................ **950.00**

**Water cooler,** cov., white glazed stoneware, 4" wing & Red Wing oval stamp, reads "Water Cooler," bailed handles, bar handled cover, 9¾" d., 3 gal. (ILLUS. bottom previous column) ............................................ **475.00**

**Water cooler,** cov., white glazed stoneware, small wing, Red Wing oval stamp, bailed handles, bar handled cover, 10¼" d., 4 gal. .......... **650.00**

**Water cooler,** cov., white glazed stoneware, 4" wing, Red Wing oval stamp, bailed handles, bar handle cover, 13½", 10 gal. ......................... **625.00**

## ROCKINGHAM WARES

*An earthenware pottery was first established on the estate of the Marquis of Rockingham in England's Yorkshire district about 1745 and occupied by a succession of potters. The famous Rockingham glaze of mottled brown, somewhat resembling tortoiseshell , was introduced about 1788 by the Brameld Brothers, and was well received. During the 1820s, porcelain manufacture was added to the production and fine quality china was turned out until the pottery closed in 1842. The popular Rockingham glaze was subsequently produced elsewhere, including*

Bennington, Vermont, and at numerous other U.S. potteries. We list herein not only wares produced at the Rockingham potteries in England, distinguishing porcelain wares from the more plentiful earthenware productions, but also include items from other potteries with the Rockingham glaze. Also see: BENNINGTON.

**Bottle,** figural "Coachman," mottled dark brown glaze, 8⅞" h. ............... **$357.00**

**Bottle,** figural Mr. Toby seated on barrel, overall mottled dark brown glaze, 9¼" h. ................ **77.00**

**Mixing bowl,** mottled dark brown glaze, 10¾" d., 4¾" h. (wear & interior flakes) .................. **115.00**

**Pitcher,** 7" h., cylindrical body w/molded rim & pinched spout, angled handle, mottled dark brown glaze .................................................. **72.00**

**Pitcher,** 7½" h., cov., squatty bulbous body tapering to flat rim w/pinched spout, flat cover w/knob finial, C-form handle, mottled dark brown glaze (chip on lid & minor flakes on pitcher).............................................. **127.00**

**Pitcher,** 10" h., cov., cylindrical body tapering to rim, domed cover w/knob finial, relief-molded sheaf & grain design, integral spout, applied relief-molded handle (small flakes & lid has chips on underside of lip) ........... **220.00**

**Pitcher,** 11½" h., mottled dark brown glaze, 19th c. ..................................... **345.00**

**Plates,** 8" d. rayed centers w/scalloped rims, mottled dark brown glaze, pr. ............................... **220.00**

**Teapot,** cov., relief-molded figure of a Chinaman on each side, swan's neck spout & applied curved handle, 9½" h. (chips).................................... **165.00**

**Umbrella stand,** cylindrical brown & white relief-molded tree bark body, w/relief-molded ivy branch & leaves, red interior, 20½" h. .......................... **110.00**

**Vegetable dish,** open, oblong, octagonal w/wide flanged rim, mottled dark brown glaze 10⅜" l. (wear & minor edge flakes).............. **137.00**

## ROOKWOOD

*Considered America's foremost art pottery, the Rookwood Pottery Company was established in Cincinnati, Ohio in 1880, by Mrs. Maria Nichols Longworth Storer. To* accurately record its development, each piece carried the Rookwood insignia, or mark, was dated, and, if individually decorated, was usually signed by the artist. The pottery remained in Cincinnati until 1959 when it was sold to Herschede Hall Clock Company and moved to Starkville, Mississippi, where it continued in operation until 1967.

*A private company is now producing a limited variety of pieces using original Rookwood molds.*

**Book ends,** model of horse head, deep celadon green glaze, impressed "M.H. McDonald," 1954, 6¼" h., pr. ....................................... **$275.00**

**Book ends,** model of an owl, matte ivory glaze, No. 2655, 6" h., pr. ........ **288.00**

**Book ends,** Rookwood Rook on book, matte blue glaze, No. 2274, 1921, 7" h., pr............................ **400.00 to 425.00**

**Clock w/relief-molded panther on base,** glossy black, No. 7039, 1950, 6 x 7 x 8".......................................... **550.00**

**Dish,** round, four-footed, square rim handles, decorated w/carved florals w/dripping matte glazes of red, yellow & purple over a mottled blue ground, No. 2080, 1917, C.S. Todd, 3 x 6½"..................................... **450.00**

**Ewer,** wide flattened base & long corseted neck w/shaped rim, decorated w/dogwood blossoms in yellow w/green leaves on a shaded orange to brown ground, Standard glaze, No. 715, 1894, Mary Nourse, 5¾" d., 6¼" h. ................................. **468.00**

**Jar,** cov., jeweled porcelain, wide ovoid body tapering to a short cylindrical neck w/fitted flat cover, decorated w/an overall thick Butterfat glaze w/a finely dotted design of large blue & brown birds & large trees w/red & purple blossoms amid green foliage, lemon yellow ground, No. 2818, 1928, E. T. Hurley........ **15,400.00**

**Jar,** cov., the squat body resting on three leafy feet, blossom-molded lid, rich matte brown glaze, No. 2016, 1912, 4½" d., 2¼" h. ........................ **330.00**

**Jar,** cov., green Coramandel glaze, No. 6286, Edward Abel, 5" h. .......... **275.00**

**Mug,** slightly tapering cylindrical body w/loop handle, decorated w/ear of corn & husk in yellow & brown, Standard glaze, impressed & incised artist initials, Elizabeth H. Lincoln, 1899, No. 587c, 3" d., 4⅝" h.,........... **173.00**

*Rookwood
Tea Set*

**Pitcher,** 4¼" h., 5¼" w., tri-cornered, decorated w/a stylized incised Greek key band in red on a feathered Matte green ground, No. 341F, Anna Marie Valentien.......................................... **303.00**

**Plaque,** rectangular, decorated w/a mountainous landscape w/a lake & birch trees in the right foreground, Vellum glaze, Edward T. Hurley, 1946, in original frame, 11¾" w., 8¾" h. ........................................... **3,450.00**

**Plaque,** porcelain, rectangular, decorated in underglaze w/a Venetian boating scene, in shades of blue, turquoise & pink, Vellum glaze, w/original gilt frame, 1926, Carl Schmidt, 14¼ x 16⅜" .......... **12,650.00**

**Tea set:** cov. teapot, creamer & cov. sugar bowl; each w/spherical bodies on four feet, decorated w/yellow & brown pansies & green stems under a greenish brown Standard glaze, the creamer w/loop handle & pinched spout, w/wicker-wrapped swing bail handle, No. 616, Rookwood logo & artist's initials, ca. 1900, Caroline Steinle, the teapot spout repaired, 6" d., 4¾" h.,3 pcs. (ILLUS. above) ................................ **173.00**

**Tea tile,** embossed Phoenix bird, blue & white Matte glaze, No. 2047, 1925, 6" sq........................................ **175.00**

**Tea tile/trivet,** embossed Phoenix bird, multicolored Vellum glaze, No. 2047, 1921, 6" sq. ...................... **250.00**

**Tea tile/trivet,** embossed duck, multicolored Vellum glaze, No. 3301, 1924, 6" sq........................................ **250.00**

**Tea tile/trivet,** embossed parrot, multicolored Vellum glaze, No. 3077, 1929, 6" sq........................................ **250.00**

**Vase,** 3½" h., 2¾" d., miniature, porcelain, urn-shaped, decorated w/delicately painted yellow flowers & brown branches on a peach shading to cream ground, uncrazed, No. 662?, 1943, Margaret McDonald ...................................... **495.00**

**Vase,** 4¾" h., 4" d., bulbous body w/a molded flat mouth, embossed w/leaves in red on a light blue semi-matte ground, No. 7031, 1945, Wilhelmina Rehm ............................ **385.00**

**Vase,** 5½" h., 3" d., cylindrical, deeply incised arrowroot leaves & blossoms, deep dark green Matte glaze, No. 924, 1904, Rose Fescheimer...................................... **413.00**

**Vase,** 5¾" h., 2¾" d., tapering cylinder, decorated w/pink roses, green leaves & brown thorny stems on a grey shading to cream ground, Vellum glaze, No. 950F, 1905, Fred Rothenbusch .................................... **825.00**

**Vase,** 6½" h., 7" d., squatty bulbous body w/flat narrow rim, decorated w/white, yellow & pink Dogwood on a bluish green ground, Vellum glaze, Rookwood logo, artist initials, No. 906C, V, ca. 1907, Edward Diers (ILLUS. right, top next page) ......... **1,380.00**

**Vase,** 6½" h., 2½" d., cylindrical w/tapering rim, decorated w/butterflies on a brown to gold ground, Standard glaze, No. 941E, 1906, William Hentschel ................... **495.00**

**Vase,** 7¼" h., 5" d., ovoid w/wide mouth, decorated w/yellow & pink oak leaves & yellow acorns on a grey shading to cream ground, Iris glaze, No. 606D, 1908, Lenore Asbury ............................................. **1,320.00**

*Rookwood Vases*

**Vase,** 7½" h., 3½" d., cylindrical, scene of grey Canadian geese flying over celadon green tall grass, on a shaded bluish grey to yellow ground, Vellum glaze, nearly uncrazed, No. 952E, 1911, Kataro Shirayamadani.............................. **7,150.00**

**Vase,** 7½" h., 3½" d., expanding cylinder w/rounded shoulder & wide mouth, panoramic landscape w/tall brown trees against a meandering blue river, blue & bright green foliage, purple mountains & a light blue sky, Vellum glaze, No. 2039, 1916, Patty Conant........................ **2,750.00**

**Vase,** 7½" h., 3½" d., tapering cylindrical sides w/a flaring base, the low angled shoulder tapering to a wide, flat mouth, decorated w/a winter landscape scene at twilight w/a shaded peach sky & bluish green trees, Vellum glaze, No. 1356E, 1917, Fred Rothenbusch................ **1,375.00**

**Vase,** 8" h., 4" d., ovoid w/short flaring rim, continuous landscape scene of trees w/green & brown foliage by a river, against a shaded blue sky, Vellum glaze, uncrazed, No. 2544, 1930, Edward Diers...................... **2,310.00**

**Vase,** 8½" h., 3½" d., cylindrical w/gently sloping shoulder & wide mouth, decorated w/daffodils & green leaves on a brown to gold ground, Standard glaze, No. 932D, 1905, Carrie Steinle.......................... **605.00**

**Vase,** 8½" h., 5½" d., ovoid w/flaring foot & short neck, decorated w/incised stylized flowers & leaves in green, blue & brown on a deep burgundy to purple ground, mottled Matte glaze, No. 1044, 1912, Charles Todd.................................... **880.00**

**Vase,** 8¾" h., 4½" d., slender waisted cylindrical form w/a flat, flaring rim, decorated w/large pink flowers & green leaves on a bright yellow ground in a mottled Wax Matte glaze, No. 1357D, 1926, Elizabeth Barrett.............................................. **385.00**

**Vase,** 9½" h., 3¼" d., shouldered cylindrical body w/a low flaring mouth, incised w/stylized peacock feathers in green & blue glaze, Matte glaze, 1920, Elizabeth N. Lincoln ..... **550.00**

**Vase,** 9½" h., 3¾" d., tapering cylindrical body w/slightly flared rim, molded stylized roses under a Butterfat blue, green & red Matte glaze, No. 1660D, 1911, William Hentschel........................................ **550.00**

**Vase,** 10" h., slightly swelled cylindrical body w/short cylindrical neck w/flat rim, decorated w/light pink grapes & green vine on a green shaded to cream & yellow ground, Iris glaze, Rookwood logo, artist's initials, No. 786 C. W., ca. 1900, Sara Sax (ILLUS. above left)......... **1,150.00**

**Vase,** 10" h., waisted cylindrical form w/cupped drip pan & short cylindrical socket, teal ground, ca. 1924, No. 1356C (glaze skip on base) ....... **250.00**

**Vase,** 10" h., 4½" d., tapering cylinder w/narrow everted rim, decorated

w/incised stylized flowers drooping
down from the rim, dark blue against
a matte purple ground, mottled
Matte glaze, No. 1658D, 1912,
W. Hentschel ................................. **1,320.00**

**Vase,** 10¼" h., 3¾" d., slightly flaring
cylindrical body w/a shoulder
tapering to a short cylindrical neck,
decorated w/paper whites against a
shaded bluish grey to yellow ground,
Iris glaze, No. 946W, 1908, Sara
Sax ................................................. **4,400.00**

**Vase,** 10½" h., 3½" d., gently swelled
cylindrical body w/closed rim,
decorated w/large purple irises on
tall green stems on a shaded black
to lavender & green ground, Iris
glaze, No. 821, 1907, Sallie E.
Coyne ............................................ **3,575.00**

**Vase,** 11" h., 4" d., cylindrical w/short
collared neck, relief stepped panels
at each side, decorated w/yellow
daffodils & green leaves on a yellow
to green ground, Wax Matte glaze,
No. 2934, 1927, Elizabeth Lincoln .. **1,100.00**

**Vase,** 11" h., 4" d., gently swelled tall
cylindrical body, decorated w/large
soft pink roses on thorny green
stems on a shaded blue to ivory
ground, Vellum glaze, No. 951,
1927, Frederick Rothenbusch .......... **303.00**

**Vase,** 12" h., baluster-form body
w/flaring rim, shaded tan to grey
ground decorated w/dark red
dogwood blossoms, dark green
leaves & branches, fluorescent blue
highlights at lower half, Standard
glaze, No. 2272, 1924, Sara Sax
(minor glaze scratch) ..................... **2,530.00**

**Wall pocket,** wide flattened oblong
form w/a flat rim, embossed w/ivy in
green against a brown butterfat
ground, Matte glaze, No. 1389,
1921, 6" w., 8½" h............................ **330.00**

# ROSE MEDALLION - ROSE CANTON

*The lovely Chinese ware known as rose
Medallion was made through the past century
and into the present one. It features
alternating panels of people and flowers or
insects with most pieces having four
medallions with a central rose or peony
medallion. The ware is called Rose Canton if
flowers and birds or insects fill all the panels.
Unless otherwise noted, our listing is for Rose
Medallion ware.*

*Rose Medallion Bowl*

**Bowl,** 8¾" rectangular....................... **$176.00**

**Bowl,** 14½" d., exterior w/two
rectangular panels of figures within
gilt fret borders & two ogee shaped
panels of figures, the interior w/five
figural panels within gilt fret borders,
19th c. (ILLUS. above)................. **1,955.00**

**Canister w/slightly domed lid,**
5⅛"sq., 5⅝" h. ................................ **935.00**

*Rose Medallion Garden Seat*

**Garden seat,** barrel-shaped w/various
figural panels alternating w/floral
panels, decorated w/bands of raised
gold knobs & pierced circles, 19th c.,
minor enamel & gilt wear, 18¾" h.
(ILLUS.) ........................................ **2,300.00**

**Jar,** cov., bulbous ovoid body tapering
to a flat base, domed lid, 10" h. ........ **440.00**

**Plates,** 8½" d., set of 4...................... **209.00**

**Plates,** 9¾" d., pr. ............................... **66.00**

**Platter,** 16¼" l. (wear & minor flaking) .. **275.00**

**Serving dish,** kidney-shaped, 10¾" l. ... **385.00**

**Vases,** 10⅜" h., cylindrical body
tapering slightly to a long neck w/a
flared rim pr. (minor damage) ........ **1,210.00**

# ROSEVILLE

*Roseville Pottery Company operated in Zanesville, Ohio from 1898 to 1954 after having been in business for six years prior to that in Muskingum County, Ohio. Art wares similar to those of Owens and Weller Potteries were produced. Items listed here are by patterns*

*Roseville*

*Roseville Mark*

## APPLE BLOSSOM

*White apple blossoms in relief on blue, green or pink ground; brown tree branch handles.*

**Basket w/circular handle,** green ground, No. 309-8", 8" h... **$235.00 to 250.00**
**Basket w/circular handle,** pink ground, No. 309-8" .......... **185.00 to 200.00**
**Basket,** hanging-type, blue ground, 8" h. (no chains) ................................ **260.00**
**Basket,** hanging-type, pink ground, 8" ....................................................... **183.00**
**Bowl,** 4" d., green ground, No. 300-4"... **80.00**
**Bowl,** 4" d., pink ground, No. 333-4" .............................. **100.00 to 110.00**
**Bowl,** 6½" d., 2½" h., flat handles, pink ground, No. 326-6" ...................... **83.00**
**Bowl,** 10" d., green ground, No. 329-10" ......................................... **62.00**
**Bowl,** blue ground, No. 330 ................ **185.00**
**Candleholders,** squatty, green ground, No. 351-2", 2" h., pr. .............. **70.00**
**Console bowl,** blue ground, No. 330 ... **185.00**
**Console set:** 12" bowl & pair of 2" h. candleholders; blue ground, Nos. 331-12" & 351, 3 pcs. ...................... **225.00**
**Creamer & open sugar bowl,** blue ground, pr. ......................................... **155.00**
**Ewer,** No. 317-7", 7" h. ....................... **100.00**
**Ewer,** pink ground, No. 318-15", 15" h. .............................. **450.00 to 500.00**
**Jardiniere,** two-handled, green ground, No. 302-5", 5" h. .................... **94.00**
**Teapot,** cov., blue or green ground, No. 371-P ....................... **250.00 to 300.00**
**Vase,** 7" h., blue ground, No. 373-7" .............................. **145.00 to 155.00**
**Vase,** bud, 7" h., base handles, flaring rim, green ground, No. 379-7" ............ **90.00**
**Vase,** 7" h., asymmetrical rim & handles, pink ground, No. 382-7" .......... **80.00 to 85.00**

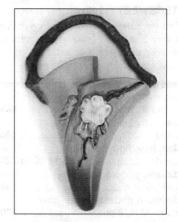

*Apple Blossom Wall Pocket*

**Vase,** 18" h., floor-type, pink ground, No. 393-18" ..................................... **475.00**
**Wall pocket,** conical w/overhead handle, blue ground, No. 366-8", 8" h. ................................................. **230.00**
**Wall pocket,** conical w/overhead handle, pink ground, No. 366-8¼", 8½" h. (ILLUS. above) ...... **285.00 to 290.00**

## BANEDA (1933)

*Band of embossed pods, blossoms and leaves on green or raspberry pink ground.*

**Bowl,** 10" d., 3½" h., two-handled, raspberry pink ground ...... **300.00 to 325.00**
**Jardiniere,** two-handled, raspberry pink ground, 4" h. .............................. **243.00**
**Jardiniere,** green ground, 7" h. ................................. **565.00 to 600.00**
**Urn,** footed, green ground, 6" h. ......... **425.00**
**Urn,** small rim handles, raspberry pink ground, 7" h. ...................................... **475.00**
**Vase,** 4½" h., tiny rim handles, sharply canted sides, raspberry pink ground, No. 603-4" ....................... **465.00 to 500.00**
**Vase,** 5½" h., rounded base w/sharply canted sides w/two handles at rim, raspberry pink ground ...... **235.00 to 250.00**
**Vase,** 6" h., two-handled, elongated ovoid, green ground No. 588-6"........ **375.00**
**Vase,** 7" h., two-handles at shoulder, cylindrical, green ground... **325.00 to 350.00**
**Vase,** 7" h., two handles at shoulder, cylindrical, raspberry pink ground ..... **450.00**
**Vase,** 9" h., cylindrical w/short collared neck, handles rising from shoulder to beneath rim, green ground ............................. **750.00 to 800.00**

## BITTERSWEET (1940)

*Orange bittersweet pods and green leaves on a grey blending to rose, yellow with terra cotta, rose with green or solid green bark-textured ground; brown branch handles.*

**Basket** w/pointed overhead handle & conforming rim, grey ground, No. 809-8", 8" h. ...................... **148.00**

**Basket,** hanging-type, grey ground ............................................. **140.00**

**Basket,** hanging-type, yellow ground ............................ **215.00 to 225.00**

**Jardiniere,** green ground, No. 801-6", 6" h. ...................................... **138.00**

**Jardiniere & pedestal base,** grey ground, 8" h., 2 pcs. .......................... **900.00**

**Pedestal base,** green ground ............................ **275.00 to 300.00**

**Vase,** 10" h., handles at midsection, scalloped rim, green ground, No. 885-10". ..................................... **120.00**

**Vases,** bud, 7" h., green ground, No. 879-7", pr. ................................. **150.00**

**Wall pocket,** curving conical form w/overhead handles continuing to one side, green ground, No. 866-7", 7" h. ................................................. **280.00**

## BLACKBERRY (1933)

*Band of relief clusters of blackberries with vines and ivory leaves accented in green and terra cotta on a green textured ground.*

**Basket,** hanging-type, 6½" d., 4½" h. .............................. **520.00 to 550.00**

**Basket,** No. 336-8", 8" h. (professional repair to handle only) .. **595.00**

**Bowl,** 8" d., tiny rim handles ............... **350.00**

**Jardiniere,** two-handled, 8" d., 6" h. .... **525.00**

**Jardiniere & pedestal base,** overall 28" h., 2 pcs. ................................. **3,550.00**

*Blackberry Vase*

**Vase,** 6" h., semi-ovoid base continuing to wide neck .................... **300.00**

**Vase,** 6" h., two handles at midsection (ILLUS. above) ................. **425.00 to 450.00**

**Vase,** 6" h., two-handled ..................... **535.00**

**Vase,** 8" h., two-handled, ovoid w/short collared neck ....................... **695.00**

**Vase,** 12½" h., 8¼" d., handles rising from shoulder to rim ...................... **1,220.00**

## BLEEDING HEART (1938)

*Pink blossoms and green leaves on shaded blue, green or pink ground.*

**Console bowl,** green ground, No. 382-10" (ILLUS. below) .............. **120.00**

**Pitcher,** 8" h., asymmetrical w/high arched handle, blue ground, No. 1323 .......................................... **550.00**

**Rose bowl,** pink ground, No. 377-4", 4" h. ................................................. **155.00**

**Vase,** double bud, 4" h., gate-form, No. 140-4". ..................................... **150.00**

**Vase,** 6½" h., base handles, green ground, No. 964-6" ........................... **139.00**

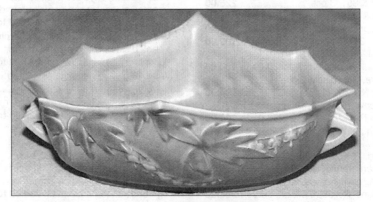

*Bleeding Heart Console Bowl*

**Vase,** 8" h., base handles, green
ground, No. 969-8" ........................... **200.00**

**Wall pocket,** angular pointed
overhead handle rising from
midsection, blue ground,
No. 1287-8", 8½" h. ........................... **400.00**

### BUSHBERRY (1948)

**Basket w/low overhead handle,**
asymmetric rim, russet ground,
No. 372-12", 12" h. ........................... **350.00**

**Basket,** hanging-type w/original
chains, blue ground, No. 465-5",
7" ...................................................... **400.00**

**Basket,** hanging-type w/original
chains, russet ground, No. 465-5",
7" h. ................................................. **350.00**

**Bowl,** 4" h., two-handled, globular,
green ground, No. 411-4" ................... **70.00**

**Bowl,** 4" h., two-handled, globular,
russet ground, No. 411-4" .................. **80.00**

**Bowl,** 10" d., blue ground, No. 415-10" .. **150.00**

**Candleholders,** large flaring handles,
russet ground, No. 1147, 2" h., pr....... **88.00**

**Console bowl,** green ground,
No. 1-10", 10" l.............................. **180.00**

**Console bowl,** russet ground,
No. 1-10", 10" l.............................. **170.00**

**Console bowl,** russet ground,
No. 415-10", 10" d. .......................... **143.00**

**Console bowl,** end handles, russet
ground, No. 385-10", 13" l... **100.00 to 115.00**

**Cornucopia-vase,** russet ground,
No. 154-8", 8" h. .............................. **130.00**

**Cornucopia-vase,** double, russet
ground, No. 155-8", 6" h... **100.00 to 115.00**

**Ewer,** russet ground, No. 2-10",
10" h. ............................................... **200.00**

**Ewer,** cut-out rim, russet ground,
No. 3-15", 15" h. ............... **365.00 to 400.00**

**Flower frog,** russet ground, No. 45 .... **130.00**

**Jardiniere,** two-handled, russet
ground, No. 657-4", 4" h. .................... **90.00**

**Flowerpot w/saucer,** russet ground,
No. 658-5", 5" h. .............................. **230.00**

**Jardiniere,** russet ground, No. 657-3",
3" h. ................................................. **60.00**

**Jardiniere & pedestal base,** russet
ground, No. 657-8", 2 pcs. .. **865.00 to 900.00**

**Pedestal,** russet ground..................... **238.00**

**Pitcher,** water, blue ground, No. 1325
(chip repair) ..................................... **263.00**

**Pitcher,** water, russet ground,
No. 1325 ......................................... **400.00**

**Sand jar,** russet ground, No. 778-14",
14" h. ............................................ **1,350.00**

**Umbrella stand,** double handles, blue
ground, No. 779-20", 20½" h. ........... **580.00**

**Urn,** two-handled, russet ground,
No. 411-6", 6" h. ............... **120.00 to 130.00**

**Vase,** 4" h., conical w/tiny rim
handles, russet ground, No. 28-4" ...... **50.00**

**Vase,** double bud, 4½" h., gate-form,
green ground, No. 158-4½" (ILLUS.
below)................................................. **175.00**

**Vase,** 6" h., asymmetrical side
handles, cylindrical w/low foot,
russet ground, No. 29-6".................... **130.00**

**Vase,** 6" h., two-handled, russet,
No. 30-6"............................................ **110.00**

**Vase,** 6 " h., pedestal base, russet,
No. 156-6".......................................... **110.00**

**Vase,** 7" h., two-handled, russet
ground, No. 31-7" ............................. **150.00**

**Vase,** 7" h., high-low handles,
cylindrical, low foot, green ground,
No. 32-7"............................................ **155.00**

*Bushberry Double Bud Vase*

**Vase,** 7" h., high-low handles,
cylindrical, low foot, russet ground,
No. 32-7"........................................... **130.00**

**Vase,** 8" h., russet ground, No. 33-8".. **130.00**

**Vase,** 8" h., cylindrical w/flattened disc
base above low foot, large curving
angular handles, blue ground,
No. 34-8"........................................... **195.00**

**Vase,** 8" h., pedestal base, squared
side handles, compressed body
w/wide neck, russet ground,
No. 157-8"......................................... **130.00**

**Vase,** 12½" h., large asymmetrical
side handles, bulging cylinder
w/flaring foot, green ground,
No. 38-12"......................................... **265.00**

**Vase,** 14½" h., asymmetrical side
handles, russet ground, No. 39-14".. **420.00**

**Wall pocket,** high-low handles,
green ground, No. 1291-8",
8" h................................... **230.00 to 250.00**

## CARNELIAN I (1910-15)

*Matte glaze with a combination of two colors
or two shades of the same color with the darker
dripping over the lighter tone or heavy and
textured glaze with intermingled colors and some
running.*

**Vase,** 7" h., slightly compressed
globular body w/wide slightly flared
neck, angled handles from lower
sides to base of rim, dark & light
blue.................................................... **135.00**

## CARNELIAN II (1915)

*Matte glaze with a combination of two
colors or two shades of the same color with the
darker dripping over the lighter tone or heavy
and textured glaze with intermingled colors
and some running.*

**Planter,** oblong, footed, w/heavy
molded ribs evenly spaced around
sides, angled loop handles, 3 x 8".... **105.00**

**Urn,** purple & rose, 5" h................. **200.00**

**Urn,** green & red, 8" h....................... **400.00**

**Vase,** 6" h., arched handles,
compressed globular form, blue &
green ................................................ **142.00**

**Vase,** 7" h., expanding cylinder,
sharply defined shoulder w/small
handles, intermingled shades of
green or raspberry pink, each........... **230.00**

**Vase,** 7" h., large handles, blue &
green .............................. **150.00 to 200.00**

**Vase,** 10" h., canted sides w/short
sharp shoulder, flat pierced handles
rising from shoulder to rim,
intermingled shades of green .......... **145.00**

**Wall pocket,** intermingled shades of
pink & green, 8" h............. **265.00 to 285.00**

## CLEMATIS (1944)

*Clematis blossoms and heart-shaped green
leaves against a vertically textured ground*

**Basket w/overhead handle,** pedestal
base, blue ground, No. 389-10",
10" h. ................................................ **190.00**

**Basket w/overhead handle,** pedestal
base, green ground, No. 389-10",
10" h. ................................................ **155.00**

**Bowl,** 5" h., No. 667-5" ........................ **90.00**

**Bowl,** 8" d., No. 457-8" ........................ **75.00**

**Bowl,** 10" d., two-handled, brown or
green ground, No. 6-10"... **100.00 to 125.00**

**Candlesticks,** green ground, No.
1159-4½", 4½" h., pr......................... **65.00**

**Compound vase** (triple opening
style), brown & gold ground,
No. 192-5", 5" h. ................................ **75.00**

**Creamer,** blue ground, No. 5 ............... **65.00**

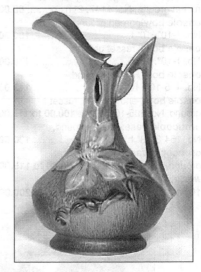

*Clematis Ewer*

**Ewer,** brown ground, No. 17-10",
10" h. (ILLUS.) ................................. **125.00**

**Ewer,** brown ground, No. 16-8", 8" h.... **190.00**

**Flower arranger,** brown ground,
No. 50, 4½" h..................................... **55.00**

**Flower arranger,** base handles, three
openings for flowers, blue ground,
No. 102-5", 5½" h. ............... **60.00 to 70.00**

**Flowerpot w/saucer,** blue ground,
No. 668-5", 5½" h. ............................ **115.00**

**Jardiniere,** green ground, No. 667-5",
5" h. .................................................... **70.00**

**Vase,** double bud, 5" h., two cylinders joined by a single clematis blossom, brown ground, No. 194-5"... **85.00 to 100.00**

**Vase,** 6" h., two-handled, blue ground, No. 103-6"........................................ **125.00**

**Vase,** 7" h., blue ground, No. 105-7"..... **80.00**

**Vase,** 7" h., green ground, No. 105-7" .. **90.00**

**Vase,** 7⅞" h., 5½" d., bulbous body, low side handles, tall neck, blue ground, No. 106-7" ............................ **65.00**

**Vase,** 9" h., brown ground, No. 110-9" .. **125.00**

**Vase,** 14" h., green ground, No. 26-14"........................................ **395.00**

**Wall pocket,** angular side handles, blue ground, No. 1295-8", 8½" h. ..... **179.00**

**Wall pocket,** angular side handles, brown ground, No. 1295-8", 8½" h. .. **140.00**

**Wall pocket,** angular side handles, green ground, No. 1295-8", 8½" h. .............................. **155.00 to 200.00**

## COLUMBINE (1940s)

*Columbine blossoms and foliage on shaded ground—yellow blossoms on blue, pink blossoms on pink shaded to green and blue blossoms on tan shaded to green.*

**Basket w/overhead handle,** blue ground, No. 366-8", 8" h... **190.00 to 200.00**

**Book end planters,** tan shaded to green ground, No. 8, 5" h., pr. .......... **295.00**

**Bowl,** 3" h., squatty w/small handles at shoulder, pink ground, No. 655-3" .. **75.00**

**Candlestick,** No. 1145-2½", 2½" h....... **38.00**

**Console bowl,** stepped handles rising from rim, tan ground, No. 404-10" ..................... **100.00 to 125.00**

**Jardiniere,** two-handled, blue ground, No. 655-3", 3" h. ................................ **66.00**

**Rose bowl,** two-handled, blue ground, No. 400-6", 6" d. .............................. **195.00**

**Urn-vase,** blue ground, No. 150-6", 6" h. .................................................... **98.00**

**Urn-vase,** pink ground, No. 150-6", 6" h. .................................................. **135.00**

**Vase,** 7" h., tan ground, No. 16-7" ........ **85.00**

**Vase,** 12" h., angular handles at midsection, flat disc base, brown ground, No. 25-12" .......... **290.00 to 295.00**

**Wall pocket,** squared flaring mouth, conical body w/curled tip, blue ground, No. 1290-8", 8½" h. ............. **348.00**

**Wall pocket,** squared flaring mouth, conical body w/curled tip, pink ground, No. 1290-8", 8½" h. ............. **310.00**

**Wall pocket,** squared flaring mouth, conical body w/curled tip, tan ground, No. 1290-8", 8½" h. ............. **495.00**

## COSMOS (1940)

*Embossed blossoms against a wavy horizontal ridged band on a textured ground—ivory band with yellow and orchid blossoms on blue, blue band with white and orchid blossoms on green or tan.*

**Basket w/overhead handle,** blue ground, No. 357-10", 10" h. .............. **300.00**

**Basket w/pointed overhead handle,** pedestal base, tan ground, No. 358-12", 12" h. .......... **340.00 to 350.00**

**Bowl,** 8" d., green ground, No. 370-8".. **150.00**

**Bowl,** 12" d., low, tan ground, No. 373-12"...................................... **100.00**

**Console set:** 10" bowl & pair of candlesticks; green ground, No. 371-10", 3 pcs. .......................... **525.00**

**Jardiniere,** two-handled, blue or green ground, No. 649-6", 6" h., each ........ **225.00**

**Rose bowl,** blue ground, No. 375-4", 4" h. .................................................. **150.00**

**Rose bowl,** green ground, No. 376-6", 6" h. .................................................. **295.00**

**Urn-vases,** blue ground, No. 135-8", 8" h., pr. ................................................ **210.00**

**Vase,** double bud, two slender cylinders joined by bridge, No. 133-4½" ............ **155.00**

**Vase,** 4" h., two-handled, globular base & wide neck, tan ground, No. 944-4" .... **85.00**

**Vase,** 5" h., loop handles rising from footed base, chalice-form, blue ground, No. 945-5" .......................... **115.00**

**Vase,** 5" h., loop handles rising from footed base, chalice-form, green ground, No. 945-5" .......................... **50.00**

**Vase,** 6" h., base handles, blue ground, No. 947-6" .......................... **175.00**

**Wall pocket,** circular overhead handle, blue ground, No. 1285-6", 6½" h. .............................. **360.00 to 375.00**

**Wall pocket,** double, tan ground, No. 1286-8", 8½" h. ......................... **500.00**

## CREMONA (1927)

*Relief-molded floral motifs including a tall stem with small blossoms and arrowhead leaves, wreathed with leaves similar to Velmoss or a web of delicate vines against a background of light green mottled with pale blue or pink with creamy ivory.*

**Vase,** 5" h., pink ground, No. 352-5"..... **90.00**

## DAHLROSE (1924-28)

*Band of ivory daisy-like blossoms and green leaves against a mottled tan ground.*

**Bowl,** 10" oval, two-handled .............. **125.00**

**Jardiniere,** tiny rim handles, 6" d., 4" h........................................................ **175.00**

**Vase,** 8" h., two handles rising from midsection to rim ............................. **160.00**

## DAWN (1937)

*Incised spidery flowers—green ground with blue-violet tinted blossoms, pink or yellow ground with blue-green blossoms, all with yellow centers.*

**Rose bowl,** tab handles at sides, square base, yellow ground, No. 315-4", 4" d. .............................. **175.00**
**Vase,** 8" h., slender cylinder w/tab handles below rim, square foot, pink ground, No. 828-8" .......................... **165.00**

## DOGWOOD II (1928)

*White dogwood blossoms & black branches against a smooth green ground.*

*Dogwood Basket*

**Basket,** oval, open overhead branch handle, 6" h. (ILLUS.) ...................... **175.00**

## DONATELLO (1915)

*Deeply fluted ivory and green body with wide tan band embossed with cherubs at various pursuits in pastoral settings.*

**Ashtray,** 3" h. ........................................ **75.00**
**Compote,** 5" h., bowl w/slightly curved sides on flared stem ............. **75.00 to 85.00**
**Compote,** 9" d. ..................................... **150.00**
**Jardiniere,** No. 575-7", 7" h. ............... **165.00**
**Jardiniere,** 8" h. ............................... **200.00**
**Jardiniere,** 9" h. ............................... **210.00**
**Jardiniere & pedestal base,** 8" h., jardiniere & 15" h. pedestal, 2 pcs. (ILLUS. top next column) .................. **700.00**
**Vase,** 10" h., expanding cylinder ......... **150.00**
**Vase,** 12" h., two-handled, green ground, No. 112-12" ......................... **165.00**

*Donatello Jardiniere & Pedestal*

## FERRELLA (1930)

*Impressed shell design alternating with small cut-outs at top and base; mottled brown or mottled turquoise and red glaze.*

**Bowl,** 9½" d., 4¼" h., deep flaring sides w/rolled rim, on a flared foot, the bowl rim w/a band of small pierced triangles above a band of larger pierced ovals, pierced triangles also around the foot, turquoise & red glaze, w/flower frog, 2 pcs. ................................................ **438.00**
**Bowl,** 12" d., 7" h., low foot, brown glaze, No. 212-12 x 7" ...................... **600.00**
**Vase,** 5" h., two-handled, turquoise & red glaze, No. 500-5" ....... **410.00 to 425.00**
**Vase,** 9" h., sharply compressed globular base, large handles rising from midsection to below rim, brown glaze ................................................. **465.00**
**Vase,** 9" h., two-handled, ovoid w/collared neck, brown glaze, No. 507-9" ........................................ **475.00**

## FOXGLOVE (1940s)

*Sprays of pink and white blossoms embossed against a shaded matte finish ground.*

**Console bowl,** blue ground, No. 422-10", 10" l. ............. **105.00 to 115.00**
**Console bowl,** pink ground, No 423-12", 12" l. .............................. **95.00**

**Console bowl,** blue ground,
No. 425-14", 14" l............................ **220.00**
**Ewer,** pink ground, No. 4-6½", 6½" h... **160.00**
**Ewer,** green ground, No. 5-10", 10" h. .. **225.00**
**Flower pot** w/attached saucer, blue
ground, No. 660-5", 5" h. ................. **130.00**
**Jardiniere,** two-handled, blue ground,
No. 569-3", 3" h. ............................. **55.00**
**Jardiniere,** blue ground, No. 659-5",
5" h. ................................................ **125.00**

*Foxglove Jardiniere & Pedestal*

**Jardiniere & pedestal base,** blue
ground, jardiniere 8" h., 2 pcs.
(ILLUS.) ........................................... **850.00**
**Rose bowl,** two-handled, green
ground, No. 418-4", 4" h. .................. **135.00**
**Tray,** open rim handles, shaped oval,
blue ground, 11" l............................. **175.00**
**Tray,** open rim handles, shaped oval,
pink ground, 11" l............................. **130.00**
**Vase,** 4" h., angular side handles, pink
ground, No. 42-4" .............................. **85.00**
**Vase,** 8" h., blue ground, No. 48-8"..... **140.00**

## FREESIA (1945)

*Trumpet-shaped blossoms and long slender
green leaves against wavy impressed lines—
white and lavender blossoms on blended green;
white and yellow blossoms on shaded blue or
terra cotta and brown.*

**Basket w/low overhead handle,** blue
ground, No. 390-7", 7" h. .................. **200.00**
**Basket w/low overhead handle,**
green ground, No. 390-7", 7" h. ........ **165.00**

*Freesia Vase*

**Basket,** hanging-type, blue ground,
No. 471-5" ...................... **220.00 to 230.00**
**Bowl,** 14" d., blue or green ground,
No. 468-12", each............................ **145.00**
**Bowl,** 16½" l., two-handled, green
ground, No. 469-14" ......................... **150.00**
**Cookie jar,** cov., two-handled, blue
ground, No. 4-8", 10" h. ................... **438.00**
**Cookie jar,** cov., two-handled, terra
cotta ground, No. 4-8", 10" h. .......... **485.00**
**Creamer,** green ground, No. 6-C ......... **75.00**
**Ewer,** squatty, green ground,
No. 19-6", 6" h. ............................... **120.00**
**Ewer,** blue ground, No. 20-10", 10" h... **210.00**
**Ewer,** terra cotta ground, No. 20-10",
10" h. .............................................. **140.00**
**Jardiniere,** tiny rim handles, blue
ground, No. 669-4", 4" h. ................... **95.00**
**Jardiniere,** tiny rim handles, green
ground, No. 669-4", 4" h. ................... **85.00**
**Jardiniere,** rim handles, green or terra
cotta ground, No. 669-6", 6" h.,
each ................................. **210.00 to 225.00**
**Jardiniere & pedestal base,** blue
ground, No. 669-8", 2 pcs................. **825.00**
**Pitcher,** 10" h., swollen cylinder,
green ground, No. 20-10" ................. **163.00**
**Vase,** bud, 7" h., handles rising from
compressed globular base, long
slender tapering neck, green or terra
cotta ground, No. 195-7",
each ................................... **70.00 to 80.00**
**Vase,** 7" h., two-handled, fan-shaped,
terra cotta, No. 200-7" ..................... **125.00**
**Vase,** 8" h., globular base & flaring
rim, handles at midsection, blue
ground, No. 122-8" .......................... **175.00**

**Vase,** 9½" h., pointed handles at midsection, blue or green ground, No. 123-9", each .............................. **195.00**

**Vase,** 10½" h., No. 125-10" (ILLUS. top previous page) ............................ **151.00**

**Vase,** floor-type, blue or terra cotta ground, No. 129-18", each.. **475.00 to 500.00**

**Vase,** 10½" h., expanding cylinder w/handles rising from raised base, green ground, No. 125-10" .............. **150.00**

**Vase,** 15" h., two-handled, terra cotta ground, No. 128-15" ........................ **385.00**

**Vase,** 18" h., blue ground, No. 129-18" ..................................... **625.00**

**Wall pocket,** angular handles, green ground, No. 1296-8", 8½" h. ............. **201.00**

**Window box,** two-handled, terra cotta ground, No. 1392-8", 10½" l. ............ **100.00**

## FUCHSIA (1939)

*Coral pink fuchsia blossoms and green leaves against a background of blue shading to yellow, green shading to terra cotta or terra cotta shading to gold.*

**Candleholders,** blue ground, No. 1132, 2" h., pr. (ILLUS. below) ......... **105.00**

**Candlestick,** domed base, tubular form raised on ring, blue ground, No. 1133-5", 5½" h. .......................... **245.00**

**Ewer,** green ground, No. 902-10", 10" h. ................................. **300.00**

**Flower frog,** blue ground, No. 37 .............................. **110.00 to 125.00**

**Jardiniere,** two-handled, terra cotta ground, No. 645-3", 3" h. .................... **80.00**

**Jardiniere,** two-handled, blue ground, No. 645-4", 4" h. .............................. **150.00**

**Jardiniere,** blue ground, No. 645-7", 7" h. ............................................ **495.00**

**Jardiniere & pedestal base,** blue ground, overall 24" h., 2 pcs. (ILLUS. top next column) ................. **925.00**

**Pitcher w/ice lip,** 8" h., terra cotta ground, No. 1322-8" ......... **400.00 to 425.00**

*Fuchsia Jardiniere & Pedestal*

**Vase,** 6" h., ovoid w/handles rising from shoulder to rim, green ground, No. 892-6" ........................................ **120.00**

**Vase,** 8" h., handles rising from flat base to shoulder, terra cotta ground, No. 897-8" ........................................ **200.00**

**Vase,** 8" h., footed bulbous base w/tapering cylindrical neck, loop handles, blue ground, No. 898-8" ..... **295.00**

**Vase,** 8" h., globular w/large angular handles, blue ground, No. 91-8" ....... **175.00**

**Vase,** 9" h., two-handled, terra cotta ground, No. 900-9" .......................... **250.00**

**Vase,** 12" h., two-handled rising from above base to neck, blue ground, No. 903-12" ...................................... **95.00**

**Vase,** 18" h., floor-type, blue ground, No. 905-18" ..................................... **914.00**

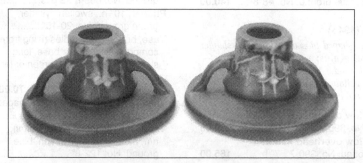

*Fuchsia Candleholders*

## FUTURA (1928)

*Varied line with shapes ranging from Art Deco geometrics to futuristic. Matte glaze is typical although an occasional piece may be high gloss.*

**Pot,** square body w/canted sides on a low footed square base, relief-molded flowering branch decoration, mottled blue & green, 3½" h. ............ **290.00**

**Vase,** 6" h., rectangular handles at midsection, cylindrical w/short tapering ridged neck, terra cotta & green, No. 381-6" ............................ **425.00**

**Vase,** 6¼" h., rectangular pillow-shape, No. 81-5 x 1½ x 5" ................ **475.00**

**Vase,** 7" h., sharply canted base, handles rising from shoulder to below rim of long cylindrical stepped neck, grey-green & tan, No. 382-7" .. **245.00**

**Vase,** 7" h., spherical body w/short cylindrical neck, square slanted base, No. 387-7" ............................................. **550.00**

*Futura Vase*

**Vase,** 7" h., 5½" d., high domed & stepped beehive-form body below a wide & flaring neck joined by two short strap handles to the shoulder, shaded cream to blue body w/green leaves around the body, unmarked, No. 403-7" (ILLUS.) .......... **700.00 to 720.00**

**Vase,** 8" h., 3¾" d., star-shaped slender tapering body on stepped circular base, No. 385-8" ................. **475.00**

**Vase,** 8" h., upright rectangular form on rectangular foot, stepped neck, long square handles, No. 386-8" ...... **725.00**

**Vase,** 8" h., No. 386-8" ....... **530.00 to 550.00**

**Vase,** 8" h., ovoid w/short collared neck, lightly embossed floral branch at shoulder, incised rings at midsection, deep rosy beige shading to sand white & black to beige w/touch of blue at branch, No. 428-8" ........................... **400.00**

**Vase,** triangular shaped body tapering to stepped round base, leafy branch design, No. 388-9" ........................... **650.00**

**Vase,** 9¼" h., 5¼" d., angular handles rising from bulbous base to rim, sharply stepped neck, shaded dark to light green high-gloss glaze, w/paper label, No. 389-9" ................ **700.00**

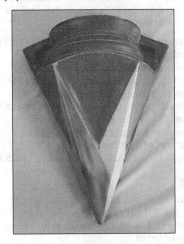

*Futura Wall Pocket*

**Wall pocket,** canted sides, angular rim handles, geometric design in blue, yellow, green & lavender on brown ground, No. 1261-8", 6" w., 8¼" h. (ILLUS.) ................ **435.00 to 475.00**

## GARDENIA (1940s)

*Large white gardenia blossoms and green leaves over a textured impressed band on a shaded green, grey or tan ground.*

**Bowl,** 3" d., green ground, No. 657-3" .. **59.00**

**Bowl,** 10" d., grey ground, No. 628-10" ... **95.00**

**Bowl,** 12" d., green ground, No. 630-12" ................................................... **145.00**

**Console bowl,** grey ground, No. 632-11", 11" l. ............................. **145.00**

**Ewer,** globular base, tan ground, No. 616-6", 6" h. ............................. **65.00**

**Jardiniere & pedestal base,** grey ground, 8" h. .................................... **750.00**

**Vase,** 8" h., grey ground, No. 684-8" .. **140.00**

**Vase,** 8" h., tan ground, No. 684-8" .... **165.00**

## IMPERIAL (1924)

*Brown pretzel-twisted vine, green grape leaf and cluster of blue grapes in relief on green and brown bark-textured ground.*

**Basket w/overhead handle,** straight
sides, 6" h. .......................................... **125.00**
**Bowl,** 7" d., pierced rim handles,
rounded sides, No. 71-70..... **50.00 to 75.00**
**Bowl,** 9" d., two-handled....................... **80.00**
**Bowl,** 10" d., 4" h., two-handled............ **62.00**

## IMPERIAL II (1924)

*Varied line with no common characteristics. Many of the pieces are heavily glazed with colors that run and blend.*

**Bowl,** 12½" d., 5" h., blue ground ....... **275.00**
**Candleholders,** deep dished base,
slender candle nozzle, No. 1077-4",
4" h. ................................ **200.00 to 220.00**
**Vase,** 5" h., tapering ovoid ringed
body ................................. **200.00 to 225.00**
**Vase,** 7" h., hemispherical w/sloping
shoulder & short collared neck, blue
glaze w/white trim at neck,
No. 474-7" ........................................ **425.00**

## IRIS

*White or yellow blossoms and green leaves on rose blending with green, light blue deepening to a darker blue or tan shading to green or brown.*

**Book ends,** blue ground, No. 5, pr. .... **265.00**
**Bowl,** 5" d., two-handled, rose
ground, No. 359-5" ............................ **95.00**
**Candlesticks,** rose ground, No. 1134,
pr. ...................................................... **110.00**
**Cornucopia-vase,** rose ground,
No. 131-6", 6" ................................... **125.00**
**Rose bowl,** rose ground, No. 358-6",
6" h. ................................................... **220.00**
**Vase,** 4" h., base handles, rose
ground, No. 914-4" ............................ **65.00**
**Vase,** 4" h., base handles, tan ground,
No. 914-4"........................................ **110.00**
**Vase,** 6½" h., two handles rising from
shoulder of globular base to
midsection of wide neck, blue
ground, No. 917-6" ........................... **110.00**
**Vase,** 6½" h., No. 917-6".................... **107.00**
**Vase,** bud, 7" h., two-handled, tan
ground, No. 918-7" ........................... **170.00**
**Vase,** 7" h., blue ground, No. 919-7"... **175.00**
**Vase,** 10" h., blue ground,
No. 927-10"....................................... **310.00**

**Vase,** 15" h., two large handles rising
from shoulder to rim, blue ground,
No. 929-15"....................................... **850.00**

## IXIA (1930s)

*Embossed spray of tiny bell-shaped flowers and slender leaves—white blossoms on pink ground; lavender blossoms on green or yellow ground.*

**Bowl,** 4" d., pointed closed handles at
rim, green ground, No. 326-4" ......... **135.00**
**Bowl,** 7" d., green ground, No. 329-7".. **125.00**
**Candleholders,** two-light, green
ground, No. 1127, 3" h., pr. ............. **110.00**
**Flower frog,** yellow ground, No. 34 ...... **90.00**
**Vase,** 8½" h., tall cylindrical body
w/stepped buttress handles up the
sides from the round foot, green or
yellow ground, No. 856-8" ............... **135.00**
**Vase,** 8½" h., tall cylindrical body
w/stepped buttress handles up the
sides from the round foot, pink
ground, No. 856-8" ........................... **100.00**
**Vase,** 12" h., closed handles,
cylindrical, green ground,
No. 864-12"....................................... **265.00**
**Vase,** 12" h., closed handles,
cylindrical, yellow ground,
No. 864-12" ..................... **290.00 to 300.00**

## JONQUIL (1931)

*White jonquil blossoms and green leaves in relief against textured tan ground; green lining.*

*Jonquil Jardiniere & Pedestal*

*Jonquil Vase*

**Basket** w/pointed overhead handle
rising from shoulder, 9" h. ................. **375.00**
**Bowl,** 3" h., large down-turned
handles, No. 523-3" ......... **130.00 to 150.00**
**Bowl,** 4" d. pink ground, No. 289-4" .... **175.00**
**Bowl,** 4¾" d., 4½" h., two-handled ...... **125.00**
**Jardiniere & pedestal base,** overall
29" h., 2 pcs. (ILLUS. bottom
previous page) ............................. **1,900.00**
**Urn-vase,** large side handles, No.
525-5", 5" h. (ILLUS. above) ............. **150.00**
**Vase,** 6½" h., large handles, bulbous
base ................................................. **380.00**
**Vase,** 6½" h., wide ovoid body w/side
handles ............................................. **300.00**
**Vase,** 8" h., ovoid body tapering to a
flaring neck, down-turned shoulder
handles, No. 529-8" ......................... **325.00**
**Vase,** 9½" h., slender handles at
midsection ....................................... **150.00**
**Vase,** 12" h., two handles beneath
flared rim, slightly ovoid ................... **495.00**

### JUVENILE (1916 on)

*Transfer-printed and painted on creamware with nursery rhyme characters, cute animals and other motifs appealing to children.*

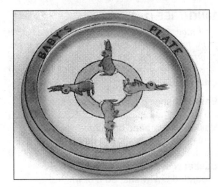

*Juvenile Feeding Dish*

**Cup,** sunbonnet girl ............................ **150.00**
**Feeding dish w/rolled edge,** nursery
rhyme, "Little Jack Horner," 6" d. ...... **125.00**
**Feeding dish w/rolled edge,** sitting
rabbits, 6½" d. .................................... **93.00**
**Feeding dish w/rolled edge,** nursery
thyme, "Hickory, Dickory, Dock,"
8" d. (slight decal wear) ................... **135.00**
**Feeding dish w/rolled edge,**
standing rabbits, 8" d. (ILLUS.
bottom previous column) ................... **88.00**
**Pitcher,** 3½" h., chicks ....................... **85.00**
**Plate,** 8" d., sunbonnet girl ................. **200.00**

### LAUREL (1934)

*Laurel branch and berries in low-relief with reeded panels at the sides. Glazed in deep yellow, green shading to cream or terra cotta.*

**Vase,** 6" h., tapering cylinder w/wide
mouth, closed angular handles at
shoulder, terra cotta, No. 667-6" ....... **190.00**
**Vase,** 6" h., angular shoulder handles,
terra cotta, No. 668-6" ...................... **170.00**
**Vase,** 8" h., deep yellow, No. 672-8" ... **225.00**
**Vase,** 9¼" h., terra cotta, No. 674-9¼" .. **220.00**

### LUFFA (1934)

*Relief-molded ivy leaves and blossoms on shaded brown or green wavy horizontal ridges.*

**Console bowl,** green ground, 14" l.
(nick to handle) ................................. **150.00**
**Jardiniere,** green ground, 8" h. .......... **550.00**
**Jardiniere & pedestal base,** green,
overall 24½" h., 2 pcs. .................... **1,000.00**
**Sand jar,** 14" h. ............................... **1,500.00**
**Vase,** 6" h., two-handled, cylindrical,
brown ground .................................... **186.00**
**Vase,** 7" h., 7" w., bulbous, brown
ground .............................................. **155.00**
**Vase,** 8" h., angular rim handles,
canted sides, brown ground ............. **295.00**
**Vase,** 8½" h., tapering cylinder w/two
handles rising from shoulder to
beneath rim, brown ground .............. **265.00**
**Vase,** 8½" h., tapering cylinder w/two
handles rising from shoulder to
beneath rim, green ground .............. **325.00**

### MAGNOLIA (1943)

*Large white blossoms with rose centers and black stems in relief against a blue, green or tan textured ground.*

**Basket,** hanging-type, green ground,
No. 469-5" ........................................ **225.00**

*Magnolia Cider Set*

**Bowl,** No. 449-10", 10" l......................... **95.00**

**Bowl,** 10" d., two-handled, blue or tan
ground, No. 450-10", 10" l., each...... **150.00**

**Candlesticks,** angular handles rising
from flat base to midsection of stem,
blue ground, No. 1157-4½", 5" h., pr.... **75.00**

**Cider set:** 7" pitcher & four 3" mugs;
green ground, Nos 132-7" & 3-3",
5 pcs. (ILLUS. above)...................... **775.00**

**Cornucopia-vase,** green ground,
No. 184-6", 6" h. ................................. **85.00**

**Creamer,** blue or tan ground, No. 4-C,
each.................................................... **75.00**

**Flowerpot w/saucer,** blue or green
ground, No. 666-5", 5" h., each ........ **125.00**

**Jardiniere,** No. 665-3", green ground,
3" h. .................................................... **55.00**

**Jardiniere,** two-handled, tan ground,
No. 665-4", 4" h. ................................. **80.00**

**Sugar bowl,** blue ground, No. 4-S........ **50.00**

**Tea set:** cov. teapot, creamer & sugar
bowl; blue ground, Nos. 4, 4C & 4S,
3 pcs. ............................................... **325.00**

**Tea set:** cov. teapot, creamer & sugar
bowl; green ground, Nos. 4,
4C & 4S, 3 pcs................................. **250.00**

**Vase,** 6" h., two-handled, green
ground, No. 87-6" .............................. **95.00**

**Vase,** 8" h., globular w/large angular
handles, blue ground, No. 91-8"....... **195.00**

**Vase,** 8" h., blue ground, No. 92-8"....... **99.00**

**Vase,** 10" h., green ground,
No. 95-10"........................................ **175.00**

**Vase,** 15" h., two-handled, bulbous, blue
ground (ILLUS. top next column)....... **229.00**

**Vase,** 16" h., floor-type, green ground,
No. 99-16"........................................ **495.00**

*Magnolia Vase*

## MING TREE (1949)

*Embossed twisted bonsai tree topped with puffy foliage—pink-topped trees on mint green ground, green tops on white ground and white tops on blue ground; handles in the form of gnarled branches.*

**Basket,** hanging-type, blue ground,
6" h. ................................................. **200.00**

**Basket** w/overhead branch handle,
rounded body w/shaped rim, green
ground, No. 508-8", 8" h. ................. **145.00**

**Basket** w/overhead branch handle,
rounded boy w/shaped rim, white
ground, No. 508-8" ........................... **165.00**

**Basket** w/overhead branch handle, ruffled rim, green ground, No. 509-12", 13" h. ............... **275.00**

**Console set:** 10" l. bowl & pair of candleholders; green ground, Nos. 528 & 551, 3 pcs. .............. **210.00**

**Planter,** blue ground, No. 568-8", 4 x 8½". ............... **65.00**

**Vase,** 6½" h., single branch handle, green or white ground, No. 572-6". ............... **100.00 to 110.00**

**Wall pocket,** overhead branch handle, blue ground, No. 566-8", 8½" h. ......... **255.00**

**Window box,** blue or green ground, No. 569-10", 4 x 11", each ............... **115.00**

## MONTACELLO (1931)

*White stylized trumpet flowers with black accents on a terra cotta band—light terra cotta mottled in blue or light green mottled and blended with blue backgrounds.*

**Basket,** squatty cushion form body w/wide cylindrical neck w/flaring rim, high pointed loop handle from shoulder to shoulder ............... **115.00**

**Vase,** 4" h., sharply compressed globular base, handles rising from shoulder to rim, blue ground, No. 555-4". ............... **175.00**

**Vase,** 5" h., two handles at mid-section, green ground, No. 556-5". .... **295.00**

**Vase,** 7" h., ovoid w/shoulder handles & collared neck, terra cotta ground, No. 562-7". ............... **475.00**

**Vase,** 10½" h., expanding cylinder w/small base handles, terra cotta ground, No. 565-10" ............... **575.00**

## MORNING GLORY (1935)

*Stylized pastel morning glory blossoms and twining vines in low relief against a white or green ground.*

**Basket** w/high pointed overhead handle, globular body, green ground, 10½" h. ............... **725.00**

**Bowl-vase,** two-handled, white ground, 7" d., 4¼" h. ............... **325.00**

## MOSS (1930s)

*Spanish moss draped over a brown branch with green leaves against a background of ivory, pink or tan shading to blue.*

**Bowl,** 4" d., pink ground, No. 289-4". ... **150.00**

**Candlesticks,** angular handles at midsection, blue or tan ground, No. 1107-4½", 4½" h., pr., each ......... **65.00**

**Vase,** 6" h., large open angular handles, pink ground, No. 774-6" ............... **220.00 to 250.00**

**Vase,** 6" h., angular handles, blue ground, No. 775-6" ............... **135.00**

**Vase,** pillow-type, 8" h., pink shading to green, No. 781-8" ............... **245.00**

**Vase,** 9" h., pink ground, No. 783-9" ... **350.00**

## PEONY (1942)

*Peony blossoms in relief against a textured swirling ground—yellow blossoms against rose shading to green, brown shading to gold or gold with green; white blossoms against green.*

*Peony Vase*

**Basket w/overhead handle,** green ground, No. 378-10", 10" h. ............... **230.00**

**Basket w/overhead handle,** rose ground, No. 378-10", 10" h. ............... **220.00**

**Book ends,** gold ground, No. 11, 5½" h., pr. ............... **245.00**

**Cornucopia-vase,** rose ground, No. 170-6", 6" h. ............... **150.00**

**Console bowl,** gold ground, No. 4-10", 10" l. ............... **295.00**

**Ewer,** gold ground, No. 8-10", 10" h. .. **310.00**

**Ewer,** rose ground, No. 7-6", 6" h. ...... **120.00**

**Jardiniere,** gold ground, No. 661-6", 6" h. ............... **295.00**

**Model of a conch shell,** rose ground, No. 436, 9½" w. ............... **130.00**

**Mug,** green ground, No. 2-3½", 3½" h. . **115.00**

**Teapot,** cov., rose ground, No. 3 ........ **185.00**

**Tea set:** cov. teapot, creamer & sugar bowl; green ground, Nos. 3, 3C & 3S, the set ............... **335.00**

**Tray,** single rim handle, rose ground,
8" sq. ............................................. **110.00**
**Tray,** gold ground, 11" l. ...................... **125.00**
**Vase,** 4" h., base handles, green
ground, No. 57-4" ............................. **60.00**
**Vase,** 7" h., gold ground, No. 60-7" ....... **85.00**
**Vase,** 7" h., rose ground, No. 60-7" .... **155.00**
**Vase,** 8" h., No. 62-8" ...................... **155.00**
**Vase,** 9" h., gold ground, No. 64-9" ..... **125.00**
**Vase,** 10" h., handles rising from
midsection to below flaring rim, rose
ground, No. 66-10" (ILLUS. previous
page) ............................................. **225.00**
**Vase,** 18" h., gold ground, No. 70-18" ... **495.00**

## PINE CONE (1931)

*Realistic embossed brown pine cones and green pine needles on shaded blue, brown or green ground. (Pink is extremely rare.)*

*Pinecone Jardiniere & Pedestal*

**Ashtray,** brown ground, No. 499,
4½" l. .............................................. **140.00**
**Basket w/overhead branch handle,**
disc base, flaring rim, green ground,
No. 338-10", 10" h. ......................... **325.00**
**Basket w/overhead branch handle,**
boat-shaped, brown ground,
No. 410-10", 10" h. ......................... **425.00**
**Basket w/overhead branch handle**
rising from midsection of cylindrical
body w/shaped base, disc foot,
green ground, No. 353-11", 11" h. ..... **375.00**

**Basket,** hanging-type, brown ground,
No. 352-5", 5" h. ............................. **345.00**
**Bowl,** 9" d., blue ground, No. 321-9" .. **390.00**
**Candleholder,** blue ground, 2½" h. .... **180.00**
**Jardiniere,** two-handled, globular,
blue ground, No. 632-3", 3" h. .......... **170.00**
**Jardiniere,** blue ground, No. 632-4",
4" h. .............................................. **265.00**
**Jardiniere,** two-handled, blue ground,
No. 632-6", 9" d., 6½" h. .................. **335.00**
**Jardiniere,** brown ground, 12" h. ...... **2,250.00**
**Jardiniere & pedestal base,** green
ground, No. 402-8", jardiniere 8" h.,
overall 25" h., 2 pcs. ...................... **1,575.00**
**Jardiniere & pedestal base,** blue
ground, No. 632-10", jardiniere
10" h., 2 pcs. (ILLUS. previous
column) .......................................... **1,800.00**
**Pitcher,** 9" h., brown ground, No. 415-9" .. **395.00**

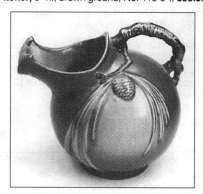

*Pine Cone Pitcher*

**Pitcher,** brown ground, No. 1321
(ILLUS.) ........................... **550.00 to 575.00**
**Planter,** single side handle rising from
base, blue ground, No. 124-5", 5" h. .. **178.00**
**Planter,** single side handle rising from
base, brown ground, No. 124-5",
5" h. .............................................. **151.00**
**Planter,** green ground, No. 261-6" ...... **275.00**
**Planter,** green ground, No. 456-6",
6" l. ............................................... **140.00**
**Plate,** wall-type, blue ground .............. **195.00**
**Plate,** wall-type, brown ground ........... **475.00**
**Rose bowl,** green ground, No. 261-6",
6" d. .............................................. **150.00**
**Sand jar,** blue ground, No. 776-14",
14" h. ............................................ **2,700.00**
**Sand jar,** green ground, No. 776-14",
14" h. ............................................ **1,600.00**
**Umbrella stand,** blue ground,
No. 777-20", 10" h. ......................... **2,400.00**
**Vase,** 6" h., blue ground, No. 748-6" ... **208.00**
**Vase,** 7" h., blue ground, No. 704-7" ... **255.00**

**Vase,** 7" h., green ground, No. 704-7".. **250.00**
**Vase,** 7" h., asymmetrical branch
handles, square base, blue ground,
No. 745-7"........................................ **325.00**
**Vase,** 7" h., No. 841-7"...................... **245.00**
**Vase,** 7" h., brown ground, No. 907-7" .. **100.00**
**Vase,** 8" h., brown ground, No. 114-8" .. **300.00**
**Vase,** 8" h., brown ground, No. 842-8" .. **615.00**
**Vase,** 8" h., green ground, No. 844-8" ... **290.00**
**Vase,** 8" h., pillow-type, brown
ground, No. 845-8" ......................... **250.00**
**Vase,** 8½" h., No. 490-8".................... **225.00**
**Vase,** 9" h., brown ground, No. 705-9".. **325.00**
**Vase,** 10" h., blue ground,
No. 709-10".................................... **435.00**
**Vase,** 10" h., green ground,
No. 709-10".................................... **325.00**
**Vase,** 10" h., blue ground, No. 711-10" .. **600.00**
**Vase,** 10" h., brown ground,
No. 711-10".................................... **395.00**
**Vase,** 10" h., conical w/base handles,
green ground, No. 747-10" .............. **285.00**
**Vase,** 12" h., blue ground,
No. 712-12".................................... **475.00**
**Vase,** 18½" h., floor-type, two-handled,
low foot, ovoid w/short neck & flaring
rim, No. 913-18"......... **1,250.00 to 1,300.00**
**Wall brackets,** brown ground, pr........ **550.00**
**Wall pocket,** double, brown ground,
No. 1273-8", 8½" h. ......................... **550.00**
**Wall pocket,** double, green ground,
No. 1273-8", 8½" h. ......................... **450.00**
**Wall pocket,** bucket-shaped, brown
ground .................................................. **655.00**
**Window box,** brown ground,
No. 431-15", 15" l., 3½" h. ............... **175.00**
**Window box,** green ground,
No. 431-15", 15" l., 3½" h. ............... **165.00**

## POPPY (1930)

*Embossed full-blown poppy blossoms, buds
and foliage—yellow blossoms on green, white
blossoms on blue or soft pink blossoms on a
deeper pink.*

**Basket,** hanging-type, two-handled,
blue ground, No. 358-5"................... **275.00**
**Bowl,** 5" d., blue ground, No. 336-5" .. **115.00**
**Candlesticks,** blue ground,
No. 1129-10", 10" h., pr. .................. **250.00**
**Ewer,** ornate cut-out lip, pink ground,
No. 866-10", 10" h. ........... **200.00 to 225.00**
**Jardiniere,** green, No. 642-6", 6" h..... **275.00**
**Jardiniere,** pink ground, No. 642-6",
6" h. .................................................. **225.00**
**Jardiniere,** loop handles at rim, green
ground, No. 335-6", 6½" h. ............... **220.00**

**Vase,** 6½" h., two-handled, ovoid,
blue ground, No. 867-6"................... **110.00**
**Vase,** 8" h., two-handled, pink ground,
No. 871-8"........................................ **225.00**

## PRIMROSE (1932)

*Cluster of long-stemmed blossoms and pod-
like leaves in relief on blue, pink or tan ground.*

**Jardiniere & pedestal base,** pink
ground, No. 634-10",
2 pcs.......................... **1,455.00 to 1,500.00**
**Vase,** 8" h., ovoid w/slender neck,
angular handles at shoulder, blue
ground, No. 767-8" ......................... **365.00**
**Wall pocket,** angular side handles,
blue ground, No. 1277-8", 8½" h. ..... **425.00**
**Bowl,** 10" d., turquoise blue ground,
No. 728-10"...................................... **100.00**

## ROSECRAFT (1916)

*Untrimmed classic shapes; glossy glazes.*

**Vase,** 7" h., compressed globular
form, arched handles, glossy black,
No. 311-7"........................................ **150.00**
**Vase,** 12" h., black glossy glaze,
No. 182-12"....................................... **225.00**

## SILHOUETTE (1952)

*Recessed shaped panels decorated with floral
designs or exotic female nudes against a combed
background.*

**Bowl,** 10" d. rose ground, No. 728-10".. **115.00**
**Candleholders,** sloping base, waisted
stem, florals, white, No. 751-3",
3" h., pr. ........................................... **130.00**
**Cornucopia-vase,** florals, tan,
No. 721-8", 8" h. ............................. **100.00**
**Cornucopia-vase,** florals, rose,
No. 721-8, 8" h.................................. **80.00**
**Ewer,** bulging base, florals, white,
No. 716-6", 6" h. ............................... **70.00**
**Rose bowl,** female nudes, tan,
No. 742-6", 6" h. ............................. **361.00**
**Vase,** 7" h., fan-shaped, female
nudes, tan, No. 783-7" ..... **330.00 to 375.00**
**Vase,** 8" h., urn-form, tapering ovoid
body raised on four angled feet on
a round disc base, wide slightly
flaring mouth, turquoise blue, No.
763-8".............................................. **425.00**
**Vase,** 14" h., globular base
w/expanding cylindrical neck w/fluted
rim, foliage, rose, No. 789-14".......... **225.00**

## SNOWBERRY (1946)

*Clusters of white berries on brown stems with green foliage over oblique scalloping, against a blue, green or rose background.*

**Ashtray,** round, shaded green ground, No. 1AT .............................. **110.00**

**Basket w/low pointed overhead handle,** shaded blue ground, No. 1BK7", 7" h................................ **161.00**

**Basket w/low pointed overhead handle,** shaded green ground, No. 1BK7", 7" h............................... **190.00**

**Basket w/overhead handle** curving from base to beneath rim on opposite side, curved rim, shaded green ground, No. 1BK-12", 12½" h. ............................................. **365.00**

**Book ends,** shaded rose ground, No. 1BE, pr....................... **200.00 to 220.00**

**Bowl,** 6" d., two-handled, green ground, No. 1BL1-6" ......................... **90.00**

**Candleholders,** squatty w/angular handles at shoulder, shaded blue ground, No. 1CS1-2", 2" h., pr. .......... **60.00**

**Console bowl,** pointed end handles, shaded green ground, No. 1BL1-10", 10" l...................................................... **100.00**

**Creamer & sugar bowl,** angular side handles, shaded rose ground, Nos. 1C & 1S, pr............................. **130.00**

**Jardiniere & pedestal base,** shaded rose ground, No. 1J-8", overall 25" h., 2 pcs....................................... **990.00**

**Pedestal base,** pink ground, 1P-8", 8" h. .................................................... **350.00**

**Rose bowl,** two-handled, shaded green ground, No. 1RB-5", 5" d. ....... **110.00**

**Vase,** 6" h., angular handles at midsection, shaded blue ground, No. 1V-6" ......................................... **95.00**

**Vase,** bud, 7" h., single base handle, asymmetrical rim, shaded rose ground, No. 1BV-7"........................... **60.00**

**Vase,** 9" h., base handles, shaded blue ground, No. 1V1-9" .................. **215.00**

**Vase,** 12" h., shaded green ground, No. 1V1-12" ...................................... **225.00**

**Vase,** 12" h., shaded rose ground, No. 1V1-12" ...................................... **215.00**

**Vase,** 12½" h., two-handled, ovoid w/flaring mouth, shaded rose ground, No. 1V1-12" ....................... **225.00**

**Vase,** 12" h., rose ground, No. 1V2-12" ...................................... **300.00**

**Vase,** 15" h., two-handled, shaded blue ground, No. 1V-15" .................. **450.00**

**Window box,** rose ground, No. 1WX-8", 8" l............................. **150.00**

## SUNFLOWER (1930)

*Long-stemmed yellow sunflower blossoms framed in green leaves against a mottled green textured ground.*

**Jardiniere,** 6" h................................... **900.00**

**Jardiniere & pedestal base,** 29" h., 2 pcs. ............................................. **5,500.00**

**Urn,** globular w/small rim handles, 4" h. ...................................................... **326.00**

**Urn,** straight sided, 5" h...................... **415.00**

*Sunflower Vase*

**Vase,** 5" h., two-handled, bulbous (ILLUS.) ............................ **325.00 to 350.00**

**Vase,** 5" h., cylindrical w/handles at midsection ....................................... **495.00**

**Vase,** 6" h., cylindrical w/tiny rim handles............................. **440.00 to 500.00**

**Vase,** 6" h., cylindrical body w/sharply angled rim handles ........................... **395.00**

**Wall pocket,** curved openwork double handle, 7½" h................................ **850.00**

## TUSCANY (1927)

*Simple forms with gently curving handles ending in leaf and grape clusters. Mottled finish found in shiny pink with pale bluish green leaves, overall greyish blue or dull turquoise.*

**Console bowl,** mottled pink, 14½" l...... **95.00**

**Flower frog,** mottled pink, 3" h. ........... **71.00**

**Vase,** 6" h., squared form w/large handles rising from the low foot to the flaring rim, mottled pink .............. **200.00**

**Vase,** 9" h., two-handled, globular base, short wide neck, mottled pink ... **135.00**

**Vase,** 9" h., two-handled, globular base, short wide neck, mottled dull turquoise......................................... **160.00**

**Vase,** 10" h., shoulder handles, bulbous, mottled green ..................... **125.00**

**Wall pocket,** long open handles, rounded rim, mottled pink, 8" h. ......... **225.00**

## WATER LILY (1940s)

*Water lily blossoms and pads against a horizontally ridged ground. White lilies on green lily pads against a blended blue ground, pink lilies on a pink shading to green ground or yellow lilies against a gold shading to brown ground.*

**Cookie jar,** cov., angular handles, blended blue ground, No. 1-8", 8" h. ................................. **345.00 to 375.00**

*Water Lily Cookie Jar*

**Cookie jar,** cov., angular handles, pink shading to green ground, No. 1-8", 8" h. (ILLUS.) ..................... **400.00**

**Ewer,** flared bottom, gold shading to brown ground, No. 10-6", 6" h. ......... **105.00**

**Ewer,** compressed globular base, gold shading to brown ground, No. 11-10", 10" h. ............................ **225.00**

**Ewer,** swollen cylindrical form on flat base, blended blue ground, No. 12-15", 15" h. .................... **370.00 to 400.00**

**Model of a conch shell,** gold shading to brown ground, No. 445-6", 6" h. (ILLUS. top next column) ... **110.00 to 120.00**

**Pedestal base,** brown ground, 16½" h. ... **258.00**

**Urn-vase,** blended blue ground, No. 175-8", 8" h. ............................... **85.00**

**Vase,** 6" h., cylindrical w/large angular side handles, blended blue ground, No. 72-6" ........................................... **90.00**

**Vase,** 6" h., waisted form w/large angular handles at mid-section, gold shading to brown ground, No. 73-6" ... **95.00**

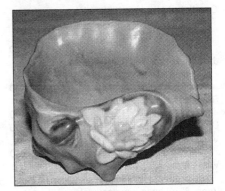

*Water Lily Conch Shell*

**Vase,** 6" h., gold shading to brown ground, No. 174-6" ............................. **75.00**

**Vase,** 8" h., two-handled, gold shading to brown, No. 76-8" ............. **155.00**

**Vase,** 8" h., two-handled, pink shading to green ground, No. 77-8" ............... **185.00**

**Vase,** 9" h., two large handles at midsection, low foot, gold shading to brown ground, No. 78-9" .................. **125.00**

**Vase,** 14" h., angular side handles, pink shading to green ground, No. 82-14" ...................................... **450.00**

**Vase,** 18" h., two-handled, ovoid w/wide mouth, pink shading to green ground, No. 85-18" .......................... **580.00**

## WHITE ROSE (1940)

*White roses and green leaves against a vertically combed ground of blended blue, brown shading to green or pink shading to green.*

**Basket** w/low pointed overhead handle, blended blue ground, No. 362-8", 7½" h. ............................. **166.00**

**Bowl,** 6" d., handled, pink shading to green ground, No. 389-6" .................. **95.00**

**Bowl,** 10" d., two-handled, pink shading to green ground, No. 392-10" ..................................... **155.00**

*White Rose Candleholder*

**Candleholders,** two-handled, low, pink shading to green ground, No. 1141, pr. (ILLUS. of one, bottom previous page) .................... **113.00**

**Jardiniere,** spherical, two-handled, brown shading to green ground, No. 653-8", 8" h. ............................. **775.00**

**Rose bowl,** blue ground, No. 388-7", 7" h. ................................................. **195.00**

**Urn-vase,** No. 147-8", 8" h.................. **225.00**

**Vase,** bud, 7" h., pink shading to green, No. 995-7" ............................ **100.00**

**Vase,** 8" h., base handles, blended blue ground, No. 984-8".................... **174.00**

**Vase,** 8" h., base handles, pink shading to green ground, No. 984-8".. **275.00**

**Vase,** 8½" h., handles rising from globular base to rim, blended blue, No. 985-8"........................................ **166.00**

**Vase,** floor-type, 15" h., blue ground (repair) ............................................. **270.00**

## WINCRAFT (1948)

*Shapes from older lines such as Pine Cone, Cremona, Primrose and others, vases with an animal motif, and contemporary shapes. High gloss glaze in bright shades of blue, tan, yellow, turquoise, apricot and grey.*

**Basket w/low overhead handle,** shaped rim, narcissus-type blossoms & foliage in relief on blue ground, No. 208-8", 8" h. .................. **140.00**

**Basket w/low overhead handle,** shaped rim, glossy chartreuse shading to brown, No. 208-8", 8" h... **175.00**

**Basket,** hanging-type, mottled glossy blue & green ..................................... **155.00**

**Book ends,** glossy tan, No. 259, 6½" h., pr. ...................................... **125.00**

**Bowl,** 10" d., glossy blue ground, No. 227-10"........................................ **75.00**

**Bowl,** 10" l., canoe-form w/high shaped ends, glossy blue or tan ground, No. 231-10", each.. **130.00 to 140.00**

**Bowl,** 12" d., tan ground, No. 228-12".. **100.00**

**Coffeepot,** cov., blue ground, No. 250-P ...................................... **300.00**

**Ewer,** branch handle, glossy blue, No. 217-6", 6" h. ............................. **55.00**

**Teapot,** cov., blue, No. 271-P ............. **120.00**

**Tea set:** cov. teapot, creamer & sugar bowl; glossy green ground, No. 271, 3 pcs. ................................................. **175.00**

**Vase,** 6" h., green or tan, No. 241-6", each ..................................... **50.00 to 70.00**

## WISTERIA (1933)

*Lavender wisteria blossoms and green vines against a roughly textured brown shading to deep blue ground, rarely found in only brown.*

**Urn,** brown ground, No. 629-4", 4" h... **290.00**

**Urn,** brown ground, No. 632-5", 5" h... **375.00**

**Vase,** 4" h., squatty, angular handles on sharply canted shoulder, No. 629-4"........................................ **262.00**

**Vase,** 6" h., ovoid w/small handles at shoulder, brown ground, No. 630-6" .. **270.00**

**Vase,** 7" h., angular handles at shoulder, blue ground, No. 634-7".... **595.00**

**Vase,** 7" h., angular handles at shoulder, brown ground, No. 634-7" .. **340.00**

**Wall pocket,** flaring rim, blue ground, 8" h. ............................................. **1,074.00**

## ZEPHYR LILY (1946)

*Deeply embossed day lilies against a swirl-textured ground. White and yellow lilies on a blended blue ground; rose and yellow lilies on a green ground; yellow lilies on terra cotta shading to olive green ground.*

*Zephyr Lily Basket*

**Basket w/overhead handle,** low foot, green ground, No. 393-7", 7" h. (ILLUS.) .......................................... **169.00**

**Basket w/asymmetrical overhead handle & rim,** green ground, No. 394-8", 8" h. ............................. **150.00**

**Book ends,** green ground, No. 16, pr... **180.00**

**Bowl,** 6" d., green ground, No. 472-6" .. **125.00**

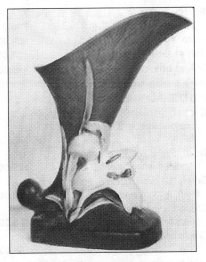

*Zephyr Lily Cornucopia Vase*

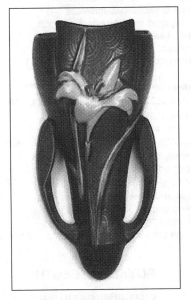

*Zephyr Lily Wall Pocket*

**Bowl,** 12" l., terra cotta ground,
No. 478-12"..................................... **133.00**

**Console bowl,** green, No. 478-12,
12" l.................................................. **165.00**

**Cornucopia-vase,** blue ground,
No. 203-6", 6" h. (ILLUS. above) ........ **95.00**

**Creamer & sugar bowl,** blue ground,
Nos. 7C 7 S, pr.................. **90.00 to 100.00**

**Ewer,** blue ground, No. 22-6", 6" h. .... **125.00**

**Flowerpot w/saucer,** green ground,
No. 672-5"......................................... **70.00**

**Jardiniere & pedestal base,** blue
ground, jardiniere 8" h., 2 pcs........ **1,150.00**

**Jardiniere & pedestal base,** green
ground, No. 671-8", overall 25" h.,
2 pcs. ............................................. **700.00**

**Tea set:** cov. teapot, creamer & sugar
bowl; blue ground, Nos. 7T, C & S,
3 pcs. ............................................. **235.00**

**Tea set:** cov. teapot, creamer & sugar
bowl; green ground, Nos. 7T, C & S,
3 pcs. ............................................. **260.00**

**Vase,** 6½" h., fan-shaped, base
handles, blue ground, No. 205-6" ..... **175.00**

**Vase,** 6½" h., fan-shaped, base
handles, brown ground, No. 205-6" .. **150.00**

**Vase,** 6½" h., fan-shaped, base
handles, green ground, No. 205-6"... **125.00**

**Vase,** bud, 7½" h., handles rising from
conical base, slender expanding
cylinder w/flaring rim, terra cotta
ground, No. 201-7" ............................ **80.00**

**Vase,** bud, 7½" h., handles rising from
conical base, slender expanding
cylinder w/flaring rim, blue ground,
No. 201-7"....................................... **125.00**

**Vase,** 15" h., two-handled, blue
ground, No. 141-15" ......... **310.00 to 350.00**

**Vase,** 15" h., two-handled, terra cotta
ground, No. 141-15........................... **250.00**

**Wall pocket,** blue ground,
No. 1297-8", 8" h. (ILLUS. above) .... **210.00**

## ROSE WARES

*Three different gaudy-type patterns of rose-decorated wares, once popular with the Pennsylvania "Deutsch" (Germans) that settled in the southeastern part of that state, are sought out by collectors who are willing to pay high prices for these early wares made in England, circa 1810-30. King's Rose pattern has an orangish red rose placed off center and green to yellow leaves and is quite a bold design. Queen's Rose pattern has a pink bloom and the remaining portions of the design are more delicate. Adams' Rose, named after its maker, William Adams has a border of two red roses and is a slightly later production. The superb shapes and the vivid decoration of this scarce and expensive ware has a cheery appeal entirely its own.*

**Bowl,** 9½" d., 4¼" h., scalloped rim,
Adams' Rose patt. (chips) .............. **$715.00**

**Cup & saucer,** handleless, Adams'
Rose patt., red, green & black, ca.
1820 (pinpoint flakes) ...................... **126.00**

**Cups & saucers,** handleless, scalloped rims, Adams' Rose patt., slight variation in pattern, saucers marked "Adams," six sets, 12 pcs. (minor chips.) .................................. **1,155.00**

**Plates,** 9½" d., Adams' Rose patt., slight variation in pattern, marked "Adams," set of 6 (very minor flakes)... **429.00**

**Plates,** 9½" d., Adams' Rose patt., slight variation in pattern, marked "Adams," set of 6 ............................ **495.00**

**Platter,** 15¼" l, Adams' Rose patt., marked "Adams" (stains & minor crazing) ............................................. **577.00**

**Vegetable bowl,** cov., molded rim & finial designs, Adams' Rose patt., marked "Adams," 12½" l. (lid has edge chip) ..................................... **2,550.00**

# ROYAL BAYREUTH

*Good china in numerous patterns and designs has been made at the Royal Bayreuth factory in Tettau, Germany, since 1794. Listings below are by the company's lines, plus miscellaneous pieces. Interest in this china remains at a peak and prices continue to rise. Pieces listed carry the company's blue mark except where noted otherwise*

## DEVIL & CARDS

**Ashtray** ............................................ **$130.00**
**Ashtray,** two cards ............................. **325.00**
**Ashtray w/match holder** .................... **150.00**
**Candleholder** .................................... **495.00**
**Creamer,** 3¾" h ................................. **350.00**
**Mug** w/blue rim .................................. **395.00**

*Devil & Cards Pitcher*

**Pitcher,** water, 7¼" h. (ILLUS. bottom previous column) ............................. **750.00**
**Plate,** 6" d ......................................... **500.00**
**Salt shaker** ....................................... **150.00**
**Stamp box,** cov., 3½" l. ..................... **595.00**

## MOTHER-OF-PEARL

**Basket,** reticulated rim, ornate handle, rose decoration, 3¾ x 4" oval, 4¼" h. ................................................ **125.00**
**Bowl,** 5½" d., grape cluster mold, pearlized white finish ........................ **125.00**
**Bowl,** 10" oval, handled, figural poppy mold, apricot satin finish .................. **550.00**
**Creamer,** grape cluster mold, pearlized white ................................. **125.00**
**Creamer,** Murex Shell patt., spiky form ........................................................ **65.00**
**Cup & saucer,** demitasse, Oyster & Pearl mold ........................................ **350.00**
**Hatpin holder,** figural poppy mold, pearlized white finish ........................ **450.00**
**Humidor,** cov., Murex Shell patt. ........ **725.00**
**Nappy,** grape cluster mold, pearlized white finish, 6 x 7" ............................ **150.00**
**Toothpick holder,** Murex Shell patt., pearlized finish ................................. **150.00**

## ROSE TAPESTRY

**Basket,** two-color roses, 3" h. ............. **300.00**
**Basket,** two-color roses, 4¼" w., 3¾" h. ................................................ **435.00**
**Bell,** gold loop handle, three-color roses, 3¼" h ...................................... **350.00**
**Box,** cov., pink & white roses, 2½" sq. .. **150.00**
**Box,** cov., shell-shaped, 3 x 5½" ......... **350.00**
**Cake plate,** three-color roses, free-form fancy rim w/gold beading, 9½" w. ................................................ **395.00**
**Cake plate,** pierced gold handles, three-color roses, 10½" d. ............... **495.00**
**Candy dish,** three-color roses, 8" oval ................................................ **300.00**
**Clock,** three-color roses ...................... **865.00**
**Creamer,** two-color roses, 3½" d., 4" h. .. **365.00**
**Creamer & cov. sugar bowl,** two-color roses, pr. ..................................... **525.00**
**Cups & saucers,** demitasse, three-color roses, pr. .................................. **275.00**
**Dessert set:** large cake plate & six matching small serving plates; three-color roses, 7 pcs. ........................... **975.00**
**Dish,** handled, clover-shaped, decorated w/yellow roses, 5" w. ....... **120.00**

*Rose Tapestry Hair Receiver*

**Hair receiver,** cov., footed, two-color roses, 4" d., 2½" h. (ILLUS.) ............ **295.00**

**Hatpin holder,** 4½" h. ......................... **550.00**

**Match holder,** wall hanging-type, a bulbous rounded pouch w/a wide arched backplate w/hanging hole, white & pink roses ........................... **250.00**

**Model of a Victorian lady's high-heeled shoe,** three-color roses ........ **350.00**

**Nappy,** open-handled, three-color roses, 5" d....................................... **195.00**

**Plaque,** pierced to hang, large pink roses................................................ **535.00**

**Plate,** 7" d., three-color roses............. **225.00**

*Rose Tapestry Powder Box*

**Powder box,** cov., footed, three-color roses, 4" d., 2½" h. (ILLUS. bottom previous column) ........................................... **275.00**

**Salt shaker,** pink roses...................... **215.00**

**Sugar bowl,** cov., two-handled, one-color rose, 3½" d., 3¼" h. ................. **295.00**

## SUNBONNET BABIES

**Ashtray,** babies cleaning ................... **250.00**

**Creamer,** babies ironing, 3" h. ........... **175.00**

*Sunbonnet Babies Creamer*

**Creamer,** babies fishing (ILLUS) ........ **200.00**

**Creamer & open sugar bowl,** boat-shaped, babies fishing on sugar, babies cleaning on creamer, pr. ....... **450.00**

**Mug,** babies washing ......................... **300.00**

## TOMATO ITEMS

**Tomato creamer,** cov., small.................................... **45.00 to 50.00**

**Tomato creamer,** cov., large............. **145.00**

**Tomato creamer & cov. sugar bowl,** creamer 3" d., 3" h., sugar bowl 3½" d., 4" h., pr. (ILLUS. below) ....... **105.00**

*Tomato Creamer & Sugar Bowl*

**Tomato cup & saucer,** demitasse ..... **125.00**
**Tomato mustard jar,** cov. ...... **55.00 to 60.00**
**Tomato pitcher,** water ....................... **395.00**
**Tomato teapot,** cov., small .. **315.00 to 325.00**

## MISCELLANEOUS

**Ashtray,** figural elk ............. **230.00 to 275.00**
**Ashtray,** figural lobster ...................... **150.00**
**Basket** w/reticulated handles,
    decorated w/white roses, 7¾" l.,
    3½" h. ............................................... **85.00**
**Bowl,** 5 x 10", footed, handled, figural
    poppy, apricot satin finish ................ **650.00**
**Bowl,** 8" l., 4" h., figural lobster ........... **195.00**
**Box,** cov., shell-shaped, Little Boy
    Blue decoration ............................... **225.00**
**Box,** cov., shell-shaped, Little Jack
    Horner decoration, 5½" d. ............... **250.00**
**Candleholder,** penguin decoration ..... **335.00**
**Candy dish,** figural lobster ................ **115.00**
**Candy dish w/turned over edge,**
    nursery rhyme scene w/Little Miss
    Muffett ................................................ **90.00**
**Cracker jar,** cov., figural lobster ........ **575.00**
**Creamer,** figural Bird of
    Paradise ......................... **355.00 to 400.00**
**Creamer,** figural crow, brown bill &
    eyes (rare) ....................................... **230.00**
**Creamer,** figural elk head, shades of
    brown & cream, 3½" d., 4¼" h. ......... **225.00**
**Creamer,** figural monk,
    brown .............................. **765.00 to 800.00**
**Creamer,** figural owl .......... **455.00 to 500.00**
**Creamer,** figural parakeet... **200.00 to 225.00**
**Creamer,** figural pig, grey ................. **600.00**
**Creamer,** figural platypus ................ **1,100.00**
**Creamer,** figural robin (ILLUS. below)... **175.00**

*Figural Robin Creamer*

**Creamer,** figural water buffalo,
    souvenir of Portland, Oregon ........... **300.00**
**Creamer,** stirrup-type, figural ibex
    head ................................................. **625.00**
**Creamer & cov. sugar bowl,** figural
    pansy, lavender, pr. ......................... **305.00**
**Creamer & cov. sugar bowl,** figural
    grape cluster, purple, pr. .. **120.00 to 150.00**
**Hair receiver,** cov., decorated w/a
    scene of a Dutch boy & girl, 3¼" h. .... **80.00**
**Hatpin holder,** figural owl .................. **725.00**
**Humidor,** cov., figural gorilla, black... **1,450.00**
**Model of a man's shoe,** black oxford... **125.00**

*Figural Elk Beer Mug*

**Mug,** beer, figural elk, 5¾" h.
    (ILLUS.) ............................ **520.00 to 550.00**
**Mug,** figural clown ............................. **495.00**
**Mustard jar,** cov., figural
    lobster ............................. **140.00 to 150.00**
**Mustard jar,** cov., figural shell ........... **160.00**
**Pin tray,** triangular, "tapestry" portrait
    decoration of lady wearing large
    purple plumed hat, 5 x 5 x 5" ........... **225.00**
**Pitcher,** 3½" h., nursery rhyme scene
    w/Little Boy Blue .............................. **210.00**
**Pitcher,** 5" h., Arab w/horse
    decoration ........................................... **75.00**
**Pitcher,** milk, 5" h., figural elk ............. **200.00**
**Pitcher,** milk, figural coachman ......... **650.00**
**Pitcher,** milk, figural Dachshund dog .. **400.00**
**Pitcher,** milk, figural eagle ................. **450.00**
**Pitcher,** milk, 5½" h., figural fish head .. **235.00**
**Pitcher,** milk, figural lamplighter ........ **400.00**
**Pitcher,** milk, figural red & white
    parrot handle ................................... **448.00**
**Pitcher,** milk, figural oak
    leaf ................................. **400.00 to 425.00**

*Tray with Girl & Geese Scene*

**Pitcher,** milk, figural St. Bernard dog,
unmarked.......................................... **375.00**

**Pitcher,** water, 7" h., figural
elk..................................... **515.00 to 525.00**

**Pitcher,** water, figural coachman........ **750.00**

**Plate,** 9½" d., "tapestry," landscape
scene w/deer by a river .................... **190.00**

**Relish dish,** open-handled, footed,
ruffled edge, cow scene decoration,
8" l.................................................. **150.00**

**Shaving mug,** figural elk .................... **550.00**

**Stamp box,** cov., colorful scene of
Dutch children..................................... **95.00**

**Sugar bowl,** cov., figural lobster,
3¾" h. .............................. **100.00 to 125.00**

**Sugar bowl,** cov., figural poppy, red,
unmarked.......................................... **150.00**

**Teapot,** cov., child's, decorated w/a
scene of hunters, 3¾" h. ...................... **70.00**

**Teapot,** cov., child's, boy & donkey
decoration, green, unmarked, 4" h. .. **185.00**

**Teapot,** cov., figural orange ................ **475.00**

**Toothpick holder,** figural elk, 3" h...... **225.00**

**Toothpick holder,** figural poppy, red.. **275.00**

**Toothpick holder,** decorated w/scene
of girl w/two chickens........................... **50.00**

**Toothpick holder,** three-handled,
Harvest scene decoration................. **150.00**

**Toothpick holder,** three-handled,
Hunt scene decoration, 3" h.
(ILLUS. top next column).................. **265.00**

**Tray,** decorated w/scene of girl
w/geese, molded rim w/gold trim,
9 x 12¼" (ILLUS. top of page) .......... **320.00**

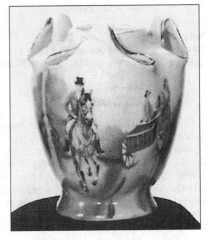

*Toothpick Holder with Hunt Scene*

**Vase,** 5¼" h., ovoid body w/short
cylindrical neck, medallion portrait
framed w/gold band in incised leaf
design w/enamel trim........................ **170.00**

**Vase,** 5½" h., tear drop-shaped,
colorful floral decoration ..................... **95.00**

**Vase,** 7¾" h., mercury & floral finish,
ca. 1919, artist-signed & signed "Kgl.
Priv. Tettan" ..................................... **150.00**

**Vase,** 9½" h., peacock decoration,
open work on neck & at base, ornate
scroll handles, lavish gold trim
(ILLUS. top next page) .................... **740.00**

**Vase,** miniature, ball-shaped, footed,
silver rim, Arab scene decoration ..... **110.00**

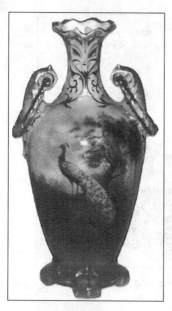

*Vase with Peacock*

**Wall pocket,** depicts a jester & "Many
Kiss the Child for the Nurses SAKE,"
green ground, signed "NOKE," 9" h... **650.00**

## ROYAL WORCESTER

*This porcelain has been made by the Royal
Worcester Porcelain Co. at Worcester,
England, from 1862 to the present. For earlier
porcelain made in Worcester, see
WORCESTER. Royal Worcester is
distinguished from those wares made at
Worcester between 1751 and 1862 that are
referred to as only Worcester collectors.*

*Royal Worcester Marks*

**Bowl,** 9¼" l., shell-shaped, No. 1274,
artist-signed ..................................... **$85.00**

**Creamer & cov. sugar bowl,** floral &
leaf decoration outlined in gold,
creamer 3¼" h., sugar bowl 4¼" h.,
No. 1253, artist-signed, pr. ............... **125.00**

**Dinner service:** twelve dinner plates,
twelve soup plates, twelve luncheon
plates, ten cups, eleven stands &
eleven dessert plates; Cradley patt.,
each piece decorated w/plums within
blue & puce scrollwork borders &
trellis-molded rims, printed factory
mark & "1865" in red, dinner plates
10¼" d., the set (one cup handle
broken, one stand restored) .......... **1,150.00**

**Figure,** "August," 5" h....................... **125.00**

*Goosie, Goosie Gander Figure*

**Figure,** "Goosie, Goosie Gander,"
5¾" h. (ILLUS.) ................................. **175.00**

**Figure,** "Hindu," No. 838, 7½" h.......... **450.00**

**Figure,** "November," designed by
F. Doughty, No. 3417, 7" h. ............. **225.00**

**Figure,** "Saturday," boy, designed by
F. Doughty. No. 3524, 1954 ............. **350.00**

**Figure,** "Saturday's Child Work's Hard
For A Living," young girl knitting w/a
cat, 5½" h....................................... **125.00**

**Figure of a Scotsman,** enamel & gilt-
decorated, printed & impressed
marks, ca. 1883, 6" h........................ **374.00**

**Figure,** "Siamese" ............................... **250.00**

**Figure,** "Sunday," boy, designed by
F. Doughty, No. 3256, 1938 ............. **300.00**

**Figure,** "Sweet Anne," designed by
F. Doughty, No. 3630 ......................... **95.00**

**Jam jar,** cov., h.p. scene of bird in
flight, embossed border at base,
silver plated lid & handles, artist-
signed, W. Stinton, Locke & Co........ **525.00**

**Model of a bird,** Phoebe & flame vine, modeled as a parent bird w/an insect in its beak, perched on the flame vine, modeled by Dorothy Doughty, overglaze black factory mark, 10" h. .................................... **259.00**

**Models of birds,** Canyon Wrens w/wild lupen, each bird perched on a rock by flowering lupen, modeled by Dorothy Doughty, overglaze black factory marks, 8½" h........................ **489.00**

**Models of birds,** a pair of Scarlet Tanagers, each modeled perched amid oak leaves & branches, overglaze black factory marks, 11" & 12" h., pr..................................... **1,093.00**

**Pitcher,** 5" h., pink w/intricate gilt trim, ca. 1890s ............................................. **85.00**

**Pitcher,** 7" h., overall floral & leaf decoration, outlined in gold gilt, No. 1094, artist-signed, ca. 1892...... **175.00**

**Vase,** 10¼" h., faience, stork in flight w/two scenes of ducks in pond, modeled by James Hadley ............... **495.00**

**Vase,** 9¾" h., squatty bulbous base below tapering reticulated panels w/neck ring below a tall slender gently flaring neck w/further reticulated panels, ivory & gold, marked "G & Co." ............................ **275.00**

**Vase,** 10½" h., bulbous body tapering to narrow neck, reticulated rim, decorated w/leaves & ferns w/gold trim..................................................... **225.00**

**Vase,** 10¾" h., double gourd-form w/large bulbous base below smaller bulbous reticulated neck tapering to tall slender slightly flaring rim ivory & gold w/polychrome floral enameling, marked "Bailey, Banks & Biddle, Phila." .............................................. **302.00**

**Vases,** 6½" h., two-handled, recticulated, raised floral decoration, No. 982, artist-signed, pr. ................. **225.00**

## R.S. PRUSSIA & RELATED WARES

*Ornately decorated china marked "R.S. Germany" and "R.S. Prussia" continues to grow in popularity. According to Clifford J. Schlegelmilch in his book, Handbook of Erdmann and Reinhold Schlegelmilch— Prussia—Germany and Oscar Schlegelmilch— Germany, Erdmann Schlegelmilch established a porcelain factory in the Germanic provinces at Suhl, in 1861. Reinhold, his younger*

*brother, worked with him until 1869 when he established another porcelain factory in Tillowitz, upper Silesia. China bearing the name of this town is credited to Reinhold Schlegelmilch. It also customarily bears the phrase "R.S. Germany." Now collectors seek additional marks including E.S. Germany, R.S. Poland and R.S. Suhl. Prices are high and collectors should beware the forgeries that sometimes find their way to the market. Mold names and numbers are taken from Mary Frank Gaston's books on R.S. Prussia.*

*We illustrate three typical markings, however, there are several others. The "R.S. Prussia" mark has been reproduced in decal form so buy with care.*

*R.S. Prussia Marks*

## R.S. GERMANY

**Candy basket,** oval w/twisted handle, orchid decoration w/gold trim, 4 x 8".............................................. **$125.00**

**Candy dish,** two-handled, floral decoration......................................... **28.00**

**Cheese & cracker dish,** pink orchid decoration, 8⅝" d., artist-signed ......... **85.00**

**Chocolate pot,** decorated w/large apricot & white flowers on shaded ground, 10½" h. ............................... **115.00**

**Chocolate set:** tall cov. chocolate pot & four matching cups & saucers; decorated w/dogwood & pine on cream satin ground, 9 pcs. ........... **295.00**

**Creamer,** decorated w/red roses on ivory & green ground, gold trim on shaped handle & ruffled rim, 3" h. ...... **30.00**

**Creamer,** cov., floral & leaf decoration, 3⅝" h.............................. **65.00**

**Dish,** open, oval, handled, pink & yellow roses decoration, 13" l. ............ **48.00**

**Dresser set:** cov. powder box, cov. hair receiver & hatpin holder on rectangular tray; decorated w/white, peach & pink roses & green leaves, the set............................................... **200.00**

**Hatpin holder,** floral decoration w/gold trim ......................................... **77.00**

**Hair receiver,** cov., floral decoration .... **33.00**

**Lettuce bowl,** Mold 12, center decoration of Irises, pearl lustre finish, 9" d. ...................................... **475.00**

**Luncheon set:** cov. teapot, creamer, cov. sugar bowl, eight cup-fitted luncheon trays, eight cups; (Medallion mold), decorated w/red roses on grey lustre ground, 19 pcs. ......................... **200.00**

**Salt & pepper shakers,** decorated w/delicate pink roses, pr. .................... **85.00**

**Toothbrush holder,** hanging-type, decorated w/two-color roses & lavish gold trim ......................................... **125.00**

**Vase,** 4¾" h., bulbous body tapering to short cylindrical neck, portrait of woman w/holly wreath in hair (salesman's sample) - IV, Pl. 718..... **175.00**

**Wall pocket,** figural slipper, flow blue w/blue floral decoration, gold trim, 7" h. ................................................ **150.00**

## R.S. PRUSSIA

*R. S. Prussia Bowl*

**Berry set:** master bowl & six sauce dishes; Mold 82, wide gold band & insets, pink ground w/roses, 7 pcs. .. **715.00**

**Bowl,** 10" d., Carnation mold, decorated w/yellow & white magnolia blossoms, teal green & cream ground w/gold trim (ILLUS. above) ................. **395.00**

**Cake plate,** open-handled, Mold 305, lily-of-the-valley decoration, satin finish, 9¼" h. ..................................... **260.00**

**Cake plate,** open-handled, Mold 251, white & pink roses decoration, band of dark gold w/lighter gold lilies on top at rim, 12" d. ............................. **320.00**

**Cake plate,** open-handled, fan border, decorated w/pink & yellow rose garlands on white ground, unmarked, 12" d. .............................. **75.00**

**Cake plate,** open-handled, Iris mold, decorated w/scattered pink poppies, satin finish........................................ **600.00**

**Cake plate,** open-handled, Iris mold, decorated w/roses, unmarked ......... **120.00**

**Cake plate,** open-handled, Point & Clover mold, decorated w/roses & mixed florals .................................... **185.00**

**Celery tray,** Plume mold, floral decoration on green ground ............ **125.00**

**Chocolate pot,** cov., Mold 540, pink & white floral decoration...................... **66.00**

**Chocolate set:** cov. chocolate pot, six cups & saucers; floral decoration, satin finish ground, the set............. **2,500.00**

**Coffeepot,** cov., demitasse, Mold 474, floral decoration, 9" h....................... **625.00**

**Cracker jar,** cov., Mold 517, silver plated lid, rim & ornate handle, decorated w/pink roses, green leaves, shadow foliage & slightly embossed flowers toward top trimmed in gold, cream shading to tan ground, unmarked, 5¾" d., 7" h. .. **225.00**

*R. S. Prussia Cracker Jar*

**Cracker jar,** cov., Mold 644, cylindrical body w/multiple lobed base, silver plated lid, rim & handle, decorated w/pink & yellow roses & small white flowers, embossed scroll designs & fans around top, lavender blue mother-of-pearl satin finish, unmarked, 5⅝" d., 7½" h. (ILLUS.)... **245.00**

**Creamer & cov. sugar bowl,** Carnation mold, unmarked, pr. ......... **325.00**

**Dresser tray,** Carnation mold, lavender edge trim, poppies decoration w/pearlized finish, 7 x 11½".............................................. **395.00**

**Hatpin holder,** Mold 731, lobed upright body w/flaring rim & scroll-molded & scalloped base, decorated w/pink roses on a shaded green & white ground, 4¾" h. ......................... **200.00**

**Plate,** 7" d., scalloped, swan scene, gold trim ......................................... **500.00**

*Plate with Dice Players Scene*

**Plate,** 9⅛" d., pierced to hang, Dice Players scene, deep rose, cream & green border w/lavish gold & dainty floral trim, embossed gold beaded edge (ILLUS.) ................................... **450.00**

**Serving plate,** open-handled, overall floral decoration gold trim, beaded border ............................................. **135.00**

**Shaving mug w/beveled mirror,** Stippled Floral mold (Mold 525), roses decoration on green ground.... **595.00**

**Sugar bowl,** Mold 507, pink roses decoration on green satin ground....... **65.00**

**Tea set:** cov. teapot, creamer & cov. sugar bowl; Stippled Floral mold (Mold 525), clematis decoration w/lavish gold trim, 3 pcs. ................. **550.00**

**Tea set:** cov. teapot, creamer & cov. sugar bowl; decorated w/surreal dogwood, enameled gold stems, soft green pearlized finish, 3 pcs. ............ **595.00**

**Tray,** Icicle mold, dark green hanging basket decoration ............................ **400.00**

**Vase,** 6⅜" h., 2¾" d., footed ovoid body tapering to short cylindrical neck w/flaring rim, decorated w/pheasant scene on shades of green & cream w/colored pheasant, shadow foliage, unmarked, faint hairline on top edge (ILLUS. top next column) ............................................. **125.00**

*Vase with Pheasant Scene*

## OTHER MARKS

**Bowl,** large, open, divided, w/center handle, double portrait decoration of Goddess of Fire & Girl with Swallows (Prov. Saxe - E.S. Germany) ............ **275.00**

**Cake plate,** split handles, decorated w/large pink & white roses on shaded satin finish ground, 10" d. (R.S. Suhl) ....................................... **125.00**

**Candleholder,** flaring socket above a squatty bulbous tapering cylindrical shaft on a flaring foot, pink floral decoration, 4¾" h. (Prov. Saxe - E.S. Germany) ......................................... **135.00**

**Match holder,** hanging-type w/striker on base, decorated w/portrait of woman w/daisy crown in long brown hair (E.S. Prussia) ........................... **110.00**

**Planter,** wide bulbous body on a short pedestal foot, decorated w/a wide band of pink flowers trimmed w/gold, 6½" d., 6¾" h. (R.S. Poland)............. **235.00**

**Plate,** 5¼" d., decorated w/sitting bull on white background (Royal Saxe - E.S. Germany) ................................... **70.00**

**Sandwich server w/center handle,** scalloped rim, lavender & pink roses w/gold trim, 11" d., 8" to top of handle (R.S. Poland) ....................... **515.00**

**Serving plate w/center handle,** decorated w/multicolored poppies, 8½" d., 3¾" h. (E. Schlegelmilch - Thuringia) ....................................... **100.00**

**Vase,** 6" h., ovoid body tapering to a slightly flared rim, decorated w/golden pheasants (R.S. Tillowitz - Silesia) .................................... **260.00**

**Vase,** 6" h., wide bulbous body w/short cylindrical neck, decorated w/white & brown pheasants (R.S. Tillowitz - Silesia) ............................. **260.00**

**Vase,** 9" h., bulbous ovoid body tapering to tall slender neck w/flaring rim, decorated w/Melon Eaters scene (R.S. Suhl) ............................ **815.00**

**Vase,** 10" h., decorated w/cottage scene, gold handles & rim (R.S. Poland) ............................................ **640.00**

**Vase,** 10" h., cylindrical body tapering to a short, slightly flared neck, angled handles from rim to shoulder, decorated w/full figure portrait scene of lady w/peacock on one side, lady w/doves on other side, gold trim, turquoise tapestry finish (E.S. Germany - Prov. Saxe) ..................... **675.00**

**Vase,** 10" h., slightly tapering cylindrical body w/ornate shoulder handles & scalloped rim, decorated w/scene of sheepherder & flock, mill in background, gold handles & rim (R.S. Poland) .................................... **640.00**

## SHAWNEE

*The Shawnee pottery operated in Zanesville, Ohio, from 1937 until 1961. Much of the early production was sold to chain stores and mail-order houses including Sears, Roebuck, Woolworth and others. Planters, cookie jars and vases, along with the popular "Corn King" oven ware line, are among the collectible items which are plentiful and still reasonably priced. Reference numbers used here are taken from Mark E. Supnick's book,* Collecting Shawnee Pottery, The Collector's Guide to Shawnee Pottery *by Duane and Janice Vanderbilt, or* Shawnee Pottery—An Identification & Value Guide *by Jim and Bev Mangus.*

**Bank,** figural Bulldog......................... **$160.00**

**Bank-cookie jar combination,** figural Smiley Pig, No. 61 ........................... **410.00**

**Bank-cookie jar combination,** figural Winnie Pig, chocolate-colored base .. **441.00**

**Cookie jar,** "Corn King" line, figural ear of corn, No. 66 (ILLUS. top next column) ............................................. **167.00**

*Corn King Cookie Jar*

**Cookie jar,** figural Dutch Boy, blue tie, striped pants ..................................... **164.00**

**Cookie jar,** figural Dutch Boy, marked "Great Northern No. 1025".............. **165.00**

**Cookie jar,** figural Dutch Girl, marked "Great Northern, No. 1026".............. **295.00**

**Cookie jar,** figural Dutch Girl, decorated w/a tulip .......................... **165.00**

**Cookie jar,** figural elephant, pink, No. 60 ................................................ **175.00**

**Cookie jar,** figural Jo Jo the Clown, No. 12.............................. **280.00 to 300.00**

**Cookie jar,** figural Puss 'n Boots (ILLUS. below) ................ **165.00 to 200.00**

**Cookie jar,** figural Sailor Boy............. **140.00**

*Puss 'n Boots Cookie Jar*

**Cookie jar,** figural Smiley Pig, blue neckerchief, gold trim ...................... **406.00**

**Cookie jar,** figural Smiley Pig, decorated w/shamrocks.................... **230.00**

**Cookie jar,** figural Winnie Pig, decorated w/clover leaves ............... **345.00**

**Figurine,** model of a Pekinese dog....... **58.00**

**Lamp,** Oriental man, 8½" h. .................. **20.00**

**Pitcher,** ball-type, Pennsylvania Dutch patt........................................................ **91.00**

**Pitcher,** figural Chanticleer Rooster, w/flower decals & gold trim ............... **177.00**

**Pitcher,** figural Little Bo Peep, flowers & gold trim, No. 47 ........................... **146.00**

**Pitcher,** figural Little Boy Blue, No. 46... **108.00**

**Pitcher,** figural Winnie Pig, blue floral decoration........................................ **225.00**

**Planter,** model of a water trough, No. 716 ............................................. **17.00**

**Planters,** figural boy & figural girl at fence, gold trim, No. 581, pr. .............. **30.00**

**Salt & pepper shakers,** Basket of Fruit line, No. 82, small, pr.................. **28.00**

**Salt & pepper shakers,** figural Cottage, pr....................................... **299.00**

**Salt & pepper shakers,** figural duck, 3¼" h., pr. ...................................... **29.00**

**Salt & pepper shakers,** figural Dutch Boy & Girl, large, pr. .......................... **93.00**

**Salt & pepper shakers,** figural Muggsey Dog, small, pr...................... **62.00**

**Salt & pepper shakers,** figural Muggsey Dog, large, pr.... **130.00 to 140.00**

**Salt & pepper shakers,** figural Owl, pr. ..................................................... **25.00**

**Salt & pepper shakers,** figural Sailor Boy & figural Little Bo Peep, pr........... **25.00**

**Salt & pepper shakers,** figural Smiley Pig, blue neckerchief, gold trim, large, pr. ............................................... **80.00**

**Salt & pepper shakers,** figural Smiley Pig, red neckerchief, large, pr............. **66.00**

**Salt & pepper shakers,** figural Winnie & Smiley Pig, heart decoration, large, 5" h., pr. .................................. **120.00**

**Salt & pepper shakers,** figural Puss 'n Boots, gold trim, pr. ...... **100.00 to 115.00**

**Sugar bowl,** cov., model of a bucket, marked "Great Northern USA 1042"... **40.00**

**Teapot,** cov., "Corn King" line, 30 oz., No. 75 (ILLUS. top next column) ........ **84.00**

**Teapot,** cov., figural Granny Ann, coral apron......................................... **98.00**

**Teapot,** cov., Pennsylvania Dutch patt. .................................... **70.00 to 75.00**

*Corn King Teapot*

**Teapot,** cov., Sunflower patt., 6½" h..... **70.00**

**Vase,** 9" h., Bow Knot patt., green glaze, No. 819 ................................... **20.00**

## SHELLEY CHINA

*Members of the Shelley family were in the pottery business in England as early as the 18th century. In 1872 Joseph Shelley formed a partnership with James Wileman of Wileman & Co. who operated the Foley China Work. The Wileman & Co. name was used for the firm for the next fifty years, and between 1890 and 1910 the words "The Foley" appeared above conjoined "WC" initials.*

*Beginning in 1910 the Shelley family name in a shield appeared on wares, although the firm's official name was still Wileman & Co. The company's name was finally changed to Shelley in 1925 and then Shelley China Ltd. after 1965. The firm changed hands in the 1960s and became part of the Doulton Group in 1971.*

*At first only average quality earthenwares were produced but in the late 1890s new shapes and better quality decorations were used.*

*Bone china was introduced at Shelley before World War I and these fine dinnerwares became very popular in the United States and are increasingly popular today with collectors. Thin "eggshell china" teawares, miniatures and souvenir items were widely marketed during the 1920s and 1930s and are sought-after today.*

*Shelley Mark*

**Candy dish,** Blue Rock patt............... $35.00

**Coffee/tea service,** Glorious Devon
patt., 25 pcs. ................................. 1,250.00

**Coffeepot,** cov., Dainty White patt.
w/gold trim ...................................... 200.00

**Creamer & cov. sugar bowl,**
Primrose patt., pr. ............................. 60.00

**Creamer & cov. sugar bowl,** Rose
patt., pr. ........................................... 85.00

**Cup & saucer,** Blue Daisy patt. ............ 55.00

**Cup & saucer,** Campanula patt., six-
flute shape ........................................ 50.00

**Cup & saucer,** Daffodil Time patt. ........ 45.00

**Cup & saucer,** Dainty Blue patt. ........... 48.00

**Cup & saucer,** Heavenly Blue patt. ...... 55.00

**Cup & saucer,** Melody patt. .................. 45.00

**Cup & saucer,** Regency patt., six-
flute shape ........................................ 45.00

**Cup & saucer,** White Rose patt. ........... 50.00

**Gravy boat & underplate,** Dainty
White patt., six-flute shape, 2 pcs. ...... 90.00

**Plate,** 6" d., Blue Rock patt. ................ 20.00

**Plate,** 8" d., Blue Rock patt. ................ 30.00

**Plate,** dinner, 10½" d., Dainty Blue
patt. .................................................... 100.00

**Plate,** dinner, 10½" d., Dainty White
patt., six-flute shape ........................... 65.00

**Sauce dish,** Blue Rock patt. ................. 25.00

**Soup plate w/flanged rim,** Dainty
White patt., six-flute shape, 8" d. ........ 55.00

**Tray,** Regency patt., fluted, 5½" oval .... 55.00

**Vegetable bowl w/flanged rim,** open,
Dainty White patt., six-flute shape,
10" oval ............................................... 65.00

# SLIPWARE

*This term refers to ceramics, primarily redware, decorated by the application of slip, or semi-liquid paste made of clay. Such wares were made for decades in England and Germany and elsewhere on the Continent, and in the Pennsylvania Dutch country, and elsewhere in the United States. Today, contemporary copies of early Slipware items are featured in numerous decorator magazines and offered for sale in gift catalogs.*

**Bowl,** 13½" d., 2⅝" h., wide shallow
sides w/coggled rim, redware
w/three-line yellow slip decoration
(wear & edge chips) ........................ $825.00

**Charger,** coggle wheel rim embellished
w/yellow slip pretzel decoration, ca.
1825-1880, Smith Pottery, Norwalk,
Connecticut, 12½" d. ..................... 2,070.00

**Dish,** coggle wheel rim centering a
yellow slip quill decoration, ca. 1850-
1912, Simon Singer, Haycock
Township, Bucks County
Pennsylvania, 9⅝" d. .................... 1,840.00

*Slipware Dish*

**Dish,** coggle wheel rim embellished
w/criss-cross decoration &
highlighted w/yellow slip & daubs of
green glaze, 19th c., Pennsylvania,
minor rim chips, 13" d. (ILLUS.)..... 3,220.00

**Jar,** cylindrical body w/molded rim,
dark brown ground, decorated in
cream slip on front w/stylized tree
flanked by a serpent-and-staff motif
& on the reverse w/a cluster of
stylized tulips beneath a squiggle-
banded border, a single row of
cream dots around rim, 19th c.
6⅝" h., (minor chips & some
hairlines on rim, chips & abrasion to
side of body) ..................................... 230.00

**Loaf dish,** rectangular, w/coggle wheel
rim & yellow triple quill zig-zag slip
decoration, 19th ca., Pennsylvania,
11½ x 16", 3" h. .............................. 2,185.00

**Loaf dish,** slip decoration w/"Phebe"
in center, 12¾" l. ............................ 2,185.00

**Loaf dish,** slip decoration w/"Emeline"
in center, 14½" l. ............................ 1,495.00

**Model of a cat,** seated w/head turned
to the left, hollow-molded, covered in
a thick brown glaze stopping above
the footrim & trailed in cream slip
w/facial details, on the left side of the
body w/swirls following the contours
of the animal's flank & on the reverse
w/a series of horizontal squiggles,
19th c., tip of left ear & front left foot
restored, 5¾" h. (ILLUS. top next
page).................................................... 287.00

*Slipware Cat Model*

**Plate,** 8¾" d., coggle wheel rim, yellow slip decoration w/daubs of green glaze on a red body w/clear lead glaze, 19th c., Pennsylvania ...**1.265.00**

**Plate,** 9" d., slip decorated w/"N B" in center (glaze loss) ............................ **489.00**

**Plate,** 9¼" d., circular, redware decorated w/yellow slip squiggly band around flaring rim .................... **495.00**

**Plate,** 10" d., slip decorated "Apple Pie" in center (glaze loss, chips) ....... **690.00**

*Slipware Plate with Bird*

**Plate,** 13½" d., coggled edge, decorated w/figure of a spotted bird w/elongated tail, perched in a leafy branch, comb-trailed wavy lines above & below, ca. 1820 (ILLUS.) ........................... **11,500.00**

**Puzzle jug,** ovoid body tapering to wide cylindrical neck w/tubular handle & rim w/three nozzles, decorated in raised cream slip &

"1870" surrounded by vertical squiggles & dots, the neck pierced w/a heart flanked by quatrefoils & S-scrolls against a cream-dotted ground, rim & nozzles decorated w/cream dots, ca. 1870, 7½" h. (nozzles each broken & re-glued)..... **345.00**

**Whistle,** model of a plump bird w/wings, beak & eyes decorated in cream slip, cream-speckled plumage, perched on a horizontal bar joined to a lower bar protruding from the sides of a conical base, applied & molded w/raised florets heightened in cream slip, 19th c., 9⅜" h. (head & beak restored, two pairs of accompanying small birds missing from the ends of each horizontal bar).................................. **287.00**

# SPATTERWARE

*This ceramic ware takes its name from the "spattered" decoration, in various colors, generally used to trim pieces handpainted with rustic center designs of flowers, birds, houses, etc. Popular in the early 19th century, most was imported from England.*

*Related wares, called "stick spatter," had free-hand designs applied with pieces of cut sponge attached to sticks, hence the name. Examples date from the 19th and early 20th century and were produced in England, Europe and America.*

*Some early spatter-decorated wares were marked by the manufacturers, but not many. 20th century reproductions are also sometimes marked, including those produced by Boleslaw Cybis in the 1940s which sometimes have 'CYBIS' impressed.*

**Cup & saucer,** handleless, decorated w/purple spatter rims ..................... **$220.00**

**Cup & saucer,** handleless, Peafowl patt. in red, blue, yellow & black, green varies, very minor flakes (ILLUS. below)................................. **330.00**

*Peafowl Cup & Saucer*

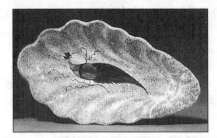

*Peafowl Shell-shaped Dish*

**Dish,** shell-shaped, Peafowl patt., the scalloped body molded w/flowerheads on the handle, in blue, red, green & black, peafowl on branch against a powder blue spattered ground, ca. 1840, impressed "ADAMS" & flowerhead mark, restorations & hairline to rim, 9" l. (ILLUS.) ................. **287.00**

**Hot water jug,** cov., barrel-shaped, slightly domed lid w/knob finial, large C-scroll handle, Peafowl Patt., in blue, green, red & black against a blue spattered ground, the gently domed cover w/three floral sprigs beneath a ball knop, ca. 1840, 7⅝" h., hairline to rim of cover (ILLUS. top next column) ..................................... **460.00**

**Pitcher,** 11¼" h., footed bulbous ovoid paneled body w/arched spout & C-form handle, overall blue spatter .. **165.00**

**Plate,** 9½" d., center decoration of star in green, red & white inside larger white star, on blue spatter (wear, red is flaked & back surface is very flaked) ..... **55.00**

**Plate,** multicolored decoration in center w/blue border, ca. mid-19th c., impressed "Villeroy & Boch" ............... **50.00**

**Platter,** 13⅝" l., canted rectangular, Peafowl Patt., blue, red, green & black on blue spattered ground, ca. 1840 (some flaking & repainting to blue enamel, staining on underside) .. **690.00**

**Platter,** 15¾" l., Rainbow spatter, a red & green bull's eye center decoration (edge wear & minor stains) ............................................ **2,255.00**

**Saucer,** Peafowl patt., free-hand bird in red, blue, yellow & black, green spatter background, 4½" d. (minor stains) ............................................... **193.00**

**Teabowl & saucer,** Dove patt., blue, yellow, green & black, Staffordshire blue spatter border, ca. 1840 incised marks, teabowl 4" d., saucer 5⅝" d. (hairline to bowl) ............................... **575.00**

*Spatterware Hot Water Jug*

**Toddy plate,** center design of viola in purple, green, yellow ochre & black, red spatter design border w/blue stripe, 5¾" d. ................................... **176.00**

**Vegetable dish,** canted rectangular, Peafowl patt., blue, green, red & black against a blue spatter ground, ca. 1840, impressed "ADAMS" mark, 10½" l (chips & hairline to rim) .......... **930.00**

**Waste bowl,** Peafowl patt. decoration in red, yellow, blue & black, 4⅞" d., (stains) ............................................. **303.00**

### STICK & CUT SPONGE

**Cup & saucer,** handleless, each w/a wide border band w/red cut sponge stylized blossoms, flanked by narrow blue stripes ......................................... **83.00**

**Plate,** 8½" d., centered w/purple, green, yellow & black viola blossom, cut sponge border made up of blue blossoms & red stripe ......................... **32.00**

**Soup plate w/flanged rim,** "gaudy" decoration of free-hand flowers & center flower, swag design on rim, 9⅜" d. (wear & minor damage) ......... **465.00**

# SPONGEWARE

*Spongeware's designs were spattered, sponged or daubed on in colors, sometimes with a piece of cloth. Blue on white was the most common type, but mottled tans, browns and greens on yellowware were also popular. Spongeware generally has an overall pattern with a coarser look than Spatterwares, to*

*Spongeware Mixing Bowl*

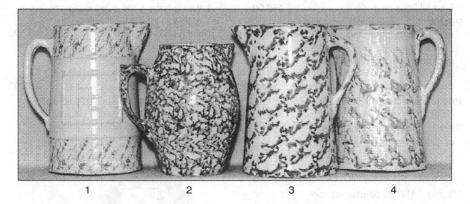

| 1 | 2 | 3 | 4 |

*Spongeware Pitchers*

*which it is loosely related. These wares were extensively produced in England and America well into the 20th century.*

**Bowl,** 7½" d., 4" h., blue & brown on yellowware, interior label "It pays to mix with G.J. Schneider, Garner, Iowa" (small rim flakes & short hairline in base ................................. **66.00**

**Butter crock,** cylindrical w/wire bail & wooden handle, blue on white, 5¼" d., (shallow flake on bottom edge, lid is a close mismatch) .......................... **220.00**

**Mixing bowl,** decorated w/bands of blue on white, 12" d., 6" h. (ILLUS. top) ................................................... **330.00**

**Pitcher,** 5¾" h., ovoid body tapering to a flat rim w/wide arched spout, C-form handle, brown & green on yellowware (small broken blister near spout) ......................................... **83.00**

**Pitcher,** 6¼" h., baluster-form body w/molded shoulder & neck, small rim spout & C-form handle, blue on cream (small lip chip & repaired chip on bottom edge) .............................. **110.00**

**Pitcher,** 7⅛" h., slightly tapering cylindrical w/small rim spout, C-form handle & molded vintage band at rim, brown & blue on cream (chips on table ring)..................................... **50.00**

**Pitcher,** 7⅝" h., bulbous ovoid w/flat rim & pinched spout, C-form handle, overall blue sponging on white, small edge flakes (ILLUS. No. 2, bottom)................................. **330.00**

**Pitcher,** 7½" h., bulbous body tapering to a wide flaring neck w/pinched spout, C-form handle, blue & brown sponging & brown stripes on cream (lip chip) ................. **83.00**

**Pitcher,** 8" h., spherical w/arched spout & C-form handle, overall blue sponging on white w/three blue bands around middle ........................ **330.00**

**Pitcher,** 8¾" h., cylindrical body tapering slightly to narrow molded rim, pinched spout & C-form handle, molded basketweave pattern w/fruit, overall blue sponging on white, firing crack at top of handle (ILLUS. No. 4, bottom previous page) ........................ **495.00**

**Pitcher,** 8⅞" h., cylindrical body tapering slightly to flat rim w/pinched spout, C-form handle, overall blue sponging on white, minor crazing & broken blisters near rim (ILLUS. No. 3, bottom previous page) ............ **330.00**

**Pitcher,** tankard, 8⅞" h., blue on white w/molded flower (chip on base & small flake on spout) ..................... **468.00**

**Pitcher,** 9" h., cylindrical w/pinched spout & C-form handle, molded bands & swastika (Indian good luck) in a rectangle, bottom edge has chips (ILLUS. No. 1, bottom previous page) ................................................. **110.00**

**Pitcher,** tankard, 9" h., blue on white (very minor edge flakes) ................... **341.00**

**Pitcher,** tankard, 9⅛" h., brown & blue on white, molded bands w/diamond lattice (minute chip on edge of bottom & hairlines in handle are "in the making") ...................................... **77.00**

**Pitcher,** 11⅛" h., baluster-shape w/scalloped rim & wide arched spout, C-scroll handle, overall blue sponging on white .............................. **99.00**

**Pitcher,** water, 11¼" h., bulbous body tapering to slightly flaring neck, pinched spout, C-form handle, blue on white w/blue bands around base (hairlines in base) ........................... **369.00**

**Teapot,** cov., ovoid body w/attached spout & C-form handle, bluish green on white, 6½" h. (small chips) ........... **385.00**

**Wash bowl,** blue on white, 14¾" d., 4¼" h. .............................................. **149.00**

# STAFFORDSHIRE FIGURES

*Small figures and groups made of pottery were produced by the majority of the Staffordshire, England potters in the 19th century and were used as mantel decorations or "chimney ornaments," as they were sometimes called Pairs of dogs were favorites and were turned out by the carload, and 19th century pieces are still available. Well-painted reproductions also abound and collectors are urged to exercise caution before investing.*

**Bust of Washington,** blue coat & ochre vest w/purple decoration, marbleized plinth, ca. mid-19th c., 8¼" h. .................................... **$715.00**

**Dog,** reclining figure, hollow creamware, lightly highlighted in splotches of reddish brown enamel, ca. 1790-1820, 4" l., 3" h. (invisible restorations to base & the top of animal's head) ................................ **148.00**

**Dogs,** greyhounds or whippets, highlighted in a reddish brown, brown & black enamel, ca. 1850-80, 4" h., pr. (one w/a small shallow flake on base & the other w/a glaze separation on the front portion of base) ................................................ **137.00**

**Dogs,** poodles, stocky white animals w/sanded coats, painted muzzles, marked "England," ca. 1900, 4¾" h., facing pr. ........................................... **165.00**

**Dogs,** poodles, seated animals w/two puppies at their feet, white w/sanded coats & enameled facial trim, oval blue base w/gilt trim, 19th c., 5½" h., pr. (crazing) ..................................... **715.00**

*Staffordshire Figure of a Spaniel*

**Dogs,** Spaniel, seated animal in white w/large copper lustre spots & painted facial features & long neck chain, minor crazing & short hairlines, 12½" h., facing pr. (ILLUS. of one) .............................................. **412.00**

**Dogs,** whippets, seated animals on oval bases, white w/red spots & painted muzzles, 5½" h., facing pr.... **715.00**

**Figure of Benjamin Franklin,** standing, wearing a blue coat, green scarf, red trousers & a sprig-decorated vest, was once titled "Washington" in applied enamel, which has faded, 15" h. .................. **970.00**

**Figure of Benjamin Franklin,** standing, wearing a blue coat & aqua & maroon decorated vest, ca. mid-19th c., mistitled "Washington" in raised letters, highlighted in gold, 15½" h. (restored)......................... **1,210.00**

**Figure,** pearlware, "Demosthenes," standing w/right arm outstretched, decorated w/lavender, yellowish tan, brown & flesh-tone enamels, attributed to Enoch Wood, ca. 1790-1820, 19" h. (restorations to corners of the base, the plinth, to one thumb & a finger & the outstretched arm has been re-attached) ..................................... **2,475.00**

**Figure group,** a man & woman, wearing kilts, standing over a clock face 6" h. (some glaze wear to hats).............................................. **110.00**

**Lamb on mound,** sanded coat, 3" l. (tight hairline in base) ....................... **70.00**

**Lions,** standing on stepped canted rectangular base, each w/shaded buff-colored body w/brown mane & glass eyes, one forepaw resting on a large brown ball, late 19th - early 20th c., 13½" l., pr. (one set of glass eyes missing).................................... **345.00**

**Rabbit,** long-eared bunny on grass base, decorated w/white, black, pink, brown & green enamels ca. 1850-70, 3¼" l., 2¼" h. (short, faint hairline on underside of base) .......... **247.00**

**Spill vase,** figural squirrel w/large busy tail, perched on a branch, holding a nut, decorated w/black, reddish brown, green, pink & yellow enamels, ca. 1850-70, 6" h. .............. **467.00**

**Spill vase,** flatback, "Robin Hood," figures of one man seated, dog w/black spots nearby & man standing, holding a yellow club, each wearing period dress, blue & red feathers in hats, black & orange boots, vase decorated w/green leaves & red grapes, orange interior 15" h. (annealing cracks, otherwise perfect) ........................................... **192.00**

## STAFFORDSHIRE TRANSFER WARES

*The process of transfer-printing designs on earthenwares developed in England in the late 18th century and by the mid-19th century most common ceramic wares were decorated in this manner, most often with romantic European or Oriental landscape scenes, animals or flowers. The earliest such wares were printed in dark blue but a little later light blue, pink, purple, red, black, green and brown were used. A majority of these wares were produced at various English potteries right up till the turn of the century but French and other European firms also made similar pieces and all are quite collectible. The best reference on this area is Petra Williams'* book Staffordshire Romantic Transfer Patterns—Cup Plates and Early Victorian China *(Fountain House, East, 1978). Also see: HISTORICAL & COMMEMORATIVE WARES.*

**Cake stand,** footed, Chinoisere patt., scene of two hunters & deer on the bank, two peddlers crossing a bridge, unmarked, probably Spode or Davenport, 12¼" d., 3¾" h. (tiny unseen flake on foot rim & a long faint hairline off the rim) .................. **$358.00**

**Cup plate,** scene of fruits & birds, dark blue, Stubbs, 4¼" d. ................... **99.00**

**Cup plate,** pagoda w/palm tree scene (double transfer), dark blue, impressed mark, Clews, 3½" d. .......... **66.00**

**Cup plates,** Canova patt., lavender, Mayer, 4" d., pr. ................................ **413.00**

**Cuspidor,** handled, hand-held, short side spout, European landscape scene, brown, ca. 1844, 5¼" d., 3" h... **77.00**

*Hindoo Village Gravy Tureen*

**Gravy tureen,** cov., scene of Hindoo Village patt., Oriental Scenery series, dark blue, base cleaned, otherwise brilliant & perfect, Hall, 6¾" h. (ILLUS. bottom previous page)...................... **358.00**

**Gravy tureen,** cover, ladle & undertray, Tyrolean patt., green transfer-printed scene of couple watching grazing goats on undertray, other pieces show Swiss? scenery, William Ridgway (1" l. hairline off the ladle hole on the cover).................... **303.00**

**Pitcher,** 4¾" h., Chinoiserie design, overall dark blue w/figures highlighted in orange, yellow, red & green polychrome, underglaze "Opaque China" mark, Riley ............. **220.00**

**Plate,** 5¾" d., center w/black transfer-printed poem titled "Against Lying," yellow, green, blue & red trim, embossed floral border....................... **66.00**

**Plate,** 6⅛" d., Beehive patt., dark blue, underglaze mark, Ralph Stevenson & Williams (faint scratching) ......................................... **94.00**

**Plate,** 7" d., center scene of English manor, horseback rider in foreground, Crocus border, medium dark blue, unknown maker ................. **94.00**

**Plate,** 7¼" d., blue transfer-printed center scene of two girls w/sheep, embossed border of flowers & scrolls w/red, black, blue & green enamel trim....................................... **72.00**

**Plate,** 7¾" d., center scene of a leopard on rocky ground, trees & mountains in background, Zoological series, dark blue, Wood, impressed mark.................................................. **413.00**

**Plate,** 8¼" d., Beehive patt., dark blue, underglaze mark, glaze rubbing on extreme edge of rim, Ralph Stevenson & Williams (ILLUS. top next column).................. **171.00**

**Plate,** 9⅜" d., ironstone, light blue transfer-print of Yale College, 19th c., England (some discoloration) ..................................... **58.00**

**Plate,** 10" d., Lion patt., Quadrupeds series, dark blue, Hall ...................... **303.00**

**Platter,** 11" oval, brown transfer center scene of the camel cage, Zoological series, Clews, underglaze mark................................................ **303.00**

**Platter,** 15½" octagonal, Ontario Lake Scenery patt., light blue, Heath, impressed & underglaze marks (some light mellowing around stilt marks)............................................... **198.00**

*Beehive Pattern Plate*

**Platter,** 16¼" l. w/matching 13⅜" strainer, Chinese Marine patt. scene, dark blue, maker unknown, probably Davenport (platter has a few short knife marks of the side of the well, strainer is perfect)............................. **705.00**

**Platter,** 21" l., light blue transfer-printed scene of deer & cottages, impressed "Rogers" ......................... **798.00**

**Platter,** well & tree-type, 21⅝" l., blue transfer-printed river scene, ca. 19th c. (knife scratches) .................. **690.00**

**Platter strainer,** oval, stylized Oriental scene w/grasshopper, medium blue, Spode, underglaze mark .................. **385.00**

**Soup tureen undertray,** octagonal, handled, mulberry transfer-printed center scene of mountainside castle on lake, unknown maker (outstanding restoration to a rim chip & an unseen chip glued in on the reverse) ............... **99.00**

**Vegetable dish,** cov., square w/cut corners, domed cover, blue transfer-printed fruit pattern, dark blue, second quarter 19th c., 11¼"............ **748.00**

**Vegetable dish,** open, oblong, Shells patt., overall transfer of various shells, medium dark blue, unmarked but probably Spode or Davenport, 11¼" w., 2⅛" h. (unseen chip on foot rim)......... **204.00**

**Waste bowl,** basket of flowers decoration, medium dark blue, Clews, underglaze "Stone China" mark, 5½" d., 3⅜" h. .......................... **99.00**

# STONEWARE

*Stoneware is essentially a vitreous pottery, impervious to water even in its unglazed state, that has been produced by potteries all over the world for centuries. Utilitarian wares such as crocks, jugs, churns and the like, were the most common productions in the numerous potteries that sprang into existence in the United States during the 19th century. These items were often enhanced by the application of a cobalt blue oxide decoration. In addition to the coarse, primarily salt-glazed stonewares, there are other categories of stoneware known by such special names as basalt, jasper and others.*

*Decorated Stoneware Churn*

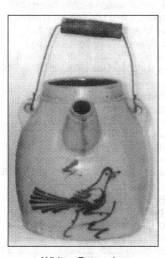

*Whites Batter Jug*

**Batter jug,** bulbous ovoid body tapering to short wide molded rim, cobalt blue slip-quilled long-tailed running bird, unsigned, attributed to Whites, Utica, New York, original wire bail handle w/wooden handgrip, few minor surface chips, ca. 1870, 1 gal., 9" h. (ILLUS.) .................... **$1,210.00**

**Batter jug,** bulbous ovoid body w/short wide neck, brushed cobalt blue accents at spout & handles & impressed label "W. Roberts Binghamton, N.Y.," wire bail handle w/wooden handgrip, ca. 1860, 6 qt., 9½" h. (two very minor surface chips) .................................................. **290.00**

**Bowl,** 12" d., 6½" h., cobalt blue brushed flower, impressed "Chollar, Darby & Co. Cortland," New York, ca. 1840, 2 gal. (minor surface wear at rim) .............................................. **877.00**

**Butter churn,** w/original dasher & guide, slightly tapering cylindrical form w/molded rim, applied eared handles, cobalt blue slip-quilled stylized bird on plume below "2," unsigned, ca. 1860, 2 gal., 13" h. ..... **847.00**

**Butter churn,** slightly swelled cylindrical body w/molded rim & applied eared handles, cobalt blue dotted leaf decoration, impressed "E.& L.P. Norton & Co. Bennington, VT.," ca. 1870, 2 gal, 13½" h. (glued 6" line in back) .................................. **605.00**

**Butter churn,** w/original dasher guide., slightly swelled cylindrical sides tapering to molded, slightly flared rim & applied eared handles, one of a kind cobalt blue decoration featuring large basket of flowers sitting on a table, impressed "Haxstun & Co. Fort Edward, N.Y.," 6" stabilized line on back, ca. 1880, 3 gal, 15" h. (ILLUS. above) .......... **2,970.00**

**Butter churn,** slightly swelled cylindrical sides tapering to ring neck slightly flared molded rim, applied eared handles, dark tan w/cobalt blue slip-quilled tree decoration & blue accent at handles, unsigned, probably Ohio origin, ca. 1860, 3 gal., 16½" h. (a few minor surface chips) .................................. **176.00**

**Butter churn,** original dasher guide, slightly swelled cylindrical sides tapering to molded rim, applied eared handles, cobalt blue slip-quilled large running bird & floral decoration, impressed "Whites Utica," New York w/blue accent, ca. 1870, 5 gal., 18" h. (orange peeled thick overglaze in the making, minor design fry spots, glaze line in base at back) .......................................... **1,485.00**

**Butter churn,** slightly swelled cylindrical sides tapering to wide, slightly flared molded rim, applied eared handles, cobalt blue detailed double flower decoration, intricately shaded to add a three-dimensional appearance, impressed "T. Harrington Lyons," Lyons, New York, ca. 1860, 5 gal., 18½" h. (professional restoration to tight lines in front & back) .............................................. **2,904.00**

**Butter churn,** slightly swelled cylindrical sides tapering to wide slightly flared molded rim, applied eared handles, cobalt blue slip-quilled life-like dotted & alert partridge surrounded w/large tree, flower & ground cover, impressed "John Burger Rochester," ca. 1860, 5 gal., 19" h. (professional restoration to lines on side & back) .................. **5,566.00**

**Butter churn,** slightly swelled cylindrical sides tapering to wide slightly flared molded rim, applied eared handles, cobalt blue slip-quilled fat chicken pecking corn, unsigned, attributed to Brady & Ryan, Ellenville, New York, ca. 1885, 6 gal., 18½" h. (8" glued crack in back, some minor surface chips in rim) .................................................. **938.00**

**Cake crock w/undecorated lid,** cylindrical w/applied eared handles, cobalt blue brushed floral decoration, front & back, impressed "J. Swank & Co Johnstown, PA," ca. 1870, 1½ gal., 7" h. (glued line on side & in the base, minor surface chips on lid, un-uniformed clay colors of grey & brown) ................................................ **242.00**

**Cake crock,** slightly waisted cylindrical body w/molded rim & applied eared handles, impressed "W.A. Macquoid & Co. Pottery Works Little 12th St. New York," flanked by cobalt blue slip-quilled flower & leaves, ca. 1870, 2 gal., 6" h. ................................................. **825.00**

**Crock,** cylindrical w/ringed neck & molded rim, applied eared handles, cobalt blue brushed flower & accents at ears, impressed "Cowden & Wilcox

Harrisburg, PA.," ca. 1870, 1 gal., 6½" h. (virtually undetectable 2" tight lines front & back, some overglazing in the front) ........................................ **254.00**

**Crock,** ovoid w/molded rim & applied eared handles, cobalt blue slip-quilled tornado-like design, impressed "Geddes, N.Y.," ca. 1840, 1 gal., 8¼" h. (some design fry & very minor base chip on back).......... **154.00**

**Crock,** ovoid w/wide slightly flared rim & applied eared handles, brushed cobalt blue flower, impressed "M. Tyler Albany," New York, ca. 1830, 1 gal., 9" h. (5" age spider on back & a few minor surface chips)............... **198.00**

**Crock,** cylindrical w/molded rim & applied eared handles, cobalt blue slip-quilled paddletail running bird, looking back, impressed "N.A. White & Son, Utica, N.Y." & "1½," ca. 1885, 1½ gal., 7¾" h. (tight freeze crack & lines throughout, stabilized & not detracting)....................................... **385.00**

**Crock,** cylindrical w/molded rim & applied eared handles, cobalt blue slip-quilled stylized running bird decoration, impressed "S. Hart Fulton," ca. 1870, 2 gal., 9" h. (full length glued crack in back)............... **315.00**

**Crock,** cylindrical w/molded rim & applied eared handles, cobalt blue brushed floral decoration, impressed "N. Clalr Athens, N.Y.," ca. 1890, 2 gal., 9" h....................................... **194.00**

*Crock with Bird on Twig*

**Crock,** cylindrical w/molded rim & applied eared handles, cobalt blue slip-quilled bird on twig, impressed "West Troy, N.Y. Pottery," very minor stain spots, ca. 1870, 2 gal., 9" h. (ILLUS.) ................................... **514.00**

**Crock,** cylindrical w/molded rim & applied eared handles, cobalt blue brushed vase of flowers, impressed "Somerset Potters' Works," ca. 1885, 2 gal., 9½" h. (some staining, 3" tight thru line in back, .... **109.00**

**Crock,** cylindrical w/molded rim & applied eared handles, cobalt blue slip-quilled chicken pecking corn decoration, unsigned, attributed to Brady & Ryan, Ellenville, New York ca. 1885, 2 gal., 9½" h. ..................... **575.00**

**Crock,** cylindrical w/molded, slightly flared rim, applied eared handles, cobalt blue slip-quilled delicate triple flower on leafy branch decoration, impressed "Cortland" & "2" above design, ca. 1870, 2 gal., 10" h. ......... **363.00**

**Crock,** ovoid w/molded rim & applied eared handles, cobalt blue slip-quilled large parrot on plume, impressed "F.B. Norton & Co. Worcester, Mass." & "2" above design, ca. 1870, 2 gal., 11" h. ...... **1,650.00**

**Crock,** wooden cover, cylindrical, tapering to wide flared rim, applied eared handles, cobalt blue brushed flower & accents at handles, impressed "H. & G. Nash Utica," New York, ca. 1835, 2 gal., 12½" h. (minor surface chips & 7" thru line on back)........................................... **220.00**

**Crock,** cylindrical w/molded, slightly flared rim, applied eared handles, cobalt blue brushed scene w/chickens, trees & pasture w/"Athens 1892" signed in script below scene, impressed "N. Clark Athens, N.Y.," ca. 1892, 3 gal., 10" h. .................... **1,980.00**

**Crock,** cylindrical w/molded rim & applied eared handles, cobalt blue brushed hops & "3" & impressed "J. Fisher & Co. Lyons, N.Y.," ca. 1880, 3 gal., 10" h. (very minor glaze spider & 1" tight line on side) .......... **278.00**

**Crock,** cylindrical w/molded rim & applied eared handles, cobalt blue slip-quilled stylized plume flower decoration, impressed "Edmunds & Co.," ca. 1860, 3 gal., 10¼" h. (some stain spots) ...................................... **121.00**

**Crock,** cylindrical w/molded rim & applied eared handles, cobalt blue slip-quilled decoration of dotted deer, pine tree & fence, impressed "J. & E. Norton & Co. Bennington, Vt.," ca. 1859, 3 gal., 10½" h. (professional restoration to surface chips at rim & to right ear) ............. **4,840.00**

**Crock,** cylindrical w/molded rim & applied eared handles, cobalt blue slip-quilled grape cluster on leafy vine, impressed "O.L. & A.K. Ballard, Burlington, VT," ca. 1860, 3 gal., 10½" h. (insignificant hairline in back)................................................. **308.00**

**Crock,** ovoid body w/short cylindrical rim, applied eared handles, cobalt blue incised flower on one side & cobalt blue pigeon on reverse, blue accents at ears, unsigned, attributed to Croluis, Manhattan Wells, ca. 1835, approx. 3 gal., 14" h. (minor chips at base & glaze chips from age & use) ... **938.00**

**Crock,** cylindrical w/molded rim & applied eared handles, cobalt blue slip-quilled paddletail bird decoration, impressed "N.A. white & Son Utica, N.Y.," ca. 1885, 4 gal., 11" h. (two rim chips) ................................................. **605.00**

**Crock,** cylindrical w/rolled molded rim & applied eared handles, cobalt blue slip-quilled large floral & vase decoration, impressed "J. & E. Norton & Co. Bennington, VT.," ca. 1859, 4 gal., 11" h. (some glaze flakes all around the base & touching the blue, 3" tight hairline in back)................................................. **787.00**

**Crock,** cylindrical w/molded rim & applied eared handles, cobalt blue brushed waterfall-like design, impressed "M. Woodruff Cortland," New York, ca. 1870, 4 gal, 11" h. (professional restoration to thru lines on side & back) ................................ **495.00**

**Crock,** cylindrical w/molded rim & applied eared handles, thick cobalt blue slip-quilled spotted dog standing & looking back, ground cover, impressed "E.W. Hale Boston" & "4," ca. 1870, 4 gal., 11¼" h. (some design fry to thick blue)................................................. **3,740.00**

**Crock,** cylindrical w/molded rim & applied eared handles, cobalt blue brushed floral decoration, impressed "C. Hart Sherburne," ca. 1870, 4 gal., 11½" h. (overall staining & minor glaze spider) ......................... **145.00**

**Crock,** cylindrical w/ring-molded rim & applied eared handles, cobalt blue brushed double tulip decoration, impressed "W. E. Welding Brantford, Ont." & "4," ca. 1880, 4 gal., 11½" h. (minor stone pings in back) ............. **165.00**

**Crock,** cylindrical w/molded rim & applied eared handles, cobalt blue slip-quilled stylized snowflake, impressed "C.L. & A.K. Ballard Burlington, VT.," ca. 1870, 4 gal., 12" h. (some overall staining) .......... **393.00**

**Crock,** wide ovoid body w/molded, slightly flared rim, applied eared handles, cobalt blue slip-quilled running rabbit decoration, impressed "Norton & Fenton Bennington, VT.," ca. 1840, 4 gal., 14½" h. (extensive professional restoration to glaze flaking throughout) ........................... **726.00**

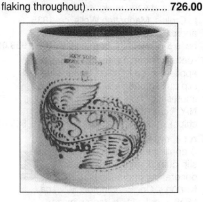

*Crock with Banner*

**Crock,** cylindrical w/molded rim & applied eared handles, cobalt blue slip-quilled detailed winged banner surrounding "S & M," impressed "New York Stoneware Co. Fort Edward, N.Y.," a specialty order piece, ca. 1870, 5 gal., insignificant glaze spider in front, 12½" h. (ILLUS.) ......................... **877.00**

**Crock,** cylindrical w/molded rim & applied eared handles, cobalt slip-quilled large wreath design w/"5" in center, impressed "John Burger Rochester," New York, ca. 1855, 5 gal., 13" h...................... **523.00**

**Crock,** cylindrical w/molded rim & applied eared handles, cobalt slip-quilled dog standing on grass w/basket in mouth, squiggles, w/"6" above dog, impressed "S. Hart Fulton, N.Y.," ca. 1860, 6 gal., 13" h. (professional restoration to glaze imperfections in back & side)............ **2,200.00**

**Crock,** cylindrical w/ring molded rim, applied eared handles, cobalt blue slip-quilled large daisy & leaves, impressed "Burger & Lang Rochester, N.Y." & "6," ca. 1870, 6 gal., 14½" h................................. **468.00**

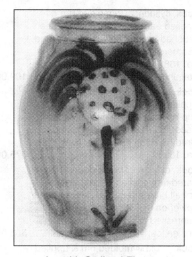

*Jar with Stylized Flower*

**Jar,** cylindrical sides tapering to a thick flaring rim, cobalt blue slip-quilled bullseye-type leaves & two stylized flowers under impressed "1/2," unsigned, attributed to M. Woodruff, Cortland, N.Y., ca. 1870, ½ gal., 7½" h.................................................. **575.00**

**Jar,** bulbous ovoid body w/molded rim & applied eared handles, cobalt blue slip-quilled long-tailed incised bird above "M. Vail" in blue script, cobalt blue slip-quilled large flower on reverse, unsigned, probable vendor name & maker is attributed to upstate New York, ca. 1830, ½ gal., 8" h. (minor chip at base)............... **1,485.00**

**Jar,** bulbous ovoid body w/narrow molded rim, applied eared handles, cobalt blue brushed bold stylized flower, blue accents at ears & handles incised "3" accented on back, unsigned, possibly N. Clark Lyons, New York, minor overall staining & surface wear at rim, ca. 1830, 3 gal., 14" h. (ILLUS. above) ....................... **908.00**

**Jar,** bulbous ovoid body w/narrow molded rim, applied eared handles, cobalt blue brushed swag decoration highlighting handles & neck, front & back, impressed "C. Crolius Manufacturer New York," ca. 1835, approx. 4 gal., 17" h. (professional restoration to age lines throughout) ... **484.00**

**Jug,** bulbous ovoid, tapering to a short cylindrical neck w/molded rim, applied strap handle, decorated w/a simple brushed cobalt blue floral design, impressed "G. F. Brayton & Co. Utica, N.Y.," ca. 1830, 1 gal., 10½" h. (overall age staining) ........... **290.00**

**Jug,** semi-ovoid w/molded rim, applied strap handle, cobalt blue brushed double floral decoration w/blue accents at the handle, impressed "Campbell, Penn Yan," ca. 1850, 1 gal., 10½" h. (few minor surface chips) ................................... **484.00**

*Jug with Brushed Plume*

**Jug,** semi-ovoid w/molded rim, applied strap handle, cobalt blue brushed double plume decoration w/blue accent at handle, impressed "Nichols & Boynton Burlington, VT.," ca. 1855, 1 gal., 11" h. (ILLUS.) ....... **385.00**

**Jug,** semi-ovoid w/molded rim, applied strap handle, cobalt blue slip-quilled Christmas tree, impressed "Whites Utica," New York, ca. 1870, 1 gal., 11" h. (thru line in handle) ............................................... **97.00**

**Jug,** semi-ovoid w/molded rim, applied strap handle, cobalt blue slip-quilled flamingo on stump, impressed "Whites Utica," New York, ca. 1870, 1 gal., 11" h. (minor surface chips in back & professional restored spout chip) ......................... **342.00**

**Jug,** semi-ovoid w/molded rim, applied strap handle, cobalt blue slip-quilled circular designed floral

decoration w/blue accent at handle, impressed "Cowden & Wilcox Harrisburg, PA.," ca. 1870, 2 gal., 13" h. (tight age lines at base in front & minor glaze spider cracks on side) ... **218.00**

**Jug,** bulbous ovoid w/molded rim, applied strap handle, cobalt blue incised long-tailed bird on branch decoration & blue accent at handle base, impressed "I. Seymour Troy," New York, ca. 1825, 14" h. (surface chip at spout) ................... **2,530.00**

**Jug,** semi-ovoid w/molded rim & applied strap handle, cobalt blue slip-quilled "1862" above line design, impressed "O.L. & A.K. Ballard, Burlington, VT" & "2," ca. 1862, 2 gal., 14" h. ................................ **1,018.00**

**Jug,** semi-ovoid w/molded rim & applied strap handle, cobalt blue slip-quilled bird on branch & "2" & impressed "T. Harrington Lyons," (T. Harrington is stamped upside down), Lyons, New York, ca. 1860, 2 gal., 13½" h. (professional restoration to freeze line at base) .......................... **908.00**

**Jug,** semi-ovoid w/molded rim & applied strap handle, cobalt blue slip-quilled dotted, running bird on floral branch, impressed "W. Roberts Binghampton, N.Y.," ca. 1860, 2 gal., 14" h. (stack marks front & back, tight age spider cracks on side) ................ **393.00**

*Jug with Bird on Plume*

**Jug,** semi-ovoid w/molded rim & applied strap handle, cobalt blue slip-quilled bird on plume decoration, impressed "J.S. Taft & Co. Keene, N.H.," ca. 1870, 2 gal., tight hairline in handle, very minor surface chip at spout, 14" h. (ILLUS. bottom previous page) ................................. **938.00**

**Jug,** bulbous semi-ovoid w/molded rim & applied strap handle, cobalt blue slip-quilled thick ribbed flower, impressed "F. Stetzenmeyer & Co. Rochester, N.Y.," ca. 1860, 2 gal., 14½" h. ........................................ **1,694.00**

**Jug,** semi-ovoid w/molded rim & applied strap handle, heavy cobalt blue slip-quilled stylized flower decoration, impressed "W.A. Lewis Galesville N.Y.," ca. 1860, 3 gal., 15½" h. (professional restoration to tight line on one side) ...................... **363.00**

**Jug,** semi-ovoid w/molded rim & applied strap handle, impressed cobalt blue script advertising "J. E. O'Keefe Oswego, N.Y." & impressed "J. Fisher & Lyons, N.Y.," ca. 1880, 3 gal., 15½" h. (repair to base chip in front) ................................................. **121.00**

**Jug,** semi-ovoid w/molded rim, applied strap handle, artistic cobalt blue slip-quilled detailed bird sitting on floral branch, impressed "J. & E. Norton & Co. Bennington, VT.," ca. 1859, 3 gal, 15½" h. (full length glued thru line in back) .................. **4,889.00**

**Jug,** semi-ovoid w/molded rim, applied strap handle, cobalt blue slip-quilled daffodil & leaf decoration, impressed "N. Clark & Co. Rochester" New York & "3," ca. 1850, 3 gal., 17" h. ......... **2,970.00**

**Jug,** semi-ovoid w/molded rim, applied strap handle, cobalt blue slip-quilled snowflake decoration, impressed advertising mark "T.S. Angel & Son, Wholesale & Retail Groceries Provisions & C No. 32 Court Street Watertown," unsigned, ca. 1860, 4 gal., 16½" h. (very minor design fry & stone ping) ................ **1,210.00**

**Pitcher,** 9½" h., squatty bulbous body tapering to a wide slightly flared rim w/pinched spout, applied strap handle, cobalt blue slip-quilled poppy decoration, impressed "Whites Binghamton," New York minor glaze run on side, ca. 1860, 1 gal. (ILLUS. top next column) ..... **1,513.00**

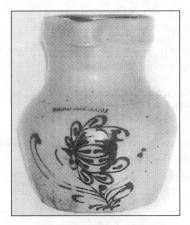

*Squatty Stoneware Pitcher*

**Preserving jar,** w/original lid, cylindrical body tapering to slightly flared molded rim, cobalt blue slip-quilled "1/2 Gallon" in script, unsigned, attributed to M. Woodruff, Cortland, N.Y., ca. 1870, ½ gal., 7½" h. (a few very minor surface rim chips & very minor glaze spider crack in front) .................................. **198.00**

**Preserving jar,** cylindrical body tapering to slightly flared molded rim, unique cobalt blue slip-quilled swirl designs, unsigned, attributed to M. Woodruff, Cortland, N.Y., ca. 1870, ½ gal., 7½" h ..................................... **308.00**

**Preserving jar,** slightly tapering cylindrical body w/slightly flared rim, elaborate cobalt blue slip-quilled dotted basket of blowers, center bullseye design, impressed "Ithaca N.Y.," attributed to Macumber & Tannahill, ca. 1870, 2 gal., 10½" h. (shallow rim chip in back & minor surface chips at ears) ...................... **770.00**

**Preserving jar,** cov., slightly tapering cylindrical w/slightly flared rim, applied eared handles, cobalt blue slip-quilled stylized floral decoration, impressed "A.O. Whittemore Havana, N.Y.," ca. 1870, 2 gal., 10½" h. ............................................. **132.00**

**Preserving jar,** cylindrical w/rolled molded rim, applied eared handles, cobalt blue slip-quilled stylized orchid decoration, impressed "Whites Utica, N.Y.," ca. 1870, 2 gal., 11" h. (professional restoration to age line on one side) ................... **206.00**

*Preserving Jar with Flower*

**Preserving jar,** cylindrical w/molded rim & applied eared handles, cobalt blue slip-quilled flower, impressed "C.W. Braun Buffalo, N.Y.," ca. 1870, 2 gal., 11½" h. (minor, tight glaze line at back).......................... **194.00**

**Preserving jar,** cylindrical w/slightly flared molded rim, applied eared handles, cobalt blue slip-quilled double flower decoration, impressed "W. A. Macquoid & Co. New York Little West 12th St.," ca. 1870, 2 gal., 11½" h................................. **339.00**

**Preserving jar,** cov., slightly tapering cylindrical body w/ring neck & molded rim, applied eared handles, cobalt blue slip-quilled geometric design, impressed "Haxstun Ottman & Co. Fort Edward, N.Y." & "2" above design, ca. 1880, 2 gal., 11½" h. ........................................... **154.00**

**Preserving jar,** slightly tapering cylindrical w/molded rim & applied eared handles, thick, rich cobalt blue slip-quilled double flower decoration, impressed "F. Stetzenmeyer Rochester, N.Y.," ca. 1860, 3 gal., professional restoration to age lines throughout, 14" h. (ILLUS. above) .......................... **1,573.00**

**Preserving jar,** slightly tapering cylindrical body w/molded rim & applied eared handles, cobalt blue slip-quilled stylized floral decoration, impressed "West Troy, N.Y. Pottery," ca. 1870, 4 gal., 14" h. (some staining & glaze flake on side) .......... **454.00**

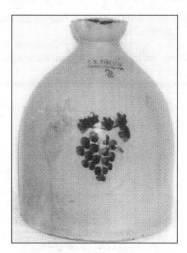

*Unusual Stoneware Syrup Jug*

**Preserving jar,** cylindrical w/rolled molded rim, applied eared handles, cobalt blue slip-quilled large leaf decoration, unsigned, attributed to Jordan, N.Y., ca. 1850, 4 gal., 15½" h. (professional restoration to 6" line by right ear, uneven bottom) ................... **545.00**

**Syrup jug,** semi-ovoid w/slightly flared pinched rim applied strap handle, slip-quilled cobalt blue grape cluster on leafy stem, impressed mark "A.K. Ballard Burlington, VT.," some minor surface wear & surface chips on spout, ca. 1870, 2 gal., 12½" h. (ILLUS. above) ................................ **726.00**

**Water cooler,** barrel-shaped w/elaborate heavy cobalt blue brushed floral design decorating entire front surface, unsigned, possibly Remmey, ca. 1830, 3 gal., 13" h. (insignificant surface chips at rim) ................................................. **696.00**

# WATT POTTERY

*Founded in 1922, in Crooksville, Ohio, this pottery continued in operation until the factory was destroyed by fire in 1965. Although stoneware crocks and jugs were the first wares produced, by 1935 sturdy kitchen items in yellowware were the mainstay of production. Attractive lines like Kitch-N-Queen (banded) wares and the hand-painted Apple, Cherry and Pennsylvania Dutch (tulip) patterns were popular throughout the country.*

*Today these hand-painted utilitarian wares are "hot" with collectors.*

*A good reference book for collectors is* Watt Pottery, An Identification and Value Guide, *by Sue and Dave Morris (Collector Books, 1993).*

*Watt Pottery mark*

**Baker,** Tear Drop patt., rectangular, No. 85, 9" w. ................................... **$800.00**

**Baker,** cov., Apple patt., No. 66, 7¼" d. ............................................. **125.00**

**Baker,** cov., Apple patt., No. 96, 8½" d. ............................................. **100.00**

**Baker,** cov., Apple patt., No. 600, 7" d. . **120.00**

**Baker,** cov., Cherry patt., No. 54, 8½" d. ............................................. **110.00**

*Morning Glory Baker*

**Baker,** cov., Morning Glory patt., No. 94, 8½" d. (ILLUS.) .................... **275.00**

**Baker,** cov., Open Apple patt., No. 96, 8½" d. ............................................. **300.00**

**Bean pot,** cov., brown, No. 76, 6½" h... **15.00**

**Bean pot,** cov., Double Apple patt., No. 76, 6½" h. ................................... **350.00**

**Bean pot,** cov., Starflower patt., No. 76, 6½" h. ................................... **175.00**

**Bean pot,** cov., Tear Drop patt., No. 76, 6½" h. ................................... **110.00**

**Bean cup,** Apple patt., No. 75, 2¼" h., 3½" d. ............................................. **250.00**

**Bean cup,** Starflower patt., No. 75, 3½" d., 2¼" h. ..................................... **40.00**

**Bowl,** 5¼" d., 2½" h., Apple patt., No. 05 ................................................. **60.00**

**Bowl,** 5½" d., 2" h., Apple patt., No. 74 ................................................. **35.00**

**Bowl,** 6¼" d., 3" h., Apple patt., No. 06 ................................................. **50.00**

**Bowl,** 6¼" d., 2½" h., Apple patt., No. 60 ................................................. **90.00**

**Bowl,** 7¼" d., 3½" h., Apple patt., No. 66 ................................................. **50.00**

**Bowl,** 8" d., 1½" h., Apple patt., No. 44 ................................................. **200.00**

**Bowl,** 9½" d., 4" h., Apple patt., No. 73 ................................................. **75.00**

*Apple Pattern Spaghetti Bowl*

**Bowl,** spaghetti, 13" d., 3½" h., Apple patt., No. 39 (ILLUS.) ...................... **135.00**

**Bowl,** 9½" d., 4" h., Autumn Foliage patt., No. 73 ................................... **85.00**

**Bowl,** 7¼" d., 3" h., Cherry patt., No. 53 ................................................. **35.00**

**Bowl,** 8¼" d., 3¼" h., Cherry patt., No. 54 ................................................. **35.00**

**Bowl,** 5½" d., 2" h., Crosshatch patt. (ILLUS. below) ................................... **75.00**

*Small Crosshatch Bowl*

*Open Apple Bowls*

**Bowl,** 5¼" d., 2½" h., Double Apple patt., No. 05 ..................................... **90.00**

**Bowl,** 6¼" d., 3" h., Double Apple patt., No. 06 ..................................... **70.00**

**Bowl,** 4¼" d., 2" h., Open Apple patt., No. 04 (ILLUS. far left, above).......... **125.00**

**Bowl,** 5¼" d., 2½" h., Open Apple patt., No. 05 (ILLUS. second from left, above) ..................................... **125.00**

**Bowl,** 6¼" d., 3" h., Open Apple patt., No. 06 (ILLUS. second from right, above)............................................. **125.00**

**Bowl,** 7 ¼" d., 3" h., Open Apple patt., No. 07 (ILLUS. far right, above)........ **125.00**

**Bowl,** 8" d., 1½" h., Rio Rose patt., No. 44 ................................................ **25.00**

**Bowl,** spaghetti, 13" d., 3½" h., Rio Rose patt., No. 39................................ **90.00**

**Bowl,** 6¼" d., 2½" h., Rooster patt., No. 60 .............................................. **100.00**

**Bowl,** 7¼" d., 3½" h., Rooster patt., No. 66 ................................................ **90.00**

**Bowl,** 8¼" d., 3¼" h., Silhouette patt., No. 54 ............................................... **30.00**

**Bowl,** 6¼" d., 2¼" h., Starflower patt., No. 52 ............................................... **30.00**

**Bowl,** 7¼" d., 3" h., Starflower patt., No. 53 ............................................... **35.00**

**Bowl,** 6¼" d., 3" h., Tear Drop patt., No. 06 ............................................... **40.00**

**Bowl,** 7¼" d., 3" h., Tear Drop patt., No. 07 ............................................... **40.00**

**Bowl,** spaghetti, 13" d., 3½" h., Tear Drop patt., No. 39 ........................... **375.00**

**Bowl,** spaghetti, 13" d., 3½" h., Tulip patt., No. 39 ..................................... **350.00**

**Bowl,** 4" d., 1½" h., Tulip patt., No. 602 ............................................ **250.00**

**Bowl,** 5" d., 2" h., Tulip patt., No. 603... **225.00**

**Canister,** cov., Apple patt., No. 81, 6½" d. ............................................... **450.00**

**Canister,** cov., Apple patt., No. 72, 7¼" d. ............................................... **450.00**

**Canister,** cov., Dutch Tulip patt., No. 82, 5" d. ...................................... **500.00**

**Canister,** cov., Starflower patt., No. 81, 6½" d. ................................... **325.00**

**Canister,** cov., Tear Drop patt., No. 72, 7¼" d. ...................................... **400.00**

**Carafe,** cov., Apple patt., No. 115, 10½" h. .......................................... **2,500.00**

*Starflower Carafe*

**Carafe,** cov., Starflower patt., No. 115, 10½" h. (ILLUS.) ............................ **1,500.00**

**Casserole,** cov., Apple patt., No. 05, 5" d. ................................................. **150.00**

**Casserole,** cov., Dutch Tulip patt., w/French handle, No. 18, 5" d. ......... **300.00**

**Casserole,** cov., Rooster patt., No. 05, 5" d. ...................................... **185.00**

**Chip-N-Dip set,** Apple patt., No. 110 & 120 bowls, the set ........................ **300.00**

**Cookie jar,** cov., Apple patt., No. 503, 8" h. .................................................. **425.00**

Cookie jar, cov., Apple patt., No. 92,
10" h. .............................................. **900.00**

Cookie jar, cov., Autumn Foliage
patt., No. 503, 8" h. ........................ **250.00**

Cookie jar, cov., Double Apple patt.,
No. 503, 8" h. ................................. **375.00**

Cookie jar, cov., "Goodies," No. 59,
8½" h. ............................................ **300.00**

Cookie jar, cov., "Goodies," No. 72,
9½" h. ............................................ **250.00**

Cookie jar, cov., Moonflower patt.,
No. 21, 7½" h. ................................ **200.00**

Cookie jar, cov., Morning Glory patt.,
brown, No. 95, 10" h. ..................... **350.00**

*Silhouette Cookie Jar*

Cookie jar, cov., Silhouette patt.,
No. 21, 7½" h. (ILLUS.) ................... **135.00**

Cookie jar, cov., Starflower patt.,
No. 21, 7½" h. ................................ **200.00**

Creamer, Autumn Foliage patt.,
No. 62, 4¼" h. ................................ **250.00**

Creamer, Double Apple patt., No. 62,
4¼" h. ............................................ **500.00**

Creamer, Morning Glory patt., yellow,
No. 97, 4¼" h. ................................ **600.00**

Creamer, Open Apple patt., No. 62,
4¼" h. ......................................... **1,000.00**

Creamer, Rooster patt., No. 62, 4¼" h.
(ILLUS. far left, top next page) ........... **225.00**

Creamer, Starflower patt., five-petal,
No. 62, 4¼" h. ................................ **250.00**

Cruet set, cov., Bisque patt., 7½" h. ...... **50.00**
Cruet set, cov., Speckled patt., 7½" h. .. **65.00**
Grease jar, cov., Apple patt., No. 01,
5" h. ............................................... **300.00**

Grease jar, cov., Starflower patt.,
No. 47, 5" h. ................................... **275.00**

Ice bucket, cov., Apple patt., No. 59,
7" h. ............................................... **250.00**

*Starflower Ice Buckets*

Ice bucket, cov., Starflower patt.,
four- or five-petals, No. 59, 7" h.,
each (ILLUS. of two) ........................ **185.00**

Ice tea keg, cov., plain, 11" h. ............... **90.00**

Mixing bowls, nesting, Apple patt.,
deep, Nos. 63, 64 & 65, 4" to 5¾" d.,
each .................................................. **60.00**

Mixing bowls, nesting, Banded patt.,
5" to 12" d., each ................. **15.00 to 25.00**

Mixing bowls, nesting, Eagle patt.,
ribbed, Nos. 5, 7, 8 & 9, 5" to 9" d,
each (ILLUS. below) ........................ **125.00**

Mixing bowls, nesting, Reduced
Apple patt., deep, Nos. 61, 63, 64 &
65, 4" to 5¾" d., each ........................ **75.00**

Mixing bowls, nesting, Rooster patt.,
5" to 9" d., each ................................ **65.00**

Mug, Apple patt., No. 701, 3" h. .......... **500.00**

Mug, Autumn Foliage patt., No. 121,
3" h. ............................................... **200.00**

Mug, Starflower patt., No. 501, 4½" h. ... **90.00**

Pie plate, Apple patt., No. 33, 9¼" d. ... **125.00**

Pie plate, Rio Rose patt., No. 33,
9¼" d. ............................................ **150.00**

Pitcher, 6½" h., Apple patt., No. 16 .... **100.00**

*Eagle Pattern Mixing Bowls*

*Rooster Pitchers and Creamer*

*Apple Pattern Salt & Pepper Shakers*

**Pitcher,** 8" h., Apple patt., No. 17 ....... **275.00**
**Pitcher,** 6½" h., Autumn Foliage patt.,
No. 16 ............................................... **75.00**
**Pitcher,** 8" h., Autumn Foliage patt.,
No. 17 ............................................. **160.00**
**Pitcher,** 5¼" h., Cherry patt., No. 15... **150.00**
**Pitcher,** 6½" h., Cross Hatch patt.,
No. 16 ............................................. **175.00**
**Pitcher,** 8" h., Cherry patt., No. 17...... **250.00**
**Pitcher,** 5¼" h., Double Apple patt.,
No. 15 ............................................. **325.00**
**Pitcher,** 6½" h., Dutch Tulip patt.,
No. 16 ............................................. **225.00**
**Pitcher,** refrigerator, 8" h., Dutch Tulip
patt., No. 69 ..................................... **650.00**
**Pitcher,** 5¼" h., Rio Rose patt.,
No. 15 ............................................. **275.00**
**Pitcher,** 5¼" h., Rooster patt., No. 15
(ILLUS. top center left) ..................... **125.00**
**Pitcher,** 6½" h., Rooster patt., No. 16
(ILLUS. top center right) ................... **135.00**
**Pitcher,** refrigerator, 8" h., Rooster
patt., No. 69 (ILLUS. top right).......... **500.00**
**Pitcher,** 8" h., Silhouette patt., No. 17... **175.00**
**Pitcher,** 5¼" h., Starflower patt., five-
petal, No. 15 ...................................... **65.00**

**Pitcher,** refrigerator, 8" h. Starflower
patt., No. 69 ..................................... **550.00**
**Pitcher,** 5¼" h., Tear Drop patt.,
No. 15 ............................................... **60.00**
**Pitcher,** 6½" h., Tear Drop patt.,
No. 16 ............................................. **125.00**
**Pitcher,** 6½" h., Tulip patt., No. 16...... **150.00**
**Pitcher,** 8" h., Tulip patt., No. 17......... **300.00**
**Plate,** 10" d., Apple patt. .................... **400.00**
**Plate,** 8½" d., Rio Rose patt................. **25.00**
**Platter,** 12" d., Apple patt., No. 49 ...... **350.00**
**Platter,** 12" d., Cherry patt., No. 49..... **150.00**
**Platter,** 15" d., Rio Rose patt.,
No. 31 ............................................. **100.00**
**Salt & pepper shakers,** barrel-
shaped, Apple patt., 4" h., the set
(ILLUS. bottom center) ..................... **450.00**
**Salt & pepper shakers,** hourglass-
shaped, Apple patt., with or without
raised "S" & "P", 4" h, the set
(ILLUS. bottom left & right) .............. **225.00**
**Salt & pepper shakers,** hourglass-
shaped, Starflower patt., four-petal
4" h., the set...................................... **250.00**
**Salt & pepper shakers,** barrel-shaped,
Rooster patt., 4" h., the set ................ **500.00**

*Autumn Foliage Teapot*

**Salt & pepper shakers,** hourglass-shaped, Tear Drop patt., 4" h., the set ..................................................... **225.00**

**Sugar bowl,** cov., Apple patt., No. 98, 4½" h. ................................................ **400.00**

**Sugar bowl,** cov., Rooster patt., No. 98, 4½" h. .................................. **500.00**

**Teapot,** cov., Autumn Foliage patt., No. 505, 5" h. (ILLUS. above) ........ **1,800.00**

**Teapot,** cov., Brown Banded patt., No. 112, 6" h. .................................. **600.00**

**Water coolers,** stoneware, Eagle or Acorn patt. ....................................... **200.00**

# WEDGWOOD

*Reference here is to the famous pottery established by Josiah Wedgwood in 1759 in England. Numerous types of wares have been produced through the years to the present.*

## BASALT
**Creamer & cov. sugar bowl,** h.p. coat of arms, impressed "Wedgwood - England" ........................................ **$75.00**

**Model of a bulldog,** standing, w/glass eyes, impressed mark, ca. 1913, 4¾" l. ................................................ **489.00**

**Pitcher,** 3" h., Kenlock Ware, bulbous ovoid body tapering to a wide short cylindrical neck w/long pinched spout, C-scroll handle, enamel-decorated w/large colorful iris blossoms & leaves, impressed & painted marks, ca. 1900 .................. **431.00**

**Pitcher,** tankard, 6¼" h., cylindrical body decorated w/white relief bust portraits of Franklin & Washington, black ground, impressed "Wedgwood England" (wear & stains) .................. **303.00**

**Tumbler,** tapering cylindrical form w/flaring ringed foot, engine-turned design, inscribed on base "A.L.G. 3.2.23," impressed marks, 1923, 4" h. .............................................. **115.00**

## CREAMWARE
**Chestnut basket,** cov., pierced body w/double-twisted handles & floral finial, impressed marks, ca. 1874, 9¼" w. handle to handle .................. **575.00**

**Coffeepot,** cov., pear-shaped body w/swan's-neck spout, strap handle & domed cover w/knob finial, black transfer-printed decoration of a figural landscape on each side, one side w/"The Shepherd," the other w/"The Tea Party," ca. 1760s, 8¾" h. (spout shortened & reglued, cover rim restoration) ................................. **413.00**

**Dinner service:** cov. gravy tureen w/attached undertray, eight 9¾" plates, six 9¾" d. soup plates, three 7¼" w. oval shallow bowls, three 6⅛" w. shallow trays, two 12¼" w. serving dishes; enamel decoration consisting of a green line border encircling a decoration of shaded green bellflowers joined by a magenta vine, tureen lid has cabbage leaf design around finial, impressed "Wedgwood" plus a single letter, single number or double letter, 22 pcs. (one 9¾" plate has unseen chip under rim, three have enamel loss on green border—some severe, one 7¼" w. oval bowl has a small glaze rub on rim, tureen undertray has three faint hairlines) ........................ **1,100.00**

**Platter,** oval 18¾" l., polychrome decorated transfer-printed foliated decoration, spiral border, impressed mark, ca. 1865 ................................. **546.00**

**Platter,** 19¾" l., colorful mosaic design of scrolls, flowers & geometric figures in center & border, blue, purplish red, yellow, black, grey & brown, impressed "Wedgwood....ABR" (either 1863 or 1889) ...................................... **77.00**

## JASPER WARE
**Box,** cov., white relief classical figures on green, 2½" ..................................... **60.00**

**Box,** cov., white relief classical figures on green, 2 x 3½", marked "Made in England" ............................................. **55.00**

**Cachepot & liner,** squatty rounded sides w/a wide flat bottom & slightly rolled rim, raised on three knob feet, black relief classical scene around the body, narrow leaf rim band, on yellow, ca. 1930, 5⅝" d., 2 pcs. ........ **546.00**

**Candlesticks,** the long bell-form socket w/flaring rim raised on a narrow neck on a ring connector above a short cylindrical shaft w/widely flaring round foot, the socket w/a white relief upright leaf band, the base w/a white relief band of classical figures & trees & a looping scroll rim band, on dark blue, mid-19th c., 4¾" h., pr. ..................... **345.00**

**Candlesticks,** cylindrical shaft w/flaring cupped rim & widely flaring foot, white relief classical figures & trees on shaft, white relief looping scrolls on the foot, on black, ca. 1900, 7¾" h., pr. (rim chip) .............. **403.00**

*Wedgwood Cheese Dish*

**Cheese dish,** cov., high domed cover on a round base w/wide flanged rim, the cover w/a white relief band of classical ladies & children w/a leaf band around the top, angled loop handle, flanged rim w/matching white relief leaf band, on dark blue, late 19th c. (ILLUS.) ......................... **431.00**

**Ewer,** classical baluster-form w/slender neck & wide tricorner rim, on domed round foot, white relief standing classical figures on dark blue, applied white rim & high arched white handle ending in a molded female mask head, ca. 1873, 8¾" h. ..................................... **460.00**

**Jardiniere,** three-color, wide bulbous tapering waisted body w/wide flaring rim & thick footring, white ground applied w/lilac trophies suspended below small rams' heads between green floral festoons & foliate top & base borders, late 19th c., 5¼" h. (staining)............................................ **345.00**

*Wedgwood Pitcher*

**Pitcher,** 5½" h., rope handle, white relief classical figures on dark blue, grape leaf border, marked "England" (ILLUS.) ............................................ **135.00**

**Plaque,** oval, white relief grouping of classical figures titles & dated "Justice and Liberty - 1914-1919," impressed mark & marked "Sgt. C. Bevington R.G. Artillery," framed, ca. 1919, plaque 3½ x 4⅜" ..................... **403.00**

**Plaque,** rectangular, white relief classical scene of Dancing Hours, on black, framed, mid-19th c., 17½" l., 5½" h. ............................... **1,150.00**

**Plaque,** rectangular, white relief classical scene of Dancing Hours, on black, mid-19th c., framed, 7½" l. .................................................. **403.00**

**Plaque,** rectangular, white relief classical scene of Dancing Hours, on green, impressed mark, early 19th c., 18¼" l. (edge chips, firing lines to relief) ..................................... **575.00**

**Spill vases,** black relief classical figures on yellow, early 20th c., 5⅝" h., pr. ......................................... **518.00**

**Tea set:** cov. teapot, cov. sugar bowl & creamer, each w/a squatty bulbous body, the teapot w/a short spout & C-form handle, sugar w/small scroll handles, teapot & sugar bowl w/white relief classical figures on dark blue, the creamer has "The Young Seamstress" & "The Reading Lesson" in white relief, teapot 4½" d., 4½" h., cov. sugar bowl 4⅛" d., 3⅞" h, creamer 3½" d., 2¾" h., 3 pcs. ..................................... **325.00**

**Tea set:** cov. teapot, cov. sugar bowl & creamer; each w/a squatty bulbous footed body, the teapot w/a short spout & C-form handle, sugar w/small scroll handles, white relief classical figural scenes on yellow, early 20th c., teapot 4¾" h., 3 pcs. ... **546.00**

**Tobacco jar,** cov., cylindrical w/a wide bulbous rim & base band, the high domed cover w/swelled rim band & inverted acorn finial, the base w/a white relief band of classical putti in a landscape, oak leaf rim bands, on light blue, ca. 1895, 9½" h. (rim chip on cover) ............................................ **375.00**

**Vase,** cov., 8" h., egg-form body raised on a short pedestal & square foot, the body & cover w/white relief narrow stripes w/a border band of ribbon-tied swags, molded white relief Bacchus head handles w/loops, inverted acorn finial, ca. 1963 .......................................... **633.00**

**Vase,** bud, 5½" h., white relief classical figures on green .................. **60.00**

**Vase,** 6½" h., three-color, classical urn-form w/a short cylindrical neck w/rolled rim & mounted w/upright scroll handles, on a short pedestal on a square foot, white ground applied w/lilac & green leaf swags around the body & leaf bands on neck & base of the body, altered impressed mark, late 19th c. (cover missing) .......................................... **805.00**

**Vase,** 13" h., three-color, bulbous classical baluster-form w/a slender cylindrical neck w/rolled rim & raised on a low pedestal on a thick square foot, white ground w/lilac & green applied relief medallions & floral swags & trophy designs around the body, long leaf bands on the neck & base of body, late 19th c. (cover missing, foot rim chip repairs) ........ **1,380.00**

**Vases,** 7¾" h., classical baluster-form w/short neck & rolled rim, raised on a domed flaring round foot, the body w/white relief large classical figures & lion mask handles w/ring handles, foliate bands on the rim, shoulder & foot, on light blue, 1865-67, pr. (relief loss on one) ...................................... **403.00**

## MISCELLANEOUS

**Bowl,** 4¾" d., Fairyland Lustre, leapfrogging elves exterior decoration, elves on a branch interior decoration ............................ **665.00**

**Bowl,** 6⅜" d., Dragon Lustre, octagonal, mottled blue exterior, mother-of-pearl lustre interior w/ornament center & paneled Oriental landscape border, No. Z4829, printed mark, ca. 1920 .................................... **374.00**

**Bowl,** 8¼" d., Hummingbird Lustre, deep rounded sides on a footring, mottled blue exterior, orange interior, ca. 1920 .......................................... **546.00**

**Bust of Robert Burns,** parian, modeled by E.W. Wyon, ca. 1860, 14" h. .............................................. **690.00**

**Cracker jar,** cov., barrel-shaped, terra cotta ground .................................... **275.00**

**Cracker jar,** cov., cylindrical, white relief classical figures on dark blue, silver plated ball-footed base, rim, cover & bail handle, ca. 1920, marked "Wedgwood - England" ........ **425.00**

**Fish set:** platter & four matching plates; majolica, swimming seals decoration, 5 pcs. ......................... **2,750.00**

**Pitcher,** 9" h., relief-molded grapes & leaves on green ground, Etruria, England .............................................. **95.00**

**Plate,** 9" d., scene of "Old Meeting House, Hingham, Mass.," white on blue .................................................. **125.00**

**Plate,** 10" d., "December" w/griffin, polychrome decorated border ........... **195.00**

**Plate,** bread & butter, Yale patt. .............. **7.00**

**Plate,** "Sugaring," wood engraving of the New England series, Clare Leighton ................................................ **95.00**

**Vase,** 7½" h., Victoriaware, classic form w/green ground decorated w/salmon-colored floral swags terminating in white ram heads & encircling trophy medallions, late 19th c. (missing cover) ..................... **316.00**

**Vase,** 8¾" h., Dragon Lustre, baluster-shaped w/short neck & flaring rim, mottled blue ground, shape No. 2355, No. Z4829, ca. 1920 ........ **431.00**

# WELLER

*The Weller Pottery was established by Samuel A. Weller in 1872 and operated until 1945. Originally located in Fultonham, Ohio, the factory moved to Zanesville in 1882. A wide range of lines, both of art pottery and commercial quality, were produced over the years and we list a sampling here*

*Reference books on Weller include* The Collectors Encyclopedia of Weller Pottery, by Sharon & Bob Huxford (Collector Books, 1979) and All About Weller by Ann Gilbert McDonald (Antique Publications, 1989)

## AURELIAN (1898-1910)

Similar to Louwelsa line but brighter colors and a glossy glaze.

*Aurelian Lamp Base*

**Lamp base,** spherical body on four small feet, decorated w/roses in yellow & brown, yellow & green leaves & brown stems against a dark brown ground, artist-signed, "E. Abel," overall 23" h. (ILLUS.) .... **$935.00**

**Vase,** 7" h., globular body w/short molded neck, decorated w/pale green iris & long leaves on abstract background of dark brown, caramel, vivid yellow & light green glaze, decorated by Madge Hurst, incised mark, "D, #557, 3" (several flakes, minor scratches) .............................. **413.00**

**Vase,** 7" h., trumpet-form w/decoration of pansies w/yellow, green & brown blossoms on green leaves & stems, brown, green, yellow & orange ground .................... **275.00**

**Vase,** 10½" h., wide ovoid body w/short flared rim, decorated w/large iris blossom w/yellow, tan, caramel, green & brown curling petals on long olive yellow & brown stems & leaves, abstract dark brown, yellow, caramel & green ground, incised artist's initials & "Aurelian" in script, impressed "Weller" (ILLUS. left, top next column)............ **1,430.00**

*Aurelian Vase with Blossoms*

**Vase,** 17" h., slender ovoid body w/tapering neck & slightly flared rim, large iris blossoms w/yellow, tan, orange, caramel, light green, teal & brown curling petals on long stems & leaves of olive, dark green & caramel against an abstract dark brown, yellow, orange & pale green ground, artist-signed "MP" on side, minor scratches to side, hairline in bottom (ILLUS. above right) .......... **1,100.00**

*Aurelian Vase with Trumpet Neck*

**Vase,** 40" h., baluster-form body w/trumpet neck, decorated w/rose blossoms in vivid yellow, caramel, peach & tan, detailed thorned stems

& leaves in dark & light green, brown, olive & ivory against an abstract background of dark brown, orange, mustard, green, yellow & caramel, signed, "Hattie Mitchell '99" on side & incised "Aurelian, X49" (ILLUS. bottom previous page).... **15,400.00**

**BALDIN (about 1915-20)**

*Rustic designs with relief-molded apples and leaves on branches wrapped around each piece.*

**Bowl,** 4" d., blue................................ **358.00**
**Pedestal base,** ivory glaze, 23½" h.... **209.00**
**Vase,** 5½" h., wide bulbous body w/short molded rim, red & yellow apple decoration on brown & green ground ............................................. **176.00**
**Vase,** 6" h, 10" d., squatty bulbous body w/flared rim, red & yellow apple decoration on brown & green ground.. **297.00**
**Vase,** 7" h., bulbous base, glossy glaze, experimental ............................ **72.00**
**Vase,** 9½" h., wide cylindrical body flaring at base & rim, apple decoration in rose & yellow, green & brown matte ground (base chips) ..... **132.00**

**BARCELONA (late 1920s)**

*Colorful Spanish peasant-style designs on buff ground.*

**Ewer,** ovoid body w/slender neck & strap handle, 6" h.............................. **128.00**
**Pitcher,** 6" h., globular body tapering to short flaring rim w/pinched spout, angled handle from mid-section to rim, yellow, rose, blue & caramel floral decoration, marked "Weller" .... **143.00**

**BLOSSOM (mid-late 1930s)**

*Pale pink flowers & green leaves on blue or green matte glazed ground.*

**Vase,** 8" h., footed cylindrical body tapering to closed rim, angled handles, green ground........................ **88.00**

**BRIGHTON (1915)**

*Various bird or butterfly figurals colorfully decorated and with glossy glazes.*

**Flower frog,** model of a bird on branch base, 6" h.............................. **176.00**

**Model of a parrot,** green, pink & yellow on stand, 8" h......................... **770.00**
**Model of a kingfisher on stump base,** blue, black, yellow, orange, green, brown, cream, aqua & tan, 9" h. ...................................................... **231.00**
**Model of a woodpecker on tree branch,** 9" h. .................................... **319.00**

**BOUQUET (late 1930s)**

*Various molded flowers in color against a light blue, green or ivory ground on simple shapes often accented by lightly molded ribbing.*

**Bowl-vase,** No. B-3, 4½" h., three-footed, short bulbous body w/short flaring neck ....................................... **125.00**

**CHASE (late 1920s)**

*White relief fox hunt scenes usually on a deep blue ground.*

*Chase Vase*

**Vase,** 7" h., spherical body w/flaring rim, relief fox hunting scene on orange ground (ILLUS.).................... **165.00**
**Vase,** 12" h., wide cylindrical w/gently flared base & rim, relief fox hunting scene on a cobalt blue ground ......... **605.00**

**CLARMONT (ca. 1920)**

*Generally rounded forms molded with horizontal ribbing or wide bands often molded with abstract florals. Decorated with an overall dark brown glaze.*

**Candlesticks** w/side handles, 8" h., pr. ...................................................... **180.00**

**Vase,** 5" h., inverted double gourd
body, double-loop handles ................. **55.00**

**Vase,** 6" h., inverted pear shape
w/flaring foot, shoulder handles,
beaded edge band w/center design
of molded flowers & leaves on
trailing vine ....................................... **66.00**

## CLAYWOOD (ca. 1910)

*Etched designs against a light tan ground,
divided by dark brown bands. Matte glaze.*

**Cuspidor,** lady's .................................. **95.00**

**Vase,** 3" h., etched floral decoration ..... **75.00**

**Vase,** 10¼" h., etched grapes............. **110.00**

## COPPERTONE (late 1920s)

*Various shapes with an overall mottled
green glaze. Some pieces with figural frog or
fish handles. Models of frogs also included.*

**Cigarette stand,** model of a frog on
lily pad, green & brown mottled
glaze ................................................. **468.00**

**Model of a frog & lily pads,** 14" h. .... **375.00**

**Pitcher,** 7½" h., wide ovoid body
composed of molded lily pad leaves
tapering to the shaped rim, large
figural fish handle, ink-stamped mark
& "MD - 19" ...................................... **938.00**

**Sprinkler w/original fittings,** figural
frog, 8 x 12" ................................. **1,950.00**

**Vase,** 6" h., tapering cylindrical shape .. **195.00**

**Vase,** 6½" h., trumpet-form w/flaring
foot.................................................... **187.00**

## CORNISH (1933)

*Various shapes with large leaves & small
berry clusters pendent from the rims against
slightly mottled, variously colored semigloss
grounds.*

**Vase,** 8½" h., blue ............................... **99.00**

## DICKENSWARE 2nd Line early 1900s)

*Various incised "sgraffito" designs usually
with a matte glaze.*

**Jardiniere,** wide bulbous body
tapering slightly to short cylindrical
neck w/slightly flaring rim, floral
decoration in yellow, pink & green on
shoulder corners, dark brown glaze,
unmarked, 9" h. (some glaze
roughness)....................................... **286.00**

**Jug,** squatty bulbous body w/handle
from shoulder to rim, bridge scene
w/"The Mt. Vernon Bridge Co, Mt.
Vernon, O," artist's initials "UJ,"
5½" h. ............................................... **550.00**

**Mug,** incised bust portrait of "Black
Bird," artist's initials "UJ," 6" h.......... **395.00**

**Mug,** incised bust portrait of "Fox
Tail," initialed "FS," 5½" h. ............... **385.00**

**Pitcher,** spherical jug-type w/short
angled spout & loop handle at top,
decorated w/peach & ivory ear of
corn, green & yellow husk & leaves,
olive, orange & brown glaze (minor
scratches to side) ............................. **165.00**

**Vase,** 4" h., two-handled, decorated
w/Viking ship w/incised rigging in
black, yellow & white on deep teal
waves, greyish green ground .......... **286.00**

**Vase,** 4½" h., cylindrical, incised
decoration of peasant man & woman
w/hats & canes in violet, black, grey,
peach & ivory on a grey to white
background, artist-signed (lid may
be missing) ...................................... **220.00**

**Vase,** 7" h., 8" d., squatty bulbous
body tapering to short flaring rim,
decorated w/green, brown & yellow
leaves & berries, brown branches,
dark olive/brown ground (minor
scratches to side) ............................. **165.00**

*Dickensware Vase*

**Vase,** 7½" h., ovoid body w/narrow molded rim, incised American Indian chief w/feathered headdress & breast plate in white, cocoa, brown, yellow, pink & teal against a tan, green & brown ground, incised "Ghost Bull" on side .......................... **523.00**

**Vase,** 8¾" h., 4" d., baluster-form, decorated w/an incised continuous landscape scene w/a golfer putting, against a shaded light blue & brown matte ground, impressed mark .......................................... **1,760.00**

**Vase,** 9" h., swelled cylindrical body w/flaring rim & slightly flared foot, incised portrait of American Indian chief "Black Heart," signed on side "Anthony Dunlavy, 1901" (ILLUS. bottom previous page) .............................. **2,200.00**

**Vase,** 11" h., cylindrical body w/narrow molded rim, incised scene of monk kneeling at altar, grey, yellow, blue, caramel & black against rich chocolate brown ground................. **1,650.00**

**Vase,** 11" h., wide ovoid body tapering to short cylindrical neck w/flaring rim, incised decoration of monk singing & playing a lute in brown, tan, white, black & pink on brown & olive ground, incised artist's initials................................... **440.00**

## DICKENSWARE 3rd LINE (1904)

*Similar to Eocean line. Various fictional characters molded and slip-painted against pale background colors. Glossy glaze.*

**Mug,** two-handled, scene of a gentleman smoking a pipe, wearing a frilly jabot, his hair pulled back & tied w/a ribbon, light blue ground, 4" h. ............................................... **395.00**

**Mug,** cylindrical w/angular handle, figure of "Master Belling" pictured, 5" h. ................................................. **350.00**

## DRESDEN (ca. 1907)

*Slip decoration of dark blue windmills, sailboats and Dutch boys and girls against a blue or green matte ground.*

**Vase,** 10½" h., cylindrical w/a Dutch harbor scene w/sailboats & windmills, shaded blue ground (ILLUS. top next column)................. **715.00**

*Dresden Vase*

## EOCEAN and EOCEAN ROSE (1898-1925)

**Vase,** 3" h., 6" d., squatty bulbous body w/wide rounded shoulder & small molded mouth, floral decoration of single large blossom in deep wine, rose & ivory, pale green leaves & stems against a dark olive shading to pale green ground........... **176.00**

**Vase,** 5½" h., wide cylindrical body w/rounded shoulder & closed rim, decorated w/large berries in deep wine & pink on pale green & greyish green thorny stems & leaves against a dark olive, ivory & pink ground (minute chip to side) ........................ **176.00**

**Vase,** 6½" h., spherical body tapering to a short cylindrical neck & flat rim, decorated w/a large blossom in deep wine & pink w/green center, greyish green stems & leaves on a dark green to grey ground ....................... **946.00**

**Vase,** 8" h., ovoid body tapering to closed rim, jonquil decoration, deep wine & rose center, surrounded by white petals, green & white leaves & stems against a green to ivory ground .............................................. **358.00**

**Vase,** 8½" h., waisted cylindrical body, decorated w/white, pink & green jonquil blossoms w/white, green & brown stems & leaves against a pale grey ground w/rose highlights (ILLUS. top next page) ................... **413.00**

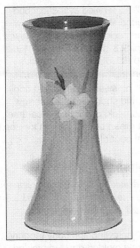

*Eocean Vase with Blossoms*

*Eocean Vase with Sea Gulls*

**Vase,** 10" h., wide expanding cylinder tapering to wide closed rim, decorated w/sea gulls soaring over tossing waves, birds of white & grey against a medium green shading to lighter green ground (ILLUS.) ........ **1,100.00**

**Vase,** 10" h., slender ovoid body w/molded rim, decorated w/berries & blossoms in deep wine & white, thorny branches of green, white & rose on dark green, white & pink ground ............................................ **605.00**

**Vase,** 10½" h., cylindrical body slightly swelling to round shoulder & tapering to narrow molded rim, decorated w/blossoms in blue, bluish

grey & violet w/orange & rose centers, vertical stems & leaves of grey & green on green to ivory ground ............................................. **825.00**

**Vase,** 12" h., swelled cylindrical shouldered body w/closed rim, decorated w/blossoms & buds in deep wine & pink w/greyish green leaves & stems on dark brown, pale green & ivory ground ....................... **297.00**

**Vase,** 14½" h., inverted trumpet form w/six open handles rising from shoulder to rim, decorated w/cluster of large grapes in purple & lavender & white & olive, greyish green & white grapes on dark green & lavender stems w/large curling leaves, dark green to ivory ground, artist-signed, "Ferrell" on side (water marks) .......................................... **1,870.00**

### ETNA (1906)

*Similar to Eocean line but designs are molded in low-relief and colored.*

**Vase,** 4" h., 8" d., wide squatty cushion-form base tapering to wide molded rim, decorated w/three pansies, pink & white, yellow & cream & violet, lavender & yellow, all w/caramel centers, against a grey to ivory ground ..................................... **176.00**

**Vase,** 14" h., cylindrical body w/short molded rim, decorated w/pink & white rose blossoms on thorny pale grey stems, dark green & ivory leaves against a dark grey, ivory & pale grey ground ............................. **495.00**

### FLORETTA (1904)

*Low-relief molded flowers and fruit decorated in underglaze brown & pastel colors. Glossy glaze.*

**Vase,** 4½" h., ovoid body tapering to a rolled rim, small loop shoulder handles, molded floral design around rim, dark brown glaze, impressed mark "#37" (minor glaze scratches) .......................................... **66.00**

**Vase,** 7" h., footed ovoid body w/tapering shoulders w/small tab handles below a swelled lobed neck, decorated w/dark shading to light orange flowers & green leaves against dark brown glaze, impressed mark "#41" ....................................... **110.00**

*Floretta Vase*

**Vase,** 12" h., slightly swelled ovoid body w/round shoulder tapering to narrow molded rim, decorated w/green, brown & yellow molded grape cluster, surrounded by vines at center, dark brown & orange ground (ILLUS.) ............................... **231.00**

### GLENDALE (early to late 1920s)

*Various relief-molded birds in their natural habitats, life-like coloring.*

**Vase,** 7½" h., footed, slightly flaring cylindrical body, decorated w/caramel, pink, green & blue birds & nest in treetop (hairline) ............... **220.00**

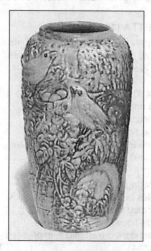

*Glendale Vase*

**Vase,** 8" h., swelled cylindrical body w/a round shoulder to the narrow molded neck, decorated w/yellow, blue, pink & green birds & nest in treetop (ILLUS. bottom previous column) ............................................. **468.00**

**Vase,** 8" h., swelled cylindrical body w/a round shoulder to the narrow molded neck, decorated w/caramel, pink & green birds & nest in treetop (partial paper label) .......................... **413.00**

### GREENBRIER (early 1930s)

*Hand-made shapes with green underglaze covered with flowing pink overglaze marbleized with maroon striping.*

**Vase,** 6" h., cylindrical body tapering to narrow molded rim, marbleized green, grey & burgundy ...................... **55.00**

**Vase,** 15½" h., slender ovoid body w/wide cylindrical neck & flared rim, covered overall in grey, violet & vivid green matte glaze ............................. **358.00**

### GREORA (early 1930s)

*Various shapes with a bicolor orange shaded to green glaze splashed overall with brighter green. Semigloss glaze.*

**Vase,** 5" h., bulbous, footed base below a tall widely flaring neck ........... **59.00**

### HUDSON (1917-34)

*Underglaze slip-painted decoration.*

*Hudson Lamp*

**Bowl,** 6½" d., 3" h., wide bulbous w/low incurved sides, decorated w/pink, yellow, orange, brown & cream blossoms on dark blue ground, artist mark........................... **187.00**

**Lamp,** swelled cylindrical body on flaring foot, short slightly flaring rim, decorated w/large cream & pink flowers w/yellow centers on a grey to cream ground, 28" h. overall (ILLUS. bottom previous page).......... **440.00**

**Tile,** scene of seaside castle in cream, rose, tan, grey & pink on brush-covered ground of green, pink, blue, yellow, cream, orange, brown & ivory, bordering choppy water of pink, blue & green w/distant blue & green sailboat against a pastel blue, lavender & pink sky w/pink & white clouds, framed in wide wooden frame, artist-signed "Timberlake" lower right corner, ink mark reads "The S.A. Weller Co., Zanesville, Ohio", 6" sq. ................................... **4,950.00**

**Vase,** 6" h., bulbous base on narrow foot ring, wide cylindrical neck w/molded rim, angled handles from mid-section to rim, decorated w/yellow, pink, blue, brown & lavender blossoms on pale green leaves, black berries & outlining on pink to blue ground (base chip) ........ **230.00**

**Vase,** 6" h., swelled cylindrical body tapering to narrow molded rim, decorated w/yellow, brown, pink & ivory iris blossom on green stems & leaves, shaded blue ground, artist's initials "DL" on side .......................... **605.00**

**Vase,** 7" h., swelled cylindrical body w/narrow molded rim, decorated w/white dogwood blossoms w/yellow centers, brown branch w/green leaves on shaded blue ground, artist's initials "DL" ........................... **358.00**

**Vase,** 9" h., swelled cylindrical body w/narrow molded rim, decorated w/white & pale blue blossoms on swirling green, blue & pink leaves & stems on a blue to pink ground, signed "Pillsbury" on side ................. **770.00**

**Vase,** 9" h., trumpet-form w/swelled foot, decorated w/blue, peach, yellow, ivory & pink blossoms on green & cream stems & leaves against a dark blue to pale pink ground, signed "Timberlake" on side, impressed "Weller" (ILLUS. top next column) ............................................. **495.00**

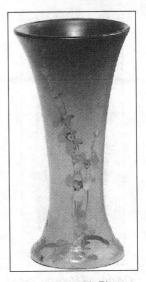

*Hudson Vase with Blossoms*

**Vase,** 9½" h., squatty bulbous body tapering to wide tall cylindrical neck, decorated w/black grapes & vines on a yellow, pink & pale blue wide band from mid-section of body to base of neck, dark blue ground .................... **220.00**

**Vase,** 9½" h., swelled cylindrical shouldered body w/a short rounded neck w/flat rim, decorated w/pink, white & burgundy blossoms w/yellow & black centers on leaves & stems in greyish green & pale blue on a wide band backed by a royal blue matte glaze, (base chip) ............................. **176.00**

**Vase,** 10" h., cylindrical, tapering slightly toward the base & narrow molded rim, decorated w/large iris blossom & bud in yellow, ivory, pink, blue & caramel w/pale green stems & leaves, all outlined in black against a blue to pale yellow ground, signed "Timberlake," impressed "Weller" ..... **880.00**

**Vase,** 10½" h., flaring foot w/bulbous body tapering to wide tall cylindrical neck w/slightly flared rim, floral decoration of large white & grey blossoms w/rose highlights on brown branches w/greyish green & white leaves against vivid blue to light blue ground, initialed "HP," incised "Weller" ............................................. **715.00**

**Vase,** 12½" h., footed cylindrical body tapering to a short widely flaring rim, decorated w/clusters of violet, lavender, white, yellow & rose

*Cylindrical Hudson Vase*

blossoms w/greyish green & pale
green leaves, all outlined in black on
a pink to pale green ground, signed
"Pillsbury" on the side (ILLUS.).......... **715.00**
**Vase,** 13" h., flaring footed swelled
cylindrical body tapering to trumpet
neck, floral decoration of pink &
white blossoms & buds w/yellow &
caramel centers on greyish green &
white branches w/broad, curled
leaves, pastel pink shading to green
ground, signed "McLaughlin" &
impressed "Weller" .......................... **550.00**

*Hudson Vase with a Blue Jay*

**Vase,** 13½" h., tapering cylindrical
body, decorated w/blue jay in blue,
pink, rose, black & white perched on
brown branch surrounded by long
narrow leaves of green, yellow &
pink, blue matte ground, impressed
"Weller," several small flakes at base
(ILLUS. bottom previous column) ..... **825.00**

## IVORY (1910 to late 1920s)

*Ivory-colored body with various shallow
embossed designs with rubbed-on brown
highlights.*

**Vase,** 13" h., waisted cylindrical form,
molded w/nude figures around the
center, molded wreaths & swags on
top & base border ............................ **120.00**
**Umbrella stand,** cylindrical
w/embossed scrolling, 19½" h. ......... **250.00**

## JAP BIRDIMAL (1904)

*Stylized Japanese-inspired figural bird or
animal designs on various solid colored
grounds.*

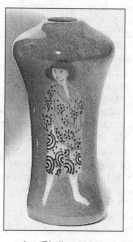

*Jap Birdimal Vase*

**Pitcher,** tankard, 11½" h., geisha girl
in robe of caramel w/black, white &
yellow highlights, carrying a ivory &
black parasol, green & yellow grass
& background of trees w/brown
trunks & green & white leaves, light
blue ground, incised "Weller
Faience" ........................................... **990.00**
**Vase,** 6½" h., waisted cylindrical body
w/short round shoulder tapering to

small flat neck, detailed decoration of Oriental girl in blue & tan w/squeezebag highlights in orange & black, greyish green ground, artist's initials "VMH" on side, impressed "99, 5" (ILLUS. bottom previous page) .............................................. **660.00**

**Vase,** 7" h., trumpet-form body, w/flat rim, geisha girl in brown robe w/black & white floral design, blue & black sash & brown, black & white parasol, large butterflies, dragonflies & beetles in ivory, yellow, black & caramel, deep teal ground, incised "Weller Rhead Faience, 525" (repair to rim) .............................................. **440.00**

**Vase,** 13" h., squatty bulbous base tapering to tall cylindrical neck w/flat rim, geisha girl in detailed blue, mustard, black & white hat & robe carrying black stringed instrument stands atop clumps of green grass & white daisies w/yellow centers, all on a rich caramel ground, squeezebag decoration of stylized overlapping olive & white circles surrounds rim, artist's initials "VMH," impressed "471, 5" ........................................ **2,420.00**

## KNIFEWOOD (late Teens)

*Pieces feature deeply molded designs of dogs, swans, and other birds and animals or flowers in white or cream against dark brown grounds.*

**Jardiniere,** squatty bulbous body w/wide flat rim, decorated w/molded blue & yellow birds sitting on branches w/cherries, 6" h. ............... **385.00**

**Vase,** 3½" h., wide cylindrical body tapering to flat closed rim, decorated w/molded swans & water flowers on rust glaze ........................................ **132.00**

**Vase,** 4½" h., squatty ovoid bulbous body w/a wide flat mouth, molded decoration of yellow daisies & blue butterflies on black ground .............. **143.00**

## KLYRO (early to late 1920s)

*Most pieces feature molded wood framing around panels topped by double pink blossoms and dark purple berries against a finely ribbed ground, often trimmed in tan, brown, cream or olive green.*

**Vase,** 6" h., fan-shaped, green, unmarked........................................... **95.00**

**Planter,** footed, fruit & floral decoration, tan ground w/brown trim & lattice openwork on top, 3½ x 8" ... **150.00**

## L'ART NOUVEAU (1903-04)

*Various figural and floral-embossed Art Nouveau designs.*

**Vase,** 11" h., cylindrical body w/molded peach roses at top, light to dark green matte glaze .................... **286.00**

**Vase,** 13" h., squared waisted cylindrical base swelled at the top & tapering to a closed rim, molded at the top w/peach & caramel poppies w/yellow & green centers against a pale peach & green ground matte glaze (small scratch to side) ............ **220.00**

## LASA (1920-25)

*Various landscapes on a banded reddish and gold iridescent ground.*

**Vase,** 5¼" h., bulbous base w/tapering cylindrical neck, trees & mountains landscape scene ............ **220.00**

*Lasa Vase*

**Vase,** 8½" h., 3¾" d., cylindrical tapering toward base & toward wide, flaring rim, landscape w/bare trees before a lake w/mountains in the distance, golden, reddish & green iridescence (ILLUS.) ........................ **413.00**

**Vase,** 9" h., slightly ovoid cylindrical body tapering slightly to a wide flat rim, landscape w/trees against the iridescent ground ............................ **450.00**

## LOUWELSA (1896-1924)

*Hand-painted underglaze slip decoration on dark brown shading to yellow ground; glossy glaze.*

*Louwelsa Mantel Clock*

**Candlestick,** yellow & orange rose decoration, 9" h. (small chip) ............. **99.00**

**Clock,** mantel or shelf, a wide domed case flattened at the front & back, swelled sides tapering down to rounded feet & an undulating front base, the round white enameled dial w/black Arabic numerals framed by a brass bezel, the case decorated w/mustard & yellow blossoms on olive stems & leaves against a shaded dark brown ground, 4½" d., 11½" w., 10" h. (ILLUS. above) ..... **1,320.00**

**Pitcher,** tankard, 12½" h., decorated w/cluster of large grapes in dark green, medium green & ivory, brown twisting branches & vines on an olive to brown ground, artist's initials "ER" on side (minute flakes at rim) ... **176.00**

**Pitcher,** tankard, 12½" h., portrait of spaniel in brown, salmon, ivory, tan & blue on beige shaded to green ground, signed "A. Haubrich" on side (repaired chips)................................ **523.00**

**Pitcher,** tankard, 17" h., portrait of elk in brown, tan, salmon, cream, grey & green on pink shading to green ground, signed "A. Haubrich" on side ................................................ **1,320.00**

**Vase,** 5" h., 8" w., "genie"-shaped bulbous body, short cylindrical neck, two handles rising from mid-section of body to edge of rim, three-footed, artist-signed ..................................... **695.00**

**Vase,** 5" h., swelled cylindrical body w/flat shoulder & narrow molded rim, decorated w/olive green palm trees against a brown, olive & orange ground .............................................. **154.00**

**Vase,** 6½" h., waisted double gourd w/very small short cylindrical neck & flared rim, decorated w/pansies in black, caramel, ivory, peach & green against a caramel to brown ground (chip at lip) ...................................... **88.00**

**Vase,** 8½" h., swelled cylindrical body, short flaring neck & molded rim, decorated w/yellow, tan & brown pansy on green vines w/large leaves, green, caramel & brown ground .............................................. **220.00**

**Vase,** 10" h., squatty bulbous base tapering to tall slender cylindrical neck w/flat flaring rim, base decorated w/yellow & peach pansies, impressed mark "86, 6"...................... **358.00**

**Vase,** 12" h., expanding cylinder w/short molded neck, decorated w/rose blossom, buds & thorned stem in yellow & olive w/hanging seed pods of caramel, tan & ivory, dark brown, olive & orange glaze, artist's initials "HM" on side............... **770.00**

*Louwelsa Vase*

**Vase,** 13" h., swelled cylindrical body
w/short slightly flared rim, decorated
w/portrait of Native American chief
w/long hair, two-feathered
headdress & necklace of claws &
beads all in shades of brown,
caramel, yellow & tan w/greyish
green accents, dark brown ground,
artist's initials on side (ILLUS. bottom
previous page) .............................. **1,980.00**

**Vase,** 14½" h., cylindrical w/narrow
molded rim, decorated w/large iris
blossoms & buds in yellow, caramel
& white w/green leaves & stems on
green to brown ground, signed
"Hurst" on side (line at rim) .............. **242.00**

## MARBLEIZED (Bo Marblo, 1915)

*Simple shapes with swirled "marbleized"
clays, usually in browns & blues.*

*Marbleized Jardiniere & Pedestal*

**Compote,** swirled orange, black,
brown & cream, 8" h. .......................... **66.00**

**Jardiniere & pedestal,** swirls of pink,
white & brown on pale yellow ground,
jardiniere w/very wide squatty
tapering body w/rolled rim & flaring
foot, impressed "Weller," repairs to
rim & base on both, 18" w., overall
10½" h., 2 pcs. (ILLUS. above).......... **209.00**

**Vase,** 8½" h., flaring foot below
expanding cylindrical body w/slightly
bulbous neck & flaring rim, model of
two frogs at base, swirled brown &
cream glaze ...................................... **77.00**

**Vase,** 14" h., tall, very slender
cylindrical body w/a slightly flaring
foot, swirled orange, black & cream
ground ............................................ **121.00**

## MARVO (mid-1920s-33)

*Molded overall fern and leaf design on
various matte background colors.*

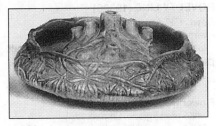

*Marvo Console Bowl with Flower Frog*

**Console bowl w/flower frog,** low
squatty form bowl w/incurved rim,
decorated w/molded dark green &
brown leaves, frog of molded
branches, scratches to interior of
bowl, bowl 11" d., frog 6" d., 2 pcs.
(ILLUS.) .......................................... **143.00**

**Vase,** double bud, 4½" h., cylindrical
vases joined by openwork lattice
bars.................................................. **84.00**

**Vase,** double bud, 5" h., tapering
cylindrical vases joined by molded
fern & leaf panel, green ground ......... **72.00**

## MATT WARE (ca. 1905)

*Various forms decorated with veined,
streaked, or mottled glazes, often with figures
molded in high- and low-relief.*

**Vase,** 5" h., wide cylindrical body
w/round shoulder & short tapering
neck w/flat rim, decorated w/fish
swimming among bubbles &
seaweed, teal glaze (minute flakes) ... **275.00**

**Vase,** 7" h., slightly tapering cylindrical
body w/a flat rim flanked by high
angled loop handles, carved
w/stylized broad spade designs in
deep teal & pale blue against a
cocoa brown matte ground, artist-
signed .............................................. **825.00**

**Vase,** 9½" h., double-gourd form
w/three tiny loop handles at the
shoulder, medium grey decoration of
broad buckeye leaves, stems &
buckeye pods around the ovoid base
section & banded decoration above

& below the shoulder, against a pale
grey matte ground, signed & artist-
initialed ........................................... **715.00**

**Vase,** 12½" h., trumpet-form,
decorated w/large blossoms in
peach, tan, blue, green & brown
w/dark green stems & leaves against
a caramel ground............................ **605.00**

## NOVELTY LINE (1930S)

**Bowl,** 1½" d., squatty bulbous body
w/molded rim, h.p. angel head,
matte rust ground ............................ **77.00**

**Dish,** Louisiana Purchase Exposition
commemorative, grey matte ground,
5" d. .................................................. **44.00**

**Flower frog,** female nude w/scarf,
white matte glaze, unmarked,
8½" h.,............................................ **231.00**

**Model of a camel,** glossy green
glaze, Weller script signature, 4" h. .... **99.00**

**Vase,** 2" h., bulbous body w/cylindrical
neck & flat rim, h.p. angel head, rust
matte ground ..................................... **88.00**

## OAK LEAF (before 1936)

*Molded oak leaves on one side and acorns
on the other; various background colors, matte
glaze.*

**Basket,** bulbous body w/overhead
twisted branch handle, tan leaves on
brown ground, Shape G-1, 7½" h. ...... **85.00**

## PANELLA (late 1930s)

*Pansies or nasturtiums in relief on various
shaded background colors. Matte glaze.*

**Wall pocket,** conical w/widely flaring
rim, decorated w/relief-molded
pansies, shaded green ground .......... **90.00**

## PARAGON (about 1935)

*Simple shapes with incised overall pointed
leaves and round blossoms.*

**Vase,** 6¾" h., 5½" d., globular w/short
wide neck, decorated w/incised
flowers & overlapping leaves,
mustard matte glaze ......................... **165.00**

## PUMILA (early 1920s-'28)

*Panels of large lily pad leaves form an
eight-scallop top. Bowls in the form of water
lily blossoms. Matte glazes in green, yellows
and browns.*

**Vase,** 12" h., trumpet-form w/flared
foot, green & brown ground (base
chips) ................................................ **99.00**

## ROMA (1912-late 1920s)

*Cream-colored ground decorated with
embossed floral swags, bands or fruit clusters.*

**Window box,** banded decoration of
pale red grapes & plums on green
leaves & stems, 8½ x 14½", 7½" h. ... **385.00**

## ROSEMONT -1st Line (late teens to late 1920s)

*Incised and colored birds on branches or
flowers against a solid black or white
background all with a glossy glaze.*

**Jardiniere,** cylindrical w/slightly
flaring rim, decorated w/blue birds
among pink blossoms & pale green
branches, black ground, 8½" d.,
7" h. ................................................. **297.00**

**Vase,** 9" h., wide ovoid body tapering
to short, slightly flaring neck,
decorated w/cockatoos in lavender,
rose & ivory on black ground (minor
scratches to side) ............................ **413.00**

## SABRINIAN (late 1920s)

*Seashell body with sea horse handle. Pastel
colors. Matte finish. Middle period.*

**Ewer,** shell-shaped body w/figural
seahorse handle, 9" h...................... **250.00**

## SICARDO (1902-07)

*Various shapes with iridescent glaze of
metallic shading in greens, blues, crimson,
purple or coppertone decorated with vines,
flowers, stars or free-form geometric lines.*

**Vase,** 4½" h., tapering ovoid body
decorated w/floral design on deep
red ground w/purple & gold
highlights, unmarked ........................ **825.00**

**Vase,** 4½" h., wide mouth on twisted
bulbous body w/four prominent ribs,
floral design in blue, green & gold on
deep glossy red glaze...................... **660.00**

**Vase,** 4½" h., baluster-form body
w/narrow molded rim, iridescent
floral decoration in vivid green &
violet, artist-signed (base chip)........ **523.00**

**Vase,** 4½" h., wide bulbous body
tapering slightly to a flat mouth, four
small round feet, iridescent floral
decoration, artist-signed (hairline) .... **264.00**

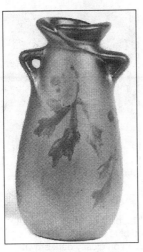

*Ovoid Sicardo Vase*

*Double-gourd Sicardo Vase*

**Vase,** 5" h., bulbous ovoid body tapering to short flaring rim, small angled handles twisting at rim, floral design w/iridescent glaze, signed "Sicard Weller" (ILLUS.) ................... **660.00**

**Vase,** 5½" h., squatty bulbous base tapering to tall slightly tapering sides w/flat mouth, iridescent floral decoration, artist-signed (drilled) ...... **385.00**

**Vase,** 5½" h., ovoid body tapering to closed rim, iridescent floral decoration, artist-signed ................... **495.00**

**Vase,** 7" h., wide ovoid body w/narrow molded rim, twisting cyclamen decoration, blue, silver & red iridescent glaze, artist-signed on side ................................................. **660.00**

**Vase,** 7½" h., ovoid body tapering to a short molded mouth, leaf & berry design, purple & green iridescent glaze, artist-signed on side .............. **935.00**

**Vase,** 7½" h., slender corseted cylindrical body w/cushion foot, landscape scene w/pine tree decoration in orange, violet & gold iridescence ..................................... **275.00**

**Vase,** 7½" h., slightly tapering cylindrical body w/a flat wide shoulder to a short molded mouth, floral decoration on multicolored iridescent glaze, artist-signed on side ............................................... **1,100.00**

**Vase,** 9" h., swelled cylindrical body w/narrow neck & flared rim, decorated w/iridescent stylized green & purple leaf design, artist-signed ................................................. **715.00**

**Vase,** 10" h., waisted double-gourd form, fleur-de-lis design in green & rose, purple, green & blue iridescent glaze, artist-signed on side & base (ILLUS.) ....................................... **1,650.00**

**Vase,** 11" h., ovoid lobed body tapering to a bulbous lobed & incurved scalloped rim, iridescent floral design in red, blue & green w/platinum highlights, artist-signed on side & bottom........................... **2,640.00**

*Sicardo Vase*

**Vase,** 12" h., bulbous ovoid body tapering to a short cylindrical neck, floral decoration, pink, green, blue & purple, iridescent glaze, artist-signed on base & side (ILLUS. bottom previous page) .............................. **2,420.00**

## SILVERTONE (1928)

*Various flowers, fruits or butterflies molded on a pale purple-blue matte pebbled ground.*

**Basket,** fan-shaped, w/overhead branch handle, decorated w/molded grape cluster & leaves on vine, 13" h. ........................................... **1,195.00**

**Vase,** 7" h., squatty bulbous base tapering to flaring rim ........................ **210.00**

**Vase,** 8" h., baluster-form body w/heavy loop handles below a short neck w/ruffled rim, large molded pink poppy blossom on green stem & a pale blue butterfly ............................. **595.00**

**Vase,** 12" h., trumpet-form w/flared foot, decorated w/large calla lilies in white & pale blue w/caramel centers, green stems & leaves, mottled lavender & blue ground ................... **358.00**

## STELLAR

*Hand slip-decorated with blue stars in a "Comet" design. White background, matte finish. Middle period.*

**Vase,** 5½" h., 6½" d., wide squatty ovoid body raised on a small flared footring & tapering to a wide flat mouth, blue stars on a white ground, marked............................................. **715.00**

**Vase,** 5¾" h., 5" d., bulbous ovoid body w/a wide shoulder & short wide cylindrical neck, decorated overall w/five- and six-point white stars on a black matte ground, decorated by Hester Pillsbury, artist's initials on the side, base incised "Weller Pottery" ........................................... **495.00**

## TURADA

*Early line with glossy black, dark brown or mottled tan and black ground decorated around the middle or the rim with a delicate slip-trailed scroll band usually in white or dark pink. On some pieces the band is domed and pierced.*

*Turada Vase*

**Vase,** 6" h., pillow-form on four feet w/raised blue & white stylized decoration on glossy dark brown glaze (ILLUS.).................................... **176.00**

## TURKIS (early 1930s)

*Simple shapes decorated with overall glossy drip glazes in mottled yellowish green against a red ground.*

**Vase,** 5" h., bulbous body w/short cylindrical neck, twisted form in green yellow & red.............................. **66.00**

## WARWICK (1929)

*Molded brown tree bark ground molded with dark brown branches with small pink blossoms and green three-leaf sprigs*

**Vase,** 7" h., circular w/overhead handle .............................................. **132.00**

**Vase,** 10" h., bulbous ovoid body w/twisted branches forming handles at rim................................................ **121.00**

## WOODCRAFT (1917)

*Rustic designs simulating the appearance of stumps, logs and tree trunks. Some pieces are adorned with owls, squirrels, dogs and other animals.*

**Bowl,** 5" d., molded tree trunk w/fox & cubs peeking out of trunk opening.... **319.00**

**Bowl,** 6" d., 3½" h., molded w/design of a seated squirrel amid tree branches.................................... **108.00**

**Flower frog,** model of a crab, 5" w. ...... **88.00**

**Mug,** cylindrical tree trunk form w/three small molded foxes peeking

*Woodcraft Planter*

out of trunk opening, double loop branch handle, large loop above smaller loop, 6" h. ............................. **358.00**

**Planter,** cylindrical tree trunk form w/three small foxes peeking out at side, molded twigs across the top, 5½" h. (ILLUS. above) ..................... **250.00**

**Vase,** 8" h., flattened fan shape, molded w/a fruiting tree ................... **140.00**

**Vase,** 9" h., wide ovoid container tapering to a slender trunk base framed by three slender open branch legs ..................................... **190.00**

**Vase,** bud, 10½" h., slender tree trunk-form molded w/fruit, the stubs of branches forming openings at the top ...................................................... **100.00**

**Vase,** 13½" h., tree trunk-form w/molded owl peering from hole in trunk, branches form tiny open handles near rim ............................. **605.00**

## WHIELDON-TYPE WARES

*The Staffordshire potter, Thomas Whieldon, first established a pottery at Fenton in 1740. Though he made all types of wares generally in production in the 18th century, he is best known for his attractive, warm-colored green, yellow and brown mottled wares molded in the form of vegetables, fruit and leaves. He employed Josiah Spode as an apprentice and was briefly in partnership with Josiah Wedgwood. The term Whieldon ware is, however, a generic one since his wares were unmarked and are virtually indistinguishable from other similar wares produced by other potters during the same period.*

**Plate,** 9¼" d., gently scalloped flanged rim, the rim molded w/panels of lattice, dot & basketweave, mottled 'tortoiseshell' glaze, ca. 1770 (surface wear) ................................. **$402.00**

**Teapot,** cov., spherical body w/small inset cover w/blossom finial, finely ribbed serpentine spout & D-form handle, mottled streaky translucent polychrome glazes, ca. 1760, 3¾" h. (spout & handle damage, cover & interior rim chips) ............................. **345.00**

**Teapot,** cov., creamware, drum-shaped w/inset cover w/knob finial, swan's neck spout w/molded leaf decoration & large loop handle, overall mottled blue, yellow & green tortoiseshell glaze, 5½" h. (small chip on edge of cover & several unseen chips on flange of cover & base has a long meandering crack around the body & through the spout) ................................................. **312.00**

## WILLOW WARES

*This pseudo-Chinese pattern has been used by numerous firms throughout the years. The original design is attributed to Thomas Minton about 1780 and Thomas Turner is believed to have first produced the ware during his tenure at the Caughley works. The blue underglaze transfer print pattern has never been out of production since that time. An Oriental landscape incorporating a bridge, pagoda, trees, figures and bird, supposedly tells the story of lovers fleeing a cruel father who wished to prevent their marriage. The Gods, having pity on them changed them into birds enabling them to fly away and seek their happiness together.*

**BLUE**

**Bowl,** 7¼" d., Mason, England ............ **$50.00**

**Bowl,** 7½" oval, England ....................... **35.00**

**Butter dish,** cov., Allerton, England ..... **95.00**

**Butter pat,** Booth's, England, 3" sq. ..... **25.00**

**Cake stand,** unmarked, England ........ **225.00**

**Cracker jar,** cov., w/cane handles, Old Willow patt., Adderley, England... **150.00**

**Creamer & cov. sugar bowl,** individual size, Booth's, England, pr... **65.00**

*Blue Willow Platter*

**Creamer & cov. sugar bowl,** John Steventon, England, pr. ...................... 65.00

**Dish,** Grimwades, England, 5 x 8" oval ...................................................... 25.00

**Dresser box,** cov., Booth's, England, 4 x 5" ................................................... 135.00

**Gravy boat,** unmarked, 4⅛" h. ............. 66.00

**Gravy boat,** Grimwades, England, 8" l. ...................................................... 35.00

**Gravy boat,** Ridgeway, England.......... 60.00

**Gravy boat w/attached underplate,** Allerton, England. ............................... 75.00

**Gravy boat w/attached undertray,** Booth's, England ................................. 85.00

**Pitcher,** 7" h., Booth's, England.......... 120.00

**Pitcher,** Allerton, England.................. 135.00

**Plate,** 6½" d., England .......................... 8.00

**Platter,** 11 x 13", Allerton, England (ILLUS.) ............................................ 150.00

**Platter,** 11 x 15", Grimwades, England ......................................... 150.00

**Platter,** 13 x 16", unmarked ............... 150.00

**Teapot,** cov., gold trim, Gibson, England ......................................... 100.00

**Vegetable bowl,** cov., unmarked, England ......................................... 125.00

**Vegetable bowl,** cov., Allerton, England ......................................... 225.00

## YELLOW-GLAZED EARTHENWARE

*In the past this early English ware was often referred to as "Canary Lustre," but recently a more accurate title has come into use.*

*Produced in the late 18th and early 19th centuries, pieces featured an overall yellow glaze, often decorated with silver or copper lustre designs or black, brown or red transfer-printed scenes.*

*Most pieces are not marked and today the scarcity of examples in good condition keeps market prices high.*

**Cup & saucer,** handleless, crudely h.p. w/four-petal orange flowers & green leaves, black rims (few enamel flakes, tiny rim flake on cup) ............. $385.00

**Mug,** child's, cylindrical, sepia transfer-printed design of an oval leafy ring around a picture of a carriage & "A New Carriage - For Ann," early 19th c., 2¼" h. ................. 518.00

**Mug,** child's, cylindrical, yellow ground decorated w/a wide h.p. band of stylized leaves & blossoms in pink lustre & green & orange enamel, 2½" h. ............................................... 209.00

**Pitcher,** 5¾" h., ovoid body tapering to a short cylindrical flat rim, red transfer-printed Hogarth figure at a table over a poem concerning drinking, reverse has transfer-printed scene of lovers w/him pledging to protect her (in poem form), silver resist lustre border ............................ **99.00**

## YELLOWWARE

*Yellowware is a form of utilitarian pottery produced in the United States and England from the early 19th century onward. Its body texture is less dense and vitreous (impervious to water) than stoneware. Most, but not all, yellowware is unmarked and its color varies from deep yellow to pale buff. In the last 19th and early 20th centuries bowls in graduated sizes were widely advertised. Still in production, yellowware is plentiful and still reasonably priced.*

**Bowl,** 4¼" d., 2" h., w/three white bands ............................................... **$95.00**
**Bowl,** 7 x 14", brown & white bands ... **120.00**
**Bowl,** 12" d., w/three brown bands ....... **40.00**
**Coffeepot,** cov., relief-molded berries on blue, brown & green running glaze, 10" h. (crazing & surface & glaze flakes in several areas) ........... **330.00**
**Pitcher,** 9½" h., relief-molded bust of beardless Lincoln, log cabin, axe in wood & crossed rifles over stump, white glaze (hairlines & small chips)... **275.00**
**Pitcher,** 10½" h., relief-molded Columbia w/shield under star decorated banner, white w/black & blue daubs & dots ............................. **385.00**

## CHARACTER COLLECTIBLES

*Numerous objects made in the likeness of or named after comic strip and comic book personalities or characters abounded from the 1920s to the present. Scores of these are now being eagerly collected and prices still vary widely. Also see: LUNCH BOXES, POP CULTURE COLLECTIBLES, RADIO & TELEVISION MEMORABILIA and TOYS.*

**Betty Boop fan,** silk & ivory, hand painted w/four images, early 1930s ... **$295.00**

*Broom Hilda Glass*

**Betty Boop figure,** bisque, playing a violin, 3¼" h. ..................................... **150.00**
**Broom Hilda glass,** enameled, shows Broom Hilda & other characters, reads "The Sunday Funnies" across bottom (ILLUS. above) ...................... **82.00**
**Buck Rogers advertisement,** 25th Century Holster, Rocket Pistol, Helmet & Combat Set, red, black & grey graphics, dated 1934, the set ..... **77.00**
**Buck Rogers badge,** "Solar Scout"...... **65.00**
**Buck Rogers Liquid Helium Water Pistol,** No. XZ-44, copper finished metal, Daisy Mfg. Co., w/original orange box stamped "New Copper Lacquer," ca. 1936, 7½" l................. **350.00**
**Buck Rogers manual,** 1933............... **150.00**
**Buck Rogers Movie Jector film,** in original box ........................................ **95.00**

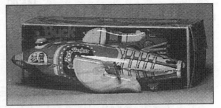

*Buck Rogers Rocket Cruiser*

**Buck Rogers toy, rocket,** "Interplanetary Rocket Cruiser," windup tin, lithographed in red w/yellow & green accents w/central fin & spark case intact, in original box, 1930s, 12" l. (ILLUS.)............. **1,950.00**

*Bugs Bunny Animation Cel*

**Bugs Bunny animation cel,** Bugs reclines atop a sign reading "Back in 15 Minootsa" while chomping on a carrot, gouache on full celluloid applied to a non-matching watercolor background inscribed "Sc 29-1160," 10 x 12½" (ILLUS.) .. **1,840.00**

**Bullwinkle "Soaky" container,** molded plastic w/painted details, in the shape of Bullwinkle wearing stripped full-length swimsuit, 11" h. (some wear on antlers) ...................... **32.00**

**Charlie Chaplin figure,** lead, hand painted, 2½" h. ............................... **120.00**

**Charlie Chaplin game,** board-type, the words "Chasing Charlie" above graphic of Chaplin being chased by a driverless roadster, ca. 1920s, manufactured by Spears Games, England, box measures 7¼ x 10" ..... **375.00**

**Charlie Chaplin pencil box,** tin, marked "Beautebox, CANCO," 8" l. **120.00**

**Dennis the Menace lamp,** composition, Dennis playing drums w/Ruff on large drum base, ca. 1961 ............................................. **145.00**

**Dick Tracy badge,** "Lieutenant" & "Secret Service Patrol" ...................... **45.00**

**Dick Tracy book,** pop-up-type, "Capture of Boris Arson," w/three pop-up illustrations, copyright 1935 .. **288.00**

**Dick Tracy camera,** Bakelite, black, reads "Dick Tracy" around lens, Seymore Products Co., shows some wear, 5" l. (ILLUS. bottom) ................ **30.00**

**Dick Tracy flashlight,** molded plastic, top of flashlight in the shape of Dick Tracy's head, on original card, dated 1975 ..................................................... **24.00**

**Dick Tracy plate,** dinner, square, "Mugg & Tracy," shows Dick Tracy looking at wrist radio watch & Mugg on top of police car w/buildings in background ....................................... **120.00**

*Dick Tracy Two-way Radios*

**Dick Tracy wrist radios,** two-way electronic units, two complete stations, in original colorful box, Remco, 1950, pr. (ILLUS.) ................ **175.00**

**Dick Tracy Jr. pistol,** "Click"-type, black aluminum, decorated w/three synthetic rubies & official decal, Louis Marx & Co., w/original box ...... **120.00**

**Dionne Quintuplets advertisement book,** "Country Doctor," Lysol, 1937 ... **45.00**

*Dick Tracy Camera*

**Dionne Quintuplets book,** "Story of Dionne Quintuplets," Whitman, 1935 ... **22.00**

**Dr. Seuss animation cel,** "How the Grinch Stole Christmas," depicts the Grinch leaning to the left w/his hands in his 'pockets,' gouache on celluloid, signed "For Irene and her children— Dr. Seuss" at lower left & "Art (?) Chuck Jones" inscribed on lower right, image size 10", 9 x 12" ......... **1,035.00**

**Dr. Seuss animation cel,** "How the Grinch Stole Christmas," the Grinch, dressed as Santa, beckons, gouache on celluloid, ca. 1966, 7½ x 9½" ..................................... **1,035.00**

**Dr. Seuss animation cel,** "The Cat in the Hat," the Cat in the Hat plays piano & sings to the young boy & girl, gouache on celluloid, 8½ x 12".. **3,737.00**

**Felix the Cat figure,** jointed wood w/leather ears, marked "Pat Sullivan, Pat June 23, 1925," Schoenhut, 8½" h. .............................................. **104.00**

**Felix the Cat toy,** car, wood construction w/painted details, Felix is sitting in roadster w/grill marked "Speedy Felix," has makers decal of Geo. Borgfeldt & Co., patent date of 1925, 12" l. (arms replaced) ............. **250.00**

*Green Hornet Glass*

**Green Hornet glass,** enameled, shows The Green Hornet fighting above "Green Hornet" (ILLUS.) .......... **55.00**

**Huckleberry Hound game,** board-type, "Huckleberry Hound Western Game," color graphics on box of Huck & other characters from show, includes board, spinner, four game pieces & instructions, by Milton Bradley, 1959, the set........................ **25.00**

**Katzenjammer Kids game,** "Hockey," 1950s.................................................... **42.00**

**Li'l Abner tumbler set:** includes illustrations of Abner, Daisy Mae, Mammy Yokum, Pappy Yokum, Lonesome Polecat, Schmoos, Unwashable Jones; clear glass, United Features Syndicate, 1949, 4¾" h., set of 7................................. **133.00**

**Nancy & Sluggo birthday card,** colorful graphics, ca. 1930................... **28.00**

**Olive Oyl marionette,** composition hands & feet w/rubber face, Gund...... **95.00**

**Olive Oyl pony tail holder,** 1958, mint on card....................................... **35.00**

**Orphan Annie manual,** in original mailer, 1936............................... **40.00**

**Peanuts animation cel,** "You're in Love Charlie Brown," shows Lucy looking curiously at Linus, who lies on the sidewalk holding his head & smiling, gouache on celluloid, 10½ x 12½"................................... **1,150.00**

**Pepe & Kitty animation cell,** Pepe embraces the ever reluctant feline, gouache on celluloid, w/Warner Bros. Pictures, Inc., copyright label along bottom, 1950s, 10 x 12" ....... **3,162.00**

**Popeye bank,** china head................... **300.00**

**Popeye book ends,** wood w/decal, pr.. **15.00**

**Popeye candy mold,** tin....................... **25.00**

**Popeye Christmas card,** Hallmark, 1934................................................... **24.00**

**Popeye costume,** cardboard, in envelope w/comic strip, Motorola premium.............................................. **45.00**

**Popeye pencil box,** copyright 1934 ..... **78.00**

**Rocky & Bullwinkle animation cel,** commericial production set up depicting Rocky & Bullwinkle, gouache on celluloid, ca. 1970, 9 x 10"................................................ **862.00**

**Skippy figure,** celluloid, w/jointed arms, 1930s, 5½" h........................... **165.00**

**Smokey the Bear bank,** plaster, 9" h. .. **125.00**

**Spark Plug toy,** advertising, features Spark Plug in bathtub on wheels, "AC Spark Plugs," rare .................... **300.00**

**Steve Canyon scarf & goggles,** on die-cut display card............................. **85.00**

**Superman bank,** turnover-type, windup, lithographed tin & chrome, Superman holds tank above heads & turns over, Marx, pre-World War II... **646.00**

**Superman billfold,** 1966 ..................... **45.00**

*Ideal Superman Doll*

**Superman doll,** composition & wood w/cloth cape, jointed wood, Ideal Toy Corporation, ca. 1930s, 13" h. (ILLUS.) ............................................ **825.00**

**Superman radio,** molded plastic, in the shape of Superman's torso w/his right arm raised, AM only, w/original box, dated 1973, (battery compartment cover missing) ............. **45.00**

**Superman scrapbook,** 1940s ............ **150.00**

**Superman toy,** swim fins, "Kiddie Paddlers," in original box, pr. .............. **94.00**

**Superman valentine,** 1940 ................... **60.00**

**Terry & the Pirates book,** "Terry & the Pirates," Caniff, 1946, hard cover w/dust jacket ...................................... **40.00**

*Tom and Jerry Animation Art*

**Tom and Jerry animation art,** model sheet depicting Jerry in twenty-two various poses & expressions, graphite & blue pencil on paper, 9 x 14" (ILLUS.) ............................. **1,035.00**

**Yellow Kid toy,** cast iron, featuring the Kid in a goat-drawn cart w/one

hand extended, the other gathering in his yellow tunic, 7½" ..................... **733.00**

**Yogi Bear costume,** parade-type ....... **150.00**

# CHILDREN'S BOOKS

*The most collectible children's books today tend to be those printed after the 1850s and, while age is not completely irrelevant, illustrations play a far more important role in determining the values. While first editions are highly esteemed, it is the beautiful illustrated books that most collectors seek. The following books all in good to fine conditions, are listed alphabetically. Also see: BIG LITTLE BOOKS, COMIC BOOKS and DISNEY COLLECTIBLES*

**"Animal Stories,"** by Thornton Burgess, illustrations by Harrison Cady, 1942 ...................................... **$75.00**

**"Boy Aviators in Africa,"** by Lawtop, 1910 ..................................................... **18.00**

**"Journey Through Space,"** pop-up type, 1952 .......................................... **60.00**

**"Mother Goose's Melodies,"** by James Miller, New York, illustrated w/h.p. engravings, maroon cloth wrap w/gold engraved illustration of Mother Goose, 1869, 96 pp., 5½ x 7" ................................................ **135.00**

**"Our Holidays Recitation & Exercises,"** McLaughlin, illustrated, 1906 ................................................... **20.00**

**"Our New Friends,"** Dick & Jane, 1946 ..................................................... **40.00**

**"Peter Pan,"** illustrated by Best, 1931 .. **50.00**

**"Push Out & Paste Without Paste,"** Saalfield Publishing Co., Akron, Ohio, 1946, 8¾ x 11" ........................... **8.00**

**"The Tale of Peter Rabbit,"** Just Right Edition, enlarged, 1926 .......... **125.00**

**"When Peter Rabbit Went to School,"** 1921 ...................................................... **110.00**

# CHILDREN'S DISHES

*During the reign of Queen Victoria, dollhouses and accessories became more popular and as the century progressed, there was greater demand for toys which would subtly train a little girl in the art of homemaking.*

## GLASSWARE

**These items have been reproduced.*

**Berry set,** Baby Flute patt.: 1 x 3½" main berry bowl & six 1 x 3½" berry bowls; pressed glass, twenty-point ray in base w/ten fluted panels on main berry, sixteen point rayed design in base of small berry, clear, set of 7 .......................... **$300.00 to 390.00**

**Berry set,** Inverted Strawberry patt.: 1⅝" main berry bowl & six ½" berry bowls; pressed glass, Cambridge, clear, rare, set of 7 .......... **200.00 to 275.00**

*__Berry set,__ Lacy Daisy patt.: 1⅝" main berry bowl & six 1" berry bowls; pressed glass, United States Glass Company, amber, blue or green, set of 7, each ...................... **300.00 to 490.00**

**Berry set,** Oval Star patt., No. 300: 2" main berry bowl & six 1" berry bowls; pressed glass, Indiana Glass Company, clear, set of 7... **125.00 to 175.00**

**Berry set,** Pattee Cross patt.: 1¾" main berry bowl & six 1" berry bowls; pressed glass, set of 7 ..... **125.00 to 175.00**

**Lemonade or water set,** Cambridge No. 1 patt.: 3⅛" pitcher & six 1⅞" tumblers; pressed glass, clear, set of 7 ...................................... **75.00 to 150.00**

**Lemonade or water set,** cobalt blue blown glass w/h.p. white enameled thistle decoration: 4¾" pitcher & six 1¼" tumblers; probably European, rare, set of 7 .................... **500.00 to 700.00**

*__Lemonade or water set,__ Galloway patt.: 3⅞" pitcher & six 2" tumblers; pressed glass, clear, set of 7 ..................................... **75.00 to 150.00**

**Lemonade or water set,** Hobbs patt.: pitcher & six tumblers; colored pressed glass, set of 7 ..... **500.00 to 700.00**

**Lemonade or water set,** Little Jo patt.: 3¾" pitcher & six 2" tumblers; colored pressed glass, Westmoreland, set of 7.................................... **300.00 to 550.00**

**Lemonade or water set,** Mary Gregory decoration enameled on clear glass: 4½" pitcher & six 2½" tumblers; rare, set of 7 .......................... **475.00 to 500.00**

**Lemonade or water set,** Michigan patt.: 4" pitcher & six 2⅛" tumblers; pressed glass, clear or colored, set of 7 ................................ **150.00 to 175.00**

**Lemonade or water set,** enameled Moser glass: 1¾" pitcher & two 1½" tumblers; colored, Europe, set of 3 ................................ **475.00 to 600.00**

**Lemonade or water set,** Oval Star patt., No. 300: 4¼" pitcher, six 2⅜" tumblers & tray; pressed glass, Indiana Glass Co., clear, set of 8 ................................ **300.00 to 400.00**

**Lemonade or water set,** Petite Hobnail patt.: 4¾" pitcher & six 2³⁄₁₃" tumblers w/tray; colored pressed glass, set of 8 .............. **1200.00 to 1500.00**

**Lemonade or water set,** Rex (Fancy Cut) patt.: 3½" pitcher & six 1½" tumblers; pressed glass, clear, set of 7 ................................. **175.00 to 275.00**

**Stein set,** Monk patt.: 2⅞" stein & six or four 2⅛" steins; pressed glass, clear, the set.................... **150.00 to 300.00**

**Table set,** Acorn patt.: 4" cov. butter, 4¾" cov. sugar, 3⅜" creamer & 3⅛" spooner; pressed glass, possibly Crystal Glass Company, clear, 4 pcs............................... **750.00 to 800.00**

*Austrian Sugar Bowl*

**Table set,** Austrian patt.: 4" cov. butter, 4¾" cov. sugar, 3⅜" creamer & 3⅛" spooner, pressed glass, Greentown, clear, 4 pcs. (ILLUS. of sugar) ............................ **500.00 to 800.00**

**Table set,** Bead & Scroll patt.: 4" cov. butter, 4" cov. sugar, 3" creamer & 2½" spooner; pressed glass, clear or clear w/decoration, 4 pcs... **375.00 to 550.00**

**Table set,** Beaded Swirl patt.: 2½" cov. butter, 3¾" cov. sugar, 2⅝" creamer & 2⅜" spooner; colored pressed glass, 4 pcs. ....... **500.00 to 900.00**

**Table set,** Braided Belt patt.: 2½" cov. butter, 3½" cov. sugar, 2⅝" creamer & 2⅝" spooner; pressed glass, 4 pcs.............................. **800.00 to 1000.00**

**Table set,** Button Arches patt.; 3¾" cov. butter, 2⅝" cov. sugar, creamer & spooner; pressed glass, George Duncan & Sons, clear or ruby-stained, 4 pcs. ................... **500.00 to 900.00**

**Table set,** Buzz Star patt., No. 15101: 5⅝" cov. butter, 3⅜" cov. sugar, 3⅜" creamer & 2¼" spooner; pressed glass, United States Glass Company, clear, common, 4 pcs. ........ **100.00 to 150.00**

**Table set,** Cambridge Colonial patt., No. 2630: 2⅛" cov. butter, 3" cov. sugar, 2⅜" creamer & 2⅛" spooner; pressed glass, clear, 4 pcs. ............................ **100.00 to 150.00**

**\*Table set,** Chimo or Oneata patt.: 2⅜" cov. butter, 3" cov. sugar, 2" creamer & 2⅛" spooner; pressed glass, Riverside Glass Co., clear, rare, 4 pcs. ....................... **375.00 to 400.00**

**Table set,** Clear and Diamond Panels patt.: 2⅞" cov. butter, 3½" cov. sugar, 2¾" creamer & 2⅜" spooner; pressed glass, blue or green, 4 pcs., each ................................ **175.00 to 300.00**

**Table set,** Cloud Band patt.: 3¾" cov. butter, 2½" cov. sugar, 4" creamer & 2⅜" spooner; pressed glass, Gillinder, milk glass, 4 pcs... **450.00 to 700.00**

**Table set,** Dewdrop or Dot patt.: 2⅝" cov. butter, 4" cov. sugar, 3" creamer & 2⅝" spooner; colored pressed glass, Columbia Glass Company, 4 pcs. .............. **450.00 to 800.00**

**Table set,** Doyle No. 500 patt.: 2¼" cov. butter, 3⅝" cov. sugar, 2½" creamer, 2⅜" spooner & tray; pressed glass, Doyle and Company, clear, 5 pcs. ...................... **250.00 to 375.00**

**Table set,** Euclid or Rexford patt.: 2⅝" cov. butter, 2¾" cov. sugar, 3¼" creamer & 2¼" spooner; pressed glass, clear, 4 pcs. ........... **100.00 to 150.00**

**Table set,** Fine Cut Star and Fan patt.: 2¾" cov. butter, 3⅛" cov. sugar, 2⅜" creamer & 2¼" spooner; pressed glass, clear, 4 pcs............... **125.00 to 175.00**

**Table set,** Hobnail with Thumbprint Base patt., No. 150: 2" cov. butter, 4" cov. sugar, 3⅜" creamer & 2⅞" spooner, 7⅜" tray; pressed glass, Doyle and Company, clear, 4 pcs.............................. **375.00 to 400.00**

**Table set,** Horizontal Threads patt.: 2" cov. butter, 3⅜" cov. sugar, 2¼" creamer & 2⅛" spooner; pressed glass, clear w/red staining, rare, 4 pcs.............................. **300.00 to 400.00**

**\*Table set,** Lamb patt.: 3⅛" cov. butter, 4⅜" cov. sugar, 2⅞" creamer & 2¾" spooner; pressed glass, clear, reproduced in color, 4 pcs. .. **400.00 to 575.00**

**Table set,** Mardi Gras patt., D. & M. No. 42: 4½" cov. butter, 4½" cov. sugar, 2⅞" creamer & 2¾" spooner; pressed glass, Duncan and Miller Company, clear, 4 pcs. .... **500.00 to 775.00**

**Table set,** Menagerie patt.: 2⅜" cov. turtle-shaped butter, 4¼" cov. bear-shaped sugar, 3¾" owl-shaped creamer & 2⅝" fish-shaped spooner; pressed glass, Bryce Higbee, amber or blue, 4 pcs., each... **3,000.00 to 3,800.00**

**Table set,** Michigan patt., No. 15077: 3¾" cov. butter, 4¾" cov. sugar, 2⅞" creamer & 3" spooner; pressed glass, clear w/red & green trim, 4 pcs.............................. **475.00 to 575.00**

**Table set,** Nursery rhyme patt.: 2⅝" cov. butter, 4" cov. sugar, 2½" creamer & 2½" spooner; pressed glass, clear, 4 pcs. ........... **300.00 to 375.00**

**Table set,** Pennsylvania patt., No. 15048: 3½" cov. butter, 4" cov. sugar, 2½" creamer & 2½" spooner; pressed glass, United States Glass Company, clear, 4 pcs. .... **300.00 to 375.00**

**Table set,** Plain Pattern, No. 13: 2⅛" cov. butter, 3⅜" cov. sugar, 2½" creamer & 2¼" spooner; pressed glass, King Glass Company, clear w/frosted ribbon, 4 pcs. ... **800.00 to 1,000.00**

**Table set,** Plain Pattern No. 13: 2⅛" cov. butter, 3⅜" cov. sugar, 2½" creamer & 2¼" spooner; pressed glass, King Glass Company, milk glass, 4 pcs. ..................... **600.00 to 900.00**

**Table set,** Rex or Fancy Cut patt.: 2⅜" cov. butter, 3⅛" cov. sugar, 2¼" creamer & 2¼" spooner; pressed glass, Co-Operative Glass Company, clear, 4 pcs. ....................... **150.00 to 175.00**

**Table set,** Rooster patt., No. 140: 3¼" cov. butter, 4½" cov. sugar, 3⅜" creamer & 3⅛" spooner; pressed glass, King Glass Company, clear, 4 pcs.............................. **600.00 to 800.00**

*Stippled Diamond Table Set*

**Table set,** Sawtooth patt.: 3" cov. butter, 5" cov. sugar, 3½" creamer & 3⅛" spooner; pressed glass, clear, 4 pcs. ............................... **150.00 to 175.00**

**Table set,** Stippled Diamond patt.: 2¼" cov. butter, 3⅛" cov. sugar, 2¼" creamer & 2⅛" spooner; pressed glass, clear, 4 pcs. (ILLUS.) .......................... **500.00 to 675.00**

**Table set,** Stippled Raindrop and Dewdrop patt.: 2" cov. butter, 3⅛" cov. sugar, 2¼" creamer & 2⅛" spooner; colored pressed glass, 4 pcs. ............................. **800.00 to 1,200.00**

**Table set,** Stippled Vine and Beads patt.: 2½" cov. butter, 3⅛" cov. sugar, 2½" creamer & 2⅛" spooner; pressed glass, clear, 4 pcs. ............................. **400.00 to 500.00**

**Table set,** Style (Madora or Arrow-Head-In-Ovals) patt.: 2½" cov. butter, 3⅛" cov. sugar, 2⅜" creamer & 2¼" spooner; pressed glass, Higbee Company, ca. 1908-1918, clear, 4 pcs. ...................... **125.00 to 175.00**

**Table set,** Sultan patt.: 3¾" cov. butter, 4½" cov. sugar, 2½" creamer & 2½" spooner; pressed glass, McKee Glass Company, clear, 4 pcs. ............................... **500.00 to 600.00**

**Table set,** Sultan patt.: 3¾" cov. butter, 4½" cov. sugar, 2½" creamer & 2½" spooner; pressed glass, McKee Glass Company, frosted green, 4 pcs. ................... **800.00 to 900.00**

**Table set,** Sweetheart patt.: 2" cov. butter, 3" cov. sugar, 2⅜" creamer & 2" spooner; pressed glass, Cambridge, clear, common, 4 pcs. ............................. **100.00 to 175.00**

**\*Table set,** Thumbleina (or Flattened Diamond) patt.: 2½" cov. butter, 2¼" cov. sugar, 2⅜" creamer & 2¼" spooner; pressed glass, clear, 4 pcs. ............................. **125.00 to 175.00**

**Table set,** Twist patt., No. 137: 2½" cov. butter, 3⅞" cov. sugar, 2⅞" creamer & 2½" spooner; pressed glass, Albany Glass Company, frosted clear, 4 pcs. .......... **300.00 to 400.00**

**Table set,** Twist patt., No. 137: 2½" cov. butter, 3⅞" cov. sugar, 2⅞" creamer & 2½" spooner; pressed glass, Albany Glass Company, opalescent, 4 pcs. ......... **800.00 to 1,200.00**

**Table set,** Wee Branches patt.: 2" cov. butter, 3" cov. sugar, 2¼" creamer & 2⅜" spooner; pressed glass, clear, 4 pcs. ........... **500.00 to 700.00**

## CERAMIC WARES

### French Toy Ware

**Chamber set:** pitcher, bowl, toothbrush holder, plus other pieces; porcelain, decorated w/roses, in original presentation box, the set (ILLUS. top next page) ......................... **1,800.00 to 2,200.00**

**Dinner service,** earthenware, French Cartoons or French Lifestyle decorations, Sarreguemines, large dinner service ................ **800.00 to 1,000.00**

**Dinner service,** faience, floral decoration, the set ......... **800.00 to 1,800.00**

**Dinner service,** faience, floral decoration w/roosters, the set .............................. **1,500.00 to 2,800.00**

*Boxed French Chamber Set*

*Boxed Tea & Stew Set*

**Dinner service,** earthenware, Kate Greenaway decoration, Sarreguemines ........... **1,800.00 to 2,500.00**

***Pots de Crémé* (cream pot),** cup, cov. & underplate; porcelain, w/color & trim, Old Paris, rare, set of 12 ........................... **1,800.00 to 2,800.00** with matching dinner service ........................ **3,500.00 to 5,000.00**

**Tea set,** porcelain, decorated w/children, marked Haviland, rare, the set ........................ **1,800.00 to 2,500.00**

**Tea set,** porcelain, decorated w/portraits of French Women, the set ................................. **800.00 to 1,000.00**

**Tea set,** porcelain, Red Riding Hood decoration, the set...... **1,500.00 to 1,800.00**

**Tea & stew set:** cov. teapot, cov. sugar, creamer, two cups, plate, cov. stew tureen, platter, stew bowls w/underplates; earthenware, decorated w/peasant man & woman, top of box labeled "La Dinette de Mes Poupées," Quimper, w/original box, the set (ILLUS. top next column) ...................... **1,000.00 to 2,000.00**

**Washstand set:** divided bowl, pitcher & two other pieces; porcelain, Red Riding Hood decoration, the set ............................ **2,500.00 to 2,800.00**

## British Ware

**Chamber set,** earthenware, Dresden Flowers patt., possibly Spode or Copeland, marked "Improved Stone China," the set ................. **500.00 to 800.00**

**Dessert set,** earthenware, Servants patt., Flow Blue transfer of gardener watering plants & a servant drawing water from a well, ca. 1830-1850, the set ........................ **1,000.00 to 1,800.00**

**Dessert set:** 3 x 5¼" compote, two 4" serving plates, 3¾" plates; earthenware, Poonah patt., marked "GFB" on some pieces, ca. 1842-1858, the set .............. **1,000.00 to 1,800.00**

**Dessert set:** 3½ x 5½" compote, 5" oval dish, 4¼" square dish, 4 x 4½" server, 4" plates; earthenware, Flow Blue, some marked by Edge Malkin, ca. 1873, the set........ **1,800.00 to 2,500.00**

**Dinner service,** earthenware, Bridgless patt., rare, the set ......... **2,800.00 to 3,200.00**

**Dinner service:** cov. soup tureen, cov. sauce tureen, two serving dishes, plates of various sizes; earthenware, Willow Ware patt., blue, ca. 1820 to 1830 (ILLUS. top next page) ................. **2,000.00 to 3,000.00**

*Early Willow Ware Dinner Service*

**Dinner service,** earthenware, Flow Blue Hopberry patt, Charles Meigh & Sons, ca. 1835-1849, the set ............................ **2,000.00 to 2,800.00**

**Dinner service,** earthenware, Milkmaid patt., Spode, ca. 1814, the set ............................ **3,000.00 to 3,800.00**

**Dinner service:** 2" sauceboat, 4⅛" soup, 3" l. shell shaped servers, 2¼" & 3¼" tureens, 3" h. cov. vegetable, 2⅛", 2¾" & 3¾" plates; earthenware, Chinese red & cobalt blue decoration w/various shades of orange, red & blue, ca. 1850, the set... **2,800.00 to 3,200.00**

**Dinner service:** 3½" large tureen, 2½" small tureen, 2¾" ladle, 1" salad bowl, 2" cov. vegetable; earthenware, Abbey Ruins patt., ca. 1827-1843, rare, the set .................. **2,400.00 to 3,400.00**

**Dinner service:** 3½", 4" & 4¼" nest of platters, 2½" & 3½" tureens, 2" cov. vegetable, 3¼" soup, 1 x 2½" salad bowls, 2¾" & 3" plates; earthenware, Flowing Berries & Flowers patt., Hackwood, ca. 1827-1843, the set ............................ **1,500.00 to 2,000.00**

**Dinner service:** 3½", 4" & 4¼" nest of platters, 2½" & 3½" tureens, 3¼" cov. vegetable, 2" oval open vegetable, 3¼" sauceboat, 2¾" ladle, 1 x 2½" salad bowls, 2½", 2¾" & 2" plates; earthenware, Kite Flyers patt., pictures young boy flying kite w/an old man by a gravestone, probably Hackwood, ca. 1827-1843, the set ....................... **2,800.00 to 3,500.00**

**Dinner service:** 3", 3½", 4", 4¼" & 5" platters, 3¼", 3½", 5" & 5⅛" tureens, 4½" & 5" tureen underplate, 2½" open compote, 2½" cov. vegetables, 2½" cov. server, 2½ x 3¼" server, 1¾" sauce, 3" & 3½" ladles, 2¼", 2½", 3", 3¾" & 4" plates; earthenware, Seeweed with Arrows patt., Charles Meigh, Old Hall Pottery, Hanley, Staffordshire Potteries, ca. 1851-1861, the set ....... **500.00 to 800.00**

**Dinner service:** 4½", 5½" & 6½" tureens, 2½" & 4½" soups, 4" ladle, 3⅝" & 4½" plates; earthenware, Rosemond patt., Bishop and Stonier, ca. 1891-1900, the set ..... **500.00 to 800.00**

**Dinner service:** 4½" & two 5⅛" platters, 4½", 5½" & 6½" tureens, 2½" sauce, 4" ladle, 4½" soups, 3⅝" & 4½" plates; earthenware, Pembroke patt., Bishop and Stonier, ca. 1890-1900, the set .............................. **500.00 to 800.00**

**Dinner service:** 4¾" & 5¾" platters, 3" cov. footed tureen w/5" underplate, 4¼" cov. vegetable, 2½" cov. vegetable, 4" soups, 2¾" & 3" oval server, 2½", 3¼" & 4" plates; earthenware, Blue Marble patt., ca. 1850, the set ......... **1,500.00 to 2,000.00**

**Dinner service:** 4¼", 4½" & 5½" platters, 3¼", 3½" & 4¼" tureens, 4¼", 4½", 5½" & 5¾" tureen underplates, two 2½" & 2¾" cov. vegetables, 3½" soups, two 1¾" sauces, 4½" wine cooler, 3", 3½" & 4½" ladles, 2", 3", 3¼" & 3¾" plates;

earthenware, Athens patt., marked "Davenport," w/impressed anchor mark, the set .................... **600.00 to 900.00**

**Dinner service:** 4¼", 4½" & 5" platters, 3½", 3¼", 3½" & 4¼" tureens, 4¼", 4½" & 5¾" tureen underplates, 1¾" open vegetable, 2½" & 2¾" cov. dishes, two 1¾" sauces, 3½" soups, 3", 3½" & 4½" ladles, 2½", 3", 3¼" & 3¾" plates; earthenware, Chinese Bells patt., black transfer, ca. 1835, the set ............................ **1,200.00 to 1,800.00**

**Dinner service:** 4¼", 4½" & 5" platters, 3¼", 3½" & 4¼" tureens, 3½", 4¼", 4½" & 5¾" tureen underplates, 4½" open vegetable, 2½" & 3½" cov. dishes, two 1¾" sauces, 3½" soups, 3", 3½" & 4½" ladles, 2½", 3", 3¼" & 3¾" plates; earthenware, Asiatic Birds patt., Charles Meigh, ca. 1835-1849, the set ............................ **1,000.00 to 1,800.00**

**Dinner service:** 4¼", 4¾", 5¼" & 6½" platters, 3" & 4½" tureens, 2½" cov. vegetable, 2¼" sauce, 2½" wine cooler, 3⅞" soups, 5" ladle, 2¾", 3½" & 3⅞" plates; earthenware, flow blue Forget-Me-Not patt., ca. 1840-1860, the set .......................... **3,000.00 to 3,800.00**

**Dinner service:** 4⅛", 4⅞" & 5¼" platters, 3½" tureen, 3" cov. vegetable, 3¾" soups, 2⅞", 3" & 3¾" plates; earthenware, English Views patt., Spode, ca. 1830, the set ............................ **5,000.00 to 6,000.00**

**Dinner service:** 4¾" & 5⅝" platters, 3¾" & 4⅞" tureens, 3" cov. vegetable, 5¼ x 6⅛" & 3¾ x 4⅝" serving plates, 4⅛" serving dish, 2" salad bowls, 1¾" sauce boat, 3½" soups, 2¾" & 3½" plates; earthenware, Dresden Flowers patt., possibly Spode or Copeland, marked "Improved Stone China," the set............. **1,500.00 to 2,000.00**

**Dinner service:** 4 x 5½" & 3 x 3¾" tureens, 2½ x 3⅝" cov. vegetable, 3⅜" soup, 2½", 2⅝" & 3½" plates; earthenware, Queen of Sheeba patt., Spode, ca. 1830, rare, the set ............................ **3,000.00 to 3,800.00**

**Dinner service:** 4", 4½", 5", 6", 7" platters, 2½ x 3½" tureen, 4½" vegetable server, 1½ x 3½" footed server, 2" sauce, 5" ladle; earthenware, Souvenir (Friendship) patt., ca. 1830-1840, the set ............................ **2,000.00 to 2,800.00**

**Dinner service:** 5", 6¼", 7" & 8" nest of platters, two 2½" cov. servers, 1¾" h. open ruffled bowl, 3¾" soup, 3¾" & 4½" plates; earthenware, Rhodesia patt., Ridgway, ca. 1900-1915, the set .. **1,200.00 to 1,800.00**

**Tea set,** earthenware, Rosemond patt., Bishop and Stonier, ca. 1891-1900, the set ..... **500.00 to 600.00**

**Tea set,** earthenware, "Gaudy Welsh," cobalt blue & orange flowers w/gold accents, ca. 1861-1867, the set ............................ **1,000.00 to 1,800.00**

**Tea set,** earthenware, Asiatic Birds patt., flow blue, Charles Meigh, ca. 1835-1849, the set ........................ **2,000.00 to 2,800.00**

**Tea set,** earthenware, Blue Marble patt., Flow Blue, ca. 1850, the set ............................ **1,000.00 to 1,900.00**

**Tea set,** earthenware, Mandarin patt., Blue Willow decoration, Copeland, ca. 1860-1875, the set ..... **400.00 to 700.00**

**Tea set:** 2¾" cov. teapot, 2¾" cov. sugar, 2¼" creamer, 1¾" cups, 4¼" saucers; earthenware, Milkmaid patt., Spode, ca. 1814, the set ............................ **1,800.00 to 2,500.00**

**Tea set:** 3" cov. teapot, 2¾" cov. sugar, 1¾" cups, 4¼" saucers, 3 x 5" waste bowl; earthenware, Cottage Girl patt., puce w/pearl lustre glaze & gold trim, ca. 1840, the set ................ **500.00 to 800.00**

**Tea set:** 3¼" cov. teapot, 2¾" cov. sugar, 2" creamer, 2" cups, 4¼" saucers, 2 x 3½" waste bowl; earthenware, Farm patt., marked "Imperial D.M. & Sons," David Methven & Sons, Scotland, ca. 1840-1930, the set ..... **400.00 to 600.00**

**Tea set:** 3⅛" cov. teapot, 1½" open sugar, 2⅛" creamer, 1¾" cups, 4⅛" saucers, 4⅛" plates, 5½" serving plate; earthenware, Blue Willow patt., marked by Collingwood, ca. 1890-1900s, the set.... **300.00 to 500.00**

**Tea set:** 3½" cov. teapot, 2½" cov. sugar, 1⅞" cups, 4¼" saucers; earthenware, Manor House patt., ca. 1820s, the set....... **2,000.00 to 2,800.00**

**Tea set:** 3¾" cov. teapot, 1¾" cups, 5" saucers; earthenware, Gipsey (sic) patt., attributed to Hackwood, ca. 1840, the set............... **600.00 to 900.00**

**Tea set:** 3¾" cov. teapot, 3¾" cov. sugar, 2¼" creamer, 1¼" & 2¼" cups, two 3½" saucers, 4½" plates;

earthenware, Elongated Lip patt.,
helmet-shaped pieces, ca. 1830,
rare, the set ................ **2,000.00 to 3,000.00**

**Tea set:** 3¾" cov. teapot, 3" cov.
sugar, 2" creamer, 2¼" cups,
4¾" saucers, 5" plates, 2½" waste
bowl; earthenware, Goat Girl patt.,
signed C.E. & M Co., Cork, Edge,
Malkin & Co., ca. 1873-1903,
the set ............................. **500.00 to 800.00**

**Tea set:** 3⅝" cov. teapot, 3⅜" cov.
sugar, 2¼" creamer, 1¾" cups,
4½" saucers; earthenware, Dresden
Flowers patt., possibly Spode or
Copeland, marked "Improved Stone
China," the set .................. **600.00 to 800.00**

**Tea set:** 3⅞" cov. teapot, 3⅝" cov.
sugar, 2½" creamer, 1½" & 1¾"
cups, 4" & 4½" saucers, 2⅝" &
4⅜" plates, 2⅝" waste bowl;
earthenware, Caledonia patt.,
ca. 1842, the set............... **400.00 to 900.00**

**Tea set:** 4" cov. teapot, 1½" cov.
sugar, 2¼" creamer, 1¾" cups,
4" saucers, 2½" l. spoons;
earthenware, Forget-Me Not, patt.,
shell-thin fluted body w/plump
elongated bodies, maker & date
unknown, the set .............. **500.00 to 800.00**

**Tea set:** 4" cov. teapot, 3½" cov.
sugar, 2½" creamer, 1⅞" cups,
4½" saucers, 5¼" plates;
earthenware, Ruins patt., blue
transfer, Davenport, ca. 1850,
the set ........................... **900.00 to 1,200.00**

**Tea set:** 4" cov. teapot, 3½" cov.
sugar, 4½" saucers, 5¼" plates;
earthenware, Chinese patt., marked
"Davenport" on bottom of teapot,
ca. 1844, the set......... **2,000.00 to 3,000.00**

**Tea set:** 4" cov. teapot, 3¼" cov.
sugar, 2½" creamer, 2" cups, 4½"
saucers, 5 x 5¼" serving plates,
2½ x 4½" waste bowl; earthenware,
Animals patt., Copeland, ca. 1860,
the set .......................... **900.00 to 1,500.00**

**Tea set:** 4" cov. teapot, 3¾" cov. sugar,
2" creamer, 2" cups, 4½" saucers,
5" plates, 1¾" handless cups, 1¾ x
4½" waste bowl; earthenware,
Chinese Bells patt., found in mulberry
& black & white, Charles Meigh,
ca. 1850, the set............... **800.00 to 1,200.00**

**Tea set:** 4" cov. teapot, 3¾" cov. sugar,
3" creamer, 1⅞" cup, 2" cup, two
saucers, 2⅞ x 4½" waste bowl, 6"
plates; earthenware, Acorn patt., in

blue, brown & lavender, w/King of
Prussia-type finials, Ridgway,
ca. 1850-1860, the set .. **500.00 to 1,000.00**

**Tea set:** 4" cov. teapot, 3¾" cov.
sugar, 3" creamer, 1⅞" cup, 2" cup,
two saucers, 2⅞ x 4½" waste bowl,
6" plates; earthenware, Gaudy Flow
with Flowers patt., transfer design of
flowers on flow blue, h.p. in pink,
yellow & green w/rust trim, w/King of
Prussia-type finials, Ridgway,
ca. 1850-1860, the
set ................................. **500.00 to 1,000.00**

**Tea set:** 4" cov. teapot, 3¾" cov.
sugar, 3" creamer, 1⅞" cup, 2" cup,
two saucers, 2⅞ x 4½" waste bowl,
6" plates; earthenware, Persia patt.,
in orange, brown & rust, w/King of
Prussia-type finials, Ridgway,
ca. 1850-1860, the set .. **500.00 to 1,000.00**

**Tea set:** 4" cov. teapot, 4" cov. sugar,
1⅞" cups, 4½" saucers; earthenware,
Zebra patt., ca. 1830-1840, the
set ..................................... **600.00 to 800.00**

**Tea set:** 4¼" cov. teapot, 3½" cov.
sugar, 2½" creamer, 1½" cups, 4½"
saucers; earthenware, Beehive patt.,
shows an urn & beehive w/floral
border, teapot has extended flange,
possibly Ridgway, ca. 1840-1850,
the set ...................... **1,200.00 to 2,000.00**

**Tea set:** 4¼" cov. teapot, 3¾" cov.
sugar, 2½" creamer, 1¾" cups, 4½"
saucers, 5" plates, 2½ x 4½" waste
bowl; earthenware, flow blue,
decorative urn surrounded by
touches of color, foliage & flowers,
No. 26, J&R Goodwin, ca. 1845, the
set ............................. **1,000.00 to 1,800.00**

Other colors & designs..... **400.00 to 600.00**

**Tea set:** 4¼" cov. teapot, 4¼" cov.
sugar, 4" creamer, 2½" cups, 5"
saucers, 5¼" plates, 2½" waste
bowl; earthenware, Old Mother
Hubbard patt., ca. 1870-1890, the
set .................................... **500.00 to 900.00**

**Tea set:** 4¼" cov. teapot, 3¾" cov.
sugar, 3⅓" creamer, 2" cups, 2"
saucers, 3" plates; earthenware,
Hey! Diddle Diddle patt., solid color,
ca. 1888, the set............ **800.00 to 1,000.00**

**Tea set:** 4¼" cov. teapot, 2½" open
sugar, 2¾" creamer, 2" cups, 4½"
saucers, 4¼" plates, 2½ x 4" waste
bowl; earthenware, Cinderella patt.,
comes in rose, blue & brown,
Ridgway, ca. 1889-1900, the
set .................................... **500.00 to 800.00**

**Tea set:** 4¼" cov. teapot, 3⅞" cov. sugar, 1½" & 1¾" cups, 4½", 4⅜" & 5" saucers, 4" & 5" plates; earthenware, Girl with Goat patt., Cork, Edge & Malkin, Newport Pottery, Burslem, Staffordshire Potteries, ca. 1850-1871, the set .................................. **500.00 to 700.00**

**Tea set:** 4¼" cov. teapot, 3⅝" handless cov. sugar, 3⅝" cups, 4½" saucers, 4⅞" plates, 2½ x 4¼" waste bowl; earthenware, Lea Flower patt., ca. 1840, the set......... **1,000.00 to 1,800.00**

**Tea set:** 4½" cov. teapot, 1¾ x 3" open sugar, 2½" creamer, 1½" cups, 4" saucers, 2⅛ x 3½" waste bowl; earthenware, Rhodesia patt., Ridgway, ca. 1900-1915, the set .................................. **500.00 to 700.00**

**Tea set:** 4½" cov. teapot, 4¼" cov. sugar, 3½" creamer, 2" cups, 4¾" d. saucers, 4" d. individual plates, 7" d. serving plate; earthenware, Alcock Blue patt., all over powder blue w/gold enhancement w/twig finials, the set .................. **500.00 to 900.00**

**Tea set:** 4¾" cov. teapot, 3⅜" cov. sugar, 2¼" creamer, 1¾" h. cups, 4½" saucers, 5" plates, 2¾" waste bowl; earthenware, Amherst Japan patt., Minton, ca. 1854, rare, the set ............................ **2,000.00 to 2,800.00**

**Tea set:** 4⅜" cov. teapot, 3¼" open sugar, 3¼" creamer, 2¼" cups, 4½" saucers, 2⅛ x 4" waste bowl; earthenware, Pembroke patt., Bishop, Stonier, ca. 1890-1900, the set .................................. **500.00 to 600.00**

**Tea set:** 5" cov. teapot, 4½" cov. sugar, 3¼" creamer, 2" cups, 4¼" saucers, 5" plates; earthenware, May patt., set comes in brown, rose, green & blue, ca. 1870-1880, the set .................................. **175.00 to 250.00**

**Tea set:** 5" cov. teapot, 4½" cov. sugar, 3¼" creamer, 2" cups, 4¼" saucers, 5" plates; earthenware, w/sponge design, ca. 1870-1880, the set ............................ **500.00 to 800.00**

**Tea set:** 5" cov. teapot, 4½" cov. sugar, 3¼" creamer, 2" cups, 4¼" saucers, 5" plates; earthenware, Octagon Blue Willow patt., ca. 1870-1880, the set ..... **400.00 to 600.00**

**Tea set:** 5" cov. teapot, 4½" cov. sugar, 3¼" creamer, 2" cups, 4¼" saucers, 5" plates; earthenware, Wagon Wheel patt., heavy flow blue treatment w/gold trim, ca. 1870-1880, the set............................. **400.00 to 600.00**

**Tea set:** 5" cov. teapot, 4½" cov. sugar, 3¼" creamer, 2" cups, 4¼" saucers, 5" plates; earthenware, Dahlia patt., ca. 1870-1880, the set ............................ **1,800.00 to 2,000.00**

**Tea set:** 5" cov. teapot, 5" cov. sugar, 3¼" creamer, 2" cups, 4½" saucers; earthenware, Dotted Swiss patt., pink, green or brown dots, mid-Victorian, the set ............. **500.00 to 800.00**

**Tea set:** 5" domed cov. teapot, 3" cov. teapot, 3¾" cov. tea kettle, 3½" creamer, 1¼" taza, 1¼" handless cups, 3¼" saucers; earthenware, Leeds Feathered Edge patt., ca. 1750, the set ............... **5000.00 and up**

**Tea set:** 5½" cov. teapot, 4¾" cov. sugar, 3" creamer, 2" cups, 4¼" saucers, 2¾ x 3½" waste bowl; earthenware, all over sheet paint, Barrow & Co., ca. 1855, the set .................................. **500.00 to 800.00**

**Tea set:** 5½" cov. teapot, 5¼" cov. sugar, 3½" creamer, 2" cups, 4¾" saucers, 5¼" plates; earthenware, decorated w/bud finial sheet print, teapot w/ring handle, ca. 1840-1860, the set ............................ **400.00 to 800.00**

**Tea set:** 6" cov. coffeepot, 4¼" cov. teapot, 3⅝" cov. sugar, 2¾" creamer, 1¾" cups, 4½" saucers, 5" plates, 2½" waste bowl; earthenware, decorated w/flow blue bars, strap handles, Scott Brothers, Nr. Edinburgh, Scotland, ca. 1786-1796, the set ............. **2,000.00 to 2,800.00**

## German Toy Ware

**Chamber Set,** porcelain, Buster Brown decoration, the set ............................ **1,000.00 to 1,500.00**

**Chocolate set:** 5" cov. chocolate pot, six 2" cups, six 4¼" saucers; porcelain, decorated w/swags of white flowers & chained together w/green foliage, each piece w/R.S. Prussia red mark, turn-of-the-century, rare w/marks, set of 13 ......................... **2,000.00 to 2,500.00**

**Dessert set,** porcelain, floral decorations, marked "Prov. E.S. Saxe Germany," ca. 1900-1920, in original box, the set......... **600.00 to 900.00**

**Dinner set,** porcelain, floral decorations, marked "Prov. E.S. Saxe Germany," ca. 1900-1920, in original box, the set ....... **800.00 to 1,500.00**

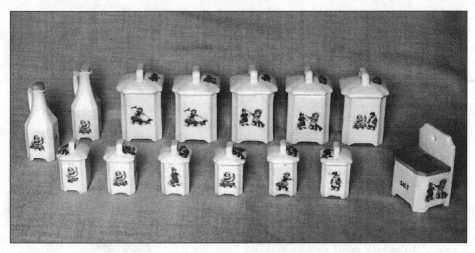

*Rare German Spice Set*

**Grater,** porcelain, Blue Onion patt.,
ca. 1920 ........................... **300.00 to 475.00**

**Spice set:** five large cov. canisters,
six small cov. canisters, two handled
bottles w/cork stoppers, cov. salt
container; porcelain, all w/children
doing various chores, salt marked
"SALT" w/wooden cov., rare, set of
14 (ILLUS. above) ........ **900.00 to 1,500.00**

**Tea set,** doll-sized, porcelain,
decorated w/roses w/green accent,
R.S. Prussia, ca. 1915-1920, the
set ................................... **500.00 to 800.00**

**Tea set:** cov. teapot, cov. sugar, cups,
saucer, plates; porcelain, Prussia
decals, Four Seasons patt.,
ca. 1900-1920, the set ... **800.00 to 1,000.00**

**Tea set,** porcelain, decorated
w/roses & gold trim w/decorative
collared bases, R.S. Prussia, ca.
1915-1925, w/original box, rare, the
set ............................ **1,800.00 to 2,500.00**

**Tea set,** porcelain, decorated w/swan
motif, R.S. Prussia, turn-of-the-
century, rare, the set .. **1,500.00 to 2,500.00**

**Tea set,** porcelain, Blue Onion patt.,
ca. 1920, w/original box, the
set ................................... **400.00 to 800.00**

**Tea set,** porcelain, Robinson Crusoe
patt., very rare, the set.. **1,000.00 to 1,800.00**

**Tea set,** porcelain, Sheepherder patt.
No. 1, w/pink flowering tree, R.S.
Prussia, turn-of-the-century, the
set ............................ **1,500.00 to 2,000.00**

**Tea set,** porcelain, white roses
against green diagonal slashes,
R.S. Prussia, ca. 1920, the
set ................................... **400.00 to 700.00**

**Tea set:** cov. teapot, open sugar,
creamer, cups & saucer, plates;
porcelain, Cook and Peary at North
Pole patt., Prussia, very rare, the
set ............................ **3,000.00 to 4,000.00**

**Tea set:** 4" cov. bulbous teapot, cov.
squatty sugar, squatty creamer, 2"
cups, 4" saucer; porcelain, w/red &
green roses on lime green gound,
R.S. Prussia, ca. 1900-1920, the
set ................................... **500.00 to 800.00**

**Tea set:** 4" cov. teapot, 2¾" cov.
sugar, 2½" creamer, 1⅛" cups, 3"
saucer, 3" plates; porcelain,
decorated w/baby red roses,
marked, R.S. Prussia, turn-of-the-
century, the set.......... **1,800.00 to 2,500.00**

**Tea set:** 4¼" cov. teapot, 3½" cov.
sugar, 3½" creamer, 2¾" cups, 4⅛"
saucer; porcelain, Indians patt.,
teapot w/rope twist handle, possibly
E. Bohne Söhne, turn-of-the-century,
rare, the set ............... **1,000.00 to 1,500.00**

**Tea set:** 4¾" cov. teapot, 2¾" cov.
sugar, 3¼" creamer, 2" cups, 3¾"
saucer, 4¼" plates; porcelain,
Florence Girls patt., ca. 1890-1900,
the set ........................... **500.00 to 700.00**

**Tea set:** 5" cov. teapot, 3" cov. sugar,
2¼" creamer, 1¾" cups, 3¾" saucer,

5¼" plates; porcelain, decorated w/castle, mill or cottage on cobalt blue ground, R.S. Prussia, late 19th c., the set........... **1,500.00 to 1,800.00**

**Tea set:** 5¾" cov. teapot, 3½" cov. sugar, 3" creamer, 2" cups, 4¼" saucer, 5¼" plates; porcelain, Happifats patt., Beyer & Bock, Volkstedt-Rudolstadt, turn-of-the-century, the set................. **400.00 to 700.00**

**Tea set:** 6½" cov. teapot, 3½" cov. sugar, 2½" creamer, 4¼" saucer, 6" plates; porcelain, Swallows and Scenes patt., R.S. Prussia, ca. 1885-1900, the set..... **2,000.00 to 3,000.00**

**Tea set:** 6" cov. teapot, 4" cov. sugar, 3¾" creamer, 1¾" cups, 4¼" saucer; porcelain, floral decorations, marked "Prov. E.S. Saxe Germany," ca. 1900-1920, in original box, the set ................................... **500.00 to 700.00**

*Paper cone Cornucopia*

# CHRISTMAS COLLECTIBLES

*Christmas collecting is extremely popular today, with both old and new Christmas-related pieces being sought by collectors around the country. In the following listing we present a selection of old and scarce Christmas collectibles which are especially desirable and can sometimes be quite expensive.*

## Artificial & Feather Trees

**Tree,** green, miniature, 6".................... **$95.00**

**Tree,** green w/candleholders, square white & red base, 36"........................ **350.00**

**Tree,** green w/frosted ends, red berries, 54" ...................................... **650.00**

## Candy Containers

**Basket,** brass, 3"................................... **35.00**

**Basket,** silver metal, 4" ......................... **50.00**

**Boot,** papier-mâché, American............. **15.00**

**Cornucopia,** paper cone, tinsel & Santa scraps on front (ILLUS. top next column) ..................................... **135.00**

**Heart,** pressed cardboard, red ............ **125.00**

**Santa in basket,** celluloid head, waxed string basket, Japan .............. **125.00**

**Santa,** glass, celluloid head ................. **85.00**

**Santa,** glass, stooped over chimney ... **225.00**

**Snowman,** papier-mâché, German ...... **65.00**

## Paper Ornaments

**Cross,** w/angel head............................. **25.00**

**Children,** decorating tree w/toys & elaborate tinsel trim, 14" .................. **100.00**

*Homecrafted Paper Ornament*

**Homecrafted,** paper cut-out bust portrait of Victorian lady mounted on a rounded net ground trimmed w/small gold stars, late 1800s (ILLUS.) ............................................ **125.00**

**Santa head,** w/tinsel holder, 4"............. **15.00**

**Victorian boy,** w/tinsel, 7" ................... **65.00**

## Dresden Paper Ornaments

**Birdcage,** gold, flat, 5" ........................... **65.00**
**Birdcage,** gold, three-dimensional, 3" ... **125.00**
**Dog,** brown w/black features, three-
    dimensional, 5" ................................. **295.00**
**Goat,** gold, flat, 4" ............................. **125.00**
**Horse,** gold, flat, 4" ............................. **85.00**
**Owl head,** gold & black, three-
    dimensional, 2" ................................. **125.00**
**Polar bear,** white, three-dimensional,
    3" ...................................................... **375.00**
**Rabbit,** gold, flat, 4" ............................. **85.00**
**Santa,** gold, flat, 4" ............................. **170.00**

## Spun Glass Ornaments

**Angel head,** in circle, Dresden trim,
    comet tail, 7" ..................................... **170.00**
**Angel,** glass torso, w/spun glass circle
    & Dresden trim, 5" ............................. **265.00**
**Angels,** in half circle, 6" ....................... **85.00**

*Wax Angel Ornament*

## Pressed Cotton Ornaments

**Apple,** white & pink, 4" ......................... **40.00**
**Baby,** in cotton bunting, 5" ................. **100.00**

*Moon Spun Glass Ornament*

**Moon,** in colored spun glass circle,
    5" (ILLUS.) ........................................ **120.00**
**Santa,** double sided, in circle, 5" .......... **50.00**
**Victorian lady,** on clip, 6" ................... **175.00**

## Wax & Waxed Ornaments

**Angel,** wax, 4" .................................... **125.00**
**Angel,** wax body & wings, 6", each
    (ILLUS. top next column) ................. **300.00**
**Angel,** wax, tree top, 7" ...................... **675.00**
**Boy in swing,** string holder, 4" .......... **550.00**
**Christ child,** in wooden oval, 3" ......... **295.00**

*Girl with Cat Ornament*

**Girl holding cat,** paper top & cotton
    skirt, 4" (ILLUS.) ............................... **150.00**
**Miss Liberty,** paper top & cotton skirt,
    14" .................................................... **200.00**
**Lemon,** 3" ............................................. **35.00**
**School girl,** paper face & book, 4" ..... **150.00**
**Santa,** paper face, 4" .......................... **150.00**
**Skier,** bisque face, 3" .......................... **175.00**

*Glass Bird Ornaments*

## Glass ornaments

**American clear,** World War II.............. **10.00**
**Apple,** venetian dew, pink, 3" .............. **45.00**
**Bear,** w/muff, pink, 4"........................... **95.00**
**Bird on glass log,** 4" (ILLUS. above
center).................................................. **265.00**
**Bird,** eagle, on clip, 4"........................ **195.00**
**Bird,** eagle standing, 4" (ILLUS. above
right) ..................................................... **325.00**
**Bird,** owl, pink w/black eyes, 3" ........... **20.00**
**Bird,** owl standing, 4" (ILLUS. above
left)....................................................... **125.00**
**Bird,** peacock, 5"................................... **65.00**
**Bird,** peacock, on clip, 5" ...................... **35.00**
**Butterfly,** spun glass wings, 3".......... **275.00**
**Candle,** on clip, 4"................................. **75.00**
**Christ head,** three sided, 2"............... **550.00**
**Church,** 3"............................................. **25.00**
**Clock,** wall w/paper face, 4".................. **65.00**
**Dog,** seated, gold & pink, 3" (ILLUS.
below right) ......................................... **95.00**
**Dog,** begging, white & black, 3" ........... **80.00**
**Fantasy ornament,** pine cones ........... **85.00**
**Father Christmas,** on clip, early, 4" ... **175.00**
**Fish,** 5"................................................. **85.00**
**Frog,** singing, 4" (ILLUS. below left) ... **150.00**
**Grape cluster,** individual grapes, 6"..... **65.00**

*Frog & Dog Ornaments*

*Kugel Grape Cluster*

**Goldilocks,** 4".................................... **120.00**
**Indian head,** full headdress, 4"........... **450.00**
**Jack o' Lantern,** gold, 3".................... **145.00**
**Keystone Cop,** on clip, 5".................. **275.00**
**Kugel,** grape cluster, cobalt blue, 4"
(ILLUS. top this column) .................. **450.00**
**Kugel,** round, cobalt blue, 3"................ **55.00**
**Kugel,** round, red, 4"........................... **550.00**
**Los Angeles zeppelin,** painted flags
(ILLUS. top next page) ..................... **325.00**
**Mushroom,** on clip, white & red, 3" ...... **35.00**
**Pickle,** straight, green, 5".................... **130.00**
**Pine cone,** curved red, 4" .................... **10.00**
**Policeman,** blue w/stick, 5"................. **185.00**
**Rose,** pink, w/venetian dew, 3"............. **25.00**
**Santa,** in chimney, 3" ........................... **55.00**
**Santa,** chenille legs, 5"....................... **185.00**
**Santa,** double sided, on ball, 6" .......... **110.00**
**St. Nicholas,** w/bag, on clip, 5"........... **300.00**
**Songbird,** on clip, 7"............................. **15.00**
**Spider on web,** Czechoslovakia, 6" ... **295.00**

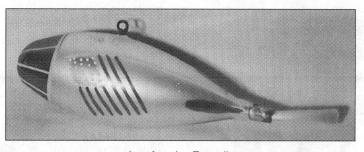

*Los Angeles Zeppelin*

**Squirrel,** gold & red, 3" ......................... 45.00
**Stork,** on clip, open beak, 5" ................. 65.00
**Strawberry,** unsilvered, red, 3" ............ 95.00
**Teapot,** gold, 2" .................................... 10.00
**Tomato,** unsilvered, red, 3" ................... 95.00
**Uncle Sam,** top hat, wire-wrapped, 5" .. 355.00
**Watermelon slice,** 4" .......................... 150.00

### Italian Glass Ornaments
**Alpine Skier,** 5" ................................. 125.00
**Billy the Kid,** 5" ................................. 100.00
**Captain Hook,** 6" ............................... 120.00
**Lucy,** 4" ............................................. 100.00

### Early Lighting Devices
**Candle holder,** counterbalance, w/tin
  birds on each side ........................... 185.00
**Candle holder,** counterbalance,
  w/glass fruit at bottom ...................... 95.00
**Candle holder,** pinch-on, embossed ...... 2.00
**Christmas light,** quilted milk glass ....... 65.00

*Purple Quilted Christmas Light*

**Christmas light,** quilted purple
  (ILLUS.) ............................................. 60.00
**Christmas light,** glass, cranberry ....... 225.00
**Lantern,** metal w/glass panels,
  square .............................................. 55.00
**Reflector,** foil & tinsel, Germany .......... 10.00

### Electric light Bulbs
**Banana,** milk glass ............................... 35.00
**Clown,** clear glass, early European .... 120.00
**Clown,** on ball, milk glass .................... 40.00
**Bird,** milk glass, blue ........................... 10.00
**Bubble light,** working ............................ 5.00
**Bulbs,** clear, early carbon tipped ........... 7.00
**Dresden,** grapes, 4" ............................. 85.00
**Dresden,** Santa, 6" ............................. 195.00
**Elephant,** milk glass, w/trunk up .......... 45.00
**Matchless star,** double row points ....... 50.00
**Monkey w/rose,** early European ......... 95.00
**Rose,** clear glass, early European ........ 35.00
**Rose,** milk glass ................................... 12.00

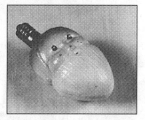

*Santa Double-sided Bulb*

**Santa,** double-sided, milk glass
  (ILLUS.) ............................................. 15.00
**Santa in chimney,** milk glass .............. 15.00
**Snowman,** milk glass ........................... 10.00
**Steamship,** milk glass, blue & red ........ 40.00
**Boxed set,** bubble, NOMA ................... 40.00

### Santa Figures
**Belsnickel,** blue, 14" ...................... 1,250.00
**Bisque,** miniature, w/two children ......... 95.00
**Celluloid,** in sleigh w/two reindeer,
  Japan, 8" .......................................... 85.00
**Celluloid,** painted details, Irwin, 8"
  (ILLUS. top next page) ................... 120.00
**Celluloid,** in cardboard sleigh w/six
  reindeer, American, 12" ..................... 85.00
**Cotton,** composition face, Japan, 8" ... 125.00

*Celluloid Santa*

*German Santa Figure*

**German,** candy container, red flannel coat, black composition boots, 22" (ILLUS.) ............................................ **3,800.00**

**German,** in sled, two cloth coated reindeer in front, 26" ...................... **3,700.00**

**Japan,** on paper skis, pack on back, 4" ...................................................... **55.00**

**Plaster,** bank, in stuffed chair, 5" .......... **85.00**

## Postcards

**Children,** decorating tree ...................... **10.00**

**Hold to light,** Santa w/toys ................ **225.00**

**Real photo,** decorated tree .................. **40.00**

**Santa riding polar bear** ...................... **20.00**

**Silk,** Santa standing w/sack of toys ...... **45.00**

## Christmas Advertising

*Advertising Buttons*

**Button,** celluloid, Santa w/airplane ....... **95.00**

**Buttons,** celluloid, Santa w/pack, each (ILLUS. above) ........................... **65.00**

**Candy box,** Santa, Christmas chocolates ........................................ **175.00**

**Coca-Cola,** standing Santa, ca. 1950s ................................................. **75.00**

**Page's Ice Cream,** Santa ................... **370.00**

**Pail,** Santa w/reindeer, 4" ................... **495.00**

**Trade card,** blue Santa holding small Christmas tree (ILLUS. below) ........... **65.00**

**Trade card,** Santa w/children, Woolsom ............................................. **75.00**

*Santa Trade Card*

*Windup Santa Toys*

## Greeting Cards

Booklet, "Visit of the Angels," 1908 ...... 40.00
Fold-out, three-layer, Father
    Christmas ........................................ 155.00
Fold-over, airbrush, Santa, 1910 ......... 25.00
Fold-over, Santa w/flag, World War II-
    era ...................................................... 5.00
Silk fringed, double sided, Rose .......... 15.00

## Cookie Molds, Candy Molds & Cookie Cutters

Christmas tree, cookie cutter .............. 10.00
Santa, candy mold, 11" ...................... 135.00
Santa, w/pack, ice cream mold ............. 75.00
Santa, cookie cutter, early, 6" .............. 75.00

## Games, Puzzles & Toys

Battery-operated, Santa w/bell,
    Japan ............................................... 185.00
Jack-in-the-box, Santa, late 1930s .... 190.00
Sleigh w/Santa, Hubley, 17" ............ 1,500.00
Windup, Santa on reindeer, Japan
    (ILLUS. left) ..................................... 175.00
Windup, Santa on skis, Japan
    (ILLUS. right) ..................................... 95.00

## Putz (Nativity) Related Materials

Animals, celluloid, assorted, Japan ...... 15.00
Animals, celluloid, assorted, German... 20.00

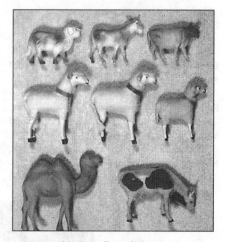

*Various Putz Animals*

Deer, celluloid, Japan, 4" ...................... 15.00
Deer, celluloid, Occupied Japan, 8" ...... 40.00
Figures, human, composition,
    German .............................................. 40.00
House, wood w/cardboard roof,
    German .............................................. 35.00
House, cardboard, small, Japan ........... 15.00
Sheep, composition head, wood body,
    6" ..................................................... 125.00
Trees, brush, medium, Japan ................. 8.00
Trees, sponge, German ......................... 15.00

## Miscellaneous Christmas Items

*Beaded Chains on a Tree*

*Gauze Santa Mask*

**Beaded chains,** glass, elaborately shaped beads, German, 36" (ILLUS.) ............................................ **200.00**

**Beaded chains,** glass, Japan, 36"........ **15.00**

**Fence,** wood, green & red, American, 12" sq................................................. **135.00**

**Fence,** wood w/wicker & tin, nine sections, two gates ........................... **225.00**

**Mask,** gauze, Santa, ca. 1930s, Japan (ILLUS. top next column)..................... **45.00**

**Nativity set,** plaster of Paris, German, 6" figures, complete ........... **200.00**

**Snow baby figure,** china, on wooden skis ..................................................... **95.00**

**Snow baby figure,** china, riding red airplane .............................................. **250.00**

**Snow baby figure,** china, w/Santa Claus ................................................. **300.00**

**Stocking,** lithographed Santa, 22"...... **225.00**

**Suit,** Father Christmas w/papier-mâché mask, early 1900s................. **650.00**

**Tree stand,** cast iron, shaped bark....... **95.00**

**Tree stand,** cast iron, w/seven light sockets, American ............................. **55.00**

*Various Snow Baby Figures*

# CIRCUS COLLECTIBLES

*Clyde Beaty & Cole Bros. Circus Poster*

**Poster,** "Clyde Beaty & Cole Bros. Circus," shows woman w/dogs doing tricks on horses, red, blue, yellow, brown & black graphic, "Globe Poster Corp. Chicago, Litho U.S.A. CF 550," very minor creasing, 20½" w., 28" h. (ILLUS.) .................. **$94.00**

**Poster,** "Cole Bros. Big Railroad Circus," shows various circus performers under the 'big top,' red, blue, yellow graphic w/red & black lettering, "Litho in U.S.A., Another U.S. Poster No. 41121 6-5," 29" w., 16" h. (thumbtack marks & fold down middle) ............................................. **132.00**

**Poster,** "Ringling Bros. and Barnum & Bailey Circus," blue w/yellow lettering, marked "1945 Ringling Bros. and Barnum & Bailey Combined Shows, Inc." at bottom 21" w., 28" h. (minor wear) .............. **154.00**

**Poster,** "Ringling Bros. and Barnum & Bailey Circus," full color poster reads "Ringling Bros. and Barnum & Bailey Circus - Circus World" above circle w/various scenes from the circus, all above "Stupendously Grand - The Greatest Place on Earth," marked "Copyright 1973 Ringling Bros.," 22" w., 28" h. (minor edge wear) ........ **22.00**

**Poster,** "Russell Bros. 3 Ring Circus," shows dogs doing various tricks, blue, yellow, orange, brown & red graphic, 20½" w., 28" h. (ragged edges)................................................. **61.00**

**Poster,** "Russell Bros. 3 Ring Circus," shows two tigers in the wild, yellow, red & blue graphic w/white lettering, paper date add-on has been removed, 20" w., 28" h. (thumbtack holes) ................................................. **17.00**

# CLOCKS

**Animated,** Haddon, electric, rocking granny, cream & red ...................... **$160.00**

**Animated,** Mastercrafter, electric, swinging playmates ......................... **190.00**

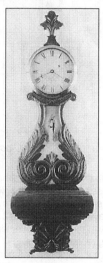

*Carved Mahogany Lyre Banjo Clock*

**Banjo,** John Anderson, Peekskill, New York, mahogany, carved Prince of Wales finial circular brass bezel w/glass door above dial w/Arabic numerals, signed "John Anderson, Peekskill, New York," supported by feather-like carvings, baluster shaped throat w/reverse-painted panel of a woman holding a lyre, cradled by feather-like carvings, all on slightly bulging rectangular bracket w/shell carvings below (ILLUS.) ........................................... **748.00**

**Banjo,** Stephen Smith, Massachusetts, Federal Mahognay & églosimé case, surmounted by a cast metal eagle finial above glazed door opening to a white-painted dial inscribed "Stephen Smith," the églosimé throat panel decorated w/a wingspread eagle & shield in polychrome, brass sidearms flanking, the églosimé box door painted w/a house by a river, ca. 1825, 4 x 9¾", 33" h. (throat panel cracked) .............................. **2,645.00**

*Mahogany Banjo Clock*

**Banjo,** Waltham Clock Co., Waltham, Massachusetts, mahogany, eagle finial above circular glass door over painted dial w/Arabic numerals, eight-day weight driven movement, above long rectangular reverse-painted throat decorated w/American eagle w/shield above rectangular base decorated w/nautical scene centered by American eagle w/shield, all flanked by "Lake Erie - Perry's Victory - Sept. 10th, 1813," 20th c. (ILLUS.) ................................ **920.00**

**Bracket,** Edward Foster, London, George III, mahogany case, the raised caddy top w/brass carrying handle above an arched glazed door & sides on molded plinth, the silvered dial engraved w/scrolling foliage w/regulation ring in the arch & spring suspension regulating rise & fall, the dial signed "Edward Foster London," the brass backplate engraved w/scrolling acanthus, mid-18th c., 12" h............................ **4,140.00**

**Bracket,** Ollivart and Botsford, Manchester, England, mahogany & gilt metal, pineapple finials & classic pilasters, brass dials, eight-day chime mechanism struck on gongs ........... **1,035.00**

*Seth Thomas Calendar Clock*

**Calendar wall clock,** Seth Thomas Clock Co., Thomaston, Connecticut, oak case, regulator, angular crest carved w/center shell decoration topped w/ball finial all flanked by scrolls above rectangular frieze carved w/small balls above rectangular glass door covering painted metal clock dial w/Roman numerals & calendar dial w/Arabic numerals, spring driven movement, late 19th c. (ILLUS.) ...................... **1,725.00**

**Calendar wall clock,** Waterbury Clock Co., Waterbury, Connecticut, walnut case, figure-eight form w/dial w/Roman numerals above & calendar dial w/Arabic numerals below, eight-day spring driven movement, late 19th c. (ILLUS. top next page)........................................ **863.00**

**Carriage,** Boston Clock, Co., Boston, Massachusetts, original case, sold by Rand & Crane, Boston Massachusetts................................. **489.00**

**Dwarf,** pine case, the horizontal reeded crest surmounted by a swan's-neck pediment & three acron finials, on turned colonnettes centering an églosimé painted dial w/Arabic numerals depicting a sunset in polychrome floral spandrels, the waisted case below w/reeded door grained to simulate crotch mahogany on a moled & reeded base similarly grained ending in bracket feet, ca. 1820, 7¼ x 11", 4' h. (repairs, bonnet lacks glazed panel) ...................... **6,900.00**

*Waterbury Calendar Clock*

**Grandfather,** Caleb Davis, Woodstock, Virginia, Federal inlaid walnut case, the hood w/swan's-neck crest ending in inlaid floral rosettes & surmounted by three urn-and-steeple finials, the tympanum board inlaid w/two suspended inlaid bellflowers w/leaves, the arched hinged door below opening to a white-painted dial w/phases of the moon including depictions of a ship at sea & a farm scene, a calendar date register below centering the inscription "Caleb Davis," turned colonnettes flanking the waisted case below, inlaid w/scrolled vines & bellflowers or turnips above an oval-inlaid door flanked by intersecting line-inlaid canted corners, the oval-inlaid base flanked by similarly decorated canted corners, on ogee bracket feet, ca. 1800, 11⅛ x 19½", 8' 8" h.............. **17,250.00**

**Grandfather,** Daniel Munroe, Concord, Massachusetts, Federal mahogany inlaid case, the curved hood w/delicate scrollwork flanked by brass ball finials above two colonnettes flanking painted face w/Roman numerals below painted scene, surrounded by w/four elaborately scrolling spandrels, labeled "Dan'l Munroe Concord," the waisted case below w/long line inlay above square base w/further inlay on ogee bracket feet, case probably made by William Munroe, Daniel's brother, w/original old finish, 89" h. (ILLUS. top next column) ............. **74,000.00**

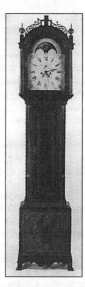

*Daniel Munroe Grandfather Clock*

*Colonial Revival Grandfather Clock*

**Grandfather,** J.E. Caldwell & Co., Boston, Massachusetts, Colonial revival, mahogany case, broken arch pediment centered w/brass squatty urn-form spandrel, flanked by two like brass spandrels, arched hood, two columns flanking glass door over phases of the moon above metal dial w/Arabic numerals & seconds bit, waisted case w/columns flanking beveled glass door above brass weight driven movement w/chimes struck on gong, spaneled base w/carved paw feet, late 19th c. (ILLUS. bottom previous page) ........................................... **2,645.00**

**Grandfather,** Payton Dana, Providence, Rhode Island, Queen Anne block-and-shell carved stained maple case, the arched molded crest flanked by fluted urn-and-flame finials on flaring columnar supports centering an arched glazed door opening to a brass dial w/Roman & Arabic numerals & the inscription in the arched reserve "Payton Dana Providence," w/an incised tulip & leaves, the waisted case below fitted w/an arched blocked door carved w/seven-lobe convex shell centering an inverted C-scroll, the base mounted w/concentric square panels, on ogee bracket feet, ca. 1750-80, 10 x 19", 6' 10" h. (rear left foot restored & patch to base panel) ..... **6,325.00**

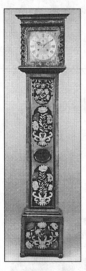

*William & Mary Grandfather Clock*

**Grandfather,** William & Mary style, walnut & marquetry case, the formerly rising flat top hood w/molded cornice supported on twisted columns w/a 10" square dial w/Roman numerals, w/silvered chapter ring enclosing a seconds ring & date aperture on matted center & w/winged cherub spandrels, bearing the signature "Daniel Quare London," the movement w/five ringed knopped

pillars, anchor escapement striking the hours by means of outside count wheel, all above the trunk w/concave molding & door inset w/panels of floral marquetry & oval lenticle w/similarly inlaid plinth & bun feet, case & movement restored, England, 78" h. (ILLUS. previous column) ........................................ **3,450.00**

**Schoolhouse wall clock,** Seth Thomas Clock Co., Thomaston, Connecticut, mahogany case, octagonal frame, paper dial w/eight-day movement, calendar timepiece, short drop w/black & gold tablet, early 20th c. ..................................... **259.00**

*Mahogany Carved Shelf or Mantel Clock*

**Shelf or mantel,** Sylvester Clark for Hills Wells & Co., Straitsville, Connecticut, Classical style mahogany case, crestrail intricately carved w/leaves & a bowl of fruit above two paneled door w/decorated lower panel, door opens to white face w/roman numerals & leaf spandrels, w/brass eight-day Salem bridge-type movement, all on scroll feet, minor imperfections, 6 x 17½", 31½" h. (ILLUS.) ........................................ **3,565.00**

**Shelf or mantel,** "Chauncey Jerome," rectangular upright ogee mahogany veneer case w/a two-panel glazed door, the upper pane over the painted metal dial w/Roman numerals, the lower tall panel w/a reverse painted scene of a willow tree & Gothic buiding, brass works, paper label inside, mid-19th c., 24¾" h. (dial wear) ........................... **220.00**

**Shelf or mantel,** "Sessions," pressed oak case w/a wide & high crown-form crest w/scrolled leaf ears above overall pressed florals over the arched glazed door opening to a dial w/Roman numerals above scrolled gilt trim, bands of pressed scrolls down the sides of a raised footed base w/further pressed scrolls, w/pendulum & key, ca. 1900, 23" h. ......................... **138.00**

**Shelf or mantel,** Ansonia Clock Co., Ansonia, Connecticut, oak gingerbread case, arched crest centered by carved portrait medallion of a young woman w/long hair below a ray-like headpiece flanked by carved scrolls all flanked by baluster shaped knobs above arched hood above columns behind carved cherubs all backed by rectangular mirrors, all flanking curved glass door over dial w/Roman numerals, eight-day time & strike movement, w/regulator, all on curved base centered w/carved winged decoration, late 19th c. ......... **259.00**

**Shelf or mantel,** Ansonia Clock Co., Ansonia, Connecticut, china, polychrome floral & green scroll motif on a cream ground, porcelain enameled dial, front escapement, late 19th c. ....................................... **288.00**

**Shelf or mantel,** Ansonia Clock Co., Ansonia, Connecticut, Royal Bonn china case, gilt highlights on greyish green ground, porcelain enameled dial, front escapement ...................... **403.00**

*Mahogany Mirror Clock*

**Shelf or mantel,** C & C. L. Ives, Bristol, Connecticut, Classical mahogany triple decker mirror case, top w/roundels flanking scalloped cornice stenclied w/leaves & fruit above hinged door opening to white face w/Roman numerals w/eight-day brass wagon spring driven movement, above mirror flanked by colonnettes above door decorated w/government buildings all on ball feet, ca. 1831, minor imperfections, 36½" h. (ILLUS. bottom previous column) ......................................... **3,680.00**

**Shelf or mantel,** E. Ingraham Clock Co., Bristol, Connecticut, pressed oak case, cupid & anvil motif w/paper dial w/eight day & strike movement ......................................... **115.00**

*Empire-style Shelf or Mantel Clock*

**Shelf or mantel,** Empire-style, gilt-metal & porcelain, high arched case topped by pointed disc w/gilt-metal knob finial above ornate openwork gilt-metal scrolls & banding above the round white porcelain dial w/Roman numerals above h.p. panel painted w/putti flanked by decorated porcelain colonettes, the whole raised on an angular stepped gilt-metal band above a scroll-cast gilt-metal apron & outswept scroll legs, France, mid-19th c. (ILLUS.) ......... **1,035.00**

**Shelf or mantel,** globe-type, Theodore R. Timby, Baldwinsville, New York, walnut case, the arched molded cornice centering a drum form finial above a globe set within a printed shapter ring, the globe

*Walnut Globe Shelf or Mantel Clock*

*Brass Shelf or Mantel Clock*

inscribed "Joslin's Six Inch Terrestrial Globe...1860," above a molded base containing glazed door enclosing a circular dial, globe by Gilman Joslin, Boston, Massachusetts, ca. 1865, 14" w., 26¾" h. (ILLUS.) ................. **3,737.00**

**Shelf or mantel,** Kroeber, New York, brass, rectangular case embossed w/leaf-like decorations, topped w/four baluster-shaped knobs at corners surrounding carrying handle, porcelain dial w/Roman numerals w/outside escapement, eight-day time & strike movement, all on ball feet, late 19th c. (ILLUS. top next column) ............................................. **345.00**

**Shelf or mantel,** Munger & Benedict, Auburn, New York, mahogany veneer Empire style case w/a leaf-varved crest centered by a basket of fruit & flanked by corner blocks above stenciled floral-decorated panels flanking the glazed door opening to a signed dial w/Roman numerals above a tall glazed door w/reverse-painted decoration of an eagle in an oval flanked by colonnettes at the sides, on carved scroll front feet, old finish, brass works w/weights, pendulum & key, paper label inside, ca. 1830-40, 39¾" h. .......................................... **2,640.00**

**Shelf or mantel,** Birge & Fuller, Bristol, Connecticut, mahogany Gothic-style double steeple case, w/eight-day brass wagon spring movement, ca. 1845, 27" h. (minor imperfections) .................................. **862.00**

**Steeple,** Smith & Taylor, New York, mahogany veneer, steeple-form case painted dial, frosted metal tablet w/floral motif, w/paper label of Smith & Taylor, mid-19th c. ............. **173.00**

---

# CLOTHING

*Recent interest in period clothing, uniforms and accessories from the 18th, 19th and through the 20th century compels us to include this category in our compilation. While style and fabric play an important role in the values of older garments of previous centuries, designer dresses of the 1920s and '30s, especially evening rowns, are enhanced by the original label of a noted courturier such as Worth or Adrian. Prices vary widely for these garments which we list by type, with infant's and children's apparel so designated.*

**Ball gown,** strapless, pale pink taffeta w/cummerbund waist & tiered skirt trimmed w/pink silk fringed & scalloped embroidered ribbons, size 6, 1950s .................................... **$80.00**

**Cape,** black velvet cut to ivory satin in a pattern of peonies & other flowers, the ruffled collar & jabot of finely pleated black silk chiffon, w/black chenille & braid frogs, size 6, turn-of-the-century ....................................... **258.00**

**Capelet,** beige wool woven in faint red & black w/a paisley inspired design, trimmed at the neck & hem w/red, black & white variegated chenille fringe, late 19th c. ............................ **143.00**

**Cardigan,** cashmere, black w/black velvet floral appliqués & jet bead embroidery, 1950s ............................ **200.00**

**Cardigan set,** grey cashmere, the cardigan trimmed w/bands of intricately folded grosgrain ribbon, 1950s, 2 pcs. ..................................... **345.00**

**Corset,** pail blue satin embroidered in white w/enlarged cross-stitch, marked "Not Genuine Unless Stamped R&G," 1870s (some discoloration) ................................... **258.00**

**Dinner jacket,** cotton velvet printed w/a small geometric pattern in shades of lavender, black & white, labelled "Emilio Pucci by Ermenegildo Zegna," 1960s.................................................. **200.00**

**Dress,** figured olive silk, w/wide neckline, horizontally tucked yoke, long curved sleeves tucked below shoulder & full skirt smocked at waist, 1840s (some spots & tears)...... **172.00**

**Dress,** lingerie-type, girl's, composed of bands of cream embroidered net, trimmed at one side of the hem w/a peach silk bow, 1910s (bow damaged) ......................................... **46.00**

**Dress,** lingerie-type, girl's, cream gauze trimmed w/floral embroidery & narrow net ruffles............................... **28.00**

**Evening dress,** strapless, of two shades of turquoise silk satin, w/draped cummerbund bodice & full gently pleated skirt, size 6, 1950s (some dirt & missing button from back) ................................................. **115.00**

**Evening dress,** summer, sheer silk printed w/orange & pink roses & greenery against a cream ground, the handkerchief hem & removable cape collar edged w/black lace, size 6, late 1920s ................................... **200.00**

**Hat,** lady's, black lace decorated w/Forget-Me-Nots, small, ca. 1870-80........................................ **55.00**

**Hat,** lady's, flat black straw hat w/velvet ribbon & rose colored underbrim, ca. 1870-80 ..................... **65.00**

**Hat,** lady's, off-the-face style, purple velvet trimmed w/silk flowers & ostrich plumes in shades of purple, labelled (partly illegible) "The Parrisian...Ltd...London," late 19th c. (some fading)........................ **69.00**

**Hat,** lady's, purple horshair trimmed w/pink velvet posies, ca. 1920............ **86.00**

**Hat,** lady's, tall brown straw hat w/velvet undertrim, w/plume, ca. 1870-80........................................ **65.00**

**Jacket,** blue embroidered silk, decorated w/figural roundels in color & scattered mythical beasts, birds, carp & flowers primarily in lavender, blue & green, China, 38" l............. **3,901.00**

**Jacket,** lady's, black velvet embroidered w/bright coral sequins & crystal beads & sewn down the underside of the sleeves & at the hem w/long ombre black & tan fringe, size 6, 1920s (losses)............ **115.00**

**Jacket,** velvet & floral brocade w/silk fringe, ca. 1870-80............................. **72.00**

**Nightgown & robe,** nightgown trimmed at the yoke w/white cotton, front of robe trimmed w/shired bands & broderie anglaise, 1870s, the pair (some small stains)........................... **345.00**

**Petticoat,** white batiste embroidered w/flowering vines, turn-of-the-century............................................... **28.00**

**Petticoat,** white batiste w/camisole bodice & deep hem of Irish crocheted lace & embroidery anglaise, size 6, 1910s..................... **115.00**

**Robe,** Ikat style, woven in shades of burgundy, teal, yellow & cream & lined w/an assortment of prints, late 19th c. ....................................... **230.00**

**Sandals,** lady's, platform-type, black suede trimmed w/self flowers & black calf piping, labelled "Styled by Thomas Cort Ltd. New York Bonwit Teller Fifth Avenue," 1940s ................ **34.00**

**Shawl,** Art Deco style, silk brocade woven w/stylized flowers in black, gold & shades of pink & turquoise, 1920s................................................. **400.00**

**Shawl,** cream silk painted w/flowers within heart shaped grapevines in shades of ochre, green, purple & grey w/knotted silk fringes, 1930s .... **172.00**

**Shawl,** triangular, black Chantilly lace worked w/ribbon tied sprays of flowers, mid-19th c., 54 x 120".......... **80.00**

**Shirt,** men's, red polished cotton, printed w/Mickey Mouse, Daffy Duck, Donald Duck & Goofy dodging rockets, w/curved pointed collar & French cuffs, labelled "Peculiar to Mr. Fish 17, Clifford Street London W.I.," 1960s ..................................... **115.00**

**Shoes,** spectator-type, natural linen & brown calf topstitched in cream, marked "I. Miller Beautiful shoes Made in New York," 1930s ................. **34.00**

**Suit,** child's, gaberdine, sailor suit, full-dress style, w/cap, size 3-4 ........... **65.00**

**Suit,** lady's, navy ribbon knit, the single breasted jacket w/notched lapel collar, short sleeves, narrow self belt & simulated pocket flaps, one sleeve embroidered w/a jeweled crown, w/skirt, size 6, 1930s, 2 pcs. ................. **200.00**

**Suit,** lady's, Navy wool shantung, the long fitted jacket of half shantung & half shantung eyelet fastening down the front w/long teardrop-shaped rhinestone buttons, w/skirt, labelled, size 6, 1940s, 2 pcs. ........................... **86.00**

**Suit,** lady's, Navy wool, the long fitted jacket embroidered at the long flat collar & slanted hip pockets w/iridescent peacock blue beads, w/skirt, size 6, 1940s, 2 pcs. ............. **316.00**

**Suit,** lady's, pale taupe wool, hip bone length, single breasted jacket w/small shawl collar & paddle shape appliqué detail, w/skirt, labelled "Adrian Original, Nan Duskin Philadelphia," size 8, 1940s, 2 pcs. ......................... **115.00**

*Velvet Tea Robe*

**Tea robe,** emerald green velvet appliquéd in paler green wool outlined w/green cord in a design of scrolling flowers, w/high collar,

straight front w/hidden closure, long flared sleeves, bustle fullness at the back, lined w/quilted dark green silk satin, size 6, late 19th c. (ILLUS.)..... **316.00**

**Vest,** men's, black silk satin embroidered at the shawl collar & down front w/flowers in rust, green, yellow & white, 19th c. (altered)........ **230.00**

**Vest,** men's, brocade, cream ribbed silk woven w/satin finish flowering vines, single breasted w/shawl collar, back buckle engraved "G.CIE. Paris 1852," 19th c. ......................... **230.00**

# COCA-COLA ITEMS

*Coca-Cola promotion has been achieved through the issuance of scores of small objects throught the years. These, together with trays, signs and other articles bearing the name of this soft drink, are now sought by many collectors.*

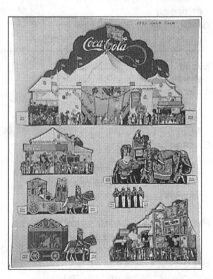

*1930 Circus Cut-out*

**Advertisement,** 1930, colorful seven-piece cut-out circus scenes, including the big top, refreshment stand, elephants, lions & "The Big Show," minor wear (ILLUS.) ........... **$140.00**

**Advertisement,** ca. 1930, Toonerville Town cut-out scenes including a boat, railroad tracks, house &

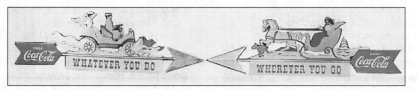

*Coca-Cola Advertisement*

general store, w/"Notice To All Members of the Scorpions Club" on reverse, 15" w., 10¼" h. (bottom right corner missing, small tear middle right & some spotting) .......... **176.00**

**Advertisement,** cardboard, shows Uncle Remus talking to young boy, reads "When dey found dat - delicious drink dey... - 'Just laffed at de sun'" above & "Uncle Remus and the - happy Animals" below, 6" w., 7" h. .................................. **495.00**

**Advertisement,** cardboard, done in green, brown, grey, red, cream & yellow & reads "Take home a carton - at popular KING SIZE price! - Coca-Cola - 12 oz...Serves 2 - King Size" above young woman measuring a bottle above "Get value, lift, and good taste, too!," 16" w., 27½" h..................................... **39.00**

**Advertisement,** die-cut tin & cardboard, in the form of two windmills facing each other, one w/old car w/passengers & the other w/an open sliegh pulled by a horse, left reads "Drink Coca-Cola - Whatever You Do," the right "Wherever You Go - Drink Coca-Cola," 48" w., 14½" h. (ILLUS. top) .................................. **1,210.00**

**Bank,** plastic, model of vending machine, marked "Drink Coca-Cola - Play - Refreshed - 5¢ - Ice Cold" w/six-pack of bottles, in original box, the set (top of box torn) .................... **500.00**

**Baseball glove,** 1920s, leather, strap marked "Drink Coca-Cola in Bottles," rare .................................. **965.00**

**Blotter,** 1916, Coca-Cola chewing gum, reads "Material Quality Flavor - Best Sanitary - Factory Methods Package" above "Made to Chew" flanked by two packs of gum all above "Franklin-Caro Co., Richmond, Va." (bend to lower right corner) .......................................... **2,475.00**

**Bookmark,** 1906, celluloid, pictures an owl reading a book marked "What Shall We Drink - Drink Coca-Cola 5¢" ................................................. **1,100.00**

**Calendar,** 1922, shows young woman holding a glass of Coke at a baseball game, July sheet only, matted & framed ......................................... **1,599.00**

**Cigarette lighter,** table-type, gold metal stamped w/red Coca-Cola logo, by Cygnos, in original box........ **478.00**

**Clock,** electric wall-type, Art Deco-style, wood w/metal face, red, white, cream & gold, paint drip, hand loose, 36" w., 18" h. (ILLUS.) ...................... **550.00**

*Art Deco-style Wall Clock*

*Electric Coca-Cola Clock*

**Clock,** electric wall-type, square, metal frame w/domed glass cover, green face w/Arabic numerals surrounding "Drink Coca-Cola" 'fish tail' logo, 1960s, 15" sq. (ILLUS.) ..... **125.00**

**Clock,** electric wall-type, round, painted metal, red & burgundy w/cream lettering reads "Drink - Coca-Cola," 17½" d. ........................ **154.00**

**Cooler,** "Vendo 39" ........................ **1,000.00**

**Cooler,** "Vendo 81" ........................ **1,250.00**

**Cooler,** "Vendolater 117" ................... **450.00**

**Cooler,** "Vendolator 27" w/stand, working condition .......................... **1,500.00**

**Coupon,** reads "Good For Two Glasses - This card entitles you and a friend to one glass each - A Delicious Beverage - Brain & Nerve Tonic - Present this at J.F. Dawson's," ca. 1890s, 3 x 5" (corner bent, two edge tears) .............................................. **3,775.00**

**Coupon,** soda jerk w/glass, 1940s ....... **28.00**

*Coca-Cola Dispenser*

**Dispenser,** metal, red container w/cream embossed lettering "Drink Coca-Cola Ice Cold," top lifts to refill, paint loss to lettering & scratches, 10½ x 16", 22" h. (ILLUS.) ......................... **400.00 to 500.00**

**Door push,** porcelain, red w/white lettering reading "Thanks Call Again - Coca-Cola," 11½" h., 4" w. (minor chipping to edges) ........................... **187.00**

**Gum wrapper,** "Coca-Cola Spearmint Flavor Gum," Franklin-Caro Co., ca. 1906, w/original gum, rare ...... **3,281.00**

**Knife,** pocket-type, red lettering on white pearlized sides reads "Drink Coca-Cola in Bottles 5¢" ................... **150.00**

**Knife,** table, silver, reads "Coca-Cola" on handle, 1920s ............................. **135.00**

**Match strike,** porcelain, red w/yellow & white, reads "Drink Coca-Cola - Strike Matches Here" above strike area, ca. 1938, 4½" sq ..................... **671.00**

**Menu,** 1902, paper, soda fountain-type, shows a turn-of-the-century woman holding up a glass of Coke, 4⅛ x 6⅛" (edge tear & edge crease) ............................................ **2,100.00**

**Menu board,** plastic, red, blue, white gold & black, top reads "Enjoy frozen - Coca-Cola," includes several rows of white plastic letters, 13¼" w., 14" h. ...................................................... **77.00**

**Menu board button,** plastic, red, black & white, circle reads "Drink Coca-Cola" w/a glass of Coke at the bottom, used as advertisement for center of menu board, 12" w., 14" h. .. **132.00**

**Needle holder,** die-cut cardboard, in the form of a full color bottle, opens to reveal full pack of needles on one side & "Comp. of Bogalusa Coca-Cola" on the other, rare ................... **816.00**

**Pencil box,** w/ruler, blotter & fountain pen, ca. 1937, the set ........................ **98.00**

**Playing Cards,** 1943, Airline Spotter, World War II, full deck ........................ **55.00**

**Radio,** model of a cooler, red Bakelite case, 1949-53, 7 x 9½ x 12" ............. **700.00**

**Sign,** counter-top light-up motion-type, reads "Pause and Refresh" next to moving waterfall to the left of "Drink Coca-Cola" all above "Please Pay When Served," 1950s, 9 x 20" ....... **1,157.00**

*Rare Coca-Cola Sign*

**Sign,** fiber, round, red ground w/raised white lettering reading "Pause... - Go refreshed - Coca-Cola" above gold wings below gold hand holding Coke bottle, early 1940s, 9½" d. (ILLUS.) .................... **935.00**

**Sign,** painted tin, white, red & green round sign reads "Enjoy Coca-Cola - while we check Your Tires," 17" d. (scratches & denting) ......................... **94.00**

*Coca-Cola Syrup Dispenser Front & Back*

**Sign,** painted tin, done in red, cream & green lettering reads "Enjoy Big King Size - Coca-Cola - Ice Cold Here" to the left of red, green, burgundy & green Coca-Cola bottle, 27½" w., 19½" h................................ **176.00**

**Sign,** painted tin, red, yellow & cream rectangular sign reads "Take a case home - Today - $1.00 plus deposit - Coca-Cola - Delicious and - Refreshing," 19½" w., 27½" h. (minor scrathces) ............................. **176.00**

**Sign,** porcelain, reads "Drink Coca-Cola - Pause Refresh - Lunch," 25½" h., 28" w. (chipping & touch-up on 'C' in 'Cola') ................................. **204.00**

**Signs,** cardboard, "All Time Sports Favorite," rectangular signs each featuring a sports celebrity, set includes Ty Cobb, Willie Hoppe, Red Grange, Man O' War, Gene Tunney, Ned Day, Colonel Lady M, Bobby Jones, Helene Madison & Don Budge, 1947, 13 x 15", set of 10 ... **2,310.00**

**Spoon,** silver plate, reads "Coca-Cola" on handle, 1920s, small (tarnishing)........................................ **125.00**

**Spoon,** silver plate, reads "Coca-Cola" on handle, 1920s, large (tarnishing)........................................ **110.00**

**Stamp holder,** 1900, celluloid, in the shape of envelope w/"The Coca-Cola Co. Atlanta Georgia" in script on front & "Drink Delicious Refreshing Coca-Cola" in script on reverse, w/calendar, 1½ x 2½" ...... **1,512.00**

**Syrup dispenser,** soda fountain-type, ceramic, cov. syrup bowl & base w/brass spigot, embossed scrollwork outlined in gold, Wheeling Pottery Co., 1896, some wear to logo, minor staining, repaired hairline crack around lower body, overall 18" h. (ILLUS. front & back) .................... **2,200.00**

**Thermometer,** round wall-type, metal framed w/domed glass cover, red ground w/white lettering "Drink - Coca-Cola - in Bottles," 1950s, 12" d. (some wear) .......................... **100.00**

**Thermometer,** metal, painted, embossed bottles flank the thermometer all above embossed letters read "Drink Coca-Cola," 7" w., 16" h. (denting & scratching) ........... **263.00**

**Thermometer,** tin, red & white cigar-shaped marked "Drink - Coca-Cola - Sign of Good Taste" at top & "Refresh Yourself" at bottom, 8" w., 30½" h. (surface scuffs, scratches & fading)............................................... **215.00**

**Toy,** dispenser, molded red plastic body w/white lettering reading "Drink - Coca-Cola," includes bottle tap & one plastic glass, 6 x 9 x 9" (shows some wear) ........................................ **48.00**

**Toy truck,** "Bubby-L" Mack truck w/clear trailer showing eight filled Coke boxes w/bottles, ca. 1960s........ **95.00**

**Toy truck,** Marx, pressed steel, red truck w/yellow back w/Sprite Boy decal on each door, model No. 991, 20" l.................................................... **665.00**

**Trade card,** early 1890s, shows Coca-Cola Girl at soda fountain, promotional advertising on the reverse side, 3½ x 5½" (two bent corners, minor edge tear, piece of tape on front, minor peeling on back) ..................... **3,800.00**

**Tray,** change, 1931 ............................ **300.00**

**Tray,** 1914, Betty (some edge chipping) ......................................... **475.00**

*1922 Summer Girl Tray*

**Tray,** 1922, Summer Girl, 10½ x 13¼" rectangle (ILLUS.) ........................... **562.00**

**Tray,** 1929, Girl in Yellow Swimsuit holding bottle, red border, 10½ x 13¼" rectangle ...................... **225.00**

**Tray,** 1941, Girl Ice Skater, 10½ x 13¼" rectangle ...................... **233.00**

**Tray,** 1958, shows wicker cart filled w/food & Coca-Cola, 10½ x 13¼" rectangle (has small wear spot on front) ................................................ **22.00**

**Tray,** 1961, shows pansy garden w/hand pouring glass of Coke, rim reads "Be Really Refreshed" at top & bottom, 10½ x 13¼" rectangle ............ **25.00**

# COFFEE GRINDERS

## Primitive Coffee Grinders

**Box mill,** w/brass hopper & Moravian base w/drawer, 5" open hopper (ILLUS. top next column) ............... **$150.00**

**Box mill,** w/pewter hopper, signed "WW Weaver" on crank, 6½ x 7" top .................................................... **150.00**

*Moravian Base Box Grinder*

**Iron mill,** mounted on wooden handle, signed "ADAMS," 14" l. ..................... **120.00**

## Side Mills

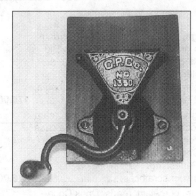

*Charles Parker Side Mill*

**Side mill,** w/wood back, "H. Wilson's Improved Patent Mill" ......................... **80.00**

**Side mill,** w/wood block, "C.P. (Charles Parker) Co. No. 1350" (ILLUS. above) .................................. **80.00**

**Side mill,** w/wood block, elaborately decorated, "Parker No. 370" ............. **120.00**

**Side mill,** cast iron, elaborate scroll decorations, embossed "Standard No. 221, Patent June 11, 1878, LF&C," Landers, Frary & Clark ......... **240.00**

## Box Mills

**Box mill,** iron covered hopper, iron top embossed "L&S Franco-American," 6 x 6" top (ILLUS. top next page) .......................................... **90.00**

**Box mill,** tall wood box w/handle, crank embossed "Logan & Strobridge," 6 x 6½" top ................... **140.00**

*Franco-American Mill*

*Universal Box Mill*

*European Box Mill*

**Box mill,** tall metal box, well marked green label reads "Universal 110 Coffee Mill Pat. Feb. 14, 1905 Landers, Frary & Clark, New Britain, Conn, USA," missing wire handle (ILLUS. middle)................................... **60.00**

**Box mill,** brass decorative box mill w/raised covered hopper, Europe, 5 x 5" top (ILLUS. bottom previous column)............................................. **150.00**

**Box mill,** wood box mill, raised covered hopper, iron top embossed "Arcade Mfg. Co. Favorite Mill"......... **120.00**

*Quick Grinder*

**Box mill,** wood box w/side handle, iron top & covered hopper, embossed crank & label reads "LF&C 1100 Quick Grinder" (ILLUS.) ...................... **150.00**

**Box mill,** wood box w/iron top & handle, Arcade's King No. 930, unmarked, 6 x 6" top........................... **80.00**

**Box mill,** tall wood box w/side handle & well marked label "Sun No. 1080," 6½ x 6½" top..................................... **100.00**

**Box mill,** circular tin mill w/twist-off canister below, Bronson-Walton Monitor, 6½ x 6½" base...................... **80.00**

**Box mill,** tall box mill, door w/tin dish, iron top, cover & handle, labeled, marked "Parker Victor No. 541," 6 x 6" top......................................... **200.00**

**Box mill,** wood box w/iron top & handle, WH Co. (Wrightsville Hardware) Colonial No. 1707, unmarked............................................. **50.00**

**Box mill,** wood box w/raised iron hopper, laebel reads "No. 125 - Coffee Mill - Steel Alloy Grinders - The Sun Manufacturing Co., Columbus, Ohio, U.S.A." (ILLUS. top next page) ........... **100.00**

**Box mill,** wood box, iron cover w/geared halves, Parker National, unmarked, 6 x 6" top........................... **90.00**

**Box mill,** wood box w/raised britannia hopper, marked "Peck, Stow & Wilcox (PS&W) No. 1006" ............... **100.00**

*Sun Coffee Mill*

## Upright Mills

**Upright mill,** cast iron, open hopper, black w/faint markings, marked "Enterprise No. 1," pat. 1873, 12" h. (ILLUS. below) .................................. **240.00**

*Enterprise Upright Mill*

*Progresso Mill*

**Upright mill,** cast iron, wooden drawer & tin covered hopper, crank w/gears, embossed "Progresso P.G.O.," 14" h. (ILLUS. bottom previous column) ............................. **380.00**

**Upright mill,** cast iron, eagle perched atop covered hopper, tin catcher & double wheels, original red, blue & gold paint, patent dates, 15" wheels embossed "Star Mill, Philadelphia" (ILLUS. below) ............................... **1,200.00**

**Upright mill,** cast iron, double 17" wheels, pivoting cover on hopper w/eagle, original paint & decals, embossed w/1873 & 1898 patent dates, Enterprise No. 7 (ILLUS. bottom this column) ....................... **1,000.00**

*Store Model Star Mill*

*Enterprise No. 7 Mill*

*Upright English Mill*

**Upright mill,** cast iron, brass hopper & single 18" wheel, original paint, embossed patent date, marked "Z Parkes Vortex No. 1," England (ILLUS.) ............................ **450.00**

**Upright mill,** cast iron, drawer, covered hopper & double wheels, original green paint, decals & labels, 18" wheels embossed "Landers, Frary & Clark, New Britain, Conn. U.S.A.," Crown No. 20 ..................... **950.00**

**Upright mill,** cast iron, pivoting cover w/sread winged eagle, double 15" wheels, original red paint, embossed "Elgin National Coffee Mill, Woodruff & Edwards Co. Elgin, Ill.," model No. 44 (missing tin catcher, eagle replaced)........................................ **900.00**

## Wall Canister Mills

**Wall canister mill,** ceramic canister w/glass cup, blue windmill scene painted on canister, marked "H.T.," A. Troesser (ILLUS. top next column) ........................................... **140.00**

**Wall canister mill,** glass canister & cup, "Arcade" embossed on jar & cap, Arcade No. 25, 16" h.................. **90.00**

**Wall canister mill,** steel canister w/iron cup, canister gold-embossed, Arcade Royal (ILLUS. middle next column)........................................... **250.00**

**Wall canister mill,** tin black on red lithographed canister, pictures tall building w/directions on side of canister, Grand Union Tea Co., 13" h. including cup ......................... **210.00**

*Painted Ceramic Mill*

*Gold-colored Arcade Mill*

*Universal Canister Mill*

**Wall canister mill,** glass canister &
cup, assembly rotates to fill, jar
embossed "Universal No. 24," LF&C
(ILLUS. bottom previous page)......... **150.00**

**Wall canister mill,** steel canister
w/glass window, w/label, Bronson-
Walton Oplex, missing cup & lid ....... **190.00**

*Metal & Wood Cylindrical Mill*

*Wood Wall Mount Mill*

**Wall canister mill,** wood box
w/engraved cast-iron front, marked
"Telephone Mill - Arcade Mfg. Co.,"
missing cup (ILLUS.) ........................ **400.00**

**Wall canister mill,** wood & cast-iron,
glass front & iron cup, Arcade X-Ray,
14" h................................................. **200.00**

## Miscellaneous

*Red Electric Mill*

**Clamp-on mill,** iron w/bell-shaped
open hopper w/tin cup, black w/gold
trim, embossed "Spong & Co."
(ILLUS. bottom previous column) ....... **80.00**

**Cylindrical mill,** metal & wood, dome
cover over hopper, slotted bottom,
engraved "F B" (ILLUS. top) ............. **150.00**

**Electric mill,** aluminum hopper & tin
catch can, red w/gold & black trim,
Hobart ¼ horsepower (ILLUS. bottom) **180.00**

**Miniature mill,** cast iron, double-
wheel, red body w/gold wheels,
unmarked 4" h. .................................. **50.00**

**Wall mount,** child's, ceramic cannister
w/glass cup, w/"Café" painted on
cannister, Germany, 5" h. ................. **300.00**

*Spong & Co. Clamp-on Mill*

*Corn & Coffee Mill*

**Wall mount,** corn & coffee mill, cast iron, single 17" wheel, embossed "Parker's Patent, Feb 7, 1860" (ILLUS.) ........................................... **450.00**

**Wall mount mill,** cast iron, open hopper, Enterprise No. 0 ................... **70.00**

# COMIC BOOKS

*Comic books, especially first or early issues of a series, are avidly collected today. Prices for some of the scarce ones have reached extremely high levels. Prices listed below are for copies in fine to mint condition.*

**Bonanza,** four color, Dell Publishing Co., No. 1283 ................................... **$40.00**

**Deputy Dawg,** four color, Dell Publishing Co., No. 1299 .................... **20.00**

**Fury,** four color, Dell Publishing Co., No. 1296, March 1962 ........................ **13.00**

**Huckleberry Hound,** four color, Dell Publishing Co., No. 3, 1960 ................ **13.00**

**I Spy,** Gold Key, No. 1, August 1966 (near mint condition) ........................ **115.00**

**Moon Pilot,** four color, Dell Publishing Co., No. 1313 ................................... **18.00**

**National Velvet,** four color, Dell Publishing Co., No. 1312 .................... **12.00**

**Rat Patrol,** Dell Publishing Co., No. 2 .. **25.00**

**Top Cat,** Dell Publishing Co., No. 2 ...... **12.00**

**Unknown Worlds,** American Comics Group/Best Syndicate Features, No. 14 ................................................. **10.00**

# COMMEMORATIVE PLATES

*Limited editions commemorative and collector plates rank high on the list of collectible items. The oldest and best-known of these plates, those of Bing & Grondahl and Royal Copenhagen, retain leadership in the field, but other companies are turning out a variety of designs, some of which have been widely embraced by the growing numbers who have made plate collecting a hobby. Plates listed below are a representative selection of fine porcelain, glass and other plates available to collectors.*

## ANRI

### Christmas

**1971,** St. Jakob in Groden................. **$34.00**
**1972,** Pipers at Alberobello ................. **45.00**
**1973,** Alpine Horn............................... **100.00**
**1974,** Young Man & Girl ...................... **56.00**
**1975,** Christmas in Ireland .................. **70.00**
**1976,** Alpine Christmas ....................... **95.00**
**1977,** Legend of Heiligenblut............... **83.00**
**1978,** The Klockler Singers ................. **89.00**
**1979,** The Moss Gatherers of Villnoess ............................................. **65.00**
**1980,** Wintry Church-going in Santa Christina ............................................... **80.00**
**1981,** Santa Claus in Tyrol ................. **105.00**
**1982,** Star Singers............................... **116.00**
**1983,** Unto Us a Child Is Born............. **116.00**
**1984,** Yuletide in the Valley................. **88.00**
**1985,** Good Morning, Good Cheer ................................. **75.00 to 100.00**

## BAREUTHER

### Christmas

**1967,** Stiftskirche................................. **50.00**
**1968,** Kappl ............................................ **14.00**
**1969,** Christkindlesmarkt........................ **17.00**
**1970,** Chapel in Oberndorf..................... **9.00**
**1971,** Toys for Sale ................................ **8.00**
**1972,** Christmas in Munich.................... **19.00**
**1973,** Christmas Sleigh Ride.................. **7.00**
**1974,** Church in the Black Forest.......... **10.00**
**1975,** Snowman ..................................... **22.00**
**1976,** Chapel in the Hills ....................... **19.00**
**1977,** Story Time.................................... **13.00**

| | |
|---|---|
| **1978,** Mittenwald | **10.00** |
| **1979,** Winter Day | **10.00** |
| **1980,** Miltengerg | **21.00** |
| **1981,** Walk in the Forest | **16.00** |
| **1982,** Bad Wimpfen | **25.00** |
| **1983,** The Night Before Christmas | **26.00** |
| **1984,** Zeil on the River Main | **25.00** |
| **1985,** Winter Wonderland | **28.00** |
| **1986,** Market Place in Forchheim | **27.00** |
| **1987,** Decorating the Tree | **21.00** |
| **1988,** St. Coloman Church | **44.00** |
| **1989,** Sleigh Ride | **44.00** |
| **1990,** The Old Forge in Rothenburg | **27.00** |

### Mother's Day

| | |
|---|---|
| **1969,** Dancing | **21.00** |

*1970 Bareuther Mother's Day Plate*

| | |
|---|---|
| **1970,** Mother & Children (ILLUS.) | **9.00** |
| **1971,** Doing the Laundry | **12.00** |
| **1972,** Baby's First Step | **10.00** |
| **1973,** Mother Kissing Baby | **19.00** |
| **1974,** Musical Children | **13.00** |
| **1975,** Spring Outing | **10.00** |
| **1976,** Rocking Cradle | **13.00** |
| **1977,** Noon Feeding | **15.00** |
| **1978,** Blind Man's Bluff | **20.00** |
| **1979,** Mother's Love | **13.00** |
| **1980,** First Cherries | **15.00** |
| **1981,** Playtime | **16.00** |
| **1982,** Suppertime | **16.00** |
| **1983,** On Farm | **16.00** |
| **1984,** Village Children | **25.00** |
| **1985,** Sunrise | **21.00** |
| **1986,** Playtime | **33.00** |
| **1987,** Pets | **19.00** |
| **1988,** Busy Afternoon | **21.00** |
| **1989,** Ring Around the Rosy | **42.00** |
| **1990,** Watching the Rainbow | **30.00** |

# BELLEEK

## Christmas

| | |
|---|---|
| **1970,** Castle Caldwell | **64.00** |
| **1971,** Celtic Cross | **44.00** |
| **1972,** Flight of the Earls | **31.00** |
| **1973,** Tribute to W. B. Yeats | **31.00** |
| **1974,** Devenish Island | **200.00** |
| **1975,** The Celtic Cross | **55.00** |
| **1976,** Dove of Peace | **50.00** |
| **1977,** Wren | **55.00** |

## Irish Wildlife Christmas

| | |
|---|---|
| **1978,** A Leaping Salmon | **47.00** |
| **1979,** Hare at Rest | **47.00** |
| **1980,** Hedgehog | **50.00** |
| **1981,** Red Squirrel | **50.00** |
| **1983,** Red Fox | **58.00** |

# BING & GRONDAHL

## Christmas

*1918 Bing & Grondahl Christmas Plate*

| | |
|---|---|
| **1895** | **5,171.00** |
| **1896** | **1,571.00** |
| **1897** | **1,411.00** |
| **1898** | **624.00** |
| **1899** | **1,212.00** |
| **1900** | **803.00** |
| **1901** | **348.00** |
| **1902** | **285.00** |
| **1903** | **280.00** |
| **1904** | **115.00** |
| **1905** | **129.00** |
| **1906** | **67.00** |
| **1907** | **94.00** |
| **1908** | **64.00** |
| **1909** | **77.00** |
| **1910** | **76.00** |

| | |
|---|---|
| 1911 | 72.00 |
| 1912 | 77.00 |
| 1913 | 77.00 |
| 1914 | 66.00 |
| 1915 | 111.00 |
| 1916 | 66.00 |
| 1917 | 64.00 |
| 1918 (ILLUS. previous page) | 64.00 |
| 1919 | 57.00 |
| 1920 | 65.00 |
| 1921 | 57.00 |
| 1922 | 56.00 |
| 1923 | 54.00 |
| 1924 | 63.00 |
| 1925 | 63.00 |
| 1926 | 63.00 |
| 1927 | 95.00 |
| 1928 | 57.00 |
| 1929 | 61.00 |
| 1930 | 78.00 |
| 1931 | 76.00 |
| 1932 | 75.00 |
| 1933 | 61.00 |
| 1934 | 58.00 |
| 1935 | 57.00 |
| 1936 | 62.00 |
| 1937 | 74.00 |
| 1938 | 110.00 |
| 1939 | 152.00 |
| 1940 | 152.00 |
| 1941 | 193.00 |
| 1942 | 163.00 |
| 1943 | 137.00 |
| 1944 | 79.00 |
| 1945 | 116.00 |
| 1946 | 68.00 |
| 1947 | 92.00 |
| 1948 | 74.00 |
| 1949 | 71.00 |
| 1950 | 101.00 |
| 1951 | 85.00 |
| 1952 | 84.00 |
| 1953 | 82.00 |
| 1954 | 83.00 |
| 1955 | 89.00 |
| 1956 | 109.00 |
| 1957 | 116.00 |
| 1958 | 80.00 |
| 1959 | 103.00 |
| 1960 | 114.00 |
| 1961 | 85.00 |
| 1962 | 53.00 |
| 1963 | 67.00 |
| 1964 | 32.00 |
| 1965 | 32.00 |
| 1966 | 30.00 |

| | |
|---|---|
| 1967 | 25.00 |
| 1968 | 20.00 |
| 1969 | 14.00 |
| 1970 | 15.00 |
| 1971 | 16.00 |
| 1972 | 15.00 |
| 1973 | 15.00 |
| 1974 | 13.00 |
| 1975 | 15.00 |
| 1976 | 21.00 |
| 1977 | 14.00 |
| 1978 | 17.00 |
| 1979 | 23.00 |
| 1980 | 27.00 |
| 1981 | 23.00 |
| 1982 | 28.00 |
| 1983 | 30.00 |
| 1984 | 27.00 |
| 1985 | 33.00 |

## Mothers's Day

| | |
|---|---|
| 1969, Dog & Puppies | 305.00 |
| 1970, Birds & Chicks | 11.00 |
| 1971, Cat & Kitten | 8.00 |
| 1972, Mare & Foal | 10.00 |
| 1973, Duck & Ducklings | 14.00 |
| 1974, Bear & Cubs | 13.00 |
| 1975, Doe & Fawns | 14.00 |
| 1976, Swan Family | 15.00 |
| 1977, Squirrel & Young | 15.00 |
| 1978, Heron | 16.00 |
| 1979, Fox & Cubs | 36.00 |

*1980 Bing & Grohdahl Mother's Day Plate*

| | |
|---|---|
| 1980, Woodpecker & Young (ILLUS.) | 25.00 |
| 1981, Hare & Yound | 26.00 |
| 1982, Lioness & Cubs | 27.00 |
| 1983, Raccoon & Young | 26.00 |
| 1984, Stork & Nestlings | 39.00 |
| 1985, Bear with Cubs | 26.00 |
| 1986, Elephant with Calf | 29.00 |
| 1987, Sheep with Lambs | 56.00 |

## Jubilee

**1915,** Frozen Window .......................... **114.00**
**1920,** Church Bells ................................. **45.00**
**1925,** Dog Outside Window .................. **83.00**
**1930,** The Old Organist ...................... **109.00**
**1935,** Little Match Girl ...................... **568.00**
**1940,** Three Wise Men ..................... **1,525.00**
**1945,** Royal Guard Amalienborg Castle .. **117.00**
**1950,** Eskimos .................................... **122.00**
**1955,** Dybbol Mill ............................... **125.00**
**1960,** Kronborg Castle ......................... **89.00**
**1965,** Churchgoers ............................... **53.00**
**1970,** Amalienborg Castle ..................... **10.00**
**1975,** Horses Enjoying Meal ................ **27.00**
**1980,** Happiness over Yule Tree .......... **26.00**
**1985,** Lifeboat at Work .......................... **38.00**

## FURSTENBERG

### Christmas

**1971,** Rabbits ...................................... **19.00**
**1972,** Snowy Village ............................ **19.00**
**1973,** Christmas Eve ............................ **24.00**
**1975,** Deer Family ................................ **12.00**
**1976,** Winter Birds ............................... **22.00**

### Mother's Day

**1972,** Hummingbird .............................. **21.00**
**1973,** Hedgehogs ................................. **12.00**
**1974,** Doe with Fawn ........................... **14.00**
**1976,** Koala Bear ................................. **14.00**

## GORHAM—NORMAN ROCKWELL

### Christmas

**1974,** Tiny Tim ..................................... **22.00**
**1975,** Good Deeds ............................... **24.00**
**1976,** Christmas Trio ............................ **19.00**
**1978,** Planning Christmas Visits ........... **19.00**
**1979,** Santa's Helpers .......................... **15.00**
**1980,** Letter to Santa ........................... **23.00**
**1981,** Santa Plans His Visit .................. **19.00**
**1982,** The Jolly Coachman .................... **20.00**
**1983,** Christmas Dancers ..................... **28.00**
**1984,** Christmas Medley ....................... **28.00**
**1985,** Home for the Holidays ................ **25.00**
**1987,** The Homecoming ........................ **25.00**

### Four Seasons

**1971,** A Boy & His Dog, set
   of 4 ................................. **185.00 to 200.00**
**1972,** Young Love, set of 4 ................ **142.00**
**1973,** The Ages of Love, set of 4 ........ **167.00**
**1974,** Grandpa & Me, set of 4 ............. **91.00**

**1975,** Me & My Pal, set of 4 ............... **132.00**
**1976,** Grand Pals, set of 4 .................. **128.00**
**1977,** Going on Sixteen, set of 4 .......... **71.00**
**1978,** The Tender Years, set of 4 ......... **64.00**
**1979,** A Helping Hand, set of 4 ............ **58.00**
**1980,** Dad's Boy, set of 4 ................... **111.00**
**1980,** Landscape Series, set of 4 .......... **95.00**
**1981,** Old Timers, set of ...................... **72.00**
**1982,** Life with Father, set of 4 ............ **50.00**
**1983,** Old Buddies, set of 4 ................. **75.00**

## HAVILAND & CO.

### Christmas

**1970,** A Partridge in a Pear Tree .......... **43.00**
**1971,** Two Turtle Doves ....................... **42.00**
**1972,** Three French Hens .................... **22.00**
**1973,** Four Colly Birds ......................... **23.00**
**1974,** Five Golden Rings ...................... **22.00**
**1975,** Six Geese A'Laying .................... **26.00**
**1976,** Seven Swans A'Swimming .......... **24.00**
**1977,** Eight Maids A'Milking ................. **25.00**
**1978,** Nine Ladies Dancing .................. **51.00**
**1979,** Ten Lords A'Leaping .................. **26.00**
**1980,** Eleven Pipers Piping .................. **65.00**
**1981,** Twelve Drummers Drumming ...... **42.00**
**12 Days of Christmas,**
   set ................................... **500.00 to 600.00**

### Mother's Day

**1973,** Breakfast ..................................... **4.00**
**1974,** The Wash .................................... **5.00**
**1975,** In the Park ................................. **13.00**
**1976,** To Market .................................... **9.00**
**1977,** Wash Before Dinner .................. **10.00**
**1978,** An Evening at Home ................. **11.00**
**1979,** Happy Mother's Day .................... **5.00**
**1980,** A Child & His Animals ................ **15.00**

## HAVILAND & PARLON

### Christmas

**1972,** Madonna & Child (Raphael) ....... **25.00**
**1973,** Madonnina (Feruzzi) ................. **50.00**
**1974,** Cowper Madonna & Child
   (Raphael) .................................... **35.00**
**1975,** Madonna & Child
   (Murillo) ............................ **40.00 to 50.00**
**1976,** Madonna & Child (Botticelli) ....... **28.00**
**1977,** Madonna & Child (Bellini) ........... **33.00**
**1978,** Madonna & Child (Fra Filippo
   Lippi) ......................................... **30.00**
**1979,** Madonna of the Eucharist
   (Botticelli) ................................... **90.00**

## Mother's Day

**1975,** Laura & Child ............... 20.00 to 25.00
**1976,** Pinky & Baby ............................. 10.00
**1977,** Amy & Snoopy........................... 10.00

## Tapestry Series

**1971,** The Unicorn in Captivity ............. 61.00
**1972,** Start of the Hunt ......................... 26.00
**1973,** Chase of the Unicorn.................. 55.00
**1974,** End of the Hunt .......................... 60.00
**1975,** The Unicorn Surrounded ............. 52.00
**1976,** The Unicorn is Brought to the
Castle .............................................. 40.00

## The Lady & The Unicorn

**1977,** To My Only Desire...................... 20.00
**1978,** Sight ........................................... 24.00
**1979,** Sound ........................................ 25.00
**1980,** Touch ......................................... 27.00
**1981,** Scent ......................................... 25.00
**1982,** Taste .......................................... 32.00

# HUMMEL (GOEBEL WORKS)

## Annual

**1971,** Heavenly Angel ........................ 434.00
**1972,** Hear Ye, Hear Ye ....................... 40.00
**1973,** Globe Trotter .............................. 68.00
**1974,** Goose Girl .................................. 43.00
**1975,** Ride into Christmas .................... 43.00
**1976,** Apple Tree Girl ........................... 32.00
**1977,** Apple Tree Boy........................... 48.00
**1978,** Happy Pastime ........................... 35.00
**1979,** Singing Lesson........................... 31.00
**1980,** School Girl.................................. 37.00
**1981,** Umbrella Boy............................... 40.00
**1982,** Umbrella Girl .............................. 93.00
**1983,** The Postman ............................. 140.00
**1984,** Little Helper ............................... 49.00
**1985,** Chick Girl.................................... 72.00
**1986,** Playmates.................................. 106.00
**1987,** Feeding Time ............................ 271.00

## Anniversary

**1975,** Stormy Weather .......................... 60.00
**1980,** Spring Dance.............................. 95.00
**1985,** Auf Wiedersehen...................... 134.00

# LALIQUE (GLASS)

## Annual

**1965,** Deux Oiseaux (Two Birds) ....... 797.00
**1966,** Rose de Songerie (Dream
Rose) ................................. 75.00 to 100.00

*1968 Lalique Plate*

**1967,** Ballet de Poisson
(Fish Ballet) ................................... 108.00
**1968,** Gazelle Fantaisie Gazelle
Fantasy (ILLUS. above).................. 180.00
**1969,** Papillon (Butterfly) ..................... 73.00
**1970,** Paon (Peacock) .......................... 75.00
**1971,** Hibou (Owl) ................................ 68.00
**1972,** Coquillage (Shell) ...................... 55.00
**1973,** Petit Geai (Jayling) ...................... 81.00
**1974,** Sous d'Argent (Silver Pennies) ... 74.00
**1975,** Duo de Poisson (Fish Duet) ...... 100.00
**1976,** Aigle (Eagle) .............................. 85.00

# LENOX

## Boehm Bird Series

**1970,** Wood Thrush............................... 98.00
**1971,** Goldfinch ................................... 80.00
**1972,** Mountain Bluebird ....................... 49.00
**1973,** Meadowlark ................................ 42.00
**1974,** Rufous Hummingbird.................... 60.00
**1975,** American Redstart....................... 53.00
**1976,** Cardinals ................................... 52.00
**1977,** Robins ....................................... 54.00
**1978,** Mockingbirds ............................. 62.00
**1979,** Golden-Crowned Kinglets ........... 85.00
**1980,** Black-Throated Blue Warblers .... 95.00
**1981,** Eastern Phoebes........................ 95.00

## Boehm Woodland Wildlife Series

**1973,** Raccoons ................................... 41.00
**1974,** Red Foxes.................................. 33.00
**1975,** Cottontail Rabbits ....................... 31.00
**1976,** Eastern Chipmunks ..................... 34.00
**1977,** Beaver........................................ 55.00
**1978,** Whitetail Deer.............................. 46.00
**1979,** Squirrels .................................... 73.00
**1980,** Bobcats ..................................... 54.00
**1981,** Martens ..................................... 89.00
**1982,** Otters......................................... 103.00

## LIHS-LINDNER

### Christmas
1972, Little Drummer Boy...................... 16.00
1973, Little Carolers ............................ 9.00
1974, Peach on Earth............................ 9.00
1975, Christmas Cheer ....................... 11.00
1976, Joy of Christmas....................... 11.00
1977, Holly-jolly Christmas................... 19.00
1978, Holy Night.................................. 10.00

## LLADRO

### Christmas
1971, Caroling ................................... 100.00
1972, Carolers..................................... 21.00
1973, Boy & Girl ................................. 55.00
1974, Carolers..................................... 45.00
1975, Cherubs..................................... 45.00
1976, Christ Child................................ 60.00
1977, Nativity Scene ........................... 65.00

### Mother's Day
1971, Kiss of the Child ........................ 37.00
1972, Bird & Chicks............................. 30.00
1973, Mother & Children ..................... 20.00
1974, Mother Nursing ............ 50.00 to 75.00
1975, Mother & Child........................... 24.00
1976, Tender Vigil ............................... 24.00
1977, Mother & Daughter..................... 25.00

## ORREFORS (Glass)

### Annual Cathedral Series
1970, Notre Dame Cathedral................. 20.00
1971, Westminster Abbey ..................... 30.00
1972, Basilica di San Marco.................. 25.00
1973, Cologne Cathedral ...................... 61.00
1974, Temple Rue de la Victoire, Paris... 49.00
1975, Basilica di San Pietro, Rome........ 36.00
1976, Christ Church, Philadelphia.......... 36.00
1977, Masjid-E-Shah............................ 81.00
1978, Santiago de Compostela............. 57.00

### Mother's Day
1971, Flowers for Mother ..................... 16.00
1972, Mother & Children ...................... 17.00
1973, Mother & Child............................ 16.00
1974, Mother & Child............................ 15.00
1975, Child's First Steps ...................... 46.00
1976, Children & Puppy ....................... 18.00
1977, Child & Dove .............................. 18.00
1978, Mother & Child............................ 18.00

## PICKARD

### Lockhart Wildlife Series
1970, Woodcock & Ruffed Grouse,
 pr. ................................... 200.00 to 225.00
1971, Green-Winged Teal & Mallard,
 pr. ................................... 150.00 to 175.00
1972, Mockingbird & Cardinal, pr. ...... 125.00
1973, Wild Turkey & Ring-Necked
 Pheasant, pr. ............................... 179.00
1974, American Bald Eagle................ 600.00
1975, White-Tailed Deer ..................... 100.00
1976, American Buffalo........................ 97.00
1977, Great Horned Owl ...................... 66.00
1978, American Panther...................... 129.00
1979, Red Fox..................................... 68.00
1980, Trumpeter Swan........................ 140.00

## PORSGRUND

### Christmas
1968, Church Scene............................. 55.00
1969, Three Kings................................. 8.00
1970, Road to Bethlehem....................... 8.00
1971, A Child is Born............................. 8.00
1972, Hark, the Herald Angels Sing.......... 7.00
1973, Promise of the Savior .................... 9.00
1974, The Shepherds............................. 6.00
1975, Jesus on the Road to the Temple ... 9.00
1976, Jesus & the Elders........................ 7.00
1977, Draught of the Fish ........................ 8.00

### Traditional Norwegian Christmas
1978, Guests Are Coming ...................... 9.00
1979, Home for Christmas ...................... 9.00
1980, Preparing for Christmas ............. 10.00
1981, Christmas Skating ...................... 11.00
1982, White Christmas ......................... 13.00

### Father's Day
1971, Fishing...................................... 10.00
1972, Cookout ...................................... 8.00
1973, Sledding ..................................... 5.00
1974, Father & Son ............................... 4.00
1975, Skating ....................................... 6.00
1976, Skiing......................................... 5.00
1977, Soccer ....................................... 5.00
1978, Canoeing .................................... 5.00
1979, Father & Daughter........................ 8.00
1980, Sailing........................................ 4.00
1981, Building a Ship ............................ 5.00
1982, Father & Daughter........................ 7.00
1983, Father's Day................................ 6.00
1984, Tree Planting............................... 8.00

## Mother's Day

**1970,** Mare & Foal ................................. 8.00
**1971,** Boy & Geese ............................... 7.00
**1972,** Doe & Fawn ............................... 7.00
**1973,** Cat & Kittens ............................. 4.00
**1974,** Boy & Goats ............................. 5.00
**1975,** Dog & Puppies ........................... 6.00
**1976,** Girl & Calf ................................. 8.00
**1977,** Boy & Chickens .......................... 8.00
**1978,** Girl & Pigs ................................. 6.00
**1979,** Boy & Reindeer .......................... 6.00
**1980,** Girl & Lambs ............................. 10.00
**1981,** Boy & Birds ............................... 6.00
**1982,** Girl & Rabbits ........................... 12.00
**1983,** Mother & Kittens ........................ 12.00
**1984,** By the Pond ............................... 6.00

# RED SKELTON

## Freddie the Freeloader Series (Crown Parian)

**1979,** Freddie in the Bathtub .............. 145.00
**1980,** Freddie's Shack ......................... 70.00
**1981,** Freddie on the Green ................. 77.00
**1982,** Love That Freddie ........ 50.00 to 60.00

## Famous Clown Series (Fairmont)

**1976,** Freddie the Freeloader ............. 283.00
**1977,** W. C. Fields ............................... 55.00
**1978,** Happy ........................... 45.00 to 55.00
**1979,** The Pledge ................................ 47.00

## Freddie's Adventures Series (Crown Parian)

**1981,** Captain Freddie .......................... 43.00
**1982,** Bronco Freddie ........................... 33.00
**1983,** Sir Freddie ................................. 36.00
**1984,** Gertrude & Heathcliffe ............... 45.00

# RORSTRAND

## Christmas

**1968,** Bringing Home the
  Tree ................................ 300.00 to 350.00
**1969,** Fisherman Sailing Home ............ 13.00
**1970,** Nils with His Geese .................... 13.00
**1971,** Nils in Lapland (ILLUS. top next
  column) ..................................... 19.00
**1972,** Dalecarlian Fiddler ...................... 12.00
**1973,** Farm in Smaland ........................ 46.00
**1974,** Vadstena ................................... 40.00
**1975,** Nils in Vastmanland ................... 16.00
**1976,** Nils in Uppland .......................... 13.00
**1977,** Nils in Varmland ........................ 11.00

*1971 Rorstrand Christmas Plate*

**1978,** Nils in Fjallbacka ........................ 21.00
**1979,** Nils in Vaestergoetland .............. 25.00
**1980,** Nils in Halland ........................... 30.00
**1981,** Nils in Gotland ........................... 28.00
**1982,** Nils at Skansen in Stockholm ...... 33.00
**1983,** Nils in Oland ............................. 32.00
**1984,** Nils in Angermanland ................. 37.00
**1985,** Nils in Jamtland ......................... 40.00
**1986,** Nils in Karlskrona ....................... 39.00

## Father's Day

**1971,** Father & Child ........................... 10.00
**1972,** Meal at Home ............................. 7.00
**1973,** Tilling Fields .............................. 7.00
**1974,** Fishing ..................................... 7.00
**1975,** Painting .................................... 7.00
**1976,** Plowing .................................... 6.00
**1977,** Sawing ..................................... 7.00
**1978,** Self-Portrait ............................. 15.00
**1979,** Bridge ..................................... 16.00
**1980,** My Etch-Nook ........................... 15.00

## Mother's Day

**1971,** Mother & Child ........................... 12.00
**1972,** Shelling Peas ............................ 10.00
**1973,** Old Fashioned Picnic ................. 11.00
**1974,** Candle Lighting ......................... 10.00
**1975,** Pontius on Floor .......................... 8.00
**1976,** Apple Picking ............................ 10.00
**1977,** Kitchen .................................... 10.00
**1978,** Azalea ..................................... 14.00
**1979,** Studio Idyll ............................... 14.00
**1980,** Lisbeth .................................... 15.00
**1981,** Karin with Brita ......................... 29.00
**1982,** Brita ........................................ 30.00
**1983,** Little Girl .................................. 29.00
**1984,** Mother & Crafts ......................... 31.00

# ROSENTHAL

## Christmas

| | |
|---|---|
| 1910 | 370.00 |
| 1911 | 104.00 |
| 1913 | 106.00 |
| 1915 | 119.00 |
| 1916 | 123.00 |
| 1923 | 75.00 |
| 1926 | 108.00 |
| 1927 | 108.00 |
| 1928 | 110.00 |
| 1929 | 135.00 |
| 1930 | 63.00 |
| 1931 | 109.00 |
| 1933 | 125.00 |

*1934 Rosenthal Christmas Plate*

| | |
|---|---|
| 1934 (ILLUS.) | 125.00 |
| 1935 | 85.00 |
| 1936 | 84.00 |
| 1937 | 110.00 |
| 1938 | 97.00 |
| 1939 | 110.00 |
| 1942 | 200.00 |
| 1944 | 176.00 |
| 1945 | 240.00 |
| 1946 | 150.00 |
| 1949 | 110.00 |
| 1950 | 110.00 |
| 1951 | 250.00 |
| 1952 | 95.00 |
| 1953 | 120.00 |
| 1954 | 120.00 |
| 1955 | 118.00 |
| 1956 | 124.00 |
| 1957 | 115.00 |
| 1958 | 115.00 |
| 1959 | 110.00 |

| | |
|---|---|
| 1960 | 115.00 |
| 1961 | 83.00 |
| 1962 | 81.00 |
| 1963 | 77.00 |
| 1964 | 80.00 |
| 1965 | 69.00 |
| 1966 | 88.00 |
| 1967 | 75.00 |
| 1968 | 88.00 |
| 1969 | 77.00 |
| 1970 | 73.00 |
| 1971 | 52.00 |
| 1972 | 52.00 |
| 1973 | 49.00 |
| 1974 | 37.00 |
| 1975 | 49.00 |
| 1976 | 38.00 |
| 1977 | 50.00 |
| 1978 | 48.00 |
| 1979 | 72.00 |
| 1980 | 99.00 |
| 1981 | 110.00 |
| 1982 | 133.00 |
| 1983 | 148.00 |
| 1984 | 148.00 |

## Wiinblad Christmas

| | |
|---|---|
| 1971, Maria & Child | 600.00 |
| 1972, King Caspar | 175.00 to 200.00 |
| 1973, King Melchior | 186.00 |
| 1974, King Balthazar | 258.00 |
| 1975, The Annunciation | 138.00 |
| 1976, Angel with Trumpet | 118.00 |
| 1977, Adoration of the Shepherds | 132.00 |
| 1978, Angel with Harp | 121.00 |
| 1979, Exodus from Egypt | 90.00 to 100.00 |
| 1980, Angel with Glockenspiel | 131.00 |
| 1981, Christ Child Visits Temple | 148.00 |
| 1982, Christening of Christ | 143.00 |

## Hibel Nobility of Children Series

| | |
|---|---|
| 1976, La Contessa Isabella | 78.00 |
| 1977, La Marquis Maurice-Pierre | 78.00 |
| 1978, Baronesse Johanna-Maryke Van Vollendam Tot Marken | 95.00 |
| 1979, Chief Red Feather | 101.00 |

# ROYAL BAYREUTH

## Christmas

| | |
|---|---|
| 1972, Carriage in the Village | 25.00 to 30.00 |
| 1973, Snow Scene | 15.00 |
| 1974, Old Mill | 13.00 |
| 1975, Forest Chalet "Serenity" | 9.00 |

**1976,** Christmas in the Country ............. 10.00
**1977,** Peach on Earth ............................. 8.00
**1978,** Peaceful Interlude ...................... 25.00
**1979,** Homeward Bound ....................... 18.00

### Mother's Day
**1973,** Consolation ................................. 20.00
**1974,** Young Americans ........................ 79.00
**1975,** Young Americans II .................... 25.00
**1976,** Young Americans III ................... 40.00
**1977,** Young Americans IV .................. 25.00
**1978,** Young Americans V ..................... 16.00
**1979,** Young Americans VI ................... 30.00
**1980,** Young Americans VII ................. 33.00
**1981,** Young Americans VIII ................. 23.00
**1982,** Young Americans IX ................... 27.00

## ROYAL COPENHAGEN

### Christmas

*1922 Royal Copenhagen Christmas Plate*

| | |
|---|---|
| **1908** | 2,932.00 |
| **1909** | 148.00 |
| **1910** | 99.00 |
| **1911** | 122.00 |
| **1912** | 122.00 |
| **1913** | 117.00 |
| **1914** | 130.00 |
| **1915** | 139.00 |
| **1916** | 97.00 |
| **1917** | 84.00 |
| **1918** | 83.00 |
| **1919** | 83.00 |
| **1920** | 75.00 |
| **1921** | 78.00 |
| **1922** (ILLUS. above) | 75.00 |
| **1923** | 67.00 |
| **1924** | 97.00 |

| | |
|---|---|
| **1925** | 89.00 |
| **1926** | 69.00 |
| **1927** | 116.00 |
| **1928** | 78.00 |
| **1929** | 78.00 |
| **1930** | 103.00 |
| **1931** | 98.00 |
| **1932** | 93.00 |
| **1933** | 130.00 |
| **1934** | 126.00 |
| **1935** | 174.00 |
| **1936** | 158.00 |
| **1937** | 201.00 |
| **1938** | 246.00 |
| **1939** | 329.00 |
| **1940** | 330.00 |
| **1941** | 293.00 |
| **1942** | 285.00 |
| **1943** | 456.00 |
| **1944** | 195.00 |
| **1945** | 341.00 |
| **1946** | 153.00 |
| **1947** | 204.00 |
| **1948** | 176.00 |
| **1949** | 187.00 |
| **1950** | 139.00 |
| **1951** | 284.00 |
| **1952** | 109.00 |
| **1953** | 132.00 |
| **1954** | 130.00 |
| **1955** | 153.00 |
| **1956** | 133.00 |
| **1957** | 101.00 |
| **1958** | 93.00 |
| **1959** | 99.00 |
| **1960** | 128.00 |
| **1961** | 115.00 |
| **1962** | 157.00 |
| **1963** | 60.00 |
| **1964** | 42.00 |
| **1965** | 43.00 |
| **1966** | 31.00 |
| **1967** | 23.00 |
| **1968** | 21.00 |
| **1969** | 20.00 |
| **1970** | 26.00 |
| **1971** | 16.00 |
| **1972** | 16.00 |
| **1973** | 18.00 |
| **1974** | 20.00 |
| **1975** | 14.00 |
| **1976** | 20.00 |
| **1977** | 16.00 |
| **1978** | 19.00 |
| **1979** | 38.00 |
| **1980** | 23.00 |

| | |
|---|---|
| 1981 | 22.00 |
| 1982 | 41.00 |
| 1983 | 37.00 |
| 1984 | 32.00 |
| 1985 | 47.00 |
| 1986 | 45.00 |
| 1987 | 47.00 |
| 1988 | 43.00 |
| 1989 | 50.00 |

## Mother's Day

| | |
|---|---|
| 1971, American Mother | 78.00 |
| 1972, Oriental Mother | 39.00 |
| 1973, Danish Mother | 38.00 |
| 1974, Greenland Mother | 30.00 |
| 1975, Bird in Nest | 35.00 |
| 1976, Mermaids | 33.00 |
| 1977, The Twins | 25.00 |
| 1978, Mother & Child | 26.00 |
| 1979, A Loving Mother | 8.00 |
| 1980, An Outing with Mother | 14.00 |
| 1981, Reunion | 15.00 |
| 1982, Children's Hour | 14.00 |

## Motherhood Series

| | |
|---|---|
| 1982, Mother Robin & Her Young Ones | 18.00 |
| 1983, Mother Cat & Kitten | 20.00 |
| 1984, Mare with Foal | 17.00 |
| 1985, Mother Rabbit with Bunny | 23.00 |
| 1986, Dog & Puppies | 26.00 |
| 1987, Goat & Kid | 33.00 |

# ROYAL DOULTON

## Beswick Christmas Series

| | |
|---|---|
| 1972, Christmas in England | 23.00 |
| 1973, Christmas in Mexico | 24.00 |
| 1974, Christmas in Bulgaria | 39.00 |
| 1975, Christmas in Norway | 45.00 |
| 1976, Christmas in Holland | 46.00 |
| 1977, Christmas in Poland | 39.00 |
| 1978, Christmas in America | 27.00 |

## Victorian Christmas

| | |
|---|---|
| 1977, Skater | 13.00 |
| 1978, Victorian Girl | 13.00 |
| 1979, Sleigh Ride | 14.00 |
| 1980, Santa's Visit | 18.00 |
| 1981, Carolers | 17.00 |
| 1982, Santa's Visit | 17.00 |

## Mother & Child Series

| | |
|---|---|
| 1973, Colette & Child | 278.00 |
| 1974, Sayuri & Child | 71.00 |
| 1975, Kristina & Child | 37.00 |
| 1976, Marilyn & Child | 48.00 |
| 1977, Lucia & Child | 37.00 |
| 1978, Kathleen & Child | 43.00 |

# SCHMID HUMMEL

## Christmas

| | |
|---|---|
| 1971, Angel | 23.00 |
| 1972, Angel with Flute | 14.00 |
| 1973, The Nativity | 57.00 |
| 1974, The Guardian Angel | 11.00 |
| 1975, Christmas Child | 12.00 |
| 1976, Sacred Journey | 12.00 |
| 1977, Herald Angel | 10.00 |
| 1978, Heavenly Trio | 12.00 |
| 1979, Starlight Angel | 12.00 |
| 1980, Parade into Toyland | 17.00 |
| 1981, A Time to Remember | 15.00 |
| 1982, Angelic Procession | 19.00 |
| 1983, Angelic Messenger | 19.00 |
| 1984, A Gift from Heaven | 21.00 |
| 1985, Heavenly Light | 17.00 |
| 1986, Tell the Heavens | 17.00 |
| 1987, Angelic Gifts | 21.00 |

## Mother's Day

| | |
|---|---|
| 1972, Playing Hooky | 11.00 |
| 1973, Little Fisherman | 38.00 |
| 1974, Bumblebee | 8.00 |
| 1975, Message of Love | 15.00 |
| 1976, Devotion for Mother | 10.00 |
| 1977, Moonlight Return | 16.00 |
| 1978, Afternoon Stroll | 15.00 |
| 1979, Cherub's Gift | 15.00 |
| 1980, Mother's Little Helpers | 17.00 |
| 1981, Playtime | 11.00 |
| 1982, The Flower Basket | 16.00 |
| 1983, Spring Bouquet | 20.00 |
| 1984, A Joy to Share | 23.00 |
| 1985, A Mother's Journey | 20.00 |
| 1986, Home from School | 19.00 |
| 1987, Mother's Little Learner | 23.00 |

# SPODE

## Christmas

| | |
|---|---|
| 1970, Partridge in a Pear Tree | 30.00 |
| 1971, In Heaven the Angels Singing | 28.00 |
| 1972, We Saw Three Ships A'Sailing | 18.00 |
| 1973, We Three Kings of Orient Are | 33.00 |
| 1974, Deck the Halls | 35.00 |
| 1975, Christbaum | 35.00 |
| 1976, Good King Wenceslas | 17.00 |

**1977,** The Holly & The Ivy ...................... 21.00
**1978,** While Shepherds Watched .......... 25.00
**1979,** Away in a Manger........................ 21.00
**1980,** Bringing in the Boar's Head......... 25.00
**1981,** Make We Merry ........................... 47.00

## VAL ST. LAMBERT (Glass)

### Old Masters Series

*1972 Gainsborough Plate*

**1968,** Rubens & Rembrandt, pr. ........... 53.00
**1969,** Van Gogh & Van Dyck, pr. .......... 62.00
**1970,** DaVinci & Michelangelo, pr. ....... 76.00
**1971,** El Greco & Goya, pr. ................. 61.00
**1972,** Reynolds & Gainsborough, pr.
    (ILLUS. of Gainsborough above) ........ 62.00

## WEDGWOOD

### Christmas
**1969,** Windsor Castle ......................... 106.00
**1970,** Christmas in Trafalgar Square .... 36.00
**1971,** Picadilly Circus, London ............. 33.00
**1972,** St. Paul's Cathedral.................... 46.00
**1973,** Tower of London ........................ 62.00
**1974,** Houses of Parliament................. 22.00
**1975,** Tower Bridge ............................. 52.00
**1976,** Hampton Court .......................... 19.00
**1977,** Westminster Abbey .................... 22.00
**1978,** Horse Guards.............. 25.00 to 50.00
**1979,** Buckingham Palace.................... 32.00
**1980,** St. James Palace ....................... 29.00
**1981,** Marble Arch............................... 26.00
**1982,** Lambeth Palace ......................... 59.00
**1983,** All Souls, Langham Palace ......... 55.00
**1984,** Constitution Hill ........................ 45.00
**1985,** The Tate Gallery........................ 53.00
**1986,** Albert Memorial ....................... 135.00

**1987,** Guildhall .................................... 75.00
**1988,** The Observatory, Greenwich ...... 70.00

### Mother's Day
**1971,** Sportive Love ............................ 20.00
**1972,** Sewing Lesson............. 15.00 to 20.00
**1973,** Baptism of Achilles .................... 14.00
**1974,** Domestic Employment .............. 23.00
**1975,** Mother & Child........................... 20.00
**1976,** The Spinner............................... 13.00
**1977,** Leisure Time.............................. 24.00
**1978,** Swan & Cygnets........................ 19.00
**1979,** Deer & Fawn ............................. 29.00
**1980,** Birds ........................................ 29.00

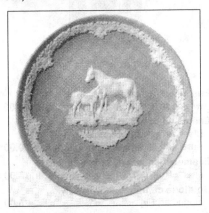

*1981 Wedgwood Mother's Day Plate*

**1981,** Mare & Foal (ILLUS.) ................. 30.00
**1982,** Cherubs with Swing.................... 21.00
**1983,** Cupid & Butterfly ........................ 19.00
**1984,** Cupid & Music ........................... 23.00
**1985,** Cupid & Doves ........................... 31.00
**1986,** Cupids at Play ........................... 32.00
**1987,** Anemones ................................. 36.00
**1988,** Tiger Lily................................... 29.00

# COMPACTS & VANITY CASES

**Bakelite compact,** w/black enameled
    floral design on the cover ................ $40.00
**Enameled compact,** Art Deco style,
    black w/diamonds, cylindrical shape
    highlighted by diamond-set bands &
    monogram, suspended from a black
    link chain w/finger ring (ILLUS. top next
    page) ............................................ 1,725.00

*Art Deco Enameled Compact*

**Enameled compact,** lavender
w/silhouette of woman in bonnet ........ **45.00**

**Enameled compact,** reads "God
Bless America" & pictures an
American flag w/48 stars .................... **20.00**

**Enameled compact,** silver & green
enamel, ca. 1920, Richard Hudnut ..... **15.00**

**Goldtone compact,** Art Deco style,
triangular, Elgin ................................. **25.00**

**Gold & gemstone vanity case,** Art
Deco style, polished surface w/a
band of calibre-cut sapphires,
diamonds & emeralds, on a link
chain ............................................ **1,725.00**

# COOKBOOKS

*Cookbook collectors are usually good cooks
and will buy important new cookbooks as well
as seek out notable older ones. Many early
cookbooks were published and given away as
advertising premiums for various products
used extensively in cooking. While some rare,
scarce first edition cookbooks can be very
expensive, most collectible cookbooks are
reasonably priced. We list our advertising
cookbooks alphabetically by names of the
companies which produced them.*

**Advertising,** "A Jell-O Year - 1924 -
America's Most Famous Desert,"
Jell-O Gelatin, paper covers,
16 pp. ................................................ **$15.00**

*"Mr. Ham" Morrell Booklet*

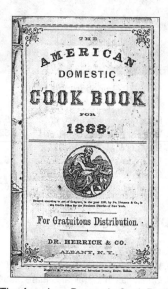

*"The American Domestic Cook Book"*

**Advertising,** "Dainty Deserts for
Dainty People," Knox Gelatin, New
York, 1924 ........................................... **6.00**

**Advertising,** "Elsie's Cook Book,"
Borden Co., New York, 1952 ............. **12.00**

**Advertising,** "Mr. Ham Goes To
Town," Morrell Ham Co.,1939, paper
covers, 14 pp. (ILLUS. top) ...... **5.00 to 8.00**

**"Alice's Restaurant Cookbook,"** A.
Brock, w/record ................................. **30.00**

**"The American Domestic Cook
Book for 1868,"** Dr. Herrick & Co.,
Albany, New York, paper-covered
almanac-style (ILLUS. bottom) ........... **15.00**

"Betty Crocker's Picture Cook Book," B. Crocker, Minnesota, 1950, spiral-bound, first edition .......... 25.00

"Celebrated Actor-Folk's Cookeries," Rowland, New York, 1916 .................................................... 75.00

"Clairvoyant Reminiscences and Herbal Recipes," T.W. Pomroy, New York, 1887 ................................ 40.00

"Cross Creek Cookery," M.K. Rawlings, New York, 1942 ................ 25.00

"Danbury Fair Cookbook," Danbury Merchants, Connecticut, 1888 ........... 75.00

"The Expert Waitress: A Manual for Kitchen, Pantry and Dining Room," Sprinsteed, New York, 1894 ................ 75.00

"For the Discriminating Hostess," E. Caron, New York, 1925, limited/inscribed copy ........................ 35.00

"General Foods Cookbook," 5th edition, 1937 ...................................... 20.00

"The Hotel St. Francis Cookbook," V. Hirtzler, Chicago, 1919 ................. 100.00

"Home Menu Cookbook," 1935, hardcover ............................................. 12.00

"How to Cook It," V. McDonald, intro by Duncan Hines, Missouri, 1949, w/dust jacket ...................................... 10.00

"The June Platt Cook Book," J. Platt, New York, 1958, w/dust jacket .............. 9.00

"The Kitchen and Fruit Gardener," Philadelphia, 1844 ........................... 150.00

"Modern Priscilla Cook Book," Priscilla Publishing Co., Boston, 1924, includes membership certificate .. 11.00

"Mrs. Rorer's Phildelphia Cookbook," S.T. Rorer, Philadelphia, 1886 ........................... 65.00

"New Orleans Recipes," Mammy on cover, 1953, softcover ...................... 12.00

"The Orange Bowl Cookbook," The Orange Bowl Committee, Miami, 1983, w/dust jacket ........................... 35.00

"Royal Cookbook," *Parents Magazine*, New York, 1971, illustrated ................... 10.00

"Rumford Recipe Book," 1907 .......... 49.00

"Table Topics," J. Street, New York, 1959, w/dust jacket ........................... 15.00

"The Taste of Madeleines," E. Culshaw, London, 1963, w/dust jacket ..................................................... 8.00

"The Whys of Cooking," J.M. Hills, Ohio, 1919 ......................................... 8.00

# COOKIE JARS

*All sorts of charming and whimsical cookie jars have been produced in recent decades and these are increasingly collectible today. Many well-known American potteries such as McCoy, Hull and Abingdon produced cookie jars and they are included in those listings. Below we are listing cookie jars produced by other companies.*

*Current reference books for collectors include:* The Collectors Encyclopedia of Cookie Jars *by Fred and Joyce Roerig (Collector Books, 1991);* Collector's Encyclopedia of Cookie Jars, Book II *by Fred and Joyce Roerig (Collector Books, 1994); and* The Complete Cookie Jar Book *by Mike Schneider (Schiffer, Ltd. 1991). Also see: CERAMICS, CHARACTER COLLECTIBLES and DISNEY COLLECTIBLES*

## AMERICAN BISQUE

Bear with cookies ............................. $66.00
Bear with hat ........................................ 84.00
Bear with honey ................................. 454.00
Blackboard Boy ................................. 350.00
Blackboard Clown ............................ 174.00
Carousel ............................................. 100.00
Casper the Friendly Ghost .............. 983.00
Cheerleaders, flasher-type ................ 420.00
Chef ...................................................... 113.00
Chef with Cookie Tray ....................... 495.00
Chick, yellow w/brown coat ................. 57.00
Clown on Stage, black cutrains, flasher-type ..................................... 324.00
Clown, standing ................................... 55.00
Cookie Truck ...................................... 112.00
Cowboy Boots .................................... 170.00
Davy Crocket, standing, name across chest ............................... 450.00 to 500.00
Davy Crocket ..................................... 395.00
Donald Duck, sitting ........................... 495.00
Dutch Boy ............................................. 95.00
Dutch Girl ............................................. 49.00
Farmer Pig ......................... 75.00 to 100.00
French Poodle, blue decoration .......... 95.00
Kids Watching TV, "Sandman Cookies," flasher-type ...................... 380.00
Kitten & Beehive ................................. 60.00
Kittens on Ball of Yarn ...................... 95.00
Lady Pig ............................. 50.00 to 100.00
Magic Bunny ...................................... 123.00
Majorette ............................................ 295.00
Milk Wagon, w/"Cookie & Milk" ......... 114.00

Mr. Rabbit ......................................... 193.00
Pennsylvania Dutch Girl ................. 500.00
Pig Dancer ........................................ 142.00
Pot Belly Stove ............................... 100.00
Ring the Bell for Cookies .................. 85.00
Rooster .............................................. 55.00
Rubbles House ............................. 1,040.00
Saddle Blackboard ........... 175.00 to 225.00
Sadiron ............................................ 165.00
Soldier ............................................. 100.00
Train Engine, white ........................ 100.00
Treasure Chest ............................... 170.00
Tugboat, blue, light brown & green .... 345.00
Umbrella Kids ................................. 330.00
Yogi Bear ......................................... 460.00

## BRUSH - MC COY

Baby Davy (Crocket) ........................ 653.00
Clown bust ....................................... 319.00
Clown, full figure, brown pants .......... 225.00
Cookie House ................................... 110.00
Covered Wagon ............................... 585.00
Cow, w/cat finial, brown ..................... 117.00
Davy Crocket, brown ........................ 300.00
Davy Crockett, gold decoration .......... 850.00
Elephant w/Ice Cream Cone,
   wearing baby hat .............................. 390.00
Formal Pig ....................................... 300.00
Granny, green dress .......... 300.00 to 350.00
Humpty Dumpty ............... 325.00 to 375.00
Little Red Riding Hood, large ........... 840.00
Nite Owl ............................. 75.00 to 110.00
Panda Bear ...................... 250.00 to 350.00
Puppy Police ..................... 650.00 to 700.00
Red Riding Hood, marked "Littl Red
   Ridding Hood" (sic) on skirt .............. 750.00
Squirrel with Top Hat ....................... 200.00
Teddy Bear, w/feet together .............. 165.00
Three Bears, tree stump
   finial ................................. 100.00 to 145.00
Treasure Chest ............................... 180.00

## CALIFORNIA ORIGINALS

Bert & Ernie Fine Cookies, No. 977 .. 325.00
Big Bird, No. 976 ............................. 115.00
Christmas Tree ................................ 530.00
Clown on elephant ........................... 200.00
Count (The) ...................................... 610.00
Dog, No. 458 ...................................... 35.00
Eeyore ............................................. 600.00
Frog .................................................... 35.00
Gumball Machine ............................... 72.00
Koala Bear ......................................... 82.00
Pinocchio with Fish Bowl ............. 1,600.00
Raggedy Ann ..................................... 56.00
Santa Claus, standing, No. 871 .......... 520.00

Woody Woodpecker in Tree House,
   copyright by Walter Lantz ................. 800.00
Cow Jumped Over the
   Moon ........................... 250.00 to 300.00
4 x 4 Pick-up Truck ........................... 295.00
Hippo ................................................. 75.00
Jeep ................................................. 395.00
Leprechaun Pot ................................. 75.00
School Bus, large ............................. 195.00
Van ...................................... 50.00 to 150.00
Volkswagon ...................... 250.00 to 300.00

## METLOX

Barrel of Apples ................................. 50.00
Bassett Dog ..................................... 650.00
Bear with Bow, "Beau" ....................... 72.00
Bear with Sombrero (Pancho) ............. 80.00
Brownie Scout (cover restored) ...... 1,200.00
Bucky Beaver .................... 200.00 to 300.00
Bunch of Grapes .............................. 285.00
Calico Cat, lime green ...................... 128.00
Chicken (Mother Hen) ....................... 197.00
Clown, standing, black & white outfit .. 183.00
Corn ................................................. 140.00
Cow with Butterfly, purple ............... 511.00
Dinosaur, "Dino," blue ...................... 175.00
Dinosaur, "Mona" ............................. 180.00
Dog, Fido ......................................... 123.00
Duck with Raincoat (Puddles) ............. 55.00
Eggplant .......................................... 170.00
Grapes ............................................. 255.00
Grapefruit ........................................ 365.00
Jolly Chef ........................................ 550.00
Kitten Head with Hat, "meows" when
   hat tipped ......................... 75.00 to 100.00
Lamb's head with Hat ......... 75.00 to 125.00
Lion, seated ..................................... 350.00
Little Piggy ...................................... 380.00
Mammy, yellow polka dots ................. 460.00
Mrs. Rabbit, w/carrot ....................... 140.00
Nun ............................................... 1,025.00
Owls on Stump ................................ 210.00
Parrot ............................................... 350.00
Pear .................................. 125.00 to 225.00
Pelican Coach (U.S. Diving Team) .... 240.00
Penguin (Frosty) ................................ 74.00
Raccoon ........................................... 140.00
Raggedy Andy .................................. 167.00
Raggedy Ann ................................... 175.00
Rose Blossom ................... 475.00 to 500.00
Rose ................................................. 492.00
Scottie Dog, black ............ 100.00 to 150.00
Squash .............................. 175.00 to 200.00
Standing Santa ................................ 650.00
Tomato ............................................. 250.00
Watermelon ...................... 250.00 to 375.00

**Water Sheaf with Ribbon** .................... 77.00
**Woodpecker on Acorn** ...................... 450.00

## MOSAIC TILE
**Mammy,** blue dress ........................... 575.00
**Mammy,** peach dress w/green trim
   (professional repair) ......................... 950.00
**Mammy,** yellow dress ........................ 560.00
**Mammy,** white dress & apron w/blue
   & yellow trim ................................... 695.00

## NAPCO
**Chef's head** ........................ 325.00 to 375.00
**Cinderella** ...................................... 280.00
**Little Red Riding Hood** ..................... 250.00
**Spaceship** ................................... 1,150.00
**Black Chef,** w/"Cooky" on front .......... 395.00
**Mammy** .......................................... 630.00
**Panda Bear** .................................... 125.00

## POTTERY GUILD
**Boy with fruit** ................................. 173.00
**Dutch Girl** ........................................ 67.00

*Elsie the Cow Cookie Jar*

**Elsie in Barrel** (ILLUS.) ...... 200.00 to 300.00
**Rooster** ............................................ 90.00

## REGAL
**Barn,** Old MacDonald Line ................. 300.00
**Churn Boy** ...................................... 230.00
**Davy Crockett** .................. 500.00 to 550.00
**Dutch Girl** ...................................... 687.00
**French Chef** ................................... 420.00
**Hubert the Lion** ............................ 1,020.00
**Kraft-T-Bear** (Kraft Marshmallows) .... 180.00

**Little Miss Muffet** .............. 250.00 to 295.00
**Little Red Riding Hood** ..................... 320.00
**Little Red Riding Hood,** closed basket,
   petticoat showing under skirt ........... 635.00
**Tobys Cookies** (Chef Head) .......... 1,150.00

## ROBINSON RANSBOTTOM
**Chef with Bowl of Eggs** ................... 123.00
**Cow Jumped Over the Moon** (Hi
   Diddle Diddle) ................................. 270.00
**Dutch Girl** ....................................... 345.00

*Ol' King Cole Cookie Jar*

**Ol' King Cole** (ILLUS.) ...................... 325.00
**Peter Pumpkin Eater** ........................ 275.00
**Sailor Jack** ...................................... 275.00
**Sheriff Pig** ......................... 65.00 to 100.00
**Snowman** ........................................ 720.00
**Tigers** ............................................... 80.00
**Whale** ............................................. 740.00

## SIERRA VISTA
**Clown Head,** colored glaze ................. 30.00
**Elephant** ......................................... 200.00
**Cookie Barn** ...................................... 20.00

## TREASURE CRAFT
**Football** ............................................ 40.00
**Football with Coach** ......... 250.00 to 350.00
**Mrs. Potts,** Disney, USA .................... 75.00
**Pinocchio** ........................... 55.00 to 120.00
**Rose Petal Place Tree of
   Knowledge** ................................. 1,500.00
**Snowman and Glass** ........................ 225.00
**Truck,** red ....................................... 215.00

## TWIN WINTON

**Bambi,** beside stump .......................... 115.00
**Churn & Kittens** ................................ 95.00
**Cooky Catcher Truck** ......................... 85.00
**Dutch Girl** .......................................... 90.00
**Hotei** (Buddha) .................. 100.00 to 120.00
**Keystone Kop,** w/matching salt &
   pepper shakers .................................. 89.00
**Modern Head** (small scuff) ................. 400.00
**Pirate Fox** ......................................... 150.00
**Poodle a Counter** (rim chip)................ 50.00
**Raccoon** ............................................. 90.00
**Rooster**............................................... 80.00
**Rubber Ducky** ................................... 140.00

## VANDOR

**Baseball**............................................. 145.00
**Carmen Mooranda**............................. 378.00
**Corcagator** ........................................ 125.00
**Howdy Doody,** head .......................... 480.00
**Howdy Doody in Bumper
   Car** ................................... 325.00 to 400.00
**Juke Box,** auxiliary wall
   box .................................. 225.00 to 295.00
**Mona Lisa**............................................ 55.00
**Popeye,** head...................................... 325.00

## MISCELLANEOUS

**Agatha,** Sigma .................................... 375.00
**Barney and Bam-Bam,** "JD 1992," JD
   James ................................................ 350.00
**Beny,** marked on box "Henry James
   Design," distributed in England, 1990
   Hanna Barbera Productions, Inc. ...... 350.00
**B-Flat Williams,** Alfano Art Pottery
   USA ................................................... 225.00
**Bear,** Avon Cosmetics .......................... 50.00
**Bernadine,** N. S. Gustin ....................... 89.00
**Big Boy Hamburger,** Elias Brothers,
   Warren, Michigan, Wolfe Original
   limited edition of 250, 1992.............. 650.00
**Buddha,** DeForest of California ............ 85.00
**C-3PO,** Roman Ceramics ... 500.00 to 550.00
**Cat Head,** Lefton ............................... 115.00
**Cat on Stool,** Sigma ........................... 150.00
**Children on Drum,** Yona Original ...... 495.00
**Chipmunk,** No. 514, DeForest ............ 145.00
**Christmas Reindeer,** Japan................. 40.00
**Circus Dolly,** Starnes......... 650.00 to 750.00
**Clown with Drum,**
   Pfaltzgraff ........................ 525.00 to 595.00
**Cookie Chef,** unmarked, Marsh
   Industries ......................................... 125.00
**Cow,** tan, Otagari, 1982...................... 45.00
**Cow Beach Woody car,** Otagari.......... 30.00

**Crackpot's Old Southern Mammy,**
   "Dinah - Hand Painted, Made in
   USA," Erwin Pottery........................... 85.00
**Cross-eyed Bird**................................. 525.00
**Daisy Mae in Barrel,** Imperial
   Porcelain, Paul Webb design ........... 695.00
**De-Lee Child Chef,** Lee, Hollywood,
   California ......................................... 500.00
**Dog House,** Starnes .......................... 225.00
**Emmett Kelly, Jr.,** Flambro ................ 600.00
**Fireman Beaver,** Sigma ...................... 295.00
**Fireman Dog,** Sigma ........................... 400.00
**Fred Flinstone,** "JD 1992," JD James.. 350.00
**Garfield on Cookies,**
   Enesco ........................... 225.00 to 350.00
**German Gentleman,** "Made in West
   Germany 3802".................................. 250.00
**Gone With the Wind Mammy,** 2nd
   edition, Hamilton Gifts, a division of
   Enesco .............................................. 210.00
**Grandma Bell,** J. C. Miller ................... 70.00
**Hershel Hippo,** Fitz & Floyd................ 60.00
**Howdy Doody Head,** Puriton ............ 690.00
**Humpty Dumpty,** Maddux of
   California ......................... 300.00 to 325.00
**Jazz Singer,** Clay Art, San Francisco,
   made in Phillipines............................ 135.00
**Juke Box,** Himark................................ 80.00
**Kabuki Dancer,** Sigma ...................... 230.00
**Keebler Elf,** Fitz & Floyd...................... 55.00
**Kermit in TV,** Sigma ........................... 450.00
**Kliban Cat,** Sigma ............................. 375.00
**Krazy Kritters Kat,** Sigma.................. 275.00
**Lady Fat Cat,** Sigma........................... 225.00
**Lady Head,** Lefton ............................. 275.00
**Lady with Cat,** Animals & Company .. 975.00
**Last Elephant Beat (The),** Sigma ...... 200.00
**Lil' Sprout,** Pilsbury............................. 60.00
**Little Black Girl,** Spears.................... 350.00
**M&M Cookie Jar,** Haeger.................. 165.00
**Mammy,** stamped "Made in Japan" .... 600.00
**Man with Ice Pack on Head,** Nasco .... 85.00
**Mercedes,** Expressive Designs, made
   in Taiwan, 1986 .............................. 240.00
**Mexican Bandito**................................. 65.00
**Milk Bone Dog Biscuts,**
   Roman........................... 85.00 to 100.00
**Mrs. Tibbgy Winkle,** Sigma ............. 425.00
**Monkey,** DeForest of
   California .......................... 75.00 to 95.00
**Old Lady in Shoe,** Pfaltzgraff............ 165.00
**Oliver Hardy,** Cumberland Ware,
   Roman Ceramics, Mayfield,
   Kentucky...................................... 1,700.00
**Paddington Bear,** Toscany .............. 850.00
**Peter Max,** Sigma, made in Japan...... 295.00

**Pig Goody Bank,** DeForest of
California .......................................... 125.00
**Pig with Apple,** Marsh Ceramics ....... 100.00
**Pirate on Chest,** Starnes of California.. 600.00
**Planetary Pal,** Sigma ........ 245.00 to 295.00
**Pound Puppy,** Tonka Corporation ....... 70.00
**Queen of Hearts,** Fitz & Floyd............ 120.00
**R2-D2,** Roman Ceramics ................... 160.00
**Rabbit in Hat,** DeForest of California ... 125.00
**Rag Doll,** Starnes of California .......... 160.00
**Raggedy Ann,** The Bobbs Merrill
Company, Ltd., Posner.................... 600.00
**Rio Rita,** Fitz & Floyd........................ 115.00
**Rocking Chair Granny,** Carol Gifford
Originals ...................................... 130.00
**Rockingham Mammy,** paper label
reads "Sasparilla Decodesigns
N.Y.C N.Y. copyright 1980
Japan" ............................. 275.00 to 300.00
**Romper Room,** "DO-BEE, E-2200"
stamped on bottom, Laurel Sales,
Cleveland, Ohio, made in Japan ..... 425.00
**Santa Claus at Desk,** "Alberta Mold
Co." on bottom of jar.......................... 95.00
**Santa Claus Head,** unmarked ............. 95.00
**Santa Claus in Easy Chair,**
unmarked............................................ 85.00
**School House,** Gilner....................... 200.00
**Scottie,** "Macia/NAC USA" incised
into bottom....................................... 65.00
**Sherman on the Mount,** American
Greeting Corporation, Cleveland,
Ohio, made in Korea ....... 425.00 to 475.00
**Snoopy and Woodstock,** United
Features Syndicate, Inc. .. 100.00 to 150.00
**Snoopy Chey,** United Features
Syndicate, made in Japan ............... 245.00
**Space Cadet,** unmarked.................... 100.00
**Spuds bust,** blue sweater w/"Mr.
Cookie" sign, Taiwan........ 150.00 to 175.00
**Star Wars,** Sigma ............................. 140.00
**Tar Baby,** Shirley Corl ...................... 165.00
**Tat-L-Tale,** Helen Hutula Original ....... 623.00
**Top Cat,** marked on box "Henry
James Design," distributed in
England, 1990 Hanna Barbera
Productions, Inc............................. 225.00
**Topo Gigio,** Maria Perego, distributed
by Ross Products Inc., New York ..... 145.00
**Tri-Star Mammy,** Erwin Pottery............ 90.00
**Watermelon Mammy,** Carol Gifford ... 200.00
**W. C. Fields,** "Cumberland Ware" ...... 900.00
**Whistler (The),** "The Collection of
Rose".............................................. 115.00
**Windmill,** F.A.P. Co............................. 30.00
**Winking Santa,** Lefton China ............. 110.00
**Woody Woodpecker Head,** Enesco.. 1,500.00
**Ziggy,** Korea ................................... 312.00

# CURRIER & IVES PRINTS

*This lithographic firm was founded in 1835 by Nathaniel Currier with James M. Ives becoming a partner in 1857. Current events of the day were portrayed in the early days and the prints were hand-colored. Landscapes, vessels, sport and hunting scenes of the West all became popular subjects. The firm was in existence until 1906. All prints listed are hand-colored unless otherwise noted. Numbers at the end of the listings refer to those used in Currier & Ives Prints—An Illustrated Checklist, by Frederick A. Conningham (Crown Publishers).*

**American Country Life,** May
Morning, after F. F. Palmer, large
folio, N. Currier, 1855 (121) ........ **$2,300.00**
**American Country Life,** October
Afternoon, after F. F. Palmer, large
folio, N. Currier, 1855 (122) .......... 2,300.00
**American Farm Scenes No. 3,** after
F.F. Palmer, large folio, 1853, in
period frame (repaired tears)............ 977.00
**American Homestead—Spring,**
small folio, 1869 (170) ..................... 400.00
**American Mountain Scenery,** large
folio, 1868 (179).............................. 419.00
**American Whalers Crushed in the
Ice,** "Burning The Wrecks to avoid
danger to other Vessels," small folio,
undated, framed (traces of old
staining, mat staining in margins) .. 1,610.00
**Ann,** small folio, full-length portrait of
woman wearing red cape on a plain
background, N. Currier, 1848 (230) .... 85.00
**Awful Conflagration of the Steamboat
Lexington in Long Island Sound,**
N. Currier, small folio, undated,
framed 12¾ x 20¾" ....................... 4,312.00
**Battle of Antietam (The),** MD, Sept.
17th, 1862, small folio, undated
(384) ................................................. 210.00
**Bear Hunting—Close Quarters,**
small folio, undated, amtted, unframed
(light mat staining, crease & small
paper loss to bottom margin) ......... 1,955.00
**Beautiful Empress (The),** small folio,
head & shoulders portrait of
Empress Eugenie, Empress of
France, undated (455) ........................ 39.00
**Beauty of the South (The),** small
folio, three-quarters length portrait,
vignette, undated (470)...................... 70.00

**Birth of Our Savior (The),** small folio, 1867 (534) ........................................ **20.00**

**Brave Wife (The),** small folio, undated (651) ................................................ **100.00**

**Brother and Sister,** small folio, upright, under tree w/brook alongside, N. Currier, undated (706) .................................................. **90.00**

**Capitol at Washington,** small folio, N. Currier, undated (792) ................. **285.00**

**Capture of Andre,** 1780, small folio, N. Currier, 1845 (804) ...................... **215.00**

**Chicago in Flames—Scene at Randolph Street Bridge,** small folio, undated (1027) ......................... **560.00**

**Christ in the Garden of Gethsemane,** small folio, undated (1061) .................. **20.00**

**Clipper Ship in a Hurricane (A),** small folio, undated (1155) .............. **630.00**

**Clipper Ship "Nightengale,"** large folio, N. Currier, 1854 (1159) ........ **5,100.00**

**"Crack" Sloop in A Race to Winward (A),** large folio, 1882, framed, 1281 (scuff in the sky at right, small crease in the sky at left, new nicks, pinholes & small creases in extreme sheet edges) ............... **1,380.00**

**"Crack Team" at a Smashing Gait (A),** large folio, labeled from Kennedy Galleries, New York on reverse, 1869, in period-style frame, 1282 (subtle toning & staining, loss to lower left corner) ......................... **977.00**

**Darktown Elopement (The),** "Skip softly lub...," small folio, 1885, framed, 1384 (minor margin stain) ... **138.00**

**Darktown Fire Brigade (The)—To the Rescue,** small folio, black comic scene, 1884 (1396) .......................... **255.00**

**Dartmouth College,** small folio, one of the earliest Currier prints, published in 1834, N. Currier, undated (1446) .. **3,050.00**

**Declaration of Independence (The),** July 4th, 1776, small folio, Washington seated to right of table, N. Currier, undated (1531) ............... **215.00**

**Deer in the Woods,** small folio, undated (1538) ............................... **250.00**

**English Winter Scene (An),** small folio, undated, framed, 1745 (margins folded over, short margin tears, pale staining, some foxing) ..... **345.00**

**Express Train (The),** small folio, 1870, framed, 1792 (staining, colors somewhat faded, tiny holes in margin) ............................................. **2,300.00**

**Fairy Isle (The),** small folio, undated (1816) ................................................. **95.00**

**Family Register,** small folio, N. Currier, 1846 (1848) ...................... **50.00**

**Flower Vase (The),** small folio, N. Currier, 1848 (2049) .................... **125.00**

**Gold Mining in California,** small folio, 1871, framed, 2412 (pale staining & foxing) ....................... **2,300.00**

**Golden Fruits of California,** large folio, 1869, framed, 2414 (two pin holes just in the image at sides, tiny nicks in extreme sheet edges) ....... **1,840.00**

**Grand National Whig Banner,** small folio, N. Currier, 1852 (2515) ........... **205.00**

**Great West (The),** small folio, 1870, framed, 2658 (tiny hole in center, pale staining & foxing, tiny tear in margin) ........................................ **1,265.00**

**Harvesting,** small folio, undated (2749) ................................................. **250.00**

**High Bridge at Harlem, N.Y. (The),** small folio, N. Currier, 1849, framed, 2811 (repaired margin hole, long crease to margin, some paper loss in margin) ................................ **575.00**

**Home in the Wilderness (A),** small folio, 1870, framed, 2861 (pale staining & foxing, tiny paper loss to margin) ............................................ **920.00**

**Home of the Deer (The),** medium folio, undated, framed, 2867 (subtle toning, annotations along lower margin) ............................................. **345.00**

**Home on the Mississippi (A),** small folio, 1871, 2876 (ILLUS. top next page) ................................................. **565.00**

**I Will Not Ask to Press that Cheek,** small folio, young man serenading young lady w/the mumps, 1875 (3019) ................................................. **189.00**

**Ice-Boat Race on the Hudson,** small folio, undated, framed, 3021 (two long creases, pale staining & tiny margin tears) ................................. **2,875.00**

**In Memory of,** small folio, woman & boy, N. Currier, 1846 (3057) ............... **45.00**

**Ingleside Winter (The),** small folio, undated, framed, 3112 (small surface losses, pale staining) ........... **690.00**

**Kitties Among the Roses,** small folio, 1873 (3352) ....................................... **140.00**

**Lake George, NY,** small folio, two deer in foreground, undated (3407) .. **250.00**

**Maple Sugaring—Early Spring in the Northern Woods,** small folio,

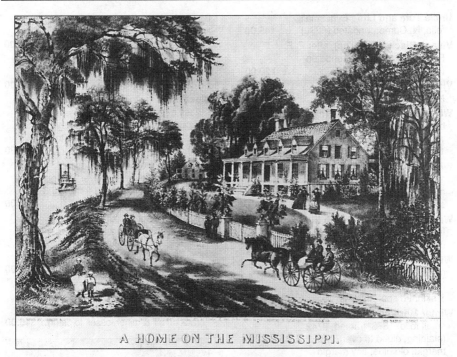

*A Home On the Mississippi*

1872, framed, 3975 (pale staining & foxing, tiny paper loss & pin holes to margin) .......................................... **1,840.00**

**New England Home (A),** small folio, undated, matted & framed (4417)..... **220.00**

**Perry's Victory On Erie Lake,** small folio, undated, framed, 4754 (faded colors, pale staining & foxing, small margin tear, some creasing) ............. **633.00**

**Pioneer Cabin of the Yo-Se-mite (The),** small folio, undated, framed, 4785 (unobtrusive toning, creases) ............................................ **316.00**

**Prairie Fires of the Great West,** small folio, 1871, framed, 4895 (pale staining, small paper losses in margin) ........................................ **1,150.00**

**Providence and Stonington Steamship Co.'s Steamer—Rhode Island,** after C.R. Parsons, large folio, 1877, framed, 4967 (unobtrusive toning, subtle staining along edges) ............................................. **1,840.00**

**Pursuit (The),** after A. F. Tait, large folio, N. Currier, 1856 (4974) ......... **2,750.00**

**Railroad Suspension Bridge (The)— Near Niagara Falls...,** medium folio, 1856, framed, 5056 (pale staining) .. **1,035.00**

**Sale of the Pet Lamb (The),** after William Collins, Esq. R.A., medium folio, N. Currier, undated, framed (some staining, small tears & losses in margin)......................................... **518.00**

**Skating Scene—Moonlight,** small folio, 1868 (5546)........................... **1,295.00**

**Snowy Morning (A),** after F. F. Palmer, medium folio, 1864, framed, 5582 (faded colors, pale light staining, small tears, paper loss & creases in margin) ........................ **3,105.00**

**Squirrel Shooting,** small folio, undated, framed, 5681 (staining, soft creases, minor defects) ................... **173.00**

**Summer Fruits,** medium folio, 1861, matted & framed, 5857 (minor stains & spot on margin) ........................... **302.00**

**Through to the Pacific,** small folio, 1870, framed, 6051 (touched spot in image, pale staining & foxing, soft creases, ink stamps on reverse).... **1,150.00**

**Tree of Life (The),** small folio, N. Currier, undated (6134) ................... **125.00**

**Trotting Gelding "St. Julien,"** small folio, 1881 (6177)............................. **290.00**

**Unbolted!,** small folio, undated (6278) .. **235.00**

**Uncle Tom and Little Eva,** small folio, N. Currier, undated (6280) ....... 145.00

**Village Blacksmith (The),** after F. F. Palmer, medium folio, undated (6460) .............................................. 720.00

**Virgin Mary (The),** small folio, N. Currier, 1849 (6471)...................... 20.00

**Wild Duck Shooting—On the Wing,** bareheaded hunter, hat on ground w/powder horn in it, small folio, 1870 (6671) ..................................... 580.00

**Wild Turkey Shooting,** small folio, 1871, framed, 6677 (trimmed margins, small margin tear, pale staining, soft creases)....................... 575.00

**William Penn's Treaty with the Indians,** small folio, N. Currier, undated (6697) ............................... 240.00

**Winter Morning,** after F. F. Palmer, medium folio, 1861, framed, 6740 (margins trimmed, light staining, split & skinned spot margins) ................ 1,265.00

**Winter Morning in the Country,** small folio, 1873, framed, 6742 (staining, glued to overmat in margin, old glue, tiny margin stains) ............................................ 1,380.00

**Winter Sports—Pickerel Fishing,** small folio, 1872, framed, 6747 (staining, minor margin soiling)...... 2,300.00

**Woodlands in Winter,** small folio, undated, matted & framed (6779)..... 330.00

**Yacht "Puritan" of Boston,** large folio, 1885 (6810).......................... 1,400.00

**Young Housekeeper (The),** small folio, full-length portraits, N. Currier, undated (6856) ................................. 89.00

# DECOYS

*Decoys have been utilized for years to lure flying water fowl into target range. They have been made of carved and turned wood, papier-mâché, canvas and metal, and some are in the category of outstanding folk art and command high prices.*

**Black breasted plover,** solid construction w/applied painted tin wings, glass eyes, appears to retain original paint, mounted on a black base, attributed to Alfred Gardiner, Hinngham, Massachusetts, ca. 1910 ......... $1,380.00

**Black duck,** cork body w/painted pine head, glass eyes, attributed to Al Lang, Stratford, Connecticut............ 431.00

**Black duck,** hollow block, old worn working paint w/glass eyes, 16⅝" l. (minor age cracks)........................... 138.00

**Black duck,** hollow construction, glass eyes, attributed to Harry V. Shourds, Tuckerton, New Jersey (areas of repaint & small chips to tail)...................................................... 345.00

**Black duck,** hollow construction, glass eyes, Delaware River Region (areas of repaint, weight removed & old repair to bill) ............................... 287.00

**Black duck,** hollow-carved in the Delaware River style, glass eyes, possible original paint, attributed to Tony Bianco, Bordentown, New Jersey ................................................ 402.00

**Black duck,** hollow-carved w/glass eyes, appears to retain original paint, Delaware River Region (stress crack on bill & minor losses to paint)... 345.00

*Virginia Black Duck Decoy*

**Black duck,** hollow-carved, raised 'V' feather carving w/carved ridge on back, carved eyes, original paint, Arthur Cobb, Cobb Island, Virginia, minor paint wear, well-done bill replacement, light shot marks, hairline cracks (ILLUS.) ................ 8,500.00

**Black duck,** primitive relief carving, old repaint w/original paint beneath, glass eyes, 17½" l............................. 83.00

**Black duck,** solid construction w/glass eyes, relief carved primary feathers & retains its original paint, impressed "Prnie 70," possibly New York state ....................................... 575.00

**Bluebill,** repaint w/glass eyes, bottom stenciled "John Beverly New Baltimore," 14½" l. (shot scars) .......... 50.00

**Bluebill,** sleeper, old working repaint, glass eyes, on plexi-glass stand, East Coast, 11" l.............................. 28.00

*"Carriage House" Bluebill Drake*

**Bluebill drake,** hollow construction, "Carriage House," raised & carved wings w/head slightly turned, original paint, maker unknown, Illinois River region, minor paint wear (ILLUS.)..... **700.00**

**Bluebill drake bobtail,** old working paint & glass eyes, attributed to Fred Plichta, Gibralter, Michigan, ca. 1930, 13" l. (shot scars)............... **50.00**

**Canvasback drake,** marked w/initials "J.D.M.," retains Elliston weight, by Robert Elliston, Bureau, Illinois, ca. 1890, rare (second coat of paint)....................................... **3,750.00**

**Canvasback hen,** hollow-carved, retains original paint, ca. 1930, by Charles Bergman, Astoria, Oregon, rare .............................................. **3,250.00**

**Crow,** solid construction w/tack eyes, retains original paint, attributed to Herters Decoy Company ................. **230.00**

*Rare Curlew Decoy*

**Curlew,** retains original paint, ca. 1910, Mason Decoy Factory, rare (ILLUS.) ........................................ **2,750.00**

**Dove,** retains original paint, tack eyes, ca. 1910, Mason Decoy Factory (minor paint wear, heavy shot damage) .......................................... **600.00**

**Elder Drake,** solid construction w/inlet head, grasping a mussel in his beak, retains original paint, possibly Maine (some losses, large stress cracks on back).................................................. **575.00**

*Brook Trout Decoy*

**Fish,** Brook trout, by Jim Nelson, Michigan, 7" (ILLUS.)........................ **358.00**

**Goldeneye drake,** old repaint, by Douge Jester, Chincoteague, Virgina, (paint worn, cracks in neck, tiny sliver of wood missing from neck, several tiny dents).................. **400.00**

**Mallard,** worn repaint, glass eyes, attributed to the Schmidt Family, Michigan (age crack in block & repaired split in neck) ........................ **72.00**

**Red head drake,** hollow block, old repaint, glass eyes, branded "Hall," attributed to Chris Smith, Algonac, Michigan, ca. 1924, 13½" l. ................ **88.00**

**Red head drake,** solid construction w/carved primary feathers, glass eyes, appears to retain much of its original paint, attributed to Elmer Crowell, East Harwich, Massachusetts (stress cracks to neck)................................................. **460.00**

*Redbreasted Merganser Drake Decoy*

**Redbreasted merganser drake,** leather crest, tack eyes & long thin bill, Massachusetts, ca. 1880-90 (ILLUS.) ........................................ **4,500.00**

**Robin snipe,** retains original paint, ca. 1910, Mason Decoy Factory.... **1,900.00**

**Snow goose,** hollow-carved construction w/relief-carved primary feathers, glass eyes, retains original paint, possibly Michigan (areas of paint loss, large check on bottom, bill damaged) .................................... **402.00**

**Yellowlegs,** relief-carved wing & carved eyes, retains original paint, by Odediah Verity, Seaford, New York, ca. 1860s (minor paint wear, hairline crack to one side, lightly hit by shot)........................................... **3,500.00**

# DISNEY COLLECTIBLES

*Scores of objects ranging from watches to dolls have been created showing Walt Disney's copyrighted animated cartoon characters, and an increasing number of collectors now are seeking these, made primarily by licensed manufacturers.*

**Alice in Wonderland movie cel,**
gouache on celluloid applied to watercolor production background from one of the opening scenes, shows Alice looking on as the White Rabbit clutches his umbrella & pocket watch, 1951, 9 x 11".......... **$4,887.00**

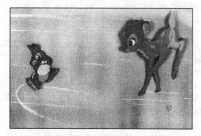

*Bambi & Thumper Animation Cell*

**Bambi & Thumper movie cel,**
gouache on celluloid applied to an airbrushed Courvoisier background, shows Bambi & Thumper sliding on ice, 1942, 6½ x 9" (ILLUS.)............ **3,737.00**

**Bambi lamp,** figural, ceramic, base is figure of Bambi below shade w/image of Bambi & Thumper, Walt Disney Production, 14" h. (shade w/some cracking)............................ **223.00**

**Cinderella & Prince toy,** windup plastic Cinderell & Prince Charming dancing, manufactured by Irwin, copyright Walt Disney Productions, 5" h., mint in box .............................. **175.00**

**Davy Crocket billfold,** mint in box ....... **70.00**

**Davy Crockett horseshoe set,** hard rubber, 1950s, mint in original box ..... **95.00**

**Disney characters cookie jars,** turn-around-type, Mickey-Minnie, Dumbo-Pluto, Dumbo-Dumbo, Jose Carioca-Donald Duck, American Bisque, ca. 1944-54, set of 4 (ILLUS. bottom) .............................. **322.00**

**Disney characters pencil box,** w/images of long-billed Donald Duck & nephews, Mickey & Minnie Mouse, by Dixon............................................ **115.00**

**Disneyland toy,** windup, "Casey Jr. Train," w/black engine & one each blue, green & yellow cars, decorated w/Disney characters, 12" l., 2½" h., the set............................................. **120.00**

*Donald Duck Animation Cell*

**Donald Duck animation cel,** from "Der Fuehrer's Face," gouache on celluloid applied to an airbrushed background, early promotional cel of Donald speaking angrily into the phone, Walt Disney signature on mat at lower right, 1943, 8½ x 10½" (ILLUS.) ...................................... **2,587.00**

**Donald Duck animation cel,** from "Donald's Penguin," gouache on trimmed celluloid applied to air-brushed Courvoisier background, the penguin Tootsie sits w/folded arms looking angrily away from Donald who eyes him suspiciously, 1939, 8½ x 9¼"............................ **2,875.00**

*Disney Characters Cookie Jars*

*Early Donald Duck Book*

**Donald Duck book,** "Walt Disney's Donald Duck," first Donad Duck book, Whitman Publishing, 1935, linen-like covers & text, color illustrations, 9½ x 13" (ILLUS. top) ..... **77.00**

**Donald Duck figure,** bisque, riding a scooter, Japan, 1930s, 3½" h. .......... **150.00**

**Donald Duck night light,** lithographed tin & paper, Micro Lite Co. of New York, copyright Walt Disney Enterprises, 1938, 3¾" h. ..... **259.00**

**Donald Duck puppet,** push-up-type, Gabriel, 1977 ..................................... **18.00**

**Donald Duck tape measure,** celluloid........................................... **450.00**

*Donald Duck on Trapeze Toy*

**Donald Duck toy,** windup celluloid, "Donald Duck on Trapeze," George Borgfeldt Co., 1930s (ILLUS. bottom previous column) .............................. **500.00**

**Donald Duck toy,** windup, painted composition, "Walking Donald Duck," Donal Duck wearing a sailor suit & hat, Lewis & Scott Mfg. Co., Plantsville, Connecticut, Geo. Borgfeldt distributors, w/original box, 10½" h. (small cracks, ox in poor condition) ...................................... **1,150.00**

**Dumbo movie cel,** gaouche on celluloid applied to an airbrushed Courvoisier background, a large image of Dumbo holding onto a happy Timothy Mouse's tail w/his trunk, a Courvoisier Galleries label on the back, together w/a copy of "Walt Disney's Dumbo of the Circus," Garden City Publishing, 1941, cel 8½ x 11", 2 pcs. ............. **3,737.00**

**Dumbo pitcher,** 6" h., marked "Walt Disney Productions," made by Leeds China ................................................. **110.00**

**Dwarf Dopey figure,** 3¼" h. ................. **38.00**

**Dwarf Dopey puppet,** hand-type, composition head, Walt Disney Enterprises ...................................... **125.00**

**Dwarfs Bashful,** Doc, Sneezy, Happy, Sleepy & Dopey movie cell, from "Snow White and the Seven Dwarfs," gouache on trimmed celluloid applied to a wood veneer Courvoisier background, shows the Dwarfs standing & guiltily hiding their hands behind their backs, 1937, 9 x 12½"...................................... **6,900.00**

**Fantasia concept drawing,** graphite on paper, depicting a Centaur pleading his case to a reluctant Centaurette, from Pastoral Symphomy sequence, 1940, 8½ x 12"........................................... **920.00**

**Fantasia movie cel,** gouache on celluloid applied to Courvoisier airbrushed background, two dewdrop fairies perform the Dance of the Sugar Plum Fairy from The Nutcracker Suite sequence, a "WDP" stamp at lower right & Walt Disney Productions label on the back, 1940, 4¾ x 5½".................... **2,185.00**

**Fantasia movie cel,** gouache on trimmed celluloid applied to an airbrushed Courvoisier background, ostrich ballerina Madame Upanova stands in the third position holding up a cornucopia of fruit, 1940, 7½ x 8½".................................... **3,450.00**

*Lady & the Tramp Glass*

**Ferdinand the Bull soap figure** .......... **58.00**

**Ferdinand the Bull toy,** windup, lithographed tin, w/cloth flowers in his mouth, rubber tail, Line-Mar, 5" l.. **200.00**

**Goofy Bank,** hard plastic, in the shape of Goffy's head w/coin slot in back & trap on bottom, Walt Disney Productions, 12" h. ............................ **66.00**

**Jungle Book movie cel,** gouache on celluloid, Baloo stands staring straight ahead, w/gold Disneyland label on back, signed by Frank Thomas & Ollie Johnston on mat, ca. 1967, 6 x 8".............................. **1,610.00**

**Lady & the Tramp glass,** enameled, shows Lady & the Tramp on one side w/two Siamese cats on the other, reads "Walt Disney's Lady and the Tramp," marked "© Walt Disney - Productions" (ILLUS. above) ................ **35.00**

**Mary Poppins spoon,** silver plate, figural handle, 1964, 6" l. .................... **20.00**

**Mickey Mouse "birthday cake" candle holders,** ca. 1935, in original package ........................................... **150.00**

**Mickey Mouse book,** "The Miracle Maker," 1948 ..................................... **45.00**

**Mickey Mouse brush & comb set,** wooden, tin & plastic, wood & lithographaed brush & "Superior" plastic comb, in original box, box 4 x 5½", 2" h. .................................... **115.00**

**Mickey Mouse doll,** musical, plush, hard rubber & chalkware, plush body has music box in chest & chalkware head rolls in circles, plays Mickey Mouse theme, Gund, ca. 1950s, 15" h. ................................................. **256.00**

**Mickey Mouse doll,** stuffed cloth, standing Mickey of velveteen, w/pie-cut eyes & dressed in red shorts, orange shoes & yellow gloves, Steiff, Germany, 1930s, 7" h. (ear button, tag & tail missing) ........................ **1,150.00**

**Mickey mouse doll,** stuffed cloth, cotton sateen w/oil painted face, felt ears, gloves & shoes, tan sateen shorts, America, 1930s, 11½" h. (some fabric wear & discoloration, tail missing)...................................... **460.00**

**Mickey Mouse doll,** stuffed cloth, swivel head, black felt pie-eyes, painted facial features, string whiskers, felt ears, unjointed cloth body, white hands w/three fingers & a thumb, orange composition feet, black rubber tail, probably Knickerbocker, 1930s, 12⅝" h. (some fabric & composition damage) ........................ **200.00**

**Mickey Mouse figure,** hard rubber, Seiberling, 1930s, 6" h. (overall age cracks) ............................................. **220.00**

**Mickey Mouse figure,** velvet, leather cloth-applied eyes, mustard yellow gloves, greyish green short pants w/mother of pearl buttons front & back, rust colored shoes, Steiff, Germany, metal button in left ear, original cardboard chest tag, early 1930s, 6" h...................................... **1,955.00**

**Mickey Mouse game,** "Mickey Mouse Coming Home," Marks Bros., 1934 .... **95.00**

**Mickey Mouse game,** "Mickey Mouse Scatterball," lithographed cardboard, w/spinning top & small wooden game balls, 1930s, 11½" sq., 1¾" h. ............. **86.00**

**Mickey Mouse magazine,** "Radio Mirror," April 1937 issue, Mickey Mouse & Donald Duck on cover ....... **100.00**

**Mickey Mouse movie projector,** model No. E-18, w/four .16 mm films, Keystone Mfg. Co., 1930s, in original box (box in fair condition) ..... **230.00**

**Mickey Mouse nutcracker,** painted cast iron, Mickey in a nutcracker uniform, mouth opens & closes to crack nuts, in original box, 13" h......... **94.00**

**Mickey Mouse string holder,** chalkware, original paint ................... **265.00**

**Mickey Mouse teaspoon,** silver plate, Branford, 1935.................................. **30.00**

**Mickey Mouse toothbrush holder,** bisque, jointed arms, colorful painted trim, w/toothbrush, Japan, 1930s, 5" h. ................................................. **316.00**

*Lionel Mickey Mouse Circus Train*

**Mickey Mouse toy,** jointed wood,
w/green pants, "Fun-E-Flex," 1930s,
4½" h. (damage to head & both
ears) .................................................. **230.00**

**Mickey Mouse toy,** jointed wood,
w/red pants, "Fun-E-Flex," 1930s,
4½" h. ............................................... **288.00**

**Mickey Mouse toy,** jointed wood,
"Fun-E-Flex," decal on bottom reads
"Geo. Borgfeldt & Co., Nifty - A Fun-
E-Flex Toy," 1930s, 7" h. (half of ear
missing) ........................................... **460.00**

*Mickey Mouse Rocking Toy*

**Mickey Mouse toy,** rocking-type, the
cut-out sides w/a silhouetted picture
of Mickey stooped over & running
w/a landscape background, curved
bottoms to sides w/child's seat
between, cracking, soiling & some
veneer missing (ILLUS.) ...................... **83.00**

**Mickey Mouse toy,** windup,
lithographed tin, "Circus Train," red
0-4-0 locomotive & tender w/Mickey
shoveling, Mickey Mouse Band car,
Mickey Mouse Dining Car & Circus
Car, Lionel No. 1536, ca. 1930s
(ILLUS. top) ................................. **2,200.00**

**Mickey Mouse watch,** blue face,
ca, 1948 (working condition)............. **125.00**

**Mickey Mouse wrist watch,** original
model, round dial, yellow-gloved
minute & hour hand & three Mickey
figures on subsidiary seconds dial,

*Mickey Mouse Wrist Watch*

original metal band w/Mickey
figures, works patented "July' 18 -
Nov. 14, 1922," made in U.S.A.,
Ingersoll, 1933, w/original box, box
has some wear (ILLUS.) .................. **545.00**

**Mickey Mouse Club newsreel
projector,** projector w/paper label
on side reading "Mickey Mouse Club
Newsreel - with sound," shows
Mickey, Minnie & Donald w/Mickey
Mouse Club logo in lower left corner,
battery-operated, together w/three
records & film slide, ca. 1950s, the
group ................................................. **77.00**

**Mickey Mouse Club phonograph
player** .............................................. **375.00**

**Mickey & Minnie Mouse animation
cel,** gouache on celluloid,
promotional cel depicting Minnie
relaying some important news to
Mickey, ca. 1930s, 10 x 12"........... **2,185.00**

**Mickey & Minnie Mouse salt &
pepper shakers,** Leeds China
Company, 1940s, pr. .......................... **45.00**

*Mickey & Minnie Hand Car*

**Mickey & Minnie Mouse toy,** windup, tin & composition, "Mickey Mouse Hand Car," red tin hand car w/painted composition Mickey & Minnie on each end of center handle, w/eight pieces of track, Lionel, ca. 1933, w/original box, slight staining & fading to box, 7½" l., 6" h. (ILLUS.) ..................... **2,185.00**

**Minnie Mouse toy,** jointed wood, "Fun-E-Flex," 1930s, 4" h. ................ **115.00**

**Peter Pan corkscrew,** figural, brass, ca. 1950s .......................................... **35.00**

**Pinocchio figure,** carnival-type, chalkware, 14½" h. ............................. **95.00**

**Pinocchio teaspoon,** silver plate, Duchess Silverplate, ca. 1939 ........... **20.00**

**Pluto animation cel,** "Private Pluto," gouache on celluloid, Pluto marches proudly to the right w/his eyes closed & helmet on, 7½ x 9½" ......... **747.00**

**Pluto glass,** enameled, shows Pluto w/musical instruments & musical notes, reads "Pluto" at bottom, marked "1937 W.D. Ent." (ILLUS. top next column) ............................. **154.00**

**Pluto toy,** mechanical tin, "Mystery Pluto," figure of crouched Pulto w/rubber ears & two wheels for hind legs, toy is activated by pushing down red metal tail, Louis Marx & Co., dated 1938, w/original box, 10" l. ................................................... **550.00**

**Pluto toy,** push-up, mint in box ..................................... **75.00 to 100.00**

**Pluto toy,** wooden & felt, "Pluto the Pup Fun-E-Flex," wooden body w/felt ears, copyright Walt Disney Enterprises, 1930s, 7" l. ..................... **316.00**

**Seven Dwarfs dolls,** each w/painted mask faces, fabric bodies, in felt & cotton costumes, Ideal Novelty & Toy Co., ca. 1937, 10¼" h., set of 7 (one tag torn, some paint loss on hands, slight wear on faces) ............ **805.00**

*1937 Pluto Glass*

**Sleeping Beauty movie cel,** gouache on celluloid applied to a pan watercolor production background w/production overlays, Briar Rose dances w/Prince Phillip in the lush, green forest, 1959, 11½ x 28½" .. **11,500.00**

**Snow White bank,** dime register-type, lithographed tin, dated 1939 ............. **140.00**

**Snow White cookie jar,** marked "Treasure Craft" ................................ **49.00**

**Snow White figure,** ceramic, Enesco Co. ................................................ **1,200.00**

**Snow White movie cel,** gouache on trimmed celluloid applied to a polka-dot Courvoisier background, Snow White sits up in bed w/two drowsy rabbits by her side, 1937, 7 x 7¾" .... **6,325.00**

**Snow White & the Seven Dwarfs figures,** bisque, made in Japan, Geo. Borgfeldt Corp. distributors, 1938, in original box, Snow White 3¼" h., set of 8 ................................. **567.00**

**Snow White & the Seven Dwarfs game,** board-type, "The Game of Snow White and the Seven Dwarfs," folding board, fourty-nine wooden game pieces, dice & instructions, Milton Bradley Co., 1937, 9½ x 19¼", 1¾" h. ............................ **230.00**

**Tinkerbell pin,** flasher-type, souvenir from Walt Disney World, 1972 ............ **15.00**

**Ugly Duckling cel (The),** gouache on trimmed celluloid applied to an airbrushed Coourvoisier background, the Ugly Duckling swims happily along, 1939, 6 x 7½" ....................... **1,495.00**

**Walt Disney cartoon theater,** w/outer shipping carton (near mint condition) ........................................... **130.00**

**Wendy (from Peter Pan) movie cel,**
gouache on celluloid applied to a
publication background, Wendy sings
Michael to sleep, 1953, 10" sq........ **1,955.00**

**Zorro figure,** plastic, all black figure
complete w/ hat, mask & silver
sword & whip on rearing horse,
Louis Marx & Co., the group............. **145.00**

---

# DOLL FURNITURE & ACCESSORIES

**Bed,** Murphy-type, hardwood, the
scroll-cut crestrail above a pair of tall
paneled doors above two long line-
incised drawers below, line-incised
ends, the back folds-down to form
bed frame, ca. 1900 (ILLUS.
bottom) ........................... **$475.00 to 600.00**

**Carriage,** Art Deco-style, wicker
w/chrome fenders ............................ **250.00**

**Desk,** Victorian "patent"-type, walnut,
the superstructure w/a stepped &
spindle-trimmed crestrail above a
pair of glazed cupboard doors
opening to shelves; the lower desk
section w/an S-scroll desk rolltop
opneing to a fitted interior above a
rank of four drawers on one side & a
swing-out compartment of small

*Miniature Wooton Desk*

drawers & letter files on the other,
paneled ends, William S. Wooton,
Indianapolis, Indiana, ca. 1875
(ILLUS.)................... **8,000.00 to 12,000.00**

**Dollhouse,** one room w/attic & front
porch, original label, Schoenhut,
11 x 14".......................................... **450.00**

**Dough keeper,** cov., tin, rounded
w/flaring sides & base, loop end
handles, ca. 1900 (ILLUS. on
shelf, top next page)......... **375.00 to 575.00**

*Doll-size
Murphy Bed*

*Hoosier Cabinet & Accessories*

**Hoosier cabinet,** painted wood, cupboard doors & drawers w/metal flour sifter & pull-out work shelf, marked (ILLUS.) ......... **2,800.00 to 3,500.00**

---

# DOLLS

*Also see: STEIFF TOYS & DOLLS*

**A.B.G. (Alt, Beck & Gottschalck) bisque shoulder head girl,** marked "698 - #10," light blue sleep eyes, mulit-stroke brows, brown h.h. (human hair) wig, closed mouth w/accent line, pink kid body w/bisque lower arms, gussets at elbows, hips & knees, wearing a pale pink dress, underclothing, socks & shoes, 17" (kid upper arms extensively repaired & reattached, hip gussets mended, left knee gusset mended) ............................. **$400.00**

**A.B.G. bisque turned shoulder head girl,** marked "698 - 8," set brown eyes, feathered brows, brown h.h. wig, closed mouth, kid body w/bisque lower arms, pin joints at hips, gussets at knees, cloth lower legs, wearing an old drop-waist dress, underclothing, socks & shoes, 17" (general wear & aging on body, repair on left knee gusset) ............... **350.00**

**Alexander (Madame) Alexander-kins** bent-knee girl walker marked "Alex." on back, hard plastic head attached to walking mechanism, blue sleep eyes w/molded lashes, original blond wig in original set, closed mouth, hard plastic body w/jointed knees & walking mechanism, wearing tagged pink ballerina outfit & matching shoes, comes w/blue & white dotted romper, turquoise dress, panties & pinafore, pink dress w/white panties & slip, pink & white striped dress, all tagged, pink & white straw hat, white socks & shoes, unplayed-with, 8", the group ........................................ **405.00**

**Alexander (Madame) Carmen,** composition head w/blue sleep eyes w/real lashes, single stroke brows, original black mohair wig, closed mouth, five-piece composition body, wearing original tagged clothing, panties, green snap shoes, hat w/fruit & beaded necklaces, 14" (general crazing on face & body, tiny flake off nose finish, some flakes on body, age soil on clothing) ............... **245.00**

**Alexander (Madame) Dionne Quintuplets,** each w/composition head, painted brown side-glancing eyes, single stroke brows, molded & painted brown hair, closed mouth, five-piece composition toddler body w/straight legs, each wearing tagged organdy dress w/matching bonnet, one-piece underwear combination, socks & center-snap shoes, w/original gold pins w/name, 7½", set of 5 (fine general crazing, some flaking & cracks on various dolls, some shoe repair or replacement, Cecile's name pin missing) ............ **1,000.00**

**Alexander (Madame) Prince Charles,** hard plastic head attached to walking mechanism, blue sleep eyes w/molded lashes, single stroke brows, original blond wig, closed mouth, hard plastic child body w/jointed knees, wearing tagged white shirt, blue shorts, jacket & cap, socks & shoes, tag on clothing reads "Alexander-kins - by Madame Alexander - Reg. U.S. Pat. Off. N.Y. U.S.A.," in original box, 8" (cheek color yellowed) ................................. **525.00**

**Alexander (Madame) Tommy Bangs,** marked "Tommy Bangs - © Madame Alexander, New York,

U.S.A." on clothing tag, hard plastic head w/blue sleep eyes w/real lashes, single stroke brows, original synthetic blond wig, closed mouth, five-piece hard plastic body, wearing original pale green pants, white shirt, dark green felt jackets & cap, rose-colored tie, socks & shoes, 14" (spotty fading on pants) ................... **600.00**

**A.M. bisque head "Just Me" toddler,** marked "Just Me 310 7/0," weighted blue 'googlie' eyes looking left, replaced brown h.h. wig, five-piece straight-leg composition body, wearing a chine silk dress, later shoes & socks & straw hat, 9½" (dress poor) ................................. **1,150.00**

**A.M. bisque head Oriental baby,** marked "353 - 10," weighted brown glass eyes, closed mouth, painted dark hair, straight-leg fabric body w/composition hands, wearing Oriental clothes comprising of tan satin pants, lack brocade tunic & gold silk vest, 9¾" (vest fragile) ........ **805.00**

**A.M. bisque head character girl,** marked "323 3/0," weighted blue 'googlie' eyes looking right, closed smiling mouth, old curly blond mohair wig, five-piece straight-leg composition body, wearing original white gauze dress, underwear, socks & white shoes, 11½" (tiny chip near inner corner left lower eyelid) ........................................... **1,035.00**

**A.M. bisque flange head "Dream Baby,"** marked "A.M. - Germany - 341/4," blue sleep eyes, softly blushed brows, painted upper & lower lashes, lightly molded & softly blushed hair closed mouth, cloth body w/celluloid hands, wearing a white baby dress, slip & lacy bonnet, 17" (light rubs, few minor inherent discolorations in hair, some fill added to body around neck) ............. **350.00**

**A.M. bisque socket head girl,** marked "Armand Marseille - Germany - 390 - A.16. M.," set brown eyes w/real lashes, feathered brows, blond h.h. wig, open mouth w/accented lips & four upper teeth, jointed wood & composition body, wearing an antique white child's two-piece white dress w/lace inserts, underclothing, socks & shoes, 36" (tooth cracked off & replaced, arms repainted, surface cracks & touch-up on torso, lower legs repainted) ......... **700.00**

**Bahr & Proschild head character girl,** marked "686 3/0," weighted left-glancing 'googlie' brown eyes, closed slightly smiling mouth, old brown mohair wig, five-pieced straight-limb composition body w/'starfish' hands, wearing original printed gauze dress w/pleated front, lace & ribbon trim, socks, brown leather shoes & later peach silk bonnet, 10" (wig sparse) ............... **1,955.00**

**Bahr & Proschild bisque socket head girl,** marked "224 - 12," set brown eyes, feathered brows, painted upper & lower lashes, open mouth w/accented lips & four upper teeth, brown h.h. wig, pierced ears, jointed wood & composition body w/straight wrists, wearing a green plaid taffeta dress, underclothing, socks & shoes, 21" (tiny flake at each earring hole, minor firing line behind each ear, minor repair & touch-up at neck socket, elbows & knees) ................... **725.00**

**Barbie,** "#1 Barbie," brunette hair in original ponytail, red lips, hoop earrings & white rimmed sunglasses w/blue lenses, finger & toe paint, wearing black & white one piece knit swimsuit (hair slightly fuzzy, some touch-ups, some discoloration to body) ............................................. **4,100.00**

**Barbie,** "#3 Barbie," brunette hair in original ponytail, blue eyeliner, full red lips, nostril paint, pearl earrings, finger & toe paint, wearing black & white one-piece knit swimsuit & black open-toed shoes, w/#3 pedestal stand, pink cover booklet & neck insert (some discoloration, two holes in swimsuit, box worn) .......... **1,700.00**

**Barbie,** "#4 Barbie," brunette hair in original ponytail, full red lips, nostril paint, finger & toe paint, wearing black & white one piece knit swimsuit (hair slightly fuzzy, some light staining, swimsuit loose) ........... **235.00**

**Barbie,** "#5 Barbie," blond hair in original ponytail, full red lips, nostril paint, finger & toe paint, wearing black & white one piece knit swimsuit w/black wire stand, box insert & yellow cove booklet, slight staining & scratching, box has age discoloration (ILLUS. top next page) ..................... **180.00**

*#5 Barbie Doll*

**Barbie,** "#5 Barbie," titian hair in
original ponytail, full red lips, nostril
paint, pearl earrings, finger & toe
paint wearing original black & white
one piece knit swimsuit (top of hair
soiled, light stains, swimsuit slightly
worn)................................................ **450.00**

**Barbie,** "35th Anniversary Barbie Gift
Set," ca. 1993, Keepsake Collection,
blond, w/replica of 'Easter Parade' &
'Roman Holiday' outfits, never
removed from the box, the set.......... **100.00**

*Sears Blossom Beautiful Barbie*

**Barbie,** "Blossom Beautiful Barbie,"
Sears Department Store, ca. 1992,
original outfit, stand, shoes &
jewelry, used for display, missing
box (ILLUS. bottom previous
column)............................................ **265.00**

**Barbie,** "Blue Rhapsody Barbie,"
Porcelain Series, ca. 1986, No.
03230, includes stand, certificate &
styrofoam insert in box (box worn) ... **350.00**

**Barbie,** "Bubblecut Barbie," ca. 1961-
62, blond, light pink lips w/tint of
white, finger & toe paint, wearing
'Let's Dance' dress .......................... **105.00**

**Barbie,** "Bubblecut Barbie," ca. 1964,
blond, coral lips, pearl earrings,
finger & toe paint, wearing red one-
piece swimsuit & red open-toed
shoes, gold wire stand, white cover
booklet in cellophane bag, in original
box w/insert (some discoloration,
"Venus" written on lower back, box
worn, "1962" written on lower flap) ... **200.00**

*Color Me Magic Barbie*

**Barbie,** "Color Me Magic Barbie," ca.
1966, raised letter issue, dark red
hair w/barrette, bright pink lips, faint
cheek blush, nostril paint, finger
paint & toe paint, original swimsuit
w/belt & scarf, aqua mules, in

original plastic box/closet w/purple plastic hanger & closet bracket, barrettes & ribbons, netting, color changer A & B, brush w/sponge end, Color Magic booklet & Exclusive Fashions Book 1, hair is slightly fuzzy, booklet have age discoloration, box worn, the set (ILLUS. bottom previous page)......... **800.00**

**Barbie,** "Empress Bride," Bob Mackie Series, ca, 1992, complete, includes cardboard shipping box ................... **750.00**

**Barbie,** "Enchanted Evening Barbie," Porcelain Series, ca. 1987, No. 0044986, includes stand, certificate & styrofoam insert in box (box slightly worn)..................................... **175.00**

**Barbie,** "Gold Barbie," Bob Mackie Series, ca. 1990, complete, includes cardboard shipping box, doll has been removed from box................... **650.00**

**Barbie,** "Greek Barbie," International Series, ca. 1985, never removed from the box (box slightly damaged) .. **55.00**

**Barbie,** "Happy Holidays Barbie," 1988, first issue, red dress w/gold glitter, never removed from the box (box worn)........................................ **575.00**

**Barbie,** "Happy Holidays Barbie," 1989, white dress w/fur trim, w/ornament, never removed from the box, ornament on front of box creased, box discolored) .................. **200.00**

**Barbie,** "Happy Holidays Barbie," 1990, fuchsia dress w/silver design, w/ornament, never removed from the box (plastic window in box creased)............................................ **100.00**

**Barbie,** "Happy Holidays Barbie," 1991, green velvet dress w/sequins, never removed from the box (box slightly discolored) ........................... **160.00**

**Barbie,** "Happy Holidays Barbie," 1992, silver dress w/pearls, sequins & glitter, never removed from the box...................................................... **95.00**

**Barbie,** "Happy Holidays Barbie," 1993, red dress w/gold trim, sequins & glitter, never removed from the box...................................................... **85.00**

**Barbie,** "India Barbie," International Series, ca. 1981, never removed from the box (box slightly damaged) ....................................... **125.00**

**Barbie,** "Italian Barbie," International Series, ca. 1979, never removed from the box (box slightly damaged) ....................................... **175.00**

**Barbie,** "Live action Barbie," ca. 1973, blond, rooted eyelashes, pink lips, cheek blush, wearing original outfit, w/wrist tag, in original plastic 'baggie' package (top of package slightly worn)..................................... **155.00**

**Barbie,** "Living Barbie," ca. 1970, brunette, rooted eyelashes, pink lips, cheek blush, wearing original silver & gold metallic swimsuit (some fading, swimsuit slightly worn) ........... **70.00**

**Barbie,** "Masquerade Ball," Bob Mackie Series, complete, includes cardboard shipping box ................... **325.00**

**Barbie,** "Neptune Fantasy," Bob Mackie Series, ca. 1992, complete, includes cardboard shipping box ...... **800.00**

**Barbie,** "Parisian Barbie," International Series, ca. 1979, never removed from the box (box slightly damaged) ........................................ **100.00**

**Barbie,** "Platinum Barbie," Bob Mackie Series, ca. 1991, complete, includes cardboard shipping box ...... **575.00**

**Barbie,** "Queen of Hearts," Bob Mackie Series, ca. 1994, complete, includes cardboard shipping box ...... **200.00**

**Barbie,** "Royal Barbie," International Series, ca. 1979, never removed from the box (box slightly damaged) ........................................ **165.00**

**Barbie,** "Russian Barbie," International Series, ca. 1988, never removed from the box (box slightly damaged) ......................................... **35.00**

**Barbie,** "Satin Nights Barbie," Service Merchandise Department Store, ca. 1992, never removed from the box (box slightly damaged) .................... **115.00**

**Barbie,** "Solo in the Spotlight," Porcelain Series, ca. 1990, No. 03013, includes stand, certificate & styrofoam insert in box .................... **120.00**

**Barbie,** "Starlight Splendor Barbie," Bob Mackie Series, ca. 1991, Black, complete, includes cardboard shipping box ..................................... **650.00**

**Barbie,** "Walk Lively Barbie," ca. 1971, never removed from the box (box slightly worn)............................ **165.00**

**Barrois (E.) bisque swivel head fashion lady,** marked "E. Depose B.," cup-and-saucer swivel head on a bisque shoulder plate, set cobalt blue eyes, multi-stroke brows, blond mohair wig, closed smiling mouth w/accented lips, kid body w/gussets at elbows, hips & knees, wearing

*Bawo & Dotter Character Lady*

possibly original brown striped dress w/white blouse, underclothing, socks, shoes & bonnet, 19" (fine firing line on shoulder plate & back of head at neck, right eye cracked, fingers on right hand replaced) ...... **3,050.00**

**Bawo & Dotter Ltd. bisque head character lady,** marked "#213 Germany," long delicate face w/painted brows & blue paperweight eyes, blond wig, delicate molded blushed closed mouth, composition body, redressed in period clothing, small eye flake, 21" (ILLUS. above) ........................................... **6,500.00**

**Belton-type bisque socket head black lady,** marked "179. 6," set brown eyes, feathered brows, original black skin wig, pierced ears, closed mouth, jointed wood & composition body w/straight wrists, wearing an antique red & white dress, underclothing, socks & red high-button boots & carrying a black antique silk bonnet, 14" (few tiny wig pulls, some repaint on body) ......... **2,700.00**

**Belton-type bisque socket-head girl,** marked "137 - 8," brown paperweight eyes, feathered brows, pierced ears, brown h.h. wig, open-closed mouth w/outlined lips & white space between lips, concave area on top of head w/two stringing holes, jointed wood & composition body w/straight wrists, wearing an old pink dress trimmed w/lace & tucks, underclothing, socks & new shoes, 16" (body finish worn & aged) ........ **1,600.00**

**Bierschenk (Fritz) bisque character head lady,** marked "FB 616," well-rendered face w/strong features, intaglio eyes, open-closed mouth w/molded & painted upper teeth, five-piece straight-limb shapely body w/ arms slightly bent, brown h.h. wig, redressed in peach pink satin & net long gown w/matching ribbon trim, old white leather lace-up ankle boots, underwear & straw hat, 13" ................................................. **2,875.00**

**Bisque girl,** marked "3/0," bisque socket head w/set blue eyes, single stroke brows, painted lashes, original blond mohair wig, open mouth w/four tiny upper teeth, five-piece composition body w/molded & painted socks & brown two-strap shoes, wearing original white print dress, underclothing & tiny lace-trimmed straw bonnet, 5" (minor firing line behind ear, painted finish on stockings cracked & lifting, bottom left foot cracked) ................... **365.00**

**Bisque girl,** marked "293 - 8/0 - SC," bisque socket head w/blue sleep eyes, single stroke brows, original blond mohair wig, open mouth w/four upper teeth, five-piece all-bisque body jointed at shoulders & hips, molded & painted white socks & black two-strap shoes, wearing probably original white net dress & underclothing, 6½" (eyelids need to be rewaxed, one leg darker but matches, end off one finger, patches of kid glued to left hip joint) ............... **340.00**

**Bisque shoulder head "Highland Mary" lady,** marked "13," painted blue eyes w/red accent line, single stroke brows, molded & painted blond hair w/bangs & ears partially exposed, closed mouth, cloth body w/kid lower arms, striped cloth lower legs w/leather feet for boots, wearing a plum taffeta dress & underclothing, 27" (rear torso patched & repaired, kid arms deteriorating, light wear on back of head) .................................... **400.00**

**Borgfeldt bisque head "Gladdie" character doll,** incised "Gladdie - Copyriht (sic) Helen W. Jensen," weighted brown eyes, open smiling mouth w/four upper teeth & tongue, molded & painted hair, fabric body w/celluloid hands, brown leather integral boots, in old white shirt & blue wool pants, German, ca. 1929 17½" (ILLUS. top next page) ......... **2,587.00**

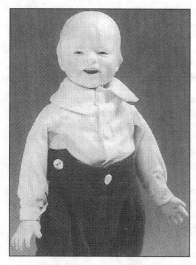

*Borgfeldt "Gladdie" Doll*

*Bru Bisque Bébé Doll*

**Bru bisque shoulder Bébé doll,** incised w/circle & dot mark & "Bru Jne - 5," fixed brown glass eyes, brown h.h. wig, pierced ears, open/closed mouth w/molded & painted upper teeth, head swiveling on long shoulder plate w/molded breasts incised "Depose," w/bisque lower arms, gusseted white leather body, dressed in pale blue satin lace trimmed short dress w/pleated skirt, wig replaced, slight rub on nose & cheeks, 15½" (ILLUS.) ................. **12,650.00**

**Bru bisque head girl,** marked "Bru Jne 5," brown fixed paperweight eyes outlined in black, lids shaded plum, closed mouth, pierced ears, blond mohair wig over cork pate, jointed composition legs, redressed in pale green satin frock w/lace trim on front & yoke, socks & old marked Bru brown leather shoes, sleeves, furry hat w/ostrich feather plume & green satin trim, muff holding a small metal mesh bag & decorative parasol w/blue satin canopy, 16½" (left pinkie restored) .................... **13,800.00**

**Bru Jne bisque socket head girl,** marked "Bru Jne. 9," blue paperweight eyes, feathered brows, mauve blush over eyes, brown h.h. wig, pierced ears, closed mouth w/accented lips & small white space between lips, kid body w/wooden lower arms & legs, wearing a pale bluish green silk dress, matching gloves, underclothing, socks & shoes, 24" (nearly invisible ¼" line at corner of right eye, minor firing lines behind ears, small chip on shoulder

**Bru bisque swivel head girl,** marked "2," fixed blue paperweight eyes, closed pale mouth, pierced ears, blond mohair wig, kid body w/bisque lower arms, kid lower legs, redressed in maroon & cream satin frock, underwear, socks, brown leather shoes & matching hat, 11½" (bisque slightly grainy on cheeks) ........................................ **6,325.00**

**Bru Jne bisque socket head girl,** marked "Bru Jne 4," blue paperweight eyes, multi-stroke brows, pierced ears, cork pate w/original blond mohair wig, closed mouth, jointed composition body w/straight wrists, redressed in antique royal blue fabric dress trimmed w/white lace, matching velvet bonnet, underclothing, blue mesh socks & antique shoes, 14" (small chip on lower right ear lobe, crazing on body) ........................... **4,500.00**

**Bru bisque shoulder head fashion lady,** marked "D," fixed pale blue eyes painted slightly smiling closed mouth, pierced ears, blond mohair wig over cork pate, gusseted kid body, delicate bisque hands, wearing original *eau de nil* & maroon two-piece day dress, green jacket, full maroon skirt w/underwear including hoop bustle, straw hat, socket & old light brown leather boots, 14½" ................................. **4,025.00**

plate, paint flaking off wooden arms & legs, small spots of discoloration on kid arms, dress fabric falling apart) .......................................... **13,000.00**

**Buddy Lee hard plastic boy,** marked "Buddy Lee" on back, hard plastic head w/stiff neck, painted black eyes, single stroke brows, painted upper lashes, molded painted hair, closed smiling mouth, hard plastic body jointed at shoulders only, molded & painted black boots, wearing original Lee denim shirt & bib overalls, red kerchief, Lee denim hat, 12" (facial color pale, light wear on boots) .......................................... **315.00**

**Bye-Lo Baby,** bisque flange head marked "Copr. Grace S. Putnam - Made in Germany," blue sleep eyes, softly blushed brows, lightly molded & softly blushed hair, closed mouth, cloth body w/"frog" legs, celluloid hands, wearing original dress, slip, diaper & socks, crocheted bonnet, 11" head circumference, 12" ............. **375.00**

**China head "Dolley Madison" lady,** painted black hair w/molded bow & band on the back, painted blue eyes w/red accent line, single stroke brows, closed mouth w/accent line, cloth body w/wooden hands, striped lower legs & black leather feet to represent boots, redressed in peach & pale blue antique fabric, fancy trim & underclothing, 24" (light color wear on back of head, general soil & aging on body, hand paint flaking).... **275.00**

**China head lady,** 'covered wagon'-type, brown painted eyes, small painted mouth, center-part black hair molded w/short side curls, fabric body w/leather lower arms w/separately stitched fingers, wearing original white cotton gown w/lace trim at neck & sleeves, layers of white underwear, original high brown leather boots w/four-button closures, mid-19th c., 25" (kiln flaws on face)................................. **805.00**

**China head lady,** painted brown eyes w/red accent line, molded & painted black flat-top hair, accented nostrils, closed smiling mouth, cloth body w/china lower arms & lower legs w/flat feet, wearing black velvet two-piece outfit trimmed w/ecru lace, underclothing, 25" (few spots of glaze missing on back of head, two flakes off hair, light wear on fingers & feet) .............................................. **425.00**

**China head lady,** painted blue eyes w/red accent line, single stroke brows, molded & painted wavy center part hair w/exposed ears, closed mouth w/red accent line between lips, cloth body w/leather lower arms, wearing an antique brocade satin two-piece dress, underclothing & socks, 27" (lower leather arms deteriorating & are repaired, body shows aging & soil, upper torso & lower legs recovered) ...................................... **250.00**

**China head wigged lady,** marked w/impressed symbols, shoulder head w/light pink tint, painted blue eyes w/red accent line, single stroke brows, molded eyelids, closed mouth, solid dome w/a dark human hair wig, cloth body w/kid arms, individually stitched fingers & applied thumbs, well redressed w/old silk fabric, underclothing, socks & shoes, 28" (cloth body recovered & maybe partially replaced, left wrist mended, thumb coming off, fingers on right hand damaged) ............................ **2,200.00**

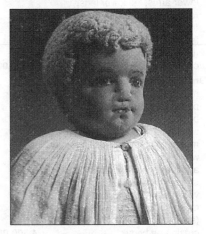

*"Beecher Baby" Doll*

**Cloth "Beecher Baby,"** painted stockinet, painted face w/blue eyes, molded nose, ears & lips, blond yarn hair, chubby body, in oversized dotted cotton baby gown, some holes & soiling, ca. 1900, 24½" (ILLUS.) ......................................... **2,587.00**

**Cloth "Tweedle Dee" & "Tweedle Dum" dolls,** each face w/ink painting, black head eyes, applied ears & noses, cotton fabric pants, brown wool short jacket w/four brass

*"Tweedle Dee & Tweedle Dum" Dolls*

*Painted Cloth Doll*

*Dressel Bisque Head Doll*

buttons, wool beanies, mitten hands, names printed on each collar, England, early 20th c., mouths worn, 13½", pr. (ILLUS.) .......................... **1,495.00**

**Cloth girl doll,** flat oil-painted head w/blue eyes, rouged cheeks, painted hair, the head stitched in four pieces, fabric body, oil-painted hands, unclothed early 20th c., 28½" (ILLUS. top next column) .............. **1,610.00**

**D•I•P bisque head girl,** marked "Geschutzt - S & Co. - Germany" in green circle, blue sleep eyes, feathered brows, painted upper lashes, blond h.h. wig, closed mouth, jointed composition toddler body w/straight wrists & jointed knees, wearing a white lace-trimmed dress, underclothing, socks & shoes, 14½" (faint inherent line under left eye, two fingers repaired) .............. **1,600.00**

**Dressel (Cuno & Otto) bisque head lady,** incised "1469," w/weighted blue glass eyes, closed mouth, brown mohair wig, adult form jointed composition body w/molded bust, long limbs, feet shaped to wear her original white leather low heeled shoes, in floral printed chiffon-trimmed dress, German, ca. 1920s, dress frail, 14" (ILLUS. bottom next column) ........................................ **1,725.00**

**Effanbee "Patricia,"** composition head w/green sleep eyes w/real lashes, single stroke brows, brown h.h. wig, closed "rosebud" mouth, five-piece composition body, wearing original red dress, matching one-piece underclothing, red velvet hat, socks & shoes, 14" (few small flakes on fingers & light crazing on legs) ................................................. **600.00**

**Effanbee "Patsy,"** composition head, brown sleep eyes w/real lashes, single stroke brows, molded & painted brown hair, closed rosebud mouth, five-piece composition body, wearing original yellow dress, matching one-piece underwear & sunbonnet, sunsuit w/matching sunbonnet, dress, robe & four coats (clothing probably made from a Patsy pattern), 14" (lashes worn, fingers touched-up, one finger damaged & some flaking) ................. **600.00**

**Elite bisque socket head character boy,** marked "Dep. Elite - D.1," molded German helmet on head, blue "googlie" set eyes, feathered brows, molded & painted hair, open smiling mouth, jointed wood & composition body w/straight wrists, wearing a felt German soldier uniform w/red trim, gold buttons, new socks & shoes, 10½" (tiny inherent cut in back of head, touch-up on upper torso, soil on body finish) ............................................ **2,100.00**

**Francie (Barbie's friend),** "Growin' Pretty Hair," ca. 1971, blond hair in original set w/'growing section,' rooted eyelashes, pink lips, cheek blush, bendable legs, wearing original dress (light coloring, dress slightly worn)...................................... **80.00**

*Bisque French Fashion Doll*

**French Fashion,** swivel bisque shoulder head incised "2" on edge of shoulder plate, fixed light blue glass eyes, closed mouth, pierced ears, original blond curly mohair wig over cork pate, gussetted kid body, kid hands w/separately stitched fingers, in original clothing comprising faded green silk two piece day dress w/large cross-over collar, full skirt w/bustled back, w/lace & metal thread trim, layers of cotton underwear, brown leather four button boots, complete w/black leather & green silk handbag, wooden handled parasol w/cream silk canopy, matching straw & green silk ribbon hat, ca. 1875, 15½" (ILLUS. previous column) .............. **3,162.00**

**French Fashion,** bisque shoulder head marked "B 4 S," blue glass eyes, closed mouth, blond mohair wig over cork pate, leather-over-wood body w/bisque lower arms, jointed at waist, redressed in chine silk two-piece bustled gown, underwear, pin, necklace w/fan-shaped locket, old black lace-up boots w/heel & straw hat, 16½" (eyes reset, old hairline on forehead) ..................................... **2,587.00**

*Gaultier Bisque "Bébé" Doll*

**Gaultier (Francois) bisque head "Bébé" doll,** incised "F 1 G," pale blue paperweight eyes outlined in black & shadowed w/pink, nicely painted lips, pierced ears, pale bisque, replaced blond skin wig over old cork pate, jointed wood & composition body, redressed in red wool drop waist dress, flannel & cotton underwear, black socks & brown leather lace up boots w/brown rosettes at toes, French, ca. 1880, hands flaking & poor, 16½" (ILLUS.) ......................................... **4,025.00**

**Goebel (W.) bisque socket head girl,** mark w/a crown over "WG" entwined - 120 4/0 Bavaria," wide brown sleep eyes, single stroke brows, brown h.h. wig, open mouth w/four upper teeth, jointed wood & composition body, wearing a little yellow organdy dress trimmed w/embroidered flowers, matching under garment, knit undershirt & panties, socks & antique shoes, 12½" (some face rubs, eyelid wax worn, general body wear) ................ **285.00**

**Greiner papier-mâché head lady,** marked "Greiner's Patent Heads - No. 12 - Pat. March 30th '58" on label on back of shoulder plate, painted blue eyes, single stroke brows, molded & painted black hair w/curls around face, closed mouth, cloth body jointed at shoulders, elbows, hips & knees, wearing red plaid dress trimmed w/black velvet ribbon, underclothing, red socks & brown leather shoes, 32" (light touch-up on nose & some other areas, light cracks & crazing to face & shoulder plate, cloth deteriorated on front torso) .............................. **1,000.00**

**Handwerck (Heinrich) bisque socket head girl,** marked "Germany - Heinrich Handwerck - Simon & Halbig - 1," brown sleep eyes w/remnants of real lashes, molded & feathered brows, pierced ears, original blond mohair wig, open mouth w/accented lips & two upper teeth, jointed wood & composition body, wearing an antique pale pink dress, underclothing, socks & shoes, 17½" (minor firing line behind ears, chip on one earring hole, light wear) ................................................ **450.00**

**Handwerck (Heinrich) bisque head girl,** marked "Germany - Heinrich Handwerck - Simon & Halbig - 3," blue sleep eyes w/"fur" eyebrows, original brown mohair wig, open mouth w/four upper teeth, pierced ears, jointed wood & composition body, wearing a white eyelet dress, matching slip, underclothing, pink socks, old black shoes, ecru wool cape w/pink trim, peach velvet hat w/ribbon & feathers, w/original box bottom w/"pillows" of excelsior & tissue paper & a paper label at one end reading "Genuine Handwerck Doll - Handwerck's Bebe

Cosmopolite...," 22" (eyes reset too close, small inherent spot on forehead, body finish "washed") ....... **775.00**

**Handwerck (Heinrich) bisque socket head girl,** marked "119-13 - Handwerck -5 - Germany," brown sleep eyes, feathered brows, pierced ears, brown h.h. wig, open mouth w/accented lips & four upper teeth, jointed wood & composition body, wearing a pale peach taffeta dress, underclothing, socks & high-button boots, 27" (minor flake at earring hole, crack in finish of lower rear torso) .............................................. **750.00**

**Handwerck (Heinrich) bisque socket head girl,** marked "109-15 - DEP. - Germany - Handwerck - 6," blue sleep eyes, feathered brows, pierced ears, original brown mohair wig, open mouth w/accented lips, jointed wood & composition body, wearing an antique white child's dress, underclothing, pink socks, black high-top shoes, 29" (small sliver off bisque at crown in back, firing line at top of right ear, tiny firing line at right earring hole) ....... **1,400.00**

**Handwerck (Heinrich) bisque socket head girl,** marked "16 - 99 - DEP - Germany - Handwerck - 7," brown sleep eyes, molded & feathered brows, replaced brown synthetic wig open mouth w/accented lips & four upper teeth, wearing a blue antique child's dress, slip, socks & high-button shoes, 32" (minor firing line below left ear, normal wear, one little finger repaired) ....................................... **1,000.00**

**Hertel, Schwab & Co. bisque head "Our Fairy" character girl,** marked "222/28," weighted blue 'googlie' eyes, pug nose, open-closed smiling mouth w/molded upper teeth, cropped strawberry blond mohair wig, straight-limbed all-bisque body w/legs jointed, hands w/fingers spread, wearing original peach gauze short dress w/short sleeves, matching silk hair bow, 11" (missing right index finger) ......................... **2,587.00**

**Hertel, Schwab & Co. bisque socket head baby,** marked "173 - 6," blue "googlie" sleep eyes looking to side, feathered brows, painted upper & lower lashes, brown mohair wig, closed smiling mouth, bent-limb composition baby body, wearing white baby dress made from old dress, underclothing, booties & pink crocheted bonnet, 16" (minor firing line on top of right ear, minor cracks in finish of body) ............................ **5,500.00**

**Heubach (Gebruder) all-bisque character girl,** marked "10490 - 3," intaglio brown eyes looking left, open-closed mouth w/two painted teeth, molded brown hair w/three molded blue hair ribbons, fixed head, straight-limb all-bisque body w/molded painted white socks & brown shoes, bent arms, wearing original off-white cotton dress w/matching ribbon trim & underwear, 9" ................................................. **2,070.00**

**Heubach (Gebruder) bisque head "Baby Stuart,"** marked "7977," molded bonnet decorated w/transfers of flowers, blue intaglio eyes, closed mouth, five-pierced curved-limb composition body, wearing a long cotton baby gown, 9" (gown worn) ...................................... **805.00**

*Heubach Character Doll*

**Heubach (Gebruder) bisque head character girl,** incised "7246 w/sun mark" pink bisque head w/weighted blue glass eyes (probably reset), closed mouth, replacement wig, jointed wood & composition body, wearing blue cotton front-buttoning sailor collar dress, underwear, straw hat, German, ca. 1912, 10¾" (ILLUS.) ........................................ **1,610.00**

**Heubach (Gebruder) bisque shoulder head character baby,** marked "3 - Heubach -Germany - 8306," blue intaglio eyes, single stroke brows, molded & brush-stroked hair, open-closed smiling mouth w/four upper & two lower teeth, blue cloth body jointed at shoulders & hips, wearing a white shirt trimmed w/red edging, red corduroy pants, underclothing, socks & shoes, 13" (body worn & soiled, mended & patched at top of torso & arms) ............................................... **450.00**

**Heubach (Gebruder) bisque head character boy,** marked "7602" w/sun mark, pensive face w/intaglio blue eyes, closed mouth, flocked hair, jointed composition body, wearing red felt pants, blue felt greatcoat w/gold buttons, black belt, blue wool cap, black shoes & w/a toy trumpet & tin drum 14½" (hair sparse)........................................... **1,035.00**

**Heubach (Gebruder) bisque head character girl,** marked "7768," 'Coquette' face w/intaglio blue side-glancing eyes, large open-closed smiling mouth w/molded teeth, dimpled cheeks, molded hair w/blue hair ribbon, jointed wood & composition body, wearing white dress w/pleated skirt, cotton & flannel underwear, later socks & white shoes, 17" ............................. **1,955.00**

**Horsman Co. all-bisque "SHEbee" character girl,** marked "150," wide blue painted eyes, closed downturned mouth, dome head, fixed on body molded w/an undershirt, jointed arms & legs, molded oversized pink shoes, wearing a short red & white houndstooth check dress, 8½" (one thumb repaired, over painting on shoes) ........................................... **1,150.00**

**Jumeau (E.) bisque head girl,** marked "Depose E 3 J" & "H," blue paperweight eyes, closed mouth, pierced ears, blond mohair wig over cork pate, eight ball-joint wood & composition body w/blue Jumeau stamp on back, redressed in purple satin dress w/vertically pleated front panel, pink ribbon & lace trim, cotton underwear, pink silk hat, old black socks & old brown shoes, 11" (slightly grainy bisque).................. **4,600.00**

**Jumeau (E.) bisque socket head
black girl,** marked "3," brown
paperweight eyes, heavy feathered
brows, long painted lashes, black
mohair wig, pierced ears, open
mouth w/six upper teeth, jointed
wood & composition body w/jointed
wrists, wearing an antique white
dress w/lace inserts & tucks,
underclothing, socks & shoes, 12"
(rub on end of nose, chips at earring
holes, body shows wear & paint
flakes on hands & knee joints) ...... **2,000.00**

**Jumeau (E.) bisque socket head
girl,** marked "Deposé - E 5 J,"
oversized bulbous blue paperweight
eyes, heavy feathered brows,
painted lashes, original blond mohair
wig, pierced ears, closed mouth
w/accented lips & white space
between lips, wearing factory-
original peach hat & dress trimmed
w/gold metal decorations at neck &
low belt, trimmed w/lace, lower skirt
lined w/pleated piece matching
pleated original slip, replaced
underpants, socks & shoes that
coordinate w/the dress, 13" (tiny
firing line on right side of crown) .... **4,500.00**

*Jumeau "Portrait" Doll*

**Jumeau (E.) bisque head "portrait"
doll,** incised "6x" & "L" in red ink
above, fixed pale blue paperweight
eyes, closed well painted mouth,
pierced ears, goatskin wig, eight ball
jointed wood & composition body
w/straight wrists, buttocks stamped
"Jumeau Medialle d'Or," wearing old

sailor suit comprising blue wool
pants, cream wool shirt w/blue
embroidered detail, blue wool cap,
old two-toned leather shoes, 14¼"
(ILLUS.) ......................................... **5,750.00**

**Jumeau (E.) bisque head girl,**
marked "7," fixed brown paperweight
eyes, closed mouth, pierced ears,
blond mohair wig over skin base &
cork pate, eight ball-jointed wood
body w/oval paper label for "Grand
Bazar Mahaut, Cherbourg," straight
wrists, redressed in pink silk & net
dress w/matching ribbon trim socks
& marked "Deposé" brown leather
shoes & matching bonnet, 15¾" h.
(one shoe sole missing)................ **5,175.00**

**Jumeau (E.) bisque socket head
girl,** marked "Depose - Tete Jumeau
- Bte. S.G.D.G.- 7," large brown
paperweight eyes, heavy feathered
brows, pierced ears, brown h.h. wig,
closed mouth w/accented lips,
jointed wood & composition body
w/jointed wrists, wearing a beige
antique coat-dress, underclothing,
mesh stockings, antique shoes,
brown furry felt hat trimmed in pale
blue, body marked "Jumeau -
Medaille d'Or - Paris," 18" (½"
inherent cut in bisque from crown in
back, few kiln specks on face, arms
& lower legs repainted & flaking,
upper torso damaged around
neck).............................................. **2,300.00**

*Jumeau Bisque "Bébé" Doll*

**Jumeau (E.) bisque head "Bébé"
doll,** stamped in red "Depose Tete
Jumeau Bte S.G.D.G. 9," large

brown fixed glass eyes, closed mouth, applied pierced ears & blond mohair wig over cork pate, jointed wood & composition baby w/blue Jumeau stamp on buttocks, straight wrists, pull-string 'mama' mechanism (inoperative), redressed in maroon velvet coat, underwear, old brown leather shoes w/maroon rosettes, lace bonnet, fingers rubbed, 20" (ILLUS.) ........................................ **4,312.00**

**Jumeau (E.) bisque head "long face" girl,** marked "10," bulbous deep blue paperweight eyes, heavy feathered brows, painted upper & lower lashes, pierced applied ears, brown h.h. wig, closed mouth w/accented lips, well redressed in royal blue taffeta French-style dress, matching hat, underclothing, socks & high-button boots, 21" (faint inherent reddish line under right eye, wear at all joints w/some plastic wood fill, some touch-up & flakes) ............... **7,900.00**

*Jumeau "Triste Bebe"*

**Jumeau (E.) bisque head "Triste Bebe,"** marked "12," large paperweight brown eyes, brown h.h. wig & blushed open mouth, on jointed composition body, outfitted in fine antique lace dress w/matching hat, signed "Jumeau," faint hairline crack at temple (ILLUS.) ............... **9,700.00**

**K (star) R celluloid socket head baby,** marked "K ★ R - 728/28," blue glass sleep eyes, feathered brows, painted upper & lower lashes, blond mohair wig, open mouth w/two upper teeth & wobble tongue, composition bent-limb baby body, wearing a white shirt, blue bib pants, socks & shoes, 10" ......................................... **325.00**

**K (star) R bisque head character girl,** marked "30 - 101," blue-painted eyes, closed mouth, replaced blond wig, jointed wood & composition body, wearing original white gauze dress w/lace yoke & trim on sleeves, underwear, cream socks & brown leather shoes, 11½" (one thumb repaired) ........................................ **2,587.00**

*K ★ R Bisque Character Boy*

**K (star) R bisque head character boy,** incised "102/30," painted blue eyes, closed mouth w/dark painted line between lips, molded & painted brown hair, jointed wood & composition body, in white short sleeved pleated front cotton shirt & later clothes, German, ca. 1909, some retouching on body, repairs at knee joints, 11¾" (ILLUS.) .......... **24,150.00**

**K (star) R (Kammer & Reinhardt) bisque head character boy,** marked "115 - 38," dome head w/weighted blue eyes, closed pouty mouth, dimpled chin, jointed wood & composition body, redressed in a white corded cotton jacket w/large collar, short pants, socks & black shoes, 15" (slight rubbing on hands) .......................................... **4,887.00**

**K (star) R bisque socket head girl,** marked "Simon & Halbig - K ★ R - 46," blue flirty sleep eyes w/real lashes, molded & feathered brows, pierced ears, original brown mohair wig, open mouth w/accented lips & four upper teeth, jointed wood & composition body, nicely redressed in a white lace-trimmed dress, underclothing, socks & shoes, 17" (small flake on earring holes) .......... **750.00**

**K (star) R bisque head character boy,** marked "101 - 46," painted blue eyes, closed mouth, replaced brown synthetic wig, redressed in white shirt, maroon velvet jacket & black velvet pants, 18" ........................... **4,312.00**

**K (star) R bisque socket head baby,** marked "X - K ★ R -22 - Germany - 50," blue sleep eyes w/real lashes, feathered brows, original brown h.h. wig, open mouth w/two upper teeth & wobble tongue, composition bent-limb baby body w/non-working crier, wearing an old white baby dress, new underclothing & booties, 21" (washed finish on upper body, some finish chipping & wear) ............ **600.00**

**K (star ) R bisque head "Mein Liebling" character girl,** marked "1174 - 58," weighted brown glass eyes, closed mouth, brown h.h. wig, jointed wood & composition body, wearing a cream dotted Swiss dress, later blue wool coat, short blue & white socks & white leather shoes, 22½" ............................................. **5,750.00**

**K (star) R bisque socket head girl,** marked "192 - 18," blue sleep eyes, feathered brows, original blond h.h. wig, open mouth w/outlined lips & four upper teeth, jointed composition body, redressed in dark brown & red plaid corduroy dress, rust silk bonnet, antique underclothing, socks & shoes, 28" (inherent dark speck left of mouth & side of face, minor firing lines, hands repainted & do not match, body wear & minor repair) ........................................... **1,400.00**

**Ken (Barbie's friend),** ca. 1964, painted brunette crew cut, pink lips, wearing red swim trunks, striped jacket & cork sandals w/red straps,

in box w/black wire stand & two blue cover booklets (some touch-ups, box discolored) ........................................ **70.00**

**Kestner (J.D.) bisque socket head baby,** marked "B made in Germany 6 - J.D.K. - 211," brown sleep eyes, feathered brows, original blond mohair wig, open-closed mouth w/accented lips, original plaster pate, composition bent-limb Kestner baby body, wearing an antique white long christening dress, underclothing & bonnet, 11" (touch-up on lower arms & one leg) ............................... **400.00**

**Kestner (J.D.) bisque character head boy,** marked "221," weighted brown 'googlie' eyes, smiling closed mouth, straight eyebrows, original brown mohair cropped wig over plaster pate, jointed wood & composition body, wearing original off-white side-button jacket & matching short pants, white belt w/large buckle, socks, silk shoes, wide-brimmed straw hat w/brown grosgrain ribbon, 11" (hands rubbed, one index finger gone) ................... **4,887.00**

**Kestner (J.D.) bisque socket head baby,** marked "F - made in Germany - 10,247 - J.D.K.," brown sleep eyes, feathered brows, painted upper & lower lashes, original brown mohair wig, open mouth w/two upper teeth & wobble tongue, bent-limb composition baby body w/original finish, wearing original long white baby dress, underclothing & lacy bonnet, 13" (tiny rub on left ear, discoloration in a few areas of the body) ............................................. **1,300.00**

**Kestner (J.D.) bisque socket head girl,** marked "6," set blue eyes, feathered brows, brown h.h. wig, open mouth w/accented lips & four upper teeth, jointed composition body w/straight wrists, wearing a fine antique white skirt, navy blue wool jacket, new socks, antique French-type shoes & a hat, 14½" (few kiln specks, wear on fingers) ................. **675.00**

**Kestner (J.D.) bisque head "Das Wunderkind" character girl,** w/four separate heads, first head marked "182," w/brown weighted eyes, closed mouth & original brown mohair wig, on a jointed composition body dressed in a floral-print cream gauze dress w/lace trim & pink ribbon trim, socks & shoes, the second head marked "179," w/blue weighted eyes, open-closed mouth w/molded tongue, original blond mohair wig, third head marked "183," w/blue weighted eyes, open closed mouth w/molded teeth, original blond mohair wig & fourth head marked "171," w/weighted blue eyes, open mouth w/upper teeth, all contained in original maroon paper-covered cardboard sectioned box w/lithographed label on the lid, ca. 1910, 14½" ................................. **12,650.00**

*Kestner "Bru-type" Doll*

**Kestner (J.D.) bisque head "Bru-type" doll,** incised "10" at rear head rim, full face w/weighted brown glass eyes, open/closed mouth w/molded & painted upper teeth, blond mohair wig over replaced pate, jointed wood & composition body w/straight wrists, appropriately redressed in pink & cream satin frock w/pink hair ribbons, cotton underwear, socks, old brown leather shoes, holding a tiny all bisque baby, German, ca. 1890, minor repairs & retouching to hands & body joints, 15" (ILLUS.).. **3,450.00**

**Kestner (J.D.) bisque head girl,** marked "F," set bluish grey threaded eyes, multi-stroke brows, closed mouth w/accent line between lips, original blond mohair wig, kid body w/bisque lower arms, gussets at elbows, hips & knees, wearing a pale peach taffeta dress, underclothing, socks, shoes & frilly bonnet, 16" (kid arms darker than body, some fingers chipped, body w/wear, patches & repairs) .............. **550.00**

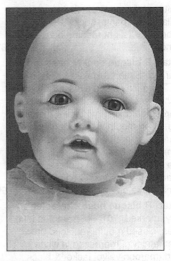

*Kestner "Hilda" Character Doll*

**Kestner (J.D.) bisque head "Hilda" character doll,** incised "Hilda - J D K Jr 1914 Ges Gesch N. 1010 Made in 16 Germany," fixed blue eyes, eye lids outlined w/black, dome head w/brushstroked hair, five-piece curved limb composition body, in simple white cotton gown, fingers & hands slightly worn, 20" (ILLUS.) ...................................... **4,312.00**

**Kley & Hahn bisque head toddler,** marked "Germany - K & H (in banner) - 525 - 6," solid dome bisque socket head w/blue intaglio eyes, feathered brows, lightly molded & brushed hair, open-closed mouth, quality jointed composition toddler body w/joints at elbows & knees, wearing a one-piece knit union suit, 15" (light rub each cheek, light touch-up on hands)............................................ **1,050.00**

**Kruse (Kathe) No. 1 girl,** marked "Kathe Kruse - 9245" on bottom of left foot, molded & painted head w/painted blue eyes w/radiating irises & white highlight, closed pouty mouth, painted brown hair w/three pate seams, cloth body jointed at shoulders & hips, wide hips, sewn-on thumbs, wearing rose dress, matching bonnet & shoes, one-piece underclothing, socks, 16" (overall light head wear, touch-up on face, dent in one cheek & at front hairline, light discoloration & aging on arms & legs)................................................ **1,900.00**

*Kathe Kruse Doll*

**Kruse (Kathe) cloth doll,** painted
brown eyes & hair, jointed body
w/wide hips, head composed of five
sections, legs of five sections, hands
w/separately stitched thumbs,
wearing original blue cotton short-
sleeved dress w/matching cap,
socks & underwear, foot stamped
"Kathe Kruse" & "R.H. Macy,"
German, ca. 1920, small scratch
through paint surface on left cheek,
slight rubbing on face & end of nose,
16½" (ILLUS.) ................................ **1,610.00**

**Lenci girl,** pressed felt swivel head,
painted blue side-glancing eyes,
single stroke brows, blond mohair
wig, closed mouth, cloth torso w/felt
arms & legs, tag on skirt reads
"Lenci - Made in Italy," wearing
original felt outfit w/shawl & apron,
felt hat, underclothing, socks &
leather shoes, 17" .......................... **1,050.00**

**Lenci baseball player boy,** molded
felt face w/brown side glancing eyes,
medium brown inserted hair,
wearing a bright pink felt shirt, beige
short pants, knitted socks, brown
leather shoes, beige cap w/blue
brim, complete w/baseball hat
w/leather-bound grip, leather
catcher's mitt, late 1920s 17½"
(some minor damage on clothes) .. **3,450.00**

**Lori bisque head baby,** marked "D -
Lori - 2 - Geschutzt - S & Co. -
Germany," solid dome bisque socket
head w/blue sleep eyes, feathered
brows, painted upper & lower

lashes, lightly molded & painted hair,
open-closed mouth, jointed wood &
composition Kestner baby body,
wearing an antique white shirt
w/large embroidered collar, brown
corduroy pants, reddish orange
corduroy coat, socks & shoes,
23" ................................................ **1,600.00**

*Marthe Chase "Little Nell"*

**Martha Chase "Little Nell" painted
fabric doll,** blue painted eyes,
applied ears, brown painted hair in
double bun at the back, painted
fabric body, wearing underwear,
original printed wool skirt, muslin
blouse, white apron, wool cape,
ca. 1930, 15½" (ILLUS.) ............... **1,610.00**

**Midge (Barbie's freind),** ca. 1964,
blond, pink lips, finger paint, toe
paint, wearing 'Orange Blossom'
outfit, includes yellow sheath dress
w/lace overskirt, white nylon long
gloves & white mules (dress is
slightly soiled) ................................... **50.00**

**Orsini bisque head baby,** marked
"Copr. by J.J. Orsini - Germany,"
painted flange head w/blue sleep
eyes w/real lashes, feathered brows,
original brown mohair wig, open
smiling mouth w/two upper teeth &
wobble tongue, heavy cloth baby
body w/composition lower arms,
wearing original pink lace-trimmed
dress, matching bonnet,
underclothing, socks & black shoes,
24" (light lip wear, lower arms
flaking, body soiled) ......................... **800.00**

**Papier-mâché "Motschmann Baby,"**
Japanese crying baby-type doll
w/dark pupilless glass eyes, closed
mouth, dome head, papier-mâché
body w/fabric jointing, stomach
w/bellows squeeker (inoperative), in
old white cotton baby gown
w/pintuck & lace insert detailing,
short sleeves, Germany, ca. 1860,
27" (repainting on head & body, one
foot detached).................................. **575.00**

**Papier-mâché shoulder doll,** blue
painted eyes, hair molded into puff
of short curls to either side of face &
three central puffs on crown
composed of small braids,
replacement leather body w/carved
lower arms, in old brown printed
dress, German, ca. 1840s, 21" h.
(piece missing from back shoulder,
tip of nose chipped, spots of wear on
hair, surface rubbed) ........................ **977.00**

**Papier-mâché shoulder head lady,**
painted blue eyes, black hair molded
w/a triangular puff over each ear &
concave bun at top of head, fabric-
covered wood torso, fabric arms,
painted wood lower arms, jointed
wood legs w/painted dark blue ankle
boots, unclothed, Germany, ca.
1830s, 22" (some restoration to left
side of shoulder plate, retouching on
side of face, some surface cracking
on shoulder plate).......................... **2,875.00**

**Ravca (Bernard) Rabbi doll,** needle
sculpture stockinet head, deep set
painted eyes, painted brows, closed
mouth, original mohair hair & long
beard, excelsior over wire armature
body, needle sculptured stockinet
hands, wearing original grey pants,
white shirt, long black coat, brown
socks, black velvet cap & holding a
purple satin "Story of Esther" scroll,
signature card & "made in France"
label on coat, seated on a chair
which is stamped twice "Made in
France," 18" (several tiny holes,
some shelf dust & fading to coat) ..... **225.00**

**Schmidt (Bruno) bisque head**
"Wendy" character girl, marked
"2033 BSW (in heart)," weighted
brown eyes, closed mouth, brown
mohair wig, jointed wood &
composition body, wearing cotton
underwear & floral printed dress,
socks, pink shoes & a straw hat, 11"
(old hairline in forehead, hands
flaking & poor) .............................. **3,450.00**

**Schoenau & Hoffmeister bisque
socket head girl,** marked "7 -
Germany - S - PB (in star) H - 9,"
blue sleep eyes, molded & feathered
brows, blond mohair wig, open
mouth w/accented lips & four upper
teeth, jointed wood & composition
body, wearing a pink dotted Swiss
jumper, white blouse, underclothing,
pink socks & new shoes
w/deteriorated antique shoes
accompanying, 25" (head sits high in
neck socket, tiny fleck on upper left
eye, firing line from crown in back to
hole to tie eye weights, some small
repairs) ........................................... **220.00**

**Schoenhut girl,** carved wood
w/painted brown eyes, closed mouth,
light brown mohair bobbed wig,
spring-jointed wood body w/stocking
groove at thigh, wearing an old white
gauze dress, underwear, white hose
& white leather shoes, ca. 1915,
18½" (areas of flaking paint,
retouching on face, one thumb
repaired, repairs to dress) ................ **575.00**

**S.F.B.J. (Société Francaise de
Fabrication de Bebes & Jouets)
bisque head girl,** marked "3," fixed
blue eyes, open mouth w/teeth,
pierced ears, original brown mohair
wig, jointed wood & composition
body, wearing factory cotton
chemise, old socks & blue leather
shoes size 3 w/bee mark, 12".......... **805.00**

**S.F.B.J. character toddler boy,**
marked "#227," blue paperweight
eyes, smiling mouth showing teeth &
applied brown flocked hair on jointed
composition body, dressed in blue
cape over red & white checked
pleated dress w/matching hat,
wearing brown stockings & black
shoes, 14"..................................... **1,600.00**

**S.F.B.J. bisque head character
baby,** marked "X - S.F.B.J. - 236,"
dark brown pupilless sleep eyes,
feathered brows, brown h.h. wig,
open-closed smiling mouth w/two
upper teeth, composition bent-limb
baby body, wearing a fine antique
white lace-trimmed baby dress,
underclothing & booties, 24" (chip &
hairline from crown on back of head,
few small specks in bisque, repaint
on lower legs, touch-up on hands) ... **850.00**

**Shirley Temple,** marked "Shirley
Temple" on head & "13" on back,
composition head w/hazel sleep

eyes w/real lashes, feathered brows, original blond mohair wig, open mouth w/six teeth, five-piece composition child body, wearing original tagged pink organdy dress, original underclothing, socks & shoes, 13" (missing hair ribbon, light wear to lips, chip off left big toe, small holes in dress) .......................... **675.00**

**Shirley Temple,** composition, original wig, dress, underclothes, socks & shoes, ca. 1930s, 18" ....................... **495.00**

**Simon & Halbig bisque head girl,** marked "979," fixed blue eyes, open mouth w/upper teeth, pierced ears, dimpled chin, replaced red wig, jointed wood & composition body w/straight wrists, redressed in old cream silk gown, underwear & matching bonnet, 9" .......................... **920.00**

**Simon & Halbig bisque socket head girl,** marked "S&H 1279 - DEP.-Germany - 3½," blue sleep eyes, molded & feathered brows, dimples in cheeks & chin, brown h.h. wig, pierced ears, open mouth w/triangular accent on lower lip, jointed wood & composition French body, wearing an antique white lace-trimmed dress, underclothing, socks & lace-up boots, 13" (small flake at left earring hole, flaking on torso & hands)............................................. **1,500.00**

**Simon & Halbig bisque socket head Oriental lady,** marked "Simon & Halbig - Germany - 1329 - 4," head w/olive skin tone, brown sleepy eyes, lightly molded & feathered brows, original black mohair wig, open mouth w/four upper teeth, jointed wood & composition body w/yellowish tint, wearing elaborate sewn-on Japanese kimono outfit, 17" (rather large flake at front of neck opening, tiny firing line at edge of left rim, wig pulls & color wear around wig) ................................................. **1,200.00**

**Simon & Halbig bisque head character girl,** incised "IV," weighted blue glass eyes, closed mouth w/full lips pierced ears, replaced light brown real hair wig, jointed wood & composition body in white embroidery dress & underwear, straw hat, German, ca. 1910, kiln spots on face, 18" (ILLUS. top next column)............. **19,550.00**

*Simon & Halbig Character Girl*

**Simon & Halbig bisque socket head girl,** marked "S 9 H 1009 - DEP - St.," brown bisque head w/brown paperweight eyes, heavy feathered brows, pierced ears, black h.h. wig, open mouth w/four upper teeth, jointed wood & composition French body w/jointed wrists & marked w/an Eiffel Tower mark & "Paris Bebe - Depose" on the back, wearing an antique red wool dress, underclothing, socks & shoes, 19" (couple minor firing cracks inside edge of crown, minor firing line behind left ear, lips touched-up) .... **2,100.00**

**Simon & Halbig bisque head girl,** marked "S & H 1279 - DEP - Germany - 14½," blue sleep eyes w/molded & feathered brows, pierced ears, dimples in cheeks & chin, brown wig, open mouth w/accented lips & four upper teeth, jointed wood & composition body, wearing an antique white dress, underclothing, socks & shoes, 33" (minor flakes at earring holes, very fine line on front of crown, hands well repainted, some body touch-up) ...................................... **3,100.00**

**Steiner Figure C bisque head boy,** incised "Sie C 2/0," fixed bright blue spiraled eyes, delicately painted closed mouth, pierced applied ears, goatskin wig, jointed wood & composition body w/straight wrists bearing blue stamped caduceus

*Steiner Bisque Figure C Doll*

mark & initials "J St," wearing old blue wool sailor suit w/corded trim, cotton chemise, blue socks, original brown leather shoes marked "EC" & "00," sailor cap reading "Sans Succi" on band & bearing "Au Nain Bleu" sticker inside, 12" (ILLUS.) ............ **5,750.00**

**Steiner poured bisque head girl,** marked "J. Steiner, Bte. S G D G Paris Fi re A 6," blue fixed paperweight eyes, closed mouth pierced ears, remains of original skin wig, replaced blond mohair ringletted wig, jointed wood & composition body w/Steiner label on back & straight legs, redressed in aqua silk gown w/cream lace trim & edge piping, matching hat, cotton underwear, socks & old brown leather shoes, approximately 13" .. **3,162.00**

**Steiner pressed bisque head girl,** marked "Steiner Bte. S. G.D.G. Bourgoin" & incised "Ste C 1," pale round face w/fixed light blue eyes w/pink eyeshadow, closed mouth, pierced ears, blond h.h. wig over cork pate, jointed wood & composition body w/straight wrists, wearing a corded cotton white dress w/button front closing, underwear, old cream satin hat w/lace & ribbon trim, old blue shoes marked w/size number 3, 16" (kiln flecks on cheeks, shoes poor)...................**3,737.00**

**Steiner Figure C bisque socket head girl,** marked "Figure C No. 2 - J. Steiner Bte. S.G.D.G. - Paris," blue paperweight eyes, feathered brows, mauve blush over eyes, pierced ears, original purple pate w/brown h.h. wig, closed mouth w/accented lips, jointed composition body w/jointed wrists marked "Le Petit Parisian - J. St. Bte. S.G.D.G. - J.B. Succr Paris" on left hip, wearing a pale blue dress trimmed w/embroidery & lace, blue velvet coat, underclothing, socks & white high-button boots, 19" (¼" firing line at crown) ....................................... **6,000.00**

**Steiner Figure A bisque head girl,** marked "J.Steiner - Bte. S.G.D.G. - Paris - FRE A 17" socket head w/deep blue paperweight eyes, feathered brows, pierced ears, brown h.h. wig, closed mouth, stamped " Le Petit Parisian, Bebe Steiner" on left hip, jointed composition body w/straight wrists, wearing possibly original flower print factory dress, underclothing, socks, high lace shoes & a ribbon-trimmed straw bonnet labeled "Cibus, 20 Rue Vivienne," 25" (tiny pinpoint fleck on lower left eye, lower arms repainted, some wear)...................................**5,300.00**

**Swaine & Co. bisque head character baby,** marked "D.V 4," weighted blue glass eyes, closed mouth, dome head w/painted hair, curved-limb composition baby body, 13½" (body surface rubbed in places)............................................**920.00**

**Terri Lee girl,** marked "Terri Lee" on head & back, hard plastic head w/painted large brown eyes, painted upper & lower lashes, closed mouth, original synthetic blond wig, five-piece hard plastic body, wearing probably original gold lamé skating outfit w/fur trim, ice skates trimmed w/gold bells & replaced gold hat, 16" (snaps on outfit resewn, cheek color pale) .................................................**175.00**

**Volland (P.F.) Co. Raggedy Ann,** cloth doll w/painted face w/linear smiling mouth, lower lashes indicated w/black dots, black button eyes, triangle nose, brown yarn hair, legs finishing in black cloth shoes, integral red & white horizontally striped knee-high hose, in old cream

*Volland Raggedy Ann Doll*

orange printed cotton dress, white apron, Volland, ca. 1920, wear & repair at eyes, seam repairs at other areas of body, costume frail 36" h (ILLUS.) ........................................ **2,875.00**

**Wax over Papier-mâché head girl,** domed head w/thin coating of wax, pupilless dark glass set eyes, rouged cheeks, nailed-on dark brown h.h. wig, open mouth w/upper & lower bamboo teeth, kid leather body w/separately stitched fingers, hip gussets, wearing a white cotton dress w/printed red flowers, cotton underwear, cream hose & old straw slippers, France, ca. 1840, 21" (costume frail, retouching at eyebrow & mouth) ........................... **575.00**

**Wright (R. John) "Patrick" w/bear,** marked "R. John Wright - Patrick - Little Friends - No. 089/250 - R. John Wright Dolls Inc. - Cambridge, N.Y." on clothing tag, pressed felt swivel head w/painted brown eyes, single stroke brows, original curly mohair wig, closed mouth, five-piece felt body jointed at shoulders & hips, wearing tagged plaid shirt, bib overalls w/"RJW" buttons, wool socks, leather shoes & holding original small felt jointed bear, in original box w/Limited Edition certificate, 18" .................................. **775.00**

**Zeller (Fawn) bisque shoulder head "Jackie Kennedy"** marked "Jackie Kennedy - By Fawn Zeller 1965," painted brown eyes, feathered brows, molded & painted brown hair,

closed mouth, cloth body w/graceful bisque lower arms & lower legs, wearing original peach taffeta long dress, underclothing, matching slippers & short fur jacket, 17½" ....... **500.00**

# DOORSTOPS

*All doorstop listed are flat-back cast-iron unless otherwise noted. Most names are taken from* Doortops—Identification & Values, *by Jaenne Bertoia (Collector Books, 1985)*

**Amish man,** bearded man w/green shirt, black hat, vest & pants, standing on brown base, purple shirt variation, 3¾ x 8½" ........................ **$175.00**

**Amish woman,** wearing green blouse, mate to Amish man ............. **175.00**

**Dog,** French Bulldog, full figure, original black & white paint, Hubley, National Foundry & others, 6¾ x 7⅝" (some touch up) ................................. **55.00**

**Girl with Bonnet,** young girl w/short dress & pentalets, holding wide-brimmed bonnet by her side, oval base, 5¼" w., 8" h. (blue dress variation) ....................................... **1,100.00**

**Rabbit with Top Hat,** dapper animal wearing top hat, vest & tailcoat, on mound base, Albany Foundry, worn, 4¾" w., 9⅞" h. (brown rabbit variation) ........................................... **204.00**

**Windmill,** marked "10 Cape Cod," National Foundry, 6⅞" w., 6¾" h. ...... **150.00**

# DRUGSTORE & PHARMACY ITEMS

*The old-time corner drugstore, once a familiar part of every American town, has now given way to the modern, efficient pharmacy. With the steamlining and modernization of this trade many of the early tools and store adjuncts have become outdated and now fall into the realm of "collectibles." Listed here are a variety of tools, bottles, display pieces and other ephemera once closely associated with the druggist's trade. Also see: SIGNS & SIGNBOARDS*

*Druggist Advertisement*

**Advertisement,** hardboard, two
embossed apothecary jars flanking
"Your Druggust is more than a
merchant - He is trained by profession
to guard the health of your family all
hours of the day and night. Protect the
welfare of your druggist...Buy all drug
products at your drugstore.," in white
& gold letering, dedicated by Johnson
& Johnson Backplasters, minor
soiling, 12½" h., 20½" w. (ILLUS.) ....... **$83.00**

**Apothecary bottle,** opium, ribbed
cylindrical body w/smooth base &
tooled lip, original glass stopper,
cobalt blue w/white & orange enamel
reading "Tinct. - Opii - Poison,"
English, ca. 1890-1910, 5⅝" ............. **275.00**

**Apothecary bottle,** cylindrical body
w/scarred base & flared lip, original
blown & ground stopper, clear glass
w/white, black & gold label reading
"Dentifrice," English, ca. 1890-1910,
8⅝" h. ................................................. **231.00**

**Apothecary bottle,** cylindrical body
w/smooth base & polished & ground
lip, original internal ground glass
spout & lid which fits over outside of
lip rather than inside, amber w/white,
black, red & gold label under glass
reading "Tinct. - Chl. Et Morph - '85
Poison'," English, ca. 1880-1910,
8⅝" ..................................................... **275.00**

**Apothecary bottles,** cased, eight
glass bottles w/scales & weights,
w/mahogany case, England,
ca. 1840, the set (ILLUS. top next
column) ............................................... **319.00**

**Cabinet,** label dispensing, oak,
dispensed sixty different labels, label
reads "Rohrer Brug Store, Clyde,
Ohio," American, ca. 1915-1925,
8 x 23", 19½" h. ............................... **385.00**

*Cased Apothecary Bottles*

# FABERGÉ

*Carl Fabergé (1846-1920) was goldsmith
and jewler to the Russian Imperial Court and
his creations are recorginzed as the finest of
their kind. He made a number of enamel
fantasies, including Easter eggs, for the
Imperial family and utilized precious metals
and jewels in other work.*

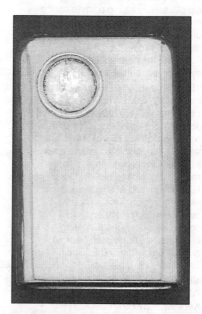

*Silver Fabergé Cigarette Case*

**Beaker,** silver & enamel, enameled translucent salmon over a guiloché gound, w/molded lip, marked w/initials of Workmaster Anders Nevalainen, "K. Fabergé" in Cyrillic w/Imperial warrant & 88 standard, 2" h. .......................................... **$2,587.00**

**Brooch,** gold & jeweled, in the form of a wheel, the border set w/diamonds, the central diamond surrounded by rubies, marked w/initials of Workmaster August Hollmig & 56 standard, St. Petersburg, Russia, ca. 1900 ...................................... **4,600.00**

**Cigarette case,** silver, open at one end, set w/silver coin of 1784, marked w/initials of Workmaster Anders Nevalainen, "Fabergé" in Cyrillic & 88 standard, 3" l. (ILLUS. bottom previous page) ............................... **1,955.00**

**Cigarette case,** silver & enamel, enameled translucent royal blue over guilloché ground, cover mounted w/a gold coin of the reign of Tsarina Elizabeth, bordered by diamonds, w/diamond set thumbpiece, ca. 1900, marked w/initials of Workmaster August Hollmig & 88 standard, 3¾" l. ........ **5,750.00**

**Kovsh,** silver & shaded enamel, the front enameled *en plain* w/a sumptuosly attired couple, the surround enameled w/stylized foliate & vegetable forms in subdued tones of blue & green, marked "K. Fabergé" in Cyrillic w/Imperial warrant & 88 standard, 4¾" l. ........................ **8,625.00**

**Match striker,** gold, in the form of a miniature book w/matted finish, one side w/striking surface, the flint holder w/cabochon sapphire finial, marked w/Cyrillic initials "K.F." & 56 standard, Moscow, ca. 1910, 1¾" h. .............. **1,380.00**

**Model of a mouse,** amethystine, carved in crouching position, the eyes set w/red stone cabochons, the long tail curved over its back, ca. 1900, 1¼" l. ............................. **1,955.00**

**Pendant,** enamel & gold, egg-shaped, enameled translucent purple over a guilloché ground & applied w/a cap of gold scrolls, marked w/Cyrillic initials of Workmaster Michael Perchin & 56 standard, St. Petersburg, ca. 1900, ½" l. ................................................ **3,450.00**

**Pendant,** rock crystal, gold enamel & jeweled, egg shaped, the frosted rock crystal egg decorated w/roundels enameled translucent red, green, yellow & blue, each roundel centered by a diamond, marked w/initials of Workmaster Henrik Wigstrom, St. Petersburg, ca. 1900, ⅝" h. ............................. **5,175.00**

# FIREARMS

**Pistol,** flintlock, brass capped butt & trigger gaurd, band marked "I.F." w/"GR" proofmarks, Vrenon, England, ca. 18th c., imperfections, 19¼" l. (ILLUS. top right, below).. **$1,840.00**

**Pistol,** flintlock, brass capped butt & trigger guard, w/swivel ramroad, "V" & "CP" proofmarks, England, ca. 19th c., imperfections, 15¾" l. (ILLUS. bottom right, below) ............ **345.00**

**Pistols,** brass capped butts & trigger guards, marked "W Ketland" w/London proofmarks, W. Ketland, England, ca. 1800, imerfections, 13½" l, pr. (ILLUS. top & bottom left, below) .................................... **1,265.00**

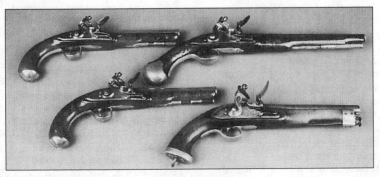

*Grouping of Pistols*

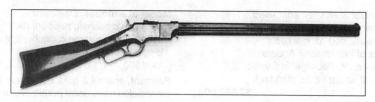

*Canadian Henry Rifle*

**Pistols,** dueling, engraved trigger
guards, tangs & lock plates,
octagonal barrels, in original fitted
case w/powder can, indistinct paper
lael on interior of case, W. Parker,
holborn, London, ca. 1800, 15½" l.
(imperfections) .............................. **2,760.00**

*Paris Exposition Dueling Pistols*

**Pistols,** dueling, engraved, made
exclusively for 1849 Paris Industrial
Exposition, w/case, case 10 x 18½",
pr. (ILLUS.) .................................. **16,500.00**

**Revolver,** Colt Navy Model 1815, Civil
War era ............................................ **825.00**

**Rifle,** factory engraved w/elaborate
scrolls, Henry, No. 2295, rear sight
missing (ILLUS. of engraving, top next
column) ....................................... **18,700.00**

**Rifle,** Henry, no. 467, marked "Robt.
S. Denee - Bath - C.W.," Center West
Ontario, Canada (ILLUS. top) ......... **24,200.00**

**Rifle,** Kentucky half-stock, percussion
lock, curly maple stock w/brass
patch box & silver inlays, left-
handles, barrel 36" l., overall 52" l. .... **248.00**

**Rifle,** Kentucky half-stock, percussion
lock, maple stocks w/painted 'curl,'
barrel 35" l., overall 51½" l. (some
damage) .......................................... **220.00**

**Rifle,** Kentucky half-stock, percussion
lock, walnut stock w/brass patch
box, 34½ l., barrel, overall 48½" l. ..... **385.00**

*Engraving on No. 2295 Rifle*

**Rifle,** maple, the stock carved w/the
letter "V," the iron lock fitted w/a
leather cover, mid 19th c., 58½" l. .... **575.00**

**Shotgun,** w/deluxe walnut stocks,
marked "M.1853," Sharps,
no. 10671 ...................................... **5,775.00**

**Shotgun,** w/deluxe walnut stocks,
marked "M.1853," Sharps,
no. 93411 ....................................... **7,700.00**

# FIREPLACE &
# HEARTH ITEMS

**Andirons,** cast iron, cast in the half-
round bull dogs w/amber glass eyes,
impressed "3008," 20th c., 17¼",
pr. ................................................ **$1,840.00**

**Andirons,** cast iron, cast in the half-
round cats w/green glass eyes,
20th c., 16", pr. (ILLUS. top next
page) ............................................... **402.00**

**Andirons,** cast iron, each cast in the
half round w/the head of a satyr
w/pierced eyes & mouth, on two
scrolled legs & hooved feet, painted
black heightened w/gilt, 20th c.,
11⅜" h., pr. .................................... **1,035.00**

**Andirons,** cast iron, full-bodied owls
sitting atop two curled snakes on
rectangular base, pr. (ILLUS. bottom
next page) ..................................... **3,300.00**

**Andirons,** cast iron, molded in the
half-round dolphins, one marked
"B&H," 20th c., 14¼", pr. .................. **862.00**

*Cast-iron Cat Andirons*

*Cast-iron Owls Andirons*

**Andirons,** cast iron, sunflowers, each surmounted by a sunburst centering a smiling face, the serpentine support below raised on shaped feet, ca. 1880, 16½" h., 9½" l., pr. ...................................... **3,335.00**

**Andirons,** Chippendale, brass & wrought iron, each having an urn finial above a tapered columnar standard decorated w/simulated rope, the lower section fluted, the plinth base below decorated w/a stylised flowerhead, the skirt decorated w/swags & bellflowers, on spurred arch supports ending in claw-and-ball feet, attributed to Daniel King, Philadelphia, Pennsylvania, last quarter 18th c., 15½" l., 26½" h., pr. (log supports reduced) ................... **5,750.00**

**Bellows,** turtle-back-type, red paint w/basket of flowers in multicolored gilt & black, brass nozzle, 18" l. (releathered, some wear) ................ **275.00**

*Pine & Mahogany Fire Box*

**Fire box,** carved & painted pine & mahogany, the open square form w/turned columnar supports & turned finials decorated w/incised hearts & tulips on a blue painted ground, the back w/a swan's neck cresting incised w/the date "1861," the whole raised on turned feet, Pennsylvania or Virginia, cover missing, 7¼ x 7⅜", 3½" h. (ILLUS.) .............................. **1,610.00**

**Fireplace set,** cast brass & steel, Federal style, the andirons w/turned finials above faceted top and ball-form support w/a hexagonal standard below on a circular plinth & spurred arched legs ending in slipper feet w/matching miniature leg stops behind, the tools comprising a shovel & tongs w/faceted & ball-form handles above continuing to steel implements, attributed to John Molineux, Boston, Massachusetts, ca. 1800, andirons 21", the set ...... **4,600.00**

**Trivet,** brass & wrought iron, the projecting columnar handle attached to a shield-shaped platform, pierced & decorated w/a blacksmith anvil, forging hammers & a horseshoe, the projecting hook support w/a medial attachment decorated w/a kettle teapot, probably Maryland or Virginia, first quarter 19th c., 17½" l. ................. **747.00**

# FISHING COLLECTIBLES

## BOOKS & PAPER ITEMS

**Book,** "Fly Tying," by Wm, Sturgis, 1940, on color illus., Scribner .......... **$20.00**

**Book,** "North American Game Fishes," by F. LaMonte, 1945, many color plates, Doubleday .................... **15.00**

*Shakespeare Revolution Bait Box*

**Box,** marked "Shakespeare Revolution
Bait - For Large and Small Mouth
Bass this Bait is almost a Sure Thing
- Pat. Feb. 5 1901-April 9, 1901 -
Made By William Shakespeare Jr.
Kalamazoo, Michigan," empty
(ILLUS.) ............................................ **522.00**

## LURES

*Millers "Reversible" minnow*

*Winchester Wooden Five-Hook Minnow*

**Florida Shiner Bait Co. "The Florida
Shiner,"** wood, handmade,
w/original box.................................... **825.00**
**Millers "Reversible,"** minnow,
wooden, ca. 1913 (ILLUS. middle).. **3,630.00**
**South Bend "Truck-Oreno,"**
w/wooden prop at front, ca. 1939 ..... **908.00**
**Wagtail Wobbler,** baby size ............ **1,100.00**
**Wagtail Wobbler,** fat body ................ **575.00**
**Winchester "Bait Minnow,"** wood,
five-hook, in original box marked
"Winchester - Bait - Minnow"
w/graphic of fish being caught,
1920s (ILLUS. bottom) ................ **1,815.00**

## REELS

*Two A.L. Walker Reels*

**A.L. Walker,** trout-type, TR-2 (ILLUS.
right) ................................................ **840.00**
**A.L. Walker,** trout-type, TR-3 (ILLUS.
left)................................................... **715.00**
**B.F. Meek,** bait casting-type, German
silver, size No. 8 (ILLUS. below) ... **3,190.00**
**Edward Vom Hoffe,** "Perfection" trout
type, size No. 1 ............................. **4,400.00**
**Edward Vom Hoffe,** "Restigouche,"
salmon-type, w/original box .......... **1,650.00**
**George Gates,** trout-type, patent,
ca. 1885...................................... **1,980.00**
**Hardy Bougle,** trout-type, England.. **3,245.00**

*B.F. Meek Reel*

*Heddon No. 4-15 Reel*

**Heddon,** bait casting-type, No. 4-15
(ILLUS.) ........................................ **1,430.00**
**Heddon,** "Pal," No. P-41 ...................... **65.00**
**Heddon,** "Winona" ............................... **95.00**

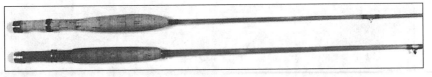

*Payne Bamboo Trout Rods*

*Two Turtle Creels*

**Kovalovsky,** big game-type,
saltwater, Hollywood California ..... **1,155.00**

**Meek & Milam,** casting-type, brass,
No. 1 ............................................. **3,080.00**

**Ustonson & Peters,** brass, London,
ca. 1850, rare ............................... **3,520.00**

## RODS

**Payne,** trout rod, bamboo, 6'
(ILLUS. top, top of page).............. **4,400.00**

**Payne,** trout rod, bamboo, 7½'
(ILLUS. bottom, top of page) ......... **2,970.00**

**Payne,** trout rod, model No. 96, 6' ... **5,060.00**

**Payne,** trout rod, parabolic model,
7' 1"............................................... **5,060.00**

## MISCELLANEOUS

**Bait trap,** "McSwain Jr Roaches
Minnow Bait Trap" (embossed),
cylindrical glass jar w/flat side
w/eight molded feet & funnel-like
opening, wire bail handle, ground
mouth w/zinc cap, smooth base,
1880-1900, greenish aqua, 12¼" h.
(two body fissures near the base) ...... **99.00**

**Creel,** Adirondack ........................... **1,100.00**

**Creel,** splint rattan body, w/unusual lid
design ............................................... **800.00**

**Creel,** split rattan body Turtle
trademark (ILLUS. middle left)....... **1,485.00**

**Creel,** split rattan body w/leather
covering corners & around trim,
turtle trademark (ILLUS. middle
right) ............................................. **1,430.00**

**Painting,** oil, a swirling fly hooked
salmon, by W. M. Brackett, ca. 1901,
20 x 32" (ILLUS. below)................. **2,420.00**

*Painting by W.M. Brackett*

# FRAKTUR

*Fraktur paintings are decorative birth and marriage certificates of the 18th and 19th centuries and also include family registers and similar documents. Illuminated family documents, birth and baptismal certificates, religious texts and rewards of merit, in a particular style, are known as "fraktur" because of the similarity to the 16th century type-face of that name. Gay watercolor borders, frequently incorporating stylized birds, hand-lettered documents, which were executed by local ministers, school masters or itinerant penman. Most are of Pennsylvania Dutch origin.*

*Pennsylvania Vorschrift*

**Baptismal certificate,** for Jacob Hubler, pen & ink & watercolor on paper, four red, yellow & green parrots, each in one corner surrounded by checkerboard tulips, all surrounding orange outlined inscription in German, by Daniel Otto, Center County, Pennsylvania, dated 1817, 13½ x 16".................. **$8,625.00**

**Birth announcement,** for Johannes Lentzen, pen & ink & watercolor on paper, two orange turreted castles each above two orange & blue birds & two tulips, centered by rectangle containing German inscription above four tulips surrounding American Eagle in cirlce, dated 1778, 12 x 15"............................ **11,500.00**

**Birth announcement,** for Micheal Gabriel, pen & ink & watercolor on paper, simple reddish brown border surrounding large tulip blossom surrounded by star-shaped blossoms w/leaf & flower vines all growing out of heart inscribed "Micheal Gabriel was born the 27th of September 1814," all done in shades of reddish brown, yellow, blue, green & dark green, backed w/a penmanship exercise signed "Jacob Stoner," 4⅜ x 6⅝" (ILLUS. bottom)................................ **2,300.00**

*Birth Announcement*

**Birth announcement,** for Salome Larhmann, pen & ink & watercolor on paper, simple red & yellow outlined heart flanked by tulips & two birds all done in red, yellow & green, inscription inside heart, in German, dated 1795, 8 x 13"....................... **2,300.00**

**Birth announcement,** pen & ink & watercolor paper, for Maria Magdelena Moll, blue pots w/yellow handles in the lower corners flanking stylized flowers, vines w/red & yellow stylized flowers & pomegranates growing out of the tops on the pots, all surrounding German text, by Arnold Hoevelmann, dated 1761, 12½ x 16"............................................ **920.00**

**Birth & baptismal certificate,** for Johannes Zöller, pen & ink & watercolor, decortaed w/blue winged flying angels, stylized birds & flowering vines, all surrounding German inscription, Cocalico Township, Lancaster, Pennsylvania, American school, dated 1788, 12½ x 15¼"...................................... **668.00**

**Vorschrift,** pen & ink & watercolor on paper, red, yellow & green strapwork lettering enclosing a lady smelling a flower above German inscription flanked by stylized tulips, American school, probably from Bucks or Montgomery County, Pennsylvania, 8¼ x 13½".................................... **6,900.00**

**Vorschrift,** pen & ink & watercolor on paper, simple green border surrounding stylized flowers flanking scrolls, strapwork lettering reading "Ich Kome Dann," above German inscription surrounded by dark green rectangle above inscription of alphabet, American school, dated 1803, 8¼ x 13" (ILLUS. top previous page) ........................................... **1,955.00**

# FRATERNAL ORDER COLLECTIBLES

*Also see: BARBERIANA*

**Eastern Star fan,** folding-type, celluloid, 1916.................................. **$60.00**

**Eastern Star spoons,** sterling silver, pr. ....................................................... **47.00**

**Fraternal Order of the Eagles badge,** enameled, red, white & blue, San Jose, 3 pcs. .............................. **25.00**

**G.A.R. (Grand Army of the Republic) medal,** brass, from 28 camp, September 1894, Pittsburgh, Pennsylvania, two-piece .................... **23.00**

**G.A.R. program,** 1895, 29th encampment..................................... **85.00**

*Knights of Columbus Chapter Sword*

**G.A.R. program,** 1895, Louisville Encampment w/full page Schlitz......... **75.00**

**G.A.R. program,** Military & Civil War Program, Boston, Massachusetts, 1873.................................................... **33.00**

**Knights of Columbus Texas chapter sword,** w/belt, buckle, decorative trim, name engraved on blade, E. A. Armstrong Mfg., Chicago (ILLUS. above)............................................... **250.00**

**Masonic ashtray,** brass, emblem in center, eye, hammer, trowel, 5½" d.... **76.00**

**Masonic ashtray,** ornate brass, "Damascus Temple, Rochester, N.Y.".. **15.00**

**Masonic book,** "Encyclopedia of Freemasonry," 1921, two vols. ........... **45.00**

**Masonic pin,** ornate, large w/purple ribbon, man in the moon carved moonstone, ca. 1905 ...................... **125.00**

**Odd Fellows parade axe,** paint decorated wood, America, ca. 19th c., 10¼" w., 33" h. (minor imperfections) ................................. **862.00**

**Shrine champagne,** pressed glass, "1909 Louisville, Ky. Pittsburg, PA," gold & silver swords on side of stem, gold & amber leaves on base .......... **135.00**

**Shrine champagne,** pressed glass, "New Orleans - Syria," alligator on each side, 1910, 4½" h. .................... **135.00**

# FRUIT JARS

**BBGM Co (monogram),** Ball Bro's Glass Mfg. Co. Buffalo N.Y. insert, ground mouth w/milk glass insert & zinc band, smooth base, 1870-90, aqua, ½ pt. (midget) ...................... **$523.00**

**BBGM Co (monogram),** Ball Bro's. Glass Mfg. Co. Buffalo N.Y. insert, ground mouth w/metal band & milk glass insert, smooth base, 1870-90, cylindrical, golden amber, qt. (spur on large "C") ................................. **4,675.00**

**Buckeye 1,** cylindrical ground mouth w/colorless glass lid, smooth base, 1860-80, aqua, qt. (iron clamp missing) ............................................. **55.00**

**Burns Mf'g Co. -** Limt - North East, Pa - Patd. Nov. 27th 83 - Patd. June 29th 1884 (inscription embossed on five lines), ground mouth w/colorless glass lid, smooth base,1880-1900, aqua, qt. (no wire bail, where wire bail connected on either side of mouth one of insert holes is broken through w/small adjacent bruise) ...... **495.00**

**Chief (The),** ground mouth w/original tin lid, smooth base, 1870-80, aqua, ½ gal. ...................................... **300.00**

**Cohansey Glass Mfg. Co. Pat. Feb 12 1867,** base embossed, ground mouth w/metal lid & soldered wire clamp, smooth base, 1860-80, aqua, pt. ......................................... **55.00**

**Dandy (The),** ribbed shoulder, clear, pt. ......................................... **55.00**

**Dandy (The),** ribbed shoulder, clear turning to amethyst, ½ pt. (some inside stain) ...................................... **45.00**

**Dexter (surrounded by fruit),** cylindrical, ground mouth w/glass lid & zinc band, smooth base, 1860-80, aqua, qt. (lid has ¼" chip, metal band is damaged) ............................. **33.00**

**Free-blown fruit jar,** cylindrical, applied wax sealer mouth, possibly Lockport Glass Works, pontil scar, 1850-60, blue w/faint amber striation in the neck, approximately 2 qt., 10" h. ........................................... **5,500.00**

**Free-blown fruit jar,** cylindrical, wide outward rolled collared mouth, pontil scar, possibly Lockport Glass Works, w/metal Willoughby stopple,

1850-60, light sapphire blue, approximately 1 qt, 6½" (⅛" flake on bottom side of rolled mouth) ......... **4,875.00**

**Gilberds Improved (embossed star) Jar,** glass lid, wire clamp extending vertically around jar, smooth base, aqua, qt. ............................................. **143.00**

**Glenny (W.H.) Son & Co. Importers of Queensware,** No. 162 Main Street, Buffalo, N.Y., cylindrical, applied mouth w/Kline stopper, smooth base, 1860-80, aqua, qt. (stopper is damaged, embossing slightly weak) .................................... **120.00**

**Globe,** glass lid, wire & iron clamp, metal band around neck, ground lip, apple green, ½ gal. (good embossing) ...................................... **125.00**

**Hero (above cross),** glass lid & wire bail, aqua, pt. (minor flakes, light spots) ..................................... **55.00**

**Mason's CFJ Co (Monogram) Improved Butter Jars,** cylindrical, ground mouth w/glass lid & zinc screw band, smooth base, 1870-90, aqua, 9" h. ....................................... **154.00**

**Mason's CFJ Co (Monogram) Improved Butter Jars,** cylindrical, ground mouth w/glass lid & zinc screw band, smooth base, 1870-90, clear, 5" h. ........................................ **154.00**

**Mason's CFJCo Patent Nov. 30 1858,** ground lip, zinc lid, light olive-green, qt. ....................................... **45.00**

**"Mason's" Improved (The),** cylindrical, ground mouth w/original glass insert & metal screw band, "H-123" on smooth base, 1870-80, medium amber, ½ gal. ...................... **145.00**

**Mason's Patent Nov. 30th 1858,** ground mouth w/zinc cap, smooth base, yellowish amber, ½ gal. .......... **110.00**

**Mason's Patent Nov. 30th 1858,** ground mouth w/zinc cap, smooth base, deep amber, ½ gal. ................. **220.00**

**Mason's Patent Nov. 30th 1858,** ground mouth, smooth base, 1870-80, yellowish olive, qt. (no zinc lid, lettering is light) ............................... **675.00**

**Mason's Patent Nov. 30th 1858,** reversed S, ground lip, yellowish green, ½ gal. (light stain) .................. **55.00**

**Millville,** cylindrical, applied collared mouth w/glass lide & iron yoke clamp, smooth base, 1860-80, aqua, ½ pt. (lid has ¼" flake off edge) ........ **198.00**

*Salem Fruit Jar*

*Stone & Co. Fruit Jar*

**Myers Test Jar,** cylindrical, ground mouth w/tin lid & brass clamp, smooth base, 1860-80, aqua, qt. (tin lid has some rusting) ...................... **110.00**

**Salem (The) Jar,** Holz Clark & Taylor Salem N.J., cylindrical, ground lip, w/original glass screw stopper, "Pat. Applied For" on smooth base, 1865-75, aqua, minor inside haze, qt. (ILLUS. above) ............................... **950.00**

**Stone (A.) & Co. Philada.,** Manufactured by Cunninghams & Co., Pittsburgh PA, (inscription embossed on five lines), shouldered cylindrical w/applied applied wax seal ring, iron pontil, aqua, slight staining, stress cracks in wax seal ring, qt. (ILLUS. top next column) ..... **475.00**

**Trademarks Mason's CJFCo. Improved,** aqua, qt. (at GM changes to light olive-green w/amber swirls) .. **175.00**

**Triumph, No. 1,** cylindrical, sheared mouth w/hand formed wax seal channel, smooth base, blown in three-piece mold, 1865-75, aqua, qt. (light haze) ...................................... **625.00**

**Triumph, No. 2,** cylindrical, sheared mouth w/hand formed wax seal channel, smooth base, blown in three-piece mold, 1865-75, aqua, qt. (light haze) ...................................... **675.00**

*Van Vliet Fruit Jar*

**Van Vliet Jar of 1881 (The),** "Pat. May 3d 1881" on glass lid, ground mouth w/wire & metal yoke, smooth base, 1881-85, aqua, qt. (ILLUS. bottom) ............................................. **750.00**

**Whitmore's Patent,** cylindrical, ground mouth w/glass lid & wire bail, smooth base, 1860-80, aqua, qt. (⅜" chip on lid) ................................. **176.00**

# FURNITURE

Furniture made in the United States during the 18th and 19th centuries is coveted by collectors. American antique furniture has a European background, primarily English, since the influence of the Continent usually found its way to America by way of England. If the style did not originate in England, it came to America by way of England. For this reason, some American furniture styles carry the name of an English monarch or an English designer. However, we must realize that, until recently, little research has been conducted and even less published on the Spanish and French influences in the areas of the California missions and New Orleans.

After the American revolution, cabinetmakers in the United States shunned the prevailing styles in England and chose to bring the French styles of Napoleon's Empire to the United States and we have the uniquely named "American Empire" style of furniture in a country that never had an emperor.

During the Victorian period, quality furniture began to be mass-produced in this country with its rapidly growing population. So much walnut furniture was manufactured, the vast supply of walnut was virtually depleted and it was of necessity that oak furniture became fashionable as the 19th century drew to a close.

For our purposes, the general guidelines for dating will be:

Pilgrim Century - 1620-85
William & Mary - 1685-1720
Queen Anne - 1720-50
Chippendale - 1750-85
Federal - 1785-1820
    Hepplewhite - 1785-1820
    Sheraton - 1800-20
American Empire (Classical) - 1815-40
Victorian - 1840-1900
    Early Victorian - 1840-50
    Gothic Revival - 1840-90
    Rococo (Louis XV) - 1845-70
    Renaissance - 1860-85
    Louis XVI - 1865-75
    Eastlake - 1870-95
    Jacobean & Turkish Revival - 1870-95
    Aesthetic Movement - 1880-1900
Art Nouveau - 1890-1918
Turn-of-the-Century - 1895-1910
Mission (Arts & Crafts movement) - 1900-15
Art Deco - 1925-40

All furniture included in this listing is American unless otherwise noted. Also see: GARDEN FOUNTAINS & ORNAMENTS, ROYCROFT ITEMS and SHAKER COLLECTIBLES.

## BEDS

**Biedermeier twin beds,** figured mahogany veneer, a gently arched headboard flanked by squatty turned finials above heavy paneled stiles flanking crock-grain veneered panels,

*Curly Maple Low Poster Bed*

turned tapering short legs on casters, original side rails, Europe, first half 19th c., 38 × 72", 45" h., pr. (some veneer damage ...................................$605.00

**Classical country-style four-poster rope bed,** curly maple & poplar, the headboard w/a molded & arched center crest flanked by incurved scrolls between the headposts w/knob- and ring-turned finials, a lower rail joins nine simple turned spindles to the upper arched headboard, the footboard w/matching posts joined by a ring-turned blanket rail above a wide arched flat rail over the round rope rail w/knobs, original side rails, old mellow refinishing, 50 × 70", 4' 9½" h. (minor edge damage).... **330.00**

**Classical country-style low poster rope bed,** curly maple, the headboard w/a rolled crest ending in acorn turnings above a wide panel & flanked by tapering paneled posts w/urn turnings supporting acorn finials, the matching footboard w/a slightly lower crestrail, on oblong knob feet on casters, New England, ca. 1820 (ILLUS. bottom previous page) ................................................. **880.00**

*Classical Tall Poster Bed*

**Classical country-style tall poster tester bed,** cypress, the headboard w/a heavy paneled crest bar ending

*West Indian Tall Poster Bed*

in bold acorn terminals above a wide shaped panel flanked by tall paneled posts topped by tapering cylindrical segments supporting acorn finials which support the large flaring tester frame, matching footposts joined by a plain flat rail, orignal side rails, tapering cylindrical legs w/ring-turned ankles, Louisiana, early 20th c. (ILLUS. top previous page) .. **1,210.00**

**Classical tall poster bed,** carved mahogany, the headboard w/a scalloped & leafy scroll-carved crest flanked by tall posts w/baluster-turned finials over ropetwist-turned sections over short urn-form turnings & a fluted section above the lower square posts raised on ring-turned ankles & oblong knob feet, matching footboard w/only a rail between the posts, original side rails, West Indies, ca. 1830, 58½ × 75", 8' 2½" h. (ILLUS. bottom previous page) ............................ **4,180.00**

**Country-style hired man's bed,** single size, pine, low headboard w/a triangular crestrail between heavy block- and knob-turned posts, heavy knob-turned legs, slightly lower footboard w/wide solid board end between block posts on knob-turned legs, old dark finish over red, original side rails w/new canvas tacked-on to form mattress, 19th c., 26 × 73", headboard 28¾" h. ........................... **110.00**

**Federal country-style tall poster canopy bed,** turned birch, the flaring octagonal headposts centring an arched pine headboard, the footposts w/ring-turned & flaring standard & urn-form supports, a circular plinth below on turned tapering legs ending in tapering feet, w/arched tester, headboard of later date, New England, ca. 1820, 45 × 80", 5' 5" h. (ILLUS. top next column)......................................**2,070.00**

**Federal country-style tall poster bed,** tiger stripe maple, a low arched headboard flanked by tall baluster-, rod- and ring-turned posts w/knob finials & ending in baluster-turned legs, matching turned footposts, original siderails, old finish, New England, early 19th c., 48½ × 79¼", 6' 10" h.......................................... **2,415.00**

*Federal Turned Birchwood Bed*

**Federal country-style tall poster tester bed,** painted, wide headboard w/flat top & scroll-cut ends between tall knob- and ring-turned posts w/pointed finials, matching footposts, original side rails & tester, original red paint w/black accents, northern New England, 1825-35, 52 × 77", 6' 1" h. (no canopy)........................ **3,335.00**

**Federal tall poster canopy bed,** cherry, a plain rounded headboard flanked by square tapering posts & on square tapering legs, the end posts w/baluster- and urn-turned sections & raised on slender turned tapering legs w/long peg feet, an arched wooden canopy framework joining the posts, original siderails w/added metal brackets, New England, ca. 1810, 52 × 69", 6' 9" h. (refinished)........................ **3,105.00**

**Federal tall poster canopy bed,** curly maple, the low gently arched pine headboard between plain simple turned tapering posts w/ring-turnings & pegs at the top, the foot posts w/spirally-carved turnings & matching finials, the posts supporting a high arched canopy frame, appears to retain original finish, New England, ca. 1820, 51¾" × 76" (ILLUS. top next page) ...................................... **1,725.00**

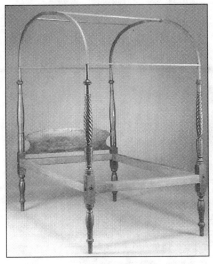

*Federal Curly Maple Canopy Bed*

*New England Canopy Bed*

**Federal tall poster canopy bed,**
maple, the low arched headboard
between plain turned & tapering
posts w/ring-turned peg finials, on
plain turned tapering legs on casters,
the footboard w/a plain rail between
vase- and tall baluster-turned reeded
posts w/matching finials & tapering
ring-turned legs on casters, old

refinish, New England, ca. 1815,
57 × 81", 7' 3" h. (ILLUS. bottom
previous column) ........................... **3,738.00**

**Federal tall poster tester bed,**
carved cherry, a wide gently arched
headboard flanked by reeded &
acanthus-carved headposts, the
footposts matching, turned tapering
feet, original siderails, w/tester,
probably Pennsylvania, ca. 1820,
55" w., 6' 6" h. ............................... **4,600.00**

**Federal tall poster canopy bed,**
turned birch, the low flat-topped pine
headboard w/rounded corners
between plain tapering turned
headposts & reeded & ring-turned
footposts, baluster-turned legs
w/flattened ball feet, New England,
ca. 1815, w/arched canopy tester,
53" w., 6' 5" h. ............................... **3,162.00**

**Federal Revival style four poster
double bed,** cherry, the high
broken-scroll arched headboard
centering a turned urn finial
between baluster- and ring-turned
posts w/ball finials, the footboard
w/a baluster- and ring-turned upper
rail connecting the slightly shorter
foot posts, double base rails at the
footboard & original side rails, short
baluster-turned legs w/knob feet,
early 20th c. (ILLUS. top next
page) ......................................... **1,100.00**

**Mission-style (Arts & Crafts
movement) double bed,** oak, the
headboard w/a narrow horizontal
slat above a wide horizontal board &
a lower slat between round-topped
rectangular posts, slight lower
matching footboard, original side
rails, original finish, branded
signature of Gustav Stickley, Model
No. 922, early 20th c., 59 × 78",
4' 10" h. ...................................... **4,675.00**

**Mission-style (Arts & Crafts
movement) single bed,** oak, the tall
headboard & slightly shorter
footboard w/peaked crestrails
between square posts, wide flat
siderails, square legs, red decal
mark of Gustav Stickley, Model No.
912, ca. 1909, 42½" w., headboard
4' 2¾" h. ...................................... **2,070.00**

*Federal Revival Double Bed*

*Mission Oak Bed*

**Mission-style (Arts & Crafts movement) three-quarter size bed,** oak, the head- and footboards w/a flat thin crestrail over wide double panels over arched aprons, square side posts forming the legs, original side rails, pegged "knock-down" construction, white decal label of L. & J.G. Stickley, Model No. 83, ca. 1915, 46" w., 4' 3" h. (ILLUS.) ....... **2,300.00**

**Mission-style (Arts & Crafts movement) three-quarter-size bed,** oak, the headboard w/nine square spindles beneath a horizontal rail, original finish, branded mark of Gustav Stickley, 44 × 75", 4' 1" h. (some veneer damage) ................... **522.50**

**Victorian half-tester bed,** Renaissance Revival substyle, carved walnut, the tall headboard w/a raised center on the crestrail centering scroll-carved details above further carved scrolls at the sides & below all above a frieze band of teardrop devices over an burl-veneered oblong panel & two lower rectangular panels all between molded side posts w/scroll-carved brackets supporting the half-tester w/a scroll-carved crestrail matching the headboard & lined w/fabric, the low footboard w/a flat crestrail over a band of teardrop devices over a rectangular burl panel between molded stiles, original side rails, ca. 1870, 63½ × 81", 9' 11" h. (ILLUS. top next page)................... **4,400.00**

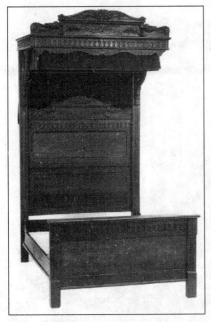

*Victorian Half-tester Bed*

**Victorian double bed,** Rococo substyle, carved rosewood, the low arched headboard topped by a pierce-carved crest, slightly lower matching footboard w/no crest, the wide original siderails w/scroll-carved corner brackets & raised scroll panels, ca. 1850, 61 × 74½", 4' 9" h.............................................. **1,320.00**

**Victorian tester bed,** Rococo substyle, carved mahogany, the high sharply arched headboard carved along the crest w/leafy scrolls centered by a carved fruit & leaf drop above a rectangular panel w/thin raised border banding between heavy posts formed of clusters of small columns, low serpentine-topped side rails & matching low footboard, matching foot columns, American-made, ca. 1850, tester missing (ILLUS. below) .. **4,180.00**

**Victorian tester bed,** Rococo substyle, carved walnut, the high arched headboard w/a crest of boldly carved scrolls over a wide

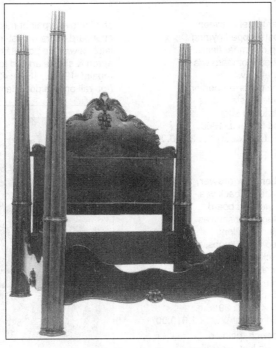

*Victorian Rococo Tester Bed*

*Victorian Walnut
Tester Bed*

plain board & lower panel between
turned paneled posts topped by ring
turnings & tapering columnar finials,
the low gently arched footboard w/a
large central roundel between
matching posts, the posts supporting
the wide cove-molded tester frame
lined w/pleated fabric, on short
double knob-turned legs, ca. 1860,
70 × 87", 8' 5" h. (ILLUS. above) ... **3,850.00**

## BENCHES

**Bucket (or water) bench w/drawer,**
painted softwood, the tall back w/a
flared crest above stepped board
sides flanking to staggered shelves
above a lower shelf over a long
drawer w/two turned wood knobs, flat
apron, tapering bracket feet, painted
dark brown to resemble mahogany
over an earlier green, probably New
England, early 19th c., some
imperfections, 13¾ × 25¾", 39¼" h.
(ILLUS. bottom next column) ......... **1,610.00**

**Bucket (or water) bench,** painted
pine, the tall back w/a low backrail
on the rectangular top above a shelf
flanked by sides curving out at the
base & a board back above a wider

shelf above a pair of raised-panel
cupboard doors w/cast-iron thumb
latches w/white porcelain knobs, flat
apron & simple angled feet, old red
repaint, 19th c., 16½ × 42", 4' 3½" h.
(top rail on one door damaged) ..... **1,870.00**

*Bucket Bench with Drawer*

*Mission Oak Hall
Bench*

**Bucket (or water) bench,** walnut &
pine, a rectangular top w/a three-
quarter low gallery w/slightly shaped
ends above two lower staggered
shelves, solid board ends w/bootjack
feet, old dark finish, square nail
construction, 19th c., 11½ × 30½",
29½" h. (some edge damage) .......... **116.00**

**Country-style bench,** pine, the
rectangular single-board plank seat
on two shaped end supports
continuing to tapering feet, 19th c.,
16¾ × 85", 19½" h. .......................... **403.00**

**Hall bench,** Mission-style (Arts &
Crafts movement), oak, high slab
ends w/gently rounded tops over a
large rounded cut-out w/three
slender square spindles & high
rounded cut-out leg openings joined
by a rectangular seat over a keyed
tenon stretcher, original rush seat,
unsigned, attributed to the Derby
Furniture Company, early 20th c.,
14 × 23", 28" h. (refinished) .............. **715.00**

**Hall bench,** Mission-style (Arts &
Crafts movement), oak, the tall
paneled back w/a flat crest flanked
by narrow side wings w/oblong cut-
outs near the top & continuing down
to low rounded arms flanking the
hinged lift-seat over a deep apron,
low cut-out end feet, original

reddish brown finish, branded
signature of Gustav Stickley, Model
No. 224, 22 × 48", 42" h. (ILLUS.
above)........................................... **9,900.00**

## BOOKCASES

*Biedermeier Burl Maple Bookcase*

**Biedermeier bookcase,** burl maple, two-part construction: the upper section w/a rectangular top w/rounded front corners & a deep cove-molded cornice above a wide frieze panel w/decorative veneering over a pair of tall single-pane glazed cupboard doors w/inner molding opening to two shelves; the lower stepped-out section w/molded edges over a case w/two small drawers above two paneled cupboard doors, on a thick molded base w/small block feet, Europe, first half 19th c., 20¾ × 56", 7' 3¼" h. (ILLUS. bottom previous page) ............................. **3,025.00**

**Mission-style (Arts & Crafts movement) bookcase,** oak, double-door, the rectangular top w/a three-quarter gallery above the slab-sided cabinet w/keyed tenons, a pair of tall twelve-pane doors w/V-shaped copper pulls opening to three shelves on each side, paper label & large red decal mark of Gustav Stickley, ca. 1905, 13 × 57¼", 4' 8" h. ........................................... **4,370.00**

**Mission-style (Arts & Crafts movement) bookcase,** oak, single-door, rectangular top overhanging a case w/a single tall glazed door flanked by columns w/capitals at the sides, the door w/three panels of four panes each above tall single panes, arched apron, arched cut-out end feet, designed by Harvey Ellis, original finish, paper label & red decal marks of Gustav Stickley, Model No. 700, early 20th c., 14 × 35", 4' 10" h. (minor splitting to exterior back).... **13,200.00**

**Mission-style (Arts & Crafts movement) bookcase,** oak, three-door, a gently rounded three-quarter gallery on the long narrow rectangular top above a case w/three tall twelve-pane glazed cupboard doors w/copper plate & ring pulls, opening to three shelves, flat apron, through-mortised top & bottom shelves & low cut-out end feet, original black finish, red decal mark of Gustav Stickley, ca. 1902, 12 × 73", 4' 8" h. ........................... **18,700.00**

**Victorian "breakfront" bookcase,** Renaissance Revival substyle, walnut & burl walnut, two-part construction: the tall upper section w/a stepped breakfront cornice w/arched & scroll-carved corner finials at the center section & the

*Victorian "Breakfront" Bookcase*

*Renaissance Revival
"Breakfront" Bookcase*

side sections, all flanking scrolled side crestrails over deep stepped cornices above narrow raised burl panels, the stepped-out center section w/a pair of tall narrow two-pane glazed doors w/oblong framing opening to adjustable shelves, the side panels w/matching shorter two-pane doors; the bottom stepped-out conforming low section w/a molded edge w/outset corners over raised pointed burl upright panels at the sides of the center section & at the outer corners, the stepped-out center section w/a pair of small paneled cupboard doors w/raised burl panels w/notched corners, the set-back side sections each w/two small drawers w/T-form drops & raised rectangular burl panels w/notched corners, on a molded conforming base, ca. 1880, some drops damaged, cornice 23 × 66", 7' 6" h. (ILLUS. bottom previous page) ............................................ **3,080.00**

**Victorian "breakfront" bookcase,**
Renaissance Revival substyle, walnut, two-part construction: the upper section w/a stepped-out wider & taller center section w/a flat convex deep stepped cornice over a fruit- and leaf-carved frieze band

over a tall single-pane curved glass door opening to four curved-front shelves & flanked by carved top blocks & spiral-twist columns & leaf-carved blocks & reeded stiles, center section flanked by set-back narrower side sections w/flat rectangular cornices over dentil-carved bands over flat single-pane glazed doors opening to three shelves & w/end blocks & columns matching the center section; the low bottom section of conforming design w/three drawers each w/a pair of stamped brass pulls, molded flat base, ca. 1880-90 (ILLUS. above) .......... **3,050.00**

**Victorian "breakfront" bookcase,**
Rococo substyle, carved mahogany, the wide stepped-out center section w/a tall arched crestrail over a pair of tall single-pane glazed doors w/ornately scroll-carved pointed-arch top borders & opening to four shelves, the set-back narrow side sections w/flat tops over deep stepped cornices above the tall narrow rectangular single-pane glazed doors w/molded edging opening to four shelves, on a deep molded flat base, England or Europe, mid-19th c., 22 × 86", 6' 9" h. (ILLUS. top next page)....... **1,870.00**

*English "Breakfront" Bookcase*

*Louis XV-Style Bureau Plat*

## BUREAUX PLAT

**Louis XV-Style,** ormolu-mounted kingwood & parquetry inlay, the rectangular top w/tooled black leather insets & ormolu edging above a deep apron w/three long drawers, each w/shaped rectangular ormolu banding around ormolu pierced scroll pulls & keyhole escutcheons, large ormolu female busts tapering to scrolls at each corner heading the cabriole legs ending in ormolu scrolled sabots, Paris, late 19th c., 36 × 69½", 30½" h. (ILLUS. bottom) ............... **6,500.00**

**Napoleon III,** brass-mounted ebony & satinwood, rectangular top w/leather inset above a case w/a long central drawer above the kneehole flanked by pairs of short drawers, on fluted tapering cylindrical legs w/turned tapering feet, third quarter 19th c., France, 57½" l., 29" h. (ILLUS. top next page) ..................................... **3,738.00**

*Napoleon III Bureau Plat*

## CABINETS

*Mission Oak China Cabinet*

**China cabinet,** Mission-style (Arts & Crafts movement), oak, a rectangular flat top slightly overhanging the case w/a single wide glazed cabinet door w/arched crestrail & original copper plate & bail pull, flanked by glazed sides w/arched crestrails, gently curved aprons, short stile feet, three interior wood shelves, original finish, Handcraft decal of L. & J.G.Stickley, Model No. 761, 16 × 36", 5' h......... **6,050.00**

**China cabinet,** Mission-style (Arts & Crafts movement), oak, the rectangular top w/a low back crest above a pair of tall eight-pane glazed cupboard doors opening to three shelves, four panes on each end, flat apron, square stile legs, original finish, red decal mark of Gustav Stickley, 14 × 36", 4' 8" h. (ILLUS. previous column) .................. **5,225.00**

**China cabinet,** Mission-style (Arts & Crafts movement), oak, rectangular top w/shallow widely flaring cornice above a pair of tall leaded glass doors w/pairs of onion-form panes over twelve rectangular panes in each door, curved apron, square stile legs joined by a wide medial shelf, on casters, original dark finish, Mackmurdo feet, Tobey Furniture Company, numbered "5862," early 20th c., 18 × 44", 5' 5" h. (ILLUS. top left, next page) ................................. **2,310.00**

**China cabinet,** turn-of-the-century corner-type, oak, the tall narrow quarter-round form w/two flat-topped top backrails w/rounded ends & framing mirrors above the pair of curved glass cupboard doors, each opening to a mirrored back & four glass shelves, double-curve apron raised on short cabriole legs ending in hairy paw feet, ca. 1900 (ILLUS. bottom left, next page) ............................................ **3,600.00**

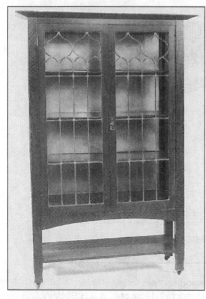

*Tobey Furniture China Cabinet*

*Ornate Oak China Cabinet*

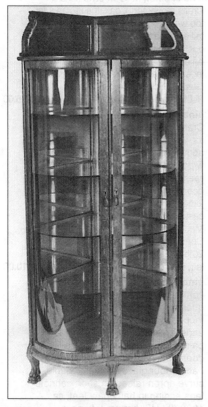

*Unique Corner China Cabinet*

*Mission Oak Liquor Cabinet*

**China cabinet,** turn-of-the-century style, oak, the large D-form piece w/a flat top over curved side cornices & a wide flat front cornice, each section w/a deep frieze band carved w/repeating rings & florettes, the wider center cornice above a pair of boldly carved caryatids & leafy scroll-carved pilasters flanking a wide curved glass door, curved glass side sections, mirror-backed interior w/four glass shelves, the wide conforming base band carved w/continuous scrolls, two large paw feet at the front, ca. 1900 (ILLUS. top right, previous page) ................................ **2,500.00**

**Display cabinet,** Oriental-style, carved teak, a high ornately pierce-carved arched dragon-form front & back crest above a round shallow drum-form cabinet w/staggered open shelves alternating w/small pairs of ornately carved doors above a tall base formed by ornately pierce-carved scrolls & dragons continuing to heavy tall scroll legs on a rectangular platform base, China or Japan, late 19th - early 20th c. ...... **2,090.00**

**Liquor cabinet,** Mission-style (Arts & Crafts movement), oak, the rectangular flip-top w/exposed dovetailed construction opens to a two-tiered copper-lined shelf over a single drawer & a single cupboard door opening to a smaller locking cabinet & open shelves, short square stile legs, red decal mark of Gustav Stickley, Model No. 86, revolving bottle rack gone, refinished, new veneer on door, 18 × 24", 43" h. (ILLUS. bottom right, previous page) .............................................. **2,640.00**

**Liquor cabinet,** Mission-style (Arts & Crafts movement), oak, rectangular top overhanging a tall case w/a pull-out tray w/hammered amber glass insert over a single long drawer above a pair of tall flat cupboard doors opening to a revolving bottle rack & accessory rack, gently arched apron, short square stile legs, original square copper pulls, original reddish brown finish, branded mark of the Charles Limbert Company, Model No. 752, early 20th c., 19 × 31", 36" h. (ILLUS. below) ................................ **6,600.00**

**Music cabinet,** Mission-style (Arts & Crafts movement), oak, low three-quarter gently rounded gallery on the rectangular top above a single tall cupboard door divided into ten panels each w/four small panes of glass & the original copper plate & ring pull, flat apron & cut-out end feet, through-tenons at top & base, lightly cleaned original finish, paper label & red decal marks of Gustav Stickley, Model No. 70, 16 × 20", 46" h. ........................ **10,500.00**

*Charles Limbert*
*Liquor Cabinet*

*Stickley Music Cabinet*

**Music cabinet,** Mission-style (Arts & Crafts movement), oak, the rectangular top w/a low three-quarter gallery above a tall narrow paneled door w/a copper plate w/V-form ring pull, opening to four shelves, branded mark of Gustav Stickley, Model No. 70, ca. 1913, 16 × 20", 47½" h. (ILLUS. right).................................... **4,370.00**

**Side cabinet,** Victorian Gothic Revival substyle, carved oak, two-part construction: the upper section w/a rectangular top w/a shallow flaring molded cornice over a central door w/wrought-iron strap hinges flanked by narrow panels all w/overall interlacing carved foliage including blossoms, thistles & acorns, door & panels divided by carved turret pilasters over a mid-molding; the lower case w/five long drawers w/ornate scrolling carving flanked by ropetwist-turned side pilasters, book leaf carving on the side panels, England, late 19th c., 19 × 35", 4' 5¾" h. (ILLUS. below)............... **1,610.00**

*Gothic Revival Side Cabinet*

**Side cabinet,** Victorian Rococo substyle, carved rosewood, the rectangular molded top w/rounded corners above a conforming case fitted w/a single drawer over a beaded frieze above a pair of cupboard doors w/pierced scrolled panels enclosing a single shelf above a base molding, on shaped reeded bracket feet w/casters, stenciled mark inside a drawer "J. AND J.W. MEEKS - MAKERS - NO. 14 VESEY ST. - NEW YORK," ca. 1850, 23 × 45½", 40½" h. .............. **2,185.00**

**Smoker's cabinet,** Mission-style (Arts & Crafts movement), oak, rectangular top overhanging a tall case w/a drawer over a long paneled door, each w/original hammered copper plate & ring bail pulls, interior w/divided compartment, light recoat over original finish, Handcraft decal mark of L. & J.G. Stickley, Model No. 26, 15 × 20", 29" h. (minor stains in top) ............................................ **3,850.00**

*Rococo Vitrine Cabinet*

**Vitrine cabinet,** Victorian Rococo substyle, carved oak, two-part construction: the upper section w/an arched top centered by a foliate-carved upright ring above a molded cornice over a frieze band carved w/scrolled panels above a pair of glazed doors w/scroll-carved muntins & borders flanked by narrow glazed corner panels & glass sides, on a molded base; the lower section w/a molding above two narrow long glazed panels at the front & smaller ones at the sides above a pair of glazed lower doors w/scroll-carved trim flanked by further angled corner glazed panels & glass sides, a scroll-carved apron continuing to short scrolled front feet, Europe, mid-19th c. (ILLUS. previous column) ............... **3,850.00**

## CHAIRS

*Bentwood Rocking Chair*

**Adirondack-style rocker w/arms,** the back w/heavy rough hickory posts & rails framing the woven rush back panel, open post arms on curved arm supports forming front legs, woven rush seat, double front & side rungs, original finish, branded Old Hickory mark, early 20th c., 37" h. (seat rewoven) ................................. **176.00**

**Art Deco rocking chair w/arms,** chrome & cushions, a rectangular tubular metal back frame w/rounded corners curving down to a comforming seat frame flanked by large open teardrop-form tubular metal arms/rockers w/two tubular supports under each padded arm & curving under the seat frame to the opposite side, red naugahyde back & seat cushions, designed by Kem Weber, manufactured by Lloyd, 26 × 39", 31" h. ............................ **1,320.00**

**Art Nouveau side chair,** carved sycamore, the arched crestrail flanked by foliate-carved ears above a row of five short baluster-turned spindles over the upholstered back panel raised above the upholstered seat on a molded seatrail & shaped & carved front legs w/scroll corner brackets & ending in paw feet, upholstered in rust & tan floral print velvet, Leon Benouville, France, ca. 1898 ........................................ **1,840.00**

**Bentwood rocking chair w/arms,** the tall oval bentwood back frame centered by five slender bent flat vertical slats flanked by rustic bark stiles above a D-shaped plank seat flanked by scrolling rustic bentwood arms over rustic legs, on curved board rockers, Amish-made, Indiana, ca. 1930, 44¾" h. (ILLUS. right previous page) ................................. **690.00**

*Chippendale Mahogany Armchair*

**Chippendale armchair,** carved mahogany, the serpentine ruffle-carved crestrail terminating in scrolled ears above a pierced vase-shaped splat centering a tassel flanked by shaped open arm rests terminating in scrolling eagle heads on curved arm supports over the

trapezoidal slip seat & gadrooned apron, on foliate-carved cabriole front legs w/ball-and-claw feet, New York, 1760-80, 38" h. (ILLUS. previous column) ........................... **7,820.00**

**Chippendale armchair,** wingback-style, mahogany, the tall upholstered back w/an arched crest above shaped side wings tapering to outscrolled arms, cushion seat, on square legs joined by an H-stretcher, Newport, Rhode Island, 1770-90, stop-fluting on front legs, old dark surface, upholstered in pale green silk damask, 44" h........................... **9,775.00**

*Chippendale "Wingback" Armchair*

**Chippendale armchair,** wingback-style, mahogany, the tall upholstered back w/a serpentine crest flanked by S-scroll long upholstered wings above the out-scrolled upholstered arms above the upholstered seat, on square molded front legs & square canted back legs all joined by box stretchers, old refinish, New England, 18th c., 45" h. (ILLUS.) ... **5,175.00**

**Chippendale armchair,** wingback-style, mahogany, the tall upholstered back w/a serpentine crest flanked by out-scrolled upholstered wings tapering to rolled arms above the cushion seat & upholstered seatrail, on square molded front legs & square canted back legs all joined by box stretchers, New England, ca. 1780 (ILLUS. top next page) ......... **5,750.00**

*Mahogany "Wingback" Armchair*

**Chippendale dining chairs,** "Gothic-back," carved mahogany, a C-scroll-carved serpentine crestrail carved w/bellflowers & acanthus leaves above a Gothic arch back comprised of pointed arches & trefoils, canted & incised stiles flanking, the molded seatrails below enclosing a slip seat cushion w/C-scroll-carved pierced leg brackets below, on square molded legs joined by flat stretchers, each w/original finish & rich brown color, Philadelphia, Pennsylvania, ca. 1770, set of 12 (some w/replaced leg brackets, one w/patch to rear foot & one w/repairs to crest, splat & one rear stile)................................ **46,000.00**

**Chippendale side chair,** carved mahogany, the serpentine ruffle-carved crestrail w/foliate-carved scrolled ears above a pierced vase-shaped splat centering a tassel over a trapezoidal upholstered slip seat & flat apron w/gadroon-carved bottom rim, on cabriole front legs w/foliate-carved knees & ending in ball-and-claw feet, New York, 1755-90, two later returns, 37¾" h. (ILLUS. bottom) ............................. **4,025.00**

*Fine Chippendale Side Chair*

**Chippendale side chair,** carved mahogany, the slightly serpentine crestrail w/small rounded ears over a pierced volute-carved splat & tapering stiles to the molded seat frame enclosing an upholstered slip seat, on shell-carved cabriole legs ending in claw-and-ball feet, Philadelphia, ca. 1770, bottom of feet slightly worn (ILLUS. below) ... **1,955.00**

*Chippendale Mahogany Side Chair*

*Virginia Chippendale Side Chair*

**Chippendale side chair,** mahogany, the back w/a simple ox-yoke crestrail ending in high squared ears above inwardly tapering stiles flanking a pierced central splat w/three long pierced panels w/small carved scrolls near the crest & small pierced circles halfway down toward the upholstered trapezoidal seat w/a wide front seatrail, on bold cabriole front legs ending in claw-and-ball feet, Virginia, 18th c., 36¼" h. (ILLUS. bottom previous column) ..... **863.00**

**Chippendale side chair,** mahogany, the serpentine crestrail ending in molded ears above gently outswept stiles flanking a pierced fan-shaped splat above the inset needlepoint upholstered seat, cabriole front legs ending in claw-and-ball feet, square back legs, all joined by rod- and block-turned stretchers, Massachusetts, late 18th c., old refinish, 36" h. ............................... **2,415.00**

**Chippendale side chairs,** ladder-back style, mahogany, a serpentine crestrail w/oblong pierced center opening & rounded corners above a back composed of three serpentine slats matching the crestrail, rectangular over-upholstered seat on square molded legs joined by flat stretchers, retains old finish, one w/a back slat repair, Philadelphia, ca. 1780, pr. (ILLUS. top next page) ... **1,955.00**

**Chippendale side chairs,** mahogany, the ox-yoke crestrail w/flaring carved ears above a scroll- and band-pierced splat over the upholstered seat, molded seat, rails, front legs & stretchers, slender curved & pierced brackets at front legs, old refinish, Boston, Massachusetts, 1750-80, 36" h., set of 4 (minor imperfections) ..... **9,200.00**

**Chippendale side chairs,** mahogany, the ox-yoke crestrail w/raised center section & flaring ears above a pierced scroll-carved splat centered by a diamond, trapezoidal slip seat upholstered in red silk damask, on cabriole front legs ending in pad feet, turned & canted rear legs, all joined by a turned H-stretcher, New York, 1755-65, old refinish, imperfections, 37½" h., pr. (ILLUS. of one, bottom left, next page) ............................... **3,738.00**

*Chippendale "Ladder-Back" Side Chairs*

*Chippendale New York Side Chair*

*Chippendale-Style Side Chair*

**Chippendale-Style side chairs,**
mahogany, the serpentine crestrail
w/a central pierced oval above the
carved & pierced flaring splat,
trapezoidal slip seat, carved
serpentine front seatrail on cabriole
front legs w/acanthus leaf-carved
knees & ending in claw-and-ball feet,
in the Philadelphia manner, bearing
label of Isidor Braverman, Boston,
Massachusetts, made in 1946, pr.
(ILLUS. of one, bottom right) ........ **3,162.00**

*Classical "Fancy" Chairs*

**Classical "fancy" side chairs,**
painted & decorated, the wide
rounded crestrail decorated w/a
green stenciled village scene above
tapering paint-trimmed stiles flanking
a vase-form splat decorated w/a large
stenciled tree above the caned seat,
on ring-, rod- and knob-turned legs
tapering to small knob feet, turned
front stretcher & plain side & rear
stretchers, all w/a wood grain-painted
dark background, New England, ca.
1840, 33½" h., pr. (ILLUS. top) .......... **690.00**

**Classical country-style side chairs,**
painted & decorated, a wide curved
crestrail above ring- and baluster-
turned stiles & a lower rail over a
seat w/a woven cane insert, rounded
front seatrail above ring- and rod-
turned front legs ending in knob feet,
simple turned rear legs, the crestrail
decorated w/various scenes of
figures in landscapes, including men
on horseback & figures on a
paddlewheel steamer, the lower rails
w/gilt scrolls, the seats trimmed
w/gilt pinstriping & decoration, New
York, ca. 1820, 31½" h., set of 6 ... **3,335.00**

**Classical side chairs,** curly maple, the
shaped crestrail w/a raised center
tablet & rounded ears above a vase-
form splat & shaped stiles curving
down to the caned seat, on simple
sabre legs w/a flat front stretcher &
turned side & rear stretchers, probably
Baltimore area, ca. 1840, old refinish,
34½" h., set of 6 (ILLUS. of three,
bottom) .............................................. **2,415.00**

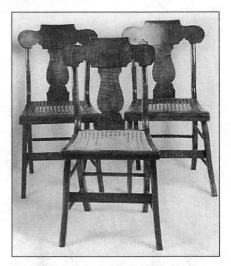

*Classical Curly Maple Side Chairs*

**Early American country-style
child's "ladder-back" highchair,**
maple & ash, the tall back w/four
arched & graduated slats between
simple turned stiles w/pointed knob
finials, shaped open arms above
the woven rush seat, on baluster-
turned arm supports continuing
down to slightly canted turned front
legs ending in knob feet, double
foot rest rungs at front, box
stretchers at middle & base of the
legs, Delaware River Valley, late
18th c., refinished, 40¾" h.
(ILLUS. top next page) ................... **920.00**

*Early "Ladder-back" Highchair*

*"Ladder-back" Armchair*

**Early American country-style "ladder-back" armchair,** painted, the tall back w/bobbin- and rod-turned stiles w/knob finials flanking the five angular arched slats, turned rod arms on knob- and rod-turned arm supports forming the front legs, woven rush seat, double sausage-turned front rungs, plain turned side & back rungs, early dark brown surface, Massachusetts, early 18th c., minor height loss, 46" h. (ILLUS. bottom previous column) ..... **1,495.00**

**Early American country-style "ladder-back" side chairs,** maple, each w/four graduated arched slats between simple turned stiles w/button finials forming the tall back above the woven rush seat, on knob- and rod-turned front legs w/knob & peg feet joined by a knob- and ring-turned front stretcher, double side rungs & plain rear legs joined by a single rung, old refinish, Berks County, Pennsylvania, 1750-70, 41" h., set of 4 (assembled set, replaced seats) ............................. **2,185.00**

**Early American country-style "ladder-back" side chairs,** painted maple & ash, the back w/tall plain round stiles w/ring & ovoid knob finials flanking three gently arched slats above the early woven hickory splint seat, plain round legs joined by plain double stretchers at the front & sides, painted Spanish brown over an earlier red, New England, late 18th c., 39½" h., set of 4 (minor imperfections) ................................... **920.00**

**Empire-Style open-arm armchairs,** ebonized & gilt-trimmed mahogany, the upright rectangular back w/a wide flat curved crestrail above the upholstered back panel flanked by down-curved carved & gilt-trimmed dolphin-form open arms, wide cushion seat over a gently curved seatrail on square tapering sabre legs, France, 19th c., pr. (ILLUS. top next page) ........................................ **937.00**

**Federal "lolling" armchair,** mahogany, the tall upholstered back w/a gently arched top above slender open downswept arms flanking the upholstered seat w/brass tack trim, square tapering front legs & gently curved square back legs all joined by flat stretchers, possibly Middle Atlantic States, ca. 1800, 41¼" h. (restoration, imperfections) ............. **920.00**

*Empire-Style Armchairs*

**Federal "wing" armchair,** mahogany, the arched upholstered back flanked by ogival wings w/slightly scrolled arms, the seat now w/a loose cushion, on ring-turned & reeded tapering legs ending in brass casters, Boston, ca. 1820 .............. **3,162.00**

**Federal country-style writing-arm armchair,** painted & decorated, the wide gently curved & rolled crestrail above tapering styles & a lower flat rail over six short arrow slats flanked on one side by an S-scroll arm & on the other by a wide rectangular writing arm on canted double supports resting in the side of the wide shaped plank seat, simple knob-turned front legs & plain round rear legs joined by box stretchers, old red w/traces of gold stenciling on crest, ca. 1830, 38" h. (splits in seat) ......... **825.00**

**Federal dining chairs,** mahogany, stepped square back w/a leaf-carved center crest above four leaf- and flowerhead-carved slender square spindles, over-upholstered seat, on square tapering legs ending in spade feet, in the New York manner, five side chairs, one armchair, set of 6 (extensive repairs) ..................... **1,610.00**

**Federal dining chairs,** tiger stripe maple, rectangular bowed tablet crest above a conforming slat flanked by tapering stiles over a trapezoidal cane seat, on sabre legs joined by stretchers, Boston, 1815-30, 33¼" h., set of 6 (repairs) ............................ **4,255.00**

*Federal Mahogany Side Chair*

**Federal side chair,** mahogany, square back w/stepped crestrail above a pair of flat columnar slender back slats flanking a central pierced urn & drapery splat, wide trapezoidal over-upholstered seat, square tapering front legs w/spade feet, probably New York, ca. 1810, old finish, minor repair, 35" h. (ILLUS.) ... **863.00**

**Federal side & armchairs,** carved mahogany, the square back w/a stepped molded crestrail over a pair of slender carved uprights flanking a

*Federal Armchair & Side Chair*

*Fine Federal Side Chairs*

slender pierced urn-form splat topped by Prince-of-Wales plumes over waterleaves & drapery swags, the bowed over-upholstered wide seat on reeded square tapering front legs ending in spade feet, the armchair w/short S-scroll arms on down-curved molded arm supports, New York, ca. 1800, armchair w/spliced front leg, restoration to three seat rails, 2 pcs. (ILLUS. top) ................................. **3,162.00**

**Federal side & armchairs,** carved mahogany, shield-form back w/triple arch crestrail above a splat w/fanned piercings flanked by bellflower-and-leaf-carved uprights, wide over-upholstered seat on square tapering reeded front legs ending in spade feet, the armchair w/slender S-scroll arms on in-curved arm supports, New York, ca. 1800, some w/repairs, nine side chairs & one armchair, set of 10 (ILLUS. of part, bottom) ...... **33,350.00**

*Federal Shield-Back Side Chairs*

*Philadelphia Shield-Back Side Chairs*

**Federal side chairs,** carved & inlaid mahogany, shield-back style w/an arched & molded crestrail above a pierced & carved splat centering a central pierced rib inlaid w/sheaves of wheat flanked by wheat-carved & pierced ribs, all above a bowed trapezoidal over-upholstered seat, on square tapering front legs joined by an H-stretcher & back stretcher, New York, 1810-25, 37¼" h., set of 4 (ILLUS. of two)............................. **8,625.00**

**Federal side chairs,** carved mahogany, shield-back style centering five slender leaf-carved uprights, the serpentine over-upholstered seat on fluted square tapering front legs ending in spade feet, probably Philadelphia, 1780-1800, pr. (ILLUS. top next column) ........................................ **8,050.00**

**Federal side chairs,** carved mahogany, the curved paneled crestrail above a double-X-form flowerhead-carved back above a balloon-form over-upholstered seat, on round reeded tapering front legs w/baluster-form feet, attributed to Duncan Phyfe or one of his contemporaries, New York, ca. 1810, each w/repairs, set of 4 (ILLUS. below) ............................... **2,875.00**

**Federal side chairs,** carved mahogany, the lyre-carved tablet-form crestrail above a back rest carved w/leaves & scrolls between reeded & scrolled stiles above a slip seat w/reeded seatrail on sabre legs, numerous repairs, New York, ca. 1820, set of 4 (ILLUS. of two, top next page)...................................... **4,025.00**

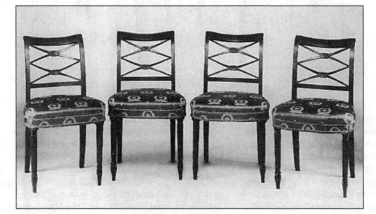

*Duncan Phyfe-type Side Chairs*

*Federal Lyre-carved Side Chairs*

**Federal side chairs,** carved mahogany, the shield-form back w/five carved & gently curved slender uprights joined at the base to a half-round fan-carved medallion, raised above the over-upholstered seat, slightly tapering front legs & square canted back legs joined by box stretchers, Philadelphia, ca. 1790, 40" h., pr. (refinish, repairs, imperfections) ............................... **4,312.50**

**Federal country-style "fancy" side chairs,** painted & decorated, a turned arched crestrail above an oval back rail decorated w/a stencilled compote filled w/fruit & flowers, woven rush seat, on ring-turned legs joined by stretchers, button feet, New England or New York, ca. 1825, set of 12 ............... **3,737.00**

**Mission-style (Arts & Crafts movement) armchair,** oak, three horizontal slats between square stiles, flat tapering arms over curved corbels to the arm supports continuing to form the front legs, original hard leather seat, wide flat front & rear rungs & double square side rungs, original finish, red decal mark & paper label of Gustav Stickley, Model No. 310½, 36" h.... **1,045.00**

**Mission-style (Arts & Crafts movement) armchair,** oak, the tall back w/a top crestrail above two

lower rails joined by five slats between the square stiles, rectangular wide bowed arms over corbels at the arm supports which continue to form the front legs, original drop-in leatherette cushion, wide flat seatrails & flat stretchers, Quaint Furniture metal tag & remnant of paper label of Stickley Brothers, Model No. 559½, refinished, 44" h. ........................... **1,100.00**

*Mission Dining Chair*

**Mission-style (Arts & Crafts movement) dining chair,** bungalow-type, oak, the gently arched crestrail above five tapering slats to a lower back rail raised above the woven rush seat over notched side rails, on square legs joined by an H-stretcher, unsigned Gustav Stickley, Model No. 1289, refinished, new rush seat, 38" h. (ILLUS.) ......................................... **1,045.00**

**Mission-style (Arts & Crafts movement) hall chair,** oak, solid board tall narrow shield-form back w/a spade-shaped cut-out, tapering rectangular plank seat on wide slab supports w/scalloped aprons & inverted heart cut-outs, joined by keyed tenons, branded mark of Charles Limbert Company, Model No. 80, 39" h. (refinished) ................. **550.00**

**Mission-style (Arts & Crafts movement) Morris child's armchair,** oak, upright adjustable back w/four slats flanked by flat slightly tapering arms on square legs, cushion seat, brass plaque on bottom reads "Quaint Furniture, Stickley Bros., Grand Rapids, Mich.," 30½" h. (some finish wear) ............... **370.00**

**Mission-style (Arts & Crafts movement) Morris armchair,** oak, the tall adjustable back w/five horizontal slats, bent flat arms over front & rear corbels over five wide slats flanking the cushion seat, seatrail & lower side rails w/through-tenon construction, cleaned original finish, branded signature of Gustav Stickley, Model No. 369, 39" h. (minor restoration) ......................... **8,800.00**

**Mission-style (Arts & Crafts movement) Morris armchair,** oak, the adjustable back w/a gently downcurved top slat over three slightly narrower slats flanked by flat arms over five vertical slats, large red decal mark of Gustav Stickley, Model No. 332, ca. 1909, 40" h. .... **6,900.00**

**Mission-style (Arts & Crafts movement) dining chairs,** oak, each w/a U-form crestrail over five vertical slats between square stiles, flat curved arms on armchairs, drop-in spring-cushion seats, some w/original leatherette, original finish, branded mark or Handcraft decal marks of L. & J.G. Stickley, 36" h., two armchairs, six side chairs, set of 8 (chip on leg of one) .................... **4,675.00**

**Mission-style (Arts & Crafts movement) rocking chair w/arms,** oak, a wide V-form crestrail between square stiles flanking five narrow slats above the flat shaped arms on front corbels on the arm supports continuing into the front legs, seat recovered in brown leather, branded mark of Gustav Stickley, Model No. 311½, 34" h. (refinished) ............ **495.00**

**Mission-style (Arts & Crafts movement) rocking chair w/arms,** oak, flat curved crestrail over three long slats flanked by square stiles above flat arms w/corbels at the arm supports which continue to form front legs, deep flat aprons, drop-in seat recovered in brown leather, branded mark of the Charles Limbert Company, Model No. 934, 39" h. (refinished)........................ **385.00**

**Mission-style (Arts & Crafts movement) rocking chair without arms,** oak, the tall back w/square stiles & two rails framing three vertical slats each inlaid w/a stylized peacock feather in copper, pewter & darker wood, a rush seat over arched aprons, on square legs w/flat stretchers, designed by Harvey Ellis, small red decal mark of Gustav Stickley & partial paper label, Model No. 337, ca. 1904, 34" h. .............. **2,760.00**

**Mission-style (Arts & Crafts movement) side chair,** oak, the tall back w/a flat crestrail & square slender stiles centered by a cluster of ten slender square spindles above the rectangular sling seat recovered w/a leather cushion, square legs & seven slender square spindles under the seat at each side joined to low stretchers, higher plain flat stretchers at front & rear, dark original finish, red decal mark of Gustav Stickley, Model No. 374, 46" h. ............................................. **4,675.00**

**Mission-style (Arts & Crafts movement) side chairs,** oak, a flat narrow crestrail w/five small long cubed spindles extending down to the back base stretcher w/exposed tenons between square stiles, woven rush seat, high front stretcher & low side stretchers, metal company tag marked "Limberts Arts & Crafts Furniture Trademark Made in Grand Rapids and Holland," made for the dining room of The Canyon Hotel in Yellowstone National Park, ca. 1910, 38½" h., pr. ................... **4,600.00**

**Modern-style side chair,** LCM-type, wide curved black wood back raised on a thin metal support above the wide curved & rolled black wood seat raised on slender curved metal legs w/small pad feet, designed by Charles Eames, made by the Herman Miller Company, ca. 1950s, 26" h. ................................................. **330.00**

**Modern-style side chair,** so-called "tongue" chair, orange fabric-cover over a sculptural foam & metal frame resembling the human tongue, designed by Pierre Paulin, manufactured by Artifort, ca. 1967, 34 × 36", 24" h. ................................ **990.00**

**Modern-style side chairs,** molded plastic, the arched rolled back flaring down to rolled closed arms continuing to gently rounded seatrail

& removable blue cushion seat, molded as a single unit & resting upon a slender tapering plastic pedestal w/a widely flaring disc foot, designed by Eero Saarinen, manufactured by Knoll, ca. 1950-60, 18 × 26", 31" h., set of 6 (minor marks)............................................ **825.00**

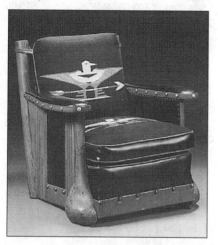

*Molesworth Fir Armchair*

**Molesworth (Thomas) armchair,** burled fir, heavy slightly canted back posts supporting the back cushion of black leather w/a Chimayo weaving depicting a red & white thunderbird flanked by upholstered paddle arms on heavy fir supports w/bulbous bases flanking the matching seat cushion & black & red leather-upholstered aprons, ca. 1945, 32" h. (ILLUS.) ........................................ **18,400.00**

**Queen Anne armchair,** wingback-style, the padded arched crestrail flanked by shaped upholstered wings continuing to vertically scrolling arms above a bowed seat w/seat cushion, on cabriole front legs ending in pad feet & square rear legs joined by a block-and arrow-turned H-stretcher, 18th c., 46" h. (ILLUS. top next column).......... **1,955.00**

**Queen Anne country-style armchair,** painted hardwood, the simple ox-yoke crestrail raised on baluster- and knob-turned stiles flanking a tapering carved splat to a lower rail flanked by slender shaped arms on baluster-turned arm supports flanking the woven rush seat, tapering cylindrical front legs ending in pad feet, back stiles form

back legs & all legs joined by box stretchers, attributed to Nathaniel Dominy, East Hampton, New York, 1770-1820, imperfections, 43" h. (ILLUS. bottom) ............................... **863.00**

*Queen Anne "Wingchair"*

*Queen Anne Country Armchair*

*Rare Newport Side Chair*

**Queen Anne country-style corner chair,** curved molded crestrail ending in rounded hand grips & supported on three baluster-turned supports joined by arched slats, replaced woven rush seat, ring- and baluster-turned front leg ending in a pad foot, plain turned back legs, some old red paint, New England, late 18th c., 28½" h. (paint imperfections) .................................. **920.00**

**Queen Anne side chair,** carved & painted, ox-yoke crestrail w/carved scrolls above a slender vase-form splat raised above a woven rush seat, baluster- and block-turned front legs joined by a knob- and ring-turned stretcher & terminating in Spanish feet, old raw umber & sienna graining, Massachusetts, 1730-50, 41" h. ............................. **1,840.00**

**Queen Anne side chair,** maple, simple ox-yoke crest w/rounded corners above gently curved stiles flanking a vase-form splat above the old woven rush seat, on baluster-, ring- and block-turned front legs joined by a bulbous knob- and ring-turned front stretcher, on knob front feet, curved square back legs, early stained surface, New England, 18th c., 41" h. (imperfections) ........ **1,150.00**

**Queen Anne side chair,** painted, the yoke crestrail above a solid vasiform splat flanked by cylindrical tapering ring- and baluster-turned stiles above a trapezoidal rush seat, on turned tapering legs joined by stretchers, the front stretcher w/ball- and bobbin-turnings, on pad feet, New York, 1740-60, 40¼" h. .............. **575.00**

**Queen Anne side chair,** walnut, the ox-yoke crestrail ending in scroll-carved ears above the reverse-curved splat, upholstered seat above a wide seatrail w/serpentine bottom edge, raised on cabriole front legs encing in raised pad feet, old finish, Philadelphia, Pennsylvania, 1740-70, 39" (minor perfections) .......... **2,645.00**

**Queen Anne side chair,** walnut, the ox-yoke crestrail w/a raised center & rounded corners on tapering turned stiles flanking the tall simple vase-form splat, the over-upholstered seat on cabriole front legs ending in pad feet & turned & shaped rear legs all joined by a block- and baluster-turned H-stretcher, refinished, repairs, Newport, Rhode Island, 1740-60, 42" h. (ILLUS. top previous column) ....................................... **19,550.00**

*Philadelphia Side Chair*

**Queen Anne side chairs,** walnut w/some curl, the arched & scalloped crestrail w/rounded corners continuing to molded incurved stiles flanking a scroll-cut vase-form splat over the reupholstered slip seat in the balloon-form seat frame, on cabriole front legs ending in pad feet & square canted back legs, Philadelphia, 18th c., old finish, pr. (ILLUS. of one, bottom previous page) .......................................... **19,800.00**

**Queen Anne side chairs,** walnut, simple ox-yoke crest w/rounded corners above the tall stiles flanking a simple vase-form splat, upholstered inset seat w/a scalloped front apron, on cabriole front legs ending in pad feet, turned stretchers joining all the legs, Massachusetts, ca. 1750, 39¾" h., pr. (old finish, minor imperfections) ................... **13,800.00**

**Queen Anne-Style wingback armchair,** the arched tall upholstered back flanked by two shaped tapering upholstered wings to out-scrolled upholstered arms over the upholstered seat w/curved seatrail, on cabriole front legs w/leafy scroll-carved knees & ending in claw-and-ball feet, 20th c. reproduction w/old crewel designs applied to newer linen, 4' 2½" h. (wear & fraying in places) ................ **330.00**

*Victorian Child's Armchair*

**Victorian armchair,** child's, Renaissance Revival substyle, mahogany, the high back w/a rose-, foliate & scroll-carved pierced crestrail w/scrolled ears above four slender baluster- and knob-turned spindles between slender bobbin-turned rails flanked by knob- and baluster-turned stiles over the padded turned arms w/knob hand grips over knob-turned arm supports flanking the upholstered seat, the flat seatrail joined to corner blocks raised on baluster- and ring-turned front legs w/peg feet, square rear legs, original condition w/old horsehair stuffing, ca. 1860-70 (ILLUS. bottom previous column) ..... **825.00**

*Gothic Revival Armchair*

**Victorian armchair,** Gothic Revival substyle, walnut, the Gothic-arched & spired open crestrail above a row of four spearpoint spindles flanked by pointed stiles above the padded open arms over the wide upholstered seat, slightly curved seatrail above slightly cabriole front legs & square canted rear legs all on casters, probably Philadelphia, ca. 1840-50 (ILLUS.) ............................ **935.00**

*Hunzinger "Patent" Armchair*

*Rococo Rosewood Desk Chair*

**Victorian armchair,** "patent"-type, walnut, canted bamboo-turned stiles continuing down to form front legs & topped by large beehive-turned finials, angled turned spindle arms joining canted bamboo-turned armrests continuing to form rear legs, the front & rear legs joined by bamboo-turned stretchers, the framework supporting a tapestry-style upholstered back w/a design of an urn framed by a large floral bouquet, the swelled upholstered seat w/matching upholstery & tassel fringe, stamped "Patent April 18, 1876" & "Pat. March 30, 1869," by Hunzinger, highlighted w/ebonized trim, ca. 1880, 33½" h. (ILLUS.) ....... **863.00**

**Victorian armchair,** Rococo substyle, walnut, the high balloon back w/a pierced leafy scroll-carved crestrail continuing down & tapering in above the tufted upholstered back & closed tufted arms, serpentine molded arm supports continuing to demi-cabriole front legs on casters & a serpentine molded seatrail, ca. 1860, 39" h. ...... **440.00**

**Victorian ballroom chairs,** Rococo substyle, walnut, rounded balloon-back w/a leaf- and fruit-carved center crest above three slender baluster- and ring-turned spindles above a lower scalloped rail over the upholstered seat, simple flat cabriole front legs, ca. 1850, set of 6 ............ **770.00**

**Victorian desk chair,** Rococo substyle, carved & laminated rosewood, the cartouche-form back w/pointed top ears & incurving frame around the upholstered back panel flanked by gently curved open arms on incurved arm supports flanking the wide upholstered seat, the seat swiveling on a pedestal raised on four down-scrolling legs on casters, attributed to John Henry Belter, ca. 1850 (ILLUS.) ................................. **9,900.00**

**Victorian dining chairs,** Rococo substyle, carved & laminated walnut, the arched & pointed padded & upholstered crest above a crestrail carved as facing pairs of dolphins w/their tails forming the stiles & their heads & leafy scrolls forming the pierced back, upholstered seat above a curved seatrail centered by a scroll-carved cartouche & continuing to demi-cabriole front legs ending in paw feet on casters, back-swept rear legs also ending in paw feet on casters, attributed to John Henry Belter, New York, New York, ca. 1850s, set of 8 ...................... **10,450.00**

**Victorian side & armchairs,** Rococo substyle, carved & laminated rosewood, each w/a tall balloon-form back w/a high arched crest boldly carved w/a cluster of fruits & flowers above an arched & scroll-carved crestrail continuing down to pierce-

*"Fountain Elms" Chairs*

*"Stanton Hall" Side Chairs*

carved sides of scrolls & floral vines framing the tufted upholstered oval back panel over the rounded upholstered seat, the armchair w/shaped & molded open arms continuing to incurved arm rests, each w/a serpentined front seatrail centered by a floral-carved cluster, on demi-cabriole front legs & curved square back legs all on casters, "Fountain Elms" patt., John Henry Belter, New York, New York, ca. 1850, armchair 44" h., set of 3 (ILLUS. top) .................................. **22,000.00**

**Victorian side chairs,** Victorian Rococo substyle, laminated & carved rosewood, the tall balloon-form back w/an arched, scroll-carved crestrail centered by a large fruit & floral carved cluster flanked by pierce-carved grapevines continuing down to form the sides framing the oval tufted upholstered back panel, raised on scrolls above the rounded upholstered seat w/a serpentine scroll-carved seatrail on demi-cabriole molded front legs & curved & canted rear legs, "Stanton Hall" patt., John J. Meeks, New York, New York, ca. 1850, 42" h., pr. (ILLUS. bottom previous page)...... **2,750.00**

*Carved Rosewood Side Chairs*

**Victorian side chairs,** Rococo substyle, carved & laminated rosewood, the balloon-form back w/an arched pierced & scroll- and floral-carved crest continuing down to pierced undulating sides framing the oval upholstered back panel raised on scrolls above the rounded upholstered seat w/a serpentine finger-molded seatrail continuing into demi-cabriole front legs & curved square rear legs, front legs on casters, ca. 1850, set of 4 (ILLUS. of two) .............................. **2,200.00**

**Victorian slipper chair,** Rococo substyle, rosewood, the tall slender balloon back w/a long molded horizontal C-scroll crest & molded incurved stiles framing the upholstered back panel above the low upholstered seat w/balloon-form seatrail, raised on carved cabriole front legs w/scroll feet on casters, square canted rear legs on casters, ca. 1850, 40½" h.............................. **880.00**

*Rococo Slipper Chair*

**Victorian slipper chairs,** Rococo substyle, carved & laminated rosewood, the tall balloon-form pierced & carved back w/a leaf-carved cartouche crest flanked by down-curved ropetwist bands over the swelled back composed of ornate C-scrolls centered by a carved grape cluster, all above the low, rounded upholstered seat on scroll-carved demi-cabriole front legs flanking a scroll-carved front apron & turned gently curved rear legs, on casters, New York, New York, ca. 1850, 41" h., pr. (ILLUS. of one) .... **2,200.00**

**Wicker armchair,** woven willow, a squared tightly woven back above broad flat arms over diamond-lattice panels, deep front & side aprons w/diamond-lattice panels w/solid woven borders, a pale moss green finish, w/cushion back & seat, unmarked Gustav Stickley, Model No. 64, ca. 1909, 33" h. ................. **5,750.00**

**William & Mary "banister-back" armchair,** carved maple, the high half-round crestrail carved as a sunburst between ring- and rod-turned stiles w/button finials flanking five split banisters resting on a wide lower rail w/a deeply scalloped bottom edge, shaped arms ending in scrolled hand holds raised on baluster-turned arm supports continuing down to form block- and baluster-turned front legs ending in scroll feet, woven rush seat, plain double rungs at front & sides, refinished, pieced feet, Connecticut, 1780-1800, 4' ½" h. (ILLUS. below).. **2,760.00**

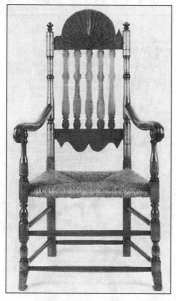

*William & Mary Armchair*

*William & Mary Side Chair*

*Windsor Highchair*

**William & Mary "banister-back" side chair,** carved & painted, the high arched pierced scroll-carved crest between corner blocks w/turned acorn finials on the rod- and knob-turned stiles flanking four split banisters on a shaped lower rail, woven rush seat on block- and baluster-turned front legs w/button feet joined by a double-knob-and-ring-turned front stretcher & turned side stretchers to the square back legs, old burnt sienna grain-painting over black, Massachusetts, early 18th c., 4' h. (ILLUS. bottom previous column) ......................................... **6,325.00**

**William & Mary "crooked-back" side chair,** maple, the tall narrow back w/a stepped & arched crestrail above gently backswept molded stiles flanking a long central upholstered panel, the trapezoidal upholstered seat raised on block- and baluster-turned front legs joined by a slender knob- and ring-turned stretcher, flat stretchers at the sides & back, square slightly canted back legs continuing from back stiles, original leather-upholstered seat, old surface, Boston area, 1740-50, 44" h. .......................................... **25,300.00**

**William & Mary side chair,** carved & painted, the tall narrow back w/an arched pierced & scroll-carved crest flanked by turned ball finials above block- and ring- and rod-turned stiles flanking four half-spindles, woven rush seat, on block- and knob-turned front legs ending in ball-and-pad front feet, square back legs, old black paint, Massachusetts, 1710-50, 46½" h. (very minor imperfections) ............................... **7,475.00**

**Windsor "bow-back" highchair,** turned wood, the bowed crestrail above five plain spindles extending through a medial rail that continues to form the flat shaped arms raised on a plain spindle & a canted bamboo-turned arm support, shaped plank saddle seat raised on tall canted bamboo-turned legs joined by a swelled H-stretcher, original black paint, New England, ca. 1790, 33" h. (ILLUS. top right, previous page) ............................ **19,550.00**

**Windsor "bow-back" side chairs,** bowed continuous crestrail above a back w/eight slender bamboo-turned spindles above the shaped saddle seat, canted bamboo-turned legs joined by a bamboo-turned H-stretcher, old refinish, Massachusetts, 1790-1810, 38½" h., set of 6 ......... **10,350.00**

**Windsor "bow-back" side chairs,** painted, the incised bowed crestrail above eight bamboo-turned tapering

spindles over a shaped saddle seat, on bamboo-turned legs joined by a swelled H-stretcher, overall brown paint, underside of each seat stamped "T.C.HAYWARD," attributed to Thomas Cotton Hayward, Charlestown, Massachusetts, 1770-1800, 37¾" h., pr. (ILLUS. bottom)..... **863.00**

*Windsor Side Chair*

*Windsor "Bow-back" Side Chairs*

**Windsor "braced bow-back" side chair,** the arched, incised crestrail above nine plain turned spindles & two back-brace spindles above the shaped saddle seat, on canted baluster- and ring-turned legs joined by a swelled H-stretcher, inscribed "J-Caldwell," New York City, ca. 1790, refinished, 35" h. (ILLUS. top right, previous page) .................. **633.00**

**Windsor "braced bow-back" side chair,** the arched crestrail surrounding nine simple turned spindles w/a pair of flared brace spindles at the back, a shaped saddled seat on canted baluster-turned legs joined by a swelled, turned H-stretcher, New York, 1780-1800, 37" h. (refinished, minor imperfections) ................................. **690.00**

*Hayward Windsor Armchair*

**Windsor "comb-back" armchair,** the arched crestrail w/rounded ears & faceted lower edge above five slender spindles & an arched back rail w/two extra spindles all of which terminate below w/swelled shafts centered by a rear rail w/carved knuckle hand holds above canted baluster- and ring-turned arm supports, on a wide oblong shaped shaped raised on canted baluster- and ring-turned legs joined by a

swelled H-stretcher, Thomas Cotton Hayward, Charlestown, Massachusetts, 1770-1800 (ILLUS. previous column) ........................ **4,830.00**

*Windsor "Comb-back" Armchair*

**Windsor "comb-back" armchair,** the shaped crestrail w/volute-carved ears above eight tall tapered spindles continuing through the U-shaped back rail that continues to form shaped arms ending in flared hand holds, the peaked elliptical shaped seat on baluster- and ring-turned canted legs joined by a swelled H-stretcher, black paint, probably New England, ca. 1790 (ILLUS.) ............ **4,888.00**

**Windsor "comb-back" armchair,** the yolk-shaped crestrail raised on seven slender spindles continuing through the arched backrail which terminates at a flat medial rail continuing to form the shaped arms w/hand holds resting on two additional short spindles & canted baluster- and ring-turned arm supports above the rounded shaped seat, raised on canted baluster- and ring-turned legs joined by a swelled H-stretcher, old worn brown repaint w/gold striping over red & green, late 18th c., Connecticut (ILLUS. top next page) ................................. **11,000.00**

*Rare Windsor "Comb-back"*

*Windsor Rocking Chair*

**Windsor "comb-back" rocking chair,** the long gently rounded crestrail above six short spindles raised on a stepped wider crestrail over seven plain turned spindles flanked by tapering 'rabbit-ear' stiles,

S-scroll arms over a spindle & canted arm supports, wide oblong shaped seat raised on bamboo-turned canted legs on rockers & joined by bamboo-turned box stretchers, old Spanish brown paint w/natural arms, restoration, early 19th c., New England, 44" h. (ILLUS. bottom previous column) ..... **748.00**

*Windsor "Continuous-arm" Armchair*

**Windsor "continuous-arm" armchair w/brace back,** the arched crestrail continuing down to slightly flaring arms all above eleven graduated turned spindles & w/two brace spindles at the back of the shaped saddle seat, on baluster- and ring-turned canted legs joined by a swelled H-stretcher, old green paint, minor repair, probably Rhode Island, ca. 1780, 37" h. (ILLUS.).... **2,185.00**

**Windsor "fan-back" side chair,** painted, narrow gently arched & curved crestrail above slender baluster-turned stiles flanking seven plain spindles above the shaped saddle seat raised on canted baluster- and ring-turned legs joined by a baluster- and ring-turned H-stretcher, New England, late 18th c., old black paint, 37½" h. ................ **4,600.00**

**Windsor "fan-back" side chair,**
painted, narrow serpentine crestrail
above seven plain turned flared
spindles between canted simple
baluster-turned stiles above the
shaped saddle seat, on canted
baluster- and ring-turned legs joined
by a swelled H-stretcher, old black
paint, New England, early 19th c.,
34½" h. (minor imperfections)........... **460.00**

**Windsor "fan-back" side chair,**
shaped & curved crestrail w/rolled
ears above slender baluster-turned
stiles flanking seven spindles above
the shaped saddle seat raised on
canted ring- and baluster-turned legs
joined by an "H" stretcher, old black
paint w/later gold striping,
Connecticut, ca. 1770-90, 37" h. ..... **1,092.00**

*Late Windsor Rocker*

*Windsor "Fan-back" Side Chair*

**Windsor "fan-back" side chair,** the
cupid's-bow crestrail w/upturned
ears above six tapering spindles &
two bracing back spindles flanked by
baluster- and ring-turned canted
stiles over the shaped saddle seat,
on baluster- and ring-turned widely
canted legs joined by a swelled H-
stretcher, Connecticut, 1780-1800,
36" h. (ILLUS.) .............................. **7,475.00**

*Windsor Child's Chair*

**Windsor "flat-crest" rocking chair,**
the wide rectangular flat crestrail
above a tall back w/seven plain turned
spindles between plain round stiles,
flattened S-scroll arms on two short
spindles & a canted turned arm
support, oblong dished seat on canted
bamboo-turned legs joined by
bamboo-turned box stretchers, on
rockers, brown & black rosewood
graining & dark-stained arms,
imperfections, northern New England,
ca. 1835, 45" h. (ILLUS. top)............. **230.00**

**Windsor "sack-back" child's armchair,** painted, the arched crestrail above five tapering spindles, the U-shaped back rail forming slightly flaring hand holds above canted baluster- and ring-turned arm supports, the oblong shaped plank seat on baluster- and ring-turned canted legs joined by a swelled H-stretcher, painted red, feet slightly shortened, Philadelphia, ca. 1785 (ILLUS. bottom previous page) ................................................ **977.00**

**Windsor "sack-back" armchair,** ash, poplar & maple, arched crestrail above seven graduated spindles over a medial rail continuing to form arms w/carved hand-grip knuckles above baluster- and ring-turned arm supports over the wide shaped saddle seat on canted baluster- and ring-turned legs joined by an H-stretcher, probably Connecticut, ca. 1780, old refinish, 36½" h. (repairs).. **978.00**

**Windsor "sack-back" armchair,** painted, the arched crestrail over seven slender spindles, the U-shaped back rail continuing to arms w/scrolled hand holds raised on canted baluster- and ring-turned arm supports, wide oblong shaped seat raised on baluster- and ring-turned canted legs joined by a swelled H-stretcher w/ring-turned central rung, probably Massachusetts, ca. 1780, several coats of early red paint, imperfections, 38" h. (ILLUS. top next column)..... **5,175.00**

*Windsor "Sack-back" Armchair*

**Windsor "sack-back" armchair,** turned & painted, the arched crestrail above seven tapered spindles, the U-shaped back rail continuing to form shaped hand holds on baluster- and ring-turned arm supports, wide oblong peaked plank seat on canted baluster- and ring-turned legs joined by a swelled H-stretcher, painted dark green, ca. 1785 ........................................ **2,645.00**

**Windsor "step-down" side chairs,** painted & decorated, the stepped crestrail above slender curved stiles

*"Step-down" Windsor Side Chairs*

*Windsor "Thumb-back"*
*Side Chairs*

flanking seven slender spindles above the shaped saddle seat, on slightly canted bamboo-turned legs joined by box stretchers, original black paint w/floral leaf decoration on the crest & stiles, New England, early 19th c., 36" h., pr. (minor paint wear)............................................. **1,150.00**

**Windsor "step-down" side chairs,** painted & decorated, the wide gently curved crestrail w/stepped & curved top above canted & bamboo-turned stiles flanking six bamboo-turned spindles, shaped saddle seat on canted bamboo-turned legs joined by a bamboo-turned H-stretcher, incised "G. Gammon - Warranted," w/indistinct rosewood graining & gold stenciling on the crest, Halifax, Nova Scotia, ca. 1800, 35½" h., set of 6................................................ **6,900.00**

**Windsor "step-down" side chairs,** the "stepped" narrow crestrail above seven slender curved spindles between flattened tapering back-curved stiles, shaped plank seat on canted bamboo-turned legs joined by turned box stretchers, original black paint w/wear & indistinct stenciling on the crest, New England, early 19th c., 36" h., pr. (ILLUS. bottom previous page)...... **2,645.00**

**Windsor "thumb-back" side chairs,** the wide flat & gently curved crestrail over four swelled slender knob-turned spindles flanked by tapering back-curved stiles, shaped plank seat on canted bamboo-turned legs joined by box stretchers, painted red, orange & brown w/metallic &

green stenciling in a grapevine design on the crestrail, one front stretcher missing, imperfections, New England, early 19th c., set of 4 (ILLUS. of two).............................. **1,725.00**

## CHESTS & CHESTS OF DRAWERS

**Apothecary chest,** hanging-type, walnut, a rectangular top w/a narrow flaring cornice above a case of forty-eight small square drawers w/beveled edges & small ivory knobs arranged in eight rows of six drawers each, flat base, square nail construction, some names written in ink inside some drawers, 19th c., cornice 3½ x 25¾", 15¾" h. (some knobs replaced) ............................ **1,128.00**

**Apothecary chest,** poplar, rectangular top above two stacks of five drawers each, porcelain pulls & raised on porcelain casters, old dark finish, 19th c., 18¼ x 24", 26¼" h. (drawer dividers removed, some edge damage, pulls mismatched & some loose) ................................................. **396.00**

**Art Deco chest of drawers,** macassar, burled maple & lacquer, a large free-standing round mirror above the chest w/a rectangular top w/rounded front edge above a case of five graduated drawers w/two bands of black lacquer forming raised pulls down the center front, blond burled maple base w/inset maccasar strip, on a narrow raised base, designed by Gilbert Rohde, manufactured by the Herman Miller Company, 1930s, 18" d. mirror, chest 18 x 33", 42½" h. (metal refinished) ......................... **1,760.00**

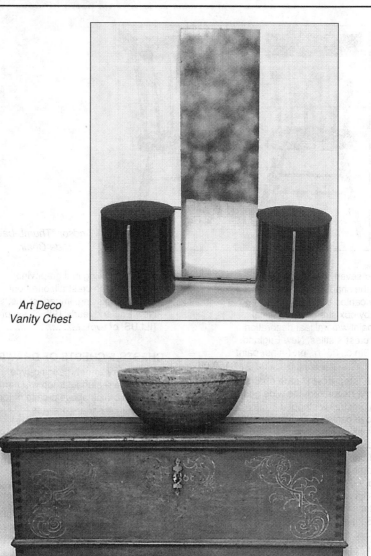

*Art Deco
Vanity Chest*

*Fine Chippendale Blanket Chest*

**Art Deco vanity chest,** macassar, a
tall narrow vertical rectangular mirror
supported by horizontal brushed
steel rods between two round stacks
of three drawers each w/macassar
veneer & a stripe of blond wood
forming handles, designed by Gilbert
Rohde, manufactured by Herman
Miller, refinished, ca. 1934, 21 × 85",
5' 6" h. (ILLUS. top) ...................... **2,310.00**

**Blanket chest,** child's, painted pine,
rectangular hinged top lifting above
a deep well, wide board sides,
bootjack cut-out ends, red paint,
New England, 19th c., 9 × 19",
12" h. (minor imperfections)........... **1,725.00**

**Blanket chest,** Chippendale country-
style, walnut, the rectangular top
w/molded edge opening to a deep
well w/a till w/lid & two secret

compartments, the dovetailed case decorated on the front w/leafy scroll designs flanking a central design around the keyhole escutcheon w/scrolls & the markings "I.D. 1768," molded mid-molding above molded base on short ogee bracket feet, Pennsylvania (ILLUS. bottom previous page) ............................ **15,400.00**

**Blanket chest,** country-style, painted & decorated, six-board construction, the rectangular hinged lid w/molded edges opening to a deep well w/lidded till, molded base on a deep serpentine apron & plain bracket feet, overall simulated rosewood graining, Scoharie County, New York, early 19th c., 17¼ × 41", 23" h. (imperfections) ........................ **575.00**

**Blanket chest,** country-style, painted & decorated pine, rectangular top w/molded edge hinged & opening to a deep well w/a lidded till above a case w/a row of three small drawers across the bottom, molded base on plain bracket feet, overall original red & black graining w/dark painted base, probably New York state, ca. 1820s, 20 × 46¼", 24½" h. (replaced drawer brasses, surface imperfections, feet repair) ................. **748.00**

**Blanket chest,** country-style, painted & decorated pine, rectangular top w/molded edge opening to a deep well above a single long drawer w/round brass pulls at the base, bootjack ends, original old painted yellow ground w/brown graining, New England, early 19th c., 16 × 40¾", 31½" h. (minor imperfections) ......... **1,840.00**

**Blanket chest,** Federal country-style, pine, rectangular hinged top w/molded edge opening to a well w/a lidded till above the dovetailed case over a mid-molding above a pair of overlapping drawers w/original simple bail handles across the bottom, molded base raised on simple tall French feet, old mellow refinishing, early 19th c., 24 × 49½", 30¾" h. (hinges replaced, various repairs) ...... **495.00**

**Blanket chest w/drawers,** Federal country-style, painted & decorated pine, the rectangular hinged top w/molded edge opening to a two-lidded till & deep well, a thin mid-molding above two drawers w/chamfered edges & two turned wood knobs each at the bottom, the molded base raised on short baluster-turned legs, decorated overall w/original red & yellow wood graining imitating mahogany, surface imperfections, Pennsylvania, early 19th c., 20 × 47¼", 33" h. (ILLUS. below) ................................................. **690.00**

**Blanket chest w/drawers,** Pilgrim Century, painted, the rectangular hinged thumb-molded top opening to a deep well above a conforming case fitted w/a long drawer across the bottom w/two sets of raised moldings forming false drawer fronts, the front case edges applied w/raised molding trim above a mid-molding & the base drawer, on plank feet, inscribed in ink on the back "1719" & branded on the back "BB" & under a top "SB," painted red, New England, 20 × 47¼", 33⅜" h. (ILLUS. top next page) ................. **6,325.00**

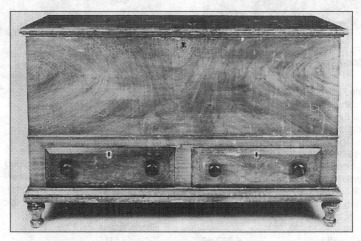

*Federal Painted Blanket Chest*

*Pilgrim Century Blanket Chest*

**Chest over drawer,** child's, grain-painted, rectangular top lifting above a deep well over a long drawer at the base, recessed side panels, turned wooden knobs on drawer, short turned & tapering feet, original smoke-grained surface, New England, ca. 1830s, 16 × 31", 24" h. (minor surface imperfections) ..................... **1,495.00**

*Chippendale "Bow-front" Chest*

**Chippendale "bow-front" chest of drawers,** carved mahogany, the rectangular top w/bowed front & molded edges above a conforming case w/four long graduated cockbeaded drawers w/two oval brasses & brass keyhole escutcheons, molded base raised on short scroll-cut cabriole legs w/claw-and-ball feet, rich brown color, appears to retain original brasses, Masscahusetts, ca. 1790, 23¼ × 41¾", 33½" h. (ILLUS.).................. **8,050.00**

**Chippendale chest of drawers,** mahogany, rectangular top w/molded edges above a case w/four long cockbeaded drawers w/butterfly brasses & keyhole escutcheons, molded base, ogee bracket feet w/double-scroll cut corners, Norwich, Connecticut, 18th c., old refinish, 20 × 38", 33" h. (repairs) ............................................ **8,050.00**

*Chippendale Maple Chest of Drawers*

**Chippendale chest of drawers,** maple, rectangular thumb-molded top above a case of four reverse-graduated long drawers w/butterfly pulls & keyhole escutcheons, molded base on tall ogee bracket feet, Rhode Island, ca. 1785, 17 × 40½", 39" h. (ILLUS.) ................................ **2,875.00**

**Chippendale "reverse serpentine" chest of drawers,** mahogany, the rectangular top w/molded edges & reverse serpentine front above a comforming case w/four long graduated cockbeaded drawers w/pierced butterfly brasses & keyhole escutcheons, molded base, ogee bracket feet, Boston, late 18th c., original brasses, 19 × 34", 33" h. ......................................... **25,300.00**

*Chippendale "Serpentine-front" Chest*

*Connecticut Chippendale Chest*

**Chippenale "serpentine-front" chest of drawers,** cherry, the oblong top w/serpentine front & thumb-molded edges above a conforming case w/four long graduated drawers w/simple bail pulls & oval brass keyhole escutcheons, fluted quarter-columns down the front corners, molded base on tall ogee bracket feet, Connecticut, ca. 1790, 21 × 43½", 34½" h. (ILLUS. above left) ... **9,200.00**

**Chippendale "serpentine-front" chest of drawers,** cherry, the oblong top w/serpentine front & thumb-molded edges above a conforming case w/four long cockbeaded drawers w/simple bail pulls & oval brass keyhole escutcheons, molded base on tall scroll-cut bracket feet, original brasses, old refinishing, late 18th c. (ILLUS. above right) ................... **11,000.00**

**Chippendale "serpentine-front" chest of drawers,** mahogany, the

*Fine Chippendale "Serpentine-front" Chest of Drawers*

rectangular top w/a molded serpentine front above a case of four long cockbeaded flat graduated drawers w/butterfly pulls & keyhole escutcheons, molded base raised on double-scroll-cut ogee bracket feet, possibly original brasses, minor imperfections, New London County, Connecticut, ca. 1780, refinished, 22 × 38", 32" h. (ILLUS. bottom previous page) ........................................... **27,500.00**

*Chippendale Cherry Chest-on-Chest*

**Chippendale chest-on-chest,** bonnet-top-style, cherry, two-part construction: the upper section w/a broken-scroll bonnet w/a wide molded cornice & three slender urn-forn finials above a case w/two pairs of small drawers flanking a deep central drawer w/a carved pinwheel & knob above four long graduated drawers; the lower case w/a mid-molding over three long graduated drawers on a molded base w/ogee bracket feet, old replaced brasses, old refinish, damages to some drawer edges, Connecticut, 1760-90, 19 × 39", 7' 3" h. (ILLUS.) ......... **12,650.00**

*Rare Connecticut Chest-on-Chest*

**Chippendale chest-on-chest,** bonnet-top-style, cherry, two-part construction: the upper section w/a broken-scroll bonnet w/a wide molded cornice & three knob-and-flame-turned finials above two small drawers flanking a deeper fan-carved center drawer above four long graduated drawers all flanked by spiral edge carving; the lower section w/a mid-molding above four long graduated drawers flanked by spiral edge carving, molded base on simple bracket feet, original brasses & keyhole escutcheons, original finish, minor imperfections, Connecticut River Valley, 1780-95, 20 × 41", 7' 6" h. (ILLUS.) ............ **57,500.00**

**Chippendale chest-on-chest,** carved mahogany, two-part construction: the upper section w/a rectangular top w/a deep flaring cornice over three short & three long graduated molded drawers, fluted canted corners flanking; the lower section w/hinged pull-out writing section opening to reveal valanced pigeonholes over small drawers, three long graduated drawers below, the molded base raised on claw-and-ball feet, appears to retain original finish & rich brown color & rare "pinetree" brasses, New York, ca. 1775, 24 × 50", 6' 7½" h. ........ **20,700.00**

**Chippendale chest-on-chest,** carved walnut, two-part construction: the upper section w/a high broken-scroll swan's-neck crest fitted w/a turned urn and flame center finial & matching corner finials above a case w/a deep fan-carved center drawer flanked by two curved-top smaller drawers over three long graduated drawers; the lower section w/a mid-molding above a case with four long graduated drawers on a molded apron raised on scroll-cut tall bracket feet & a center drop, Massachusetts or New Hampshire, some original butterfly brasses, old refinish, late 18th c., 23 × 41", 7' 5½" h. (imperfections) ............................ **13,800.00**

**Chippendale chest-on-chest,** cherry, two-part construction: the upper section w/a rectangular top w/a cove-molded cornice above a case w/five long graduated drawers w/simple bail pulls; the lower section w/a mid-molding above a case w/four long graduated drawers w/simple bail pulls, molded flat base, early red-stained surface, original brasses, New England, ca. 1800, 19 × 38", 5' 8" h. (base missing, minor imperfections) ..................... **4,600.00**

**Chippendale chest-on-chest,** flat-top-style, maple, two-part construction: the upper section w/a flat rectangular top w/a deep cove-molded cornice above a case of five long graduated drawers w/butterfly brasses & keyhole escutcheons; the lower section w/a mid-molding over a case of four long graduated drawers w/matching brasses, molded base on short cabriole legs ending in claw-and-ball feet, New England, last quarter 18th c. (ILLUS. top next column) ................. **9,200.00**

**Chippendale tall chest of drawers,** cherry, rectangular top above a cove-molded cornice above a case of six long graduated thumb-molded drawers w/butterfly brasses & keyhole escutcheons, molded base on tall bracket feet, probably Connecticut River Valley, late 18th c., 17 × 37", 4' 5" h. (old refinish, replaced brasses, imperfections) ... **1,725.00**

*Chippendale Maple Chest-on-Chest*

*Chippendale Curly Maple Tall Chest*

**Chippendale tall chest of drawers,** curly maple, the rectangular top w/a deep cove-molded cornice above a case w/six long graduated drawers w/simple bail pulls & oval keyhole escutcheons, molded base on tall scroll-cut bracket feet, old dark finish, top drawers lined w/1803 Massachusetts newspaper, original brasses & two original locks, New England, late 18th - early 19th c. (ILLUS. bottom previous page).... **13,200.00**

**Chippendale tall chest of drawers,** mahogany, a rectangular top w/a deep flaring molded cornice above a tall case fitted w/a row of three small thumb-molded drawers over five long graduated drawers flanked by fluted quarter columns above a molded base, on ogee bracket feet, appears to retain original oval brasses, Philadelphia, 1760-80, 22 × 43½", 5' 4¾" h. (restorations to feet) ................... **5,750.00**

**Chippendale tall chest of drawers,** maple, a rectangular top w/a cove-molded cornice above a case of seven long graduated drawers each w/a simple bail pull & oval brass keyhole escutcheon, molded base on tall bracket feet, probably Massachusetts, ca. 1790, 17¼ × 36¾", 4' 9¼" h. (old refinish, old replaced brasses, restoration) ........................................ **5,462.50**

**Chippendale tall chest of drawers,** walnut, the rectangular top above a deep simple coved cornice above a row of three small drawers over a pair of drawers above four long graduated drawers all w/butterfly brasses & the long drawers w/brass keyhole escutcheons, molded base on tall scroll-cut ogee bracket feet, reeded quarter columns down the front corners, Pennsylvania, late 18th c., cornice 22¾ × 40⅜", 5' 11¾" h. (some old repairs & replacements, replaced brasses, refinished) .......... **6,325.00**

**Chippendale country-style chest of drawers,** cherry, plain rectangular top above a case w/four long flush graduated drawers w/butterfly pulls, molded base on shaped bracket feet, w/a brush slide, ca. 1780, 19 × 45", 39" h. ............................ **1,540.00**

**Chippendale country-style chest of drawers,** red birch, rectangular top above a case of four long drawers each w/oval brasses & brass keyhole escutcheons, on tall bracket feet, Concord, New Hampshire, early 19th c., original surface & pulls, 18 × 38", 37" h. ............................. **3,450.00**

**Chippendale country-style chest of drawers,** stained maple, rectangular top above a case w/four long graduated drawers w/oval brass keyhole escutcheons, molded base, tall scroll-cut bracket feet, old red stain, Masschusetts or New Hampshire, late 18th c., 20½ × 38¾", 37½" h. (no brasses, imperfections) ............................... **3,220.00**

*Chippendale-Style Chest of Drawers*

**Chippendale-Style "block-front" chest of drawers,** mahogany, the rectangular top w/a molded edge above a blocked case w/four long drawers, each w/outer blocked sections flanking a concave center section, each section topped by a bold shell carving, butterfly brasses & keyhole escutcheons, on a conforming molded base on ogee bracket feet, in the Newport, Rhode Island manner, 18½ × 35½", 34½" h. (ILLUS. above) ............................. **5,462.00**

*Small Classical Chest of Drawers*

**Classical chest of drawers,**
mahogany & mahogany veneer, the
rectangular top w/a high flat backrail
w/raised corner blocks, the top
above a long ogee-front drawer
overhanging two deep long drawers
w/early small glass knobs flanked by
heavy ogee-cut pilasters, flat apron
& C-scroll front feet & square back
feet, ca. 1840, small size (ILLUS.
bottom previous page) ..................... **605.00**

**Classical chest of drawers,**
mahogany & mahogany veneer, the
rectangular top fitted w/a raised
frame w/a row of three small
handkerchief drawers, the end two
each w/two small wooden knobs &
the center one w/an ogee front, the
top above a case w/a long ogee-
front drawer slightly overhanging
three long graduated drawers
w/wooden knobs flanked by heavy
ogee pilasters, heavy C-scroll front
legs & baluster- and knob-turned
rear legs w/peg feet, ca. 1830,
21 × 43½", 45¼" h. .......................... **770.00**

*Late Classical Chest of Drawers*

**Classical chest of drawers,**
mahogany & mahogany veneer, a
large horizontal rectangular mirror
frame raised & swiveling between
long S-scroll supports on a
rectangular tiered top w/two narrow
drawers w/small round brass pulls

on a rectangular top above a long
ogee-fronted drawer overhanging a
case w/two long, deep drawers
w/round brass pulls & flanked by
free-standing columns w/scroll-
carved capitals, flat apron raised on
leaf-carved hairy paw front feet, ca.
1830-40 (ILLUS. previous column) ... **825.00**

*Duncan Phyfe-type Classical Chest*

**Classical chest of drawers,**
mahogany, the rectangular top
w/rounded corners above a
conforming case fitted w/a deep
cockbeaded long drawer w/oval inlay
over three graduated cockbeaded
long drawers flanked by reeded inset
colonettes, the case w/panelled
sides, on short tapering ring-turned
legs w/ball feet, appears to retain
original lion head-and-ring brasses,
attributed to Duncan Phyfe, New
York, 1810-20, 21 × 45½", 45" h.
(ILLUS.) ........................................ **4,370.00**

**Classical chest of drawers,**
rosewood veneer, cherry & bird's-
eye maple, the top fitted w/a
rectangular mirror swiveling between
two curved uprights w/a shaped
base resting atop a row of three
small handkerchief drawers set-back
on the rectangular top w/outset front
corners over corner blocks flanking a
long round-fronted drawer slightly
overhanging a case of two deep,
long drawers flanked by free-
standing turned columns on blocks,
flat apron, baluster- and-ring-turned
front legs, Orange, Massachusetts,
old refinish, old brass pulls, ca. 1835,
20¼ × 41¼", 5' 3" h. (ILLUS. top next
page) ............................................. **1,955.00**

*Maple Veneered Classical Chest of Drawers*

**Classical country-style chest of drawers,** curly maple, rectangular top above a case w/two deep large square drawers flanking a stack of two small drawers in the center & slightly overhanging three long graduated drawers all w/simple turned wood knobs, flat apron w/corner blocks raised on short heavy turned tapering legs w/knob feet, good figure throughout, ca. 1830, 20¼ × 43½", 46¾" h. (refinished) ....................................... **990.00**

**Classical country-style chest of drawers,** painted poplar, rectangular top above a deep top drawer w/two brass pulls w/clear ribbed glass inserts overhanging three long graduated drawers w/matching pulls flanked by columnar pilasters decorated w/gold stenciled leaves & classical designs, old alligatored red finish, ebonized legs & pilasters, baluster-turned legs w/knob feet w/added casters, ca. 1830, top 20¾ × 42", 4' 1½" h. ...................... **1,100.00**

**Classical country-style chest of drawers,** painted & decorated, the scrolled splashboard above a rectangular top over a conforming case w/a long drawer overhanging a case w/three long graduated drawers flanked by ring-and-baluster-turned colonettes w/square block bases, on ring-turned legs w/compressed ball feet, the whole grain-painted & outlined w/green & yellow, appears to retain original round brass pulls, Maine, 1830-40, 23¼ × 43¼", 45" h. (ILLUS. below) ............................ **10,925.00**

*Rare Decorated Classical Chest of Drawers*

**Country-style blanket chest,** six-board construction, grain-painted, the rectangular top w/a molded edge opening to a well w/lidded till, the top & sides w/overall early graining simulating tiger stripe maple, on short turned double-knob feet, Pennsylvania, 1830-40, 20 × 42", 24" h. (imperfections)...................... **805.00**

*Painted & Decorated Chest of Drawers*

**Country-style chest of drawers,** painted & decorated, the rectangular top centering a painted ship within an oval reserve above a pair of short drawers over three long drawers, on compressed ball feet, the entire surface painted brown & embellished w/yellow line trim & yellow leafy scrolls & the inscription "1871 - THE LIBERTY - 800 TONS - FALMOUTH," New England, 18 × 39", 43" h. (ILLUS.) .............................. **1,295.00**

**Dower chest,** Chippendale country-style, painted poplar, rectangular top w/molded edges opening to a deep well above a mid-molding over two long drawers flanking a small drawer across the bottom, molded base on ogee bracket feet, painted blue w/salmon red contrasting molding, old butterfly brasses on the drawers, Pennsylvania, late 18th c., 22¾ × 49", 29" h........... **4,600.00**

**Federal "bow-front" chest of drawers,** mahogany veneer, rectangular top w/bowed front above a conforming case w/four long cockbeaded drawers w/turned wood knobs, shaped apron & French feet, old refinish, New England, ca. 1800, 22 × 41", 37" h. (old replaced knobs, minor imperfections) ......... **2,415.00**

**Federal chest of drawers,** birch, bird's-eye maple & mahogany veneer, the rectangular top above a case of four long drawers w/cross-banded veneer & cockbeading outlining each & w/oval brass pulls & keyhole escutcheons, double-scallop apron & slender French feet, old brass stamped "WJ," Rutland, Middlebury, Vermont area, 1817, 19 × 40", 37" h. (minor imperfections).................................... **2,530.00**

**Federal chest of drawers,** carved mahogany & mahogany veneer, a curved & scroll-ended crestboard above a rectangular top w/a bowed front & ovolu front corners above carved cornucopia & rope-twist columns flanking four long cockbeaded bowed drawers w/rosette & bail pulls, on baluster- and ring-turned legs w/knob feet, coastal North Shore, Massachusetts, ca. 1820, 22½ × 42", 44½" h. (old refinish, imperfections) ................. **2,070.00**

**Federal chest of drawers,** cherry & maple, the rectangular top above a conforming case fitted w/a long deep drawer over three long graduated drawers, on ring-turned tapering feet, 1800-15, 19 × 41", 41½" h. ..... **1,380.00**

**Federal chest of drawers,** cherry, rectangular top w/beaded edges above a case w/four long graduated thumb-molded drawers w/oval brasses & brass keyhole escutcheons raised on slender French feet, old surface, original brasses, Wakefield, New Hampshire, 17 × 36", 36" h. .............................. **2,990.00**

**Federal chest of drawers,** flame birch & mahogany veneer, rectangular top w/ovolu outset front corners above turned columns w/reeded & knob-turned segments centered by a tall spiral-turned segment all flanking four long drawers w/banded edging & oval brasses, on short turned & tapering legs ending in small knob feet, old refinish, eastern Massachusetts or southern New Hampshire, ca. 1810, 20 × 40", 36" h. (replaced brasses, imperfections) ................. **1,610.00**

**Federal chest of drawers,** inlaid cherry, rectangular top w/outset ovolu corners above finely reeded outset columns flanking four long mahogany-veneered drawers w/pairs of oval brasses, on baluster-turned legs w/knob feet, inlaid escutcheons, original brasses stamped "HJ," old refinish, Athol, Massachusetts, attributed to Spooner and Fitch, ca. 1810, 19 × 42", 41" h. (minor imperfections) .................................. **1,840.00**

**Federal chest of drawers,** inlaid cherry, rectangular top w/herringbone-inlaid edges above a case w/four long cockbeaded drawers each w/two round brass pulls above an inlaid zipper base band above a fishtail-carved apron centered by an inlaid oval, on plain bracket feet, probably central Massachusetts, ca. 1810, 20 × 42¾", 41½" h. (old refinish, replaced brasses, minor imperfections) ...... **1,725.00**

**Federal chest of drawers,** inlaid cherry, a rectangular top above a pair of drawers w/light veneer banding, bone-inlaid keyhole escutcheons & old lacy pressed glass pulls above three long graduated matching drawers, on short ring-turned legs, northern New England, ca. 1820, 21 × 40", 45" h. (refinished, imperfections) ... **1,955.00**

**Federal chest of drawers,** inlaid mahogany, rectangular top above four long cockbeaded drawers w/original oval brasses stamped "HJ," brass keyhole escutcheons, scalloped apron on French feet, old refinish, Connecticut, ca. 1810, 18 × 41", 35" h. (imperfections) ...................... **1,610.00**

**Federal chest of drawers,** mahogany & mahogany veneer, the rectangular top w/ovolu front corners above bamboo-turned corner columns flanking four long beaded drawers w/stringing, inlay & oval brass pulls, & inlaid keyhole escutcheons, sawtooth-cut apron, tapering baluster-turned legs, New Hamshire, 1815-25, 20 × 41½", 37" h. (refinished, imperfections) ............. **1,150.00**

**Federal country-style chest of drawers,** cherry, small tall upright case w/a rectangular top above four long graduated drawers each w/two turned wood knobs, on short baluster-turned legs w/knob feet,

underside of top drawer colorfully signed in four colors w/flourishes "Made in 1830, Clara M. Ilger," old refinishing, early 19th c., top 16 × 22½", 31¾" h. (top drawer missing lock, filled age crack in top, pulls mismatched) ......................... **1,705.00**

**Federal country-style chest of drawers,** painted & decorated, rectangular hinged top opening to a deep well over two long drawers w/round brass knobs & keyhole escutcheons, raised on knob- and ring-turned short legs tapering to peg feet, overall burnt sienna & mustard putty paint & green sponging in combination w/red & black paint simulating mahogany, Massachusetts, ca. 1825-35, 18 × 40", 40½" h. (old replaced brasses, minor imperfections) ................... **31,050.00**

**Federal country-style tall chest of drawers,** painted & decorated, a rectangular top above a cove-molded cornice over a case w/six long graduated drawers w/simple bail pulls & brass oval keyhole escutcheons, molded base on tall scroll-cut bracket feet, faux grained to resemble bird's-eye maple, probably New Hampshire, late 18th c.,18½ × 38", 4' 3¾" h. (replaced brasses) ........................................ **4,312.00**

**Mission-style (Arts & Crafts movement) chest of drawers w/mirror,** oak, a large rectangular mirror frame swiveling between tapering square uprights on a backrail over the rectangular top overhanging the case w/a pair of drawers over three long graduated drawers all w/hammered copper plates w/ring pulls, flat apron, short stile feet, butterfly joint construction, original light finish, red decal mark of Gustav Stickley, Model No. 905, 23 × 48", 5' 6" h. ............................. **7,700.00**

**Pilgrim Century chest over drawer,** oak, joined construction w/a rectangular hinged top w/breadboard ends lifting above a deep well, the front divided into four panels separated by reeded pilasters above a long drawer across the bottom w/three panels & four short pilasters, double-paneled ends, short stile legs, old finish, minor imperfections, New England, ca. 1700, 22 × 48½", 32¾" h. (ILLUS. top next page) ..... **4,312.00**

*Pilgrim Century Chest over Drawer*

**Pilgrim Century chest over drawer,**
pine, joined & paneled, the
rectangular top hinged & opening to
a deep well, the front w/three
recessed panels & paneled sides, a
long drawer at the bottom front fitted
w/two small turned wood knobs, on
knob- and conical-turned short legs,
old refinish, Hampshire County,
Massachusetts, 1710-30, 19 × 38",
35½" h. (replaced pulls)................. **5,175.00**

*Queen Anne Chest of Drawers*

**Queen Anne tall chest of drawers,**
maple, the rectangular top w/a deep,
flaring coved cornice above a case
w/five long graduated drawers
w/butterfly pulls & keyhole
escutcheons, molded base on short
cabriole legs ending in raised pad
feet, old brasses, refinished,
imperfections, Massachusetts or
New Hampshire, late 18th c.,
17¼ × 36", 4' 1¾" h. (ILLUS. bottom
previous column) .......................... **3,335.00**

**Sugar chest,** walnut, rectangular top
opening to a deep well, the front w/a
butterfly keyhole escutcheon above a
long recessed panels over two small
drawers at the bottom w/small round
brass pulls & oval keyhole
escutcheons, on ring- and rod-turned
legs w/button feet, southeastern
United States, replaced brasses,
restoration, ca. 1820, 15½ × 35",
34" h. (ILLUS. top next page) .......... **1,092.00**

**Victorian chest of drawers,**
Aesthetic Movement substyle, inlaid
& ebonized walnut, a tall vertical
rectangular mirror plate w/a gently
arched frame crest carved w/stylized
blossoms & a band of buttons
flanked by corner blocks w/turned
button finials & continuing down to
form turned & paneled stiles flanked
at the base w/curved panels w/end
stiles & finials, raised above a

*Early Southern Sugar Chest*

rectangular white marble top above a case w/a pair of narrow molded drawers above two long molded drawers, all w/angular bail handles, the top drawers w/carved stylized blossoms, reeded stiles on the base & paneled ends, on button feet, signed by Herter Brothers, New York, ca. 1870, 24½ x 54½", 6' 10¾" h. (ILLUS. below) ............. **2,090.00**

*Victorian Renaissance Revival Chest*

**Victorian chest of drawers,**
Renaissance Revival substyle, rosewood, the tall superstructure w/an arched & scroll-carved crestrail centered by a large carved bulbous urn finial above a florette-carved block & flanked by a molded cornice

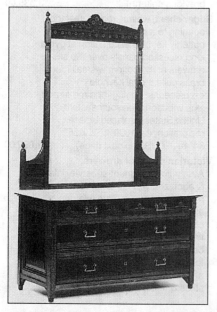

*Aesthetic Movement Chest of Drawers*

above scroll-carved corners & side stiles w/small candle shelves w/carved bracket supports all framing the tall arch-topped mirror & resting on a molded base w/two tiny handerchief drawers at the sides, all resting on the rectangular inset white marble top w/molded edges above a case w/a long narrow paneled drawer slightly overhanging two long drawers w/molded banding surrounding the two, the sides w/narrow molded panels & the wide molded base centered by a scroll-carved cartouche, on small block feet, ca. 1860, 23 × 49", 8' 3½" h. (ILLUS. right previous page) .......... **1,650.00**

*Victorian Rococo Chest of Drawers*

**Victorian chest of drawers,** Rococo substyle, walnut, the tall superstructure w/a high arched & scroll-carved crest w/bold fruit carving flanked by broken-scrolls continuing to carved scrolls above the tall round-topped mirror plate swiveling between the carved supports ending in incurved leafy C-scrolls on block supports & resting atop the rectangular white marble top w/outset front corners & molded edges, the case w/scroll- and-panel-

carved outset angled corners flanking three long graduated drawers each w/a raised oval band framing two turned wood knobs & a central keyhole escutcheon, molded base on narrow disc front feet, on casters, ca. 1850-60, 21 × 75¼" (ILLUS. previous column) .............. **1,100.00**

**William & Mary chest of drawers,** country-style, painted, joined construction, rectangular top w/a molded edge above a narrow cornice over molded side bands flanking four long reverse-graduated drawers w/small butterfly brasses & keyhole escutcheons, molded base on short square feet, old black paint, Deerfield, Massachusetts, ca. 1700-15, 19 × 36" h, 38" h. (imperfections, loss of height) ........................................ **3,450.00**

## CRADLES

**Country-style cradle on stand,** painted & decorated, original blue painted w/red striping & gilt-stenciled decoration, stamped "Ford, Johnson and Co. Manufacturers Michigan 76," third quarter 19th c., 24 × 50", 29½" h. .............................................. **633.00**

**Country-style hooded cradle on rockers,** painted pine, canted sides, original blue paint, New England, late 18th c., 45" l., 28" h. (minor imperfections) .................................. **431.00**

## CUPBOARDS

**Corner cupboard,** Chippendale architectural-type, pine, one-piece construction, flat crest w/central keystone & corner capitals above full-length pilasters flanking a pair of tall, arched glazed doors w/H-hinges opening to four shaped shelves & a coved shell-carved top all above a pair of short pilasters flanking a small paneled door w/H-hinges & thumb-latch, flat base, traces of old color, Connecticut, ca. 1750, 23 × 65", 7' 6" h. (restored) .......................... **5,750.00**

**Corner cupboard,** Chippendale, pine, two-part construction: the upper section w/a flat top & a molded cornice w/three blocked sections over pilasters & a central keystone above a pair of arched, fielded panelled cupboard doors opening to an interior fitted w/two scalloped shelves, the whole flanked by fluted

*Chippendale Corner Cupboard*

pilasters w/molded capitals & bases;
the lower section w/a stepped mid-
molding above a pair of raised panel
cupboard doors opening to a fitted
interior flanked by outset paneled
pilasters w/molded capitals & block
bases, Pennsylvania or Maryland,
1760-80, 31¾ × 55¾", 8' 2½" h.
(ILLUS.)......................................... **3,450.00**

**Corner cupboard,** country-style,
cherry, one-piece construction, a flat
top w/a narrow cove-molded poplar
cornice above a pair of six-pane
glazed cupboard doors opening to
two shelves above a pair of small
drawers w/wooden knobs above a
pair of paneled cupboard doors
opening to a shelf, flat apron w/simple
short cut-out feet, mid-19th c., cornice
51 × 54½", 6' 7" h. (old varnish mostly
removed, top doors need to be
reattached) .................................... **1,595.00**

**Corner cupboard,** country-style,
cherry, two-part construction: the
upper section w/molded swan's-neck
pediment centering three urn finials
above a conforming case fitted w/an
arched glazed door enclosing four
shelves, the lower section w/a pair of
paneled cupboard doors opening to
a single shelf, on bracket feet,
19th c., 24½ × 43", 7' 10¾" h......... **4,370.00**

**Corner cupboard,** country-style,
poplar w/greyish color, one-piece
construction, the flat top w/a cove-
molded cornice above a single long
six-pane glazed cupboard door
opening to two shelves above a
short paneled door, flat apron &
simple cut-out feet, original cast-iron
thumb latches, 19th c., 38 × 41¼",
7' 1" h. (one porcelain knob on latch
gone, some edge damage)............ **1,760.00**

**Corner cupboard,** country-style,
walnut, one-piece construction, the
flat top w/a deep cove-molded
cornice above a pair of tall raised-
panel cupboard doors w/glass knob
fitted into former keyhole above a
pair of small drawers w/porcelain
knobs above another pair of raised
panel cupboard doors w/original
cast-iron thumb latch w/porcelain
knob, scalloped apron, all doors &
drawers w/unusual chamfered
edging, old varnish finish, 19th c.,
cornice 45½ × 48½", 7' 8¼" h. (one
end of cornice damaged & needs
reattaching)...................................... **990.00**

*Federal "Architectural" Corner Cupboard*

**Corner cupboard,** Federal, architectural-type, painted pine, one-piece construction, the very tall case w/a flat top w/a flaring stepped cornice above a wide frieze band carved w/a Greek key design above a narrow raised molding framing the pair of arched, geometrically-glazed cupboard doors w/fan-carved panels in the upper corners, the doors opening to four scalloped shelves, a mid-molding above a pair of short raised-panel doors, flat cut-down base, bottom doors poorly constructed replacements, old olive tan grained repaint, early 19th c., 58½" w., 8' 6" h. (ILLUS. bottom previous page) ........ **3,300.00**

*Federal Cherry Corner Cupboard*

**Corner cupboard,** Federal country-style, cherry, one-piece construction, the flat top w/a narrow coved cornice above a single long twelve-pane glazed cupboard door opening to three shelves above a thin mid-molding over a wide two-panel cupboard door, doors w/wooden knobs, scalloped apron & simple bracket feet, early 19th c. (ILLUS.) ........................................ **3,450.00**

**Corner cupboard,** Federal country-style, cherry, two-part construction: the upper section w/a molded cornice above a wide frieze band over a pair of tall two-panel cupboard doors w/a small square panel over a long rectangular panel, all w/edge molding, the sides w/matching panels; the lower section w/a pair of paneled cupboard doors w/a thumb latch & flanked by paneled sides, molded flat base, New England, old refinish, minor imperfections, ca. 1810, 20½ x 42", 6' 10" h. .......................................... **2,530.00**

*Federal Pine Corner Cupboard*

**Corner cupboard,** Federal country-style, pine & poplar, two-part construction: the upper section w/a flat top & wide coved cornice above a single tall twelve-pane glazed door opening to three shelves; the lower section w/a mid-molding above a pair of paneled cupboard doors, molded base on scroll-cut bracket feet, probably New York State, ca. 1815, 21 x 42", 7' 3" h. (ILLUS.) .... **4,887.00**

**Corner cupboard,** Federal country-style, pine, one-piece construction, the flat top w/a cove-molded cornice above a dentil-carved frieze band & narrow raised molding above a pair of six-pane glazed cupboard doors opening to two shelves above a wide stepped mid-molding above a pair of paneled cupboard doors, molded base & cut-out bracket feet, old mellow refinishing, interior painted light blue, early 19th c., 48½ × 50½", 6' 2½" h. (pieced repairs & some replacements, edge damage & replaced hardware)........................ **1,430.00**

**Corner cupboard,** Federal country-style, walnut, one-piece construction, a flat top w/a narrow molded cornice above a pair of tall eight-pane glazed doors opening to three shelves above a pair of paneled cupboard doors above a scroll-cut apron, old refinish, probably Pennsylvania, ca. 1820, 19 × 48", 6' 9" h. (minor imperfections).................................. **1,840.00**

**Corner cupboard,** Federal, cherry, two-part construction: the upper section w/a cove-molded cornice above a long hinged, fifteen-pane glazed cupboard door opening to blue-painted shelves carved w/plate grooves; the lower section w/a mid-molding over a pair of hinged paneled doors opening to a shelf, Pennsylvania, ca. 1820, 21 × 43¼", 7' 10½" h....................................... **7,475.00**

**Hanging corner cupboard,** Chippendale, walnut, the scalloped gallery w/a small corner shelf above a dentil-carved cornice over a conforming case w/a raised-panel cupbard door opening to a scalloped shelf above a drawer, molded base,

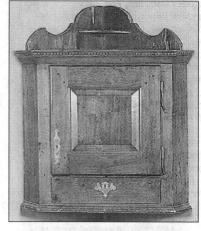

*Chippendale Hanging Cupboard*

long scrolled brass keyhole escutcheon on the door & a butterfly escutcheon on the drawer, Pennsylvania, 1760-80, 19½ × 34¾", 40" h. (ILLUS. above) ...................... **3,450.00**

**Hanging wall cupboard,** painted & decorated pine, one-piece construction, the rectangular top w/a overhanging flat cornice above a cupboard door w/a recessed panel, on a conforming shaped base, grain-painted overall, New England, early 19th c., 10 × 24", 36" h...................... **805.00**

*Early Painted Hutch Cupboard*

**Hanging wall cupboard,** pine, a rectangular top above a deep stepped cornice over wide face boards framing the single raised-panel cupboard door opening to an interior shelf & secret compartment all above a mid-molding over a long drawer beside a short drawer above a scrolled bracket base, old mellow refininishing, ghost images of original decoration, Pennsylvania, late 18th - early 19th c., cornice 16¾ × 31", 47" h. (larger drawer restored, interior shelf replaced) ........................................... **770.00**

**Hanging wall cupboard,** walnut, a rectangular top w/low backrail above a case w/wide front stiles flanking a double-paneled door w/a beaded frame, the door w/a small panel over a tall panel, flat base, old dark finish, 19th c., cornice 8½ × 28¾", 35" h. ..... **880.00**

**Hutch cupboard,** country-style, painted & decorated, the tall back w/scallop-cut sides flanking to two shelves above a rectangular top w/molded edges above a pair of raised-panel cupboard doors w/oval wood knobs, molded base on simple bracket feet, overall red & orange wood graining simulating mahogany except the door panels which simulate maple w/moldings in old red, the single-shelved interior painted old bluish green, pulls old replacements, surface imperfections, Canada or northern New England, ca. 1840, 15⅜ × 54½", 5' 8¾" h. (ILLUS. bottom previous page) .................. **5,462.00**

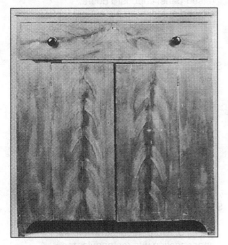

*Painted Jelly Cupboard*

**Jelly cupboard,** country-style, painted & decorated pine, rectangular top above a single long drawer w/two turned wood knobs over a pair of narrow flush doors opening to two shelves, gently arched bracket feet, overall red & yellow graining simulating mahogany, surface imperfections, probably New York State, late 19th c., 15⅜ × 48½", 4' 8" h. (ILLUS. bottom previous column) ................................. **1,035.00**

**Jelly cupboard,** poplar, primitive country style w/a flat thin rectangular top above a case w/a pair of tall narrow one-board doors w/thumb latches between wide stiles, high angled bracket feet, old dark finish, interior w/old yellow enamel paint w/newspaper adhering to shelves, 19th c., 15¼ × 43¼", 5' 6½" h. ............................... **550.00**

*French Pewter Cupboard*

**Pewter cupboard,** French Provincial, cherry, the rectangular top w/a narrow molded cornice above a scalloped frieze band above three open shelves w/plate guard bars above a stepped-out top above a pair of paneled cupboard doors w/long pierced brass keyhole escutcheons, flat apron, short stile legs, France, ca. 1780, 25 × 52", 6' 4" h. (ILLUS.) ............................ **2,420.00**

*Painted & Decorated Pie Safe*

**Pie safe,** painted & decorated, the pointed-arch splashboard w/a medial shelf on small ring-turned supports above a rectangular top w/rounded edges overhanging a conforming case fitted w/two drawers w/molded edges & two wood knobs each over a pair of double-panel cupboard doors each w/two white-painted & punch-decorated tulip tin panels, opening to an interior fitted w/two shelves, shaped bracket feet, restoration to splashboard, 19th c., 17 × 47¾", 4' 3" h. (ILLUS.) .......... **2,185.00**

**Pie safe,** pine, a rectangular top above a deep simple coved cornice over a pair of tall two open-panel doors missing their cheese cloth or screen, interior w/three shelves, raised on wide board end legs on shoe feet, cut-out & carved details on the doors, attributed to the Amana Colonies, Iowa, late 19th c., cornice 13 × 42", 5' 4½" h. (some edge damage & repair) .................... **413.00**

**Pie safe,** walnut, a rectangular top w/rounded front corners above a pair of drawers w/turned wooden knobs overhanging a pair of two-panel cupboard doors w/each panel filled w/a matching punched tin panel decorated w/Masonic symbols including an arch, compass & "G," the doors opening to two shelves & flanked by half-round turned pilasters down the front sides, pairs of matching punched tin panels in the sides, flat apron, raised on

turned peg feet, Pennsylvania, first half 19th c., refinished, 18 × 42¾", 44½" h. ......................................... **1,450.00**

**Pie safe,** poplar, flat rectangular top above a case w/eight front pierced tin panels arranged in two rows, the center four in a pair of two-panel cupboard doors, all w/a large circle & star design centered by blossoms in each corner, three pierced panels at each end for a total of fourteen tin panels, raised on tall square tapering legs, mortised & pinned construction, refinished, 19th c., top 18½ × 50¾", 4' 3½" h..................... **2,475.00**

**Step-back hutch cupboard,** stained butternut & poplar, one-piece construction, a rectangular flat top above a tall open upper section w/three shelves above the stepped-out lower section w/a pair of small drawers above a pair of flat cupboard doors, flat apron & angled bracket feet, old red stain, 19th c., 20 × 44", 6' 6" h. (rodent holes in doors, drawers good replacements, some damage on side feet) .......... **1,100.00**

**Step-back wall cupboard,** cherry & poplar, two-part construction: the upper section w/a rectangular top w/a flaring cornice w/a bold carved gadrooned frieze band above a pair of six-pane glazed cupboard doors opening to two shelves above an open pie shelf; the stepped-out lower section w/a pair of drawers w/wooden knobs above a pair of raised-panel cupboard doors, shaped apron w/simple cut-out feet, found in Richland County, Ohio, mid-19th c., cornice 15 × 50½", 7' h. (refinished)..................................... **1,980.00**

**Step-back wall cupboard,** cherry, two-part construction: the upper section w/a rectangular molded cornice above a dentil-molded frieze band over a pair of glazed mullioned cupboard doors opening to two shelves; the stepped-out lower section w/three small drawers above a pair of paneled cupboard doors opening to a shelf, molded base, 19th c., 18¾ × 54¼", 6' 6½" h. ........ **1,725.00**

**Step-back wall cupboard,** Classical country-style, pine w/traces of old graining, two-part construction: the upper section w/a rectangular top w/a flaring coved cornice above a pair of four-pane glazed cupboard doors w/brass thumb latches & wood knobs opening to two shelves above a pair of shallow drawers each w/two wood knobs; the widely stepped-out lower section w/a pair of round-fronted long drawers flanking a small square center drawer above two pairs of paneled cupboard doors flanked by free-standing columns at the sides, flat apron w/corner blocks raised on short double-knob turned feet, found in southern Pennsylvania, ca. 1830-50, cornice 15¼ × 59¼", 7' 2" h. ..... **2,200.00**

*Painted Ohio Step-back Cupboard*

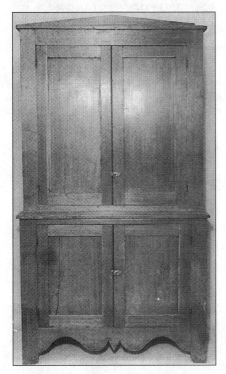

*Walnut Step-back Cupboard*

**Step-back wall cupboard,** country-style, walnut, one-piece construction, the rectangular top w/a pointed front cornice board above a pair of tall paneled doors w/origianl brass thumb latch above a stepped-out lower section w/a pair of shorter paneled cupboard doors w/original brass thumb latch, deeply scalloped apron & bracket feet, old finish, crack in one bottom door panel, one end of crest damaged, mid-19th c., 13¾ × 44¼", 6' 6¼" h. (ILLUS.) ............. **1,320.00**

**Step-back wall cupboard,** country-style, painted, two-piece construction: the upper section w/a rectangular top w/a flaring stepped cornice above a pair of six-pane glazed cupboard doors opening to two shelves above an open pie shelf flanked by tiny square drawers; the stepped-out lower section w/a row of three drawers w/wooden knobs over a pair of paneled cupboard doors w/cast-iron thumb latches w/porcelain knobs, flat apron & scroll-cut bracket feet, found in Wayne County, Ohio, attributed to Mennonite craftsmen, mid-19th c. (ILLUS.) ...................................... **24,200.00**

**Step-back wall cupboard,** painted poplar, two-part construction: the upper section w/a rectangular top w/a flaring stepped cornice above a pair of tall paneled doors w/cast-iron thumb latch; the stepped-out lower section w/a pair of drawers w/wooden knobs above a pair of paneled cupboard doors, old red repaint w/yellow drawers & door panels trimmed w/vining floral borders, scalloped apron w/low cut-out feet, 19th c., cornice 14½ × 46", 6' 8½" h. (apron & feet replaced, repairs) ......... **853.00**

*Step-back "Jackson press" Cupboard*

**Step-back wall cupboard,** painted wood, one-piece construction, the rectangular top w/plain rim above a pair of tall flat cupboard doors opening to a white & blue painted interior fitted w/three shelves above a stepped-out lower section w/a single cupboard door opening to a white-painted interior w/a shelf, exterior painted blue, on bootjack legs, Pennsylvania, 19th c., 18½ × 40", 6'¼" h. ................................... **1,380.00**

**Step-back wall cupboard,** pine, two-part construction: the upper section w/a rectangular stepped cornice above a conforming case fitted w/a pair of recessed-panel cupboard doors enclosing two shelves; the lower section w/three small drawers over a pair of recessed-panel cupboard doors opening to a single shelf, on bracket feet, 19th c., 21 × 54", 6' 11¼" h. ........................ **2,300.00**

**Step-back wall cupboard,** walnut, two-part construction: the upper section w/a rectangular top w/a deep flat & flaring cornice above a pair of tall paneled cupboard doors w/original brass thumb latch opening to shelves above a low open pie shelf; the stepped-out lower section

w/a pair of paneled cupboard doors w/original repaired brass thumb latch opening to a shelf, flat apron, curved cut-out bracket feet, old mellow finish, 19th c., cornice 15 × 53¼", 6' 2¾" h. (pieced repair at hinges & one end of cornice) ....................... **2,310.00**

**Step-back wall cupboard,** country-style, walnut, so-called "Jackson press," two-part construction: the upper section w/a rectangular top w/flat cornice above a pair of six-pane glazed cupboard doors opening to two shelves on a molded base; the stepped-out lower section w/a pair of paneled cupboard doors w/turned wood knobs, flat apron w/scroll-cut bracket feet, ca. 1840 (ILLUS. top previous column) ........ **1,100.00**

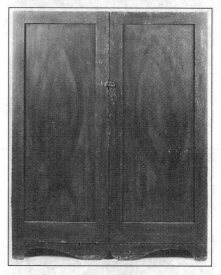

*Painted Pine Wall Cupboard*

**Wall cupboard,** country-style, painted pine, rectangular top over two long paneled doors w/a metal latch & keyhole escutcheon, scalloped apron w/bracket feet, early red & black graining simulating rosewood, interior w/sectioned shelving, restoration, height loss, Maine, mid-19th c., 13 × 37¼", 4' h. (ILLUS.) ................... **489.00**

**Wall cupboard,** Federal country-style, painted, rectangular top w/molded edge above a case w/two tall paneled doors opening to an interior fitted w/two shelves, molded base on scroll-cut bracket feet, painted red, New York, ca. 1840, 19 × 33", 39½" h. (ILLUS. bottom next page)............. **2,300.00**

*George III Welsh Cupboard*

*Small Federal Wall Cupboard*

**Welsh cupboard,** oak, the long rectangular top w/a coved cornice above a deeply scalloped frieze band above shaped sides & a closed back framing three long shelves above the stepped-out lower case w/a molded edge above a row of three beaded drawers w/two small

brass ring pulls & keyhole escutcheons each, a mid-molding above a widely scalloped apron raised on columnar-turned front supports on a thick platform rectangular base, George III period, England, late 18th - early 19th c., 66" w., 6' 8" h. (ILLUS. above)....... **3,740.00**

## DESKS

**Art Deco desk,** lacquered wood, rectangular top featuring a geometric design in white eggshell lacquer, on a double pedestal base of burnt orange lacquer, each pedestal w/two drawers above a cabinet, signed in the lacquer "JEAN DUNAND," France, ca. 1925, 25½ × 45", 29" h. (ILLUS. top next page) ................ **66,300.00**

**Chippendale "block-front" slant-front desk,** carved mahogany, a narrow rectangular top above the rectangular hinged molded slant lid opening to a baize-lined writing surface w/crossbanded border, the interior comprising two tiers of blocked- and fan-carved small drawers centering valanced pigeonholes & a fan-carved prospect door, document drawers flanking, the

*Rare Art Deco Desk*

*Chippendale "Block-front" Desk*

case below w/four blocked long graduated drawers, the molded base w/a fan-carved center pendant continuing to blocked bracket feet, rich old reddish brown patina, appears to retain original brasses & keyhole escutcheons, Boston, ca. 1760, 20½ × 40½", 41" h. (ILLUS. bottom)............................ **17,250.00**

**Chippendale country-style slant-front desk,** maple, a narrow rectangular top above a wide,

hinged slant-front opening to an interior fitted w/pigeonholes & small drawers, the lower case w/three long drawers w/batwing brass pulls, on a molded base w/scroll-cut bracket feet, old refinish, Connecticut, late 18th c., 18⅝ × 36", 39" h. (replaced brasses, repairs) .......... **2,300.00**

**Chippendale country-style slant-front desk,** painted maple, a narrow rectangular top above a rectangular slant lid w/breadboard ends opening

*Painted Chippendale Desk*

to a stepped valanced multi-drawer interior, the lower case w/slide supports & four long graduated drawers w/oval brasses & keyhole escutcheons, molded base & shaped bracket feet, old red paint & varnish, old eagle-stamped brasses, minor imperfections, New England, late 18th c., 18 × 35¾", 43½" h. (ILLUS.) ........................................ **7,475.00**

**Chippendale "oxbow serpentine" slant-front desk,** mahogany, a narrow rectangular top above the hinged slant lid opening to an interior fitted w/a row of pigeonholes surrounded by small drawers, all above slide supports & a serpentine-front case w/four long graduated drawers w/butterfly pulls & keyhole escutcheons, molded base, tall ball-and-claw feet, Massachusetts, late 18th c., 21⅔ × 42", 43" h. (old refinish, replaced brasses, imperfections) ............................... **3,105.00**

**Chippendale slant-front desk,** figured mahogany, a narrow rectangular top above a rectangular hinged slant lid opening to an interior fitted w/small drawers over valanced pigeonholes centering a hinged prospect door opening to two small drawers, four graduated cockbeaded drawers below, on bracket feet, appears to retain original butterfly brasses, New York, ca. 1785, 21⅞ × 45¾", 43" h. .................................. **4,025.00**

**Chippendale slant-front desk,** cherry, narrow rectangular top above a wide slant lid opening to an interior fitted w/arched pigeonholes flanking a fan-carved prospect door over small drawers, all above pull-out slide supports & four long graduated drawers w/butterfly pulls & oval keyhole escutcheons, molded base on scroll-cut ogee bracket feet, Connecticut River Valley, late 18th c., 20 × 37", 46" h. (old refinish, replaced brasses, minor imperfections) ....... **9,200.00**

**Chippendale slant-front desk,** cherry, a narrow rectangular top above the wide hinged slant-front opening to a compartment fitted w/small drawers & pigeonholes above a case w/four long drawers each w/butterfly brasses & keyhole escutcheons, molded base on tall ogee bracket feet, Connecticut, ca. 1780, 18⅛ × 38", 44" h. (refinished, replaced brasses, minor imperfections) ............................... **3,737.50**

**Chippendale slant-front desk,** curly maple, a narrow rectangular top above a wide rectangular hinged molded lid opening to an interior fitted w/valanced pigeonholes w/small drawers centering a prospect door opening to two pigeonholes & a small drawer, all above four long graduated molded drawers each w/butterfly brasses & keyhole escutcheons, on a molded base w/reduced bracket feet, probably Rhode Island, ca. 1785, 18 × 36", 37" h. (lacks lower section of feet, patches to drawer lips) .................... **6,900.00**

*Chippendale Curly Maple Desk*

**Chippendale slant-front desk,** curly maple, a narrow rectangular top above a rectangular slant lid w/breadboard ends opening to a fitted interior, above pull-out support slides & four long graduated drawers, all w/butterfly brasses & keyhole escutcheons, molded base on tall bracket feet, New England, late 18th c. (ILLUS. bottom previous page) ............................................. **9,200.00**

**Chippendale slant-front desk, mahogany,** the narrow rectangular top above a wide slant lid opening to a compartment w/a row of arched pigeonholes flanking a shell-carved prospect door above small convex & concave drawers, above slide supports & four long molded drawers, molded base & scroll-cut bracket feet, Newport, Rhode Island, 18th c., 20 × 40½", 41½" h. (restored, replaced brasses, refinished) ...................................... **2,990.00**

**Chippendale slant-front desk,** maple, a narrow rectangular top above the rectangular slant lid opening to an interior fitted w/a row of pigeonholes above two tiers of small drawers, the lower case w/pull-out support slides & four long graduated drawers w/butterfly

*Chippendale Maple Desk*

brasses & keyhole escutcheons, molded base on scroll-cut bracket feet, original brasses, refinished, minor imperfections, Rhode Island, late 18th c., 17¼ × 35½", 40" h. (ILLUS. above) ............................ **4,888.00**

**Classical writing desk,** mahogany, rectangular top w/inset leather writing surface above two ranks of two small drawers flanking the shaped kneehole apron, raised on heavy tapering ring- and columnar-

*Painted Sewing Desk*

turned legs ending in disc feet, marked w/stenciled label of "Stephan Smith, No. 51 & 53, Cornhill, Boston," ca. 1840, 26½ × 48", 29½" h. .......................... **935.00**

**Country-style sewing desk,** painted, a high gently arched crest board behind a tiered stack of small drawers w/a single top center drawer over a pair of drawers over a row of four drawers over a pair of longer drawers, all w/turned wood knobs, the overhanging rectangular top above a single long drawer w/two wood knobs, on simple rod-turned legs, old brown paint w/orange drawer fronts, original pulls, imperfections, attributed to Ezra Haskell, Sweden, Maine, 1860-70, 18½ × 36⅛", 40½" h. (ILLUS. bottom previous page) .................. **3,738.00**

**Country-style slant-front "Plantation" desk,** walnut two-piece construction: the upper section w/a rectangular top over a deep coved cornice above a pair of tall doors each w/a single pane of glass opening to one shelf & flanking a center section w/a stack of three small drawers over an open compartment; the lower section w/a top rail above the wide

hinged slant-front w/breadboard ends opening to a divided interior, raised on tall slender tapering turned legs w/ring-turned segments at the top & ending in ring-turned peg feet, mid-19th c., base 26¾ × 37¾", 5' 4" h. (one door w/pieced repair at hinges, refinished) ........................................ **1,017.50**

**Country-style slant-front desk,** cherry, a narrow top above a wide hinged slant front opening to a well fitted w/pigeonholes & five dovetailed small drawers above an apron w/pull-out slide supports flanking a long drawer w/two wooden knobs, raised on baluster-, ring- and knob-turned tapering legs ending in peg feet, 19th c., 23 × 37½", 38¼" h. (refinished, some replacements in interior, repairs & hinge rail restored) ........................................ **1,540.00**

**Federal "butler's" desk,** cherry, the rectangular top above a wide fall-front opening to an interior fitted w/two rows of pigeonholes & seven small drawers w/the fall-front forming the writing surface, a pair of veneer-banded cupboard doors below flanked by reeded stiles, on short turned & tapering legs w/knob feet, ca. 1820, 20¾ × 48", 46¼" h. (ILLUS. below) .. **1,100.00**

*Federal "Butler's" Desk*

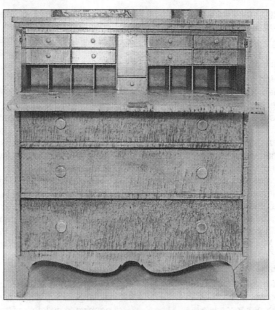

*Federal Curly Maple "Butler's" Desk*

**Federal "butler's" desk,** inlaid cherry, a rectangular top above a deep hinged-front drawer opening to an interior fitted w/small drawers, valanced pigeonholes, an inlaid prospect door & a felt-lined writing surface, the drawer front w/banded border inlay & a large central inlaid diamond, a narrow middle drawer w/banded inlay above a pair of short central band-inlaid doors flanked by narrow band-inlaid bottle drawers, on reeded & ring-turned legs w/peg feet, oval & round brasses, old refinish, northern Windsor County, Vermont, 1810-15, 20 × 43", 43" h. (minor imperfections)........... **3,220.00**

**Federal country-style "butler's" desk,** curly maple, a rectangular top above a flat fall-front false drawer opening to an interior fitted w/two groups of four small drawers over four pigeonholes flanking a central prospect door over a small drawer, all above three long graduated drawers, deeply scalloped apron on French feet, refinished, replaced turned wood pulls, age cracks, minor repairs, early 19th c., 18¾ × 40¾", 46¾" h. (ILLUS. above) ................. **3,190.00**

**Federal country-style school desk,** maple & softwood, a narrow top above double wide hinged slant lids w/breadboard ends opening to a well, front of desk w/two iron locks & three brass escutcheon plates, raised on ring-, rod & knob-turned legs w/knob feet, 19th c., 24 × 50", 32" h. (interior lock removed, refinished)........................................ **300.00**

*Federal Country Slant-front Desk*

**Federal country-style slant-front desk,** inlaid mahogany, a narrow rectangular top above a hinged slant lid opening to an interior fitted w/two sets of four small drawers over four arched pigeonholes flanking a central prospect door, above slide supports & four long graduated drawers each w/delicate herringbone ivory inlay around the edges & diamond-form ivory inlaid keyhole escutcheons, simple bail pulls, a flat apron w/a wider diamond-inlaid band, raised on short ring-turned legs w/large ball feet, Southern United States, ca. 1800, 37 × 41", 47" h. (ILLUS. bottom previous page)............................... **2,750.00**

**Federal country-style "stand-up" desk,** painted & decorated, an arched crestrail w/scroll-cut ends above a slant-front opening to a fitted interior & well above a pair of beaded reverse-graduated drawers w/round brass knobs, double-paneled ends, shaped apron & tall slender tapering legs, original grain-painted surface, original brasses, probably Canada, second quarter 19th c., 14 × 29", 46" h. (minor losses) ......................................... **6,900.00**

*Federal Lady's Desk*

**Federal lady's writing desk,** inlaid mahogany, two-part construction: the upper section w/a rectangular top w/band inlaid edge above a conforming case fitted w/two band-inlaid cupboard doors opening to a fitted interior w/one cockbeaded shelf over four short drawers flanked by two cockbeaded pigeonholes; the

lower section w/a rectangular band-inlaid top opening to a baize-lined writing surface fitted w/a long reserve & three inkwells all above two cockbeaded long graduated drawers flanked by veneered panels on double tapering inlaid square legs w/cuffs, Massachusetts, 1800-20, 20 × 35½", 4' 4⅞" h. (ILLUS. bottom previous column) .......................... **3,220.00**

*Federal Slant-front Desk*

**Federal slant-front desk,** walnut, a narrow rectangular top above a wide slant lid opening to an interior fitted w/six small drawers over eight arched pigeonholes flanking a central prospect door, all above a pair of slide supports & four long cockbeaded graduated drawers w/oval brasses & keyhole escutcheons, figured veneer on the drawer fronts, curved apron continuing to French feet, old finish, minor imperfections, probably Pennsylvania, ca. 1800, 20 × 41", 44¼" h. (ILLUS.) ........................... **2,760.00**

**Mission-style (Arts & Crafts movement) desk,** oak, rectangular top w/carved Arts & Crafts designs around the edge & on the square legs ending in short block feet, the case w/two stacks of two drawers each w/a short drawer over a deep drawer flanking a long center drawer over an arched apron above the kneehole fitted w/a lower shelf stretcher, brass plate & bail handle pulls, original finish, unsigned, early 20th c., 30 × 50", 29" h. (some stains on top, one pull missing) ........ **440.00**

**Mission-style (Arts & Crafts movement) desk,** oak, rectangular top overhanging a case over two stacks of two small drawers w/metal plates & bail pulls flanking a central drawer over a kneehole, on square legs joined by end stretchers, Quaint Furniture tag of the Stickley Brothers, 28 × 42", 30" h. (overall roughness, one pull missing) ............ **467.50**

**Mission-style (Arts & Crafts movement) desk,** oak, rectangular top above a case w/two stacks of two drawers each w/hammered copper plate & bail pulls flanking the kneehole & a longer center drawer without a pull, on slender square legs, original finish on base, top refinished, red decal mark of Gustav Stickley, Model No. 710, early 20th c., 29 × 48", 30" h ................... **1,650.00**

*Mission Drop-front Desk*

**Mission-style (Arts & Crafts movement) drop-front desk,** oak, the rectangular top w/a three-quarter gallery w/gently arched sides above the wide rectangular drop front opening to pigeonholes, above a pair of short drawers above three long drawers all w/V-shaped hammered copper pulls, flat apron & cut-out end feet, branded mark & partial paper label of Gustav Stickley, Model No. 729, ca. 1912, 15 × 36½", 45¼" h. (ILLUS.) ..................................... **3,450.00**

**Queen Anne slant-front desk on frame,** cherry, a narrow rectangular top above a slant lid opening to an interior fitted w/six pigeonholes & four small drawers flanking a central prospect door carved w/a sunburst over a small drawer, all above slide supports & four long graduated drawers w/butterfly pulls & keyhole escutcheons, flat apron w/two small drops, short cabriole front legs ending in angled pad feet, damages to drawer edges, Norwich, Connecticut, ca. 1750, 19¾ × 34¾", 45¾" h. (ILLUS. below) ................. **5,463.00**

*Queen Anne Desk on Frame*

**Schoolmaster's desk,** country-style, painted & decorated pine & poplar, a low shaped crestrail over a narrow shelf above the wide slant-front w/breadboard ends opening to pigeonholes above a long drawer w/two wooden knobs, raised on baluster- and ring-turned legs w/peg feet, old worn greyish yellow graining on a white ground w/earlier dark red showing through in some areas, ca. 1850-70, 22½ × 33", 36¼" h. (some edge wear, pieced drawer repair & lock missing) ........... **743.00**

**Victorian Eastlake substyle cylinder-front desk,** walnut & burl walnut, an elaborately carved crested gallery above two short drawers, the cylinder front enclosing a fitted interior w/two short drawers, over a base w/three drawers & a cupboard, on bun feet, ca. 1870, 19¾ × 34½", 4' 10¼" h. ................. **1,100.00**

*Gothic Revival Desk*

**Victorian Gothic Revival writing desk,** carved mahogany, a rectangular molded top w/inset writing surface & circular reserve overhanging an apron fitted w/a long drawer on bracket feet, the front w/scrolling carved leaves, the rear scroll- and leaf-carved above quarter columns w/Corinthian capitals, the sides w/deep relief-carved foliate medallion & pierced D-shaped side openings w/exposed mortise-and-tenon joints, designed by Leopold Eidlitz for the New York State Assembly Chamber, manufactured by Weller, Brown and Mesmer, Buffalo, New York, ca. 1879, cracks in top & lining missing, 24 × 26½", 30¾" h. (ILLUS. top previous column) ........................... **1,150.00**

**Victorian Renaissance Revival substyle writing desk,** walnut & burl walnut, the wide rectangular top w/molded edge inset w/a brown leather writing surface w/tack trim, the apron w/two long drawers w/narrow burl panels w/line-incised stars & round keyhole escutcheons w/similar burl panels along the sides, w/heavy block- and column-turned cross-form end legs w/boldly carved leaf trim & a central forked support on a ring-turned column, the legs & support joined by a scalloped & fan-carved cross stretcher, on casters, ca. 1870, 32 × 51¾", 30" h. (ILLUS. below) .............................. **3,105.00**

## GARDEN & LAWN

**Armchairs,** classical-style w/a gently curved crestrail over a pierced design of crossed arrows above a pierced splat w/a classical figure standing amid foliage, curved square open arms above the wood slat seat, square tapering legs, 19th c., pr. (ILLUS. of one, top left next page)..................................... **2,300.00**

*Victorian Renaissance Revival Writing Desk*

*Classical Garden Armchair*

*Lyre-back Garden Armchair*

**Armchairs,** the gently curved crestrail w/a pierced rose cluster finial above the pierced back w/a large lyre framed w/leafy scrolls, the crestrail continuing down to form narrow flat arms w/rolled hand grips above pierced leafy scroll sides, oblong pierced seat w/pierced scroll apron band, on molded flattened cabriole legs w/flared feet, the legs joined by slender cross-bars, painted, 19th c., pr. (ILLUS. of one, top right) ............ **880.00**

**Armchairs,** upright back w/arched pierced scroll crest above a pierced back composed of ornate tight scrolls flanked by S-scroll arms over openwork scrolls flanking the pierced rectangular seat, scalloped front apron, on pierced scroll sides supported by four looped-scroll short legs, painted white, ca. 1870-90, pr. .. **550.00**

**Benches,** stone, a shaped rectangular back centering a cartouche, scrolled arm brackets, the rectangular seat w/a wide curved lappet-carved band, raised on heavy blocks carved at the front w/scrolls & paw feet, 19th c., pr. (ILLUS. of one, below)............. **8,625.00**

*Stone Garden Bench*

*Gothic-style Garden Settee*

*Medallion-back Garden Settee*

**Settee,** fern design, the gently arched back composed of entwined scrolling fern fronds tapering slightly to rounded arms above the pierced seat, on flaring legs composed of ferns, painted white, seat labeled "Mfg. by the Kramer Bros Fdy Co. Dayton, O.," 19th c., 58" l. (worn & weathered paint).............................................. **880.00**

**Settee,** Gotchic Revival-style, the flat bar crestrail above a back composed of pierced Gothic trefoils & quatrefoils, down-curved arms w/arched bands of trefoils, pierced rectangular seat, undulating Gothic pierced apron, on simple bar legs w/corner & end braces, late 19th c., 4' 9 ½" l. (ILLUS. top)................... **2,300.00**

**Settee,** the back composed of four large pierced oval medallions w/scrolled crests & each centering a different figure, each medallion separated by leaf & flower bands, pierced scroll arms, wooden slat seat, on scrolled H-form end legs w/knob feet, painted white, 19th c., 5' 8" l. (ILLUS. bottom).................. **2,875.00**

## HALL RACKS & TREES

**Hall rack,** bentwood, an oval bentwood frame w/a ring-turned cross bar supporting five S-scroll bentwood hooks, medium brown finish, three hook ends missing, in the style of Thonet of Austria, unmarked, early 20th c., 7 × 37", 12" h. (ILLUS. below)......................... **83.00**

**Hall rack,** Mission-style (Arts & Crafts movement), oak, a long top flat rail above a hat shelf over wide rails between double upright square posts joined by short stretchers & raised on shoe feet & joined by double rails at the base, original finish, custom built for the L. & J.G. Stickley Factory, Fayetteville, New York, signed, 22 × 101", 6' h. (small screws added) .............................. **2,200.00**

**Hall rack,** Victorian Renaissance Revival substyle, walnut & burled walnut, a reticulated crest above a rectangular mirror over a marble top shelf above a small drawer, metal umbrella trays on each side of base, late 19th c., 10½ × 27¼", 7' 2" h. ...... **715.00**

**Hall tree,** Classical-style, carved mahogany, the turned tapering standard w/a leaf-and-acorn finial raised on a ring-turned & acanthus leaf-carved section on a tripod base w/bold leaf-carved animal paw feet on casters, seven brass hooks, one hook broken, probably New York, ca. 1830, 7' 2" h. (ILLUS. next column, left) ................................... **3,737.00**

**Hall tree,** Mission-style (Arts & Crafts movement), oak, a single square slightly swelled pole w/a corbeled cruciform base, original finish, Handcraft label of L. & J.G. Stickley, early 20th c., 25" w., 6' h. (ILLUS. next column, right) ........................... **825.00**

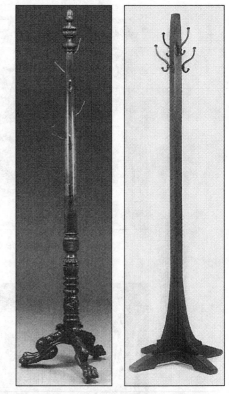

*Classical Hall Tree*        *Stickley Hall Tree*

## HIGHBOYS & LOWBOYS

### HIGHBOYS

**Chippendale "flat-top" highboy,** maple w/old mahogany stain, two-part construction: the upper section w/a rectangular top above a deep coved cornice & a dentil-carved band above two pairs of small drawers flanking a deep pinwheel-carved center drawer above four

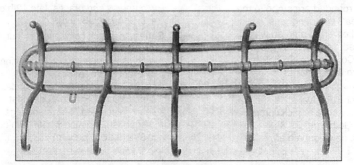

*Bentwood Hall Rack*

long graduated drawers; the lower section w/a mid-molding above two long shallow drawers above a pair of square drawers flanking a wider fan-carved central drawer above the apron boldly carved w/facing scrolls & continuing to shaped corner braces at the cabriole legs ending in claw-and-ball feet, backboards of base initialed & dated "1792," Dunlap School (ILLUS. below) .... **25,300.00**

*Queen Anne Cherry Highboy*

*Chippendale Highboy*

**Queen Anne "bonnet-top" highboy,** cherry, two-part construction: the upper section w/a broken-scroll top centering three urn-turned finials, the corner finials on reeded blocks all above a row of three drawers w/a deep fan-carved center drawer flanked by two small drawers above a case of four long thumb-molded graduated drawers; the lower section w/a long shallow drawer above a row of three drawers w/a large fan-carved center drawer flanked by two smaller drawers above a scalloped apron w/two turned pendent drops, on cabriole legs ending in pad feet, Connecticut, ca. 1760, butterfly brasses appear to be original, old refinish, 20¼ x 37½", 6' 9½" h. (restored bonnet added) ... **8,050.00**

**Queen Anne "bonnet-top" highboy,** carved cherry, two-part construction: the upper section w/a broken-arch swan's-neck pediment decorated w/three flame-turned finials above a case w/a pair of small drawers flanking a deeper shell-carved drawer above four long graduated drawers; the lower section w/a mid-molding above a case w/a pair of drawers above a row of three deeper drawers, the center one shell-carved, scalloped apron continuing to cabriole legs ending in raised pad feet, altered, Connecticut, 18th c., 20 x 37", 6' 9½" h. (ILLUS.) .......... **5,462.00**

**Queen Anne "flat-top" highboy,** cherry, two-part construction: the upper section w/a rectangular top w/a deep flaring stepped cornice above a case of five long graduated thumb-molded drawers; the lower section w/a mid-molding above a case w/a long shallow drawer above a row of three drawers w/a pair of deep drawers flanking a smaller central drawer above a scroll-cut apron continuing to cabriole legs ending in pad feet, Long Island, New York, 1760-80, 19 x 36½", 6' 1¾" h. (refinished, imperfections) ................................. **8,050.00**

**Queen Anne "flat-top" highboy,**
curly maple, two-part construction:
the upper section w/a molded cornice
above a convex secret drawer, two
short & three molded graduated long
drawers above a projecting molding;
the lower section w/three short
molded drawers, the scroll-cut
shaped skirt continuing to cabriole
legs ending in pad feet, 18th c.,
21½ × 39¼", 8' ½" h. ..................... **9,775.00**

**Queen Anne "flat-top" highboy,**
figured maple, two-part construction:
the upper section w/a rectangular
top w/a deep flaring molded cornice
above a conforming case fitted
w/five thumb-molded long graduated
drawers; the lower section w/a mid-
molding over a long narrow drawer
over a row of three drawers w/two
deep drawers flanking a narrow
central drawer all over a deeply
scalloped apron w/a fan-shaped
center drop, on cabriole front legs &
cylindrical back legs ending in pad
feet, Stonington, Connecticut,
1740-60, 20⅛ × 38¾", 5' 11¾" h. .. **17,250.00**

**Queen Anne "flat-top" highboy,**
maple, pine & chestnut, two-part
construction: the upper section w/a
flat top w/deep flaring, stepped
cornice above a pair of drawers over
three long graduated drawers; the
lower section w/a wide stepped mid-
molding above a row of three
drawers w/two deep drawers w/edge
molding flanking a small center
drawer w/molding along the bottom
edge, a deeply scalloped apron
continuing to cabriole legs ending in
raised pad feet, probably
Massachusetts, ca. 1750, 20 × 37",
5' 5" h. (replaced brasses, refinished,
minor imperfections) ..................... **6,325.00**

**Queen Anne "flat-top" highboy,**
maple, two-part construction: the
rectangular top w/a stepped flaring
cornice above a case w/a pair of
drawers above four long graduated
thumb-molded drawers; the lower
section w/a mid-molding above a
pair of deep square drawers flanking
a shallow center drawer above the
deeply scalloped apron, cabriole
legs ending in pad feet, probably
Connecticut, 1740-60, 19½ × 39",
6' ½" h. (ILLUS. top next column) .. **11,500.00**

*Queen Anne Maple Highboy*

LOWBOYS

**Chippendale lowboy,** carved
mahogany, the rectangular thumb-
molded top w/notched front corners
above one long & three short
molded drawers, the deeper center
drawer carved w/a fluted,
flowerhead-carved, punchwork-
decorated shell flanked by acanthus
leaves, fluted quarter columns
flanking, the shaped skirt below
continuing to shell-carved cabriole
legs ending in claw-and-ball feet,
Philadelphia, Pennsylvania, ca.
1765, retains original pierced brass
handles & escutcheon plate,
21⅜ × 37", 30½" h. ..................... **76,750.00**

**Queen Anne lowboy,** carved maple,
the rectangular molded top above a
pair of drawers over a row of three
smaller drawers, the center drawer
shell-carved, all w/butterfly
brasses, deeply scalloped skirt,
angular cabriole legs ending in
ribbed pad feet, mellow old patina,
small size, Connecticut, 1750-70,
24 × 31", 30" h. (old repair to
right front leg) ......................... **25,300.00**

*Victorian
Upholstered
Bourne*

*European
Classical Daybed*

## LOVE SEATS, SOFAS & SETTEES

**Bourne,** the three-part central raised down-swept tufted upholstered back above the wide three-lobed tufted upholstered seat, raised on tapering ring-turned legs, ca. 1850 (ILLUS. top) ..................................................... **880.00**

**Daybed,** Classical-style, burl walnut, the head- and footboards of equal height, each w/an arched & stepped crestrail above a wide panel flanked by round posts w/simple mushroom finials, on short ring-turned legs w/peg feet, wide shaped siderails, Europe, ca. 1830, 40 × 77", 38" h. (ILLUS. bottom) ................................ **358.00**

**Daybed,** Mission-style (Arts & Crafts movement), oak, an angled headrest w/tapering curved sides to the wide flat sides & footboard, short square legs, original drop-in cushions recovered in leather, original finish, branded mark of the Charles Limbert Company, Model No. 850, 30 × 80", 25" h. ............................................. **1,100.00**

**Fainting couch,** Victorian, giltwood & upholstery, a high slightly canted tufted upholstered back at one end above the long tufted upholstered seat, a molded giltwood seatrail & tapering reeded round legs on casters, worn upholstery, England, ca. 1850 (ILLUS. top next page) ....... **770.00**

**Recamier,** Classical, mahogany, the scrolled crest w/flowerhead terminal above a padded seat w/bolection molded seatrail & scrolled ends, on bolection-molded bracket legs

*English Victorian Fainting Couch*

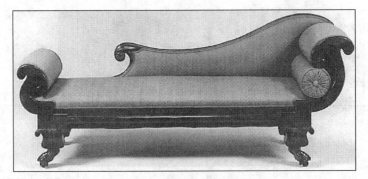

*New York Classical Recamier*

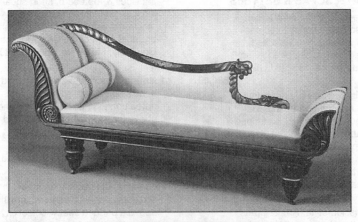

*Rare Decorated Recamier*

w/animal paw feet on casters, New York, ca.1830, 83½" l., 34¾" h. (ILLUS. middle previous page) ...... **1,610.00**

**Recamier,** painted, carved & stenciled mahogany, the shaped crest stenciled w/gilt foliage & terminating in a stylized carved grotesque mask, the arm supports carved w/stylized waterleaves, the molded & stenciled seatrail raised on bulbous acanthus-carved & ring-turned legs on brass casters, New York City, 1826-30, 7' 2" l. (ILLUS. bottom previous page) .......................................... **18,400.00**

**Settee,** Adirondack-style, the back w/rough-hewn stick posts & rails framing the woven hickory back panel, open stick arms on curved rough-hewn front arm supports continuing as front legs, rewoven hickory seat, original finish, branded Old Hickory mark, early 20th c., 25 × 45", 35" h. ................................ **605.00**

**Settee,** Art Nouveau, the serpentine rectangular padded eared back w/outscrolling arms & serpentine padded seat, decorated along the crestrail w/boldly carved clusters of flowers framed by wavy designs continuing around the side wings & down the arm frames w/scroll-carved hand grips & arm supports, the curved seatrail w/a boldly carved central leafy blossom flanked by undulating waves, on scroll-carved cabriole legs ending in scroll feet on casters, upholstered in worn foliate gold silk brocade, attributed to S. Karpen & Bros., Chicago, ca. 1900, 31 × 56", 44" h. (ILLUS. top) ............. **1,495.00**

*Karpen Art Nouveau Settee*

*Boston Classical Settee*

**Settee,** Classical, carved mahogany veneer, a rolled & carved flat crestrail w/carved florette terminals above the curved, outswept rails over the upholstered back flanked by outswept upholstered arms w/scrolled leaf-carved arm supports flanking the upholstered seat w/a flat paneled seatrail raised on carved cornucopia brackets over the carved animal paw feet on casters, old surface, Boston, 19th c., 20½ × 53½", 32" h. (ILLUS. bottom previous page) ............................... **2,070.00**

**Settee,** Federal country-style, painted, the long flat & wide crestrail raised on three simple turned stiles also joined by two narrower lower rails flanked by S-scroll arms on turned arm supports flanking the long plank seat, on six simple turned & slightly canted legs joined at the front & rear by flat stretchers & round end stretchers, old worn reddish brown repaint, ca. 1830-50, 60" l ................. **357.50**

**Settee,** Federal, carved mahogany, the flat crestrail comprised of three carved rectangular inset panels carved w/a pair of reserves carved w/drapery swags tied w/bowknots & a central reserve carved w/bellflowers centering an oval reserve decorated w/arrows tied w/a bowknot, the reeded arms & baluster-turned reeded arm supports w/closed arms flanking the bowed over-upholstered seat, flowerhead-carved dyes

flanking, on turned tapering reeded legs ending in brass casters, New York, ca. 1805, 5' 5" l .................... **11,500.00**

**Settee,** Mission-style (Arts & Crafts movement), oak, a wide V-form crestrail above twelve slats between square stiles over flat shaped arms over curved corbels on the square front arm supports continuing to form the front legs, original leather seat w/tacks, original finish, red decal mark & paper label of Gustav Stickley, Model No. 212, 25 × 47", 36" h ........ **3,300.00**

**Settee,** Queen Anne-Style, mahogany, the tall upholstered back w/an undulating crestrail above the curved & shaped open arms on shepherd's-crook arm supports flanking the upholstered seat w/an undulating seatrail, raised on four scroll-carved cabriole legs ending in pad feet, celedon velvet upholstery, good antique finish, England, 19th c. (ILLUS. below) .............................. **2,530.00**

**Settee,** Windsor, painted wood, the long flat narrow rectangular crestrail above numerous bamboo-turned spindles flanked by scrolled end arms over two spindles & a canted arm support flanking the wide plank seat raised on five pairs of canted bamboo-turned legs joined by plain box stretchers, old red stain w/black seat, minor imperfections, signed "J.C. Hubbard Boston, J.M. White Boston," ca. 1840, 18 × 95½", 30¾" h. (ILLUS. top next page) ..... **1,955.00**

*Queen Anne-Style Settee*

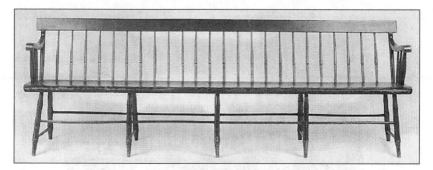

*Painted Windsor Settee*

*Fine Art Nouveau Sofa*

**Settle,** country-style, pine, the tall closed curved back w/narrow crestrail over four wide boards flanked by shaped one-board sides w/rounded hand grips above the long board seat over a five-panel base w/two small hinged doors, flat base, old mellow refinishing, late 18th - early 19th c., 69" l., 5' 8" h. (minor base damage, one arm w/old nailed split) .................................. **3,190.00**

**Settle,** Mission-style (Arts & Crafts movement), oak, the "crib-style" piece w/wide flat even crest & arm rails above thirteen vertical slats in the back, the canted sides w/five slats under each arm, large red decal mark of Gustav Stickley, Model No. 207, ca. 1904, 34 × 71", 39" h. .......................................... **29,900.00**

**Sofa,** Art Nouveau, carved mahogany, the heavy molded rectangular back frame continuing down to rounded arms & centered by a large realistically-carved semi-nude maiden w/her arms stretched across the top, two upholstered panels in the back continuing to upholstered arms over the upholstered seat above the wide flat molded seatrail, stylized carved floral clusters at the end of the seatrail above the short molded square legs ending in casters, probably manufactured by the Tobey Furniture Company, Chicago, ca. 1906, 6' l. (ILLUS. bottom) ....... **6,325.00**

**Sofa,** Chippendale-Style, camel-back-type w/serpentine crestrail on the upholstered back above out-scrolled upholstered arms flanking the long cushion seat, upholstered seatrail, raised on five square loop-carved legs joined by flat front stretchers

*Chippendale-Style Sofa*

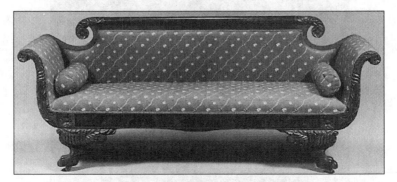

*Carved Mahogany Classical Sofa*

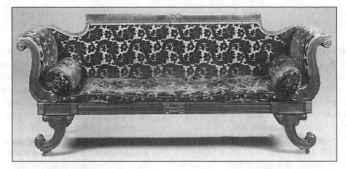

*Sabre-leg Classical Sofa*

pierced w/oval openings, flat side stretchers, covered in blue damask, probably England, early 20th c. (ILLUS. top) .................................. **1,540.00**

**Sofa,** Classical, box-style, carved mahogany, the flat slightly pointed crestrail ending in rounded ears above the upholstered back over upholstered arms w/downswept reeded & acanthus leaf-carved arm

supports flanking the upholstered seat on a wide straight rounded seatrail, on lobed & turned heavy feet ending in brass casters, possibly Boston, early 19th c., 5' 6" l. ........... **4,070.00**

**Sofa,** Classical, carved mahogany, a long flat bar crestrail w/rolled ends carved w/leaves & a floral rosette above curved side rails over the upholstered back flanked by outswept upholstered arms w/leaf-carved arm supports continuing to a long paneled seatrail w/florette-carved blocks at each end above the cornucopia-carved brackets over hairy paw feet on casters, ca. 1830, 85" l. (ILLUS. middle previous page) ......... **2,530.00**

**Sofa,** Classical, carved mahogany, the long wide & flat crestrail gently rolled & divided by reeded bars into three panels above the upholstered back flanked by shaped & reeded arm rails over upholstered panels & terminating in pierced reeded scrolls w/spiral-turned supports, long cushion seat, flat seatrail raised on baluster- and ring-turned front legs, probabaly Philadelphia, ca. 1810, on casters, 74" l., 36" h. (imperfections) ............. **1,955.00**

**Sofa,** Classical, carved mahogany, the long flat paneled crestrail centering a leaf-carved reserve flanked by outscrolled arms w/scrolled panel-and-roundel-carved arm supports flanking the upholstered seat, flat reeded, paneled & leaf-carved seatrail raised on paneled & roundel-carved sabre legs on casters, appears to have original finish, probably New York, ca. 1825, 89" l. (ILLUS. bottom previous page) ............................. **1,725.00**

**Sofa,** Classical, ormolu-mounted, carved & figured mahogany, the flat convex crotch-figured crestrail centering ormolu mounts in the form of a central female mask flanked by flowers & leafage, scroll arms & free-standing tapered columns flanking, the flat molded seatrail flanked by

ormolu dyes, on reeded vase-form feet on casters, New York, ca. 1830, 6' 8" l. ............................................. **5,462.00**

**Sofa,** Federal, carved mahogany, narrow reeded crestrail flanking a central panel carved w/a bowknot & sheaves of wheat as well as triglyphs, reeded & scrolled arms above upholstered sides, tapering reeded columnar arm supports above paterae-carved corner blocks flanking the upholstered seat, turned tapering & reeded front legs, square back legs, on casters, New York City, ca. 1810, 78½" l., 36" h. (old refinish, 20th c. gold upholstery w/bolsters, repairs) ........................ **3,450.00**

**Sofa,** Federal, painted & decorated, the shaped crestrail w/fruit- and foliate-stenciled decoration & rosette terminals above a padded back & outwardly scrolling arms over a padded seat w/gardrooned seatrail, on fluted sabre legs w/brass hairy paw feet, first quarter 19th c., 92⅓" l., 35½" h. ............................................. **575.00**

**Sofa,** Modern-style, the long, low flat upholstered back & even end arms fitted w/three upholstered back cushions & three seat cushions, flat upholsterd apron raised on a narrow wooden frame & flat slat legs decorated w/the Taliesin design, original frame finish, older reupholstering in a striped cream & yellow fabric, designed by Frank Lloyd Wright for the Heritage Henredon Company, paper label, 1950s, 34 × 99", 27" h. .................. **2,310.00**

*Victorian "Louis XV" Substyle Sofa*

**Sofa,** Victorian Rococo "Louis XV" substyle, carved rosewood, the long serpentine crestrail carved in the center w/a high arched crest centered by a large shell framed by leafy scrolls, rounded crest corners w/further leaf carving continuing around the oblong molded frame enclosing the wide upholstered back panel, padded arms w/molded & curved arm supports flanking the long upholstered seat above a triple-serpentine front seatrail raised on four demi-cabriole legs, each seatrail section centered by a large carved shell flanked by scrolls, American-made, ca. 1850, 33 × 80", 46" h. (ILLUS. bottom previous page) ......... **660.00**

**Sofa,** Victorian Rococo substyle, carved rosewood, the triple-serpentine crestrail carved at the center & ends w/arched boldly carved blossom & leaf clusters, the crestrail continuing down the sides to the upholstered half-arms flanking the upholstered back, molded & curved arm supports above the undulating molded & scroll-carved seatrail centered by a large blossom & leaf cluster, on demi-cabriole front legs on casters & canted square back legs, good dark finish, ca. 1850, 38 × 85", 41¾" h. (ILLUS. top) ........ **2,640.00**

**Sofa,** Victorian Rococo substyle, carved & laminated rosewood, the triple-serpentine crestrail carved at

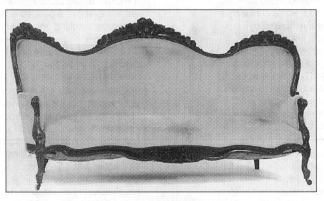

*Fine Rosewood Victorian Rococo Sofa*

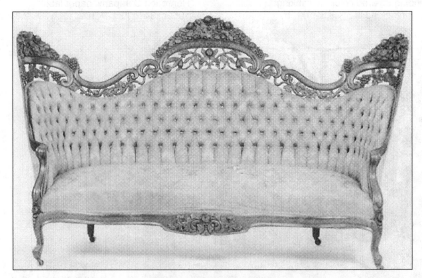

*Belter "Tuthill King" Sofa*

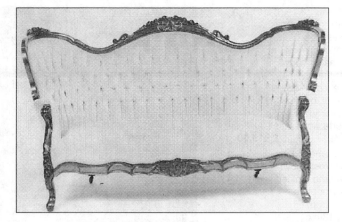

*Victorian Rococo*
*Walnut Sofa*

the center & curved ends w/high arched fruit, leaf & blossoms clusters above a scroll-carved rail over a pierce-carved band of fruiting grapevines above the long tufted upholstered back curving to form half-arms w/molded & curved arm supports flanking the upholstered seat, the molded slightly serpentine seatrail centered by a leafy scroll-carved reserve, on demi-cabriole legs on casters, "Tuthill King" patt., by John Henry Belter, New York, ca. 1850, 86" l., 4' 3" h. (ILLUS. bottom previous page) ............................. **42,900.00**

**Sofa,** Victorian Rococo substyle, carved walnut, the triple-serpentine crestrail carved at the center & curved ends w/leafy scrolls & a central cartouche above the tufted upholstered back, the curved ends continuing to form upholstered half-arms w/curved & molded arm supports, the serpentine & panel-carved seatrail centered by a cartouche & scroll-carved reserve, demi-cabriole front legs, ca. 1850 (ILLUS. top) ...................................... **990.00**

**Sofa,** Victorian Rococo substyle, walnut, triple-back style, the arched center section of crestrail carved w/a large blossom flanked by leafy scrolls, the arched end sections carved w/blossom & leaf clusters, the crestrail continuing down to closed upholstered arms flanking the tufted upholstered back & seat, molded curved arm supports above molded demi-cabriole front legs & the serpentine seatrail carved at the center w/a large blossom flanked by leaf clusters, ca. 1850, 80" l .............. **990.00**

*Victorian Overstuffed "Tête-a-tête"*

**Tête-a-tête,** Victorian overstuffed-style, a pair of rounded seats facing in opposite directions & joined by a wide pierced scroll-carved center S-form rail supporting oval upholstered back panels & round overstuffed upholstered seats w/wide tasseled fringe, worn original upholstery, mid-19th c. (ILLUS.) ......................... **880.00**

**Wagon seat,** country-style, maple & ash, the rush seat raised on supports, New England, old refinish, 19th c., 30" h. (minor imperfections)... **805.00**

**Wagon seat,** ladder-back country-style, refinished hardwoods, double-back form w/each section w/two rounded slats between three rod- and ring-turned stiles w/turned button finials flanked by turned rod arms w/baluster- and rod-turned arm supports continuing to form front legs & topped by wide mushroom-form hand grips, third turned leg in center under new woven blue tape seat, plain turned double rungs at front & sides, 19th c., 41" l., 35" h..... **605.00**

## MIRRORS

**Chippendale wall mirror,** mahogany & gilt gesso, arched crest cut w/declicate scrolls framing a relief-carved spread-winged eagle above scroll-carved ears over the rectangular mirror plate, scroll-cut base drop w/scrolled ears, original finish, Massachusetts, early 19th c., 20¼ × 40" (minor imperfections, one lower ear off) .................................. **2,415.00**

**Chippendale wall mirror,** mahogany, high arched & stepped crest above short serrated ears over the molded frame & rectangular mirror plate above a scroll-cut base drop, probably England, late 18th c., 17 × 35½" (refinished) ................... **1,150.00**

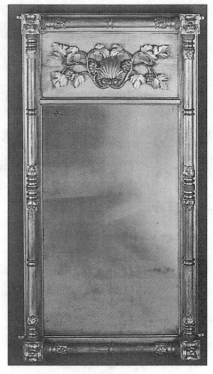

*Classical Giltwood Wall Mirror*

*Classical Girandole Mirror*

**Classical girandole mirror,** giltwood, the circular frame enclosing a convex mirror surmounted by a feather-carved cartouche flanked by carved scrolling leaf & acorns above a scrolling leaf- and acorn-carved pediment, 19th c., 21 × 41" (ILLUS. left) ................................. **3,680.00**

**Classical overmantel mirror,** gilt gesso, rectangular frame w/a

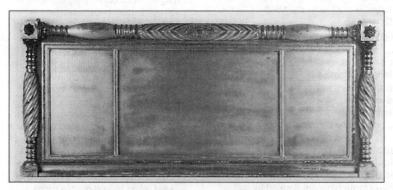

*Classical Overmantel Mirror*

crestrail carved w/half-round ring-turned balusters centered by a section of carved herringbone w/a central almond reserve w/an oval blossom, square top corner blocks w/florettes above the ring- and spiral-turned baluster-form side pilasters on foot blocks, flat molded base rail, the mirror plate divided into three sections w/two smaller flanking a longer center section, northeastern United States, ca. 1820, minor imperfections, 69⅜" l., 29⅜" h. (ILLUS. bottom previous page) ........................................... **1,093.00**

**Classical wall mirror,** carved giltwood, the rectangular frame w/a ring-turned & acanthus-carved pediment above a frieze embellished w/a scalloped carved shell over a rectangular frame enclosing a rectangular mirror flanked by ring-turned & acanthus-carved balusters on square corner blocks w/carved florettes, Philadelphia, ca. 1820-30, 31½ × 60½" (ILLUS. top right previous page) ............................... **2,990.00**

**Classical wall mirror,** the long rectangular frame composed of half-round ring-turned columns between corner blocks mounted w/rosettes, the upper section w/original reverse-painted colorful basket of fruit framed by leafy sprigs over the long rectangular mirror plate, gold repaint on frame, ca. 1830, 15½" w., 34" h. (wear & touch-up on painting, repaired corner break) ...................... **352.00**

**Classical-Style wall mirror,** eglomisé & parcel-gilt, the rectangular gilt & ebonized split-baluster frame w/ebonized corner blocks centering applied rosettes centering an eglomisé panel depicting a woman flanked by curtains above a rectangular mirror plate, late 19th c., 15¾ × 31¾" ......... **207.00**

**Early American country-style wall mirror,** carved hardwood, the high crest pierce-carved w/a bold scrolled tulip-shape above a pair of large inverted hearts over a dentil-carved band above the rectangular mirror plate w/molded edging & notched top corners & rounded bottom corners, the frame base w/pointed down-curved ears & a wide curved base centered by a carved four-leaf pinwheel, Pennsylvania Dutch, 19th c. (ILLUS. top next column).... **33,000.00**

*Pennsylvania Dutch Wall Mirror*

**Federal country-style dressing mirror,** painted & decorated, a nearly square mirror plate in a molded framed swiveling between slender uprights set upon a D-form base w/a single drawer & raised on small knob feet, painted cream w/outlining in red & grey pinstriping, the top w/painted foliate designs in mustard brown & red, the drawer front w/a polychrome floral design, Massachusetts or New Hampshire, ca. 1810, 10 × 17¾", 19¼" h. (minor imperfections) ................................ **1,092.50**

**Federal dressing mirror,** mahogany & mahogany veneer, the scrolled cresting above a rectangular inlaid frame on tapering posts & trestle feet, probably New England, ca. 1790, 5 × 10¾", 16½" h. .................. **489.00**

**Federal overmantel mirror,** giltwood, the flat wide flaring crestrail carved w/four beaded swags joined by scroll-carved cartouches above a molded frieze band over an egg-and-dart-carved narrow band above the three-part mirror plate w/two narrow plates flanking a large central plate, each plate separated by a narrow spiral-turned rail, the mirror flanked by slender ring-turned free-standing colonettes w/simple spiral-carved vines & resting on carved base blocks flanking the molded

*Federal Overmantel Mirror*

bottom rail w/a narrow beaded band, early 19th c., 67½" l., 41¾" h. (ILLUS. above) .............................. **1,210.00**

**Federal wall mirror,** mahogany & eglomisé, a carved gilt broken swan's-neck pediment w/rosette terminals centering a gilt flowering urn finial above an eglomisé panel depicting a farm scene over a rectangular mirror plate within a molded gilt surround & line-inlaid frame flanked by gilt floral & foliate spandrels above a shaped pendant, probably New York, 1790-1810, 24 × 53½" ..................................... **1,495.00**

*Fine Federal Wall Mirror*

**Federal wall mirror,** giltwood & eglomisé, the projecting spherule-mounted cornice above an eglomisé panel decorated w/flowers & leaves in gold & black on a white & robin's-egg blue ground, a beveled mirror plate below flanked by fluted pilasters w/upper & lower capitals in the form of Egyptian masks & feet, bears the pencilled inscription on the back of the eglomisé panel reading "James Dionne (?) sold this glass to Madam Dobree July th 16 1808," 26¾" w., 43" h. (ILLUS. bottom previous column) ....... **3,450.00**

**Georgian wall mirror,** walnut & gilt gesso, the arched & scroll-cut crest centered by a large round gilt gesso leaf & shell device above the long rectangular mirror plate w/notched upper corners & gilt liner, base drop w/scroll-cut designs flanking a smaller gilt gesso device flanked by a pair of brass candlearms, probably England, 1750-80, old finish, 20¼", 42" h. (minor imperfections) ........... **4,312.50**

**Mission-style (Arts & Crafts movement) wall mirror,** a long gently rounded crestrail w/through-tenon construction above wide board sides & bottom rail, iron hooks at each side & two at the bottom, cleaned original finish, signed by L. & J.G. Stickley, Model No. 65, 40" l., 27" h. .............. **2,750.00**

**Mission-style (Arts & Crafts movement) wall mirror,** rectangular wide board sides w/through-tenons at each corner, original glass, original finish, numbered mark of Stickley Brothers, Model No. 7507, early 20th c., 39" l., 27" h................. **770.00**

*French Regence Dressing Mirror*

*Queen Anne Wall Mirror*

**Regence dressing mirror,** walnut, the arched beveled mirror within a comforming frame w/rounded crest & carved w/delicate foliate scrolling vines centered at the top by a Hoho bird, first quarter 18th c., France, 17¼ × 21⅛" (ILLUS. above) .......... **3,737.00**

**Victorian cheval mirror,** Gothic Revival substyle, carved rosewood, the tall Gothic arch frame pierce-carved at the top w/scrolls centered by a quatrefoil below a pointed finial, the molded frame around the tall rectangular mirror w/a pointed top swiveling between tall spiral-twist-turned uprights over tripartite outswept scalloped & molded legs w/pierced Gothic trefoils & joined by a scalloped stretcher w/pointed drops, attributed to Alexander Roux, New York, New York, ca. 1850 (ILLUS. top next page)....... **2,750.00**

**Victorian cheval mirror,** Rococo substyle, mahogany, a tall rectangular molded frame w/a rounded crestrail swivels between tall S-scroll uprights set on rectangular blocks raised on outswept scroll feet, ca. 1850 .......... **825.00**

**Queen Anne wall mirror,** walnut & parcel gilt, the shaped scroll-cut crest w/carved & gilded shell within a central circular opening above a rectangular beveled mirror plate w/a gilt surround & molded, veneered frame, America or England, ca. 1740, 15⅛ × 30⅞" (ILLUS.) .......... **2,185.00**

*Gothic Revival Cheval Mirror*

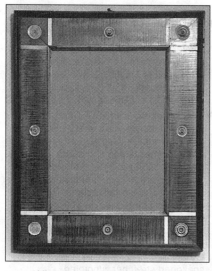

*Victorian Country-style Mirror*

**Victorian country-style wall mirror,**
inlaid curly maple, the wide flat
maple frame w/a narrow black outer
molding & an inner yellow molding
framing the rectangular mirror plate,
the maple inlaid w/bone & ivory bars
& roundels, 19th c. (ILLUS.) .......... **5,500.00**

**Victorian overmantel mirror,**
giltwood, the wide rectangular frame
w/rounded corners centered at the
top by a high pierced scroll-carved
crest, molded large floral, leaf & fruit
clusters at top corners & pierced
long leafy scrolls at bottom corners,
mid-19th c., 67" w., 4' 11" h. .......... **2,200.00**

## PARLOR SUITES

**Art Deco:** sofa, a pair of armchairs &
a pair of side chairs; parcel-gilt
mahogany, each piece w/a gently
arched crestrail above the
upholstered back, upholstered
arms w/rectangular pierced arm
supports w/a lattice design & a
central gilt floral bouquet, molded
seatrails & square tapering legs,
the side chairs w/an arched &
molded back w/a pierced lattice slat
w/gilt floral bouquet above the
upholstered seat, grey textured
fabric, in the manner of Maurice
Dufrene, France, ca. 1925, sofa 69" l.,
5 pcs. (ILLUS. of part, top next
page) ........................................ **13,800.00**

**Louis XVI-Style:** settee, pair of
open-arm armchairs & four side
chairs; giltwood, each piece w/a
gently arched crestrail w/a ribbon
band design & a small central floral
crest, the ribbon design continuing
around the panel enclosing the
upholstered back, padded arms on
curved & carved arm supports
flanking the upholstered seat,
matching carved seatrail design,
turned tapering & reeded front legs
& square slightly curved back legs,
late 19th c., the set (ILLUS. middle,
next page) .................................... **1,540.00**

**Victorian Baroque-style:** a settee, two
armchairs & two side chairs;
mahogany, each piece w/a wide
curved & rolled crestrail center by a
large boldly carved oval cartouche
framed by leafy scrolls above the
tufted upholstered back, the down-
curved arms terminating in hand grips
carved as realistic ladies' heads
above leaf-carved supports flanking
the upholstered seat, plain seatrails,
squared simple cabriole front legs
ending in paw feet on casters, square
slightly curved rear legs on casters,
ca. 1900, armchair 41" w. (ILLUS. of
part, bottom next page).................... **3,575.00**

*Art Deco Parlor Suite*

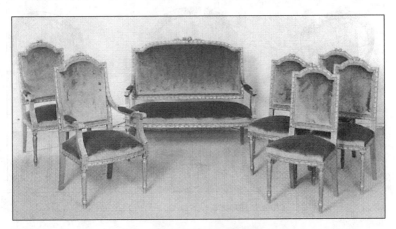

*Louis XVI-Style Parlor Suite*

*Victorian Baroque Parlor Suite*

*Renaissance Revival Parlor Suite*

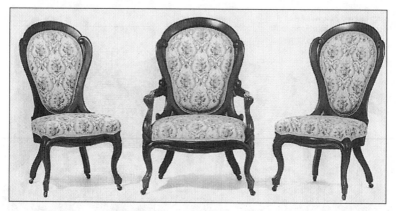

*Victorian Rococo Rosewood Parlor Suite*

*Wicker Settee & Armchair*

**Victorian Renaissance Revival
substyle:** sofa, armchair & two side
chairs; walnut & burl walnut, each
piece having ornately carved arched
crestrails centered w/carved
medallions of Roman soldiers, the
sofa back divided by distinctive
carved architectural urns, the arms
ending in carved bearded heads, on
ring- and trumpet-turned reeded
front legs on casters, ca. 1875, the
set (ILLUS. of part, top previous
page) .............................................. **8,800.00**

**Victorian Rococo substyle:** a sofa,
armchair & two side chairs; carved &
laminated rosewood, each piece w/a
tapering oval balloon back w/a
simple scroll-carved frame around
the upholstered panel, the armchair
w/curved & molded open arms
continuing to incurved arm supports,
curved & molded seatrails continuing
to semi-cabriole front legs, square
back-swept rear legs, on casters,
attributed to John Henry Belter,
NewYork, ca. 1850, the set (ILLUS.
of part, middle previous page) ....... **8,250.00**

**Wicker:** a sofa, pair of armchairs,
rocking armchair, occasional table, &
planter; the seating pieces w/wide
tightly woven rolled crestrails
continuing down to form flat arms all
above open diamond-lattice woven
backs & sides, armchair backs
upholstered, seats w/cushions, the
aprons w/a wide tightly woven band
above a diamond-lattice band, tightly
woven side panels, on short
wrapped legs, natural finish, all
bearing metal labels for the Paine
Furniture Co., Boston, the upholstery
of Chinese raw silk w/an additional
small bolt of fabric, ca. 1910, the set
(ILLUS. of part, bottom previous
page) .............................................. **4,312.00**

## SCREENS

**Fire screen,** Federal, painted
mahogany, a large nearly square
wooden frame surrounding a
needlework panel of a basket of
flowers, adjusting on a slender
tapering columnar standard on a
tripod base w/three spider legs,
minor imperfections, New England,
ca. 1800, 22½" w., 4' 4" h. (ILLUS. top
next column) ...................................... **546.00**

*Federal Fire Screen*

*Victorian Rococo Fire Screen*

*Pair of Chinese Wallpaper Screens*

**Fire screen,** Victorian Rococo substyle, carved rosewood, a molded rectangular frame trimmed around the sides w/pierced leafy scrolls & centered at the top by a carved urn of flowers, the frame holding two pencil drawings under glass, one depicting a romantic landscape, the other an old mill, adjusting on a ring-turned column w/a ribbed baluster-knop above the tripod base w/three scroll-carved legs, ca. 1850, 31¾" w., 45½" h. (ILLUS. bottom previous page)......... **935.00**

*French Wallpaper Screen*

**Folding screen,** four-fold, Zubrie wallpaper, the four panels forming a continuous landscape scene of Neoclassical ruins w/figures in a garden, France, 19th c., each panel 23½" w., 5' 10" h. (ILLUS. bottom previous column) .......................... **3,450.00**

**Folding screens,** four-fold, painted wallpaper, decorated w/a continuous scene of exotic birds, flowering vines & bamboo on a sea green ground, the reverse covered in rattan weave, China, 18th c. paper, each panel 15¾" w., 8' 2" h., pr. (ILLUS. top)....... **5,175.00**

## SECRETARIES
**Chippendale secretary-bookcase,** carved cherry, two-part construction: the upper section w/a rectangular top w/a molded dentil-carved cornice above a pair of tall hinged cockbeaded doors centered by three fluted pilasters & opening to shaped shelves, a pair of candle slides below; the lower section w/hinged molded slant lid carved at the center w/a large stop-fluted fan & opening to an interior fitted w/valanced pigeonholes over small drawers centering fluted document drawers, the lower case w/a narrow drawer flanked by slide supports above

*Rare Chippendale Cherry Secretary*

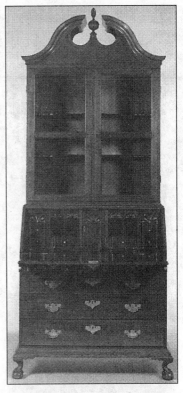

*Newport Chippendale Secretary*

three, long graduated molded drawers, the lower two carved in the center w/a fan, the molded base continuing into claw-and-ball feet, all drawers w/oval brass pulls, attributed to Ephriham Munson, Woodbury, Connecticut, ca. 1785,19½ × 39", 6' 11" h. (ILLUS. above left) ...................... **23,000.00**

**Chippendale secretary-bookcase,** walnut, two-part construction: the upper section w/a molded swan's-neck pediment centering a flaming urn finial above a pair of four-pane glazed doors opening to two shelves; the lower section w/a hinged slant lid opening to a fitted interior w/a slide-lid writing compartment & central shell-carved prospect door enclosing three concave blocked drawers flanked on either side by two shell-carved valanced drawers over two pigeonholes above a convex blocked drawer flanked by a shell-carved drawer above two drawers,

all above a case w/slide supports & four long graduated drawers, molded base, on short cabriole legs w/claw-and-ball feet, feet replaced, Newport, Rhode Island, 1760-80, 23½ × 40¾", 7' 7½" h. (ILLUS. above right) ................................ **34,500.00**

**Classical country-style secretary-bookcase,** curly maple, two-part construction: the upper section w/a flat rectangular top w/a flat projecting cornice above a pair of Gothic-glazed tall cupboard doors opening to shelves; the stepped-out lower section w/a pull-out writing compartment & hinged lid opening to reveal valanced pigeonholes & small drawers centering a line-inlaid prospect door opening to a small valanced drawer, overhanging a case w/three long graduated drawers flanked by free-standing ring-turned columns, on stepped block feet, New York State, ca. 1835, 22¼ × 49¾", 6' 11¾" h. (ILLUS. top next page) ................. **5,175.00**

*Classical Curly Maple Secretary*

*Country Federal Secretary*

**Classical secretary-bookcase, mahogany,** two-part construction: the upper section w/a high coved plain cornice above a pair of tall two-pane glazed cupboard doors opening to two shelves; the lower section w/a long drawer above a fold-down leather-lined writing surface above a long support drawer fitted w/inkwells above a pair of paneled cupboard doors trimmed w/molding, scalloped apron on bracket feet, ca. 1830, 21¾ × 46⅞", 7' 4⅜" h. ....................................... **2,200.00**

**Federal country-style secretary-bookcase,** painted poplar, two-part construction: the upper section w/a rectangular top w/a deep flaring cove-molded cornice above a pair of four-panel glazed cupboard doors w/fake curved mullions opening to three shelves; the stepped-out lower section w/a narrow rectangular top above a wide slant lid opening to an interior fitted w/small drawers surrounding a central arched pigeonhole, the case below w/three long drawers w/oval brass pulls, scalloped apron & simple bracket feet, old brownish red paint, original hardware, early 19th c., top 14 × 41½", 6' 11¼" h. (ILLUS. bottom) ............................................... **3,520.00**

**Federal secretary-bookcase,** figured maple inlaid mahogany, two-part construction: the upper section w/a shaped crest surmounted by three turned urn finials centering a rectangular bird's-eye reserve, above a pair of diamond-glazed cupboard doors opening to two shelves; the projecting lower section centering a hinged fall-down writing section opening to two small drawers & a hinged baise-lined writing surface opening to reveal a well, two small drawers flanking w/a single long drawer below, the subtly arched figured skirt continuing to ring-turned reeded tapering legs ending in slightly swelled feet, probably Massachusetts, ca. 1810, 21 × 42", 7' 3¼" h. .......................... **7,475.00**

**Federal secretary,** bird's-eye maple, mahogany & wavy birch, two-part construction: the upper section w/a rectangular top above a narrow flaring cornice above a pair of wide doors w/light & dark inlaid panels flanking a small central door w/light inlay above a row of three narrow drawers; the stepped-out lower section w/a fold-down writing surface above a case w/slide supports & four long graduated drawers w/light inlay banding & simple turned wood knobs, scalloped apron, baluster- and ring-turned short legs, refinished, imperfections, Massachusetts or New Hampshire, ca. 1820, 20½ × 41¼", 5'½" h. (ILLUS. below) ...................... **1,725.00**

**Federal secretary-bookcase,** curly maple-inlaid mahogany, two-part construction: the upper section w/a rectangular top w/a molded, reeded cornice above a pair of Gothic-glazed cupboard doors opening to a shelf, tapered pilasters at the sides & two narrow drawers below; the stepped-out lower section w/a hinged writing flap above two long drawers flanked by reeded three-quarter round columns, on ring-turned legs joined by end stretchers, on casters, New England, ca. 1815, 25½ × 36½", 5' 2½" h. (ILLUS. top next column) ................................. **6,325.00**

*Fine Federal Secretary*

*New England Federal Secretary*

*Inlaid Cherry Secretary*

**Federal secretary-bookcase,** inlaid cherry, two-part construction: the upper section w/a rectangular top w/a deep coved cornice above a pair of tall doors w/rectangular scalloped inset panels opening to sectioned beaded shelves; the stepped-out lower section w/a hinged slant lid opening to an interior fitted w/small drawers & valanced pigeonholes, all above pull-out slide supports & four long graduated drawers w/banded inlay, old refinish, restored, Middle Atlantic States, ca. 1810, 20¾ × 40¼", 6' 11½" h. (ILLUS. bottom previous page) .................................................. **3,105.00**

**Federal secretary-bookcase,** inlaid mahogany, three-part construction: the upper section w/three urn finials above a shaped pediment w/central arch w/a veneered oval reserve over a molded cornice w/band-inlay above two glazed doors w/inlaid interlacing mullions opening to an interior fitted w/two shelves; the mid-section w/a

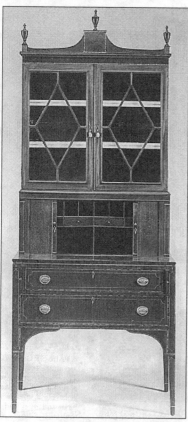

*Three-part Federal Secretary*

mid-molding over tambour doors flanked by line- and band-inlaid panels & opening to an interior fitted w/eight pigeonholes above four short drawers over two pigeonholes; the lower section w/a rectangular molded hinged top opening to a baize-lined writing surface above two line- and band-inlaid long drawers over line- and band-inlaid shaped skirt, on double tapering square line- and band-inlaid legs w/cuffs, North Shore, Massachusetts, 1790-1810, 19½ × 36", 7' 1½" h. (ILLUS. bottom previous column) ........................... **10,925.00**

**Federal secretary-bookcase,** inlaid mahogany, two-part construction: the upper section w/an angular arched crestrail w/a large center block supporting a upright block finial flanked by C-scrolls & topped by a pointed brass ball, the corner blocks w/matching brass balls all above a frieze band over a pair of tall diamond-glazed cupboard doors opening to two shelves over a row of pigeonholes; the lower section w/a fold-out hinged writing surface w/inlaid edge banding above a case w/slide supports & three long line-inlaid drawers w/oval brass pulls, on square tapering legs w/inlay, northern New England, early 19th c., 19 × 39", 6' 2½" h. (replaced brasses, old refinish, imperfections).................... **2,645.00**

**Federal secretary-bookcase,** mahogany veneer, two-part construction: the upper section w/a crown-form crest w/a high center block curving down to small corner blocks above a molded cornice over a pair of geometrically-glazed cupboard doors opening to shelves; the lower, slightly stepped-out section w/a molded edge above a case of four long cockbeaded drawers w/simple turned wood knobs & keyhole escutcheons, curved apron continuing to tall gently outswept French feet, Massachusetts,1790-1810, 20½ × 40½", 5' 10¼" h. (old refinish, imperfections) ............................... **4,600.00**

**Victorian "Golden Oak" side-by-side secretary-bookcase,** oak, a high flat crestboard on one side of the top w/an arched fan-carved center crest flanked by flat cornices over a shaped board w/applied scroll carving all

*Ornate "Golden Oak" Side-by-side Secretary*

beside a narrow high, arched crestrail w/leafy scroll carving on the other side of the top above a shield-form long mirror, the left side of the cabinet w/a curved-glass cupboard door opening to four wooden shelves & flanked by narrow beaded edge bands, the right side w/a small nearly square scroll-pierced panel beside the mirror & below an incurved shelf supported by a small spiral-turned spindle above a small drawer, all

above a wide slant lid w/swagged scroll carving & opening to a fitted interior above a curve-fronted drawer over two flat drawers, all w/pierced brass pulls, shaped apron w/delicate scrolls, on short shaped bracket feet, ca. 1900 (ILLUS. top previous column) .......................... **1,500.00**

## SIDEBOARDS

**Art Deco sideboard,** zebrawood, a rectangular form w/four cupboard doors, each opening to a shelves interior, on V-shaped supports w/gilt-bronze square accents & feet, Andre Leleu, France, 18 × 89", 33½" h. (ILLUS. below) .............................. **9,200.00**

**Art Nouveau sideboard,** mahogany, the superstructure w/a gently arched crestrail above a long open shelf supported on curved & carved brackets flanking a long rectangular mirror above the rectangular top w/a molded edge over a case w/a pair of small paneled drawers flanking a long center paneled drawer, all w/long looped ormolu handles, the end drawers above square open compartments over short paneled doors flanking a large paneled central door, the molded, gently curving apron on molded bracket feet, Louis Majorelle, France, ca. 1900, 20 × 62", 5' 1" h. (ILLUS. top next page) ................................ **2,530.00**

**Classical server,** cherry & curly maple, a low three-quarter gallery w/scroll-cut ends in curly maple above the curly maple rectangular top over a single long drawer w/mahogany flame veneer, on block- and ring-turned legs w/knob

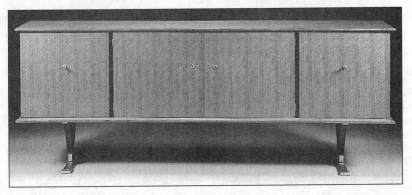

*Art Deco Sideboard*

*Art Nouveau Sideboard*

*Philadelphia Classical Sideboard*

feet, drawer w/two opalescent lacy glass pulls, old finish, ca. 1830, 19¾ × 35¼", 28" h. plus gallery (minor veneer damage & repair) ..... **880.00**

**Classical sideboard,** mahogany, a central arched splashboard flanked by raised square end platforms w/coved sides on square plinths on the rectangular top, the case w/outset end sections consisting of a short drawer w/round brass & ring pull above a long paneled cupboard door flanking the inset center section w/a long paneled drawer w/two pulls above a pair of paneled cupboard doors, free-standing columns down the front sides w/leaf-carved capitals, carved paw feet & a reeded shaft, the conforming molded base raised on four baluster-turned & leaf-carved front legs & two plain back legs, attributed to Joseph Berry, Philadelphia, ca. 1815, 24 × 77", 4' 7" h. (ILLUS. bottom) ................ **3,300.00**

*Classical "Grecian" Sideboard*

**Classical sideboard,** mahogany, an architectural "Grecian" pedimented & galleried backsplash flanked by shaped low sides on the rectangular top above a row of three round-fronted drawers w/round brass knobs above single paneled end doors flanking a pair of paneled center doors all separated by free-standing columns, molded base raised on four scrolled leaf-carved legs on animal paw feet, Philadelphia, ca. 1825 (ILLUS. top) ................................... **2,200.00**

**Federal server,** cherry, rectangular top w/reeded edges above an apron w/two drawers w/round brass pulls flanked by three incised lines at each end, raised on slender ring-, rod- and baluster-turned legs ending in ringed peg feet, New England, early 19th c., 18 × 32", 34½" (refinished, restoration, replaced brasses) ........................................ **1,150.00**

**Federal server,** mahogany & mahogany veneer, rectangular top above a deep case w/a pair of short drawers above a very deep long drawer all w/oval brass pulls, on baluster- and ring-turned legs w/peg feet, early 19th c., 21 × 35½", 37½" h. (age cracks, veneer repairs, back leg repaired, replaced brasses) ...... **1,320.00**

**Federal sideboard,** bird's-eye maple & cherry, a tall backboard w/rounded corners tapering down to scrolls above the rectangular top w/outset ovolu front corners over outset reeded columns flanking the case w/a row of two short drawers flanking a long drawer above a row of four small cupboard doors above two long drawers across the bottom, each drawer w/bird's-eye maple veneering and the doors w/additional mahogany banding, early lacy glass pulls, on ring- and baluster-turned legs, Vermont, 1815-25, 18 × 42", 44½" h. (refinished, minor imperfections)..... **2,645.00**

**Federal sideboard,** inlaid & figured mahogany, serpentine-front, the oblong top w/a line-inlaid edge & serpentine front above a conformingly-shaped case w/a pair of concave hinged cupboard doors w/fan-inlaid corners centering three long convex drawers w/line-inlaid banding, on line-inlaid square double-tapering legs ending in cross-banded cuffs, deep honey-brown color, now fitted w/rare oval eagle-decorated brasses & earlier Queen Anne style keyhole escutcheons, New England, ca. 1800, 28 × 66", 38¾" h. (ILLUS. below) ......................................... **6,900.00**

*Federal Serpentine Sideboard*

*Federal-Style Inlaid Mahogany Sideboard*

*Early French Canadian Buffet*

**Federal sideboard,** inlaid mahogany, a rectangular top w/a stepped-out center section flanked by curved side sections above a conforming case w/a curved-front drawer over a curved-front cupboard door at each end & three small drawers over a pair of flat cupboard doors in the center section, all edges w/line-inlay, drawers w/oval brasses except the center one which is centered by an inlaid oval reserve, on square tapering legs w/line-inlay, New England, ca. 1790, 24½ x 68", 40½" h. (refinished, replaced brasses, minor imperfections) ....... **8,050.00**

**Federal-Style sideboard,** inlaid mahogany, a low stepped & rounded crestrail above the rectangular top w/a D-form front above a case w/small curved end drawers w/line-inlay above long curved cupboard doors w/similar inlay flanking a central flat-fronted section w/a stack of two long, line-inlaid drawers above a pair of wide line-inlaid cupboard doors, all doors & drawers w/oval brasses, raised on four turned, reeded & tapering legs ending in brass paw feet, carrying the label of "Ernest N. Hagen, 213 East 26th Street," New York, ca. 1890, 72" l., 43" h. (ILLUS. top) ..... **4,675.00**

**French Canadian buffet,** pine, the rectangular top above a pair of raised-panel cupboard doors, each raised panel w/notched corners, curved iron hinges & an oval iron keyhole escutcheon on one door, flat base, old refinish, imperfections, French Canada, 18th c., 14¾ x 49½", 33" h. (ILLUS. bottom)............ **518.00**

*Stickley Brothers Sideboard*

a single long drawer w/two wood knobs, raised on square legs joined by a medial shelf, original finish, red decal mark of Gustav Stickley, 20 × 48", 44" h. (veneer chips on side, some top stains).................... **1,750.00**

**Mission-style (Arts & Crafts movement) sideboard,** oak, the low paneled splashboard w/a plate rail between pointed stiles above the rectangular top overhanging the case w/a pair of long narrow paneled end doors w/hammered copper butt hinges flanking a pair of short drawers above two long drawers all w/hammered copper plate & bail pulls, flat apron w/corner corbels, square stile legs, fine original finish, Stickley Brothers, Model No. 8869, 22 × 60", 46" h. (ILLUS. top).......... **2,860.00**

*18th Century French Provincial Buffet*

**French Provincial buffet,** poplar, the rectangular top above a row of three thumb-molded drawers over a pair of large paneled doors, simple metal hardware, scalloped apron & short curved front legs, France, ca. 1760, 24 × 71", 44" h. (ILLUS.)................ **2,200.00**

**Mission-style (Arts & Crafts movement) server,** oak, a low back rail on the rectangular top over a narrow apron w/a pair of small drawers flanking a long center drawer all w/hammered copper plate & bail pulls, on slender square legs joined by a medial shelf, original finish, remnant of decal mark of L. & J.G. Stickley, Model No. 741, early 20th c., 18 × 44", 40" h. ................ **3,300.00**

**Mission-style (Arts & Crafts movement) server,** oak, a plate rail on the narrow rectangular top overhanging a case w/a pair of drawers w/turned wood knobs above

*Limbert Mission Oak Sideboard*

*Victorian Rococo Server*

*Victorian Eastlake Sideboard*

**Mission-style (Arts & Crafts movement) sideboard,** oak, the superstructure w/a gently arched top above an open rectangular shelf raised on incurved brackets flanking a long rectangular mirror above the rectangular top w/rounded front

corners overhanging the case w/corner corbels flanking a pair of drawers above small paneled end doors flanking three small central drawers all above a long bottom drawer, original copper hardware, original finish, Charles Limbert Co., Model No. 1443½, 23 × 60", 4' 10" h. (ILLUS. bottom previous page) ....... **8,250.00**

**Neo-Classical sideboard,** fruitwood, a rectangular top above a molded edge above a row of four small drawers w/molded edging above two pairs of paneled cupboard doors w/molded interior edging, molded base raised on short square tapering legs, Europe, early 19th c., 20¼ × 80", 40" h. ................................................. **3,960.00**

**Victorian server,** Rococo substyle, rosewood, the tall superstructure w/a scalloped & scroll-carved crestrail w/central pierced cartouche & urn-turned end finials above two tiered open shelves each backed by two narrow rectangular mirrors w/notched corners & supported by S-scroll supports above the rectangular white marble top over a deep scalloped & scroll-carved apron w/a long drawer w/a central shell-carved reserve raised on double C-scroll supports for the two open, tiered lower shelves, each backed by a pair of rectangular mirrors w/notched corners, the lower shelf w/a shaped front & raised on scrolled, leaf-carved short front legs & square back legs all on casters, ca. 1850, 18¼ × 43", 5' 5¼" h. (ILLUS. top previous column) ......... **2,200.00**

**Victorian sideboard,** Eastlake substyle, walnut & burl walnut, the tall superstructure w/a flat coved crestrail above a long panel & long shaped brackets over a large rectangular mirror flanked by scroll-carved side panels w/a small open shelf above a recessed panel above a long open shelf w/reeded square supports above a recessed long burl panel over the rectangular grey marble top, the lower case w/a pair of long paneled end cupboard doors w/carved rosette bands & a burl panel flanking a stack of four long line-incised & burled central drawers all above a long burled base drawer, the drawers w/butterfly & bail brasses, blocked side stiles ending in block feet on casters, ca. 1880-90 (ILLUS. bottom previous column)................. **1,600.00**

## STANDS

**Bookstand,** Mission-style (Arts & Crafts movement), oak, rectangular slab sides w/half-round cut-outs at the top flanking a V-form book trough over a lower open shelf, arched aprons & arched cut-out end feet, keyed tenon construction, original finish, unsigned but similar to Gustav Stickley Model No. 74, 10 × 27", 31" h. ................................. **550.00**

*English Victorian Bookstand*

**Bookstand,** Victorian, inlaid mahogany, the tall tiered top w/four revolving shelves surmounted by a reeded turned finial, each shelf w/inlaid false book bindings separating openings, on a deep round base w/a flush drawer raised on a bulbous baluster-turned standard on a tripod base w/three downswept legs ending in brass animal paw caps & casters, repairs, lacking one caster, England, third quarter 19th c., 27½" d., 5' 8" h. (ILLUS.) ........................................ **7,475.00**

**Candlestand,** Chippendale, carved walnut, the hinged dished top tilting above a birdcage mechanism & spirally-fluted flaring standard raised on a tripod base w/leaf- and bellflower-carved cabriole legs

*Chippendale Candlestand*

ending in claw-and-ball feet, Pennsylvania, ca. 1760, 22¾" d., 27¾" h. (ILLUS.) ........................... **1,380.00**

**Candlestand,** Chippendale, carved walnut, the round dished top tilting & revolving on a birdcage mechanism above a compressed-ball & rod-turned pedestal on a tripod base w/cabriole legs ending in claw-and-ball feet, Philadelphia, ca. 1765, 20¾"d., 27" h. (old repair to lower section of pedestal) ...................... **4,887.00**

*Walnut Chippendale Candlestand*

*Federal Mahogany
Canterbury*

**Candlestand,** Chippendale, walnut, the round two-board dished top tilting above a baluster- and ring-turned standard on a tripod base w/cabriole legs ending snake feet, Pennsylvania, late 18th c. (ILLUS. bottom previous page).............................. **5,225.00**

**Candlestand,** Classical, cherry & walnut, rectangular top w/notched corners tilting above a baluster- and ring-turned pedestal on a triangular platform w/three long outswept C-scroll feet, Pennsylvania, ca. 1830-40 ..................... **330.00**

**Candlestand,** Classical, cherry, oblong top tilting above a double-bulb- and rod-turned pedestal, the lower bulb carved w/swirled reeding above another band of swirled reeding above the tripod base w/long slender S-scroll legs, Connecticut, ca. 1820, 15 × 20", 28" h. (old refinish, imperfections)... **1,725.00**

**Candlestand,** Federal country-style, cherry, square top w/undulating edges above a heavy turned columnar pedestal on a tripod base w/spider legs, original surface, New Hampshire, ca. 1810, 14" sq., 28" h. (minor surface wear) .............. **920.00**

**Candlestand,** Federal tilt top, mahogany, rectangular top w/angled corners above a baluster- and ring-turned pedestal above a tripod base w/spider legs & tapering block feet, crossbanded veneer outlining the top, old surface, Boston or Concord, Massachusetts, 1800-10, 15 × 23", 29" h. ........................................... **1,495.00**

**Candlestand,** Federal tilt-top, mahogany veneered cherry & birch, the octagonal oblong top w/checkered line-inlaid border tilting above a chip-carved urn-form standard, on line-inlaid arched square tapering legs ending in crossbanded cuffs, Northeastern Shore, New England, ca. 1810, 15 × 22", 29" h. (some leg repair) ........................... **2,070.00**

**Candlestand,** Federal, ormolu-mounted mahogany, shaped oblong top tilting above a turned flaring baluster- and urn-form pedestal raised on three downcurving reeded legs ending in ormolu hairy paw feet, New York, ca. 1815, 18½ × 26", 29½" h. (crack to one leg) ........................ **2,587.00**

**Candlestand,** Federal, painted birch, thin rectangular top w/notched corners above a knob-topped columnar pedestal on a tripod base w/spider legs, painted red, attributed to Lieutenant Samuel Dunlap, New Hampshire, late 18th - early 19th c., 16⅛ × 16½", 26½" h. (old refinish, imperfections) ................................ **2,875.00**

**Canterbury (music stand),** Federal, mahogany, of rectangular form surmounted by pointed ball finials, the upper section fitted w/four transverses, the case below w/a single drawer on ring-turned feet ending in brass casters, appears to retain original finish, American ca. 1820, 15 × 22", 21" h. (ILLUS. above)............................................. **3,450.00**

*Victorian Folio Stand*

**Folio stand,** Victorian Aesthetic Movement substyle, carved & ebonized walnut, the tall back w/a serrated crestrail w/a central carved palmette & carved ears above carved slats over a large rounded arch enclosing a pierce-carved flower-filled urn above a band of small turned spindles all raised on three stiles above the lower rectangular case, the case w/a narrow rectangular top above a rectangular door carved w/corner florettes in blocks & two central blocks w/roundels, the case raised above a front wide slat pierce-carved w/two crosses & supported at the bottom by four ring- and baluster-turned angled spindles joining the ring- and block-turned heavy front legs to the slender turned & canted rear legs, late 19th c. (ILLUS.)....... **1,320.00**

**Kettle stand,** Chippendale, cherry, round dished top w/slightly rounded tightly scalloped apron raised on a ring-, rod- and urn-turned pedestal ending in a tripod base w/cabriole

legs ending in snake feet, old refinish, ca. 1800, 12½" d., 27" h. (minor imperfections).................... **2,645.00**

**Magazine stand,** Mission-style (Arts & Crafts movement), oak, the three-quarter gallery top w/an open back rail flanked by solid board ends w/a curved front cut-outs flanking the top shelf over three lower shelves flanked by two slats on each side & three slats down the back, square stile legs, cleaned original finish, paper label & red decal mark of Gustav Stickley, 15 × 20", 36" h. .... **1,540.00**

**Magazine stand,** Mission-style (Arts & Crafts movement), oak, slab sides w/through-tenon construction & half-round cut-outs at the top flanking four open shelves, arched front apron & arched cut-out end feet, cleaned original finish, brand signature of Gustav Stickley, Model No. 79, 10 × 14", 40" h. (some wear to shelves) .................................... **1,430.00**

**Magazine stand,** Mission-style (Arts & Crafts movement), oak, tapering slab sides flanking four open shelves, low arched front apron, arched cut-out side feet, through-tenon construction, original finish, Handcraft label of L. & J.G. Stickley, Model No. 47, 15 × 18", 42" h........ **1,870.00**

*Classical Nightstand*

**Nightstand,** Classical, mahogany & mahogany veneer, the rectangular top above a single flush drawer overhanging a single paneled door w/small wood knob flanked by free-standing columns on outset blocks, raised on heavy knob feet, ca. 1840, 17⅝ × 22⅞", 31⅝" h. (ILLUS.).......... **605.00**

*Art Deco Rosewood
Nightstands*

**Nightstands,** Art Deco, rosewood,
each of rectangular form raised on a
grooved base, one w/two open bays,
the other w/a cabinet below two
drawers w/ball-shaped brass pulls,
each piece w/a border design of brass
nailheads, one stand marked on the
base "FRANCE ETRANGER..."
w/the third word obscured, André
Sornay, France, 1930s, 10¾ × 16",
23¾" h., pr. (ILLUS. top) ................ **6,325.00**

**Plant stand,** Mission-style (Arts &
Crafts movement), oak, the square
top w/a raised open railing, on
square legs joined by end stretchers
& a medial shelf, original finish, decal
mark of the Lakeside Craftshop, early
20th c., 15" sq., 28" h. ........................ **319.00**

**Plant stand,** Mission-style (Arts &
Crafts movement), oak, square top
widely overhanging a deep apron
w/arched bottom rims supported by
four flaring square legs w/a
cruciform base, unsigned Stickley
Brothers, Model No. 131, 14" sq.,
34" h. (refinished) .......................... **1,045.00**

**Plant stand,** Mission-style (Arts &
Crafts movement), oak, the round
top over four wide bowed flat legs
w/a round lower shelf & a cross-
stretcher base, refinished, slightly
shortened, unsigned Charles
Limbert Company, Model No. 244,
13" d., 29¾" h. (ILLUS. bottom)..... **1,650.00**

**Telephone stand,** Mission-style (Arts
& Crafts movement), oak,
rectangular top above a narrow
arched apron above an open shelf,

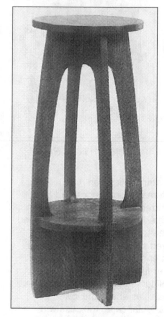

*Mission Plant Stand*

on tall slender square tapering legs
joined by side stretchers, original
light finish, branded mark of the
Charles Limbert Company, Model
No. 261, 15 × 18", 30" h.................... **413.00**

**Umbrella stand,** Mission-style (Arts &
Crafts movement), oak, tapering
cylindrical slatted sides supported by
three iron hoops w/iron rivets,
recoated original finish, unsigned
Gustav Stickley, Model No. 100,
12" d., 24" h. ................................. **1,980.00**

**Umbrella stand,** Mission-style (Arts & Crafts movement), oak, cylindrical form w/vertical slats riveted to internal metal bands at top, middle & base, burned-in mark reads "Oak Craft, Portland, Michigan," original finish, early 20th c., 10½" d., 27" h. ... **413.00**

**Washstand,** Classical, carved mahogany, nearly square lift-lid above a well above a single door w/wooden knob over a small drawer all flanked by half-round acanthus-carved columns, raised on ring- and acanthus-turned legs ending in knob feet, New York, ca. 1820-25 ............ **715.00**

*New York Classical Washstand*

**Washstand,** Classical, mahogany, the high rounded & scroll-cut three-quarter gallery above the bow-fronted top w/a pierced central basin hole above two tiny drawers w/round brass pulls, the top raised on square S-scroll front supports & spiral-turned back supports on a rectangular medial shelf w/incurved front over a conforming drawer w/round brass florette & ring pull, on ring- and baluster-turned legs w/peg feet, original brasses, New York, ca. 1820 (ILLUS.) ................................. **880.00**

**Washstand,** country-style, painted & decorated softwood, a scalloped splashboard across the back w/scrolled brackets at the front of top supporting turned towel bars above

the rectangular top over a single drawer, raised on simple turned supports w/ring-turned sections at the top & base above the medial shelf w/shaped front, on short baluster-turned legs w/knob feet, overall orangish yellow graining w/black banding & red striping around the edges & on the drawer front, ca. 1850-1880, 18¼ × 30", 34" h. (some wear, some towel rod & splashboard repairs, split in shelf) .... **180.00**

**Washstand,** Federal, corner-style, inlaid mahogany, shaped splashboards & small quarter-round shelf above a bowed top fitted to hold a wash bowl & accessories above line-inlaid supports over a medial shelf w/central small drawer flanked by two faux drawers, on line-inlaid slightly splayed legs joined by a shaped stretcher, New England, ca. 1800, 14¾ × 22½", 40½" h. ........ **805.00**

*Federal Washstand*

**Washstand,** Federal, mahogany & inlaid mahogany veneer, the high three-quarter galleried splashback w/down-swept sides flanking a narrow shelf above the rectangular top pierced w/a large central basin hole & two smaller front holes over a case w/a rectangular tambour door w/small brass knob above a narrow cockbeaded drawer w/a small brass knob, on square tapering legs, old refinish, replaced brasses, minor imperfections, probably Massachusetts, ca. 1800, 18¼ × 18½", 41" h. (ILLUS. right previous page) ............................ **1,495.00**

**Writing stand,** Classical, figured mahogany, the hinged rectangular thumb-molded top opening to a well w/ratcheted baize-lined writing surface above two graduated drawers, spirally-reeded legs & turned tapering feet joined by a platform shelf, the feet w/brass caps & casters, ink stains on top, New York, ca. 1820, 16 × 22½", 30¼" h. (ILLUS. top next column) ... **2,300.00**

**Art Deco stand,** marble, the long octagonal top w/fluted apron on a slender tapering post raised on a stepped & fluted base, white & green marble, impressed & incised "FRANCE," ca. 1925, 14¼ × 24⅜", 29¼" h. (ILLUS. bottom next column) .. **747.00**

**Federal country-style one-drawer stand,** painted birch, rectangular top above an apron w/a single drawer w/a round florette brass knob, on square tapering legs, original red-washed surface, Maine or New Hampshire, early 19th c. ................... **690.00**

**Federal country-style one-drawer stand,** painted & decorated, the square top painted w/a brown grained central panel w/notched corners outlined in black surrounded by yellow overhanging an apron w/a single drawer w/a turned wood knob also painted w/a brown grained panel trimmed in black, the remainder of the apron & square tapering legs in yellow outlined in black, minor surface imperfections, New England, ca. 1825, 18" sq., 27" h. (ILLUS. top next page) ........ **4,600.00**

**Federal country-style one-drawer stand,** painted pine, rectangular top above an apron w/a single drawer w/a brass pull, on square tapering legs, original red surface, New England, early 19th c., 15 × 19", 28" h. (minor surface imperfections) ............................. **546.00**

**Federal country-style one-drawer stand,** tiger stripe maple & cherry, the rectangular top w/knotched & rounded corners widely overhanging the apron w/a single tiger stripe maple drawer w/an oval pull, on square tapering legs, original pull, old refinish, Connecticut River Valley, early 19th c., 20 × 24", 26" h. ............................................. **2,760.00**

*Classical Writing Stand*

*Art Deco Marble Stand*

*Fine Decorated Federal Stand*

**Federal one-drawer stand,** inlaid cherry, nearly square top w/a bowed front above a conforming apron w/a cockbeaded crossbanded drawer flanked by wavy birch panels, replaced wooden knob, on slender square tapering legs, probably western Massachusetts, ca. 1800, 17½ × 17¾", 26½" h. (old refinish, minor imperfections) ........ **2,530.00**

**Federal one-drawer stand,** tiger stripe maple & bird's-eye maple veneer, the rectangular top overhanging an apron w/a single drawer w/bird's-eye maple veneer & a florette brass knob, raised on slender delicately ring- and tapering rod-turned legs ending in peg feet, northern New England, ca. 1815-25, old surface, 18 × 18", 29" h............ **1,610.00**

**Federal country-style two-drawer stand,** curly maple, rectangular top overhanging a deep apron w/two drawers w/early pressed glass knobs, on slender ring- and rod-turned legs w/ball feet, New England, 1800-15, 18¾ × 21¾", 28¾" h. (ILLUS. top next column).. **1,610.00**

**Federal country-style two-drawer stand,** tiger stripe maple, a rectangular top above a deep case w/two narrow drawers w/original clear lacy pressed glass pulls, on ring-, knob- and rod-turned legs

ending in knob feet, old refinish, New England, ca. 1820, 16 × 19", 28" h. (minor imperfections) ......... **1,495.00**

*Federal Two-drawer Stand*

*Fine Federal Stand*

**Federal two-drawer stand,** figured mahogany, the rectangular top above a deep case w/two drawers w/round brass pulls raised on ring-turned & reeded tapering legs joined by a medial shelf w/incurved front above baluster-turned feet on brass casters, small patch to center of top, New York, ca. 1825, 16½ × 23¾", 29¼" h. (ILLUS.) ........................... **3,162.00**

**Federal two-drawer stand,** inlaid mahogany, rectangular top above two narrow graduated line-inlaid drawers, on square tapering legs, appears to retain its orignal finish & rich brown color, New England, ca. 1810, 15½ × 17¾", 28⅞" h. ........... **2,300.00**

**Federal country-style three-drawer stand,** wavy birch & tiger stripe maple, nearly square top above a deep case w/three tiger stripe maple drawers each w/an original round brass pull, on slender turned legs w/a ring-turned segment above a long baluster-turned leg ending in a baluster-form peg foot, old refinish, New Hampshire, early 19th c., 18 × 18", 29" h. .............................. **2,300.00**

## STOOLS

**Egyptian Revival stool,** walnut, Thebes-type, the down-curved slatted seat w/vertical, diagonal & horizontal spindle supports on four shaped turned legs, attributed to Liberty and Company, England, early 20th c., 17" sq., 14" h. (refinished, repairs).......................... **495.00**

**Footstool,** country-style, walnut, the oblong top w/rounded ends above oblong apron boards w/rounded & chip-carved decorated ends, raised on canted bookjack ends, refinished, 7¼ × 14", 7½" h. .............................. **110.00**

**Jacobean joint stool,** oak, rectangular top w/molded edges & rounded corners above a deep line-incised apron w/scroll-cut bottom edge between canted legs w/top blocks over rod- and ring-turned legs to lower blocks joined by rectangular stretchers, on ring- and oblong-knob

feet, England, old dark finish, 17th century style, 10¾ × 18¼", 17¾" h. (damage, repair, feet ended out) ...... **413.00**

**Mission-style (Arts & Crafts movement) stool,** oak, rectangular top recovered in leather over arched seatrails & square legs joined by through-tenon stretchers, original finish, remnant of Eastwood paper label of Gustav Stickley, Model No. 300, early 20th c., 17 × 21", 16" h.... **2,420.00**

**Mission-style (Arts & Crafts movement) stool,** oak, the rectangular top recovered in old leather, square legs joined at sides by single wide slats & at end by double narrow rungs, original finish, Handcraft decal mark of L. & J.G. Stickley, Model No. 391, early 20th c., 14 × 19", 18" h. (one side rung replaced, tears in leather)................. **275.00**

**Mission-style (Arts & Crafts movement) stool,** oak, the upholstered rectangular top w/square tack trim, on square post legs joined by stretchers, large "Craftsman" paper label & small red decal marks of Gustav Stickley, Model No. 300, ca. 1911, 16 × 20", 15¼" h. ............................................ **920.00**

**Victorian footstools,** inlaid satinwood, the rectangular upholstered top w/incurved sides w/a molded rim & canted corners above arched aprons inlaid along the bottom edge w/sawtooth bands, on reeded faux agate feet, minor cracks & chips, mid-19th c., 12¼" l., pr. (ILLUS. of one, below)................. **977.00**

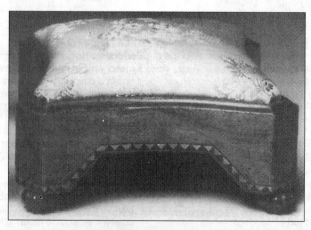

*Inlaid Victorian Footstool*

*Victorian Piano Stool*

**Victorian piano stool,** Rococo substyle, carved rosewood, a low open C-scroll back carved w/a leafy blossom sprig above the adjustable rectangular upholstered seat w/serpentine edges above a base w/a shaped skirt w/a scroll-carved border band & four cabriole legs w/boldly leaf-carved knees & floral vines down to the scroll-carved feet, the legs joined by a medial shelf w/incurved sides centered by a leaf-carved, baluster-turned post, worn velvet upholstery, mid-19th c. (ILLUS.) ........................................ **3,200.00**

## TABLES

**Adirondack-style side table,** square three-board top raised on four rough-hewn hickory legs joined by a stick stretcher near the top & stick cross-stretcher w/center post near the bottom, metal tag & branded Old Hickory marks, early 20th c., 24" w., 28" h. (refinished top, recoat over base) ................................................ **413.00**

**Art Deco center table,** galuchat & mahogany, the oval top covered in galuchat radiating from the center to the stepped, molded curving rim, supported on four curved & fluted legs scrolled at the top, resting on a carved oval plinth, Andre Groult, France, ca. 1925, 32 × 46", 29½" h. (ILLUS. below) ............................ **14,950.00**

**Art Deco dining table,** extension-type, mahogany & marquetry, the richly grained rounded rectangular top centering a geometric & lozenge marquetry design, molded edge above a shaped apron, supported by tapered legs ending in brass-capped feet, no leaves, Jules Leleu, France, 39 × 79½", 29½" h. ........................ **1,725.00**

**Art Deco dining table,** oval walnut veneer top raised on four flat black lacquer wooden legs joined by three narrow circular square faux burled stretchers, designed by Walter D. Teague, made by the Hastings Company, unmarked, 41 × 50", 30" h. (top refinished) .................... **1,870.00**

**Art Deco side table,** mahogany & wrought iron, the circular mahogany top raised on an open, waisted iron

*Rare Art Deco
Center Table*

base composed of four flat bars joined by a central ring & connected at the base w/a large flat ring, Pierre Chareau, ca. 1926, 21¾" d., 24¼" h. (ILLUS. top next column) ............ **10,925.00**

**Art Nouveau side table,** carved & marquetry hardwood, the oblong scallop-edged top inlaid w/a spray of wildflowers & foliage, raised on molded outcurved supports to a lower, larger matching open shelf similarly decorated & raised on shaped & molded splayed legs, marquetry signature "Gallé," Emile Gallé, ca. 1900, 24 × 36", 30" h. (ILLUS. bottom next column) ......... **2,760.00**

**Baroque center table,** walnut & oak, the rectangular top w/molded, rounded edges above side braces & a deep ogee apron, raised on four heavy columnar legs w/scrolled capitals & bulbous reeded bases on pedestal bases joined by wide, flat stretchers, on squatty bun feet, England or Flanders, ca. 1700, 33 × 49", 29" h. (ILLUS. below) ..... **1,320.00**

**Chippendale card table,** serpentine-front style, mahogany, the hinged rectangular top w/serpentine edges & beaded rim folding above a conforming apron w/pierced lattice corner brackets at the square, molded Marlboro legs, one replaced bracket, possibly Rhode Island, 1780-1800, 32 × 33½" open, 28¼" h. (ILLUS. top next page) .................. **3,450.00**

**Chippendale dressing table,** carved mahogany, rectangular top w/molded edge overhanging a case

*Art Deco Side Table*

*Gallé Side Table*

*Early Baroque Center Table*

*Chippendale Card Table*

*Chippendale Dressing Table*

w/a long drawer w/butterfly pulls & matching keyhole escutcheons above a row of three smaller, deeper drawers, the center w/a carved half-round indentation & matching pulls above a scalloped apron w/two pendant drops w/acorn finials, cabriole legs w/foliate-carved knees ending in claw-and-ball feet, probably Massachusetts, ca. 1750, replaced brasses (ILLUS.) ........... **17,250.00**

**Chippendale drop-leaf dining table,** mahogany, the rectangular top flanked by a pair of drop leaves, shaped end aprons, on cabriole legs ending in claw-and-ball feet, legs swing-out to support leaves, Massachusetts, ca. 1800, top center 17" w., extended 48 × 48", 27" h. (refinished, imperfections) ............. **1,495.00**

**Chippendale Pembroke table,** mahogany, rectangular top flanked by serpentine-edged drop leaves above an apron w/a cockbeaded end drawer w/butterly brass, square molded legs, New England, late 18th c., 32 × 37", 28" h. (old refinish, imperfections) ............................... **1,265.00**

**Chippendale Pembroke table,** mahogany, rectangular top flanked by hinged rectangular leaves centering a drawer w/pierced fretwork brasses, raised on square chamfered legs joined by a pierced flat cross stretcher, warm brown color, Rhode Island, ca. 1770, extended 18¼ × 32½", 28¼" h. (leg brackets replaced) ........................ **2,300.00**

*Chippendale Pembroke Table*

**Chippendale Pembroke table,** mahogany, the rectangular top flanked by two rectangular hinged drop leaves above a plain apron, raised on fluted & chamfered square legs, repairs, Rhode Island, 1765-90, 18 × 29", 27½" h. (ILLUS.).......... **748.00**

**Chippendale Pembroke table,** walnut, rectangular top flanked by rectangular drop leaves, apron w/a single end drawer w/a teardrop pull, on square reeded legs w/block feet joined by cross-stretchers, old finish, probably Maryland, 18th c., 17 × 31", 28" h. (repairs) ................................ **1,150.00**

**Chippendale side table,** carved & figured mahogany, the rectangular top w/thumb-molded edges above a single long cockbeaded drawer w/ornate brass bail handles & keyhole escutcheons above pierced C-scroll carved brackets heading the square molded legs, Philadelphia or Mid-Atlantic States, ca. 1780, 24 × 35", 30" h............................................. **12,650.00**

*Chippendale Tea Table*

**Chippendale tea table,** tilt-top, the wide round top tilting above a ring- and baluster-turned pedestal above the tripod base w/three cabriole legs ending in claw-and-ball feet, old refinish, imperfections, Massachusetts, 18th c., 32" d., 28" h. (ILLUS. above) ................. **1,955.00**

**Chippendale tilt-top tea table,** mahogany, octagonal top above a birdcage tilting mechanism above the ring-turned columnar pedestal above the tripod base w/cabriole legs ending in snake feet, Middle Atlantic States, ca. 1780, 18¾ × 23¾", 28" h. (refinished, restoration) .................... **1,093.00**

**Classical breakfast table,** carved & figured mahogany, the rectangular top flanked by two D-form crotch-figured drop leaves above a plain frieze on a ring-turned & waterleaf-carved standard, on four acanthus-carved downcurving legs ending in carved animal paw feet, New York City, ca. 1840, extended 39 × 51", 29" h. .............................................. **920.00**

**Classical breakfast table,** carved mahogany & mahogany veneer, the wide rectangular top flanked by D-form drop leaves w/notched corners above an apron w/a long cockbeaded drawer w/a brass ring pull on one side & a matching faux drawer on the opposite side, raised on a bulbous carved pedestal above

*Classical Breakfast Table*

the quadrapartite base w/four outswept leaf-carved & reeded legs ending in brass paw caps & casters, very minor imperfections, New York, ca. 1815-20, 25 × 37½", 28½" h. (ILLUS.) ........................................ **4,313.00**

**Classical breakfast table,** mahogany & mahogany veneer, a rectangular top flanked by two wide D-form drop leaves over ogee end aprons, raised on a square urn-form pedestal on a heavy cross-form platform w/rounded ends raised on bun feet on casters, attributed to Joseph Meeks, ca. 1830, open 42¾ × 56⅜", 29¼" h. ............................................. **770.00**

**Classical card table,** carved mahogany & mahogany veneer, a rectangular fold-over top w/a bowed center section flanked by florette-carved corner blocks, raised on double leaf-carved lyre-form supports w/brass strings set on a quadrepartite platform raised on four molded downswept legs ending in brass paws on casters, old finish, Pennsylvania or New York, ca. 1815, 17¾ × 35¼", 29½" h. (imperfections) .............................. **2,070.00**

**Classical card table,** carved mahogany, the hinged rectangular top w/rounded corners & reeded edges above a conforming apron w/a thin rope-twist-carved border, raised on a thick ovoid pedestal w/swirled ribbed sections centered by a band of large beads & a gadrooned base band, raised on a quadrapartite base w/a ringed & gadrooned thick disc framed by four scrolled & outswept legs ending in brass animal paws on casters, old refinish, minor imperfections, Boston, ca. 1825-35, 19⅝ × 35½", 28¾" h. (ILLUS. top next column).. **1,265.00**

**Classical card table,** carved mahogany, the rectangular hinged top w/rounded front corners above a conforming apron raised on four tall, slender outswept carved cornucopia above a small oval-shaped platform raised on four acanthus leaf-carved legs ending in hairy paw feet on casters, New York, 1815-25, 29¾" h. (ILLUS. middle next column) ......... **2,300.00**

**Classical center table,** mahogany & mahogany veneer, the rectangular white marble top w/serpentine sides above a conforming deep apron raised on four heavy squared S-scrolls resting on a thick platform base on C-scroll feet, ca. 1840, 34½ × 35", 27¾" h. (ILLUS. bottom next column) ..................................... **715.00**

**Classical center table,** mahogany, a round white marble top above a conforming apron raised on a hexagonal pedestal w/a flat section above a swelled section resting on a tripartite base w/C-scroll feet, ca. 1835, 35¾"d., 28" h. ...................... **1,045.00**

**Classical center table,** mahogany, rectangular white marble top w/canted corners above a conforming bolection-molded apron w/a molded frieze band, on lyre-form supports joined by a shaped marble inset medial shelf, on scrolled feet, ca. 1830, 21¼ × 46⅓", 28¾" h. ..... **4,025.00**

*Classical Card Table*

*New York Classical Card Table*

*Marble-top Center Table*

*Classical Dining Table*

*Inlaid Classical Center Table*

**Classical center table,** rosewood-inlaid figured maple & cherry, the twelve-sided top inlaid at the center w/a rosewood stellar device above a conformingly-shaped convex frieze & massive vase-form cherry pedestal, the four-part shaped plinth base inlaid w/stars & moons & raised on tapered turned feet, probably Pennsylvania, ca. 1830, 39¾" w., 28¾" h. (ILLUS.) ............. **4,312.00**

**Classical dining table,** a rectangular top flanked by wide D-form drop leaves above a deep flat apron, raised on six spiral-turned legs w/peg feet on casters, four legs swing-out to support the leaves, old refinish, alterations, imperfections, New England, ca. 1830, 43¾ × 71¼" extended, 28" h. (ILLUS. top) .......... **690.00**

**Classical dining table,** drop-leaf style, mahogany, rectangular top flanked by two wide D-shaped drop leaves above a curved veneered apron, raised on knob- and ring-turned legs w/long fluted central sections, peg feet on casters, ca. 1825, 29" h. ..................................... **660.00**

**Classical pier table,** mahogany, the rectangular black marble top above a conforming bolection-molded apron, above scrolled bracket supports & a mirrored back joined by a platform base w/shaped front, on shaped tapering feet w/casters, Philadelphia, 1820-30, 20 × 42", 37¼" h. .......................................... **1,093.00**

*Classical Side Table*

**Classical side table,** mahogany & mahogany veneer, the D-form white marble top above a conforming apron, raised on four slender squared S-scroll supports resting on a narrow waisted platform raised on C-scroll feet, bears the label of "Samuel Waterbury Cabinet Ware Rooms, New York City," ca. 1830-40, 19 × 35½", 28½" h. (ILLUS. bottom previous page) ..................... **825.00**

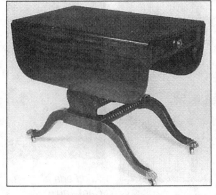

*Classical Sofa Table*

**Classical sofa table,** mahogany & mahogany veneer, the rectangular top flanked by two wide D-form drop leaves, the apron w/a cockbeaded drawer at each end, each w/a round brass pull, raised on vase-form splats joined by double bobbin-turned stretchers raised on four downswept molded legs ending in brass paw feet on casters, probably New York, 1820-40, old refinish, 36⅛ × 39¾" extended, 31¼" h. (ILLUS.) ........................................ **4,025.00**

**Classical work table,** mahogany & mahogany veneer, a nearly square top flanked by wide drop leaves w/rounded corners flanking a deep apron w/three narrow drawers each w/pairs of round brass pulls & inlaid metal keyhole escutcheons, raised on legs w/a ring-turned short section above a long rope-twist turned section on ring-turned peg feet on casters, probably Massachusetts, ca. 1825, 18 × 18¼", 29¼" h. (refinished, replaced brasses) ....... **1,840.00**

**Country-style card table,** cherry, rectangular hinged top above a swing-out support leg w/a small drawer fitted into the inner rail behind that leg, the apron w/a gadroon-carved lower edge & raised on square tapering legs w/blocked ankles, Connecticut, 1765-90, 16⅝ × 36" h, 29" h. (refinished, minor imperfections) ............................... **2,415.00**

**Country-style "trestle" table,** painted, the yellow-painted rectangular top above four black-painted crossed sawbuck legs joined by a cylindrical stretcher, 19th c., 19¼ × 53", 29" h. ............................... **460.00**

**Country-style work table,** painted pine, rectangular top w/breadboard ends & scrubbed finish widely overhanging a deep apron w/a long drawer w/a wooden knob raised on square tapering legs, the base w/red paint, original surfaces, New Hampshire, late 18th c., 27 × 41⅜", 28" h. (minor imperfections) ........... **2,760.00**

**Federal card table,** inlaid cherry, D-form hinged top w/a flat center section flanked by rounded sections all w/line-inlay & opening above a conforming apron inlaid w/line blocks & a series of large cross-forms, raised on square tapering legs w/pendant inlays, New England, early 19th c., 17½ × 36", 29½" h. (old refinish, minor imperfections) ................................. **3,737.00**

**Federal card table,** inlaid cherry, the rectangular hinged fold-over top w/serpentine edges above a conforming apron inlaid in the front center w/an oval paterae & w/scroll-cut brackets at the corners of the front square, tapering legs, probably Connecticut, ca. 1800, 17 × 32", 28½" h. (refinished, restoration) .... **2,760.00**

**Federal card table,** inlaid mahogany, bow-front style w/the oblong top w/crossbanded edge above a conformingly-shaped hinged leaf swiveling to reveal a well above a crossbanded apron & four baluster- and ring-turned supports, the plinth base on four reeded downswept legs ending in brass animal paw feet on casters, probably Rhode Island, ca. 1810, 17½ × 35¾", 29" h. (ILLUS. top next page) ................. **2,875.00**

**Federal card table,** inlaid mahogany, the D-shaped hinged top w/inlaid edge fitted w/a concealed drawer above a conforming line-inlaid apron, the dies inlaid w/paterae within oval reserves, on line-inlaid square tapering legs, two swinging as gate supports, warm brown patina, left rear leg repaired, restorations to small drawer, New England, ca. 1800, 17¾ × 35¾", 29" h. (ILLUS. middle next page) ... **2,645.00**

*Inlaid Federal Card Table*

*Federal D-shaped Card Table*

*Federal "Bow-front" Card Table*

**Federal card table,** mahogany & wavy birch inlay, a D-form hinged top w/a reeded edge forming two points at the front above a comforming apron w/birch inlay, raised on four slender ring- and rod-turned legs ending in peg feet, possibly New Hampshire, ca. 1810, old refinish, minor imperfections, 19½ x 39", 29¼" h. (ILLUS. top next page) ............................................. **2,300.00**

**Federal card table,** inlaid mahogany, bow-front style w/the oblong top w/crossbanded edge & rounded center section, above a conformingly-shaped hinged leaf swiveling to reveal a well above a crossbanded frieze & four ring-turned supports on a plinth raised on reeded downcurving legs ending in brass animal paw feet on brass casters, New England, probably Rhode Island, ca. 1810, 17½ x 35¾", 29" h. (ILLUS. bottom previous column) .......................... **2,875.00**

**Federal dining table,** three-part, mahogany veneer, two D-shaped end sections w/a wide drop leaf at the back edge flanking the rectangular center section w/two wide drop leaves, on ring-, knob- and rod-turned tapering legs ending in ball feet, Boston, Massachusetts, ca. 1800, old refinish, 59 x 161", 29" h. (repairs) .............................. **4,600.00**

**Federal dining table,** three-part, mahogany, comprised of two D-

*Federal Mahogany & Wavy
Birch Card Table*

*Decorated Federal
Dressing Table*

shaped end sections flanking a rectangular center section w/two hinged drop leaves above a plain apron on square tapering legs, probably New England or New York State, ca. 1800, extended 53½ x 120", 28¾" h. (patches to several legs & skirt) .................................. **3,162.00**

**Federal dressing table,** cherry & mahogany veneer, the rectangular top w/molded edges & rounded front corners above a case w/small deep veneer-banded drawers flanking a shallow veneer-banded center drawer above an arched apron, all w/round brass knobs & flanked by reeded pilasters, fan-carved large corner brackets below the drawers,

raised on rope-twist turned legs w/ring- and knob-turned sections at the top & base, on tapering ring-turned peg feet, early 19th c., 20 x 35¼", 43" h. (minor repairs)... **2,310.00**

**Federal dressing table,** country-style, painted & decorated basswood, the low scroll-ended splashboard above a stepped case fitted w/a pair of shallow drawers over a rectangular top above a conforming apron fitted w/a long drawer, turned wooden knobs, on ring- and baluster-turned tapering legs, decorated overall w/red & black grain painting imitating mahogany, Yarmouth, Maine, 1830-40, 18½ x 37", 35½" h. (ILLUS. bottom) .............................................. **690.00**

**Federal country-style dressing table,** painted & decorated, rectangular top above an apron w/a single drawer, on bamboo-turned legs, decorated in burnt sienna w/black pinstripping, probably New England, ca. 1830, 17¾ x 31½", 29¾" h. (imperfections)................. **1,265.00**

**Federal library table,** carved mahogany, the rectangular top flanked by wide shaped leaves w/wide rounded corners above an apron w/a drawer at one end w/a round brass pull & a faux drawer at the opposite end, rounded knob drops at each corner of the apron, raised on shaped end splat supports joined by a round stretcher above the pairs of downswept molded legs on casters, Philadelphia, ca. 1820, 40 x 51" open, 28" h. (ILLUS. below)...................... **1,725.00**

*Federal Library Table*

*Federal Pembroke Table*

**Federal Pembroke table,** inlaid mahogany, the rectangular top w/gently bowed & molded ends flanked by hinged D-form drop leaves w/band inlay above a bowed apron w/a single drawer w/a brass rectangular plate & bail pull, raised on line-inlaid square tapering legs ending in crossbanded cuffs, some inlay repair, New York, ca. 1800, 32 x 43" open, 28½" h. (ILLUS. bottom previous column) .............. **3,450.00**

**Federal Pembroke table,** mahogany, rectangular top flanked by two drop leaves above an apron w/a single end drawer, on square tapering legs, New England, ca. 1820, 29 x 36", 29" h. ................................................ **517.00**

**Federal sewing table,** figured mahogany, a rectangular top flanked by deep D-form drop leaves flanking a case w/two cockbeaded drawers above a sewing bag slide, all w/two large round brass pulls, on ring-turned & reeded tapering legs ending in knob & peg feet on brass casters, probably Boston, Massachusetts, ca. 1820, extended 17⅛ x 35¼", 30¼" h. ....... **2,587.00**

*Federal Work Table*

**Federal work table,** carved mahogany, the rectangular top w/outset rounded corners w/molded roundels over two graduated cockbeaded drawers w/round brass knobs flanked by engaged ring- and baluster-turned colonettes, on spiral-turned tapering legs w/compressed ball feet, on casters, wear & slight damage to the top, Salem, Massachusetts, 1800-20, 20" w., 29" h. (ILLUS.).................... **1,380.00**

*Boston Federal Work Table*

*Figured Mahogany Work Table*

**Federal work table,** figured mahogany, the rectangular top w/outset rounded corners above two cockbeaded drawers w/wooden knobs & fitted w/dividers, three-quarter round ring-turned columns flanking, on star-punch-decorated reeded legs ending in ringed ankles & tapered peg feet on brass casters, Salem, Massachusetts, 19½ × 22", 29¾" h. (ILLUS.) ............................ **2,070.00**

**Federal work table,** inlaid mahogany, rectangular top w/outset rounded corners above bobbin-turned columns flanking two narrow crossbanded & crotch-figured drawers, on slender ring-turned & reeded tapering legs ending in delicate vase-form feet, warm reddish brown color, Massachusetts, ca. 1810, 15⅛ × 20", 29" h. ........................ **3,737.00**

**Federal work table,** mahogany, rectangular top above three graduated drawers w/small pressed glass knobs raised on turned & reeded legs joined by a shaped medial shelf raised on ring- and knob-turned legs ending in brass caps & casters, New York, ca. 1810, 16½ × 22½", 30" h. (minor repairs) ........................................ **3,737.00**

**Federal work table,** mahogany, the rectangular top above a pair of shallow cockbeaded drawers w/small round brass knobs, the upper drawer fitted w/a divided well, on slender ring-turned & reeded tapering legs ending in peg feet w/casters, old finish, warm brown color, Boston, Massachusetts, ca. 1800, 16¾ × 22", 29½" h. (ILLUS.) .............................. **5,462.00**

**French Provincial farmhouse table,** chestnut, the long rectangular top widely overhanging a deep apron w/a single end drawer & single short side drawer, each w/a small turned wood knob, on square legs joined by flat box stretchers, some edge damage, France, ca. 1800, 39 × 66", 32" h. (ILLUS. top next page) ........ **1,100.00**

**"Harvest" table,** Mission-style (Arts & Crafts movement), oak, the wide, long rectangular top widely overhanging double square leg supports at the ends & middle w/a high double stretcher w/keyed tenons, on long tapering shoe feet, branded mark of L. & J.G. Stickley, ca. 1925, 47½ × 144½", 30" h. (ILLUS. middle next page) ........... **14,950.00**

**"Harvest" table,** pine & birch, long narrow rectangular top flanked by two wide drop leaves w/rounded corners, raised on simple baluster-

*French Farmhouse Table*

*Mission "Harvest" Table*

and ring-turned legs old refinish, probably New England, ca. 1830, 40 × 81", 27¾" h. ........................... **4,945.00**

**Hutch (or chair) table,** painted pine, a round top tilting above four square uprights over the square box seat w/hinged lid, on shoe feet, scrubbed top, early red paint on base, Connecticut River Valley, 18th c., 46"d., 28¼" h. (imperfections) ....... **5,750.00**

**Hutch (or chair) table,** painted, the round multi-board top tilting above shaped end supports & a boxed seat, double flat cross stretchers at the base, old red paint, imperfections, New England, early 18th c., 44½" d., 27" h. (ILLUS. bottom next column) .. **8,625.00**

**Mission-style (Arts & Crafts movement) dining table,** oak, drop-leaf style, a narrow rectangular top

w/rounded ends flanked by two wide half-round drop leaves over an apron & swing-out gate legs, original finish, Quaint Furniture tag of the Stickley Brothers, early 20th c., open 36" d., 28" h. ................................. **1,650.00**

*Early Hutch Table*

**Mission-style (Arts & Crafts movement) dining table,** oak, round split top raised on five slightly tapered square posts on a cruciform base, original finial, signed by L. & J.G. Stickley, Model No. 716, w/four 12" w. leaves, 48"d., 29" h. (minor stains on top) ................................ **6,600.00**

**Mission-style (Arts & Crafts movement) library table,** oak, a rectangular top widely overhanging an apron w/two long drawers w/square copper pulls over gently arched aprons, on heavy square legs w/curved corbels & through-mortised end stretchers joined by a wide medial shelf, original finish, branded mark of the Charles Limbert Company, Model No. 1141, early 20th c., 32 × 48", 29" h. ................. **2,530.00**

**Mission-style (Arts & Crafts movement) side table,** oak, a square top overhanging solid sides each w/two small square cut-outs, notched feet, branded mark of the Charles Limbert Company, Model No. 234, early 20th c., 16" sq., 18" h. (refinished)..................................... **2,860.00**

**Mission-style (Arts & Crafts movement) side table,** oak, the square top w/cut corners inset w/an octagonal green-glazed Grueby pottery tile, flush tenons at top corners above square legs joined by a notched cross stretcher w/through-tenon construction, original finish, paper label & branded mark of Gustav Stickley, Model 53T, 17" sq., 22" h.. **11,000.00**

**Mission-style (Arts & Crafts movement) side table,** oak, the rectangular top inlaid w/stylized peacock feathers in pewter, copper & darker wood above an apron w/one drawer over a shelf stretcher near the base, on square legs, designed by Harvey Ellis, red decal mark of Gustav Stickley, ca. 1904, 20 × 30", 30¼" h. (lacking a piece of copper in inlay) ............................. **5,175.00**

**Modern-style side table,** hardwood, rectangular top w/molded edges raised on square supports above a lower shelf over a single drawer w/incised finger pull, raised on low foot rails, the base rim decorated w/the Taliesin design, designed by Frank Lloyd Wright for the Heritage Henredon Company, original finish, "FLW" red monogram mark, 1950s, 21 × 27", 23" h. ............................. **1,210.00**

**Queen Anne card table,** mahogany, rectangular hinged top w/wide, rounded turret-like corners, the apron w/a small thumb-molded drawer w/round brass knob, on cabriole legs ending in high pad feet, old refinish, Boston, Massachusetts, 1730-60, 11⅝ × 26", 29" h. (pull replaced, imperfections) ............ **134,500.00**

*Queen Anne Dining Table*

**Queen Anne dining table,** curly maple, the narrow rectangular top w/rounded ends flanked by wide D-form hinged drop leaves above the arched end aprons, on nearly straight cabriole legs ending in pad feet, old minor repair to skirt, New England, ca. 1765, 48½ × 55" open, 27¾" h. (ILLUS.) ............................ **5,750.00**

**Queen Anne dining table,** painted cherry & birch, narrow rectangular top w/rounded ends & flanked by two deep half-round drop leaves, scalloped end aprons, on cabriole legs ending in cushioned pad feet, painted red, probably Connecticut River Valley, 18th c., 36 × 40½", 28½" h. (minor imperfections)...... **20,700.00**

**Queen Anne dressing table,** carved walnut, rectangular top w/thumb-molded edges & cusped corners above a deep case w/a pair of drawers above a pair of deep square drawers flanking a small central drawer all above a deeply scalloped apron, on cabriole legs ending in trifid feet, Philadelphia, Pennsylvania, 1730-50, 23½ × 34", 27¼" h. ........ **20,700.00**

**Queen Anne drop-leaf dining table,** mahogany, the rectangular top w/gently rounded ends flanked by

*Queen Anne Work Table*

*English Regency Dining Table*

two D-shaped hinged leaves above a shaped skirt on circular tapering legs ending in pad feet, probably Newport, Rhode Island, ca. 1735, one hinge stamped "W.S.," probably by William Seaver of Newport, Rhode Island, extended 41¾ × 50", 27⅛" h. (minor repairs & patch to top at hinge) ........ **2,415.00**

**Queen Anne tea table,** cherry, the circular dished top tilting & revolving above a birdcage support over a tapering compressed ball-turned pedestal, on a tripod base w/cabriole legs ending in peaked slipper feet, Connecticut, 1740-60, 34½" d., 29½" h. .......................................... **1,610.00**

**Queen Anne tea table,** tray-top-style, cherry, the rectangular top w/thumb-molded raised edge above an apron w/cyma-shaped projecting molding continuing to cabriole legs ending in pad feet, minor patch to one top molding, Connecticut, ca. 1765, 21¼ × 27⅞", 28" h. (ILLUS. bottom) ......................................... **39,100.00**

*Rare Queen Anne Tea Table*

**Queen Anne work table,** pine & oak, the wide rectangular thumb-molded top w/end braces above a deep apron w/a single drawer w/old replaced butterfly brass, old refinish, Pennsylvania, 1760-80, 33 × 55½", 30" h. (ILLUS. top) ......................... **2,760.00**

*New England Tavern Table*

*Victorian Rococo Center Table*

**Regency dining table,** two-pedestal, inlaid mahogany, the rectangular top w/rounded corners & reeded edges above two columnar turned supports on tripod bases w/outswept reeded sabre legs ending in brass box casters, w/two leaves, restoration, England, second quarter 19th c., 50½ × 100½" open, 27½" h. (ILLUS. middle previous page) ...... **4,600.00**

**Regency tilt-top tea table,** figured & turned mahogany, oblong molded top tilting above a ring-turned standard, on downcurving legs, England, ca. 1820, 14 × 17", 28" h. ..................... **1,725.00**

**Tavern table,** country-style, pine & maple, the rectangular top w/breadboard ends widely overhanging an apron w/one large drawer w/small wooden knob, on square, slightly tapering legs, old refinish, New England, ca. 1800, 28½ × 44", 27" h. ................. **1,150.00**

**Tavern table,** painted maple & pine, the rectangular top w/canted corners above an apron w/a long drawer w/a small turned wood knob, on baluster-turned legs joined by box stretchers, retains old paint, missing ball feet, New England, mid-18th c., 28½ × 57", 25½" h. (ILLUS. top).... **2,185.00**

**Victorian center table,** Rococo substyle, carved rosewood, the round white marble top w/molded edge above a deep apron w/a scalloped & scroll-carved bottom edge, raised on four squared S-scroll legs joined by serpentine cross stretchers centered by a turned compressed urn-form finial & drop, ca. 1850, 36"d., 27¾" h. (ILLUS. bottom)............................. **1,760.00**

*Rococo "Turtle-top"
Center Table*

*Ornate Belter
"Turtle-top"
Center Table*

**Victorian "turtle-top" center table,**
Rococo substyle, "turtle-top"-style,
carved rosewood, the oblong shaped
colorful marble top above a
conforming apron carved w/blossom
& leafy scroll-carved reserves, raised
on four cabriole legs carved at the
knees w/blossom & leafy-scroll
pendent swags & ending in button-
carved feet on casters joined by
molded & scroll-carved serpentine
cross stretchers centered by a large
turned & paneled urn-form finial &
ball-turned drop, attributed to John
Henry Belter, New York, ca. 1850,
28 × 38", 27¾" h. (ILLUS. top)........ **7,700.00**

**Victorian "turtle-top" center table,**
Rococo substyle, "turtle-top"-style,
carved & laminated rosewood, the
oblong shaped black marble top above
a deep conforming arched apron pierce-
carved w/ornate fruiting grapevines
centered by large rose & leaf clusters,
raised on cabriole legs ornately carved
at the knees w/scrolls & grape clusters
continuing to the scrolled feet on casters
joined by S-scroll-carved cross
stretchers centered by a large flower-
filled carved urn above a knob-turned
drop, attributed to John Henry Belter,
New York, ca. 1850, 29 × 41", 28" h.
(ILLUS. bottom) .............................. **35,750.00**

**Victorian "turtle-top" center table,**
Rococo substyle, rosewood, the
oblong shaped white marble top
above a deep paneled & scroll-carved
serpentine apron raised on four ornate
scroll-, leaf- and fruit-carved cabriole
legs ending in scroll feet & joined by
boldly carved S-scroll stretchers w/a
central urn filled w/a large cluster of
fruit, on casters, attributed to
Alexander Roux, New York, New
York, ca. 1850, 32 × 46", 29" h. ...... **6,600.00**

**Victorian "turtle-top" center table,**
Rococo substyle, walnut, the oblong
shaped top w/molded rim above a
conforming undulating apron raised
on four S-scroll supports joined at
the center by a short column w/a
turned bun finial, raised on short
scroll- and leaf-carved S-scroll legs,
ca. 1850, 40 × 54¼", 29¼" h. ........ **1,200.00**

**Victorian dressing table,** Rococo
substyle, carved rosewood, "duchesse"
form, the tall superstructure w/a scroll-
carved delicate arched frame around
the arched & molded swiveling mirror
frame, pierced scroll-carved side
brackets above a small handkerchief
drawer at each side of the scalloped D-
form colorful scagliola top above a
conforming leafy scroll-carved apron
supported on four leaf-carved slender
cabriole legs w/scroll feet on casters
joined by pierced serpentine cross
stretchers centered by a turned
handled urn finial, in the manner of
James & William McCracken, probably
New Orleans, ca. 1850 (ILLUS. top
next column) ...................................... **2,860.00**

**Victorian dressing table,** Rococo
substyle, carved rosewood,
"duchesse" form, the tall
superstructure w/an oval molded &
scroll-carved mirror frame w/a high,
arched pierce-carved crest of vines &
leaves swiveling between ornate
pierced & scroll-carved serpentine
supports resting on the serpentine D-
form white marble top w/molded
edges above the ornate serpentine
scroll-carved apron w/a central
cartouche raised on four cabriole legs
ornately carved & molded w/floral &
leaf bands on casters joined by
pierced scroll-carved serpentine
cross stretchers centered by a flower-
filled urn finial & turned drop, ca. 1850
(ILLUS. bottom next column) ............. **9,000.00**

*Rosewood Rococo Dressing Table*

*Rococo "Duchesse" Dressing Table*

*Victorian Baroque Side Table*

**Victorian side table,** Baroque style, tray-top form, the oblong dished tray top w/scalloped & carved edges & scroll-carved rim drops removable from the base formed by end supports carved in full-relief as nude winged female figures above scroll-carved legs w/hoof feet above arched cross feet joined by a knob-turned & carved cross-stretcher, an oblong medial shelf w/a carved border & scroll-carved rim drops, some minor repair, 19th c., 32" h. (ILLUS.) ........................ **1,210.00**

**Wicker side table,** oval wood top w/applied wicker apron, top supported by a diamond-shaped base flaring at bottom & supported by wicker-wrapped wooden feet, painted white, early 20th c., 24½ × 40¼", 31" h. (paint wear) ....... **110.00**

*William & Mary "Butterfly" Table*

**William & Mary "butterfly" table,** maple, the narrow rectangular top w/rounded ends flanked by D-form drop leaves supported by swing-out "butterfly" wings, wide canted apron & blocks above the canted double-baluster- and ring-turned legs ending in blocks joined by box stretchers, on worn button feet, refinished, restored, New England, 18th c., 28 × 33", 24¾" h. (ILLUS. bottom previous column) ........................ **1,150.00**

**William & Mary tavern table,** maple, a round top overhanging a deep apron raised on four baluster- and knob-turned legs joined by low flat stretchers, worn knob feet, old natural surface on the top, dark red-painted base, New England, 18th c., 23⅜ × 26¾", 24¼" h. (minor imperfections) ............................... **6,325.00**

**William & Mary tavern table,** painted, a rectangular top w/breadboard ends widely overhanging an apron w/a single long drawer & scroll-cut front rim, raised on baluster- and disc-turned legs joined by rectangular base stretchers at the base blocks, old red paint, Newbury, Massachusetts, early 18th c., 25½ × 39", 26½" h. (loss of height, added casters) .................... **9,200.00**

## WARDROBES & ARMOIRES

*Late Classical Armoire*

**Armoire,** Classical, mahogany & mahogany veneer, the flat rectangular top overhanging an arched frieze panel above a pair of recessed Gothic arch-paneled tall doors opening to a fitted interior & flanked by tall free-standing columns down the sides on outset blocks, flat apron, raised on short ring- and bulbous knob-turned legs w/smaller brass ball feet, ca. 1830 (ILLUS. previous page) ............................. **4,950.00**

**Armoire,** Federal, mahogany, the wide rectangular top w/upright crestrail above a stepped cornice over a beaded frieze band above a pair of tall double-paneled doors w/ivory diamond-inlaid keyhole escutcheons, beaded bands framing the outer case, double-paneled sides, flat apron raised on short ring- and knob-turned legs w/brass paw feet, Louisiana, ca. 1810 (ILLUS. below) ............................................. **4,125.00**

*French Fruitwood Armoire*

*Louisiana Federal Armoire*

**Armoire,** French Provincial, fruitwood, the molded flat cornice over a molded frieze band above two molded & paneled doors w/square panels at the top & bottom flanking oblong central panels, the interior fitted w/a single drawer, a molded & scalloped apron, chamfered front corners & short block feet, France, 19th c., 27 × 62", 7' 3" h. (ILLUS. top next column) ................................... **2,420.00**

*French Oak Armoire*

**Armoire,** French Provincial, painted oak, the molded cornice above a fan- and scroll-carved frieze band over a pair of tall doors w/scroll carving framing two shaped rectangular pierced panels fitted w/wire grillwork, a deep fan- and scroll-carved apron on short shaped legs, France, 19th c., 20½ × 65", 7' 7" h. (ILLUS.)............ **3,630.00**

*Dutch Rococo Armoire*

**Armoire,** Rococo, pine, the arched & boldly scroll-carved crestrail w/a raised center leafy scroll-carved finial w/a flat top above lower flanking similarly carved finials over a scalloped frieze above a pair of tall, wide scallop-topped cupboard doors w/scroll-trimmed oblong panels & long pierced brass keyhole escutcheons, the chamfered front corners w/scroll-carved sections at the top & base, the lower section w/a mid-molding over a stepped "bombe" form base w/three long convex- and concave-fronted drawers w/pierced brass pulls & keyhole escutcheons, the wide molded apron w/a curved wide central panel w/scroll carving, raised on blocked paw-form feet, Holland, late 18th - early 19th c. (ILLUS. top) ....... **3,335.00**

**Armoire,** Victorian Rococo substyle, mahogany & mahogany veneer, the arched & scroll-carved crestrail centered by a high pierced & scroll-carved crest w/a center button & flanked by outset rounded ends above a conforming frieze panel over a gently arched thin molding over a single tall door w/an arched & molding-trimmed mirrored door flanked by thin reeded quarter-columns ending in scroll-carved base blocks above the scalloped apron & short demi-cabriole legs, diminutive size, mid-19th c. (ILLUS. top next column) .............. **1,500.00**

*Diminutive Rococo Armoire*

*Ornate Single-door Armoire*

**Armoire,** Victorian Rococo substyle, carved rosewood, single-door-type, the arched & molded crestrail topped by an ornately pierce-carved crest w/entwined scrolling vines & blossoms & flanked by flattened end sections w/squatty turned urn-form finials, the upper frieze panel decorated w/bold relief-carved scrolls & leafy vines flanked by outset paneled corner blocks over the single tall, wide mirrored door w/delicate scroll-carving across the top, flanked by side stiles w/scroll-carved top & base drops, the door opening to an interior fitted w/maple veneering & three cedar shelves & a cased belt of two drawers, the base section w/paneled corner blocks flanking a long paneled drawer w/scroll carving above a deep molded base w/blocked ends over a narrow scroll-carved scalloped apron & turned disc feet, ca. 1850, 22½ × 44¼", 9' 1" h. (ILLUS. bottom previous page) .............................. **7,000.00**

**Armoire,** Victorian Rococo substyle, mahogany & mahogany veneer, double-door-type, the domed top above a conforming cove-molded cornice band above a pair of dome-topped tall doors w/scroll-carved bands along the top & raised veneer panels, rounded front corners, on a flat molded conforming base, ca. 1850 (ILLUS. below) ............... **2,200.00**

*Rococo Mahogany Armoire*

*Fine New York Rococo Armoire*

**Armoire,** Victorian Rococo substyle, carved mahogany, double-door-type, the flat molded double crestrail centered by arched, scroll-carved crests w/central large bottons above a double frieze panel separated by three ring-turned outset captials w/lobed squatty turned finials, a lower frieze rail above the two long mirrored doors w/gently arched molded panels & scroll-carved trim, the doors flanked by three long, slender spiral-twist colonettes, maple interior, the base w/a pair of long paneled drawers w/round pulls flanked by outset angled blocks over flaring block feet, original finish, New York, mid-19th c., 28 × 78", 8' 2" h. (ILLUS.) ........................................ **4,125.00**

**Kas (American version of the Netherlands Kast or wardrobe),** painted pine, the flat top w/a wide flaring stepped cornice w/angled corners above a conforming swelled frieze band above paneled canted corners flanking the large single double-raised panel door w/S-scroll iron keyhole escutcheon, a mid-molding above a wide base panel w/a secret compartment w/access through a sliding front panel, original blue paint w/red & green sponged panels & solid red moldings, one end has added date "1858," original hinges & escutcheon, some moldings replaced, touched-up

*European Painted Kas*

repair on red moldings, turned feet replaced, lock missing, Europe, late 18th - early 19th c., cornice 25 × 58¾", 6' h. (ILLUS.).................... **990.00**

**Wardrobe,** Victorian Renaissance Revival substyle, walnut, a rectangular top w/flaring stepped cornice above a frieze band of carved undulating rounded drops over a pair of tall paneled doors w/serpentine top to panels & inset w/long mirrors, line-incised bands down the sides, a mid-molding above a pair of line-incised drawers w/stamped brass & bail pulls, on thin block feet on casters, ca. 1880, 19¾ × 58", 7' 6½" h. ...................... **1,650.00**

**Wardrobe,** Victorian Renaissance Revival substyle, walnut & burl walnut, an arched & pierce-carved crest framing an anthemion-carved finial above a carved cornice & a pair of tall doors above a drawered base, raised burl panels, ca. 1875... **1,320.00**

**Wardrobe,** Victorian Renaissance Revival substyle, mahogany, the broken-scroll arched pediment centered by a large scroll-carved cartouche w/a central carved "S," the top corners w/large squatty turned urn-form finials, arched triangular frieze panels above a thin molding above a pair of tall paneled doors w/scroll-carved top arches, a base

molding above a pair of plain drawers over the molded base w/a scroll-carved scalloped apron & bracket feet, probably New Orleans, ca. 1860 (ILLUS. below) ................................ **2,420.00**

*Renaissance Revival Wardrobe*

*Walnut Renaissance Revival Wardrobe*

**Wardrobe,** Victorian Renaissance Revival substyle, walnut & burl walnut, the high pedimented crest w/a flat-topped central panel w/a long raised cartouche flanked by slanted molded cornice sections over narrow raised triangular burl panels above a deep rounded cornice above a frieze band w/three narrow indented panels above a pair of double-paneled doors each w/an arched raised burl panel at the top & a rectangular raised burl panel below, the sides w/two long, narrow oval indented panels flanking a center round panel, the lower section w/a pair of drawers w/raised oblong burl panels & teardrop pulls, the case demountable, flat apron, original hardware, ca. 1875-85, cornice 22¼ × 61½", 8' 3½" h. (ILLUS. bottom previous page) .................................. **1,870.00**

## WHATNOTS & ETAGERES

*Federal Etagere*

**Etagere,** Classical, birch, a stack of six thin rectangular open shelves each supported by four slender tapering columns, on short block feet, original translucent red stain, New England, early 19th c., 13¼ × 18", 5' ½" (minor imperfections) ............. **2,300.00**

**Etagere,** Federal, mahogany, two open square shelves raised on simple ring-turned supports w/ball finials above a tall base cabinet w/a pull-out writing surface above a long paneled door, molded base on casters, old finish, probably New England, ca. 1830, 17 × 18", 4' 10½" h. (ILLUS. bottom previous column) ........................... **1,840.00**

*New York Rococo Etagere*

**Etagere,** Victorian Rococo substyle, carved rosewood the tall superstructure w/a scroll-carved arched crestrail centered by an inset gilt-bronze satyr mask above the arched tall rectangular mirror flanked by graduated pierce-carved scrolling sides supporting a shaped open candleshelf on each side & w/scrolling front supports on the D-shaped top w/outset rounded posts separating the curving paneled sides & the curved paneled central drawer, the lower cabinet w/an open shelf forming two compartments at each side & topped by ornately pierce-carved top brackets flanking the curved central long door, the door w/a large raised oval-band reserve framing an ornate scroll-carved cartouche w/urn finial & further carved w/scrolls at each corner, the conforming molded base raised on four disc feet, New York, ca. 1850, 20 × 59", 6' 11" h. (ILLUS) ............. **7,150.00**

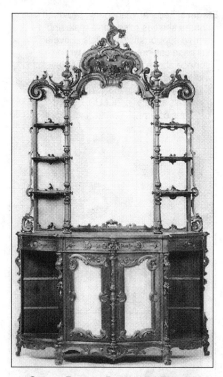

*Ornate Rococo Rosewood Etagere*

*Meeks Rosewood Etagere*

**Etagere,** Victorian Rococo substyle, carved rosewood, the very tall & wide superstructure w/an ornately carved arched central crest w/detailed scrolls & carved florals topped by a large C-scroll finial all above scrolling side crestrails w/tall turned finials, the crestrails above a wide arched central rectangular mirror flanked by narrow tall mirrors fronted by three half-round scroll-trimmed open shelves on knob-and rod-turned supports, scroll-carved trim down the outer edges, the superstructure resting on a D-form case w/a flat-front outset central section flanked by quarter-round side sections, the central section w/a long scroll- and cartouche-carved narrow drawer above a pair of tall mirrored doors w/ornate scroll-carved framing, each side section w/two quarter-round shelves, scrolled edge trim on all sections, the scalloped & scroll-carved apron on short scrolled feet, attributed to Meeks of New York, ca. 1850, 22 x 64", 9' 2" h. (ILLUS.) ........................... **17,600.00**

**Etagere,** Victorian Rococo substyle, carved & laminated rosewood, the tall superstructure w/a high pierced & arched scroll-carved crest centering an oval panel w/carved roses above ornate pierced scrolls above smaller pierced & scroll-carved crests, the high arched central frieze band w/scalloped carving over a setback tall arched mirror flanked by long S-scroll side framing enclosing narrow shaped mirrors backing a small half-round open shelf & a larger open lower shaped shelf each w/slender ring-and rod-turned supports w/heavy S-scroll-carved supports at the bottom & resting on the long D-form serpentine white marble top, the top above a deep curved, pierced & scroll-carved apron divided by four heavy cabriole legs boldly carved w/scrolls & floral clusters & ending in scroll feet, the incurved legs supporting an open shelf at each side & a long base shelf all backed by mirrored sections, attributed to J. & J.W. Meeks, New York, mid-19th c. (ILLUS.) ........................................ **28,600.00**

*Belter Rosewood Etagere*

**Etagere,** Victorian Rococo substyle, rosewood, an ornate arched center crest topped by bold leaf & grape carving above a tall arch-topped mirror flanked by narrow side mirrored panels each w/two small rounded open shelves w/scroll-carved brackets & flanked by slender reeded columns, each side section topped by a high pierced & scroll-carved crest, the superstructure resting on a serpentine white marble top above a lower case divided into three sections by four bold serpentine grape-carved pilasters, the center section w/a serpentine-front drawer w/flower & leaf carving above a two-paneled cupboard door w/mirrors in each panel, the side sections each w/a quarter-round open shelf backed by a narrow rectangular mirror, deep conforming molded base w/scroll carving & thin disc front feet, raised on four casters, stenciled mark w/"J.H. Belter & Co. - 547 - Broadway," New York, New York, ca. 1850, 16 × 49", 7' 6" h........................................ **33,000.00**

**Etagere,** Victorian Rococo substyle, carved & laminated rosewood, the tall arched superstructure w/a wide arched crestrail pierce-carved overall w/bold scrolls & fruit clusters & a central cartouche all above the tall arched central mirror flanked by narrower, shorter side mirrors fronted by tiered, shaped open

shelves w/S-scroll carved or columnar supports & resting on the low base w/a long serpentine white marble top over a deep conforming apron w/scroll-carved reserves, on low disc feet on casters, attributed to John Henry Belter, New York, ca. 1850 (ILLUS. top left)................ **17,600.00**

*Victorian Rococo Whatnot*

**Whatnot,** Victorian Rococo substyle, carved rosewood, the three-quarter low galleried top pierce-carved w/delicate scrolls on the narrow rectangular top shelf above three graduated rectangular open shelves backed by a large mirror & supported on graduated large S-scrolls, the rectangular base w/a wide apron carved w/a band of scrolls, on scroll-carved bracket feet, ca. 1850 (ILLUS.) ............................ **770.00**

---

# GAMES & GAME BOARDS

*Also see: CHARACTER COLLECTIBLES, DISNEY ITEMS and RADIO & TELEVISION COLLECTIBLES*

**Anagrams,** Milton Bradley, original box ....................................................**$30.00**

**Arabian Nights,** National Games,
ca. 1950 ...............................................**25.00**

**Batman board game,** from TV show,
includes plastic figure, board, insert,
& control board, Milton Bradley,
1966, box 15½ x 18" ........................**110.00**

**Big Battle punch board game,**
unused, 1930s, 7 x 9" .........................**28.00**

**Chess set,** carved ivory, in natural &
brown stained ivory, both w/crowned
king & queens, former w/bishops as
officers in tall hats, latter as Africans
w/togas, sea horse knights, tower
rooks, baluster pawns w/florette
knop, Germany, late 18th c., 32 pcs.
(two pawns replaced) .....................**3,335.00**

**Chess set,** carved ivory, the baluster
kings & queens w/crowns & finials,
the bishops as horse heads, rook
towers & pawn knops, w/wood
storage box, French, early 19th c.,
32 pcs. (white king damaged, white
knight repaired)...............................**1,610.00**

**Chess set,** silver & oxidized silver,
pieces in the form of 17th century
style figures, the kings w/orbs &
scepters, German, 20th c., 32 pcs. ....**1,840.00**

**Chess set,** silver, partly gilded, pieces
in the form of medieval figures,
w/fitted case, English, 1975,
32 pcs. ...........................................**1,150.00**

**"Game of the District Messenger
Boy,"** folding game board, metal
figures, tokens, teetotum,
McLoughlin Brothers, copyright 1886
(some edge wear)..............................**115.00**

*Painted Game Wheel*

**Game wheel,** wood & metal, painted
in green, red, black & gold w/a large
central star, the border w/bands of
alternating red, black & green
panels, minor chips to paint, 20th c.,
36" d. (ILLUS.) ...............................**2,070.00**

**Golf Jr. board game,** complete
w/metal ball markers, spinner,
scoreboard & instructions .................**250.00**

**Huggin' the Rail board game,**
complete w/six matching race cars,
lane locator, die & gameboard,
A Sell Right Game .............................**66.00**

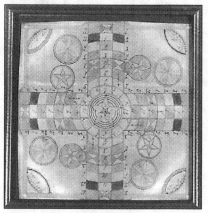

*19th Century Parcheesi Board*

**Parcheesi,** watercolor, pen & ink on
paper, American school, 19th c.,
12 x 12½" (ILLUS.) ...........................**402.00**

**Pop-up Store board game,** board
has pop-up parts, complete, Bradley
(box corners are taped) .....................**37.00**

**Ticker the Wall St. board game,**
complete w/chips, stocks &
certificates, vinyl playing board &
box, Glow Productions Co. (wear
to box).............................................**176.00**

**Tiddley Winks,** w/original box, Milton
Bradley ............................................**20.00**

**Walt Disney's Adventureland board
game,** complete, Walt Disney
Productions, by Parker Brothers,
dated 1965 (some wear).....................**27.00**

# GARDEN FOUNTAINS & ORNAMENTS

*Ornamental garden or yard fountains,
urns and figures often enhanced the formal
plantings on spacious lawns of mansion-sized
dwellings during the late 19th and early 20th
century. While fountains were usually
reserved for the lawns of estates, even modest
homes often had a latticework arbor or cast-
iron urn in the yard. Today garden enthusiasts*

*look for these ornamental pieces to lend the aura of elegance to their landscaping.*

**Bell,** wrought iron, decorated w/leaf-tip scrolls, 27½" h. ..........................**$575.00**

**Bench,** cast iron, w/rectangular double paneled back depicting putti terms centering a lyre, after a design by Karl Fredrich Schinkel, 48" l.......**1,610.00**

**Bench,** marble, the arm supports formed as sphinxes, 7' l. ................**6,900.00**

**Bench,** stone, 6' 3" l. ...........................**977.00**

**Birdbath,** bronze, figural, depicting a nude female emerging from water holding a bird high above her head, ca. 1900, 36" h...............................**4,600.00**

**Birdbath,** lead & stone, figural, lead figure of a cherub supporting shell, raised on a stone pedestal, 47" h. ..**1,610.00**

**Birdbath,** stone, the scalloped welled top above a tiered base, 30½" h......**1,265.00**

**Figure of a archer,** bronze, the nude male on one knee w/drawn bow & arrow, 45" l.....................................**5,750.00**

**Figure of a boy,** painted stone, a young smiling bare foot black boy wearing hat, jacket buttoned at top & rolled-up pants, seated on stone slab, 4' 1½" l., 33" h. ......................**4,312.00**

*Stone Figure of Bacchus*

**Figure of Bacchus,** stone, depicting a young Bacchus standing in front of tree stump, mounted on square pedestal base, 5' 1" (ILLUS.) .........**1,610.00**

**Fountain,** stone, baluster-shaped standard carved w/masks, swags & figural terms, raised on a square base carved w/figures, lyres & shields, ending in paw feet supporting font, early 20th c., 5' h...........................**10,925.00**

*Limestone Wall Fountain*

**Fountain,** wall-type, limestone, the gadrooned bowl raised on scrolled tri-part base surmounted by a scrolled plaque centering a satyrs mask, drilled for water nozzle, 6' 2" (ILLUS.) .......................................**12,650.00**

**Greenhouse,** miniature, painted iron & glass, domed paneled removable top above a conforming base, Coldbrookdale, ca. 1840, 24" h. .....**1,092.00**

**Gueridons,** marble & cast iron, the circular marble top raised on a circular fluted standard ending in a triform base w/fish head feet, 20" d., 28" h. ..............................................**2,875.00**

**Jars,** limestone, classical-style, tear-drop shaped, each carved w/continuous band of rosettes, vitruvian scrolls & foliage supported by twisted wrought-iron base, 41½" h., pr.....................................**9,775.00**

*Granite Chinese Lantern*

*Model of a Bronze Elephant*

**Lantern,** granite, Chinese-style, carved w/zodiac motifs, China, 7' 8" (ILLUS. bottom previous page).......**6,037.00**

**Model of a frog,** bronze, 24" h. ........**1,380.00**

**Model of a greyhound,** cast iron, the recumbent dog w/paws outstretched, head up & ears raised, 4' 3".............**2,587.00**

**Model of an elephant,** bronze, the standing elephant w/long tusks & trunk raised, 34½" h. (ILLUS. above)............................................**1,840.00**

**Model of a hound,** cast iron, the standing hound w/tail raised, 4' 1" h............................................**4,025.00**

**Models of falcons,** cast iron, each majestically perched on stepped bases, 33" h., pr..............................**6,900.00**

**Models of turtles,** polychrome clay, each w/head raised, 35", pr. ...........**3,680.00**

**Planters,** clay, ovoid shape, each decorated w/winged allegorical figures, each flanked w/scrolled handles, 24", pr..............................**6,900.00**

**Pump & vessel,** cast iron, the circular leaf-cast standard fitted w/an iron pump & nozzle, together w/a cast-iron floral decorated rectangular vessel, 19th c., pump 4' 5" h...........**2,415.00**

**Table,** Victorian, marble & cast iron, with a rectangular marble top above a standard cast w/dolphins ending in triform scrolled legs, 40" l., 30" h. ...**2,587.00**

**Table,** wrought iron & granite, the granite top raised on wrought-iron scrolled legs, 5' 1" h........................**2,300.00**

**Urns,** cast iron, compana form, flaring rim w/lappet decorations tapering to bulbous gadrooned section w/loop handles on plinth foot on square base, 24" h., pr. (ILLUS. of one, top next column) .....................................**2,587.00**

*Cast-iron Garden Urns*

**Urns,** cast iron, each spiral-fluted body flanked by loop handles ending in masks, on square bases, late 19th c., 25½" h., pr. .......................**3,450.00**

**Urns,** cov., Neoclassical-style, marble, w/continuous vitruvian bands w/a gadrooned bass, covers w/knob finials, 27" h., pr. ............................**8,050.00**

**Urns,** marble, compana form, the base w/gadrooned bands, on square base, 28" h., pr. ............................**10,350.00**

**Wall planter,** wrought iron, decorated w/leaf tips & scrolls, 32" h.................**747.00**

*Marble & Wrought-iron Well Head*

**Well head,** marble & wrought iron, carved w/foliage, birds & masks, fitted w/a copper liner surrounded by an elaborate wrought-iron superstructure (ILLUS.) .................**4,025.00**

# GLASS

Also see: *Antique Trader Books* American Pressed Glass & Bottles Price Guide *and* American & European Decorative & Art Glass Price Guide.

## AGATA

*Agata was patented by Joseph Locke of the New England Glass Company in 1887. The application of mineral stain left a mottled effect on the surface of the article. It was applied chiefly to the Wild Rose (Peach Blow) line but sometimes was applied as a border on a pale opaque green. In production for a short time, it is scarce. Items listed below are of the Wild Rose line unless otherwise noted.*

**Bowl,** 5½" d., 2¾" h., upright deeply ruffled sides .................................... **$865.00**

**Vase,** 6¼" h., Green Opaque, fourteen-rib gently tapering ovoid body w/flared rim, New England Glass Co. ......................................... **518.00**

## AMBERINA

*Amberina Mark*

*Amberina was developed in the late 1880s by the New England Glass Company and a pressed version was made by Hobbs, Brockunier & Company (under license from the former). Another unlicensed pressed version was also made by the Gillinder factory in Philadelphia. A similar blown ware, called Rose Amber, was made by the Mt. Washington Glass Works. Amberina-Rose Amber shades from amber to deep red or fuchsia and cut and plated (lined with creamy white) examples were also made. The Libbey Glass Company briefly revived blown Amberina using modern shapes, in 1917.*

**Berry set:** 9" sq., 2½" h. master bowl & six 5" sq., 1⅜" h. sauce dishes; pressed Daisy & Button patt., attributed to Hobbs, Brockunier & Co., the set (minor rim chips) .............................. **$345.00**

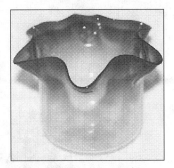

*Ruffled Amberina Bowl*

**Bowl,** 3¾" d., 2¾" h., cylindrical body w/a deeply ruffled fuchsia rim (ILLUS.) ........................................... **295.00**

**Bowl,** squatty rounded base w/waisted sides to a widely flaring rim, light vertical molding, Mt. Washington ...... **225.00**

**Creamer,** spherical swirled pattern-molded body w/a wide cylindrical neck w/pinched spout, applied angled amber handle w/end curl, 3½" d., 5" h. ..................................... **135.00**

**Cruet w/original bubble stopper,** spherical body in Inverted Thumbprint patt., slender cylindrical neck w/a tricorner mouth, applied amber handle, 3½" d., 6" h. ................ **250.00**

**Finger bowl,** Hobnail patt., squared rim on squatty rounded body, 4⅜" d., 2¾" h. ............................................... **125.00**

**Pitcher,** 8⅞" h., 5¼" d., tapering ovoid body w/a swirled rib design, wide cylindrical neck w/pinched spout, applied amber handle ...................... **245.00**

**Pitcher,** Plated Amberina, bulbous ovoid body tapering to a tricorner mouth, applied ruby handle, creamy white lining .................................. **10,000.00**

*Plated Amberina Tankard Pitcher*

*Various Amberina Vases*

**Pitcher,** Plated Amberina, tankard-type, small pinched spout, applied amber handle (ILLUS. bottom previous page) .............................. **12,000.00**

**Pitcher & tumbler,** pitcher 6½" h., 2½" d., the pitcher w/a footed ovoid body in the Inverted Thumbprint patt. tapering to a cylindrical neck w/a small pinched spout, applied angled amber handle, matching footed 3⅜" h. tumbler, 2 pcs. ...................... **185.00**

**Sugar bowl,** cov., pressed Daisy & Button patt., cylindrical bucket-style w/tab rim handles & flattened fitted cover w/knob finial, base in all-amber, 5½" h. (flake on cover) ......... **540.00**

**Vase,** 6⅜" h., 4⅛" d., melon-lobed ovoid body tapering to a widely flaring four-ruffle neck, h.p. w/dainty white & yellow flowers & green leaves (ILLUS. above left) ............... **245.00**

**Vase,** 7⅛" h., 3¾"d., cylindrical body w/a narrow cushion foot, pattern-molded swirled rib design, h.p. soft pink flowers & green leaves, gilt rim (ILLUS. above right) ........................ **245.00**

**Vase,** 8⅝" h., 7"d., wide spherical body in the Hobnail patt., tapering to a lightly ribbed upright oval neck, raised on pale amber applied pad feet................................................... **265.00**

**Vase,** jack-in-the-pulpit-style, 12" h., 5½" d., tall tapering ovoid body in the Inverted Thumbprint patt., the wide rolled rim w/a fluted edge & a pull-up back peak, on an applied amber foot (ILLUS. above center) .... **245.00**

**Water set:** 9½" h., 4" d. tankard pitcher & four 3¾" h. tumblers; all in the Inverted Thumbprint patt., the

pitcher w/a flat angle-cut rim & applied angled amber handle, the set .............................................. **395.00**

## APPLIQUÉD

*Simply stated, this is an art glass form with applied decoration. Sometimes master glass craftsmen applied stems or branches to an art glass object and then added molded glass flowers or fruit specimens to these branches or stems. At other times a button of molten glass was daubed on the object and a tool pressed over it to form a prunt in the form of a raspberry, rosette or other shape. Always the work of a skilled glassmaker, applied decoration can be found on both cased (two-layer) and single layer glass. The English firm of Stevens and Williams was renowned for the appliquéd glass they produced.*

**Pitcher,** 6¾" h., footed ovoid shaded cobalt blue body tapering to a cylindrical neck w/pinched spout, applied w/two large red strawberries & green leafy stems, applied angled amber thorn handle ...................... **$345.00**

**Vase,** 4½" h., 3¼" d., opaque white spherical body w/a wide trumpet-form neck, applied w/a large blue blossom w/amber center & stem & two green leaves, raised on amber wishbone feet (ILLUS. right, top next page) ......... **78.00**

**Vase,** 4⅞" h., 5" d., squatty bulbous lime green body tapering toward the base & up to a flattened flaring rim, applied w/two large crystal daisy-like flowers w/white opalescent petals & applied clear leaf & branches .......... **195.00**

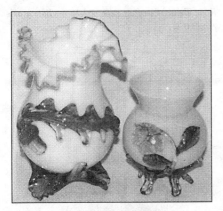

*Two Appliquéd Vases*

**Vase,** 5" h., 3¼" d., tapering cylindrical amber body in the Inverted Thumbprint patt., applied w/large light blue leaves & branches & two sapphire blue plums, applied leaf feet ............................................. **145.00**

**Vase,** 6¾" h., 4¾" d., tapering ovoid opaque white body w/a tri-lobed & fluted rolled rim w/an applied amber band, the body applied w/a large wrapped cranberry leaf & large amber acorn, on applied amber leaf feet (ILLUS. above left) ..................... **135.00**

**Vase,** 7" h., 4⅞" d., opaque white baluster-form body tapering to a deeply ruffled & crimped wide mouth w/applied amber rim band, the body applied w/a large amber leaf & bellflower, on an applied amber crimped foot ..................................... **135.00**

*Tall Appliquéd Vase*

**Vase,** 15" h., 5" d., tall slender baluster-form body in pale green opalescent w/a molded swirl design, applied w/a large peach center & opalescent-edged petals on a large pale pink stem & long serrated leaves (ILLUS. bottom previous column) ............................................. **650.00**

**Vases,** stick-type, 16" h., 4½" d., tall slender cylinder in orange w/opalescent raised thorny nubs & applied yellowish green leaves & branches trimmed in gold, small applied trumpet-form vases at the base, applied curled green leaf feet ................................................. **895.00**

## ART GLASS BASKETS

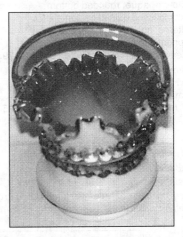

*Cased Art Glass Basket*

**Cased,** white exterior, dark shaded rose pink interior, the tall waisted footed body applied around the sides w/a large amber & cranberry ruffled leaf, amber edging on the crimped & ruffled rim, applied amber handle, 6½" d., 7¾" h. (ILLUS.) ...... **$295.00**

**Spangled,** the interior w/spattered yellow, gold, green, white, pink & mica flecks, the white exterior w/melon ribbing, deeply ruffled & crimped rim, applied clear reeded handle, 6½ x 7", 6½" h. ..................... **195.00**

**Spatter,** the bulbous exterior w/upright crimped rim decorated w/pink, aqua, maroon & gold spattering, white lining, applied clear high thorn handle, 5" d., 6¾" h. (ILLUS. top next page) ......................................... **175.00**

*Spatter Art Glass Basket*

**Yellow opaque,** rounded bottom
w/embossed quilted design
alternating w/three-rib bands to the
upright crimped & ruffled rim, applied
clear pointed handle, 4½" d., 5¼" h.... **79.00**

**Yellow opaque,** nearly spherical body
w/Hobnail patt. & incurved crimped
rim, applied clear thorn handle, 5" d.,
6" h. ................................................. **195.00**

# BACCARAT

*Baccarat glass has been made by
Cristalleries de Baccarat, France, since 1765.
The firm has produced various glassware of
excellent quality and paperweights. Baccarat's*

*Rose Teinte is often referred to as Baccarat's
Amberina.*

*Baccarat Candlestick*

**Candlestick,** square foot supporting a
round shaft & squared socket, Rose
Teinte Pinwheel patt., marked,
3⅝" w., 8¼" h. (ILLUS.) .................. **$195.00**

**Cologne bottle w/original patterned
ball stopper,** spherical body w/a
short flaring neck, Rose Teinte
Pinwheel patt., 2⅞" d., 5" h................ **95.00**

**Cologne bottle w/original patterned
ball stopper,** spherical body w/a
short flaring neck, Rose Teinte
Pinwheel patt., 3⅝" d., 6¼" h........... **110.00**

*Baccarat Rose Teinte Pinwheel Dresser Set*

**Dresser set:** 10¼" h. bottle w/stopper, two 4½" h. tumblers, a 4⅜" d., 5" h. cov. bowl & a 9¼ x 13¼" rectangular tray; Rose Teinte Pinwheel patt., the set (ILLUS. bottom previous page).... **450.00**

**Ice bucket,** slightly tapering cylindrical body w/a brass rim band & brass swing handle, Rose Teinte Swirl patt., 5¼" d., 5⅜" h. ......................... **175.00**

**Jar w/original top,** cylindrical, Rose Teinte Swirl patt., signed, 2½" d., 3½" h. ............................................ **110.00**

**Perfume bottle w/stopper,** "Subtilité" by Houbigant, clear glass modeled as a seated figural Buddha, w/original ringed copper stopper & tassel, 3½" h. ................................. **316.00**

**Perfume bottles w/patterned ball stoppers,** cylindrical w/flattened shoulder to a short cylindrical neck w/flared rim, Rose Teinte Swirl patt., 5½" h., pr. ....................................... **173.00**

## BRIDE'S BASKETS & BOWLS

*These berry or fruit bowls were popular late Victorian wedding gifts, hence the name. They were produced in a variety of quality art glasswares and sometimes were fitted in ornate silver plate holders.*

**Cased bowl,** blue shaded exterior w/two pull-up sides w/the crimped rim applied w/an amber band, white interior, fitted in a brass basket w/a pair of tall looped woven handles continuing down to the basketweave woven flaring base w/a looped border, bowl 14" w., overall 16" h. (ILLUS. top next column) ............... **$795.00**

*Bride's Bowl in Brass Basket*

**Cased bowl,** shallow cupped form w/peach satin interior decorated w/enameled white butterflies among flowering branches, white exterior, smooth rim, raised in an ornate silver plate footed stand w/scroll handles & marked Reed & Barton, bowl 10¼" d., overall 4½" h. ............. **173.00**

**Cased bowl,** pink interior, white exterior w/two sides pulled-up w/a crimped & ruffled rim w/an applied clear rim band, the exterior decorated w/heavy gold leafy blossoming branches, satin finish, 7⅝ x 11¼", 5" h. ............................... **395.00**

**Cased bowl,** purple shaded to white interior w/flattened sides & a crimped rim, decorated w/sprays of dainty flowers & leaves in color, white exterior, 10¾" d., 3½" h. .................... **265.00**

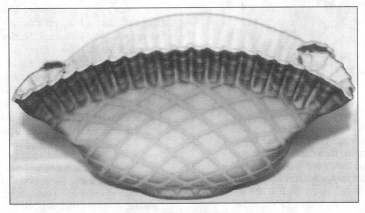

*Blue Mother-of-Pearl Bowl*

**Mother-of-pearl satin bowl,** shaded dark blue Diamond Quilted exterior w/two sides pulled up to the crimped & ruffled rim, white interior, 6 x 9½", 4⅝" h. (ILLUS. bottom previous page) ............................................... **695.00**

**Pale green bowl,** pleated shell-form w/two turned-in tabs at one side, satin ground decorated w/dainty white flowers, 10¾" d., 3¾" h. .......... **300.00**

# BRISTOL

*A number of glasshouses operated in Bristol, England over the years and they produced a variety of wares. Today, however, the generic name Bristol refers to a type of semi-opaque glass, often accented with ornate enameling. Such wares were produced in England, Europe and America in the 19th and early 20th centuries.*

**Cracker jar w/silver plate cover,** rim & swing bail handle, barrel-shaped turquoise blue body decorated w/h.p. white, pink & gold daisy-like flowers & green leaves, resilvered fittings, 4½" d., 6¾" h. ..................... **$195.00**

*Bristol Ewer*

**Ewers,** footed tapering ovoid body w/a cylindrical cupped neck & pinched spout, applied blue handle, decorated around the center w/a wide gold band & lacy gold sprays w/small white & pink or blue blossoms, gilt trim at rim & handle, 2⅝" d., 5¼" h., pr. (ILLUS. of one)................................................. **135.00**

**Mantel lustres,** apple green w/satin finish, wide rounded top bowl w/the rim notch-cut in seven wide points above the slender shaft to a smaller bulbous medial section above the thick disc foot, the rim hung w/seven long facet-cut pointed clear prisms, the lustre decorated around the top w/a gilt band & clusters of pointed gold leaves, delicate gilt trim on the lower sections, 4½" d., 9⅝" h., pr. .... **395.00**

*Bristol Stick Vase*

**Vase,** stick-type, glossy opaque turquoise blue, the slender cylindrical bowl raised on a ringed short pedestal & disc foot, the base in gold & the bowl decorated overall w/heavy gold leafy blossom branches, 1⅜" d., 3⅝" h. (ILLUS.) ...... **36.00**

# BURMESE

*Burmese is a single-layer heat-reactive glass that shades from pink to pale yellow. It was patented by Frederick S. Shirley and made by the Mt. Washington Glass Co. A license to produce the glass in England was granted to Thomas Webb & Sons, which called its articles Queen's Burmese. Gunderson Burmese was made briefly about the middle of this century, and the Pairpoint Crystal Company is making limited quantities at the present time.*

**Bowl,** 4" d., 2½" h., squatty bulbous body w/a wide flat rim, raised on a short foot, the sides decorated w/a blue butterfly & reddish blossoms on slender vines trimmed in gold, attributed to Webb ......................... **$585.00**

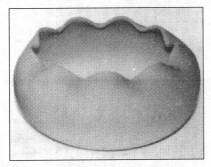

*Burmese Finger Bowl*

**Bowl,** 4¼" d., 3⅛" h., squatty bulbous body w/an upright short six-sided neck, decorated w/lavender five-petal blossoms w/green & brown leaves, satin finish, unsigned Webb .. **395.00**

**Ewer,** tall ovoid body tapering to a tall, pointed upright spout, w/an applied loop handle & disc foot, satin finish, Mt. Washington, 6" h. ............. **950.00**

**Finger bowl,** 4½" d., 2" h., wide squatty bulbous body w/incurved crimped rim, satin finish, Mt. Washington (ILLUS. above) ............. **225.00**

**Rose bowl,** miniature, spherical body w/an eight-crimp top, satin finish, unsigned Webb, 2⅜" d., 2⅛" h. ........ **175.00**

**Toothpick holder,** bulbous ovoid body tapering to a short six-sided neck, satin finish, 2½" d., 2½" h........ **195.00**

**Toothpick holder,** bulbous squatty base w/a flaring squared neck, decorated w/lavender blossoms & green & brown leaves, satin finish, attributed to Webb, 2½" d., 2⅞" h..... **325.00**

**Toothpick holder,** footed ovoid body w/a short cylindrical neck, decorated w/lavender blossoms & green & brown leaves, satin finish, attributed to Webb, 2¼" d., 3" h........................ **350.00**

**Vase,** 2½ h., 2½" d., scalloped rim, glossy finish, marked Webb.............. **525.00**

**Vase,** 3⅝" h., 3" d., squatty bulbous base w/a slightly flaring tall cylindrical neck topped by a fluted & crimped rim, glossy finish, unsigned Webb ..... **195.00**

**Vase,** 3⅝" h., 3⅜" d., spherical body w/a short six-sided neck, decorated w/green ivy leaves in two shades of green & tan, satin finish, unsigned Webb (ILLUS. right, top next column)............................................. **395.00**

*Decorated Burmese Vases*

**Vase,** 8¼" h., 4" d., footed bottle-form w/tall cylindrical neck, decorated w/green & brown leaves & red flower buds, satin finish, unsigned Webb (ILLUS. left) ..................................... **650.00**

**Vase,** 10¼" h., stick-type w/rounded bulbous base & slender neck, decorated w/raised gold flower & vine decoration, satin finish, unmarked Webb .......................... **1,100.00**

**Vase,** 10¼" h., trumpet-form body w/a gently ruffled rim, raised on a ringed pedestal on a disc foot, Bryden-Pairpoint ......................................... **288.00**

## CAMBRIDGE

*The Cambridge Glass Company was founded in Ohio in 1901. Numerous pieces are now sought, especially those designed by Arthur J. Bennett, including Crown Tuscan. Other productions included crystal animals, "Black Amethyst," "blanc opaque," and other types of colored glass. The firm was finally closed in 1954. It should not be confused with the New England Glass Co., Cambridge, Massachusetts.*

**NEAR CUT**

*Various Cambridge Marks*

**Ashtray,** Statuesque line, Carmen (ruby red) bowl, clear Nude Lady stem ................................ **$310.00**

**Ashtray,** Statuesque line, pink bowl, clear Nude Lady stem ...................... **499.00**

**Ashtray,** Statuesque line, Royal Blue (dark blue) bowl, clear Nude Lady stem ................................. **399.00**

**Basket,** handled, Amethyst, w/Farberware holder, 5½" .................. **45.00**

**Bell,** etched Diane patt., Crystal ......... **150.00**

**Bonbon,** Decagon line, green, 5½" w... **25.00**

**Bonbon,** underplate & spoon, handled, etched Rose Point patt., Crystal, 6" d., the set .......................... **65.00**

**Bonbon,** square, footed, pressed Caprice patt., Moonlight (pale blue).... **65.00**

**Bonbon,** square, handled, pressed Caprice patt., Moonlight, 4" w. ............. **33.00**

**Bonbon,** square, two-handled, pressed Caprice patt., Moonlight, 6" w. ...................................................... **48.00**

**Bowl,** 5" d., etched Apple Blossom patt., Moonlight .................................. **20.00**

**Bowl,** fruit, 5" d., crimped, pressed Caprice patt., Moonlight.................... **125.00**

**Bowl,** fruit, 5½" d., bell shaped, Decagon line, green .......................... **17.00**

**Bowl,** 6" d., footed, Decagon line, green ................................................. **24.00**

**Bowl,** 6¾" d., flat rim, Decagon line, green ................................................. **24.00**

**Bowl,** pickle, 9" d., etched Apple Blossom patt., yellow .......................... **38.00**

**Bowl,** 9½" d., pickle, etched Rose Point patt., Crystal ............................. **90.00**

**Bowl,** salad, 10" d., footed, pressed Alpine Caprice patt., Moonlight......... **250.00**

**Bowl,** 10½" d., footed, belled, pressed Caprice patt., Moonlight.................... **100.00**

**Bowl,** 11" d., footed, etched Rose Point patt., Crystal ............................ **225.00**

**Bowl,** 12" d., handled, Caprice patt., Moonlight ..................................... **75.00**

**Bowl,** 12" d., flat rim, Decagon line, black ...................................................... **65.00**

**Bowl,** 12" d., footed, etched Rose Point patt., Crystal ............................ **150.00**

**Bowl,** 12½" d., footed, belled, pressed Caprice patt., Moonlight.................... **120.00**

**Bowl,** 13" d., Decagon line, green ...... **110.00**

**Brandy,** Statuesque line, Amethyst bowl, frosted Nude Lady stem, 1 oz... **159.00**

**Brandy,** Statuesque line, Carmen bowl, frosted Nude Lady stem .......... **120.00**

*Statuesque Line Brandy*

**Brandy,** Statuesque line, Forest Green (dark green) bowl, clear Nude Lady stem ................................................... **120.00**

**Brandy,** Statuesque line, Forest Green bowl, frosted Nude Lady stem ............ **159.00**

**Brandy,** Statuesque line, Mandarin Gold (medium yellow) bowl, clear Nude Lady stem (ILLUS. above) ...... **159.00**

**Butter dish,** cov., etched Apple Blossom patt., pink, 5½" d. ................. **75.00**

**Butter dish,** cov., round, etched Rose Point patt., Crystal, 5½" d. ................ **200.00**

**Cake plate,** handled, etched Wildflower patt., Crystal, 13½" d. ........................... **34.00**

**Candlestick,** Rosalie etching (No. 731), Amber, 4" h. ............................................. **28.00**

**Candlesticks,** etched Apple Blossom patt., yellow, 4" h., pr. ....................... **75.00**

**Candlesticks,** pressed Caprice patt., Crystal, 2½" h., pr. ............................. **22.00**

**Candlesticks,** etched Cleo patt., pink, 4" h., pr. ............................................. **95.00**

**Candlesticks,** Decagon line, black, 4" h. pr. ............................................... **55.00**

**Candlesticks,** Decagon line, Cobalt Blue (clear medium blue), 4" h., pr. .... **95.00**

**Candlesticks,** Decagon line, green, 4" h., pr. ................................................ **65.00**

**Candlesticks,** two-light, keyhole stem, etched Rose Point patt., Crystal, 6" h., pr. ................................. **185.00**

**Candlesticks w/ram's head,** etched Rose Point patt., Crystal, 4" h., pr. ... **240.00**

**Candy box,** cov., three-part, etched Chantilly patt., Crystal........................ **95.00**

**Candy dish,** cov., three-footed, pressed Caprice patt., Crystal, 6" d. .... **22.00**

**Candy dish,** cov., three-footed, pressed Caprice patt., Moonlight........ **55.00**

**Candy dish,** cov., three-part, etched Chantilly patt., sterling silver base, Crystal ................................................ **82.00**

**Candy dish,** cov., footed, Mt. Vernon line, Crystal, 1 lb. ............................... **65.00**

**Champagne,** etched Apple Blossom patt., yellow........................................ **25.00**

**Champagne,** etched Diane patt., Crystal ................................................ **24.00**

**Champagne,** Statuesque line, Cobalt Blue bowl, clear Nude Lady stem ..... **185.00**

**Cigarette box,** etched Apple Blossom patt., Topaz..................................... **195.00**

**Cigarette box,** cov., etched Rose Point patt., Crystal ............................ **225.00**

**Cigarette box,** Statuesque line, Amber top, clear Nude Lady stem .... **450.00**

**Cigarette box,** Statuesque line, Amethyst top, clear Nude Lady stem .. **400.00**

**Cigarette box,** Statuesque line, Cobalt Blue top, clear Nude Lady stem................................................ **550.00**

**Cigarette box,** Statuesque line, Gold Krystol top, clear Nude Lady stem.... **450.00**

**Cigarette/card holder,** etched Apple Blossom patt., Cobalt Blue .............. **125.00**

**Cigarette holder,** triangular, pressed Caprice patt., Moonlight...................... **60.00**

**Cigarette set:** box & four ashtrays; pressed Caprice patt., Moonlight........ **90.00**

**Claret,** etched Chantilly patt., Crystal, 4½ oz. .................................................. **32.00**

**Claret,** etched Diane patt., Crystal, 4½ oz. .................................................. **65.00**

**Claret,** Statuesque line, Amethyst bowl, clear Nude Lady stem .............. **85.00**

**Claret,** Statuesque line, Carmen bowl, clear Nude Lady stem...................... **125.00**

**Claret,** Statuesque line, Crystal bowl, clear Nude Lady stem........................ **75.00**

**Claret,** Statuesque line, Emerald Green (light green) bowl, clear Nude Lady stem ......................................... **79.00**

**Claret,** Statuesque line, Forest Green bowl, clear Nude Lady stem .............. **85.00**

**Claret,** Statuesque line, Royal Blue bowl, clear Nude Lady stem ............. **139.00**

**Cocktail,** etched Apple Blossom patt., yellow, 3 oz..................................... **28.00**

*Cocktail in Farberware Holder*

**Cocktail,** pressed Caprice patt., Moonlight, 3½ oz. ............................. **55.00**

**Cocktail,** Amber, in Farberware holder, 5⅝" h., 3 oz. (ILLUS. above) .. **11.00**

**Cocktail,** Statuesque line, Amber bowl, clear Nude Lady stem ............. **110.00**

**Cocktail,** Statuesque line, Amethyst bowl, clear Nude Lady stem ............. **110.00**

**Cocktail,** Statuesque line, Pistachio (delicate pastel green) bowl, clear Nude Lady stem ............................... **165.00**

**Cocktail,** Statuesque line, yellow bowl, clear Nude Lady stem ............. **125.00**

**Cocktails,** Gloria patt., clear, set of 6 .. **110.00**

**Cocktail shaker,** Pristine line, Crystal .. **75.00**

**Compote,** 5" d, etched Apple Blossom patt., Moonlight ................... **25.00**

**Compote,** 7" d., etched Apple Blossom patt., green........................ **95.00**

**Compote,** 7" d., pressed Caprice patt., Moonlight ................................. **50.00**

**Compote,** 7" d., Decagon line, green ... **65.00**

**Cordial,** etched Apple Blossom patt., yellow.................................................. **95.00**

**Cordial,** Amethyst bowl, in Faberware holder, 1 oz....................................... **20.00**

**Cordial,** Statuesque line, Amber bowl, clear Nude Lady stem...................... **650.00**

**Cordial,** Statuesque line, Amethyst bowl, clear, Nude Lady stem ............ **150.00**

**Cordial,** Statuesque line, Carmen bowl, clear Nude Lady stem ............. **650.00**

**Creamer & sugar bowl,** pressed Caprice patt., Moonlight, pr. .............. **55.00**

**Creamer & sugar bowl w/undertray,** individual size, Caprice patt., Moonlight, 3 pcs. .............................. 45.00

**Creamer & sugar bowl,** etched Chantilly patt., Crystal, pr. ................. 42.00

**Creamer & sugar bowl,** Decagon line, green .......................................... 38.00

**Creamer & sugar bowl,** Decagon line, Moonlight, pr. ............................. 35.00

**Creamer & sugar bowl,** Mt. Vernon line, Crystal, pr. ................................. 24.00

**Crown Tuscan ashtray,** round, 4" d. ... 25.00

**Crown Tuscan ashtray,** round, 6" d. ... 40.00

**Crown Tuscan bowl,** 11" oval ............. 55.00

**Crown Tuscan cigarette box,** cov., No. 101 ............................................... 50.00

**Crown Tuscan cocktail,** Statuesque line, Nude Lady stem ....................... 129.00

**Crown Tuscan model of a swan,** 3" l. ....................................................... 38.00

**Crown Tuscan model of a swan,** gold trim, 9" l. ...................................... 95.00

**Crown Tuscan vase,** bud, 10" h., footed ................................................. 25.00

**Cruet w/stopper,** oil, pressed Caprice patt., Moonlight, 5 oz. ....................... 350.00

**Cup & saucer,** pressed Caprice patt., Crystal ............................................... 14.00

**Cup & saucer,** pressed Caprice patt., Moonlight ......................................... 40.00

**Cup & saucer,** Decagon line, green ..... 11.00

**Cup & saucer,** Decagon line, Moonlight ......................................... 17.00

**Cup & saucer,** etched Diane patt., Crystal ............................................... 30.00

**Cup & saucer,** etched Rose Point patt., Crystal ...................................... 35.00

**Decanter w/stopper,** etched Apple Blossom patt., Carmen, 12 oz. ........... 75.00

**Decanter set:** decanter w/stopper & six 2 oz. tumblers; etched Apple Blossom patt., Topaz, the set .......... 800.00

**Figure flower holder,** "Bashful Charlotte," Moonlight, 11" h. .............. 185.00

**Figure flower holder in bowl,** "Bashful Charlotte," etched bowl w/gold rim, pink, 8" h. ....................... 140.00

**Figure flower holder,** "Draped Lady," blue, 8½" h. (ILLUS. top next column) ................................................. 250.00

**Figure flower holder,** "Draped Lady," Crystal, 8½" h. ..................................... 100.00

**Figure flower holder,** "Draped Lady," yellow, 8½" h. ................... 200.00 to 250.00

**Figure flower holder** w/high base, "Rose Lady," Crystal, 9¾" h. ............. 205.00

*Draped Lady Flower Holder*

**Figure flower holder** w/high base, "Rose Lady," frosted green, 9¾" h.... 210.00

**Figure flower holder,** "Two-Kid," Amber, 8¾" h. .................................... 180.00

**Flower holder,** Blue Jay, Crystal, 5¼" h. ............................................... 102.00

**Flower holder,** Heron, Crystal, 9" h. .... 60.00

**Flower holder,** Sea Gull, Crystal, 8" h. ................................................. 45.00

**Goblet,** water, etched Apple Blossom patt., Crystal, 8 oz. ............................ 25.00

**Goblet,** water, etched Chantilly patt., Crystal ............................................... 30.00

**Goblet,** etched Portia, Crystal, 7½" h. ... 25.00

**Goblet,** etched Rose Point patt., Crystal, 10 oz. .................................... 25.00

**Goblet,** water, Gadroon line (No. 3500), etched Rose Point patt., Crystal, 10 oz. .................................... 30.00

**Goblet,** Statuesque line, Carmen bowl, clear Nude Lady stem ............. 225.00

**Goblet,** Statuesque line, green bowl, clear Nude Lady stem, 8¾" h. .......... 175.00

**Goblet,** banquet, Statuesque line, Royal Blue bowl, clear Nude Lady stem ................................................... 650.00

**Goblet,** water, etched Wildflower patt., Crystal ............................................... 25.00

**Ice bucket,** etched Cleo patt., pink ....... 95.00

**Ice bucket,** etched Diane patt., Amber ............................................... 200.00

**Ice bucket,** w/chrome handle, etched Rose Point patt., Crystal .................. **110.00**

**Ivy ball,** pressed Caprice patt., Moonlight, 5" ...................................... **295.00**

**Ivy ball,** Statuesque line, Amethyst bowl, frosted Nude Lady stem .......... **249.00**

**Ivy ball,** Statuesque line, Forest Green bowl, clear Nude Lady Stem .. **210.00**

**Ivy ball,** Statuesque line, Royal Blue bowl, clear Nude Lady stem ............. **295.00**

**Lamp,** figural Buddha, green .............. **375.00**

**Lemon plate,** pressed Caprice patt., Crystal, 6½" d. ..................... **12.00**

**Lemon plate,** pressed Caprice patt., Moonlight, 6½" d. ............................... **26.00**

**Marmalade jar,** cov., etched Chantilly patt., Crystal, silver plate cover & base ................................ **100.00 to 145.00**

**Marmalade jar,** cov., etched Rose Point patt., Crystal ............................ **139.00**

**Martini pitcher,** etched Rose Point patt., Crystal, 32 oz. ........................... **495.00**

**Mayonnaise dish w/liner & ladle,** etched Apple Blossom patt., pink, the set ............................................... **145.00**

**Mayonnaise dish w/liner,** Decagon line, green, 2 pcs. .............................. **45.00**

**Nut bowl,** footed, etched Rose Point patt., Crystal ...................................... **70.00**

**Oil bottle w/stopper,** etched Apple Blossom patt., Moonlight, 2 oz. .......... **75.00**

**Oil bottle w/stopper,** etched Apple Blossom patt., yellow, 6 oz. ............... **60.00**

**Oil bottle w/stopper,** pressed Caprice patt., Crystal ......................... **55.00**

**Oyster cocktail,** blown Caprice patt., Moonlight, 4½ oz. .............................. **68.00**

**Oyster cocktail,** etched Rose Point patt. ...................................................... **35.00**

**Parfait,** blown Caprice patt., Moonlight, 5 oz. ............................... **225.00**

**Pitcher,** handled, etched Apple Blossom patt., pink, 12½" h. ............... **85.00**

**Pitcher,** etched Apple Blossom patt. (No. 1205), yellow............................ **395.00**

**Pitcher,** ball-shaped, pressed Caprice patt., Crystal, 80 oz. .......................... **150.00**

**Pitcher,** ball-shaped, pressed Caprice patt., Moonlight, 32 oz. .................... **295.00**

**Pitcher,** ball-shaped, pressed Caprice patt., Moonlight, 80 oz. .................... **290.00**

**Pitcher,** pressed Caprice patt., Doulton style #178, Moonlight, 90 oz. ....................... **4,300.00 to 4,600.00**

**Plate,** 6" d., Decagon line, green .......... **10.00**

**Plate,** 6" d., Decagon line, Moonlight ...... **6.00**

**Plate,** 6" d., etched Diane patt., Crystal ............................................. **15.00**

**Plate,** 6" d., etched Elaine patt., Crystal ............................................. **15.00**

**Plate,** 6½" d., etched Apple Blossom patt., Carmen ...................................... **12.00**

**Plate,** 7" d., etched Diane patt., Crystal ............................................. **17.00**

**Plate,** 8" d., etched Rose Point patt., Crystal ............................................. **40.00**

**Plate,** 8¼" d., Decagon line, green ....... **10.00**

**Plate,** luncheon, 8½" d., pressed Caprice patt., Crystal ......................... **12.00**

**Plate,** 8½" d., Mt. Vernon line, Crystal .. **10.00**

**Plate,** 8¾" d., Decagon line, green ....... **19.00**

**Plate,** dinner, 9" d., Decagon line, Moonlight ............................................. **60.00**

**Plate,** 9¼" d., etched Apple Blossom patt., Moonlight ..................... **30.00**

**Plate,** grill, 10" d., etched Apple Blossom patt., yellow...................... **55.00**

**Plate,** dinner, 10¼" d., etched Apple Blossom patt., Heatherbloom (delicate orchid) ............................... **125.00**

**Plate,** cabaret, 11½" d., four-footed, pressed Caprice patt., Moonlight........ **75.00**

**Plate,** sandwich, 12½" d., two-handled, etched Apple Blossom patt., yellow......................................... **45.00**

**Plate,** 14" d., four-footed, pressed Caprice patt., Moonlight.................... **110.00**

**Plate,** cabaret, 14" d., four-footed, pressed Caprice patt., Moonlight........ **85.00**

**Platter,** 12" d., Decagon line, green...... **60.00**

**Platter,** 12½" d., etched Apple Blossom patt., pink ............................ **33.00**

**Relish,** four-part, etched Apple Blossom patt., Crystal...................... **65.00**

**Relish,** two-part, Decagon line, green, 8½" .................................................... **35.00**

**Relish,** five-part, etched Diane patt., Crystal ............................................. **60.00**

**Relish,** three-part, clover-shaped, three-handled, Mt. Vernon line, Crystal, 8" ............................................ **25.00**

**Relish,** two-part, etched Rose Point patt., Crystal, 6" ................................. **25.00**

**Relish,** three-part, etched Rose Point patt., Crystal, 6½" .............................. **40.00**

**Relish,** three-part, footed, etched Rose Point patt., Crystal, 10".............. **47.00**

**Relish,** three-part, etched Rose Point patt., Crystal, 11" ................................. **70.00**

**Relish dish,** four-part, Amethyst, in Faberware holder............................ **48.00**

**Relish dish,** etched Rose Point patt., Crystal, 12", 6 pcs............................ **395.00**

**Relish dish,** etched Rose Point patt., Crystal, 4½ x 15" ............................ **200.00**

**Salt & pepper shakers w/chrome tops,** flat base, etched Rose Point patt., Crystal, pr. ................................. **45.00**

**Salt & pepper shakers w/chrome tops,** footed, etched Rose Point patt., Crystal, pr. ................................. **75.00**

**Server,** center-handled, etched Cleo patt., pink ............................. **48.00**

**Server,** center-handled, Decagon line, green .................................... **28.00**

**Sherbet,** etched Apple Blossom patt., yellow, 6 oz......................... **20.00**

**Sherbet,** tall, blown Caprice patt., blue, 6 oz. ...................... **20.00**

**Sherbet,** Decagon line, Moonlight ........ **35.00**

**Sherbet,** etched Rose Point patt., Crystal ................................. **20.00**

**Sherbet,** Stradivari/Regency line, Crystal ................................. **10.00**

**Sherbet,** etched Wildflower patt., Crystal ................................. **17.00**

**Sugar shaker w/original top,** Decagon line, green ........................ **145.00**

**Toothpick holder,** Colonial line, Cobalt blue ........................................ **30.00**

**Tumbler,** footed, pressed Caprice patt., Moonlight, 3 oz. ...................... **195.00**

**Tumbler,** footed, etched Apple Blossom patt., Topaz, 5 oz. ................ **22.00**

**Tumbler,** juice, pressed Caprice patt., Moonlight, 5 oz. .............................. **135.00**

**Tumbler,** juice, footed, pressed Caprice patt., Moonlight, 5 oz. ............ **40.00**

**Tumbler,** flat, pressed Caprice patt., Moonlight, 5 oz. .............................. **48.00**

**Tumbler,** footed, pressed Caprice patt., Moonlight, 5 oz. ....................... **60.00**

**Tumbler,** old fashioned, pressed Caprice patt., Moonlight, 7 oz. .......... **140.00**

**Tumbler,** footed, pressed Caprice patt., Crystal, 10 oz........................ **20.00**

**Tumbler,** water, footed, pressed Caprice patt., Moonlight, 10 oz........... **35.00**

**Tumbler,** footed, etched Cleo patt., blue, 10 oz. ....................................... **55.00**

**Tumbler,** footed, Decagon line, Moonlight, 10 oz. ............................. **28.00**

**Tumbler,** etched Rose Point patt., Crystal, 10 oz...................................... **27.00**

**Tumbler,** pressed Caprice patt., Moonlight, 12 oz. ............................. **58.00**

**Tumbler,** iced tea, two-footed, pressed Caprice patt., Moonlight, 12 oz. .......... **45.00**

**Tumbler,** footed, Decagon line, Moonlight, 12 oz. ............................. **43.00**

**Tumbler,** Forest Green, in Farberware holder, 12 oz. ................. **28.00**

**Tumbler,** iced tea, etched Diane patt., Crystal, 5½" h., 15 oz. ....................... **60.00**

**Tumbler,** iced tea, footed, etched Apple Blossom patt., yellow............... **35.00**

**Tumbler,** juice, footed, etched Apple Blossom patt., green.......................... **30.00**

**Tumbler,** juice, footed, etched Apple Blossom patt., yellow......................... **24.00**

**Tumbler set:** various colors, in Faberware holders; 12 oz., 5" h., 6 pcs. ................................................. **110.00**

**Vase,** 4½" h., pressed Caprice patt., Moonlight..................................... **175.00**

**Vase,** 5½" h., pressed Caprice patt., Moonlight..................................... **150.00**

**Vase,** 6½" h., globe-form, etched Rose Point patt., Crystal.................. **180.00**

**Vase,** 7" h., footed, Mt. Vernon line, Crystal ................................................. **30.00**

**Vase,** 7" h., sweet pea-type (tall, slender w/ruffled rim), Rubina (ruby top blending to yellowish green) ....... **125.00**

**Vase,** 10" h., etched Rose Point patt. (No. 1242), Crystal ............ **200.00**

**Vase,** 10" h., slender, etched Rose Point patt. (No. 274), Crystal ............ **85.00**

**Vase,** 12" h., gold-rimmed, etched Rose Point patt., Crystal.................. **185.00**

**Whiskey,** two-footed, pressed Caprice patt., Moonlight, 2½ oz. .................... **225.00**

**Wine,** etched Apple Blossom patt., yellow................................................ **40.00**

**Wine,** Decagon line, Cobalt blue.......... **40.00**

**Wine,** Decagon line, Moonlight ............ **35.00**

**Wine,** etched Diane patt. Crystal, 2½ oz. .................................................. **45.00**

**Wine,** etched Rose Point patt., Crystal, 3½ oz..................................... **55.00**

**Wine,** Mt. Vernon patt., Crystal, 3 oz. ... **14.00**

**Wine,** Statuesque line, Amber bowl, clear Nude Lady stem...................... **325.00**

**Wine,** Statuesque line, Royal Blue bowl, clear Nude Lady stem ............ **395.00**

## CARNIVAL GLASS

*Earlier called Taffeta glass, the Carnival glass now being collected was introduced early in this century. Its producers gave it an iridescence that attempted to imitate that of some Tiffany glass. Collectors should look for books by leading authorities Donald E. Moore, Sherman Hand, Marion T. Hartung, Rose M. Presznick and Bill Edwards.*

### ACANTHUS (Imperial)

**Bowl,** 7" d., green .............................. $20.00
**Bowl,** 7" d., marigold............................ 48.00
**Bowl,** 7½" d., purple............................ 80.00
**Bowl,** 7¾" d., marigold......................... 45.00
**Bowl,** 7¾" d., smoky............................. 50.00
**Bowl,** 8" to 9" d., green ........................ 87.00
**Bowl,** 8" to 9" d., marigold .................. 106.00
**Bowl,** 8" to 9" d., purple ....................... 95.00
**Bowl,** 8" to 9" d., smoky ........................ 79.00
**Plate,** 9" to 10" d., marigold ................ 194.00
**Plate,** 9" to 10" d., smoky.................... 250.00
**Plate,** chop, marigold......... 110.00 to 140.00

### ADVERTISING & SOUVENIR ITEMS

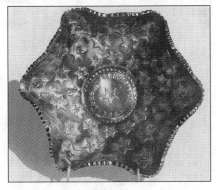

*"Bernheimer Brothers" Bowl*

**Basket,** "Feldman Bros. Furniture, Salisbury, Md.," open edge, marigold............................................. 68.00
**Basket,** "John H. Brand Furniture Co., Wilmington, Del.," marigold ................ 60.00
**Basket,** "Miller's Furniture," marigold.... 85.00
**Bell,** souvenir, BPOE Elks, "Atlantic City, 1911," blue ........................... 2,000.00
**Bell,** souvenir, BPOE Elks, "Parkersburg, 1914," blue.............. 1,250.00
**Bonbon,** "Isaac Benesch," Holly Sprig patt., purple..................................... 350.00

**Bowl,** "Isaac Benesch," 6¼" d., purple (Millersburg) .................... 400.00 to 450.00
**Bowl,** "H. Mayday & Co., 1910," 8½" d., Wild Blackberry patt., purple ............................. 190.00 to 350.00
**Bowl,** "Bernheimer Brothers," blue (ILLUS. bottom previous column) ..................... 1,500.00 to 1,750.00
**Bowl,** "Central Shoe Store," purple..... 185.00
**Bowl,** "Dreibus Parfait Sweets," ruffled, smoky lavender ................... 400.00
**Bowl,** "Horlacher" green..................... 110.00
**Bowl,** "Horlacher" marigold ............... 120.00
**Bowl,** "Horlacher" Butterfly patt., purple........................................... 125.00
**Bowl,** "Horlacher" Peacock Tail patt., green ..................................................... 94.00
**Bowl,** "Horlacher" Peacock Tail patt., purple................................................... 60.00
**Bowl,** "Horlacher" Thistle patt., green.... 175.00
**Bowl,** "Horlacher" Thistle patt., purple ................................. 80.00 to 95.00
**Bowl,** "Horlacher" Vintage patt., marigold ............................................. 130.00
**Bowl,** "Morris Smith" ruffled, purple............................................ 1,250.00
**Bowl,** "Ogden Furniture Co." purple.... 225.00
**Bowl,** "Sterling Furniture" purple......... 600.00
**Bowl,** souvenir, BPOE Elks, "Atlantic City, 1911" blue, one-eyed Elk ......... 954.00
**Bowl,** souvenir, BPOE Elks, "Detroit, 1910" blue, one-eyed Elk.................. 550.00
**Bowl,** souvenir, BPOE Elks, "Detroit, 1910" green, one-eyed Elk ............... 900.00
**Bowl,** souvenir, BPOE Elks, "Detroit, 1910" ruffled, green ...................... 500.00
**Bowl,** souvenir, BPOE Elks, "Detroit, 1910" purple, one-eyed Elk ............. 385.00
**Bowl,** souvenir, BPOE Elks, "Detroit, 1910" purple, two-eyed Elk (Millersburg) ................................... 775.00
**Bowl,** souvenir, "Brooklyn Bridge," marigold .......................... 350.00 to 400.00
**Bowl,** souvenir, "Brooklyn Bridge" unlettered, marigold ......... 475.00 to 500.00
**Bowl,** souvenir, "Millersburg Courthouse," purple........................ 655.00
**Bowl,** souvenir, "Millersburg Courthouse," unlettered, purple..... 1,000.00
**Card tray,** "Fern Brand Chocolates," turned-up sides, purple, 6¼" d......... 175.00
**Card tray,** "Isaac Benesch," Holly Whirl patt., marigold........................ 102.00
**Dish,** "Compliments of Pacific Coast Mail Order House, Los Angeles, California" ............................................. 700.00
**Hat,** "Arthur O'Dell," green .................. 75.00

**Hat,** "General Furniture Co.," 1910,
Peacock Tail patt., green ................... **75.00**
**Hat,** "Horlacher," Peacock Tail patt.,
green ................................................... **70.00**
**Hat,** "John Brand Furniture," green ....... **42.00**
**Hat,** "John Brand Furniture," open
edge, marigold ................................... **45.00**
**Hat,** "Miller's Furniture - Harrisburg,"
basketweave, marigold ...................... **75.00**
**Paperweight,** souvenir, BPOE Elks,
green .................................................. **625.00**
**Paperweight,** souvenir, BPOE Elks,
purple (Millersburg) .......... **600.00 to 700.00**
**Plate,** "Ballard, California," purple
(Northwood) ..................................... **900.00**
**Plate,** "Bird of Paradise," purple .......... **500.00**
**Plate,** "Brazier Candies," w/handgrip,
6" d., purple ..................... **500.00 to 600.00**
**Plate,** "Campbell & Beesley,"
w/handgrip, purple ........................ **1,250.00**
**Plate,** "Central Shoe," flat, purple ..... **1,200.00**
**Plate,** "Davidson Chocolate Society,"
6¼" d., purple ................................. **500.00**
**Plate,** "Dreibus Parfait Sweets,"
6¼" d., purple ................................. **400.00**
**Plate,** "Eagle Furniture Co.," purple  .. **750.00**
**Plate,** "Fern Brand Chocolates,"
6" d., purple ..................................... **800.00**
**Plate,** "Gervitz Bros., Furniture &
Clothing," w/handgrip, 6" d.,
purple .......................... **1,300.00 to 1,500.00**
**Plate,** "Greengard Furniture Co.,"
purple ................................................ **625.00**
**Plate,** "E. A. Hudson Furniture Co.,"
7" d., purple (Northwood) ................. **500.00**
**Plate,** "Jockey Club," w/handgrip,
6" d., purple ..................................... **500.00**
**Plate,** "Old Rose Distillery," Grape &
Cable patt., stippled, 9" d., green ..... **370.00**
**Plate,** "Roods Chocolate, Pueblo,"
purple ................................................ **750.00**
**Plate,** "Season's Greetings - Eat
Paradise Soda Candies," 6" d.,
purple ................................................ **178.00**
**Plate,** "Morris N. Smith," purple .......... **250.00**
**Plate,** "Spector's Department Store,"
Heart & Vine patt., 9" d.,
marigold .......................... **600.00 to 900.00**
**Plate,** "Utah Liquor Co.," w/handgrip,
6" d., purple  ................................. **1,800.00**
**Plate,** "We Use Brocker's," 7" d.,
purple ................................................ **495.00**
**Plate,** souvenir, BPOE Elks, "Atlantic
City, 1911," blue .............. **800.00 to 900.00**
**Plate,** souvenir, BPOE Elks,
"Parkersburg, 1914," 7½" d., blue.. **2,000.00**
**Plate,** "E. A. Hudson Furniture Co.,"
w/handgrip, purple ........................ **1,450.00**
**Vase,** "Howard Furniture," Four Pillars
patt., green ....................................... **65.00**

## APPLE BLOSSOMS

**Bowl,** 5" d., marigold ............................ **40.00**
**Bowl,** 5½" d., purple ............................. **43.00**
**Bowl,** 6" d., marigold ............................ **22.00**
**Bowl,** 6" d., deep, purple ...................... **30.00**
**Bowl,** 7" d., collared base, marigold ..... **34.00**
**Bowl,** 7" d., collared base, peach
opalescent .......................... **75.00 to 110.00**
**Bowl,** 7" d., collared base, purple ......... **78.00**
**Bowl,** 7" d., ribbon candy rim,
marigold .............................. **30.00 to 45.00**
**Bowl,** 7" d., ribbon candy rim, white.... **135.00**
**Bowl,** 9" d., three-in-one edge, peach
opalescent ....................................... **130.00**
**Rose bowl,** marigold ............................. **65.00**
**Tumbler,** enameled, blue ...................... **85.00**
**Water set:** pitcher & one tumbler;
enameled, blue, 2 pcs. .................... **200.00**

## APRIL SHOWERS (Fenton)

**Vase,** 8" h., green ................................. **40.00**
**Vase,** 8" h., marigold ............................ **50.00**
**Vase,** 8½" h., Peacock Tail interior,
purple ................................................. **85.00**
**Vase,** 9" h., piecrust edge, blue ............ **60.00**
**Vase,** 10" h., blue ................................. **50.00**
**Vase,** 10" h., teal ................................. **65.00**
**Vase,** 10½" h., Peacock Tail interior,
blue .................................................... **75.00**

*April Showers Vase*

**Vase,** 11" h., blue (ILLUS.).................... **80.00**
**Vase,** 11" h., Peacock Tail interior,
green .................................................. **80.00**
**Vase,** 11" h., Peacock Tail interior,
purple ................................................. **55.00**
**Vase,** 11½" h., marigold ........................ **38.00**
**Vase,** 12" h., blue ................................. **65.00**
**Vase,** 12" h., green ............................... **65.00**

**Vase,** 12" h., Peacock Tail interior,
marigold.............................................. **35.00**
**Vase,** 12" h., Peacock Tail interior,
purple ............................ **55.00 to 60.00**
**Vase,** 12" h., vaseline ........................ **110.00**
**Vase,** green.......................................... **45.00**
**Vase,** purple opalescent ..... **700.00 to 750.00**

## BASKET (FENTON'S OPEN EDGE)

**Amber**........................... **200.00 to 250.00**
**Amberina**.................................... **200.00**
**Amberina,** w/two rows, two sides
turned up ...................................... **125.00**
**Aqua**................................. **100.00 to 125.00**
**Aqua,** w/two rows, jack-in-the-pulpit
shape ............................. **100.00 to 125.00**
**Aqua,** w/two rose, two sides turned up .. **110.00**
**Aqua,** two sides turned up ................... **80.00**
**Aqua opalescent** .............. **225.00 to 250.00**
**Black amethyst** .............................. **365.00**
**Blue**.................................................... **59.00**
**Blue,** jack-in-the-pulpit shape .............. **75.00**
**Blue,** w/two rows................................. **45.00**
**Celeste blue** ...................................... **91.00**
**Green** ................................................. **53.00**
**Green,** four sides turned up ............... **225.00**
**Green,** hat shape ............................... **200.00**
**Green,** jack-in-the-pulpit shape.......... **300.00**
**Green,** low sides ................................ **200.00**
**Ice blue,** w/two rows, open edge,
six ruffled ....................................... **500.00**
**Ice blue,** w/three rows........................ **550.00**
**Ice green**........................................... **240.00**
**Ice green,** w/three rows...... **350.00 to 400.00**
**Lavender** ........................................... **110.00**
**Marigold,** 5" h., w/applied crystal
handle.............................................. **75.00**
**Marigold** ............................. **35.00 to 45.00**
**Marigold,** jack-in-the-pulpit shape ........ **35.00**
**Marigold,** w/two rows........................... **41.00**
**Purple** ............................................... **110.00**
**Red**.................................................... **425.00**
**Red,** hat shape .................. **450.00 to 500.00**
**Red,** jack-in-the-pulpit
shape ............................. **450.00 to 525.00**
**Red,** w/two rows, small ....... **325.00 to 350.00**
**Reverse Amberina**............................ **650.00**
**Vaseline**.............................................. **87.00**
**Vaseline,** jack-in-the-pulpit shape,
small ............................................... **125.00**
**Vaseline,** plain interior ...................... **275.00**
**Vaseline,** w/marigold overlay,
small ............................................... **275.00**
**Vaseline,** w/two rows, large ................. **64.00**
**White,** round ....................................... **55.00**
**White,** square...................................... **75.00**
**White,** w/two rows................................ **18.00**

**White,** w/two rows, four sides
turned up ........................................ **110.00**
**White,** 6" ............................. **200.00 to 225.00**
**White,** 9" d. .......................................... **95.00**

## BEADED SHELL (Dugan or Diamond Glass Co.)

*Beaded Shell Mug*

**Berry set:** master bowl & four footed
sauce dishes; purple, 5 pcs. ............. **195.00**
**Bowl,** master berry, marigold............... **54.00**
**Bowl,** 8½" d., footed, purple............... **165.00**
**Butter dish,** cov., purple..................... **160.00**
**Creamer,** marigold ............................. **65.00**
**Creamer,** purple.................................. **64.00**
**Mug,** blue........................... **150.00 to 200.00**
**Mug,** marigold .................................. **105.00**
**Mug,** purple (ILLUS. above).................. **80.00**
**Mug,** purple, souvenir ........................ **150.00**
**Mug,** vaseline, souvenir ....................... **50.00**
**Mug,** white...................................... **1,000.00**
**Pitcher,** water, marigold..................... **300.00**
**Pitcher,** water, purple ........................ **530.00**
**Sauce dish,** marigold............................ **30.00**
**Sauce dish,** purple .............................. **42.00**
**Spooner,** footed, marigold .................... **54.00**
**Sugar bowl,** cov., marigold................... **55.00**
**Sugar bowl,** open, marigold ................ **45.00**
**Table set,** marigold, 4 pcs. ................. **275.00**
**Table set,** purple, 4 pcs. ..................... **525.00**
**Tumbler,** blue .................................... **134.00**
**Tumbler,** lavender ................................ **80.00**
**Tumbler,** marigold ................................ **48.00**
**Tumbler,** purple...................... **70.00 to 75.00**
**Water set:** pitcher & one tumbler;
purple, 2 pcs. ................................... **550.00**
**Water set:** pitcher & six tumblers;
marigold, 7 pcs. ............................... **700.00**

## BIRD WITH GRAPES

*Bird with Grapes Wall Vase*

**Wall vase,** marigold, 7½" w.,
8" h. (ILLUS.) ...................................... **97.00**

## BLACKBERRY (Fenton)

**Basket,** aqua....................................... **150.00**
**Basket,** amber ...................................... **85.00**
**Basket,** blue.......................................... **42.00**
**Basket,** clambroth................................. **45.00**
**Basket,** green ...................................... **100.00**
**Basket,** marigold.................................. **58.00**
**Basket,** purple ..................... **95.00 to 120.00**
**Basket,** red........................ **300.00 to 600.00**
**Basket,** smoky w/marigold overlay ....... **75.00**
**Bowl,** 5" d., purple................................ **30.00**
**Bowl,** 7" d., ruffled, marigold................. **30.00**
**Bowl,** 7" d., purple................................ **80.00**
**Bowl,** 7" d., red .................................. **185.00**
**Bowl,** 8" to 9" d., ruffled, green ............. **90.00**
**Bowl,** 8" to 9" d., ruffled, marigold ........ **50.00**
**Bowl,** 8" to 9" d., ruffled, purple ............ **58.00**
**Bowl,** 10" d., ruffled, blue.................... **650.00**
**Bowl,** 10" d., ruffled, green ................. **125.00**
**Bowl,** 10" d., ruffled, purple................. **125.00**

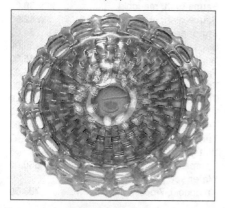

*Blackberry Plate*

**Bowl,** nut, open edge, Basketweave
exterior, purple................................... **60.00**
**Cuspidor,** blue............................... **2,700.00**
**Plate,** openwork rim, marigold
(ILLUS. bottom previous
column) ........................... **500.00 to 525.00**
**Plate,** openwork rim, white... **500.00 to 750.00**
**Vase,** whimsey, open edge, blue
opalescent ....................................... **900.00**
**Vase,** whimsey, open edge,
marigold.......................................... **650.00**

## BLACKBERRY SPRAY

**Basket,** medium, red........................... **300.00**
**Bonbon,** marigold ............................... **30.00**
**Bonbon,** red...................................... **300.00**
**Bowl,** 7" d., marigold............................ **20.00**
**Bowl,** 7" d., red ................................. **245.00**
**Compote,** 5½" d., green ...................... **42.00**
**Compote,** 5½" d., marigold................... **38.00**
**Compote,** 5½" d., purple...................... **95.00**
**Hat shape,** amber .............................. **108.00**
**Hat shape,** Amberina ........ **300.00 to 350.00**
**Hat shape,** amethyst opalescent ........ **295.00**
**Hat shape,** aqua .................................. **58.00**
**Hat shape,** jack-in-the-pulpit, crimped
rim, aqua........................................... **150.00**
**Hat shape,** aqua opalescent.............. **475.00**
**Hat shape,** jack-in-the-pulpit, aqua
opalescent ...................................... **300.00**
**Hat shape,** blue .................................. **39.00**
**Hat shape,** jack-in-the-pulpit, crimped
rim, blue............................................. **69.00**
**Hat shape,** blue opalescent............... **585.00**
**Hat shape,** jack-in-the-pulpit, crimped
rim, clambroth.................................... **27.00**
**Hat shape,** green................. **75.00 to 150.00**
**Hat shape,** ice green
opalescent...................... **300.00 to 350.00**
**Hat shape,** jack-in-the-pulpit, lime
green w/marigold overlay ................. **35.00**
**Hat shape,** lime green opalescent ...... **325.00**
**Hat shape,** marigold ............................ **39.00**
**Hat shape,** milk white w/marigold
overlay ............................................... **145.00**
**Hat shape,** purple ............................... **53.00**
**Hat shape,** red ................................... **307.00**
**Hat shape,** red slag ........... **575.00 to 600.00**
**Hat shape,** Reverse Amberina ........... **450.00**
**Hat shape,** vaseline ............................ **72.00**
**Hat shape,** jack-in-the-pulpit, crimped
rim, vaseline ........................ **70.00 to 75.00**
**Hat shape,** vaseline w/marigold
overlay ............................................... **54.00**
**Hat shape,** white................................. **800.00**

## BUTTERFLIES (Fenton)

**Bonbon,** blue ....................................... **65.00**
**Bonbon,** green...................................... **55.00**

*Butterflies Bonbon*

*Cherry or Cherry Circles Bonbon*

**Bonbon,** marigold ................................. 40.00
**Bonbon,** purple (ILLUS. above) ............ 62.00

## BUTTERFLY & FERN (Fenton)

**Pitcher,** water, blue............................ 538.00
**Pitcher,** water, green ......................... 425.00
**Pitcher,** water, marigold ..... 325.00 to 350.00
**Pitcher,** water, purple ......................... 385.00
**Tumbler,** amber ................................... 45.00
**Tumbler,** blue ...................................... 54.00
**Tumbler,** green .................................... 56.00
**Tumbler,** marigold .............................. 44.00
**Tumbler,** pastel marigold..................... 35.00
**Tumbler,** purple ................................... 50.00
**Water set:** pitcher & four tumblers;
  blue, 5 pcs...................... 800.00 to 850.00
**Water set:** pitcher & four tumblers;
  purple, 5 pcs.................... 650.00 to 700.00
**Water set:** pitcher & five tumblers;
  marigold, 6 pcs. ............................. 800.00
**Water set:** pitcher & six tumblers;
  green, 7 pcs.................................... 850.00

## CAROLINA DOGWOOD

**Bowl,** 8½" d., blue
  opalescent........................ 400.00 to 425.00
**Bowl,** 8½" d., marigold......................... 65.00
**Bowl,** 8½" d., milk white w/marigold
  overlay ............................ 200.00 to 250.00
**Bowl,** 8½" d., peach opalescent ......... 145.00
**Bride's bowl,** peach opalescent......... 325.00
**Plate,** 8½" d., peach opalescent ......... 475.00

## CATTAILS & WATER LILY - See Water Lily & Cattails Pattern

## CHERRY or CHERRY CIRCLES (Fenton)

**Bonbon,** two-handled, aqua .............. 280.00
**Bonbon,** two-handled, blue ............... 100.00
**Bonbon,** two-handled,
  marigold .............................. 45.00 to 50.00

**Bonbon,** two-handled, purple .............. 50.00
**Bonbon,** two-handled, red
  (ILLUS. above) ............................. 7,250.00
**Bowl,** 5" d., fluted, blue........................ 33.00
**Bowl,** 5" d., marigold............................ 32.00
**Bowl,** 5" d., purple............................... 40.00
**Bowl,** 6" d., ruffled, marigold............... 40.00
**Bowl,** 7" d., three-footed, marigold ....... 40.00
**Bowl,** 7" d., three-footed, peach
  opalescent w/plain interior ................ 90.00
**Bowl,** 8" to 9" d., marigold ................... 30.00
**Bowl,** 8" to 9" d., white......................... 70.00
**Bowl,** 10" d., vaseline w/marigold
  overlay ............................................. 75.00
**Bowl,** 10" d., ruffled, white ................. 100.00
**Card tray,** aqua................................. 125.00
**Plate,** 6" d., blue................................ 100.00
**Plate,** 6" d., marigold........................... 40.00
**Plate,** 6" d., Orange Tree exterior,
  marigold ........................................... 80.00
**Plate,** 6" d., purple ............. 200.00 to 250.00
**Plate,** 7" d., marigold ......... 150.00 to 200.00
**Plate,** chop, white............................... 500.00

## CHERRY CIRCLES - See Cherry (Fenton) Pattern

## CIRCLED SCROLL (Dugan or Diamond Glass Co.)

**Berry set:** master bowl & three sauce
  dishes; purple, 4 pcs........................ 275.00
**Berry set:** master bowl & four sauce
  dishes; marigold, 5 pcs. ..................... 75.00
**Bowl,** master berry, marigold............... 35.00
**Bowl,** master berry, purple................... 75.00
**Bowl,** small, triangular-shaped,
  marigold ........................................... 50.00
**Creamer,** marigold .............................. 65.00
**Creamer,** purple................................. 110.00
**Pitcher,** water,
  marigold ................... 1,000.00 to 1,200.00
**Plate,** chop, smoky blue.................. 1,900.00
**Sauce dish,** marigold........................... 35.00
**Sauce dish,** purple .............................. 38.00

*Circled Scroll Tumbler*

**Spooner,** marigold .............................. 125.00
**Spooner,** purple .................................... 63.00
**Tumbler,** clambroth ............................. 75.00
**Tumbler,** marigold (ILLUS. above) ..... 200.00
**Tumbler,** purple .................................. 450.00
**Vase,** 7" h., purple .............. 300.00 to 325.00
**Vase,** 7½" h., marigold ......................... 60.00
**Vase,** 7½" h., purple ........................... 145.00
**Vase,** 9" h., marigold ........................... 78.00
**Vase,** hat-shaped, marigold ................. 66.00
**Vase,** hat-shaped, purple .................. 110.00
**Vase,** jack-in-the-pulpit shape,
  blue .................................................. 100.00
**Water set:** pitcher & six tumblers;
  marigold, 7 pcs ............................. 1,150.00
**Whimsey,** jack-in-the-pulpit shape,
  marigold .......................................... 125.00

### COMET or RIBBON TIE (Fenton)

*Comet Bowl*

**Bowl,** 8" to 9" d., blue .......................... 65.00
**Bowl,** 8" to 9" d., green ....................... 45.00
**Bowl,** 8" to 9" d., ribbon candy rim,
  lavender ............................................ 88.00
**Bowl,** 8" to 9" d., marigold (ILLUS.
  bottom previous column) .................. 45.00
**Bowl,** 8" to 9" d., purple ...................... 62.00
**Bowl,** ribbon candy rim, green ............. 88.00
**Plate,** 9" d., ruffled, blue..................... 400.00
**Plate,** 9" d., ruffled, marigold.............. 200.00
**Plate,** 9" d., ruffled, purple.................. 250.00
**Plate,** 9" d., red ............................... 1,500.00

### CORN BOTTLE

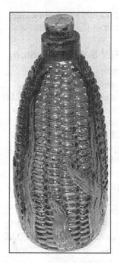

*Corn Bottle*

**Green**................................. 225.00 to 250.00
**Ice green** .......................... 250.00 to 275.00
**Marigold** .......................................... 248.00
**Smoky** (ILLUS.)................. 250.00 to 300.00

### CORNUCOPIA

**Candlestick,** ice blue............................ 75.00
**Candlestick,** white............................... 85.00
**Candlesticks,** ice blue, pr................... 115.00
**Candlesticks,** white, pr. ...................... 88.00
**Vase,** 5" h., marigold............................ 25.00

### CRACKLE

**Automobile vase w/bracket,**
  marigold............................................. 25.00
**Automobile vases,** marigold, pr.
  (no brackets) ..................................... 20.00
**Bowl,** 7½" d., marigold.......................... 18.00
**Candy jar,** cov., marigold...................... 25.00
**Cuspidor,** marigold.............................. 59.00

**Plate,** 6" d., marigold............................. 40.00
**Plate,** 7½" d., marigold......................... 13.00
**Plate,** 8" d., marigold............................. 20.00
**Plate,** 9½" d., purple............................. 40.00
**Plate,** chop, 12" d., marigold................. 45.00
**Rose bowl,** low, marigold..................... 28.00
**Salt & pepper shakers w/original
    tops,** light blue, pr. ............................ 35.00
**Tumbler,** green....................................... 37.00
**Tumbler,** dome-footed, marigold ......... 12.00
**Vase,** fan-shaped, marigold ................. 24.00
**Wall pocket,** marigold........................... 28.00
**Water set:** pitcher & six footed
    tumblers; marigold, 7 pcs. ................ 135.00

## DAISIES & DRAPE VASE (Northwood)

**Aqua** ..................................................... 173.00
**Aqua opalescent**................................ 557.00

*Daisies & Drape Vase*

**Cobalt blue** (ILLUS.) .......................... 900.00
**Green**.............................................. 4,500.00
**Ice blue** ......................................... 1,200.00
**Ice green**....................................... 1,500.00
**Marigold** ........................................... 700.00
**Purple** .............................................. 800.00
**White**................................................. 250.00

## DANDELION, PANELED (Fenton)

**Pitcher,** water, blue............................. 450.00
**Pitcher,** water, green .......................... 713.00
**Pitcher,** water, marigold...................... 448.00
**Pitcher,** water, purple ........ 400.00 to 500.00
**Tumbler,** blue ....................................... 46.00
**Tumbler,** green...................................... 70.00
**Tumbler,** marigold ................................ 40.00
**Tumbler,** purple .................................... 40.00
**Water set:** pitcher & six tumblers;
    blue, 7 pcs. ...................................... 950.00
**Water set:** pitcher & six tumblers;
    green, 7 pcs. ................................. 1,012.00

**Water set:** pitcher & six tumblers;
    marigold, 7 pcs. .............................. 550.00
**Water set:** pitcher & six tumblers;
    purple, 7 pcs. ................................. 650.00

## DIAMOND & RIB VASE (Fenton)

**Vase,** 5½" h., marigold....................... 125.00
**Vase,** 6" h., green ................................ 40.00
**Vase,** 7" h., green ................................ 25.00
**Vase,** 7" h., marigold............................ 25.00
**Vase,** 7" h., purple................................ 34.00
**Vase,** 8" h., green ................................ 22.00
**Vase,** 8" h., white ................................ 75.00
**Vase,** 9" h., green ................. 30.00 to 35.00
**Vase,** 9½" h., green............................. 90.00
**Vase,** 10" h., blue................................. 53.00
**Vase,** 10" h., green............................... 40.00
**Vase,** 10" h., marigold.......................... 35.00
**Vase,** 10" h., purple .............. 30.00 to 35.00
**Vase,** 10" h., white ............................... 85.00
**Vase,** 11" h., aqua................................ 40.00
**Vase,** 11" h., blue................................. 55.00
**Vase,** 11" h., green............................... 38.00
**Vase,** 11" h., ice green......................... 80.00
**Vase,** 11" h., marigold.......................... 70.00
**Vases,** 11" h., purple, pr....................... 63.00
**Vase,** 12" h., blue................................. 32.00
**Vase,** 12" h., green .............................. 26.00
**Vase,** 12" h., purple.............................. 33.00
**Vase,** 13" h., blue................................. 35.00
**Vase,** 14½" h., blue.............................. 32.00
**Vase,** 15" h., marigold.......................... 55.00
**Vase,** 16" h., green ............................ 390.00
**Vase,** 16" h., marigold.......................... 20.00
**Vase,** 16" h., purple .............. 50.00 to 75.00
**Vase,** 16½" h., blue............................ 110.00
**Vase,** 19" h., purple.............................. 95.00
**Vase,** 19" h., funeral, purple............. 1,150.00
**Vase,** 20" h., marigold........................ 300.00
**Vase,** funeral, green......................... 1,500.00

## DIAMOND LACE (Imperial)

**Bowl,** 8" to 9" d., clambroth ................. 65.00
**Bowl,** 8" to 9" d., marigold ................... 40.00
**Bowl,** 8" to 9" d., purple.......... 65.00 to 75.00
**Bowl,** 10" d., purple.............................. 73.00
**Pitcher,** water, purple ........................ 300.00
**Sauce dish,** marigold, 5" d. ................. 25.00
**Sauce dish,** purple, 5" d. ..................... 35.00
**Tumbler,** marigold .............................. 425.00
**Tumbler,** purple .................................... 53.00
**Water set:** pitcher & four tumblers;
    purple, 5 pcs.................... 425.00 to 450.00

## DIVING DOLPHINS FOOTED BOWL
   (Sowerby)

**Aqua blue,** embossed scroll interior ... 325.00
**Marigold,** embossed scroll interior ..... 110.00
**Marigold** ........................................... 150.00
**Purple** .............................................. 500.00

## DRAGON & LOTUS (Fenton)

**Bowl,** 7" to 9" d., three-footed,
blue .................................. **60.00 to 65.00**
**Bowl,** 7" to 9" d., three-footed, green.... **85.00**
**Bowl,** 7" to 9" d., three-footed,
lavender ......................................... **125.00**
**Bowl,** 7" to 9" d., three-footed, lime
green opalescent ............................ **500.00**
**Bowl,** 7" to 9" d., three-footed,
purple................................................. **70.00**
**Bowl,** 8" to 9" d., collared base,
amber .............................. **200.00 to 225.00**
**Bowl,** 8" to 9" d., collared base,
blue ............................... **95.00 to 125.00**
**Bowl,** 8" to 9" d., collared base,
green ............................................... **146.00**
**Bowl,** 8" to 9" d., collared base, lime
green ............................................... **325.00**
**Bowl,** 8" to 9" d., collared base, lime
green opalescent............. **500.00 to 550.00**
**Bowl,** 8" to 9" d., collared base,
marigold............................................. **70.00**
**Bowl,** 8" to 9" d., collared base,
moonstone.................................... **1,100.00**
**Bowl,** 8" to 9" d., collared base,
peach opalescent ........................... **500.00**
**Bowl,** 8" to 9" d., collared base,
purple ............................ **145.00 to 150.00**

*Dragon & Lotus Bowl*

**Bowl,** 8" to 9" d., collared base,
red (ILLUS.)................ **1,500.00 to 1,575.00**
**Bowl,** 9" d., ice cream shape, collared
base, amber.................................... **170.00**
**Bowl,** 9" d., ice cream shape, collared
base, aqua opalescent .................. **2,750.00**
**Bowl,** 9" d., ice cream shape,
collared base, blue .......................... **102.00**
**Bowl,** 9" d., ice cream shape, collared
base, marigold .................................. **75.00**
**Bowl,** 9" d., ice cream shape, collared
base, moonstone w/peach marigold
overlay .......................................... **1,250.00**

**Bowl,** 9" d., ice cream shape, collared
base, purple ..................................... **145.00**
**Bowl,** 9" d., ice cream shape, collared
base, red........................................ **2,500.00**
**Bowl,** 9" d., ice cream shape, collared
base, Reverse Amberina .................. **700.00**
**Bowl,** 9" d., marigold............................ **92.00**
**Bowl,** 9" d., three-in-one edge,
green ................................................ **148.00**
**Bowl,** ice cream shape, spade-footed,
purple................................................ **100.00**
**Bowl,** ruffled, blue................ **90.00 to 100.00**
**Bowl,** ruffled, spatula-footed,
green ................................................ **130.00**
**Bowl,** ruffled, lavender ....................... **195.00**
**Bowl,** ruffled, marigold........... **60.00 to 65.00**
**Bowl,** ruffled, marigold opalescent...... **675.00**
**Bowl,** ruffled, flat, peach opalescent... **450.00**
**Bowl,** ruffled, purple ............................. **88.00**
**Bowl,** marigold w/vaseline base ........ **190.00**
**Bowl,** moonstone .......................... **1,700.00**
**Bowl,** vaseline................................. **200.00**
**Bowl,** ruffled, Bearded Berry
exterior, amber ............................... **133.00**
**Bowl,** three-in-one edge, lavender...... **295.00**
**Bowl,** smoky ...................................... **425.00**
**Nut bowl,** marigold ............................ **225.00**
**Plate,** 9" d., marigold...................... **2,600.00**
**Plate,** collared base,
blue .......................... **1,500.00 to 2,000.00**
**Plate,** collared base, ruffled,
marigold ........................................ **2,200.00**
**Plate,** edge turned up, blue................. **250.00**
**Plate,** spatula-footed, marigold .......... **638.00**

## EMBROIDERED MUMS (Northwood)

*Embroidered Mums Bowl*

**Bonbon,** stemmed, white ............... **1,088.00**
**Bowl,** 8" to 9" d., amber................... **1,000.00**
**Bowl,** 8" to 9" d., ruffled, aqua
opalescent ..................................... **3,400.00**
**Bowl,** 8" to 9" d., blue ....................... **405.00**
**Bowl,** 8" to 9" d., ruffled, blue .......... **1,350.00**

**Bowl,** 8" to 9" d., blue, electric
iridescence ...................... **600.00 to 625.00**
**Bowl,** 8" to 9" d., ice
blue ................................ **900.00 to 925.00**
**Bowl,** 8" to 9" d., ice
green .............................. **850.00 to 900.00**
**Bowl,** 8" to 9" d., marigold ................. **500.00**
**Bowl,** 8" to 9" d., ruffled, marigold ...... **285.00**
**Bowl,** 8" to 9" d., pastel marigold ........ **500.00**
**Bowl,** 8" to 9" d., purple (ILLUS.
bottom previous page) ..................... **375.00**
**Bowl,** aqua ..................................... **1,400.00**
**Bowl,** lavender ............................... **1,600.00**
**Bowl,** lime green opalescent ............ **1,800.00**
**Bowl,** piecrust rim, sapphire blue ..... **2,700.00**
**Plate,** ice green .............................. **2,267.00**

## FARMYARD (Dugan)

*Farmyard Bowl*

**Bowl,** green ..................................... **6,000.00**
**Bowl,** peach opalescent .................. **9,000.00**

**Bowl,** purple ................................... **2,600.00**
**Bowl,** fluted, purple ......................... **3,900.00**
**Bowl,** ribbon candy rim,
purple (ILLUS. previous
column) ..................... **4,000.00 to 4,500.00**
**Bowl,** square, purple ....................... **2,900.00**
**Plate,** 10" d., purple ......................... **6,000.00**

## FENTONIA

**Berry set:** master bowl & four sauce
dishes; marigold, 5 pcs. ................... **175.00**
**Bowl,** master berry, blue ................... **263.00**
**Bowl,** master berry, marigold ............... **55.00**
**Butter dish,** cov., footed, blue ........... **150.00**
**Butter dish,** cov., footed,
marigold ......................................... **138.00**
**Creamer,** blue ................................... **100.00**
**Creamer,** marigold ............................... **60.00**
**Pitcher,** water, marigold ..................... **225.00**
**Sauce dish,** claw feet, blue ................. **44.00**
**Sauce dish,** claw feet, marigold ........... **22.00**
**Spooner,** blue ..................................... **85.00**
**Spooner,** marigold ............................... **60.00**
**Sugar bowl,** cov., blue ....................... **115.00**
**Table set:** creamer, cov. sugar bowl
& spooner; blue, 3 pcs. .................... **350.00**
**Table set,** marigold, 4 pcs. ................. **350.00**
**Tumbler,** blue ..................................... **73.00**
**Tumbler,** marigold ............................... **47.00**
**Water set:** pitcher & two tumblers;
marigold, 3 pcs. ............................... **623.00**
**Water set:** pitcher & three tumblers;
marigold, 4 pcs. ............................... **492.00**
**Water set:** pitcher & six tumblers;
blue, 7 pcs. (ILLUS. below) ............. **800.00**

*Fentonia Water Set*

*Floral & Grape Water Set*

## FLORAL & GRAPE (Dugan or Diamond Glass Co.)

**Pitcher,** water, blue ............ **300.00 to 350.00**
**Pitcher,** water, green ......................... **275.00**
**Pitcher,** water, marigold...................... **110.00**
**Pitcher,** water, purple ......................... **200.00**
**Pitcher,** water, white .......................... **475.00**
**Pitcher,** water, variant, white .............. **750.00**
**Tumbler,** black amethyst ...................... **80.00**
**Tumbler,** blue ...................................... **40.00**
**Tumbler,** green .................................. **175.00**
**Tumbler,** marigold ................................ **28.00**
**Tumbler,** purple .................................... **53.00**
**Tumbler,** white ........................ **75.00 to 85.00**
**Water set:** pitcher & six tumblers;
  blue, 7 pcs.(ILLUS. above) .............. **490.00**
**Water set:** pitcher & six tumblers;
  marigold, 7 pcs. ................ **300.00 to 375.00**
**Water set:** pitcher & six tumblers;
  white, 7 pcs...................................... **750.00**
**Whimsey,** hat-shaped (from tumbler
  mold), marigold.................................. **80.00**

## FLUTE (Northwood)

**Pitcher,** milk, marigold ......................... **20.00**
**Pitcher,** water, clambroth.................... **175.00**
**Salt dip,** footed, individual size,
  marigold............................................. **40.00**
**Salt dip,** footed, individual size,
  vaseline ............................................. **45.00**
**Salt dip,** master size, blue ................... **45.00**
**Salt dip,** master size, marigold ............. **51.00**
**Salt dip,** master size, vaseline.............. **95.00**
**Salt set:** master salt dip & four footed
  open salts; marigold, 5 pcs. .............. **140.00**
**Sugar bowl**........................................... **70.00**
**Tumbler,** dark marigold ........................ **95.00**

**Tumbler,** marigold ............................... **48.00**
**Tumbler,** marigold, variant................... **85.00**
**Vase,** 13" h., funeral, marigold............. **35.00**
**Vase,** funeral, green............................ **175.00**

## FOUR FLOWERS - See Pods & Posies Pattern

## GARDEN PATH

*Garden Path Variant Plate*

**Berry set:** master bowl & six sauce
  dishes; white, 7 pcs. ......................... **350.00**
**Bowl,** 6" d., peach opalescent,
  variant ............................................... **60.00**
**Bowl,** 6" d., ruffled, purple.................... **45.00**
**Bowl,** 6" d., ruffled, white..................... **45.00**
**Bowl,** 8" to 9" d., marigold ................... **68.00**
**Bowl,** 9" d., ice cream shape,
  marigold............................................. **60.00**

**Bowl,** 9" d., ice cream shape, purple .. **700.00**
**Bowl,** 10" d., ruffled,
marigold .............................. **75.00 to 95.00**
**Bowl,** 10" d., ruffled, peach
opalescent ....................................... **282.00**
**Bowl,** 10" d., ruffled,
white ............................... **300.00 to 325.00**
**Bowl,** fruit, peach opalescent,
variant............................................ **550.00**
**Bowl,** white, variant............................ **120.00**
**Plate,** 6" d., peach opalescent ............ **625.00**
**Plate,** 6" d., white .............................. **260.00**
**Plate,** 6½" d., white ............................ **400.00**
**Plate,** 7" d., peach opalescent ............ **500.00**
**Plate,** chop, 11" d., peach
opalescent ................................... **4,200.00**
**Plate,** chop, 11" d., purple............... **7,500.00**
**Plate,** peach opalescent, variant
(ILLUS. bottom previous page)......... **500.00**
**Sauce dish,** peach opalescent ............ **80.00**
**Sauce dish,** purple ............................. **75.00**

### GOD & HOME

**Pitcher,** blue ................................... **2,265.00**
**Tumbler,** blue ..................................... **150.00**
**Water set:** pitcher & six tumblers;
blue, 7 pcs. ................. **2,500.00 to 3,000.00**

### GRAPE & CABLE

**Banana boat,** amber.......................... **300.00**
**Banana boat,** blue.............. **400.00 to 450.00**
**Banana boat,** banded rim, stippled,
blue .......................... **1,000.00 to 1,200.00**
**Banana boat,** green........................... **352.00**
**Banana boat,** stippled, green ............. **400.00**
**Banana boat,** ice blue ........ **550.00 to 600.00**
**Banana boat,** purple........................... **265.00**
**Banana boat,** white ........... **650.00 to 685.00**
**Berry set:** master bowl & four sauce
dishes; purple, 5 pcs......................... **425.00**
**Berry set:** master bowl & five sauce
dishes; green, 6 pcs. ........................ **250.00**
**Bonbon,** two-handled, blue w/electric
iridescence ...................................... **295.00**
**Bonbon,** two-handled, stippled, blue .. **225.00**
**Bonbon,** two-handled, green............... **74.00**
**Bonbon,** two-handled, stippled,
green .............................. **100.00 to 125.00**
**Bonbon,** two-handled, marigold ........... **75.00**
**Bonbon,** two-handled, stippled,
marigold............................................. **50.00**
**Bonbon,** two-handled, purple .............. **88.00**
**Bonbon,** two-handled, white ............. **620.00**
**Bowl,** 5" d., ball-footed, aqua
opalescent (Fenton)........................... **45.00**
**Bowl,** 5" d., blue (Fenton) .................... **64.00**
**Bowl,** 5" d., green ............................... **93.00**
**Bowl,** 5" d., marigold........................... **38.00**
**Bowl,** 5" d., purple............................... **79.00**

**Bowl,** 6" d., ruffled, purple.................... **40.00**
**Bowl,** 6" d., red (Fenton) ................... **360.00**
**Bowl,** 6½" d., marigold......................... **38.00**
**Bowl,** 7" d., ice cream shape, aqua
(Fenton) .......................................... **300.00**
**Bowl,** 7" d., ice cream shape, ice
green ............................................... **315.00**
**Bowl,** 7" d., ruffled, vaseline (Fenton)... **48.00**
**Bowl,** 7" d., spatula-footed, green
(Fenton) ............................................ **85.00**
**Bowl,** 7" d., scalloped, Basketweave
exterior, purple.................................. **75.00**
**Bowl,** 7" sq., four sides turned up,
marigold............................................. **58.00**
**Bowl,** 7½" d., ball-footed, amber
(Fenton) ............................................ **90.00**
**Bowl,** 7½" d., ball-footed, aqua
(Fenton) ............................................ **96.00**
**Bowl,** 7½" d., ball-footed, blue (Fenton).. **65.00**
**Bowl,** 7½" d., ball-footed, green
(Fenton) ............................................ **42.00**
**Bowl,** 8" d., red (Fenton).................... **550.00**
**Bowl,** 8" d., ruffled, green ................... **65.00**
**Bowl,** 8" d., ruffled, vaseline ............... **65.00**
**Bowl,** 8½" d., crimped edge,
scalloped, green ............................... **85.00**
**Bowl,** 8½" d., ruffled, stippled, green.... **275.00**
**Bowl,** 8½" d., ruffled, stippled, ribbed
back, green ..................................... **495.00**
**Bowl,** 8½" d., scalloped, purple
(Northwood) ...................................... **95.00**
**Bowl,** 8¾" d., ruffled rim, purple........... **94.00**

*Grape & Cable Bowl*

**Bowl,** 8" to 9" d., piecrust rim, aqua
opalescent, Northwood (ILLUS.) ..... **3,900.00**
**Bowl,** 8" to 9" d., piecrust rim, blue
w/electric iridescence ...................... **300.00**
**Bowl,** 8" to 9" d., piecrust rim,
stippled, blue ................................... **303.00**
**Bowl,** 8" to 9" d., piecrust rim,
green ................................................ **105.00**
**Bowl,** 8" to 9" d., piecrust rim,
Basketweave exterior, green ........... **236.00**

**Bowl,** 8" to 9" d., piecrust rim, ice
blue .................................................. **1,000.00**
**Bowl,** 8" to 9" d., spatula-footed,
ruffled, purple (Northwood) ... **75.00 to 100.00**
**Bowl,** 8" to 9" d., stippled,
blue ................................... **375.00 to 400.00**
**Bowl,** 8" to 9" d., stippled, ruffled
w/Basketweave exterior, marigold .... **300.00**
**Bowl,** berry, 9" d.,
clambroth ........................... **75.00 to 100.00**
**Bowl,** berry, 9" d., green .................... **120.00**
**Bowl,** berry, 9" d., ice green............. **1,100.00**
**Bowl,** berry, 9" d., marigold.................. **95.00**
**Bowl,** berry, 9" d., purple ...................... **76.00**
**Bowl,** berry, 9" d., teal blue................. **125.00**
**Bowl,** 9" d., Basketweave exterior,
green ................................................... **78.00**
**Bowl,** orange, 10½" d., footed,
stippled, blue .................... **800.00 to 875.00**
**Bowl,** orange, 10½" d., footed,
clambroth........................................... **350.00**
**Bowl,** orange, 10½" d., footed,
stippled, blue w/electric iridescence
(Northwood) ..................... **800.00 to 825.00**
**Bowl,** orange, 10½" d., footed,
green ................................ **300.00 to 350.00**
**Bowl,** orange, 10½" d., footed, ice
blue ................................................. **1,250.00**
**Bowl,** orange, 10½" d., footed, ice
green .......................... **950.00 to 1,150.00**
**Bowl,** orange, 10½" d., footed,
marigold .......................... **175.00 to 225.00**
**Bowl,** orange, 10½" d., footed,
stippled, marigold ............................ **400.00**
**Bowl,** 11" d., ice cream shape,
green ............................... **750.00 to 850.00**
**Bowl,** 11" d., ice cream shape,
Basketweave exterior, green ......... **1,250.00**
**Bowl,** 11" d., ice cream shape,
ice blue ..................... **2,100.00 to 2,750.00**
**Bowl,** 11" d., ice cream shape, ice
green ......................... **1,200.00 to 1,500.00**
**Bowl,** 11" d., ice cream shape,
marigold............................................ **418.00**
**Bowl,** 11" d., ice cream shape,
Basketweave exterior,
marigold ......................... **150.00 to 200.00**
**Bowl,** 11" d., ice cream shape,
purple ............................. **300.00 to 325.00**
**Breakfast set:** individual size
creamer & sugar bowl; green, pr....... **172.00**
**Breakfast set:** individual size
creamer & sugar bowl; marigold, pr.. **140.00**
**Breakfast set:** individual size
creamer & sugar bowl; purple,
pr. ...................................... **200.00 to 250.00**
**Bride's basket,** purple.................... **2,975.00**
**Butter dish,** cov., amber.................. **115.00**
**Butter dish,** cov., green.................... **180.00**
**Butter dish,** cov., purple.................... **250.00**

**Candle lamp,** green .......... **650.00 to 700.00**
**Candle lamp,** marigold....... **500.00 to 550.00**
**Candle lamp,** purple........... **500.00 to 600.00**
**Candle lamp shade,** green .............. **750.00**
**Candle lamp shade,** marigold........... **210.00**
**Candle lamp shade,** purple............... **575.00**
**Candlestick,** green............................ **120.00**
**Candlestick,** marigold ......................... **72.00**
**Candlestick,** purple............ **150.00 to 175.00**
**Candlesticks,** blue, pr. ...................... **275.00**
**Candlesticks,** green, pr...................... **223.00**
**Candlesticks,** marigold, pr. ............... **235.00**
**Candlesticks,** purple, pr. ................... **243.00**
**Card tray,** green ............................... **350.00**
**Card tray,** horehound ........................ **80.00**
**Card tray,** marigold............................ **120.00**
**Card tray,** purple................................. **80.00**
**Cologne bottle w/stopper,**
green.............................. **250.00 to 275.00**
**Cologne bottle w/stopper,** ice blue... **950.00**
**Cologne bottle w/stopper,**
marigold............................................ **215.00**
**Cologne bottle w/stopper,**
purple ............................. **200.00 to 275.00**
**Cologne bottle w/stopper,** sapphire
blue.................................................. **795.00**
**Cologne bottle w/stopper,**
white.............................. **625.00 to 650.00**
**Cologne bottle w/stoppers,**
marigold, pr....................................... **450.00**
**Compote,** cov., large, green.............. **425.00**
**Compote,** cov., large, marigold ....... **1,450.00**
**Compote,** cov., small,
purple ............................. **350.00 to 400.00**
**Compote,** cov., large, purple .............. **450.00**
**Cracker jar,** cov., blue ...................... **500.00**
**Cracker jar,** cov., ice green ............... **800.00**
**Cracker jar,** cov., marigold ................ **425.00**
**Cracker jar,** cov., purple ................... **613.00**
**Cracker jar,** cov., white...................... **875.00**
**Creamer,** green.................................. **125.00**
**Creamer,** marigold ............................... **90.00**
**Creamer,** purple................................... **89.00**
**Creamer,** individual size, green ........... **65.00**
**Creamer,** individual size, marigold........ **65.00**
**Creamer,** individual size, purple .......... **75.00**
**Creamer & sugar bowl,** amber, pr..... **195.00**
**Creamer & sugar bowl,** green, pr...... **145.00**
**Creamer & sugar bowl,** marigold, pr. .. **75.00**
**Creamer & cov. sugar bowl,** purple,
pr. ...................................................... **278.00**
**Cup & saucer,** marigold ..................... **250.00**
**Cup & saucer,** purple ........................ **320.00**
**Cuspidor,** amber ............................. **3,000.00**
**Cuspidor,** purple.............................. **3,000.00**
**Decanter w/stopper,** whiskey,
marigold............................................ **540.00**
**Decanter w/stopper,** whiskey,
purple................................................ **825.00**

**Dish,** blue, 6" d..................................... **54.00**
**Pitcher,** water, 8¼" h., green.............. **413.00**
**Pitcher,** water, 8¼" h., marigold ......... **208.00**
**Pitcher,** water, 8¼" h., purple ............. **295.00**
**Pitcher,** tankard, 9¾" h., green........ **1,500.00**
**Pitcher,** tankard, 9¾" h., ice
   green............................................. **2,400.00**
**Pitcher,** tankard, 9¾" h., marigold ...... **540.00**
**Pitcher,** tankard, 9¾" h., purple .......... **600.00**
**Pitcher,** smoky..................................... **600.00**
**Plate,** 5" to 6" d., purple (Northwood) ... **167.00**
**Plate,** 7½" d., turned-up handgrip,
   green ............................................. **145.00**
**Plate,** 7½" d., turned-up handgrip,
   marigold ........................... **75.00 to 100.00**
**Plate,** 7½" d., turned-up handgrip,
   purple.............................................. **163.00**
**Plate,** 8" d., clambroth.......................... **850.00**
**Plate,** 8" d., footed, green (Fenton) .... **185.00**
**Plate,** 8" d., green (Northwood)........... **140.00**
**Plate,** 8" d., footed, marigold................ **92.00**
**Plate,** 8" d., footed, purple (Fenton).... **110.00**
**Plate,** 8" d., footed, purple ................... **84.00**
**Plate,** 8" d., purple .............. **225.00 to 275.00**
**Plate,** 9" d., blue.................................. **250.00**
**Plate,** 9" d., spatula-footed, blue ......... **150.00**
**Plate,** 9" d., stippled, blue ................... **600.00**
**Plate,** 9" d., stippled, green................. **302.00**
**Plate,** 9" d., stippled, green,
   variant ............................ **500.00 to 750.00**
**Plate,** 9" d., stippled, ice blue........... **1,700.00**
**Plate,** 9" d., stippled, marigold ............ **120.00**
**Punch bowl & base,** blue, 11" d.,
   2 pcs. .............................................. **395.00**
**Punch bowl & base,** green, 11" d.,
   2 pcs. .............................................. **600.00**
**Punch bowl & base,** marigold, 11" d.,
   2 pcs. .............................................. **250.00**
**Punch bowl & base,** purple, 11" d.,
   2 pcs. .............................................. **450.00**
**Punch cup,** marigold ............................. **28.00**
**Punch cup,** purple ................................. **29.00**
**Punch cup,** white .................................. **60.00**
**Punch set:** 11" bowl & six cups; blue,
   7 pcs. ............................................ **1,500.00**
**Punch set:** 11" bowl & six cups;
   white, 7 pcs..................................... **1,750.00**
**Punch set:** 11" bowl, base & six
   cups; stippled, blue, 8 pcs. .............**2,800.00**
**Punch set:** 11" bowl, base & six
   cups; marigold, 8 pcs. ...... **450.00 to 500.00**
**Punch set:** 14" bowl & ten cups; ice
   green, 11 pcs...................................**2,300.00**
**Punch set:** 14" bowl, base & five
   cups; purple, 7 pcs. .......................... **895.00**
**Punch set:** 14" bowl, base & six
   cups; marigold, 8 pcs........................ **585.00**
**Punch set:** 14" bowl, base & six
   cups; white, 8 pcs. ..........................**3,500.00**

**Punch set:** 14" bowl, base & eight
   cups; blue, 10 pcs..........................**2,300.00**
**Punch set, master:** 17" bowl, base &
   six cups; purple, 8 pcs. .................. **2,000.00**
**Punch set, master:** 17" bowl, base &
   eight cups; green, 10 pcs. ............. **3,800.00**
**Punch set, master:** 17" bowl, base &
   fourteen cups; purple, 16
   pcs............................ **2,450.00 to 2,500.00**
**Spooner,** green................................... **125.00**
**Spooner,** ice green ............................. **200.00**
**Spooner,** marigold ................................ **61.00**
**Spooner,** purple .................................... **95.00**
**Sugar bowl,** cov., green ....................... **85.00**
**Sugar bowl,** cov., marigold................... **85.00**
**Sugar bowl,** cov., purple ..................... **130.00**
**Sugar bowl,** individual size,
   green ...................................................... **60.00**
**Sugar bowl,** individual size, marigold... **35.00**
**Sugar bowl,** individual size, purple....... **67.00**
**Sweetmeat jar,** cov., marigold......... **1,800.00**
**Sweetmeat jar,** cov., purple............... **250.00**
**Table set:** cov. sugar bowl, spooner
   & cov. butter dish; marigold, 3 pcs. .. **185.00**
**Table set:** cov. sugar bowl,
   creamer & spooner; purple,
   3 pcs................................ **475.00 to 525.00**
**Table set:** cov. sugar bowl, creamer,
   spooner & cov. butter dish; green,
   4 pcs. .............................................. **525.00**
**Tumbler,** green...................... **55.00 to 65.00**
**Tumbler,** ice green ............. **700.00 to 800.00**
**Tumbler,** marigold ................................. **32.00**
**Tumbler,** stippled, marigold .................. **60.00**
**Tumbler,** purple ..................................... **50.00**
**Tumbler,** stippled, purple....................... **50.00**
**Tumbler,** smoky...................................... **30.00**
**Tumblers,** green, set of 6 ................... **300.00**
**Tumblers,** purple, set of 6 .................. **160.00**
**Tumbler,** tankard, green..... **200.00 to 225.00**
**Tumbler,** tankard, marigold .................. **52.00**
**Tumbler,** tankard, stippled, marigold .... **65.00**
**Tumbler,** tankard, purple........ **45.00 to 55.00**
**Tumbler,** tankard, stippled, purple........ **89.00**
**Tumblers,** tankard, purple, set of 6 ..... **263.00**
**Water set:** pitcher & six tumblers;
   blue, 7 pcs. ..................................... **550.00**
**Water set:** pitcher & six tumblers;
   green, 7 pcs. ............. **1,050.00 to 1,075.00**
**Water set:** pitcher & six tumblers;
   ice green, 7 pcs. ........................... **2,400.00**
**Water set:** pitcher & six tumblers;
   marigold, 7 pcs. ................ **475.00 to 500.00**
**Water set:** pitcher & six tumblers;
   purple, 7 pcs...................... **575.00 to 600.00**
**Water set,** tankard pitcher &
   five tumblers; marigold, 6 pcs. ........ **1,650.00**
**Whimsey compote** (sweetmeat
   base), green ..................................... **175.00**

## GRAPE & GOTHIC ARCHES (Northwood)

**Berry set:** master bowl & six sauce
  dishes; marigold, 7 pcs. ..................... **140.00**
**Bowl,** master berry, blue ..................... **85.00**
**Bowl,** master berry, marigold .............. **43.00**
**Butter dish,** cov., blue ........................ **250.00**
**Butter dish,** cov., green ..................... **225.00**
**Butter dish,** cov., marigold .................. **75.00**
**Creamer,** blue .................................. **83.00**
**Creamer,** green ................................. **200.00**
**Creamer,** marigold .............................. **45.00**
**Creamer,** purple ................................. **85.00**
**Creamer & spooner,** blue, 2 pcs. ......... **90.00**
**Creamer & cov. sugar bowl,**
  marigold, pr. ...................................... **100.00**
**Creamer & open sugar bowl,**
  marigold, pr. ...................................... **85.00**
**Pitcher,** water, blue ........... **350.00 to 375.00**
**Pitcher,** water, green ......................... **235.00**
**Pitcher,** water, marigold ..................... **190.00**
**Sauce dish,** aqua ................................. **25.00**
**Sauce dish,** blue ................................ **30.00**
**Sauce dish,** green ............................... **35.00**
**Sauce dish,** marigold .......................... **15.00**
**Sauce dish,** pearl pastel milk white ...... **38.00**
**Spooner,** blue .................................... **65.00**
**Spooner,** green ................................... **175.00**
**Spooner,** green w/gold ........................ **50.00**
**Spooner,** marigold ............................... **45.00**
**Sugar bowl,** cov., blue ........................ **100.00**
**Sugar bowl,** cov., green ...................... **96.00**
**Sugar bowl,** cov., marigold ................... **55.00**
**Sugar bowl,** cov., purple ...................... **90.00**
**Sugar bowl,** open, blue ........................ **40.00**
**Table set:** creamer, cov. sugar bowl
  & spooner; blue, 3 pcs. ..................... **500.00**
**Table set,** blue, 4 pcs. ........ **350.00 to 450.00**
**Table set,** marigold, 4 pcs. ................. **300.00**
**Tumbler,** amber ................................... **50.00**
**Tumbler,** blue ........................ **45.00 to 50.00**
**Tumbler,** clambroth ........................... **150.00**
**Tumbler,** green ................................... **77.00**
**Tumbler,** marigold .............................. **37.00**
**Tumbler,** pearl pastel milk
  white .............................. **125.00 to 150.00**
**Tumbler,** purple ................................... **50.00**
**Water set:** pitcher & four tumblers;
  blue, 5 pcs. ...................................... **550.00**
**Water set:** pitcher & six tumblers,
  green, 7 pcs. ..................................... **700.00**
**Water set:** pitcher & six tumblers,
  marigold, 7 pcs. ................................ **545.00**
**Water set:** pitcher & six tumblers,
  purple, 7 pcs. ................... **600.00 to 650.00**

## HEART & VINE

**Bowl,** 8" to 9" d., blue ......... **100.00 to 125.00**
**Bowl,** 8" to 9" d., ribbon candy rim,
  blue .................................................. **125.00**

*Heart & Vine Bowl*

**Bowl,** 8" to 9" d., green ...................... **150.00**
**Bowl,** 8" to 9" d., ribbon candy rim,
  green (ILLUS.) ................................... **150.00**
**Bowl,** 8" to 9" d., marigold ................... **75.00**
**Bowl,** 8" to 9" d., ribbon candy rim,
  marigold ............................................. **100.00**
**Bowl,** 8" to 9" d., purple ..................... **150.00**
**Bowl,** 8½" d., ribbon candy rim,
  purple ................................................ **100.00**
**Plate,** 9" d., blue ............................... **500.00**
**Plate,** 9" d., marigold .......................... **250.00**
**Plate,** 9" d., purple ............................ **450.00**

## HEARTS & FLOWERS (Northwood)

**Bowl,** 8" to 9" d., aqua
  opalescent ................. **1,000.00 to 1,500.00**
**Bowl,** 8" to 9" d., blue ........................ **600.00**
**Bowl,** 8" to 9" d., piecrust rim, blue ..... **500.00**
**Bowl,** 8" to 9" d., piecrust rim, blue
  w/electric iridescence ................... **1,175.00**
**Bowl,** 8" to 9" d., piecrust rim, ice
  blue .................................. **550.00 to 650.00**
**Bowl,** 8" to 9" d., piecrust rim, ice
  green ............................................. **2,600.00**
**Bowl,** 8" to 9" d., piecrust rim,
  marigold .......................... **450.00 to 550.00**
**Bowl,** 8" to 9" d., piecrust rim,
  purple ............................. **350.00 to 375.00**
**Bowl,** 8" to 9" d., piecrust rim, white
**Bowl,** 8" to 9" d., ruffled, aqua ........... **600.00**
**Bowl,** 8" to 9" d., ruffled, blue ............. **402.00**
**Bowl,** 8" to 9" d., ruffled, green ........... **700.00**
**Bowl,** 8" to 9" d., ruffled, ice
  blue ................................. **400.00 to 425.00**
**Bowl,** 8" to 9" d., ruffled, ice
  green ............................ **800.00 to 1,000.00**
**Bowl,** 8" to 9" d., ruffled,
  marigold .......................... **350.00 to 375.00**
**Bowl,** 8" to 9" d., ruffled,
  purple ............................. **400.00 to 425.00**
**Bowl,** 8" to 9" d., ruffled,
  white ............................... **200.00 to 225.00**

**Bowl,** 8" d., white............... **350.00 to 400.00**
**Compote,** 6¾" h., aqua
opalescent........................ **600.00 to 625.00**
**Compote,** 6¾" h., blue...................... **350.00**
**Compote,** 6¾" h., blue
opalescent..................................... **1,500.00**
**Compote,** 6¾" h., blue w/electric
iridescence ...................................... **270.00**
**Compote,** 6¾" h.,
green ........................ **2,250.00 to 2,700.00**
**Compote,** 6¾" h., ice blue ................. **850.00**
**Compote,** 6¾" h., ice green............... **933.00**
**Compote,** 6¾" h., lime
green ........................ **1,500.00 to 2,000.00**
**Compote,** 6¾" h.,
marigold ........................... **200.00 to 225.00**
**Compote,** 6¾" h., moonstone.......... **5,000.00**
**Compote,** 6¾" h., purple .... **500.00 to 525.00**
**Compote,** 6¾" h., sapphire blue......... **895.00**
**Compote,** 6¾" h., white...... **150.00 to 175.00**
**Plate,** green ................. **1,500.00 to 1,700.00**
**Plate,** ice blue .............. **4,000.00 to 4,500.00**
**Plate,** ice green ............................... **3,900.00**
**Plate,** marigold ............................... **1,000.00**

*Hearts & Flowers Plate*

**Plate,** purple (ILLUS.) ...................... **1,000.00**
**Plate,** white ..................................... **2,500.00**

## HOBSTAR (Imperial)

**Berry set:** master bowl & six sauce
dishes; marigold, 7 pcs. ..................... **53.00**
**Bowl,** 10¾" d., marigold........................ **35.00**
**Butter dish,** cov., green...................... **245.00**
**Butter dish,** cov., marigold ................ **105.00**
**Butter dish,** cov., purple..................... **130.00**
**Celery vase,** two-handled, marigold..... **75.00**
**Compote,** green.................................... **60.00**
**Compote,** marigold ............................... **50.00**
**Compote,** purple.................................. **110.00**
**Cracker jar,** cov., green........................ **90.00**
**Cracker jar,** cov., marigold .................. **70.00**
**Creamer,** green.................................... **80.00**

*Hobstar Pickle Castor*

**Creamer,** marigold................................ **40.00**
**Creamer,** purple.................................... **75.00**
**Humidor,** cov., marigold ....................... **98.00**
**Pickle castor,** cov., marigold,
complete w/silver plate frame
(ILLUS. above) ................................ **450.00**
**Punch set:** bowl, base & twelve cups,
marigold, 14 pcs. ............................. **300.00**
**Spooner,** marigold ................................ **35.00**
**Spooner,** purple.................................... **90.00**
**Sugar bowl,** cov., green ....................... **70.00**
**Sugar bowl,** cov., marigold................... **50.00**
**Table set,** marigold, 4 pcs. ................. **200.00**
**Table set:** creamer, cov. sugar bowl,
spooner, cov. butter & cracker jar;
marigold, 5 pcs. ............................... **185.00**

## HOLLY WHIRL or HOLLY SPRIG
## (Millersburg, Fenton & Dugan)

**Bowl,** 6" w., tricornered, amethyst ...... **125.00**
**Bowl,** 6" w., tricornered, green............. **85.00**
**Bowl,** 6" w., tricornered, marigold....... **295.00**
**Bowl,** 6" w., tricornered, purple........... **125.00**
**Bowl,** 6" d., ruffled, marigold................. **95.00**
**Bowl,** 6" d., ruffled, purple.................... **93.00**
**Bowl,** 7" d., ruffled, blue....................... **40.00**
**Bowl,** 7" d., green ................................ **60.00**
**Bowl,** 7" d., marigold............................ **55.00**
**Bowl,** 7" d., ruffled, purple ...... **55.00 to 60.00**
**Bowl,** 7" d., vaseline .......................... **650.00**
**Bowl,** 7" w., tricornered, marigold....... **160.00**
**Bowl,** 7½" w., tricornered, purple.......... **98.00**
**Bowl,** 8" d., ice cream shape,
marigold, variant ............................... **68.00**
**Bowl,** 8" d., ice cream shape, white.... **110.00**
**Bowl,** 8" w., tri-cornered, green ............ **98.00**
**Bowl,** 8" to 9" d., ruffled, blue .............. **50.00**
**Bowl,** 8" to 9" d., green ........................ **80.00**
**Bowl,** 8" to 9" d., marigold...... **70.00 to 75.00**

Bowl, 8" to 9" d., peach opalescent ...... 75.00
Bowl, 8" to 9" d., purple ........ 75.00 to 100.00
Bowl, 9" w., tricornered, purple .......... 105.00
Bowl, 10" d., ruffled, marigold .............. 50.00
Bowl, 10" d., ruffled,
  purple ............................. 100.00 to 125.00
Card tray, two-handled, marigold ......... 93.00
Hat shape, green, 6" ............................ 38.00
Nappy, single handle, marigold ............ 45.00
Nappy, single handle, peach
  opalescent (Dugan) .......................... 62.00
Nappy, single handle, purple
  (Dugan) ......................... 75.00 to 100.00
Nappy, tricornered, green (Dugan) ....... 98.00
Nappy, tricornered, marigold
  (Millersburg) ................................... 110.00
Nappy, tricornered, purple
  (Dugan) ........................................... 100.00
Nappy, tricornered, purple
  (Millersburg) ..................... 175.00 to 200.00
Nappy, two-handled, amethyst
  (Millersburg) ..................................... 68.00
Nappy, two-handled, green
  (Dugan) ............................ 75.00 to 100.00
Nappy, two-handled, green
  (Millersburg) ..................................... 80.00
Nut dish, two-handled, green ............... 75.00
Nut dish, two-handled, marigold .......... 64.00
Nut dish, two-handled, purple ............. 84.00
Rose bowl, blue.................................. 300.00
Rose bowl, small, marigold ................ 325.00
Rose bowl, small, vaseline................. 400.00
Sauceboat, peach opalescent
  (Dugan) ........................................... 135.00
Sauce dish, purple, 5½" d.
  (Millersburg) ................................... 145.00
Sauce dish, marigold, 5¾" d. ............. 125.00
Sauce dish, green, 6½" d.
  (Millersburg) ..................... 100.00 to 125.00
Sauce dish, deep, purple .................. 350.00

### INVERTED FEATHER (Cambridge)

*Inverted Feather Cracker Jar*

Compote, jelly, marigold...................... 70.00
Cracker jar, cov., green
  (ILLUS.) ........................... 200.00 to 250.00

Cracker jar, cov., purple .................... 750.00
Creamer, marigold .............................. 70.00
Parfait, marigold ................................. 95.00
Pitcher, milk, marigold ....................... 750.00
Pitcher, milk, pastel marigold ............ 475.00
Pitcher, water, tankard, marigold ..... 4,000.00
Tumbler, green ................................. 750.00
Tumbler, marigold .............. 450.00 to 500.00

### INVERTED THISTLE (Cambridge)

Bowl, 11" d., green ............................ 275.00
Bowl, purple...................................... 300.00
Compote, 8" h., ruffled, green ........... 550.00
Creamer, purple................................. 130.00
Pitcher, milk, purple........................ 2,500.00
Pitcher, water, marigold.................. 2,000.00

*Inverted Thistle Pitcher*

Pitcher, water, purple (ILLUS.) ........ 2,000.00
Plate, chop, purple .......................... 1,750.00
Tumbler, purple ................................. 225.00
Water set: pitcher & six tumblers;
  purple, 7 pcs.............. 3,500.00 to 4,300.00
Whimsey, tricornered, green
  (made from celery) .......................... 650.00

### LEAF CHAIN (Fenton)

Bowl, 5" d., ruffled, marigold................. 45.00
Bowl, 6" d., ruffled, red ...................... 613.00
Bowl, 7" d., ruffled, Amberina ............. 450.00
Bowl, 7" d., ruffled, green ................... 113.00
Bowl, 7" d., ruffled, ice green............. 950.00
Bowl, 7" d., aqua ............... 125.00 to 150.00
Bowl, 7" d., blue................................ 56.00
Bowl, 7" d., green .............................. 45.00
Bowl, 7" d., lavender.......................... 150.00
Bowl, 7" d., marigold............................ 49.00
Bowl, 7" d., red............. 1,000.00 to 1,200.00
Bowl, 7" d., vaseline ......................... 100.00
Bowl, 7" d., vaseline w/marigold
  overlay .............................................. 60.00

**Bowl,** 7" d., white ................................. 66.00
**Bowl,** 8" d., ice cream shape, blue ..... 120.00
**Bowl,** 8" d., ice cream shape,
  clambroth ......................................... 160.00
**Bowl,** 8" d., ice cream shape, green... 145.00
**Bowl,** 8" d., ice cream shape, white.... 150.00
**Bowl,** 8" to 9" d., aqua ........................ 165.00
**Bowl,** 8" to 9" d., clambroth ................. 64.00
**Bowl,** 8" to 9" d., green ........................ 75.00
**Bowl,** 8" to 9" d., light blue ................... 80.00
**Bowl,** 8" to 9" d., marigold ................... 57.00
**Bowl,** 8" to 9" d., purple ....................... 84.00
**Bowl,** 8" to 9" d., vaseline ................... 95.00
**Bowl,** 8" to 9" d., white ........................ 88.00
**Bowl,** ruffled, purple ............................ 213.00
**Plate,** 7" to 8" d., blue ......................... 175.00
**Plate,** 7" to 8" d., marigold ................. 185.00
**Plate,** 9" d., blue ................................. 180.00
**Plate,** 9" d., clambroth ........ 125.00 to 150.00
**Plate,** 9" d., green ............................... 165.00
**Plate,** 9" d., ice green ......................... 225.00

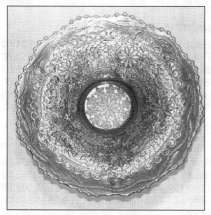

*Leaf Chain Plate*

**Plate,** 9" d., marigold (ILLUS.) ............ 500.00
**Plate,** 9" d., pastel marigold ............... 350.00
**Plate,** 9" d., purple .............................. 240.00
**Plate,** 9" d., white ............... 195.00 to 225.00

## LITTLE FLOWERS (Fenton)

**Berry set:** master bowl & four sauce
  dishes; blue, 5 pcs. ......................... 200.00
**Berry set:** master bowl & four sauce
  dishes; purple, 5 pcs. ...................... 240.00
**Berry set:** master bowl & six sauce
  dishes; green, 7 pcs. ....................... 250.00
**Berry set:** master bowl & six sauce
  dishes-; marigold, 7 pcs. .................. 195.00
**Bowl,** 6" d., ice cream shape,
  blue ..................................... 30.00 to 40.00
**Bowl,** 6" d., ruffled, vaseline ................ 35.00
**Bowl,** 6½" d., marigold ......................... 20.00
**Bowl,** 6½" d., purple ............................. 65.00

**Bowl,** 8" to 9" d., blue ......................... 100.00
**Bowl,** 8" to 9" d., green ......................... 45.00
**Bowl,** 8" to 9" d., marigold ................... 58.00
**Bowl,** 8" to 9" d., purple ....................... 92.00
**Bowl,** 8" to 9" d., red ......................... 2,500.00
**Bowl,** 10" d., amber ............................. 75.00
**Bowl,** 10" d., blue ............................... 110.00
**Bowl,** 10" d., green .............................. 75.00
**Bowl,** 10" d., ruffled, green ................ 143.00
**Bowl,** 10" d., ruffled, lavender ............ 116.00
**Bowl,** 10" d., ruffled, marigold .............. 75.00
**Bowl,** 10" d., purple .............................. 95.00
**Bowl,** 10" d., ruffled,
  purple ............................. 100.00 to 125.00
**Bowl,** 10" d., spatula-footed, red ...... 2,500.00
**Bowl,** 11" d., marigold .......................... 67.00
**Nut bowl,** blue ..................................... 75.00
**Nut bowl,** marigold ............................... 65.00
**Plate,** 6" d., marigold ......................... 450.00
**Plate,** chop, footed, marigold ............. 400.00
**Sauce dish,** 5" d., aqua ...................... 100.00
**Sauce dish,** 5" d., blue ......................... 43.00
**Sauce dish,** 5" d., green ...................... 25.00
**Sauce dish,** 5" d., marigold ................. 34.00
**Sauce dish,** 5" d., purple ..................... 89.00

## LOTUS & GRAPE (Fenton)

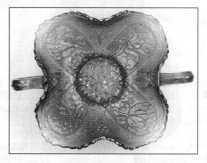

*Lotus & Grape Bonbon*

**Bonbon,** two-handled, blue .. 95.00 to 125.00
**Bonbon,** two-handled, celeste blue
  (ILLUS.) ........................................... 185.00
**Bonbon,** two-handled, green ................ 90.00
**Bonbon,** two-handled, marigold ........... 40.00
**Bonbon,** two-handled, purple ............. 225.00
**Bonbon,** two-handled, red ............. 1,338.00
**Bonbon,** two-handled, teal blue .......... 350.00
**Bonbon,** two-handled, vaseline ............ 90.00
**Bowl,** 5" d., footed, blue ...................... 40.00
**Bowl,** 5" d., footed, green .................... 67.00
**Bowl,** 5" d., footed, marigold ................ 45.00
**Bowl,** 5" d., footed, purple .................... 45.00
**Bowl,** 6" d., footed, blue ...................... 65.00
**Bowl,** 7" d., footed, marigold ................ 44.00
**Bowl,** 7½" d., ice cream shape, blue .... 65.00
**Bowl,** 8" d., collared base, ruffled,
  marigold on vaseline ......................... 75.00

Bowl, 8" d., ruffled, blue........................ 93.00
Bowl, 8" to 9" d., blue .......................... 93.00
Bowl, 8" to 9" d., green......................... 95.00
Bowl, 8" to 9" d., marigold ................... 95.00
Bowl, 8" to 9" d., purple ..................... 105.00
Bowl, 8½" d., ice cream shape,
    Persian blue.................................... 400.00
Bowl, 9" d., ruffled, blue....................... 80.00
Bowl, ruffled, blue.............................. 150.00
Plate, 9" d., blue ............................. 1,400.00
Plate, 9" d., green ........................... 1,200.00
Plate, 9" d., purple............................ 360.00

## MANY FRUITS (Dugan)

*Many Fruits Punch Bowl & Base*

Punch bowl, 9¾" d., marigold ............. 180.00
Punch bowl, 9¾" d., purple ................. 335.00
Punch bowl & base, marigold, 2 pcs... 400.00
Punch bowl & base, purple, 2 pcs.
    (ILLUS.) .............................................. 715.00
Punch bowl & base, white, 2 pcs. ....... 765.00
Punch cup, blue..................................... 41.00
Punch cup, green ................................... 35.00
Punch cup, marigold ............................. 21.00
Punch cup, purple .................................. 28.00
Punch cup, white.................................... 70.00
Punch set: bowl & six cups; marigold,
    7 pcs. .................................................. 400.00
Punch set: bowl, base & six cups;
    purple, 8 pcs.............. 1,000.00 to 1,025.00
Punch set: bowl, base & six cups;
    white, 8 pcs.................................... 1,600.00

## MILADY (Fenton)

Pitcher, water, blue ......... 900.00 to 1,000.00
Pitcher, water, marigold..................... 675.00
Tumbler, blue ....................................... 85.00
Tumbler, green..................................... 675.00
Tumbler, marigold ................................ 67.00
Tumbler, purple ................................... 116.00
Tumblers, blue, set of 6..................... 550.00

*Milady Water Set*

Water set: pitcher & six tumblers;
    blue, 7 pcs. (ILLUS.)......................... 800.00

## NESTING SWAN (Millersburg)

Bowl, 9" d., green ............................... 524.00
Bowl, 9" d., marigold........................... 450.00
Bowl, 10" d., amber ............................ 325.00
Bowl, 10" d., green............. 300.00 to 325.00
Bowl, 10" d., marigold ........ 200.00 to 225.00
Bowl, 10" d., purple ............................ 325.00

## NU-ART HOMESTEAD PLATE
   (Imperial)

Amber................................................ 1,500.00
Blue.................................................... 5,250.00
Emerald green ................................. 3,000.00
Green................................. 750.00 to 850.00
Helios.................................................... 395.00
Lavender .............................................. 900.00
Marigold ............................................... 400.00
Purple ................................ 825.00 to 850.00
White..................................................... 758.00

## PALM BEACH (U.S. Glass Co.)

Berry set: master bowl & six sauce
    dishes; white, 7 pcs. ......................... 275.00
Bowl, 5" d., four turned-in sides,
    marigold............................................... 90.00
Bowl, 8½" d., marigold.......................... 50.00
Butter dish, cov., white ...................... 250.00
Creamer, marigold ................................ 68.00
Creamer, white ..................................... 80.00
Pitcher, water, marigold...................... 450.00
Pitcher, water, white .......................... 700.00
Rose bowl, amber ............................... 125.00
Rose bowl, marigold........................... 213.00
Rose bowl, marigold w/Goofus
    finish ................................................. 213.00
Rose bowl, white .................................. 75.00

**Rose bowl,** w/Gooseberry interior,
white ................................................ **225.00**
**Sauce dish,** marigold........................... **30.00**
**Sauce dish,** white .............................. **77.00**
**Spooner,** marigold .............................. **80.00**
**Spooner,** white ................................. **100.00**
**Sugar bowl,** cov., honey amber ........ **158.00**
**Sugar bowl,** cov., marigold................. **75.00**
**Table set,** white, 4 pcs. ...................... **700.00**
**Tumbler,** amber................................ **200.00**
**Tumbler,** marigold ............................ **210.00**
**Tumbler,** white .................. **190.00 to 200.00**
**Vase,** marigold, large .......................... **65.00**
**Vase,** white, oval .............................. **125.00**
**Water set:** pitcher & three tumblers;
white, 4 pcs. .................................. **842.00**
**Water set:** pitcher & five tumblers;
amber, 6 pcs. ................................. **405.00**
**Water set:** pitcher & six tumblers;
marigold, 7 pcs. .............................. **475.00**
**Whimsey banana boat,** amber ........... **60.00**
**Whimsey banana boat,** marigold,
6".......................................... **75.00 to 90.00**
**Whimsey banana boat,** purple,
6"...................................................... **120.00**
**Whimsey vase,** purple........................ **400.00**
**Whimsey vase,** white ........................ **450.00**

### PEACOCK & DAHLIA (Fenton)

**Bowl,** 6" d., ice cream shape,
marigold.............................................. **45.00**
**Bowl,** 6" d., ice cream shape,
vaseline............................................. **100.00**
**Bowl,** 6¼" d., ice cream shape,
green ................................................ **120.00**
**Bowl,** 6½" d., 2" h., scalloped edge,
green ................................................ **125.00**
**Bowl,** 7" d., ice cream shape,
vaseline ........................... **175.00 to 200.00**
**Bowl,** 7" d., ruffled, aqua opalescent .. **138.00**
**Bowl,** 7" d., ruffled, blue ..... **100.00 to 125.00**
**Bowl,** 7" d., ruffled, marigold................. **61.00**
**Bowl,** 7" d., ruffled, purple ................... **70.00**
**Bowl,** 7" d., vaseline ......................... **150.00**
**Bowl,** 7½" d., aqua ............................ **125.00**
**Bowl,** 7½" d., purple w/blue base ....... **100.00**
**Bowl,** 8" d., footed, green ..................... **49.00**
**Plate,** 7½" d., marigold....................... **550.00**
**Plate,** 8½" d., marigold....................... **312.00**
**Sauce dish,** marigold........................... **25.00**

### PEACOCK AT FOUNTAIN (Northwood)

**Berry set:** master bowl & two sauce
dishes; ice blue, 3 pcs. ................ **640.00**
**Berry set:** master bowl & three sauce
dishes; blue, 4 pcs. ...................... **300.00**
**Berry set:** master bowl & four sauce
dishes; purple, 5 pcs. ................... **450.00**

**Berry set:** master bowl & five sauce
dishes; ice blue, 6 pcs. ................. **650.00**
**Berry set:** master bowl & five sauce
dishes; marigold, 6 pcs. ................ **185.00**
**Bowl,** fruit, blue w/electric
iridescence ................................. **2,700.00**
**Bowl,** master berry, blue.................... **325.00**
**Bowl,** master berry, green ................. **600.00**
**Bowl,** master berry, ice blue .............. **380.00**
**Bowl,** master berry, marigold............. **125.00**
**Bowl,** master berry, purple................. **225.00**
**Bowl,** master berry, white... **240.00 to 250.00**
**Bowl,** orange, three-footed, aqua
opalescent ................................. **1,100.00**
**Bowl,** orange, three-
footed, blue ................. **1,045.00 to 1,075.00**
**Bowl,** orange, three-footed, green........ **525.00**
**Bowl,** orange, three-footed,
ice green ......................................... **288.00**
**Bowl,** orange, three-footed, lavender ... **525.00**
**Bowl,** orange, three-footed,
marigold............................. **250.00 to 275.00**
**Bowl,** orange, three-footed,
purple................................. **450.00 to 475.00**
**Butter dish,** cov., blue ...................... **200.00**
**Butter dish,** cov., green...................... **500.00**
**Butter dish,** cov., marigold ................ **210.00**
**Butter dish,** cov., purple .................... **275.00**
**Butter dish,** cov., white ..................... **380.00**
**Compote,** aqua opalescent ............. **3,100.00**
**Compote,** blue .................................. **587.00**
**Compote,** ice blue .......................... **1,550.00**
**Compote,** ice green ........................ **1,650.00**
**Compote,** marigold ........................... **575.00**
**Compote,** purple ............... **800.00 to 825.00**
**Compote,** white .............................. **625.00**
**Creamer,** blue .................................. **105.00**
**Creamer,** marigold ............................. **65.00**
**Creamer,** purple .................. **75.00 to 100.00**
**Pitcher,** water, blue ........... **500.00 to 550.00**
**Pitcher,** water, green.... **1,500.00 to 1,750.00**
**Pitcher,** water, ice blue ................... **1,600.00**
**Pitcher,** water, ice green.................. **2,600.00**
**Pitcher,** water, marigold..................... **288.00**
**Pitcher,** water, purple ......... **350.00 to 400.00**
**Pitcher,** water, white..... **1,000.00 to 1,025.00**
**Punch bowl & base,** blue, 2 pcs. ..... **2,300.00**
**Punch bowl & base,** ice blue,
2 pcs. ......................................... **8,000.00**
**Punch bowl & base,** ice green,
2 pcs. ......................................... **9,500.00**
**Punch bowl & base,** marigold, 2 pcs. .. **900.00**
**Punch bowl & base,** purple,
2 pcs. ........................... **1,400.00 to 1,425.00**
**Punch cup,** aqua opalescent........... **1,400.00**
**Punch cup,** blue ................................. **50.00**
**Punch cup,** blue w/electric
iridescence ...................................... **95.00**
**Punch cup,** ice blue........................... **125.00**
**Punch cup,** ice green ........................ **525.00**

*Peacock at Fountain Punch Set*

**Punch cup,** lavender ............................ 88.00
**Punch cup,** marigold ........................... 38.00
**Punch cup,** purple ................. 40.00 to 45.00
**Punch cup,** white ............... 95.00 to 100.00
**Punch cups,** white, set of 6 ............... 750.00
**Punch set:** bowl, base & four cups;
     marigold, 6 pcs. ................ 825.00 to 875.00
**Punch set:** bowl, base & five cups;
     ice green, 7 pcs. .......................... 10,750.00
**Punch set:** bowl, base & six cups;
     purple, 8 pcs. .................................. 1,750.00
**Punch set:** bowl, base & six cups;
     ice blue, 8 pcs. ............................... 7,000.00
**Punch set:** bowl, base & six cups;
     white, 8 pcs. (ILLUS. above) ......... 6,000.00
**Sauce dish,** aqua ................................. 23.00
**Sauce dish,** blue ................................... 40.00
**Sauce dish,** ice blue ........... 100.00 to 150.00
**Sauce dish,** marigold ............................ 31.00
**Sauce dish,** purple ............................... 37.00
**Sauce dish,** teal blue ......................... 100.00
**Sauce dish,** white ................................ 50.00
**Spooner,** blue ..................................... 150.00
**Spooner,** blue w/electric
     iridescence ...................................... 250.00
**Spooner,** green .................................... 185.00
**Spooner,** ice blue ............................... 280.00
**Spooner,** marigold ................................ 76.00
**Spooner,** purple .................................. 130.00
**Spooner,** white .................................... 183.00
**Sugar bowl,** cov., blue ........................ 125.00
**Sugar bowl,** cov., ice blue .................. 265.00
**Sugar bowl,** cov., marigold .................. 85.00
**Sugar bowl,** cov., purple ...................... 85.00
**Sugar bowl,** cov., white ...................... 180.00

**Table set:** cov. butter dish, sugar
     bowl & spooner; purple, 3 pcs. ......... 350.00
**Table set,** ice blue, 4 pcs. ............... 2,600.00
**Table set,** marigold, 4 pcs. ................. 505.00
**Table set,** purple, 4 pcs. ...... 450.00 to 500.00
**Tumbler,** amber .................................... 89.00
**Tumbler,** blue ......................... 55.00 to 60.00
**Tumbler,** green ................................... 325.00
**Tumbler,** ice blue .............. 350.00 to 400.00
**Tumbler,** lavender .............................. 125.00
**Tumbler,** marigold ................. 40.00 to 50.00
**Tumbler,** purple ..................... 50.00 to 60.00
**Tumbler,** smoky .................................... 75.00
**Tumbler,** teal blue .............................. 139.00
**Tumbler,** white ................... 200.00 to 225.00
**Tumblers,** blue, set of 6 ..................... 360.00
**Water set:** pitcher & six tumblers;
     blue, 7 pcs. ................. 1,045.00 to 1,075.00
**Water set:** pitcher & six tumblers; blue
     w/electric iridescence, 7 pcs. ......... 1,600.00
**Water set:** pitcher & six tumblers;
     marigold, 7 pcs. ............... 500.00 to 550.00
**Water set:** pitcher & six tumblers;
     purple, 7 pcs. .................... 800.00 to 825.00
**Water set:** pitcher & six tumblers;
     white, 7 pcs. .............. 2,100.00 to 2,125.00

**PEACOCK TAIL (Fenton)**

**Berry set:** 9" d. bowl & four 5" d.
     bowls; green, 5 pcs. .......................... 140.00
**Bonbon,** two-handled, blue .... 18.00 to 35.00
**Bonbon,** two-handled, green ............... 80.00
**Bonbon,** two-handled, marigold
     (ILLUS. top next page) ...................... 37.00
**Bonbon,** two-handled, purple .............. 65.00

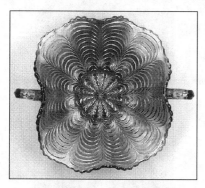

*Peacock Tail Bonbon*

**Bonbon,** tricornered, green .................. 55.00
**Bonbon,** tricornered, marigold.............. 23.00
**Bonbon,** tricornered, purple.................. 40.00
**Bowl,** 4" d., marigold............................ 40.00
**Bowl,** 5" d., ruffled, green ....... **20.00 to 25.00**
**Bowl,** 5" d., ruffled, marigold................ 24.00
**Bowl,** 5" d., ruffled, purple.................... 28.00
**Bowl,** 6" d., blue.................................. 45.00
**Bowl,** 6" d., ruffled, marigold ............... 30.00
**Bowl,** 6" d., ruffled, peach
 opalescent ....................................... 700.00
**Bowl,** 6" d., ruffled, purple.................... 40.00
**Bowl,** 6" d., ruffled, red ................... 1,850.00
**Bowl,** 7" d., ribbon candy rim, amber.... 40.00
**Bowl,** 7" d., ruffled, blue...................... 55.00
**Bowl,** 7" d., green ................................ 35.00
**Bowl,** 7" d., purple............................... 37.00
**Bowl,** 7" d., red ................................... 575.00
**Bowl,** 8" d., green ................................ 75.00
**Bowl,** 8" d., purple............................... 40.00
**Bowl,** 9" d., blue.................................. 48.00
**Bowl,** 9" d., green ................................ 49.00
**Bowl,** 9" d., crimped, green.................. 55.00
**Bowl,** 9" d., crimped, marigold............. 50.00
**Bowl,** 9" d., ribbon candy rim, electric
 green ............................................... 175.00
**Bowl,** 9" d., ribbon candy rim, green... 125.00
**Bowl,** 9" d., ribbon candy rim, purple .... 50.00
**Bowl,** 9" sq., ribbon candy rim,
 purple.............................................. 475.00
**Bowl,** 10" d., ribbon candy rim, green .. 225.00
**Bowl,** 10" d., green ............................... 75.00
**Bowl,** 10½" d., marigold........................ 47.00
**Bowl,** ice cream, green ........................ 35.00
**Bowl,** ice cream, purple ....................... 25.00
**Bowl,** ice cream, red ........................... 600.00
**Compote,** 6" d., 5" h., blue ................. 40.00
**Compote,** 6" d., 5" h., green... **75.00 to 85.00**
**Compote,** 6" d., 5" h.,
 marigold .......................... **95.00 to 125.00**
**Compote,** 6" d., 5" h., marigold
 variant.............................................. 90.00
**Compote,** 6" d., 5" h., purple ............... 88.00

**Plate,** 6" d., blue ................ **195.00 to 225.00**
**Plate,** 6" d., green ............................. 100.00
**Plate,** 6" d., marigold.......................... 275.00
**Plate,** 6" tricornered, panels exterior,
 purple ............................. **125.00 to 150.00**
**Plate,** 9" d., marigold....................... 1,250.00
**Whimsey,** hat-shaped, blue................. 27.00
**Whimsey,** hat-shaped, green .............. 75.00
**Whimsey,** hat-shaped, w/advertising,
 green ................................................. 75.00
**Whimsey,** hat-shaped, marigold........... 10.00
**Whimsey,** hat-shaped, purple.............. 25.00

## PERSIAN MEDALLION (Fenton)

**Berry set:** master bowl & four small
 sauce dishes, blue, 5 pcs. ............... 145.00
**Berry set:** master bowl & six small
 sauce dishes, purple,
 7 pcs............................... **300.00 to 325.00**
**Bonbon,** two-handled, amber .............. 60.00
**Bonbon,** two-handled, Amberina........ 250.00
**Bonbon,** two-handled,
 aqua .............................. **250.00 to 300.00**
**Bonbon,** two-handled, blue .... **65.00 to 70.00**
**Bonbon,** two-handled, celeste blue .... 500.00
**Bonbon,** two-handled, green .............. 100.00
**Bonbon,** two-handled, lavender .......... 60.00
**Bonbon,** two-handled,
 marigold ............................ **55.00 to 65.00**
**Bonbon,** two-handled, purple... **50.00 to 60.00**
**Bonbon,** two-handled, red ............... 1,000.00
**Bonbon,** two-handled, vaseline ......... 225.00
**Bowl,** 5" d., aqua ............... **125.00 to 150.00**
**Bowl,** 5" d., blue .................... **45.00 to 55.00**
**Bowl,** 5" d., green ................................ 45.00
**Bowl,** 5" d., marigold............................ 35.00
**Bowl,** 5" d., purple............................... 67.00
**Bowl,** 5" d., red ................................... 250.00
**Bowl,** 5" d., white ................................ 60.00
**Bowl,** 6" d., ruffled, aqua...................... 95.00
**Bowl,** 6" d., ruffled, green .................. 120.00
**Bowl,** 6" d., ruffled, marigold................ 33.00
**Bowl,** 7" d., green ................................ 75.00
**Bowl,** 7" d., marigold............................ 45.00
**Bowl,** 7" d., ice cream shape, purple .... 33.00
**Bowl,** 7" d., ribbon candy rim, marigold .. 40.00
**Bowl,** 7" d., ribbon candy rim, purple .... 75.00
**Bowl,** 8" to 9" d., fluted, blue.............. 100.00
**Bowl,** 8" to 9" d., ice cream shape,
 green ............................................... 155.00
**Bowl,** 8" to 9" d., ribbon candy rim,
 blue.................................................... 80.00
**Bowl,** 8" to 9" d., ribbon candy rim,
 green .................................................. 55.00
**Bowl,** 8" to 9" d., marigold ................... 50.00
**Bowl,** 8" to 9" d., purple ....................... 65.00
**Bowl,** 8" to 9" d., ribbon candy rim,
 purple................................................. 95.00

**Bowl,** 8" to 9" d., ruffled rim,
red ............................... **900.00 to 1,175.00**
**Bowl,** 9" d., ruffled, green .................... **75.00**
**Bowl,** 9½" d., footed, Grape & Cable
exterior, blue ................... **250.00 to 300.00**
**Bowl,** 9½" d., purple............................ **100.00**
**Bowl,** ice cream, 10½" d., purple .......... **55.00**
**Bowl,** 10½" d., fluted, blue.................... **85.00**
**Bowl,** 10½" d., ruffled, green .............. **100.00**
**Bowl,** large, salad, blue...... **400.00 to 425.00**
**Bowl,** orange, blue.............................. **130.00**
**Bowl,** orange, marigold........................ **100.00**
**Bowl,** orange, purple........................... **185.00**
**Bowl,** three-in-one rim, blue .............. **100.00**
**Compote,** 6½" d., 6½" h., blue ............. **90.00**
**Compote,** 6½" d., 6½" h., clambroth .... **90.00**
**Compote,** 6½" d., 6½" h., green ......... **274.00**
**Compote,** 6½" d., 6½" h.,
marigold ............................... **75.00 to 80.00**
**Compote,** 6½" d., 6½" h.,
purple ................................. **75.00 to 100.00**
**Compote,** 6½" d., 6½" h., white.......... **625.00**
**Compote,** ribbon candy rim, cobalt
blue..................................................... **275.00**
**Compote,** ribbon candy rim, purple .... **325.00**
**Compote,** three-in-one rim, purple ..... **575.00**
**Hair receiver,** blue ............. **145.00 to 165.00**
**Hair receiver,** green ............................. **95.00**
**Hair receiver,** marigold ......... **60.00 to 70.00**
**Hair receiver,** white ............................ **125.00**
**Plate,** 6½" d., blue .............. **100.00 to 125.00**
**Plate,** 6½" d., green ............................ **200.00**
**Plate,** 6½" d., marigold ........... **60.00 to 70.00**
**Plate,** 6½" d., purple............................ **175.00**
**Plate,** 6½" d., red slag......................... **500.00**
**Plate,** 6½" d., white ............................ **130.00**
**Plate,** 7" d., blue.................................. **125.00**
**Plate,** 7" d., marigold............................ **87.00**
**Plate,** 7½" d., blue.............................. **100.00**
**Plate,** 7¾" d., blue.............................. **300.00**
**Plate,** 8" d., marigold............................ **55.00**
**Plate,** 9" d., blue ................. **250.00 to 300.00**
**Plate,** 9" d., clambroth........................ **195.00**
**Plate,** 9" d., green ............................... **115.00**
**Plate,** 9" d., marigold.......................... **275.00**
**Plate,** 9" d., purple................................ **75.00**
**Plate,** 9" d., white ............................ **2,800.00**
**Plate,** chop, 10½" d., blue... **400.00 to 425.00**
**Plate,** chop, 10½" d., purple............. **2,300.00**
**Plate,** chop, 10½" d., white ................ **225.00**
**Rose bowl,** blue .................................. **150.00**
**Rose bowl,** clambroth.......................... **300.00**
**Rose bowl,** marigold.............................. **73.00**
**Rose bowl,** purple ................................. **60.00**
**Rose bowl,** white............... **130.00 to 135.00**

## PIPE HUMIDOR (Millersburg)

**Green** (ILLUS. top next column) ...... **6,500.00**
**Marigold** ......................................... **5,000.00**

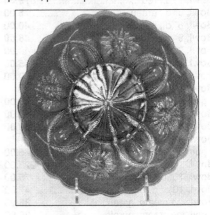

*Pipe Humidor*

## PODS & POSIES or FOUR FLOWERS (Dugan)

**Bowl,** 6" d., peach opalescent .............. **68.00**
**Bowl,** 6" d., purple................................. **55.00**
**Bowl,** 8" to 9" d., green ....................... **160.00**
**Bowl,** 8" to 9" d., marigold ................... **45.00**
**Bowl,** 8" to 9" d., purple ..................... **115.00**
**Bowl,** 10" d., shallow, ruffled, lavender.. **225.00**
**Bowl,** 10" d., peach
opalescent........................ **150.00 to 200.00**
**Bowl,** 10" d., purple ............ **125.00 to 150.00**
**Plate,** 6" d., peach opalescent ............ **164.00**
**Plate,** 6" d., purple.............................. **295.00**
**Plate,** 6" to 7" d., w/exterior
pattern, peach opalescent ............... **102.00**

*Pods & Posies Plate*

**Plate,** 9" d., green (ILLUS.) ................ **790.00**
**Plate,** 9" d., purple.............................. **500.00**
**Plate,** chop, 11" d., peach
opalescent .................... **450.00 to 475.00**
**Plate,** chop, 11" d.,
purple ........................ **1,000.00 to 1,075.00**

## POPPY SHOW (Northwood)

**Bowl,** 7" d., purple................................. **52.00**
**Bowl,** 7½" d., ruffled, marigold............. **30.00**

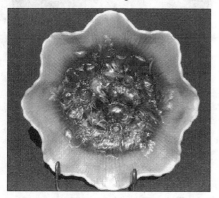

*Poppy Show Bowl*

**Bowl,** 8" to 9" d., aqua opalescent
   (ILLUS.) ........................................ **18,500.00**
**Bowl,** 8" to 9" d., blue ......................... **600.00**
**Bowl,** 8" to 9" d., clambroth ............... **190.00**
**Bowl,** 8" to 9" d., blue w/electric
   iridescence ...................................... **750.00**
**Bowl,** 8" to 9" d., green ................... **1,300.00**
**Bowl,** 8" to 9" d., ice blue................ **1,700.00**
**Bowl,** 8" to 9" d., ice green ............. **2,400.00**
**Bowl,** 8" to 9" d., marigold .. **500.00 to 525.00**
**Bowl,** 8" to 9" d., white....................... **375.00**
**Plate,** blue...................................... **3,000.00**
**Plate,** blue w/electric iridescence..... **1,750.00**
**Plate,** green.................................... **5,800.00**
**Plate,** ice blue.............. **1,600.00 to 2,000.00**
**Plate,** ice green............. **3,800.00 to 4,200.00**
**Plate,** marigold................................ **1,100.00**
**Plate,** pastel marigold ..................... **1,000.00**
**Plate,** purple ................ **1,200.00 to 1,275.00**
**Plate,** white .........................**600.00 to 620.00**

## RIPPLE VASE

**Marigold,** 5½" h. ................................ **100.00**
**Amber,** 7½" h.......................................... **77.00**
**Amber,** 10" h........................................... **60.00**
**Amber,** 11½" h......................................... **45.00**
**Amber,** 15¼" h......................................... **81.00**
**Aqua,** 10" h........................................... **125.00**
**Aqua,** 11" h........................................... **200.00**
**Aqua,** 12" h............................................. **78.00**
**Aqua**.................................. **145.00 to 150.00**
**Green,** 6" h.............................................. **95.00**
**Green,** 8¼" h........................................... **60.00**
**Green,** 9½" h........................................... **85.00**
**Green,** 10" h........................................... **25.00**
**Green,** 11" h........................................... **30.00**
**Green,** 13" h........................................... **45.00**
**Green,** 14½" h......................................... **75.00**

*Ripple Vase*

**Green,** 15½" h....................................... **125.00**
**Green,** 18¾" h....................................... **163.00**
**Green,** funeral, mid-size..................... **175.00**
**Ice green,** 14½" h. ............. **200.00 to 245.00**
**Marigold,** 5" h. ...................................... **70.00**
**Marigold,** 6" h................... **100.00 to 150.00**
**Marigold,** 6½" h. .................................... **45.00**
**Marigold,** 8" h. ...................................... **29.00**
**Marigold,** 9½" h.................... **25.00 to 30.00**
**Marigold,** 10½" h. .................................. **40.00**
**Marigold,** 12" h. .................................... **45.00**
**Marigold,** 15" h. .................................... **45.00**
**Marigold,** funeral, 16½" h. ................... **58.00**
**Marigold,** 17" h. .................................... **65.00**
**Marigold,** funeral, 17½" h. ................. **200.00**
**Marigold,** 20" h. (ILLUS.
   above) ........................... **150.00 to 200.00**
**Purple,** 8" h............................................ **40.00**
**Purple,** 8½" h........................................ **150.00**
**Purple,** 10" h.......................................... **50.00**
**Purple,** 11" h.......................................... **83.00**
**Purple,** 11½" h...................................... **175.00**
**Purple,** 13" h......................................... **145.00**
**Purple,** 16" h.......................................... **45.00**
**Purple**.................................................... **49.00**
**Smoky,** 12" h.......................................... **86.00**
**Smoky,** 13" h.......................................... **25.00**
**Teal blue,** 6¾" h..................................... **50.00**
**Teal blue,** 10½" h.................................. **100.00**
**Teal blue,** 11½" h.................................. **150.00**
**White,** 8" h............................................ **155.00**
**White,** 9" h............................................ **130.00**
**White,** 9½" h. ...................... **175.00 to 200.00**

## SAILBOATS (Fenton)

**Bowl,** 5" d., amber ............................ **250.00**
**Bowl,** 5" d., ruffled, Amberina ............ **400.00**
**Bowl,** 5" d., aqua ................. **90.00 to 100.00**
**Bowl,** 5" d., ruffled, blue....................... **53.00**

Bowl, 5" d., clambroth............................ 40.00
Bowl, 5" d., green ............................... 125.00
Bowl, 5" d., marigold............................. 27.00
Bowl, 5" d., ice cream shape,
  marigold ......................................... 40.00
Bowl, 5" d., purple............................... 120.00
Bowl, 5" d., ruffled, red....... 500.00 to 500.00
Bowl, 5" d., vaseline........... 200.00 to 225.00
Bowl, 6" d., blue.................................. 50.00
Bowl, 6" d., ruffled, green ................... 105.00
Bowl, 6" d., ruffled, marigold................ 33.00
Bowl, 6" d., Orange Tree exterior,
  marigold......................................... 60.00
Bowl, 6" d., ruffled, purple.................. 150.00
Bowl, ice cream shape, vaseline ........ 475.00
Bowl, ruffled, blue ................................ 55.00
Bowl, ruffled, green.............................. 55.00
Bowl, ruffled, vaseline......................... 250.00
Compote, blue ................................... 220.00
Compote, marigold .............................. 75.00
Compote, marigold w/frosted stem....... 34.00
Dish, square, marigold....................... 115.00
Goblet, water, green........... 250.00 to 350.00
Goblet, water, marigold ...................... 130.00
Goblet, water, purple .......................... 300.00
Plate, 6" d., blue................................ 195.00
Plate, 6" d., marigold .......... 400.00 to 450.00
Wine, blue............................. 80.00 to 90.00
Wine, marigold..................................... 32.00
Wine, vaseline.................................... 125.00

## SKI STAR (Dugan)

Banana bowl, peach opalescent ........ 190.00
Banana bowl, purple ............................ 92.00
Basket, peach opalescent ................... 520.00
Berry set: master bowl & six sauce
  dishes; peach opalescent, 7 pcs. ..... 400.00
Bowl, 5" d., peach opalescent ............. 40.00
Bowl, 5" d., fluted, peach opalescent ... 35.00
Bowl, 5" d., ruffled, peach opalescent .. 45.00
Bowl, 5" d., ruffled, purple.................... 50.00
Bowl, 6" d., ruffled, peach opalescent .. 65.00
Bowl, 7" d., ruffled, purple.................... 75.00
Bowl, 8" d., ruffled, purple .. 425.00 to 450.00
Bowl, 8" to 9" d., dome-footed, peach
  opalescent ..................................... 100.00
Bowl, 8" to 9" d., dome-footed, purple .. 130.00
Bowl, 10" d., marigold........................... 62.00
Bowl, 10" d., peach
  opalescent........................... 80.00 to 90.00
Bowl, 10" d., purple............................ 250.00
Bowl, 11" d., peach
  opalescent.................... 100.00 to 150.00
Bowl, 11" d., purple ............ 165.00 to 175.00
Bowl, tricornered, dome-footed,
  peach opalescent (ILLUS.
  top next column).............. 100.00 to 125.00
Plate, 6" d., crimped rim, peach
  opalescent...................... 150.00 to 200.00

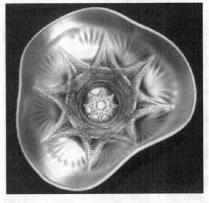

*Ski Star Bowl*

Plate, 7" d., candy ribbon rim, deep,
  peach opalescent ............................... 65.00
Plate, 8½" d., dome-footed,
  w/handgrip, peach opalescent.......... 148.00
Plate, 8½" d., dome-footed,
  w/handgrip, purple ........................... 295.00

## STAG & HOLLY

Bowl, 7" d., spatula-footed,
  blue ................................ 150.00 to 175.00
Bowl, 7" d., spatula-footed, green....... 150.00
Bowl, 7" d., spatula-footed, marigold .... 55.00
Bowl, 7" d., spatula-footed, purple........ 78.00
Bowl, 7" d., spatula-footed, red........ 2,500.00
Bowl, 8" d., footed, ice cream shape,
  blue................................................ 188.00
Bowl, 8" d., footed, ice cream shape,
  green ............................................. 200.00
Bowl, 8" d., footed, ice cream shape,
  marigold............................................ 99.00
Bowl, 8" d., footed, ice cream shape,
  purple............................................. 300.00
Bowl, 8" to 9" d., spatula-footed,
  green ............................................. 228.00
Bowl, 8" to 9" d., spatula-footed,
  lavender .......................... 175.00 to 200.00
Bowl, 8" to 9" d., spatula-footed,
  marigold .............................. 80.00 to 90.00
Bowl, 8" to 9" d., spatula-footed,
  peach opalescent ......................... 1,900.00
Bowl, 8" to 9" d., spatula-footed,
  purple............................................. 167.00
Bowl, 10" to 11" d., three-footed,
  amber ............................................. 450.00
Bowl, 10" to 11" d., three-footed,
  Amberina ........................................ 838.00
Bowl, 10" to 11" d., three-footed,
  aqua ............................................... 800.00
Bowl, 10" to 11" d., three-footed,
  blue ................................ 350.00 to 400.00

**Bowl,** 10" to 11" d., three-footed, cobalt blue ........................................ **125.00**
**Bowl,** 10" to 11" d., three-footed, green .............................................. **425.00**
**Bowl,** 10" to 11" d., three-footed, marigold ......................... **150.00 to 200.00**
**Bowl,** 10" to 11" d., three-footed, purple .............................. **375.00 to 400.00**
**Bowl,** 10" to 11" d., three-footed, vaseline ........................................... **500.00**
**Bowl,** 11" d., flat, amber..................... **750.00**
**Bowl,** 11" d., flat, blue w/electric iridescence ...................................... **450.00**
**Bowl,** 11" d., flat, green .............. **1,250.00**
**Bowl,** 11" d., flat, marigold.. **100.00 to 125.00**
**Bowl,** 11" d., ruffled, blue................... **241.00**
**Bowl,** 11" d., ruffled, green w/marigold overlay........................... **250.00**
**Bowl,** 12" d., ice cream shape, blue ................................. **325.00 to 350.00**
**Bowl,** 12" d., ice cream shape, green ............................................... **170.00**
**Bowl,** 12" d., ice cream shape, marigold ........................... **100.00 to 125.00**
**Bowl,** ice cream shape, spatula-footed, smoky ............................. **475.00**
**Bowl,** spatula-footed, green............... **100.00**
**Bowl,** spatula-footed, red............................ **1,325.00 to 1,375.00**
**Plate,** 9" d., marigold........................... **900.00**
**Plate,** chop, 12" d., three-footed, marigold ........................... **750.00 to 850.00**
**Rose bowl,** blue, large...................... **995.00**
**Rose bowl,** marigold, large................. **280.00**
**Rose bowl,** marigold, giant... **400.00 to 425.00**

## STRAWBERRY (Northwood)

**Berry set:** master bowl & four sauce dishes; marigold, 5 pcs. .................... **165.00**
**Bowl,** 5" d., fluted, blue .......................... **35.00**
**Bowl,** 5" d., marigold.............................. **28.00**
**Bowl,** 5" d., fluted, purple ...................... **40.00**
**Bowl,** 6" d., green................................... **65.00**
**Bowl,** 7" d., green................................... **56.00**
**Bowl,** 7" d., marigold ............................. **50.00**
**Bowl,** 7" d., purple.................................. **33.00**
**Bowl,** 8" to 9" d., stippled, blue ............. **925.00**
**Bowl,** 8" to 9" d., stippled, ice green .. **1,100.00**
**Bowl,** 8" to 9" d., stippled, purple ............................... **200.00 to 250.00**
**Bowl,** 8" to 9" d., ruffled, Basketweave exterior, green ................. **125.00 to 150.00**
**Bowl,** 8" to 9" d., ruffled, Basketweave exterior, marigold ............................... **60.00**
**Bowl,** 8" to 9" d., ruffled, Basketweave exterior, purple ................. **100.00 to 125.00**
**Bowl,** 8" to 9" d., ruffled, white......... **1,350.00**
**Bowl,** 8" to 9" d., blue .......................... **80.00**
**Bowl,** 8" to 9" d., piecrust rim, stippled, blue ................................... **425.00**

**Bowl,** 8" to 9" d., piecrust rim, green .. **125.00**
**Bowl,** 8" to 9" d., marigold ................... **40.00**
**Bowl,** 8" to 9" d., purple...... **125.00 to 175.00**
**Bowl,** 9" d., piecrust rim, marigold ........ **70.00**
**Bowl,** 9" d., ruffled, stippled, ribbed exterior, purple............................. **1,000.00**
**Bowl,** 9" d., stippled, ribbed exterior, marigold ........................... **165.00 to 175.00**
**Bowl,** 10" d., Basketweave exterior, green ............................................... **190.00**
**Bowl,** 10" d., ice green........................ **700.00**
**Bowl,** 10" d., marigold.......................... **65.00**
**Bowl,** 10" d., Basketweave exterior, marigold ............................................ **125.00**
**Bowl,** 10" d., purple............................. **110.00**
**Bowl,** 10" d., Basketweave exterior, purple................................................ **170.00**
**Plate,** 6" to 7" d., w/handgrip, green ... **210.00**
**Plate,** 6" to 7" d., w/handgrip, marigold.. **75.00**
**Plate,** 6" to 7" d., w/handgrip, purple... **105.00**
**Plate,** 9" d., green .............................. **135.00**
**Plate,** 9" d., lavender.......................... **135.00**
**Plate,** 9" d., marigold .......................... **145.00**
**Plate,** 9" d., pastel marigold ............... **125.00**
**Plate,** 9" d., purple ............. **220.00 to 250.00**
**Plate,** Basketweave exterior, green ............................... **200.00 to 275.00**
**Plate,** Basketweave exterior, marigold ........................... **150.00 to 200.00**
**Plate,** Basketweave exterior, purple ... **213.00**
**Plate,** stippled, Basketweave exterior, green ............................................... **400.00**
**Plate,** stippled, green ........................ **600.00**
**Plate,** stippled, marigold .. **800.00 to 1,000.00**
**Plate,** stippled, purple ..................... **1,500.00**

## SWIRL HOBNAIL (Millersburg)

*Swirl Hobnail Cuspidor*

**Cuspidor,** marigold ............ **750.00 to 800.00**
**Cuspidor,** purple (ILLUS.).. **700.00 to 900.00**
**Rose bowl,** green .............................. **500.00**
**Rose bowl,** marigold ......... **200.00 to 300.00**
**Rose bowl,** purple .............. **275.00 to 325.00**
**Vase,** green ........................ **200.00 to 300.00**
**Vase,** marigold ................................... **200.00**
**Vase,** purple....................... **250.00 to 350.00**

## THISTLE (Fenton)

Banana boat, amber........................... 170.00
Banana boat, blue.............. 325.00 to 350.00
Banana boat, blue w/electric
    iridescence ..................................... 500.00
Banana boat, celeste blue................. 350.00
Banana boat, green............................ 285.00
Banana boat, marigold....... 160.00 to 175.00
Banana boat, purple .......... 350.00 to 400.00
Bowl, 7" d., marigold............................ 47.00
Bowl, 7" d., purple................................ 45.00
Bowl, 7½" d., ice cream shape,
    purple .................................. 75.00 to 85.00
Bowl, 8" d., three-in-one edge, purple .. 85.00
Bowl, 8" to 9" d., ruffled, amber .......... 125.00
Bowl, 8" to 9" d., ribbon candy rim,
    blue...................................................... 80.00
Bowl, 8" to 9" d., ruffled, blue .............. 83.00
Bowl, 8" to 9" d., flared, green ............ 108.00
Bowl, 8" to 9" d., ribbon candy rim,
    green ................................. 90.00 to 100.00
Bowl, 8" to 9" d., ruffled,
    green ................................... 80.00 to 90.00
Bowl, 8" to 9" d., ruffled, lavender ........ 45.00
Bowl, 8" to 9" d., ribbon candy rim,
    marigold............................................... 70.00
Bowl, 8" to 9" d., ruffled, marigold ........ 56.00
Bowl, 8" to 9" d., ribbon candy rim,
    purple .................................. 65.00 to 75.00
Bowl, 8" to 9" d., ruffled, purple ............ 95.00
Bowl, 9" d., fluted, green...................... 95.00
Bowl, 9" d., ice cream shape, purple .... 65.00
Bowl, 9" d., piecrust rim, marigold ...... 160.00
Bowl, ruffled, aqua.............................. 600.00
Bowl, three-in-one edge, marigold...... 104.00
Bowl, three-in-one edge, purple ........... 45.00
Centerpiece bowl, blue...................... 380.00
Creamer, footed, marigold.................... 25.00
Plate, 9" d., blue, .......... 2,500.00 to 3,000.00

*Thistle Plate*

Plate, 9" d., green (ILLUS.).............. 3,000.00
Plate, marigold................................ 3,500.00
Plate, purple.................................... 3,700.00
Vase, 6" h., green ................................ 75.00
Vase, 6" h., marigold............................ 30.00

## TROUT & FLY (Millersburg)

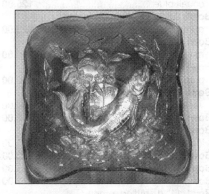

*Trout & Fly Bowl*

Bowl, ice cream shape,
    green ............................... 750.00 to 800.00
Bowl, ice cream shape, lavender..... 1,350.00
Bowl, ice cream shape,
    marigold .......................... 450.00 to 500.00
Bowl, ice cream shape, purple ........... 600.00
Bowl, ribbon candy rim, green ........... 712.00
Bowl, ribbon candy rim, lavender .... 1,400.00
Bowl, ribbon candy rim, marigold ....... 350.00
Bowl, ribbon candy rim, purple ........... 575.00
Bowl, ruffled, green ............ 450.00 to 500.00
Bowl, ruffled, lavender..................... 1,800.00
Bowl, ruffled, marigold........ 400.00 to 475.00
Bowl, ruffled, marigold, satin finish ..... 385.00
Bowl, ruffled, pastel marigold, satin
    finish .................................................. 500.00
Bowl, ruffled, purple ........... 550.00 to 600.00
Bowl, ruffled, purple, satin finish......... 675.00
Bowl, square, green ..... 1,225.00 to 1,275.00
Bowl, square, marigold (ILLUS.
    above)................................................ 650.00
Bowl, square, purple........................... 825.00

## VENETIAN GIANT ROSE BOWL (Cambridge)

*Venetian Giant Rose Bowl*

**Green** (ILLUS. bottom previous
page) ............................................ **1,200.00**
**Marigold** ...................................... **1,700.00**

## WATER LILY & CATTAILS

**Banana boat,** blue............. **150.00 to 185.00**
**Banana boat,** marigold ...................... **140.00**
**Banana boat,** purple .......................... **110.00**
**Bonbon,** two-handled, marigold,
large................................................ **50.00**
**Bowl,** 5" d., marigold............................ **32.00**
**Bowl,** 9" d., marigold............................ **80.00**
**Bowl,** 9" d., purple.............................. **60.00**
**Butter dish,** cov., marigold ................ **156.00**
**Dish,** three turned-up sides, marigold,
6" d. ............................................... **29.00**
**Pitcher,** water, marigold...................... **548.00**
**Plate,** 6" d., marigold............................ **55.00**
**Rose bowl,** blue.................................... **75.00**
**Rose bowl,** marigold............................. **30.00**
**Sauce dish,** marigold............................ **12.00**
**Sauce dish,** footed, vaseline
w/marigold overlay.............................. **75.00**
**Spooner,** marigold................................. **50.00**
**Sugar bowl,** cov., marigold.................... **75.00**
**Table set:** cov. sugar bowl, creamer,
spooner & cov. butter dish;
marigold, 4 pcs. .............................. **535.00**
**Toothpick holder,** marigold ................. **65.00**
**Tumbler,** blue .............................. **2,700.00**
**Tumbler,** marigold ................. **25.00 to 35.00**
**Tumbler,** purple ................................... **23.00**
**Tumblers,** marigold, set of 6.............. **240.00**
**Water set:** pitcher & six tumblers;
marigold, 7 pcs. .............................. **765.00**
**Whimsey,** marigold............................... **38.00**
**Whimsey,** purple.................................. **55.00**

## WISHBONE (Northwood)

**Bowl,** 7" d., three-footed, ruffled rim,
marigold.............................................. **50.00**
**Bowl,** 7" d., three-footed, ruffled rim,
purple ............................. **130.00 to 140.00**
**Bowl,** 8" to 9" d., footed, aqua
opalescent .................................... **1,300.00**
**Bowl,** 8" to 9" d., footed, blue ............. **300.00**
**Bowl,** 8" to 9" d., footed, clambroth ...... **90.00**
**Bowl,** 8" to 9" d., footed,
green.............................. **100.00 to 125.00**
**Bowl,** 8" to 9" d., footed, ice blue..... **2,200.00**
**Bowl,** 8" to 9" d., footed, ice green .. **1,650.00**
**Bowl,** 8" to 9" d., footed, lavender ...... **200.00**
**Bowl,** 8" to 9" d., footed, lime green ..... **80.00**
**Bowl,** 8" to 9" d., footed, marigold ........ **71.00**
**Bowl,** 8" to 9" d., footed, pastel
marigold.............................................. **85.00**
**Bowl,** 8" to 9" d., footed,
purple .............................. **115.00 to 150.00**
**Bowl,** 8" to 9" d., footed, white............ **550.00**

*Wishbone Plate*

**Bowl,** 10" d., footed, blue ... **500.00 to 600.00**
**Bowl,** 10" d., piecrust rim, blue
w/electric iridescence ................... **2,300.00**
**Bowl,** 10" d., piecrust rim,
green ................................. **225.00 to 250.00**
**Bowl,** 10" d., piecrust rim, Basketweave
exterior, green ..................... **900.00 to 975.00**
**Bowl,** 10" d., piecrust rim,
marigold ........................... **150.00 to 200.00**
**Bowl,** 10" d., piecrust rim,
Basketweave exterior, marigold ....... **115.00**
**Bowl,** 10" d., ruffled, green ................ **145.00**
**Bowl,** 10" d., ruffled, marigold............. **150.00**
**Bowl,** 10" d., ruffled, Basketweave
exterior, purple ................................ **125.00**
**Bowl,** 10" d., piecrust rim, purple........ **130.00**
**Bowl,** 10" d., footed, ruffled,
purple ............................... **125.00 to 135.00**
**Bowl,** 10" d., footed, piecrust rim,
smoky ............................................ **1,300.00**
**Bowl,** 10" d., footed, piecrust rim,
white ................................................. **750.00**
**Bowl,** 11 d., flat, green......................... **125.00**
**Bowl,** footed, clambroth ..................... **115.00**
**Epergne,** ice blue............................. **3,500.00**
**Epergne,** green ................................... **675.00**
**Epergne,** marigold............. **400.00 to 450.00**
**Epergne,** purple................. **450.00 to 500.00**
**Epergne,** white ................................. **1,875.00**
**Pitcher,** water, green ...................... **1,800.00**
**Pitcher,** water, marigold.................. **1,500.00**
**Pitcher,** water, purple ... **1,050.00 to 1,100.00**
**Plate,** 6½" d., purple............................ **85.00**
**Plate,** 8½" d., three sides turned up,
marigold.............................................. **40.00**
**Plate,** 8½" d., footed, marigold............ **475.00**
**Plate,** 8½" d., footed, purple (ILLUS.
above)................................................ **300.00**
**Plate,** 8½" d., footed, tricornered,
green ................................................. **675.00**

**Plate,** 8½" d., footed, tricornered,
purple .............................. **350.00 to 400.00**
**Plate,** chop, 11" d., marigold ............... **500.00**
**Plate,** chop, 11" d., purple ................... **645.00**
**Tumbler,** green ................................. **180.00**
**Tumbler,** marigold ............. **100.00 to 125.00**
**Tumbler,** purple ................................. **135.00**

### ZIG ZAG (Millersburg)

**Bowl,** 9½" d., marigold ....................... **168.00**
**Bowl,** 9½" d., green ........................... **420.00**
**Bowl,** 10" d., green ............. **250.00 to 275.00**
**Bowl,** 10" d., marigold ........................ **185.00**
**Bowl,** 10" d., purple ........... **230.00 to 240.00**
**Bowl,** 10" w., tricornered, piecrust
rim, green ...................................... **200.00**
**Bowl,** 10" w., tricornered, marigold .... **275.00**
**Bowl,** 10" w., tricornered, purple ........ **430.00**
**Bowl,** 10", ribbon candy rim, green ...... **95.00**
**Bowl,** 10" d., three-in-one rim, purple... **325.00**
**Bowl,** ribbon candy rim, marigold ....... **220.00**
**Bowl,** ribbon candy rim,
purple ............................. **250.00 to 300.00**
**Tumbler,** green ................................. **15.00**

**(End of Carnival Glass Listings)**

# CHRYSANTHEMUM SPRIG, BLUE

*The Chrysanthemum Sprig pattern, originally called "Pagoda," was one of several patterns produced by the Northwood Glass Company at the turn-of-the-century in their creamy white Custard glass (which see). A limited amount of this pattern was also produced in a blue opaque color, sometimes erroneously called 'blue custard.'*

*Blue Chrysanthemum Sprig Butter Dish*

**Berry set,** master berry bowl & six
sauce dishes, 7 pcs. ................... **$1,195.00**
**Bowl,** berry, individual........................ **115.00**
**Butter dish,** cov. (ILLUS. bottom
previous column) ......................... **1,250.00**
**Celery dish** .................................... **1,150.00**
**Compote,** jelly................................. **500.00**
**Creamer** ........................... **325.00 to 400.00**
**Cruet w/original stopper** .. **975.00 to 1,200.00**
**Spooner** ........................... **295.00 to 350.00**
**Sugar bowl,** cov. ............................. **585.00**
**Tumbler** ............................................ **115.00**

# CORALENE

*Coralene is a method of decorating glass, usually satin glass, with the use of beaded-type decoration customarily applied to the glass with the use of enamels, which were melted. Coralene decoration has been faked with the use of glue.*

*Fine Coralene Pitcher*

**Pitcher,** 6¼" h., 4" d., spherical base
w/a wide cylindrical neck w/an
upright pointed spout, deep orangish
red decorated w/large coralene
water lilies & leaves around the
base, applied amber rigaree band
around the base of the neck &
applied amber handle, marked
"Patent" (ILLUS.) ........................... **$225.00**
**Vase,** 4" h., ovoid cased butterscotch
yellow body & white lining w/a
diamond & fleur-de-lis pattern
between the layers & the surface
decorated w/coralene beading ......... **316.00**

*Coralene "Seaweed" Vase*

**Vase,** 8" h., 3⅝" d., tall ovoid body w/a trumpet neck, shaded blue satin ground decorated w/"seaweed" coralene beading (ILLUS.)............... **450.00**

**Vase,** 11¼" h., bulbous ovoid body tapering to a tall slender cylindrical neck, dusty rose satin at the top shading to white & then turquoise blue at the base, completely covered w/patchwork panels each filled w/delicate starburst or blossom designs ........................................... **890.00**

# CRANBERRY

*Gold was added to glass batches to give this glass its color on reheating. It has been made by numerous glasshouses for years and is currently being reproduced. Both blown and molded articles were produced. A less expensive type of cranberry was made with the substitution of copper for gold.*

**Bowl,** 8" d., 1½" h., the clear center encasing a silver coin surrounded by wide cranberry sides & an applied ruffled pale blue border band, applied clear low foot..................... **$225.00**

**Box w/fitted cover,** rounded form w/twelve cut panels around the sides of the base & cover, each panel outlined in gold & filled w/gold squiggles & dots, applied clear facet-cut knob finial, 2⅝" d., 3⅛" h. .......................................... **110.00**

*Decorated Cranberry Box*

**Box w/hinged cover,** round, squatty rounded body & domed cover, the cover decorated in delicate gold w/a cross-form framing leafy scrolls & framed by leafy blossom clusters, dainty gold flowers & leaves around the sides of the base, 3¼" d., 2⅞" h. (ILLUS.) ........................................... **185.00**

**Box w/hinged cover,** round, squatty tapering body w/metal fittings for the hinged, domed cover, the top & sides enamel-decorated w/gold & white buds & large gold flowers, buds & leaves outlined in white, 3⅞" d., 3⅜" h. .................................. **235.00**

**Celery vase,** cylindrical body w/lightly ruffled rim, Inverted Thumbprint patt., h.p. w/flowers & butterflies, fitted in a pedestal-based fancy silver plate stand w/loop side handles, overall 10¼" h. ................ **640.00**

**Creamer,** the ovoid body facet-cut on the upper & lower halves w/ten panels, the panel-cut neck w/a high arched spout & scalloped rim, applied cut cranberry handle, 3½" d., 4½" h. .. **165.00**

**Cruet w/clear bubble stopper,** bulbous body tapering to a tall cylindrical neck w/ringed rim, applied clear spun rope handle w/flower print at base & applied clear wafer foot, 2¾" d., 6¼" h. .................................. **110.00**

**Cruet w/clear facet-cut stopper,** footed spherical body tapering to a slender cylindrical neck w/a cupped rim, the sides decorated w/large pink & white flowers & small yellow blossoms & green leaves, gold trim, applied clear handle, 3½" d., 7⅛" h. (ILLUS. top next page) .................... **195.00**

*Decorated Cranberry Cruet*

**Cup & saucer,** the flaring cylindrical cup w/applied gold loop handle, both the cup & saucer decorated w/heavy gold lacy pointed panels & flowers & foliage, saucer 5⅛" d., cup 3⅛" d., 2¼" h. .............................................. **245.00**

**Decanter w/clear bubble stopper,** the clear applied foot supporting a bulbous optic ribbed body tapering to a slender cylindrical ringed neck w/small clear spout, applied clear ropetwist handle w/a flower print at its base, 4¾" d., 11" h. ...................... **195.00**

**Decanter w/clear facet-cut stopper,** the double-gourd form body w/dimpled sides on the lower section, each body section decorated w/lacy gold scrolls framing stylized reddish flowers & gold dots, 3¾" d., 11¼" h. ................. **225.00**

**Decanter w/tall clear facet-cut stopper,** the applied clear foot supporting a bulbous body tapering to a tall slender "stick" neck w/a flaring rim, the sides of the lower body decorated w/ornate lacy gold scrolls & garlands w/dainty blue & gold flowers, gold trim on the foot, 4½" d., 12⅜" h. ............................... **225.00**

**Jam pot w/silver plated lid,** rim & handle, slighting tapering bulbous body, hole in the lid for jam spoon, 3¾" d., 3½" h. ................................. **110.00**

**Pitcher,** miniature, 2" h., 1¼" d., footed ovoid body tapering to a wide spout, decorated in blue, white & pink w/gold diamonds around the top & small flowers hanging down, applied clear handle w/white trim ..... **125.00**

**Pitcher,** cov., tankard-type, the wide slightly tapering cylindrical optic ribbed body topped by a wide silver plate collar & spout & hinged low domed cover, applied clear handle, 5" d., 11" h. ....................................... **295.00**

**Rose bowl,** miniature, twelve-crimp rim, "Jewell," decorated w/airtraps in a zipper-like design, 2½" d., 2" h. ..... **135.00**

**Salt dip,** round, decorated w/white enamel lacy scrolls & white dots w/gold trim, 2⅞" d., 1¾" h. ................... **75.00**

**Scent bottle,** lay-down-type, double-ended w/a screw-on silver cap on one end & a hinged silver cap at the other, the cylindrical body w/narrow cut panels, ⅞" d., 4" l. ...................... **185.00**

**Sugar bowl,** cov., footed nearly spherical body w/a fitted domed cover w/a clear applied knob finial, clear wafer foot, 3⅞" d., 6¼" h. .......... **110.00**

**Vase,** 5⅛" h., 3¾" d., footed wide optic ribbed ovoid body tapering to a tricorner rim, the sides applied w/a large clear blossom on a leafy stem on three sides, clear applied foot ..... **165.00**

*Decorated Cranberry Vases*

**Vase,** 8¼" h., 4" d., footed bulbous optic ribbed body tapering to a tall cylindrical neck w/a rolled & scalloped rim, the sides decorated w/heavy gold roses, buds & leaves, probably Webb (ILLUS. right) .......... **225.00**

**Vase,** 10⅝" h., 3⅝" d., a cushion-form base tapering to a tall optic ribbed body w/a flat angle-cut mouth, decorated w/dainty lacy white flowers & branches winding up the sides (ILLUS. left) ............................. **165.00**

## CROWN MILANO

*This glass, produced by the Mt. Washington Glass Company late last century, is opal glass decorated by painting and enameling. It appears identical to a ware term Albertine, also made by Mt. Washington. Some pieces carried a special trade-mark on the bottom.*

*Crown Milano mark*

*Crown Milano Cracker Jar*

**Cracker jar w/silver plate cover,** ruffled rim & bail handle, squatty bulbous body decorated w/gold & orange roses & leaves on a white ground, the lid decorated w/a small figural turtle (ILLUS.) .................. **$1,200.00**

**Creamer & cov. sugar bowl,** each of squatty bulbous form tapering to a narrow neck, the sugar bowl w/small loop handles & the shoulder & a bulbous domed cover w/knob finial, the creamer w/a high curved spout & applied handle, each decorated w/sprays of blue cornflowers, purple asters, pink & yellow roses & red wild roses on a soft beige ground w/heavy gilt trim, sugar 4¾" h., creamer 4¼" h., pr. (hairline in base of sugar) .............. **1,250.00**

*Tall Crown Milano Lamp*

**Lamp,** banquet-style, spherical ball shade on a metal ring & burner above a small squatty bulbous font w/ribbed scroll upturned handles above the tall slender shaft flaring to a wide squatty bulbous base, shiny opaque ground decorated down the side of the base w/a wide gilded ribbon of glass & h.p. on the shade & base w/floral bouquets & scrolls w/a gilt lattice background at the lower section of the base, marked, all original, 38" h. (ILLUS.) ........... **12,650.00**

**Vase,** cov., 10½" h., wide ovoid body w/a small high, domed cover w/a ribbed & pointed finial, the body decorated w/large green & brown ivy leaves & vines w/lighter tan swirled designs on the cover & around the base all on a creamy white ground, unmarked ...................................... **2,285.00**

**Vase,** 4¾" h., squatty bulbous body tapering to a short rolled neck flanked by small loop handles, decorated w/gilded wild roses over a peach & amber leafy ground w/folded gold rim handles, unsigned Mt. Washington (ILLUS. right, top next page) ........................................ **575.00**

**Vase,** 8" h., squared bulbous spherical body w/a short cylindrical neck w/rolled rim flanked by ribbed S-scroll handles, decorated w/gold enameled

*Fine Crown Milano Vases*

oak leaves & acorns over a shadowy amber patterned background, stamped mark in blue (ILLUS. left)...... **920.00**

**Vase,** 14" h., tall slender ovoid body w/a very slender & slightly flaring tall neck, decorated w/lilacs highlighted w/heavy matte gold scrolls & a cross design on the neck ........................ **1,725.00**

## CRUETS

**Amber,** mold-blown, footed bulbous body tapering to a cylindrical neck w/a tricorner rim, the sides decorated w/clusters of pink flowers & gold leaves, original blue teardrop stopper, applied blue handle, 3⅜" d., 6½" h. (ILLUS. left, top next page) .............. **$195.00**

**Amber,** blown, nearly spherical body tapering to a slender cylindrical neck w/a ringed rim, the sides finely engraved w/ferns, leaves, a butterfly & a wasp, original facet-cut stopper, applied blue handle, 4½" d., 9" h. ...... **195.00**

**Amber & white,** blown, bulbous body tapering to a slender cylindrical neck w/a tricorner rim, the amber body overlaid w/a stretched white spatter effect, amber bubble stopper, applied reeded amber rope handle, 3¾" d., 8¾" h. (ILLUS. center, top next page) ......................................... **150.00**

**Amethyst,** blown, the tall, slender conical body w/a wide tricorner rim, the sides decorated w/heavy gold large leaves, stem & cherry cluster all outlined in white, amethyst teardrop stopper, applied amethyst handle, 3" d., 9¾" h. ......................... **195.00**

**Blue,** mold-blown, the ringed ovoid body tapering to a tall cylindrical neck w/an arched spout, an applied amber neck ring w/white dots, the body decorated w/colored florals & leaves, ringed amber bubble stopper, applied amber handle, 3½" d., 9" h. (ILLUS. right, top next page) .......................... **195.00**

**Cranberry,** blown, the bulbous body tapering to a slender cylindrical neck & pointed spout decorated overall w/delicate threading, clear bubble stopper, clear applied reeded handle, 3½" d., 7" h. ......................... **110.00**

**Cranberry,** mold-blown, the tall cylindrical body w/a squatty swelled shoulder w/a short cylindrical neck & cupped rim, the shoulder decorated w/dainty yellow blossom clusters & white leaves, clear ringed stopper, applied clear handle, 3½" d., 8⅜" h... **195.00**

*Green Decorated Cruet*

*A Group of Decorated Cruets*

**Green,** mold-blown, the tapering ovoid body w/a tall slender cylindrical neck w/pinched spout, the shoulder decorated w/white blossom clusters & leaves, green teardrop stopper, applied green handle, 3¼" d., 8¼" h. (ILLUS. bottom previous page)........... **95.00**

**Green,** mold-blown, wide squatty bulbous cylindrical body tapering to a tall cylindrical neck w/a tricorner rim, the sides decorated w/almond-shaped dainty white blossom panels framing gold bands, tall ringed clear bubble stopper, applied clear reeded handle, 4¼" d., 10⅜" h. .................... **100.00**

**Green,** mold-blown, a cushion foot supports the ovoid body tapering to a swelled shoulder & cylindrical neck w/a long arched spout, the sides decorated w/clusters of white blossoms & gold stems & line banding, gold bands around neck & rim, tall steeple-style facet-cut green stopper, applied green handle, 3¼" d., 11¾" h. ................................. **110.00**

## CUSTARD GLASS

*This ware takes its name from its color and is a variant of milk white glass. It was produced largely between 1890 and 1915 by the Northwood Glass Co., Heisey Glass Company, Fenton Art Glass Co., Jefferson Glass Co., and a few others. There are twenty-one major patterns and a number of minor ones. The prime patterns are considered*

*Argonaut Shell, Chrysanthemum Sprig, Inverted Fan and Feather, Louis XV and Winged Scroll. Most custard glass patterns are enhanced with gold and some have additional enameled decoration or stained highlights. Unless otherwise noted, items in this listing are fully decorated.*

### *Northwood*

*Custard Northwood Script Mark*

### ARGONAUT SHELL (Northwood)

*Argonaut Shell Butter Dish*

**Bowl,** master berry or fruit, 10½" l., 5" h. ............................... **$185.00 to 225.00**
**Butter dish,** cov. (ILLUS.) .. **300.00 to 375.00**
**Compote,** jelly, 5" d., 5" h. .................. **140.00**

Creamer............................................. 150.00
Cruet w/original stopper.................. 850.00
Pitcher, water ................................... 430.00
Sauce dish, gold trim, decorated.......... 55.00
Spooner............................................ 150.00
Sugar bowl, cov. ............................. 185.00
Toothpick holder.............. 325.00 to 425.00
Tumbler .......................................... 110.00
Water set, pitcher & six tumblers,
　7 pcs. ........................................... 900.00

## BEADED CIRCLE (Northwood)

Butter dish, cov............................... 460.00
Creamer ......................... 150.00 to 175.00
Cruet w/original stopper................... 650.00
Pitcher, water.................... 600.00 to 650.00
Spooner ........................... 100.00 to 150.00
Sugar bowl, cov. ............................. 175.00
Tumbler ........................................... 130.00

## BEADED SWAG (Heisey)

Butter dish, cov................................ 110.00
Goblet................................................. 60.00
Goblet, souvenir .................................. 70.00
Sauce dish .......................................... 25.00
Sauce dish, souvenir........................... 45.00
Sugar bowl, open ................................ 45.00
Wine.................................................... 48.00
Wine, souvenir .................................... 65.00

## CARNELIAN - See Everglades Pattern

## CHERRY & SCALE or FENTONIA (Fenton)

Berry set, master bowl & six sauce
　dishes, 7 pcs.................................. 395.00
Bowl, master berry or fruit ................ 115.00
Butter dish, cov................................ 235.00
Creamer.............................................. 95.00
Spooner............................................ 110.00
Tumbler .............................................. 75.00

## CHRYSANTHEMUM SPRIG (Northwood's Pagoda)

*Chrysanthemum Sprig Master Berry Bowl*

Berry set, master bowl & six sauce
　dishes, 7 pcs.................................. 520.00
Bowl, master berry or fruit, 10½" oval,
　decorated (ILLUS. bottom previous
　column)........................................... 165.00
Butter dish, cov................................ 297.00
Celery vase ...................................... 755.00
Compote, jelly, decorated .. 100.00 to 125.00
Compotes, jelly, goofus trim, set of 7 ... 385.00
Compote, undecorated........................ 52.00
Condiment tray................. 570.00 to 610.00
Creamer ........................... 100.00 to 150.00
Cruet w/original stopper... 300.00 to 400.00
Pitcher, water, decorated ................... 457.00
Pitcher, water, undecorated .............. 225.00
Salt & pepper shakers w/original
　tops, decorated w/gold trim.............. 145.00
Sauce dish ............................ 50.00 to 60.00
Sauce dish, blue trim......................... 140.00
Spooner............................. 100.00 to 150.00
Sugar bowl, cov., decorated... 175.00 to 250.00
Sugar bowl, cov.,
　undecorated .................... 150.00 to 180.00
Table set, cov. sugar bowl, creamer,
　cov. butter dish & spooner, 4 pcs. .... 740.00
Toothpick holder w/gold trim & paint,
　signed.............................. 250.00 to 350.00
Toothpick holder, undecorated ......... 175.00
Tumbler.............................. 75.00 to 100.00
Water set, pitcher & six tumblers,
　7 pcs................................ 675.00 to 775.00

## DIAMOND MAPLE LEAF (Dugan)

*Diamond Maple Leaf Sugar Bowl*

Bowl, master berry............................ 145.00
Banana boat...................................... 235.00
Butter dish, cov. ............... 300.00 to 350.00
Creamer............................................ 145.00
Sugar bowl, cov., w/gold trim
　(ILLUS. above) .............................. 275.00
Water set, pitcher & six tumblers,
　7 pcs. ............................................. 700.00

## DIAMOND WITH PEG (Jefferson)

**Butter dish,** cov. ............... 250.00 to 275.00
**Creamer,** individual size ...................... 30.00
**Creamer,** individual size, souvenir........ 85.00
**Creamer**............................................... 60.00
**Mug,** souvenir ......................... 35.00 to 45.00
**Napkin ring**........................................ 145.00
**Pitcher,** 5½" h. .................................... 140.00
**Pitcher,** tankard, 7½" h. ...................... 250.00
**Pitcher,** tankard, 7½" h., souvenir ...... 230.00

*Diamond with Peg Pitcher*

**Pitcher,** water, tankard, decorated
   (ILLUS.) ............................................ 395.00
**Salt shaker w/original top**................... 60.00
**Spooner**............................................... 95.00
**Sugar bowl,** cov. ................ 125.00 to 150.00
**Toothpick holder** ................................. 75.00
**Tumbler** ............................................... 75.00
**Tumbler,** souvenir................................. 39.00
**Whiskey shot glass** ............................. 45.00
**Wine,** souvenir......................... 55.00 to 70.00

## EVERGLADES or CARNELIAN (Northwood)

**Bowl,** master berry or fruit,
   footed ............................. 165.00 to 185.00
**Compote,** jelly .................... 250.00 to 275.00
**Creamer**............................................. 120.00
**Sauce dish** .......................................... 60.00
**Spooner**............................................. 130.00
**Sugar bowl,** cov. (ILLUS. top next
   column) ............................................. 175.00
**Table set,** 4 pcs .................................. 850.00
**Tumbler** ............................................. 105.00

*Everglades Sugar Bowl*

## FAN (Dugan)

*Fan Master Berry Bowl*

**Bowl,** master berry or fruit
   (ILLUS.) ........................... 175.00 to 200.00
**Creamer**............................................... 90.00
**Ice cream dish** .................................... 50.00
**Pitcher,** water ..................................... 290.00
**Sauce dish** .......................................... 60.00
**Spooner**............................................... 65.00
**Tumbler**................................. 65.00 to 70.00
**Tumblers,** set of 6 ............................. 400.00

## FLUTED SCROLLS or KLONDYKE (Northwood)

**Berry set:** master berry, two
   decorated sauces & four
   undecorated sauces; 7 pcs............... 375.00
**Bowl,** master berry or fruit, footed ...... 145.00
**Creamer**............................................... 65.00
**Spooner**............................................... 48.00

## GENEVA (Northwood)

**Banana boat,** four-footed, 11"
   oval..................................... 95.00 to 125.00
**Banana boat,** four-footed, green
   stain, 11" oval .................................. 145.00

**Bowl,** master berry or fruit, oval,
8½" d., four-footed ............................. **90.00**

**Bowl,** master berry or fruit, round,
8½" d., three-footed ......................... **135.00**

**Butter dish,** cov. ............... **175.00 to 250.00**

**Compote,** jelly...................................... **75.00**

**Creamer** ............................ **80.00 to 100.00**

**Cruet w/original stopper**... **250.00 to 350.00**

**Pitcher,** water ................................... **223.00**

*Geneva Salt Shaker*

**Salt & pepper shakers w/original
tops,** pr. (ILLUS. of one) .................. **241.00**

**Sauce dish,** oval................................... **43.00**

**Sauce dish,** round .............................. **40.00**

**Spooner**.............................................. **92.00**

**Sugar bowl,** open ................................ **75.00**

**Syrup pitcher w/original top**............. **275.00**

**Table set,** 4 pcs.................. **450.00 to 500.00**

**Toothpick holder,** decorated ............. **125.00**

**Toothpick holder,** decorated, green
stain, goofus trim ............................. **238.00**

**Tumbler** .............................................. **48.00**

**Tumbler** w/green trim .......................... **55.00**

### GEORGIA GEM or LITTLE GEM (Tarentum)

**Bowl,** master berry or fruit,
decorated ......................... **100.00 to 125.00**

**Bowl,** master berry or fruit,
undecorated...................................... **65.00**

**Butter dish,** cov.,
decorated ......................... **175.00 to 200.00**

**Butter dish,** cov., undecorated........... **100.00**

**Creamer,** decorated............................. **95.00**

**Creamer & cov. sugar
bowl,** souvenir, pr. ............. **75.00 to 125.00**

**Creamer & open sugar bowl,**
breakfast size, decorated, pr. ............. **95.00**

**Creamer & open sugar bowl,**
breakfast size, souvenir, pr................ **90.00**

**Cruet** w/original stopper..................... **295.00**

**Pitcher,** water, undecorated.. **150.00 to 200.00**

**Sauce dish,** decorated ......................... **35.00**

**Spooner**.............................................. **62.00**

**Sugar bowl,** cov., decorated ............. **105.00**

**Sugar bowl,** cov., undecorated ........... **45.00**

**Sugar bowl,** open, breakfast size......... **42.00**

**Sugar bowl,** open breakfast size,
souvenir ............................................ **38.00**

**Table set,** decorated,
4 pcs............................... **350.00 to 450.00**

*Georgia Gem Toothpick Holder*

**Toothpick holder** (ILLUS.).................. **22.00**

**Tumbler,** souvenir............................... **35.00**

### GRAPE & GOTHIC ARCHES (Northwood)

**Goblet**................................................ **66.00**

**Sugar bowl,** cov., blue stain .............. **195.00**

**Table set,** 4 pcs. ................................ **375.00**

**Tumbler** .............................................. **58.00**

**Vase,** 10" h. ("favor" vase made from
goblet mold)....................................... **75.00**

**Vase,** ruffled hat shape ........................ **55.00**

### INTAGLIO (Northwood)

**Berry set,** 9" d. master berry bowl,
compote-style, footed & six sauce
dishes, 7 pcs.................................... **392.00**

**Bowl,** fruit, 7½" d. master berry bowl,
compote-style, footed ...................... **127.00**

**Bowl,** master berry w/green
decoration........................................ **165.00**

**Butter dish,** cov. .............. **200.00 to 260.00**

**Butter dish,** cov., gold w/blue
decoration........................................ **130.00**

**Butter dish,** cov., gold w/green
decoration........................................ **295.00**

**Compote,** jelly................................... **115.00**

**Creamer & cov. sugar bowl,** pr......... **275.00**

**Cruet** w/original stopper.................... **310.00**

*Intaglio Tumbler*

**Pitcher,** water .................................. 373.00
**Salt shaker w/original top**.................. 98.00
**Salt & pepper shakers w/original
tops,** pr............................................ 200.00
**Table set,** green stain, 4 pcs. ............. 540.00
**Tumbler** (ILLUS. above) ...................... 60.00
**Tumbler,** blue decoration...................... 85.00

## INVERTED FAN & FEATHER
(Northwood)

*Inverted Fan & Feather Sugar Bowl*

**Berry set,** master bowl & six sauce
dishes, 7 pcs. .................. 600.00 to 700.00
**Bowl,** master berry or fruit, 10" d.,
5½" h., four-footed............ 200.00 to 250.00
**Butter dish,** cov................................. 216.00
**Compote,** jelly .................... 425.00 to 525.00
**Creamer** .............................. 90.00 to 120.00
**Pitcher,** water ...................................... 650.00
**Punch cup**........................................... 265.00
**Salt & pepper shakers w/original
tops,** pr............................................ 495.00
**Sauce dish** ........................................... 59.00
**Spooner**.............................................. 137.00
**Sugar bowl,** cov. (ILLUS.
above) ............................. 200.00 to 285.00

**Table set,** 4 pcs................... 800.00 to 850.00
**Toothpick holder**.............. 600.00 to 650.00
**Tumbler** ............................................... 100.00

## JACKSON or FLUTED SCROLLS WITH
FLOWER BAND (Northwood)

**Bowl,** master berry or fruit .................... 85.00
**Creamer**................................................ 85.00
**Pitcher,** water, undecorated ............... 275.00
**Salt shaker w/original top,**
undecorated...................................... 58.00
**Salt & pepper shakers w/original
tops,** pr. ........................................... 135.00
**Tumbler** ................................................ 41.00
**Water set,** pitcher & four tumblers,
5 pcs................................ 365.00 to 385.00

## LOUIS XV (Northwood)

**Bowl,** master berry or fruit w/gold trim... 295.00
**Bowl,** berry or fruit, 7¾ x 10" oval....... 132.00
**Butter dish,** cov. ............... 150.00 to 200.00
**Creamer** ................................. 65.00 to 85.00
**Cruet w/original stopper**.................. 450.00
**Pitcher,** water .................... 200.00 to 250.00
**Sauce dish,** footed, 5" oval.................. 40.00
**Spooner** ................................. 50.00 to 75.00
**Sugar bowl,** cov. ............... 120.00 to 175.00
**Table set,** 4 pcs................. 500.00 to 550.00
**Tumbler**................................. 50.00 to 70.00

## MAPLE LEAF (Northwood)

*Maple Leaf Butter Dish*

**Banana bowl** ...................................... 175.00
**Butter dish,** cov. (ILLUS.) .................. 290.00
**Compote,** jelly .................... 425.00 to 450.00
**Creamer**.............................................. 160.00
**Pitcher,** water ...................................... 395.00
**Sauce dish** ........................................... 80.00
**Spooner**.............................................. 125.00
**Sugar bowl,** cov. ............... 200.00 to 225.00
**Toothpick holder** .............................. 650.00
**Tumbler** ................................................ 90.00

## NORTHWOOD GRAPE, GRAPE & CABLE or GRAPE & THUMBPRINT

*Northwood Grape Humidor*

Banana boat...................................... 325.00
Bowl, 6½" d., ruffled rim, nutmeg stain.. 40.00
Bowl, 7½" d., ruffled rim....................... 42.00
Bowl, master berry or fruit, 11" d.,
  ruffled, footed.................................... 445.00
Butter dish, cov................................. 250.00
Cologne bottle w/original stopper ... 538.00
Cracker jar, cov., two-
  handled ........................... 575.00 to 600.00
Creamer ............................. 125.00 to 150.00
Creamer & open sugar bowl,
  breakfast size, pr. ............. 100.00 to 125.00
Dresser tray ...................... 275.00 to 325.00
Dresser tray, nutmeg decoration........ 150.00
Humidor, cov. (ILLUS. above)............ 650.00
Pin dish ............................................. 165.00
Plate, 8" d............................................ 55.00
Plate, 8" w., six-sided............................ 65.00
Punch cup ............................................ 75.00
Sauce dish, flat..................................... 30.00
Sauce dish, footed ............................... 40.00
Spooner.............................................. 135.00
Sugar bowl, cov. ................................. 150.00
Sugar bowl, open, breakfast size......... 62.00
Tumbler .............................................. 47.00
Water set, pitcher & six tumblers,
  7 pcs. ............................................ 1,250.00
Plate, 7½" d.......................................... 60.00

## PUNTY BAND (Heisey)

Creamer, individual size, souvenir........ 35.00
Cuspidor, lady's .................................. 75.00
Mug, souvenir ...................................... 55.00
Mug, 4½" h........................................... 29.00
Toothpick holder, souvenir.................. 45.00
Tumbler, floral decoration, souvenir..... 45.00

## RIBBED DRAPE (Jefferson)

Compote, jelly.................................... 150.00

Creamer........................................... 125.00
Pitcher, water .................................... 255.00
Sauce dish ......................................... 35.00
Sauce dishes, set of 6........................ 250.00
Spooner............................................. 115.00
Sugar bowl, cov. ................................ 185.00
Toothpick holder w/rose decoration.. 195.00
Tumbler .............................................. 82.00

## RING BAND (Heisey)

Berry set, master bowl & six sauce
  dishes, 7 pcs.................................... 482.00
Butter dish, cov................................. 223.00
Compote, jelly ................... 145.00 to 175.00
Condiment tray ................................. 150.00

*Ring Band Pitcher*

Pitcher, water (ILLUS.)....... 300.00 to 375.00
Salt shaker w/original top,
  undecorated....................................... 50.00
Sauce dish .......................................... 38.00
Spooner ............................................. 120.00
Sugar bowl, cov. ................ 150.00 to 175.00
Syrup pitcher w/original
  top....................................... 325.00 to 365.00
Toothpick holder, decorated .............. 115.00
Toothpick holder, undecorated............ 85.00
Toothpick holder, souvenir................... 75.00
Tumbler, decorated .............................. 75.00
Tumbler, undecorated .......................... 70.00
Water set, pitcher & four tumblers,
  decorated, 5 pcs. ............................. 895.00

## VICTORIA (Tarentum)

Butter dish, cov. ................ 275.00 to 325.00
Celery vase ........................ 150.00 to 200.00
Spooner, decorated............................ 130.00
Spooner, undecorated.......................... 70.00
Vase, bud........................... 300.00 to 350.00

## WINGED SCROLL or IVORINA VERDE (Heisey)

**Berry set,** master bowl & four sauce dishes, undecorated, 5 pcs.............. **275.00**

**Berry set,** master bowl & five sauce dishes, 6 pcs.................................. **445.00**

**Bowl,** fruit, 8½" d., undecorated.......... **120.00**

*Winged Scroll Butter Dish*

**Butter dish,** cov. (ILLUS.) .. **190.00 to 220.00**
**Celery vase** ........................................ **350.00**
**Cigarette jar** ...................................... **160.00**
**Creamer,** decorated............................ **102.00**
**Cruet w/original stopper,** undecorated ....................................... **100.00**
**Match holder**...................... **190.00 to 225.00**
**Pitcher,** water, 9" h., bulbous.............. **230.00**
**Pitcher,** water, tankard, decorated ..... **338.00**
**Pitcher,** water, tankard, undecorated ... **230.00**
**Salt & pepper shakers w/original tops,** pr......................................... **150.00**
**Sauce dish,** 4½" d. ............................... **36.00**
**Spooner**.............................................. **82.00**
**Sugar bowl,** cov., decorated .............. **225.00**
**Sugar bowl,** cov., undecorated ........... **95.00**
**Table set,** cov. butter dish, creamer & spooner, 3 pcs. ................................. **250.00**
**Toothpick holder** .............................. **129.00**
**Tumbler** .............................................. **69.00**

## MISCELLANEOUS PATTERNS

### DELAWARE

**Berry set,** master bowl & five sauce dishes, 6 pcs.................................... **190.00**
**Creamer,** individual size ...................... **45.00**
**Creamer w/rose decoration**............... **67.00**
**Card tray,** 5" ..................................... **145.00**
**Pin tray** w/blue decoration ................... **75.00**
**Pin tray** w/green decoration, 7" ........... **70.00**
**Pin tray,** w/rose stain, 4½".................. **68.00**
**Punch cup** ........................................... **40.00**

**Ring tree,** 4" h. .................... **80.00 to 100.00**
**Spooner**.............................................. **65.00**
**Sugar bowl,** breakfast size.................. **45.00**
**Tumbler** w/blue decoration .................. **70.00**
**Tumbler** w/green decoration................ **52.00**

### PEACOCK AND URN

**Bowl,** master berry............................ **200.00**
**Ice cream bowl,** master...................... **320.00**
**Ice cream bowl,** master w/nutmeg stain, 9¾" d. .................... **300.00 to 375.00**
**Ice cream dish,** individual w/nutmeg stain .............................................. **55.00**

### VERMONT

**Butter dish,** cov................................ **104.00**
**Candlestick,** finger-type......... **50.00 to 70.00**
**Celery vase** ...................................... **225.00**
**Creamer** w/blue decoration.................. **97.00**
**Creamer** w/green & pink florals ........... **95.00**
**Salt shaker w/original top,** enameled decoration............................ **78.00**
**Salt & pepper shakers w/original tops,** blue decoration, pr. ................. **135.00**
**Spooner**.............................................. **95.00**
**Spooner** w/green decoration ............... **75.00**
**Toothpick holder** w/blue trim & enameled decoration....................... **95.00**
**Toothpick holder** w/green decoration .. **135.00**
**Tumbler**............................... **75.00 to 100.00**
**Tumbler** w/blue decoration .................. **72.00**
**Vase** w/enameled decoration............. **135.00**

### WILD BOUQUET

**Bowl,** master berry............................ **225.00**
**Butter dish,** cov................................ **565.00**
**Creamer** ........................... **100.00 to 125.00**
**Cruet w/original stopper,** w/enameling & gold trim ............... **1,000.00**
**Sauce dish,** undecorated .................... **42.00**
**Sauce dish,** small, grey, rare............. **295.00**
**Spooner** w/gold trim & colored decoration....................................... **165.00**
**Spooner,** undecorated......................... **72.00**
**Toothpick holder,** decorated ............. **475.00**
**Tumbler,** undecorated ......................... **86.00**

### OTHER MISCELLANEOUS PIECES:

**Alba,** sugar shaker w/original lid ......... **125.00**
**Basket** (Northwood) w/nutmeg stain..... **62.00**
**Beaded Cable,** rose bowl w/nutmeg stain................................................ **88.00**
**Beaded Scroll,** butter dish, cov., enameled floral top .......................... **175.00**
**Blackberry Spray,** hat-shape, ribbon candy edge ....................................... **35.00**

**Butterfly & Berry,** vase, 7" h............... 25.00
**Canadian,** compote ............................. 30.00
**Chrysanthemum,** tray, 8½ x 4½"......... 38.00
**Circled Scroll,** sauce dish, round,
  green opalescent ................................. 25.00
**Creased Bale,** condiment set
  w/original tops.................................... 125.00
**Cut Block,** sugar bowl, open,
  individual size .................................... 35.00
**Dandelion,** mug w/nutmeg stain......... 135.00
**Drapery,** vase, 10" h., w/nutmeg stain .. 48.00
**Drapery,** vase, 12" h., w/nutmeg stain.. 45.00
**Finecut & Roses,** rose bowl
  w/nutmeg stain ................................... 63.00
**Footed Wreath,** bowl............................ 85.00
**Fruits & Flowers (N),** bowl, 7¼" d.,
  flared.................................................... 65.00
**Gothic Arches,** goblet......................... 35.00
**Grape Arbor,** hat-shape w/nutmeg
  stain..................................................... 42.00
**Grape Arbor,** vase, 3¾" h ................... 85.00
**Grape Arbor,** vase, No. 200 ................ 40.00
**Heart,** salt........................................... 45.00
**Honeycomb,** cordial ............................ 70.00
**Honeycomb,** wine ............................... 60.00
**Horse Medallion,** bowl, grapes ext.,
  6½" d. .................................................. 50.00
**Horse Medallion,** bowl, green stain,
  7" d. ..................................................... 60.00
**Iris,** cruet w/original stopper,
  undecorated...................................... 285.00
**Jefferson Optic,** salt shaker
  w/original lid, roses decoration,
  souvenir ............................................... 35.00
**Jefferson Optic,** berry set: master
  bowl & six sauces; rare..................... 350.00
**Jefferson Optic,** butter dish, cov.......... 50.00
**Jefferson Optic,** creamer................... 150.00
**Jefferson Optic,** pitcher, tankard,
  souvenir ............................................. 275.00
**Jefferson Optic,** salt dip w/rose
  decoration............................................ 65.00
**Jefferson Optic,** spooner .................... 65.00
**Jefferson Optic,** sugar bowl, cov. ........ 90.00
**Jefferson Optic,** table set, bases
  w/gold, 4 pcs....................................... 350.00
**Jefferson Optic,** toothpick holder,
  souvenir ............................................... 40.00
**Jefferson Optic,** tumbler...................... 30.00
**Lacy Medallion,** tumbler...................... 38.00
**Ladder w/Diamond,** butter dish, cov.... 85.00
**Ladder w/Diamond,** creamer ............... 60.00
**Ladder w/Diamond,** spooner ............... 60.00
**Ladder w/Diamond,** sugar bowl, cov. .. 70.00
**Lamp,** kerosene, finger-type, greenish
  colored, embossed tulip design ........ 185.00
**Lion,** plate, 7" d., w/green
  stain............................... 100.00 to 200.00

**Little Shrimp,** salt shaker w/original
  top....................................................... 45.00
**Lotus,** nappy, handled, 6½".................. 35.00
**Lotus & Grape,** bonbon, green stain.... 65.00
**Lotus & Grape,** bonbon, nutmeg
  stain ................................................... 110.00
**Lotus & Grape,** bonbon, handled,
  red stain............................................... 45.00
**Lotus & Grape,** nappy, handled........... 65.00
**Many Lobes,** sugar shaker w/original
  top....................................................... 95.00
**Melon Rib,** lamp base.......................... 55.00
**Nine Panels,** lamp, miniature .............. 65.00
**Panelled Teardrop,** sugar shaker
  w/original lid...................................... 140.00
**Pansy,** pitcher, milk............................. 48.00
**Peacock & Dahlia,** plate, 7¾" d., flat,
  w/green stain........................................ 75.00
**Peacock & Urn,** ice cream bowl,
  9⅔" d., nutmeg stain ........ 250.00 to 275.00
**Pineapple & Fan,** pitcher, 5½" h.,
  souvenir ............................................... 65.00
**Pods & Posies,** butter dish, cov.,
  w/gold trim ........................................ 125.00
**Prayer Rug,** nappy, two-handled,
  ruffled, w/nutmeg stain, Imperial,
  6" d. ..................................................... 35.00
**Poppy,** relish tray, nutmeg stain .......... 42.00
**Ribbed Thumprint,** toothpick holder,
  w/floral decoration .............................. 82.00
**Ribbed Thumbprint,** tumbler,
  souvenir ............................................... 70.00
**Rings & Beads,** pitcher, 2¾" h.,
  souvenir ............................................... 25.00
**Rings & Beads,** toothpick holder,
  souvenir ............................................... 45.00
**Shell & Scroll,** spooner, 3½ x 4¼" h. .. 150.00
**Singing Birds,** mug ............................. 85.00
**Smocking,** bell w/original clapper......... 45.00
**Spool,** spooner .................................... 32.00
**Strawberry,** compote............................ 75.00
**Sunset,** toothpick holder ...................... 99.00
**Three Fruits,** bowl, 6¾" d., flared rim,
  nutmeg stain ........................................ 95.00
**Three Fruits,** plate............................... 95.00
**Tiny Thumbprint,** goblet, souvenir....... 60.00
**Tiny Thumbprint,** pitcher, 5" h.,
  souvenir ............................................... 30.00
**Tiny Thumbprint,** table set, 4 pcs...... 650.00
**Tiny Thumbprint,** toothpick holder,
  souvenir ............................................... 85.00
**Trailing Vine,** sauce dish, footed......... 30.00
**Trailing Vine,** spooner, blue................. 65.00
**Twigs,** plate ........................................ 70.00
**Water Lily,** cracker jar, cov................. 185.00
**Woven Cane,** salt shaker w/original
  lid ........................................................ 30.00

## CUT GLASS

*Cut glass most eagerly sought by collectors is American glass produced during the so-called "Brilliant Period" from 1880 to about 1915. Pieces listed below are by type of article in alphabetical order.*

*Hawkes, Hoare, Libbey and Straus Marks*

## BOWLS

**Egginton signed,** Dryden patt., deep bowl, 10" d. .................................. **$550.00**

**Egginton signed,** Spartan patt., deeply cut w/clusters of hobstars, 10¼" d. ........................................ **2,000.00**

**Egginton signed,** Trellis patt., 3½" h., 9" d. .................................................. **3,600.00**

**Fruit,** blown, heavy & well cut in cane, hobstars, strawberry diamond & fans 10" d. ................................................ **600.00**

**Fruit,** dentil edge, Arcadia patt., checkerboard, diamonds & hobstars, 6" d. .................................................. **150.00**

**Fruit,** Pairpoint's Victoria patt., clear & heavy blank, oblong (small chip) ...... **300.00**

**Fruit,** three hobstars w/fine strawberry cutting creating a ribbon effect from center out, 9" d. ................................ **600.00**

**Hawkes' Patt. No. 1189,** crimped rim, 8½" d. ................................................ **950.00**

**Hawkes' Sunburst patt.,** 8" d. ........... **237.00**

**Hawkes signed,** chain of hobstars, strawberry diamond & cane, 4½ x 10½" ...................................... **275.00**

**Hoare signed,** Kohinoor patt., low, 10" d. .............................................. **3,200.00**

**Hoare signed,** thirteen miniature hobstars creating a star, alternating hobstar & prism & file, low sides, 8" d. .................................................. **170.00**

**Hobstar,** fan & beading cutting, 9" d... **150.00**

**Libby's Glenda (Laurent) patt.** w/double X-cut vesicas, beading, fan, hobnail, stars & strawberry diamond motifs, heavy & brilliant blank, 8" d., 4" h. ............................... **200.00**

**Libby signed,** eight hobstars & geometric cutting, low, 8" d. .............. **150.00**

**Libby signed,** hobstar variation, 7" d.... **150.00**

**Libby signed,** six hobstars w/prism panels, 8" d. ....................................... **170.00**

**Libby signed,** vesica star center w/daisy & feathers design, 9" d. ....... **300.00**

**Pine tree design** cutting, low sides, 9" d. ................................................... **275.00**

**Salad,** hobstars, cane, vesicas & strawberry diamond, 9" h. ................. **150.00**

*Tomato Bowl*

**Tomato w/13" underplate,** well cut in notched cross bars & hobstars, 11" d., 2 pcs. (ILLUS. of one) ........ **2,900.00**

**Tuthill's Rex patt.,** two-handled, low, 12" w. from handle to handle ......... **1,350.00**

**Tuthill signed,** 1000 Eye patt., 8½" d., 3" h. .................................... **1,200.00**

**Tuthill signed,** Rex patt., serrated top, chain of hobstars w/strawberry diamond above cane vesicas, 8¼" d. ........................................... **3,250.00**

## BOXES

**Jewel,** top cut w/center hobstar surrounded by alternating zipper cut bands & small hobstars in diamonds, low base cut w/fans alternating w/zipper bands, bottom cut w/24-point hobstar, round, 6" d. (hinge repair) ............................................. **225.00**

**Powder,** buzzstar cutting, 4½" d. .......... **90.00**
**Powder,** hobstar on top & base, 4" d. .. **180.00**
**Powder,** overall hobstar & diamond,
4" d. ................................................. **275.00**

## CANDLESTICKS & CANDLEHOLDERS

**Hawkes signed,** satin engraved,
Steuben blanks w/green base,
12" h., pr. .......................................... **600.00**
**Hawkes signed,** Sinclaire patt.,
amber, 12" h., pr. .............................. **200.00**
**Candelabra,** prism-cut body w/four
removable arms & a center candle
socket, elaborate silver plate base
w/embossed face at feet, matching
snuffer, 26" h. ............................... **1,550.00**

## CLOCKS

**Clock,** arch-shaped, Sinclair signed,
intaglio floral cutting, 5" h. ................. **175.00**
**Clock,** cross-cut diamond top
w/etched daisy w/works, 5½" h. ......... **150.00**
**Clock,** Harvard top & base w/daisy
w/works, 5½" h. ............................... **170.00**
**Clock,** hobstar & slanted prism, star
ray on back w/works, 9½" h. ............. **350.00**
**Clock,** triple notched w/daisy w/works,
5" h. ................................................. **120.00**

## CREAMERS & SUGAR BOWLS

**Heart patt.,** oval-shaped, pr. ............... **250.00**
**Hobstar & beaded vesicas,** oval-
shaped, pr. ........................................ **180.00**
**Hobstar & prism w/rayed base,** pr. .... **130.00**
**Hobstar,** strawberry & diamond &
prism, pr. ........................................... **110.00**
**Hobstars,** flashed fans w/bottom cut
in petals, pr. ..................................... **125.00**
**Sunburst patt.,** pedestal, extremely
heavy, 3½" h., pr. .............................. **200.00**

## DECANTERS

**Cordial,** J. Hoare's Croesus patt,
sterling stopper w/attached sterling
chain ............................................. **2,200.00**
**Harvard patt.,** triple notched neck,
11" h. ............................................... **500.00**
**Libbey's Jewel patt.,** 12¼" h.
decanter w/stopper & four 4½" h.
stems, 5 pcs. .................................... **615.00**
**Two large oval hobstars** surrounded
w/rows of smaller stars, triple
lapidary neck, 13" h. ......................... **525.00**

## DISHES, MISCELLANEOUS

**Butter,** cov., hobstars, cane & fans .... **425.00**
**Celery,** Bergen's Caprice patt., 13" l..... **90.00**
**Celery,** hobstars & slanted prisms,
11" l..................................................... **80.00**
**Celery,** large hobstar in center
w/prism cutting all around, 11½" l. ... **110.00**
**Celery,** Russian & Buttons patt. w/two
hobstars, 11½" l. ................................ **75.00**
**Cheese,** cov., hobnails & buzzstars,
2 pcs. ............................................... **300.00**
**Dish,** engraved w/three birds perched
on vine of wild roses, 7½ x 10"...... **1,050.00**
**Heart-shaped,** Heart patt., 6¾" w....... **190.00**
**Olive,** Eulalia patt., 7½" l. .................. **225.00**
**Relish,** Egginton signed, Trellis patt.,
4 x 13" l. ....................................... **3,600.00**

## JARS

*Brilliant Cut Tobacco Jar*

**Horseradish,** cov., pinwheel & cross-
cut diamond w/cut hollow stopper,
5½" h. .............................................. **150.00**
**Mustard,** cov., prisms, fans &
hobstars design ............................... **100.00**
**Sweetmeat,** cov., strawberry diamond
cutting, handled, 4" h. ...................... **160.00**
**Tobacco,** cov., Tiffany & Co. signed,
hobstars, cross-cut diamond,
strawberry diamond & fans............... **450.00**
**Tobacco,** cov., Dorflinger's
Honeycomb patt., 3" d., 6" h. ............ **225.00**
**Tobacco,** cov., silver-mounted
canister-form w/hobstar & oval

cutting, matching stopper, silver marked "(cross) sterling 925-1000 fine," small chip on base, silver dent at side, 9½" d., 6" h. (ILLUS. previous page) .............................. **690.00**

## LAMPS

**Parlor lamp,** mushroom-shaped shade w/floral etching & cane-cut rim band, on metal shade ring hung w/faceted spearpoint prisms, electrical fitting on slender matching baluster-shaped shaft stem, on domed foot, engraved w/matching florals ................................................ **523.00**

**Table lamp** w/11" mushroom-shaped shade, hobstars, strawberry diamond & fans, 18" h. .................. **3,700.00**

*Hobstar Cut Table Lamp*

**Table lamp** w/honeycomb shaft above hobstar & fan-cut base w/conforming 12" d. mushroom cap shade, accompanied by cut glass prisms, some wear to glass, plating worn, 20½" h. (ILLUS.) .................. **1,840.00**

## PERFUME & COLOGNE BOTTLES

**Cologne,** bulbous-shaped, buzzstars & cane, 6½" h. ............................... **140.00**

**Cologne,** Dorflinger's Hobnail & Lace patt., ruby cut to clear ................... **1,800.00**

**Cologne,** Dorflinger's Hobnail & Lace patt., w/faceted stopper, 8½" h. ........ **300.00**

**Cologne,** flutes at neck w/cross cut diamond motif, 5" h. .......................... **120.00**

**Cologne,** hobstars & notched "V's," teardrop stopper, 7" h. ...................... **220.00**

**Cologne,** hobstars & strawberry diamond, 6½" h. ................................ **200.00**

**Cologne,** palms & hobstars, 7" h. ........ **325.00**

**Perfume,** lay-down-type, icicle-shaped w/notched rib design w/sterling twist-off lid, 3¼" l. .............. **95.00**

## PITCHERS

**Champagne,** overall cutting of hobstars, cross bars, stars & cane w/24-point hobstar base & hollow diamond-cut handle, 14" h. .............. **175.00**

**Champagne,** tankard, heavy blank w/overall hobstars & fans w/triple mitred handle, 14" h. ...................... **1,200.00**

**Cider,** hobstar & cane cutting, double notched handle, 7" h. ...................... **250.00**

**Tankard,** miniature, Libbey signed, cut in bull's-eye & cross-cut diamond, 5½" h. ............................... **275.00**

**Water,** clear swirls & double mitre cane w/clear handle & feathered rays in bottom, 9½" h. ...................... **190.00**

**Water,** Pitkin & Brooks signed, intaglio-cut, pears & berry w/triple notched handle, 7½" h. .................... **600.00**

**Water,** Sinclaire signed, Russian & Fruit patt. ........................................ **475.00**

**Water,** vesica bead w/hobstar, strawberry diamond & fan, 10" h. ...... **250.00**

## PLATES

**7" d.,** J. Hoare signed, Hindoo patt. ..... **175.00**

**7" d.,** Libbey signed, Colonna patt., set of 8 ............................................. **170.00**

**7" d.,** Libbey signed, Ellesmere patt. .. **412.00**

**10" d.,** Sinclaire's Assyrian & Lace patt. ................................................. **1,700.00**

**11½" d.,** cane cutting w/large scalloped edge ............................... **2,500.00**

*Large Plate with Hobstars*

**14½" d.,** hobstar encircled w/cross-cut diamond-square surrounded by eight hobstars w/serrated edge (ILLUS. bottom previous page)...................... **3,565.00**

## PUNCH BOWLS

**Egginton's Cluster patt.,** 12" d., 2 pcs. ............................................ **1,500.00**

**Five large shooting stars** on bowl & base, 12" d., 2 pcs. ........................... **975.00**

**Hobstars** between vessica w/cane-cut panels, scalloped rim w/notched edges, on flaring matching pedestal base, twelve matching handled punch cups & ladle stand, ca. 1900, fine cut. 16" d., 16½" h., 14 pcs. .... **6,600.00**

**Parshe & Co.'s Empire patt.,** bowl & stand, 2 pcs. ................................. **1,600.00**

**Thirty-four point hobstars** w/chains of hobstars & fans around top of bowl, 7½" h., 12½" d. ..................... **3,500.00**

## SPOONERS

**Hobstars base,** prism cut, 4¼" h. ...... **200.00**

**Hobstars,** cane & strawberry diamond w/ray base, 4½" h. ........................... **250.00**

**Hobstars & crosses,** 4½" h. ............. **100.00**

**Hobstars & notched** fans w/center ray on each side, two notched handles, hob-cut foot pedestal, 5" h. .................................................. **425.00**

**Hobstars & strawberry diamond,** 4" h. ..................................................... **150.00**

**Libbey signed,** hobstars, prism & strawberry diamond, 4½" h. .............. **225.00**

**Salesman's sample,** notched prism cutting w/three cut notched handles & fancy rim, 3" h. ............................. **145.00**

## TRAYS

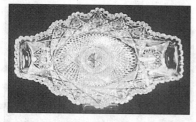

*Boat-shaped Ice Cream Tray*

**Bread,** Libbey signed, four large vesicas w/hobstar & cane, 3 x 6 x 11" ......................................... **325.00**

**Card,** Sinclaire signed, cross-cut diamond base w/intaglio border, 6" l. .... **300.00**

*Russian-cut Ice Cream Tray*

**Celery,** Bird in Cage patt., dentil edges, 4½ x 12" l. ........................... **550.00**

**Cheese & cracker,** Meriden's Thalia patt., 10" d. ...................................... **100.00**

**Dresser,** cross-cut diamond bands & hobstars, 10" ..................................... **175.00**

**Hawkes signed,** Panel patt. No. 11, round, 11" d. .................................. **4,250.00**

**Hawkes signed,** sharp diamond border pierced by bull's-eyes, fluted sides around a rayed star center, round, 14" ...................................... **100.00**

**Ice cream,** Duncan patt., 10½" w., 18" l.................................................. **3,900.00**

**Ice cream,** Egginton's Cluster patt., 7 x 13"............................................. **1,900.00**

**Ice cream,** oblong, boat-shaped w/large almond-shaped hobstar in center, sides cut w/bands of diamonds framing small hobstar, squared end handles w/hobstar, scalloped & serrated rim, 16½" w., 9½" l. (ILLUS. bottom previous column) ..................... **978.00**

**Ice cream,** oblong, boat-shaped, overall Russian-cut, 17¾" w., 1¼" l. (ILLUS. above) .................................................. **690.00**

**Ice cream,** 32-point hobstars surrounded by feathered design, 7½ x 14¾"........................................ **275.00**

**Ice cream,** three finely cut 32-point hobstars & four smaller hobstars, 10 x 17"........................................ **1,400.00**

*Libbey Signed Tray*

**Libbey signed,** daisy & vesica cut center, soft turned edges w/Greek Key border, handled, 13" l. (ILLUS. bottom previous page)...... **1,400.00**

## VASES

**Egginton's Trellis patt.,** sharp cutting on sparkling white & brilliant blank, 16" h.................................. **11,500.00**

**Flower-form shape,** notched prism flares, hobstars, fans, design, 24-point hobstar base, 12" h................. **475.00**

**Hoare signed,** beading on four sides, 8" h. ....................................................... **210.00**

**Libbey signed,** Sultana patt., cut in intersecting painted ovals, topped by a fan to join hobstars, extremely heavy, 10" h...................................... **625.00**

**Panels of sunburst & hobstars,** heavy, 10" h...................................... **175.00**

**Sinclaire's Adam patt.,** 9½" h............ **475.00**

**St. Louis diamond & hobstars** w/beautiful cross bands of basketweave, 12" h. ........................ **375.00**

*Tulip Vase*

**Tulip,** deep notched prisms creating grass effect around large cut tulips, 14" h. (ILLUS.) ................................. **900.00**

## MISCELLANEOUS

**Cake plate,** Tuthill signed, Vintage patt., four-footed, 9" d. ...................... **500.00**

**Cordial set,** Dorflinger's Renaissance patt., cobalt blue cut to clear, 6 pcs. . **350.00**

**Epergne,** four-lily, Meriden's Alhambra patt. (ILLUS. top next column)...................................... **16,000.00**

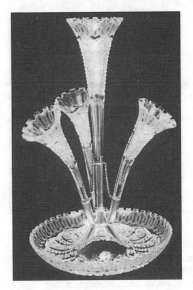

*Four-Lily Epergne*

**Finger bowl,** hobstars & cane, w/star-cut base, 5" d.................................... **110.00**

**Finger bowl set,** Dorflinger's Renaissance patt., cobalt blue cut to clear, 4 pcs. ..................................... **275.00**

**Goblet,** J. Hoare's Croesus patt. ........ **250.00**

**Goblet set,** water, Libbey signed, Colonna patt., teardrop stems, 6⅜" h., 8 pcs................................. **1,000.00**

**Inkwell w/sterling silver hinged lid,** heavy glass cut w/small hobstars & geometric cutting, 4 x 4 x 5" ............. **425.00**

**Loving cup,** hobstars & strawberry diamond, three-handled, 6" d., 7" h. ................................................ **1,500.00**

**Mayonnaise set:** bowl & underplate; pinwheels & fans cutting, 2 pcs. ....... **175.00**

**Milk jug,** Russian patt. on heavy clear blank, step-cutting on spout, triple notched handle ................................. **525.00**

**Rose bowl,** miniature, Bergen's Electric patt., three handled, sparkling clear ................................... **250.00**

**Rose bowl,** Dorflinger's Sultana patt., 7" d. ................................................... **800.00**

**Salad fork & spoon,** sterling w/cross-cut diamond & fans, handles cut in strawberry diamond, 2 pcs. ............. **650.00**

**Sherbet,** Dorflinger's Renaissance patt., cobalt blue cut to clear............... **48.00**

**Tumbler set,** hobstars & fans w/cross-cut diamond in star points on extra heavy blanks, 4 pcs. ............. **55.00**

*Two-handled Urn*

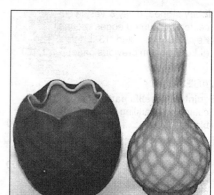

*Rose Bowl & Vase*

**Urn,** bulbous-shaped, flared neck, hobstars & cane, extremely heavy, on massive square pedestal foot, 11" h. ........................................... **1,500.00**

**Urn,** deep cutting of hobstars, notched prism & cross-cut diamond on extremely heavy blank, two triple-notched handles, pegged feet (ILLUS.) ....................................... **1,550.00**

**Vase,** 6¼" h., 2⅞" d., footed bulbous double-gourd body, heavenly blue Diamond Quilted patt., white lining (ILLUS. above right) ........................ **118.00**

**Vase,** 7½" h., 3⅜" d., footed bulbous bottle-form vase w/'stick' neck, dark blue Diamond Quilted patt., white lining ................................................ **125.00**

## CUT VELVET

This mold-blown, two-layer glassware is usually lined in white with a colored exterior with a molded pattern. Pieces have a satiny finish, giving them a 'velvety' appearance. The Mt. Washington Glass Company was one of several firms which produced this glass.

**Rose bowl,** six-crimp rim, ovoid form, cased deep blue in the Diamond Quilted patt., white lining, 3⅜" d., 3¾" h. (ILLUS. left, top next column) ......................................... **$145.00**

**Vase,** 4¾" h., 2¾" d., footed squatty bulbous body tapering to a ringed shoulder & tall, slender cylindrical neck, heavenly blue embossed rib design, white lining ............................ **85.00**

**Vase,** 5¾" h., 3⅛" d., footed bulbous body w/a tall 'stick' neck, heavenly blue Diamond Quilted patt. w/twisted design on the neck, white lining ....... **100.00**

**Vase,** 6" h., 3⅜" d., footed squatty bulbous body tapering to a tall 'stick' neck, light blue Diamond Quilted patt., white lining ................................. **95.00**

## DAUM NANCY

This fine glass, much of it cameo-cut, was made by Auguste and Antonin Daum, who founded a factory in 1875 in Nancy, France. Most of their cameo and enameled glass was made from the 1890s into the early 20th century.

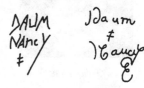

*Daum Marks*

**Cameo lamp,** the pointed mushroom-shaped shade raised on a slender baluster-form base w/a sloping round foot, the tricorner shade pinched at each corner, base & shade in frosted amber overlaid in dark purple & etched w/a wooded river landscape scene, base & shade signed, shade 7" d., overall 16½" h. ........................................ **$7,475.00**

*Daum Thistle Vase*

**Cameo vase,** 5½" h., 5¼" d.,
  irregularly tooled rim on the lobed
  ovoid body, mottled pink, red &
  yellow layered in maroon & black &
  acid-etched w/a tree-lined waterfront
  scene w/sailboats & mountains in
  the distance, signed...................... **1,265.00**

**Cameo vase,** 13½" h., footed baluster-
  form body w/slightly flaring wide
  mouth, mottled yellow, green & red
  overlaid in black & cameo-etched &
  wheel-finished w/leafy vines & grape
  clusters, signed on the side............ **1,610.00**

**Light fixture,** ceiling-type, a wide
  deeply dished bowl-form in thick
  mottled blue, yellow & orange, drilled
  & mounted w/three chains w/light
  socket fittings, signed, 18¼" d. ......... **978.00**

**Vase,** 9½" h., tall baluster-form body
  on a cushion foot w/applied handles
  from the rim to the shoulder, pink,
  yellow & frosted clear bands of color
  w/etched long-stemmed blossoms
  enamel-painted blue, black & base,
  marked on base in gold (ILLUS.
  above)........................................... **4,600.00**

**Vase,** 11" h., slender baluster-form
  body tapering to a swelled neck
  w/flaring rim, applied handles from
  neck swell to shoulder, plain &
  frosted clear decorated *en grisaille*
  w/a lowlands landscape w/windmills
  on the reverse, marked in gold on
  the base....................................... **2,875.00**

**Vase,** 11½" h., cushion base tapering
  to a tall swelled cylindrical body,
  emerald green double-etched w/a
  raised lion rampant trimmed in gold
  enamel, inscribed mark on the
  base ............................................. **1,725.00**

# DEPRESSION

  *The phrase "Depression Glass" is used by
collectors to denote a specific kind of transparent
glass produced primarily as tablewares, in
crystal, amber, blue, green, pink, milky-white,
etc., during the late 1920s and 1930s when this
country was in the midst of a financial
depression. Made to sell inexpensively, it was
turned out by such producers as Jeannette,
Hocking, Westmoreland, Indiana and other
glass companies. We compile prices on all the
major Depression Glass patterns. Collectors
should consult Depression Glass references for
information on those patterns and pieces which
have been reproduced.*

### ADAM, Jeannette Glass Co., 1932-34 (Process-etched)

*Adam Candlestick*

| | |
|---|---:|
| **Ashtray,** clear, 4½" sq. ...................... | **$11.00** |
| **Ashtray,** green, 4½" sq. ...................... | **22.00** |
| **Ashtray,** pink, 4½" sq. ...................... | **27.00** |
| **Bowl,** dessert, 4¾" sq., green.............. | **14.00** |
| **Bowl,** dessert, 4¾" sq., pink ................ | **16.00** |
| **Bowl,** cereal, 5¾" sq., green................ | **44.00** |
| **Bowl,** cereal, 5¾" sq., pink .................. | **39.00** |
| **Bowl,** nappy, 7¾" sq., green................ | **23.00** |
| **Bowl,** nappy, 7¾" sq., pink ................. | **23.00** |
| **Bowl,** cov., 9" sq., green..................... | **68.00** |
| **Bowl,** cov., 9" sq., pink........................ | **63.00** |
| **Bowl,** 9" sq., green.............................. | **28.00** |
| **Bowl,** 9" sq., pink ................................ | **19.00** |
| **Bowl,** 10" oval vegetable, green .......... | **25.00** |
| **Bowl,** 10" oval vegetable, pink............. | **30.00** |
| **Butter dish,** cov., green..................... | **297.00** |
| **Butter dish,** cov., pink ......................... | **85.00** |
| **Butter dish,** cov., w/Sierra patt., pink .. | **495.00** |
| **Cake plate,** footed, green, 10" sq. ........ | **26.00** |
| **Cake plate,** footed, pink, 10" sq........... | **26.00** |
| **Candlestick,** green, 4" h...................... | **29.00** |
| **Candlestick,** pink, 4" h. (ILLUS. above).. | **41.00** |

Candlesticks, green, 4" h., pr.............. 91.00
Candlesticks, pink, 4" h., pr. ............... 86.00
Candy jar, cov., green .......................... 93.00
Candy jar, cov., pink ........................... 88.00
Coaster, clear, 3¼" sq. ....................... 14.00
Coaster, green, 3¼" sq....................... 19.00
Coaster, pink, 3¼" sq. ........................ 19.00
Creamer, green................................... 19.00
Creamer, pink ..................................... 19.00
Cup & saucer, green ............................ 26.00
Cup & saucer, pink................................ 29.00
Pitcher, 8" h., 32 oz., cone-shaped,
   clear.................................................. 35.00
Pitcher, 8" h., 32 oz., cone-shaped,
   green ................................................. 43.00
Pitcher, 8" h., 32 oz., cone-shaped,
   pink.................................................... 40.00
Pitcher, 32 oz., round base, clear......... 19.00
Pitcher, 32 oz., round base, pink.......... 45.00
Plate, sherbet, 6" sq., green.................. 8.00
Plate, sherbet, 6" sq., pink................... 8.00
Plate, salad, 7¾" sq., green ................ 14.00
Plate, salad, 7¾" sq., pink................... 15.00
Plate, salad, round, pink ...................... 60.00
Plate, salad, round, yellow ................. 110.00
Plate, dinner, 9" sq., green.................... 24.00
Plate, dinner, 9" sq., pink ..................... 30.00
Plate, grill, 9" sq., green....................... 17.00
Plate, grill, 9" sq., pink......................... 20.00
Platter, 11¾" l., green........................... 27.00
Platter, 11¾" l., pink............................. 26.00
Relish dish, two-part, green, 8" sq. ...... 20.00
Relish dish, two-part, pink, 8" sq.......... 20.00
Salt & pepper shakers, footed,
   green, 4" h., pr. ................................. 88.00
Salt & pepper shakers, footed, pink,
   4" h., pr. ............................................ 74.00
Sherbet, green, 3" h............................. 36.00
Sherbet, pink, 3" h. .............................. 27.00
Sugar bowl, cov., green ....................... 29.00
Sugar bowl, cov., pink.......................... 44.00
Tumbler, cone-shaped, green,
   4½" h., 7 oz...................................... 25.00
Tumbler, cone-shaped, pink, 4½" h.,
   7 oz. .................................................. 28.00
Tumbler, iced tea, green, 5½" h., 9 oz. .. 48.00
Tumbler, iced tea, pink, 5½" h., 9 oz..... 62.00
Vase, 7½" h., green.............................. 50.00
Vase, 7½" h., pink .............................. 250.00
Water set: pitcher & six tumblers;
   pink, 7 pcs. ..................................... 162.00

## AMERICAN SWEETHEART, MacBeth - Evans Glass Co., 1930-36 (Process-etched)

Berry set: 9" bowl & six sauce
   dishes; Cremax, 7 pc. ........................ 50.00
Bowl, berry, 3¾" d., pink...................... 52.00
Bowl, cream soup, 4½" d., Monax ...... 120.00

Bowl, cream soup, 4½" d., pink ............ 84.00
Bowl, cereal, 6" d., Cremax ................... 8.00
Bowl, cereal, 6" d., Monax .................. 14.00
Bowl, cereal, 6" d., Monax "smoke"
   w/black edge..................................... 25.00
Bowl, cereal, 6" d., pink ....................... 16.00
Bowl, berry, 9" d., Cremax.................... 29.00
Bowl, berry, 9" d., Monax..................... 63.00
Bowl, berry, 9" d., pink......................... 47.00
Bowl, soup w/flanged rim, 9½" d.,
   Monax................................................ 75.00
Bowl, soup w/flanged rim, 9½" d.,
   pink.................................................... 66.00
Bowl, 11" oval vegetable, Monax.......... 76.00
Bowl, 11" oval vegetable, pink.............. 65.00
Console bowl, blue, 18" d. ................. 850.00
Console bowl, Monax, 18" d. ............. 425.00
Creamer, footed, blue ......................... 95.00
Creamer, footed, Monax ...................... 12.00
Creamer, footed, pink .......................... 15.00
Creamer, footed, ruby red.................. 106.00
Cup, ruby red ...................................... 82.00
Cup & saucer, Monax .......................... 12.00
Cup & saucer, pink .............................. 20.00
Cup & saucer, ruby red ...................... 109.00
Lamp shade, Monax........................... 560.00
Pitcher, 7½" h., 60 oz., jug-type,
   pink.................................................. 615.00
Pitcher, 8" h., 80 oz., pink.................. 532.00
Plate, bread & butter, 6" d., Monax........ 5.00
Plate, bread & butter, 6" d., pink ............ 5.00
Plate, salad, 8" d., blue ...................... 110.00
Plate, salad, 8" d., Monax ..................... 9.00
Plate, salad, 8" d., pink ....................... 11.00
Plate, salad, 8" d., ruby red................. 63.00
Plate, luncheon, 9" d., Monax .............. 10.00
Plate, dinner, 9¾" d., Monax............... 26.00
Plate, dinner, 9¾" d., pink................... 35.00
Plate, dinner, 10¼" d., Monax............. 20.00
Plate, chop, 11" d., Monax.................. 15.00
Plate, salver, 12" d., Monax ................ 19.00

*Pink Salver*

**Plate,** salver, 12" d., pink (ILLUS. bottom previous page) .......................... **25.00**

**Plate,** salver, 12" d., ruby red .............. **170.00**

**Plate,** 15½" d., w/center handle, Monax ................................................ **215.00**

**Plate,** 15½" d., w/center handle, ruby red ...................................................... **242.00**

**Platter,** 13" oval, Monax ........................ **66.00**

**Platter,** 13" oval, pink ............................ **51.00**

**Salt & pepper shakers,** footed, Monax, pr. ................................................ **325.00**

**Salt & pepper shakers,** footed, pink, pr ...................................................... **217.00**

**Sherbet,** footed, pink, 3¾" h. ................. **20.00**

**Sherbet,** footed, Monax, 4¼" h. ............. **20.00**

**Sherbet,** footed, pink, 4¼" h. ................. **16.00**

**Sherbet,** metal holder, clear ................. **14.00**

**Sugar bowl,** cov., Monax, rare ........... **265.00**

**Sugar bowl,** open, blue ......................... **90.00**

**Sugar bowl,** open, Monax .................... **10.00**

**Sugar bowl,** open, pink ......................... **13.00**

**Sugar bowl,** open, ruby red ................... **90.00**

**Tidbit server,** two-tier, Monax .............. **71.00**

**Tidbit server,** two-tier, pink ................... **56.00**

**Tidbit server,** three-tier, Monax .......... **158.00**

**Tidbit server,** three-tier, ruby red ....... **545.00**

**Tumbler,** pink, 3½" h., 5 oz. ................... **81.00**

**Tumbler,** pink, 4¼" h., 9 oz. ................... **73.00**

**Tumbler,** pink, 4¾" h., 10 oz. ................. **94.00**

**Water set:** 7½" h. pitcher & four 9 oz. tumblers; pink, 5 pcs. ......................... **525.00**

**BUBBLE, Bullseye or Provincial, Anchor-Hocking Glass Co., 1940-65 (Press-mold)**

*Bubble Ruby Red Pitcher*

**Berry set:** master bowl & eight sauce dishes; clear, 9 pcs. ............................ **18.00**

**Bowl,** berry, 4" d., blue ........................... **16.00**

**Bowl,** berry, 4" d., clear .......................... **4.00**

**Bowl,** berry, 4" d., green ........................ **9.00**

**Bowl,** berry, 4" d., milk white .................. **4.00**

**Bowl,** berry, 4" d., pink ........................... **15.00**

**Bowl,** fruit, 4½" d., blue ......................... **9.00**

**Bowl,** fruit, 4½" d., clear ......................... **4.00**

**Bowl,** fruit, 4½" d., green ....................... **7.00**

**Bowl,** fruit, 4½" d., milk white ................. **4.00**

**Bowl,** fruit, 4½" d., ruby red .................... **9.00**

**Bowl,** cereal, 5¼" d., blue ..................... **12.00**

**Bowl,** cereal, 5¼" d., clear ...................... **8.00**

**Bowl,** cereal, 5¼" d., green .................... **11.00**

**Bowl,** soup, 7¾" d., blue ........................ **13.00**

**Bowl,** soup, 7¾" d., clear ........................ **8.00**

**Bowl,** soup, 7¾" d., pink ......................... **9.00**

**Bowl,** 8⅜" d., blue ................................. **15.00**

**Bowl,** 8⅜" d., clear .................................. **8.00**

**Bowl,** 8⅜" d., green ............................... **15.00**

**Bowl,** 8⅜" d., milk white .......................... **7.00**

**Bowl,** 8⅜" d., pink .................................. **7.00**

**Bowl,** 8⅜" d., ruby red ........................... **20.00**

**Candlesticks,** clear, pr. ......................... **15.00**

**Creamer,** blue ...................................... **33.00**

**Creamer,** clear ....................................... **6.00**

**Creamer,** green...................................... **12.00**

**Creamer,** milk white ................................ **4.00**

**Cup & saucer,** blue ................................. **6.00**

**Cup & saucer,** clear ................................ **4.00**

**Cup & saucer,** green .............................. **11.00**

**Cup & saucer,** milk white ........................ **3.00**

**Cup & saucer,** ruby red .......................... **12.00**

**Dinner service,** four dinner plates, four cups & saucers, four 5½" d. bowls, creamer & sugar bowl, green, 18 pcs. .............................................. **190.00**

**Dinner service** for four w/serving pieces, blue, 31 pcs. ......................... **200.00**

**Lamp,** clear ........................................... **34.00**

**Lamps,** clear (electric), pr. .................... **56.00**

**Pitcher w/ice lip,** 64 oz., clear ............. **65.00**

**Pitcher w/ice lip,** 64 oz., ruby red (ILLUS. bottom previous column) ....... **53.00**

**Plate,** bread & butter, 6¾" d., blue .......... **4.00**

**Plate,** bread & butter, 6¾" d., clear ......... **2.00**

**Plate,** bread & butter, 6¾" d., green........ **4.00**

**Plate,** dinner, 9⅜" d., blue...................... **7.00**

**Plate,** dinner, 9⅜" d., clear...................... **5.00**

**Plate,** dinner, 9⅜" d., green .................. **20.00**

**Plate,** dinner, 9⅜" d., ruby red ............. **18.00**

**Plate,** grill, 9⅜" d., blue ......................... **18.00**

**Plate,** grill, 9⅜" d., clear ......................... **8.00**

**Platter,** 12" oval, blue............................ **12.00**

**Platter,** 12" oval, clear............................ **12.00**

**Sugar bowl,** open, blue ......................... **16.00**

**Sugar bowl,** open, clear .......................... **6.00**

**Sugar bowl,** open, green ...................... **11.00**

**Sugar bowl,** open, milk white ................. **5.00**

**Tidbit server,** two-tier, blue ................. **44.00**

**Tumbler,** juice, clear, 6 oz. ..................... **7.00**

**Tumbler,** juice, ruby red, 6 oz. ............... **8.00**

**Tumbler,** old fashioned, clear, 3¼" h., 8 oz. ....................................................... **6.00**

**Tumbler,** old fashioned, ruby red,
3¼" h., 8 oz. .......................................... **14.00**
**Tumbler,** water, clear, 9 oz. ..................... **7.00**
**Tumbler,** water, ruby red, 9 oz. .............. **9.00**
**Tumbler,** iced tea, clear, 4½" h., 12 oz. .... **16.00**
**Tumbler,** iced tea, ruby red, 4½" h.,
12 oz. .................................................. **12.00**
**Tumbler,** lemonade, clear, 5⅞" h.,
16 oz. .................................................. **14.00**
**Tumbler,** lemonade, ruby red, 5⅞" h.,
16 oz. .................................................. **17.00**
**Water set:** pitcher & eight tumblers;
ruby red, 9 pcs. ................................. **130.00**

### CAMEO or Ballerina or Dancing Girl, Hocking Glass Co. 1930-34 (Process-etched)

**Bowl,** sauce, 4¼" d., clear ..................... **5.00**
**Bowl,** cream soup, 4¾" d., green........ **165.00**
**Bowl,** cereal, 5½" d., clear..................... **6.00**
**Bowl,** cereal, 5½" d., green................... **33.00**
**Bowl,** cereal, 5½" d., yellow................. **29.00**
**Bowl,** salad, 7¼" d., green................... **58.00**
**Bowl,** large berry, 8¼" d., green .......... **38.00**
**Bowl,** soup w/flange rim, 9" d., green ... **56.00**
**Bowl,** 10" oval vegetable, green .......... **24.00**
**Bowl,** 10" oval vegetable, yellow ......... **44.00**
**Butter dish,** cov., green...................... **193.00**
**Cake plate,** three-footed, green, 10" d.. **24.00**
**Cake plate,** handled, green, 10½" d. .... **35.00**
**Candlestick,** green, 4" h. ...................... **43.00**
**Candlesticks,** green, 4" h., pr............. **114.00**
**Candy jar,** cov., green, 4" h. ................ **71.00**
**Candy jar,** cov., yellow, 4" h. .............. **124.00**

*Green Cameo Candy Jar*

**Candy jar,** cov., green, 6½" h.
(ILLUS.) ............................................ **180.00**
**Compote,** mayonnaise, 5" d., 4" h.,
cone-shaped, green............................ **32.00**
**Compote,** mayonnaise, 5" d., 4" h.,
cone-shaped, pink ............................. **21.00**
**Console bowl,** three-footed, green,
11" d. .................................................. **73.00**

**Console bowl,** three-footed, pink,
11" d. .................................................. **49.00**
**Console bowl,** three-footed, yellow,
11" d. .................................................. **95.00**
**Cookie jar,** cov., green ......................... **49.00**
**Creamer,** green, 3¼" h. ......................... **20.00**
**Creamer,** yellow, 3¼" h......................... **19.00**
**Creamer,** green, 4¼" h. ......................... **23.00**
**Creamer,** pink, 4¼" h. ........................... **65.00**
**Cup & saucer,** green ............................. **16.00**
**Cup & saucer,** yellow ............................. **9.00**
**Decanter,** no stopper, green................. **60.00**
**Decanter w/stopper,** green, 10" h...... **141.00**
**Decanter w/stopper,** green frosted,
10" h .................................................. **36.00**
**Domino tray,** clear, 7" d. ...................... **85.00**
**Domino tray,** green, 7" d...................... **155.00**
**Domino tray,** pink, 7" d........................ **185.00**
**Goblet,** wine, green, 4" h. ..................... **63.00**
**Goblet,** water, green, 6" h. .................... **51.00**
**Goblet,** water, pink, 6" h. ..................... **163.00**
**Ice bowl,** tab handles, green, 5½" d.,
3½" h. ................................................ **177.00**
**Jam jar,** cov., closed handles, green,
2" ...................................................... **196.00**
**Juice set:** pitcher & six tumblers;
green, 7 pcs....................................... **162.00**
**Pitcher,** syrup or milk, 5¾" h., 20 oz.,
green ................................................. **207.00**
**Pitcher,** syrup or milk, 5¾" h., 20 oz.,
yellow.................................................. **32.00**
**Pitcher,** juice, 6" h., 36 oz., green........ **55.00**
**Pitcher,** water, 8½" h., 56 oz.,
jug-type, clear.................................... **35.00**
**Pitcher,** water, 8½" h., 56 oz.,
jug-type, green................................... **52.00**
**Plate,** sherbet (or ringless saucer),
6" d., clear ........................................... **2.00**
**Plate,** sherbet (or ringless saucer),
6" d., green .......................................... **4.00**
**Plate,** sherbet (or ringless saucer),
6" d., yellow ......................................... **3.00**
**Plate,** salad, 7" d., clear ......................... **4.00**
**Plate,** luncheon, 8" d., green................. **11.00**
**Plate,** luncheon, 8" d., yellow................. **9.00**
**Plate,** 8½" sq., green............................ **43.00**
**Plate,** 8½" sq., yellow......................... **310.00**
**Plate,** dinner, 9½" d., green ................. **19.00**
**Plate,** dinner, 9½" d., yellow................... **8.00**
**Plate,** sandwich, 10" d., green ............. **17.00**
**Plate,** sandwich, 10" d., pink ............... **60.00**
**Plate,** dinner, 10½" d., rimmed, green .. **12.00**
**Plate,** 10½" d., closed handles, green .. **15.00**
**Plate,** 10½" d., closed handles, yellow.. **26.00**
**Plate,** grill, 10½" d., green...................... **8.00**
**Plate,** grill, 10½" d., yellow ..................... **7.00**
**Plate,** grill, 10½" d., closed handles,
green ................................................... **89.00**
**Plate,** grill, 10½" d., closed handles,
yellow.................................................... **7.00**

Platter, 12", closed handles, green....... 19.00
Platter, 12", closed handles, yellow...... 40.00
Relish, footed, three-part, green, 7½"... 26.00
Salt & pepper shakers, green, pr. ...... 67.00
Salt & pepper shakers, pink, pr......... 950.00
Saucer w/cup ring, green.................. 181.00
Sherbet, green, 3⅛" h........................... 15.00
Sherbet, pink, 3⅛" h. ........................... 83.00
Sherbet, yellow, 3⅛" h. ......................... 38.00
Sherbet, thin, high stem, green, 4⅞" h... 32.00
Sherbet, thin, high stem, yellow, 4⅞" h. .. 39.00
Sugar bowl, open, green, 3¼" h........... 17.00
Sugar bowl, open, yellow, 3¼" h.......... 15.00
Sugar bowl, open, green, 4¼" h........... 25.00
Sugar bowl, open, pink, 4¼" h. ............ 81.00
Tumbler, juice, footed, green, 3 oz....... 64.00
Tumbler, juice, green, 3¾" h., 5oz........ 27.00
Tumbler, water, clear, 4" h., 9 oz.......... 10.00
Tumbler, water, green, 4" h., 9 oz. ...... 23.00
Tumbler, water, pink, 4" h., 9 oz.......... 95.00
Tumbler, footed, green, 5" h., 9 oz....... 29.00
Tumbler, footed, pink, 5" h., 9 oz........ 45.00
Tumbler, footed, yellow, 5" h., 9 oz. ..... 14.00
Tumbler, green, 4¾" h., 10 oz. ............. 22.00
Tumbler, yellow, 4¾" h., 10 oz. ........... 83.00
Tumbler, green, 5" h., 11 oz. ................ 28.00
Tumbler, yellow, 5" h., 11 oz. .............. 58.00
Tumbler, footed, green, 5¾" h., 11 oz.. 58.00
Tumbler, green, 5¼" h., 15 oz. ............. 61.00
Vase, 5¾" h., green.............................187.00
Vase, 8" h., green ................................ 34.00
Water bottle, dark green "White
    House Vinegar" base, 8½" h.............. 19.00
Water set: pitcher & six tumblers;
    green, 7 pcs. .................................... 215.00
Dinner set: service for six, green,
    46 pcs. ............................................. 400.00

## CHERRY BLOSSOM
### Jeannette Glass Co., 1930-38
### (Process-etched)

*Cherry Blossom Pitcher*

Berry set: master bowl & six sauce
    dishes; Delphite, 7 pcs. ..................... 84.00
Bowl, berry, 4¾" d., Delphite ............... 14.00
Bowl, berry, 4¾" d., green ................... 17.00
Bowl, berry, 4¾" d., pink...................... 17.00
Bowl, cereal, 5¾" d., green.................. 38.00
Bowl, cereal, 5¾" d., pink .................... 37.00
Bowl, soup, 7¾" d., green.................... 58.00
Bowl, soup, 7¾" d., pink ...................... 69.00
Bowl, berry, 8½" d., Delphite ................ 38.00
Bowl, berry, 8½" d., green .................... 42.00
Bowl, berry, 8½" d., pink....................... 48.00
Bowl, 9" d., two-handled, Delphite........ 29.00
Bowl, 9" d., two-handled, green............ 44.00
Bowl, 9" d., two-handled, pink .............. 45.00
Bowl, 9" oval vegetable, Delphite ......... 38.00
Bowl, 9" oval vegetable, green ............. 42.00
Bowl, 9" oval vegetable, pink............... 42.00
Bowl, fruit, 10½" d., three-footed,
    green ................................................. 73.00
Bowl, fruit, 10½" d., three-footed,
    pink ................................................... 76.00
Butter dish, cov., green....................... 79.00
Butter dish, cov., pink ......................... 82.00
Cake plate, three-footed, green,
    10¼" d. .............................................. 25.00
Cake plate, three-footed, pink, 10¼" d.... 28.00
Coaster, green..................................... 12.00
Coaster, pink ....................................... 15.00
Creamer, Delphite ............................... 19.00
Creamer, green.................................... 18.00
Creamer, pink ...................................... 19.00
Cup & saucer, Delphite ....................... 24.00
Cup & saucer, green ........................... 26.00
Cup & saucer, pink.............................. 22.00
Mug, green, 7 oz. ............................... 167.00
Mug, pink, 7 oz.................................... 180.00
Pitcher, 6¾" h., 36 oz., overall patt.,
    Delphite (ILLUS. previous column)..... 83.00
Pitcher, 6¾" h., 36 oz., overall patt.,
    green ................................................. 58.00
Pitcher, 6¾" h., 36 oz., overall patt.,
    pink ................................................... 56.00
Pitcher, 8" h., 36 oz., footed,
    cone-shaped, patt. top, Delphite......... 66.00
Pitcher, 8" h., 36 oz., footed,
    cone-shaped, patt. top, green............. 55.00
Pitcher, 8" h., 36 oz., footed,
    cone-shaped, patt. top, pink ............... 49.00
Pitcher, 8" h., 42 oz., patt. top, green... 57.00
Pitcher, 8" h., 42 oz., patt. top, pink ..... 55.00
Plate, sherbet, 6" d., Delphite ................ 9.00
Plate, sherbet, 6" d., green .................... 7.00
Plate, sherbet, 6" d., pink...................... 9.00
Plate, salad, 7" d., green...................... 20.00
Plate, salad, 7" d., pink ........................ 22.00
Plate, dinner, 9" d., Delphite ................ 21.00
Plate, dinner, 9" d., green ..................... 23.00
Plate, dinner, 9" d., pink........................ 22.00
Plate, grill, 9" d., green......................... 25.00

Plate, grill, 9" d., pink ........................... 23.00
Platter, 11" oval, Delphite .................... 29.00
Platter, 11" oval, green ........................ 33.00
Platter, 11" oval, pink........................... 42.00
Platter, 13" oval, green ....................... 59.00
Platter, 13" oval, pink........................... 66.00
Platter, 13" oval, divided, green........... 52.00
Platter, 13" oval, divided, pink ............. 68.00
Salt & pepper shakers, green, pr. .. 1,085.00
Sandwich tray, handled, Delphite,
    10½" d. ............................................ 25.00
Sandwich tray, handled, green,
    10½" d. ............................................ 26.00
Sandwich tray, handled, pink, 10½" d. .. 23.00
Sherbet, Delphite................................. 12.00
Sherbet, green..................................... 17.00
Sherbet, pink ....................................... 16.00
Sugar bowl, cov., clear........................ 15.00
Sugar bowl, cov., Delphite .................. 35.00
Sugar bowl, cov., green....................... 32.00
Sugar bowl, cov., pink.......................... 35.00
Sugar bowl, open, Delphite.................. 19.00
Sugar bowl, open, green...................... 15.00
Sugar bowl, open, pink ....................... 12.00
Tumbler, patt. top, green, 3½" h.,
    4 oz.................................................. 26.00
Tumbler, patt. top, pink, 3½" h.,
    4 oz.................................................. 22.00
Tumbler, juice, footed, overall patt.,
    Delphite, 3¾" h., 4 oz. ...................... 18.00
Tumbler, juice, footed, overall patt.,
    green, 3¾" h., 4 oz. .......................... 17.00
Tumbler, juice, footed, overall patt.,
    pink, 3¾" h., 4 oz. ............................ 16.00
Tumbler, footed, overall patt.,
    Delphite, 4½" h., 8 oz. ...................... 22.00
Tumbler, footed, overall patt., green,
    4½" h., 8 oz...................................... 35.00
Tumbler, footed, overall patt., pink,
    4½" h., 8 oz...................................... 28.00
Tumbler, patt. top, green, 4¼" h., 9 oz.. 22.00
Tumbler, patt. top, pink, 4¼" h., 9 oz.... 21.00
Tumbler, footed, overall patt.,
    Delphite, 4½" h., 9 oz. ...................... 22.00
Tumbler, footed, overall patt.,
    green, 4½" h., 9 oz. .......................... 31.00
Tumbler, footed, overall patt., pink,
    4½" h., 9 oz...................................... 31.00
Tumbler, patt. top, green, 5" h., 12 oz.. 58.00
Tumbler, patt. top, pink, 5" h., 12 oz..... 67.00
Water set: pitcher & six tumblers;
    green, 7 pcs. .................................... 165.00
Water set: pitcher & six tumblers;
    pink, 7 pcs. ...................................... 126.00

JUNIOR SET:
Creamer, Delphite................................ 43.00
Creamer, pink ...................................... 41.00
Cup, Delphite ....................................... 31.00

Cup, pink............................................... 35.00
Cup & saucer, Delphite....................... 42.00
Cup & saucer, pink.............................. 43.00
Cup, saucer & plate, pink, 3 pcs. ......... 30.00
Plate, 6" d., Delphite ........................... 12.00
Plate, 6" d., pink.................................. 12.00
Sugar bowl, Delphite........................... 42.00
Sugar bowl, pink .................................. 40.00
14 pc. set, Delphite............................. 311.00
14 pc. set, pink ................................... 270.00

## COLONIAL or Knife & Fork, Hocking Glass Co., 1934-39 (Press-mold)

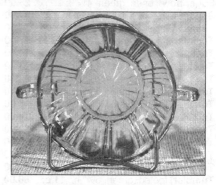

*Colonial Cream Soup Bowl*

Bowl, berry, 3¾" d., pink....................... 52.00
Bowl, berry, 4½" d., clear...................... 5.00
Bowl, berry, 4½" d., green ................... 14.00
Bowl, berry, 4½" d., pink...................... 14.00
Bowl, cream soup, 4½" d., clear.......... 35.00
Bowl, cream soup, 4½" d., green
    (ILLUS.) ........................................... 60.00
Bowl, cream soup, 4½" d., pink ............ 48.00
Bowl, cereal, 5½" d., clear................... 33.00
Bowl, cereal, 5½" d., green.................. 66.00
Bowl, cereal, 5½" d., pink .................... 31.00
Bowl, soup, 7" d., clear........................ 22.00
Bowl, soup, 7" d., green....................... 63.00
Bowl, soup, 7" d., pink......................... 54.00
Bowl, 9" d., clear................................. 18.00
Bowl, 9" d., green ............................... 26.00
Bowl, 9" d., pink.................................. 25.00
Bowl, 10" oval vegetable, clear............. 17.00
Bowl, 10" oval vegetable, green .......... 33.00
Bowl, 10" oval vegetable, pink............. 24.00
Butter dish, cov., clear........................ 34.00
Butter dish, cov., green....................... 51.00
Butter dish, cov., pink ......................... 250.00
Celery or spooner, clear...................... 62.00
Celery or spooner, green .................... 114.00
Celery or spooner, pink....................... 118.00
Creamer or milk pitcher, clear, 5" h.,
    16 oz................................................ 16.00
Creamer or milk pitcher, green, 5" h.,
    16 oz................................................. 23.00

Creamer or milk pitcher, pink, 5" h.,
16 oz. ............................................. **25.00**
Cup & saucer, clear ........................... **9.00**
Cup & saucer, green ......................... **15.00**
Cup & saucer, milk white ...................... **9.00**
Cup & saucer, pink............................. **16.00**
Goblet, cordial, clear, 3¾" h., 1 oz. ........ **15.00**
Goblet, cordial, green, 3¾" h., 1 oz. ..... **29.00**
Goblet, wine, clear, 4½" h., 2½ oz. ........ **15.00**
Goblet, wine, green, 4½" h., 2½ oz. ..... **23.00**
Goblet, cocktail, clear, 4" h., 3 oz. ........ **14.00**
Goblet, cocktail, green, 4" h., 3 oz. ........ **27.00**
Goblet, claret, clear, 5¼" h., 4 oz. ........ **15.00**
Goblet, claret, green, 5¼" h., 4 oz. ....... **25.00**
Goblet, clear, 5¾" h., 8½ oz. ............... **18.00**
Goblet, green, 5¾" h., 8½ oz. .............. **31.00**
Goblet, pink, 5¾" h., 8½ oz. ................. **18.00**
Mug, green, 4½" h., 12 oz................... **750.00**
Pitcher, ice lip or plain, 7" h., 54 oz.,
clear .................................................. **29.00**
Pitcher, ice lip or plain, 7" h., 54 oz.,
green ................................................. **52.00**
Pitcher, ice lip or plain, 7" h., 54 oz.,
pink ................................................... **49.00**
Pitcher, ice lip or plain, 7¾" h.,
68 oz., clear ..................................... **27.00**
Pitcher, ice lip or plain, 7¾" h.,
68 oz., green..................................... **61.00**
Pitcher, ice lip or plain, 7¾" h.,
68 oz., pink........................................ **57.00**
Plate, sherbet, 6" d., clear .................... **6.00**
Plate, sherbet, 6" d., green .................... **6.00**
Plate, sherbet, 6" d., pink...................... **6.00**
Plate, luncheon, 8½" d., clear ................ **5.00**
Plate, luncheon, 8½" d., green................ **9.00**
Plate, luncheon, 8½" d., pink ................ **10.00**
Plate, dinner, 10" d., clear.................... **26.00**
Plate, dinner, 10" d., green ................... **57.00**
Plate, dinner, 10" d., pink..................... **60.00**
Tumbler, whiskey, clear, 2½" h.,
1½ oz. .............................................. **11.00**
Tumbler, whiskey, green, 2½" h.,
1½ oz. .............................................. **12.00**
Tumbler, whiskey, pink, 2½" h.,
1½ oz. .............................................. **12.00**
Tumbler, cordial, footed, clear,
3¼" h., 3 oz. ..................................... **12.00**
Tumbler, cordial, footed, green,
3¼" h., 3 oz. ..................................... **23.00**
Tumbler, cordial, footed, pink, 3¼" h.,
3 oz. ................................................. **16.00**
Tumbler, juice, green, 3" h., 5 oz.......... **24.00**
Tumbler, juice, pink, 3" h., 5 oz. ........... **17.00**
Tumbler, footed, clear, 4" h., 5 oz. ....... **13.00**
Tumbler, footed, green, 4" h., 5 oz. ...... **35.00**
Tumbler, footed, pink, 4" h., 5 oz.......... **26.00**
Tumbler, water, clear, 4" h., 9 oz.......... **14.00**
Tumbler, water, green, 4" h., 9 oz. ....... **21.00**
Tumbler, water, pink, 4" h., 9 oz........... **19.00**
Tumbler, footed, clear, 5¼" h., 10 oz. .. **23.00**
Tumbler, footed, green, 5¼" h., 10 oz.. **44.00**

Tumbler, footed, pink, 5¼" h., 10 oz..... **39.00**
Tumbler, clear, 5⅛" h., 11 oz. .............. **19.00**
Tumbler, green, 5⅛" h., 11 oz. ............. **29.00**
Tumbler, pink, 5⅛" h., 11 oz. ............... **35.00**
Tumbler, iced tea, green, 12 oz........... **32.00**
Tumbler, iced tea, pink, 12 oz. ............ **45.00**
Tumbler, lemonade, green, 15 oz. ....... **72.00**
Tumbler, lemonade, pink, 15 oz. ......... **60.00**

### DIANA, Federal Glass Co., 1937-41 (Press-mold)

*Diana Amber Bowl*

Ashtray, green, 3½" d............................ **3.00**
Bowl, cereal, 5" d., amber.................... **11.00**
Bowl, cereal, 5" d., clear ....................... **4.00**
Bowl, cereal, 5" d., pink ......................... **9.00**
Bowl, cream soup, 5½" d., amber......... **14.00**
Bowl, cream soup, 5½" d., clear............. **4.00**
Bowl, cream soup, 5½" d., pink ........... **22.00**
Bowl, salad, 9" d., amber (ILLUS.) ....... **14.00**
Bowl, salad, 9" d., clear ......................... **6.00**
Bowl, salad, 9" d., pink ........................ **19.00**
Bowl, 12" d., scalloped rim, amber ....... **11.00**
Bowl, 12" d., scalloped rim, clear........... **9.00**
Bowl, 12" d., scalloped rim, pink .......... **15.00**
Candy jar, cov., round, amber .............. **33.00**
Candy jar, cov., round, clear ................ **14.00**
Candy jar, cov., round, pink.................. **35.00**
Coaster, amber, 3½" d......................... **13.00**
Coaster, clear, 3½" d............................ **6.00**
Coaster, pink, 3½" d............................. **7.00**
Console bowl, amber, 11" d.................. **15.00**
Console bowl, clear, 11" d...................... **6.00**
Console bowl, pink, 11" d..................... **27.00**
Creamer, oval, amber ............................ **9.00**
Creamer, oval, clear .............................. **3.00**
Creamer, oval, pink............................... **6.00**
Cup, demitasse, clear ............................ **6.00**
Cup, demitasse, pink ........................... **33.00**
Cup & saucer, demitasse, clear ............. **9.00**
Cup & saucer, demitasse, pink ............ **41.00**
Cup & saucer, amber ............................. **9.00**
Cup & saucer, clear ............................... **4.00**
Cup & saucer, pink............................... **18.00**
Plate, bread & butter, 6" d., amber......... **2.00**

Plate, bread & butter, 6" d., clear ............ 2.00
Plate, bread & butter, 6" d., pink ............. 3.00
Plate, dinner, 9½" d., amber .................. 9.00
Plate, dinner, 9½" d., clear..................... 5.00
Plate, dinner, 9½" d., pink..................... 16.00
Plate, sandwich, 11¾" d., amber .......... 13.00
Plate, sandwich, 11¾" d., clear............... 7.00
Plate, sandwich, 11¾" d., pink.............. 22.00
Platter, 12" oval, amber ...................... 15.00
Platter, 12" oval, clear........................... 7.00
Platter, 12" oval, pink........................... 18.00
Salt & pepper shakers, amber, pr. ...... 89.00
Salt & pepper shakers, clear, pr........... 22.00
Salt & pepper shakers, pink, pr........... 79.00
Saucer, demitasse, pink ...................... 19.00
Sherbet, amber...................................... 9.00
Sherbet, pink ...................................... 11.00
Sugar bowl, open, oval, amber ............. 8.00
Sugar bowl, open, oval, clear................ 2.00
Sugar bowl, open, oval, pink............... 12.00
Tumbler, amber, 4⅛" h., 9 oz. ............. 26.00
Tumbler, clear, 4⅛" h., 9 oz. .............. 27.00
Junior set: six cups, saucers & plates
 w/round rack; clear, set ................... 109.00
Child's Cup, clear.................................. 5.00
Child's cup & saucer, clear.................. 8.00
Child's cup & saucer, pink ................. 45.00

## DOGWOOD or Apple Blossom or Wild Rose, MacBeth-Evans, 1929-32 (Process-etched)

Bowl, cereal, 5½" d., green.................. 28.00
Bowl, cereal, 5½" d., pink .................. 26.00
Bowl, berry, 8½" d., Cremax................ 31.00
Bowl, berry, 8½" d., green.................. 85.00
Bowl, berry, 8½" d., Monax.................. 44.00
Bowl, berry, 8½" d., pink.................... 54.00
Bowl, fruit, 10¼" d., green ............... 181.00
Bowl, fruit, 10¼" d., pink.................... 370.00
Cake plate, heavy solid foot, pink,
 11" d. .................................................. 72.00
Cake plate, heavy solid foot, green,
 13" d. .................................................. 99.00
Cake plate, heavy solid foot, pink,
 13" d. ................................................ 112.00
Creamer, thin, green, 2½" h.............. 39.00
Creamer, thin, pink, 2½" h. ............... 18.00
Creamer, thick, footed, pink, 3¼" h...... 18.00
Cup & saucer, Cremax........................ 35.00
Cup & saucer, green ........................... 39.00
Cup & saucer, pink.............................. 20.00
Pitcher, 8" h., 80 oz., American
 Sweetheart-style, pink ...................... 565.00
Pitcher, 8" h., 80 oz., decorated,
 green ................................................ 415.00
Pitcher, 8" h., 80 oz., decorated,
 pink .................................................. 183.00
Plate, bread & butter, 6" d., green.......... 6.00
Plate, bread & butter, 6" d., pink ............ 8.00
Plate, luncheon, 8" d., clear.................. 4.00

Plate, luncheon, 8" d., green.................. 9.00
Plate, luncheon, 8" d., pink ................... 7.00
Plate, dinner, 9¼" d., pink.................... 32.00
Plate, grill, 10½" d., overall patt. or
 border design only, green.................. 17.00
Plate, grill, 10½" d., border design,
 pink .................................................. 17.00
Plate, grill, 10½" d., overall patt., pink .. 19.00
Plate, salver, 12" d., Monax ................. 18.00
Plate, salver, 12" d., pink ..................... 29.00
Platter, 12" oval, pink........................... 481.00
Sherbet, low foot, green ....................... 40.00
Sherbet, low foot, pink ......................... 29.00
Sugar bowl, open, thin, green, 2½" h... 40.00
Sugar bowl, open, thin, pink, 2½" h. .... 18.00
Sugar bowl, open, thick, footed, pink,
 3¼" h. .................................................. 16.00
Tumbler, decorated, pink, 3½" h.,
 5 oz.................................................... 280.00
Tumbler, decorated, green, 4" h.,
 10 oz.................................................... 80.00
Tumbler, decorated, pink, 4" h., 10 oz.. 32.00
Tumbler, decorated, green, 4¾" h.,
 11 oz.................................................. 116.00
Tumbler, decorated, pink, 4¾" h.,
 11 oz.................................................... 50.00
Tumbler, decorated, pink, 4¾" h.,
 11 oz., w/original box, set of 6 ......... 500.00
Tumbler, decorated, pink, 5" h.,
 12 oz.................................................... 56.00
Tumbler, molded band, pink................. 18.00
Water set: decorated pitcher &
 six decorated tumblers; pink, 7 pcs. . 298.00

## DORIC, Jeannette Glass Co.,1935-38 (Press-mold)

Bowl, berry, 4½" d., green ..................... 9.00
Bowl, berry, 4½" d., pink........................ 9.00
Bowl, cereal, 5½" d., green.................. 68.00
Bowl, cereal, 5½" d., pink ................... 57.00
Bowl, large berry, 8¼" d., green .......... 19.00
Bowl, large berry, 8¼" d., pink............. 21.00
Bowl, 9" d., two-handled, green........... 14.00
Bowl, 9" d., two-handled, pink ............. 16.00
Bowl, 9" oval vegetable, green............. 36.00

*Doric Vegetable Bowl*

**Bowl,** 9" oval vegetable, pink
  (ILLUS. bottom previous page).......... 26.00
**Butter dish,** cov., green........................ 80.00
**Butter dish,** cov., pink .......................... 58.00
**Cake plate,** three-footed, green, 10" d.. 24.00
**Cake plate,** three-footed, pink, 10" d. ... 22.00
**Candy dish,** three-section, Delphite,
  6"........................................................ 10.00
**Candy dish,** three-section, green, 6".... 12.00
**Candy dish,** three-section, pink, 6" ........ 8.00
**Candy jar,** cov., green, 8" h................. 35.00
**Candy jar,** cov., pink, 8" h.................... 34.00
**Coaster,** green, 3" d............................. 18.00
**Coaster,** pink, 3" d. ............................. 19.00
**Creamer,** green, 4" h. .......................... 14.00
**Creamer,** pink, 4" h. ............................ 12.00
**Cup & saucer,** green ........................... 13.00
**Cup & saucer,** pink.............................. 12.00
**Pitcher,** 6" h., 36 oz., green................. 38.00
**Pitcher,** 6" h., 36 oz., pink.................... 31.00
**Pitcher,** 7½" h., 48 oz., footed, pink.... 425.00
**Plate,** sherbet, 6" d., green ..................... 5.00
**Plate,** sherbet, 6" d., pink ...................... 4.00
**Plate,** salad, 7" d., green...................... 17.00
**Plate,** salad, 7" d., pink ........................ 17.00
**Plate,** dinner, 9" d., green ..................... 19.00
**Plate,** dinner, 9" d., pink ....................... 13.00
**Plate,** grill, 9" d., green ......................... 15.00
**Plate,** grill, 9" d., pink .......................... 16.00
**Platter,** 12" oval, green ......................... 27.00
**Platter,** 12" oval, pink........................... 20.00
**Relish tray,** green, 4 x 4"...................... 12.00
**Relish tray,** pink, 4 x 4" ........................ 13.00
**Relish tray,** green, 4 x 8"...................... 18.00
**Relish tray,** pink, 4 x 8" ........................ 18.00
**Relish or serving tray,** green, 8 x 8" ... 18.00
**Relish or serving tray,** pink, 8 x 8" ...... 19.00
**Relish,** square inserts in metal holder,
  green .................................................. 37.00
**Relish,** square inserts in metal holder,
  pink..................................................... 48.00
**Relish set:** two 4 x 4" dishes & one
  4 x 8" dish on 8 x 8" undertray;
  green, 4 pcs...................................... 46.00
**Salt & pepper shakers,** green, pr. ........ 37.00
**Salt & pepper shakers,** pink, pr. ........... 34.00
**Sandwich tray,** handled, green, 10" d.. 20.00
**Sandwich tray,** handled, pink, 10" d. ... 16.00
**Sherbet,** footed, Delphite........................ 6.00
**Sherbet,** footed, green ......................... 14.00
**Sherbet,** footed, pink ........................... 15.00
**Sugar bowl,** cov., green ....................... 17.00
**Sugar bowl,** cov., pink.......................... 21.00
**Tumbler,** green, 4½" h., 9 oz. ............... 85.00
**Tumbler,** pink, 4½" h., 9 oz................... 63.00
**Tumbler,** footed, green, 4" h., 10 oz. ..... 52.00
**Tumbler,** footed, pink, 4" h., 10 oz. ....... 55.00
**Tumbler,** footed, green, 5" h., 12 oz. .... 90.00
**Tumbler,** footed, pink, 5" h., 12 oz. ....... 82.00

**DORIC & PANSY, Jeannette Glass Co.,
1937-38 (Press-mold)**

**Bowl,** berry, 4½" d., clear....................... 8.00
**Bowl,** berry, 4½" d., pink........................ 9.00
**Bowl,** berry, 4½" d., ultramarine .......... 17.00
**Bowl,** large berry, 8" d., clear............... 25.00
**Bowl,** large berry, 8" d., pink................ 19.00
**Bowl,** large berry, 8" d., ultramarine ..... 68.00
**Bowl,** 9" d., handled, ultramarine.......... 39.00
**Butter dish,** cov., ultramarine............. 488.00
**Creamer,** pink ...................................... 32.00
**Creamer,** ultramarine.......................... 160.00
**Cup,** ultramarine ................................. 19.00
**Cup & saucer,** clear ............................ 15.00
**Cup & saucer,** pink................................ 7.00

*Doric & Pansy Cup & Saucer*

**Cup & saucer,** ultramarine (ILLUS.)..... 10.00
**Plate,** salad, 7" d., ultramarine ............. 32.00
**Plate,** dinner, 9" d., ultramarine............. 36.00
**Salt & pepper shakers,** ultramarine,
  pr. ..................................................... 385.00
**Saucer,** ultramarine ............................... 5.00
**Sugar bowl,** open, pink ........................ 32.00
**Sugar bowl,** open, ultramarine............. 138.00
**Tray,** handled, ultramarine, 10"............. 26.00
**Tumbler,** ultramarine, 4½" h., 9 oz. ...... 73.00

PRETTY POLLY PARTY DISHES

**Creamer,** pink ...................................... 31.00
**Creamer,** ultramarine........................... 34.00
**Cup & saucer,** pink............................... 36.00
**Cup & saucer,** ultramarine ................... 46.00
**Plate,** pink ............................................. 8.00
**Plate,** ultramarine................................. 13.00
**Sugar bowl,** pink .................................. 34.00
**Sugar bowl,** ultramarine ....................... 41.00
**14 piece set,** pink ............................... 285.00

**ENGLISH HOBNAIL, Westmoreland
Glass Co., 1920s-40s (Handmade - not
true Depression)**

**Ashtray,** clear, various shapes............. 12.00
**Ashtray,** green, various shapes............ 22.00
**Basket,** handled, clear, 5" h................. 20.00

Bowl, nappy, 4½" d., amber.................. 8.00
Bowl, nappy, 4½" d., clear...................... 9.00
Bowl, nappy, 4½" d., green.................. 12.00
Bowl, nappy, 4½" d., ice blue ............... 43.00
Bowl, nappy, 4½" d., pink ...................... 9.00
Bowl, nappy, 4½" d., turquoise............ 18.00
Bowl, nappy, 4½" sq., clear ................... 5.00
Bowl, nappy, 4½" sq., green.................. 8.00
Bowl, nappy, 4½" sq., pink .................. 12.00
Bowl, cream soup, 4¾" d., clear............ 6.00
Bowl, cream soup, 4¾" d., green.......... 20.00
Bowl, 6" d., amber ................................. 9.00
Bowl, 6" d., clear.................................... 9.00
Bowl, 6" d., green ................................. 10.00
Bowl, nappy, 6" sq., green.................... 14.00
Bowl, grapefruit, 6½" d., clear.............. 14.00
Bowl, fruit, 8" d., two-handled, footed,
   clear.................................................. 22.00
Bowl, fruit, 8" d., two-handled, footed,
   cobalt.............................................. 120.00
Bowl, fruit, 8" d., two-handled, footed,
   green ................................................ 37.00
Bowl, fruit, 8" d., two-handled, footed,
   turquoise.......................................... 44.00
Bowl, nappy, 8" d., amber ................... 29.00
Bowl, nappy, 8" d., clear...................... 13.00
Bowl, nappy, 8" d., green..................... 30.00
Bowl, nappy, 11" d., blue..................... 38.00
Bowl, 12" d., canted sides, turquoise.... 77.00
Bowl, 12" d., flared, clear..................... 28.00
Bowl, 12" d., flared, green ................... 40.00
Bowl, 12" d., flared, turquoise.............. 30.00
Candlesticks, amber, 3½" h., pr.......... 18.00
Candlesticks, blue, 3½" h., pr. ............. 34.00
Candlesticks, clear, 3½" h., pr. ............ 15.00
Candlesticks, green, 3½" h., pr........... 28.00
Candlesticks, pink, 3½" h., pr. ............. 29.00
Candlesticks, turquoise, 3½" h., pr...... 67.00
Candlesticks, amber, 8½" h., pr........... 68.00
Candlesticks, clear, 8½" h., pr. ........... 58.00
Candlesticks, green, 8½" h., pr............ 56.00
Candlesticks, pink, 8½" h., pr. ............. 40.00
Candlesticks, turquoise, 8½" h., pr...... 61.00
Candy dish, cov., cone-shaped,
   amber, ½ lb....................................... 45.00
Candy dish, cov., cone-shaped,
   clear, ½ lb......................................... 34.00
Candy dish, cov., cone-shaped,
   cobalt blue, ½ lb. ............................ 252.00
Candy dish, cov., cone-shaped,
   green, ½ lb........................................ 61.00
Candy dish, cov., cone-shaped,
   pink, ½ lb. ........................................ 42.00
Candy dish, cov., urn-shaped, green,
   15" h. .............................................. 300.00
Celery tray, clear, 12" l. ...................... 12.00
Cigarette box, cov., clear.................... 36.00
Cigarette box, cov., pink..................... 24.00
Cologne bottle, amber........................ 47.00
Cologne bottle, blue ........................... 38.00

Cologne bottle, clear .......................... 27.00
Cologne bottle, pink............................ 24.00
Cologne bottle, turquoise ................... 36.00
Cologne bottles w/stoppers, blue, pr. .. 55.00
Cologne bottles w/stoppers, cobalt
   blue, pr.............................................. 91.00
Creamer, flat or footed, amber............. 24.00
Creamer, flat or footed, blue ................ 38.00
Creamer, flat or footed, clear ................ 9.00
Creamer, flat or footed, green.............. 19.00
Creamer, flat or footed, pink ................ 14.00
Cup & saucer, demitasse, clear........... 24.00
Cup & saucer, demitasse, pink ........... 39.00
Cup & saucer, clear .............................. 9.00
Cup & saucer, green............................ 35.00
Cup & saucer, pink............................... 20.00
Cup & saucer, turquoise ..................... 23.00
Decanter w/stopper, clear, 20 oz. ....... 29.00
Dish, cov., three-footed, amber ........... 60.00
Dish, cov., three-footed, clear.............. 33.00
Dish, cov., three-footed, green ............ 57.00
Dresser set: cov. puff box & two
   cologne bottles; green, 3 pcs........... 102.00
Egg cup, clear ..................................... 17.00
Goblet, cordial, clear, 1 oz.................... 16.00
Goblet, wine, clear, 2 oz. ..................... 13.00
Goblet, cocktail, amber, 3 oz. .............. 15.00
Goblet, cocktail, clear, 3 oz. ................ 10.00
Goblet, cocktail, green, 3 oz. ............... 16.00
Goblet, cocktail, pink, 3 oz. ................. 15.00
Goblet, cocktail, turquoise, 3 oz. ........ 23.00
Goblet, claret, blue, 5 oz...................... 27.00
Goblet, claret, clear, 5 oz...................... 7.00
Goblet, claret, cobalt blue, 5 oz. .......... 18.00
Goblet, blue, 6¼ oz. ............................ 37.00
Goblet, clear, 6¼ oz. ........................... 16.00
Goblet, cobalt blue, 6¼ oz. ................. 35.00
Goblet, green, 6¼ oz. .......................... 22.00
Goblet, pink, 6¼ oz. ............................ 18.00
Goblet, turquoise, 6¼ oz. .................... 44.00
Goblet, water, clear, 8 oz. ..................... 8.00
Goblet, water, green, 8 oz. ................... 25.00
Goblet, water, ice blue, 8 oz. ............... 50.00
Hat, high, clear..................................... 15.00
Ice tub, clear ........................................ 65.00
Lamp, electric, clear, 6¼" h. ................ 38.00
Lamp, electric, pink, 6¼" h................... 55.00
Lamp, electric, amber, 9¼" h. .............. 71.00
Lamp, electric, blue, 9¼" h. ................. 85.00
Lamp, electric, clear, 9¼" h. ................ 27.00
Lamp, electric, green, 9¼" h. .............. 99.00
Lamp, electric, pink, 9¼" h................. 109.00
Marmalade jar, cov., clear ................... 34.00
Marmalade jar, cov., green .................. 35.00
Marmalade jar, cov., pink .................... 33.00
Oil bottle, clear, 2 oz. .......................... 45.00
Parfait, footed, round, clear ................. 19.00
Pitcher, 23 oz., clear............................ 67.00
Pitcher, ½ gal., straight sides, clear ... 164.00

Pitcher, ½ gal., straight sides, green .. **235.00**
Plate, sherbet, 5½" or 6½" d., clear ........ **5.00**
Plate, sherbet, 5½" or 6½" d., green ....... **4.00**
Plate, sherbet, 5½" or 6½" d., pink ......... **3.00**
Plate, 7¼" d., clear.................................. **5.00**
Plate, luncheon, 8" round or square,
 green .................................................. **11.00**
Plate, luncheon, 8" round or square,
 ice blue ............................................. **25.00**

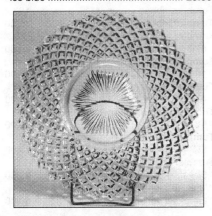

*English Hobnail Plate*

Plate, luncheon, 8" round or square,
 pink (ILLUS.)........................................ **9.00**
Plate, dinner, 10" d., amber ................. **18.00**
Plate, dinner, 10" d., clear.................... **16.00**
Plate, dinner, 10" d., green .................. **19.00**
Puff box, cov., clear.............................. **28.00**
Puff box, cov., green ............................ **35.00**
Relish dish, three-part, clear, 8" oval ... **29.00**
Relish dish, green, 8" oval ................... **24.00**
Rose bowl, clear, 4" .............................. **15.00**
Rose bowl, clear, 6" .............................. **21.00**
Salt & pepper shakers, amber, pr. ....... **72.00**
Salt & pepper shakers, clear, pr.......... **30.00**
Salt & pepper shakers, green, pr. ....... **74.00**
Salt & pepper shakers, turquoise, pr... **110.00**
Salt dip, footed, blue, 2" ...................... **13.00**
Salt dip, footed, clear, 2" ....................... **8.00**
Salt dip, footed, pink, 2"....................... **15.00**
Salt dip, footed, turquoise, 2" .............. **17.00**
Saucer, demitasse, clear ..................... **10.00**
Sherbet, footed, amber......................... **13.00**
Sherbet, footed, clear ............................ **7.00**
Sherbet, footed, green.......................... **16.00**
Sherbet, footed, ice blue...................... **23.00**
Sherbet, footed, pink ........................... **12.00**
Sugar bowl, open, footed or flat, clear ... **9.00**
Sugar bowl, open, footed or flat,
 green .................................................. **16.00**
Sugar bowl, open, footed or flat, pink .. **19.00**
Tumbler, whiskey, clear, 1½ oz.............. **8.00**
Tumbler, whiskey, clear, 3 oz............... **13.00**
Tumbler, clear, 3¾" h., 5 oz. ................ **12.00**

Tumbler, green, 3¾" h., 5 oz. ................ **7.00**
Tumbler, footed, clear, 7 oz................... **8.00**
Tumbler, footed, green, 7 oz. .............. **15.00**
Tumbler, amber, 3¾" h., 9 oz. ............... **6.00**
Tumbler, clear, 3¾" h., 9 oz. ............... **12.00**
Tumbler, green, 3¾" h., 9 oz. ................ **8.00**
Tumbler, pink, 3¾" h., 9 oz................... **8.00**
Tumbler, footed, clear, 9 oz.................. **9.00**
Tumbler, iced tea, clear, 4" h., 10 oz.... **11.00**
Tumbler, iced tea, ice blue, 4" h.,
 10 oz.................................................. **48.00**
Tumbler, iced tea, clear, 5" h., 12 oz.... **14.00**
Tumbler, iced tea, pink, 5" h., 12 oz..... **12.00**
Tumbler, footed, clear, 12½ oz............. **19.00**
Tumbler, footed, green, 12½ oz. .......... **15.00**
Vase, 7¼" h., amber.............................. **85.00**
Vase, 7¼" h., green............................... **55.00**
Vase, 7¼" h., pink ............................... **101.00**

### (OLD) FLORENTINE or Poppy No. 1 Hazel Atlas Glass Co., 1932-35 (Process-etched)

Ashtray, green, 5½".............................. **22.00**
Ashtray, pink, 5½" ............................... **27.00**
Bowl, berry, 5" d., clear........................ **11.00**
Bowl, berry, 5" d., green ...................... **11.00**
Bowl, berry, 5" d., pink......................... **10.00**
Bowl, berry, 5" d., yellow...................... **13.00**
Bowl, cereal, 6" d., clear...................... **20.00**
Bowl, cereal, 6" d., green..................... **33.00**
Bowl, cereal, 6" d., pink ....................... **20.00**
Bowl, cereal, 6" d., yellow.................... **35.00**
Bowl, 8½" d., clear................................ **22.00**
Bowl, 8½" d., green............................... **24.00**
Bowl, 8½" d., pink................................. **36.00**
Bowl, 8½" d., yellow.............................. **29.00**
Bowl, cov. vegetable, 8½" oval, clear ... **47.00**
Bowl, cov. vegetable, 8½" oval, green.. **36.00**
Bowl, cov. vegetable, 8½" oval, pink .... **55.00**
Bowl, 9½" oval vegetable, green .......... **24.00**
Bowl, 9½" oval vegetable, yellow ......... **28.00**
Butter dish, cov., clear ....................... **118.00**
Butter dish, cov., green .................... **117.00**
Butter dish, cov., pink ....................... **145.00**
Butter dish, cov., yellow...................... **153.00**
Coaster-ashtray, yellow, 3¾" d............ **26.00**
Creamer, plain rim, clear ....................... **8.00**
Creamer, plain rim, green .................... **11.00**
Creamer, plain rim, pink....................... **15.00**
Creamer, ruffled rim, cobalt blue .......... **60.00**
Creamer, ruffled rim, green................... **23.00**
Creamer, ruffled rim, pink .................... **22.00**
Cup & saucer, clear .............................. **9.00**
Cup & saucer, green ............................ **12.00**
Cup & saucer, pink............................... **14.00**
Nut dish, handled, ruffled rim, pink....... **18.00**
Nut dish, handled, ruffled rim, yellow ... **18.00**
Pitcher, 6½" h., 36 oz., footed, clear .... **37.00**
Pitcher, 6½" h., 36 oz., footed, green... **43.00**
Pitcher, 6½" h., 36 oz., footed, pink...... **44.00**

*Florentine Pitcher & Tumblers*

**Pitcher,** 6½" h., 36 oz., footed,
yellow............................................. **47.00**
**Pitcher,** 7½" h., 48 oz., clear
(ILLUS. back).................................. **63.00**
**Pitcher,** 7½" h., 48 oz., green.............. **75.00**
**Pitcher,** 7½" h., 48 oz., pink.............. **125.00**
**Pitcher,** 7½" h., 48 oz., yellow ........... **154.00**
**Plate,** sherbet, 6" d., clear...................... **4.00**
**Plate,** sherbet, 6" d., green .................... **6.00**
**Plate,** sherbet, 6" d., pink ...................... **5.00**
**Plate,** salad, 8½" d., clear ...................... **7.00**
**Plate,** salad, 8½" d., green..................... **9.00**
**Plate,** salad, 8½" d., yellow.................. **12.00**
**Plate,** dinner, 10" d., clear.................... **13.00**
**Plate,** dinner, 10" d., green ................... **17.00**
**Plate,** dinner, 10" d., pink..................... **27.00**
**Plate,** dinner, 10" d., yellow.................. **21.00**
**Plate,** grill, 10" d., clear ....................... **11.00**
**Plate,** grill, 10" d., green....................... **12.00**
**Plate,** grill, 10" d., pink........................ **16.00**
**Plate,** grill, 10" d., yellow..................... **13.00**
**Platter,** 11½" oval, clear....................... **11.00**
**Platter,** 11½" oval, green ...................... **16.00**
**Platter,** 11½" oval, pink........................ **19.00**
**Platter,** 11½" oval, yellow ..................... **24.00**
**Salt & pepper shakers,** footed,
clear, pr........................................... **36.00**
**Salt & pepper shakers,** footed,
green, pr.......................................... **39.00**
**Salt & pepper shakers,** footed,
yellow, pr. ........................................ **52.00**
**Sherbet,** footed, clear, 3 oz. .................. **8.00**
**Sherbet,** footed, green, 3 oz. ............... **10.00**
**Sherbet,** footed, pink, 3 oz.................... **9.00**
**Sherbet,** footed, yellow, 3 oz. .............. **10.00**
**Sugar bowl,** cov., green ....................... **27.00**
**Sugar bowl,** cov., pink.......................... **41.00**
**Sugar bowl,** cov., yellow ....................... **30.00**
**Tumbler,** footed, green, 3¼" h., 4 oz. ..... **8.00**

**Tumbler,** juice, footed, clear, 3¾" h.,
5 oz. (ILLUS. of two, front)................. **14.00**
**Tumbler,** juice, footed, green, 3¾" h.,
5 oz.................................................. **16.00**
**Tumbler,** juice, footed, pink, 3¾" h.,
5 oz.................................................. **19.00**
**Tumbler,** juice, footed, yellow, 3¾" h.,
5 oz.................................................. **19.00**
**Tumbler,** ribbed, clear, 4" h., 9 oz. ....... **14.00**
**Tumbler,** ribbed, green, 4" h., 9 oz. ...... **16.00**
**Tumbler,** ribbed, pink, 4" h., 9 oz.......... **15.00**
**Tumbler,** water, footed, green,
4¾" h., 10 oz..................................... **23.00**
**Tumbler,** water, footed, pink, 4¾" h.,
10 oz................................................ **25.00**
**Tumbler,** water, footed, yellow,
4¾" h., 10 oz..................................... **19.00**
**Tumbler,** iced tea, footed, green,
5¼" h., 12 oz..................................... **19.00**
**Tumbler,** iced tea, footed, pink,
5¼" h., 12 oz..................................... **18.00**
**Tumbler,** iced tea, footed, yellow,
5¼" h., 12 oz..................................... **22.00**
**Water set:** jug-type pitcher & six footed
tumblers; yellow, 7 pcs. ..................... **60.00**

**FLORENTINE or Poppy No. 2, Hazel
Atlas Glass Co., 1932-35 (Process-
etched)**

**Bowl,** berry, 4½" d., clear........................ **9.00**
**Bowl,** berry, 4½" d., green .................... **12.00**
**Bowl,** berry, 4½" d., pink....................... **15.00**
**Bowl,** berry, 4½" d., yellow ................... **18.00**
**Bowl,** cream soup, plain rim, 4¾" d.,
clear................................................. **9.00**
**Bowl,** cream soup, plain rim, 4¾" d.,
green ................................................ **13.00**
**Bowl,** cream soup, plain rim, 4¾" d.,
pink.................................................. **15.00**
**Bowl,** cream soup, plain rim, 4¾" d.,
yellow................................................ **23.00**
**Bowl,** 5½" d., yellow............................. **41.00**
**Bowl,** cereal, 6" d., green....................... **23.00**
**Bowl,** cereal, 6" d., yellow..................... **35.00**
**Bowl,** 8" d., clear................................. **20.00**
**Bowl,** 8" d., green ............................... **24.00**
**Bowl,** 8" d., pink.................................. **31.00**
**Bowl,** 8" d., yellow............................... **29.00**
**Bowl,** cov. vegetable, 9" oval, clear...... **47.00**
**Bowl,** cov. vegetable, 9" oval, green..... **49.00**
**Bowl,** cov. vegetable, 9" oval, yellow.... **63.00**
**Bowl,** 9" oval vegetable, green ............ **23.00**
**Bowl,** 9" oval vegetable, yellow ........... **21.00**
**Butter dish,** cov., clear......................... **92.00**
**Butter dish,** cov., green......................... **99.00**
**Butter dish,** cov., yellow..................... **135.00**
**Candlesticks,** green, 2¾" h., pr........... **54.00**
**Candlesticks,** yellow, 2¾" h., pr........... **55.00**
**Candy dish,** cov., clear........................ **89.00**
**Candy dish,** cov., green ..................... **115.00**

**Candy dish,** cov., pink........................ **107.00**
**Candy dish,** cov., yellow .................... **147.00**
**Coaster,** clear, 3¼" d. ........................... **10.00**
**Coaster,** green, 3¼" d........................... **12.00**
**Coaster,** pink, 3¼" d. ............................ **18.00**
**Coaster,** yellow, 3¼" d. .......................... **19.00**
**Coaster-ashtray,** clear, 3¾" d. ............. **17.00**
**Coaster-ashtray,** green, 3¾" d............. **18.00**
**Coaster-ashtray,** yellow, 3¾" d........... **23.00**
**Coaster-ashtray,** green, 5½" d............. **19.00**
**Coaster-ashtray,** yellow, 5½" d........... **32.00**
**Compote,** 3½", ruffled, clear................ **24.00**
**Compote,** 3½", ruffled, cobalt blue ....... **50.00**
**Compote,** 3½", ruffled, pink.................. **17.00**
**Condiment set:** creamer, cov. sugar
    bowl, salt & pepper shakers &
    8½" d. tray; yellow, 5 pcs. ................. **148.00**
**Creamer,** clear....................................... **7.00**
**Creamer,** green....................................... **9.00**
**Creamer,** yellow.................................... **11.00**
**Cup & saucer,** clear .............................. **9.00**
**Cup & saucer,** green ............................ **13.00**
**Cup & saucer,** pink............................... **12.00**

*Florentine Cup & Saucer*

**Cup & saucer,** yellow (ILLUS.).............. **13.00**
**Custard cup,** clear................................. **37.00**
**Custard cup,** yellow ............................. **77.00**
**Gravy boat,** yellow................................ **47.00**
**Gravy boat w/platter,** yellow,
    11½" oval............................................ **87.00**
**Pitcher,** 6¼" h., 24 oz., cone-shaped,
    yellow................................................ **134.00**
**Pitcher,** 7½" h., 28 oz., cone-shaped,
    clear.................................................... **23.00**
**Pitcher,** 7½" h., 28 oz., cone-shaped,
    green .................................................. **40.00**
**Pitcher,** 7½" h., 28 oz., cone-shaped,
    yellow.................................................. **28.00**
**Pitcher,** 7½" h., 48 oz., straight sides,
    clear.................................................... **52.00**

**Pitcher,** 7½" h., 48 oz., straight sides,
    yellow................................................ **168.00**
**Pitcher,** 8¼" h., 76 oz., clear ............... **58.00**
**Pitcher,** 8¼" h., 76 oz., green............... **85.00**
**Pitcher,** 8¼" h., 76 oz., pink................ **234.00**
**Plate,** sherbet, 6" d., clear ..................... **3.00**
**Plate,** sherbet, 6" d., yellow.................... **5.00**
**Plate,** 6¼" d., w/indentation, yellow ...... **25.00**
**Plate,** salad, 8½" d., clear ...................... **7.00**
**Plate,** salad, 8½" d., green...................... **8.00**
**Plate,** salad, 8½" d., yellow .................... **9.00**
**Plate,** dinner, 10" d., clear ..................... **11.00**
**Plate,** dinner, 10" d., green ................... **15.00**
**Plate,** dinner, 10" d., yellow .................. **12.00**
**Plate,** grill, 10¼" d., clear ...................... **12.00**
**Plate,** grill, 10¼" d., green...................... **14.00**
**Plate,** grill, 10¼" d., yellow .................... **11.00**
**Platter,** 11" oval, clear............................ **11.00**
**Platter,** 11" oval, green .......................... **16.00**
**Platter,** 11" oval, yellow ......................... **18.00**
**Platter,** 11½", for gravy boat, yellow ..... **43.00**
**Relish dish,** three-part or plain, clear,
    10" ...................................................... **13.00**
**Relish dish,** three-part or plain,
    green, 10" ........................................... **22.00**
**Relish dish,** three-part or plain,
    pink, 10".............................................. **24.00**
**Relish dish,** three-part or plain,
    yellow, 10" .......................................... **33.00**
**Salt & pepper shakers,** clear, pr.......... **36.00**
**Salt & pepper shakers,** green, pr ........ **41.00**
**Salt & pepper shakers,** yellow, pr ....... **45.00**
**Sherbet,** clear ........................................ **9.00**
**Sherbet,** yellow..................................... **10.00**
**Sugar bowl,** cov., clear.......................... **24.00**
**Sugar bowl,** cov., yellow ....................... **31.00**
**Sugar bowl,** open, clear .......................... **8.00**
**Sugar bowl,** open, green......................... **9.00**
**Tray,** yellow, 8½" d.................................. **86.00**
**Tumbler,** footed, clear, 3¼" h., 5 oz. .... **12.00**
**Tumbler,** footed, yellow, 3¼" h., 5 oz. .. **16.00**
**Tumbler,** juice, clear, 3½" h., 5 oz......... **9.00**
**Tumbler,** juice, green, 3½" h., 5 oz....... **12.00**
**Tumbler,** juice, pink, 3½" h., 5 oz. ....... **14.00**
**Tumbler,** juice, yellow, 3½" h., 5 oz...... **17.00**
**Tumbler,** footed, clear, 4" h., 5 oz. ....... **11.00**
**Tumbler,** footed, yellow, 4" h., 5 oz. ..... **15.00**
**Tumbler,** blown, clear, 3½" h., 6 oz....... **16.00**
**Tumbler,** water, clear, 4" h., 9 oz.......... **10.00**
**Tumbler,** water, green, 4" h., 9 oz. ....... **12.00**
**Tumbler,** water, pink, 4" h., 9 oz........... **16.00**
**Tumbler,** water, yellow, 4" h., 9 oz. ...... **19.00**
**Tumbler,** footed, green, 4½" h., 9 oz. ... **20.00**
**Tumbler,** footed, yellow, 4½" h., 9 oz. .. **30.00**
**Tumbler,** blown, clear, 5" h., 12 oz. ...... **19.00**
**Tumbler,** blown, green, 5" h., 12 oz...... **16.00**
**Tumbler,** iced tea, clear, 5" h., 12 oz.... **24.00**
**Tumbler,** iced tea, green, 5" h.,
    12 oz.................................................... **36.00**

**Tumbler,** iced tea, yellow, 5" h.,
12 oz. ................................................. **40.00**
**Vase (or parfait),** 6" h., clear ............... **25.00**
**Vase (or parfait),** 6" h., green............... **37.00**
**Vase (or parfait),** 6" h., yellow.............. **56.00**
**Water set:** cone-shaped pitcher &
six tumblers; yellow, 7 pcs. ................. **80.00**

### HOMESPUN or Fine Rib, Jeannette Glass Co., 1939-49 (Press-mold)

**Bowl,** 4½" d., closed handles................ **11.00**
**Bowl,** cereal, 5" d................................. **20.00**
**Bowl,** berry, 8¼" d. .............................. **16.00**
**Butter dish,** cov. ................................... **53.00**
**Coaster-ashtray** ...................................... **9.00**
**Creamer,** footed...................................... **8.00**
**Cup & saucer** ........................................ **14.00**
**Plate,** sherbet, 6" d.................................. **7.00**
**Plate,** dinner, 9¼" d .............................. **17.00**
**Platter,** 13", closed handles .................. **19.00**
**Tumbler,** straight, 3⅞" h., 9 oz. ............ **27.00**
**Tumbler,** footed, 4" h., 5 oz. ................... **8.00**
**Tumbler,** water, 4" h., 9 oz. ................... **22.00**
**Tumbler,** footed, 6¼" h., 9 oz. ............... **8.00**
**Tumbler,** iced tea, 5¼" h., 13 oz........... **30.00**
**Tumbler,** footed, 6½" h., 15 oz. ............ **23.00**

CHILD'S TEA SET:

**Cup & saucer,** clear ............................ **24.00**
**Cup & saucer,** pink............................... **21.00**
**Plate,** clear ............................................ **7.00**
**Plate,** pink ........................................... **12.00**
**Teapot,** cov., pink ................................ **72.00**
**Teapot,** cov., pink ................................ **59.00**
**14 piece set,** pink ............................... **285.00**

### MADRID, Federal Glass Co., 1932-39 (Process-etched)

**Ashtray,** amber, 6" sq......................... **264.00**
**Ashtray,** green, 6" sq.......................... **195.00**
**Bowl,** cream soup, 4¾" d., amber ........ **14.00**
**Bowl,** sauce, 5" d., amber...................... **5.00**
**Bowl,** sauce, 5" d., blue ...................... **35.00**
**Bowl,** sauce, 5" d., clear ....................... **5.00**
**Bowl,** sauce, 5" d., green ...................... **9.00**
**Bowl,** sauce, 5" d., pink ...................... **11.00**
**Bowl,** soup, 7" d., amber ..................... **14.00**
**Bowl,** soup, 7" d., blue ........................ **20.00**
**Bowl,** soup, 7" d., clear ......................... **5.00**
**Bowl,** soup, 7" d., green....................... **16.00**
**Bowl,** salad, 8" d., amber .................... **14.00**
**Bowl,** salad, 8" d., blue ....................... **46.00**
**Bowl,** salad, 8" d., clear ........................ **9.00**
**Bowl,** salad, 8" d., green ..................... **16.00**
**Bowl,** large berry, 9⅜" d., amber ......... **22.00**
**Bowl,** large berry, 9⅜" d., pink ........... **24.00**
**Bowl,** salad, 9½" d., deep, amber......... **33.00**
**Bowl,** 10" oval vegetable, amber .......... **15.00**

**Bowl,** 10" oval vegetable, blue............. **34.00**
**Bowl,** 10" oval vegetable, green ........... **19.00**
**Butter dish,** cov., amber...................... **67.00**
**Butter dish,** cov., clear ....................... **51.00**
**Butter dish,** cov., green...................... **81.00**
**Cake plate,** amber, 11¼" d. ................. **15.00**
**Cake plate,** pink, 11¼" d...................... **12.00**
**Candlesticks,** amber, 2¼" h., pr........... **20.00**
**Candlesticks,** clear, 2¼" h., pr. ........... **15.00**
**Candlesticks,** pink, 2¼" h., pr. ............. **22.00**
**Console bowl,** flared, amber, 11" d...... **13.00**
**Console bowl,** flared, clear, 11" d. ....... **14.00**
**Console bowl,** flared, pink, 11" d. ........ **17.00**
**Console set:** bowl & pair of
candlesticks; amber, 3 pcs. ................. **37.00**
**Console set:** bowl & pair of
candlesticks; iridescent, 3 pcs. ........... **35.00**
**Console set:** bowl & pair of
candlesticks; pink, 3 pcs. .................... **36.00**
**Cookie jar,** cov., amber ....................... **44.00**
**Cookie jar,** cov., clear......................... **33.00**
**Cookie jar,** cov., pink .......................... **38.00**
**Creamer,** amber...................................... **7.00**
**Creamer,** green..................................... **11.00**
**Cup & saucer,** amber ............................. **9.00**

*Madrid Cup & Saucer*

**Cup & saucer,** blue (ILLUS.) ............... **23.00**
**Cup & saucer,** clear ............................... **9.00**
**Cup & saucer,** green ........................... **12.00**
**Cup & saucer,** pink ............................. **13.00**
**Gelatin mold,** amber, 2⅛" h. ............... **11.00**
**Gravy boat & platter,** amber............. **500.00**
**Hot dish coaster,** amber, 5" d............. **39.00**
**Hot dish coaster,** clear, 5" d. ............. **32.00**
**Hot dish coaster w/indentation,**
amber ................................................. **35.00**
**Hot dish coaster w/indentation,**
clear.................................................... **28.00**
**Hot dish coaster w/indentation,**
green .................................................. **37.00**
**Jam dish,** amber, 7" d. ......................... **19.00**
**Jam dish,** blue, 7" d............................. **33.00**
**Jam dish,** clear, 7" d............................ **10.00**
**Jam dish,** green, 7" d. ......................... **25.00**
**Lazy susan,** walnut base w/seven
clear hot dish coasters .................... **871.00**
**Pitcher,** juice, 5½" h., 36 oz., amber..... **37.00**

**Pitcher,** 8" h., 60 oz., square, amber.... **45.00**
**Pitcher,** 8" h., 60 oz., square, blue ..... **160.00**
**Pitcher,** 8" h., 60 oz., square, clear ...... **22.00**
**Pitcher,** 8" h., 60 oz., square, green ... **132.00**
**Pitcher,** 8" h., 60 oz., square, pink........ **34.00**
**Pitcher,** 8½" h., 80 oz., jug-type,
  amber ..................................................... **55.00**
**Pitcher,** 8½" h., 80 oz., jug-type,
  green ..................................................... **188.00**
**Pitcher w/ice lip,** 8½" h., 80 oz.,
  amber ..................................................... **54.00**
**Plate,** sherbet, 6" d., amber ................. **3.00**
**Plate,** sherbet, 6" d., blue.................. **12.00**
**Plate,** sherbet, 6" d., green ................. **5.00**
**Plate,** sherbet, 6" d., pink.................... **4.00**
**Plate,** salad, 7½" d., amber ................. **9.00**
**Plate,** salad, 7½" d., blue .................. **18.00**
**Plate,** salad, 7½" d., green ................. **9.00**
**Plate,** luncheon, 8⅞" d., amber ........... **7.00**
**Plate,** luncheon, 8⅞" d., blue ........... **18.00**
**Plate,** luncheon, 8⅞" d., clear ............. **6.00**
**Plate,** luncheon, 8⅞" d., green .......... **13.00**
**Plate,** dinner, 10½" d., amber.............. **37.00**
**Plate,** dinner, 10½" d., blue.................. **65.00**
**Plate,** dinner, 10½" d., clear............... **21.00**
**Plate,** dinner, 10½" d., green ............. **34.00**
**Plate,** grill, 10½" d., amber.................... **19.00**
**Plate,** grill, 10½" d., clear ..................... **9.00**
**Plate,** grill, 10½" d., green.................... **17.00**
**Platter,** 11½" oval, amber ..................... **15.00**
**Platter,** 11½" oval, blue...................... **29.00**
**Platter,** 11½" oval, clear........................ **7.00**
**Platter,** 11½" oval, green ..................... **19.00**
**Relish plate,** amber, 10½" d................. **15.00**
**Relish plate,** clear, 10½" d. ................. **7.00**
**Relish plate,** pink, 10½" d. .................. **18.00**
**Salt & pepper shakers,** amber,
  3½" h., pr. ............................................. **45.00**
**Salt & pepper shakers,** clear,
  3½" h., pr. ............................................. **41.00**
**Salt & pepper shakers,** green,
  3½" h., pr. ............................................. **64.00**
**Salt & pepper shakers,** footed,
  amber, 3½" h., pr. ................................. **73.00**
**Salt & pepper shakers,** footed, blue,
  3½" h., pr. ........................................... **200.00**
**Salt & pepper shakers,** footed,
  green, 3½" h., pr. ................................. **81.00**
**Sherbet,** amber...................................... **8.00**
**Sherbet,** blue ...................................... **15.00**
**Sherbet,** clear ....................................... **7.00**
**Sherbet,** green...................................... **10.00**
**Sugar bowl,** cov., amber ...................... **45.00**
**Sugar bowl,** cov., clear........................ **33.00**
**Sugar bowl,** cov., green ........................ **9.00**
**Tumbler,** juice, amber, 3⅞" h., 5 oz...... **14.00**
**Tumbler,** juice, blue, 3⅞" h., 5 oz......... **34.00**
**Tumbler,** footed, amber, 4" h., 5 oz..... **19.00**
**Tumbler,** amber, 4½" h., 9 oz............... **13.00**
**Tumbler,** blue, 4½" h., 9 oz. ............... **24.00**

**Tumbler,** green, 4½" h., 9 oz. .............. **24.00**
**Tumbler,** pink, 4½" h., 9 oz.................. **15.00**
**Tumblers,** amber, 4½" h., 9 oz.,
  w/box, set of 24 ................................. **325.00**
**Tumbler,** footed, amber, 5¼" h.,
  10 oz..................................................... **25.00**
**Tumbler,** footed, clear, 5¼" h.,
  10 oz..................................................... **14.00**
**Tumbler,** footed, green, 5¼" h.,
  10 oz..................................................... **34.00**
**Tumbler,** amber, 5½" h., 12 oz. ........... **18.00**
**Tumbler,** blue, 5½" h., 12 oz. .............. **21.00**
**Tumbler,** green, 5½" h., 12 oz. ............. **35.00**
**Water set:** 60 oz. pitcher & six 9 oz.
  tumblers; green, 7 pcs. .................... **197.00**

## MAYFAIR or Open Rose, Hocking
## Glass Co., 1931-37 (Process-etched)

**Bowl,** cream soup, 5", pink ................... **45.00**
**Bowl,** cream soup, 5", pink frosted ....... **26.00**
**Bowl,** cereal, 5½", blue........................ **49.00**
**Bowl,** cereal, 5½", pink ........................ **24.00**
**Bowl,** vegetable, 7", blue ..................... **53.00**
**Bowl,** vegetable, 7", pink ..................... **27.00**
**Bowl,** vegetable, 7", pink frosted .......... **18.00**
**Bowl,** 9½" oval vegetable, blue............. **70.00**
**Bowl,** 9½" oval vegetable, pink............. **32.00**
**Bowl,** 9½" oval vegetable, yellow ....... **175.00**
**Bowl,** 10", cov. vegetable, blue.......... **130.00**
**Bowl,** 10", cov. vegetable, pink.......... **113.00**
**Bowl,** 10", open vegetable, blue .......... **72.00**
**Bowl,** 10", open vegetable, pink .......... **29.00**
**Bowl,** 10", open vegetable, pink
  frosted................................................. **12.00**
**Bowl,** 11¾" d., low, blue ...................... **80.00**
**Bowl,** 11¾" d., low, green..................... **36.00**
**Bowl,** 11¾" d., low, pink....................... **55.00**
**Bowl,** 11¾" d., low, yellow ................. **350.00**
**Bowl,** fruit, 12" d., deep, scalloped,
  blue ..................................................... **88.00**
**Bowl,** fruit, 12" d., deep, scalloped,
  green ..................................................... **34.00**
**Bowl,** fruit, 12" d., deep, scalloped,
  pink ...................................................... **55.00**
**Butter dish,** cov., blue ........................ **306.00**
**Butter dish,** cov., green ....................... **34.00**
**Butter dish,** cov., pink ......................... **68.00**
**Cake plate,** footed, blue, 10" .............. **67.00**
**Cake plate,** footed, pink, 10"............... **26.00**
**Cake plate,** handled, blue, 12" ............ **63.00**
**Cake plate,** handled, green, 12" .......... **30.00**
**Cake plate,** handled, pink, 12" ............ **39.00**
**Cake plate,** handled, pink frosted,
  12" ....................................................... **32.00**
**Candy jar,** cov., blue........................... **282.00**
**Candy jar,** cov., pink............................ **54.00**
**Candy jar,** cov., pink frosted ............... **38.00**
**Celery dish,** blue, 10" l. ....................... **50.00**
**Celery dish,** pink, 10" l. ....................... **39.00**
**Celery dish,** two-part, blue, 10" l. ........ **60.00**

**Celery dish,** two-part, pink, 10" l. ....... **168.00**
**Cookie jar,** cov., blue........................... **299.00**
**Cookie jar,** cov., green ...................... **541.00**
**Cookie jar,** cov., pink........................... **54.00**
**Cookie jar,** cov., pink frosted............... **29.00**
**Creamer,** footed, blue........................... **76.00**
**Creamer,** footed, green...................... **135.00**
**Creamer,** footed, pink .......................... **25.00**
**Creamer,** footed, pink frosted .............. **16.00**
**Cup,** blue............................................... **53.00**
**Cup,** pink............................................... **16.00**
**Cup & 5¾" underplate,** blue................ **66.00**
**Cup & 5¾" underplate,** pink................ **33.00**
**Cup & saucer w/cup ring,** pink............ **38.00**
**Decanter w/stopper,** pink, 10" h.,
    32 oz................................................... **170.00**
**Decanter,** no stopper, pink, 10" h.,
    32 oz..................................................... **86.00**
**Goblet,** pink, 4" h., 2½ oz. ................... **61.00**
**Goblet,** wine, pink, 4½" h., 3 oz............ **73.00**
**Goblet,** cocktail, pink, 4" h., 3½ oz. ..... **80.00**
**Goblet,** claret, pink, 5¼" h., 4½ oz........ **75.00**
**Goblet,** water, pink, 5¾" h., 9 oz........... **57.00**
**Goblet,** water, thin, blue, 7¼" h., 9 oz.... **200.00**
**Goblet,** water, thin, pink, 7¼" h., 9 oz. .. **121.00**
**Pitcher,** juice, 6" h., 37 oz., blue ......... **158.00**
**Pitcher,** juice, 6" h., 37 oz., clear.......... **15.00**
**Pitcher,** juice, 6" h., 37 oz., pink ........... **52.00**
**Pitcher,** juice, 6" h., 37 oz., yellow...... **950.00**
**Pitcher,** 8" h., 60 oz., jug-type, blue.... **204.00**

*Mayfair Pitcher*

**Pitcher,** 8" h., 60 oz., jug-type,
    pink (ILLUS.)........................................ **53.00**
**Pitcher,** 8½" h., 80 oz., jug-type,
    blue.................................................... **238.00**
**Pitcher,** 8½" h., 80 oz., jug-type,
    pink .................................................... **110.00**
**Plate** (or saucer), 5¾", blue ................. **24.00**
**Plate** (or saucer), 5¾", pink.................. **12.00**
**Plate,** sherbet, 6½" d., pink.................. **13.00**
**Plate,** sherbet, 6½ d., off-center
    indentation, blue ............................... **26.00**

**Plate,** sherbet, 6½ d., off-center
    indentation, pink ............................... **13.00**
**Plate,** luncheon, 8½", blue ................... **51.00**
**Plate,** luncheon, 8½", green................... **8.00**
**Plate,** luncheon, 8½", pink ................... **27.00**
**Plate,** luncheon, 8½", yellow............... **72.00**
**Plate,** dinner, 9½", blue........................ **78.00**
**Plate,** dinner, 9½", pink........................ **51.00**
**Plate,** dinner, 9½", yellow.................... **117.00**
**Plate,** grill, 9½", blue .......................... **59.00**
**Plate,** grill, 9½", pink .......................... **37.00**
**Platter,** 12" oval, open handles, blue...... **68.00**
**Platter,** 12" oval, open handles, clear..... **15.00**
**Platter,** 12" oval, open handles, green ... **25.00**
**Platter,** 12" oval, open handles, pink ...... **26.00**
**Platter,** 12" oval, open handles,
    yellow................................................. **241.00**
**Platter,** 12½" oval, closed handles,
    yellow................................................. **200.00**
**Relish,** four-part, blue, 8⅜" ................... **61.00**
**Relish,** four-part, pink, 8⅜" .................. **36.00**
**Salt & pepper shakers,** flat, blue, pr.. **313.00**
**Salt & pepper shakers,** flat, pink, pr. .... **63.00**
**Salt & pepper shakers,** flat, yellow,
    pr. .................................................... **1,175.00**
**Sandwich server w/center handle,**
    blue, 12"............................................... **80.00**
**Sandwich server w/center handle,**
    green, 12" ........................................... **33.00**
**Sandwich server w/center handle,**
    pink, 12"............................................... **45.00**
**Sandwich server w/center handle,**
    pink frosted, 12"................................... **23.00**
**Saucer w/cup ring,** blue........................ **22.00**
**Saucer w/cup ring,** pink........................ **39.00**
**Sherbet,** flat, blue, 2¼" h. ................... **133.00**
**Sherbet,** flat, pink, 2¼" h. ................... **153.00**
**Sherbet,** footed, pink, 3" h. ................... **15.00**
**Sherbet,** footed, blue, 4¾" h. ............... **88.00**
**Sherbet,** footed, pink, 4¾" h. ............... **75.00**
**Sugar bowl,** open, footed, blue ............ **81.00**
**Sugar bowl,** open, footed, pink ............ **28.00**
**Sugar bowl,** open, footed, pink frosted .. **16.00**
**Tumbler,** whiskey, pink, 2¼" h., 1½ oz. .. **73.00**
**Tumbler,** juice, footed, pink, 3¼" h.,
    3 oz..................................................... **80.00**
**Tumbler,** juice, blue, 3½" h., 5 oz. ...... **100.00**
**Tumbler,** juice, pink, 3½" h., 5 oz. ........ **39.00**
**Tumbler,** water, blue, 4¼" h., 9 oz....... **111.00**
**Tumbler,** water, pink, 4¼" h., 9 oz........ **28.00**
**Tumbler,** footed, blue, 5¼" h., 10 oz. .. **151.00**
**Tumbler,** footed, pink, 5¼" h., 10 oz..... **37.00**
**Tumbler,** water, blue, 4¾" h., 11 oz.... **139.00**
**Tumbler,** water, pink, 4¾" h., 11 oz.... **128.00**
**Tumbler,** iced tea, pink, 5¼" h.,
    13½ oz................................................. **45.00**
**Tumbler,** iced tea, footed, blue,
    6½" h., 15 oz...................................... **183.00**
**Tumbler,** iced tea, footed, pink,
    6½" h., 15 oz........................................ **39.00**

**Vase,** 5½ x 8½", sweetpea,
  hat-shaped, blue .............................. 113.00
**Vase,** 5½ x 8½", sweetpea,
  hat-shaped, pink ............................. 160.00
**Water set:** pitcher & six tumblers;
  pink, 7 pcs. ..................................... 150.00
**Wine set:** decanter, five wines, pink,
  6 pcs ............................................... 525.00

## MISS AMERICA, Hocking Glass Co., 1935-38 (Press-mold)

**Bowl,** berry, 4½" d., green .................... 10.00
**Bowl,** berry, 6¼" d., clear....................... 9.00
**Bowl,** berry, 6¼" d., green .................... 18.00
**Bowl,** berry, 6¼" d., pink ..................... 22.00
**Bowl,** fruit, 8" d., curved in at top,
  clear .................................................... 39.00
**Bowl,** fruit, 8" d., curved in at top,
  pink ..................................................... 78.00
**Bowl,** fruit, 8¾" d., deep, clear.............. 36.00
**Bowl,** fruit, 8¾" d., deep, pink ............... 62.00
**Bowl,** 10" oval vegetable, clear............. 14.00
**Bowl,** 10" oval vegetable, pink............. 29.00
**Butter dish,** cov., clear ....................... 198.00
**Butter dish,** cov., pink ........................ 442.00
**Cake plate,** footed, clear, 12" d. .......... 27.00
**Cake plate,** footed, pink, 12" d. ........... 44.00
**Candy jar,** cov., clear, 11½" h. ............. 58.00
**Candy jar,** cov., pink, 11½" h............... 137.00
**Celery tray,** clear, 10½" oblong............ 14.00
**Celery tray,** pink, 10½" oblong ............. 27.00
**Coaster,** clear, 5¾" d. ........................... 15.00
**Coaster,** pink, 5¾" d. ............................. 28.00
**Compote,** 5" d., clear .......................... 15.00
**Compote,** 5" d., pink............................. 26.00

*Miss America Creamer*

**Creamer,** footed, clear (ILLUS.).............. 8.00
**Creamer,** footed, pink ........................... 18.00
**Cup & saucer,** clear ............................. 12.00
**Cup & saucer,** pink.............................. 30.00

**Goblet,** wine, clear, 3¾" h., 3 oz. ......... 18.00
**Goblet,** wine, pink, 3¾" h., 3 oz. ........... 73.00
**Goblet,** juice, clear, 4¾" h., 5 oz.......... 20.00
**Goblet,** juice, pink, 4¾" h., 5 oz. ........... 79.00
**Goblet,** water, clear, 5½" h., 10 oz. ..... 19.00
**Goblet,** water, green, 5½" h., 10 oz. ..... 14.00
**Goblet,** water, pink, 5½" h., 10 oz........ 42.00
**Pitcher,** 8" h., 65 oz., clear .................. 54.00
**Pitcher,** 8" h., 65 oz., pink.................. 117.00
**Pitcher w/ice lip,** 8½" h., 65 oz., clear... 57.00
**Pitcher w/ice lip,** 8½" h., 65 oz.,
  pink.................................................... 126.00
**Plate,** sherbet, 5¾" d., clear.................. 5.00
**Plate,** sherbet, 5¾" d., pink.................. 9.00
**Plate,** 6¾" d., green ............................. 8.00
**Plate,** salad, 8½" d., clear ...................... 7.00
**Plate,** salad, 8½" d., pink ..................... 22.00
**Plate,** dinner, 10¼" d., clear................. 14.00
**Plate,** dinner, 10¼" d., pink................. 27.00
**Plate,** grill, 10¼" d., clear ...................... 9.00
**Plate,** grill, 10¼" d., pink ..................... 23.00
**Platter,** 12¼" oval, clear...................... 14.00
**Platter,** 12¼" oval, pink ...................... 28.00
**Relish,** four-part, clear, 8¾" d .............. 11.00
**Relish,** four-part, pink, 8¾" d................. 23.00
**Relish,** divided, clear, 11¾" d. .............. 19.00
**Relish,** divided, pink, 11¾" d. ............... 13.00
**Salt & pepper shakers,** clear, pr.......... 28.00
**Salt & pepper shakers,** green, pr. ..... 268.00
**Salt & pepper shakers,** pink, pr........... 59.00
**Sherbet,** clear ........................................ 7.00
**Sugar bowl,** open, footed, clear ............ 8.00
**Sugar bowl,** open, footed, pink ........... 18.00
**Tumbler,** juice, clear, 4" h., 5 oz. .......... 16.00
**Tumbler,** juice, ice blue, 4" h., 5 oz. ..... 15.00
**Tumbler,** juice, pink, 4" h., 5 oz. ........... 46.00
**Tumbler,** water, clear, 4½" h.,
  10 oz.................................................... 18.00
**Tumbler,** water, green, 4½" h.,
  10 oz.................................................... 14.00
**Tumbler,** water, pink, 4½" h., 10 oz...... 29.00
**Tumbler,** iced tea, clear, 6¾" h.,
  14 oz.................................................... 26.00
**Tumbler,** iced tea, pink, 6¾" h.,
  14 oz.................................................... 79.00
**Water set:** pitcher & six tumblers;
  pink, 7 pcs. ....................................... 195.00

## MODERNTONE, Hazel Atlas Glass Co., 1934-43, late 1940s & early 1950s (Press-mold)

**Ashtray w/match holder,** cobalt
  blue, 7¾" d........................................ 217.00
**Ashtray w/match holder,** pink,
  7¾" d. ................................................. 58.00
**Bowl,** cream soup, 4¾" d., amethyst .... 17.00
**Bowl,** cream soup, 4¾" d., cobalt
  blue..................................................... 21.00
**Bowl,** cream soup, 4¾" d., platonite ....... 6.00
**Bowl,** berry, 5" d., amethyst.................. 21.00

**Bowl,** berry, 5" d., cobalt blue .............. **23.00**
**Bowl,** berry, 5" d., platonite .................... **6.00**
**Bowl,** cream soup w/ruffled rim, 5" d.,
amethyst ......................................... **12.00**
**Bowl,** cream soup w/ruffled rim,
5" d., cobalt blue ............................... **59.00**
**Bowl,** cream soup w/ruffled rim,
5" d., platonite .................................. **7.00**
**Bowl,** cereal, 6½" d., cobalt blue .......... **85.00**
**Bowl,** cereal, 6½" d., platonite ............... **6.00**
**Bowl,** soup, 7½" d., amethyst ............... **10.00**
**Bowl,** soup, 7½" d., cobalt blue .......... **130.00**
**Bowl,** soup, 7½" d., platonite ............... **12.00**
**Bowl,** large berry, 8¾" d., amethyst ...... **44.00**
**Bowl,** large berry, 8¾" d., cobalt blue ... **57.00**
**Bowl,** large berry, 8¾" d., platonite ........ **9.00**
**Butter dish w/metal lid,** cobalt blue... **109.00**
**Cheese dish w/metal lid,** cobalt blue,
7" d. ............................................... **430.00**
**Creamer,** amethyst .............................. **11.00**
**Creamer,** platonite .............................. **6.00**
**Cup & saucer,** amethyst...................... **15.00**

*Moderntone Cup & Saucer*

**Cup & saucer,** cobalt blue (ILLUS.) ..... **15.00**
**Cup & saucer,** platonite......................... **7.00**
**Custard cup,** amethyst........................ **13.00**
**Custard cup,** cobalt blue ..................... **16.00**
**Plate,** sherbet, 5⅞" d., amethyst............ **6.00**
**Plate,** sherbet, 5⅞" d., cobalt blue ......... **7.00**
**Plate,** salad, 6¾" d., amethyst ............... **5.00**
**Plate,** salad, 6¾" d., cobalt blue ............ **9.00**
**Plate,** salad, 6¾" d., platonite ............... **4.00**
**Plate,** luncheon, 7¾" d., amethyst ......... **9.00**
**Plate,** luncheon, 7¾" d., cobalt blue...... **11.00**
**Plate,** luncheon, 7¾" d., platonite .......... **5.00**
**Plate,** dinner, 8⅞" d., amethyst............. **11.00**
**Plate,** dinner, 8⅞" d., cobalt blue .......... **18.00**

**Plate,** dinner, 8⅞" d., platonite............. **19.00**
**Plate,** sandwich, 10½" d., amethyst...... **48.00**
**Plate,** sandwich, 10½" d., cobalt
blue................................................ **54.00**
**Plate,** sandwich, 10½" d., platonite....... **19.00**
**Platter,** 11" oval, amethyst................... **18.00**
**Platter,** 11" oval, cobalt blue................ **43.00**
**Platter,** 11" oval, platonite..................... **8.00**
**Platter,** 12" oval, amethyst................... **41.00**
**Platter,** 12" oval, cobalt blue.............. **105.00**
**Platter,** 12" oval, platonite................... **14.00**
**Salt & pepper shakers,** cobalt blue,
pr. .................................................. **44.00**
**Salt & pepper shakers,** platonite, pr.... **13.00**
**Sherbet,** amethyst .............................. **12.00**
**Sherbet,** cobalt blue............................ **13.00**
**Sherbet,** platonite ................................ **4.00**
**Sugar bowl,** open, amethyst ............... **11.00**
**Sugar bowl,** open, cobalt blue............... **9.00**
**Sugar bowl,** open, platonite .................. **5.00**
**Sugar bowl w/metal lid,** cobalt blue .... **45.00**
**Tumbler,** whiskey, clear, 1½ oz............. **7.00**
**Tumbler,** whiskey, cobalt blue, 1½ oz. . **42.00**
**Tumbler,** whiskey, platonite, 1½ oz. ..... **12.00**
**Tumblers,** whiskey, cobalt blue, 1½ oz.
w/handled chrome rack, set of 6........ **200.00**
**Tumbler,** juice, cobalt blue, 5 oz........... **43.00**
**Tumbler,** juice, platonite, 5 oz. ............. **11.00**
**Tumbler,** water, cobalt blue, 4" h., 9 oz. .. **34.00**
**Tumbler,** water, platonite, 4" h., 9 oz...... **8.00**
**Tumbler,** iced tea, amethyst, 12 oz. ..... **67.00**

LITTLE HOSTESS PARTY SET

**Creamer,** 1¾" h., dark........................... **13.00**
**Creamer,** 1¾" h., pastel ...................... **17.00**
**Cup,** 1¾" h., dark .............................. **11.00**
**Cup,** 1¾" h., pastel............................. **11.00**
**Cup & saucer,** dark ............................ **17.00**
**Cup & saucer,** pastel ............................ **9.00**
**Plate,** 5¼" d., dark.............................. **11.00**
**Plate,** 5¼" d., pastel ........................... **10.00**
**Sugar bowl,** 1¾" h., dark...................... **13.00**
**Sugar bowl,** 1¾" h., pastel .................. **15.00**
**Teapot,** cov., 3½" h., dark..................... **99.00**
**Teapot,** cov., 3½" h., pastel ................. **60.00**
**Tea set,** pastel, 12 pcs...................... **110.00**
**Tea set,** dark, 14 pcs. ...................... **133.00**
**Tea set,** pastel, 14 pcs. ...................... **87.00**
**Tea set,** dark, 16 pcs. ...................... **224.00**
**Tea set,** pastel, 16 pcs........................ **245.00**

**NUMBER 612 or Horseshoe, Indiana
Glass Co., 1930-33 (Process-etched)**

**Bowl,** berry, 4½" d., green ................... **21.00**
**Bowl,** cereal, 6½" d., yellow................. **22.00**
**Bowl,** salad, 7½" d., green................... **19.00**
**Bowl,** salad, 7½" d., yellow.................. **23.00**
**Bowl,** large berry, 9½" d., green .......... **37.00**

*No. 612 Butter Dish*

**Bowl,** large berry, 9½" d., yellow .......... **33.00**
**Bowl,** 10½" oval vegetable, green ........ **19.00**
**Bowl,** 10½" oval vegetable, yellow ....... **26.00**
**Butter dish,** cov., green (ILLUS.) ....... **550.00**
**Candy in metal holder,** motif on lid,
   green ................................................. **165.00**
**Candy in metal holder,** motif on lid,
   pink .................................................... **175.00**
**Creamer,** footed, green ......................... **15.00**
**Creamer,** footed, yellow ......................... **14.00**
**Cup & saucer,** yellow .......................... **14.00**
**Pitcher,** 8½" h., 64 oz., green ............. **288.00**
**Pitcher,** 8½" h., 64 oz., yellow ............ **346.00**
**Plate,** sherbet, 6" d., green ................... **6.00**
**Plate,** sherbet, 6" d., yellow................... **7.00**
**Plate,** salad, 8⅜" d., green..................... **9.00**
**Plate,** salad, 9⅜" d., green................... **13.00**
**Plate,** salad, 9⅜" d., yellow................... **12.00**
**Plate,** dinner, 10⅜" d., green ............... **18.00**
**Plate,** grill, 10⅜" d., green.................... **76.00**
**Plate,** sandwich, 11" d., green .............. **17.00**
**Platter,** 10¾" oval, green ..................... **21.00**
**Platter,** 10¾" oval, yellow ..................... **22.00**
**Relish,** three-part, footed, green.......... **22.00**
**Relish,** three-part, footed, yellow .......... **30.00**
**Sherbet,** green...................................... **14.00**
**Sherbet,** yellow ..................................... **15.00**
**Sugar bowl,** open, footed, green.......... **13.00**
**Sugar bowl,** open, footed, yellow ......... **15.00**
**Tumbler,** green, 4¼" h., 9 oz. .............. **45.00**
**Tumbler,** footed, green, 9 oz. .............. **22.00**
**Tumbler,** footed, yellow, 9 oz. .............. **21.00**
**Tumbler,** footed, green, 12 oz. ............. **79.00**
**Tumbler,** footed, yellow, 12 oz. .......... **103.00**

## OLD CAFE, Hocking Glass Co., 1936-40 (Press-mold)

**Bowl,** berry, 3¾" d., clear...................... **4.00**
**Bowl,** berry, 3¾" d., pink........................ **6.00**
**Bowl,** nappy, 5" d., handled, clear ......... **4.00**
**Bowl,** nappy, 5" d., handled, pink .......... **8.00**
**Bowl,** cereal, 5½" d., pink .................... **11.00**
**Bowl,** cereal, 5½" d., ruby.................... **15.00**

**Bowl,** 9" d., handled, pink ...................... **8.00**
**Bowl,** 9" d., handled, ruby..................... **13.00**
**Candy dish,** clear, 8" d.......................... **8.00**
**Candy dish,** pink, 8" d. ......................... **10.00**
**Candy dish,** ruby, 8" d.......................... **13.00**
**Cup & saucer,** pink............................... **13.00**
**Cup & saucer,** ruby cup, clear
   saucer................................................. **10.00**
**Lamp,** pink ............................................ **13.00**
**Olive dish,** clear, 6" oblong .................. **6.00**
**Pitcher,** 6" h., 36 oz., clear .................. **25.00**
**Pitcher,** 6" h., 36 oz., pink.................... **74.00**
**Pitcher,** 8" h., 80 oz., pink.................. **104.00**
**Plate,** sherbet, 6" d., pink .................... **12.00**
**Plate,** dinner, 10" d., clear.................... **20.00**
**Plate,** dinner, 10" d., pink .................... **30.00**
**Sherbet,** low foot, clear.......................... **4.00**
**Sherbet,** low foot, pink ......................... **10.00**
**Tumbler,** juice, clear, 3" h...................... **6.00**
**Tumbler,** juice, pink, 3" h. ..................... **14.00**
**Tumbler,** juice, ruby, 3" h. ...................... **7.00**
**Tumbler,** water, pink, 4" h..................... **14.00**
**Tumbler,** water, ruby, 4" h. ................... **14.00**
**Vase,** 7¼" h., clear................................. **9.00**

## OYSTER & PEARL, Anchor Hocking Glass Corp., 1938-40 (Press-mold)

**Bowl,** 5¼" heart-shaped, w/handle,
   clear..................................................... **9.00**
**Bowl,** 5¼" heart-shaped, w/handle,
   pink...................................................... **9.00**
**Bowl,** 5¼" heart-shaped, w/handle,
   white w/green ....................................... **8.00**
**Bowl,** 5¼" heart-shaped, w/handle,
   white w/pink.......................................... **9.00**
**Bowl,** 5½" d., w/handle, clear ................ **9.00**
**Bowl,** 5½" d., w/handle, ruby ............... **13.00**
**Bowl,** 6½" d., handled, pink ................. **12.00**
**Bowl,** 6½" d., handled, ruby................. **19.00**
**Bowl,** fruit, 10½" d., clear.................... **18.00**
**Bowl,** fruit, 10½" d., pink...................... **29.00**
**Bowl,** fruit, 10½" d., ruby...................... **45.00**
**Bowl,** fruit, 10½" d., white w/green ....... **13.00**
**Candleholder,** pink, 3½" h.................... **11.00**
**Candleholders,** clear, 3½" h., pr. ......... **18.00**
**Candleholders,** pink, 3½" h., pr. .......... **17.00**
**Candleholders,** ruby, 3½" h., pr........... **41.00**
**Candleholders,** white w/green,
   3½" h., pr. ........................................... **13.00**
**Candleholders,** white w/pink,
   3½" h., pr. ........................................... **14.00**
**Plate,** sandwich, 13½" d., clear............ **13.00**
**Plate,** sandwich, 13½" d., pink............. **29.00**
**Plate,** sandwich, 13½" d., ruby............. **36.00**
**Relish,** divided, clear, 10¼" oval............. **8.00**
**Relish,** divided, pink, 10¼" oval............ **13.00**

*Green Parrot Butter Dish*

## PARROT or Sylvan, Federal Glass Co., 1931-32 (Process-etched)

Bowl, berry, 5" sq., amber .................... 19.00
Bowl, berry, 5" sq., green ..................... 21.00
Bowl, soup, 7" sq., amber .................... 31.00
Bowl, soup, 7" sq., green..................... 41.00
Bowl, large berry, 8" sq., green ........... 58.00
Bowl, 10" oval vegetable, amber ......... 45.00
Bowl, 10" oval vegetable, green ........... 55.00
Butter dish, cov., green (ILLUS.
   above)............................................... 336.00
Creamer, footed, green......................... 49.00
Cup & saucer, amber ........................... 38.00
Cup & saucer, green ............................. 61.00
Hot plate, green, scalloped edge........ 875.00
Jam dish, amber, 7" sq........................ 31.00
Plate, sherbet, 5¾" sq., amber............. 19.00
Plate, salad, 7½" sq., green ................. 36.00
Plate, dinner, 9" sq., amber.................. 37.00
Plate, dinner, 9" sq., green................... 52.00
Plate, grill, 10½" sq., amber ................. 29.00
Plate, grill, 10½" sq., green .................. 31.00
Platter, 11¼" oblong, amber................. 45.00
Platter, 11¼" oblong, green .................. 46.00
Salt & pepper shakers, green, pr. ..... 242.00
Sherbet, footed, cone-shaped,
   amber ................................................. 19.00
Sugar bowl, cov., green ..................... 171.00
Sugar bowl, open, amber...................... 19.00
Sugar bowl, open, green....................... 34.00
Tumbler, green, 4¼" h., 10 oz. ............. 98.00
Tumbler, footed, amber, 5½" h.,
   10 oz...................................................139.00
Tumbler, footed, cone-shaped,
   amber, 5¾" h. .................................... 112.00
Tumbler, footed, cone-shaped,
   green, 5¾" h. ..................................... 124.00

## PRINCESS, Hocking Glass Co., 1931-35 (Process-etched)

*Pink Princess Candy Jar*

Ashtray, green, 4½"............................... 68.00
Ashtray, pink, 4½" ................................ 22.00
Bowl, berry, 4½", green ........................ 22.00
Bowl, berry, 4½", pink........................... 24.00
Bowl, cereal, 5", green........................... 29.00
Bowl, cereal, 5", pink ............................ 28.00
Bowl, cereal, 5", yellow......................... 31.00
Bowl, salad, 9" octagon, green ............. 41.00
Bowl, salad, 9" octagon, pink................ 38.00
Bowl, salad, 9" octagon, yellow .......... 109.00
Bowl, 9½" hat shape, green.................. 39.00
Bowl, 9½" hat shape, pink .................... 36.00
Bowl, 10" oval vegetable, green ........... 26.00

Bowl, 10" oval vegetable, pink............. 29.00
Bowl, 10" oval vegetable, yellow ......... 55.00
Butter dish, cov., green........................ 89.00
Butter dish, cov., pink ......................... 96.00
Cake stand, green, 10"......................... 22.00
Cake stand, pink, 10" .......................... 28.00
Candy jar, cov., green ......................... 58.00
Candy jar, cov., pink (ILLUS. bottom
   previous page)..................................... 62.00
Coaster, green, 4"................................ 32.00
Coaster, pink, 4" ................................. 20.00
Coaster, yellow, 4" .............................. 78.00
Cookie jar, cov., green ......................... 56.00
Cookie jar, cov., pink ........................... 59.00
Creamer, oval, amber........................... 13.00
Creamer, oval, green ............................ 15.00
Creamer, oval, yellow ........................... 15.00
Cup & saucer, amber .............................. 9.00
Cup & saucer, green ............................. 14.00
Cup & saucer, pink............................... 19.00
Cup & saucer, yellow ........................... 11.00
Dinner service: six each 9½" dinner
   plates, 10 oz. footed tumblers, cups
   & saucers plus creamer & cov.
   sugar bowl; amber, 26 pcs. ............. 220.00
Pitcher, 6" h., 37 oz., jug-type, green ... 49.00
Pitcher, 6" h., 37 oz., jug-type, pink...... 56.00
Pitcher, 8" h., 60 oz., jug-type, green ... 54.00
Pitcher, 8" h., 60 oz., jug-type, pink...... 53.00
Pitcher, 8" h., 60 oz., jug-type,
   yellow................................................. 90.00
Plate, sherbet, 5½", green ..................... 9.00
Plate, sherbet, 5½", pink ...................... 10.00
Plate, sherbet, 5½", yellow..................... 4.00
Plate, salad, 8", green........................... 13.00
Plate, salad, 8", pink ............................ 13.00
Plate, salad, 8", yellow............................ 9.00
Plate, dinner, 9", amber ........................ 12.00
Plate, dinner, 9", green ......................... 23.00
Plate, dinner, 9", pink ........................... 22.00
Plate, dinner, 9", yellow........................ 15.00
Plate, grill, 9", amber ............................. 7.00
Plate, grill, 9", green............................. 11.00
Plate, grill, 9", pink .............................. 13.00
Plate, grill, 9", yellow.............................. 7.00
Plate, grill, 10½", closed handles,
   green ................................................. 11.00
Plate, grill, 10½", closed handles,
   pink.................................................... 13.00
Plate, grill, 10½", closed handles,
   yellow ................................................... 6.00
Plate, sandwich, 11¼", handled,
   green ................................................. 16.00
Plate, sandwich, 11¼", handled,
   pink.................................................... 24.00
Platter, 12" oval, closed handles,
   green ................................................. 25.00
Platter, 12" oval, closed handles,
   pink.................................................... 25.00

Platter, 12" oval, closed handles,
   yellow................................................. 52.00
Relish, green, 7½" ............................... 103.00
Relish, pink, 7½"................................. 300.00
Relish, yellow, 7½" ............................... 75.00
Relish, divided, green, 7½".................... 27.00
Relish, divided, pink, 7½" ..................... 24.00
Salt & pepper shakers, green, 4½" h.,
   pr....................................................... 54.00
Salt & pepper shakers, pink, 4½" h.,
   pr. ..................................................... 49.00
Salt & pepper shakers, yellow,
   4½" h., pr. .......................................... 69.00
Salt & pepper (or spice) shakers,
   green, 5½" h., pr. ................................ 41.00
Saucer, green ........................................ 9.00
Sherbet, footed, green .......................... 19.00
Sherbet, footed, pink ............................ 21.00
Sherbet, footed, yellow ......................... 24.00
Sugar bowl, cov., amber ....................... 23.00
Sugar bowl, cov., green ........................ 29.00
Sugar bowl, cov., pink........................... 44.00
Sugar bowl, cov., yellow ....................... 27.00
Sugar bowl, open, amber ........................ 9.00
Sugar bowl, open, pink frosted ............... 6.00
Sugar bowl, open, yellow ........................ 9.00
Tumbler, juice, green, 3" h., 5 oz.......... 28.00
Tumbler, juice, pink, 3" h., 5 oz. .......... 27.00
Tumbler, juice, yellow, 3" h., 5 oz........ 23.00
Tumbler, water, green, 4" h., 9 oz. ....... 28.00
Tumbler, water, pink, 4" h., 9 oz.......... 26.00
Tumbler, footed, green, 5¼" h.,
   10 oz.................................................. 31.00
Tumbler, footed, pink, 5¼" h.,
   10 oz.................................................. 28.00
Tumbler, footed, green, 6½" h.,
   12½ oz................................................ 84.00
Tumbler, footed, pink, 6½" h.,
   12½ oz................................................ 85.00
Tumbler, footed, yellow, 6½" h.,
   12½ oz................................................ 21.00
Tumbler, iced tea, green, 5¼" h.,
   13 oz.................................................. 43.00
Tumbler, iced tea, pink, 5¼" h.,
   13 oz.................................................. 34.00
Tumbler, iced tea, yellow, 5¼" h.,
   13 oz.................................................. 25.00
Vase, 8" h., green ................................ 32.00
Vase, 8" h., pink .................................. 36.00
Vase, 8" h., pink frosted ...................... 20.00
Water set: pitcher & four tumblers;
   green, 5 pcs. ..................................... 113.00

## QUEEN MARY or Vertical Ribbed Hocking Glass Co., 1936-49 (Press-mold)

Ashtray, clear, 2 x 3¾" oval................... 3.00
Ashtray, clear, 3½" d............................. 6.00

*Queen Mary Cup & Saucer*

Ashtray, ruby, 3½" d. .............................. 8.00
Bowl, nappy, 4" d., clear ........................ 3.00
Bowl, nappy, 4" d., pink ......................... 5.00
Bowl, nappy, 4" d., single handle,
  clear ...................................................... 5.00
Bowl, nappy, 4" d., single handle, pink ... 7.00
Bowl, berry, 5" d., clear ........................... 6.00
Bowl, berry, 5" d., pink ............................ 5.00
Bowl, 5½" d., two-handled, clear ........... 4.00
Bowl, 5½" d., two-handled, pink .......... 16.00
Bowl, cereal, 6" d., clear ........................ 7.00
Bowl, cereal, 6" d., pink ....................... 22.00
Bowl, nappy, 7" d., clear ........................ 8.00
Bowl, nappy, 7" d., pink ........................ 17.00
Bowl, large berry, 8¾" d., clear .............. 9.00
Bowl, large berry, 8¾" d., pink ............. 12.00
Butter (or jam) dish, cov., clear .......... 31.00
Butter (or jam) dish, cov., pink .......... 119.00
Candlesticks, two-light, clear,
  4½" h., pr. .......................................... 16.00
Candy dish, cov., clear .......................... 23.00
Candy dish, cov., pink ........................... 33.00
Celery (or pickle) dish, clear,
  5 x 10" oval .......................................... 8.00
Celery (or pickle) dish, pink,
  5 x 10" oval ........................................ 17.00
Cigarette jar, clear, 2 x 3" oval .............. 7.00
Coaster, clear, 3½" d. ............................. 3.00
Coaster, pink, 3½" d. .............................. 4.00
Coaster-ashtray, clear, 4¼" sq. ............. 4.00
Coaster-ashtray, pink, 4¼" sq. .............. 9.00
Compote, 5¾" d., clear ........................... 7.00
Creamer, oval, clear ............................... 5.00
Creamer, oval, pink ............................... 10.00
Cup & saucer, clear (ILLUS. above) ...... 8.00
Cup & saucer, pink ................................ 10.00
Plate, sherbet, 6" d., clear ...................... 3.00
Plate, sherbet, 6" d., pink ....................... 6.00
Plate, 6⅝" d., clear ................................. 4.00
Plate, 6⅝" d., pink ................................ 10.00

Plate, salad, 8½" d., clear ...................... 5.00
Plate, dinner, 9¾" d., clear .................... 15.00
Plate, dinner, 9¾" d., pink .................... 49.00
Plate, sandwich, 12" d., clear ................ 9.00
Plate, sandwich, 12" d., pink ................ 20.00
Plate, serving, 14" d., clear .................. 11.00
Relish, three-part, clear, 12" d. ............. 11.00
Relish, three-part, pink, 12" d. ............... 7.00
Relish, four-part, clear, 14" d. ............... 10.00
Salt & pepper shakers, clear, pr. ......... 22.00
Sherbet, footed, clear ............................. 5.00
Sherbet, footed, pink .............................. 8.00
Sugar bowl, open, oval, clear ................ 5.00
Sugar bowl, open, oval, pink ................ 11.00
Table set: individual size creamer &
  sugar bowl, pair of salt & pepper
  shakers & tray; clear, boxed set of
  5 pcs. ................................................. 30.00
Tumbler, juice, pink, 3½" h., 5 oz. ........ 11.00
Tumbler, water, clear, 4" h., 9 oz. .......... 7.00
Tumbler, water, pink, 4" h., 9 oz. .......... 11.00
Tumbler, footed, clear, 5" h., 10 oz. ..... 25.00
Tumbler, footed, pink, 5" h., 10 oz. ........ 59.00

### ROULETTE or Many Windows, Hocking Glass Co., 193-39 (Press-mold)

Bowl, fruit, 9" d., green ........................ 18.00
Cup & saucer, green .............................. 9.00
Pitcher, 8" h., 64 oz., green .................. 30.00
Pitcher, 8" h., 64 oz., pink ................... 27.00
Plate, sherbet, 6" d., green .................... 4.00
Plate, luncheon, 8½" d., clear ............... 4.00
Plate, luncheon, 8½" d., green .............. 6.00
Plate, sandwich, 12" d., green ............. 14.00
Sherbet, green ........................................ 6.00
Sherbet, pink .......................................... 3.00
Tumbler, whiskey, green, 2½" h.,
  1½ oz. ................................................ 10.00
Tumbler, whiskey, pink, 2½" h., 1½ oz. .. 14.00
Tumbler, juice, clear, 3¼" h., 5 oz. ......... 3.00
Tumbler, juice, green, 3¼" h., 5 oz. ...... 18.00
Tumbler, juice, pink, 3¼" h., 5 oz. .......... 9.00
Tumbler, Old Fashioned, pink,
  3¼" h., 7½ oz. .................................... 19.00
Tumbler, water, green, 4⅛" h., 9 oz. .... 25.00
Tumbler, water, pink, 4⅛" h., 9 oz. ....... 19.00
Tumbler, footed, clear, 5½" h., 10 oz. .. 18.00
Tumbler, footed, green, 5½" h., 10 oz. .. 23.00
Tumbler, iced tea, clear, 5⅛" h., 12 oz.. 16.00
Tumbler, iced tea, green, 5⅛" h., 12 oz... 23.00
Tumbler, iced tea, pink, 5⅛" h., 12 oz... 19.00

### ROYAL LACE, Hazel Atlas Glass Co., 1934-41 (Process-etched)

Bowl, cream soup, 4¾" d., blue ........... 39.00
Bowl, cream soup, 4¾" d., clear ........... 13.00
Bowl, cream soup, 4¾" d., green.......... 26.00
Bowl, cream soup, 4¾" d., pink ........... 27.00

**Bowl,** berry, 5" d., blue ......................... 35.00
**Bowl,** berry, 5" d., clear......................... 13.00
**Bowl,** berry, 5" d., pink.......................... 28.00
**Bowl,** berry, 10" d., blue......................... 75.00
**Bowl,** berry, 10" d., clear...................... 73.00
**Bowl,** berry, 10" d., pink........................ 34.00
**Bowl,** 10" d., three-footed, rolled
  edge, blue........................................ 500.00
**Bowl,** 10" d., three-footed, rolled
  edge, clear......................................... 29.00
**Bowl,** 10" d., three-footed, rolled
  edge, pink........................................... 50.00
**Bowl,** 10" d., three-footed, ruffled
  edge, clear......................................... 38.00
**Bowl,** 10" d., three-footed, ruffled
  edge, green ........................................ 65.00
**Bowl,** 10" d., three-footed, ruffled
  edge, pink........................................... 71.00
**Bowl,** 10" d., three-footed, straight
  edge, blue........................................... 71.00
**Bowl,** 10" d., three-footed, straight
  edge, pink........................................... 39.00
**Bowl,** 11" oval vegetable, blue.............. 61.00
**Bowl,** 11" oval vegetable, clear............ 18.00
**Bowl,** 11" oval vegetable, green .......... 33.00
**Bowl,** 11" oval vegetable, pink.............. 34.00
**Butter dish,** cov., blue ........................ 565.00
**Butter dish,** cov., clear ......................... 63.00
**Butter dish,** cov., green........................ 26.00
**Butter dish,** cov., pink ........................ 161.00
**Candlesticks,** rolled edge, blue, pr...... 231.00
**Candlesticks,** rolled edge, clear, pr....... 49.00
**Candlesticks,** ruffled edge, blue, pr..... 149.00
**Candlesticks,** ruffled edge, clear, pr. .... 28.00
**Candlesticks,** ruffled edge, pink, pr. ..... 46.00
**Candlesticks,** straight edge, blue, pr. .... 90.00
**Candlesticks,** straight edge, clear, pr. ... 32.00
**Cookie jar,** cov., amethyst.................... 100.00
**Cookie jar,** cov., blue (ILLUS. top next
  column) .............................................. 420.00
**Cookie jar,** cov., clear............................. 40.00
**Cookie jar,** cov., green .......................... 92.00
**Cookie jar,** cov., pink ............................. 61.00
**Creamer,** footed, blue ........................... 56.00
**Creamer,** footed, clear ........................... 11.00
**Creamer,** footed, green ......................... 27.00
**Creamer,** footed, pink ........................... 21.00
**Cup & saucer,** blue................................ 46.00
**Cup & saucer,** clear................................ 13.00
**Cup & saucer,** green .............................. 26.00
**Cup & saucer,** pink................................. 25.00
**Pitcher,** 48 oz., straight sides, blue .... 180.00
**Pitcher,** 48 oz., straight sides, clear ..... 39.00
**Pitcher,** 8" h., 64 oz., without ice lip,
  blue...................................................... 195.00
**Pitcher,** 8" h., 64 oz., without ice lip,
  pink ..................................................... 103.00
**Pitcher,** 8" h., 68 oz., w/ice lip,
  clear...................................................... 40.00
**Pitcher,** 8" h., 68 oz., w/ice lip, pink...... 98.00

*Royal Lace Cookie Jar*

**Pitcher,** 8" h., 86 oz., without ice lip,
  pink ...................................................... 78.00
**Pitcher,** 8½" h., 96 oz., w/ice lip,
  clear...................................................... 60.00
**Pitcher,** 8½" h., 96 oz., w/ice lip,
  green .................................................. 150.00
**Plate,** sherbet, 6" d., blue..................... 13.00
**Plate,** sherbet, 6" d., green .................. 10.00
**Plate,** sherbet, 6" d., pink...................... 9.00
**Plate,** luncheon, 8½" d., blue ............... 37.00
**Plate,** luncheon, 8½" d., green ............. 17.00
**Plate,** luncheon, 8½" d., pink ............... 19.00
**Plate,** dinner, 9⅞" d., blue.................... 45.00
**Plate,** dinner, 9⅞" d., clear................... 18.00
**Plate,** dinner, 9⅞" d., green ................. 29.00
**Plate,** dinner, 9⅞" d., pink.................... 29.00
**Plate,** grill, 9⅞" d., blue ........................ 27.00
**Plate,** grill, 9⅞" d., clear ........................ 9.00
**Plate,** grill, 9⅞" d., green...................... 26.00
**Plate,** grill, 9⅞" d., pink ........................ 19.00
**Platter,** 13" oval, blue............................ 51.00
**Platter,** 13" oval, clear............................ 15.00
**Platter,** 13" oval, green ......................... 38.00
**Platter,** 13" oval, pink............................ 35.00
**Salt & pepper shakers,** blue, pr.......... 302.00
**Salt & pepper shakers,** clear, pr.......... 42.00
**Salt & pepper shakers,** green, pr. ..... 120.00
**Salt & pepper shakers,** pink, pr........... 74.00
**Sherbet,** footed, blue ............................ 47.00
**Sherbet,** footed, clear ........................... 11.00
**Sherbet,** footed, green.......................... 26.00
**Sherbet,** footed, pink ............................ 17.00
**Sherbet in metal holder,** amethyst....... 34.00
**Sherbet in metal holder,** blue.............. 27.00
**Sherbet in metal holder,** clear............... 9.00
**Sherbet in metal holder,** green ............. 6.00
**Sugar bowl,** cov., blue.......................... 215.00
**Sugar bowl,** cov., clear.......................... 23.00
**Sugar bowl,** cov., green ........................ 63.00
**Sugar bowl,** cov., pink........................... 58.00

**Sugar bowl,** open, blue ........................ 34.00
**Sugar bowl,** open, clear ......................... 9.00
**Sugar bowl,** open, green...................... 20.00
**Toddy or cider set:** cookie jar
   w/metal lid & six roly-poly tumblers;
   blue, 7 pcs. ..................................... 125.00
**Toddy or cider set:** cookie jar
   w/metal lid, seven roly-poly tumblers
   & metal tray; amethyst, 9 pcs. .......... **125.00**
**Tumbler,** blue, 3½" h., 5 oz. ................. 49.00
**Tumbler,** clear, 3½" h., 5 oz. ............... 13.00
**Tumbler,** green, 3½" h., 5 oz. .............. 28.00
**Tumbler,** blue, 4⅛" h., 9 oz. ................. 41.00
**Tumbler,** clear, 4⅛" h., 9 oz. ............... 12.00
**Tumbler,** green, 4⅛" h., 9 oz. .............. 30.00
**Tumbler,** pink, 4⅛" h., 9 oz. ................. 19.00
**Tumbler,** blue, 4⅞" h., 10 oz. ............. 119.00
**Tumbler,** pink, 4⅞" h., 10 oz. .............. 35.00
**Tumbler,** blue, 5⅜" h., 12 oz. .............. 84.00
**Tumbler,** clear, 5⅜" h., 12 oz. ............. 21.00
**Tumbler,** green, 5⅜" h., 12 oz. ............ 42.00
**Tumbler,** pink, 5⅜" h., 12 oz. .............. 38.00
**Water set:** 68 oz. pitcher & six 9 oz.
   tumblers; blue, 7 pcs. ...................... 360.00

## ROYAL RUBY, Anchor Hocking Glass Co., 1939-60s (Press-mold)

**Ashtray,** 4½" sq. ..................................... 5.00
**Bowl,** berry, 4¼" d. ................................. 7.00
**Bowl,** 4¾" sq. ........................................ 5.00
**Bowl,** 5¼" d. .......................................... 11.00
**Bowl,** 6½" d., scalloped .......................... 8.00
**Bowl,** 7⅜" sq. ....................................... 13.00
**Bowl,** soup, 7½" d. ............................... 12.00
**Bowl,** 8" oval vegetable ........................ 35.00
**Bowl,** berry, 8½" d. ............................... 21.00
**Bowl,** popcorn, 10" d., deep................. 43.00
**Bowl,** salad, 11½" d............................... 32.00
**Creamer,** flat .......................................... 8.00
**Creamer,** footed...................................... 8.00
**Cup & saucer,** round ............................... 7.00
**Cup & saucer,** square ............................. 7.00
**Goblet,** ball stem.................................... 10.00
**Juice set,** 22 oz. tilted pitcher & six
   5 oz. tumblers, 7 pcs. ......................... 67.00
**Pitcher,** 22 oz., tilted or upright............. 34.00
**Pitcher,** 3 qt., tilted or upright ............... 42.00
**Plate,** sherbet, 6½" d ............................. 5.00
**Plate,** salad, 7" d. ................................... 6.00
**Plate,** luncheon, 7¾" d. ........................... 6.00
**Plate,** 8⅜" sq. ........................................ 7.00
**Plate,** dinner, 9" d................................. 12.00
**Plate,** 13¾" d ....................................... 23.00
**Playing card or cigarette box,**
   divided, clear base............................. 59.00
**Popcorn set,** 10" d. serving bowl &
   six 5¼" d. bowls, 7 pcs. ................... 125.00
**Popcorn set,** 10" d. serving bowl &
   eight 5¼" d. bowls, 9 pcs. ................ 125.00

**Punch set,** punch bowl, base &
   twelve cups, 14 pcs. ......................... **114.00**
**Sherbet,** footed ....................................... 8.00
**Sugar bowl,** flat ...................................... 7.00
**Sugar bowl,** footed .................................. 6.00
**Sugar bowl w/slotted lid,** footed ......... 17.00
**Tumbler,** cocktail, 3½ oz. ....................... 9.00
**Tumbler,** juice, 5 oz. ............................... 6.00
**Tumbler,** water, 9 oz................................ 5.00
**Tumbler,** water, 10 oz. ............................ 8.00
**Tumbler,** iced tea, footed, 6" h., 12 oz. .. 12.00
**Tumbler,** iced tea, 13 oz. ........................ 9.00
**Vase,** 4" h., ball-shaped ......................... 4.00
**Vase,** 5" h., ball-shaped ....................... 10.00
**Vase,** bud, 5½" h., ruffled top................. 7.00
**Vase,** 6½" h., bulbous ............................ 6.00
**Vase,** various styles, large ................... 14.00
**Wine,** footed, 2½ oz. ............................. 11.00

## SANDWICH, Anchor Hocking Glass Co., 1939-64 (Press-mold)

**Berry set:** master bowl & eight sauce
   dishes; clear, 9 pcs. ......................... 30.00
**Bowl,** 4⁵⁄₁₆" d., clear .............................. 5.00
**Bowl,** 4⁵⁄₁₆" d., green ............................. 3.00
**Bowl,** berry, 4⅞" d., amber ..................... 5.00
**Bowl,** berry, 4⅞" d., clear ..................... 13.00
**Bowl,** berry, 4⅞" d., pink ........................ 7.00
**Bowl,** 5¼" d., scalloped, amber ............. 6.00
**Bowl,** 5¼" d., scalloped, clear................ 7.00
**Bowl,** 5¼" d., ruby ................................ 18.00
**Bowl,** cereal, 6½" d., amber.................. 14.00
**Bowl,** cereal, 6½" d., clear ................... 31.00
**Bowl,** 6½" d., smooth or scalloped,
   amber ................................................. 6.00
**Bowl,** 6½" d., smooth or scalloped,
   clear .................................................... 7.00
**Bowl,** 6½" d., smooth or scalloped,
   green ................................................. 41.00
**Bowl,** salad, 7" d., clear .......................... 9.00
**Bowl,** salad, 7" d., green ....................... 52.00
**Bowl,** 8" d., scalloped, clear.................. 11.00
**Bowl,** 8" d., scalloped, pink .................. 19.00
**Bowl,** 8" d., scalloped, ruby ................. 45.00
**Bowl,** 8½" oval vegetable, clear............. 6.00
**Bowl,** salad, 9" d., amber..................... 22.00
**Bowl,** salad, 9" d., clear ....................... 19.00
**Butter dish,** cov., clear ......................... 43.00
**Cake plate,** 13" d., clear ....................... 33.00
**Cookie jar,** cov., amber ........................ 34.00
**Cookie jar,** cov., clear........................... 33.00
**Cookie jar,** green (no cover made)....... 17.00
**Creamer,** green..................................... 26.00
**Cup & saucer,** amber .............................. 6.00
**Cup & saucer,** clear ................................ 5.00
**Cup & saucer,** green ............................. 31.00
**Custard cup,** clear................................... 5.00
**Custard cup,** ruffled, clear.................... 15.00
**Custard cup,** green .................................. 4.00

*Sandwich Punch Set*

**Custard cup liner,** clear...................... 12.00
**Pitcher,** juice, 6" h., clear...................... 61.00
**Pitcher,** juice, 6" h., green ................. 165.00
**Pitcher w/ice lip,** 2 qt., clear ............... 72.00
**Pitcher w/ice lip,** 2 qt., green ............ 260.00
**Plate,** dessert, 7" d., amber.................... 8.00
**Plate,** dessert, 7" d., clear...................... 9.00
**Plate,** 8" d., clear.................................... 5.00
**Plate,** dinner, 9" d., amber ..................... 9.00
**Plate,** dinner, 9" d., clear..................... 16.00
**Plate,** dinner, 9" d., green .................... 88.00
**Plate,** snack, 9" d., clear ........................ 5.00
**Plate,** sandwich, 12" d., amber ........... 15.00
**Plate,** sandwich, 12" d., clear............... 32.00
**Punch bowl,** clear ............................... 17.00
**Punch bowl,** white............................... 10.00
**Punch bowl & base,** clear.................... 38.00
**Punch bowl & base,** opaque white ...... 23.00
**Punch set:** punch bowl & six cups;
    clear, 7 pcs. (ILLUS. above) .............. 65.00
**Punch set:** punch bowl, base &
    ten cups; opaque white, 12 pcs. ......... 45.00
**Sherbet,** footed, clear ............................ 8.00
**Sugar bowl,** cov., clear......................... 20.00
**Sugar bowl,** cov., green ....................... 23.00
**Sugar bowl,** open, clear ......................... 5.00
**Sugar bowl,** open, green....................... 26.00
**Tumbler,** juice, clear, 3 oz. ..................... 8.00
**Tumbler,** juice, green, 3 oz..................... 4.00
**Tumbler,** clear, 5 oz............................... 6.00
**Tumbler,** green, 5 oz. ............................. 4.00
**Tumbler,** water, clear, 9 oz. .................... 8.00
**Tumbler,** water, green, 9 oz. ................... 4.00
**Tumbler,** footed, amber, 9 oz. .............. 24.00

**Tumbler,** footed, clear, 9 oz................. 26.00
**Water set:** 36 oz. pitcher & six
    tumblers; green, 7 pcs. .................... 106.00

### SPIRAL, Hocking Glass Co., 1928-30 (Press-mold)

*Spiral Pitcher*

**Bowl,** berry, 8" d., green ...................... 12.00
**Creamer,** flat or footed, green................ 8.00
**Cup & saucer,** green ............................. 7.00
**Ice or butter tub,** green........................ 26.00
**Pitcher,** 7⅝" h., 58 oz., green (ILLUS.) .. 32.00
**Plate,** sherbet, 6" d., green .................... 4.00

**Plate,** luncheon, 8" d., green.................. **4.00**
**Platter,** 12" l., oval, green .................... **21.00**
**Preserve,** cov., green .......................... **29.00**
**Sandwich server,** w/center handle,
    green ................................................ **28.00**
**Sherbet,** green.................................... **5.00**
**Sherbet,** pink ...................................... **4.00**
**Sugar bowl,** flat or footed, green............ **7.00**
**Tumbler,** water, green, 5" h., 9 oz. ....... **12.00**

## SWANKY SWIGS, early 1930s to early 1940s (Kraft cheese glasses)

**Antique No. 1,** black, blue, brown,
    green, orange or red ........................... **4.00**
**Band** No. 1........................................... **4.00**
**Band** No. 2........................................... **4.00**
**Band** No. 3........................................... **3.00**
**Band** No. 4........................................... **2.00**
**Bustlin' Betsy,** blue, brown, green,
    orange, red or yellow ........................ **11.00**
**Carnival,** cobalt blue or red ................... **4.00**
**Carnival,** yellow ................................... **6.00**
**Checkerboard,** blue & white................... **8.00**
**Checkerboard,** green & white ............. **25.00**
**Checkerboard,** red & white ................. **23.00**
**Circles & Dot,** blue or green.................. **7.00**
**Daisy (or Bachelor Button),** green,
    red or white...................................... **3.00**
**Forget-Me-Not,** dark blue, light blue,
    red or yellow ..................................... **6.00**
**Kiddy Kup,** black, blue, brown,
    green, orange or red........................... **7.00**
**Posy -** Cornflower No. 1, 3½" h. ............. **3.00**
**Posy -** Cornflower No. 1, 4½" h. ........... **15.00**
**Posy -** Cornflower No. 2, dark blue,
    light blue, red or yellow........................ **4.00**
**Posy -** Jonquil ...................................... **7.00**
**Posy -** Tulip ......................................... **4.00**
**Posy -** Violet........................................ **5.00**
**Sailboat No. 1** (three boats), blue ........ **12.00**
**Sailboat No. 2** (four boats), blue .......... **11.00**
**Stars No. 1,** black, blue, green, red or
    yellow............................................... **7.00**
**Texas Centennial,** black ..................... **16.00**
**Texas Centennial,** red......................... **16.00**
**Tulip No. 1,** black, dark blue, green or
    red, 3½" h. ....................................... **3.00**
**Tulip No. 1,** red or green, 4½" h. ........... **8.00**
**Tulip No. 2,** black, blue, green or red ... **16.00**
**Tulip No. 3,** dark blue, light blue or
    yellow............................................... **3.00**

## SWIRL or Petal Swirl, Jeannette Glass Co., 1937-38 (Press-mold)

**Ashtray,** pink, 5⅜" ................................ **6.00**
**Bowl,** cereal, 5¼" d., Delphite............... **13.00**
**Bowl,** cereal, 5¼" d., pink .................... **10.00**
**Bowl,** cereal, 5¼" d., ultramarine.......... **14.00**
**Bowl,** salad, 9" d., Delphite.................... **28.00**

*Ultramarine Candleholder*

**Bowl,** salad, 9" d., pink ........................ **15.00**
**Bowl,** salad, 9" d., ultramarine ................ **25.00**
**Bowl,** 9" d., rimmed, ultramarine.......... **26.00**
**Bowl,** fruit, 10" d., closed handles,
    footed, ultramarine............................. **28.00**
**Butter dish,** cov., pink .......................... **169.00**
**Butter dish,** cov., ultramarine............. **268.00**
**Candleholders,** double, pink, pr........... **24.00**
**Candleholders,** double, ultramarine,
    pr. (ILLUS. of one) .............................. **43.00**
**Candy dish,** cov., pink........................... **110.00**
**Candy dish,** cov., ultramarine ........... **149.00**
**Candy dish,** open, three-footed, pink,
    5½" d. .............................................. **12.00**
**Candy dish,** open, three-footed,
    ultramarine, 5½" d. ............................ **17.00**
**Coaster,** pink, 3¼" d., 1" h.................... **15.00**
**Coaster,** ultramarine, 3¼" d., 1" h. ....... **15.00**
**Console bowl,** footed, pink, 10½" d. .... **16.00**
**Console bowl,** footed, ultramarine,
    10½" d. ............................................. **30.00**
**Creamer,** Delphite................................ **11.00**
**Creamer,** pink ...................................... **9.00**
**Creamer,** ultramarine........................... **15.00**
**Cup & saucer,** Delphite ........................ **12.00**
**Cup & saucer,** pink................................ **12.00**
**Cup & saucer,** ultramarine ................... **19.00**
**Plate,** sherbet, 6½" d., Delphite............. **5.00**
**Plate,** sherbet, 6½" d., ultramarine.......... **6.00**
**Plate,** 7¼" d., ultramarine..................... **11.00**
**Plate,** salad, 8" d., Delphite................... **5.00**
**Plate,** salad, 8" d., pink .......................... **6.00**
**Plate,** salad, 8" d., ultramarine .............. **11.00**
**Plate,** dinner, 9½" d., Delphite ............. **12.00**
**Plate,** dinner, 9½" d., pink ................... **13.00**
**Plate,** dinner, 9½" d., ultramarine.......... **16.00**
**Plate,** sandwich, 12½" d., pink ............. **17.00**
**Plate,** sandwich, 12½" d., ultramarine... **26.00**
**Platter,** 12" oval, Delphite .................... **35.00**
**Salt & pepper shakers,** Delphite, pr. ... **95.00**

**Salt & pepper shakers,** ultramarine,
  pr. ..................................................... **40.00**
**Sherbet,** ultramarine ........................... **18.00**
**Soup bowl w/lug handles,** pink .......... **19.00**
**Soup bowl w/lug handles,**
  ultramarine....................................... **37.00**
**Sugar bowl,** open, Delphite.................. **9.00**
**Sugar bowl,** open, ultramarine ............. **15.00**
**Tumbler,** pink, 4" h., 9 oz..................... **11.00**
**Tumbler,** ultramarine, 4" h., 9 oz. ....... **30.00**
**Tumbler,** pink, 4⅝" h., 9 oz.................. **17.00**
**Tumbler,** footed, pink, 9 oz.................. **14.00**
**Tumbler,** footed, ultramarine, 9 oz. ..... **38.00**
**Tumbler,** pink, 5⅛" h., 13 oz. ............. **26.00**
**Tumbler,** ultramarine, 5⅛" h., 13 oz. .... **80.00**
**Vase,** 6½" h., pink ............................... **16.00**
**Vase,** 6½" h., ultramarine..................... **19.00**
**Vase,** 8½" h., ultramarine..................... **27.00**

## TEA ROOM, Indiana Glass Co., 1926-31 (Press-mold)

**Banana split dish,** flat, green, 7½" ...... **98.00**
**Banana split dish,** footed, clear, 7½"... **46.00**
**Banana split dish,** footed, green,
  7½" ................................................... **81.00**
**Bowl,** salad, 8¾" d., green................... **80.00**
**Bowl,** salad, 8¾" d., pink ..................... **52.00**
**Bowl,** 9½" oval vegetable, green .......... **67.00**
**Bowl,** 9½" oval vegetable, pink............. **66.00**
**Candlesticks,** green, pr........................ **69.00**
**Candlesticks,** pink, pr. ......................... **66.00**
**Celery or pickle dish,** green, 8½"........ **28.00**
**Creamer,** green, 3¼" h. ........................ **19.00**
**Creamer,** pink, 3¼" h ........................... **26.00**
**Creamer,** clear, 4" h............................. **12.00**
**Creamer,** green, 4" h. ........................... **15.00**
**Creamer,** pink, 4" h. ............................. **12.00**
**Creamer,** footed, green, 4½" h. ............ **19.00**
**Creamer,** footed, pink, 4½" h. .............. **15.00**
**Creamer,** rectangular, green................. **16.00**
**Creamer,** rectangular, pink ................... **15.00**
**Creamer & open sugar bowl** on
  center-handled tray, green ................. **61.00**
**Creamer & open sugar bowl** on
  center-handled tray, pink .................. **87.00**
**Creamer & open sugar bowl** on
  rectangular tray, green .................... **107.00**
**Creamer & open sugar bowl** on
  rectangular tray, pink ........................ **59.00**
**Cup & saucer,** green............................ **62.00**
**Cup & saucer,** pink............................... **72.00**
**Finger bowl,** green................................ **85.00**
**Finger bowl,** pink.................................. **69.00**
**Goblet,** green, 9 oz. .............................. **78.00**
**Goblet,** pink, 9 oz. ................................ **77.00**
**Ice bucket,** green .................................. **75.00**
**Ice bucket,** pink ................................... **66.00**

**Lamp,** electric, clear, 9" ...................... **123.00**
**Lamp,** electric, green, 9" ...................... **106.00**
**Mustard,** cov., clear............................. **79.00**
**Parfait,** clear ........................................ **65.00**
**Parfait,** green........................................ **64.00**
**Pitcher,** 64 oz., green ........................... **159.00**
**Pitcher,** 64 oz., pink............................. **150.00**
**Plate,** sherbet, 6½" d., green ............... **16.00**
**Plate,** sherbet, 6½" d., pink.................. **17.00**
**Plate,** luncheon, 8¼" d., green............. **32.00**
**Plate,** 10½" d., two-handled, green....... **50.00**
**Plate,** 10½" d., two-handled, pink ........ **60.00**
**Plate,** sandwich, w/center handle,
  green ................................................. **166.00**
**Plate,** sandwich, w/center handle,
  pink .................................................... **158.00**
**Relish,** divided, green ........................... **23.00**
**Relish,** divided, pink.............................. **13.00**
**Salt & pepper shakers,** green, pr. ....... **64.00**
**Salt & pepper shakers,** pink, pr........... **52.00**
**Sherbet,** low footed, green ................... **29.00**
**Sherbet,** low footed, pink ..................... **23.00**
**Sherbet,** low, flared edge, clear........... **19.00**
**Sherbet,** low, flared edge, green .......... **29.00**
**Sherbet,** low, flared edge, pink ............. **25.00**
**Sherbet,** tall footed, clear .................... **28.00**
**Sherbet,** tall footed, green ................... **43.00**
**Sherbet,** tall footed, pink ..................... **35.00**
**Sugar bowl,** cov., pink, 3" h................ **130.00**
**Sugar bowl,** cov., green, 3" h. ............ **100.00**
**Sugar bowl,** open, green, 4" h. ............ **18.00**
**Sugar bowl,** open, pink, 4" h. .............. **13.00**
**Sugar bowl,** open, footed, green,
  4½" h. ............................................... **21.00**
**Sugar bowl,** open, footed, pink,
  4½" h. ............................................... **15.00**
**Sugar bowl,** open, rectangular,
  green ................................................. **23.00**
**Sugar bowl,** open, rectangular, pink .... **12.00**
**Sundae,** footed, ruffled, clear............... **53.00**
**Sundae,** footed, ruffled, green ........... **115.00**
**Sundae,** footed, ruffled, pink
**Tray,** rectangular, for creamer &
  sugar bowl, green .............................. **48.00**
**Tray,** rectangular, for creamer &
  sugar bowl, pink................................. **53.00**
**Tray,** w/center handle, for creamer &
  sugar bowl, green ............................. **150.00**
**Tray,** w/center handle, for creamer &
  sugar bowl, pink................................ **135.00**
**Tumbler,** footed, clear, 6 oz................. **28.00**
**Tumbler,** footed, green, 6 oz. .............. **42.00**
**Tumbler,** footed, pink, 6 oz.................. **32.00**
**Tumbler,** green, 4³⁄₁₆" h., 8½ oz.......... **105.00**
**Tumbler,** pink, 4³⁄₁₆" h., 8½ oz. ........... **33.00**
**Tumbler,** footed, green, 5¼" h., 8 oz. ... **34.00**
**Tumbler,** footed, pink, 5¼" h., 8 oz...... **36.00**
**Tumbler,** footed, clear, 11 oz............... **40.00**
**Tumbler,** footed, green, 11 oz. ............. **52.00**

*Tea Room Tumbler*

**Tumbler,** footed, pink, 11 oz.
(ILLUS.) .............................................. 42.00
**Tumbler,** footed, clear, 12 oz................ 45.00
**Tumbler,** footed, green, 12 oz. ............. 63.00
**Tumbler,** footed, pink, 12 oz................. 65.00
**Vase,** 6½" h., ruffled rim, green........... 129.00
**Vase,** 6½" h., ruffled rim, pink ............. 106.00
**Vase,** 9½" h., ruffled rim, amber.......... 150.00
**Vase,** 9½" h., ruffled rim, clear.............. 21.00
**Vase,** 9½" h., ruffled rim, green........... 134.00
**Vase,** 11" h., ruffled rim, clear............. 120.00
**Vase,** 11" h., straight, green................. 152.00
**Vase,** 11" h., straight, pink ................... 95.00
**Water set:** pitcher & four tumblers;
green, 5 pcs. .................................... 225.00

## WATERFORD or Waffle, Hocking Glass Co., 1938-44 (Press-mold)

**Ashtray,** clear, 4"................................... 7.00
**Bowl,** berry, 4¾" d., clear........................ 6.00
**Bowl,** berry, 4¾" d., pink....................... 15.00
**Bowl,** cereal, 5¼" d., clear..................... 19.00
**Bowl,** cereal, 5¼" d., pink...................... 32.00
**Bowl,** berry, 8¼" d., clear........................ 9.00
**Bowl,** berry, 8¼" d., pink....................... 22.00
**Butter dish,** cov., clear .......................... 25.00
**Butter dish,** cov., pink ......................... 203.00
**Cake plate,** handled, clear, 10¼" d........ 9.00
**Cake plate,** handled, pink, 10¼" d........ 17.00
**Creamer,** oval, clear .............................. 5.00
**Creamer,** oval, pink................................ 12.00
**Cup & saucer,** clear .............................. 9.00
**Cup & saucer,** pink............................... 21.00
**Dinner service for eight:** dinner
plates, cups & saucers & 10 oz.
tumblers; clear, 32 pcs. ................... 144.00
**Goblet,** amber, 5¼" h.......................... 125.00

**Goblet,** clear, 5¼" h. ............................. 16.00
**Goblet,** clear 5½" h. (Miss America-
style) ................................................. 34.00
**Goblet,** pink 5½" h. (Miss America-
style) ................................................. 40.00
**Lamp,** clear, 4" h.................................. 29.00
**Pitcher,** juice, 42 oz., tilt-type, clear...... 26.00
**Pitcher w/ice lip,** 80 oz., clear.............. 33.00
**Pitcher w/ice lip,** 80 oz., pink............. 148.00
**Plate,** sherbet, 6" d., clear ...................... 4.00
**Plate,** sherbet, 6" d., pink........................ 8.00

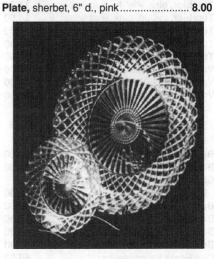

*Waterford Plates*

**Plate,** salad, 7½" d., clear (ILLUS.
front) .................................................. 6.00
**Plate,** salad, 7½" d., pink ...................... 10.00
**Plate,** dinner, 9⅝" d., clear.................... 10.00
**Plate,** dinner, 9⅝" d., pink...................... 22.00
**Plate,** sandwich, 13¾" d., clear (ILLUS.
back) .................................................. 10.00
**Plate,** sandwich, 13¾" d., pink.............. 26.00
**Relish,** five-section, clear, 13¾" d. ....... 16.00
**Salt & pepper shakers,** clear, short,
pr. ....................................................... 8.00
**Salt & pepper shakers,** clear, tall,
pr. ....................................................... 9.00
**Sherbet,** footed, clear ............................ 4.00
**Sherbet,** footed, pink ............................ 13.00
**Sugar bowl,** cov., oval, clear .................. 9.00
**Sugar bowl,** cov., oval, pink ................. 21.00
**Sugar bowl,** open, footed, clear (Miss
America-style) .................................... 2.00
**Tumbler,** footed, pink, 3½" h., 5 oz....... 12.00
**Tumbler,** footed, clear, 5" h., 10 oz. ..... 11.00
**Tumbler,** footed, pink, 5" h., 10 oz........ 19.00
**Water set:** 80 oz. pitcher & six footed
tumblers; pink, 7 pcs........................ 155.00

**(End of Depression Glass Listings)**

*Three Fine Durand Vases*

## DURAND

*Fine decorative glass similar to that made by Tiffany and other outstanding glasshouses of its day was made by the Vineland Flint Glass Works Co. in Vineland, New Jersey, first headed by Victor Durand, Sr., and subsequently by his son Victor Durand, Jr., in the 1920s.*

**Lamp base,** "King Tut" patt., small bulbous base tapering to a tall slender trumpet-form neck topped by two-socket gilt-metal electric socket fittings, the base raised on a domed gilt-metal support w/four thick scroll feet, the lamp in green iridescent w/platinum gold coiled & swirled decoration, glass 9" h., overall 27" h. ............................ **$374.00**

**Lamp base,** "King Tut" patt., simple ovoid body tapering to a trumpet neck, mounted on an octagonal gilt-metal base, gilt-metal electric fittings at the top w/two sockets, the body of golden orange iridescence w/dark olive-green pulled coils & swirls, glass 12" h., overall 20" h. ................ **374.00**

**Vase,** 6¾" h., baluster-form body w/cushion foot & short flaring neck, gold iridescent ground decorated w/five pulled feathers in yellow & white w/blue outlining, base center inscribed "Durand" in silver script (some interior stain) .......................... **575.00**

**Vase,** 7" h., baluster-form body w/flaring trumpet neck, "King Tut" patt., white pulled & hooked design over the iridescent blue ground, unsigned (ILLUS. above left) ............ **863.00**

**Vase,** 7½" h., simple baluster form w/a wide, short flaring neck, gold iridescent ground w/the exterior covered w/random gold threading (minimal thread damage) .................. **230.00**

**Vase,** 8" h., the wide squatty base centered by a widely flaring trumpet neck, lightly molded ribbing, ambergris w/bright blue iridescent finish highlighted by purplish green, base signed in silver "V. Durand 1986-8" ............................................. **748.00**

**Vase,** 8¼" h., wide bulbous baluster-form w/flattened flaring rim, "King Tut" patt., iridescent green hooked & pulled swirls on a golden orange cased to opal ground, signed "Durand" across the pontil (ILLUS. above center) ................................. **1,495.00**

**Vase,** 8½" h., swelled cylindrical body w/a rounded shoulder to the short trumpet neck, ambergris body w/overall lustrous blue iridescent random threading, unsigned (ILLUS. above right) ...................................... **403.00**

**Vases,** 4¼" h., ovoid body w/an averted rim, the iridescent gold ground decorated w/an iridescent silvery green wave design, engraved "DURAND," each drilled, pr. ............. **115.00**

## FENTON

*Fenton Art Glass Company began producing glass at Williamstown, West Virginia, in January 1907. Organized by Frank L. and John W. Fenton, the company began operations in a newly built glass factory* with an experienced master glass craftsman, Jacob Rosenthal, as their factory manager. Fenton has produced a wide variety of collectible glassware through the years, including Carnival. Still in production today, their current productions may be found at finer gift shops across the country. William Heacock's three-volume set on Fenton, published by Antique Publications, is the standard reference in this field.

*Modern Fenton Mark*

**Ashtray,** fan-shaped, Hobnail patt., yellow opalescent, 5½" d. ................. **$35.00**

**Banana bowl,** pedestal base, Silver Crest, No. 7324 ................................. **62.00**

**Barber bottle,** Coin Dot patt., cranberry opalescent ......................... **229.00**

**Basket,** Big Cookie patt., No. 1681, Jade Green, no handle ....................... **95.00**

**Basket,** Big Cookie patt., No. 1681, red, no handle ................................. **110.00**

**Basket,** handled, Hobnail patt., cranberry opalescent, 4" h. ................. **55.00**

**Basket,** handled, Hobnail patt., cranberry opalescent, 7" h. ................. **57.00**

**Basket,** Hobnail patt., milk white, 7" h. ... **18.00**

**Basket,** Peach Crest, 7" h. .................... **45.00**

**Basket,** milk white handles, Peach Crest, 10" h. ....................................... **85.00**

**Basket,** Silver Crest, No. 7251 ............. **28.00**

**Bonbon w/handle,** small, Hobnail patt., French Opalescent .................... **19.00**

**Bonbon,** Hobnail patt., yellow opalescent, 5¾" d. ......................... **20.00**

**Bonbon,** Silver Crest ........................... **15.00**

**Bowl,** berry, 5½" d., Hobnail patt., yellow opalescent ............................. **20.00**

**Bowl,** 6" d., Coin Dot patt., cranberry ... **50.00**

**Bowl,** 6" d., Coin Dot patt., green ......... **48.00**

**Bowl,** 8" d., Dragon & Lotus patt., pink ...................................................... **60.00**

**Bowl,** 8½" d., Silver Crest, No. 7338 .... **65.00**

**Bowl,** 9½" d., Silver Crest .................... **22.00**

**Bowl,** 10¼" d., shell-shaped, Peach Crest, No. 9020 ................................. **90.00**

**Bowl,** dolphin-footed, blue ................... **35.00**

**Bowl,** fruit, footed, square, Silver Crest ................................................... **70.00**

**Bowl,** sauce, Water Lily & Cattails patt., Chocolate glass ...................... **125.00**

**Cake stand,** Hobnail patt., milk white ... **30.00**

**Cake stand,** Silver Rose Crest ............. **55.00**

**Candlesticks,** No. 848, light blue, pr. ... **25.00**

**Candlesticks,** No. 848, red, pr. ............ **25.00**

**Candlesticks,** Diamond Lace patt., French Opalescent, pr. ...................... **45.00**

**Candlesticks,** cornucopia-form, Hobnail patt., blue opalescent, pr. ....... **24.00**

**Candlesticks,** Hobnail patt., plum opalescent, pr. .................................. **150.00**

**Candlesticks,** cornucopia-form, Ivory Crest, 6" h., pr. .................................. **65.00**

**Candy box,** cov., footed, Silver Crest .. **125.00**

**Compote,** 3½" d., Silver Crest ............. **10.00**

**Console set:** bowl & pair of candleholders; Diamond Lace patt., French Opalescent, the set ............... **75.00**

**Console set:** bowl & pair of candleholders; Hobnail patt., blue opalescent, 3 pcs. ........................... **125.00**

**Creamer,** No. 1924, aqua .................... **45.00**

**Creamer,** Hobnail patt., blue opalescent, 3½" h. ............................. **13.00**

**Creamer & sugar bowl,** Daisy & Button patt., white, pr. ...................... **25.00**

**Cruet w/stopper,** Hobnail patt., French Opalescent ............................ **22.00**

**Epergne,** single-lily, Hobnail patt., milk white ............................................. **40.00**

**Epergne,** single-lily, Hobnail patt., blue opaque ....................................... **65.00**

**Epergne,** single lily, Hobnail patt., pink ...................................................... **10.00**

**Hat,** Daisy & Button patt., blue opalescent ............................................ **40.00**

**Lamp,** Rib Optic patt., topaz opalescent .......................................... **225.00**

**Mayonnaise set:** bowl w/ladle & underplate; Hobnail patt., cranberry opalescent, 3 pcs. ........................... **125.00**

**Napkin ring set,** Hobnail patt., milk white, 4 pcs. ....................................... **30.00**

**Nappy,** two-handled, small, Hobnail patt., blue opalescent ....................... **12.00**

**Oil bottle w/stopper,** handled, Emerald Crest patt., No. 7269, green.. **90.00**

**Pitcher,** water, Christmas Snowflake patt., cranberry opalescent, modern... **350.00**

**Pitcher,** water, Coin Spot patt., cranberry opalescent ...................... **263.00**

**Pitcher,** water, Daisy & Fern patt., cranberry, modern ........................... **100.00**

**Pitcher,** Daisy & Fern patt., canary opalescent, satin finish, modern ....... **100.00**

**Pitcher,** Dot Optic patt., cranberry opalescent, modern .......................... **275.00**

**Pitcher,** water, Polka Dot patt., cranberry opalescent, modern .......... **130.00**

**Plate,** 6" d., Silver Crest ........................ **13.00**

**Plate,** 8" d., Lincoln Inn patt., Jade Green ................................................... **25.00**

**Plate,** 8" d., Lincoln Inn patt., pink ........ **17.00**

**Plate,** 8½" d., Silver Crest .................... **20.00**

**Plate,** 12" d., Silver Crest .................... **40.00**

**Rose bowl,** Garland patt., blue ............. **75.00**

**Salt & pepper shakers,** Georgian patt., No. 1611, ruby, pr. .................... **75.00**

**Sherbet,** Lincoln Inn patt., Jade Green 4¼" h. ................................................ **22.00**

**Sherbet,** Lincoln Inn patt., red, 4¼" h. ... **23.00**

**Sherbet w/underplate,** Persian Pearl stretch glass, clear, 2 pcs. .................. **85.00**

**Sugar shaker w/original cover,** Daisy & Fern patt., cranberry opalescent, modern .......................... **100.00**

**Sugar shaker w/original cover,** Thumbprint patt., cranberry opalescent ......................................... **75.00**

**Syrup w/original top,** Daisy & Fern patt., cranberry opalescent, modern.. **100.00**

**Top hat,** Rib Optic patt., French Opalescent, 6 x 10" ........................... **225.00**

**Tumbler footed,** Coin Dot patt. No. 1553, cranberry opalescent, modern ............................................... **40.00**

**Tumbler,** footed, Daisy & Fern, cranberry opalescent, modern ............ **50.00**

**Tumbler,** water, Hobnail patt., blue opalescent ......................................... **20.00**

**Tumbler,** iced tea, Lincoln Inn patt., cobalt blue, 12 oz. ............................... **45.00**

**Vase,** ivy, miniature, Beaded Melon patt., green .......................................... **39.00**

**Vase,** 4" h., crimped, Hobnail patt., yellow opalescent ............................... **27.00**

**Vase,** 4" h., fan-topped, Hobnail patt., yellow opalescent ............................... **37.00**

**Vase,** bud, 8" h., footed, Hobnail patt., yellow opalescent ............................... **34.00**

**Vase,** 8" h., Polka Dot patt. No. 2251, cranberry opalescent, modern ............ **95.00**

**Vase,** 12" h., fan-topped, Silver Crest ... **83.00**

**Wine,** Lincoln Inn patt., cobalt blue ....... **28.00**

## FOSTORIA

*Fostoria Glass company, founded in 1887, produced numerous types of fine glassware over the years. Their factory in Moundsville, West Virginia closed in 1986.*

**Fostoria**

*Fostoria Label*

**Appetizer set:** rectangular tray w/six inserts, American patt., clear, 10½" l. ............................................... **$275.00**

**Bonbon,** Versailles etching, blue .......... **29.00**

**Bowl,** 4" d., handled, Baroque patt., yellow ............................................... **20.00**

**Bowl,** hanky-style, 5½" d., 3" h., Heirloom patt., ruby ........................... **32.00**

**Bowl,** 8" d., Coin patt., clear ................ **22.00**

**Bowl,** oval, 9" l., Versailles etching, blue ................................................... **115.00**

**Bowl,** oval, 9½" l., Century patt., clear ................................................... **32.00**

**Bowl,** Grecian-type, oval, 10" l., scroll handles, June etching, clear ............... **65.00**

**Bowl,** 10" d., Heirloom patt., blue opalescent ......................................... **60.00**

**Bowl,** 10¾" d., Colony patt., clear ......... **35.00**

**Bowl,** 11" w., tri-cornered, American patt., clear ......................................... **40.00**

**Bowl,** 12" d., Baroque patt., yellow ....... **33.00**

**Bowl,** 12" d., Brocade etching, Grape patt., orchid ...................................... **95.00**

**Bowl,** centerpiece, 12" d., June etching, blue ..................................... **130.00**

**Bowl,** oval, 13" l., June etching, blue .. **140.00**

**Bowl,** centerpiece, 15" d., American patt., clear ....................................... **150.00**

**Bowl,** centerpiece, oval, 16" l., Heirloom patt., ruby ........................... **75.00**

**Butter dish,** cov., American patt., clear, ¼ lb. ......................................... **18.00**

**Butter dish,** w/domed cover, round, American patt., clear ...................... **110.00**

**Butter dish,** cov., Fairfax patt., green... **90.00**

**Cake plate,** handled, Century patt., Milkweed etching, 10" d .................... **25.00**

**Cake plate,** footed, Colony patt., clear, 12" d .................................... **55.00**

**Cake stand,** Carmen patt., clear, 9" d. ................................................ **45.00**

**Candelabrum,** two-light, Baroque patt., clear ........................................ **45.00**

**Candleholder,** Heirloom patt., blue opalescent, 3½" h. ........................... **30.00**

**Candleholders,** Coin patt., clear, short, pr. ........................................... **28.00**

**Candle lamp,** American patt., clear, 4 pcs. ............................................... **125.00**

**Candlestick,** two-light, American patt., clear .............................................. **130.00**

**Candlestick,** Baroque patt., clear......... **16.00**

**Candlestick,** three-light, Baroque patt., clear.............................................. **25.00**

**Candlestick,** Century patt., clear, 4½" h. .............................................. **15.00**

**Candlestick,** Colony patt., clear, 3½" h. .............................................. **10.00**

**Candlestick,** three-light, Romance etching, clear, 8" h. ............................ **85.00**

**Candlestick,** Trojan etching, yellow, 2" h. ................................................... **10.00**

**Candlesticks,** American patt., clear, pr. ........................................................ **55.00**

**Candlesticks,** Baroque patt., yellow, 5½" h., pr. .......................................... **65.00**

**Candlesticks,** three-light, Buttercup etching, clear, 8" h., pr...................... **125.00**

**Candlesticks,** three-light, Century patt., clear, 7½" h., pr. ........................ **60.00**

**Candlesticks,** Chintz etching, clear, 5½" h., pr. .......................................... **68.00**

**Candlesticks,** Coin patt., olive-green, 4½" h., pr. .......................................... **23.00**

**Candlesticks,** low, June etching, blue, pr.................................................... **90.00**

**Candlesticks,** one-light, Navarre etching, clear, pr. ............................... **50.00**

**Candlesticks,** two-light, Rambler etching, clear, pr. ............................... **45.00**

**Candle vase,** Heirloom patt., pink opalescent, 10" h. ............................... **60.00**

**Candy dish,** footed w/cover, American Patt., clear, 7" h. ........................ **75.00**

**Candy dish,** cov., three-part, Lido patt., clear...................................... **50.00**

**Cheese & cracker set,** American Patt., clear, 4" h. ............................... **60.00**

**Cigarette box,** American patt., clear .... **32.00**

**Claret,** Versailles etching, blue ........... **120.00**

**Cocktail,** oyster, American patt., clear, 4½" h. ............................................... **18.00**

**Cocktail,** Chintz etching, clear............ **24.00**

**Cocktail,** Fairfax patt., topaz, 3 oz........ **18.00**

**Cocktail,** Holly cutting, clear, 5¼" h., 3½ oz. ............................................... **14.00**

**Cocktail,** oyster, Versailles etching, yellow............................................... **19.00**

**Comport,** Century patt., clear, 4½" d.... **25.00**

**Compote,** jelly, Coin patt., amber ......... **18.00**

**Compote,** Fuchsia etching (No. 2470).. **35.00**

**Compote,** cheese, Vesper etching, green ............................................... **18.00**

**Compote,** 4¾" d., Versailles etching, yellow............................................... **30.00**

**Cookie jar,** cov., American patt., clear.. **275.00**

**Cordial,** Romance etching, clear ......... **45.00**

**Cordial,** Versailles etching, yellow........ **85.00**

**Cordial,** blank No. 5099, topaz, plain ... **20.00**

**Creamer,** Coronet patt., clear ............... **6.00**

**Creamer & open sugar bowl,** Chintz etching, clear, pr. ............................ **27.00**

**Creamer & open sugar bowl,** footed, Meadow Rose etching, clear, pr. ........ **27.00**

**Creamer & open sugar bowl,** Navarre etching, clear, pr. .................. **40.00**

**Creamer & open sugar bowl,** Versailles etching, blue, pr. ............... **72.00**

**Creamer, sugar bowl & tray,** American patt., clear, 3 pcs. ............... **20.00**

**Creamer, sugar bowl & tray,** individual size, Chintz etching, clear, 3 pcs. ................................................ **55.00**

**Cup & saucer,** demitasse, Fairfax patt., blue ....................................... **12.00**

**Cup & saucer,** footed, American patt., clear ................................................. **11.00**

**Cup & saucer,** Baroque patt., blue....... **35.00**

**Cup & saucer,** Chintz etching, clear..... **25.00**

**Cup & saucer,** Colony patt., clear ......... **7.00**

**Cup & saucer,** Fairfax patt., blue ......... **25.00**

**Cup & saucer,** footed, Fairfax patt., green ................................................. **10.00**

**Cup & saucer,** Fairfax patt., pink.......... **14.00**

**Cup & saucer,** June etching, blue ........ **45.00**

**Cup & saucer,** June etching, pink ........ **45.00**

**Cup & saucer,** Romance etching, clear................................................. **25.00**

**Decanter w/stopper,** cordial-size, American patt. (No. 2056), clear, 9 oz. .................................................. **70.00**

**Decanter w/stopper,** American patt., clear, 24 oz. ..................................... **100.00**

**Figure of St. Francis,** frosted, 13" h...... **200.00**

**Finger bowl w/liner,** Trojan etching, topaz, 2 pcs. ..................................... **45.00**

**Finger bowl w/liner,** Versailles etching, blue, 2 pcs.......................... **43.00**

**Flower float bowl,** Heirloom patt., blue opalescent, 10" l. ...................... **60.00**

**Goblet,** wine, American patt. (No. 2056), clear, 2½ oz. ................... **15.00**

**Goblet,** juice, American patt., clear, 5 oz. .................................................. **12.00**

**Goblet,** water, American patt., clear, 9 oz. .................................................. **14.00**

**Goblet,** water, hexagonal-footed, American patt., clear, 10 oz. .............. **15.00**

**Goblet,** water, American Lady patt. ...... **15.00**

**Goblet,** water, Buttercup etching, clear................................................. **15.00**

**Goblet,** water, Colony patt., clear ......... **12.00**

**Goblet,** Fairfax patt., blue, 8¼" h., 10 oz. ................................................ **35.00**

**Goblet,** Fuchsia etching, clear .............. 24.00
**Goblet,** tall, Holly cutting, clear ............ 20.00
**Goblet,** Jamestown patt., amber .......... 10.00
**Goblet,** Jamestown patt., amethyst ...... 16.00
**Goblet,** Jamestown patt., blue, 6" h. ..... 17.00
**Goblet,** Jamestown patt., blue, 9½ oz. ... 12.00
**Goblet,** Jamestown patt., pink, 10 oz. .. 17.00
**Goblet,** iced tea, footed, Jamestown
   patt., blue ......................................... 24.00
**Goblet,** June etching, rose, 6" h.,
   4 oz. ................................................ 125.00
**Goblet,** water, June etching, blue,
   10 oz. ................................................. 60.00
**Goblet,** water, Laurel cutting, clear ....... 18.00
**Goblet,** water, Lido etching, clear ......... 14.00
**Goblet,** Meadow Rose etching, clear,
   7⅝" h. ................................................ 25.00
**Goblet,** water, Midnight Rose etching,
   clear, 9 oz. ......................................... 20.00
**Goblet,** Mystic etching, green .............. 30.00
**Goblet,** water, Navarre etching, blue .... 40.00
**Goblet,** water, Navarre etching, clear,
   10 oz. ................................................. 30.00
**Goblet,** Trojan etching, topaz, 8¼" h.,
   10 oz. ................................................. 30.00
**Goblet,** Vernon etching, amethyst ........ 30.00
**Goblet,** water, Versailles etching,
   blank No. 5098, blue .......................... 43.00
**Goblet,** blank No. 5082, green
   w/spiral optic design .......................... 10.00
**Goblet,** blank No. 5098, yellow
   w/clear stem ...................................... 15.00
**Goblets,** water, American patt.,
   amber, set of 4 ................................... 56.00
**Goblet,** water, American patt., amber,
   set of 4 ............................................... 56.00
**Goblet,** magnum-style, Navarre
   etching, blue, 16 oz. ........................... 68.00
**Goblets,** Orchid etching, clear, 9 oz.,
   set of 8 ............................................. 200.00
**Grapefruit liner,** June etching, topaz ... 175.00
**Handkerchief box,** cov., American
   patt., blue ......................................... 210.00
**Hat shape,** top hat, American patt.,
   clear, 3" h. .......................................... 28.00
**Hat shape,** tall, top hat, American
   patt., clear, 4" h. ................................. 45.00
**Hurricane lamp base,** American patt.,
   clear .................................................. 75.00
**Ice bucket,** Baroque patt., blue .......... 115.00
**Ice bucket w/tongs,** Hermitage patt.,
   clear, 6" h., 2 pcs. .............................. 20.00
**Ice bucket,** Meadow Rose etching,
   clear .................................................. 110.00
**Ice bucket,** Versailles etching, pink .... 140.00
**Icer w/tomato liner,** American patt.,
   clear .................................................. 45.00

**Icer,** Hermitage patt., clear ................... 10.00
**Icer,** Versailles etching, yellow ............ 110.00
**Ice tub & underplate,** American patt.,
   clear, tub, 5⅝" d., 3¾" h., 2 pcs. ......... 45.00
**Jelly dish,** cov., American patt., clear,
   6¾" d. ................................................ 35.00
**Jewel box,** cov., American patt.,
   clear ................................................. 450.00
**Lemon dish,** American patt., clear ....... 45.00
**Lunch tray,** center handle, Romance
   etching (No. 341), clear, 11" d. ........... 32.00
**Lunch tray,** center handle, Holly
   cutting, clear, 11¼" d. ......................... 20.00
**Lunch tray,** center handle, Meadow
   Rose etching, clear, 12" d. .................. 45.00
**Mayonnaise bowl w/underplate &
   ladle,** American patt., clear, 3 pcs. ...... 33.00
**Muffin tray,** Century patt., clear. .......... 22.00
**Muffin tray,** Colony patt., clear ............ 30.00
**Napkin ring,** American patt., clear ........ 15.00
**Nappy, bowl,** handled, American
   patt., large ......................................... 25.00
**Nut bowl,** individual size, Alexis patt.,
   clear .................................................. 15.00
**Nut dish,** American patt., clear,
   3½ x 5¼" ............................................ 12.00
**Oyster cocktail,** Colony patt., clear ...... 13.00
**Parfait,** June etching, pink, 5¼ oz. ..... 125.00
**Parfait,** June etching, topaz, 5¼" h. ...... 65.00
**Pickle jar,** cov., American patt.,
   clear .......................... 350.00 to 450.00
**Pitcher,** water, Coin patt., frosted red ... 115.00
**Pitcher,** Chintz etching, clear .............. 375.00
**Pitcher,** Fairfax patt., pink ................... 225.00
**Pitcher,** June etching, clear ................. 375.00
**Pitcher,** Meadow Rose etching, clear... 400.00
**Pitcher,** Trojan etching, yellow .......... 360.00
**Pitcher,** Versailles etching, topaz ....... 300.00
**Pitcher-vase,** Heirloom patt., pink
   opalescent, 9" h. ................................ 60.00
**Pitcher-vase,** Heirloom patt., ruby,
   9" h. ................................................... 70.00
**Plate,** salad, 7" d., American patt.,
   clear .................................................... 7.00
**Plate,** 7" d., Colony patt., clear ............. 6.00
**Plate,** 7" d., Meadow Rose etching,
   clear .................................................. 16.00
**Plate,** 7¼" d., Midnight Rose etching,
   clear .................................................. 10.00
**Plate,** salad, 7½" d., Chintz etching,
   clear .................................................. 18.00
**Plate,** cream soup, 7½" d., June
   etching, pink ...................................... 30.00
**Plate,** 8" d, Heirloom, bittersweet
   (orange) ............................................. 55.00
**Plate,** 8" d., Holly patt., clear ............... 15.00

**Plate,** salad, 8½" d., American patt.,
clear ................................................... 12.00

**Plate,** salad, 8¾" d., Fairfax patt.,
topaz ..................................................... 7.00

**Plate,** 9" d., Buttercup etching, clear ..... 35.00

**Plate,** 9" d., Meadow Rose etching,
clear ................................................... 45.00

**Plate,** dinner, 9" d., Royal etching,
amber .................................................. 15.00

**Plate,** dinner, 9½" d., American patt.,
clear ................................................... 20.00

**Plate,** dinner, 9½" d., Chintz etching,
clear ................................................... 43.00

**Plate,** 9½" d., Fairfax patt., blue ............ 25.00

**Plate,** dinner, 9½" d., June etching,
blue ..................................................... 55.00

**Plate,** dinner, 10" d., Fairfax patt.,
topaz ................................................... 25.00

**Plate,** 11" d., Chintz etching, clear ........ 37.00

**Plate,** chop, 13" d., June etching, pink .. 110.00

**Plate,** torte, 14" d., Baroque patt.,
topaz ................................................... 20.00

**Plate,** torte, 14" d., Baroque patt.,
clear ................................................... 25.00

**Plate,** torte, 14" d., Holly cutting, clear .. 38.00

**Plate,** torte, 14" d., Jamestown patt.,
green .................................................. 40.00

**Plate,** torte, 14" d., Romance patt.,
clear ................................................... 23.00

**Plate,** 17" d., Heirloom patt., blue
opalescent ......................................... 75.00

**Plate,** torte, 20" l., American patt.,
clear ................................................. 100.00

**Plates,** salad, 7" d., Orchid etching,
clear, set of 8 .................................... 50.00

**Platter,** 12" oval, American patt., clear ... 35.00

**Puff box,** cov., American patt., clear .... 225.00

**Puff box,** cov., American patt., topaz .. 450.00

**Punch bowl,** American patt., clear,
14" d. ................................................ 115.00

**Punch bowl & base,** American patt.,
clear, 17" d., 2 pcs. .......................... 225.00

**Punch set:** bowl, base & eleven
cups; American patt., clear, 13 pcs. .... 350.00

**Punch set:** bowl, twelve cups & ladle;
Coin patt., clear, 14 pcs. ................... 495.00

**Relish dish,** Baroque patt., yellow,
10" ...................................................... 23.00

**Relish dish,** Hermitage patt., topaz,
8" ........................................................ 11.00

**Relish dish,** four-part, Mayfair patt.,
topaz, 8½" l. ....................................... 20.00

**Relish dish,** two-part, handled,
Midnight Rose etching, clear ............. 18.00

**Relish dish,** three-part, Navarre
etching, clear ..................................... 48.00

**Relish dish,** three-part, handled,
Romance etching, clear ..................... 45.00

**Rose bowl,** American patt., clear,
3½" h. ................................................. 15.00

**Rose bowl,** American patt., clear,
5" h. .................................................... 27.00

**Rose bowl lamp,** American patt.,
clear, 3½" .......................................... 69.00

**Salt & pepper shakers w/original
tops,** Chintz etching, clear, pr. .......... 88.00

**Salt & pepper shakers w/original
tops,** Coin Patt., red, pr. ................... 40.00

**Salt & pepper shakers w/original
tops,** Jamestown patt., pink, pr. ........ 65.00

**Salt & pepper shakers w/original
tops,** June etching, pink, pr. ............ 165.00

**Salt & pepper shakers w/original
tops,** Meadow Rose etching, clear,
pr. ..................................................... 120.00

**Salt & pepper shakers w/original
tops,** Versailles etching, green, pr. .. 100.00

**Salt & pepper shakers w/original
tops,** Versailles etching, yellow, pr. ..... 65.00

**Salver,** footed, round, American Patt.,
clear, 10" d. ........................................ 75.00

**Salver,** two-footed, Colony patt., clear .. 55.00

**Shaker set:** individual salt & pepper
shakers w/original tops & undertray;
American patt., clear, 3 pcs. .............. 18.00

**Sherbet,** flared rim, American patt.,
clear, 4½ oz. ...................................... 12.00

**Sherbet,** sundae, American patt.,
clear, 6 oz. ........................................... 8.00

**Sherbet,** Baroque patt., blue ................ 28.00

**Sherbet,** Baroque patt., topaz .............. 15.00

**Sherbet,** Century patt., clear ................ 18.00

**Sherbet,** Colony patt., clear .................. 7.00

**Sherbet,** Fairfax patt., blue, 4¼" h. .... 18.00

**Sherbet,** tall, Fairfax patt., topaz, 6 oz. .. 12.00

**Sherbet,** Hermitage patt., azure .......... 13.00

**Sherbet,** Holly cutting, clear, 4⅜" h. ..... 14.00

**Sherbet,** Holly cutting, clear, 5⅝" h.,
6 oz. ................................................... 15.00

**Sherbet,** Jamestown patt., amber.......... 7.00

**Sherbet,** Jamestown patt., blue, 4" h. .... 15.00

**Sherbet,** Jamestown patt., ruby, 4¼" h. .. 16.00

**Sherbet,** June etching, blue .................. 35.00

**Sherbet,** June etching, rose, 6" h.,
6 oz. ................................................... 40.00

**Sherbet,** Meadow Rose etching, clear .. 23.00

**Sherbet,** Midnight Rose etching,
clear, 5½ oz. ........................................ 8.00

**Sherbet,** tall, Navarre etching, clear ...... 24.00

**Sherbet,** Navarre etching, topaz, 4½" h. . 5.00

**Sherbet,** Orchid etching, clear,
5½ oz., set of 8 .................................. 85.00

**Sherbet,** tall, Romance etching, clear... **10.00**
**Sherbet,** Trojan etching, topaz, 6" h. .... **22.00**
**Sherbet,** Versailles, etching, yellow...... **20.00**
**Shrimp cocktail,** Trojan etching,
     yellow............................................. **20.00**
**Straw jar,** cov., American patt., clear.. **190.00**
**Sugar bowl,** cov., Coronet patt., clear.... **6.00**
**Sugar bowl,** open, footed, Romance
     etching, clear ..................................... **14.00**
**Sugar bowl,** open, Meadow Rose
     etching, clear ...................................... **8.00**
**Sugar pail,** Trojan etching, amber...... **100.00**
**Sugar pail,** Versailles etching, blue.... **195.00**
**Syrup w/original top,** Carmen patt.,
     clear.................................................. **135.00**
**Tidbit tray,** Navarre etching, clear,
     8" d. .................................................. **23.00**
**Tray,** pin, oval, American patt., clear .. **125.00**
**Tray,** sandwich, American patt., clear,
     12" d. ................................................. **80.00**
**Tray,** for individual creamer/sugar,
     Baroque patt., clear, 6¼" l. ................. **30.00**
**Tray,** for individual creamer/sugar,
     Century patt., clear, 7⅛" l. .................. **30.00**
**Tumbler,** American patt., clear, 8 oz. ... **15.00**
**Tumbler,** water, Buttercup etching,
     clear.................................................... **15.00**
**Tumbler,** juice, Chintz etching, clear,
     5 oz..................................................... **20.00**
**Tumbler,** iced tea, Chintz etching,
     clear, 13 oz. ........................................ **28.00**
**Tumbler,** old-fashioned, Coin patt.,
     clear, 3⅝" h........................................ **28.00**
**Tumbler,** footed, Colony patt., clear,
     5 oz..................................................... **11.00**
**Tumbler,** juice, footed, Dolly Madison
     cutting, clear ....................................... **15.00**
**Tumbler,** footed, Fairfax patt., blue,
     3" h., 2½ oz......................................... **30.00**
**Tumbler,** footed, Fairfax patt., blue,
     5 oz..................................................... **18.00**
**Tumbler,** Fairfax patt., blue, 5¼" h.,
     9 oz..................................................... **22.00**
**Tumbler,** Fairfax patt., topaz, 5¼" h.,
     9 oz..................................................... **16.00**
**Tumbler,** footed, Hermitage patt.,
     azure, 9 oz........................................... **15.00**
**Tumbler,** iced tea, footed, Holly
     cutting, clear, 12 oz.. ........................... **20.00**
**Tumbler,** water, Ingrid cutting, clear ..... **15.00**
**Tumbler,** juice, footed, Jamestown
     patt., blue, 5 oz. ................................. **19.00**
**Tumbler,** juice, footed, Jamestown
     patt., red, 5 oz..................................... **13.00**
**Tumbler,** water, Jamestown patt.,
     blue..................................................... **23.00**

**Tumbler,** iced tea, Jamestown patt.,
     blue..................................................... **25.00**
**Tumbler,** iced tea, Jamestown patt.,
     red ...................................................... **25.00**
**Tumbler,** whiskey, June etching,
     clear, 2½ oz. ....................................... **20.00**
**Tumbler,** footed, June etching, topaz,
     4½" h., 5 oz. ....................................... **30.00**
**Tumbler,** June etching, rose, 5¼" h.,
     9 oz..................................................... **45.00**
**Tumbler,** footed, Meadow Rose
     etching (No. 328), clear, 5 oz. ............ **25.00**
**Tumbler,** footed, Midnight Rose
     etching, clear, 12 oz. .......................... **20.00**
**Tumbler,** juice, Navarre etching,
     topaz, 4⅝" h........................................ **6.00**
**Tumbler,** footed, Navarre etching,
     clear, 7½" h......................................... **15.00**
**Tumbler,** iced tea, Navarre etching,
     clear, 13 oz. ........................................ **32.00**
**Tumbler,** footed, Romance etching,
     clear, 12 oz. ........................................ **28.00**
**Tumbler,** water, Versailles patt.,
     yellow.................................................. **22.00**
**Urn,** cov., Coin patt., amber................. **65.00**
**Urn,** cov., Coin patt., olive, 11½" h........ **75.00**
**Vase,** two-handled, Coronet patt.,
     clear.................................................... **45.00**
**Vase,** bud, 6" h., Colony patt., red ........ **35.00**
**Vase,** bud, 6½" h., Colony patt., clear... **15.00**
**Vase,** 7" h., flared rim, American patt.,
     clear.................................................... **70.00**
**Vase,** 7" h., flared rim, Colony patt.,
     clear.................................................... **35.00**
**Vase,** 7" h., No. 2292, green, plain ....... **30.00**
**Vase,** 8" h., straight sides, American
     patt., clear........................................... **45.00**
**Vase,** bud, 8½" h., footed, flared rim,
     American patt., clear............................ **32.00**
**Vase,** 10" h., swung-type, American
     patt., clear......................................... **175.00**
**Vase,** 10½" h., Heirloom patt. .............. **45.00**
**Vases,** 20" h., swung-type, Heirloom
     cutting, blue opalescent, pr.............. **150.00**
**Vegetable dish,** oval, American patt.,
     clear, 9" l............................................ **27.00**
**Washbowl & pitcher,** hotel-type,
     American patt., clear, the set ......... **4,800.00**
**Water bottle,** American patt., clear..... **800.00**
**Water set:** pitcher, six tumblers;
     Rosby patt., ca. 1910, clear............. **190.00**
**Whiskey decanter w/stopper,**
     American patt., clear............................ **70.00**
**Wine,** Buttercup etching, clear ............. **18.00**
**Wine,** Corsage etching, clear, 5½" h..... **20.00**
**Wine,** hexagonal-shaped base,
     American patt., clear, 4¾" h. .............. **10.00**

**Wine,** Holly cutting, clear ..................... **25.00**
**Wine,** Jamestown patt., ruby, 4¼" h. .... **20.00**
**Wine,** June etching, pink....................... **85.00**
**Wine,** Meadow Rose etching, clear,
5¼" h. ................................................ **38.00**
**Wine,** Navarre etching, clear, 5½" h. .... **20.00**

## GALLÉ

*Gallé glass was made in Nancy, France, by Emile Gallé, a founder of the Nancy School and a leader in the Art Nouveau movement in France. Much of his glass, both enameled and cameo, is decorated with naturalistic designs. The finest pieces were made in the last two decades of the 19th century and the opening years of the present one. Pieces marked with a star preceding the name were made between 1904, the year of Gallé's death, and 1914.*

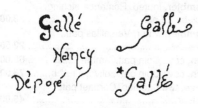

*Gallé Marks*

**Cameo vase,** 7⅝" h., gently tapering cylindrical body w/a narrow rounded shoulder to the short cylindrical neck w/a flat rim, frosted clear ground overlaid in rich honey amber & acid-etched overall w/blossoms, buds & leafy vines, highly polished surface, signed in a japanesque-style cameo signature ..................................... **$1,610.00**
**Cameo vase,** 9⅜" h., flattened oval cylindrical body in frosted clear layered in deep red maroon & etched w/feathery blossoms & butterflies in flight, signed in cameo .................. **2,300.00**
**Cameo vase,** 12¼" h., slender flattened ovoid body tapering to a short cylindrical neck, bright yellow frosted ground overlaid in violet, purple & dark brown, mold-blown & etched w/hyacinths & leaves, cameo signature..................................... **8,625.00**
**Cameo vase,** 12½" h., swelled cylindrical form in grey overlaid in purple & cut w/iris blossoms & leafage, fire-polished, signed in cameo, ca. 1900 (ILLUS. top next column)......................................... **1,840.00**

*Gallé Iris Vase*

**Vase,** 5¼" h., engraved & enameled crystal, baluster-form w/a wide disc foot, decorated w/a scene of a hunter w/a gun, hound & their prey on the front & a scrolling design on the back, in red, black & white repeating enamel borders, inscribed on the base "Emile E (cross) G Gallé - Nancy"....................................... **1,265.00**
**Vase,** 6½" h., etched, engraved & enameled cylindrical body w/a trefoil rim, bright peacock blue w/gold-accented pink & white enamel decoration on etched & wheel-carved blossoms w/seven star-forms inside the body, elaborate sunflower "Gallé" on the base w/"Modelé et decor deposé - Coompos EG" in script, some interior stain (ILLUS. below) .. **2,300.00**

*Etched & Enameled Gallé Vase*

# HEISEY

*Numerous types of fine glass were made by A. H. Heisey & Co., Newark, Ohio, from 1895. The company's trade-mark—an H enclosed within a diamond—has become known to most glass collectors. The company's name and molds were acquired by Imperial Glass Co., Bellaire, Ohio, in 1958, and some pieces have been reissued. The glass listed below consists of miscellaneous pieces and types. Also see PATTERN GLASS under Glass.*

*Heisey Diamond "H" Mark*

**Ashtray,** coaster, round, Crystolite patt., clear, 4".................................... **$8.00**

**Ashtray,** Lariat patt, clear, 4"............... **15.00**

**Ashtray,** Winged Scroll patt., green...... **75.00**

**Basket,** footed, Lariat patt., clear, 8½" h. .............................................. **175.00**

**Bowl,** nut, dolphin footed, Empress patt., Sahara (yellow)......................... **25.00**

**Bowl,** chow chow, 4" d., Pleat & Panel patt., Flamingo (pink) ......................... **18.00**

**Bowl,** preserve, 5" d., handled, Empress patt., Sahara...................... **24.00**

**Bowl,** mint, 6" d., footed, Empress patt., Moongleam (green) .................. **45.00**

**Bowl,** 6" d., Queen Ann patt., clear....... **10.00**

**Bowl,** lily, 7" d., oval, Queen Ann patt., Orchid etching, clear................ **45.00**

**Bowl,** 8" d., Lodestar patt., Dawn (light grey)............................................. **85.00**

**Bowl,** 8" d., low, footed, Rose etching, Flamingo ............................................. **65.00**

**Bowl,** nasturtium, 8" d., round, Twist patt., pink ............................................. **68.00**

**Bowl,** relish/pickle, leaf, Crystolite patt., clear............................................. **25.00**

**Bowl,** gardenia, 9" d., Queen Ann patt., Orchid etching, clear................. **60.00**

**Bowl,** 9½" d., crimped, Queen Ann patt., Orchid etching, clear.................. **60.00**

**Bowl,** 10" d., heavy silver floral overlay, Ridgeleigh patt. .................... **45.00**

**Bowl,** 10" d., Lariat patt., clear............. **50.00**

**Bowl,** 11" d., dolphin footed, Queen Ann patt., Danish Princess etching, clear.................................................. **51.00**

**Bowl,** 11" d., footed, Empress patt., clear...................................................... **40.00**

**Bowl,** 12" d., gardenia, Crystolite patt., clear...................................... **30.00**

**Bowl,** 12" d., cupped, Lariat patt., clear...................................................... **39.00**

**Bowl,** 12" d., Lariat patt., clear............. **20.00**

**Bowl,** floral, 12" d., oval, four-footed Twist patt., clear ............................... **45.00**

**Bowl,** floral, 12" d., Waverly patt., Orchid etching, clear.......................... **75.00**

**Bowl,** 13" d., flared w/applied clear lion's head decoration, Empress patt., clear...................................... **300.00**

**Bowl,** floral, 13" d., oval, Lariat patt., Moonglo cutting, clear ...................... **35.00**

**Bowl,** finger, Old Sandwich patt., clear...................................................... **15.00**

**Bowl,** finger, Old Sandwich patt., Sahara ............................................... **60.00**

**Bowl,** individual nut, handled, Rose etching, Flamingo ............................... **20.00**

**Butter dish,** cov., Orchid etching, clear, 1 lb. ...................................... **150.00**

**Butter dish,** cov., round, Plantation patt., clear, 5" d............................... **115.00**

**Cake stand,** Orchid etching, clear, 14" d. ................................................ **210.00**

**Candelabra,** two-light w/bobeche, New Era patt., clear, pr. .................... **200.00**

**Candle block,** Ridgeleigh patt., clear, 3", pr. ................................................ **47.00**

**Candlestick,** Crystolite patt., clear ....... **24.00**

**Candlestick,** Mercury patt., clear, 4" h. ..................................................... **15.00**

**Candlestick,** Mercury patt., Orchid etching, clear, 4" h. ............................ **30.00**

**Candlesticks,** Empress patt., Sahara, 6" h., pr. ............................................ **210.00**

**Candlesticks,** Empress patt., clear, 7" h., pr. .............................................. **90.00**

**Candlesticks,** two-light, Kohinoor patt., clear, pr................................... **225.00**

**Candlesticks,** one-light, Lariat patt., clear, pr............................................. **30.00**

**Candlesticks,** Mars patt., clear, 4¼" h., pr. ............................................ **60.00**

**Candlesticks,** Mercury patt., Rose etching, clear, pr. ................................. **80.00**

**Candlesticks,** Minuet etching, clear, pr. ........................................................ **95.00**

**Candlesticks,** Parallel Quarter patt. clear, 3¼" h., pr. ................................. **55.00**

**Candlesticks,** two-light, Plantation patt., clear, pr................................... **160.00**

**Candlesticks,** Ridgeleigh patt., clear, 2" h., pr. .............................................. **35.00**

*Trident Pattern Candlestick*

**Candlesticks w/bobeches,**
Ridgeleigh patt., clear, pr.................. 265.00

**Candlesticks,** two-light, Thumbprint &
Panel patt., Flamingo, pr. ................. 250.00

**Candlesticks,** No. 134 Trident,
Alexandrite (light lavender), pr....... 1,350.00

**Candlesticks,** two-light, Trident patt.,
clear, pr................................................ 65.00

**Candlesticks,** two-light, Trident patt.,
Sahara, pr. (ILLUS. of one) .............. 125.00

**Candlesticks,** No. 136 Triplex, Cobalt
Blue, pr. ......................................... 1,100.00

**Candlesticks,** three-light, Waverly
patt., Orchid etching, clear, pr. ......... 175.00

**Candy box,** cov., Coventry patt.,
Zircon (pale blue).............................. 33.00

**Candy dish,** cov., Lariat patt., clear...... 50.00

**Celery tray,** Ridgeleigh patt., clear,
12" l.................................................... 38.00

**Celery tray,** Waverly patt., Rose
etching, clear, 12" l............................ 60.00

**Champagne,** Charter Oak patt.,
Flamingo............................................. 13.00

**Champagne,** saucer-type, Colonial
patt., clear........................................... 8.00

**Champagne,** Lariat patt., clear, 6 oz. ... 11.00

**Champagne,** saucer-type, Old
Sandwich patt., Sahara, 5 oz............. 35.00

**Champagne,** saucer-type, Orchid
etching, clear ..................................... 30.00

**Champagne,** saucer-type, Rose
etching, clear, 6 oz. ........................... 35.00

**Champagne,** saucer-type, Spanish
patt., Cobalt Blue .............................. 85.00

**Champagne,** Spanish patt., Killarney
cutting, clear ...................................... 30.00

**Champagne,** Suez patt., clear, 6 oz. ..... 13.00

**Cigarette holder,** cov., footed, Orchid
etching, clear ................................... 165.00

**Cigarette holder,** cov., Rose etching,
clear.................................................. 100.00

**Claret,** New Era patt., clear, 4 oz......... 38.00

**Claret,** Orchid etching, clear, 4½ oz. ..... 135.00

**Claret,** Rose etching (No. 5072), clear.. 130.00

**Coaster,** Lariat patt., clear, 4" d............. 7.00

**Cocktail,** Crystolite patt., clear............. 25.00

**Cocktail,** Lariat patt., Moonglo cutting,
clear, 3½ oz. ...................................... 18.00

**Cocktail,** New Era patt., clear, 3½ oz. ... 22.00

**Cocktail,** Orchid etching, clear, 4 oz..... 35.00

**Cocktail,** Rose etching, clear, 4 oz....... 40.00

**Cologne bottle w/original stopper,**
Ridgeleigh patt., clear........................ 55.00

**Comport,** cheese w/14" plate, Orchid
etching, clear ................................... 195.00

**Compote,** 7" d., Charter Oak patt.,
Flamingo............................................. 75.00

**Compote,** cov., 6" d., Pleat & Panel
patt., Flamingo.................................... 95.00

**Compote,** cov., 8½" h., footed, Pleat
& Panel patt., Flamingo ..................... 95.00

**Compote,** jelly, Orchid etching, clear,
6½" h. ................................................ 43.00

**Compote,** Yeoman patt., Moongleam... 40.00

**Condiment jar,** w/sterling silver lid,
Grape patt., clear, 4½" h.................... 55.00

**Condiment set:** salt, pepper & cov.
mustard in metal holder; Victorian
etching, clear, the set ...................... 135.00

**Cordial,** Graceful patt., Orchid
etching, clear ................................... 150.00

**Cordial,** Kenilworth patt. stem
w/Sahara bowl ................................. 150.00

**Cordial,** Kenilworth patt. stem w/clear
bowl .................................................. 145.00

**Cordial,** Orchid etching (No. 5022),
clear.................................................. 135.00

**Creamer & open sugar bowl,** Rose
etching, clear, pr. ............................... 45.00

**Creamer & sugar bowl,** Crystolite
patt., cranberry-stained, pr. ............... 65.00

**Creamer & sugar bowl,** Orchid
etching, clear, pr. ............................... 55.00

**Creamer & sugar bowl w/tray,**
Queen Ann patt., Orchid etching,
clear, the set .................................... 125.00

**Cruet w/original stopper,** Crystolite
patt., clear, 3 oz. ............................... 45.00

**Cruet w/original stopper,** Plantation
patt., clear.......................................... 90.00

**Cruet w/original silver trimmed
stopper,** Saturn patt., clear .............. 48.00

**Cruet w/original stopper,** Stanhope
patt., clear........................................ 179.00

**Cup & saucer,** Crystolite patt., clear .... 27.00

**Cup & footed saucer,** Empress patt.,
Sahara............................................... 39.00

**Decanter w/stopper,** Orchid etching,
No. 4036, clear, pt. ............................ **275.00**
**French dressing bottle w/stopper,**
Ridgeleigh patt., clear ......................... **50.00**
**French dressing bottle w/stopper,**
Victorian patt., clear ........................... **50.00**
**Goblet,** Charter Oak patt., Flamingo..... **22.00**
**Goblet,** Colonial patt., clear ................. **20.00**
**Goblet,** water, No. 5003, Crystolite,
clear, 10 oz. ........................................ **28.00**
**Goblet,** footed, Gascony patt.,
Sahara, 11 oz. .................................... **95.00**
**Goblet,** Ipswich patt., clear, 10 oz. ....... **24.00**
**Goblet,** King Arthur patt., Moongleam .. **29.00**
**Goblet,** water, blown, Lariat patt.,
clear ................................................... **22.00**
**Goblet,** water, pressed, Lariat patt.,
clear, 9 oz. ......................................... **20.00**
**Goblet,** water, Minuet etching, clear,
9 oz. ................................................... **35.00**
**Goblet,** Old Glory patt., Renaissance
etching, clear ..................................... **22.00**
**Goblet,** Old Williamsburg patt., clear,
9 oz. ................................................... **15.00**
**Goblet,** Orchid etching, clear, 10 oz. .... **34.00**
**Goblet,** Park Lane patt., Briar Cliff
cutting, clear ...................................... **40.00**
**Goblet,** water, Rose etching, clear,
9 oz. ................................................... **45.00**
**Goblet,** Spanish patt., Cobalt Blue,
7½" h. ................................................. **87.00**
**Goblet,** low, Suez patt., clear, 9 oz. ...... **15.00**
**Goblet,** Wabash patt., Pied Piper
etching, clear ..................................... **25.00**
**Goblet,** Waverly patt., clear ................. **22.00**
**Goblet,** Yeoman patt., clear, 5¼" h....... **18.00**
**Goblets,** Charter Oak patt., clear,
4 pcs. ................................................. **48.00**
**Goblets,** creme de menthe, Puritan
patt., clear, 2½ oz., 5 pcs. .................. **50.00**
**Goblets,** No. 3335 w/etched stems,
8 pcs. ................................................. **195.00**
**Goblets,** Old Sandwich patt., Sahara,
5 pcs. ................................................. **90.00**
**Ice bucket,** Pillows patt., clear ........... **495.00**
**Ice bucket,** Waverly patt., clear .......... **295.00**
**Jar,** cov., crushed fruit, Greek Key
patt., clear .......................................... **650.00**
**Jar,** cov., jam, Crystolite patt., clear...... **50.00**
**Mayonnaise bowl,** Twist patt., Sahara... **45.00**
**Mayonnaise bowl,** underplate & ladle,
Rose etching, clear, 3 pcs.................... **72.00**
**Mayonnaise liner,** Lariat patt., clear .... **18.00**
**Molasses tub,** large, Punty Band
patt., clear .......................................... **125.00**
**Nut cup,** Empress patt., Flamingo ........ **26.00**
**Nut cup,** Queen Ann patt., clear ........... **15.00**

**Oil & vinegar cruets w/stoppers,**
Saturn patt., clear, the set .................. **95.00**
**Oil & vinegar cruets w/stoppers,**
Twist patt., Sahara, the set............... **125.00**
**Pitcher,** iced tea, Orchid etching,
clear, 64 oz. ....................................... **450.00**
**Pitcher,** Winged Scroll patt., emerald
green w/gold trim, large ................... **165.00**
**Pitcher set:** dolphin footed pitcher
w/six 8 oz. tumblers; Empress patt.,
Moongleam, 7 pcs. ......................... **650.00**
**Plate,** 6" d., Empress patt.,
Moongleam ........................................ **10.00**
**Plate,** 6" d., Empress patt., Sahara....... **14.00**
**Plate,** 6" d., Old Sandwich patt.,
Sahara ................................................ **20.00**
**Plate,** 6" d., square, Old Sandwich
patt., clear .......................................... **9.00**
**Plate,** salad, 7" d., Orchid etching,
clear ................................................... **20.00**
**Plate,** salad, 7" d., Waverly patt.,
Rose etching, clear ............................ **20.00**
**Plate,** 8" d., Ipswich patt., clear............. **28.00**
**Plate,** luncheon, 8" d., Minuet etching,
clear ................................................... **20.00**
**Plate,** salad, 8" d., Orchid etching,
clear ................................................... **22.00**
**Plate,** salad, 8½" d., Crystolite patt.,
clear ................................................... **17.00**
**Plate,** 9" d., square, Empress patt.,
Sahara ................................................ **20.00**
**Plate,** sandwich, 11" d., center
handle, Rose etching, clear ............. **200.00**
**Plate,** salver, 12" d., footed, Waverly
patt., Orchid etching, clear............... **225.00**
**Plate,** torte, 14" d., Rose etching,
clear ................................................... **87.00**
**Plate,** sandwich, 14" d., Waverly patt.,
Orchid etching, clear.......................... **75.00**
**Plate,** torte, 14" d., Waverly patt.,
Orchid etching, clear.......................... **80.00**
**Platter,** 14" l., center handle, Waverly
patt., Orchid etching, clear............... **250.00**
**Puff box,** cov., Crystolite patt., clear..... **75.00**
**Punch cup,** Colonial patt. (No. 341),
clear ................................................... **12.00**
**Punch cup,** Greek Key patt.,
Flamingo............................................. **30.00**
**Punch set:** bowl, 20" d. underplate,
twelve cups & ladle; Crystolite patt.,
clear, 15 pcs. ................................... **300.00**
**Punch set:** punch bowl, underplate,
nine cups; Colonial patt., clear, 11
pcs. ................................................... **275.00**
**Relish dish,** three-part, Crystolite
patt., clear, 9"..................................... **40.00**

**Relish dish,** three-part, Orchid
etching (No. 1509), clear, 7" .............. **55.00**

**Relish dish,** three-part, oval, Orchid
etching, clear, 11" l. ........................... **65.00**

**Relish dish,** two-part, oval,
Ridgeleigh patt., clear, 7".................. **35.00**

**Relish dish,** four-part, round, Waverly
patt., Rose etching, clear, 9"............. **100.00**

**Salt & pepper shakers w/original
tops,** Fandango patt., clear, pr. .......... **95.00**

**Salt & pepper shakers w/original
tops,** Plantation patt., clear, pr. .......... **65.00**

**Sherbet,** Crystolite patt., clear .............. **18.00**

**Sherbet,** Danish Princess cutting,
clear...................................................... **20.00**

**Sherbet,** Gascony patt., Sahara, 6 oz..... **50.00**

**Sherbet,** Ipswich patt., clear ................. **18.00**

**Sherbet,** blown, Lariat patt., clear,
5½ oz..................................................... **14.00**

**Sherbet,** Lariat patt., Moonglo
cutting, clear, 5½ oz. ......................... **15.00**

**Sherbet,** New Era patt., clear, 6 oz....... **16.00**

**Sherbet,** Orchid etching, clear, 6 oz. .... **30.00**

**Sherbet,** Rose etching, clear, 6 oz. ...... **30.00**

**Sherry,** Orchid etching, No. 5025,
clear, 2 oz. ........................................ **125.00**

**Sugar bowl,** Orchid etching
(No. 1519), clear.............................. **30.00**

**Sugar bowl,** cov., Pineapple & Fan
patt., clear............................................ **40.00**

**Syrup pitcher w/original top,** Punty
Band patt., clear .............................. **195.00**

**Toothpick holder,** Prison Stripe patt.,
clear.................................................... **425.00**

**Tumbler,** juice, footed, Orchid
etching, clear, 5 oz. ............................ **45.00**

**Tumbler,** juice, footed, Provincial
patt., clear............................................ **11.00**

**Tumbler,** juice, footed, Rose etching,
clear, 5 oz. .......................................... **48.00**

**Tumbler,** Empress patt., Flamingo,
8 oz...................................................... **50.00**

**Tumbler,** Empress patt., Moongleam,
8 oz...................................................... **50.00**

**Tumbler,** footed, Yeoman patt.,
Sahara, 8 oz. ....................................... **18.00**

**Tumbler,** Provincial patt., Zircon, 9 oz. .. **95.00**

**Tumbler,** iced tea, Crystolite patt.,
clear...................................................... **33.00**

**Tumbler,** iced tea, footed, Lariatt patt.,
Moonglo cutting, clear, 12 oz............... **25.00**

**Tumbler,** iced tea, Rose etching,
clear, 12 oz. ........................................ **60.00**

**Tumbler,** soda, footed, New Era patt.,
clear, 12 oz. ........................................ **25.00**

**Tumbler,** iced tea, Orchid etching,
clear, 12 oz. ........................................ **60.00**

**Tumbler,** Provincial patt., Zircon,
12 oz.................................................. **110.00**

**Tumbler,** iced tea, footed, Rose
etching, clear ...................................... **55.00**

**Vase,** 7" h., Lariat patt., clear.............. **48.00**

**Vase,** oval, 7" h., Yeoman patt.,
Moongleam........................................... **95.00**

**Vase,** 8" h., Ridgeleigh patt., Sahara .. **135.00**

**Vase,** 10" h., Saturn patt., Dawn ........ **300.00**

**Wine,** Empress patt., green ................. **40.00**

**Wine,** Fancy Loop patt., green w/gold
trim....................................................... **65.00**

**Wine,** Locket on Chain patt., clear,
early 20th c. ........................................ **57.00**

**Wine,** Minuet etching, clear, 2½ oz....... **65.00**

**Wine,** New Era patt., clear, 3 oz. .......... **38.00**

**Wine,** Orchid etching, clear, 3 oz. ......... **70.00**

**Wine,** Rose etching, clear, 3 oz. .......... **80.00**

**Wine,** Victorian patt., clear, 2½ oz. ....... **24.00**

## HISTORICAL &
## COMMEMORATIVE

*Reference numbers are to Bessie M.
Lindsey's book,* American Historical Glass.

**Battleship Maine dish,** cov.,
"Remember the Maine" inscribed on
each side of base, green, 7½" l.,
2¾" h., No. 465.............................. **$125.00**

**Battleship Wheeling dish,** cov., milk
white, 6⅜" l., 3⅝" w., 4" h., No. 470 ... **75.00**

**British Lion paperwieght,** head of
lion & front paws on round base,
Gillinder & Sons, unsigned, frosted,
2½" d., 2½" h. .................................... **220.00**

**Carpenter's Hall (Washington
Centennial patt.) bread platter,**
clear, No. 28 ....................................... **95.00**

**Constitution platter,** eagle & banner
center, clear, 12½" l., No. 43 ............. **75.00**

**Dewey (Admiral) pitcher,** bust
portrait of Dewey & flagship Olympia
reverse, w/mounted cannons,
crossed rifles, U.S. & Cuban flags &
stacks of cannon balls toward base,
clear, 9½" h., No. 400 (ILLUS. top
next page)....................................... **125.00**

**Dewey (Admiral) statuette,** bust
of Dewey, frosted, 5" h.,
No. 383...................... **120.00 to 145.00**

**Garfield Star plate,** frosted bust of
Garfield center, star border, clear,
6" d., No. 299 ................. **35.00 to 55.00**

**Garfield plate,** frosted bust of Garfield
center, 1-0-1 border, clear, 9" d.,
No. 300 ............................................... **62.00**

*Admiral Dewey Pitcher*

**Gladstone plate,** "For the Million,"
  clear, 9½" d........................................ **40.00**

**Grant Memorial plate,** bust portrait of
  Grant center, laurel wreath on
  stippled border, amber, 10" d.,
  No. 288 ............................................. **75.00**

**Knights of Labor mug,** laborer
  clasping hands w/bearded man
  wearing high hat & frock coat, handle
  w/thumbrest, inscribed "Arbitration,"
  clear, 3" d., 7" h., No. 514 ..... **45.00 to 70.00**

**Lee (Major General) Fitzhugh plate,**
  bust portrait transfer of the Major
  General center, 1-0-1 border,
  clear, 5½" d., No. 378......... **65.00 to 105.00**

**Liberty Bell Signer's platter,** clear,
  9½ x 13", No. 42.................. **65.00 to 90.00**

**Lincoln paperweight,** round w/turned
  sides & beveled rim, bust within
  frosted circle, 3⅛" d., No. 274 .......... **375.00**

**Lind (Jenny) compote,** milk white,
  8¼" d., 8" h., No. 424 ....... **125.00 to 150.00**

**Louisiana Purchase Exposition
  tumbler,** features scenes of St.
  Louis Exposition in relief, clear, 5" h.,
  No. 107 ............................................. **45.00**

**McCormick Reaper platter,** clear,
  8 x 13", No. 119 ............................ **158.00**

**McKinley plate,** bust portrait of
  McKinley center, openwork Gothic
  patt. border, milk white, 9" d.,
  No. 341 ................................ **20.00 to 40.00**

**McKinley (William B.) cup,** cov., bust
  portrait opposite handle, "Protection
  & Prosperity," clear, overall 5" h.,
  No. 335 ............................................. **85.00**

**McKinley Gold Standard tray,** full-
  length figure of McKinley standing on
  plank inscribed "Gold," w/Feather
  Duster patt. border, clear, 7¾ x 10¼",
  No. 332 ............................ **600.00 to 700.00**

**Railroad train platter,** Union Pacific
  Engine No. 350, clear, 9 x 12",
  No. 134 ............................................. **85.00**

**Rock of Ages bread tray,** clear,
  No. 236 ............................................. **75.00**

**Rock of Ages bread tray,** milk white,
  No. 236 ........................................... **165.00**

**Roosevelt (Theodore) platter,**
  frosted portrait center, Teddy bears,
  etc. border, clear, 7¾ x 10¼",
  No. 357 ........................................... **197.00**

**Three Graces plate,** "Faith, Hope &
  Charity," clear, 10" d.,
  No. 230................................ **30.00 to 55.00**

# IMPERIAL

*Imperial Glass Company, Bellaire, Ohio,
was organized in 1901 and was in continuous
production, except for very brief periods, until
its closing in June 1984. It had been a major
producer of Carnival Glass earlier in this
century and also produced other types of glass
including an Art Glass line called "Free Hand
Ware" during the 1920s and its "Jewels" about
1916. The company acquired a number of
molds of other earlier factories, including the
Cambridge and A. H. Heisey companies, and
reissued numerous items through the years.
Also see CARNIVAL GLASS under Glass.*

*Various Imperial Marks*

## CANDLEWICK PATTERN

**Ashtray,** eagle-shaped, No. 1776/1,
  clear, 6½" d..................................... **$75.00**

**Bowl,** 4¾" d., 2" h., round, two
  handled, No. 400/42B, clear, ............. **13.00**

**Bowl,** 5½" d., No. 400/53, clear ........... **90.00**

**Bowl,** sauce, 5½" d., No. 400/23,
  Viennese blue (light blue) .................. **65.00**

**Bowl,** 8½" d., No. 400/69B, clear.......... **50.00**

**Bowl,** fruit, 9" d, footed, No. 400/67B, Fuchsia cut, clear ............................ **150.00**

**Bowl,** 10½" d., bell-shaped, No. 400/63B, clear............................. **60.00**

**Bowl,** 12" d., No. 400/106B, clear........ **70.00**

**Butter dish,** cov., No. 400/144, clear, 5½"..................................................... **45.00**

**Butter dish,** cov., No. 400/276, clear .. **165.00**

**Cake plate,** birthday, seventy-two candle holes, No. 400/160, clear, 13" d. ..................................................... **550.00**

**Cake plate,** No. 400/103D, clear ........ **115.00**

**Cake plate,** No. 400/670, clear............. **65.00**

**Cake stand,** low foot, No. 400/67D, clear, 10" d........................................ **50.00**

**Candleholders,** flower, No. 400/40C, clear, pr. ..................................... **120.00**

**Candleholders,** two-light, No. 400/100, clear, pr. ..................................... **50.00**

**Candleholders,** handled, bowled-up base, No. 400/90, clear, 5" h., pr. ..... **110.00**

**Candleholders,** mushroom-form, No. 400/86, clear, pr. ......................... **60.00**

**Candleholders,** No. 400/40F, clear, 6" d., pr. ....................................... **90.00**

**Candy dish,** cov., footed, No. 400/140, clear .............................................. **310.00**

**Celery dish,** No. 400/58, clear, 8½" oval................................................ **28.00**

**Compote,** 5" d., tri-stem, No. 400/220, clear .............................................. **150.00**

**Compote,** 5½" d., No. 400/66B, clear... **32.00**

**Compote,** 8" d., No. 400-48F, clear.... **125.00**

**Creamer,** sugar bowl & tray, footed, bead handle, No. 400/30, clear, 3 pcs. ..................................................... **25.00**

**Cup & saucer,** coffee, No. 400/37, clear.................................................... **7.00**

**Cup & saucer,** tea, No. 400/35, clear..... **7.00**

**Plate,** bread & butter, 6" d., No. 400/1D, clear....................................................... **8.00**

**Plate,** salad, 7" d., No. 400/3D, clear.... **10.00**

**Plate,** salad, 8" d., No. 400/5D, clear...... **9.00**

**Puff jar,** cov. three-bead finial on lid, clear..................................................... **125.00**

**Relish dish,** three-part, No. 400/208, clear, 10" l........................................ **125.00**

**Relish tray,** three-part, No. 400/56, clear, 10½" d..................................... **70.00**

**Salad fork & spoon,** No. 400/75, clear, pr.................................................. **30.00**

**Salt & pepper shakers w/original tops,** bulbous, No. 400/96, clear, pr. ...................................................... **15.00**

**Salt & pepper shakers w/original tops,** footed, bead base, No. 400/190, clear, pr..................................... **47.00**

**Salt dip,** No. 400/61, clear, 2".............. **14.00**

**Tumbler,** old fashioned, No. 400/18, clear, 7 oz. ....................................... **23.00**

**Vase,** 8" h., beaded handle, No. 400/87C, clear............................. **28.00**

**Vase,** bud, 8½" h., footed, No. 400/28C, clear...................................................... **110.00**

## CAPE COD PATTERN

**Bottle,** condiment, No. 160/224, 6 oz., clear...................................................... **80.00**

**Bowl,** 4½" d., No. 160/1W, clear............. **9.00**

**Bowl,** baked apple, 6" d., No. 160/53X, clear ..................................................... **10.00**

**Bowl,** 11¾" d., No. 160/10B, clear........ **75.00**

**Bowl,** salad, 12" d., No. 160/75B, clear...................................................... **45.00**

**Butter dish,** cov., handled, No. 160/144, clear, 5"......................... **40.00**

**Cake plate,** four-footed, No. 160/220, clear...................................................... **75.00**

**Candy dish,** cov., No. 160/110, clear, 1 lb......................................................... **70.00**

**Celery dish,** No. 160/189, clear, 10½" oval....................................................... **45.00**

**Claret,** No. 1602, Azalea (pink), 5 oz.... **20.00**

**Claret,** No. 1602, Verde (yellowish green), 5 oz. ................................. **18.00**

**Coaster w/spoon rest,** No. 160/76, clear...................................................... **11.00**

**Cocktail,** stemmed, No. 1602, clear, 3½ oz. .................................................. **7.00**

**Compote,** cov., 6" d., footed, No. 160/140, clear ............................. **70.00**

**Cordial,** No. 1602, clear, 1½ oz............ **12.00**

**Cruet w/stopper,** No. 160/119, clear, 4 oz....................................................... **24.00**

**Cruet w/stopper,** No. 160/70, clear, 5 oz....................................................... **40.00**

**Decanter w/original stopper,** No. 160/163, clear, 30 oz. ........................ **60.00**

**Decanter w/original stopper,** No. 160/163, red, 30 oz......................... **300.00**

**Decanter w/original stopper,** handled, heavy chrome trim, clear ... **225.00**

**Decanter set:** decanter & stopper w/eight 16 oz. clarets; Verde, 9 pcs. set....................................................... **275.00**

**Desert bowl,** tab handle, No. 160/197, clear, 4½" d......................... **25.00**

**Egg cup,** No. 160/225, clear................. **35.00**

**Goblet,** water, No. 1602, clear, 9 oz. .... **10.00**

**Goblet,** water, No. 1602, Verde, 9 oz. .. **23.00**
**Goblet,** water, No. 160, clear, 14 oz. ..... **10.00**
**Horseradish jar,** cov., No. 160/226,
   clear, 5 oz. ......................................... **75.00**
**Mustard,** cov., No. 160/156, clear ........ **25.00**
**Parfait,** stemmed, No. 1602, clear,
   6 oz. ..................................................... **13.00**
**Pitcher,** clear, 64 oz............................. **60.00**
**Pitcher,** blown, clear, 80 oz. ............... **150.00**
**Plate,** salad, 8" d., No. 160/5D, clear.... **10.00**
**Plate,** salad, 8" d., No. 160/5D, Verde .. **18.00**
**Plate,** 8½" d., handled, No. 160/62D,
   clear..................................................... **30.00**
**Plate,** 11½" d., handled, No. 160/145D,
   clear ..................................................... **35.00**
**Plate,** 14" d., regular edge,
   No. 160/75D, clear.............................. **65.00**
**Punch set:** 17" tray w/punch bowl
   No. 160/20, ladle & twelve cups;
   clear, 15 pcs. ..................................... **275.00**
**Relish dish,** three-part, No. 160/55,
   clear, 9½" oval ..................................... **25.00**
**Relish,** four-part, No. 160/56, clear,
   9½" l....................................................... **40.00**
**Salt & pepper shakers w/original**
   **tops,** footed, No. 160/116, clear, pr. .. **20.00**
**Server,** No. 160/103D, clear, 11" d. ..... **110.00**
**Sherbet,** tall, No. 1602, clear, 6 oz. ........ **5.00**
**Sundae,** low, No. 1602, clear, 6 oz. ......... **5.00**
**Tumbler,** juice, No. 1600, clear, 6 oz...... **7.00**
**Tumbler,** old fashioned, No. 160,
   clear, 7 oz. ........................................... **10.00**
**Tumbler,** tea, footed, No. 1602, clear,
   12 oz.................................................... **13.00**
**Whiskey set:** decanter w/stopper &
   six matching tumblers; decanter No.
   160/212, clear, the set ...................... **155.00**
**Wine,** No. 1602, clear, 3 oz.................... **9.00**

## MISCELLANEOUS PATTERNS & LINES

**Ashtray,** square, marked "IG,"
   chocolate slag, 6" d. ........................... **22.00**
**Bowl,** 8" d., caramel slag w/satin
   finish, Rose patt., marked "IG,"........... **28.00**
**Bowl,** 9" d., red slag w/glossy finish,
   Rose patt., marked "IG" ...................... **40.00**
**Bowl,** nappy w/handle, 5" d., caramel
   slag, Floral patt., marked "IG" ............ **28.00**
**Cruet w/stopper,** caramel slag,
   Octagon patt., marked "IG" ................. **32.00**
**Jar,** cov., figural owl, green slag
   w/glossy finish, marked "IG" .............. **60.00**
**Jar,** cov., figural owl, purple slag
   w/glossy finish, marked "IG" .............. **68.00**
**Jar,** cov., figural owl, green slag
   w/satin finish, marked "IG" ................. **60.00**

**Pitcher,** green slag w/glossy finish,
   Windmill patt., marked "IG" ................ **45.00**
**Pitcher,** red slag w/glossy finish
   Windmill patt., marked "IG" ................ **45.00**
**Pitcher,** purple slag w/glossy finish,
   Windmill patt., marked "IG" ................ **45.00**
**Toothpick holder,** caramel slag,
   Octagon patt., marked "IG" ................ **10.00**

## LACY

*Lacy Glass is a general term developed by collectors many years ago to cover the earliest type of pressed glass produced in this country. "Lacy" refers to the fact that most of these early patterns consisted of scrolls and geometric designs against a finely stippled background which gives the glass the look of fine lace. Formerly this glass was often referred to as "Sandwich" for the Boston & Sandwich Glass Company of Sandwich, Massachusetts which produced a great deal of this ware. Today, however, collectors realize that many other factories on the East Coast and in the Pittsburgh, Pennsylvania and Wheeling, West Virginia areas also made lacy glass from the 1820s into the 1840s. All pieces listed are clear unless otherwise noted. Numbers after salt dips refer to listings in* Pressed Glass Salt Dishes of the Lacy Period, 1825-1850, *by Logan W. and Dorothy B. Neal.*

**Bowl,** 7⅞"d., round, Shields &
   Anchors patt., attributed to the
   Providence Flint Glass Works, ca.
   1830-35 (minor mold roughness, two
   tipped scallops)............................. **$132.00**
**Bowl,** 8⅝"d., round, Princess Feather
   patt., probably Midwestern,
   amethystine tint, ca. 1830-50 (mold
   roughness, several lightly tipped &
   one chipped scallop)....................... **198.00**

*Fan & Scroll Lacy Bowl*

**Bowl,** 9 x 10¾", oval, Fan & Scroll patt., large diamond in the center, attributed to New England, ca. 1830-45, rim chip w/loss of two scallops, four tipped scallops & usual roughness (ILLUS. bottom previous page) ................................. **385.00**

**Compote,** open, 11" d., 6¾" h., Peacock & Feather patt., wide shallow bowl attached w/a wafer to the plain flaring hexagonal pedestal base, New England area, ca. 1840 (non-disfiguring spall on side of base)............................................. **1,210.00**

**Lamps,** whale oil, a blown conical font attached w/a bladed wafer to the pressed thick cup plate base w/a scallop fan-design border, w/period double tin drop-in burners, 6⅞" h., pr. (one w/small flake on one base scallop, one w/two small flakes on two scallops) .................................. **2,200.00**

**Plate,** 9" d., round, Oak Leaves patt., New England, ca. 1835-50 (six tipped scallops).................................. **77.00**

**Plate,** 9¼" w., octagonal, Beehive patt., attributed to the Boston & Sandwich Glass Co., ca. 1830-50 (two lightly tipped scallops)................. **88.00**

**Salt dip,** cov., casket-shaped, upright S-scroll ends & reclining S-scroll feet, domed cover w/scrolls & pineapple finial, attributed to the Boston & Sandwich Glass Co., CD 2a (shallow spalls on both sides of cover)............................................. **1,100.00**

**Salt dip,** Henry Clay Train patt., sleigh-shaped w/scrolled ends flanking a center shield, the rectangular bottom w/a scene of an early train, attributed to Boston & Sandwich, HL 4 (mold roughness on scrolls) ......................................... **1,100.00**

**Salt dip,** model of a sleigh on runners, attributed to Boston & Sandwich, SH 1 (mold roughness on upper portion of highest scrolls & rear tip of one runner) .................................. **4,125.00**

**Salt dip,** sleigh-shaped, Eagle patt., pairs of eagles looking over their shoulders & flanking a shield form the sides, attributed to Boston & Sandwich, opal opaque (EE 3b) ....... **770.00**

**Salt dip,** Washington-Lafayette patt., rectangular w/scalloped rim & columnar corners, small medallions on the sides, attributed to the New England Glass Co., HL 1a (shallow spall along top rim, open bubble on base corner) ................................. **935.00**

**Sugar bowl,** cov., Gothic Arch patt., attributed to the Boston & Sandwich Glass Company, alabaster-clambroth, 5⅜" h. (minor flaking & rim roughness)................................. **385.00**

**Sugar bowl,** cov., oblong boat-shape, knobby base band below the rounded sides w/curved end ribs flanking a panel of diamond point below a curved rim band of heavy knobs, scroll end rim handles, the domed cover w/a lappet border band & florette finial, attributed to New England, ca. 1830 (severe mold roughness on cover)...................... **9,900.00**

## LALIQUE

*Fine glass, which includes numerous extraordinary molded articles, has been made by the glasshouse established by René Lalique early in this century in France. The firm was carried on by his son, Marc, until his death in 1977 and is now headed by Marc's daughter, Marie-Claude. All Lalique glass is marked, usually on or near the bottom with either an engraved or molded signature. Unless otherwise noted, we list only those pieces marked "R. Lalique" produced before the death of René Lalique in 1945.*

**R.LALIQUE**

**FRANCE**

**R LALIQUE**

**FRANCE**

*R. Lalique France N°3152*

*Lalique marks*

**Centerpiece,** illuminated, "Oiseau de Feu," a large half-round clear flat disc molded in medium-relief w/a mythological figure of a fire bird, mounted on a square bronze base cast w/stylized butterflies, molded mark on glass, base inscribed "1918" & "a928," introduced in 1922, overall 16¾" h........................... **$10,350.00**

**Figure,** "Suzanne," frosted opalescent molded in full-relief as a standing nude maiden w/outstretched arms holding lengths of drapery, molded mark, introduced in 1925 (small chip on base) ..................................... **10,062.00**

**Figure,** "Thais," molded in full-relief as a nude dancer w/outstretched arms bearing an open scarf, grey, acid-stamped mark, introduced in 1925, 8½" h. .......................................... **4,600.00**

**Perfume bottle w/stopper,** "Leurs Ames" for D'Orsay, plain grey tapering cylindrical body w/a large rounded fan-shaped stopper molded in low-relief w/two nude females amid leafy branches, unsigned, introduced in 1920, 5¼" h. ............. **2,990.00**

**Vase,** 6¼" h., "Courlis," tapering ovoid body w/a short cylindrical neck, deep amber molded in low- and medium-relief w/a flock of sandpipers amid stylized clouds above breaking waves, acid-stamped mark, introduced in 1931 ......................... **2,530.00**

**Vase,** 6¾" h., "Gui," footed bulbous ovoid body tapering to a short cylindrical neck, teal blue molded in low- and medium-relief w/mistletoe berries & leaves, retains traces of original white patina, molded mark, introduced in 1920 ......................... **3,680.00**

**Vase,** 7¼" h., "Piriac," large trumpet-form body in frosted purplish grey, molded around the lower half w/a high-relief band of swimming fish above narrow bands of molded waves around the base, inscribed mark, introduced in 1930 .............. **2,070.00**

**Vase,** 9" h., "Ceylon," swelled cylindrical shape w/flattened rim in opalescent grey, molded in low- and medium-relief w/pairs of perched lovebirds cooing beneath leafy branches, inscribed "R. LALIQUE - No. 905 - FRANCE," introduced in 1924 (chip on base) ....................... **3,162.00**

**Vase,** 9½" h., "Bacchantes," flaring cylindrical shape in frosted charcoal grey molded in high-relief w/a continuous band of cavorting nude maidens, retains traces of original white patina, inscribed mark, introduced in 1927 ......................... **4,600.00**

**Vase,** 9¾" h., "Aigrettes," ovoid body w/a wide, flat rim, frosted clear grey molded in low- and medium-relief w/a flock of swooping egrets among bulrushes, molded mark ............... **2,875.00**

*Lalique "Oran" Vase*

**Vase,** 10¼" h., "Oran," slightly tapering cylindrical form in opalescent grey molded in high-relief w/large round dahlia blossoms amid leaves, inscribed mark, introduced in 1927 (ILLUS.) .............................. **9,430.00**

## LOETZ

*Iridescent glass, some of it somewhat resembling that of Tiffany and other comtemporary glasshouses, was produced by the Bohemian firm of J. Loetz Witwe of Klostermule and is referred to as Loetz. Some cameo pieces were also made. Not all examples are signed.*

*Loetz,*
*Austria*

*Loetz mark*

**Inkwell,** a wide squatty disc-form base w/brass collar & hinge to the small domed cover, top & base in grey decorated w/salmon & silvery blue trailing about the shoulder & cover, the cover's central section w/a concentric wave-like design in silvery blue, the base section w/dripping gunmetal & opalescent meandering trailings, unsigned, 3⅜" d. ......................................... **$3,737.00**

**Vase,** 4" h., 5¾" l., squatty bulbous quatraform body of royal purple w/two applied large prunt blossoms of red, white & clear w/matching threading overall .............................. **575.00**

*Loetz Vase with Silver Overlay*

**Vase,** 7⅜" h., ovoid body w/a short flaring neck, blown emerald green cased to bright cobalt blue interior w/a swirled silvery metallic layer between, the exterior decorated w/broad scrolling silver overlay foliage & flowers (ILLUS.) .............. **2,760.00**

**Vase,** 7¾" h., simple ovoid body w/a short, wide flaring neck, amber decorated w/an overall iridescent oil spot decoration ............................. **1,380.00**

**Vase,** 8" h., gently swelled cylindrical body w/a rounded shoulder to a short cylindrical neck, dark green rainbow iridescent ground decorated w/pale green iridescent oil spot designs ......................................... **1,380.00**

*Etched Loetz Vase*

**Vase,** 8" h., ovoid body tapering to a rounded shoulder & wide short cylindrical neck, orangish amber ground etched w/delicate leaf & vine repeating panels, lustrous gold iridescent surface on the decoration & upper border (ILLUS. bottom previous column) .......................... **2,875.00**

**Vase,** 9¾" h., flattened circular cushion base tapering to a tall slender cylindrical neck w/a widely flaring rim, gold iridescent ground & the neck applied w/a large coiled snake in greenish gold iridescence & an oil-spot decorated head ............ **2,760.00**

**Vase,** 11⅝" h., cushion-footed base & tapered stem ascending to a bulbous neck w/a pinched rim, purple rainbow iridescent ground decorated w/silver iridescent oil spots, the whole overlaid w/an interlacing floral design in silver..... **3,220.00**

## MARY GREGORY

*Glass enameled in white with silhouette-type figures, primarily of children, is now termed "Mary Gregory" and was attributed to the Boston and Sandwich Glass Company. However, recent research has proven conclusively that this was not decorated by Mary Gregory nor was it made at the Sandwich plant. Miss Gergory was employed by the Boston and Sandwich Glass Company as a decorator; however, records show her assignment was the painting of naturalistic landscape scenes on larger items such as lamps and shades but never the charming children for which her name has become synonymous. Further, in the inspection of fragments from the factory site, no paintings of children were found*

*It is now known that all wares collectors call "Mary Gregory" originated in Bohemia beginning in the late 19th century and were extensively exported to England and the U.S. well into this century*

*For further information see* The Glass Industry in Sandwich, Volume 4, *by Raymond E. Barlow and Joan E. Kaiser, and the recent book,* Mary Gregory Glassware, 1880-1990, *by R. & D. Truitt.*

**Box w/hinged cover,** round, cobalt blue, white enameled girl standing in landscape, 3½" d., 2½" h. (ILLUS. top next page) ......................................... **$285.00**

*Mary Gregory Box*

**Carafe w/original hollow blown stopper,** ten-paneled base, clear, white enameled girl holding flowers, detailed w/grasses, ferns & foliage ... **265.00**

**Carafe,** no stopper, tapering cylindrical optic-ribbed body w/a rounded shoulder to the tall slender flaring neck, champagne-amber, white enameled boy holding a butterfly net w/butterfly nearby, 3½" d., 7⅝" h. .................................. **145.00**

**Cheese dish,** cov., high-domed cover, clear round base & clear cover finial, the dome in cranberry, white enameled figures of two girls & a boy, 9" h............................................ **365.00**

**Cruet w/original ball stopper,** optic ribbed spherical body w/a short cylindrical neck w/a tricorner rim, applied clear handle, lime green, white enameled young boy sitting in a chair, 5" d., 9¾" h. ......................... **235.00**

**Mug,** slightly tapering optic ribbed form, clear applied handle, dark green, white enameled young girl standing in a garden, 2⅛" d., 3¼" h.... **50.00**

**Stein w/hinged old pewter domed cover & handle,** footed ovoid optic ribbed body tapering to a tall wide cylindrical neck, emerald green, white enameled girl wearing hat & carrying a basket walking in a leafy garden, white enameled band of leaf sprigs & berry clusters around the neck, modern, ca. 1980, 2½ liter ...... **375.00**

**Tumbler,** slender slightly flaring cylindrical form w/optic ribbing, pale greenish yellow, white enameled girl standing in a garden, 2½" d., 4⅜" h.... **45.00**

**Tumbler,** flaring tall cylindrical form w/ringed base, amber, white enameled boy, 2⅝" d., 5⅛" h............. **69.00**

**Vase,** 6" h., optic ribbing, cranberry, white enameled girl holding a leafy sprig, gold trim .................................. **100.00**

*Mary Gregory Vase*

**Vase,** 7¾" h., 3" d., footed ovoid body w/a tall slightly flaring cylindrical neck, medium green, white enameled young boy walking ........... **135.00**

**Vase,** 12" h., cushion foot supporting a flaring cylindrical optic ribbed body w/an angled narrow shoulder to the widely flaring & deeply notched neck, sapphire blue, white enameled girl picking apples (ILLUS. above).... **260.00**

**Water set:** 14" h. footed tankard pitcher w/arched spout & four 6½" h. footed optic ribbed goblets; amber w/applied sapphire blue handle on pitcher & blue bases on goblets, white enameled lady standing & resting by a fence on pitcher w/white enameled boys on two goblets & girls on two others, all figures w/fleshtone faces & hands, the set... **925.00**

## McKEE

*The McKee name has been associated with glass production since 1834, first producing window glass and later bottles. In the 1850s a new factory was established in Pittsburgh, Pennsylvania, for production of flint and pressed glass. The plant was relocated in Jeannette, Pennsylvania in 1888 and operated there as an independent company almost continuously until 1951 when it sold out to Thatcher Glass Manufacturing Company. Many types of collectible glass were produced by McKee through the years including*

*Depression, Pattern, Milk White and a variety of utility kitchenwares.*

# PRESCUT

*McKee Marks*

**Bowl,** 8" d., mixing, French Ivory ........ **$16.00**
**Bowl,** fruit, 12" d., pedestal base,
   Seville Yellow ..................................... **75.00**
**Butter,** cov., large, Skokie Green ......... **55.00**
**Cake plate,** Snowflake patt., pink ......... **35.00**
**Canister,** cov., French Ivory, "Cereal"
   in red.................................................. **45.00**
**Canister,** cov., French Ivory, "Sugar"
   in red.................................................. **45.00**
**Dispenser,** cov., Skokie Green............. **50.00**
**Mug,** Tom and Jerry, milk white ............. **5.00**
**Pepper shaker,** Roman Arch-style,
   French Ivory...................................... **24.00**
**Pitcher set:** pitcher & four cups;
   Seville Yellow, the set...................... **110.00**
**Pitcher,** Yutec patt., clear .................... **45.00**
**Refrigerator box,** cov., 4 x 5", French
   Ivory.................................................. **18.00**
**Refrigerator set,** revolving-type, top
   w/fired on yellow, clear ...................... **60.00**
**Rolling pin w/wood handles,**
   clambroth white ............................... **100.00**

*Shakers, Roman Arch-style with Red Ships*

**Salt & Pepper shakers,** white w/red
   ship, Roman Arch-style, pr. (ILLUS.).. **12.00**
**Salt shaker,** Roman Arch-style,
   French Ivory...................................... **24.00**
**Salt shaker,** square, French Ivory ........ **27.00**
**Tumbler,** whiskey, w/coaster base,
   "Bottoms Up," clear w/frosted legs ..... **65.00**

**Tumbler,** whiskey, w/coaster base,
   "Bottoms Up," Skokie Green............. **100.00**

## MILK WHITE

*This is opaque white glass that resembles the color of and was used as a substitute for white porcelain. Opacity was obtained by adding oxide of tin to a batch of clear glass. It has been made in numerous forms and shapes in this country and abroad from about the first quarter of the last century. It is still being produced, and there are many reproductions of earlier pieces.*

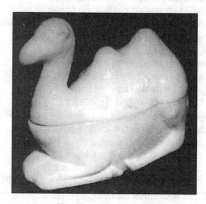

*Resting Camel Dish*

**Animal covered dish,** Camel resting,
   6¼" l. (ILLUS.) ............... **$150.00 to 200.00**
**Animal covered dish,** Cat on lacy-
   edge base, blue eyes ....................... **110.00**
**Animal covered dish,** Chicks on
   Round Basket, 4½" w., 3" h. .............. **75.00**
**Animal covered dish,** Reclining dog,
   Vallerysthal ....................................... **89.00**
**Animal covered dish,** Dove on
   basketweave base, round, marked
   "McKee," 4½" l. ................................. **350.00**
**Animal covered dish,** Duck on split
   ribbed base, Kemple.......................... **65.00**
**Animal covered dish,** Pintail Duck on
   diamond basket ................................. **55.00**
**Animal covered dish,** American Hen,
   6⅛" l. .............................. **100.00 to 200.00**
**Animal covered dish,** Hen on chick
   base, by Flaccus, 6¼" l..................... **375.00**
**Animal covered dish,** Hen on
   diamond basket, Kemple ................... **65.00**
**Animal covered dish,** Hen on
   diamond basket w/blue
   head ................................. **65.00 to 100.00**

**Animal covered dish,** Hen on oval lacy basket w/round flat eye sockets w/glass eyes, Atterbury ...................... 95.00

**Animal covered dish,** Owl Head on split-ribbed base, Atterbury............... 800.00

**Animal covered dish,** Rabbit on Egg, Vallerysthal, 3¼" l. ........................... 300.00

**Animal covered dish,** Rabbit on Split Rib base, 5½" l. .................................. 75.00

**Animal covered dish,** Robin on Nest, 6¼" d. .............................. 200.00 to 245.00

**Animal covered dish,** Rooster on wide rib base w/h.p. accents, Westmoreland Specialty Co., 5½" l. ... 50.00

**Animal covered dish,** Squirrel on split-ribbed base, McKee, 5½" l. ....... 275.00

**Animal covered dish,** Swan w/closed neck on basketweave base, 7" l., 7" h. ..................................................... 65.00

**Animal covered dish,** Swan w/raised wings & glass eyes on lacy-edge base, Atterbury, 9½" l., 6" h. .............................. 140.00 to 160.00

**Animal covered dish,** White Turtle w/snail finial ..................................... 300.00

**Bottle w/stopper,** Gargoyle head patt. ...................................................... 48.00

**Bowl,** shell-shaped, 8" d., footed, figural dolphin stem ........................... 35.00

**Candlestick,** Cruciform, 10" h. ............. 30.00

**Candy dish,** cov., kneeling nude figurine on lid w/h.p. roses & gold leafing ..................................................... 100.00

**Card case holder,** rectangular form, molded w/ornate scrolls w/heart to the side w/scroll feet ........................... 25.00

**Card tray,** double hands w/grapes at wrists, 5¾" w., 7½" l. ..................... 45.00

**Compote,** open, 7¼" h., six-sided, Scroll patt. ......................................... 65.00

**Compote,** open, 8" d., Blackberry patt. ....................................................... 75.00

**Compote,** open, 8¼" d., 8¼" h., Atlas stem, open-edge border, Atterbury..... 75.00

**Covered dish,** Covered Wagon w/five rib frame, 6" l. ................................. 125.00

**Covered dish,** Dewey Boat w/bust of Admiral w/"Dewey" embossed below, on tile base .............................. 85.00

**Covered dish,** Hand & dove on lacy-edge base, Atterbury, 8¾" l., 4¾" h. (ILLUS. top next column) .................. 165.00

**Covered dish,** Moses in the Bulrushes, 5½" ................................. 255.00

**Creamer,** Ceres patt. ........................... 55.00

*Hand & Dove Dish*

**Creamer,** Panelled Wheat patt. ............ 40.00

**Cruet w/original stopper,** Tree of Life patt. ....................................................... 35.00

**Dish in silver holder** w/Elephant heads for feet.................................... 145.00

**Dosage reminder,** clock face that fits atop a tumbler w/"Take Next Dose At," reverse embossed "Acme Tumbler Cover and Dose Indicator, Sharon Mfg. Co. Philada Pa. Pat. Appl'd For," 4" d. ................................ 38.00

**Dresser bottle w/stopper,** molded fern design, h.p. brown florals w/gold trim........................................................ 75.00

**Egg cup,** single, Blackberry patt........... 38.00

**Egg cup,** double, Birch Leaf patt. ......... 38.00

**Fruit jar,** figural Owl w/embossed eagle on milk glass insert, 6¼" h. ....... 85.00

**Inkwell,** model of a horseshoe, 4" l...... 38.00

**Match holder,** model of a pipe ............. 35.00

**Mug,** shaving, two-sided, Bird and Wheat patt. ........................................ 45.00

**Nappy w/handle,** oval, Prism patt., Atterbury, ca. 1872, 5" l. ................. 18.00

**Pepper shaker,** Johnny Bull, Atterbury, 6¼" h. .............................. 49.00

**Pickle dish,** Blackberry patt., 5½" d., 9½" l. ................................................. 38.00

**Pickle dish,** boat-shaped, "Pickle" embossed at front & "Patented Feb. 17, 1874" on bottom, 9½" l. ........ 38.00

**Pickle dishes,** fish-shaped, Atterbury, ca. 1872, 4½", pr. ............................ 150.00

**Plate,** 5¾" d., Woof-Woof, embossed face of long-haired dog in center, round w/lacy edge, Westmoreland Specialty Company, early 20th c. ....... 65.00

**Plate,** 7" d., Easter Greetings w/chick... 35.00

**Plate,** 7" d., Three Puppies sit at top, open leaf border ............................... 110.00

**Plate,** 7¼" d., Easter Greetings w/rabbit............................................... 50.00

*"No Easter Without Us" Plate*

**Plate,** 7¼" d., "No Easter Without Us"
(ILLUS.) ............................................ **30.00**

**Plate,** 7½" d., Easter Sermon............... **50.00**

**Plate,** 8¼" d., Washington portrait
w/thirteen stars around ...................... **95.00**

**Spooner,** Blackberry patt...................... **38.00**

**Spooner,** Blooming Rose patt. ............ **55.00**

**Spooner,** Sawtooth patt....................... **95.00**

**Sugar bowl,** cov., Blackberry patt. ....... **60.00**

**Sugar bowl,** cov., Blooming Rose
patt., miniature.................................. **55.00**

**Syrup pitcher w/original top,**
Coreopsis patt. w/good decoration ... **325.00**

**Syrup pitcher w/original hinged lid,**
Tree of Life patt. ................................ **75.00**

**Toothpick holder,** Button & Bulge
patt., decorated................................. **35.00**

**Toothpick holder,** figural Parrot on
brim of top hat.................................... **55.00**

**Tumbler,** Apple Blossom patt. ............. **65.00**

**Tumbler,** Beaded Swag patt................ **75.00**

**Tumbler,** Scroll patt. ............................ **25.00**

**Tumbler,** Waffle patt. ........................... **25.00**

**Vase,** 5" h. Poppy patt., poppies in
high-relief, ca. 1910 ........................... **55.00**

**Zipper side jar,** w/original lid,
threaded glass closure, Atterbury,
6⅛" h. ................................................ **40.00**

## MOSER

*Ludwig Moser opened his first glass shop
in 1857 in Karlsbad, Bohemia (now Karlovy
Vary, in the former Czechoslovakia). Here he
engraved and decorated fine glasswares
especially to appeal to rich visitors to the local
health spa. Later other shops were opened in
various cities and throughout the 19th and
early 20th century lovely, colorful glasswares,*
*many beautifully enameled, were produced by
Moser's shops and reached a wide market in
Europe and America. Ludwig died in 1916 and
the firm continued under his sons. They were
forced to merge with the Meyer's Nephews
glass factory after World War I. The
glassworks were sold out of the Moser family
in 1933.*

**Bowl,** 9" d., 5¼" h., four-sectioned,
the wide shallow form w/a flat rim
divided in the center by four arched
panels forming four compartments,
raised on applied gilt reeded scroll
feet, dark amber-topaz decorated
w/elaborate polychrome enamel
floral decoration overall w/bugs &
insects interspersed, applied beads
as grape clusters ........................ **$1,035.00**

*Moser Shaded Cologne Bottle*

**Cologne bottle w/original bubble
stopper,** cylindrical optic ribbed
bottle w/rounded shoulder & short
cylindrical neck, shaded amethyst to
clear w/dark purple stopper, gold
enameled garlands, bands & lacy
decoration, black circle Moser mark
on base, 2" d., 5" h. (ILLUS.)............ **195.00**

**Pitcher,** 6½" h., 4⅝" d., squatty
bulbous footed ringed body w/a wide
cylindrical ringed neck, applied clear
handle, clear w/a slight pearl lustre
decorated overall w/elaborate
colorful fern leaves in green, red,
gold & blue, gold trim on bands,
unmarked (ILLUS. top next page) .... **295.00**

*Elaborate Moser Pitcher*

**Vase,** 5" h., bulbous tapering body w/a flat rim & facet-cut rounded panels around the base, golden amber topaz w/an engraved wide gilt border frieze of Amazon warriors, inscribed "Moser Carlsbad Made in Czechoslov" ...................................... **345.00**

**Vase,** 6" h., "Royalit," gently flaring cylindrical form w/a flat wide mouth, light-reactive Alexandrite-type color, patterned overall w/wide polished cut swirls, stamped "Royalit Moser Karlsbad" ......................................... **230.00**

**Vase,** 13¼" h., classic baluster urn-form w/flaring foot & ringed pedestal base supported a tall ovoid body w/a trumpet neck, amethyst acid-etched around the center w/a wide gilt band of Hellenic warriors w/shields & spears, inscribed on the base "Moser Carlsbad Made in Czechoslovakia" (gilt worn) .............. **259.00**

## MT. WASHINGTON

*A wide diversity of glass was made by the Mt. Washington Glass Company of New Bedford, Massachusetts, between 1869 and 1900. It was succeeded in 1900 by the Pairpoint Corporation. Miscellaneous types are listed below.*

**Bell,** white satin enameled w/pink florals & gold trim, original clapper, 5" h. ................................. **$150.00**

**Box w/hinged cover,** round, squatty bulbous base & low domed cover joined by fancy gold-washed silver plate rim & hinge, the cover decorated w/a scene of a monk drinking a glass of red wine, shaded green ground on cover & base, artist-signed, original satin lining, 5¼" d., 3¼" h. ................................... **550.00**

**Collars & cuffs box,** cov., white opal wide, short cylindrical box in the form of two collars w/a big bow in the front, the cover decorated w/Oriental poppies in shades of pink & orange w/a silver poppy finial w/gold trim, the sides of the base also w/Oriental poppies & gold trim, the bow at the bottom front in bright blue w/white polka dots & a buckle at the back, signed on the base "Patent applied for April 10, 1894," large ................................................. **950.00**

*Mt. Washington Cracker Jar*

**Cracker jar,** cov., melon-ribbed squatty white opal body decorated w/blackberries & green leaves, silver plate rim, domed cover & scroll-trimmed bail handle, silver marked w/Pairpoint logo, 5" h. (ILLUS.) ........ **578.00**

**Cracker jar,** cov., exterior decorated w/acorns & oak leaves on a pale pink shading to pale yellow ground, white interior, silver plate rim, cover & bail handle, cover marked "No. 4404/a" ..................................... **815.00**

**Salt & pepper shakers w/original tops,** white opal, figural fig-shaped, pr. ..................................................... **325.00**

**Salt & pepper shakers w/original tops,** white opal, ribbed pillar-form, in a resilvered silver plate frame, the set ..................................................... **310.00**

**Salt & pepper shakers w/original tops,** ribbed white ground, one decorated w/oak leaves & cobalt blue dotting, the other w/oak leaves & cobalt blue dotted flowers, in a fancy footed & handled silver plate holder, the set .................................. **275.00**

**Sugar shaker w/original top,** white opal, egg-shaped, decorated w/h.p. maidenhair ferns .............................. **270.00**

**Sugar shaker w/original top,** white opal, egg-shaped, shaded yellow satin ground w/h.p. pink wild roses & green shadow leaves........................ **295.00**

**Vase,** 9" h., 5½" w., footed bottle form w/tall cylindrical neck, "Pairpoint Delft," opal white ground decorated in pink w/a scene of a windmill in a landscape w/a small figure, gold trim on the base & top ............................ **375.00**

# MULLER FRERES

*The Muller Brothers made acid-etched cameo and other fine glass at Luneville, France, starting in 1910 and until the outbreak of World War II in Europe.*

*Muller Freres Mark*

**Cameo ceiling fixture,** electrified, the large dished inverted shade suspended by three long ropetwist cords, the shade in grey shaded w/pink, turquoise & pale lemon yellow & overlaid w/dusty rose & violet & cut w/three pastoral scenes of dancing maidens & a hunter, signed in cameo, ca. 1925, 14" d.............................. **$2,875.00**

**Cameo lamp,** boudoir-type, a deep domical shade in frosted clear overlaid in blue & etched to depict a wooden pond scene w/dragonflies hovering about, on a slender tapering base w/wide disc foot w/similar coloring & etched to depict aquatic plant life, engraved signature, overall 14" h. ................. **2,760.00**

**Cameo vase,** 8¾" h., slender ovoid body w/a short swelled cylindrical neck, yellow overlaid in shades of brown & cut w/a windmill on a lake

w/numerous sailing vessels, mountains & another windmill in the far distance, ca. 1920 ................... **1,265.00**

**Cameo vase,** 15¾" h., footed trumpet-form, striated dusty pink ground overlaid in royal blue & deeply etched to depict stylized fern fronds & a scrolling design, cameo signature (small rim chip) ................. **748.00**

*Muller Vase with Village Scene*

**Cameo vase,** 16½" h., tall ovoid body w/angled shoulder to a flat, wide mouth, frosted clear overlaid in tangerine & teal blue & etched to depict a French village scene by the water in the distance & sailboats & country folk in the foreground, cameo-signed (ILLUS.).................. **4,830.00**

# NEW MARTINSVILLE

*The New Martinsville Glass Mfg. Co. opened in New Martinsville, West Virginia in 1901 and during its first period of production came out with a number of colored opaque pressed glass patterns. They also developed an art glass line they named "Muranese," which collectors refer to as "New Martinsville Peach Blow." The factory burned in 1907 but reopened later that year and began focusing on production of various clear pressed glass patterns, many of which were then decorated with gold or ruby staining or enameled decoration. After going through receivership in 1937, the factory again changed the focus of its production to more contemporary glass lines and figural animals. The firm was purchased in 1944 by the Viking Glass company (now Dalzell-Viking) and some of the long-popular New Martinsville patterns are now produced by this still active firm.*

**Basket,** Janice patt. (No. 4500 Line), clear, 12"............................................ **$40.00**

**Book ends,** Clipper Ship, clear, pr. ...... **85.00**

**Bowl,** 5½" d., handled, No. 26, clear .... **15.00**

**Bowl,** berry, 5¼" d., Moondrops patt. (No. 37 Line), red................................ **30.00**

**Candlestick,** two-light, Janice patt. (No. 4500 Line), clear, 5" h. ............... **10.00**

**Candlesticks,** Janice patt. (No. 4500 Line), clear, 6" h., pr. ......................... **24.00**

**Candlesticks,** No. 415, clear, 5" w., 6½" h., pr. .......................................... **40.00**

**Candy dish w/metal cover,** Moondrops patt. (No. 37 Line), red ............................ **95.00**

**Cheese & cracker server,** No. 26, clear ................................................ **45.00**

**Cocktail,** Moondrops patt. (No. 37 Line), cobalt blue ............................... **35.00**

**Compote,** cheese-type, No. 26, clear... **15.00**

**Compote,** Moondrops patt. (No. 37 Line), cobalt blue ............................... **45.00**

**Compote,** Moondrops patt. (No. 37 Line), red ............................................. **30.00**

**Cordial,** Moondrops patt. (No. 37 Line), amber w/silver decoration......... **25.00**

**Cordial,** Radiance patt. (No. 4200 Line), red ............................................. **25.00**

**Creamer & sugar bowl,** footed, Moondrops patt. (No. 37 Line), amber, the set...................................... **22.00**

**Creamer & sugar bowl,** individual size, Moondrops patt. (No. 37 Line), red, the set.......................................... **35.00**

**Creamer,** No. 26, clear ......................... **15.00**

**Creamer,** Janice patt. (No. 4500 Line), clear............................................. **9.00**

**Cup,** Moondrop patt. (No. 37 Line), amber ................................................... **10.00**

**Cup,** footed, Moondrops patt (No. 37 Line), red ............................................. **15.00**

**Decanter set:** decanter w/diamond band at shoulder & fanned stopper w/four pedestal-based wines w/flaring bowls & round tray; No. 15, green, 6 pcs. (ILLUS. of decanter, top next column) ............................. **125.00**

**Decanter set:** decanter w/diamond band at shoulder & fanned stopper w/four pedestal-based wines w/flaring bowls & a round tray; No. 15, red, 6 pcs. ............................ **200.00**

**Decanter set:** small decanter w/six handled shot glasses, Moondrops patt. (No. 37 Line), amber, the set.... **100.00**

*Moondrops Decanter*

**Honey jar,** cov., Radiance patt. (No. 4200 Line), blue ........................ **300.00**

**Honey jar,** cov., Radiance patt. (No. 4200 Line), red.......................... **200.00**

**Mayonnaise set:** bowl w/ladle; Radiance patt. (No. 4200 Line), blue, the set................................................. **30.00**

**Pickle dish,** Moondrops patt. (No. 37 Line), cobalt blue ................................ **55.00**

**Pitcher,** medium, Moondrops patt. (No. 37 Line), cobalt blue ................. **390.00**

**Pitcher,** Radiance patt. (No. 4200 Line), amber ....................................... **95.00**

**Plate,** 6½" d., handled, No. 26 .............. **15.00**

**Plate,** 7½" d., indented, Radiance patt. (No. 4200 Line), blue ................. **25.00**

**Punch bowl w/ladle,** Radiance patt. (No. 4200 Line), amber, the set.......... **85.00**

**Punch cup,** Radiance patt. (No. 4200 Line), light blue ................................... **12.00**

**Relish dish,** two-part, No. 26, 5¾" l...... **19.00**

**Salt & pepper shakers,** Radiance patt. (No. 4200 Line), light blue, pr. .... **85.00**

**Sherbet,** Radiance patt. (No. 4200 Line), red ............................................. **45.00**

**Sugar bowl,** Moondrops patt. (No. 37 Line), green .......................................... **10.00**

**Sugar bowl,** Radiance patt. (No. 4200 Line), red ............................................. **22.00**

**Vase,** crimped, Radiance patt. (No. 4200 Line), dark green ...................... **85.00**

**Whiskey,** Moondrops patt. (No. 37 Line), cobalt blue ................................ **17.00**

**Wine,** low-footed, Moondrops patt. (No. 37 Line), cobalt blue, 3 oz.......... **22.00**

**Wine,** Moondrops patt. (No. 37 Line), red, 4 oz................................................. **25.00**

# NORTHWOOD

*Harry Northwood (1860-1919) was born in England, the son of noted glass artist John Northwood. Brought up in the glass business, Harry immigrated to the United States in 1881 and shortly thereafter became manager of the La Belle Glass Company, Bridgeport, Ohio. Here he was responsible for many innovations in colored and blown glass. After leaving La Belle in 1887 he opened The Northwood Glass Company in Martins Ferry, Ohio in 1888. The company moved to Ellwood City, Pennsylvania in 1892 and Northwood moved again to take over a glass plant in Indiana, Pennsylvania in 1896. One of his major lines made at the Indiana, Pennsylvania plant was Custard glass (which he called "ivory"). It was made in several patterns and some pieces were marked on the base with "Northwood" in script*

*Harry and his family moved back to England in 1899 but returned to the U.S. in 1902 at which time he opened another glass factory in Wheeling, West Virginia. Here he was able to put his full talents to work and under his guidance the firm manufactured many notable glass lines including opalescent wares, colored and clear pressed tablewares, various novelties and, probably best known of all, Carnival glass. Around 1906 Harry introduced his famous "N" in circle trademark which can be found on the base of many, but not all, pieces made at his factory. The factory closed in 1925*

*In this listing we are including only the clear and colored tablewares produced at Northwood factories. Specialized lines such as Custard glass, Chrysanthemum Sprig, Blue, Carnival and Opalescent wares are listed under their own headings in our Glass category.*

*Northwood "N" in Circle Mark, ca. 1906 &
Script mark*

**Berry set:** master bowl & four sauce dishes; Leaf Medallion (Regent) patt., purple w/very good gold trim, 5 pcs. .............................................. **$150.00**

**Butter dish,** cov., Gold Rose patt....... **100.00**

**Butter dish,** cov., Memphis patt., green ................................................ **160.00**

**Butter dish,** cov., Panelled Holly patt., blue opalescent ............................... **200.00**

**Butter dish,** cov., Teardrop Flower patt., green ..................................... **160.00**

**Candy jar,** cov., shape No. 636, blue "stretch" glass .................................... **50.00**

**Ceiling shade,** four-light, marked "Luna," custard-colored w/nutmeg stain, 20" d.................................... **1,150.00**

**Compote,** jelly, Intaglio patt., green gilded ..................................................... **90.00**

**Compote,** jelly, Scroll w/Acanthus, patt., Mosaic (purple slag) ................. **50.00**

**Compote,** open, 8" d., shape No. 656, Chinese Coral.................................... **50.00**

*Northwood Peach Creamer*

**Creamer,** Peach patt., green w/gold trim (ILLUS.) ..................................... **85.00**

**Creamer,** Panelled Holly patt., blue opalescent ........................................ **120.00**

**Creamer,** Posies & Pod, green ............. **80.00**

**Epergne,** single-lily, Wide Panel patt., clear w/satin finish ............................ **85.00**

**Epergne,** four-lily, Wide Panel patt., blue opalescent .............................. **650.00**

**Fruit dish,** Grape Frieze patt., Verre D'or line, purple, 11" d. .................... **175.00**

**Pitcher,** shape No. 287, green enameled ........................................... **75.00**

**Pitcher,** water, Leaf Umbrella patt., mauve cased ................................... **455.00**

**Pitcher,** water, Paneled Sprig patt., blue opalescent ............................... **250.00**

**Rose bowl,** Beaded Cable patt.,
Mosaic ................................................ **40.00**

**Rose bowl,** Jewel (Threaded Swirl)
patt., Rubina, large ............................ **75.00**

**Salt shaker,** Panelled Sprig patt, red.. **150.00**

**Sauce dish,** Leaf Umbrella patt.,
Rose DuBarry (cased mauve), 4" d .... **45.00**

**Spooner,** Cherry & Cable patt., clear
w/purple & gold trim ........................... **45.00**

**Spooner,** Peach patt., green w/gold
trim...................................................... **95.00**

**Sugar bowl,** Memphis patt., green ..... **140.00**

**Sugar bowl,** Panelled Holly patt., blue
opalescent ......................................... **120.00**

**Sugar bowl,** cov., Teardrop Flower
patt., green ........................................ **125.00**

**Sugar shaker,** Leaf Umbrella patt.,
cranberry ............................................ **375.00**

**Tumbler,** Netted Oak patt., milk white .. **50.00**

*Memphis Tumbler*

**Tumblers,** Memphis patt., green, set
of 6 (ILLUS. of one) ........................... **150.00**

**Vase,** 7" h., Twist, shape No. 727,
Chinese Coral..................................... **55.00**

**Vase,** 9" h., Twist, shape No. 727,
Jade green.......................................... **50.00**

**Water set:** pitcher & six tumblers;
Peach patt., green w/gold trim,
7 pcs. ................................................. **400.00**

## OPALESCENT

*Presently, this is one of the most popular areas of glass collecting. The opalescent effect was attained by adding bone ash to the glass batch and then refiring the object at tremendous heat. Both pressed and mold-blown patterns are available to collectors and we distinguish the types in our listing below. Opalescent Glass from A to Z by the late William Heacock is the definitive reference book for collectors. Also see: PATTERN GLASS.*

## MOLD-BLOWN OPALESCENT PATTERNS

### COIN SPOT

**Syrup pitcher w/original top,** white .. **$120.00**

*Coin Spot Sugar Shaker*

**Sugar shaker w/original metal lid,**
ring mold, wide waist, cranberry
(ILLUS.) ............................................. **345.00**

### DAISY AND FERN

**Cruet w/original stopper,**
blue .................................... **125.00 to 150.00**

**Pitcher,** 6" h., ball-shaped,
cranberry ........................... **475.00 to 500.00**

**Sugar Shaker w/original lid,**
swirl, cranberry ................................. **395.00**

**Tumbler,** blue ......................... **50.00 to 60.00**

### HONEYCOMB

**Water set:** pitcher & six tumblers,
green, 7 pcs..................................... **550.00**

### POLKA DOT

**Pitcher set:** water pitcher & four
tumblers; cranberry, West Virginia
Glass, 5 pcs. ................................... **1,300.00**

### SEAWEED

**Barber bottle,** blue ............................. **250.00**

**Celery dish,** cranberry....................... **285.00**

**Cruet w/original stopper,**
cranberry ........................... **350.00 to 450.00**

**Pitcher,** water, tricorner top w/crimped
rim, cranberry ................................... **995.00**

## SPANISH LACE

*Spanish Lace Sugar Shaker*

**Bowl w/upturned edge,** canary ........... 95.00
**Sugar shaker w/original metal lid,**
  wide waist, cranberry (ILLUS.) ......... 215.00

## SWIRLING MAIZE

**Pitcher,** tankard, cranberry .............. 1,000.00
**Tumbler,** blue ....................................... 40.00

## PRESSED OPALESCENT PATTERNS

## ARGONAUT SHELL

*Argonaut Shell Fruit Stand*

**Berry set:** master bowl & six sauce
  dishes; white, 7 pcs. ......................... 175.00
**Fruit stand,** footed, incurved sides,
  blue (ILLUS.) ........................ 30.00 to 40.00
**Sugar bowl,** cov., blue ....... 190.00 to 200.00

## CIRCLED SCROLL

**Compote,** jelly, green ......................... 125.00
**Table set:** cov. butter, cov. sugar,
  spooner & creamer; green, 4 pcs. .... 845.00

## DRAPERY

**Berry set:** master berry & six sauces;
  blue w/gold trim, 7 pcs. ..................... 350.00
**Table set,** blue w/gold trim, 4 pcs. ...... 425.00

## EVERGLADES

*Everglades Butter Dish*

**Butter dish,** cov., blue
  (ILLUS.) ........................... 350.00 to 375.00
**Cruet w/original stopper,** canary ...... 425.00
**Spooner,** blue ...................... 90.00 to 100.00
**Water set:** pitcher & six tumblers;
  white, 7 pcs. ..................................... 650.00

## FLORA

**Butter dish,** cov., canary
  yellow .............................. 175.00 to 200.00
**Creamer,** white .................................... 45.00
**Table set,** blue, 4 pcs. ........................ 690.00

## FLUTED SCROLLS

*Fluted Scrolls Bowl*

**Bowl,** tri-cornered, three-footed, clear
  (ILLUS.) ............................................. 40.00
**Creamer,** blue ..................................... 50.00
**Sauce dish,** canary .............................. 24.00
**Tumbler,** green .................................... 48.00

## INTAGLIO

**Butter dish,** cov., blue ....................... 300.00
**Cruet w/original stopper,** blue .......... 200.00

Pitcher, water, blue............................ 325.00
Tumbler, white.................................... 45.00

## INVERTED FAN & FEATHER
Bowl, novelty, clear............................ 195.00
Rose bowl, canary.............................. 135.00

## JEWEL & FLOWER
Berry set: master bowl & six sauce
　dishes; clear w/gold & cranberry
　trim, 7 pcs. ..................................... 225.00
Cruet w/original stopper, canary ...... 750.00
Spooner, white (ILLUS.) ...................... 75.00
Table set, canary w/gold trim, 4 pcs. .. 775.00

## JEWELED HEART

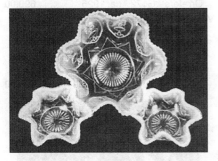

*Jeweled Heart Berry Set*

Berry set: 9" master bowl & five
　sauces, crimped rims, green,
　6 pcs. (ILLUS. of part) ..................... 150.00
Sauce dish, blue................................. 20.00
Tumbler, clear ..................................... 18.00

## PALM BEACH
Creamer & sugar bowl, blue, pr. ....... 350.00
Spooner, canary .................................. 85.00
Water set: pitcher & five tumblers;
　canary, 6 pcs. .................................. 625.00

## REGAL, Northwood's
Butter dish, cov., green ..... 175.00 to 185.00
Table set, blue, 4 pcs. ....................... 625.00
Water set: pitcher & six tumblers;
　blue, 7 pcs. ..................................... 700.00

## SCROLL WITH ACANTHUS
Butter dish, cov., blue ........................ 100.00
Compote, jelly, blue .............. 45.00 to 50.00
Spooner, blue ..................................... 85.00

## WILD BOUQUET
Bowl, master berry, blue.................... 135.00

Sauce dish, blue.................................. 45.00
Tumbler, white..................................... 45.00

## WREATH & SHELL
Berry set: master bowl & six sauce
　dishes; canary, 7 pcs. ...................... 340.00
Bowl, master berry, blue ................... 125.00
Butter dish, cov., canary ................... 185.00
Butter dish, cov., decorated, white .... 125.00
Celery dish, blue ............................... 450.00
Celery vase, canary............................ 185.00
Cracker jar, cov., canary ................... 725.00
Sauce dish, blue.................................. 40.00
Sauce dish, canary.............................. 45.00

*Wreath & Shell Spooner*

Spooner, canary (ILLUS.)..................... 85.00
Table set, blue, 4 pcs. ........................ 595.00
Toothpick holder, canary ................. 195.00
Tumbler, canary ................................. 85.00

## MISCELLANEOUS PRESSED NOVELTIES

*Winter Cabbage Bowl*

Basketweave bowl, open-edged,
　canary................................................. 22.00

**Basketweave candlesticks,** three-footed, green, 2" h., pr. ...................... **125.00**

**Leaf & Beads bowl,** 8" w., three-footed, white ..................................... **60.00**

**Beaded Cable rose bowl** .................... **40.00**

**Roulette bowl,** 7½" h., white ............... **60.00**

**Sea Spray nappy,** green ..................... **45.00**

**Spokes & Wheels,** plate, 8½" d., blue.. **35.00**

**Tree Trunk vase,** 11" h., Northwood, white ................................................. **125.00**

**Twig vase,** 7" h., Northwood, blue...... **125.00**

**Vintage bowl,** 8" d., green.................... **30.00**

**Winter Cabbage bowl,** footed, crimped rim, blue (ILLUS. bottom previous page) ................................. **40.00**

# ORREFORS

*This Swedish glasshouse, founded in 1898 for production of tablewares, has made decorative wares as well since 1915. By 1925, Orrefors had achieved an international reputation for its Graal glass, an engraved art glass developed by master glassblower Knut Berquist and artist-designers Simon Gate and Edward Hald. Ariel glass, recognized by a design of controlled air traps and the heavy Ravenna glass, usually tinted, were both developed in the 1930s. While all Orrefors glass is collectible, pieces signed by early designers and artists are now bringing high prices.*

*Orrefors*

*Orrefors Mark*

**Bowl,** 10¼" d., 5⅛" h., deep sharply tapering sides w/a beveled flat rim, internally decorated w/cobalt blue rectangles outlined in amber, engraved "ORREFORS Ravenna Nr 1682 Sven Palmquist," designed by Sven Palmquist........................... **$4,255.00**

**Bowl & underplate,** 15¼" d., 5¼" h., the wide deeply flaring bowl in clear engraved on both sides w/nude male & female figures amid scrolling foliage, the underplate w/matching engraving, inscribed "Orrefors - Gate - 147 - 29 - WE," ca. 1920, 2 pcs... **4,600.00**

**Vase,** 6" h., "Ariel," bulbous conical thick-walled clear body, the internally

decorated linear geometric bands w/controlled air bubbles piercing a dark amber ground, signed "Orrefors - Ariel Nu 4260 - Ingeborg Lundin," ca. 1963........................................ **1,150.00**

**Vase,** 6⅛" h., "Ariel," thick-walled ovoid form w/a small mouth, clear w/bright blue trapped air genre scene of nudes reclining under a still life painting in an interior setting, engraved on the base "Orrefors Sweden Ariel 573E E. Ohrstrom" .. **5,175.00**

**Vase,** 6½" h., flaring cylindrical body, etched w/a nude woman astride an oryx, the borders w/a band of oval & cross designs, the base w/flutes, designed by Simon Gate, signed "Orrefors - G172," ca. 1925 .............. **690.00**

**Vase,** 7⅛" h., footed tapering cylindrical clear body w/molded ridged rings around the lower half, engraved w/full-length nude male divers, inscribed on the base "Orrefors Lindstrand 1304 Al. KY" .... **633.00**

*Orrefors "Graal" Vase*

**Vase,** 7¼" h., "Graal," heavy thick tapering ovoid body w/small mouth, clear internally decorated as an underwater ocean scene in green & brown tones, signed "Orrefors Sweden Graal 919D Edward Hald" (ILLUS.) ........................................... **978.00**

**Vase,** 8½" h., "Ariel," thick-walled clear flattened teardrop form internally decorated w/a blue network centering a single bubble in each square, transparent blue at top, base inscribed "Orrefors Kraka No. 349 Sven Palmquist" ................. **489.00**

**Vase,** 12½" h., footed cylindrical clear body w/optically wavy sides engraved w/two nude male divers, designed by Vicke Lindstrand, signed "Orrefors L. 1348 CG. (?)," ca. 1935 ........................................ **2,875.00**

## PADEN CITY

*The Paden City Glass Manufacturing Company began operations in Paden City, West Virginia in 1916, primarily as a supplier of blanks to other companies. All wares were hand-made, that is, either hand-pressed or mold-blown. The early products were not particularly noteworthy but by the early 1930s the quality had improved considerably. The firm continued to turn out high quality glassware in a variety of beautiful colors until financial difficulties necessitated its closing in 1951. Over the years the firm produced, in addition to tablewares, items for hotel and restaurant use, light shades, shaving mugs, perfume bottles and lamps.*

**Bowl,** 9¼" d., footed, Mrs. "B" (No. 411) line, Ardith etching, yellow.. **$57.00**

**Bowl,** 9¾" d., pedestal base, Mrs. "B" (No. 411) line, Orchid Etching, pink.. **165.00**

**Bowl,** 10" d., pedestal base, Maya (No. 221) line, light blue ...................... **85.00**

**Bowl,** 11" d., Gothic Garden etching, yellow................................................ **55.00**

**Cake plate,** 11¼" d., footed, Archaic (No. 300) line, Ardith etching, green ... **72.00**

**Cake plate,** footed, Cupid etching, green ............................................... **230.00**

**Cake plate,** footed, Cupid etching, pink .................................................... **230.00**

**Cake plate,** Peacock & Rose etching, pink .................................................... **140.00**

**Candy dish,** cov., Crow's Foot (No. 412) line, red............................ **85.00**

**Candy dish,** cov., flat, Nora Bird etching, green.................................. **375.00**

**Cheese stand,** Crow's Foot (No. 890) line, red............................................. **35.00**

**Cocktail shaker,** Speak Easy, green ... **45.00**

**Compote,** Crow's Foot line, cobalt blue................................................... **50.00**

**Compote,** 6⅝" d., black Crow's Foot line w/yellow Orchid etching ............. **175.00**

**Console bowl,** low, Crow's Foot (No. 412) line, red............................... **45.00**

**Console bowl,** black Crow's Foot line w/yellow Orchid etching, 11" d......... **185.00**

**Gravy boat,** pedestal base, Crow's Foot line, red........................................ **95.00**

**Ice tub,** Peacock & Rose etching, green ................................................. **185.00**

**Mayonnaise set:** bowl w/ladle; Nora Bird etching, green, 2 pcs................. **110.00**

**Measure/reamer,** Party Line (No. 191) line, green, pt....................................... **60.00**

**Napkin holder,** Party Line (No. 191) line, green......................................... **205.00**

**Plate,** 10½" d., Peacock & Rose etching, green...................................... **75.00**

**Punch bowl set:** bowl w/seven cups; No. 555 line, clear, 8 pcs. .................. **75.00**

**Sugar bowl,** round w/handle, Nora Bird etching, pink............................... **60.00**

**Tray w/center handle,** Gazebo etching, light blue............................... **75.00**

**Tray w/center handle,** Mrs. "B" (No. 411) line, Ardith etching, 10" l............. **50.00**

**Tumbler,** cone-shaped, Party Line (No. 191) line, green, 5" h.................... **10.00**

**Tumbler,** cone-shaped, Party Line (No. 191) line, green, 5¾" h................ **10.00**

**Tumbler,** cone-shaped, Party Line (No. 191) line, green, 6¾" h................ **10.00**

**Tumbler,** flat, Crow's Foot line, amber, 9 oz........................................... **35.00**

**Vase,** 8" h., Gothic Garden etching, pink ................................................. **210.00**

**Vase,** 8" h., elliptical, Lela Bird etching, black....................................... **175.00**

**Vase,** 10" h., Peacock & Rose etching, green ................. **140.00 to 165.00**

**Vase,** 10" h., Utopia etching, black ..... **195.00**

**Vase,** 10" h., Lela Bird etching, black ................................................... **155.00**

**Vase,** 12" h., Peacock & Rose etching, green................................... **190.00**

**Vase,** short, squat, Orchid etching, black ................................................. **150.00**

## PATE DE VERRE

*Pate de Verre, or "paste of glass," was molded by very few artisans. In the pate de verre technique, powdered glass is mixed with a liquid to make a paste which is then placed in a mold and baked at a high temperature. These articles have a finely pitted or matte finish and are easily distinguished from blown glass. Duplicate pieces are possible with this technique which was used most often by French glass artists.*

Pate de Verre marks

**Bowl,** 10⅜" d., "Les Oiseaux," the circular footed bowl of mottled yellowish amber, the perimeter molded w/a band of amber cranes above flower petals radiating from the center, the underside molded w/rows of square tiles continuing to the dark amber flaring high foot, molded signature "G. Argy-Rousseau," ca. 1925 ................... **$4,600.00**

**Bust of a maiden,** in opalescent grey tinged w/lavender & mauve, cast in full-relief as a maiden w/closed eyes & stylized hair, on a walnut stand, cast mark "DECORCHEMONT," France, ca. 1925, head 6⅝" h. ...... **3,450.00**

**Dish,** round, opaque blue w/a raised black & brown beetle on the top opposite a C-form indentation, signed "A. Walter France," 4" d. .... **2,415.00**

**Paperweight,** figural, grey molded in full-relief w/two lizards perched on a leafy precipice, in shades of amber, brown, green & black, molded mark "A. Walter - Nancy - H. Bergé - SC," ca. 1925, 3½" h. .......................... **4,255.00**

**Vase,** 5¼" h., tapering cylindrical body w/a short cupped neck, unusual coloration w/molded white forsythia blossom-laden branches around the lower section against a mottled white ground speckled by amethyst, amber & green inclusions, impressed mold mark "G. Argy-Rousseau" ...................................... **4,600.00**

**Vase,** 6⅜" h., trumpet-form body on a flaring foot, molded w/clusters of raspberries & leafage around the top half, the foot cast w/three flowerheads, in mottled shades of yellow, green, rust & ochre, molded mark "A Walter - Nancy - H Bergé - SC," ca. 1925 .............................. **2,530.00**

*Rare Pate de Verre Vase*

**Vase,** 9⅜" h., "Le Jardin des Hesperides," simple ovoid form w/a wide, flat rim, molded in low-relief w/a frieze of three tunic-clad maidens in various stages of apple harvesting, above a lower band molded w/a stylized Greek key design, the maidens in red w/other shades of grey, charcoal, yellow, magenta & purple, molded mark "G. Argy-Rousseau," ca. 1926 (ILLUS.).................................... **20,700.00**

**Veilleuse (night light),** a tall ovoid molded shade of muted amberish tan decorated by three repeating honey brown blossoms separated by amethyst purple V-shaped designs, fitted upon a wrought-iron round base w/light socket & topped by a hand-wrought metal cap w/large knob finial, Argy-Rousseau, overall 8½" h. ........................................... **5,750.00**

**Vide poche (figural dish),** oblong shield-shape tray of orangish amber w/a fat bumble bee of brown & black w/green wings at one end, impressed "A. Walter," 4" l.............................. **2,600.00**

## PATTERN GLASS

*Though it has never been ascertained whether glass was first pressed in the United States or abroad, the development of the glass pressing machine revolutionized the glass industry in the United States and this country receives the credit for improving the method to make this process feasible. The first wares pressed were probably small flat plates of the type now referred to as "lacy," the intricacy of the design concealing flaws.*

*In 1827, both the New England Glass Co., Cambridge, Massachusetts and Bakewell & Co., Pittsburgh, took out patents for pressing glass furniture knobs and soon other pieces followed. This early pressed glass contained red lead which made it clear and resonant when tapped (flint). Made primarily in clear, it is rarer in blue, amethyst, olive green and yellow.*

*By the 1840s, early simple patterns such as Ashburton, Argus and Excelsior appeared. Ribbed Bellflower seems to have been one of the earliest patterns to have had complete sets. By the 1860s, a wide range of patterns was available.*

*In 1864, William Leighton of Hobbs, Brockunier & Co., Wheeling, West Virginia, developed a formula for "soda lime" glass which did not require the expensive red lead for clarity. Although "soda lime" glass did not have the brilliance of the earlier flint glass, the formula came into widespread use because glass could be produced cheaply.*

*An asterisk (\*) indicates a piece which has been reproduced.*

### ACTRESS

| | |
|---|---|
| **Bowl,** cov. | $110.00 |
| **Bowl,** 6" d., flat | 45.00 |
| **Bowl,** 6" d., footed | 50.00 |
| **Bowl,** 7" d., footed | 60.00 |
| **Bowl,** 8" d., Adelaide Neilson | 65.00 |
| **Bread tray,** Miss Neilson, 12½" l. | 70.00 to 75.00 |
| **Butter dish,** cov., Fanny Davenport & Miss Neilson | 100.00 to 125.00 |
| **Cake stand,** Maude Granger & Annie Pixley, 10" d., 7" h. | 112.00 |
| **Cake stand,** frosted stem | 150.00 to 165.00 |
| **Celery vase,** Pinafore scene | 180.00 |
| **Cheese dish,** cov., "Lone Fisherman" on cover, "The Two Dromios" on underplate (ILLUS. top next column) | 225.00 to 235.00 |
| **Compote,** cov., 6" d., 10" h. | 100.00 |
| **Compote,** cov., 7" d., 8½" h. | 155.00 |
| **Compote,** cov., 8" d., 12" h. | 175.00 to 190.00 |

*Actress Cheese Dish*

| | |
|---|---|
| **Compote,** cov., 10" d., 14½" h., Fanny Davenport & Maggie Mitchell | 200.00 to 225.00 |
| **Compote,** open, 6" d., 11" h. | 102.00 |
| **Compote,** open, 7" d., 7" h., Miss Neilson | 150.00 |
| **Compote,** open, 7" d., 7" h., Maggie Mitchell & Fanny Davenport | 110.00 |
| **Compote,** open, 8" d., 5" h. | 75.00 |
| **Compote,** open, 10" d., 6" h. | 80.00 |
| **Compote,** open, 10" d., 9" h. | 100.00 |
| **Creamer,** clear | 78.00 |
| **Creamer,** frosted | 200.00 to 250.00 |
| **Creamer,** Miss Neilson & Fanny Davenport | 84.00 |
| **Creamer & cov. sugar bowl,** pr. | 135.00 |
| **Goblet,** Lotta Crabtree & Kate Claxton | 77.00 |
| **Goblet,** frosted bowl | 97.00 |
| **Marmalade jar,** cov., Maude Granger & Annie Pixley | 110.00 |
| **Mug,** Pinafore scene | 47.00 |
| **\*Pickle dish,** Kate Claxton, "Love's Request is Pickles," 5¼ x 9¼" | 36.00 |
| **Pitcher,** water, 9" h., Miss Neilson & Maggie Mitchell | 275.00 to 325.00 |
| **Platter,** 7 x 11½", Pinafore scene | 107.00 |
| **\*Relish,** Miss Neilson, 5 x 8" | 40.00 |
| **Relish,** Maude Granger, 5 x 9" | 75.00 to 95.00 |
| **Salt shaker w/original pewter top** | 56.00 |
| **Sauce dish,** Maggie Mitchell & Fanny Davenport, 4½" d., 2½" h. | 18.00 |
| **Spooner,** Mary Anderson & Maude Granger | 80.00 |
| **Sugar bowl,** cov., Lotta Crabtree & Kate Claxton | 111.00 |

### ADONIS (Pleat & Tuck or Washboard)

| | |
|---|---|
| **Bowl,** master berry, canary yellow | 50.00 |
| **Celery** | 26.00 |
| **Compote,** cov., 8" d. | 110.00 |

Creamer, blue ...................................... 35.00
Creamer, clear ..................................... 25.00
Plate, 10" d., clear................................. 13.00
Plate, 10" d., green .............................. 35.00
Plate, 11" d., canary yellow.................. 28.00
Relish dish ............................................ 9.00
Salt shaker w/original top.................. 27.00
Sauce dish ............................................ 7.00
Sugar bowl, cov., clear......................... 28.00

## ALASKA (Lion's Leg)

Banana boat, blue
    opalescent........................ 200.00 to 250.00
Banana boat, emerald
    green ................................ 165.00 to 185.00
Banana boat, canary opalescent........ 200.00
Banana boat, canary opalescent
    w/enameling ..................................... 325.00
Berry set: master bowl & four sauce
    dishes; emerald green, 5 pcs. .......... 250.00
Berry set: master bowl & six sauce
    dishes; emerald green w/gold
    enamel decoration, 7 pcs. ............... 265.00
Bowl, 8" sq., blue opalescent
    (ILLUS. below) ................. 200.00 to 225.00
Bowl, 8" sq., canary opalescent.......... 130.00
Bowl, 8" sq., canary opalescent
    w/enameled florals............................ 200.00
Bowl, 8" sq., clear opalescent
    w/enameled florals.............................. 65.00
Bowl, 8" sq., emerald green.................. 55.00
Bowl, 8" sq., emerald green
    w/enameled florals ........... 100.00 to 125.00
Bowl, 8" sq., emerald green w/gold &
    enameling, w/silver plate stand ........ 100.00
Butter dish, cov., blue
    opalescent........................ 350.00 to 375.00
Butter dish, cov., canary
    opalescent........................ 250.00 to 300.00

Butter dish, cov., clear opalescent..... 102.00
Butter dish, cov., emerald green.......... 92.00
Butter dish, cov., emerald green
    w/enameled florals .......... 200.00 to 250.00
Celery (or jewel) tray, blue
    opalescent ...................................... 132.00
Celery tray, clear................................. 75.00
Celery tray, emerald green.................. 75.00
Celery tray, emerald green w/gold ....... 85.00
Creamer, blue opalescent.................... 75.00
Creamer, canary opalescent................ 76.00
Creamer, clear opalescent ..... 35.00 to 40.00
Creamer, emerald green...................... 48.00
Creamer, emerald green w/enameled
    florals ............................................... 70.00
Creamer & cov. sugar bowl, blue
    opalescent, pr. ................................ 220.00
Creamer & cov. sugar bowl, canary
    opalescent, pr. ................................ 175.00
Creamer & cov. sugar bowl, emerald
    green, pr. .......................................... 90.00
Cruet w/original stopper, blue
    opalescent ...................................... 260.00
Cruet w/original stopper, blue
    opalescent w/enameled florals ......... 300.00
Cruet w/original stopper, canary
    opalescent w/enameled
    florals............................. 250.00 to 300.00
Cruet w/original stopper, clear
    opalescent w/enameled florals ........... 52.00
Cruet w/original stopper, emerald
    green ............................................... 275.00
Cruet w/original stopper, emerald
    green w/enameled florals ................. 175.00
Pitcher, water, blue
    opalescent........................ 300.00 to 350.00
Pitcher, water, blue opalescent
    w/enameled florals ........... 500.00 to 525.00
Pitcher, water, canary opalescent ...... 350.00

*Alaska Bowl*

**Pitcher,** water, canary opalescent
w/enameled florals .......... **425.00 to 500.00**
**Pitcher,** water, clear opalescent
w/enameled florals & gold trim ......... **125.00**
**Pitcher,** water, emerald green
w/enameled florals........................... **285.00**
**Salt shaker w/original top,** blue
opalescent........................... **75.00 to 85.00**
**Salt shaker w/original top,** canary
opalescent........................................ **75.00**
**Salt shaker w/original top,** clear
opalescent ...................................... **25.00**
**Salt shaker w/original top,** emerald
green ............................................... **70.00**
**Salt shaker w/original top,** emerald
green w/enameling ............................ **75.00**
**Sauce dish,** blue opalescent ............... **47.00**
**Sauce dish,** canary opalescent ........... **38.00**
**Sauce dish,** canary opalescent
w/enameled florals ............... **40.00 to 50.00**
**Sauce dish,** clear opalescent .............. **30.00**
**Sauce dish,** emerald green ................. **20.00**
**Sauce dish,** emerald green
w/enameled florals & leaves............... **38.00**
**Spooner,** blue opalescent ................... **60.00**
**Spooner,** canary opalescent................ **70.00**
**Spooner,** canary opalescent
w/enameled florals........................... **112.00**
**Spooner,** clear opalescent................... **42.00**
**Spooner,** clear opalescent
w/enameled florals............................. **75.00**
**Spooner,** emerald green...................... **34.00**
**Spooner,** emerald green w/enameled
florals ............................................. **70.00**
**Sugar bowl,** cov., blue opalescent ..... **165.00**
**Sugar bowl,** cov., canary opalescent... **210.00**
**Sugar bowl,** cov., canary opalescent
w/enameled florals........................... **247.00**
**Sugar bowl,** cov., emerald green
w/enameled florals............................. **73.00**
**Table set:** cov. butter, creamer, cov.
sugar bowl & spooner; blue
opalescent, 4 pcs. ............ **600.00 to 650.00**
**Table set:** cov. butter, creamer, cov.
sugar bowl & spooner; canary
opalescent, 4 pcs............................. **700.00**
**Tumbler,** blue opalescent..................... **70.00**
**Tumbler,** blue opalescent
w/enameled florals............................. **75.00**
**Tumbler,** canary opalescent... **75.00 to 85.00**
**Tumbler,** canary opalescent
w/enameled florals............................. **80.00**
**Tumbler,** emerald green ...................... **46.00**
**Water set:** pitcher & six tumblers; blue
opalescent, 7 pcs.............................. **695.00**
**Water set:** pitcher & six tumblers;
canary opalescent, 7 pcs... **775.00 to 800.00**

**ALEXIS - See Priscilla Pattern**

**AMBERETTE - See Klondike Pattern**

## APOLLO
**Bowl,** 8" d.......................................... **22.00**
**Cake stand,** engraved, 9" d.... **45.00 to 50.00**
**Cake stand,** plain, 9" to 10½" d. ........... **50.00**
**Celery tray**...................................... **16.00**
**Celery vase** ......................... **37.00 to 45.00**
**Compote,** cov., 4¾" d., 8¾" h.............. **45.00**
**Compote,** cov., 6" d........................... **41.00**
**Compote,** cov., 8" d........................... **65.00**
**Compote,** open, 5" d........................... **25.00**
**Creamer,** engraved.............................. **57.00**
**Creamer,** plain ................................. **45.00**
**Goblet,** engraved ................................ **35.00**
**Goblet,** frosted ................................. **36.00**
**Goblet,** plain ................................... **32.00**
**Lamp,** kerosene-type, clear, 7" h. ......... **60.00**
**Lamp,** kerosene-type, blue, 8" h. ........ **225.00**
**Lamp,** kerosene-type, blue, 9" h. ........ **265.00**
**Lamp,** kerosene-type, clear, 10" h. ........ **60.00**
**Lamp,** kerosene-type, blue base
w/canary font ................................... **245.00**
**Pitcher,** water, bulbous........................ **72.00**
**Salt dip,** master size ........................... **20.00**
**Sauce dish,** flat or footed ................... **11.00**

*Apollo Spooner*

**Spooner** (ILLUS.) ................................ **40.00**
**Sugar bowl,** cov. ................................. **50.00**
**Sugar bowl,** cov., etched..................... **75.00**
**Sugar shaker w/original top**... **60.00 to 65.00**
**Syrup pitcher w/original top** .. **85.00 to 95.00**
**Toothpick holder** ............................... **28.00**
**Tray,** water ........................................ **40.00**
**Tumbler,** frosted ................................ **25.00**

## ART (Job's Tears)
**Banana stand**.................................. **100.00**
**Bowl,** 7" d., flared rim, footed............... **25.00**

Bowl, 8" sq., shallow............................ 33.00
Bowl, 8½" d............................................ 40.00
Bowl, 9¾" d............................................ 38.00
Bowl, rectangular.................................. 20.00
Butter dish, cov., clear......................... 45.00
Cake stand, 9" to 10½" d. ...... 65.00 to 70.00
Celery vase .......................................... 47.00
Compote, cov., 6" d., 10" h................... 54.00
Compote, cov., 7" d. ............................. 80.00
Compote, cov., 9" d. ............................. 60.00
Compote, open, jelly, 5" d. ................... 27.00
Compote, open, 7" d.............................. 56.00
Compote, open, 8" d., high stand......... 35.00
Compote, open, 9" d., 7¼" h. .............. 48.00
Compote, open, 10" d., 9" h. ............... 50.00
Cracker jar, cov., 7" d., 8" h. to top of
  finial ................................................... 95.00
Creamer................................................ 42.00

*Art Goblet*

Goblet (ILLUS.)...................................... 55.00
Pitcher, water, bulbous......................... 82.00
Pitcher, water, 9½" h. .......................... 150.00
Relish, clear, 4¼ x 7¾"........................ 19.00
Sauce dish, flat or footed ..................... 11.00
Spooner................................................ 27.00
Sugar bowl, cov., engraved ................. 44.00
Sugar bowl, cov., plain......................... 45.00
Sugar bowl, open ................................. 28.00
Tumbler ................................................ 30.00

## ASHBURTON

Ale glass, flint, 6½" h............................ 82.00
Bitters bottle w/original pewter lid..... 65.00
Celery vase, plain rim, flint .................. 59.00
Celery vase, scalloped rim, canary
  yellow, flint...................... 700.00 to 850.00
Celery vase, scalloped rim, clear,
  flint...................................................... 135.00

Champagne, flint .................................. 59.00
Champagne, barrel-shaped, flint .......... 85.00
Claret, flint, 5¼" h. .............................. 63.00
Cordial, clear, flint, 4¼" h. ...... 40.00 to 45.00
Cordial, non-flint .................................. 60.00
Creamer, applied handle,
  flint.............................. 250.00 to 260.00
Decanter, bar lip w/patent pewter
  stopper clear, flint ............................ 155.00
Egg cup, clambroth, flint.................... 155.00
Egg cup, clear, flint ............... 20.00 to 30.00
Egg cup, clear, non-flint....................... 15.00
Egg cup, disconnected ovals, clear...... 35.00
Egg cup, short, flint.............................. 42.00
Goblet, short, flint ................................ 42.00
Goblet, barrel-shaped, flint.... 50.00 to 55.00
Goblet, flared, flint, clear ........ 50.00 to 55.00
Goblet, flared, flint, clear w/gold, 6" h... 100.00
Goblet, non-flint ................................... 30.00
Honey dishes, 3½" d., set of 8............. 85.00
Mug, applied handle, 3" h. ................... 60.00
Mug, applied handle, 4¾" h. ................ 87.00
Pitcher, water, applied hollow handle,
  flint................................. 400.00 to 450.00
Pomade jar, cov., white opaque, flint ... 195.00
Sauce dish, flint.................................... 7.00

*Ashburton Sugar Bowl*

Sugar bowl, cov., flint
  (ILLUS.)............................. 95.00 to 135.00
Sugar bowl, cov., fiery opalescent,
  flint...................................................... 1,650.00
Tumbler, bar, flint ................................ 66.00
Tumbler, water, flint.............................. 59.00
Tumbler, water, footed ......................... 92.00
Tumbler, whiskey, applied handle,
  flint................................. 100.00 to 125.00
Wine, clear, flint ................................... 39.00
Wine, clear, knob stem ......................... 85.00
Wine w/cut design, clear w/gold trim... 125.00
Wine, peacock green, flint.................... 650.00
Wine, non-flint...................................... 31.00

**ıg cup,** coarse rib ............... 20.00 to 30.00
**ıg cup,** fine rib, single vine ............... 40.00
**ɔblet,** barrel-shaped, fine rib, single vine, knob stem .................... 55.00 to 60.00
**ɔoblet,** barrel-shaped, fine rib, single vine, plain stem .................... 35.00 to 45.00
**ɔblet,** coarse rib ............................................ 46.00
**ɔblet,** double vine ................... 65.00 to 70.00
**ɔblet,** single vine, fine rib, pale green, 5⅞" h. ...................................... 210.00
**ɔney dish,** rayed center, 3¼" d. ..... 22.00
**ɔney dish,** ringed center, 3½" d. ........ 22.00
**ɪmp,** kerosene-type, 7½" h. ...................... 200.00 to 250.00
**ɪmp,** kerosene-type, 8½" h. .............. 175.00
**ɪmp,** kerosene-type, clear font, ɔrass stem w/engraved decoration & ɪarble base, flint, 11" h. ................... 247.00
**ɪcher,** cider, double vine ................. 230.00
**ɪcher,** milk, double vine ................. 350.00
**ɪcher,** water, 8¾" h., coarse rib, ɔouble vine ............................................ 407.00
**ɪte,** 6" d., fine rib, single vine .......... 115.00
**ɪlt dip,** cov., master size, footed, ɔeaded rim, fine rib, single vine ......... 72.00
**ɪlt dip,** open, master size, footed, ɔcalloped rim, single vine ................... 48.00
**ɪuce dish,** double vine ...................... 20.00
**ɪuce dish,** single vine ....................... 21.00
**ɔooner,** clear, low foot, double vine ... 60.00
**ɔooner,** clear, scalloped rim, single ɪine ........................................ 35.00 to 40.00
**ɔooner,** cobalt blue ......................... 600.00
**ɪgar bowl,** cov., single ɪine ...................................... 100.00 to 125.00
**ɪrup pitcher w/original top,** applied ɪandle, fine rib, single vine, ɔlear ................................. 600.00 to 700.00
**ɪrup pitcher w/original top,** applied ɪandle, pale green ........................... 525.00
**ɪmbler,** bar, fine rib, single ɪine ........................................ 95.00 to 125.00
**ɪmbler,** coarse rib, double vine ........ 105.00
**ɪumbler,** fine rib, single ɪine ........................................ 65.00 to 75.00
**ɪmbler,** fine rib, single vine, banded .. 150.00
**ɪmbler,** whiskey ............................... 135.00
**ɪne,** barrel-shaped, knob stem, fine ɪib, single vine, rayed ɪase .................................... 100.00 to 125.00
**ɪne,** barrel-shaped, fine rib, double ɪine, w/cut bellflowers ...................... 325.00
**ɪne,** straight sides, plain stem, rayed ɪase ........................................ 90.00 to 100.00

**GLER**
**ɪwl,** 8" d. ............................................ 45.00
**ɪlery vase** ......................................... 77.00
**ɪampagne** .......................................... 85.00

**Cordial** ...................................................... 50.00
**Decanter** w/bar lip, qt. ......................... 105.00
**Goblet,** 6" h. .......................................... 50.00
**Lamp,** 9" .............................................. 125.00
**Lamp,** whale oil, 10" h. ......................... 175.00
**Plate,** 6" d., clear ................................... 30.00
**Salt dip,** master size, clear ................. 40.00
**Sauce dish,** clear, 4" d. ........................ 16.00
**Tumbler** ................................................. 67.00
**Tumbler,** bar, flint ................................. 45.00

## BIRD & STRAWBERRY (Bluebird)

**Berry set,** master bowl & five sauce dishes; w/color, 6 pcs. ....................... 525.00
**Berry set,** master bowl & five sauce dishes; clear w/gold, 6 pcs. ............... 175.00
**Bowl,** 5½" d., clear .................. 30.00 to 35.00
**Bowl,** 5½" d., w/color ............................ 35.00
**Bowl,** 7½" d., footed, clear .................... 62.00
**Bowl,** 7½" d., footed, w/color ............... 70.00
**Bowl,** 9" d., flat, clear ............................ 55.00
**Bowl,** 9" d., flat, w/color ....................... 75.00
**Bowl,** 9½" l., 6" w., oval, footed ........... 58.00
**Bowl,** 10" d., flat, clear ............ 60.00 to 70.00
**Bowl,** 10" d., flat, w/color & gold trim .. 115.00
**Butter dish,** cov. .................... 100.00 to 125.00
**Butter dish,** cov., w/color ... 175.00 to 225.00
**Cake stand,** 9" to 9½" d. ......... 50.00 to 60.00
***Celery tray,** 10" l. ................................. 52.00
**Compote,** cov., 6" d., low stand ............ 57.00
***Compote,** cov., 6½" d., 9½" h. ......... 145.00
**Compote,** cov., jelly ............................ 130.00
**Compote,** open, 4½" d., 5" h. ............... 47.00
**Compote,** open, 6" d., ruffled rim, w/color ................................................ 81.00
**Creamer,** clear ........................ 55.00 to 60.00
**Creamer,** w/color ................................ 115.00
**Creamer & sugar bowl** ......................... 110.00
**Dish,** heart-shaped ................. 55.00 to 60.00
**Pitcher,** water, clear ......... 300.00 to 325.00
**Pitcher,** water, w/color ........................ 345.00
**Plate,** 12" d. ........................................... 80.00
**Punch cup** ............................................. 22.00

*Bird & Strawberry Sauce Dish*

## ATLAS (Crystal Ball or Cannon Ball)

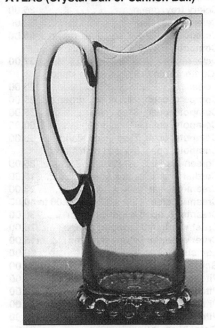

*Atlas Pitcher*

**Berry set:** master bowl & four sauce dishes; ruby-stained w/gold, 5 pcs. .... 47.00
**Bowl,** open, 6" d. ................................... 37.00
**Butter dish,** cov. ................................... 41.00
**Cake stand,** clear, 8" to 10" d. ....................................... 45.00 to 50.00
**Celery vase** .......................................... 39.00
**Champagne,** 5½" h. ................ 30.00 to 35.00
**Claret,** 4¾" h. ........................................ 37.00
**Compote,** open, 8" d., 8" h. ................. 102.00
**Cordial** ................................................... 42.00
**Creamer,** flat or pedestal base ............ 20.00
**Goblet,** engraved .................................. 30.00
**Goblet,** plain ......................................... 26.00
**Pitcher,** milk, tankard, applied handle .. 45.00
**Pitcher,** water, tankard, applied handle (ILLUS. above) ...................... 50.00
**Salt dip,** individual size ....................... 15.00
**Salt dip,** master size ............................ 21.00
**Sauce dish,** flat or footed, clear ........... 11.00
**Spooner,** clear ...................................... 40.00
**Toothpick holder** .................................. 26.00
**Tray,** water ............................................. 65.00
**Tumbler** ................................................. 19.00
**Wine** ........................................ 25.00 to 30.00

## BABY THUMBPRINT - See Dakota Pattern

## BALDER - See Pennsylvania Pattern

## BARLEY

*Barley Celery Vase*

**Bowl,** 6¼ x 8½" oval, scalloped rim ...... 16.00
**Bowl,** 10" oval ....................................... 36.00
**Butter dish,** cov. ..................... 35.00 to 40.00
**Cake stand,** 8" to 10½" d. ...... 35.00 to 40.00
**Celery vase** (ILLUS. above) ................ 41.00
**Compote,** open, 7" d., 8" h. .................. 25.00
**Compote,** open, 8½" d., 8" h. ............... 33.00
**Compote,** open, 8¾" d., 6½" h., scalloped rim .................................... 26.00
**Creamer** ................................................. 24.00
**Goblet** ................................................... 35.00
**Marmalade jar,** cov. .............................. 50.00
**Pickle castor** w/silver plate frame & tongs .................................................. 80.00
**Pitcher,** water ......................... 45.00 to 50.00
**Plate,** 6" d. ............................................. 30.00
**Platter,** 8 x 13" ....................................... 26.00
**Relish,** 8" l., 6" w. .................................. 19.00
**Relish,** handled, 9½" l., 5¼" w. .............. 16.00
**Salt shaker w/original top** ................... 23.00
**Sauce dish,** flat or footed ..................... 10.00
**Spooner** ................................................. 20.00
**Wine,** 3¾" h. ........................................... 30.00

## BASKETWEAVE

**Bread plate,** amber .............................. 30.00
**Bread plate,** blue .................................. 29.00
**Creamer,** amber .................................... 35.00
**Cup,** blue ................................................ 30.00
**Cup & saucer,** amber ............. 25.00 to 30.00
**Cup & saucer,** canary ........................... 37.00
***Goblet,** amber ...................... 14.00 to 20.00
***Goblet,** blue ........................................ 35.00
***Goblet,** canary .................................... 34.00
***Goblet,** clear ....................................... 27.00

Pitcher, milk, blue .......................... 50.00
*Pitcher, water, amber ....................... 57.00
*Pitcher, water, blue ........................ 70.00
*Pitcher, water, canary ...................... 77.00
Pitcher, water, clear ........................ 70.00
Plate, 8¾" d., handled, amber .............. 24.00
Plate, 8¾" d., handled, blue ................ 19.00
Plate, 8¾" d., handled, clear .............. 10.00
Sauce dish ................................... 8.00
*Tray, water, scenic center, amber,
   12" ...................................... 47.00
*Tray, water, scenic center, blue, 12" .. 55.00
*Tray, water, scenic center, canary,
   12" ...................................... 50.00
*Tray, water, scenic center, clear, 12" .. 55.00
Wine .......................... 16.00 to 20.00
Water set: water pitcher & two
   tumblers w/tray; blue, 4 pcs. ............ 75.00
Water set: water pitcher & three
   tumblers; canary, 4 pcs. ................ 125.00

## BEADED DEWDROP - See Wisconsin Pattern

## BEADED GRAPE (California)

*Beaded Grape Bowl*

Bowl, 5½" sq., clear ......................... 17.00
Bowl, 5½" sq., green .............. 20.00 to 25.00
Bowl, 6½" sq., green .............. 20.00 to 25.00
Bowl, 7½" sq., green ......................... 32.00
Bowl, 8" sq., clear (ILLUS. above) ........ 24.00
Bowl, 6¼ x 8½", rectangle, clear .......... 20.00
Bowl, 6¼ x 8½", rectangle, green ......... 28.00
Bowl, 9" sq., four-footed .................... 15.00
Bowls, berry, green, set of 6 .............. 212.00
Bread tray, clear, 7 x 10" ................... 20.00
Bread tray, green, 7 x 10" ...... 85.00 to 95.00
Butter dish, cov., square, clear ........... 55.00
Butter dish, cov., square,
   green .......................... 70.00 to 80.00
Cake stand, clear, 9" sq., 6" h. ........... 55.00

Cake stand, green, 9" sq., 6" h. .......... 102.00
Celery tray, green ........................... 35.00
Celery vase, clear ........................... 32.00
Compote, cov., 4⅞" sq., 6" h., green .... 55.00
Compote, cov., 6½" sq., high stand,
   clear ..................................... 37.00
*Compote, cov., 8½" sq., high stand,
   clear .................................... 125.00
Compote, open, jelly, 4" sq., green ...... 25.00
Compote, open, 6" sq., clear .............. 35.00
Compote, open, 6" sq., green .............. 60.00
Compote, open, 7" sq., high stand ...... 38.00
Compote, open, 8½" sq., high stand,
   green ..................................... 85.00
Cordial ...................................... 15.00
Creamer, clear ............................... 28.00
Creamer, green ................... 35.00 to 40.00
Creamer & open sugar bowl, pr. ........ 30.00
Cruet w/original stopper, clear ........... 70.00
Cruet w/original stopper, green ........ 115.00
Egg cup ...................................... 30.00
Goblet ....................................... 35.00
Pitcher, milk, green ........................ 150.00
Pitcher, water, round, green ............... 78.00
Pitcher, water, square, green ............. 125.00
Pitcher, water, tankard, green w/gold ... 150.00
Plate, 8" sq., green ......................... 31.00
Relish, clear, 4 x 7" ........................ 20.00
Relish, green w/gold, 4 x 7" ............... 35.00
Salt shaker w/original top, clear ........ 32.00
Salt shaker w/original top, green ........ 47.00
*Sauce dish, clear .......................... 11.00
*Sauce dish, green .......................... 15.00
Sauce dishes, clear, set of 7 ............. 100.00
Sauce dish, handled, clear ................. 15.00
Sauce dish, handled, green ................. 30.00
Spooner, clear ............................... 40.00
Sugar bowl, cov., clear ..................... 54.00
Table set, green, 4 pcs. .................... 312.00
Toothpick holder, clear ..................... 23.00
Toothpick holder, green ........ 55.00 to 60.00
*Tumbler, clear .............................. 27.00
*Tumbler, green .............................. 40.00
*Wine, clear ................................. 35.00
*Wine, green ................................. 62.00

## BEADED LOOP (Oregon, U.S. Glass Co.)

Berry set, master bowl & six sauce
   dishes, 7 pcs. ............................ 65.00
Bowl, berry, 9½" l., 6¾" w. oval, clear .. 25.00
Bread platter ................................ 21.00
Butter dish, cov., clear ..................... 46.00
Cake stand, 9" to 10½" d. ................. 46.00
Celery vase, clear, 7" h. ................... 27.00
Compote, cov., 7" d. ........................ 90.00
Compote, cov., 11" .......................... 42.00
Compote, open, jelly, clear ................ 31.00
Compote, open, 5¼" d., 4½" h., clear .. 15.00
Compote, open, 7" d., clear ............... 26.00

*Beaded Loop Goblet*

Compote, open, 7½" d., low stand,
   clear ..................................... 38.00
Creamer, clear ............................... 35.00
*Goblet (ILLUS. above) .......... 30.00 to 35.00
Goblet, w/gold trim .......................... 32.00
Mug, footed, clear ........................... 38.00
Mug, ruby-stained ............................ 25.00
Pickle dish, boat-shaped, 7¼" l. .......... 12.00
Pickle dish, boat-shaped, 9" l. ............ 15.00
Pitcher, pint, 7" h. ......................... 44.00
Pitcher, milk, 8½" h. ........................ 37.00
Pitcher, water, tankard .......... 45.00 to 50.00
Relish ....................................... 16.00
Relish, w/advertising for "Carson
   Furniture, Pittsburgh" .................... 26.00
Salt shaker w/original top .................. 25.00
Sauce dish, flat or footed, each ........... 13.00
Spooner, clear ............................... 26.00
Spooner, ruby-stained ....................... 65.00
Table set, 4 pcs. ........................... 186.00
Toothpick holder ................. 45.00 to 50.00
Tumbler, clear ............................... 49.00
Vase, small ...................... 40.00 to 45.00
Wine ............................. 55.00 to 65.00

## BEADED MIRROR

Celery vase .................................. 50.00
Goblet ........................... 20.00 to 25.00
Pitcher, water ............................... 49.00
Plate, 8" d. ................................. 27.00
Spooner ...................................... 26.00
Sugar bowl, cov. ................. 40.00 to 45.00
Tumbler .......................... 45.00 to 50.00

## BEARDED HEAD - See Viking Pattern

## BELLFLOWER

Bowl, 7½" d., 2" h. ......................... 110.00
Bowl, 8" d., 4½" h., scalloped
   rim .............................. 75.00 to 80.00

Butter dish, cov. ............................
Castor bottle w/original stopper .
Castor set, four-bottle, w/pewter
   stand .......................................
Castor set, five-bottle, single vine,
   w/pewter stand ............................
Celery vase, fine rib, single vine .....
Champagne, barrel-shaped, fine ri[b]
   knob stem, plain base ....................
Champagne, straight sides, plain
   stem, rayed base ..........................
Compote, open, 4½" d., low stand,
   scalloped rim ..................... 85.00
Compote, open, 6" d., low stand ...
Compote, open, 7" d., 5" h., fine rib
   double vine .................... 100.00
Compote, open, 7" d., low stand,
   scalloped rim ..................... 80.0[0]
Compote, open, 8" d. ...................
Compote, open, 8" d., 5" h., scallop[ed]
   rim, single vine ................. 80.0[0]
Compote, open, 8" d., 8" h., pedes[tal]
   base, single vine .........................
Compote, open, 8" d., 8" h., dome-
   footed, single vine .......................
Compote, open, 9½" d., 8½" h.,
   scalloped rim, single vine ...............
Cordial, barrel-shaped, knob stem,
   rayed base ................................
Cordial, fine rib, single vine, knob
   stem ......................................
Cordial, fine rib, single vine, plain
   stem ......................................

*Bellflower Creamer*

Creamer, fine rib, double vine, appli[ed]
   handle (ILLUS.) .............. 150.00
Creamer, fine rib, single vine, applie[d]
   handle ....................................
Decanter w/bar lip, single vine, qt. ...
Decanter w/bar lip, patent stopper,
   double vine, qt. ..........................

Sauce dish, flat or footed, clear
  (ILLUS. bottom previous
  page) ..................................... 25.00 to 30.00
Sauce dish, w/color ............................ 34.00
Spooner, clear ..................................... 49.00
Spooner, w/color ............... 100.00 to 125.00
Sugar bowl, cov., clear ....................... 65.00
Table set, clear, 4 pcs. ....... 225.00 to 250.00
Table set, w/color, 4 pcs. ... 400.00 to 450.00
Tumbler, clear ........................ 50.00 to 55.00
Tumbler, w/color .................................. 95.00
Water set: pitcher & six tumblers;
  w/color, 7 pcs. .................. 700.00 to 750.00
Wine ....................................... 55.00 to 75.00

## BLUEBIRD - See Bird & Strawberry Pattern

## BUCKLE WITH STAR

*Buckle with Star Compote*

Cake stand, 9" d. ............................... 40.00
Celery vase ....................................... 32.00
Compote, cov., 7" d. (ILLUS.) .. 70.00 to 80.00
Compote, open, 7" d., 5½" h. .............. 19.00
Compote, open, 8" d. ........................... 37.00
Compote, open, 9¼" d., high stand .... 125.00
Compote, open, 10" d., 7" h. ... 35.00 to 50.00
Creamer ............................................. 32.00
Goblet ............................................... 28.00
Relish, 5⅛ x 7¼" oval .......................... 10.00
Sauce dish, flat or footed ...................... 9.00
Spooner .............................................. 27.00
Syrup pitcher w/metal top ............... 102.00
Wine .................................................. 21.00

## BULL'S EYE WITH DIAMOND POINT

Celery vase ...................................... 180.00
Champagne ....................................... 687.00
Compote, cov., 5½" d. ......................... 50.00
Compote, open, jelly ........................... 30.00
Cordial .............................................. 357.00
Creamer, applied handle ................... 175.00
Decanter w/bar lip, pt. ....................... 209.00
Egg cup ............................................. 187.00
Goblet ............................... 100.00 to 125.00

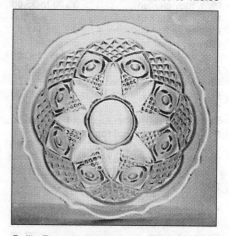

*Bull's Eye with Diamond Point Honey Dish*

Honey dish (ILLUS.) ............................ 25.00
Lamp, kerosene-type, applied strap
  handle, original burner & attached
  burner cover, 3" h. ........................... 250.00
Sauce dish ......................................... 22.00
Spooner .............................................. 91.00
Sugar bowl, cov. ............... 110.00 to 130.00
Tumbler, bar ..................................... 135.00
Tumbler, water .................................. 120.00
Tumbler, whiskey ............................... 148.00
Wine, small ....................................... 550.00

## BUTTON ARCHES

Bowl, 8" d., ruby-stained, souvenir ....... 60.00
Butter dish, cov., clear ........................ 52.00
*Butter dish, cov., ruby-stained,
  souvenir ......................................... 100.00
Compote, open, jelly, 4½" h., ruby-
  stained ............................................. 40.00
Creamer, clear .................................... 18.00
*Creamer, ruby-stained ........................ 37.00
Creamer, ruby-stained, souvenir, 3½" h. .. 30.00
Creamer, ruby-stained, souvenir,
  4½" h. ............................................. 45.00
Creamer, individual size, clambroth ...... 30.00
*Creamer, individual size, ruby-
  stained ............................................. 28.00

**Cruet w/original stopper,** ruby-
stained............................ 180.00 to 185.00
**Goblet,** clambroth ................................. 26.00
**Goblet,** clambroth, souvenir.................. 20.00
**Goblet,** clear ........................................ 24.00
***Goblet,** ruby-stained............................ 51.00
**Match holder,** clambroth, souvenir....... 35.00
**Match holder,** ruby-stained, souvenir... 13.00
**Mug,** child's, ruby-stained, souvenir...... 23.00
**Mug,** clear ............................... 20.00 to 30.00
**Mug,** ruby-stained.................... 30.00 to 35.00
**Mug,** ruby-stained, souvenir, 3½" h. ..... 27.00
**Pitcher,** tankard, 8¾" h. ...................... 117.00
**Pitcher,** water, tankard, ruby-stained,
souvenir of Pan American Exposition.. 150.00
**Punch cup,** clear ................................... 9.00
**Punch cup,** ruby-stained ...................... 19.00
**Punch cup,** ruby-stained, souvenir....... 28.00
**Salt dip** .............................................. 18.00
**Salt shaker w/original top,** clear ......... 18.00
**Salt shaker w/original top,** clear,
souvenir.................................................. 8.00
**Salt shaker w/original top,** ruby-
stained .................................................. 26.00
**Salt & pepper shakers w/original
tops,** clear, small, pr............................ 35.00
***Sauce dish,** clear ............................... 16.00
**Sauce dish,** ruby-stained..................... 30.00
**Spooner,** clear ..................................... 27.00
***Spooner,** ruby-stained......................... 42.00
**Spooner,** ruby-stained w/clear band..... 62.00
**Spooner,** ruby-stained & engraved....... 44.00
**Sugar bowl,** cov., clear........................ 45.00
***Sugar bowl,** cov., ruby-stained ........... 85.00
**Syrup pitcher w/original top,** clear... 132.00
**Syrup pitcher w/original top,** ruby-
stained .................................................. 147.00
**Syrup pitcher w/original top,** ruby-
stained, souvenir ............................... 110.00
**Table set,** ruby-stained, 4 pcs. ........... 245.00
***Toothpick holder,** ruby-stained .......... 28.00
***Toothpick holder,** ruby-stained,
souvenir ............................................... 30.00
**Tumbler,** clambroth, souvenir............... 23.00
**Tumbler,** clear ..................................... 16.00
**Tumbler,** clear w/frosted band.............. 25.00
**Tumbler,** ruby-stained .......................... 41.00
**Tumbler,** ruby-stained, souvenir........... 39.00
**Tumblers,** ruby-stained w/frosted
band, set of 6 ...................................... 210.00
**Vase,** engraved .................................... 22.00
**Water set:** pitcher & three tumblers;
ruby-stained & engraved, 4 pcs........ 150.00
**Water set:** tankard pitcher & four
tumblers; ruby-stained, 5 pcs. .......... 265.00
**Water set:** tankard pitcher & four
tumblers; ruby-stained, souvenir,
5 pcs. ................................................. 210.00

**Water set:** pitcher & five tumblers;
clear w/frosted band & gold, 6 pcs. .. **225.00**
**Water set:** tankard pitcher & five
tumblers; ruby-stained, souvenir,
6 pcs................................. **300.00 to 350.00**
**Water set:** pitcher & six tumblers;
clear, 7 pcs. ..................................... **321.00**
**Water set:** pitcher & six tumblers;
clear w/frosted band & gold, 7 pcs. .. **280.00**
**Water set:** pitcher & six tumblers;
ruby-stained, 7 pcs. ......................... **295.00**

*Button Arches Wine*

**Whiskey shot glass,** ruby-stained ....... 14.00
**Wine,** clambroth ................................... 25.00
**Wine,** clear ......................................... 30.00
**Wine,** ruby-stained .............................. 37.00
**Wine,** ruby-stained, souvenir (ILLUS.) .. 35.00

### CABLE
**Bowl,** 9" d............................................ 57.00
**Butter dish,** cov.................................... 90.00
**Celery vase** ......................................... 82.00
**Champagne**......................................... 250.00
**Compote,** open, 7" d., 5" h. ................. 51.00
**Compote,** open, 8" d., 4¾" h. .............. 67.00
**Compote,** open, 9" d., 4½" h. .............. 70.00
**Decanter w/stopper,** pt. ..................... 175.00
**Egg cup,** clambroth, flint..................... 385.00
**Egg cup,** clear (ILLUS. top next page) .. 47.00
**Goblet**............................................90.00 to 95.00
**Honey dish,** 3½" d., 1" h. ................... 15.00
**Plate,** 6" d........................................... 90.00
**Salt dip,** individual size ....................... 37.00
**Salt dip,** master size ........................... 50.00
**Sauce dish** ......................................... 26.00
**Spooner,** chartreuse green............. 1,200.00
**Spooner,** clambroth w/gilt trim............ 850.00

*Cable Egg Cup*

**Spooner,** clear...................... **35.00 to 45.00**
**Spooner,** jade green w/gilt trim........... **850.00**
**Sugar bowl,** cov ................................. **115.00**
**Tumbler,** footed ............................... **335.00**
**Tumbler,** whiskey ............................. **230.00**
**Wine** ................................ **200.00 to 225.00**

## CALIFORNIA - See Beaded Grape Pattern

## CANNON BALL - See Atlas Pattern

## CAPE COD

*Cape Cod Spooner*

**Bread platter** ....................................... **48.00**
**Compote,** cov., 8" d., 12" h................ **140.00**

**Compote,** open, 8" d., 5½" h. ............... **43.00**
**Marmalade jar,** cov.............................. **65.00**
**Pitcher,** water ...................................... **95.00**
**Plate,** 6" d............................................ **35.00**
**Plate,** 10" d., open handles.................. **52.00**
**Sauce dish,** flat or footed ..................... **16.00**
**Spooner** (ILLUS. bottom previous
    column)............................................... **35.00**

## CLASSIC

**Berry set,** master bowl & eight sauce
    dishes, 9 pcs..................................... **475.00**
**Bowl,** open, 8" hexagon, open log
    feet .................................. **100.00 to 125.00**
**Butter dish,** cov., collared
    base .................................. **125.00 to 150.00**
**Butter dish,** cov., open log
    feet .................................. **200.00 to 225.00**
**Celery vase,** collared base ................. **147.00**
**Celery vase,** open log feet................... **175.00**
**Compote,** cov., 6½" d., collared base .. **172.00**
**Compote,** cov., 6½" d., open log feet... **180.00**
**Compote,** cov., 7½" d., 8" h., open log
    feet.................................................... **220.00**
**Compote,** cov., 9" d., open log feet.... **265.00**
**Compote,** open, 7¾" d., open log
    feet.................................................... **150.00**
**Creamer,** collared base ...................... **125.00**
**Creamer,** open log feet....... **140.00 to 150.00**
**Creamer & sugar bowl,** open log
    feet, pr. ............................................ **225.00**
**Goblet**................................. **260.00 to 280.00**
**Pitcher,** milk, 8½" h., open log
    feet .................................. **450.00 to 600.00**
**Pitcher,** water, collared
    base .................................. **250.00 to 275.00**
**Pitcher,** water, 9½" h., open log feet .. **395.00**
**Plate,** 10" d., "Blaine" or "Hendricks,"
    signed Jacobus, each....................... **215.00**
**Plate,** 10" d., "Cleveland" ................... **200.00**
**Plate,** 10" d., "Logan".......... **165.00 to 225.00**
**Plate,** 10" d., "Warrior" ....................... **154.00**
**Plate,** 10" d., "Warrior," signed
    Jacobus ............................................ **185.00**
**Sauce dish,** open log feet ...... **35.00 to 40.00**
**Spooner,** collared base ........................ **95.00**
**Spooner,** open log feet....................... **120.00**
**Sugar bowl,** cov., collared base ......... **150.00**
**Sugar bowl,** cov., open log feet.......... **185.00**

## COLORADO (Lacy Medallion)

**Banana bowl,** two turned-up sides,
    blue..................................................... **35.00**
**Banana stand,** green ............. **30.00 to 35.00**
**Berry set:** 8" d. master bowl & five
    4" d. sauce dishes; green w/gold,
    6 pcs. ............................................... **160.00**
**Berry set:** master bowl & six sauce
    dishes; clear w/gold, 7 pcs. ............. **125.00**

Bowl, 4" d., blue.................................. 39.00
Bowl, 4" d., green w/gold..................... 20.00
Bowl, 5" d., ruffled rim, blue................. 35.00
Bowl, 7" d., footed, clear...................... 25.00
Bowl, 7½" d., footed, turned-up sides,
    blue w/gold .................................... 50.00
Bowl, 7½" d., footed, turned-up sides,
    green ................................................ 29.00
Bowl, 8" d., turned-up sides, blue......... 65.00
Bowl, 8" d., turned-up sides, green
    w/gold .............................................. 62.00
Bowl, 8½" d., footed, crimped edge,
    green ................................................ 40.00
Bowl, 9" d., footed, three turned-up
    sides, clear ...................................... 32.00
Bowl, 9" d., green w/gold...................... 45.00
Bowl, 9" d., footed, crimped edge,
    green ................................................ 40.00
Bowl, 10" d., footed, flared &
    scalloped rim, clear........................... 45.00
Bowl, 10" d., footed, fluted, green ........ 48.00
Bowl, violet, footed, blue...................... 38.00
Butter dish, cov., blue w/gold............ 260.00
Butter dish, cov., clear ......................... 62.00
Butter dish, cov., green ..... 100.00 to 125.00
Butter dish, cov., green w/gold ............ 84.00
Cake stand ............................................ 65.00
Cake stand, green, 7¾" d., 4" h. .......... 75.00
Cake stand, green w/gold, 9¼" d. ...... 125.00
Candy dish, clear.................. 20.00 to 30.00
Card tray, blue w/gold ........................ 120.00
Card tray, green.................... 30.00 to 35.00
Celery vase, green w/gold..................... 70.00
Cheese dish, cov., blue w/gold ............ 70.00
Compote, open, 6" d., 4" h., crimped
    rim..................................................... 22.00
Compote, open, 8" d., 7" h., beaded
    rim, green .......................... 100.00 to 125.00
Compote, open, 9½" d., 3½" h., clear
    w/gold .............................................. 87.00
Creamer, blue ....................................... 90.00
Creamer, blue, souvenir ....................... 60.00
Creamer, clear ...................................... 34.00
Creamer, green ..................... 35.00 to 45.00
Creamer, ruby-stained .......................... 54.00
Creamer, individual size,
    green .................................. 25.00 to 30.00
Creamer, individual size, green
    w/gold.................................. 35.00 to 40.00
Creamer, individual size, green
    w/gold, souvenir................................. 40.00
Creamer & sugar bowl, green, pr........ 60.00
Cup, punch, clear................................... 15.00
Cup, punch, green ................................. 28.00
Cup, punch, green, souvenir .. 20.00 to 25.00
Cup & saucer, green ............................. 45.00
Mug, green, souvenir, miniature ........... 22.00
Mug, clambroth, souvenir, decorated.... 22.00
Mug, green............................................. 30.00

*Colorado Spooner*

Mug, green, souvenir ............................ 23.00
Mug, ruby-stained ................................. 55.00
Nappy, tricornered, blue w/gold............ 47.00
Nappy, tricornered, green w/gold.......... 30.00
Pitcher, water, blue w/gold ................. 400.00
Pitcher, water, clear w/gold ............... 116.00
Pitcher, water, green w/gold............... 180.00
Rose bowl, blue..................................... 60.00
Salt shaker w/original top, ruby-
    stained, souvenir ............................... 75.00
Salt & pepper shakers w/original
    tops, green, pr.................................... 89.00
Sauce dish, blue w/gold ....................... 37.00
Sauce dish, clambroth........................... 20.00
Sauce dish, clear................................... 13.00
Sauce dish, green .................................. 15.00
Sauce dish, green w/gold...................... 24.00
Sauce dish, green, souvenir.................. 27.00
Sherbet, blue w/gold............................. 48.00
Spooner, blue w/gold ............. 50.00 to 60.00
Spooner, clear ....................................... 40.00
Spooner, green (ILLUS. above) ........... 60.00
Spooner, green w/gold .......................... 72.00
Sugar bowl, cov., clear, large............... 53.00
Sugar bowl, cov., green w/gold,
    large .................................. 75.00 to 80.00
Sugar bowl, open, individual size,
    green ................................................. 35.00
Sugar bowl, open, individual size,
    green w/gold ...................................... 20.00
Sugar bowl, open, individual size,
    green, souvenir................................... 22.00
Sugar bowl, open, individual size,
    ruby-stained....................................... 50.00
Sugar bowl, open, clear, large ............. 25.00
Sugar bowl, open, green, large............ 45.00
Table set, blue, 4 pcs. ........................ 525.00
Table set, green w/gold, 4
    pcs................................ 325.00 to 350.00
*Toothpick holder, blue w/gold............ 50.00
*Toothpick holder, clear w/gold........... 25.00
*Toothpick holder, green ...... 40.00 to 45.00

*Toothpick holder, green
w/gold .................................. 30.00 to 35.00
*Toothpick holder, green w/gold,
souvenir ............................................. 30.00
*Toothpick holder, ruby-stained,
souvenir ............................................. 55.00
Tumbler, green w/gold ......................... 45.00
Tumbler, green w/gold, souvenir .......... 30.00
Vase, 2½" h., green ............................. 45.00
Vase, 10½" h., blue .............................. 78.00
Vase, 12" h., trumpet-shaped, blue
w/gold ............................................. 112.00
Vase, 12" h., trumpet-shaped,
green ............................. 100.00 to 125.00
Vase, 12" h., trumpet-shaped, clear ...... 60.00
Vase, 14½" h., green w/gold ................. 60.00
Water set: pitcher & six tumblers;
green w/gold, 7 pcs. ......................... 450.00
Wine, clear ............................. 25.00 to 35.00
Wine, green w/gold ................. 30.00 to 40.00
Wine, green, souvenir ........................... 35.00

## CORD DRAPERY

*Cord Drapery Compote*

Berry set, master bowl & five sauce
dishes, 6 pcs. ................................... 100.00
Berry set: master bowl & six sauce
dishes; amber, 7 pcs. ...................... 450.00
Bowl, 6¼" d., footed, amber ............... 175.00
Bowl, 6¼" d., footed, clear ................... 75.00
Bowl, 6¼" d., footed, green ............... 115.00
Bowl, 7" d., flat ...................... 20.00 to 25.00
Bowl, 10" d., 3½" h. ............................ 42.00
Butter dish, cov., clear ........................ 52.00
Butter dish, cov., green ....................... 175.00
Cake stand, amber ............................. 145.00
Cake stand, clear ................................ 40.00
Cake stand, green, 10" d ..................... 55.00
Compote, cov., jelly, blue ..................... 96.00

Compote, cov., jelly, clear ................... 60.00
Compote, cov., 9" d. ............................ 70.00
Compote, open, jelly (ILLUS.
previous column) ................. 35.00 to 45.00
Compote, open, 7½" d., 5½" h. ........... 40.00
Compote, open, 8½" d., 6¼" h., clear .. 48.00
Compote, open, 8½" d., 6¼" h.,
cobalt blue ...................................... 180.00
Compote, open, fluted, 10" d.,
amber ............................................. 450.00
Creamer, blue .................................... 125.00
Creamer, clear ..................................... 40.00
Cruet w/original stopper, amber ....... 305.00
Cruet w/original stopper,
clear ................................. 80.00 to 90.00
Goblet ................................................. 85.00
Mug, clear ........................................... 40.00
Pickle dish, amber, 5¼ x 9¼" oval ....... 85.00
Pickle dish, clear, 5¼ x 9¼" oval ......... 37.00
Pickle dish, cobalt blue, 5¼ x 9¼"
oval .................................................. 75.00
Pitcher, water, amber ......................... 185.00
Pitcher, water, clear ............................. 65.00
Pitcher, water, cobalt blue ................. 225.00
Pitcher, water, green ......................... 235.00
Punch cup ............................ 15.00 to 20.00
Relish, 4 x 7" ....................................... 21.00
Salt shaker w/original top ................... 55.00
Sauce dish, flat or footed,
blue .................................. 30.00 to 40.00
Sauce dish, flat or footed, clear ........... 11.00
Spooner ............................................... 42.00
Sugar bowl, cov., amber .................... 125.00
Sugar bowl, cov., clear ........................ 60.00
Sugar bowl, cov., green ..... 100.00 to 125.00
Syrup pitcher w/original top, amber .. 300.00
Toothpick holder ................................. 95.00
Tray .................................................. 175.00
Tumbler, blue ........................ 50.00 to 75.00
Tumbler, clear ..................................... 37.00
Wine, amber ...................................... 225.00
Wine, clear ........................................... 90.00

## CROESUS

Berry set: master bowl & five sauce
dishes; green, 6 pcs. ........................ 295.00
Berry set: master bowl & six sauce
dishes; clear, 7 pcs. ......................... 300.00
Berry set: master bowl & six sauce
dishes; purple, 7 pcs. ....... 400.00 to 425.00
Bowl, 6¾" d., footed, green ............... 150.00
Bowl, 7" d., 4" h., footed, green
w/gold ............................................... 65.00
Bowl, 7" d., 4" h., footed, purple .......... 66.00
Bowl, 7" d., 4" h., footed, purple
w/gold ............................................. 225.00
Bowl, 8" d., green ................................ 87.00
Bowl, 8" d., green w/gold.... 100.00 to 125.00
Bowl, 8" d., purple ............................. 157.00

Bowl, berry or fruit, 9" d., green.......... 108.00
Bowl, berry or fruit, 9" d., purple ........ 195.00
Bowl, 10" d., footed, purple................. 155.00
*Butter dish, cov., clear........................ 98.00
*Butter dish, cov., green.... 135.00 to 150.00
*Butter dish, cov., green
  w/gold............................. 170.00 to 200.00
*Butter dish, cov., purple ... 200.00 to 225.00
Butter dish, cov., purple w/gold ........ 165.00
Celery vase, green w/gold .. 150.00 to 175.00
Celery vase, purple ........................... 300.00
Compote, open, jelly,
  green ............................... 225.00 to 275.00
Compote, open, jelly,
  purple .............................. 250.00 to 275.00
Condiment set: cruet, salt & pepper
  shakers & tray; green w/gold,
  4 pcs................................ 335.00 to 350.00
Condiment set: cruet, salt & pepper
  shakers & tray; purple w/gold,
  4 pcs................................ 375.00 to 425.00
Condiment tray, clear .......................... 27.00
Condiment tray, green .......................... 55.00
Condiment tray, purple ......................... 87.00
Cracker jar, green w/gold ................... 145.00
*Creamer, clear.................................... 60.00
*Creamer, green ................................... 82.00
*Creamer, purple ............... 145.00 to 150.00
Creamer, individual size, green,
  3" h. ................................ 135.00 to 140.00
Creamer, individual size, purple,
  3" h. ................................ 110.00 to 130.00
Creamer, individual size, purple
  w/gold, 3" h. ..................................... 170.00
Creamer & cov. sugar bowl, green,
  pr. ..................................................... 225.00
Creamer & cov. sugar bowl, purple,
  pr. ..................................................... 250.00
Creamer & cov. sugar bowl,
  individual size, green, pr.................... 325.00
Creamer & cov. sugar bowl,
  individual size, green w/gold, pr. ...... 225.00
Cruet w/original stopper, clear ......... 115.00
Cruet w/original stopper, green........ 290.00
Cruet w/original stopper, green
  w/gold, 6½" h. ................................. 150.00
Cruet w/original stopper, purple ....... 365.00
Pickle dish, green w/gold .................... 35.00
Pitcher, milk, green............................. 90.00
Pitcher, water, green.......... 235.00 to 285.00
Pitcher, water, purple ........ 400.00 to 500.00
Plate, 8" d., scalloped rim, green
  w/gold ............................................. 153.00
Plate, purple...................................... 245.00
Relish, boat-shaped, green ................. 60.00
Relish, boat-shaped, purple ................ 75.00
Salt shaker w/original top, green
  w/gold ............................................. 120.00
Salt shaker w/original top, purple..... 115.00

*Croesus Sugar Bowl*

Sauce dish, clear................................. 23.00
Sauce dish, green w/gold..................... 35.00
Sauce dish, purple w/gold ................... 44.00
*Spooner, clear.................................... 55.00
*Spooner, green ................................... 62.00
*Spooner, green w/gold ......... 80.00 to 95.00
*Spooner, purple .................................. 67.00
*Spooner, purple w/gold..... 100.00 to 125.00
*Sugar bowl, cov., clear ..................... 104.00
*Sugar bowl, cov., green...................... 95.00
Sugar bowl, cov., green w/gold.......... 185.00
*Sugar bowl, cov., purple
  (ILLUS. above) ................ 135.00 to 150.00
*Sugar bowl, cov., purple w/gold....... 190.00
Sugar bowl, individual size, green ....... 55.00
Table set: creamer, cov. sugar bowl &
  spooner; purple, 3 pcs. .................... 600.00
Table set, green w/gold, 4 pcs........... 650.00
*Toothpick holder, clear ...................... 25.00
*Toothpick holder, green...................... 60.00
*Toothpick holder, green w/gold ......... 92.00
*Toothpick holder, purple................... 165.00
Toothpick holder, purple w/gold........ 130.00
*Tumbler, green................................... 42.00
*Tumbler, green w/gold ........................ 60.00
*Tumbler, purple................................... 64.00
*Tumbler, purple w/gold ....................... 75.00
Water set: pitcher & six tumblers;
  green, 7 pcs. .................... 575.00 to 675.00
Water set: pitcher & six tumblers;
  purple, 7 pcs.................... 850.00 to 900.00

**CRYSTAL BALL - See Atlas Pattern**

## CURRIER & IVES

**Bowl,** master berry or fruit, 10" oval,
  flat w/collared base ............................ 35.00
**Bread plate,** handled, blue .................. 85.00
**Bread plate,** handled, clear ................. 45.00
**Cake stand,** amber ............................ 110.00
**Cake stand,** clear ................................ 75.00
**Compote,** cov., 7½" d., high stand ....... 90.00
**Compote,** cov., 11½" d., amber.......... 145.00
**Compote,** open, 7½" d., high stand,
  scalloped rim .................................... 50.00
**Cup & saucer,** blue ............................. 85.00
**Cup & saucer,** clear .............. 35.00 to 40.00
**Goblet,** amber ...................................... 75.00
**Goblet,** clear .......................... 20.00 to 30.00
**Lamp,** kerosene-type, 9½" h................. 80.00
**Lamp,** kerosene-type, 11" h.................. 80.00
**Pitcher,** milk........................................ 52.00
**Pitcher,** water, amber......... 145.00 to 150.00

*Currier & Ives Pitcher*

**Pitcher,** water, clear (ILLUS.) .............. 57.00
**Relish,** 10" oval ...................... 16.00 to 20.00
**Salt shaker w/original top,** blue .......... 75.00
**Salt shaker w/original top,** canary ...... 52.00
**Salt shaker w/original top,** clear ......... 30.00
**Sauce dish,** flat or footed, amber ......... 22.00
**Sauce dish,** flat or footed, blue............ 31.00
**Sauce dish,** flat or footed, clear............ 11.00
**Spooner,** blue ..................................... 50.00
**Spooner,** clear ..................................... 35.00
**Sugar bowl,** cov. ................................. 55.00
**Syrup jug w/original top,** amber ....... 210.00
**Syrup jug w/original top,** blue........... 162.00
**Syrup jug w/original top,** clear........... 50.00
**Tray,** water, Balky Mule on Railroad
  Tracks, blue, 9½" d........................... 75.00
**Tray,** water, Balky Mule on Railroad
  Tracks, clear, 9½" d........................... 50.00
**Tray,** water, Balky Mule on Railroad
  Tracks, blue, 12" d.......................... 150.00
**Tray,** water, Balky Mule on Railroad
  Tracks, canary, 12" d. ...... 100.00 to 125.00

**Tray,** water, Balky Mule on Railroad
  Tracks, clear, 12" d............................ 65.00
**Tumbler,** footed .................................. 38.00
**Water set,** pitcher & six goblets,
  7 pcs................................ 200.00 to 225.00
**Wine decanter w/original stopper** ...... 55.00
**Wine,** clear .......................................... 18.00
**Wine,** ruby-stained .............................. 85.00

## CURTAIN TIEBACK

**Bowl,** 7½" sq., flat................................ 20.00
**Bread plate** ......................................... 37.00
**Butter dish,** cov................................... 38.00
**Celery vase** ......................................... 30.00
**Compote,** cov., 7½" d., low stand........ 35.00
**Creamer**.............................................. 32.00
**Goblet**................................... 25.00 to 30.00
**Pitcher,** water .................................... 52.00
**Relish**.................................................. 10.00
**Sauce dish,** flat or footed ................... 12.00
**Spooner**............................................... 28.00
**Sugar bowl,** cov. ................................. 35.00

## DAISY & BUTTON

**Banana boat,** blue ............................... 45.00
**Banana boat,** green.............................. 30.00
**Berry set:** triangular master bowl &
  four sauce dishes; canary, 5 pcs. ..... 150.00
**Berry set:** six-sided master bowl & six
  sauce dishes; amber, 7 pcs............. 135.00
**Berry set:** master bowl & twelve
  sauce dishes; canary, 13 pcs. ......... 225.00
**Bowl,** 8" d., flat.................................... 15.00
**Bowl,** 8" w., tricornered, canary ........... 37.00
**Bowl,** 8" w., tricornered, clear.............. 45.00
**Bowl,** berry or fruit, 8½" d. ................... 35.00
**Bowl,** 9" sq., amber ............... 30.00 to 35.00
**Bowl,** 9" sq., Amberina ...................... 182.00
**\*Bowl,** 9½" oblong, amber .................. 35.00
**\*Bowl,** 10" oval, blue........................... 65.00
**Bowl,** 10 x 11" oval, 7¾" h., flared,
  canary.............................................. 95.00
**Bowl,** 12" l., 9" w., shell-shaped oval,
  blue .................................................. 75.00
**\*Bread tray,** amber .............................. 35.00
**\*Bread tray,** canary ............................. 40.00
**\*Bread tray,** clear ............................... 20.00
**\*Butter chip,** round, amber................... 12.00
**\*Butter chip,** round, blue ..................... 15.00
**\*Butter chip,** round, canary ................... 9.00
**\*Butter chip,** round, clear ..................... 6.00
**\*Butter chip,** square, amber ................. 13.00
**\*Butter chip,** square, Amberina............ 75.00
**\*Butter chip,** square, blue .................... 16.00
**\*Butter chip,** square, canary ............... 20.00
**\*Butter chip,** square, clear ................... 7.00
**\*Butter chip,** square, green.................. 14.00
**\*Butter chip,** square, purple................. 15.00

**Butter chip**, triangular, canary.............. 15.00
**Butter dish**, cov., scalloped base,
  blue..................................................... 65.00
**Butter dish**, cov., scalloped base,
  clear.................................................... 50.00
**Butter dish**, cov., square, amber........ 110.00
**Butter dish**, cov., square, apple green... 115.00
**Butter dish**, cov., square, canary ....... 120.00
**Butter dish**, cov., square, clear ......... 100.00
**Butter dish**, cov., triangular, amber...... 60.00
*****Butter dish,** cov., model of Victorian
  stove, apple green ............................ 215.00
**Cake stand**, blue ................................... 50.00
**Cake stand**, clear, 9" sq., 6" h. ............. 45.00
**Cake stand**, clear ................................. 30.00
**Canoe**, canary, 4" l.............................. 18.00
**Canoe**, apple green, 6" l. ..................... 18.00
**Canoe**, clear, 6" l.................................. 8.00
**Canoe**, amber, 8" l. ............................. 35.00
**Canoe**, Amberina, 8" l. ...................... 495.00
**Canoe**, apple green, 8" l. ..................... 32.00
**Canoe**, blue, 8" l.................................. 46.00
**Canoe**, canary, 8" l.............................. 38.00
**Canoe**, clear, 8" l................................. 25.00
**Canoe**, amber, 12" l............... 60.00 to 65.00
**Canoe**, blue, 12" l................................. 38.00
**Canoe**, canary yellow, 12" l.................. 50.00
**Canoe**, clear, 12" l............................... 25.00
**Canoe**, canary, 14" l............................ 45.00
**Canoe**, clear, 14" l............................... 25.00
**Castor set**, three-bottle, amber, clear
  & blue, in clear glass frame ............. 120.00
**Castor set**, four-bottle, blue, in glass
  frame ................................................ 375.00
**Celery tray**, flat, boat-shaped,
  4½ x 14".............................................. 90.00
**Celery tray**, Amberina, in gilt-metal
  footed holder..................................... 130.00
**Celery vase**, square ............................ 35.00
**Celery vase**, triangular, amber ............ 65.00
**Celery vase**, triangular, apple green .... 35.00
**Celery vase**, triangular, clear............... 45.00
**Cheese dish**, cov., canary ................. 165.00
**Cheese dish**, cov., clear...................... 62.00
**Compote**, cov., 8" d., high stand .......... 55.00
**Compote**, open, 8½" d., 8" h.,
  scalloped rim, clear............................. 40.00
**Creamer**, child's, amber........................ 25.00
*****Creamer,** amber ................................. 27.00
*****Creamer,** blue ..................................... 40.00
*****Creamer,** clear .................................... 18.00
**Creamer**, pedestal base, canary, 7" h. ... 30.00
*****Cruet w/original stopper,** amber ....... 100.00
*****Cruet w/original stopper,** blue............ 95.00
*****Cruet w/original stopper,** canary........ 80.00
*****Cruet w/original stopper,** clear........... 45.00
**Dish**, canary, shallow, 5½" sq................ 20.00
*****Dish,** fan-shaped, clear, 10" w.............. 35.00
**Finger bowl**, blue, 4⅜" d., 2⅞" h.
  (ILLUS. top next column) ..... 33.00 to 35.00

*Daisy & Button Finger Bowl*

*****Goblet,** amber ..................................... 40.00
*****Goblet,** blue......................................... 45.00
*****Goblet,** canary .................................... 40.00
*****Goblet,** clear ....................................... 25.00
*****Hat shape,** amber, 2½" h. ..... 25.00 to 30.00
*****Hat shape,** apple green, 2½" h............ 35.00
*****Hat shape,** blue, 2½" h. ........ 40.00 to 50.00
*****Hat shape,** canary, 2½" h................... 38.00
*****Hat shape,** clear, 2½" h...................... 17.00
*****Hat shape,** amber, from tumbler
  mold, 4" widest diameter ................... 40.00
*****Hat shape,** clear, from tumbler
  mold, 4½" widest diameter ................. 55.00
*****Hat shape,** blue, from tumbler mold,
  4¾" widest diameter ........................... 45.00
*****Hat shape,** clear, from tumbler mold,
  4¾" widest diameter ........................... 16.00
**Hat shape,** canary yellow, from
  tumbler mold, 5" widest diameter,
  3¾" h. .................................................. 48.00
**Hat shape,** clear, 8 x 8", 6" h. ............... 85.00
*****Ice cream dish,** cut corners, 6" sq. ....... 8.00
*****Match holder,** cauldron w/original
  bail handle, blue ................................. 25.00
**Match holder,** wall-hanging scuff,
  clear.................................................... 65.00
**Mustard,** amber...................... 15.00 to 20.00
*****Pickle castor,** amber insert, w/silver
  plate frame & tongs .......................... 197.00
*****Pickle castor,** canary insert, w/silver
  plate frame & tongs .......................... 185.00
*****Pickle castor,** sapphire blue insert,
  w/silver plate frame & tongs ........... 238.00
**Pitcher,** water, tankard, 9" h., amber .. 125.00
**Pitcher,** water, bulbous, applied
  handle, amethyst.............. 150.00 to 200.00
**Pitcher,** water, bulbous, applied
  handle, scalloped top, canary yellow... 100.00
**Pitcher,** water, bulbous, applied
  handle, clear ....................................... 75.00
**Plate,** 7" sq., blue ................................. 18.00
**Plate,** 9" d., canary................................ 40.00
*****Plate,** 10" d., scalloped rim, amber...... 26.00
*****Plate,** 10" d., scalloped rim, blue ......... 35.00

*Plate, 10" d., scalloped rim, canary ..... 39.00
Platter, 9 x 11½" oval, open handles,
  amber ................................... 30.00 to 35.00
Platter, 9 x 11½" oval, open handles,
  canary ................................................ 52.00
Powder jar, cov., blue .......................... 38.00
Punch cup, clear .................................... 8.00
Relish, "Sitz bathtub," amber .............. 125.00
Relish, "Sitz bathtub," canary .............. 80.00
Relish, "Sitz bathtub," clear ................. 60.00
*Rose bowl, canary ............................. 38.00
*Rose bowl, clear ................................ 17.00
*Salt dip, canoe-shaped, amber, 2 x 4" .. 19.00
*Salt dip, canoe-shaped, canary, 2 x 4"... 12.00
*Salt dip, canoe-shaped, clear, 2 x 4" .. 14.00
*Salt dip, master size, blue, 3½" d........ 18.00
*Salt dip, master size, canary, 3½" d.... 22.00
*Salt shaker w/original top, corset-
  shaped, amber.................................. 25.00
*Salt shaker w/original top, corset-
  shaped, blue .................................... 35.00
*Salt & pepper shakers w/original
  tops, blue, pr. ................................... 47.00
*Salt & pepper shakers w/original
  tops, canary, pr. ................................ 57.00
*Salt & pepper shakers w/original
  tops, clear, pr. .................................. 25.00
Salt & pepper shakers, blue &
  amber, pr., w/clear glass stand .......... 55.00
*Sauce dish, amber, 4" to 5" sq. .......... 13.00
*Sauce dish, Amberina, 4" to 5" sq. ... 115.00
*Sauce dish, blue, 4" to 5" sq. ............. 16.00
*Sauce dish, canary, 4" to 5" sq. .......... 20.00
*Sauce dish, clear, 4" to 5" sq.... 6.00 to 12.00
*Slipper, "1886 patent," amber ............. 46.00
*Slipper, "1886 patent," blue................. 47.00
*Slipper, "1886 patent," canary............. 50.00
*Slipper, "1886 patent," clear............... 40.00
*Slipper, apple green........................... 35.00
*Slipper, canary .................................. 55.00
*Spooner, amber ................................. 38.00
Spooner, Amberina, 5" h.... 110.00 to 125.00
Spooner, amethyst .............................. 35.00
Spooner, blue ..................................... 40.00
*Spooner, clear.................................... 32.00
Toothpick holder (or salt dip),
  "Bandmaster's cap," canary .. 45.00 to 55.00
Toothpick holder, fan-shaped,
  amber ............................................... 35.00
Toothpick holder, fan-shaped, blue .... 40.00
Toothpick holder, square, blue ........... 24.00
*Toothpick holder, three-footed,
  amber ............................................... 35.00
Toothpick holder, three-footed,
  Amberina ......................................... 170.00
*Toothpick holder, three-footed,
  canary ............................................... 39.00
*Toothpick holder, three-footed,
  electric blue ..................................... 55.00

Toothpick holder, urn-shaped,
  canary ............................................... 30.00
Toothpick holder, urn-shaped, clear ... 22.00
Tray, clover-shaped, amber ................. 75.00
Tray, canary, 10 x 12" .......................... 57.00
Tray, water, amber, 11" d....................... 90.00
Tray, water, triangular, canary... 75.00 to 80.00
Tumbler, water, amber ......................... 26.00
Tumbler, water, blue............................. 30.00
Tumbler, water, canary......................... 35.00
Tumbler, water, clear............................ 19.00
Waste bowl, canary.............................. 30.00
Whimsey, "cradle," amber .................... 45.00
*Whimsey, "dustpan," light blue............ 42.00
*Whimsey, "sleigh," amber, 4½ x 7¾".. 225.00
Whimsey, "wheel barrow," canary ....... 125.00
*Whimsey, "whisk broom" dish, amber... 35.00
*Whimsey, "whisk broom" dish, blue ...... 75.00
*Whimsey, "whisk broom" dish, canary .. 40.00
*Wine ................................................. 20.00

DAISY & BUTTON WITH CROSSBARS
(Mikado)
Bowl, 6 x 9", clear................................. 8.00
Bowl, 8" d., 4½" h., amber ................... 15.00
Bread tray, amber, 9 x 12" .................. 30.00
Bread tray, apple green, 9 x 12".......... 35.00
Bread tray, blue, 9 x 12"...................... 42.00
Bread tray, canary yellow, 9 x 12"........ 35.00
Bread tray, clear, 9 x 12"..................... 30.00
Butter dish, cov., amber....................... 55.00
Butter dish, cov., blue ......................... 58.00
Butter dish, cov., canary yellow ........... 60.00
Butter dish, cov., clear ........................ 45.00
Celery vase, amber ............................. 38.00
Celery vase, canary yellow................... 43.00
Celery vase, clear................................ 32.00
Compote, cov., 7" d., high stand,
  amber ............................................... 30.00
Compote, open, 7" d., low stand,
  amber ............................................... 38.00
Compote, open, 7" d., high stand,
  blue................................................... 85.00
Compote, open, 7" d., high stand,
  canary yellow ....................... 45.00 to 50.00
Compote, open, 8" d., high stand,
  amber ............................................... 45.00
Compote, open, 8" d., high stand,
  canary yellow..................................... 70.00
Creamer, amber................................... 34.00
Creamer, blue ..................................... 45.00
Creamer, canary yellow ....................... 40.00
Creamer, clear .................................... 30.00
Creamer, individual size, amber .......... 21.00
Creamer, individual size, blue.............. 24.00
Creamer, individual size, canary
  yellow................................................ 22.00
Creamer, individual size, clear............. 14.00

*Daisy & Button with Crossbars Goblet*

**Creamer & cov. sugar bowl,** amber,
pr. ........................................................ **85.00**
**Creamer & open sugar bowl,** amber ... **70.00**
**Cruet w/original stopper,** amber ....... **115.00**
**Cruet w/original stopper,** blue .......... **150.00**
**Cruet w/original stopper,** canary
yellow................................................ **125.00**
**Cruet w/original stopper,** clear .......... **55.00**
**Goblet,** amber..................................... **40.00**
**Goblet,** blue ....................................... **45.00**
**Goblet,** canary yellow ......................... **40.00**
**Goblet,** clear (ILLUS. above) .............. **32.00**
**Mug,** amber, 3" h................................ **25.00**
**Mug,** blue, 3" h. .................................. **15.00**
**Mug,** clear, 3" h. ................................. **15.00**
**Pitcher,** milk, amber............................ **44.00**
**Pitcher,** milk, blue .............................. **60.00**
**Pitcher,** milk, canary yellow ................ **45.00**
**Pitcher,** milk, clear ............................. **46.00**
**Pitcher,** water, amber ......................... **63.00**
**Pitcher,** water, canary yellow............... **80.00**
**Pitcher,** water, clear............................ **52.00**
**Relish,** amber, 4½ x 8" ....................... **30.00**
**Salt shaker w/original top,** amber....... **18.00**
**Salt shaker w/original top,** canary
yellow.................................................. **35.00**
**Salt & pepper shakers,** blue &
amber, w/clear glass stand, pr............ **85.00**
**Spooner,** amber................................... **31.00**
**Spooner,** canary yellow ....................... **30.00**
**Sugar bowl,** cov., amber ..................... **42.00**
**Sugar bowl,** cov., blue......................... **75.00**
**Syrup pitcher w/original top,** clear ..... **50.00**
**Tumbler,** amber ................................... **25.00**
**Tumbler,** blue ..................................... **30.00**
**Tumbler,** canary yellow ....................... **24.00**

**Water set:** pitcher & six tumblers;
canary yellow, 7 pcs. ....................... **250.00**
**Water set:** pitcher & eight tumblers;
amber, 9 pcs.................................... **190.00**
**Wine,** amber......................................... **20.00**
**Wine,** canary yellow ............................. **28.00**
**Wine,** clear .......................................... **25.00**

## DAKOTA (Baby Thumbprint)

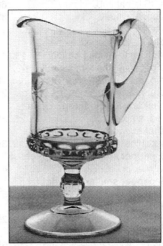

*Dakota Creamer*

**Butter dish,** cov., engraved ... **70.00 to 80.00**
**Butter dish,** cov., plain ........................ **48.00**
**Cake basket** w/metal handle, 10" d. .... **245.00**
**Cake stand,** 8" d., engraved................ **50.00**
**Cake stand,** 8" d., plain ....................... **45.00**
**Cake stand,** 9" d., engraved................ **85.00**
**Cake stand,** 9½" d. ............................. **51.00**
**Cake stand,** 10½" d.,
engraved ............................ **70.00 to 75.00**
**Cake stand,** 10½" d., plain..... **45.00 to 55.00**
**Cake stand** w/high domed cover ........ **295.00**
**Castor set**........................................... **125.00**
**Celery vase,** flat base, clear,
engraved .............................. **35.00 to 40.00**
**Celery vase,** flat base, clear, plain ....... **36.00**
**Celery vase,** pedestal base,
engraved.............................................. **48.00**
**Celery vase,** pedestal base, plain ........ **42.00**
**Cologne bottle w/original stopper,**
7" h. .................................................. **135.00**
**Compote,** cov., jelly, 5" d., 5" h. .......... **48.00**
**Compote,** cov., 6" d., high stand,
engraved ........................... **75.00 to 100.00**
**Compote,** cov., 6" d., high stand,
plain ..................................................... **58.00**
**Compote,** cov., 7" d., high stand ........ **125.00**
**Compote,** cov., 8" d., high stand,
engraved............................................ **190.00**

Compote, cov., 8" d., high stand,
plain ................................................ 72.00
Compote, cov., 9" d., high stand .......... 95.00
Compote, cov., 12" d., high stand,
engraved........................................ 145.00
Compote, open, jelly, 5" d., 5½" h.,
engraved.......................................... 32.00
Compote, open, jelly, 5" d., 5½" h.,
plain ................................................ 36.00
Compote, open, 6" d. ............. 25.00 to 35.00
Compote, open, 7" d., engraved.......... 40.00
Compote, open, 7" d., plain................. 35.00
Compote, open, 8" d., high stand ........ 39.00
Compote, open, 9" d., high stand,
engraved.......................................... 45.00
Compote, open, 10" d., high stand ....... 95.00
Creamer, table, engraved
(ILLUS. previous page) ........ 55.00 to 65.00
Creamer, table, plain ........................... 45.00
Creamer, hotel ................................... 110.00
Creamer & cov. sugar bowl, pr........... 83.00
Cruet w/original stopper, engraved .. 145.00
Dish, ice cream, flat ............................. 16.00
Goblet, clear, engraved.......... 20.00 to 30.00
Goblet, clear, plain ................. 20.00 to 25.00
Goblet, ruby-stained, engraved ........... 87.00
Goblet, ruby-stained, plain................... 65.00
Lamp, kerosene-type .......................... 120.00
Pitcher, milk, jug-type, engraved, pt. ... 190.00
Pitcher, milk, tankard, engraved,
pt. ..................................... 150.00 to 155.00
Pitcher, milk, tankard, clear, plain,
pt........................................................ 95.00
Pitcher, milk, tankard, engraved,
qt...................................................... 115.00
*Pitcher, water, tankard, engraved,
½ gal. ............................... 140.00 to 150.00
Pitcher, water, tankard, ruby-stained,
½ gal. ............................... 185.00 to 200.00
Plate, 10" d........................................... 63.00
Salt shaker w/original top, clear ......... 50.00
Salt & pepper shakers w/original
tops, clear, engraved, pr. ................. 125.00
Sauce dish, flat or footed, clear,
engraved, each .................................. 18.00
Sauce dish, flat or footed, clear, plain,
each.................................................. 10.00
Sauce dish, flat or footed, cobalt blue,
each.................................................. 55.00
Shaker bottle w/original top, 5" h. ...... 68.00
Shaker bottle w/original top, hotel
size, 6½" h. ....................................... 65.00
Spooner, engraved ............... 35.00 to 45.00
Spooner, plain ..................................... 40.00
Sugar bowl, cov., engraved .. 60.00 to 70.00
Sugar bowl, cov., plain......................... 46.00
Sugar bowl, open, engraved ............... 35.00
Table set, 4 pcs. ................................. 263.00
Tray, water, piecrust rim, engraved,
13" d. .............................................. 125.00

Tray, water, piecrust rim, plain,
13" d. ................................................ 95.00
Tray, wine, 10½" d. ............................. 105.00
Tumbler, clear, engraved ....... 35.00 to 45.00
Tumbler, clear, plain............................ 35.00
Tumbler, ruby-stained ......................... 41.00
Tumbler, ruby-stained,
souvenir............................ 25.00 to 30.00
Waste bowl, engraved.......................... 75.00
Waste bowl, plain ................................ 58.00
Wine, clear, engraved............. 30.00 to 40.00
Wine, clear, plain ................................. 27.00
Wine, ruby-stained................. 50.00 to 60.00
Wine, ruby-stained, souvenir ............... 40.00

### DEER & PINE TREE

Bowl, 5½ x 7¼", clear.......................... 45.00
Bowl, 5½ x 8", clear............... 40.00 to 45.00
Bread tray, amber, 8 x 13"..... 50.00 to 65.00
Bread tray, apple green, 8 x 13".......... 85.00
Bread tray, blue, 8 x 13"..................... 105.00
Bread tray, canary yellow, 8 x
13"..................................... 90.00 to 100.00
Bread tray, clear, 8 x 13" ....... 35.00 to 45.00

*Deer & Pine Tree Butter Dish*

Butter dish, cov. (ILLUS.) ................... 93.00
Cake stand........................ 110.00 to 125.00
Celery vase ......................................... 80.00
Compote, cov., 8" sq., high
stand ............................... 200.00 to 225.00
Compote, open, 7 x 9" high stand ........ 68.00
Creamer................................................ 63.00
*Goblet................................................. 55.00
Marmalade jar, cov............................. 220.00
Mug, child's, apple green ..................... 45.00
Mug, child's, blue ................................ 42.00
Mug, child's, clear ............................... 39.00
Mug, large, blue ................................... 55.00
Mug, large, clear .................................. 47.00
Pickle castor w/metal frame.............. 425.00
Pitcher, water ..................................... 130.00
Relish, 5½ x 8"...................................... 60.00
Sauce dish, flat or footed, clear, each.. 18.00

Spooner..............................................43.00
Sugar bowl, cov. ...............................63.00
Tray, water, handled, amber, 9 x 15"....55.00
Tray, water, handled, apple green,
9 x 15"...............................................89.00
Tray, water, handled, clear, 9 x 15" ....110.00
Waste bowl.........................................83.00

## DELAWARE (Four Petal Flower)
Banana boat, green w/gold,
11¾" l. ..............................**75.00 to 80.00**
Banana boat, rose w/gold, 11¾" l. .....120.00
Berry set: boat-shaped master bowl
& four boat-shaped sauce dishes;
clear w/rose flowers & gold,
5 pcs. ...........................150.00 to 200.00
Berry set: boat-shaped master bowl &
five boat-shaped sauce dishes; rose
w/gold, 6 pcs. ...................250.00 to 300.00
Berry set: master bowl & six sauce
dishes; rose w/gold, 7 pcs.. 300.00 to 350.00
Bowl, 8" d., clear..................................50.00
Bowl, 8" d., clear w/gold ......................39.00
Bowl, 8" d., green w/gold........40.00 to 50.00
Bowl, 9" d., scalloped rim, clear
w/gold ...............................................30.00
Bowl, 9" d., scalloped rim, green
w/gold ...............................................68.00
Bowl, 9" octagon, clear w/gold.............55.00
Bowl, 9" octagon, green w/gold ...........40.00
Bowl, 10" octagon, green
w/gold.................................90.00 to 95.00
Bride's basket, boat-shaped open
bowl, green w/gold, in silver plate
frame, 11½" oval...............................160.00
Bride's basket, boat-shaped open
bowl, rose w/gold, in silver plate
frame, 11½" oval ..............200.00 to 225.00
Bride's basket, boat-shaped open
bowl, green w/gold, miniature...........175.00
Bride's basket, rose w/gold,
miniature.............................................85.00
Butter dish, cov., clear.......................125.00
*Butter dish, cov., green w/gold.........100.00
Butter dish, cov., rose w/gold ............165.00
Celery vase, rose band w/gold.............45.00
Celery vase, green w/gold....................83.00
Celery vase, purple w/gold...................59.00
Celery vase, rose w/gold......................88.00
Claret jug, rose w/gold .......150.00 to 175.00
Creamer, clear w/gold..........................45.00
Creamer, green w/gold .........................53.00
Creamer, rose w/gold ...........................54.00
Creamer, individual size, clear w/gold.....25.00
Creamer, individual size, green w/gold.....50.00
Creamer, individual size, rose w/gold.....60.00
Creamer & cov. sugar bowl, clear, pr....75.00
Creamer & cov. sugar bowl, green
w/gold, pr..........................................135.00

Creamer & cov. sugar bowl, rose
w/gold, pr. .........................................185.00
Creamer & sugar bowl, individual
size, rose w/gold, pr..........................195.00
Cruet w/original stopper, clear .........100.00
Cruet w/original stopper, green
w/gold ...............................................185.00
Cruet w/original stopper, rose
w/gold ...............................................325.00
Marmalade dish w/silver plate holder,
green w/gold .......................................45.00
Marmalade dish w/silver plate holder,
rose w/gold .........................................85.00
Pin tray, clear ......................................15.00
Pin tray, green w/gold...........................55.00
Pin tray, rose w/gold ...............75.00 to 85.00
Pitcher, milk, green w/gold ..................85.00
Pitcher, tankard, green
w/gold ................................100.00 to 125.00
Pitcher, tankard, rose w/gold.............185.00
Pitcher, water, clear w/gold....50.00 to 75.00
Pitcher, water, green
w/gold................................125.00 to 150.00
Pitcher, water, rose w/gold..140.00 to 145.00
Pomade jar w/jeweled cover, green
w/gold ................................185.00 to 200.00
Pomade jar w/jeweled cover, rose
w/gold ...............................................335.00
Powder jar, cov., green w/copper rim...14.00
Powder jar, cov., green w/gold...........225.00
Powder jar, cov., green w/silver lid.......80.00
Powder jar, cov., rose w/gold ..............75.00
Punch cup, clear ..................................16.00
Punch cup, clear w/gold.......................30.00
Punch cup, green, souvenir .................15.00
Punch cup, green w/gold .....................35.00
Punch cup, rose w/gold........................44.00
Salt shaker w/original top, clear .........85.00
Salt shaker w/original top, rose
w/gold ...............................................110.00
Salt & pepper shakers w/original
tops, green w/gold, pr......290.00 to 300.00
Salt & pepper shakers w/original
tops, rose w/gold, pr. .......300.00 to 325.00
Sauce dish, boat-shaped, clear............14.00
Sauce dish, boat-shaped, green
w/gold...................................30.00 to 35.00
Sauce dish, boat-shaped, rose-
stained ...............................................20.00
Sauce dish, boat-shaped, rose w/gold ..38.00
Sauce dish, round, green w/gold..........23.00
Sauce dish, round, rose w/gold............21.00
Shade, gas, rose w/gold .....................295.00
Spooner, clear w/gold...........................50.00
Spooner, green......................................35.00
Spooner, green w/gold...........40.00 to 50.00
Spooner, rose........................................60.00
Spooner, rose w/gold ...........................70.00
Sugar bowl, cov., clear.........................63.00
Sugar bowl, cov., green w/gold............90.00
Sugar bowl, cov., rose w/gold .............90.00
Sugar bowl, open, clear .......................34.00

*Delaware Water Set*

**Sugar bowl,** open, green w/gold .......... 45.00
**Sugar bowl,** individual size, green
w/gold ................................................. 30.00
**Sugar bowl,** individual size, rose
w/gold ................................................. 95.00
**Table set,** green w/gold, 4 pcs............ 400.00
**Table set,** rose w/gold, 4 pcs.............. 450.00
**Toothpick holder,** clear ...................... 45.00
**Toothpick holder,** green
w/gold.................................. 65.00 to 75.00
**Toothpick holder,** rose
w/gold.............................. 120.00 to 125.00
**Tumbler,** clear w/gold .......................... 40.00
**Tumbler,** custard glass w/stained
florals.................................... 70.00 to 75.00
**Tumbler,** green w/gold.......................... 35.00
**Tumbler,** rose, souvenir........................ 25.00
**Tumbler,** rose w/gold ............. 40.00 to 50.00
**Vase,** 6" h., green w/gold ...................... 65.00
**Vase,** 7¼" h., green............................. 125.00
**Vase,** 8" h., clear ................................. 105.00
**Vase,** 8" h., green w/gold ................... 105.00
**Vase,** 8" h., rose w/gold ...................... 100.00
**Vase,** 9½" h., amethyst ....................... 100.00
**Vase,** 9½" h., green w/gold ................. 110.00
**Vase,** 9½" h., rose................................. 75.00
**Vase,** 9½" h., rose w/gold ................... 115.00
**Vase,** 12" h., rose w/gold .................... 100.00
**Water set:** water pitcher & three
tumblers; rose w/gold, 4 pcs. ............ 295.00
**Water set:** water pitcher & four
tumblers; green w/gold, 5 pcs............ 550.00
**Water set:** tankard pitcher & five
tumblers; rose w/gold, 6 pcs. ............ 600.00
**Water set:** water pitcher & six
tumblers; clear w/gold,
7 pcs................................. 145.00 to 165.00
**Water set:** water pitcher & six
tumblers; green w/gold,
7 pcs................................. 450.00 to 550.00
**Water set:** water pitcher & six
tumblers; rose w/gold, 7 pcs.
(ILLUS. above) ................................ 375.00

## DEWEY (Flower Flange)

*Dewey Creamer*

**Bowl,** 8" d., amber ................................ 45.00
**Bowl,** 8" d., clear.................................. 35.00
**Bowl,** 8" d., green ................................ 63.00
**\*Butter dish,** cov., amber .................... 85.00
**\*Butter dish,** cov., clear...................... 50.00
**\*Butter dish,** cov., green........ 70.00 to 75.00
**Butter dish,** cov., green,
miniature ............................. 75.00 to 80.00
**Creamer,** cov., clear, individual size ..... 45.00
**Creamer,** amber .................... 50.00 to 60.00
**Creamer,** canary yellow ....................... 35.00
**Creamer,** Nile green (ILLUS.
above) ............................. 250.00 to 275.00
**Creamer & cov. sugar bowl,**
individual size, canary yellow, pr. ..... 150.00
**Cruet w/original stopper,** amber....... 130.00
**Cruet w/original stopper,** canary
yellow................................................. 185.00
**Cruet w/original stopper,** clear ......... 125.00

**Cruet w/original stopper,**
green ............................. 150.00 to 200.00
**Finger bowl,** amber ............................ 35.00
**Mug,** amber ........................... 55.00 to 60.00
**Mug,** canary yellow ............................ 55.00
**Mug,** clear.............................. 30.00 to 35.00
**Mug,** green ........................... 55.00 to 60.00
**Parfait,** amber ....................................... 65.00
**Parfait,** canary yellow .......................... 65.00
**Parfait,** clear ....................................... 40.00
**Pitcher,** water, amber ........................ 110.00
**Pitcher,** water, canary yellow............. 220.00
**Pitcher,** water, clear .............. 55.00 to 65.00
**Pitcher,** water, green ......................... 145.00
**Plate,** footed, canary yellow ................. 85.00
**Plate,** footed, green............................. 65.00
**Salt shaker w/original top,** amber....... 63.00
**Sauce dish,** amber .............................. 20.00
**Sauce dish,** canary yellow................... 35.00
**Sauce dish,** green ................................ 30.00
**Spooner,** canary yellow ........................42.00
**Sugar bowl,** cov., clear....................... 35.00
**Sugar bowl,** cov., green ....................... 80.00
**Tray,** serpentine shape, amber, small... 45.00
**Tray,** serpentine shape, clear, small ..... 28.00
**Tray,** serpentine shape, Nile green,
small ................................................... 250.00
**Tray,** serpentine shape, amber, large ... 65.00
**Tumbler,** amber ................................... 60.00
**Tumbler,** canary yellow ........................ 55.00
**Tumbler,** clear ..................................... 45.00
**Tumbler,** green .................................... 45.00
**Water set:** pitcher & six tumblers;
canary yellow, 7 pcs. ........ 450.00 to 500.00
**Water set:** pitcher & six tumblers;
clear, 7 pcs....................... 300.00 to 350.00

## DIAMOND & SUNBURST

**Bowl,** cov., 8" d. ................................... 35.00
**Cake stand,** 8" d. ................................. 24.00
**Compote,** cov., 7" d., high stand ......... 48.00
**Creamer,** applied handle ..................... 33.00
**Goblet**................................................... 21.00
**Pitcher** w/applied handle, milk............. 40.00
**Sauce dish,** handled, flat, 3¾" d........... 10.00
**Spooner**................................................ 22.00
**Sugar bowl,** open.................. 30.00 to 35.00
**Toothpick holder** ................................. 40.00

## DIAMOND THUMBPRINT

**Bowl,** 7" d., footed, scalloped rim ......... 95.00
**Bowl,** 8" d., footed, scalloped rim ......... 90.00
**Celery vase**....................... 175.00 to 200.00
**Compote,** open, 7" d., low
stand .................................. 45.00 to 55.00
**Compote,** open, 7" d., low stand,
extended scalloped rim..................... 125.00
**Compote,** open, 8" d., high
stand .............................. 125.00 to 135.00

*Diamond Thumbprint Spooner*

**Compote,** open, 8" d., low
stand ................................... 80.00 to 85.00
**Compote,** open, 10½" d., high
stand ............................... 200.00 to 250.00
**Compote,** open, 11½" d., high stand.. 300.00
**Cordial,** 4" h........................................ 295.00
**\*Creamer,** applied handle ................... 200.00
**Decanter** w/bar lip, qt., 10½" h. .......... 195.00
**Decanter w/original stopper,** pt. ........ 240.00
**Decanter w/original stopper,** qt. ........ 225.00
**\*Goblet**................................................ 450.00
**Honey dish** ............................................ 23.00
**Pitcher,** water .................... 400.00 to 600.00
**Punch bowl,** scalloped rim, pedestal
base, 11½" d., 9⅛" h. ....... 225.00 to 275.00
**Sauce dish,** flat..................................... 16.00
**Sauce dish,** footed ............................... 45.00
**\*Spooner** (ILLUS. above) .................... 86.00
**\*Sugar bowl,** cov. .............................. 120.00
**Sugar bowl,** open .............................. 45.00
**\*Tumbler**.............................................. 85.00
**Tumbler,** bar, 3¾" h............................ 150.00
**Tumbler,** whiskey ............................. 150.00
**Wine**.................................................... 235.00

**DORIC - See Feather Pattern**

## DOUBLE RIBBON

**Bread plate** ......................... 40.00 to 45.00
**Butter dish,** cov. .................................. 32.00
**Compote,** cov. ....................... 80.00 to 85.00
**Creamer** ............................... 35.00 to 40.00
**Goblet**.................................. 40.00 to 45.00
**Lamp,** kerosene-type, frosted, dated
1872................................................... 135.00
**Relish**.................................................... 13.00

## EGYPTIAN

**Bowl,** 8½" d......................................... 57.00
**Bread platter,** Cleopatra center,
9 x 12" ...................................... 45.00 to 55.00
**\*Bread platter,** Salt Lake Temple
center ................................ 220.00 to 225.00
**Butter dish,** cov. ................................. 73.00
**Celery vase** ......................... 80.00 to 85.00
**Compote,** cov., 6" d., 6" h., sphinx
base ................................ 100.00 to 125.00
**Compote,** cov., 7" d., high stand,
sphinx base ................................ 195.00
**Compote,** cov., 8" d., high stand,
sphinx base ................................ 260.00
**Compote,** cov., 8" d., low stand,
sphinx base ................................ 45.00
**Creamer** ............................... 45.00 to 55.00
**Goblet**................................... 45.00 to 50.00
**Pickle dish**.......................................... 20.00
**Pitcher,** water .................... 245.00 to 255.00
**Plate,** 10" d........................................... 65.00
**Plate,** 12" d., handled........................... 85.00
**Relish,** 5½ x 8½"................................... 31.00
**Sauce dish,** flat.................................... 21.00
**Sauce dish,** footed ............................. 16.00
**Spooner** ............................... 35.00 to 45.00
**Sugar bowl,** open .............................. 32.00
**Table set,** cov. butter dish, spooner &
creamer, 3 pcs.................................. 145.00
**Table set,** 4 pcs. ................................ 295.00

## EMERALD GREEN HERRINGBONE - See Paneled Herringbone Pattern

## ENGLISH HOBNAIL CROSS - See Klondike Pattern

## ESTHER

**Berry set:** master bowl & six sauce
dishes; green, 7 pcs. ........................ 290.00
**Bowl,** 8" d., clear.................................. 35.00
**Bowl,** 8" d., green w/gold...................... 73.00
**Bowl,** 11" d., footed, clear.................... 53.00
**Butter dish,** cov., amber-stained........ 125.00
**Butter dish,** cov., clear ......................... 63.00
**Butter dish,** cov., green...................... 145.00
**Cake stand,** 10½" d., 6" h.................... 50.00
**Celery vase,** amber-stained.. 95.00 to 100.00
**Celery vase,** clear................................ 35.00
**Celery vase,** green ............................... 85.00
**Celery vase,** green w/gold.................... 55.00
**Celery vase,** ruby-stained..................... 75.00
**Compote,** cov., 8" d., high stand ........ 100.00
**Compote,** open, 4" d., amber-stained... 78.00
**Compote,** open, jelly, 5" d., amber-stained
w/enamel decoration ......... 115.00 to 125.00
**Compote,** open, jelly, 5" d., green ........ 68.00
**Creamer,** individual size, clear............ 165.00
**Creamer,** clear ..................................... 70.00

**Creamer,** green................................... 90.00
**Creamer & cov. sugar bowl,** amber-
stained, pr............................... 169.00
**Cruet w/original stopper,** clear, large.. 300.00
**Cruet w/original stopper,** green
w/gold, large .................... 145.00 to 155.00
**Cruet w/original stopper,** clear,
miniature.............................................. 30.00
**Cruet w/original stopper,** green,
miniature .......................... 200.00 to 275.00
**Cruet w/ball-shaped stopper,** clear .... 35.00
**Cruet w/ball-shaped stopper,**
green ................................. 240.00 to 250.00
**Goblet,** amber-stained......................... 95.00
**Goblet,** amber-stained w/enamel
decoration ..................................... 140.00
**Goblet,** clear ........................................ 60.00
**Pickle dish,** clear................................. 14.00
**Pitcher,** water, amber-
stained............................ 200.00 to 250.00
**Pitcher,** water, green.......... 275.00 to 325.00
**Plate,** 10¼" d........................................ 30.00
**Plate,** small, amber-stained w/enamel
decoration ....................................... 50.00
**Plate,** large, amber-stained w/enamel
decoration...................................... 139.00
**Relish,** clear, 4½ x 8½"......................... 24.00
**Relish,** green, 4½ x 8½" ....................... 36.00
**Relish,** green, 5½ x 11" ........................ 43.00
**Rose bowl,** green w/gold, 5" d.............. 40.00
**Salt shaker w/original top,** clear ......... 20.00
**Salt shaker w/original top,** green........ 72.00
**Salt & pepper shakers w/original
tops,** clear, pr. ..................................... 65.00
**Salt & pepper shakers w/original
tops,** green, pr...................................... 130.00
**Salt & pepper shakers w/original
tops,** green w/gold, pr. ..................... 100.00
**Sauce dish,** amber-stained .... 35.00 to 40.00
**Sauce dish,** clear, engraved................. 15.00
**Sauce dish,** green w/gold ...... 15.00 to 25.00
**Sauce dishes,** amber-stained, set
of 6......................................... 150.00
**Spooner,** clear ..................................... 34.00
**Spooner,** green .................................... 68.00
**Sugar bowl,** cov., green ...................... 125.00
**Toothpick holder,** amber-
stained............................ 145.00 to 155.00
**Toothpick holder,** clear ....................... 40.00
**Toothpick holder,** green........ 75.00 to 80.00
**Toothpick holder,** green
w/gold.................................. 80.00 to 85.00
**Tray,** ice cream, clear ........................... 68.00
**Tray,** ice cream, green ........................ 145.00
**Tumbler,** amber-stained......... 50.00 to 55.00
**Tumbler,** clear ...................................... 32.00
**Tumbler,** green ..................................... 55.00
**Tumbler,** green w/gold.......................... 55.00
**Wine,** amber-stained............................ 75.00
**Wine,** ruby-stained, souvenir ............... 75.00

## EXCELSIOR

Bar bottle, flint, qt. .............................. **70.00**
Cake stand, flint, 9¼" h. .................... **150.00**
Candlesticks, flint, 9½" h., pr. ............ **275.00**
Castor set, four-bottle, non-flint, in
   pewter frame ................... **225.00 to 250.00**
Celery vase, flint ................................. **78.00**
Champagne ........................................ **98.00**
Cologne bottle w/faceted stopper ...... **95.00**
Creamer, applied handle ................... **275.00**
Decanter, flared lip, pt. ...................... **95.00**
Egg cup .............................. **35.00 to 45.00**
Egg cup, double, fiery opalescent,
   flint ............................................... **295.00**
Goblet, "barrel" .................................. **38.00**
Goblet, flint .......................... **70.00 to 80.00**
Lamps, whale oil, 9¾" h. to collar,
   11¼" h. to burner, pr. ...................... **190.00**
Platter, 9¼" l. ..................................... **22.00**
Spooner, flint ..................................... **76.00**
Sugar bowl, cov. .............. **125.00 to 150.00**
Tumbler, bar, flint, 3½" h. ................... **60.00**
Tumbler, footed, flint ............. **30.00 to 40.00**
Wine, flint ........................................... **58.00**

## FEATHER (Doric, Indiana Swirl or Finecut & Feather)

*Feather Compote*

Berry set, master bowl & six sauce
   dishes, 7 pcs. .................................. **120.00**
Bowl, 6½" d. ...................................... **12.00**
Bowl, 7" oval ...................................... **18.00**
Bowl, 7 x 9" oval .................... **30.00 to 35.00**
Bowl, 7½" d., clear ............................. **35.00**
Bowl, 8" d. ............................ **20.00 to 25.00**
Bowl, 8½" oval, flat ............................ **26.00**
Butter dish, cov., clear .......... **45.00 to 50.00**
Butter dish, cov., green ..................... **210.00**
Cake stand, 8½" d. ................ **35.00 to 40.00**

Cake stand, clear, 9½" h. ....... **45.00 to 50.00**
Cake stand, green, 9½" h. .. **125.00 to 150.00**
Cake stand, 11" d. .............................. **60.00**
Celery vase, clear ................. **30.00 to 35.00**
Compote, cov., 7" d., high
   stand ................................ **135.00 to 140.00**
Compote, cov., 8½" d., high stand ..... **138.00**
Compote, open, jelly, 5" d., 4¾" h.,
   amber-stained .................................. **110.00**
Compote, open, jelly, 5" d., 4¾" h.,
   clear (ILLUS. bottom previous
   column) ............................... **20.00 to 25.00**
Compote, open, 8" d., low stand .......... **45.00**
Compote, open, 8" d., high stand ........ **40.00**
Cordial ............................................... **43.00**
Cordials, set of 6 .............................. **300.00**
Creamer, amber-stained .................... **235.00**
Creamer, clear ....................... **35.00 to 45.00**
Creamer, green .................................. **65.00**
Creamer & cov. sugar bowl, green,
   pr. ................................................... **195.00**
Cruet w/original stopper, clear ........... **39.00**
Cruet w/original stopper, green ........ **250.00**
Doughnut stand, 8" w., 4½" h. ............. **36.00**
Goblet, amber-stained ....................... **140.00**
*Goblet, clear ......................... **55.00 to 60.00**
Pickle dish ......................................... **15.00**
Pitcher, milk, clear ................. **50.00 to 60.00**
Pitcher, water, clear ........................... **63.00**
Pitcher, water, green .......................... **180.00**
Plate, 10" d., clear ................. **45.00 to 55.00**
Relish, 8¼" oval, amber-stained .......... **75.00**
Relish, 8¼" oval, clear ....................... **20.00**
Salt & pepper shakers w/original
   tops, green, pr. ................................ **225.00**
Sauce dish, flat or footed, clear .......... **12.00**
Sauce dishes, flat, clear, set of six ...... **88.00**
Sauce dish, flat or footed, green .......... **45.00**
Spooner, amber-stained ...................... **50.00**
Spooner, clear ....................... **25.00 to 30.00**
Sugar bowl, cov., clear ......... **40.00 to 45.00**
Sugar bowl, cov., green ..................... **172.00**
Sugar bowl, open, large ...................... **20.00**
Sugar bowl, open, green ...................... **50.00**
Syrup pitcher w/original top, clear ... **135.00**
Syrup pitcher w/original top, green .. **315.00**
Table set: cov. butter dish, cov. sugar
   bowl; creamer & spooner, 4 pcs. ...... **135.00**
Toothpick holder, clear ....................... **97.00**
Tumbler, clear .................................... **50.00**
Tumbler, green ................................... **85.00**
Water set: pitcher & four tumblers;
   green, 5 pcs. ..................................... **75.00**
Water set: pitcher & five goblets;
   clear, 6 pcs. ..................................... **300.00**
*Wine, clear ........................................ **35.00**
Wine, ruby-stained (1950s reproduction) .. **45.00**

**FLOWER FLANGE - See Dewey Pattern**

## FLOWER POT (Potted Plant)

*Flower Pot Creamer*

| | |
|---|---|
| Bread tray | 60.00 |
| Butter dish, cov. | 50.00 |
| Cake stand, 10½" d. | 40.00 |
| Creamer, clear (ILLUS.) | 25.00 |
| Goblet | 40.00 |
| Pitcher, milk | 40.00 |
| Pitcher, water | 48.00 |
| Salt shaker w/original top | 33.00 |
| Sauce dish | 12.00 |
| Spooner, clear | 22.00 |
| Sugar bowl, cov. | 40.00 |

## FOUR PETAL FLOWER - See Delaware Pattern

## FROSTED CIRCLE

*Frosted Circle Compote*

| | |
|---|---|
| Bowl, 8" d., 3¼" h. | 20.00 |
| Butter dish, cov. | 65.00 |
| Cake stand, 9½" d. | 48.00 |
| Champagne | 48.00 |
| Compote, open, 9" d., 6" h. | 47.00 |
| Compote, open, 9" d., 8½" h. | 60.00 to 65.00 |

| | |
|---|---|
| Compote, open, 10" d., high stand, scalloped rim (ILLUS. bottom previous column) | 55.00 |
| Creamer | 46.00 |
| Cruet w/original stopper | 43.00 |
| *Goblet | 30.00 to 35.00 |
| Pitcher, water, tankard | 80.00 |
| Plate, 7" d. | 23.00 |
| Plate, 9" | 38.00 |
| Sauce dish | 12.00 |
| Spooner | 45.00 |
| Sugar bowl, cov. | 60.00 |
| Tumbler | 26.00 |

## FROSTED LION (Rampant Lion)

| | |
|---|---|
| Bowl, cov., 3⅞ x 6⅞" oblong, collared base | 80.00 |
| Bowl, cov., 4⅝ x 7⁷⁄₁₆" oblong, collared base | 110.00 |
| *Bowl, open, oval | 62.00 |
| *Bread plate, rope edge, closed handles, 10½" d. | 81.00 |
| *Butter dish, cov., frosted lion's head finial | 90.00 |
| Butter dish, cov., rampant lion finial | 165.00 to 170.00 |
| *Celery vase, each | 70.00 |
| Cheese dish, cov., rampant lion finial | 425.00 |
| Compote, cov., 5" d., 8½" h. | 175.00 |
| Compote, cov., 6" d., 7" h., rampant lion finial | 200.00 to 250.00 |
| *Compote, cov., 6¾" oval, 7" h., collared base, rampant lion finial | 150.00 to 175.00 |
| Compote, cov., 7" d., 11" h., lion head finial | 150.00 |
| Compote, cov., 7¾" oval, low collared base, rampant lion finial | 128.00 |
| Compote, cov., 8" d., 13" h., rampant lion finial | 165.00 |
| Compote, cov., 8¼" d., high stand, frosted lion head finial | 145.00 |
| Compote, cov., 7¾ x 8½" oval, low collared base, rampant lion finial | 85.00 |
| Compote, cov., 5½ x 8¾" oval, 8¼" h., rampant lion finial | 170.00 to 180.00 |
| Compote, open, 5" d., low stand | 62.00 |
| Compote, open, 7" d., 6¼" h. | 125.00 |
| Compote, open, 7" oval, 7½" h. | 135.00 |
| Compote, open, 8" d. | 175.00 |
| Compote, open, 8" oblong, low stand | 70.00 |
| Creamer | 80.00 |
| Creamer & cov. sugar bowl, pr | 130.00 |
| *Egg cup | 90.00 |
| *Goblet | 75.00 to 80.00 |
| Marmalade jar, cov., rampant lion finial | 135.00 |
| Paperweight, embossed "Gillinder & Sons, Centennial" | 100.00 to 110.00 |

Pickle dish.......................................... 50.00
*Pitcher, water................... 475.00 to 525.00
Platter, 9 x 10½" oval, lion handles ...... 95.00
Relish.................................................. 40.00
Salt dip, cov., master size, collared
  base, rectangular.............................. 295.00
*Sauce dish, 4" to 5" d. .......... 20.00 to 25.00
Sauce dishes, 4" to 5" d., set of 6 ...... 150.00
*Spooner ............................... 55.00 to 65.00
*Sugar bowl, cov., frosted lion's head
  finial ................................................ 50.00
Sugar bowl, cov., rampant lion
  finial.................................. 100.00 to 125.00
Table set, cov. sugar bowl, creamer &
  spooner, 3 pcs. ................................ 225.00

## GALLOWAY (Mirror or misnamed Virginia

Basket, twisted handle, 5 x 8½ x
  10"...................................... 55.00 to 60.00
Berry set: master bowl & four sauce
  dishes; clear, 5 pcs. ........................... 48.00
Bowl, 9½" d., flat ................... 25.00 to 30.00
Butter dish, cov., clear ......................... 55.00
Cake stand, 9¼" d., 6" h. ....... 60.00 to 65.00
Celery vase, clear ................................ 30.00
Compote, open, 4¼" d., 6" h. ............... 33.00
Compote, open, 6¼" d., 7½" h. ............ 30.00
Compote, open, 8½" d., 7" h. ............... 60.00
Compote, open, 8¾" d., flared, rose-
  stained ............................................. 85.00
Compote, open, 10" d., 8" h.,
  scalloped rim ...................... 70.00 to 75.00
Creamer, amber-stained....................... 14.00
Creamer, clear....................... 20.00 to 25.00
Creamer, rose-stained .......................... 90.00
Creamer, individual size, clear............. 19.00
Cruet w/stopper ................................... 38.00
Goblet, clear.......................... 70.00 to 75.00
Goblet, rose-stained ............................. 60.00
Mug, 4½" d............................................ 38.00
Olive dish, 4 x 6".................................. 17.00
Pickle castor insert w/silver plate lid,
  no frame ............................................ 65.00
Pitcher, milk......................................... 70.00
Pitcher, water ...................................... 35.00
Punch bowl, 14" d. ............................. 135.00
Punch cup .............................................. 9.00
Relish, 8¼" l......................................... 17.00
Relish, ruby-stained.............................. 30.00
Salt dip, master size, scalloped rim,
  2" d. ..................................... 20.00 to 25.00
Salt & pepper shakers w/original
  tops, gold trim, 3" h., pr..................... 48.00
Sauce dish, flat or footed ..................... 13.00
Sauce dishes, rose-stained, set of 6.. 175.00
Sherbet, footed, 3¼" h.......................... 27.00
Spooner, clear ..................................... 23.00
Spooner, rose-stained .......................... 80.00

Sugar bowl, cov., clear......................... 50.00
Sugar bowl, cov., rose-stained............. 85.00
Sugar bowl, open, individual size......... 12.00
Sugar shaker w/original top ............... 35.00
Syrup pitcher w/metal spring top,
  clear................................................. 75.00
Table set, 4 pcs................ 225.00 to 275.00
*Toothpick holder, clear ..................... 26.00
*Toothpick holder, green..................... 50.00
Tray, flat, 8" d.................................... 195.00
Tumbler ............................................... 30.00
Tumbler, rose-stained ......................... 42.00
Vase, 9" h., green ................................ 30.00
Vase, 9½" h........................................... 32.00
Vase, 11" h........................................... 30.00
Vase, 14" h........................................... 25.00
Vase, 18" h........................................... 35.00
Waste bowl........................................... 38.00
Water set: pitcher & four tumblers;
  rose-stained, 5 pcs. .......................... 495.00
Water set: pitcher & six tumblers,
  clear, 7 pcs. ...................................... 195.00
Wine.................................................... 35.00

## GEORGIA - See Peacock Feather Pattern

## GOOD LUCK - See Horseshoe Pattern

## GOTHIC

Butter dish, cov. ............... 100.00 to 125.00
Castor bottle ....................................... 30.00
Castor set: mustard, cruet & shaker &
  original wire holder .......................... 165.00
Celery vase ........................................ 120.00
Champagne......................................... 195.00
Compote, open, 7" d., 3½" h. ............... 63.00
Compote, open, 8" d., 4" h. ................. 63.00
Creamer, applied handle ........ 75.00 to 80.00
Egg cup, 3½" h..................................... 45.00
Goblet................................... 55.00 to 65.00
Goblets, set of 14 .............................. 660.00
Sauce dish .......................................... 15.00
Spooner ............................................... 56.00
Sugar bowl, cov. ............................... 125.00
Tumbler................................ 100.00 to 150.00
Wine, 3¾" h. ....................... 100.00 to 125.00

## HARP

Bowl, 6" d............................................. 45.00
Bowl, 6½" d., 1½" h., ten-sided,
  opaque white .................................... 375.00
Goblet, flared sides............................. 950.00
Lamp, kerosene, hand-type w/applied
  finger grip ......................... 125.00 to 175.00
Lamp, kerosene, hexagonal font,
  shaped base, brass collar, flint,
  9½" h. .............................................. 350.00

*Harp Spooner*

**Salt dip,** master size ............................ **55.00**
**Spooner** (ILLUS. above)....................... **80.00**

## HEART WITH THUMBPRINT

**Banana boat,** 6½ x 7½"...................... **115.00**
**Banana boat,** 6½ x 11" ...... **120.00 to 125.00**
**Barber bottle w/original pewter
    stopper** ......................................... **163.00**
**Berry set,** master bowl & five sauce
    dishes, 6 pcs.................................... **135.00**
**Bowl,** 7" sq., 3½" h. ............................. **38.00**
**Bowl,** 8" d., 2" h., flared rim ................. **32.00**
**Bowl,** 9" d........................................... **38.00**
**Bowl,** 10" d., scalloped rim ................... **45.00**
**Butter dish,** cov................................... **125.00**
**Cake stand,** 9" d., 5" h. ...... **150.00 to 175.00**
**Carafe**.................................. **75.00 to 85.00**
**Card tray,** clear..................................... **19.00**
**Card tray,** green ................................... **55.00**
**Celery vase** ......................................... **74.00**
**Compote,** open, jelly, two handles,
    green ................................................ **25.00**
**Compote,** open, 7½" d., 7½" h.,
    scalloped rim ................................... **145.00**
**Compote,** open, 8½" d., high stand.... **155.00**
**Cordial,** 3" h. ...................... **200.00 to 250.00**
**Creamer** ............................................... **39.00**
**Creamer,** individual size, green w/gold... **37.00**
**Creamer & open sugar bowl,**
    individual size, clear, pr. .................... **43.00**
**Creamer & open sugar bowl,**
    individual size, green w/gold, pr. ........ **65.00**
**Cruet w/original stopper**....... **75.00 to 80.00**
**Goblet,** clear.......................... **55.00 to 65.00**
**Goblet,** green w/gold (ILLUS. top next
    column)............................................ **125.00**
**Ice bucket**............................................ **75.00**
**Lamp,** kerosene-type, clear, finger ..... **168.00**
**Lamp,** kerosene-type, clear,
    8" h.................................. **165.00 to 175.00**

*Heart With Thumbprint Goblet*

**Lamp,** kerosene-type, green, 9" h....... **250.00**
**Mustard jar** w/silver plate cover .......... **95.00**
**Mustard jar** w/silver plate cover,
    green ............................................... **110.00**
**Nappy,** heart-shaped ........................... **43.00**
**Olive dish,** clear ................................... **20.00**
**Plate,** 6" d., clear................................. **25.00**
**Plate,** 10" d........................................... **34.00**
**Plate,** 12" d........................................... **65.00**
**Punch cup,** clear ................................. **20.00**
**Punch cup,** green................................. **23.00**
**Rose bowl,** 2¼" d................................. **35.00**
**Rose bowl,** 3¾" d................................. **55.00**
**Rose bowl,** 5" d. .................................. **35.00**
**Salt shaker w/original top**................... **50.00**
**Sauce dish,** clear................................. **16.00**
**Spooner**.............................................. **55.00**
**Sugar bowl,** cov., large ....................... **95.00**
**Sugar bowl,** open ................................ **29.00**
**Sugar bowl,** open, individual size,
    clear, pewter rim ............................... **28.00**
**Sugar bowl,** open, individual size,
    green w/gold .................................... **45.00**
**Sugar bowl,** open, individual size,
    green w/gold, pewter rim ................... **40.00**
**Syrup jug w/original pewter top**....... **108.00**
**Syrup jug w/original pewter top**
    miniature, 4" h. ................ **100.00 to 125.00**
**Tray,** 4¼ x 8¼"..................................... **30.00**
**Tumbler,** water, clear w/gold ............... **47.00**
**Vase,** 6" h., trumpet-shaped, clear........ **41.00**
**Vase,** 6" h., trumpet-shaped, green ...... **75.00**
**Vase,** 8" h............................................. **45.00**
**Vase,** 10" h., trumpet-shaped .............. **65.00**
**Waste bowl**......................................... **105.00**

**Water set,** carafe & six tumblers,
7 pcs................. **300.00 to 325.00**
**Wine,** clear............................................. **49.00**
**Wine,** green w/gold ............................. **135.00**

## HEARTS OF LOCH LAVEN - See Shuttle Pattern

## HOBNAIL
**Butter dish,** cov., blue........................... **85.00**
**\*Butter dish,** cov., clear......................... **85.00**
**Celery vase,** footed, square, clear........ **20.00**
**\*Cologne bottle,** amber, 6½" h. .......... **38.00**
**Compote,** 6" h., fluted rim, blue ............. **55.00**
**\*Creamer,** fluted top, applied handle,
amber, 2 x 3" ...................................... **25.00**
**Creamer,** three-footed, blue.................. **25.00**
**\*Creamer,** individual size, amber.......... **31.00**
**\*Cruet w/original stopper,** clear,
4½" h. .................................................. **40.00**
**Egg cup,** single.................................... **29.00**
**Egg cup,** double, clear.......................... **15.00**

*Hobnail Mug*

**Mug,** amber (ILLUS.) ............................. **30.00**
**Mug,** blue .............................................. **21.00**
**Mug,** clear .............................................. **8.00**
**Pitcher,** 7" h., blue ............................... **80.00**
**Pitcher,** 8" h., square top, amber........ **235.00**
**Pitcher,** 8" h., ruby-stained .................. **45.00**
**Pitcher,** 8" h., square top, sapphire
blue...................................................... **265.00**
**Pitcher,** water, blue............................... **125.00**
**Salt shaker w/original top,**
blue ....................................... **30.00 to 35.00**
**Salt shaker w/original top,** clear ......... **17.00**
**Sauce dish,** amber, 4" sq. ...................... **5.00**
**Spooner,** ruffled rim, amber.................. **30.00**
**\*Spooner,** clear...................................... **30.00**
**Spooner,** frosted.................................... **35.00**
**\*Sugar bowl,** cov., clear ........................ **20.00**
**Sugar shaker w/original top,** blue ...... **43.00**
**\*Toothpick holder,** amber.................... **39.00**
**\*Toothpick holder,** blue ...................... **25.00**

**Toothpick holder,** canary ...... **35.00 to 45.00**
**Tray,** water, amber, 11½" d.................. **55.00**
**Tray,** water, blue, 11½" d. .................... **48.00**
**Tumbler,** amber .................................... **30.00**
**Tumbler,** seven-row, amber ................ **20.00**
**\*Tumbler,** eight-row, amber.................. **23.00**
**\*Tumbler,** ten-row, amber.................... **60.00**
**\*Tumbler,** ten-row, blue.......... **25.00 to 30.00**
**\*Tumbler,** clear .................................... **15.00**
**Tumbler,** ten-row, ruby-stained .......... **110.00**
**Tumbler,** canary .................................... **29.00**
**\*Vase,** 5½" h., cone-shaped, ruffled
rim, canary.......................................... **45.00**
**Water set:** pitcher & six tumblers,
canary, 7 pcs. ................................... **250.00**
**\*Wine,** amber ...................................... **25.00**
**\*Wine,** clear.......................................... **25.00**
**Wine,** green.......................................... **23.00**

## HOBNAIL WITH THUMBPRINT BASE
**Butter dish,** cov., child's, blue .............. **95.00**
**Creamer,** amber.................................... **31.00**
**Creamer,** blue ...................................... **35.00**
**Creamer,** child's, amber....................... **20.00**
**Pitcher,** 7" h., clear ............................. **30.00**
**Pitcher,** 7" h., ruby-stained rim ............. **65.00**
**Pitcher,** 8" h., amber ............................. **68.00**
**Pitcher,** 8" h., blue ............................... **80.00**
**Spooner,** amber.................................... **25.00**
**Spooner,** blue ...................................... **35.00**
**Waste bowl,** amber .............................. **28.00**
**Waste bowl,** blue.................................. **30.00**

## HONEYCOMB
**Ale glass**.............................................. **39.00**
**Ale glass,** New York Honeycomb......... **25.00**
**\*Butter dish,** cov., clear, non-flint......... **45.00**
**Butter dish,** cov., clear, w/gold
non-flint ............................................... **75.00**
**Cake stand,** 9" d., 5¾" h., cable
border .................................................. **35.00**
**Celery vase,** flint.................................... **60.00**
**Celery vase,** clear, non-flint.................. **24.00**
**Celery vase** w/frosted Roman Key
etching, flint ....................................... **75.00**
**Celery vase,** New York Honeycomb,
flint ...................................................... **40.00**
**Celery vase,** New York Honeycomb,
non-flint ............................................... **28.00**
**Champagne,** flint.................... **35.00 to 45.00**
**Champagne,** New York
Honeycomb ......................... **20.00 to 25.00**
**\*Champagne,** non-flint........................... **30.00**
**Claret,** flint............................................. **50.00**
**Claret,** New York Honeycomb, flint....... **45.00**
**Claret,** non-flint ..................................... **23.00**
**Compote,** cov., 6½" d., 8½" h., flint...... **45.00**
**Compote,** cov., 9¼" d., 11½" h., flint .... **90.00**
**Compote,** open, 7" d., 7" h., flint........... **55.00**
**Compote,** open, 7½" d., 5½" h., flint..... **25.00**

**Compote,** open, 8" d., 6¼" h., flint...... **110.00**
**Compote,** open, 9" d., 6" h., flint........... **75.00**
**Cordial,** New York Honeycomb, flint..... **30.00**
***Creamer,** non-flint................................ **45.00**
**Decanter** w/bar lip, flint, 10½" h.......... **110.00**
**Decanter w/original stopper,** flint,
    13" h. ................................................. **110.00**
**Egg cup,** flint........................................... **30.00**
**Egg cup,** New York Honeycomb, flint... **30.00**
**Egg cup,** non-flint ................................... **13.00**
**Goblet,** engraved ................................... **15.00**
**Goblet,** flint ............................................ **25.00**
**Goblet,** engraved, flint .......................... **65.00**
***Goblet,** non-flint.................................... **13.00**
**Goblet,** Banded Vernon Honeycomb.... **18.00**
**Goblet,** Barrel Honeycomb w/knob
    stem.................................................... **14.00**
**Goblet,** buttermilk .................................. **48.00**
**Goblet,** lady's, flint ................................ **40.00**
**Goblet,** lady's, non-flint ......................... **14.00**
**Goblet,** Laredo Honeycomb.................. **45.00**
**Goblet,** New York Honeycomb, flint...... **21.00**
**Mug,** flint................................................. **28.00**
**Mug,** child's............................................ **35.00**
**Mustard pot,** w/original pewter lid,
    etched, flint........................................ **75.00**
**Pitcher,** milk, flint ................................... **90.00**
**Pitcher,** 7¼" h., bulbous, applied
    handle ................................................ **35.00**
**Pitcher,** water, 8½" h., molded handle,
    polished pontil, flint............. **150.00 to 175.00**
**Pitcher,** water, 9" h., applied handle,
    flint .................................................... **155.00**
**Pitcher,** water, New York Honeycomb.. **120.00**
***Salt & pepper shakers w/original
    tops,** non-flint, pr. .............................. **75.00**
**Salt dip,** New York Honeycomb, flint.... **15.00**
**Sauce dish,** flint...................................... **13.00**
**Spooner,** flint .......................................... **40.00**
**Spooner,** non-flint................................... **23.00**
**Sugar bowl,** cov., flint............................ **75.00**
**Syrup pitcher w/pewter top,** flint....... **128.00**
**Tumbler,** bar ........................................... **24.00**
**Tumbler,** footed, flint............................. **35.00**
**Tumbler,** Vernon Honeycomb, flint ...... **65.00**
**Wine,** flint............................................... **32.00**
***Wine,** non-flint....................................... **11.00**
**Wine,** New York Honeycomb, flint ........ **21.00**

## HORN OF PLENTY (McKee's Comet)
**Bar bottle w/original stopper,**
    qt. ..................................... **135.00 to 145.00**
**Bowl,** 7½" d.............................................. **70.00**
**Bowl,** 8" oval ......................................... **110.00**
**Butter dish,** cov.................................... **125.00**
**Butter pat** ............................................... **16.00**
**Celery vase** .......................................... **148.00**
**Champagne** ........................ **185.00 to 195.00**
**Compote,** cov., 6¼" d., 7½" h............. **250.00**
**Compote,** open, 6" d.............................. **75.00**

*Horn of Plenty Sugar Bowl*

**Compote,** open, 6¾" d.,
    3½" h. ................................. **75.00 to 85.00**
**Compote,** open, 7" d., 3" h. ................. **123.00**
**Compote,** open, 7" d., 5½" h. ............. **225.00**
**Compote,** open, 7" d., 7½" h., waffle
    base.................................................. **110.00**
**Compote,** open, 8" d., low stand ........ **110.00**
**Compote,** open, 8" d., 6" h... **135.00 to 140.00**
**Compote,** open, 8" d., 8" h. ................ **124.00**
**Compote,** open, 9" d., low stand ........ **100.00**
**Compote,** open, 9" d., 8½" h. ............. **195.00**
**Compote,** open, 10½" d., 9¾" h. ........ **350.00**
**Creamer,** applied handle, 7" h. ........... **142.00**
**Creamer & cov. sugar bowl,** pr........ **325.00**
**Decanter,** bar lip, pt. ............................ **110.00**
**Decanter w/original stopper,** pt. ....... **150.00**
**Decanter w/original stopper,** qt. ....... **175.00**
**Dish,** 6¾ x 10", 2¼" h. ......................... **140.00**
**Egg cup,** 3¾" h. ...................................... **44.00**
***Goblet** ................................. **75.00 to 85.00**
***Hat whimsey** ....................................... **350.00**
**Honey dish** ............................................. **16.00**
***Lamp,** w/whale oil burner, all-glass,
    11" h. ............................... **200.00 to 225.00**
**Peppersauce bottle w/stopper** ......... **154.00**
**Plate,** 6" d., canary yellow................... **248.00**
**Plate,** 6" d., clear................................... **83.00**
**Relish,** 5 x 7" oval .................................. **95.00**
**Salt dip,** master size, oval ..................... **85.00**
**Sauce dish,** 3½" to 5" d....................... **15.00**
**Spooner,** 4½" h., clear........................... **82.00**
**Spooner,** clear........................................ **45.00**
**Spooner,** w/yellow-stained rim ........... **225.00**
**Sugar bowl,** cov. (ILLUS. above) ....... **120.00**
**Tumbler,** bar...................... **100.00 to 125.00**
***Tumbler,** water, 3⅝" h....................... **63.00**
**Tumbler,** whiskey, 3" h. .................... **141.00**
**Tumbler,** whiskey, handled................ **220.00**
**Tumblers,** set of six ............................ **420.00**
**Wine**...................................................... **175.00**

## HORSESHOE (Good Luck or Prayer Rug)

Bowl, cov., 5 x 8" oval, flat, triple
horseshoe finial ............................... **295.00**
Bowl, open, 7" d., footed ..................... **48.00**
Bowl, open, 5 x 8" oval, footed ............. **30.00**
Bowl, open, 6 x 9" oval ...................... **28.00**
*Bread tray, single horseshoe
handles................................. **40.00 to 50.00**
Bread tray, double horseshoe
handles ................................................ **93.00**
Butter dish, cov. .............................. **105.00**
Cake stand, 7" d. ................................ **35.00**
Cake stand, 8" d., 6½" h. ..................... **76.00**
Cake stand, 9" d., 6½" h. ..................... **69.00**
Cake stand, 10" d. ............................... **74.00**
Cake stand, 10¾" d. .......................... **127.00**
Celery vase ........................................ **61.00**
Cheese dish, cov., w/woman
churning butter in base .................... **275.00**
Compote, cov., 6" d., 10½" h. .............. **250.00**
Compote, cov., 7" d., high stand .......... **75.00**
Compote, cov., 8" d., low stand.......... **210.00**
Compote, cov., 8" d., high stand ........ **175.00**
Compote, open, 8" d., 7¾" h. .............. **30.00**
Creamer ........................... **35.00 to 45.00**
Doughnut stand................................ **95.00**
Goblet, knob stem .............................. **45.00**
Goblet, plain stem................................ **25.00**
Marmalade jar, cov. ........................... **225.00**
Pitcher, milk ...................... **125.00 to 135.00**
Pitcher, water ..................... **125.00 to 135.00**
Plate, 7" d. ......................................... **45.00**
Plate, 8" d. ......................................... **80.00**
Plate, 10" d. ....................................... **86.00**
Relish, 5 x 8" ....................................... **5.00**
Salt dip, individual size ........................ **18.00**
Salt dip, master size, horseshoe
shape ................................................ **100.00**

*Horseshoe Spooner*

Sauce dish, flat or footed, each........... **11.00**
Spooner (ILLUS. bottom previous
column) ............................................... **35.00**
Sugar bowl, cov. ................. **75.00 to 100.00**
Sugar bowl, open ................................ **30.00**
Table set, 4 pcs. ............................... **345.00**
Wine................................................. **295.00**

## INVERTED FERN

Bowl, 7" d. .......................................... **45.00**
Butter dish, cov. ................................. **85.00**
Champagne.......................................... **170.00**
Compote, open, 8" d. ............................ **33.00**
Creamer, applied handle ................... **150.00**
Egg cup................................ **30.00 to 35.00**

*Inverted Fern Goblet*

*Goblet (ILLUS.) ...................... **45.00 to 50.00**
Pitcher, water ...................................... **360.00**
Salt dip, master size, footed................. **33.00**
Sauce dish, 4" d. ................................. **14.00**
Spooner............................................... **50.00**
Sugar bowl, cov. ................................. **75.00**
Tumbler ............................................... **95.00**
Wine.................................................... **745.00**

## INVERTED LOOPS & FANS - See
## Maryland Pattern

## JACOB'S LADDER (Maltese)

Bowl, 7¼" d., footed ............................. **30.00**
Bowl, 6 x 8¾" oval, flat........................ **21.00**
Bowl, 7½ x 10¾" oval ........................... **25.00**
Bowl, 9" d., flat .................................... **40.00**
Bowl, 10" d., flat .................................. **27.00**
Butter dish, cov., Maltese Cross finial ... **55.00**
Cake stand, 8" to 12" d. ....................... **52.00**

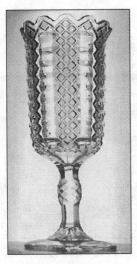

*Jacob's Ladder Celery Vase*

Celery vase (ILLUS.) ........................... 32.00
Compote, cov., 8¼" d., high stand ..... 128.00
Compote, open, 6" d., high stand ......... 24.00
Compote, open, 7" d., low stand .......... 32.00
Compote, open, 7" d., high stand ......... 35.00
Compote, open, 8" d., high stand ......... 42.00
Compote, open, 9" d., low stand .......... 52.00
Compote, open, 10" d., 5" h... 30.00 to 35.00
Compote, open, 10" d., high stand ....... 55.00
Compote, open, 13½" d., high stand .... 75.00
Creamer ............................................... 32.00
Cruet w/original stopper, footed ......... 85.00
Dish, 8" oval ........................................ 18.00
Goblet .................................................. 65.00
Honey dish, open ................................... 9.00
Marmalade jar, cov. ........... 100.00 to 135.00
Pickle castor, complete w/stand ........ 132.00
Pickle dish, Maltese Cross handle,
  clear ................................................. 18.00
Pitcher, water, applied handle ............ 185.00
Plate, 6" d., amber ............................ 105.00
Plate, 6" d., clear ................................ 35.00
Plate, 6" d., purple ............................ 110.00
Relish, Maltese Cross handles,
  5½ x 9½" oval .................................. 19.00
Salt dip, master size, footed ................ 22.00
Sauce dish, flat or footed, blue ............ 20.00
Sauce dish, flat or footed, canary ........ 72.00
Sauce dish, flat or footed, clear ............ 8.00
Spooner ................................................ 31.00
Sugar bowl, cov. .................................. 65.00
*Sugar bowl, open ................................ 26.00
Syrup jug w/metal top ....... 100.00 to 125.00
Wine ..................................................... 27.00

**JEWEL & DEWDROP - See Kansas Pattern**

**JOB'S TEARS - See Art Pattern**

**JUMBO and JUMBO & BARNUM**

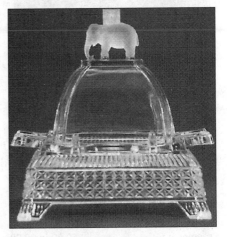

*Jumbo Butter Dish*

Butter dish & cover w/frosted
  elephant finial, oblong
  (ILLUS.) ........................... 675.00 to 700.00
Castor holder (no bottles) ................. 100.00
Compote, cov., 7⅞" d ......... 275.00 to 300.00
Creamer ............................. 235.00 to 250.00
Creamer, w/Barnum head at handle... 295.00
Marmalade jar w/Barnum head
  handles & cover w/frosted elephant
  finial .................................................. 450.00
Spoon rack ........................ 600.00 to 750.00
Sugar bowl w/Barnum head handles
  & cover w/frosted elephant
  finial ................................. 475.00 to 500.00

**KAMONI - See Pennsylvania Pattern**

**KANSAS (Jewel & Dewdrop)**
Banana bowl ........................................ 55.00
Berry set, master bowl & six sauce
  dishes, 7 pcs. .................................... 80.00
Bowl, 7½" d ......................................... 22.00
Bowl, 8½" d ......................................... 35.00
Bread tray, "Our Daily Bread,"
  10½" oval ........................................... 44.00
Butter dish, cov. .................................. 65.00
Cake stand, 8" to 10" d ....................... 48.00
Cake tray, "Cake plate," 10½" oval ....... 78.00
Celery vase .......................................... 65.00
Compote, cov., 7" d., high stand ........ 125.00
Compote, open, jelly, 5" d. .................. 42.00
Compote, open, 7" d., low stand .......... 65.00
Compote, open, 7" d., high stand ......... 88.00
Compote, open, 8" d ............................ 38.00
Compote, open, 8" d., high stand ......... 58.00

*Kansas Pitcher*

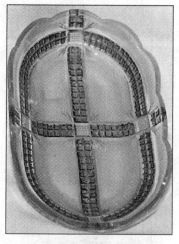

*Klondike Dish*

**Creamer** ............................... **50.00 to 60.00**
**Goblet** ...................................................... **63.00**
**Mug,** small, 3½" h. ............................... **30.00**
**Pitcher,** milk.......................................... **72.00**
**Pitcher,** water (ILLUS.) ......................... **60.00**
**Relish,** 8½" oval.................................... **26.00**
**Sauce dish,** 4" d. ................................. **11.00**
**Spooner**................................................. **70.00**
**Sugar bowl,** cov. ................................. **65.00**
**Toothpick holder** ............................... **50.00**
**Tumbler,** water, footed ........................ **58.00**
**Whiskey,** handled................................. **8.00**
**Wine,** clear ............................................ **47.00**
**Wine,** ruby-stained w/gilt trim............... **98.00**

## KENTUCKY
**Celery tray**............................................ **25.00**
**Cruet w/original stopper**....... **35.00 to 40.00**
**Nappy,** handled, green .......................... **15.00**
**Punch cup,** clear ................................... **7.00**
**Punch cup,** green .................................. **28.00**
**Sauce dish,** footed, blue w/gold .......... **32.00**
**Sauce dish,** footed, clear...................... **9.00**
**Sauce dish,** footed, green .................... **13.00**
**Toothpick holder,** clear ........................ **30.00**
**Toothpick holder,** green.................... **100.00**
**Toothpick holder,** green w/gold.......... **75.00**
**Tumbler,** green...................................... **50.00**
**Wine,** clear ............................................ **30.00**
**Wine,** green ............................. **35.00 to 45.00**

## KLONDIKE (Amberette or English Hobnail Cross)
**Berry set:** master bowl & four sauce
dishes; frosted w/amber cross,
5 pcs............................. **450.00 to 500.00**
**Bowl,** 6" sq., frosted w/amber cross ... **188.00**
**Bowl,** 7" sq., frosted w/amber cross ... **185.00**

**Bowl,** 7¼" sq., scalloped top, clear
w/amber cross ................................. **185.00**
**Bowl,** master berry or fruit, 8" sq.,
clear w/amber cross ......................... **85.00**
**Bowl,** master berry or fruit, 8" sq.,
frosted w/amber cross ..................... **250.00**
**Bowl,** 11" sq., frosted w/amber
cross ................................................ **265.00**
**Bread plate,** clear w/amber cross,
8½ x 11" oval ................................. **120.00**
**Butter dish,** cov., clear ...................... **150.00**
**Butter dish,** cov., clear w/amber
cross................................. **225.00 to 250.00**
**Butter dish,** cov., frosted w/amber
cross................................. **450.00 to 475.00**
**Butter pat,** clear w/amber cross ........... **36.00**
**Celery tray,** frosted w/amber cross,
4½ x 10⅞", 2⅞" h. .......................... **193.00**
**Celery vase,** clear w/amber cross ...... **127.00**
**Celery vase,** frosted w/amber cross ... **225.00**
**Champagne,** frosted w/amber cross ... **650.00**
**Condiment set:** tray, cruet, salt &
pepper shakers; frosted w/amber
cross, 4 pcs. ................................. **1,350.00**
**Creamer,** clear w/amber
cross.................................... **85.00 to 90.00**
**Creamer & open sugar bowl,** frosted
w/amber cross, pr. .......................... **200.00**
**Cruet w/original stopper,** clear
w/amber cross .................................. **425.00**
**Cruet w/original stopper,** frosted
w/amber cross.................. **700.00 to 750.00**
**Dish,** oval, flat, shallow, clear ............. **120.00**
**Dish,** oval, flat, shallow, clear
w/amber cross ................................. **130.00**
**Dish,** oval, flat, shallow, frosted
w/amber cross (ILLUS. above) ......... **150.00**
**Goblet,** clear .......................................... **95.00**
**Goblet,** clear w/amber cross.............. **180.00**

**Jam dish,** frosted w/amber cross,
4¾" sq., 5½" h., in silver plate
holder ........................................ **113.00**
**Lamp,** kerosene-type, clear w/amber
cross, 10" h. .................................. **155.00**
**Pitcher,** water, clear ............................ **50.00**
**Pitcher,** water, clear w/amber
cross .................................. **250.00 to 275.00**
**Punch bowl,** tulip-shaped,
pedestaled, slightly flared top ........... **475.00**
**Punch cup,** frosted w/amber
cross ................................... **95.00 to 125.00**
**Relish,** boat-shaped, clear, 4 x 9" ......... **40.00**
**Relish,** boat-shaped, clear, w/amber
cross, 4 x 9" .................................. **112.50**
**Relish,** boat-shaped, frosted w/amber
cross, 4 x 9" .................................. **146.00**
**Salt shaker w/original top,** clear
w/amber cross .................................... **69.00**
**Salt shaker w/original top,** frosted
w/amber cross ................... **75.00 to 100.00**
**Salt & pepper shakers w/original
tops,** clear, pr. ................. **135.00 to 150.00**
**Salt & pepper shakers w/original
tops,** clear w/amber cross, pr. .......... **275.00**
**Salt & pepper shakers w/original
tops,** frosted w/amber cross,
pr. .................................. **200.00 to 250.00**
**Sauce dish,** flat or footed, clear
w/amber cross .................................... **20.00**
**Sauce dish,** flat or footed, frosted
w/amber cross .................................... **69.00**
**Spooner,** clear ................................... **40.00**
**Spooner,** clear w/amber cross ............. **85.00**
**Spooner,** frosted w/amber cross ........ **250.00**
**Sugar bowl,** cov., clear ........................ **95.00**
**Sugar bowl,** cov., clear w/amber
cross, 6¾" h. .................................. **165.00**
**Sugar bowl,** open, clear w/amber
cross ................................................ **75.00**
**Sugar bowl,** open, frosted w/amber
cross .............................................. **175.00**
**Table set,** frosted w/amber cross,
4 pcs. ............................................ **950.00**
**Toothpick holder,** clear .................... **125.00**
**Toothpick holder,** clear w/amber
cross .............................................. **375.00**
**Tray,** flat, frosted w/amber cross,
5½" sq. ........................................... **100.00**
**Tray,** clear w/amber cross, 11" sq. ........ **45.00**
**Tumbler,** clear ................................... **25.00**
**Tumbler,** clear w/amber cross ............. **93.00**
**Tumbler,** frosted w/amber cross ........ **145.00**
**Vase,** 7" h., trumpet-shaped, clear ........ **35.00**
**Vase,** 8" h., trumpet-shaped, clear ........ **50.00**
**Vase,** 8" h., trumpet-shaped, clear
w/amber cross .................................. **130.00**
**Vase,** 8" h., trumpet-shaped, frosted
w/amber cross .................................. **260.00**
**Vase,** 10" h., trumpet-shaped, frosted
w/amber cross .................................. **308.00**

**LACY MEDALLION - See Colorado
Pattern**

**LIBERTY BELL**
**Bowl,** berry or fruit, 8" d., footed ........... **95.00**
**Bread platter,** "John Hancock," twig
handles, 9½ x 13½", milk white ........ **155.00**
**\*Bread platter,** "Signer's," twig
handles ............................................ **95.00**
**Bread platter,** w/thirteen original
states, twig handles, 8¼ x 13" ............ **70.00**
**Butter dish,** cov. ................................. **95.00**
**Butter dish,** cov., miniature ............... **143.00**
**Compote,** open, 8" d. ............................ **65.00**
**Creamer,** applied handle ...................... **98.00**
**Creamer,** miniature .............................. **88.00**

*Liberty Bell Goblet*

**Goblet** (ILLUS.) ...................... **40.00 to 50.00**
**Mug,** miniature, 2" h. ........................... **125.00**
**Mug,** snake handle ............. **465.00 to 480.00**
**Pickle dish,** closed handles, 1776-
1876, w/thirteen original states,
5½ x 9¼" oval .................................... **50.00**
**Pitcher,** water .................... **650.00 to 850.00**
**Plate,** 6" d., closed handles, scalloped
rim, w/thirteen original states ............. **75.00**
**Plate,** 6" d., no states, dated ... **55.00 to 65.00**
**Plate,** 8" d., closed handles,
scalloped rim, w/thirteen original
states .................................... **50.00 to 60.00**
**Plate,** 10" d., closed handles,
scalloped rim, w/thirteen original
states .............................................. **83.00**
**Relish,** shell handles, 7 x 11¼" ............. **68.00**
**Salt dip** ............................................. **55.00**
**Salt shaker w/original pewter top** ...... **90.00**
**Sauce dish** ........................... **20.00 to 25.00**
**Spooner** ............................................ **62.00**
**Sugar bowl,** cov. .............................. **110.00**

Table set, cov. butter dish, creamer,
cov. sugar bowl & spooner,
4 pcs.............................. **400.00 to 450.00**

## LINCOLN DRAPE & LINCOLN DRAPE
## WITH TASSEL

Celery vase ...................................... **90.00**
Compote, cov., 6" d., high stand
(sweetmeat) .................... **325.00 to 375.00**
Compote, open, 6¾" d., 5¼" h. ............ **85.00**
Compote, open, 7⅛" d.,
5" h. ................................. **118.00 to 125.00**
Compote, open, 7½" d., 3½" h. ............ **50.00**
Compote, open, 8" d., medium
stand.................................................. **110.00**
Compote, open, 8¼" d., 5⅛" h.,
domed foot......................................... **88.00**
Compote, open, 9" d........................... **105.00**
Creamer ............................ **125.00 to 150.00**
Egg cup................................. **55.00 to 65.00**
Goblet................................. **125.00 to 150.00**
Goblet w/tassel.................. **225.00 to 275.00**
Salt dip, master size ............................ **55.00**
Salt dip, master size, w/tassel ............ **125.00**

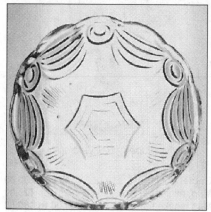

*Lincoln Drape Sauce Dish*

Sauce dish, 4" d. (ILLUS.).................... **23.00**
Spooner................................................. **75.00**
Sugar bowl, cov. .............................. **165.00**
Syrup pitcher w/original pewter top,
clear.................................................. **175.00**
Syrup pitcher w/original top, opaque
white ................................................. **600.00**

## LION, FROSTED - See Frosted Lion
## Pattern

## LION WITH CABLE - See Frosted Lion

## LION'S LEG - See Alaska Pattern

## LOG CABIN

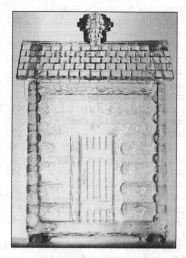

*Log Cabin Sugar Bowl*

Bowl, cov., 8 x 5¼ x 3⅝" .................... **125.00**
Butter dish, cov................................. **295.00**
Compote, cov. ................................... **350.00**
Compote, cov., "Lutteds Cough
Drops".............................................. **325.00**
*Creamer, 4¼" h. .............................. **141.00**
Creamer & cov. sugar bowl, pr......... **225.00**
Pitcher, water ................................... **325.00**
Sauce dish, flat oblong...................... **85.00**
*Spooner, clear.................................. **130.00**
Spooner, sapphire blue ..................... **395.00**
*Sugar bowl, cov., 8" h., clear
(ILLUS.)........................... **250.00 to 275.00**

## LOOP & DART

Bowl, 5 x 8" oval, round ornaments ...... **33.00**
Butter dish, cov., diamond
ornaments, non-flint........................... **38.00**
Butter dish, cov., round ornaments,
flint.................................................... **80.00**
Butter pat, round ornaments .............. **35 .00**
Celery vase, diamond ornaments......... **32.00**
Celery vase, round ornaments, flint...... **50.00**
Celery vase, round ornaments, non-
flint.................................................... **34.00**
Champagne, round ornaments, flint..... **85.00**
Compote, cov., 6½" d., high stand,
round ornaments ............................... **90.00**
Compote, cov., 7" d., 10" h., diamond
ornaments.......................................... **65.00**
Compote, cov., 8" d., 10" h., round
ornaments.......................................... **95.00**
Compote, cov., 8" d., low stand,
round ornaments ............................... **74.00**
Compote, cov., 9½" d., 11" h.............. **75.00**

**Compote,** open, 8" d., diamond
ornaments.................................... 28.00
**Creamer,** applied handle, round
ornaments.................................... 45.00
**Cup plate,** round ornaments................ 15.00
**Egg cup,** diamond ornaments ............. 20.00
**Egg cup,** round ornaments.................. 25.00
**Goblet,** diamond ornaments ................ 33.00
**Goblet,** round ornaments ....... 25.00 to 30.00
**Pitcher,** water, round ornaments ........ 125.00
**Plate,** 6" d., round ornaments ............... 35.00
**Salt dip,** master size, diamond
ornaments.................................... 28.00
**Salt dip,** master size, round
ornaments.................................... 45.00
**Sauce dish,** diamond ornaments............ 5.00
**Spooner,** diamond ornaments ............. 25.00
**Spooner,** round ornaments.................. 25.00
**Sugar bowl,** cov., diamond
ornaments.................................... 45.00
**Sugar bowl,** cov., round ornaments,
flint .............................................. 75.00
**Tumbler,** flat or footed, diamond
ornaments.................................... 25.00
**Tumbler,** flat or footed, round
ornaments.................................... 24.00
**Wine,** diamond ornaments ................... 32.00
**Wine,** round ornaments .......... 35.00 to 45.00

## LOOP & PILLAR - See Michigan Pattern

## LOOPS & DROPS - See New Jersey Pattern

## LOOPS & FANS - See Maryland Pattern

## MAINE (Stippled Flower Panels)
**Bowl,** 6" d.................................... 30.00
**Bowl,** master berry, 8½" d., clear ......... 30.00
**Bread plate**.................................. 26.00
**Butter dish,** cov............................. 68.00
**Cake stand,** 8½" d., green................... 65.00
**Compote,** open, jelly, 4¾" d. ............... 28.00
**Compote,** open, 7" d., clear................. 32.00
**Compote,** open, 7" d., green ............... 52.00
**Compote,** open, 8" d., clear.................. 35.00
**Compote,** open, 8" d., green ............... 43.00
**Creamer**..................................... 28.00
**Pitcher,** water, clear......................... 85.00
**Pitcher,** water, w/red & green stain .... 108.00
**Platter,** oval................................. 38.00
**Relish,** 7¼" l.................................. 14.00
**Salt & pepper shakers, w/original
tops,** pr. ....................................... 69.00
**Sauce dish** .................................. 13.00
**Spooner**..................................... 32.00
**Syrup pitcher w/original top,** clear ..... 70.00
**Table set,** 4 pcs. .......................... 275.00
**Toothpick holder,** clear .................... 225.00

**Toothpick holder,** pink-stained............ 95.00
**Wine,** clear................................... 38.00
**Wine,** green.................................. 65.00

## MALTESE - See Jacob's Ladder Pattern

## MARYLAND (Inverted Loops & Fans or Loops & Fans)
**Banana bowl,** flat, 5 x 11¼" ................ 40.50
**Bread platter** ................................ 25.00
**Cake stand,** 8" d............................. 42.00
**Cake stand,** 9" d............................. 65.00
**Celery vase** .................................. 30.00
**Compote,** cov., jelly ......................... 32.00
**Compote,** cov., 7" d., high stand ......... 35.00
**Compote,** open, medium ................... 28.00
**Creamer**..................................... 25.00
**Goblet**....................................... 28.00
**Pickle dish**.................................. 14.00
**Pitcher,** milk................................. 42.00
**Pitcher,** water, clear......................... 37.00
**Pitcher,** water, ruby-stained.............. 105.00
**Plate,** 7" d................................... 23.00
**Platter** ...................................... 30.00
**Relish**....................................... 30.00
**Sauce dish** .................................. 18.00
**Spooner**..................................... 29.00
**Sugar bowl,** cov. ............................ 42.00
**Syrup pitcher** ............................... 55.00
**Toothpick holder** ............................ 35.00
**Tumbler** ..................................... 29.00
**Wine**......................................... 50.00

## MASSACHUSETTS
**Banana boat,** 6½ x 8½"...................... 55.00
**Bar bottle,** bar lip, 11" h.................... 44.00
**Bar bottle,** green, 11" h. .................... 60.00
**Bar bottle w/original pewter top,**
11" h. .......................................... 80.00
**Bowl,** 6" sq.................................. 18.00
**Bowl,** 8" l., pointed sides................... 35.00
**Bowl,** master berry, 9" sq................... 32.00
**\*Butter dish,** cov., clear.................... 75.00
**Butter dish,** cov., green.................... 65.00
**Champagne**.................................. 45.00
**Cologne bottle w/stopper** ................. 48.00
**Cordial**...................................... 55.00
**Creamer**..................................... 31.00
**Creamer & open sugar bowl,**
breakfast size, pr. ............................ 35.00
**Cruet w/original stopper** .................. 41.00
**Decanter w/stopper** ........................ 88.00
**Goblet**....................................... 44.00
**Mug,** 3½" h., clear........................... 20.00
**Mug,** 3½" h., clear w/gold trim............. 24.00
**Plate,** 6" sq., w/advertising................. 90.00
**Plate,** 8" sq.................................. 34.00
**Punch cup** ................................... 14.00
**Punch cups,** set of 4 ........................ 58.00

Relish, 8½" l.............................................. 13.00
Rum jug, 5" h. ......................... 80.00 to 90.00
Sauce dish .......................................... 15.00
Spooner................................................ 20.00
Sugar bowl, cov. ................................. 35.00
Tabasco sauce bottle, no lid .............. 35.00
Table set, 4 pcs. ................................. 225.00
Toothpick holder ................................. 50.00
Tumbler, juice...................................... 17.00
Tumbler, water .................................... 25.00
Tumbler, whiskey ................................ 13.00
Vase, 6½" h., trumpet-shaped, clear..... 22.00
Vase, 6½" h., trumpet-shaped, green ... 19.00
Vase, 7" h., clear w/gold..................... 24.00
Vase, 7" h., corset-shaped................... 14.00
Vase, 9" h., trumpet-shaped, clear........ 34.00
Vase, 9" h., trumpet-shaped, green ...... 38.00
Vase, 10" h., trumpet-shaped, green .... 60.00
Whiskey shot glass, clear ................... 16.00
Wine, blue ........................................... 110.00
Wine, clear .......................................... 35.00

## MICHIGAN (Paneled Jewel or Loop & Pillar)

Bowl, 8" d., clear................................. 36.00
Bowl, 8" d., pink-stained w/gold trim..... 75.00
Bowl, 8¾" d., scalloped & flared rim..... 28.00
Bowl, 10" d........................................... 35.00
Butter dish, cov., blue-stained ........... 175.00
Butter dish, child's (1-pc) .................... 75.00
Butter dish, cov., clear ......................... 60.00
Butter dish, cov., pink-stained ........... 260.00
Butter dish, cov., yellow-stained,
  enameled florals .............. 150.00 to 175.00
Carafe, water, clear.............................. 100.00
Celery vase, clear................................. 45.00
Compote, open, jelly, 4½" d., blue-
  stained ............................................. 125.00
Compote, open, 8½" d., high stand..... 65.00
Compote, open, 8½" d., pink-stained ... 40.00
Compote, open, 9¼" d........................... 85.00
Compote, open, flared, 9¾" d., pink-
  stained, enameled florals.................. 425.00
Compote, open, 10" d........................... 55.00
Creamer, 4" h., clear ............................ 30.00
Creamer, 4" h., pink-stained ................ 95.00
Creamer, individual size, blue-stained.. 19.00
Creamer, individual size, clear............. 45.00
Creamer, individual size, enameled
  decoration......................................... 20.00
Creamer, individual size, yellow-
  stained, enameled florals................... 55.00
Cruet w/original stopper ..................... 63.00
Goblet, clear........................................ 35.00
Goblet, clear w/blue stain .................... 40.00
Goblet, clear w/gold (ILLUS. top next
  column).............................................. 40.00
Goblet, clear w/green stain, w/enamel... 49.00
Marmalade dish, silver plate base,
  spoon & cover..................................... 85.00

*Michigan Goblet*

Mug, clear ........................................... 30.00
Mug, pink-stained, gold trim................. 38.00
Mug, yellow-stained, enameled florals.. 28.00
Pitcher, miniature, clear........................ 29.00
Pitcher, water, 8" h. ............................. 48.00
Pitcher, water, tankard, 12" h., clear .... 75.00
Pitcher, water, tankard, 12" h., pink-
  stained .............................................. 248.00
Plate, tea, 6" d., yellow-stained w/pink
  florals ............................................... 25.00
Punch bowl, 8" d., 4½" h...................... 50.00
Punch cup, clear .................................. 8.00
Punch cup, enameled decoration ........ 25.00
Punch cup, pink-stained....................... 30.00
Punch cups, enameled decoration,
  set of 5............................................. 125.00
Relish, clear......................................... 18.00
Relish, pink-stained ............................. 24.00
Salt shaker w/original top, clear ........ 28.00
Salt & pepper shakers w/original
  tops, pr.............................................. 50.00
Salt & pepper shakers w/original
  tops, pink-stained, pr.......................... 48.00
Salt & pepper shakers w/original
  tops, individual size, pr. ..................... 75.00
Sauce dish, clear.................................. 13.00
Sauce dish, pink-stained ...................... 28.00
Sauce dish, yellow-stained................... 20.00
Spooner, blue-stained .......................... 125.00
Spooner, clear...................................... 40.00
Spooner, pink-stained .......................... 71.00
Spooner, clear, child's ......................... 60.00
Sugar bowl, cov., blue-stained............ 150.00
Sugar bowl, cov., clear......................... 75.00
Sugar bowl, cov., pink-stained, gold
  trim .............................. 100.00 to 125.00
Sugar bowl, cov., child's, 4¾" h. .......... 40.00
Sugar bowl, open ................................. 10.00

Sugar bowl, individual size.................. 22.00
Sugar bowl, individual size, w/pewter
  holder...................................................... 70.00
Syrup jug w/pewter top ...................... 165.00
Table set, pink-stained,
  4 pcs................................. 425.00 to 500.00
Toddy mug, clear, tall........................... 45.00
Toothpick holder, blue-stained on top
  w/yellow enameled dots ... 100.00 to 125.00
*Toothpick holder, clear....................... 38.00
Toothpick holder, clear, enameled
  florals .................................................. 45.00
Toothpick holder, pink-stained, gold
  trim...................................................... 245.00
Toothpick holder, yellow-stained ........ 55.00
Toothpick holder, yellow-stained,
  enameled florals ................................. 90.00
Tumbler, clear ...................................... 24.00
Tumbler, clear w/gold trim.................... 37.00
Tumbler, pink-stained, gold trim .......... 55.00
Tumbler, yellow-stained, enameled
  florals .................................................. 35.00
Vase, 6" h., clear................................. 35.00
Vase, 6" h., pink-stained, enameled
  florals .................................................. 38.00
Vase, 6" h., pink-stained, gold trim........ 18.00
Vase, 8" h., green-stained, white
  enameled dots ..................................... 60.00
Vase, 8" h., pink-stained ...................... 35.00
Vase, 12" h., clear................................ 24.00
Waste bowl............................................ 68.00
Water set: pitcher & three tumblers;
  yellow-stained, enameled florals,
  4 pcs. .................................................. 225.00
Water set: pitcher & six tumblers;
  clear, 7 pcs. ....................................... 195.00
Wine, blue-stained ............................... 40.00
Wine, clear............................................ 35.00
Wine, yellow-stained ............................ 43.00

## MISSOURI (Palm & Scroll)

Bowl, 8" d.............................................. 21.00
Bowl, 8¾" d., green .............................. 41.00
Butter dish, cov., green......................... 85.00
Cake stand, 9" d., 4¾" h., clear............ 40.00
Cake stand, 9" d., green....................... 48.00
Cake stand, 10" d., clear ...................... 63.00
Compote, jelly ...................................... 32.00
Creamer, clear...................................... 35.00
Creamer, green...................................... 30.00
Doughnut stand, 6" d. (ILLUS. top
  next column) ....................................... 55.00
Mug, clear ............................................ 30.00
Pitcher, milk, clear................................ 45.00
Pitcher, milk, green............................... 125.00
Pitcher, water, clear.............................. 52.00
Pitcher, water, green ............................ 113.00
Pitcher, water, tankard green .............. 70.00
Sauce dish, green ................................. 13.00

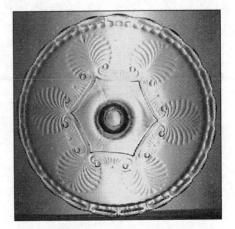

*Missouri Doughnut Stand*

Spooner, clear ...................................... 24.00
Spooner, green...................................... 40.00
Sugar bowl, cov., clear.......................... 49.00
Sugar bowl, cov., green ........................ 54.00
Syrup pitcher ........................................ 68.00
Table set, green, 3 pcs. ........................ 165.00
Table set, clear, 4 pcs. ........................ 195.00
Table set, green, 4 pcs....... 250.00 to 300.00
Tumbler, green ...................................... 35.00
Wine, clear............................................ 36.00
Wine, green............................................ 53.00

## MONKEY

Butter dish, cov. .................................. 195.00
Creamer, opalescent ............................ 600.00
Mug, amethyst ...................................... 360.00
Mug, clear ........................... 75.00 to 85.00
*Spooner, clear .................. 120.00 to 125.00
Spooner, white opalescent ................. 170.00
Sugar bowl, open .................................. 90.00

## MOON & STAR

Bowl, cov., 6" d. .................................... 26.00
*Bowl, cov., 7" d..................................... 34.00
*Bowl, master berry, 8¼" d., 4" h.......... 35.00
Bowl, fruit, 9" d., footed ...................... 35.00
Bread tray, scalloped rim, 6½ x 10¾" .. 65.00
*Butter dish, cov. .................................. 46.00
*Cake stand, 9" d.................................... 65.00
Cake stand, 10"d. ............................... 95.00
Celery vase .......................................... 29.00
*Compote, cov., 6" d., high stand ......... 60.00
*Compote, cov., 6" d., low stand .......... 50.00
Compote, cov., 7" d., 9" h.................... 45.00
Compote, cov., 7" d., 11" h.................. 70.00
Compote, cov., 13½" h. ...................... 125.00
Compote, open, 7" d., 7½" h. (ILLUS.
  top next page...................................... 30.00

*Moon & Star Compote*

Compote, open, 8" d., 8" h. ................. 58.00
Compote, open, 9" d., 6½" h. .............. 35.00
*Creamer ............................................. 52.00
*Cruet w/original stopper, applied
  handle ............................................... 125.00
*Egg cup ............................................. 35.00
*Goblet ................................. 35.00 to 45.00
Pickle dish, 8" l ................................. 15.00
*Pitcher, water, 9¼" h., applied rope
  handle ............................................... 150.00
Relish, oblong ...................................... 20.00
Salt dip, individual size, footed ............ 32.00
Salt shaker w/original top ................... 30.00
*Sauce dish, flat or footed, each ......... 14.00
*Spooner ............................................ 45.00
*Sugar bowl, cov. ................................ 60.00
*Syrup pitcher w/original top .......... 125.00
*Toothpick holder ............................... 21.00
*Tumbler, flat ...................................... 85.00
*Wine ................................................... 43.00

## NAILHEAD

Bowl, 7¾" d., 2⅝" h. ........................... 40.00
Butter dish, cov. .................................. 47.00
Cake stand, 9" to 12" d. ...................... 30.00
Cake stand, 10½" d. ............................ 50.00
Celery vase ......................................... 42.00
Compote, cov., 8½" d., 12" h. ............. 90.00
Creamer ............................................. 26.00
Goblet, plain (ILLUS. top next
  column) ............................... 30.00 to 35.00
Pitcher, water ...................... 65.00 to 75.00
Plate, 6" or 7" d. ................................. 19.00
Plate, 7" sq. ........................................ 19.00
Plate, 9" sq. ........................................ 23.00
Plate, 9" d. .......................................... 22.00
Sauce dish, 4" ...................................... 9.00
Spooner .............................................. 19.00
Sugar bowl, cov. ................................. 35.00
Tumbler, ruby-stained ......................... 35.00
Wine ................................................... 24.00

*Nailhead Goblet*

## NEW HAMPSHIRE (Bent Buckle)

Creamer, clear .................................... 30.00
Creamer, individual, 3¼" h., clear .......... 25.00
Cruet w/original stopper, clear ............ 60.00
Cruet w/original stopper, rose-
  stained ............................................. 289.00
Goblet, clear ....................................... 25.00
Goblet, rose-stained .............. 60.00 to 65.00
Mug, medium size, clear ...................... 24.00
Mug, large size, rose-stained .............. 75.00
Olive dish, diamond-shaped, 6⅝" w.,
  rose-stained ...................................... 20.00
Sauce dish, round, 4" d., rose-stained ... 14.00
Sugar bowl, cov., breakfast size,
  clear .................................................. 14.00
Sugar bowl, cov., breakfast size,
  rose-stained ...................................... 17.00
Sugar bowl, open, individual, double-
  handled, rose-stained ........................ 21.00
Toothpick holder, clear ....................... 20.00
Toothpick holder, rose-stained .......... 65.00
Tumbler, water, clear ............. 20.00 to 25.00
Vase, 6" h., thick stem, rose-stained ... 23.008
Wine, flared bowl, clear ....................... 19.00
Wine, flared bowl, rose-stained ............ 55.00

## NEW JERSEY (Loops & Drops)

Berry set, master bowl & three sauce
  dishes, 4 pcs. .................................... 75.00
Berry set, master bowl & six sauce
  dishes, 7 pcs. ................................... 175.00
Bowl, 9" d. ........................................... 28.00
Bowl, oval ........................................... 85.00
Bread plate .......................................... 28.00
Butter dish, cov., ruby-
  stained ........................... 150.00 to 200.00
Butter dish, cov., w/gold trim .............. 75.00
Carafe, water ....................................... 75.00
Celery tray, flat .................................... 25.00

Compote, open, jelly.......................... 32.00
Compote, open, 7" d., low stand ......... 32.00
Compote, open, 7" d., high stand........ 60.00
Creamer, clear ................................... 36.00
Creamer, ruby-stained .......................... 65.00
Creamer, w/gold trim ........................... 60.00
Cruet w/original stopper ................... 45.00
Goblet, clear ..................................... 33.00
Goblet, ruby-stained ........................... 195.00
Goblet, w/gold trim............................... 28.00
Pitcher, water, bulbous ...... 150.00 to 175.00
Plate, 10½"........................................ 36.00
Relish................................................ 13.00
Salt shaker w/original top................. 35.00
Sauce dish, flat................................. 11.00
Spooner, clear ................................... 28.00
Spooner, ruby-stained ......................... 65.00
Sugar bowl, cov. ............................... 53.00
Syrup pitcher w/original lid .............. 115.00
Table set, 4 pcs. ................................. 215.00
Toothpick holder, clear ...................... 49.00
Toothpick holder, w/gold trim.............. 65.00
Tumbler, clear ................................... 27.00
Vase, 8" h., green ............................... 26.00
Vase, 10" h., clear .............................. 20.00
Vase, 10" h., green .............................. 24.00
Water set, pitcher & six tumblers,
  7 pcs. ................................................... 175.00
Wine..................................................... 40.00

### OLD MAN OF THE MOUNTAIN - See Viking Pattern

### OREGON NO. 1 - See Beaded Loop Pattern

### PALM & SCROLL - See Missouri Pattern

### PANELED FORGET-ME-NOT

Bread platter, 7 x 11" oval .................. 31.00
Butter dish, cov.................................. 63.00
Cake stand, 8" d., amethyst ............... 295.00
Cake stand ......................................... 47.00
Celery vase ........................................ 40.00
Compote, cov., 7" d., 10" h.................. 81.00
Compote, cov., 8" d., high stand .......... 89.00
Compote, open, 7" d., high stand......... 50.00
Compote, open, 8½" d., high stand..... 40.00
Creamer................................................ 32.00
Cruet w/original stopper .................... 55.00
Goblet, amethyst ............................... 750.00
Goblet, clear ........................... 35.00 to 45.00
Mustard jar, cov. ............................... 40.00
Pitcher, milk, clear .............................. 60.00
Pitcher, water, amethyst.................... 175.00
Pitcher, water, clear .............. 65.00 to 70.00
Relish, handled, 4½ x 7¾"................... 21.00
Relish, scoop-shaped, 9" l. ................. 20.00
Sauce dish, flat or footed, each............ 16.00

Spooner...................................................... 40.00
Sugar bowl, cov. ................................... 35.00
Wine......................................................... 120.00

### PANELED 44 - See Reverse 44 Pattern

### PANELED HERRINGBONE (Emerald Green Herringbone or Florida)

*Paneled Herringbone Goblet*

Bowl, master berry, 9" sq., green ......... 21.00
Butter dish, cov., clear ......................... 50.00
Butter dish, cov., green......................... 73.00
Compote, open, jelly, 5½" sq., green ... 26.00
Cruet w/original stopper,
  green .............................. 100.00 to 125.00
*Goblet, clear......................................... 40.00
*Goblet, green (ILLUS.) ......................... 75.00
Pitcher, milk, green ............... 55.00 to 65.00
Pitcher, water, clear............................. 42.00
Pitcher, water, green .......................... 85.00
*Plate, 9", green................................... 35.00
Relish, 4½ x 8" oval, green................... 14.00
Sauce dish, green ............................... 8.00
Spooner, green...................................... 25.00
Syrup pitcher w/original top,
  green ............................... 150.00 to 200.00
Tumbler, green ....................................... 20.00
Wine, clear.............................................. 23.00
Wine, green.............................................. 48.00

### PANELED JEWEL - See Michigan Pattern

### PEACOCK FEATHER (Georgia)

Bonbon dish, footed ............................ 23.00
Bowl, 6 x 8" oval..................................... 28.00
Bowl, 8" d.............................................. 30.00
Butter dish, cov..................................... 40.00
Cake stand, 8½" d., 5" h...................... 31.00

Compote, open, 6" d............................ 18.00
Compote, open, 6¾" d., low stand ....... 25.00
Creamer.............................................. 23.00
Cruet w/original stopper ..................... 40.00
Goblet................................................. 25.00
Lamp, kerosene-type, low hand-type
  w/handle, 5½" h., clear ...................... 95.00
Lamp, kerosene-type, table model
  w/handle, 9" h., blue ........................ 220.00
Lamp, kerosene-type, table model
  w/handle, 9" h., clear ......................... 85.00
Lamp, kerosene-type, table model,
  10" h., amber ................................... 275.00
Lamp, kerosene-type, table model,
  12" h., amber ................................... 325.00
Mug ................................................... 40.00
Nappy, 7" d., footed ............................ 23.00
Pitcher, water ....................... 55.00 to 60.00
Relish, 8" oval..................................... 14.00
Salt & pepper shakers w/original
  tops, pr. ............................................ 85.00
Sauce dish .......................................... 13.00
Spooner .............................................. 37.00
Sugar bowl, cov. ................................. 37.00
Tumbler .............................................. 35.00
Water set, pitcher & six tumblers,
  7 pcs............................... 250.00 to 275.00

## PENNSYLVANIA (Balder or Kamoni)

Bowl, berry or fruit, 8½" d., clear
  w/gold trim ........................................ 30.00
Butter dish, cov., clear ........................ 58.00
Butter dish, cov., green ....................... 85.00
Cake stand .......................................... 45.00
Carafe ................................................ 48.00
Celery tray, 4½ x 11"............................ 28.00
Celery vase ........................................ 21.00

*Pennsylvania Creamer*

Creamer, 3" h., clear w/gold trim,
  small (ILLUS.).................................... 23.00
Creamer, 3" h., green w/gold trim,
  small ................................................. 75.00
Cruet w/original stopper .................... 44.00
Decanter w/original stopper, 10¾" h.. 75.00
Goblet, clear ....................................... 22.00

Goblet, clear w/gold............................. 30.00
Pitcher, water ...................................... 85.00
Punch cup, clear ................................. 10.00
Punch cup, clear w/gold....................... 20.00
Salt & pepper shakers w/original
  tops, pr............................................. 65.00
Sauce dish, round or square ............... 12.00
*Spooner ............................................ 21.00
Sugar bowl, cov., child's, green
  w/gold trim ...................................... 160.00
Syrup pitcher w/original top.............. 55.00
Table set, child's, 4 pcs. .................... 250.00
Table set, 4 pcs. ............................... 225.00
Toothpick holder, clear ....................... 31.00
Toothpick holder, clear w/gold ........... 69.00
Tumbler, juice, clear............................ 12.00
Tumbler, juice, set of 4 ....................... 28.00
Tumbler, water, clear............................ 23.00
Tumbler, water, clear w/gold trim ......... 25.00
Tumbler, water, ruby-stained............... 49.00
Tumbler, whiskey, clear........................ 17.00
Tumbler, whiskey, green w/gold trim.... 25.00
Vase, 5¾" h., green.............................. 60.00
Whiskey shot glass, clear ................... 13.00
Whiskey shot glass, green................... 25.00
Wine, clear............................. 10.00 to 15.00
Wine, green........................................ 32.00

## PILLOW ENCIRCLED

Bowl, 8" d., ruby-stained...................... 51.00
Celery vase, clear................................ 35.00
Creamer, clear .................................... 25.00
Cruet w/original stopper, clear
  w/enameled floral decoration.............. 35.00
Lamp, kerosene, finger-type, clear ....... 75.00
Mug .................................................... 35.00
Pitcher, water, tankard, clear............... 42.00
Pitcher, water, tankard, ruby-stained.. 102.00
Salt shaker w/original top.................. 35.00
Salt & pepper shakers w/original
  tops, ruby-stained, pr. ....................... 85.00
Sauce dish, footed, clear..................... 12.00
Spooner, ruby-stained ......................... 62.00
Sugar bowl, cov., clear......................... 40.00
Sugar bowl, cov., ruby-stained........... 125.00
Tumbler, clear ..................................... 25.00
Tumbler, ruby-stained ......................... 41.00

## PLEAT & TUCK - See Adonis Pattern

## PLUME

Berry set, 8½" sq. master bowl & five
  4½" sq. sauce dishes, 6 pcs. .............. 95.00
Bowl, cov., 8" d. .................................. 43.00
Bowl, open, 6" d.................................. 24.00
Bowl, open, 8½" sq. master berry........ 35.00
Bowl, open, 9" d.................................. 30.00
Butter dish, cov., clear ........................ 48.00
Cake stand, 9" d., high stand .............. 50.00
Celery vase, clear................................ 38.00

*Plume Goblet*

**Compote,** open, 6" d., collared base .... **36.00**
**Compote,** open, 7" d., collared base .... **40.00**
**Compote,** open, 8" d., high stand ......... **40.00**
**Creamer,** applied handle, clear............. **28.00**
**Creamer,** ruby-stained .......................... **60.00**
**Cruet w/original stopper** .................... **38.00**
***Goblet,** clear (ILLUS.) ......................... **34.00**
**Goblet,** engraved ................................. **44.00**
**Goblet,** ruby-stained &
    engraved ............................. **75.00 to 80.00**
**Pitcher,** water, bulbous, clear,
    engraved ............................................. **75.00**
**Pitcher,** water, bulbous, clear, plain ..... **65.00**
**Pitcher,** water, bulbous, ruby-
    stained ............................. **200.00 to 250.00**
**Relish**................................................... **22.00**
**Sauce dish,** flat or footed, clear........... **10.00**
**Spooner,** clear ...................................... **31.00**
**Spooner,** ruby-stained .......................... **60.00**
**Tumbler,** clear ...................................... **45.00**
**Tumbler,** ruby-stained, souvenir........... **43.00**

## PORTLAND

**Bowl,** 8" d............................................. **25.00**
**Bowl,** 10" d., flared................................ **25.00**
**Butter dish,** cov. .................................. **48.00**
**Cake stand,** 10½" .............................. **55.00**
***Candlestick**...................................... **110.00**
***Celery tray** ....................................... **25.00**
**Celery vase** ........................................ **43.00**
**Compote,** cov., 6½" d., high stand ..... **125.00**
**Compote,** cov., 7" d., high stand ........ **100.00**
**Compote,** cov., 8" d., high stand ......... **40.00**
**Compote,** open, 7" d., high stand......... **45.00**
**Cordial** ................................................. **25.00**
**Creamer**................................................ **40.00**
***Creamer,** individual size (ILLUS.
    top next column) ................................ **18.00**
**Cruet w/original stopper**....... **60.00 to 65.00**

*Portland Creamer*

**Goblet,** clear ........................................ **39.00**
**Pitcher,** water ....................................... **33.00**
**Pitcher,** water, miniature...................... **26.00**
**Punch bowl,** 15" d.,
    8½" h. .............................. **150.00 to 175.00**
**Punch cup** ............................................ **18.00**
**Salt shaker w/original top**.................. **16.00**
**Sauce dish,** 4½" d. ................................ **8.00**
**Spooner**................................................ **25.00**
**Sugar bowl,** cov. .................................. **55.00**
**Sugar shaker w/original top** .............. **58.00**
**Table set:** cov. butter dish, cov. sugar
    bowl, creamer & spooner; clear
    w/gold trim, 4 pcs............................. **350.00**
**Toothpick holder** ................................. **27.00**
**Tumbler** ................................................ **25.00**
**Vase,** 6" h., scalloped rim..................... **22.00**
**Wine**...................................................... **21.00**

**PRAYER RUG  - See Horseshoe Pattern**

## PRESSED DIAMOND

**Bowl,** berry, flat, 8" d., amber .............. **20.00**
**Butter dish,** cov., amber...................... **45.00**
**Butter dish,** cov., blue ......................... **95.00**
**Celery vase,** clear ................................ **15.00**
**Creamer,** amber, 4¾" h. ....................... **38.00**
**Creamer,** canary, 4¾" h........................ **40.00**
**Goblet,** blue ......................................... **30.00**
**Salt shaker w/original top,** tall, blue ... **48.00**
**Salt shaker w/original top,** tall, canary.. **30.00**
**Salt shaker w/original top,** tall, clear .. **15.00**
**Sauce dish,** flat, round, blue................. **25.00**
**Sauce dish,** flat, round, canary............ **23.00**
**Sauce dish,** flat, round, clear................ **7.00**
**Spooner,** flat, amber............................ **35.00**
**Spooner,** flat, blue ............................... **40.00**
**Spooner,** flat, canary ........................... **35.00**
**Spooner,** flat, clear .............................. **30.00**
**Tumbler,** water, flat, amber .................. **30.00**
**Tumbler,** water, flat, blue...................... **28.00**

## PRISCILLA (Alexis)

**Banana stand**...................................... **95.00**
**Bowl,** 8" d., 3½" h., straight sides, flat .. **38.00**

*Priscilla Sugar Bowl*

**Bowl,** 8" d., 3½" h., w/pattern on base.. **45.00**
***Bowl,** 10¼" to 10½" d. .......................... **35.00**
**Butter dish,** cov. ..................................... **95.00**
**Cake stand,** 9" to 10" d., high stand ..... **65.00**
**Compote,** cov., jelly ................ **55.00 to 60.00**
***Compote,** cov., 8" d. ........................... **100.00**
**Compote,** cov., 12" d. ........................... **145.00**
***Compote,** open, 8" d., 8" h. .................. **55.00**
***Creamer** ............................................... **45.00**
**Creamer,** individual size ...................... **28.00**
**Cup & saucer** ........................................ **32.00**
***Goblet** .................................................... **38.00**
**Pitcher,** water, bulbous ...................... **140.00**
**Plate,** 10½" d., turned-up rim ................ **25.00**
**Relish** ...................................................... **23.00**
***Sauce dish,** flat, 4½" to 5" d. ................ **25.00**
**Sauce dish,** ruby-stained ...................... **55.00**
**Spooner** ................................................... **35.00**
**Sugar bowl,** cov. (ILLUS. above) .......... **45.00**
**Sugar bowl,** cov., individual size .......... **31.00**
**Syrup pitcher w/original pewter top,**
  clear ................................. **120.00 to 125.00**
**Syrup pitcher w/original pewter top,**
  green w/gold .................................... **450.00**

*Priscilla Tumbler*

**Table set,** 4 pcs. ................ **200.00 to 225.00**
**Toothpick holder** ................................. **32.00**
**Tumbler** (ILLUS. bottom previous
  column) ............................................. **44.00**
***Wine** ..................................................... **40.00**

## RAMPANT LION - See Frosted Lion Pattern

## REVERSE 44 (Paneled 44, U.S. Glass "Athenia")

**Berry set:** master bowl & six sauce
  dishes; clear w/gold or platinum
  stain, 7 pcs. ..................................... **225.00**
**Bowl,** 8" d., shallow sides, clear
  w/gold or platinum stain ..................... **75.00**
**Butter dish,** cov., clear w/gold or
  platinum stain .................................. **155.00**
**Champagne,** clear w/platinum stain ..... **75.00**
**Compote,** jelly, clear w/gold or
  platinum stain .................................... **69.00**
**Compote,** open, 5½" d., high
  standard, clear ................................... **32.00**
**Creamer,** after dinner, clear ................. **45.00**
**Creamer,** berry, clear w/gold or
  platinum stain .................................... **95.00**
**Creamer,** table size, clear w/gold or
  platinum stain .................................... **35.00**
**Creamer,** tankard, clear w/gold or
  platinum stain .................................... **30.00**
**Cruet w/original stopper,** clear .......... **58.00**
**Goblet,** clear ......................................... **65.00**
**Goblet,** clear w/gold or platinum
  stain ................................... **75.00 to 85.00**
**Pitcher,** tankard-type, footed,
  clear ................................ **175.00 to 180.00**
**Pitcher,** tankard-type, footed, clear
  w/gold or platinum stain ................... **150.00**
**Sauce dish,** 4" d., straight sides, clear
  w/gold or platinum stain ..................... **20.00**
**Spoonholder,** handled, clear w/gold
  or platinum stain ................................ **75.00**
**Sugar bowl,** open, after dinner,
  clear ................................................... **45.00**
**Table set:** creamer, cov. sugar bowl &
  spooner; clear w/platinum stain,
  3 pcs. ............................................... **290.00**
**Toothpick holder,** footed, handled,
  clear ................................................... **35.00**
**Toothpick holder,** footed, handled,
  clear w/gold or platinum
  stain ................................... **75.00 to 85.00**
**Wines,** clear w/gold or platinum stain,
  set of 5 ............................................. **180.00**

## RIBBON (Early Ribbon)
**Bread tray** .............................................. **40.00**
**Butter dish,** cov. .................................... **73.00**
**Celery vase** ............................................ **38.00**

*Ribbon Compote*

**Compote,** cov., 8" d. (ILLUS.) ............... **96.00**
**Compote,** open, 8" d., low stand .......... **40.00**
**Compote,** open, 8" d., 8" h., frosted
　dolphin stem on dome base ............. **245.00**
**\*Compote,** open, 5½ x 8" rectangular
　bowl, 7" h., frosted dolphin stem on
　dome base ....................................... **295.00**
**Compote,** open, 8½" d., 4½" h. ............. **50.00**
**Compote,** open, 10½" d., frosted
　dolphin stem on dome base ............. **395.00**
**Creamer** ............................................. **34.00**
**Dresser bottle w/stopper** ................. **125.00**
**\*Goblet** ............................................... **31.00**
**Pitcher,** water ..................................... **120.00**
**Plate,** 7" d. ........................................... **34.00**
**Platter,** 9 x 13" .................................... **60.00**
**Sauce dish,** flat or footed .................... **13.00**
**Spooner** .............................................. **30.00**
**Sugar bowl,** cov., 4¼" d., 7¾" h. .......... **72.00**
**Table set,** 4 pcs. ................. **200.00 to 225.00**
**Waste bowl** ......................................... **43.00**

## ROMAN ROSETTE

**Bowl,** 8" d. ............................................ **24.00**
**Bread platter,** 9 x 11" ........................... **28.00**
**Butter dish,** cov., clear ......................... **55.00**
**Cake stand,** 9" to 10" d. ........................ **58.00**
**Celery vase,** ruby-stained .................... **95.00**
**Compote,** cov., 6" d., high stand .......... **70.00**
**Compote,** open, jelly, 5" d. ................... **23.00**
**Cordial** ............................................... **48.00**
**Creamer,** clear (ILLUS. top next
　column) .............................. **30.00 to 35.00**
**\*Goblet** ................................................ **51.00**
**Marmalade dish,** footed, clear ............. **24.00**
**Mug,** 3" h. ............................................. **16.00**
**Pitcher,** milk ......................................... **60.00**
**Pitcher,** water ....................................... **78.00**
**Plate,** 7" d. ............................................ **35.00**

*Roman Rosette Creamer*

**Relish,** 3½ x 8½" ................................... **13.00**
**Sauce dish** ............................ **40.00 to 50.00**
**Spooner,** clear ...................................... **26.00**
**Sugar bowl,** cov. ................................... **40.00**
**Wine,** clear ............................................ **48.00**
**Wine,** ruby-stained ................................ **65.00**

## ROYAL IVY (Northwood)

*Royal Ivy Cruet*

**Berry set:** master bowl & three sauce
　dishes; craquelle (cranberry &
　canary spatter), 4 pcs. ...................... **175.00**
**Berry set:** master bowl & six sauce
　dishes; frosted rubina crystal, 7 pcs. ... **310.00**
**Bowl,** 8" d., frosted rubina
　crystal .............................. **150.00 to 200.00**
**Bowl,** fruit, 9 d., craquelle (cranberry
　& canary spatter) .............................. **235.00**

**Bowl,** fruit, 9" d., frosted craquelle ...... **150.00**
**Butter dish,** cov., rubina
   crystal .............................. **150.00 to 175.00**
**Creamer,** clear & frosted ...................... **82.00**
**Creamer,** rubina crystal ...... **115.00 to 125.00**
**Creamer,** frosted rubina
   crystal .............................. **200.00 to 215.00**
**Cruet w/original stopper,** clear &
   frosted .............................................. **135.00**
**Cruet w/original stopper,** craquelle
   (cranberry & canary spatter) ............. **495.00**
**Cruet w/original stopper,** rubina
   crystal (ILLUS. bottom previous
   page) ................................................ **295.00**
**Cruet w/original stopper,** frosted
   rubina crystal .................... **350.00 to 375.00**
**Marmalade jar,** w/original silver plate
   lid, clear & frosted ............................ **100.00**
**Pickle castor,** frosted rubina crystal
   insert, complete w/silver plate
   frame ............................... **350.00 to 375.00**
**Pickle castor,** cased spatter
   (cranberry & canary w/white lining)
   insert, complete w/silver plate frame
   & tongs ............................. **300.00 to 350.00**
**Pitcher,** water, cased spatter
   (cranberry & canary w/white
   lining) ................................ **325.00 to 350.00**
**Pitcher,** water, clear &
   frosted .............................. **110.00 to 125.00**
**Pitcher,** water, craquelle (cranberry &
   canary spatter) .................................. **375.00**
**Pitcher,** water, rubina crystal .............. **250.00**
**Pitcher,** water, frosted rubina
   crystal .............................. **350.00 to 400.00**
**Rose bowl,** clear & frosted ................... **60.00**
**Rose bowl,** rubina crystal ..................... **78.00**
**Rose bowl,** frosted rubina crystal ....... **120.00**
**Rose bowl,** craquelle (cranberry &
   canary spatter) .................................. **180.00**
**Salt shaker w/original top,** cased
   spatter (cranberry & canary w/white
   lining) ................................................ **125.00**
**Salt shaker w/original top,** rubina
   crystal ................................................ **48.00**
**Salt shaker w/original top,** frosted
   rubina crystal ..................................... **78.00**
**Salt & pepper shakers w/original
   tops,** cased spatter (cranberry &
   canary w/white lining), pr. ................. **225.00**
**Sauce dish,** craquelle (cranberry &
   canary spatter) ..................... **50.00 to 65.00**
**Spooner,** clear & frosted ...................... **41.00**
**Spooner,** craquelle (cranberry &
   canary spatter) .................................. **150.00**
**Spooner,** rubina crystal ....................... **65.00**
**Spooner,** frosted rubina crystal ............ **80.00**
**Sugar bowl,** cov., frosted rubina
   crystal ................................................ **200.00**
**Sugar shaker w/original top,** cased
   spatter (cranberry & canary w/white
   lining) ................................................ **300.00**

**Sugar shaker w/original top,** rubina
   crystal ................................................ **130.00**
**Sugar shaker w/original top,** frosted
   rubina crystal .................... **200.00 to 250.00**
**Syrup pitcher w/original top,** cased
   spatter (cranberry & canary w/white
   lining) ................................................ **490.00**
**Syrup pitcher w/original top,** clear &
   frosted .............................. **100.00 to 150.00**
**Syrup pitcher w/original top,** frosted
   rubina crystal .................... **500.00 to 525.00**
**Toothpick holder,** cased spatter
   (cranberry & canary w/white lining) .. **145.00**
**Toothpick holder,** clear & frosted ........ **48.00**
**Toothpick holder,** craquelle
   (cranberry & canary spatter) ............. **235.00**
**Toothpick holder,** rubina crystal .......... **85.00**
**Toothpick holder,** frosted rubina
   crystal ................................................ **125.00**
**Tumbler,** cased spatter (cranberry &
   canary w/white lining) ........................ **85.00**
**Tumbler,** clear & frosted ...................... **36.00**
**Tumbler,** craquelle (cranberry &
   canary spatter) .................................... **81.00**
**Tumbler,** rubina crystal ......................... **66.00**
**Tumbler,** frosted rubina crystal ............. **70.00**
**Water set:** pitcher & five tumblers;
   clear & frosted, 6 pcs. ...................... **175.00**
**Water set:** pitcher & five tumblers;
   rubina crystal, 6 pcs. ......................... **595.00**
**Water set:** pitcher & six tumblers;
   cased spatter (cranberry & canary
   w/white lining), 7 pcs. ....................... **955.00**

## ROYAL OAK

*Royal Oak Butter Dish*

**Berry set:** master bowl & four sauce
   dishes; rubina crystal, 5 pcs. ............ **290.00**
**Bowl,** berry, 7½" d., frosted crystal ....... **65.00**
**Butter dish,** cov., frosted crystal
   (ILLUS.) ............................................. **55.00**
**Butter dish,** cov., frosted rubina
   crystal ................................................ **231.00**
**Creamer,** frosted crystal ...................... **75.00**

**Creamer,** rubina crystal ...... **150.00 to 175.00**
**Creamer,** frosted rubina
　crystal .............................. **200.00 to 225.00**
**Cruet w/original stopper,** frosted
　rubina crystal ................................... **250.00**
**Pickle castor,** rubina crystal insert,
　w/resilvered frame & tongs ............... **450.00**
**Pitcher,** 8½" h., frosted crystal............. **82.00**
**Pitcher,** water, rubina
　crystal.............................. **300.00 to 350.00**
**Salt shaker w/original top,** rubina
　crystal ............................................ **100.00**
**Sauce dish,** rubina crystal ................... **50.00**
**Spooner,** frosted crystal ....................... **48.00**
**Spooner,** frosted rubina crystal ............ **95.00**
**Sugar bowl,** cov., frosted rubina
　crystal .............................. **145.00 to 155.00**
**Sugar shaker w/original top,** frosted
　crystal .............................................. **95.00**
**Sugar shaker w/original top,** rubina
　crystal ............................................ **138.00**
**Sugar shaker w/original top,** frosted
　rubina crystal ................... **145.00 to 165.00**
**Syrup jug w/original metal lid,**
　rubina crystal ................................... **200.00**
**Table set,** frosted rubina crystal, 4 pcs. . **595.00**
**Toothpick holder,** frosted crystal......... **60.00**
**Toothpick holder,** rubina crystal........ **150.00**
**Tumbler,** frosted rubina crystal............. **84.00**

## RUBY THUMBPRINT

**Bowl,** 6½" d., engraved......................... **56.00**
**\*Bowl,** 8½" d. ...................................... **90.00**
**Bowl,** master berry or fruit,
　10" l., boat-shaped........................... **125.00**
**Butter dish,** cov., engraved............... **225.00**

*Ruby Thumbprint Celery Vase*

**Celery vase** (ILLUS.).............. **85.00 to 90.00**
**Champagne,** souvenir ......................... **45.00**
**\*Claret**................................................. **65.00**
**Compote,** open, jelly, 5¼" h. ............... **40.00**

**Compote,** open, 7" d.,
　engraved ......................... **185.00 to 190.00**
**Compote,** open, 7" d., plain............... **145.00**
**Compote,** open, 8½" d., 7½" h.,
　scalloped rim ................................... **220.00**
**Cordial,** engraved................................ **40.00**
**Creamer,** engraved.............................. **68.00**
**\*Creamer,** plain ................ **45.00 to 50.00**
**Creamer,** individual size ...................... **28.00**
**Cup,** engraved ..................................... **35.00**
**\*Cup,** plain .......................................... **24.00**
**Cup & saucer,** engraved........ **60.00 to 65.00**
**\*Cup & saucer,** plain .......................... **57.00**
**\*Goblet,** plain...................................... **40.00**
**Goblet,** souvenir ................................. **41.00**
**Pitcher,** milk, 7½" h., bulbous............. **100.00**
**Pitcher,** milk, tankard, 8⅜" h.............. **125.00**
**\*Pitcher,** water, tankard, 11" h. .......... **132.00**
**Pitcher,** water, tankard, 11" h.,
　w/engraved leaf band ....................... **180.00**
**\*Plate,** 8¼" d. ...................................... **20.00**
**Sauce dish,** boat-shaped ..................... **28.00**
**\*Sauce dish,** round.............................. **20.00**
**Sauce dish,** round, engraved .............. **48.00**
**\*Sherbet**............................................. **18.00**
**Spooner**.............................................. **65.00**
**Toothpick holder,** engraved ............... **45.00**
**Toothpick holder,** plain ......... **30.00 to 40.00**
**Tumbler,** engraved .............................. **60.00**
**\*Tumbler,** plain ................................... **39.00**
**Water set,** bulbous pitcher & six
　tumblers, w/engraved family names
　& dated 1897, 7 pcs.......................... **595.00**
**\*Wine** ................................................. **30.00**
**Wine,** engraved................................... **35.00**
**Wine,** souvenir ................................... **35.00**

## SAWTOOTH

**Butter dish,** cov., clear, flint ................. **78.00**
**\*Butter dish,** cov., clear, non-flint......... **50.00**
**Butter dish,** cov., sapphire blue,
　non-flint............................................ **230.00**
**Cake stand,** non-flint, 7½" d., 6" h........ **30.00**
**\*Cake stand,** non-flint, 9½" d., 4½" h. .. **75.00**
**Celery vase,** knob stem, flint.. **45.00 to 55.00**
**Celery vase,** knob stem, non-flint......... **33.00**
**Celery vase,** stepped pedestal base,
　notched rim, flint .............................. **125.00**
**Champagne,** knob stem, flint................ **85.00**
**Champagne,** non-flint........................... **33.00**
**Compote,** open, 7½" d., 5½" h. ............ **38.00**
**Compote,** open, 7½" d., 7½" h., flint .... **55.00**
**Compote,** open, 8" d., low stand,
　blue, flint .......................................... **250.00**
**Compote,** open, 8" d., low stand,
　canary, flint ....................................... **200.00**
**Compote,** open, 9½" d., 10" h., flint.... **100.00**
**Compote,** open, 11¼" d., 8¾" h., milk
　white, flint ......................................... **85.00**
**Creamer,** applied handle, clear,
　flint..................................... **70.00 to 75.00**

**Creamer,** applied handle, cobalt blue,
  flint ................................................... **230.00**
**Creamer,** miniature, non-flint ............... **29.00**
**Decanter w/original stopper,** flint,
  14" h. ............................................... **145.00**
**Egg cup,** cov., canary, flint ................. **193.00**
**Egg cup,** cov., clear, flint .................... **100.00**
**Goblet,** knob stem, flint......................... **35.00**
**Goblet,** knob stem, non-flint ... **20.00 to 25.00**
**Goblet,** plain stem, non-flint.................. **19.00**
**Lamp,** whale oil, w/marble base ......... **150.00**
**Pitcher,** water, applied handle, clear,
  flint .................................................... **175.00**
**Pomade jar,** cov. .................... **75.00 to 80.00**
**Salt dip,** cov., master size, footed,
  clear, flint ......................................... **100.00**
**Salt dip,** cov., master size, footed,
  milk white, flint ................................... **75.00**
**Salt dip,** cov., master size, footed,
  clear, non-flint ..................................... **35.00**
**Salt dip,** cov., master size, clear, flint ... **45.00**
**Salt dip,** cov., master size, clear, non-
  flint ...................................................... **22.00**
**Sauce dish,** clear................................. **10.00**
**Sauce dish,** flat, canary....................... **23.00**

*Sawtooth Spooner*

**Spooner,** clear, flint (ILLUS.) ................ **39.00**
**Spooner,** jagged sawtooth rim,
  sapphire blue, flint, 5½" h. ................ **700.00**
**Spooner,** clear, non-flint......... **55.00 to 65.00**
**Spooner,** cobalt blue, non-flint............. **85.00**
**Spooner,** milk white, flint ...................... **75.00**
**Tumbler,** bar, flint, 4½" h. ..................... **58.00**
**Tumbler,** bar, non-flint .......................... **33.00**
**Wine,** flint ............................................. **43.00**
**Wine,** non-flint....................................... **15.00**

### SHELL & JEWEL (Victor)
**Bowl,** 10" d., clear................................. **25.00**
**Compote,** open, 7" d., 7½" h. ............... **55.00**
**Creamer**................................................ **23.00**

*Shell & Jewel Tumbler*

**Pitcher,** milk, clear ................................ **32.00**
**Pitcher,** water, blue............................... **82.00**
**Pitcher,** water, clear.............................. **42.00**
**Pitcher,** water, green ............................ **90.00**
**Sauce dish,** clear.................................... **8.00**
**Spooner**................................................. **30.00**
**Tumbler,** amber ..................................... **24.00**
**Tumbler,** blue ........................ **35.00 to 40.00**
**Tumbler,** clear (ILLUS.) ........................ **18.00**
**Tumbler,** green ...................................... **44.00**
**Water set,** pitcher & six tumblers,
  7 pcs................................ **170.00 to 190.00**

### SHUTTLE (Hearts of Loch Laven)
**Butter dish,** cov................................... **110.00**
**Cake stand** ......................................... **105.00**
**Celery vase** .......................................... **46.00**
**Cordial,** small........................................ **31.00**

*Shuttle Creamer*

**Creamer,** tall tankard (ILLUS.).............. **30.00**
**Goblet**................................................... **60.00**
**Mug,** amber.......................................... **300.00**
**Mug,** clear ............................................. **28.00**
**Pitcher,** water ...................................... **140.00**

Salt shaker w/original top................... 60.00
Spooner, scalloped rim........................ 50.00
Tumbler ................................................. 50.00
Wine....................................................... 12.00

## S-REPEAT

Berry set, apple green.......................... 85.00
Butter dish, cov., clear....................... 125.00
Butter dish, cov., sapphire blue
  w/gold ............................................... 150.00
Compote, jelly, clear............................. 40.00
Condiment set, apple green .............. 225.00
Condiment set, clear........................... 190.00
Condiment set, sapphire
  blue ................................. 200.00 to 250.00
Condiment tray, amethyst ................... 38.00
Condiment tray, apple green .............. 55.00
*Cruet, amethyst.................................. 195.00
*Cruet, apple green............................. 110.00
Decanter w/stopper, wine, amethyst.. 155.00
Decanter w/stopper, wine, apple
  green w/gold .................................... 138.00
Decanter w/stopper, wine, sapphire
  blue w/gold ...................................... 195.00
Pitcher, green ........................................ 85.00
Punch cup, clear ................................... 16.00
Salt shaker w/original top, sapphire
  blue....................................................... 40.00
Salt & pepper shakers, apple green,
  pr. ...................................................... 103.00
Salt & pepper shakers, clear, pr.......... 38.00
Sauce dish, amethyst w/gold .............. 30.00
Sauce dish apple green w/gold ............ 28.00
Syrup pitcher w/original top ................ 70.00
*Toothpick holder, amethyst .............. 62.00
*Toothpick holder, apple green.......... 50.00
*Toothpick holder, sapphire blue ........ 55.00
Tumbler, amethyst................................ 40.00
Tumbler, sapphire blue......................... 38.00
*Wine, apple green ............................... 45.00
*Wine, sapphire blue............................ 39.00

## STATES (THE)

Bowl, 7" d., three-handled ................... 50.00
Bowl, 7½" d............................................ 23.00
Bowl, 9" d.............................................. 35.00
Butter dish, cov. ................................... 56.00
Cocktail, flared .................................... 22.00
Compote, open, 5 x 5½"....................... 34.00
Creamer.................................................. 26.00
Creamer, individual size ...................... 30.00
Creamer & sugar bowl, pr. .................. 65.00
Cruet w/stopper .................................... 55.00
Goblet.................................................... 30.00
Punch bowl, 13" d., 5½" h.................... 95.00
Punch cup .............................................. 15.00
Salt & pepper shakers w/original
  tops, pr. .............................................. 60.00
Sauce dish ............................................ 10.00

Spooner................................................. 23.00
Sugar bowl, cov. ................................... 46.00
Tumbler ................................................. 25.00
Wine, clear ............................................ 25.00
Wine, clear w/gold trim......................... 29.00
Wine, green............................................ 60.00

## SUNK HONEYCOMB (Corona)

Bowl, 8¼" d., ruby-stained w/h.p.
  floral decoration ................................. 75.00
Cake stand, ruby-stained ................... 125.00
Celery, ruby-stained.............................. 73.00
Cheese dish, cov., ruby-stained......... 170.00
Compote, cov., 7" d., 11" h. ................ 165.00
Creamer, ruby-stained, 4½" h............. 53.00
Creamer, ruby-stained, souvenir .......... 45.00
Cruet w/original stopper, clear .......... 28.00
Cruet w/original stopper, ruby-
  stained ............................................. 110.00
Cup & saucer, ruby-stained ................. 35.00
Goblet, clear ......................................... 39.00
Goblet, ruby-stained ............................ 45.00
Mug, clear, souvenir............................. 25.00
Mug, ruby-stained, 3" h........................ 41.00
Pitcher, tankard, 8¼" h........................ 150.00
Pitcher, water, bulbous, ruby-stained ... 95.00
Punch cup .............................................. 14.00
Salt dip, individual size ........................ 18.00
Salt shaker w/original top, ruby-
  stained ................................................. 38.00
Sauce dish, 4" d., ruby-stained,
  engraved............................................... 35.00
Sugar bowl, cov., hotel size, ruby-
  stained, engraved ............................. 195.00
Syrup pitcher w/original top, clear ... 135.00
Syrup pitcher w/original top, ruby-
  stained ............................................... 143.00
Table set: cov. butter dish, cov. sugar
  bowl, creamer & spooner; ruby-
  stained, 4 pcs. .................................. 350.00
Toothpick holder, ruby-stained .......... 25.00
Toothpick holder, ruby-stained,
  souvenir ............................................... 43.00
Tumbler, clear, engraved ..................... 24.00
Tumbler, ruby-stained .......................... 50.00
Water set, pitcher & six goblets,
  7 pcs. ................................................. 350.00
Wine, clear, engraved............................ 19.00
Wine, clear, plain .................................. 13.00
Wine, ruby-stained................................ 35.00
Wine, ruby-stained, engraved.............. 40.00
Wine, ruby-stained, souvenir ............... 20.00

## TEXAS (Loop with Stippled Panels)

Cake stand, 9½" to 10¾" d. .... 90.00 to 95.00
Celery vase .......................................... 75.00
Compote, open, jelly........................... 100.00
Compote, cov., 6" d., 11" h................. 200.00
Creamer................................................. 51.00

*Texas Creamer*

**\*Creamer,** individual size (ILLUS.)........ **18.00**
**Goblet,** clear .......................................... **70.00**
**Goblet,** ruby-stained ........................... **110.00**
**Relish,** handled, 8½" l. .......................... **20.00**
**Salt dip,** master size, footed, 3" d.,
  2¾" h. ................................................ **22.00**
**Sauce dish,** flat or footed ..................... **25.00**
**Spooner,** ruby-stained .......................... **95.00**
**Toothpick holder,** clear ........................ **32.00**
**Toothpick holder,** clear w/gold ............ **41.00**
**Vase,** 7½" h., trumpet-shaped, pink-
  stained ............................................... **95.00**
**Vase,** bud, 8" h. .................................... **28.00**
**Vase,** 9" h. ............................................ **35.00**
**Vase,** 10" h. .......................................... **30.00**
**\*Wine,** clear .......................................... **95.00**
**Wine,** ruby-stained ............................. **125.00**

## THREE FACE

*Three Face Lamp*

**Butter dish,** cov., engraved .. **200.00 to 225.00**
**Butter dish,** cov., plain ..................... **190.00**
**\*Cake stand,** 8" to 10½" d. .. **160.00 to 165.00**
**Celery vase** ....................... **100.00 to 125.00**
**\*Champagne** .................................... **165.00**
**Claret,** engraved ............................... **265.00**
**Claret,** plain ..................................... **152.00**
**Compote,** cov., 4½" d., 6½" h. ............. **100.00**
**\*Compote,** cov., 6" d. ........................ **125.00**
**Compote,** cov., 7" d. .......................... **285.00**
**Compote,** cov., 8" d., high stand ........ **295.00**
**Compote,** cov., 10" d. ........................ **275.00**
**Compote,** open, 6" d., high stand ......... **80.00**
**Compote,** open, 7" d., high stand ......... **90.00**
**Compote,** open, 8½" d., high
  stand .............................. **100.00 to 115.00**
**Compote,** open, 9½" d., high stand,
  engraved ........................................... **375.00**
**Compote,** open, 9½" d., high stand,
  plain ................................................. **168.00**
**Creamer** ............................................. **93.00**
**\*Creamer** w/mask spout ..................... **150.00**
**Goblet,** engraved ............................... **150.00**
**\*Goblet,** plain ......................... **40.00 to 45.00**
**\*Lamp,** kerosene-type, pedestal base,
  8" h. (ILLUS. bottom previous
  column) ............................................ **165.00**
**Marmalade jar,** cov. ........................... **225.00**
**Pitcher,** water ................................... **550.00**
**\*Salt dip** .............................................. **44.00**

## TORPEDO (Pygmy)

*Torpedo Syrup Jug*

**Bowl,** 7" d., flat, clear ........................... **24.00**
**Bowl,** 8" d., clear ................................. **33.00**
**Bowl,** 9" d., clear ................................. **32.00**
**Bowl,** 9½" d., clear ............................... **43.00**
**Butter dish,** cov. ................................. **75.00**
**Celery vase** ......................................... **40.00**
**Compote,** cov., jelly ............................. **44.00**
**Compote,** cov., 7" d., 7¼" h. ................. **65.00**

Compote, cov., 8" d., 14" h.............. **135.00**
Compote, open, jelly, 5" d., 5" h. .......... **48.00**
Compote, open, 7" d., high stand......... **52.00**
Compote, open, 8" d., high stand,
   flared rim.......................................... **110.00**
Compote, open, 8 x 10½", 8" h.,
   ruffled rim......................................... **145.00**
Creamer, collared base ....................... **55.00**
Creamer, footed................................... **38.00**
Cruet w/original faceted stopper ....... **75.00**
Cup & saucer......................... 60.00 to **65.00**
Goblet, clear......................... 50.00 to **55.00**
Goblet, ruby-stained ............................ **80.00**
Lamp, kerosene-type, hand-type
   w/finger grip, w/burner & chimney .... **125.00**
Lamp, kerosene-type, 10" h................ **140.00**
Pickle castor, silver plate cover &
   tongs ................................................ **250.00**
Pitcher, milk, 8½" h., clear................... **85.00**
Pitcher, water, tankard, 12" h. ............. **80.00**
Salt dip, individual size, 1½" d............. **26.00**
Salt dip, master size ............................ **38.00**
Salt & pepper shakers w/original
   tops, pr. .............................................. **95.00**
Sauce dish ........................................... **16.00**
Spooner ................................................ **40.00**
Sugar bowl, cov. .................................. **95.00**
Syrup jug w/original top, clear
   (ILLUS. bottom previous
   page) ................................ 95.00 to **125.00**
Syrup jug w/original top, ruby-
   stained .............................................. **250.00**
Tray, water, clover-shaped, 11¾" ......... **90.00**
Tumbler, clear, engraved ..................... **55.00**
Tumbler, clear, plain............................. **38.00**
Tumbler, ruby-stained .......................... **48.00**
Wine, clear ........................................... **90.00**
Wine, ruby-stained............................... **103.00**

## TREE OF LIFE - PORTLAND

Butter dish, cov.................................. **110.00**
Celery vase ......................................... **69.00**
Celery vase, in silver plate holder ...... **135.00**
Champagne ......................................... **75.00**
Compote, open, 7" d., high stand,
   w/applied red serpent on stem ......... **245.00**
Compote, open, 7½" d., scalloped rim... **45.00**
Compote, open, 8½" d., 5" h., signed
   "Davis"................................................ **93.00**
Compote, open, 8¾" d., in two-
   handled Meriden silver plate holder,
   bowl signed "Davis" .......................... **185.00**
Compote, open, 10" d., 6" h., signed
   "Davis" (ILLUS. top next
   column) ............................ 100.00 to **125.00**
Creamer, signed "Davis"....................... **55.00**
Creamer, blue, in silver plate
   holder ............................. 175.00 to **200.00**
Creamer, clear, in silver plate holder .... **85.00**
Creamer, cranberry, in silver plate
   holder................................................ **190.00**

*Portland Tree Of Life Compote*

Epergne, single lily, red snake around
   stem, 18" h....................................... **450.00**
*Goblet.................................................. **42.00**
Goblet, signed "Davis"........ 100.00 to **125.00**
Ice cream set, tray & six leaf-shaped
   desserts, 7 pcs. ............................... **150.00**
Mug, applied handle, 3½" h. ................ **45.00**
Pitcher, water, applied handle, clear .... **82.00**
Plate, 7¼" d.......................................... **50.00**
Powder jar, cov., red coiled snake
   finial on cover ................................... **350.00**
Salt dip, individual size, footed,
   amber ................................................. **65.00**
Salt dip, footed, "Salt" embossed in
   bowl, clear ....................................... **135.00**
Sauce dish, leaf-shaped, blue............. **18.00**
Sauce dish, leaf-shaped, clear............ **12.00**
Spooner................................................ **30.00**
Spooner, in handled silver plate
   holder w/two griffin heads................ **110.00**
Sugar bowl, cov., blue, in silver plate
   holder ............................. 175.00 to **200.00**
Sugar bowl, cov., clear, in silver plate
   holder................................................ **88.00**
Sugar bowl, cov., clear......................... **69.00**
Syrup pitcher w/original metal top,
   blue opaque..................................... **100.00**
Table set: cov. sugar bowl, creamer &
   spooner; in ornate silver plate
   holders, the set ................................ **180.00**
Toothpick holder, apple green .......... **125.00**
Tray, ice cream, clear, 14" rectangle .... **36.00**
Vase, 12" h., clear.............................. **145.00**
Waste bowl, amber ............................. **50.00**
Waste bowl, blue.................................. **52.00**
Waste bowl, blue, in ornate silver
   plate holder...................................... **175.00**
Waste bowl, clear................................. **33.00**
Waste bowl, green ............................... **45.00**

## TREE OF LIFE WITH HAND (Tree of Life
   - Wheeling)

Butter dish, cov.................................. **125.00**
Cake stand, frosted base,
   11½" d. ............................ 115.00 to **125.00**

Celery vase ............................................ 56.00
Compote, open, 5½" d., 5½" h., clear
hand & ball stem ................................. 48.00
Compote, open, 5½" d., 5½" h.,
frosted hand & ball stem ..................... 65.00
Compote, open, 7¾" d., 11" h., Infant
Samuel stand, signed "Davis".. 125.00
Compote, open, 8" d., clear hand &
ball stem .............................. 50.00 to 55.00
Compote, open, 9" d., frosted hand &
ball stem .............................................. 83.00
Compote, open, 10" d., 10" h., frosted
hand & ball stem ................................. 95.00
Creamer, w/hand & ball handle ........... 75.00
Mug, applied handle, 3" h. ................. 125.00
Pitcher, water, 9" h. ............................. 68.00
Sauce dish, flat or footed ................... 19.00
Spooner ................................................. 42.00

## U.S. COIN

*Bowl, berry, 6" d., frosted coins, plain
rim ...................................................... 450.00
Bowl, berry, 7" d., frosted quarters,
plain rim ........................... 300.00 to 350.00
Bowl, berry, 8" d., frosted half dollars,
plain rim ............................................ 400.00
Bowl, berry, 9" d., frosted dollars,
plain rim ............................................ 800.00
Bowl, berry, 6" d., frosted coins,
scalloped rim ................................... 850.00
Bowl, berry, 7" d., frosted quarters,
scalloped rim ................................... 800.00
Bowl, berry, 8" d., clear half dollars,
scalloped rim ................................... 610.00
Bowl, berry, 8" d., frosted half dollars,
scalloped rim ................................... 900.00
Bowl, berry, 9" d., frosted dollars,
scalloped rim ................................ 1,350.00
Bread tray, frosted quarters & half
dollars ............................................... 230.00
*Bread tray, frosted dollars & half
dollars .............................. 350.00 to 395.00
Butter dish, cov., clear dollars & half
dollars ............................................... 490.00
Butter dish, cov., frosted dollars &
half dollars ...................... 400.00 to 500.00
Cake plate, frosted dollars & quarters,
7" d. ................................. 400.00 to 450.00
Cake stand, clear dollars, 10" d. ......... 320.00
Cake stand, frosted dollars, 10" d. ..... 425.00
Celery tray, clear
quarters ........................... 175.00 to 185.00
Celery tray, frosted
quarters ........................... 325.00 to 350.00
Celery vase, clear quarters ............... 245.00
Celery vase, frosted
quarters ........................... 350.00 to 375.00
Champagne, flared rim, frosted half
dimes ................................................. 800.00
Claret, flared rim, frosted half dimes... 650.00

Claret, straight rim, frosted half
dimes ................................................. 650.00
Compote, cov., 6" d., high stand,
quarters on lid, twenty cent pieces
on base ............................................. 495.00
*Compote, cov., 6" d., high stand,
frosted dimes & quarters .. 350.00 to 400.00
Compote, cov., 7" d., high stand,
clear dimes & quarters ..................... 300.00

*U.S. Coin Compote*

Compote, cov., 7" d., high stand,
frosted dimes & quarters
(ILLUS.) ........................... 500.00 to 550.00
Compote, cov., 8" d., high stand,
frosted quarters & half
dollars ............................. 475.00 to 500.00
Compote, cov., 9" d., high stand,
frosted dollars ................................. 600.00
Compote, cov., 9" d., high stand,
frosted dollars & quarters ............. 1,750.00
Compote, cov., 6" d., low stand, clear
twenty cent pieces & quarters .......... 425.00
Compote, open, 7¼" d., high stand,
straight rim, frosted quarters ............ 485.00
Compote, open, 7½" d., high stand,
straight rim, frosted dimes &
quarters ............................................ 300.00
Compote, open, 7½" d., high stand,
straight rim, frosted quarters............ 495.00
Compote, open, 8¼" d., high stand,
straight rim, frosted quarters............ 523.00
Compote, open, 8½" d., high stand,
straight rim, frosted dimes &
quarters ........................... 350.00 to 400.00
Compote, open, 8½" d., high stand,
straight rim, frosted quarters............ 523.00

**Compote,** open, 9¾" d., high stand, straight rim, frosted quarters & half dollars.............................. **350.00 to 400.00**

**Compote,** open, 10½" d., straight rim, frosted quarters & half dollars........... **500.00**

**Compote,** open, 7" d., high stand, flared rim, frosted dimes & quarters ........................... **300.00 to 350.00**

**Compote,** open, 8¼" d., high stand, flared rim, frosted dimes & quarters ........................... **350.00 to 400.00**

**Compote,** open, 9½" d., high stand, flared rim, frosted quarters & half dollars ............................... **700.00**

**Compote,** open, 10½" d., high stand, flared rim, frosted quarters & half dollars ............................... **950.00**

**Compote,** open, 7¼" d., high stand, flared & scalloped rim, frosted dimes & quarters ...................... **750.00**

**Compote,** open, 6" d., low stand, flared & scalloped rim, frosted twenty cent pieces ........................... **850.00**

**Compote,** open, 7" d., low stand, straight top w/scalloped rim, frosted twenty cent pieces ........................... **450.00**

**Compote,** open, 7" d., low stand, flared & scalloped rim, frosted twenty cent pieces ........................... **525.00**

**\*Creamer,** frosted quarters ................. **400.00**

**Cruet w/original stopper,** frosted quarters, 5½" h. ................ **625.00 to 650.00**

**Epergne,** clear quarters & dollars ....... **632.00**

**Epergne,** frosted quarters & dollars.... **800.00**

**Finger bowl,** straight rim, frosted coins ................................................ **500.00**

**Finger bowl,** flared rim, frosted coins... **500.00**

**Goblet,** straight top, frosted dimes, 6½" h. .............................. **250.00 to 300.00**

**Goblet,** straight top, frosted half dollars, 7" h. ..................................... **400.00**

**Goblet,** flared top, frosted half dollars, 7" h. ................................................... **450.00**

**Lamp,** kerosene-type, square font, frosted quarters & half dollars, 8½" h. .............................. **300.00 to 350.00**

**Lamp,** kerosene-type, square font, frosted dollars & quarters, 9½" h. .............................. **400.00 to 450.00**

**Lamp,** kerosene-type, square font, frosted half dollars & dollars, 10¼" h... **500.00**

**Lamp,** kerosene-type, square font, frosted half dollars & dollars, 11" h... **550.00**

**Lamp,** kerosene-type, square font, frosted half dollars & dollars, 11½" h... **638.00**

**Lamp,** kerosene-type, round font, frosted quarters, 8" h........ **300.00 to 400.00**

**Lamp,** kerosene-type, round font, frosted quarters, 8½" h. ................... **350.00**

**Lamp,** kerosene-type, round font, frosted quarters, 9" h. ...................... **400.00**

**Lamp,** kerosene-type, round font, frosted half dollars, 9½" h. ............... **400.00**

**Lamp,** kerosene-type, round font, frosted half dollars, 10" h.. **400.00 to 450.00**

**Lamp,** kerosene-type, round font, frosted half dollars, 10½" h.............................. **400.00 to 450.00**

**Lamp,** kerosene-type, round font, frosted half dollars, 11½" h. .............. **525.00**

**Lamp,** kerosene-type, round font, frosted dollars, 11½" h. .... **750.00 to 850.00**

**Lamp,** kerosene-type, flaring font, frosted quarters, 8½" h. ................... **600.00**

**Lamp,** kerosene-type, flaring font, frosted quarters, 9" h. ...................... **600.00**

**Lamp,** kerosene-type, flaring font, frosted quarters, 9½" h. ................... **600.00**

**Lamp,** kerosene-type, flaring font, frosted quarters, 10" h. ..................... **600.00**

**Lamp,** kerosene-type, handled, frosted twenty cent pieces, 5" h........ **500.00**

**Lamp,** kerosene-type, handled, clear quarters, 5" h................... **450.00 to 500.00**

**Lamp,** kerosene-type, handled, frosted quarters, 5" h. ....................... **350.00**

**Mug,** frosted dollars ........................... **350.00**

**Pickle dish,** frosted half dollars, 3¾ x 7½" ................................. **200.00 to 225.00**

**Pitcher,** milk, frosted half dollars.............................. **600.00 to 650.00**

**Pitcher,** water, frosted dollars.............................. **600.00 to 700.00**

**Preserve dish,** clear half dollars in rim, dollars in base, 5 x 8".. **300.00 to 350.00**

**Preserve dish,** frosted half dollars in rim, dollars in base, 5 x 8" .. **300.00 to 350.00**

**Salt & pepper shakers w/original tops,** frosted coins, pr. ..... **280.00 to 300.00**

**Sauce dish,** flat, plain rim, frosted quarters, 3¾" d. ............... **120.00 to 130.00**

**Sauce dish,** flat, plain rim, clear quarters, 4¼" d. ............................. **205.00**

**Sauce dish,** flat, plain rim, frosted quarters, 4¼" d. ............................. **150.00**

**Sauce dish,** flat, scalloped rim, frosted quarters, 4" d. ...................... **350.00**

**Sauce dish,** flat, scalloped rim, frosted quarters, 4½" d. ................... **400.00**

**Sauce dish,** footed, plain top, frosted quarters ........................... **150.00 to 195.00**

**Sauce dish,** footed, scalloped rim, frosted quarters ............................... **350.00**

**Spooner,** clear quarters ..... **225.00 to 250.00**

**\*Spooner,** frosted quarters ................. **300.00**

**\*Sugar bowl,** cov., frosted quarters & half dollars...................... **350.00 to 400.00**

**Syrup jug w/original dated pewter top,** frosted coins ............. **500.00 to 550.00**

**Toothpick holder,** clear dollars.............................. **150.00 to 175.00**

*Toothpick holder,* frosted
dollars............................... **150.00 to 175.00**
**Tumbler,** frosted dime on side............ **200.00**
**Tumbler,** dollar in base, clear sides
w/clear 1879 coin ............. **200.00 to 225.00**
**Tumbler,** dollar in base, clear sides
w/frosted 1882 coin ......................... **250.00**
**Tumbler,** dollar in base, paneled
sides w/clear 1878 coin.... **150.00 to 200.00**
**Water tray,** frosted coins .................... **500.00**
**Wine,** frosted half dimes ..................... **650.00**

## VICTOR - See Shell & Jewel Pattern

## VIKING (Bearded Head or Old Man of the Mountain)

**Apothecary jar w/original stopper** ..... **75.00**
**Bowl,** cov., 8" oval ............................. **100.00**
**Bowl,** 8" sq............................................ **45.00**

*Viking Butter Dish*

**Butter dish,** cov., clear (ILLUS.).......... **115.00**
**Butter dish,** cov., frosted..................... **85.00**
**Celery vase** ......................................... **55.00**
**Compote,** cov., 7" d., low stand............ **82.00**
**Compote,** cov., 9" d., low
stand ............................... **165.00 to 175.00**
**Creamer**................................................ **60.00**
**Egg cup** ............................................... **65.00**
**Marmalade jar,** cov., footed................. **75.00**
**Mug,** applied handle............................. **63.00**
**Pickle jar w/cover** ............................... **95.00**
**Pitcher,** water, 8¾" h., clear.. **100.00 to 115.00**
**Pitcher,** water, 8¾" h., clear &
frosted ............................. **240.00 to 250.00**
**Relish**.................................................... **25.00**
**Salt dip,** master size ............................ **35.00**
**Sauce dish,** footed .............................. **18.00**
**Spooner**................................................ **30.00**
**Sugar bowl,** cov. .................................. **70.00**

## WASHBOARD - See Adonis Pattern

## WESTWARD HO

*Westward Ho Spooner*

**Bowl,** 8"............................................... **125.00**
**Bowl,** 9" oval......................................... **95.00**
**Bread platter** ...................................... **115.00**
*Butter dish,* cov. ............... **125.00 to 150.00**
*Celery vase* ......................................... **135.00**
*Compote,* cov., 4" d., low stand ........ **100.00**
**Compote,** cov., 5" d., high
stand ................................ **100.00 to 110.00**
*Compote,* cov., 6" d., low stand ........ **120.00**
**Compote,** cov., 6" d., high stand ........ **325.00**
*Compote,* cov., 4 x 6¾" oval, low
stand................................................. **150.00**
**Compote,** cov., 5 x 7¾" oval, high
stand ................................ **200.00 to 225.00**
**Compote,** cov., 8" d., low stand.......... **325.00**
**Compote,** cov., 8" d., high
stand ................................ **275.00 to 325.00**
**Compote,** cov., 5½ x 8" oval, high
stand................................................. **440.00**
**Compote,** cov., 8" d., 14" h................. **350.00**
**Compote,** cov., 6½ x 10" oval, low
stand ................................ **225.00 to 250.00**
**Compote,** open, 7" d., low stand ........ **175.00**
**Compote,** open, 9" oval, high stand ... **100.00**
*Creamer* ........................... **125.00 to 150.00**
*Goblet*................................................... **85.00**
**Marmalade jar,** cov............................. **295.00**
**Mug,** child's, clear, 2½" h.................... **250.00**
**Mug,** child's, milk white, 2½" h. ........... **175.00**
**Pickle dish,** oval ................................... **65.00**
**Pitcher,** milk, 8" h................................ **495.00**
**Pitcher,** water.................... **350.00 to 400.00**
**Platter,** 9 x 13".................................... **175.00**
**Relish,** deer handles........................... **100.00**

**Sauce dish,** footed ................ 35.00 to 40.00
**Spooner** (ILLUS. top previous
page) .............................. **100.00 to 125.00**
**\*Sugar bowl,** cov............... **125.00 to 150.00**
**\*Wine** .................................................. **225.00**

## WINDFLOWER

**Butter dish,** cov....................................... **45.00**
**Compote,** cov., 8½" d., low stand......... **70.00**
**Compote,** open, 8" d.......................... **30.00**
**Creamer** .................................................. **32.00**
**Egg cup**.............................. **30.00 to 35.00**
**Pitcher,** water ..................................... **65.00**
**Salt dip,** master size ......................... **20.00**
**Sauce dish** ............................................ **13.00**
**Spooner,** ................................................ **34.00**
**Sugar bowl,** cov. .................................. **39.00**

## WISCONSIN

*Wisconsin Pitcher*

**Banana stand,** turned-up sides,
7½" w., 4" h.......................................... **72.00**
**Bonbon,** handled, 4"............................. **24.00**
**Bowl,** 6½" d............................................ **35.00**
**Bowl,** 8" d.............................................. **36.00**
**Butter dish,** cov...................................... **93.00**
**Cake stand,** 8¼" d., 4¾" h.................... **43.00**
**Cake stand,** 9¾" d. .............................. **45.00**
**Celery tray,** flat, 5 x 10" ...................... **43.00**
**Celery vase** ........................................... **47.00**
**Compote,** cov., 10½" d. ........................ **64.00**
**Compote,** open, 6½" d., 3½" h. ............ **30.00**
**Compote,** open, 6½" d., 6½" h. ............ **26.00**
**Compote,** open, 7½" d., 5½" h. ............ **42.00**
**Compote,** open, 7" d., 4" h.,
tricornered, footed ............................ **25.00**

**Creamer,** individual size ...................... **35.00**
**Cruet w/original stopper** .................... **40.00**
**Cup & saucer** ........................................ **55.00**
**Dish,** cov., oval ...................................... **27.00**
**Doughnut stand,** 6" d........................... **40.00**
**Marmalade jar,** cov............................. **125.00**
**Mug,** 3½" h. .......................................... **34.00**
**Nappy,** handled, 4" d. .......................... **34.00**
**Pitcher,** milk........................................... **75.00**
**Pitcher,** water, 8" h. (ILLUS. previous
column)............................................... **65.00**
**Plate,** 5" sq............................................. **24.00**
**Plate,** 6½" sq.......................................... **26.00**
**Punch cup** ............................................. **17.00**
**Relish,** 4 x 8½"....................................... **20.00**
**Salt shaker w/original top**.................. **55.00**
**Sauce dish** ............................................ **12.00**
**Spooner**.................................................. **33.00**
**Sugar bowl,** cov., 5" h. ........................ **95.00**
**Sugar shaker w/original top**.. **85.00 to 95.00**
**Syrup pitcher w/original top,** 6½" h.... **75.00**
**\*Toothpick holder**................................ **41.00**
**Tumbler** .................................................. **45.00**
**Vase,** 6" h................................................ **58.00**
**Wine** ................................. **60.00 to 70.00**

## WYOMING

**Bowl,** 7" d., footed................................. **43.00**
**Cake stand,** 9" d., high stand .............. **57.00**
**Cake stand,** 10" d., high stand ............ **55.00**
**Compote,** open, 8" d., shallow bowl ..... **40.00**
**Creamer,** open, individual, tankard
shape.................................................. **30.00**
**Mug**....................................................... **65.00**
**Pitcher,** water, pressed handle, 3 pt..... **65.00**
**Relish tray** ............................................. **28.00**
**Sauce dish,** flat, round, 4" d. ............... **18.00**
**Tumbler,** water, flat............................... **25.00**

## ZIPPER

**Butter dish,** cov...................................... **39.00**
**Butter dish,** cov., ruby-stained ........... **100.00**
**Cheese dish,** cov.................................... **45.00**
**Creamer**................................................. **35.00**
**Cruet w/original stopper,** clear .......... **36.00**
**Goblet**................................................... **24.00**
**Pitcher,** milk, amber.............................. **55.00**
**Pitcher,** milk, clear................................ **55.00**
**Relish,** 6 x 9½"....................................... **45.00**
**Sugar bowl,** cov. .................................. **35.00**
**Sugar bowl,** cov., ruby-stained............. **65.00**
**Toothpick holder,** green w/gold........... **45.00**
**Wine,** clear ............................................ **30.00**
**Wine,** ruby-stained................................ **38.00**

**(End of Pattern Glass Listings)**

## PELOTON

*Made in Bohemia, Germany and England in the late 19th century, this glassware is characterized by threads or filaments of glass rolled into the glass body of the objects in random patterns. Some of these wares were then further decorated.*

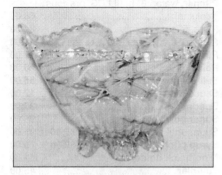

*Footed Peloton Bowl*

**Bowl,** 3 x 6¼", 4⅛" h., footed, the oblong form w/molded ribbing in white opalescent decorated w/overall pink, blue, yellow & white coconut threadings, clear applied crimped rim edging & applied clear shell feet (ILLUS.) .......................... **$295.00**

**Rose bowl,** miniature, spherical w/cased clear ribbing & six-crimp rim, decorated w/pink, blue, yellow & white small coconut threading, on applied clear wishbone feet, 2⅝" d., 2¾" h. .... **175.00**

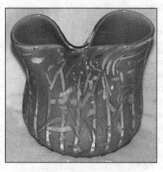

*Cased Peloton Vase*

**Vase,** 3½" h., 3 x 3⅞", rounded form w/two sides of the top rim pinched together, orchid pink cased in clear ribbing, decorated w/pink, blue, yellow & white coconut threading (ILLUS.) ........................................... **225.00**

**Vase,** 4" h., 4¾" d., squatty bulbous ribbed body tapering to a short neck w/a widely flaring tricorner rim w/folded inward edges, white cased in clear & decorated w/pink, yellow, blue & white coconut threading ........ **295.00**

**Vase,** 4⅛" h., 3¼" d., footed spherical body w/a short cylindrical neck flanked by angled handles to the shoulder, clear decorated overall w/cranberry coconut threading .......... **95.00**

## QUEZAL

*These wares resemble those of Tiffany and other glasshouses which produced lustred glass pieces in the late 19th and early 20th centuries. They were made by the Quezal Art glass and Decorating Co. of Brooklyn, New York, early in this century and until the factory's closing in the mid-1920s*

# Quezal

*Quezal mark*

**Vase,** 4½" h., ruffled rim, gold iridescent pulled-feather decoration, signed ............................................. **$375.00**

**Vase,** 6" h., "Agate," ovoid body tapering to a tall trumpet neck, opaque greyish brown w/agate-like streaks of amber, blue, aqua, green & black at the rim, signed on the base .............................................. **1,610.00**

**Vase,** 8" h., ovoid body w/a slender neck w/everted rim, overall gold iridescence, signed ........................... **483.00**

**Vase,** 12¾" h., tall baluster-form body swelled at the top & w/a short cylindrical neck, opalescent decorated w/pulled green & gold iridescent leafage & applied w/reeded gold medallions w/tendrils down the sides, unsigned, ca. 1910 ........................... **4,025.00**

**Vase,** floriform, a decorated cushion foot supporting a slender stem to the widely flaring ruffled top, iridescent gold ground decorated w/white pulled-feather design ..................... **1,900.00**

**Vase,** bulbous ovoid body tapering to a short rolled neck, bold gold pulled-feather & scroll designs on a dark colored ground w/white around the shoulder & neck, gold iridescent interior (ILLUS. top next page) ...... **2,800.00**

*Fine Quezal Vase*

## ROSE BOWLS

*These decorative small bowls were widely popular in the late 19th and early 20th centuries. Produced in various types of glass, they are most common in satin glass or spatter glass. They are generally a spherical shape with an incurved crimped rim, but ovoid or egg-shaped examples were also popular.*

*Their name derives from their reported use, to hold rose petal potpourri or small fresh-cut roses.*

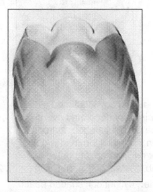

*Mother-of-Pearl Satin Rose Bowl*

**Cased satin,** shaded heavenly blue w/embossed overall flowers & leaves design, white interior, spherical body, eight-crimp top, 4" d., 3½" h. ................................... **$125.00**

**Cased satin,** shaded brown to gold, spherical body, white interior, pleated six-crimp top, attributed to Stevens & Williams, 4¼" d., 3½" h. .. **225.00**

**Cased satin,** shaded deep rose pink, dimpled spherical body, white interior, eight-crimp top, 4¾" d., 4⅞" h. .............. **100.00**

**Cased satin,** shaded blue mother-of-pearl Herringbone design, egg-shaped w/six-crimp top, white interior, 3⅜" d., 4" h. (ILLUS. bottom previous column) .............................. **175.00**

**Cased satin,** deep chartreuse green mother-of-pearl Ribbon patt., spherical body, white interior, nine-crimp top, 3½" d., 2¾" h. ................... **245.00**

**Cased satin,** shaded pink mother-of-pearl Rivulet patt., squatty rounded body w/eight-crimp top, white interior, 4½" d., 2¾" h. ...................... **195.00**

**Cranberry,** spherical body w/crystal intaglio-cut flowers on the exterior, optic ribbed interior, on three clear applied thorny ball feet, probably Stevens & Williams, clear applied berry prunt on base, 3⅜" d., 3" h. ...... **265.00**

**Green & white,** "Arboresque" line, the spherical green body w/an overall white craquelle design, ribbon candy crimped top, attributed to Stevens & Williams, 3¾" d., 3" h. ........................ **79.00**

**Pink satin,** spherical shaded body decorated w/dainty pink & yellow flowers & grasses, eight-crimp top, 3⅜" d., 4" h. ...................................... **110.00**

*Spangle Rose Bowl*

**Spangle,** cased deep rose w/mica flecks, white interior, spherical body w/eight-crimp top, 3½" d., 3⅝" h. (ILLUS.) ........................................... **110.00**

**Spangle,** cased spatter w/swirled design in maroon & pink spatter on white, gold mica flecks swirled in the opposite direction, white interior, spherical w/eight-crimp top, 3⅞" d., 3⅜" h. ................................................ **95.00**

# SATIN

*Satin glass was a popular decorative glass developed in the late 19th century. Most pieces were composed of two layers of glass with the exterior layer usually in a shaded pastel color. The name derives from the soft matte finish, caused by exposure to acid fumes, which gave the surface a "satiny" feel. Mother-of-pearl satin glass was a specialized variety wherein air trapped between the layers of glass provided subtle surface patterns such as Herringbone and Diamond Quilted. A majority of satin glass was produced in England and America but collectors should be aware that reproductions have been produced for many years*

*Satin Cracker Jar*

**Bowl,** 5" d., 3⅝" h., wide squatty bulbous body w/a high upright ruffled rim, shaded heavenly blue mother-of-pearl Herringbone patt., white interior ........................................... **$235.00**

**Cracker jar,** cov., barrel-shaped w/silver plate rim, bail handle & flat cover w/pointed finial, cased pink exterior decorated w/large gold flowers & leaves framing a scene of a fence & gate w/birds flying, white interior, 4¾" d., 6½" h. (ILLUS. above).............................................. **195.00**

**Creamer,** spherical body w/a flaring neck & oblong rim, shaded heavenly blue decorated w/dainty white & gold enameled flowers & green leaves, frosted clear applied handle, white interior, 3½" d., 4¼" h ...................... **195.00**

**Creamer,** spherical body in molded Swirl patt., wide cylindrical neck w/pinched spout, rich gold body w/frosted clear applied handle, 4" d., 5" h. .................................................. **165.00**

**Ewer,** baluster-form body w/deep lobes below a flaring neck w/a tricorner rim, angled applied frosted clear handle, shaded heavenly blue body decorated w/cream & yellow flowers & brown & green foliage, 3⅛" d., 8⅝" h. ................................. **100.00**

**Finger bowl,** wide squatty bulbous body w/incurved six-crimp rim, Rainbow mother-of-pearl in a concentric ring design w/alternating wide vertical bands of pink, blue & yellow on upper half, marked "Patent" on base, 4¼" d., 2½" h........ **750.00**

**Rose bowl,** spherical body w/eight-crimp top, shaded heavenly blue Embossed Shell & Seaweed patt., white interior, 4" d., 3¼" h................. **100.00**

**Rose bowl,** spherical body w/six-crimp top, shaded apricot mother-of-pearl Herringbone patt., white interior, 3½" d., 3¾" h. ...................... **195.00**

*Fine Satin Scent Bottle*

**Scent bottle,** cov., flattened ovoid body in ivory decorated overall w/heavy gold bamboo, maroon & green leaves all trimmed w/gold, silver neck & cap, attributed to Webb, 3¾" d., 5½" h. (ILLUS.) ......... **295.00**

**Tumbler,** cylindrical, shaded peach mother-of-pearl Diamond Quilted patt., white interior, 2¾" d., 4" h. ...... **135.00**

**Vase,** 2¾" h., 3" d., footed inverted bell-form w/incurved squared mouth, chartreuse green mother-of-pearl Ribbon patt., white interior............... **185.00**

**Vase,** 4" h., 3¾" d., bulbous lobed body w/a wide cylindrical neck flanked by applied frosted clear angled handles, shaded pink decorated w/gold enameled flowers, foliage & trim................................... **110.00**

**Vase,** 6⅝" h., 4¼" d., tapering ovoid body w/pinched-in sides tapering to a wide shoulder & short slightly tapering cylindrical neck w/flat rim, heavenly blue ground, the neck decorated w/heavy dark gold scrolls & lattice panels, the sides decorated w/pink, blue & cream floral sprigs & green leaves ..................................... **185.00**

**Vase,** 7" h., 2¾" d., footed tall ovoid melon-lobed body w/a short flaring neck w/a deeply crimped & scalloped rim, shaded heavenly blue mother-of-pearl Swirl patt., white interior, fitted on a gilt-metal ring base w/scroll feet (ILLUS. below) ..... **225.00**

*Satin Vase on Base*

**Vase,** 7¼" h., 2½" d., footed squared ovoid body w/deeply dimpled sides below the trumpet neck w/a fluted rim, shaded heavenly blue mother-of-pearl Diamond Quilted patt., white interior............................................... **165.00**

**Vase,** 8" h., 3½" d., ovoid body w/a short neck below the widely flaring & deeply fluted rim, heavenly blue mother-of-pearl Diamond Quilted patt., frosted clear top edging, white interior............................................... **250.00**

**Vase,** 9" h., 4½" d., bottle-form, spherical base w/a tall 'stick' neck, shaded deep rose to green, cream interior, attributed to Webb .............. **395.00**

**Vases,** 9½" h., 5¾" d., ovoid body tapering to a wide short cylindrical neck w/an upright crimped rim, the

base raised on three frosted clear applied pointed legs & frosted clear applied angular thorn handles from the neck to the shoulder, shaded heavenly blue mother-of-pearl Herringbone patt., pr......................... **695.00**

## SILVER DEPOSIT - SILVER OVERLAY

*Silver Deposit and Silver Overlay have been made commercially since the last quarter of the 19th century. Silver is deposited on the glass by various means, most commonly by utilizing an electric current. The glass was very popular during the first three decades of this century, and some pieces are still being produced. During the late 1970s, silver commanded exceptionally high prices and this was reflected in a surge of interest in silver overlay glass, especially in pieces marked "Sterling" or "925" on the heavy silver overlay. Pieces were produced both in this country and abroad.*

*Fine Silver Overlay Vases*

**Vase,** 2¾" h., bulbous ovoid body tapering to a wide, short flaring mouth, mold-blown iridescent blue overlaid in silver w/a scrolling poppy blossoms, Europe, ca. 1900 (ILLUS. bottom right) ................................. **$633.00**

**Vase,** 4⅜" h., footed flattened disc form w/downcurved rims, greenish opalescent overlaid in silver w/long paired scrolls up the sides flanking a

large central blossom, the short
flaring foot overlaid w/silver grillwork,
unsigned Loetz, Austria, ca. 1900 .. **2,415.00**

**Vase,** 5" h. slightly swelled cylindrical
body w/a tricorner flaring wide mouth,
sapphire blue w/silvery iridescent
surface overlaid w/elaborate Art
Nouveau-style pond lily design,
Austria, ca. 1900 (ILLUS. left,
previous page) ................................ **1,265.00**

**Vase,** 6" h., slender double-gourd
form body w/long swelled upper
section w/squared mouth, iridescent
gold ground on amber overlaid
w/silver flowering leafy vines,
marked "Sterling" on the top rim,
Europe, ca. 1900 (ILLUS. top right,
previous page) .................................. **748.00**

**Vase,** 6½" h., bulbous ovoid body
w/tall lobed panels trimmed
w/beading below the trumpet neck,
pale green ground w/swirling
iridescence, overlaid on three panels
& neck w/Art Nouveau whiplash
designs & a silver rim, unsigned
Loetz, Austria, ca. 1900 ................ **9,200.00**

**Vase,** 6⅞" h., slender ovoid body
tapering to a short flaring neck,
lemon yellow ground decorated
around the lower section w/finely
striped red & green trailings &
overall random oil spots of silvery
gold iridescence, overlaid w/stylized
iris blossoms & whiplash leafage,
unsigned Loetz, Austria, ca. 1900 ... **4,600.00**

**Vase,** 7¼" h., slightly flaring cylindrical
body w/a short waisted neck
w/flaring rim, amber iridescent
decorated w/sprays of oil spots in
blue & lavender, overlaid w/stylized
iris blossoms & whiplash leafage,
unsigned Loetz, Austria, ca. 1900 ... **6,325.00**

**Vase,** 8¾" h., gently swelled
cylindrical body w/a wide, flat mouth,
pale green decorated w/swirling
silvery bluish green iridescence & a
rose-textured ground encased in
clear, further decorated w/stylized
entrelac foliage & overlaid in silver
w/long looping scrolls, unsigned
Loetz, Austria, ca. 1900 ................ **5,750.00**

## SPANGLED

*Spangled glass incorporated particles of
mica or metallic flakes and variegated colored
glass particles imbedded in the transparent*

*glass. Usually made of two layers, it might
have either an opaque or transparent casing.
The Vasa Murrhina Glass Company of
Sandwich, Massachusetts, first patented the
process for producing Spangled glass in 1884
and this factory is known to have produced
great quantities of this ware. It was, however,
also produced by numerous other American
and English glasshouses. This type, along with
Spatter, is often erroneously called "End of
Day."*

*A related decorative glass, Aventurine,
features a fine speckled pattern resembling
gold dust on a solid color ground. Also see
ART GLASS BASKETS and ROSE BOWLS
under Glass.*

**Bowl,** 3¾" d., 3⅞" h., deep rounded
sides in cranberry cased in clear,
overall large mica flecks, applied
clear rim, large stars around the
sides & three scroll feet .................. **$145.00**

**Ewer,** footed tall ovoid body tapering
to a slender flaring neck w/a widely
rolled & ruffled tricorner rim, applied
clear thorn handle, shaded heavenly
blue ground w/large mica flecks,
2⅞" d., 7½" h. .................................. **110.00**

**Rose bowl,** spherical body w/eight-
crimp rim, blue w/white spatter &
overall mica flecks, 3⅝" d., 3⅛" h. ..... **85.00**

**Rose bowl,** spherical body w/eight-
crimp rim, deep red ground w/coral-
design overall mica flecks, 3⅝" d.,
3⅜" h. ............................................... **95.00**

**Vase,** 5¼" h., 4¼" d., bulbous ovoid
body tapering to a short neck w/four-
lobed rolled rim, pink, maroon, blue
& yellow spatter w/mica flecks, white
lining ................................................ **65.00**

**Vase,** 6" h., 3⅝" d., footed spherical
melon-lobed body w/a slender
cylindrical neck w/cupped &
scalloped rim, shaded deep rose
w/overall fine mica flecks, white
lining ................................................ **75.00**

**Vase,** 6¼" h., 3¾" d., bulbous ovoid
body tapering to a flaring four-lobed
rim, raised on four applied clear
wishbone feet, rich rose w/overall
large mica flecks ............................... **95.00**

**Vase,** 8¾" h., 4" d., footed tapering
cylindrical body w/a crimped fan-
shaped rim w/clear applied edging,
deep rose w/overall large mica
flecks, white lining .............................. **75.00**

*Ornate Spangled Vase*

**Vase,** 13½" h., 6" d., footed swelled cylindrical body w/a rounded shoulder to the wide, short cylindrical neck w/rolled rim, dark cobalt blue w/overall fine mica flecks, finely enameled w/a scene of two large birds perched on flowering branches done in blue, green, white, pink & tan, fitted on narrow gilt-metal ring on three scroll feet w/mask faces (ILLUS.)..................................... **395.00**

## STEUBEN

*Most of the Steuben glass listed below was made at the Steuben Glass Works, now a division of Corning Glass, between 1903 and about 1933. The factory was organized by T. G., noted glass designer, Frederick Carder, and others. Mr. Carder devised many types of glass and revived many old techniques.*

*Steuben Mark*

**ACID CUT BACK**

*Art Deco Acid Cut Back Vase*

**Vase,** 12" h., gently flaring cylindrical body w/an angled shoulder to the flat mouth, Pomona green overlaid in blue Aurene & acid-cut w/a dramatic Art Deco "Debut" patt., overall etched texture, No. 6904, "Steuben" fleur-de-lis mark (ILLUS) ............. **$5,750.00**

*Oriental Acid Cut Back Vase*

**Vase,** 14½" h., graceful baluster-form, the yellow ground overlaid in black & etched w/two bands of stylized foliage centering an Oriental-inspired design of a large ferocious dragon, drilled for use as a lamp (ILLUS.)..**1,380.00**

*Aurene Console Set*

## AURENE

**Center bowl,** footed deep wide sides w/a widely rolled rim, overall strong blue iridescence, No. 2606, signed "Steuben Aurene 2606," 11¼" d., 4½" h. ............................................... **863.00**

**Console set:** center bowl, flower frog & a pair of tall blossom-form candlesticks; the wide shallow bowl w/incurved & lightly scalloped rim & applied leaf & branch side handles holds a round disc-form flower frog, each candlestick w/a cylindrical tulip-form candle socket raised on a double-twist openwork stem on a disc foot, all w/blue Aurene finish, bowl inscribed "STEUBEN AURENE V959," frog unsigned, sticks signed "STEUBEN AURENE 6059," chip on base of frog, bowl 13¾" w. over handles, candlesticks 12⅜" h., the set (ILLUS. top) ............................... **4,600.00**

**Ewer,** squatty bulbous base tapering to a tall 'stick' neck w/angled spout, angled loop handle from neck to shoulder, overall gold iridescence, inscribed "Aurene 2773," 5½" h. ....... **748.00**

**Scent bottle w/teardrop stopper,** ribbed & compressed bulbous body w/everted neck, overall iridescent gold, signed, No. 1455, 5⅞" h. ......... **575.00**

**Vase,** 7½" h., flaring trumpet-form w/a ruffled rim, bright golden orange overall iridescence, No. 723, signed "Aurene 723" ................................... **489.00**

**Vase,** 11½" h., footed ovoid body tapering to a short widely flaring neck, upright applied small scroll shoulder handles, overall blue iridescence, base inscribed "Steuben" (tiny base edge chip, some surface scratches) .............. **1,150.00**

## CALCITE

*Calcite Candlesticks*

**Candlesticks,** flaring trumpet-form ring base in white w/an opal wafer, the mushroom-shaped candle socket cased in iridescent blue on the interior of the widely flaring & flattened rims, No. 3581, 6¼" h., pr. (ILLUS.) ........................................ **2,070.00**

## CINTRA

**Vase,** 7" h., bulbous ovoid footed body w/a wide closed rim, satin-finished clear body speckled throughout w/yellow inclusions, Steuben fleur-de-lis mark .............. **1,093.00**

## CLUTHRA

**Vase,** 6¼" h., bulbous ovoid body tapering to a short rolled neck, bright swirled & bubbled blue cased in clear, No. 2683 (ILLUS. top left next page) ..................................... **1,093.00**

*Small Cluthra Vase*

*Fine Cluthra Vase*

*Handled Cluthra Vase*

**Vase,** 10" h., wide ovoid body tapering to a short cylindrical neck flanked by applied clear small double-loop handles, grey shading from white to blue infused w/controlled air bubbles, No. 6898, ca. 1920s, acid-stamped "STEUBEN" w/fleur-de-lis (ILLUS.) ........................................ **2,530.00**

**Vase,** 10¾" h., footed bulbous baluster-form w/short widely rolled neck, upright applied S-scroll loop shoulder handles in white, swirled & bubbly body, No. 2959 (ILLUS. top next column) .................................. **2,900.00**

**Vase,** 11" h., 9" d., green bubbly glass, fleur-de-lis mark .................. **1,500.00**

## FLEMISH BLUE
**Candleholders,** overall "controlled bubble" decoration w/ruffled sockets & an applied foot w/threading, signed, 5½" h., pr............................. **300.00**
**Compote,** open, 6" d., 4" h. ................. **95.00**

## FLORENTIA

*Florentia Vase*

**Vase,** 7" h., footed squatty bulbous body tapering to a widely flaring rim w/an applied ring, cinnamon pink floral design w/matching collar ring, No. 6781, small interior blemish (ILLUS.) ......................................... **1,150.00**
**Vase,** 7½" h., flaring body internally decorated w/pink blossoms & silver inclusions, stamped mark..... **2,070.00**

## GOLD RUBY
**Goblet,** pilsner-form, tall bright ruby trumpet-form body atop a clear knopped stem w/a compressed air

teardrop above a short knopped stem & disc foot, engraved autograph on base "Steuben F. Carder," 7¼" h. ...... **173.00**

## GROSTESQUE

*Steuben Grotesque Vase*

**Vase,** 9" h., flaring randomly ruffled sides, footed, Ivrene ........................ **350.00**

**Bowl-vase,** 9½" l., 5½" h., fanned & pinched ruffled sides w/four pillars, crystal, No. 7277, signed "Steuben" (ILLUS.) ............................................ **345.00**

**Vase,** 11" h., amethyst flaring ruffled sides, No. 7090, ca. 1920 ................. **525.00**

## JADE

**Luncheon set:** four wines & four 8½" d. plates; green Jade wines w/Alabaster stems, green Jade plates, set of 8 ................................. **350.00**

**Vase,** 8½" h., yellow Jade, wide bulbous ovoid body in deep yellow w/a wide rounded shoulder & short cylindrical neck w/rolled rim cased in iridescent blue Aurene, lower portion etched overall w/a background of small blossomheads, No. 7014, ca. 1925 ........................................ **4,600.00**

**Vase,** 10¼" h., blue Jade, swelled cylindrical body w/narrow vertically ribbed panels to the narrow angled shoulder below the wide rolled rim, dark cobalt blue, No. 7437, fleur-de-lis mark ......................................... **3,737.00**

**Vase,** 12" h., green Jade, bulbous ovoid body w/flat rim & swirled optic rib design, No. 6215 ......................... **325.00**

**Vase/lamp base,** 12" h., green Jade, tall ovoid body w/a wide shoulder to a short rolled neck, deeply etched w/a sculptured chrysanthemum design, accompanied by original gilt-metal two-socket lamp fittings .......... **863.00**

## MIRROR BLACK

**Candlestick,** tall slender domed foot supporting a tall slender baluster-form stem w/a small waisted connector to the tall ovoid socket w/a flint white rim wrap, in the Sinclaire manner, fleur-de-lis mark, 13½" h. ............................................. **345.00**

## ORIENTAL POPPY

*Steuben Oriental Poppy Lamp*

**Lamp,** the ovoid glass shaft tapering to a slender cylindrical neck w/flattened rim, the sides in vertically striped pastel pink w/applied neck threading of Pomona green, mounted in an elaborate gilt-metal pedestal w/domed & beaded round base w/small disc feet, the top mounted w/a double swan finial, No. 8026, glass 11" h., overall 31" h. (ILLUS.) .................... **1,955.00**

## POMONA GREEN

**Bowl,** 11" d., signed ............................ **125.00**

**Candlesticks,** optic ribbed design w/a wide disc foot supporting a swelled disc below a slender baluster-form section below to round knops & the tall ovoid candle socket w/a flattened rim, No. 2959, 10" h., pr.................... **748.00**

**Center bowl w/flower frog,** bowl w/rolled rim & optic ribbing, No. 6106, signed, 2 pcs. .................. **220.00**

**Vase,** 9" h., rectangular upright form w/swirled optic ribbing, No. 6199, signed .............................................. **150.00**

*Roseline Luncheon Set*

## ROSELINE

*Roseline Center Bowl*

*Selenium Red Goblets*

**Center bowl,** deep rounded flaring sides in pink cased in clear w/applied black ball feet & a thin black applied rim band, 10⅜" d., 5" h. (ILLUS.) .................................... **316.00**

**Goblet,** footed, cased crystal ................ **50.00**

**Luncheon set:** four 10¾" d. plates, four bouillon cups & underplates & four footed dessert dishes; pink ground copper wheel-cut w/leaf bands alternating w/squares w/blossom heads, some impurities, the set (ILLUS. top) ........................................ **805.00**

## SELENIUM RED

**Goblets,** water, brilliant red w/copper wheel-engraved Vineyard patt., all marked, No. 6792, 4⅜" h., set of 12 (ILLUS. of part, next column) ............ **863.00**

**Vase,** 6¾" h., swirled optic rib design, unsigned .......................................... **125.00**

**Vase,** 7" h., footed gently flaring wide cylindrical body w/swirled optic rib design, No. 6030. ............................. **425.00**

## SILVERINA

*Silverina Vase*

**Vase,** 7" h., footed urn-form body w/a widely flaring rim, Pomona green w/silver specks & diamond-shaped air trap decoration overall, No. 6545 variant, partial fleur-de-lis mark on base (ILLUS.) .................................... **805.00**

*Topaz Stemware Set*

## SPANISH GREEN

**Candlesticks,** a high domed swirled optic ribbed foot supporting a double knop below the tall slender optic ribbed shaft below the ovoid socket w/wide rolled rim & swirled optic ribbing, No. 6110, stamped fleur-de-lis mark, 12" h., pr. ............................ **575.00**

**Stemware set:** four wines & four water goblets; tall tapering cylindrical bowl w/applied reeding around the lower half, raised on knopped tall slender stems on disc feet, applied Venetian prints, random bubbles in bowls, No. 6359, several stamped "Steuben," 6¾" & 7½" h., set of 8 (one w/base edge chip) ................... **518.00**

## TOPAZ

**Candlesticks,** a high domed foot w/optic ribbing supporting a double knop below the tall slender optic ribbed shaft supporting an ovoid optic ribbed socket w/a wide rolled rim, No. 6110, acid-stamped "Steuben," 12" h., pr. ...................... **633.00**

**Stemware set:** six champagnes & six water goblets; flaring bell-form Topaz bowls w/a diamond optic design raised on a slender Pomona green stem & applied w/trailing green prints, No. 6303, champagnes 6" h., goblets 8" h., set of 12 (ILLUS.) ....................................... **1,495.00**

## VERRE DE SOIE

**Candleholders,** diamond optic design, widely flaring disc foot supporting a short baluster-form stem below the socket w/a widely flaring down-turned rim decorated w/rose-colored threading, No. 6593, stamped "Steuben" mark, 4½" h., pr. .............. **633.00**

**Perfume bottle w/original blue stopper,** bulbous melon-ribbed body, signed, 4¾" h. ........................ **295.00**

## MISCELLANEOUS WARES

**Candelabra,** two-light, crystal, a pair of thick angled arms each supporting a cylindrical candle socket w/a flattened, flared rim, the arms joining a central tall, slender ovoid teardrop shaft & flanking a pointed teardrop finial, on a thick, round foot, No. 805, designed by George Thompson in 1952, signed "Steuben," 9⅝" h., pr. ...................... **1,035.00**

**Decanter w/stopper,** "Eagle," crystal, low squatty bulbous wide body w/deeply indented side panels, the wide shoulders tapering to a short

*Bicentennial Goblet*

*Penguin Sculpture*

cylindrical neck w/a flaring rim, the ball finial on the stopper topped w/a full-figure tall-winged bird, No. 8276, signed "Steuben" on the base, 11" h... **863.00**

**Goblet,** Bicentennial commemorative, crystal, deep bell-form bowl etched w/the Presidential Seal & "The Bicentennial of the U.S.A.," knopped stem w/a tear-shaped air bubble above the domed foot, designed by Donald Pollard & Patricia Weisberg, No. 21-200, 1975, signed "Steuben," 8⅛" h. (ILLUS. above) ...................... **690.00**

**Sculpture,** "Carrousel," a solid crystal merry-go-round w/carved horses on a striped pole, raised on a revolving turntable base to simulate a real carrousel, topped by a sterling silver banner, No. 1122, designed by Peter Aldridge, 8" h. ............................... **3,450.00**

**Sculpture,** "Crystal and Silver Ice Hunter," a large frosted arched iceberg centering a small Eskimo in a kayak w/an engraved seal below, No. 1033, designed by James Houstor, 1972, w/original red velvet-lined leather case, 5¾" h. .............. **2,990.00**

**Sculpture,** "Crystal and Silver Ice Penguin," crystal, a full-form sterling bird atop a frosted & hand-polished glass ice chunk w/engraved penguin diving toward a school of fish below, designed by James Johnson as part of the "Arctic" series," signed "Steuben," w/original red velvet & leather case, 6½" h. (ILLUS. top next column) .................................. **3,680.00**

**Sculpture,** "Trout and Fly," the crystal fish twisted in mid-jump to capture the "Royal Coachman" 18k gold fly lure, No. 1002, designed by James Houston in 1966, w/original red leather & velvet case, 9" h. ............ **1,725.00**

## STEVENS & WILLIAMS

*This long-established English glasshouse has turned out a wide variety of artistic glasswares through the years. Fine satin glass pieces and items with applied decoration (sometimes referred to as "Matsu-No-Ke") are especially sought after today. The following represents a cross-section of its wares.*

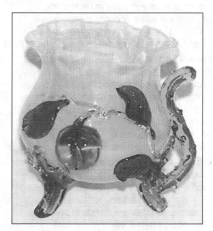

*Ornate Appliquéd Bowl*

**Bowl,** 6½" d., 7¼" h., bulbous ovoid body in soft opalescent blue tapering to a crimped & ruffled rim, applied w/a large amber peach & branches w/green leaves & raised on applied amber branch feet & a thorn handle at one side (ILLUS. bottom previous page) ............................................. **$995.00**

**Bottle w/original stopper,** footed tall tapering conical body w/greenish amber foot & body, the body applied w/tiers of crystal shells giving a Christmas tree effect, the tall matching stopper topped by an applied crystal figural peacock, 5" d., 11" h. ............................................... **495.00**

**Finger bowl & underplate,** crystal cased in royal blue & intaglio cut w/a design of a wide fruiting leafy vine around the border & a starburst in the center, the bowl w/deep rounded & gently flaring sides, smooth rim w/light notch cutting, plate 8" d., bowl, 6" d., 3" h., 2 pcs. ..................... **265.00**

**Finger bowl & underplate,** crystal cased in dark green & intaglio-cut w/wide grapevines, seven grape clusters on the bowl & vines & leaves on the underplate, the round bowl w/tapering rounded sides, plate 6½" d., bowl 4¾" d., 2½" h., 2 pcs. .... **265.00**

**Rose bowl,** quadraform rim, milk white ground decorated w/three applied amber & green acanthus leaves forming loop feet, pink interior, 4½" h. .................................. **385.00**

**Rose bowl,** creamy white exterior & pink interior, applied leaf feet & applied raspberry prunt, 4½" h. ........ **248.00**

**Tumbler,** slightly flaring cylindrical form, alternating wide vertical stripes of opaque white & chartreuse green & thin clear stripes, wide silver rim band, 3" d., 4⅞" h. ............................ **110.00**

**Vase,** 4¼" h., 2⅛" d., baluster-form w/a short cylindrical neck w/a deeply ruffled rim, white cased w/rose pink & intaglio cut w/bands of beads & a large band of stylized blossoms alternating w/leaf clusters below a wide plain band, on an applied opalescent foot (ILLUS. right, next column) .................. **225.00**

**Vase,** 5⅛" h., 2¾" d., bulbous footed base w/a tall 'stick' neck w/a deeply ruffled rim, white cased in rose pink & cut around the body w/ferns & grasses & dot & line bands around the neck, clear applied wafer foot (ILLUS. left, next column) ................ **235.00**

*Two Stevens & Williams Cut Vases*

**Vase,** 5⅜" h., 5¼" d., wide bulbous ovoid body w/a wide shoulder to the short widely flaring neck w/a flattened rim, mother-of-pearl satin Pompeian Swirl patt. in pale greenish yellow shading to deep rose red, white interior ...................... **750.00**

**Vase,** 7½" h., 4½" d., creamy white opaque body w/applied amber scallops around the rim & applied amber loop feet, clear applied flower prunt, the sides applied w/three shaded amber, cranberry & green long leaves, deep rose interior ......... **265.00**

**Vase,** 7½" h., 4½" d., footed ovoid body in opaque creamy white tapering to a flattened shaped rim applied w/a band of amber scallops, the body applied w/three large shaded green, amber & cranberry leaves curving up around the sides, deep rose interior.............................. **225.00**

**Vase,** 10½" h., slender baluster-form body w/a flaring cupped rim w/a flat edge, finely decorated w/a tall branch of green leaves & soft pink blossoms & a large blue & rose perched bird, all trimmed w/gold, thin gold lancet bands around the rim & base.................................................... **425.00**

**Vase,** jack-in-the-pulpit form, 11¾" h., 5" d., the tall slender trumpet-form body w/a deeply crimped & rolled front rim & a pulled-up back rim, the body w/alternating stripes of opaque chartreuse green & opaque white & clear, all w/a satin finish, on a wide applied crimped clear frosted flattened foot .................................... **225.00**

# TIFFANY

*This glassware, covering a wide diversity of types, was produced in glasshouses operated by Louis Comfort Tiffany, America's outstanding glass designer of the Art Nouveau period, from the last quarter of the 19th century until the early 1930s. Tiffany revived early techniques and devised many new ones.*

*Tiffany Marks*

**Bowl,** 7½" d., 1½" h., pastel line, wide shallow form w/a wide flattened & gently scalloped rim, unusual transparent central section w/bright yellow rim w/opal on the reverse & radiating colored bands from the clear center, signed "L.C.T. Favrile"... **$805.00**

**Bowl,** 8" d., 3" h., round ribbed herringbone body w/strong silvery lustre within & purple iridescent exterior, signed "L.C. Tiffany Favrile 1925" ............................................. **1,265.00**

**Bowl,** 9" d., 2½" h., pastel line, short cylindrical center flaring to a wide flattened rim, bright pink stretched rim w/wide colored bands down to the center, opal beneath, signed "L.C. Tiffany Favrile 898" .................. **863.00**

**Center bowl,** wide shallow form w/upturned low rim, ten-rib design w/lustrous gold iridescence & wheel-cut ivy leaf & vine decoration in the interior, two lady bugs intaglio-cut on the exterior, signed "L.C.T. Favrile," 12" d., 4½" h. ................................. **1,725.00**

**Compote,** open, 5" d., 2¼" h., pastel line, wide shallow bowl w/a flattened rim in pastel pink w/stretched iridescence & ten white opal stripes radiating from the center, applied clear knop stem & foot, signed "L.C.T. Favrile 1871" ........................ **690.00**

**Jar,** cov., wide cylindrical body transparent pink diamond quilted design w/opal striations, gilt-brown low dome cover w/enamel-decorated

button finial, fitted in a metal foot ring, cover impressed "Louis C. Tiffany Furnaces Inc., Favrile 137," 3¾" d., overall 4" h............................ **863.00**

**Perfume bottle w/original metal cap,** lay-down-type, amorphous tapering cylindrical body of iridescent bluish gold glass, mounted w/a signed "Tiffany & Co." 18k yellow gold rim & hinged cap enhanced w/collet-set demantoid garnet within a polychrome guilloche enamel ground accented w/four small collet-set diamonds, 4¾" l................................................ **21,850.00**

*Small Tiffany Vase*

**Vase,** 4" h., squatty bulbous ribbed body tapering to a short molded neck, overall blue iridescence, signed (ILLUS.) ................................ **450.00**

**Vase,** 8" h., footed swelled cylindrical body w/a wide compressed bulbous shoulder band tapering to a short flaring & scalloped rim, ten-rib molded body, overall gold iridescence, signed "L.C. Tiffany Favrile X165 1931 M" .... **863.00**

**Vase,** 8½" h., paperweight-type, tall slender tapering cylindrical form w/a bulbous top & incurved rim, clear decorated w/pale yellow & lemon yellow narcissus flowers above dark green stems & wide leaves, flared foot, signed "L.C.Tiffany - Favrile - 4508 J," ca. 1915 ........................... **6,037.00**

**Vase,** 9¼" h., millefiori-type, ovoid body tapering to a short cylindrical neck w/flat rim, deep red decorated w/iridescent silver millefiori blossoms & iridescent blue leafage w/scrolling vines, signed "L.C.Tiffany - Favrile - 1676 K (indistinct)," ca. 1916 ........... **5,520.00**

**Vase,** bud, 10" h., footed tall slender slightly tapering cylinder w/flaring rim, decorated w/green pointed leaf

*Unusual Tiffany Vase*

forms on a gold iridescent ground,
applied gold disc foot, signed
"L.C. Tiffany Favrile 1502-6559" .... **1,093.00**

**Vase,** 11" h., "Cypriote," tall slender
slightly tapering cylinder,
convoluted & rough-textured
surface, overall gold iridescence
w/purple & metallic overtones,
inscribed "L.C.T. 6211 B" ............... **2,300.00**

**Vase,** 11½" h., floriform, the slender
elongated stem w/a bulbed blossom
bowl striated in pulled cinnamon
brown & white organic leaf forms on
transparent ambergris crystal,
domed foot w/hooked & pulled white
border, signed "7650" .................... **6,900.00**

**Vase,** 12⅛" h., footed tall slender
ovoid body tapering to a short
cylindrical neck w/flat rim, golden
amber iridescent decorated
w/whispy finely trailed feathering &
bluish iridescent dashes, signed
L.C.T. A1833," ca. 1894 ................ **2,587.00**

**Vase,** 15⅜" h., tall slender baluster-
form body w/a short cylindrical neck &
flat rim, amber w/golden iridescence
applied w/green leaves, vines & eight
white blossoms, all wheel-engraved
w/naturalistic folds, stamens & petal
formations, signed "Louis C. Tiffany
Inc. Favrile 9672" (ILLUS. above) ... **9,200.00**

**Vase,** 15⅜" h., bulbous base tapering
slightly to a tall cylindrical body w/a
flat rim, opaque black w/pulled blue
iridescent stylized floral decoration
& blue iridized interior, signed "Louis
C. Tiffany 7498" w/a "TGD Co."
label ............................................. **5,750.00**

*Flower-form Tiffany Vase*

**Vase,** 16½" h., flower-form, the
upright flaring blossom-form bowl
w/delicate pulled-feather articulated
design within transparent green
w/lustred opal exterior, the slender
shaped stem numbered "1756" &
inserted into a gilt-bronze organic-
form base impressed "Tiffany
Studios New York - TG&D Co." &
numbered "1756" (ILLUS.) ............. **8,050.00**

## VASELINE

*This glass takes its name from its color
which is akin to that of petroleum jelly used for
medicinal purposes. Originally manufacturers
usually referred to the color as "canary." We
list miscellaneous pieces below. Also see:
OPALESCENT GLASS and PATTERN
GLASS.*

**Bowl,** Hobbs Star patt. ........................ **$80.00**

**Cracker jar,** cov., opalescent swirl,
barrel-shaped, pale coral pink leaf
applied finial, 7¾" h., 4¼" d. ............ **145.00**

**Vase,** 6¼" h., 3⅞" d., ruffled top,
Drape patt., slightly embossed .......... **80.00**

**Vase,** 4¾" h., 3⅞" d. opalescent
ruffled top, squared bulbous base
w/dimpled sides, opalescent Swirl
patt. alternating w/opalescent rice-
like design.......................................... **95.00**

**Vase,** 5¼" h., 3" d., pedestal foot,
opalescent top edge w/opalescent
Cattails patt. ...................................... **95.00**

# VENETIAN

*Venetian glass has been made for six centuries on the island of Murano, where it continues to be produced. The skilled glass artisans developed numerous techniques, subsequently imitated elsewhere. Below we list a sampling of mainly 19th and 20th century pieces.*

**Bowl,** 12½" d., 4⅝" h., "merletto"-type, deep & wide rounded oblong form w/white lacework wide bands alternating w/pale blue bands, by Archimede Seguso, ca. 1950 ...... **$1,725.00**

**Coupe,** deep rounded ribbed sides w/two sides pulled up into outswept curved points, large applied gold grape cluster handles at each side, thick ribbed disc foot, clear w/gold foil inclusions, the foot & rim w/applied opaque white ribbons, designed by Ercole Barovier, unsigned, ca. 1930, 6¼" h. ............. **4,025.00**

**Figure of a human head,** stylized balloon-form, yellow opalescent decorated w/cobalt blue hair & mustache, the bow tie in applied green, the nose a white triangle, the ears applied in yellow looped glass, mounted on a thick clear glass base, signed "J. Dubuffet - Ermanno Nason I.V.R. Di Mazzega - Murano," executed by Ermanno Nason for I.V.R. Di Mazzega, ca. 1950, 12" h. .............................................. **6,325.00**

**Figures of man & woman,** multi-colored, one a standing man in striped garment supporting a vase on his shoulder, the woman w/a matching striped garment standing & holding a glass tazza against her hip, both w/gold foil inclusions, the woman w/the company's paper label, Barovier & Toso, tallest 11⅓" h., pr. .................................... **1,955.00**

**Model of a bird,** stylized long-tailed bird w/head turned back over shoulder, on a domed glass base, heavy solid sommerso-type of olive amber & brown layered w/clear eyes, crest & beak, polished base, 21½" l., 12½" h. .............................. **230.00**

**Model of a ram's head,** solid clear sculpture of a stylized ram head w/long, curved applied amber horns swirled in an integrated wrap, foil label "Alvin Italy Murano Crafted Art Objects," 17½" h. ............................ **259.00**

**Vase,** 10" h., "inciso sommerso"-type, a large bulbous egg-shaped top raised on a thick cylindrical tall foot, the top w/a red teardrop-form encased in the center of the topaz & thick grey body incised w/horizontal lines, signed "A. Barbini," Alfredo Barbini, ca. 1962 ........................... **4,887.00**

**Vase,** 10" h., "merletto"-style, asymmetrical tapering ovoid body w/a crumpled rim, decorated w/large patches of white lacework design again a clear & bluish green ground, by Archimede Seguso, ca. 1952.... **8,625.00**

*Barovier Venetian Vase*

**Vase,** 11⅝" h., "Lenti"-type, cylindrical heavy walled cobalt blue layered in gold foil & wrapped w/wide clear strips of glass w/rounded molded protrusions, designed by Ercole Barovier, Barovier & Toso Studio (ILLUS.) ........................................ **6,900.00**

**Vase,** 15⅛" h., tall gently flaring cylindrical body w/a widely flaring rim & beveled rim, decorated w/a patchwork of large colored & opaque white panels of red, blue & gold, by Ansolo Fuga ................................. **6,900.00**

**Vase,** 16¼" h., tall ovoid curved asymmetrical form pierced low on one side w/a thick loop handle, polychrome decoration comprised of a patchwork of zanfirico canes & millefiori cane sections cased in clear, by A. VE. M. ........................ **5,750.00**

*Venini Chickens*

## VENINI

*Founded by former lawyer Paolo Venini in 1925, this Venetian glasshouse soon developed a reputation for its fine quality decorative and tablewares. Several noted designers have worked for the firm over the years and their unique pieces in the modern spirit, made using traditional techniques, are increasingly popular with collectors today. The factory continues in operation.*

**Bottle,** tall cylindrical form w/rounded base & shoulder to a short cylindrical neck w/flared rim, the body composed of three wide horizontal bands of plum, lemon yellow & moss green, designed by Tapio Wirkalla, engraved "venini tw 89," 1989, 17" h. ............. **$1,035.00**

**Candleholders,** figural, modeled as a seated male & female blackamoor in striped garments, the male w/candleholders on knees, the lady w/one on her head, the other on her lap, lady w/Venini label, designed by Fulvio Bianconi, 8" & 9" h., pr. (restoration to left foot of male)......... **575.00**

**Figure of a nude woman,** "Sirena," the stylized headless figure recumbent on her stomach, deep emerald green, designed by Fulvio Bianconi, unsigned, ca. 1950, 16⅛" l. ........................................... **5,462.00**

**Models of chickens,** a stylized hen & rooster, each hollow-bodied of ribbed opaque white threaded in colorful stripes w/applied wings, eyes, combs, tailfeathers & feet, on black disc base, acid-stamped "Venini Murano Italia," designed by Fulvio Bianconi, rooster base flawed, 6¾" h., pr. (ILLUS.)........................ **3,335.00**

**Vase,** 6" h., "pezzato"-style, wide irregular cupped form tapering sharply toward the base, clear decorated w/red, blue & teal blue irregular patches, probably designed by Fulvio Bianconi, acid-stamped "Venini - Murano - Italia," ca. 1951 .. **5,175.00**

**Vase,** 9⅝" h., cylindrical body w/irregular rim & dimpled sides, decorated w/red, green, blue & clear vertical stripes, acid-stamped "Venini - Italia - Murano," w/original paper label, probably designed by Gio Ponti, ca. 1955.............................. **5,175.00**

**Vase,** 9¾" h., "tessuto"-style, tall slightly tapering cylindrical form, pale ruby & opalescent, decorated w/wide vertical bands of pale yellow & black threading & cased in clear, the surface finely martelé, designed by Carlo Scarpa, unsigned, ca. 1940 ... **3,737.00**

**Vase,** 10" h., "vaso-a-canne"-style, slightly tapering cylindrical body w/a waisted neck below the widely flaring rim, multi-colored w/vertically striped sides composed of narrow bands of red, green, blue, amethyst & amber (ILLUS. top next page)....... **575.00**

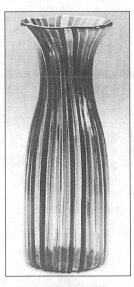

*Venini Striped Vase*

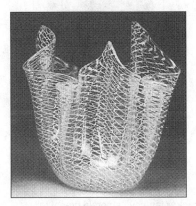
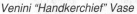

*Venini "Handkerchief" Vase*

**Vase,** 11" h., "handkerchief"-style, the
upright randomly ruffled sides in
clear decorated w/white zanfirico,
acid-stamped "venini - murano -
ITALIA," ca. 1950 (ILLUS.) ............ **2,300.00**

**Vase,** 11⅜" h., bottle-form, slender
gently tapering form w/a small mouth,
translucent cobalt blue w/three wide
applied bands of red w/slight hints of
orange, designed by Fulvio Bianconi,
unsigned, ca. 1950 ........................ **2,070.00**

**Vase,** 11½" h., tall cylindrical form in
pale marine green, the base in pale
lavender, the surface finely wheel-
carved overall w/vertical wavy lines,
designed by Carlo Scarpa, w/original
paper label, ca. 1940 .................... **2,875.00**

*Venini "Bikini" Vase*

**Vase,** 12¾" h., "murrine"-style, tall
slender tapering squared form
w/ruffled small rim, composed of
murrine sections in opaque white
w/comma-like designs overall in
black & aubergine, possibly
designed by Riccardo Licata, retains
portion of original paper label,
ca. 1953 ....................................... **5,462.00**

**Vase,** 13¾" h., "bikini" series, waisted
torso-shape w/royal blue & opaque
white swirled decoration at the top
& base, small cylindrical clear neck
& clear central section, designed by
Fulvio Bianconi, ca. 1949
(ILLUS. above).......................... **25,600.00**

## VICTORIAN COLORED GLASS

*There are, of course, many types of colored
glassware of the Victorian era and we cover a
great variety of these in our various glass
categories. However, there are some pieces of
pressed, mold-blown and free-blown Victorian
colored glass which don't fit well into other
specific listings, so we have chosen to include a
selection of them here.*

**Bowl,** 7½" d., 5½" h., squatty wide
bulbous form w/clear cased swirled
ribbing over wide stripes of pink,
blue & yellow, the short, wide
cylindrical neck decorated in gold
w/lacy white scrolls, white interior
(ILLUS. top next page) .................. **$550.00**

*Striped Overlay Bowl*

**Bowl,** 5½ x 8½", 4⅞" h., rounded body w/a deeply fluted & ruffled rim w/two sides pulled together at the center, heavenly blue cased in deep pink & w/applied clear wishbone feet, clear edging around the rim ..... **195.00**

**Bowl,** 6 x 9½", 5¼" h., footed wide cylindrical & slightly waisted body w/a tightly crimped & rolled rim, sapphire blue decorated overall w/small pink, yellow, white & peach flowers & green leaf sprigs ............... **345.00**

**Box w/hinged cover,** round, deep amethyst cylinder w/white enameled leaves around the sides & large white & small blue flowers w/a gold & blue butterfly on the flat cover, brass base band w/looped wire feet, brass hinge fittings & small ring handles, 3⅝" d., 3¾" h ...................... **225.00**

**Box w/hinged cover,** round w/tapering optic ribbed sides & a flattened domed optic ribbed cover, lime green, the cover decorated w/large daisy-like white & yellow blossoms & shaded green leaves, the sides w/small white floral sprigs, brass hinge fittings, 5¼" d., 4¾" h. (ILLUS. top next column) .................. **165.00**

**Box w/lift-off cover,** round w/low domed cover, amethyst, the cover decorated w/large gold flowers & leafy sprigs w/white & green trim, a gold band around the base, 4½" d., 3" h. .................................................. **135.00**

**Cracker jar,** cov., barrel-shaped, sapphire blue optic ribbed form decorated w/a wide center gold band & large sprays of white lily-of-the-valley & green leaves, silver plate rim, cover & swing bail handle, 4¾" d., 7¾" h. ................................. **185.00**

*Large Decorated Box*

*Green Cracker Jar*

**Cracker jar,** cov., emerald green, tall ovoid form w/lozenge-paneled sides & a domed fitted cover w/a large knob finial, the side panels alternatively decorated w/white lacy scrolls & tiny dotted blossoms trimmed in gold & w/white fans at the top & base, the cover w/white dot bands & a narrow scroll band, 4½" d., 9¼" h. (ILLUS.) .................... **165.00**

**Cruet w/original clear facet-cut stopper,** sapphire blue cylindrical optic body ribbed body w/a white flattened shoulder to the tall narrow cylindrical neck, fitted w/a wide pierced silvered metal body band & a smaller piece band at the top of the neck, the bands joined by a twisted wire handle w/knob ends, 2½" d., 7¾" h. ................................. **145.00**

*Bird-decorated Decanter*

*Fine Blue Liqueur Set*

**Decanter w/original tall teardrop stopper,** amethyst slender ovoid body raised on a low trumpet foot & tapering to a tall slender neck w/a tricorner spout, applied angled amethyst handle, the neck & shoulder decorated w/heavy gold trimmed w/white & yellow enameled flowers & green leaves on spearpoint panels, gold flower sprigs on lower body & gold trim on stopper, 3" d., 12" h.................................. **225.00**

**Decanter w/original teardrop stopper,** slightly tapering cylindrical optic ribbed body w/a rounded shoulder to a tall slender cylindrical neck w/a wide bulbous medial ring & flared rim, sapphire blue decorated w/a large spread-winged white bird w/long brown beak & legs standing in a pond & framed by a delicate floral wreath w/pink & white blossoms, 3¾" d., 12¼" h. (ILLUS. above)......... **210.00**

**Decanter w/original clear facet-cut stopper,** footed slightly flaring cylindrical body w/a wide flattened shoulder to the tall slender cylindrical neck w/a flared rim, pale amber decorated w/a large, long-billed flying tan, white & black bird above a branch of white & yellow blossoms, 3½" d., 12¾" h. ................ **195.00**

**Liqueur set:** ovoid footed diamond quilted sapphire blue decanter w/original tall clear teardrop stopper & clear applied handle, six matching mugs & a round tray; all pieces except

the tray decorated in white enamel w/large stylized white blossoms & leaves w/gilt rim trim, tray 9⅛" d., mugs 1⅞" h., decanter 3" d., 9" h., the set (ILLUS.) ........................................ **295.00**

**Pitcher,** 7¼" h., 5" d., shaded deep rose to pink spherical body w/a wide cylindrical neck w/pinched spout, applied clear reeded handle, glossy finish .................................................. **185.00**

**Pitcher,** 8⅜" h., 5½" w., squared bulbous optic ribbed body tapering gently to a wide cylindrical neck w/pinched spout, pink cased w/shaded vaseline opalescent, applied pale vaseline green handle .. **195.00**

**Sugar shaker w/original top,** Acorn patt., shaded pink opaque, 5" h. ....... **195.00**

**Tumbler,** tapering cylindrical form, rose opalescent shaded to clear, decorated w/enameled yellow & gold floral sprays, 2½" d., 3⅞" h. ................ **45.00**

**Vase,** 3½" h., 3" d., bulbous optic ribbed body in green w/a ruffled & twisted rim & an applied medial rigaree band, raised on applied vaseline large leaf-form feet ............. **65.00**

**Vase,** 4¾" h., 4" d., footed bulbous ovoid body w/a rounded shoulder to a wide short cylindrical neck flanked by applied angled handles, sapphire blue Inverted Thumbprint body decorated around the shoulder w/a white enamel delicate heart band & a Roman key neck band, amber handles ............................................... **165.00**

*Amber Vase with Flowers*

**Vase,** 7¼" h., 3" d., cobalt blue gently flaring cylindrical body w/a rounded shoulder to the tall cylindrical neck topped by a rolled & crimped tri-lobe rim, the sides decorated in white enamel w/a landscape scene w/a large two-story house & stylized trees.................................................... **88.00**

**Vase,** 8¼" h., 5" d., ovoid optic ribbed body in amber tapering to a crimped & fluted rim, the sides applied w/large clear leaves & branches & pink & white spatter flower & bud wrapped around the sides, applied clear loop feet & clear rim edging (ILLUS. above) ................................ **175.00**

## WAVE CREST

*Now much sought after, Wave Crest was produced by the C.F. Monroe Co., Meriden, Connecticut, in the late 19th and early 20th centuries from opaque white glass blown into molds. It was then hand-decorated in enamels and metal trim was often added. Boudoir accessories such as jewel boxes, hair receivers, etc., were predominant.*

# WAVE CREST WARE

*Wave Crest Mark*

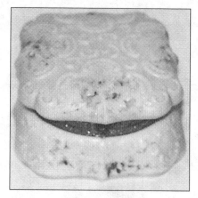

*Ornate Wave Crest Box*

**Box w/hinged lid,** Embossed Rococo mold, decorated w/pink & white roses, original lining, 5" sq., 2½" h. .............. **$350.00**

**Box w/hinged lid,** squared shaped w/overall delicate molded scrolls highlighted w/pastel blue & pink blossoms & green leaves, delicately embossed metal fittings, unlined, unsigned, 7" w., 4" h. (ILLUS.).......... **550.00**

**Box w/hinged lid,** Baroque Shell mold, decorated w/pink daisies bordered by sky blue & all outlined in lavender, 7¼" d............................... **765.00**

**Cracker jar,** cov., Tulip mold, decorated w/pink apple blossoms front & back, cream shading to blue ground ............................................... **250.00**

**Creamer & cov. sugar bowl,** Helmschied Swirl mold, lower portion in solid beige separated by enamel beading from the upper section w/pink roses, pr. ................... **630.00**

**Jardiniere,** wide bulbous smooth body w/a wide short cylindrical neck, decorated w/large clusters of chrysanthemums around the body, gilt lacy lancets around the neck, 14" d., 10" h. ..................................... **950.00**

**Syrup jug w/hinged silver plate cover & handle,** Helmschmied Swirl mold, lovely floral decoration ........... **395.00**

## WEBB

*This glass is made by Thomas Webb & Sons of Stourbridge, one of England's most prolific glasshouses. Numerous types of glass, including cameo, have been produced by this firm through the years. The company also*

*produced various types of novelty and "art"
glass during the late Victorian period. Also see
BURMESE, ROSE BOWLS, and SATIN &
MOTHER-OF-PEARL under glass.*

**Bowl,** 7½" d., 6¼" h., footed bulbous
body w/deeply dimpled sides & a
wide, short cylindrical neck, shaded
tan satin ground decorated w/long
curved black branches w/shaded
rose & yellow blossoms, gold trim .. **$295.00**

**Cameo bowl & underplate,** wide
rounded bowl in red cut w/large
white blossoms & long serrated
leaves & an insect hanging from
around the double line border, the
wide shallow underplate w/similar
decoration, unsigned, ca. 1890,
underplate 7¾" d., 2 pcs. ................... **977.00**

**Cameo vase,** 5¾" h., bulbous bottle-
form bud-type in ruby overlaid in
white & cut w/a bunch of grapes,
leaves & vine tendrils pendent from
the lip & also a moth, base
impressed "Thomas Webb & Sons -
Cameo," ca. 1900 ......................... **1,035.00**

**Cameo vase,** 10½" h., slender conical
body w/waisted inverted conical rim,
frosted red overlaid in white &
delicately carved w/passion flowers,
buds, leaves, tendrils & gently
curving vines below bands of rim
decoration, unsigned, ca. 1900 ..... **2,415.00**

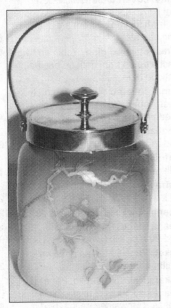

*Webb Cracker Jar*

**Cracker jar,** cov., squared body
w/dimpled sides, dark shaded blue
to pale blue glossy sides decorated
w/heavy gilt branches, blossoms &
leaves, plain silver plate rim, flat
cover & swing bail handle, 3⅜" d.,
5¼" h. (ILLUS. bottom previous
column) ............................................ **295.00**

**Ewer,** bulbous base tapering to a tall
slender neck w/a high pointed
arched spout, applied loop handle
from neck to shoulder, rare shaded
green to white satin ground
decorated w/gold enameled leaves
& branches w/three realistic apples,
numbered on the base, 4" d., 9" h. .... **425.00**

**Perfume bottle w/sterling silver
screw-off cap,** spherical body of
four shaded layers producing a
Peach Blow-type coloration,
decorated w/heavy gold prunus
blossoms & a butterfly, 5¼" h. ....... **1,520.00**

**Potpourri jar,** cov., bulbous ovoid
body w/a hinged inner lid & ornate
pierced outer lid, the body attached
to a three-footed brass base,
decorated w/multi-colored florals on
a satin opalescent ground w/a deep
aqua top border w/gold fringe,
5½" h. ............................................... **615.00**

**Vase,** 5½" h., 5½" d., footed squatty
bulbous body w/a wide, short
cylindrical neck, shaded dark gold to
pale yellow satin ground decorated
overall w/heavy gold prunus
blossoms, branches, pine needles &
a butterfly, gold foot & rim bands ...... **550.00**

**Vase,** 8" h., 4¼" d., bulbous four-
lobed body w/a tall slightly flaring
cylindrical neck, raised on four
pointed feet, opaque white
decorated w/a background of soft
blue & yellow forming zigzag panels
outlined in black, each panel
decorated w/delicate florals & scrolls
& large diamonds & scrolls on each
lobe (ILLUS. top next page) ............. **225.00**

**Vase,** 8¼" h., 6¼" d., bulbous ovoid
body tapering a wide flaring
cylindrical neck, shaded satin robin's
egg blue to pale blue w/bright yellow
overall decoration of a bird in flight
w/long branches of prunus
blossoms, berries, leaves & a large
butterfly, zigzag rim band ................ **425.00**

**Vase,** 8⅜" h., 4¼" d., footed flaring
baluster-form body w/a short flaring
neck, cased satin w/a shaded

*Ornate Webb Vase*

heavenly blue exterior decorated
w/large brown branches, gold &
green leaves & clusters of red
cherries, creamy white lining ............ **145.00**

**Water set:** 8" h. pitcher w/clear
applied reeded handle & six 3¾" h.
tumblers; all peach opalescent
w/dimpled sides & decorated w/gold
leaf vine design, marked, the set...... **750.00**

# WESTMORELAND

The Westmoreland Specialty Company
was founded in East Liverpool, Ohio in 1889
and relocated in 1890 to Grapeville,
Pennsylvania where it remained until its
closing in 1985.

During its early years Westmoreland
specialized in glass food containers and
novelties but by the turn of the century they
had a large line of milk white items and clear
tableware patterns. In 1925 the company
name was shortened to The Westmoreland
Glass Company and it was during that
decade that more colored glasswares entered
their line-up. When Victorian-style milk
glass again became popular in the 1940s and
1950s, Westmoreland produced extensive
amounts in several patterns which closely
resemble late 19th century wares. These and

their figural animal dishes in milk white and
colors are widely collected today but buyers
should not confuse them for the antique
originals. Watch for Westmoreland's "WG"
mark on some pieces. A majority of our
listings are products from the 1940s through
the 1970s. Earlier pieces will be indicated.

*Early Westmoreland Label & Mark*

**Animal covered dish,** Dove in Hand
on lacy base, copied from antique
original, milk white, 6⅜" l. .............. **$155.00**

**Animal covered dish,** oval Duck on
rimmed base, copied from antique
original, antique blue ......................... **75.00**

**Animal covered dish,** Hen on lacy
base, copied from antique original,
milk white........................................... **80.00**

**Animal covered dish,** Lovebirds on
oval base, copied from antique
original, 5¼" h., 6½" l........................ **45.00**

**Animal covered dish,** Mother Eagle
on a basket, copied from antique
original, milk white ........................... **105.00**

**Animal covered dish,** Mule-eared
Rabbit on ribbed octagonal base,
milk white, copied from antique
original, 5½" l., 4½" h......................... **65.00**

**Animal covered dish,** Robin on twig
nest, copied from antique original,
antique blue ...................................... **60.00**

**Animal covered dish,** Robin on twig
nest, copied from antique original,
green mist........................................... **40.00**

**Appetizer set,** Paneled Grape patt.,
mid-20th c., milk white, 9" d., 3 pcs. ... **65.00**

**Ashtray,** square, Beaded Grape patt.,
milk white, 4"..................................... **14.00**

**Ashtray,** square, Beaded Grape patt.,
milk white, 5"..................................... **20.00**

**Banana bowl,** Paneled Grape patt. ..... **125.00**

**Banana stand,** Paneled Grape patt.,
mid-20th c., milk white ..................... **100.00**

**Basket,** Paneled Grape patt., milk
white, 6" h. ........................................ **22.00**

**Basket,** oval, split handle, Paneled
Grape patt., crystal mist w/h.p.
Roses & Bows decoration, 6½" h. ....... **40.00**

**Basket,** handled, Paneled Grape patt., milk white, 8" h........................ **85.00**

**Basket,** ruffled, Paneled Grape patt., milk white, 8" d.............................. **65.00**

**Bowl,** cov., 4" square, Beaded Grape patt., milk white................................. **30.00**

**Bowl,** rose, 4½" d., American Hobnail patt., lilac opalescent .......................... **15.00**

**Bowl,** cov., 5" d., flared-rim, footed, Beaded Grape patt., milk white .......... **25.00**

**Bowl,** cov., 7" square, high-footed, Beaded Grape patt., milk white .......... **40.00**

**Bowl,** cov., 7" d., square-footed, Beaded Grape patt., milk white w/h.p. Roses & Ribbons decoration ... **55.00**

**Bowl,** wedding, 8" d., Paneled Grape patt., h.p. Roses & Bows decoration, milk white............................................ **80.00**

**Bowl,** 8¼" d., shallow, Paneled Grape patt.................................................... **50.00**

**Bowl,** cov., 9" h., high footed, Beaded Grape patt., trimmed in 22k gold ........ **55.00**

**Bowl,** 9" d., footed, flared, Beaded Grape patt., milk white........................ **45.00**

**Bowl,** 9" d., lipped, footed, Paneled Grape patt., milk white........................ **90.00**

**Bowl,** 9½" d., bell-shaped, Paneled Grape patt., milk white........................ **50.00**

**Bowl,** 9½" d., bell-shaped, footed, Princess Feather patt., Golden Sunset ..................................................... **65.00**

**Bowl,** wedding, 10" d., Paneled Grape patt., h.p. Roses & Bows decoration, milk white............................................ **95.00**

**Bowl,** oval, 11" w., lipped & footed, Paneled Grape patt., milk white........ **115.00**

**Bowl,** 11" d., Thousand Eye patt. ......... **40.00**

**Bowl,** oval, 12" d, footed, Paneled Grape patt., milk white...................... **100.00**

**Bowl,** 12½" d., bell-shaped, Paneled Grape patt., milk white............................ **95.00**

**Box,** cov., square, Beaded Grape (No. 1884) patt., milk white................. **35.00**

**Butter dish,** cov., Paneled Grape patt., milk white................................. **18.00**

**Butter dish,** cov., Paneled Grape patt., milk white, ¼ lb. ......................... **24.00**

**Cake plate,** pedestaled, Paneled Grape patt., milk white........................ **70.00**

**Cake salver,** flat top, pattern on underside of top, 12" d....................... **80.00**

**Cake stand,** skirted, Paneled Grape patt., milk white, 11" d...................... **70.00**

**Canape set,** Paneled Grape patt., milk white, 3 pcs. ............................. **120.00**

**Candlestick,** American Hobnail patt., milk white...................................... **15.00**

**Candlesticks,** Dolphin patt., milk white, pr. ......................................... **55.00**

**Candlesticks,** Paneled Grape patt., milk white, 4" h., pr. ............................ **20.00**

**Candy dish,** cov., Beaded Grape patt., mid-20th c., milk white, 5" d. ....... **18.00**

**Candy dish,** cov., footed, Della Robbia patt., h.p. Roses & Bows decoration, milk white ......................... **50.00**

**Candy dish,** cov., three-footed, Paneled Grape patt., milk white.......... **33.00**

**Celery vase,** Paneled Grape patt., milk white...................................... **35.00**

**Cheese dish,** cov., Paneled Grape patt., milk white............................... **60.00**

**Cigarette box,** cov., Beaded Grape patt., milk white, 4 x 6"....................... **45.00**

**Champagne,** Della Robbia patt., colored trim....................................... **23.00**

**Cocktail,** Princess Feather patt., clear....................................................... **10.00**

**Compote,** 8" d., Old Quilt patt., milk white....................................................... **15.00**

**Compote,** 9" d., crimped edge, Paneled Grape patt., milk white.......... **40.00**

**Compote,** 9" d., crimped edge, footed, Paneled Grape patt., milk white................................................... **77.00**

**Creamer & cov. sugar bowl,** Della Robbia patt., milk white, pr. ............... **21.00**

**Creamer & cov. sugar bowl,** Paneled Grape patt., 6½" h., pr. ...................... **35.00**

**Cruet w/original stopper,** Old Quilt patt., milk white................................. **20.00**

**Cruet w/original stopper,** Paneled Grape patt., milk white...................... **20.00**

**Cup & saucer,** Paneled Grape patt., milk white...................................... **22.00**

**Egg cup,** chicken w/red trim, milk white....................................................... **14.00**

**Egg cup,** two-handled chicken, footed, milk white................................. **30.00**

**Epergne,** Paneled Grape patt., almond, 3 pcs. ..................................... **275.00**

**Epergne,** single-lily, Paneled Grape patt., milk white, 9" d. bowl base w/8" h. lily........................................... **175.00**

**Fruit bowl,** crimped rim, footed, Old Quilt patt., milk white, 9" d. ................. **45.00**

**Honey dish,** cov., low footed, Beaded Grape patt., milk white ........................ **25.00**

**Goblet,** water, American Hobnail patt... **13.00**

**Goblet,** water, footed, Beaded Grape, patt., milk white, 8 oz. ......................... 30.00

**Goblet,** water, Della Robbia patt., clear ..................................................... 18.00

**Goblet,** water, Della Robbia patt., colored trim ......................................... 25.00

**Goblet,** water, Della Robbia patt., milk white .................................................. 22.00

**Goblet,** water, Paneled Grape patt., milk white .................................................. 18.00

**Goblet,** water, footed, Paneled Grape patt., clear, 8 oz. ................................. 20.00

**Gravyboat w/underplate,** Paneled Grape patt., milk white, 2 pcs. ............ 65.00

**Honey dish,** cov., low footed, Beaded Grape patt., milk white ....................... 25.00

**Honey dish,** cov., low footed, Beaded Grape patt., 22k gold decoration ....... 35.00

**Honey dish,** cov., low footed, Beaded Grape patt., Crystal Mist w/h.p. Roses & Bows decoration, 5" l. .......... 50.00

**Ivy ball,** footed, Paneled Grape patt., milk white .................................................. 40.00

**Jardiniere,** footed, Paneled Grape patt., milk white, 5" h. ......................... 25.00

**Jardiniere,** footed, Paneled Grape patt., milk white, 6½" h. ...................... 35.00

**Parfait,** scallop-footed, Paneled Grape patt., clear ..................................... 25.00

**Pickle dish,** oval, Paneled Grape patt., milk white .................................... 20.00

**Pitcher,** juice, Paneled Grape patt., milk white, pt. ..................................... 40.00

**Pitcher,** Paneled Grape patt., milk white, 16 oz. ......................... 30.00 to 40.00

**Pitcher,** Paneled Grape patt., clear, 1 qt. ..................................................... 34.00

**Planter,** Paneled Grape patt., milk white, 5 x 9" ....................................... 42.00

**Plate,** 6" d., Della Robbia patt., clear .... 10.00

**Plate,** 6¼" d., Della Robbia patt., colored trim ........................................ 12.00

**Plate,** salad, 7½" d., Della Robbia patt., clear ...................................... 20.00

**Plate,** 8" d., Paneled Grape patt., milk white .................................................. 25.00

**Plate,** 8½" d., Paneled Grape patt., milk white ............................................. 24.00

**Plate,** 9" d., Della Robbia patt., colored trim ...................................... 30.00

**Plate,** dinner, 10½" d., Paneled Grape patt., milk white ................................. 48.00

**Plate,** torte, 14" d., Thousand Eye patt. ................................................. 40.00

**Puff box,** cov., Beaded Grape patt., clear w/h.p. Roses & Bows decoration ..................................... 23.00

**Puff box,** cov., Paneled Grape patt., milk white .......................................... 45.00

**Punch bowl base,** Old Quilt patt., milk white ............................................... 35.00

**Punch bowl base,** Paneled Grape patt., milk white ................................. 55.00

**Punch set:** punch bowl & fourteen cups; Paneled Grape patt., milk white, 15 pcs. ................................ 750.00

**Salt & pepper shakers,** flat, Old Quilt patt., milk white, pr. .......................... 25.00

**Salt & pepper shakers,** footed, Paneled Grape patt., milk white, pr. ... 22.00

**Sherbet,** Della Robbia patt., milk white ................................................. 10.00

**Sherbet,** Della Robbia patt., clear........ 20.00

**Sherbet,** Princes Feather patt., Golden Sunset, 4⅝" h. ...................... 13.00

**Sherbet,** Paneled Grape patt., milk white ................................................. 18.00

**Soap dish,** Paneled Grape patt., milk white ................................................. 65.00

**Spooner,** Paneled Grape patt., milk white, 6" l. .......................................... 35.00

**Sweetmeat,** footed, Old Quilt patt., milk white ............................................. 20.00

**Toilet bottle w/stopper,** Paneled Grape patt., milk white, 5 oz. .............. 55.00

**Tumbler,** iced tea, footed, Della Robbia patt., milk white ..................... 17.00

**Tumbler,** iced tea, Paneled Grape patt., milk white ................................. 20.00

**Vase,** 6" h., Paneled Grape patt., milk white ................................................. 16.00

**Vase,** 8" h., footed, crimped, Paneled Grape patt., milk white ...................... 55.00

**Vase,** 8" h., footed, double-crimped, Paneled Grape patt., milk white.......... 85.00

**Vase,** bud, 10" h., Paneled Grape patt., clear w/h.p. Roses & Bows decoration ..................................... 20.00

**Vase,** bud, 11" h., Paneled Grape patt., milk white ................................. 32.00

**Vase,** 11½" h., footed, bell-shaped rim, Paneled Grape patt. .................... 65.00

**Vase,** 12" h., swung-type, Paneled Grape patt., milk white ...................... 95.00

**Vase,** bud, 14" h., Paneled Grape patt., h.p. Roses & Bows decoration, milk white .......................................... 19.00

**Wine,** American Hobnail patt., cobalt blue, 4½" h. ...................................... 15.00

*Celestial & Terrestrial Table Globes*

# GLOBE MAPS

**Celestial globe,** table model, w/corrections to 1850, on rosewood stand, Maley's of London, 12" d., 17" h. (damages) .......................... **$748.00**

**Celestial globe,** mounted in a mahogany ring stand w/three curved support arms above a squatty swirled gadrooned knob over a tripod base w/square cabriole legs ending in pad feet, W. S. Jones, England, ca. 1800, 17" d., 24" h. (missing stretchers & compass) .... **2,760.00**

**Celestial & terrestrial globes,** table models, each mounted within a round ring supported on baluster- and knob-turned legs joined by stretchers, each inscribed "Joslins six-inch...(celestial/terrestrial)...globe from the best authorities, Gillman Joslin, Boston, 1840," 9" d., 9½" h., pr. (ILLUS. top) ............................. **8,625.00**

**Celestial & terrestrial globes,** each colored globe mounted on a later brass equinoctial dial on a wooden baluster-turned stem & circular molded foot, terrestrial globe dated 1848, celestial globe dated 1850, by Malby's, England, 14" h., pr........... **4,600.00**

**Celestial & terrestrial globes,** each mounted in a mahogany circular median w/a molded border & raised on three spiral-turned legs joined by arched stretchers joined at the center by a ring-turned drop, Newton's, England, calculated to the years 1830 & 1843, 20" d. globes, height to median 28½", pr........... **23,000.00**

**Celestial & terrestrial globes,** Regency period, the colored globes within grass rings mounted on a mahogany base w/three curved arms supporting the ring framed & raised on turned standards above tall tripod supports w/outswept legs centering a compass in the base, Cary's, England, dated 1816, 36" h., pr. (repairs) ................................. **27,600.00**

*Bardin's Terrestrial Globe*

**Terrestrial globe,** floor model, mounted in a later mahogany stand w/a ring- and knob-turned standard & tripod base w/spider legs, by W. & T. M. Bardin, England, w/additions to 1807, 18½" h. (ILLUS.) ................. **3,738.00**

*Terrestrial Table Globe*

**Terrestrial globe,** pocket-type, w/paper covered horizon circle, published by C. Abel-Klinger, Nurnberg, Germany, 19th c., 2½" d. ................................. **1,840.00**

**Terrestrial globe,** pocket-type, the interior lined w/celestial gores, based on globe by R. Cashee, European, w/imitation fishskin case, early 19th c., 3" d. ......................... **2,990.00**

**Terrestrial globe,** school-type, on an ebonized stand w/circular foot, marked "Terrestrial School Globe," Bacon's, late 19th c., 6" d., 12" h... **1,035.00**

**Terrestrial globe,** table model, late Regency period, "Newton's New and Improved Terrestrial Globe," corrected to 1829, England, second quarter 19th c., without stand, 12" d. ............................................. **1,035.00**

**Terrestrial globe,** table model "Fitz Globe," w/double meridian, on a black painted wrought-iron base, Ginn & Heath, America, ca. 1870, 12" d., 16" h. ................................. **2,990.00**

**Terrestrial globe,** table model, the geographical globe w/detail engraved maps of the world, ship routes, longitudinal & latitudinal lines w/names of oceans, countries, states & cities rotating within a calibrated meridian w/engraved paper of astrological calendar, the stand w/tapering baluster-and-ring turned legs w/tapering cone feet joined by ring-turned X-stretchers, J. Wilson & Sons, Albany, New York, 1828, 12" d., 18" h. (ILLUS. above)........................................... **4,025.00**

**Terrestrial globe,** hand-colored in outline, w/three decorative descriptive cartouches, the water w/ships, sea monsters &

compasses, by Mattaus Greuter, Dutch, published by R.C.A., Rome, ca. 1744, without stand, 19¼" d. ...................................... **10,350.00**

**Terrestrial globe,** table model, Victorian, on an ebonized stem & turned foot, George Philip & Son, London, England, third quarter 19th c., 10" d., 17" h. .................. **20,707.00**

**Terrestrial globe,** table model, William IV era, on a mahogany fluted stem & circular foot, by J. Wyld, England, ca. 1835, 6" d., 12" h. ..... **1,725.00**

# GRANITEWARE

*This is a name given to metal (customarily iron) kitchenware covered with an enamel coating. Featured at the 1876 Philadelphia Centennial Exposition, it became quite popular for it was lightweight, attractive and easy to clean. Although it was made in huge quantities and is still produced, it has caught the attention of a younger generation of collectors and prices have steadily risen over the past few years. There continues to be a consistent demand for the wide variety of these utilitarian articles turned out earlier in this century and rare forms now command high prices.*

### Blue and White Swirl

*Blue Swirl Candlestick*

**Baking pan,** 11" w., 15" l., 2½" depth .. **$175.00**
**Berry bucket,** cov., 7" d., 6½" h. ......... **200.00**
**Bowl,** mixing, 5" d., 2¼" h. .................... **60.00**
**Candlestick,** 5" d., 2" h. (ILLUS.) ....... **650.00**

*Labeled Coffeepot*

**Coffee boiler,** cov., 10¾" d., 13" h. .... **275.00**

**Coffeepot,** cov., labeled "Cream City Tulip Ware," 6¾" d., 10½" h. (ILLUS. above) .................................. **250.00**

**Cream can,** tin cov., 6½" d., 11" h, ..... **425.00**

**Cup & saucer,** 4¼" d., 2¼" h. cup, 6" d. saucer........................................ **100.00**

**Dish pan,** round, 17¾" d., 5¼" h. ....... **125.00**

**Double boiler,** cov., 8" d., 9" h., 3 pcs. ..................................................... **275.00**

**Kettle,** cov., Berlin-style, 6¼" d., 6" h.... **200.00**

**Measuring cup,** 6¼" d., 10½" h. ........ **400.00**

**Milk pan,** 9½" d., 2" h. ......................... **50.00**

**Mold,** Turkish head turban, 9¾" d., 4¾" h. .................................................... **500.00**

**Muffin pan,** 12 cup ......................... **1,000.00**

**Mug,** railroad advertisement for C.G.W.Ry, Chicago, Great Western Railroad, 2¾" d., 2¾" h. ..................... **200.00**

**Pitcher,** 6" h., 5" d., convex ................ **300.00**

**Plate,** 9¼" d., 1" h. ................................ **75.00**

**Pudding pan,** 9¾" d., 3½" h. ................ **50.00**

**Skillet,** 10¼" d., 2" h., 8½" handle ...... **200.00**

**Skimmer,** 4¾" d., 11" handle.............. **175.00**

**Soap dish,** hanging, 6" w., 4" h., 4¼" depth.................................................... **200.00**

**Strainer,** triangular sink, 9¾" d., 2½" h. .................................................... **300.00**

**Sugar bowl,** cov., bulbous, 4½" d., 5" h. ..................................................... **500.00**

**Teakettle,** cov., wood & wire handle, 10" d., 7" h. .......................................... **300.00**

**Tea strainer,** screen bottom, 4" w., ¾" depth ......................................... **225.00**

## Blue Diamond Ware (Iris Blue & White Swirl)

*Diamond Ware Berry Bucket*

**Baking pan,** 10½" w., 14¾" l., 2¼" depth................................................... **275.00**

**Berry bucket,** cov., wood & wire handle, 6¾" d., 7¼" h. (ILLUS. above)................................................. **350.00**

**Coffeepot,** cov., goose neck, 4½" d., 8½" h. ................................................. **425.00**

**Colander,** 9¾" d., 5" h. ....................... **300.00**

**Cream can,** cov., 4" d., 7¾" h. ............ **600.00**

**Custard cup,** 4¼" d., 2¼" h.............. **100.00**

**Dipper,** Windsor, 8¾" d., 12" handle .. **125.00**

**Double boiler,** cov., 6½" d., 9" h., 3 pcs. ..................................................... **300.00**

**Funnel,** bulbous, 4¼" d., 3¼" h. ......... **225.00**

**Measuring cup,** 3" d., 4½" h. ............ **625.00**

**Mustard pot,** cov., 2¾" d., 4" h. ...... **1,000.00**

**Pitcher,** water, 7½" h., 5" d. ............... **500.00**

**Platter,** oval, 11" x 14", 1" depth......... **300.00**

**Salt shaker,** 1½" d., 3¼" h.............. **1,200.00**

**Soap dish,** hanging, 6" w., 3¼" h., 4¼" depth ......................................... **225.00**

**Tea steeper,** 3¼" d., 3½" h. ................ **375.00**

**Tumbler,** 3¼" d., 3½" h...................... **325.00**

## Brown and White Swirl

**Baking pan,** corrugated bottom, 10" w., 14" l., 2¼" depth .................. **200.00**

**Coffee biggin,** cov., tin biggin, 3½" d., 7¼" h. .............................. **2,000.00**

**Coffeepot,** cov., 6½" d., 9½" h. .......... **350.00**

**Colander,** footed, 10¼" d., 4¼" h. ...... **300.00**

**Cream can,** tin cov., 4¾" d., 9½" h. .... **600.00**

*Brown & White Cuspidor*

*Chrysolite Swirl Mixing Bowl*

**Cuspidor,** 7¾" d., 4½" h. (ILLUS.)...... **375.00**
**Double boiler,** cov., 8" d., 8½" h.,
3 pcs. ............................................. **350.00**
**Funnel,** bulbous, 6" d., 5½" h. ........... **250.00**
**Kettle,** cov., Berlin-style, wood & wire
handle, 6¼" d., 4¼" h. ..................... **300.00**
**Lunch bucket,** oval, 8½" w., 7" h.,
6¾" depth, 3 pcs. .......................... **1,000.00**
**Pail,** water, 9½" d., 8" h. ...................... **225.00**
**Pie pan,** 8¾" d., 1" h. ......................... **100.00**
**Skillet,** cast iron, 10¼" d., 2" h., 6½"
handle ............................................ **300.00**
**Spooner,** 4" d., 5¼" h. ..................... **1,100.00**

### Chrysolite and White Swirl (Dark Green and White Swirl)

**Berry bucket,** tin cov., 6" d., 5¾" h. ... **325.00**
**Bowl,** mixing, 7" d., 3¼" h. (ILLUS.
top next column) .............................. **125.00**
**Coffeepot,** cov., 5¾" d., 9½" h. .......... **375.00**
**Colander,** footed, 10½" d., 4½" h. ...... **450.00**
**Cup & saucer,** 4" d., 2" h. cup, 6" d.
saucer............................................... **125.00**

**Double boiler,** cov., 9" d. base, 7" h.,
3 pcs. (ILLUS. below) ...................... **400.00**
**Kettle,** cov., Berlin-style, 7½" d.,
5½" h. .............................................. **250.00**
**Mug,** 6" d., 5¼" h. .............................. **100.00**
**Pie pan,** 8¾" d., 1" h. ......................... **100.00**
**Pitcher,** water, 9" h., 5½" d ................. **350.00**
**Pudding pan,** 8½" d., 3" h. ................... **75.00**
**Skillet,** 10¼" d., 2" h., 8" handle ......... **275.00**
**Spoon,** 2¼" d., 15" l. handle .............. **125.00**
**Syrup,** nickel flip-top cov., 3½" d.,
7½" h. ............................................ **1,250.00**
**Teakettle,** cov., 9¾" d., 8¼" h............. **700.00**
**Wash basin,** 12" d., 3¼" h. ................. **150.00**

### Cobalt Blue and White Swirl

**Berry bucket,** tin cov., 7½" d., 7¾" h. .. **300.00**
**Candlestick,** 5¼" d., 2¼" h.................. **900.00**
**Chamber pot,** cov., 7½" d., 5¾" h.
(ILLUS. top next page) ..................... **300.00**
**Coffee boiler,** cov., 9½" d., 12" h. ...... **350.00**
**Coffeepot,** cov., wooden handle,
5½" d., 9" h. .................................... **375.00**
**Coffeepot,** cov., wooden handle,
5¾" d., 9½" h. ................................. **350.00**

*Chrysolite Double Boiler*

*Cobalt Blue Chamber Pot*

**Cream can,** cov., 5" d., 9" h................. 650.00
**Cuspidor,** 11¼" d., 5" h......................... 400.00
**Dipper,** Windsor, 5¼" d., 9½" handle ... 175.00
**Kettle,** cov., preserve, 11" d., 6½" h..... 175.00
**Ladle,** 3" d., 10" handle........................ 85.00
**Loaf pan,** 4¾" w., 9¾" l., 3" depth ...... 300.00
**Measuring cup,** 3¾" d., 4½" h. .......... 500.00
**Muffin pan,** 6 cup ............................ 1,000.00
**Muffin pan,** 8 cup ............................. 650.00
**Pie pan,** 9½" d., 1" h. ......................... 95.00
**Platter,** oval, 8" w., 12" l., 1" depth ..... 275.00
**Pudding pan,** 8½" d., 3½" h. ............... 75.00
**Skillet,** 9¾" d., 1½" h., 9½" handle ..... 300.00
**Skimmer,** ladle, 4" d., 9" handle ......... 175.00
**Soap dish,** hanging, 6" w., 3¼" h.,
　4¼" depth ...................................... 250.00
**Sugar bowl,** cov., 4½" d., 6¼" h...... 1,100.00

*Bulbous Syrup Container*

**Syrup,** cov., bulbous body w/nickel
　flip-top cover, 4¼" d., 7½" h.
　(ILLUS.) ...................................... 1,200.00
**Tea Steeper,** tin cov., 4¾" d., 4¾" h... 250.00
**Tumbler,** 3¼" d., 3½" h....................... 350.00

## Emerald Ware (Green and White Swirl)

**Bowl,** mixing, 11¼" d., 5½" h. ............. 250.00
**Coffee boiler,** cov., 8½" d., 11¾" h. ... 375.00

*Footed Emerald Colander*

**Colander,** footed, 10¼" d., 4¼" h.
　(ILLUS.) ............................................ 850.00
**Dipper,** Windsor, 6½" d., 9¼" handle .. 325.00
**Double boiler,** cov., 6¼" d., 9" h.,
　3 pcs. .............................................. 375.00
**Kettle,** lipped, preserve, 9" d., 4" h. .... 180.00
**Ladle,** 3¾" d., 10" handle.................... 180.00
**Mug,** 2¾" d., 2¾" h. ........................... 125.00
**Pail,** water, 10½" d., 9" h..................... 225.00
**Pie pan,** 9" d., 1¼" h. ........................... 90.00
**Pudding pan,** 10" d., 3¾" h. ............... 100.00
**Skillet,** 10" d., 2" h., 8" handle ........... 350.00
**Skimmer,** 5" d., 11" handle................. 225.00
**Spoon,** 2¼" d., 13" h.......................... 100.00
**Tea steeper,** cov., 4¼" d., 6¼" h. ....... 400.00

## Red and White Swirl

**Berry bucket,** tin cov., 6¼" d.,
　6½" h. ............................................ 2,000.00
**Bowl,** mixing, swirl inside & out, light
　weight, ca. 1960s, 12¼" d., 6" h. ........ 40.00
**Coffeepot,** cov., 5¼" d., 8½" h. ....... 1,400.00
**Coffeepot,** cov., goose neck,
　unattached cover, light weight, ca.
　1960s, 5" d., 8" h. ........................... 100.00
**Cream can,** tin cov., 5" d., 9¼" h. ..... 2,000.00
**Ladle,** 3½" d., 10" handle................... 400.00
**Mug,** light weight, ca. 1950s, 3¾" d.,
　3½" h. .............................................. 30.00
**Pail,** water, 11½" d., 8½" h.............. 1,600.00
**Pie pan,** 9¾" d., 1" h. ......................... 300.00
**Platter,** oval, swirl inside & out, light
　weight, ca. 1950s, 13" w., 17½" l.,
　1¼" depth ......................................... 140.00
**Pudding pan,** 8½" d., 3" h. ................. 300.00
**Skillet,** swirl inside & out, light weight,
　ca. 1960, 8" d., 1¼" h., 6" handle ....... 80.00
**Wash basin,** 12¼" d., 3½" h. .............. 600.00

## Gray (Mottled)

**Baking pan,** 12" w., 18¼" l., 2½"
　depth................................................. 60.00
**Berry bucket,** tin cov., 3¼" d., 3¼" h. .. 175.00
**Chamber pot,** cov., 7½" d., 6" h. .......... 40.00

*Pewter Trimmed Coffeepot*

**Coffee biggin,** cov., tin biggin, 3½" d.,
6½" h. ............................................... **275.00**

**Coffee flask,** cov., screw-on cover,
4½" w., 6¼" h., 2" depth .................. **275.00**

**Coffeepot,** cov., goose neck, 5¾" d.,
9¾" h. ............................................... **85.00**

**Coffeepot,** cov., bulbous body
w/goose neck spout, pewter trim,
3½" d., 5¾" h. (ILLUS. above) .......... **500.00**

**Cream can,** tin cover, mottled steel
ware, w/label, reads "EL-AN-GE,"
Boston ............................................. **225.00**

**Dipper,** 4½" d., 9" handle...................... **40.00**

**Double boiler,** cov., 7" d., 8½" h.,
3 pcs. ............................................... **70.00**

**Dust pan,** 12¾" w., 14" l. .................... **600.00**

**Kettle,** tin cov., Berlin-style, 8" d.,
6" h. .................................................. **50.00**

**Loaf pan,** 5" w., 9½" l., 3¼" depth ........ **45.00**

**Lunch bucket,** oval, 6½" w., 9" l.,
8" h., 3 pcs. ..................................... **300.00**

**Measuring Cup,** embossed "For
Household Use Only,"
w/measurement numbers, 4" d.,
5½" h. ............................................... **150.00**

**Mold,** tin cov., melon-shaped, 5" w.,
6½" l., 3¼" h. .................................... **150.00**

**Muffin pan,** 8 cup ................................ **60.00**

**Mug,** 4" d., 4" h. .................................. **35.00**

**Pail,** water, 11" d., 9" h....................... **40.00**

**Pie pan,** 7½" d., ¾" h. ........................... **25.00**

**Pitcher,** 7" h., 4½" d ........................... **125.00**

**Plate,** luncheon, 7" d. .......................... **30.00**

**Pudding pan,** 8" d., 3" h. ..................... **25.00**

**Salt box,** hanging, granite flip-top
cov., 7½" w., 11" h., 6" depth
(ILLUS. top next column) ................. **550.00**

**Salt & pepper shakers,** strap handle,
1¾" d., 3" h., pr. ............................. **1,800.00**

**Scoop,** grocer's, 5¼" w., 9¼" l. ........... **150.00**

*Hanging Salt Box*

**Skillet,** 9½" d., 2" h., 8½" handle ......... **80.00**

**Skimmer,** 3½" d., 9" handle................. **65.00**

**Spoon,** 2¼" d., 12" h............................ **30.00**

**Strainer,** toddy, perforated, shell-
shaped, w/handle, 3" d., 6" l. ............ **275.00**

**Teakettle,** cov., 8½" d., 6½" h............. **150.00**

*Teapot with Tea Strainer*

**Teapot,** tin cov., w/tea strainer,
3½" d., 5¾" h. (ILLUS.).................... **275.00**

## Solid Colors

**Berry bucket,** cov., blue, 6⅛" d.,
6¼" h. ............................................... **75.00**

**Butter carrier,** cov., oval, white
w/black trim, 8¾" w., 7" h., 6½"
depth................................................ **100.00**

**Candlestick,** solid white, scalloped
edge, 6" d., 2" h. ............................... **95.00**

**Canisters,** cov., solid blue w/white lettering "Coffee, Flour, Rice, Soda, Sugar & Tea," 4½" d., 6½" h., the set .............................................. **100.00**

**Coffee biggin,** cov., biggin, cover, & pot solid red w/black trim, 4½" d., 9½" h. .............................................. **100.00**

**Coffeepot,** cov., goose neck, solid blue, 3½" d., 5¾" h. .......................... **100.00**

**Colander,** footed, cream w/green trim, 8¾" d., 4" h. .................................. **65.00**

**Cream can,** tin cov., solid blue, 3½" d., 7" h. .................................. **125.00**

**Creamer,** solid white w/cobalt trim, 4" d., 3¾" h. .................................. **80.00**

**Custard cup,** white w/black trim, 2¼" h., 4" d. .................................. **30.00**

**Dipper,** Windsor, white w/red trim, 6¼" d., 10" handle ........................... **30.00**

**Funnel,** bulbous shape, white w/black trim, 7½" d., 4¼" h. ........................ **75.00**

**Grater,** solid blue, 3¾" d., 10" h. ........... **75.00**

**Kettle,** cov., cream w/gold trim, 10" d., 8½" h. .............................................. **30.00**

**Measuring cup,** solid blue, 3½" d., 4½" h. .............................................. **125.00**

**Mold,** ring, cream w/green trim, 10" d., 2¾" h. .............................................. **80.00**

**Muffin pan,** solid cobalt blue, 8 cup.... **175.00**

**Mug,** white w/red trim, 3" d., 3" h. ......... **25.00**

**Pie pan,** solid cobalt blue, 9½" d., 1" h. .............................................. **25.00**

**Pitcher,** water, 8" h., 5¾" d., white w/black trim........................................ **60.00**

**Plate,** 10" d., 1" h., white w/black trim ... **20.00**

**Pudding pan,** solid red w/black trim, 10" d., 3" h. ...................................... **25.00**

**Roaster,** oval, cream w/green trim, 10½" w., 17" l., 8" h. ........................... **75.00**

**Skimmer,** solid red w/black handle, 14½" l.................................................. **20.00**

**Soap dish,** hanging, solid red, 5¼" w., 5" h., 3" depth ...................................... **65.00**

**Spoon,** cream w/green handle, 2½" d., 11" l. .................................... **30.00**

**Syrup,** cov., white w/black trim, nickel flip-top cover, 3½" d., 7½" h.............. **125.00**

**Teakettle,** cov., solid red w/black trim, 8¾" d., 7½" h. ............................ **75.00**

**Teapot,** cov., bulbous body, white cobalt blue trim, 3¾" d., 4½" h............ **75.00**

**Tea steeper,** cov., solid blue, 4½" d., 5½" h. .............................................. **60.00**

**Tea strainer,** solid red, 3¾" w., 1" depth................................................. **65.00**

## Children's Items, Miniatures & Salesman's Samples

**Bowl,** child's, blue w/girl & bear, 7½" d., 1¼" h. ...................................... **40.00**

**Bread raiser,** miniature, footed solid blue, 2½" d., 1¼" h. .......................... **200.00**

**Colander,** miniature, footed, solid blue, 2¼" d., 1¾" h. .......................... **325.00**

**Colander,** miniature, footed, blue w/white specks, 2¾" d., 1¼" h. ........ **325.00**

*Graniteware Miniature Dust Pans*

**Dust pan,** miniature, blue w/white specks, 3¼" h. (ILLUS. left) ............. **160.00**

**Dust pan,** miniature, solid blue, w/handle, 4" h. (ILLUS. right)............ **160.00**

**Ladle,** miniature, white w/blue specks, 1⅛" d., 4¼" h. ...................................... **175.00**

**Mold,** miniature, solid blue, lobster flutted mold, 2½" w., 4½" h. .............. **200.00**

**Mug,** salesman's sample, brown & white swirl, 1¼" d., 1" h..................... **675.00**

**Pail,** water, salesman's sample, grey w/wooden bail handle, 3" d., 3" h...... **300.00**

**Pail,** child's, grey, embossed ABC plate, 6" d............................................. **950.00**

**Plate,** child's, white w/red trim, "Mary Had a Little Lamb," marked "Sweden," 8" d. ................................ **40.00**

**Roasting pan,** miniature, solid blue, oblong w/handle & pouring spout, 2¼" w., 4¼" l., ¾" depth .................... **95.00**

**Roasting pan,** miniature, blue w/white specks, oval, two handled, 2" w., 4" l., ½" depth .................................. **100.00**

**Sauce pan,** miniature, blue w/white specks, w/handle, 2" d., 1" depth........ **75.00**

**Skillet,** miniature, solid blue, w/handle, 3" d., ½" depth.................... **50.00**

**Spatula,** miniature, white w/blue specks, 1¼" w., 5¼" l........................ **100.00**

**Table,** child's, ABC, white trimmed in dark blue, circus ring scene & nursery rhymes, 16" w., 20" l., 17½" h. .............................................. **250.00**

**Teakettle,** cov., miniature, blue, w/lid, bell shaped, 3" d., 2½" h. .................. **400.00**

**Tea set,** miniature: cov. teapot, six cups, six saucers, creamer, cov. sugar; white & blue design, teapot 5¼" h, 17 pcs. .................... **600.00**

**Tea strainer,** miniature, solid blue, w/handle, 2¾" h. ............................. **250.00**

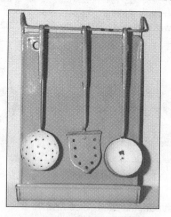

*Miniature Utensil Rack*

**Utensil rack,** miniature, solid light blue, w/three utensils, 4½" d., 6¾" h. (ILLUS.) ........................................... **500.00**

**Wash basin,** miniature, shaded blue w/floral design, "Stewart Ware," 4½" d. ............................................... **125.00**

**Wash basin,** salesman's sample, blue & white swirl, 4½" d. .......................... **125.00**

## Miscellaneous Graniteware & Related Items

**Baking pan,** Duchess Ware, large blue dots w/white & brown veins, 10¼" w., 14" l., 2¼" depth ............... **325.00**

*Covered Butter Carrier*

**Bowl,** mixing, yellow & white swirl, ca. 1950s, 9¾" d., 5" h. ........................ **30.00**

**Butter carrier,** cov., oval, aqua & white swirl, 7¾" w., 8" h., 10½" l. (ILLUS. bottom previous column) ..... **350.00**

**Canister,** cov., blue & white mottled, "Flour" in white letters, 8½" d., 10" h. ... **200.00**

**Catalog,** "Agate Iron Ware, Lalance & Grosjean Manufacturing Co.," w/price listings, dated 1889 ............. **300.00**

**Chamber pail,** cov., Bluebelle Ware, blue shading to lighter blue back to blue, 9½" d., 10¼" h. .................. **150.00**

*Duchess Ware Coffee Boiler*

**Coffee boiler,** cov., Duchess Ware, large blue dots w/white & brown veins, 10" d., 12½" h. (ILLUS.) ......... **375.00**

**Coffeepot,** tin cov., light blue & white mottled, 3½" d., 5½" h. ..................... **300.00**

**Cream can,** tin cov., Onyx Ware, brown & white mottled, 5¼" d., 9" h.. **100.00**

**Cup & saucer,** Thistle Ware, deep violet shading to a lighter violet, 4¼" d., 2¼" cup, 6" d. saucer ............. **60.00**

**Cuspidor,** blue & white mottled, 8¼" d., 5" h. ...................................... **225.00**

**Dipper,** Windsor, Shamrock Ware, dark green to a lighter green back to a dark green, 4" d., 2½" h. .................. **50.00**

**Funnel,** canning, blue & white mottled, 5¼" d., 3" h. ........................ **120.00**

**Gravy boat,** footed, blue & white mottled, 3½" w., 8" l., 4½" h.............. **350.00**

**Loaf pan,** blue & white mottled, 6" w., 11½" l., 3" depth ............................. **200.00**

**Lunch bucket,** Thistle Ware, deep violet shading to a lighter violet, round, 7¼" d., 9½" h., 3 pcs. ............ **275.00**

**Mold,** aqua & white swirl, tube-style turban, 8¼" d., 3½" h. ...................... **350.00**

*1904 Worlds Fair Mug*

**Mug,** advertising, "Worlds Fair & Exposition, St. Louis, 1904," 3" d. 2¾" h. (ILLUS.) ................................ **175.00**

**Pie pan,** Duchess Ware, large blue dots w/white & brown veins, 10" d., 1" h. ................................................ **60.00**

**Pitcher,** water, 8½" h., 6" d., Snow on the Mountain, white w/light blue swirl ................................................ **150.00**

**Plate,** 10¼" d., 1" h., yellow & white swirl, ca. 1950s .............................. **30.00**

**Sauce pan,** Bluebelle, blue shading to a light blue back to blue, lipped w/handle, 4½" d., 2½" h. ..................... **50.00**

**Scoop,** thumb, blue & white mottled, 3" d., 6" h. ........................................ **325.00**

**Skimmer,** hand-type, blue & white fine mottled, 5" w., 5¼" h. ........................ **350.00**

**Soap dish,** hanging, Onyx Ware, dark brown & white, 6" w., 3½" h., 4" depth ................................................ **60.00**

**Spoon,** blue & white mottled, 2¼" d., 13½" l. .............................................. **55.00**

**Syrup,** nickel flip-top cov., aqua & white swirl, 5" d., 8¾" h. ..................... **900.00**

**Teakettle,** cov., Thistle Ware, deep violet shading to a lighter violet, 8" d., 7½" h. ...................................... **225.00**

**Teapot,** cov., Shamrock Ware, dark green shading to lighter green back to a dark green, bulbous body, 7" d., 7¼" h. .............................................. **275.00**

**Tea steeper,** cov., Thistle Ware, deep violet shading to a lighter violet, 4" d., 4½" h. ...................................... **150.00**

# HOLIDAY COLLECTIBLES

*For collectors, Christmas offers the widest selection of desirable collectibles; however,* other national and religious holidays were also noted with the production of various items which are now gaining popularity. Halloween-related pieces such as candy containers, lanterns, decorations and costumes are the most sought-after category after Christmas. Other holidays such as Thanksgiving, Easter and the 4th of July have relatively few collectibles common for collectors. Also see: CHRISTMAS COLLECTIBLES.

## EASTER

**Candy egg box,** "Schuller Chocolate," illustrated w/rabbits & chicks, 3 x 4 x 7" ........................................... **$9.00**

## HALLOWEEN

**Costume,** Golden Princess, size 6, ca. 1940s ...................................... **20.00**

**Costume,** Little Golden Books, Pokey Little Puppy, Collegeville, w/original box ................................................ **20.00**

**Costume,** Pirate, size 4, ca, 1940s ....... **20.00**

**Cut-out set,** haunted house, 1940s, Hallmark .............................................. **25.00**

**Jack o'lantern,** cardboard, double-faced w/candle inside, originally folded, 5½ x 7" .................................. **85.00**

**Lantern,** glass & metal, metal base & handle w/painted glass pumpkin-shaped lantern, battery-operated, made in British Hong Kong, w/original box, 4½" h., 3½" w. (minor paint chips to glass, box has dents & tears) ................................................ **39.00**

**Mold,** chocolate, tin, in the shape of a witch .................................................. **45.00**

# HORN

*The hard keratinous substance that forms the horns and hoofs of animals can be worked to produce a wide range of items, both utilitarian and decorative. Powder horns are probably the most readily recognized items, but spoons, tumblers, jewelry and haircombs also abound. The horn furniture, popular in this country during the 1880s, incorporates whole animal horns of the Texas Longhorn and other steers to form the framework. Excluding furniture, most horn items, even those with scratch-carved decoration, are moderately priced.*

*Rhinoceros Horn Budai*

**Figure of Budai,** rhinoceros horn, the obese God of Happiness carved seated, his body enveloped in loosely draped robes, one hand resting on his upturned right leg, the other hidden beneath the long sleeves, his round wide face w/a jovial smile below his bald head, the base solid, 17th c., 2¾" h. (ILLUS.) .............. **$25,300.00**

**Libation cup,** irregular flaring form w/four carved *qilong* clutching the lip, the body w/a taotie mask design, w/a wide scroll handle, a *qilong* scampering up the side, on three monster mask feet, China, 17th c., 4" h. (feet reduced, chips).............. **7,450.00**

**Libation cup,** rhinoceros horn, deeply carved & undercut w/flowering prunus, gnarled pine & leafy bamboo stalks & branches, intermeshing around the sides, issuing from rockwork, one side w/a cascading waterfall, the interior rim w/a *chilong* confronting prunus branches, orangish brown, China, 17th - 18th c., 3¾" h. (splits, chips) ........................ **6,325.00**

**Libation cup,** rhinoceros horn, short irregular oblong shape, the exterior w/two carved gnarled knotty pine branches spreading over the sides & forming the foot, dark brown color, China, 17th c., 4¾" l. ..................... **2,415.00**

**Libation cup,** jug-form, elegant archaic bronze-form, raised on three finely tapered legs, delicately carved w/two roundels enclosing cloud scrolls, reserved on a dense diaper band, beneath the widely flaring rim & spout, w/two upright posts at the center of the edges, rich golden toned rhinoceros horn, China, 17th - 18th c., 5⅜" h. (legs restored) ..... **16,100.00**

**Spill vase,** of a natural contour, carved in high-relief on one side w/four Immortals & two attendants in a rocky grotto gazing at a scroll painting, beneath a calligraphic inscription, warm reddish brown, China, 18th c., 5½" (splits, age cracks) ......................................... **4,025.00**

# ICART PRINTS

The works of Louis Icart, the successful French artist whose working years spanned the Art Nouveau and Art Deco movements, first became popular in the United States shortly after World War I. His limited edition etchings were much in vogue during those years when the fashion trends were established in Paris. These prints were later relegated to the closet shelves and basements but they have now re-entered the art market and are avidly sought by collectors. Listed by their American titles, all prints are framed unless otherwise noted.

**Behind the Fan,** 1922, 14¾ x 19" (laid-down, slight margin soiling) ... **$1,450.00**

**Carmen,** 1927, 13½ x 20" ................ **1,350.00**

**Conchita,** 1929, 14 x 21" (loose sheet, glue residue, mat burn) ....... **1,380.00**

**Girl in Crinoline,** 1937, 19½ x 23½" .. **1,750.00**

**Lady of the Camellias,** 1927, 16¾ x 21" oval (loose sheet, margins trimmed) ........................................ **1,380.00**

**Pink Lady,** 1933, 8⅝ x 11⅜" .......... **1,100.00**

**Recollections,** 1928, framed, 12 x 17" ...................................... **1,200.00**

**Youth,** 1930, 15¾ x 24" (age darkened) ..................................... **2,588.00**

# ICONS

*Icon is the Latin word meaning likeness or image and is applied to small pictures meant to be hung on the iconostasis, a screen dividing the sanctuary from the main body of Eastern Orthodox churches. Examples may be found all over Europe. The Greek, Russian and other Orthodox churches developed their own styles, but the Russian contribution to this form of art is considered outstanding. The collector should be aware of reproductions.*

**Anastasis,** Russia, 19th c., 15¼ x 17¼" ................................. **$1,150.00**

*Dormition of the Holy Virgin*

**Dormition of the Holy Virgin,** finely painted, the Mother of God shown lying on her bier, the Savior holds her soul while she is depicted enthroned in heaven above within a mandala, Russia, 19th c., 13⅞ x 17½" (ILLUS.) ................. **3,737.00**

**Evangelist St. John,** the silver oklad w/a column on each side chased

w/entwined foliage, marked "Moscow, 1781," 10 x 12" ............. **2,875.00**

**Holy Trinity,** Russia, 19th c., 10½ x 12¼" ................................... **1,092.00**

**Kazan Mother of God,** w/silver oklad repoussé & chased w/scrolls & foliage, marked "1848," Russia, 11¼ x 13" ..................................... **2,587.00**

**Quadripartite,** painted w/the Kazan Virgin, St. Nicholas, St. George Slaying the Dragon & the Decollation of St. John the Baptist, Russia, 19th c., 12⅛ x 13⅞" ....................... **1,495.00**

**Raising the Cross,** Russia, 19th c., 14¾ x 17⅜" .................................. **1,380.00**

**Resurrection with Feasts,** w/metal oklad, Russia, 19th c., 17⅜ x 21" .. **1,840.00**

**St. John,** Russia, 19th c., 14 x 21" .. **1,380.00**

**Virgin of Kazan,** w/a gilded silver oklad, marked "Moscow, 1893," 9⅛ x 11" ......................................... **1,360.00**

**Virgin of Tenderness,** Russia, 19th c., 19 x 24¾" ...................................... **2,875.00**

*Vladimir Mother of God*

**Vladimir Mother of God,** Russia, 19th c., 20¼ x 27¼" (ILLUS.) ........ **2,587.00**

# INDIAN ARTIFACTS & JEWELRY

**Basket,** Makah/Nootka, pottery, polychrome, rectangular form, linear & pictorial decoration, 4½ x 10", 7" h. ................................................ **$144.00**

**Bowl,** Apache, basketry, flat base & flaring sides, woven willow & blackened devil's claw, 14" d., 4½" (stitch loss & staining) ...................... **230.00**

**Bowl,** Hopi, pottery, polychrome, low shouldered form, 10¼" d., 2⅛" h. ..... **200.00**

**Bowl,** Hopi, pottery, polychrome, shallow body, painted on interior w/stylized dot & parrot motif in dark brown & brick over an orange clay body, 9⅝" d., 2½" h. ....................... **200.00**

**Bowl,** Hopi, basketry, coiled, flat base, polychrome pictorial decoration, 8" h. ..................................... **259.00**

**Bowl,** Maidu, basketry, coiled, flat base, deep form, woven of redwood & willow, 5¼" h. ....................... **431.00**

**Bowl,** Panamint, basketry, coiled, globular form, ticked rim finish, 3¾" h. ............................................. **288.00**

**Bowl,** Pomo, basketry, coiled, shouldered oval body, woven of redbud & willow, 2¾" d., 1¼" h. ........ **230.00**

**Bowl,** San Ildefonso Pueblo, blackware, black on black, matte painted decoration painted signature on base "Tonita," 8¼" d., 3¼" h. (minor abrasions) .............................. **633.00**

**Box,** cov., San Ildefonso Pueblo, blackware, black-on-matte paint decoration, inscribed on base "Juanita," 2½ x 3¾ x 6½" (abrasions, minor clay loss) ................................ **288.00**

**Bracelet,** Navajo, silver, incised & stamped decoration, 1⅝" w. ............. **489.00**

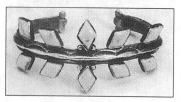

*Silver & Turquoise Navajo Bracelet*

**Bracelet,** Navajo, silver & turquoise, stamp decorated band supporting diamond-cut stones, teardrop silver beads at end, 1¼" w. (ILLUS.) ........... **431.00**

**Canteen,** Tesque Pueblo, pottery, polychrome, dark ivory slip over a red clay body, black & orange paint decoration, 9" h. .............................. **345.00**

**Concho belt,** Zuni, silver & mosaic link-type, composed of fourteen circular silver disks, each inlaid w/a stone 'rainbow man' image, composed of jet, coral & turquoise, 30" l. (minor inlay loss) ..................... **431.00**

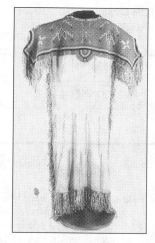

*Beaded Sioux Dress*

**Dress,** woman's, Sioux, beaded & fringed w/light blue background yoke, enhanced w/feather, arrow, cross, triangle & geometric designs in primary colors (ILLUS.) .............. **8,500.00**

**Drum,** Pueblo, wood & hide, polychrome, painted black w/shades of yellow, 6¼" h. .............................. **200.00**

*Cochiti Pueblo Figurines*

**Figure,** Cochiti Pueblo, pottery, polychrome, seated woman holding bowl, pierced ears, black & brick red paint decoration over dark cream slip, 8" h. (ILLUS. left) ...................... **920.00**

**Figure,** Cochiti Pueblo, pottery, polychrome, standing animal, pierced mouth & tail, black & brick red paint decoration over pinkish cream slip, 9½" l., 8¼" h. (ILLUS. right) ................................................ **863.00**

**Jar,** Cochiti Pueblo, pottery, polychrome, indented base, ivory slip over orange clay body, black pictorial & stylized geometric paint decoration, red painted base & inner lip, w/tag that reads "Indian Market...Golden Gate International Exposition, made by Madelina Melcher...," 6" h. .............................. **374.00**

**Jar,** San Ildefonso Pueblo, blackware, black on black, matte painted decoration, inscribed on base "Marie and Julian," 5½" h. ......................... **2,300.00**

**Moccasins,** Sioux, hide, sinew sewn, painted parfleche hard soles, decorated w/pink, white-heart red, white, apple, yellow, turquoise & navy blue beads, Reservation period........... **346.00**

*Acoma Polychrome Olla*

**Olla,** Acoma, pottery, polychrome, indented base, creamy white slip over white clay body, brick red, hatched, cross-hatched & geometric paint decoration, orange painted base & inner lip, 12" h. (ILLUS.) .... **4,600.00**

*Large Coiled Apache Olla*

**Olla,** Apache, coiled figural w/flaring cylindrical body & a flaring rim, repeating step design on the bottom, vertical stripes of connecting diamond & geometric design & repeating devil & animal figures throughout (ILLUS.) ...................... **9,200.00**

**Olla,** Cochiti Pueblo, pottery, polychrome, indented base, out-curving rim, rag-polished creamy ivory slip over an orange clay body painted w/banded geometric & stylized pictorial images of birds, deer & a hunter w/drawn bow, painted black dot over cream interior rim, painted red band near base, 6" h. (minor abrasions) .................... **575.00**

**Olla,** Zia Pueblo, pottery, polychrome, indented base, dark ivory slip over red clay body, painted in brick & black w/hatched & solid geometric & stylized foliate devices, 9¼" h. (minor surface wear)..................... **1,840.00**

**Olla,** Zia Pueblo, pottery, polychrome, indented base, dark ivory slip over red clay body, painted in black, orange & brick red w/stylized geometric, floral & parrot devices, red painted band near base & inner lip, 10½" h. (minor hairline cracks at lip, pitting & surface wear) ............. **2,415.00**

**Pin,** Zuni, silver & mosaic, in the form of a butterfly, stone against stone mosaic pattern of jet, turquoise, orange & white shell, 2 x 3" .............. **863.00**

**Pipebag,** Sioux, beaded & quilled, sinew sewn, bead stitched on both sides, Reservation period, 24" l. .... **1,150.00**

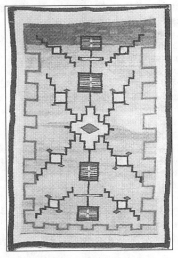

*Wool Navajo Rug*

**Rug,** Navajo, natural & aniline dyed homespun wool, woven w/a pattern of stylized Chef's blanket motifs, red, black, ivory & shaded brown, dye runs, wool loss, 37 x 52½" (ILLUS.) .. **489.00**

**Rug,** Navaho, Western Reservation, a bird centered in serrate diamonds w/feathers & serrate border, hand-carved woolen white, black, red, grey & tan, ca. 1950, 42 x 57" (stains, damaged areas) ................... 149.00

**Rug,** Navajo, Centipede patt., natural & aniline dyed homespun wool, in white, red, sand & black, 31 x 63" (soiling) ............................................. 200.00

**Rug,** Navajo, natural & aniline dyed homespun wool, black, white & shaded brown, 41 x 65" (wool loss).. 173.00

**Rug,** Navajo, natural & aniline dyed homespun wool, multicolored geometric devices against a shaded brownish grey field, 44 x 66" (wool loss & staining) ............................... 403.00

**Rug,** Navajo, natural & aniline dyed homespun & commercial wool, violet, red, black & white, 41½ x 71" (dye runs) ........................................ 690.00

**Saddle blanket,** Navajo, natural & aniline dyed homespun wool, black, white, burgundy & grey, 27½ x 38½" (wool loss soiling) ............................... 87.00

**Saddle blanket,** Navajo, woven, natural & aniline dyed homespun wool, ivory & dark brown, 28½ x 50" (wool loss & staining)........................ 173.00

**Tray,** Pima, basketry, coiled, broad flaring walls, expanding fretwork pattern, 16¾" d., 4¾" h. ................... 748.00

**Vessel,** Cochiti, figural, pottery, polychrome, animal-form, pierced mouth, black & brick red paint decoration over rag-polished creamy ivory slip, lug handle on one side, 5¼" h. ........................................... 546.00

**Weaving,** Navajo, pictorial, "Yei-bichai," natural & aniline dyed homespun wool, red, green, pale orange, dark & shaded brown against an ivory field, 39½ x 78" (minor soiling & staining) .............. 1,093.00

**Weaving,** Navajo, pictorial, "Yei-bichai," natural & aniline dyed homespun wool, 51 x 83½" (dye runs & staining)............................... 518.00

**Whimsey,** Pima, basketry, coiled stylized joined cup & saucer, 3½" h... 144.00

# IVORY

**Cricket cages,** mesh-like w/hand-carved flowers w/long sienna tassels, suspended, China, pr. .... $2,250.00

*Ivory Table Screen*

**Figure of Buddha,** seated in *dhyanasanya* & w/robe draped across one shoulder, w/downcast eyes, the hair in tight small curls, on double lotus throne w/beaded edge, China,17th c., 5½" h. ..................... 3,450.00

**Screens,** table, each of rectangular outline, depicting an immortal on lotus throne at the waters edge, another immortal approaching the shore while standing on a leaf, a stand of bamboo & rockwork in the background, a small bird in flight holding a strand of beads, the screens mirror images, China 4¾" h., 3⅞" (ILLUS. of one above).............................................. 2,990.00

**Seal box,** cov., cubical form, well-painted to a rich honey color, the removable cover carved in low-relief w/a coiled blunt-nosed dragon, the edges w/incurvate corners & beading at the lip, China, Kangxi Period, 2" h. ................................. 2,070.00

# JADE

**Bowl,** 2½" d., the rounded sides flaring up from the small flat circular base, w/incurved lip, carved w/three *chilongs* in high-relief clambering over the rim, their tails trailing around the sides, mottled greenish white, China, Song Dynasty ...... $10,350.00

**Bowl,** 4¾" d., wide shallow sides thinly carved as a flowerhead w/thin radiating & fluted petals on a flared foot, bright spinach green, China, 18th c. ........................................... **2,300.00**

**Bowls,** 4½" d., a small footring supporting the deep gently flaring sides, thin translucent pale greenish white, China, pr. ........................... **7,762.00**

**Bowls,** 5½" d., deep wide flaring sides on a thin footring, translucent greenish white, China, pr. .............. **3,450.00**

**Box,** cov., figural, model of a quail, overall incised overlapping feathers, the well-fitted body w/oval-shaped hollow cavity, the underside carved w/claws in low relief, white, China, 18th c., 4" l ................................. **16,100.00**

**Box,** cov., figural, carved as a standing crane w/the hollowed-out body forming the box, incised w/over-lapping feathers, the head turned back, a leafy *lingzhi* trailing from its open beak, two smaller cranes at its feet, mottled green w/streaks of dark brown on one side, China, 5⅞" h. .............................. **6,612.00**

**Cup,** deep rounded bowl on a small footring, the sides w/three well-carved & reticulating *chilong* grasping the vessel lip, even greenish white, Ming Dynasty, China, 3¾" w. ............................. **2,530.00**

**Dagger handle,** of tapering form, well-carved as an open-jawed horse head, the ears held back & mane swept to one side, opposite the bifurcated rim w/flowering floral sprays, pierced to receive a blade, now mounted on a lucite stand, spinach green, Moghul, China, 17th c., 4¾" l ................................. **6,900.00**

**Dish,** leaf-shaped, a scalloped grape form, issuing from a leaf stem w/an insect & a cluster of grapes on the interior & incised veins, the exterior w/faint veining, translucent icy white, China, 5" l. ....................................... **862.00**

**Dish,** thinly carved as a six-petaled blossom gently flaring from a foot rim enclosing an incised seal mark of "feng hua," the stone of pale translucent color, China, Yuan/Ming Dynasty, 6¾" d. (ILLUS. top next column) ........................................ **5,750.00**

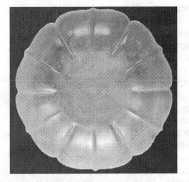

*Jade Foliate Dish*

**Figure of a Meiren,** the demure lady wearing long robes falling in pleated folds, a mantle covering the shoulders & draped over the head & the elaborate coif, wearing a double beaded necklace w/pendant, the hands clasped at the waist, the partially translucent stone in pale lavender & green, China, 7¼" h. ...... **2,530.00**

**Figure of an Immortal,** the stern faced man w/a balding head, bushy eyebrows & beard, w/long pendulous earlobes, standing wrapped in robes falling in uneven pleated folds, on a wave-form circular base, lavender & pale green, China, 8½" h. ................................. **4,370.00**

**Figure group,** a recumbent horse w/legs tucked beneath, the head outstretched w/ears laid back & mane falling on either side in wavy tufts, the tail flicked to one side, a recumbent foal to one side, icy white, China, 18th c., 3⅜" l. ........... **2,760.00**

*Jade Koro*

**Koro (incense burner),** cov., the wide & deep slightly flaring cylindrical body w/flanged rim, raised on three scrolled monster mask feet, carved around the sides w/a band of confronted archaistic birds, interrupted by three loose rings suspended from peony blossoms extending onto the rim, the domed & tiered cover reticulated w/floral & dragon cartouches, the upper tier w/six upright bloom & ring handles, beneath the reticulated dragon knob picked out in apple green, pale green, China, minute chips, 7¾" h. (ILLUS. bottom previous page)...... **5,175.00**

**Marriage bowl,** the low sides elaborately carved w/alternating registers of scrolling blooms & tall Indian lotus blossoms in high-relief interrupted by butterfly-form loop handles, the base w/a central square of trefoil palmettes enclosed by four floriform pad feet, white, China, 18th c., 8½" d............................... **9,775.00**

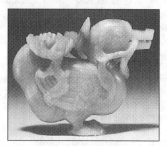

*Model of a Jade Duck*

**Model of a duck,** the stylized bird standing & holding a branch of blossoming lotus in the beak, the swept-back wings closely held to the body w/feathers depicted in archaistic-style, the greyish celedon stone w/russet patches, 17th c., 4" h. (ILLUS.) ...................................... **3,450.00**

**Model of an elephant,** realistically carved standing on a cloud scroll base, sagging under its weight, carved w/concentric folds of skin around the legs & neck, the head w/pendent ears, pointed tusks & slender trunk turned to one side, opaque pale green w/patches of white & grey, China, 17th c., 5" h. (fissures) .................................... **20,700.00**

**Stein,** cov., pale green baluster-form body w/a slip-on domed cover & double-scroll jade handle, on a short flaring ring foot w/a reeded gold mount, the handle wrapped w/gold leaves, gold baluster finial, Europe, early 20th c., 7¼" h. ...................... **4,025.00**

**Teapot,** cov., rectangular section on raised foot, carved on the long sides w/a leafy peony between borders of overlapping petals, flanked by the spout & handle elaborately carved w/scrolling foliate vines in relief, each flanked by pendent stalks, the cover w/further overlapping petals radiating from the stepped flora-form knob, translucent white, China, 18th c., 7¼" l., 4½" h................... **18,400.00**

**Vase,** 6⅝" h., archaic *gu*-form w/a lobed flaring neck, carved in high-relief w/a long sinuous scaly dragon in pursuit of a "flaming pearl," clambering up the sides amid tall *lingzhi* above foaming waves carved around the base, pale celadon green, China, 19th c. .................... **4,600.00**

**Vase,** 6¾" h., archaistic-style, footed wide ovoid body tapering to a narrow molded mouth, decorated w/a dense frieze of numerous mythical animals interweaving amid interlocking scrollwork, above a further smaller band of hooked scrolls, volutes & masks, greenish grey suffused w/white & black riveting, China, 17th c. ........................................... **6,037.00**

**Vase,** 8" h., cov., wide pear-shaped body on a narrow flaring footring, skillfully carved w/a continuous looped ropework design around the base, the thick cylindrical neck carved w/four mask-form handles w/loose rings, below a slightly flaring lipped rim, the domed cover w/an openwork sinuous three-clawed dragon amid clouds, white, China, 18th c. ........................................... **20,700.00**

**Wine cup,** gently rounded sides w/a flat rim, counter-sunk base, celadon green w/faint russet streaks, six-character Qianlong mark on base, China, 3³⁄₁₆" d. ............................... **2,300.00**

---

# JEWELRY

## ANTIQUE (1800-1920)

**Bar pin,** garnet & yellow gold (18k), Arts & Crafts-style, centered by an oval garnet within pierced mount, highlighted by grey & yellow pearl terminals, signed "Tiffany & Co." .... **$978.00**

**Bracelet,** bangle-type, sapphire & yellow gold (14k), Art Nouveau-style, the front w/five collet-set faceted sapphires within an engraved foliate mount w/platinum accents, Rikers.. **1,150.00**

**Bracelet,** bloodstone & rose gold, centered by a bloodstone carved intaglio depicting a classical figure profile, within a textured frame, completed by a three row curb link chain, Victorian .................................. **575.00**

**Bracelet,** diamond & yellow gold (14k), composed of textured circular discs, accented by an old mine-cut diamond, safety chain w/beads, Edwardian (minor dents) .................. **575.00**

**Bracelet,** diamond, enamel & gold (18k), set w/a circular set w/rose-cut diamonds within a black enamel frame on a woven mesh bracelet, suspending a beaded tassel, Victorian (some enamel loss) ........ **1,495.00**

**Bracelet,** diamond, freshwater pearl & yellow gold (18k), Art Nouveau-style, scrolling links set w/rose-cut diamonds, highlighted by pearls, French hallmarks .......................... **1,840.00**

**Bracelet,** Scottish agate, onyx & sterling silver, adjustable buckle design connected by chased silver links, each set w/banded onyx, Victorian............................................. **978.00**

**Brooch,** yellow gold (18k) & enamel, genre scene reserve, three pendants spaced w/pearls, Victorian, w/fitted box (enamel scratches) ................. **2,070.00**

**Brooch,** Art Nouveau-style plique-a-jour enamel model of a dragonfly w/wings in shades of blue enamel w/a silver gilt body & red stone eyes, European hallmark .......................... **489.00**

**Brooch,** citrine, centered by three oval citrines within an openwork scrolling vermeil mount, Victorian..... **230.00**

**Brooch,** coral & gold (14k), depicting carved nuts, berries & leaves, w/14k gold findings, Victorian, w/original fitted box ......................................... **489.00**

**Brooch,** diamond & enamel, model of a pansy, centered by an old European-cut diamond within violet enameled petals, edged in rose-cut diamonds, signed, "Tiffany & Co.," Edwardian (minor enamel loss) ..... **7,475.00**

*Arts & Crafts Brooch*

**Brooch,** garnet & yellow gold (14k), Art Nouveau-style, centered by an oval garnet within a textured winged frame accented by a seed pearl, w/attachment for pendant watch....... **259.00**

**Brooch,** moonstone & gold, Arts & Crafts-style, set w/large oval moonstone in a gold frame w/bezel-set diamonds terminals, marked "MR" for Margaret Rogers (ILLUS. above) .. **4,600.00**

**Cameo brooch,** carved shell, depicting a female profile within a pierced frame highlighted by cultured pearls & diamonds, set in platinum w/gold pin stem, Edwardian............ **1,035.00**

**Cameo brooch,** shell, depicting a lady in profile within a seed pearl frame set in yellow gold (14k), Victorian (minor solder & veining)................... **200.00**

*Cameo Brooch*

**Cameo brooch,** shell, depicting an allegorical scene of a woman, children & angels within a cobalt blue enamel & gold (18k) wiretwist mount, Victorian (ILLUS.) .............. **2,760.00**

**Cameo necklace,** carved lava, composed of oval cameo portraits of women in profile, framed & suspended from a chain in gold-fill, Victorian, 17" l. (has extra link) ......... **575.00**

**Cameo necklace,** carved onyx, depicting a lady in profile within a blue & white enamel frame w/wiretwist &

*Onyx Cameo Pendant/Brooch*

bead accents w/similar rosette link chain, yellow gold (14k) mount, Victorian, 18" l .............................. **3,335.00**

**Cameo pendant/brooch,** onyx, circular design, carved to depict a royal woman within a seed pearl, set in yellow gold (14k) mount, Victorian (ILLUS. above) ..................... **633.00**

**Cuff links,** cat's eye operculum set within a yellow gold (15k) mount, Victorian, pr. ..................................... **173.00**

**Cuff links,** jade & gold (14k), Art Nouveau-style, double hinge design, each centered by a round nephrite jade within a scrolled mount, marked "Carter, Gough & Co.," pr. ................ **200.00**

**Cuff links,** yellow gold (14k), Art Nouveau-style, single oval link design, each centered by a flower in repoussé, partial hallmark, pr. .......... **316.00**

**Earrings,** yellow gold (14k), woven knot design, each enhanced by a chased scrolling design & suspending a bead drop, marked "GB," Victorian, pr. ........................... **489.00**

*Victorian Drop Earrings*

**Earrings,** yellow gold (15k), garnet & chrysolite, textured shield shape, each highlighted by two almandine garnets flanking a chrysolite, suspending bead drop, Victorian, pr. (ILLUS. bottom previous column) ..... **633.00**

**Earrings,** black & white onyx, each designed as a banded onyx shield shape, top suspending a bead, silver gilt mounts, Victorian, pr. .................. **345.00**

*Victorian Gold Locket with Star Motif*

**Locket,** yellow gold (15k), enamel & pearl, oval design, the front centered by a blue enamel & cultured pearl star motif, the reverse w/textured engraved monogram, Victorian (ILLUS.) ............................................. **633.00**

**Locket,** yellow gold (15k), oval design, the front w/applied wiretwist accented by beadwork, Victorian (dent to back, minor bead loss) ........ **345.00**

**Locket,** diamond & yellow gold (14k), Art Nouveau-style, the front designed w/a foliate motif accented by collet-set diamonds within a scrolling frame, suspended from a banded circle link chain ................ **1,093.00**

**Necklace,** banded agate, composed of beads graduating in size from 11.4 mm to 25 mm, gold-fill clasp, Victorian, 31¼" l ............................... **978.00**

**Pendant,** citrine & silver, Arts & Crafts-style, a hammered circular design, centered by a round citrine accented by wiretwist, suspended from a fine link chain, hallmark for Theodor Fahrner, 16" l. .............. **460.00**

**Pendant,** diamond & yellow gold (18k), Art Nouveau-style, octagonal design, depicting a woman in profile highlighted by a collet-set diamond, suspended from a macramé chain, signed "Vernier" ............................... **920.00**

**Pendant/brooch,** gold (14k), shield-shape, within a foliate & scrollwork mount highlighted by a round diamond, accented by beads & black enamel, Victorian ............................. **230.00**

**Pendant/pin,** designed in the shape of a heart, surrounded by seed pearls, in a yellow gold (14k) mount, Edwardian ........................................ **345.00**

*Victorian Pansy Pin*

**Pin,** bead-set rose-cut garnets within a stylized mount in gold-fill, model of a pansy, Victorian (ILLUS.) ............... **259.00**

**Pin,** diamond, polychrome enamel, Art Nouveau-style, designed as a shell depicting a woman, with gold accents & framed by guilloche enamel in shades of blue, highlighted by rose-cut diamonds, yellow gold (18k) mount, No. 2979 ..................... **2,760.00**

**Pin,** diamond, ruby & pearl, model of a sword, scrolling handle set w/old mine-cut diamonds, accented by three round rubies & pearl terminals yellow gold (14k) mount, 6⅛" l., Edwardian ........................................ **345.00**

**Pin,** model of a butterfly w/rose-cut diamond, highlighted by two cultured pearls & red stone eyes, yellow gold (14k), knife-edge mount, w/silver accents, Edwardian .......................... **230.00**

**Ring,** circular design, pearl center surrounded by rose-cut & collet-set diamonds within a blue enamel mount, black enamel accents, in yellow gold (14k), Victorian (ILLUS. top next column) .............. **1,265.00**

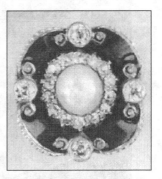

*Victorian Diamond and Pearl Ring*

**Ring,** hardstone seal, hinged beaded frame enhanced by chased shoulder & enamel accents in yellow gold, 14k (some enamel loss) ................... **230.00**

**Ring,** pearl & gold (14k), Art Nouveau-style, centered by a pink freshwater pearl flanked by two female heads ... **978.00**

**Ring,** pearl, sapphire, centered by a button pearl, flanked by calibre-cut sapphires in a platinum-topped yellow gold mount, Edwardian .......... **403.00**

## SETS

**Bracelet & earrings,** black onyx, pearl & gold (14k), faceted links set w/two pearls, Victorian, the set (nick to one earring) ................................. **690.00**

**Brooch & earrings,** applewood, depicting acorns & oak leaves w/black enamel accents set in yellow gold (18k), in original fitted box marked "Browne & Spaulding," purportedly made from the apple tree at Appomattox under which Generals Grant & Lee arranged the surrender in 1865, accompanied by documentation which includes an original letter from the jeweler, a jeweler's trade card & an auction catalog from 1908, Victorian, the set (ILLUS. top next page) ............................ **6,210.00**

**Brooch & earrings,** pietra dura, an oval brooch depicting white flowers, within a frame enhanced by applied wirework in yellow gold (18k), the matching earrings w/later backs in yellow gold (10k), Victorian, the set ............................ **805.00**

*Applewood Brooch & Earring Set*

*Pietra Dura Brooch & Earrings*

**Brooch & earrings,** pietra dura, a circular brooch depicting a fly, within a wiretwist frame in yellow gold (18k), together w/matching earrings, Victorian, the set (ILLUS.) ............. **1,265.00**

**Bracelet, brooch & earrings,** pietra dura, each designed as a foliate plaque within a frame enhanced by ropetwist in yellow gold (14k), inscription dated "1856," w/original fitted box, Victorian, the set (minor solder) ............................................... **805.00**

**Cameo brooch & earrings,** agate, each depicting the profile of a woman, within yellow gold scrolling mounts Victorian, the set (solder) .. **1,380.00**

**Pendant brooch & earrings,** garnet & yellow gold (14k), a scrolling pendant brooch enhanced by wiretwist, beadwork & foliate motifs, together w/matching earrings, Victorian, the set .............................. **690.00**

## MODERN (1920s-1960s)

**Bar pin,** diamond & platinum, Art Deco-style, centered by a collet-set diamond w/a pierced diamond-set mount ......................................... **1,495.00**

**Bar pin,** diamond & ruby, Art Deco-style, a row of square-cut rubies flanked by ten diamonds, in a platinum mount ............................. **1,610.00**

**Bar pin,** diamond, sapphire, diamond & platinum, Art Deco-style, set w/four clipped corner square diamonds centered by a row of calibre-cut sapphires within a diamond-set platinum openwork mount, French hallmark, signed "Cartier, Paris 41028" ............................................ **4,600.00**

**Bracelet,** amazonite, lapis, marcasite & sterling silver, Art Deco-style, set w/oval amazonites accented by lapis within a marcasite & silver mount, signed "Theodor Fahrner" (minor crazing) ......................................... **1,380.00**

**Bracelet,** bangle-type, sterling silver, scrolling abstract design, ca. 1960s, signed "Lobel" .................................. **317.00**

![Art Deco Diamond Bracelet]

*Art Deco Diamond Bracelet*

**Bracelet,** line-type, diamond & platinum, Art Deco-style, composed of pierced rectangular links set w/round diamonds, flanked by small diamond accents (ILLUS.) ............. **3,795.00**

**Bracelet,** line-type, onyx, diamond & platinum, Art Deco-style, composed of channel-set faceted black onyx spaced by seven round diamonds.. **2,185.00**

**Bracelet,** sterling silver link, lily pad design, marked "Danecraft" ............... **65.00**

**Bracelet,** three rows of clear stones, marked "Eisenberg" .......................... **125.00**

**Bracelet,** tourmaline, topaz, citrine, amethyst, pearls, sapphires & beryl, designed as random clusters of round, oval, emerald-cut & cabochon stones forming the links, includes, pink tourmaline, blue topaz, light blue sapphires & green beryl, in a yellow gold (14k) mount, ca. 1949............................................. **2,415.00**

**Bracelets,** pearl, enamel & yellow gold (14k), slide-type, mesh design, each w/a shield-shape slide accented by seed pearls & black enamel tracery, suspending beaded tassels, Victorian (fraying) ............... **978.00**

**Brooch,** Bakelite & Lucite, clear cameo w/black ground........................ **25.00**

**Brooch,** gold-filled, iris enamel & pave, marked "Coro"......................... **220.00**

**Brooch,** sterling silver & bronze, abstract design w/rectangular bronze element on a knife-edge mount, ca. 1960s, signed "Macchiarini" .................................. **259.00**

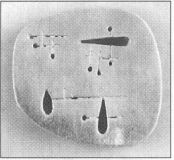

*Sterling Silver Brooch*

**Brooch,** sterling silver, pierced abstract design, Ed Wiener, ca. 1950s (ILLUS.)............................ **748.00**

**Cuff links,** crystal, ruby & yellow gold, (14k), Art Deco-style, each w/a bead set w/a collet-set cabochon ruby, pr... **374.00**

**Cuff links,** gold (14k) & diamond, Art Deco-style, each highlighted by a round diamond within an openwork square mount in yellow gold, pr.......... **518.00**

**Earrings,** gold-filled, for pierced ears, leaf-shaped, w/each having seven marquise-shaped crystals forming a long leaf, marked "Miriam Haskell," pr. ..................................................... **45.00**

**Earrings,** jadeite jade, diamond, Art Deco-style, a carved rectangular plaque surmounted by a diamond-set platinum top, pr. (veining) ........ **1,955.00**

**Necklace,** amethyst, peridot & mixed metal, textured branch design w/caged amethyst crystals, highlighted by faceted green peridot, ca. 1950s, 24" l. ............................... **863.00**

**Pendant,** sterling silver, concentric circles w/a center cabochon amethyst on a silver tongue, Georg Jensen, No. 143, ca. 1950............... **518.00**

**Pendant/brooch,** sterling silver, designed as an arc-shape top suspending a bird in flight, ca. 1950s, hallmark for Georg Jensen, No. 334 ............................................. **259.00**

**Pin,** diamond, Art Deco-style, designed as a tapering circle set w/graduating round diamonds accented by a marquise diamond bow top & green stones in a platinum mount ............................... **1,725.00**

**Pin,** diamond, onyx & platinum, Art Deco-style, bow-form, centered by a row of round diamonds edged in calibre-cut onyx in a platinum mount, signed "Tiffany & Co." .................... **3,738.00**

**Pin,** sterling silver, model of a tulip, signed "Hobe" .................................. **295.00**

**Pins,** Bakelite, orange triangles w/brass studs on butterscotch circles, 2" l., pr. ..................................... **35.00**

**Ring,** blue zircon, diamond, Art Deco-style, centered by a round zircon within a navette-shape diamond & enamel surround w/diamond shoulders, yellow gold (14k) & platinum mount, enamel loss & abraided zircon (ILLUS. top next page) ................................................... **920.00**

**Ring,** diamond solitaire, Art Deco-style, centered by a collet-set diamond, flanked by smaller diamonds, in a pierced diamond-set platinum mount .............................. **4,888.00**

**Ring,** jade, diamond & platinum, Art Deco-style, set w/an oval jade within a platinum & diamond mount......... **3,680.00**

**Ring,** lapis & diamond, Art Deco-style, large oval lapis set within a pierced diamond-set platinum mount ............ **748.00**

*Art Deco Zircon Ring*

**Ring,** sapphire, diamond & platinum, Art Deco-style, centered by a large square-cut sapphire flanked by trapezoid diamonds, in a platinum mount............................................. **2,900.00**

## SETS

**Bracelet & earrings,** large red cabachons, marked "Coro," the set. ... **35.00**

**Bracelet & earrings,** ruby, diamond & yellow gold (18k), Retro-style, a bangle bracelet of double hinged design, the top set w/ruby & diamond clusters, together w/matching earrings, French hallmarks, the set .......................... **3,220.00**

**Brooch & earrings,** ruby, diamond & gold (18k), Retro-style, the brooch designed as a reeded disc topped by an arc of channel-set rubies & round diamonds, matching earrings, the set.................................................. **3,220.00**

**Cuff links & matching shirt studs,** mother-of-pearl & gold (14k), each w/circular discs centered by a seed pearl, w/fitted box marked "Tiffany & Co.," the set..................................... **403.00**

*Sterling Silver Tie Bar*

**Cuff links & tie bar,** sterling silver, each cuff link of circular design depicting an abstract face, w/matching tie bar, signed "Ed Wiener," the set (ILLUS. of part)....... **288.00**

# JUKE BOXES

**Rock-ola "Standard" Model ST-20,** smaller glazed front revealing twenty song selections, lower grill w/red & yellow panels, in walnut veneered case, serial No. 43609, 1939, 25½ x 55½"................................. **$2,300.00**

**Wurlitzer Model 780,** 1941.............. **7,800.00**

**Wurlitzer Model 800,** glazed front revealing twenty-four song selections, features three bubble tubes in its center pilasters surrounding incandescent bulbs in its side pilasters, serial No. 461702, 1940, 27¾ x 37, 60" h................... **5,175.00**

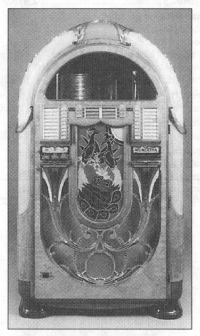

*Wurlitzer "Peacock" Jukebox*

**Wurlitzer Model 850,** glazed front revealing twenty-four song selections, the front w/two stylized peacocks, also known as "The Peacock," serial No. 786525, 1941, 26½ x 39", 65½" h. (ILLUS.) ...................................... **12,075.00**

**Wurlitzer Model 1015,** glazed front revealing twenty-four song selections, decorative front panel & plastic cylinders, walnut-veneered case, ca. 1946-47, 59" h............... **6,325.00**

# KITCHENWARES

*Also see: METALS*

*Special sections are included on Egg Beaters and Reamers following the general listings.*

**Apple parer,** The "New Lightning" geared arc-type, common.............. **$145.00**

**Apple parer,** White Mountain, screw apple parer, marked "GOODELL CO. ANTRIUM, N.H. U.S.A.," common............................................. **45.00**

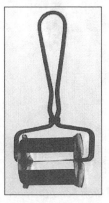

*Tin Biscuit Cutter*

**Biscuit cutter,** tin, rolls three biscuits at a time, Pat. Sept. 12, 1893, common (ILLUS.) ............................. **45.00**

**Bowl,** yellowware, miniature, 4½" d., 2" h., flat rim, body decorated w/wide blue band between two thin white bands, rare (ILLUS. below right)......... **50.00**

**Bowl,** yellowware, 4½" d., 2¾" h., rim decorated w/blue band between two thin white bands, body decorated w/blue band between two thin white bands, common (ILLUS. below left) ..... **45.00**

**Bread slicer,** wood w/iron gauge for adjusting slice thickness, iron blade & handle, marked "Arcadian Mfg. Co., Newark, N.Y.," 21" l., ca. 1885.. **155.00**

**Butter churn,** tin w/original blue paint & marked "Dazey" w/four legs & two-piece wooden lid, patent dated 1907, 23" h. ................................................. **125.00**

**Cake pan,** for bundt cake, early iron, swirled pattern around base w/twelve domes on top, 10" d., 5" h. ..................................................... **85.00**

**Can opener,** cast iron, mounted on board, William's Patent of Jan 8, 1878, rare................................ **275.00**

**Candy mold,** tin w/twelve molds, common................................................ **20.00**

**Cherry pitter,** cast iron, on three legs mounted on board, patent dated "Nov. 17, 1863"................................. **65.00**

**Cherry pitter,** cast metal, double prong, clamp-on-style, marked "GOODELL CO, ANTRIM, N.H. U.S.A.," common ............................... **45.00**

**Cherry pitter,** metal, clamp-on-style, single spring loaded pitter, "ROLLMAN MFG. CO; MOUNT JOY PA USA," common ................................................. **45.00**

**Coffeepot,** tin, squatty body, common.. **25.00**

**Cookie board,** spingerle, heavy pewter on wood backing w/eight patterns including a tulip, windmill, birds & flowers, 3¾ x 7½" .................. **60.00**

**Cookie cutters,** tin, in the shape of four animals, marked "DAVIS BAKING POWDER," set of 4, common (ILLUS. top next page)......... **92.00**

**Cookie sheet,** tin, marked "Betty Crocker 'Bisquick' Baker," common.... **25.00**

*Two Yellowware Bowls*

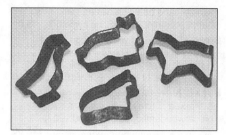

*Davis Baking Powder Cookie Cutters*

**Cornstick pan,** cast iron, marked
"Aunt Jemima Meal," five sticks .......... **30.00**

**Cornstick pan,** cast iron, seven
wheat pattern sticks ......................... **145.00**

**Culinary device,** tin, marked "HAND-
D-HAND," original box, used for
lifting hot plates, grabbing potatoes
in oven, dying garments, pat.
April 14, 1908, rare .......................... **165.00**

**Doughnut cutter,** wooden, common .... **45.00**

**Doughnut maker,** cast iron, makes
three doughnuts, marked "Cloverleaf
Doughnut form, The Ace Co. St.
Louis, Mo, Pat. 1904," 13" l. ............. **165.00**

**Egg holder,** wire, holds six eggs,
common ............................................. **35.00**

**Egg poacher,** tin, single cup, common .. **20.00**

**Egg separators,** tin, advertises
various companies, common .............. **18.00**

**Egg scale,** aluminum, marked "Acme
Grading Scale" & "pat. 6-24-24" ......... **35.00**

**Fish scaler,** tin, three grating sides,
long cylindrical handle marked "FISH
SCALER," rare ................................... **65.00**

**Flour sifter,** glass & tin, two glass
containers separated by triple
screen & held together by tin locking
bands, 8½" h. ..................................... **75.00**

**Flour sifter,** tin, child's, Hunter Flour
sifter, "PAT MAY 16, 71," 1½" h.,
rare (ILLUS. center, bottom previous
column) ............................................ **225.00**

**Flour sifter,** tin, paper label for
Hunters Flour sifter, common
(ILLUS. left, bottom previous
column) .............................................. **25.00**

**Flour sifter,** tin w/cast-iron legs,
stenciled "GEM" on side, rare
(ILLUS. right, bottom previous
column) ............................................ **185.00**

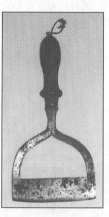

*Iron Food Chopper*

**Food Chopper,** hand-wrought iron,
wood handle, ca. 1850, common
(ILLUS.) ............................................. **85.00**

**Fruit press,** iron foundation w/screw
handle w/tin mesh hopper, marked
"Improved Fruit and Jelly Press" &
"Pat. Aug. 12, 1873," 4½" d., 6¾" h. .... **75.00**

**Grapefruit corer,** segmentor & corer,
w/large red knob handle, marked
"Karver Kutter," 3½" d. ....................... **15.00**

*Tin Flour Sifters*

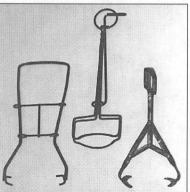

*Various Jar Lifters*

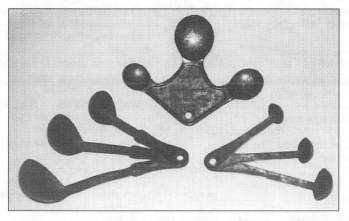

*Various Measuring Spoons*

**Jar lifter,** flat steel, common (ILLUS. right, bottom previous page) .............. **20.00**

**Jar lifter,** wire, common (ILLUS. left, bottom previous page) ........................ **15.00**

**Jar lifter,** wire, common (ILLUS. center, bottom previous page) ............ **30.00**

**Knife sharpener,** brass ends, marked "The Dewey," w/wooden box, ca. 1880 ............................................. **45.00**

**Lemon squeezer,** cast iron & white metal, marked "LF&C" (Landers Frary & Clark Co.) .............................. **40.00**

**Measuring cup,** darkened tin, 1 cup size, marked "Cottolene" .................... **20.00**

**Measuring spoons,** darkened tin, ¼ tsp., ½ tsp. & 1 tsp., marked "Rumford," 3⅝" l., the set .................... **65.00**

**Measuring spoons,** tin, 1 tsp. or 60 drops, 1 dessert or 120 drops & 1 Tbs. or 230 drops, marked "UNIVERSAL," rare, the set (ILLUS. above left) .......................................... **85.00**

**Measuring spoons,** tin, combination, ¼ tsp., ½ tsp. & 1 tsp., marked "COMPLIMENTS OF THE NEW ENGLAND ENAMELING CO.," rare (ILLUS. above center) ...................... **125.00**

**Measuring spoons,** tin, ¼ tsp. or 15 drops, ½ tsp. or 30 drops & 1 tsp. or 60 drops, marked "Original," common, the set (ILLUS. above right) ................. **50.00**

**Meat tenderizer,** rolling-type, very heavy cast-iron cylinder w/iron teeth fitted in brass yoke & wood handle ..... **28.00**

**Mold,** chocolate, darkened tin, five champagne bottles in a row, 2 pts., 7" l ...................................................... **55.00**

**Mold,** chocolate, donkey carrying baskets on his back, No. 2044, 5" l. ... **60.00**

**Mold,** chocolate, flat sheet, fourteen Father Christmas figures, marked "Booderas Ernotebruck No. 2214".... **150.00**

**Mold,** chocolate, tin, Charlie Chaplin standing w/hand in pocket, marked "Le Tang Fils no. 3696," 2 pt., 8" h. .. **180.00**

**Mold,** chocolate, tin, clown holding hands in front & wearing big shoes, 2 pt., 5" h. ........................................... **70.00**

**Mold,** chocolate, tin, four Teddy bears, marked "Anton Reiche No. 23937, Bortz Candy Co." 4 x 7" ........ **165.00**

**Mold,** chocolate, tin, four witches riding brooms, 3 pt., 9" l ..................... **85.00**

**Mold,** chocolate, tin, girl in full skirt holding flower bouquet, No. 2686, 2 pt ....................................................... **65.00**

**Mold,** chocolate, tin, two rabbits standing on either side of large woven basket, 8" l ............................... **90.00**

**Mold,** chocolate, tin, swan w/curved neck, marked "Depose Letang Fils, Paris," 2 pt., 3 x 5" ............................. **70.00**

**Mold,** chocolate, tin, two lamb figures, marked "#15542, Anton Reiche, Germany," 3 pt., 3 x 6"...................... **75.00**

**Mold,** chocolate, tin, W. C. Fields riding mini bicycle, two figures, marked "Anton Reiche, No. 25628," 6" l., 3 pcs. ........................................ **225.00**

**Mold,** pudding, darkened tin, bundt shape ornately decorated w/two tiers sides by columns topped w/flowers, No. 413, Austria ................................. **68.00**

**Nutmeg grater,** "Little Rhody," wood & knob w/original label, 5½" l............ **145.00**

**Nutmeg grater,** tin, asphaltum, wood knob, common ................................. **175.00**

**Nutmeg grater,** tin, circular, rare ........ **550.00**

**Nutmeg grater,** tin, coffin-style w/box to hold nutmeg, marked "KREAMER," common ................................................ 35.00

**Nutmeg grater,** tin, marked "PATENTED NOV 20 1855," rare ..... 375.00

**Nutmeg grater,** tin, wood knobs, marked "Pat Nov 10, 1896," common ............................................. 65.00

**Nutmeg grater,** tin & wood, Hughes, marked "FEB 27 1877," common ..... 250.00

**Nutmeg grater,** tin & wood, The Monitor, marked "MAR 19 1889," 4½" l., common ................................ 180.00

**Pan,** popover, cast iron, makes eight, Wagner Ware R1336 ......................... 65.00

*Various Pans & Molds*

**Pan,** roll, tin w/twelve molds, marked "KREAMER," common (ILLUS. center left) .......................................... 20.00

**Pan,** tin w/six molds, marked "KREAMER," common (ILLUS. center right) ......................................... 25.00

**Pan,** tin w/six molds, maybe used for pancakes, common (ILLUS. bottom) .... 40.00

**Pan/mold,** tin w/three small rectangular molds, common (ILLUS. top right) ........................................... 15.00

**Pan,** Vienna roll, makes six rolls, Griswold No. 26, Pat 958 .................... 85.00

**Sugar maple mold,** tin w/six molds, common (ILLUS. center) ................... 25.00

**Pie lifter,** cast iron, marked "PAT'D MARCH 16 1880," rare ..................... 95.00

**Pie lifter,** twisted wire, mechanical, swivels in oven to allow pie to turn & bake evenly, marked "PAT'D SE 27 '87," rare ......................................... 185.00

**Pie lifter,** wire & wood, two wire 'arms' operate like butterfly wings for lifting pie from oven, 20" l. ................. 34.00

**Pie lifter,** wire in the form of a semi-circle around a thin tin spatula w/wood handle, common .................... 75.00

**Pie lifter,** wire & tin w/adjustable wood handle, common ............................. 45.00

**Pot,** cov., cast iron, stands on three feet, holds nine quarts, w/bail handle, marked "J.M.B. Davidson & Co., Albany, N.Y." .............................. 85.00

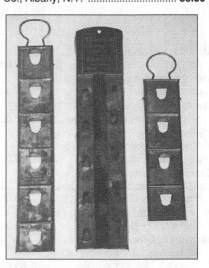

*Potato Bakers*

**Potato baker,** tin, advertising, six potato holder (placed potatoes on protrusions, kept potatoes from exploding & rolling around in oven), marked "RUMFORD," common (ILLUS. left) ..................................... 110.00

**Potato baker,** tin, advertising, ten potato holder, marked "Thayer & - Sherwood - COAL - AND - PRODUCE - Both Phones - LIVONIA, N.Y.," rare (ILLUS. center) .................. 165.00

**Potato baker,** tin, advertising, four potato holder, "COMSTOCK POTATO BAKER," rare (ILLUS. right) ................................................. 145.00

**Potato masher,** mechanical, two mashing surfaces that meet when pushed down w/spring action, A & J, 11½" ................................................. 30.00

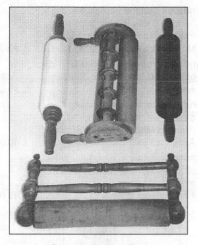

*Diverse Rolling Pins*

**Rolling pin,** china, white roller w/green handles, common (ILLUS. left) ...................................................... **30.00**

**Rolling pin,** "Roll-Rite," glass screw cap w/original instructions, 14" l. ........ **35.00**

**Rolling pin,** tin w/wood handles, common (ILLUS. right) ..................... **300.00**

**Rolling pin,** w/tin sieve insert, Harloes's "No Doe Stick," patent date Dec. 12, 1905, rare ................... **375.00**

**Rolling pin,** wood, w/slicing wheels, marked on paper label "manufactured by the Southern Pin CO, Nough TN, Patented July" (?), rare (ILLUS. center) ......................... **275.00**

**Rolling pin,** wood, handmade, w/two scroll-cut handles, common (ILLUS. bottom) ............................................. **250.00**

**Scoop,** tin, small, common ................... **10.00**

**Skillet,** "Odorless," Griswold No. 869, Patent date. Oct., 17 1893 ................. **35.00**

**Spatter lid,** domed tin w/finely pierced holes & wood finial, comes in two sizes, "Pat Jan 3 1899," common ............................................. **35.00**

**Spatula,** green, wooden handle, common ............................................. **10.00**

**Spoon,** ice cream-type w/Bakelite handle, marked "Rainbow," 11½" l. .... **25.00**

**Spoon,** tin, measuring-type w/bottle opener in handle, common (ILLUS. left, top next column) ......................... **15.00**

**Spoon,** tin, rippled egg beater spoon, marked "PAT AUG 6 1872," rare (ILLUS. right, top next column) ......... **125.00**

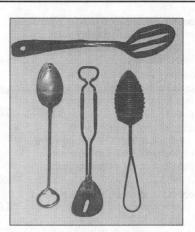

*A Group of Tin Spoons*

**Spoon,** tin, single-slotted w/bottle opener in handle, marked "GRANDMA'S LOPSIDED MIXING SPOON," common (ILLUS. center) .... **25.00**

**Spoon,** tin, whipping-type, four slotted, marked "App'd for," rare (ILLUS. top) ...................................... **25.00**

**Sugar nippers,** heavy cast iron, ca. mid-1880s, 8½" l. ............................... **125.00**

**Teakettle,** tin, slightly tapering cylindrical form, common (ILLUS. below) ................................................ **50.00**

*Tin Teakettle*

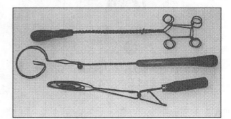

*Three Wire Toasters*

**Toaster,** wire w/wood handle, place bread between decorative wires, rare (ILLUS. center, bottom previous page) ................................................. **75.00**

**Toaster,** wire w/wood handle, place bread between decorative wires, rare (ILLUS. top, bottom previous page) ................................................. **50.00**

**Toaster,** wire w/wood handle, mechanical, pull lever to open wire circles to insert bread, common (ILLUS. bottom, bottom previous page) ................................................. **30.00**

**Vegetable strainer,** wire base, wood handle, common ................................. **18.00**

## EGGBEATERS

*Items are listed alphabetically by manufacturer or type.*

**A & J,** wood handle, metal rotary, marked "A&J Pat Oct. 9, 1923," 10¾" ...................................... **5.00 to 10.00**

**A & J,** Lady Bingo, wood handle, metal rotary, marked "Lady Bingo No. 72 A&J Pat Apl'd for Made in the U.S.A.," 10¾" ................................... **15.00**

*Super Speed A & J Spinnit Cream & Egg Whip*

**A & J,** Super Speed Spinnit egg & cream whip, wood handle, rotary turbine bottom, marked "Super Speed A&J Spinnit Cream Egg Whip," 11½" (ILLUS.) .......................... **30.00**

**Androck,** turbine beater, wood handle, rotary w/turbine dasher, marked "Turbine Beater Androck Made in USA," 11½" .......................... **20.00**

**Androck,** rotary apron beater w/clear, glass bowl, marked "Another Androck product," 5½" ....................... **35.00**

**Androck,** rotary apron beater w/clear glass bowl, marked "Androck Pat Pending Made in United States of America," 6¾" ................................... **40.00**

**Androck,** rotary open beater w/red plastic coating on beater & bowl, marked "Another Androck Product Patent Pending," 6¾" ......................... **45.00**

*Frederick Ashley's May 1, 1860 Archimedes Eggbeater*

**F. Ashley,** archimedes, wood & metal, marked "F. Ashley Patent May 1, 1860," 11½" (ILLUS.) ............ **500.00**

**Ball bearing,** cast iron, rotary w/propeller dashers, marked "Ball Bearing patd. 22, 1898 Dec. 3, 1901," 9¼" h. ................................................. **225.00**

**Christie,** cast iron, table-mount rotary w/two beater attachments, marked "Christie Knife Patented Fremont," 11½" h. ............................................. **250.00**

**Dover,** cast iron, rotary marked "Dover Egg Beater Pat. May 31st 1870," 10" h. ................................................. **65.00**

**Dover,** cast iron, rotary marked "Dover Egg Beater Pat. May 31st 1870," 16½" h. ............................................... **165.00**

**Dover,** cast iron, rotary marked "Dover Egg Beater Pat May 6th 1873," 10" h. .. **75.00**

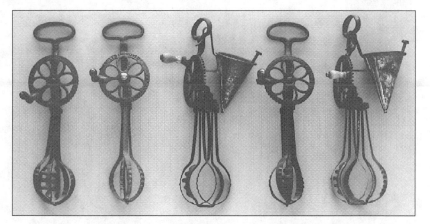

*Various Holt's Egg Beaters with Original Funnels*

**Dover,** cast iron, rotary marked "Dover Egg Beater Patd made in Boston U.S.A.," 9½" h........................ **40.00**

**Dream cream,** rotary turbine marked "The Dream Cream Trade Mark Whip Patent Kohler Die & Sp'lty Co. DeKalb, Ill U.S.A.," 10½" h. ................ **35.00**

**Eagle Precision Tool Co.,** metal squeeze w/plastic pin, marked "One-Hand Wip (sic) Eagle Precision Tool Co. Long Island, New York," 12¾" h. . **25.00**

**Hand-held,** wood handle, marked "March 24, 1868," 9½" h. .................... **35.00**

**Hand-held,** all wire, unmarked, 10½" h...... **5.00**

**Hand-held,** wire w/wood handle, unmarked, 13" h. ............................ **25.00**

**Holt-Lyon,** cast iron, rotary marked "H-L Co. No. 0 Tarrytown, N.Y.," 9" h. (ILLUS. above) .......................... **50.00**

**Holt-Lyon,** cast iron, rotary w/funnel, marked "Holt's Patented Flared Dasher Egg Beater U.S.A.," 10½" h. (ILLUS. above)..................................... **55.00**

**Holt-Lyon,** cast iron, rotary jar mount, marked "Holt's Egg Beater & Cream Whip Pat. Aug. 22-99. Apr. 3-00 USA," jar embossed "The Holt-Lyon Jar Cream Whip and Mayonnaise Mixer" .. **300.00**

**Holt-Lyon,** cast iron, rotary jar mount, marked "Holt's Improved Patented Made by Holt-Lyon CO. Tarrytown N.Y.," jar embossed "The Holt-Lyon Jar Cream Whip and Mayonnaise Mixer, The Holt-Lyon Co. Tarrytown, N.Y." ................................................. **275.00**

**Jaquette Bros.,** scissors-type, cast iron, marked "Jaquette Bros No. 3," 10½" l................................................. **350.00**

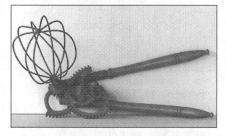

*Jaquette Bros. Scissors-type Mixer*

**Jaquette Bros.,** scissors-type, cast iron, marked "Pat." only, 20" l. (ILLUS.) ........................................... **500.00**

**Ladd,** metal rotary, marked "No. 2 Ladd Beater July 7, 1908, Oct, 1921," 12½" h.............................. **25.00**

**Ladd,** metal rotary, marked "No. 3 Ladd Ball Bearing Beater Oct. 18, 1921 Other Pats Pend," 11" h. ............ **15.00**

**Ladd,** tumbler model, metal rotary marked "Ball Bearing Ladd Beater," w/apron on jar embossed "Ladd," 12" h. ................................................. **100.00**

**Ladd,** beater held in two-part apron marked "Ladd No. 1," embossed on pedestal jar "Ladd Mixer No. 1 Feb. 15, 1916," 12½" h. .................... **200.00**

**Master,** cast-iron rotary w/unusual wire handle, marked "Master Pat. Aug. 24 09," 10½" h.......................... **250.00**

**Monroe,** cast-iron rotary, shelf mount, marked "Monroe Bro's Fitchburg, Mass. Patent April 19, 1859 & Oct. 16 1860," 10"............................ **550.00**

*P-D-&-Co. Spring Dasher Beater*

*Family Egg Beater*

**P-D-&-Co.,** cast-iron rotary w/spring dasher bottom w/"P - D - & - Co" cut-out on spokes of main gear wheel & marked "Dec 1, 1885," 10" h. (ILLUS.) .......................................... **550.00**

**S&S Hutchinson,** cast-iron rotary marked "S&S Hutchinson New York Pat Appl. for," w/glass apron on baluster shaped bowl embossed "S&S Trade Mark Reg. U.S. Pat. Off. 852 Vernon Ave. Long Island City, N.Y." .............................................. **350.00**

**Spear's,** archimedes, metal, marked "Spear's 20th Century Egg & Cream Whipper March 5, 1912 Improvements allowed Nov. 29, 1913," 12½" h. .......... **100.00**

**Spear's,** archimedes, metal, marked "20th Century Egg & Cream Whipper March 5, 1912," 12½" h. ................... **100.00**

**Taplin,** cast-iron rotary, marked "Taplin's Dover Pattern Improved Pat. April 14, 1903," 12¼" h. ............... **45.00**

**Taplin,** cast-iron rotary, marked "The Taplin Mfg. Co. New Britain Conn, U.S.A Light Running Pat. Nov. 24 '08," 10½" h. .......................... **35.00**

**Taplin,** cast-iron rotary, wood handle, marked "The Taplin Mfg. Co. New Britian Conn, U.S.A Light Running Pat. Nov. 24 '08," 15" h....................... **50.00**

**Taplin,** tin rotary, wood handle, marked "The Taplin Mfg. Co. New Britain Conn. Pat. 12-9-24 Made in USA," 11" h......................................... **15.00**

**Turner & Seymour,** cast-iron rotary, "T&S No. 20 Made in the U.S.A.," 10½" h. ............................................. **30.00**

**Turner & Seymour,** cast-iron rotary, "T&S No. 40 Made in the U.S.A.," 12¼" h. ............................................. **55.00**

**Turner & Seymour,** cast-iron rotary, marked "Family Egg Beater Pat Sep' 26 1876," 10" h. (ILLUS. above) ....... **300.00**

**Turner & Seymour,** metal rotary, marked "T&S No. 1 Pat. Nov. 28, 1916 Aug 2, 1921 Pat. Pending Made in U.S.A.," 11" h. .................. **20.00**

**Turner & Seymour,** metal rotary, wood handle, marked "Blue Swirl Pat. Nov. 28, 1916 Aug. 2, 1921 Pat. Pending Made in U.S.A. (T&S)," 12½" h. ............................................. **15.00**

## REAMERS

**Ceramic,** barrel-shaped w/reamer cover, cream ground w/multicolored flowers, marked "Universal Potteries, Inc. Oven Proof," 9" h. ...................... **125.00**

**Ceramic,** figure of a clown, red, w/black & orange on white, marked "SIGMA," ca. 1960s, 6½" h. (ILLUS. top next page)..................................... **90.00**

**Ceramic,** figure of a cream & multicolored clown w/yellow & green hat, stamped "Made in Japan" & marked "Japan," ca. 1930s-40s, 8" h. ...................................................... **75.00**

*Ceramic Clown Reamer*

**Ceramic,** Goldenrod face w/orange &
black trim, marked "Carlton Ware" &
"Made in England," 3¾" h. ............... **110.00**

**Ceramic,** green & white plaid, marked
Japan, ca. 1940s, 5½" h. ................... **45.00**

**Ceramic,** light green pig, yellow top,
marked "Marutomoware Hand
Painted Japan," 5" h. ........................ **175.00**

**Ceramic,** lustre w/red & yellow
flowers, marked "Made in Japan,"
ca. 1930s-40s, 2" h. ...........................**100.00**

*Jiffy Juicer*

**Ceramic,** maroon, marked "Jiffy Juicer
U.S. Pat 2, 755 Sept. 20, 1938,"
5¼" h. (ILLUS.) ................................... **75.00**

**Ceramic,** orange w/green leaves &
brown handle, marked "Made in
Czechoslovakia-Erphila Art Pottery,"
6" h. ..................................................... **55.00**

**Ceramic,** pink orchids w/green leaves,
unmarked, 3" h. ................................. **65.00**

**Ceramic,** pink pig w/blue & maroon
trim, 4¼" h. ........................................ **50.00**

**Ceramic,** tapering cylindrical sides
w/reamer top, white w/multicolored
flowers & sterling silver trim, marked
"France," w/underplate, 5⅜" h.,
3 pcs. ................................................. **175.00**

**Ceramic,** white, marked U.S.A. Corns
China, 4¼" d. ..................................... **60.00**

**Ceramic,** yellow pear w/green leaves
& white cone, marked "Made in
Japan," 4¾" h., 3 pcs. ......................... **55.00**

**Ceramic,** yellow, blue & red on white
ground, marked "Henroit Quimper
France 1166," ca. 1940, 4¼" d. ........ **350.00**

**Ceramic,** yellow, tan dog & blue kitten
w/red umbrella, inscribed "Orange
Juice," marked "Made in Japan
75/476," 4½" h. ................................. **65.00**

**Ceramic & metal,** white milk glass
bowl, green enamel base, marked
"Presto-Juicer," The National Electric
Appliance Corp., Bridgeport, Conn.,
7½" h. ................................................. **75.00**

**Glass,** clear, marked "Sunkist,
Oranges-Lemons," Pacific Coast
Glass Works, ca. 1916, 6" d.
(ILLUS. below) ................................... **35.00**

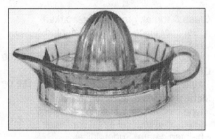

*Clear Glass Sunkist Reamer*

*Fenton Glass Reamer*

**Glass,** jade green, w/cover, Fenton
Art Glass Co., 6⅜" h. (ILLUS.) ....... **1,200.00**

**Glass,** light blue, foreign, marked
"Bayel," 4¾" d. ................................. **150.00**

**Glass,** opalescent, Fry Glass Co.,
ca. 1925-35, 6¼" d. ........................... **40.00**

**Glass,** ultramarine, Jeanette Glass
Co., 5¼" d. ....................................... **120.00**

**Glass,** white milk glass, embossed
w/fleur-de-lis, 6¼" d. .......................... **95.00**

*Servmor Juice Extractor*

**Glass & metal,** green glass, marked "Servmor Juice Extractor Patented," U.S. Glass Co., ca. 1930s, 5" h. (ILLUS.) ............................................. **75.00**

**Glass & metal,** green, Mount Joy, ca. 1929, 11" h. ..................................... **150.00**

**Metal,** hinged back handle to plunger-type mechanism above the reamer fitted on cylindrical metal container, painted cream, Super Juicer, Household Products Mfg. Co., ca. 1940s, 6" h. .................................... **25.00**

**Silver plate & oak,** England, 7¾" h. .... **200.00**

**Silver plate,** marked "Muss Bach," 4½" l. .................................................. **20.00**

---

# LAUNDRY ROOM ITEMS

The *"good old days" weren't really all that good when Monday "wash day" and Tuesday "ironing day" came around. There was a lot of hard work involved in scrubbing clothes on the washboard and smoothing out the wrinkles with the hefty flatiron or "sadiron" (sad = heavy). Today collectors can look back with some nostalgia on those adjuncts of the laundry room, curious relics of the not too distant past.*

### IRONS

**Box iron,** Bless & Drake Salamander, top lifts off by swing latch ................ **$275.00**

*Butters Box Iron*

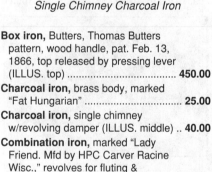

*Single Chimney Charcoal Iron*

**Box iron,** Butters, Thomas Butters pattern, wood handle, pat. Feb. 13, 1866, top released by pressing lever (ILLUS. top) ...................................... **450.00**

**Charcoal iron,** brass body, marked "Fat Hungarian" ................................. **25.00**

**Charcoal iron,** single chimney w/revolving damper (ILLUS. middle) .. **40.00**

**Combination iron,** marked "Lady Friend. Mfd by HPC Carver Racine Wisc.," revolves for fluting & smoothing, separate fluting bed ...... **325.00**

**Combination iron,** Myers, fluter/sad iron, pat. March 7, 1887 .................... **450.00**

**Little iron,** figure of a swan w/original paint, 2¾" ........................................ **175.00**

*Small Swan Iron*

*Tailor Iron with Twisted Handle*

*Soapstone Sad Iron*

**Little iron,** figure of a swan, without original paint, 2½" (ILLUS. bottom previous page) ................................... **90.00**

**Tailor iron,** advertising-type, marked "John L. Bo Bo & Co'pny, Tailors Trimmings Chicago" ........................ **250.00**

**Tailor iron,** cast iron, marked "IXL 20 lb.," w/twisted handle (ILLUS. above).... **40.00**

**Tailor iron,** marked "Ober Mfg. Co. Chargin Falls O." ............................. **125.00**

*Manville Crank Fluter*

**Fluter,** crank, cast iron, wide base w/gold painted scrolls tapering into a cylindrical neck w/knob finial, crank fluter attached to neck, marked "Manville," wood handle, Pat. 1869, paint worn (ILLUS.) ........................... **700.00**

**Fluter,** crank, marked "Dudley," Pat. Nov. 14, 1876 ................................... **450.00**

**Fluter,** rocking, marked "The Best" ....... **65.00**

**Fluter,** rolling, cast iron, marked "Shepard Hardware Co. Buffalo, NY," heated w/slug ........................... **125.00**

**Fluter,** rolling, marked "Doty," Pat. June 4, 1878 ................................... **325.00**

**Fuel iron,** Coleman, model 4A w/all accessories ......................................... **55.00**

**Polisher,** marked "Gem," heated w/slug ............................................... **275.00**

**Sad Iron,** detachable handle, Enterprise, A. C. Williams & others .... **25.00**

**Sad Iron,** cast iron, detachable wood handle, marked "Sensible," No. 2 N.R.S. & Co. ...................................... **65.00**

**Sad Iron,** porcelain finish, France ......... **85.00**

**Sad Iron,** soapstone body w/cast-iron bottom & handle, Pat. Jan 15, 1867 marked "Hoods" (ILLUS. above) ....... **225.00**

**Sleeve iron,** cast iron, long thin body, WaPak .............................................. **75.00**

### SPRINKLING BOTTLES

**Ceramic,** figural Chinaman, California Cleminsons ........................................ **24.00**

**Ceramic,** figural Mammy, marked "Pfaltzgraff" ...................................... **225.00**

**Ceramic,** figural Muggsy, Pfaltzgraff..... **80.00**

**Ceramic,** model of a clothespin ........... **98.00**

**Ceramic,** model of an iron ................... **40.00**

**Ceramic,** model of a Siamese cat......... **85.00**

**Plastic,** figure of a merry maid............. **18.00**

**Soft plastic,** model of an elephant ....... **45.00**

### WASHBOARDS

**Enamelware,** cobalt blue, National No. 197 .......................................... **125.00**

**Roller-type,** wooden frame, 4" w., 33" l.................................................. **65.00**

**Wooden,** rounded corrugated surface, 5" hewn "D" shaped handle, ca. 1810, 19" l....................................... **150.00**

---

# LAW ENFORCEMENT ITEMS

*All types of objects relating to law enforcement activities of earlier days are now being collected, just as are fire fighting mementos. The range extends from badges and insignia to leg irons and weapons. The following compilation represents a cross-section.*

**Badge,** "Patrolman Special Officer
  Calif" in blue enamel on gold &
  chrome, Sun Badge Co. .................. **$55.00**
**Iron claw,** by Argus ............................. 70.00
**Iron claw,** patent date 1869 ............... 175.00
**Handcuffs w/key,** H&R Co. ............... 275.00
**Palm disc,** lead, leather covered
  w/hand band ...................................... 75.00
**Brass knuckles** ................................... 65.00

# LIGHTING DEVICES

## LAMPS

### ALADDIN® MANTLE LAMPS

*Aladdin Chandelier*

**Chandelier,** single w/No. 3 burner &
  flame spreader, Model No. 3
  (ILLUS.) ................... **$3,500.00 to 4,000.00**
**Hanging lamp,** w/No. 7 flame
  spreader & No. 416 shade, Model
  No. 7 ................................. 600.00 to 650.00
**Parlor lamp,** satin brass, w/a 4A
  flame spreader, Model
  No. 4 (ILLUS. top next
  column) ........................... 850.00 to 900.00

*Aladdin Parlor Lamp*

*Nickel Finish Table Lamp*

**Table lamp,** brass finish, No. 8 flame
  spreader & No. 401 shade, Model
  No. 8 ............................... **400.00 to 475.00**
**Table lamp,** nickel finish, No. 601S
  shade, Model No. 12
  (ILLUS. bottom) ............... 375.00 to 475.00
**Table lamp,** nickel plated, plain foot,
  1 qt. font, Model No. 2 ...... 350.00 to 400.00
**Table lamp,** satin brass, w/a
  No. 5 flame spreader, Model
  No. 5 ............................... 225.00 to 275.00
**Vase lamp,** black, gold foot edge,
  three feet, 10¼" h. ............. 500.00 to 550.00
**Vase lamp,** Florentine, rose
  moonstone, Model No. 12, glass
  portion 8½" h. .............. 2,200.00 to 2,400.00
**Vase lamp,** red iridescent, gold foot
  edge, three feet, 10¼" h. ... 450.00 to 500.00

**Vase lamp,** tan w/brown foot edge, six
feet, 10¼" h. ..................... **150.00 to 200.00**

*The following pattern glass names are from J. W. Courter reference books on Aladdin Lamps*

*Beehive Table Lamp*

**Table lamp,** Beehive patt., ruby
crystal (ILLUS.) ............... **500.00 to 550.00**

**Table lamp,** Cathedral patt.,
clear ................................ **100.00 to 125.00**

**Table lamp,** Cathedral patt., green
moonstone ...................... **250.00 to 300.00**

**Table lamp,** Colonial patt.,
clear ................................ **100.00 to 125.00**

**Table lamp,** Colonial patt., green or
amber crystal.................... **175.00 to 200.00**

**Table lamp,** Corinthian patt., clear
font w/black, green or amber
foot ................................. **125.00 to 150.00**

**Table lamp,** Corinthian patt., green
moonstone ...................... **150.00 to 175.00**

**Table lamp,** Corinthian patt., rose
moonstone ...................... **200.00 to 250.00**

**Table lamp,** Corinthian patt., white
moonstone ...................... **175.00 to 200.00**

**Table lamp,** Diamond Quilted patt.,
white moonstone .............. **300.00 to 350.00**

**Table lamp,** Diamond Quilted patt.,
white moonstone font w/rose or
black foot.......................... **350.00 to 400.00**

**Table lamp,** Lincoln Drape patt.,
short, amber crystal, raised glass
collar at font top........... **2300.00 to 2500.00**

**Table lamp,** Lincoln Drape patt.,
short, w/flared lower stem,
Alacite ............................. **450.00 to 500.00**

**Table lamp,** Lincoln Drape patt., tall,
clear crystal, one piece of glass (no
glue joint at stem top)... **5,500.00 to 6,000.00**

**Table lamp,** Lincoln Drape patt., tall,
clear, cobalt, or ruby crystal, two-
piece, glue joint at stem
top ..................................... **80.00 to 100.00**

**Table lamp,** Majestic patt., green,
white, or rose moonstone on metallic
foot ................................. **250.00 to 300.00**

**Table lamp,** Orientale patt., silver
or rose gold, all metallic
finish................................ **150.00 to 200.00**

**Table lamp,** Simplicity patt., Alacite,
green or white enamel...... **150.00 to 175.00**

**Table lamp,** Simplicity patt., floral
decal or gold lustre ........... **350.00 to 400.00**

**Table lamp,** Treasure patt., chromium,
nickel or bronze finish....... **150.00 to 175.00**

**Table lamp,** Venetian patt., clear,
clear, stem-foot/bowl
threaded .......................... **300.00 to 350.00**

**Table lamp,** Venetian patt., clear,
rose enamel ..................... **150.00 to 200.00**

**Table lamp,** Vertique patt., rose
moonstone ...................... **400.00 to 450.00**

**Table lamp,** Vertique patt., white
moonstone ...................... **750.00 to 800.00**

**Table lamp,** Washington Drape patt.,
bell-shaped stem, clear
crystal.............................. **150.00 to 200.00**

**Table lamp,** Washington Drape patt.,
clear crystal, filigree stem... **100.00 to 125.00**

**Table lamp,** Washington Drape patt.,
green or amber crystal, bell-shaped
stem ................................ **350.00 to 400.00**

**Table lamp,** Washington Drape patt.,
green or amber crystal, filigree
stem ................................ **150.00 to 200.00**

## FAIRY LAMPS

*These are candle burning night lights of the Victorian era. Best known are the Clarke Fairy Lamps made in England, but they were also made by other firms. They were produced in two sizes, each with a base and a shade. Fairy Pyramid lamps usually have a clear glass base and are approximately 2⅞" d. and 3¼" h. The Fairy Lamps are usually at least 4" d. and 5" h. when assembled and these may or may not have an additional saucer or bottom holder to match the shade in addition to the clear base.*

## Fairy Lamps

**Amber glass shade,** frosted w/embossed swirl w/diamond quilted pattern on clear glass base marked "Clark," 4" d., 4¾" h. ......................... **165.00**

*Brass Fairy Lamp*

**Brass shade,** openwork w/figured pattern of flowers & birds on shade, colored jewels form centers of flowers, w/matching brass handled base, 3⅝" d., 4¼" h. (ILLUS.) ........... **245.00**

**Burmese glass shade,** acid finish, lush salmon pink evenly shading to yellow, decorated w/green leaves, branches & clusters of red berries, w/clear glass base marked "Clark," 4" d., 4¾" h. (ILLUS. below) ............. **650.00**

**Pearl satin glass shade,** heavenly blue swirl mother-of-pearl w/embossed swirl shade, w/clear glass base marked "Clark," 4" d., 4½" h. ............................................... **245.00**

**Verre Moiré (Nailsea)** frosted blue w/opaque white loopings glass shade w/matching base, clear cup insert marked "Clark," 6¼" d., 5¼" h. (ILLUS. top next column) ................. **695.00**

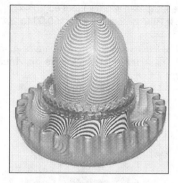

*Verre Moiré Fairy Lamp*

*Fairy Lamp Epergne*

**Verre Moiré (Nailsea)** frosted rose w/opaque white loopings glass shades w/a central shade w/a Clarke Cricklite clear base in a gilt-metal ring raised at the center of six scroll arms each w/a ring holding a matching shade & base all raised on a slender clear crystal standard w/a trumpet-form glass fitting at the top & a diamond-faceted flaring base w/a metal ring issuing four metal scroll arms each w/a suspending a small crystal vase w/a flaring faceted rim above a bulbous diamond-cut bowl & long stem, the glass base resting on a scroll-cast metal base ring w/small cloven hoof feet, overall 30" h. (ILLUS.) ............................... **3,450.00**

*Burmese Fairy Lamp*

## Figural Fairy Lamps

*Owl Head Fairy Lamp*

**Bisque,** figure of grey owl's head w/glass eyes & blue ribbon around neck, 3⅛" d., 3⅝" h. (ILLUS.) ........... **195.00**

**Porcelain,** figure of owl sitting on stack of books, brown glass eyes, German maker mark on base, electrified, 4" d., 8¾" h. ...................... **165.00**

*Flame-form Fairy Lamp*

**Ruby glass shade** in the shape of flames, on clear glass base marked "Clarke," 2¾" d., 3⅞" h. (ILLUS.) ........ **95.00**

## HANDEL LAMPS

*The Handel Company of Meriden, Connecticut (1885-1936) began as a glass and lamp shade decorating company. Following World War I they became a major producer of decorative lamps which have become very collectible today.*

**Boudoir lamp,** 7" d. domical reverse painted Teroma shade decorated w/a Dutch landscape scene w/a windmill & village, marked "Handel 5882 RG," on a slender round cast metal shaft w/flaring ribbed foot marked "Handel," 14" h. ................. **1,495.00**

**Boudoir lamp,** 8⅜" w. squared domical reverse painted shade of light grey w/an intaglio exterior finish, painted on the exterior & interior w/a pastoral landscape w/trees & a ridge in the foreground, cloudy blue sky above & background in shades of green, brown, grey, purple & peach, on a slender cast-metal standard w/squared pierced scroll-cast foot, shade signed "Handel 6154," base w/cloth Handel label, ca. 1910, 15½" h. (base depatinated) ................................... **3,162.00**

**Bridge floor lamp,** the wide bell-form harp frame suspending a socket w/a holophane clear finely ribbed pressed bell-form shade, the tall slender metal standard on a tripod base w/three low scrolled feet marked "Handel," overall 4' 10" h. .... **633.00**

**Desk lamp,** a rolled cylindrical 10" l. green Teroma glass shade cased in white adjusts in a long C-form frame raised on a curved reeded shaft adjusting above the round flaring ribbed weighted disc foot w/"Handel" fabric label, 16" h. ......................... **1,265.00**

*Handel Desk Lamp*

**Desk lamp,** a bell-form six-lobed reverse painted shape w/a 'chipped ice' finish & decorated around the lower rim w/green maidenhair ferns on a pink ground, the shade suspended from a bell-form frame above the slender ribbed copper finished standard w/a wide lobed disc foot base impressed "Handel," small rim chip on shade, wingnut replacement, overall 18" h. (ILLUS. bottom previous page) ..................................................... **805.00**

**Hall globe lamp,** spherical orangish amber shade w/painted bird on branches at front & back, original metal hardware tassel & cap painted green, 10" d. (ILLUS. below) ............ **460.00**

*Handel Hall Globe*

*Handel Lily Lamp*

**Lily table lamp,** three blossom-form shades each w/six bent panels of white opal glass forming the lily petals attached to sockets on arched stems joined at the center above curved ribbed leaves joined at the floral-form cast bronze base marked "Handel," 21" h. (ILLUS. bottom previous column) .......................... **4,600.00**

**Miniature lamp,** 6" d. conical frosted shade w/a green chain decoration outside & orangish amber inside, mounted on a three-arm 'spider' support & bronzed metal single-socket base impressed "Handel," overall 9¾" h. .................................. **345.00**

**Table lamp,** 16" d. domical reverse painted Teroma shade decorated w/lush palm trees & leafy plants around a peaceful lagoon reflecting the moon above, earthtone colors below a blue sky, signed "6971A," on a slender round cast metal shaft w/a wide disc foot, 20½" h. (base repainted) ..................................... **3,910.00**

**Table lamp,** 16" d. 'Tam O'Shanter'-form white opal open-topped shade decorated on the exterior w/an enameled decorated band of yellow daisies & brown scrolling designs, rim marked "Handel 3845," the shade in a shade ring & mounted on a slender squared cast-metal shaft on a squared foot signed "Handel," 19" h... **690.00**

**Table lamp,** 17¼" d. domical reverse painted shade in textured grey painted w/a scene of the Dutch inland sea w/windmills & sailboats in shades of yellow, pink, blue, purple, ochre, green, black & brown, on a ribbed columnar patinated metal base w/foliate-cast bands, bronze patina, shaded signed "Handel," base w/Handel fabric label, 23¼" h. ......... **2,070.00**

**Table lamp,** 18" d. conical open-topped reverse-painted shade composed of four curved frosted panels, acid-etched w/two orange exotic parrots amid broad-leafed bamboo-like grasses, signed on the rim "Handel 7686," on a cast metal slender tapering cylindrical metal base w/dished disc foot & dark finish, 24" h. .................................. **8,050.00**

**Table lamp,** 18" d. domical reverse-painted shaded w/slender stylized dark trees w/bright amber leaf accents & blueberries, rim signed "Bedigie Handel 7202," on a slender gilt-metal ribbed base w/a flaring foot, 24" h. ..................................... **7,475.00**

**Table lamp,** 18" d. domical reverse-painted shade w/a river landscape w/a fence, tall leafy trees, blue skies & purple mountains in the background, metal cap & raised on a bottle-form ribbed bronzed metal standard on a fretwork platform base, "Handel" on ring mount, 24" h. ........................................... **5,175.00**

**Table lamp,** 18" d. domical reverse-painted Teroma shade decorated in primary colors w/a wide stylized Arts & Crafts design rim band below an orangish amber top, signed at the rim "Handel 6750," mounted on a heavy cast-metal copper-finished Oriental-style vase-form base w/round pierced scroll-cast incurved foot, 24" h. (one flat inside rim shade chip) .............................................. **3,335.00**

**Table lamp,** 18¾" d. leaded glass domical shade composed of central graduated tiles in striated green & white above a border of water lilies & leafage in shades of striated red, pink, white & green, raised on a slender patinated metal shaft on a round disc foot cast w/petals & stems, black base patina, shade impressed "Handel," base w/Handel fabric label, ca. 1915, 23" h. .......... **2,300.00**

**Table lamp,** 20" d. conical leaded shade composed of deep red, yellowish orange, green & tree-branch brown w/selected opal & ripple glass arranged as pansy-like blossoms in overall brilliant display, mounted on bronzed metal base w/floral motif signed "Handel," 24" h. ........................................... **5,175.00**

*Scenic Handel Lamp*

**Table lamp,** 20" d. conical Teroma shade artistically painted w/white birches & green tree-filled river scene under blue, yellow, orange sunset sky, signed "Handel 6939" & "Handel Lamps" on ring, mounted on three-socket bronzed metal base w/threaded "Handel" label, small chip at rim edge, 23" h. (ILLUS. bottom previous column) .............. **4,313.00**

*Rare Handel Lamp*

**Table lamp,** domical reverse-painted shade decorated w/large chrysanthemum blossoms & leaves, raised on a figural-cast metal base w/a kneeling maiden holding a jug on one shoulder, complete w/original metal cap (ILLUS.)...................... **30,000.00**

## KEROSENE LAMPS

*Note: Lamps do not include burner & chimney, unless otherwise noted.*

**Hand lamp,** clear pressed glass, Cup and Saucer patt. ............... **150.00 to 175.00**

**Hand lamp,** clear pressed glass, Feathered Arch patt. font w/triple stem base......................... **175.00 to 225.00**

**Hand lamp,** clear pressed glass, plain ovoid font above domed foot, w/two loop handles connect base to font, marked "1868 Ripley & Co." .................................... **75.00 to 100.00**

**Hand lamp,** clear pressed glass, Prince Edward patt., footed ............. **150.00 to 175.00**

**Hand lamp,** clear glass, Quartered Block patt., w/handle, footed, kerosene burner & "pie crust" chimney, ca. 1880s .......... **150.00 to 200.00**

*Colored Glass Hand Lamp*

*"Non-Explosive" Tin Hand Lamp*

**Hand lamp,** clear pressed glass,
Seashell patt. .................. **100.00 to 125.00**

**Hand lamp,** clear pressed glass,
Torpedo patt. .................... **100.00 to 125.00**

**Hand lamp,** colored glass, waisted
cylindrical font w/applied handle,
kerosene burner & "pie crust" topped
chimney (ILLUS. top) ........................ **295.00**

**Hand lamp,** tin & glass, tin bottom
w/handle, kerosene burner
w/cylindrical chimney, "Non-
Explosive," Perkins and House,
ca. 1890s (ILLUS. bottom).. **100.00 to 125.00**

*Bradley & Hubbard Parlor Lamp*

**Parlor lamp,** slag green glass shade
& cylindrical glass chimney above
squatty baluster-shaped bottom
w/serpentine handles & raised ridge
in middle, w/"verde gris" finish,
signed Bradley & Hubbard, complete
(ILLUS.) ............................................ **650.00**

**Student lamp,** brass lamp w/original
nickel-plate finish, tall cylindrical
glass chimney w/cased green
shade, kerosene burner, Manhattan
Brass Co. ............................ **450.00 and up**

*Buckle Pattern Table Lamp*

**Table lamp,** clear pressed glass,
Buckle patt., angular font w/ribbed
top, tapers to columnar cast-iron
standard & square base, Atterbury &
Co., ca. 1860s .................. **125.00 to 150.00**

*Chicago Table Lamp*

*Ring Punty Kerosene Lamps*

**Table lamp,** clear pressed glass, Chicago patt., ribbed font w/plain center band on columnar standard on domed foot, named for the 1893 Chicago World's Fair (ILLUS. top) ...................... **100.00 to 150.00**

**Table lamp,** clear pressed glass, Daisy and Button patt., w/matching base ................................ **150.00 to 175.00**

**Table lamp,** clear pressed glass, Ella patt., squatty ovoid font above baluster standard w/domed foot, machine-made, one-piece, ca. after 1910 ...................................... **45.00 to 60.00**

**Table lamp,** clear pressed glass, Four Petal patt., w/blue glass base ................................. **350.00 to 450.00**

**Table lamp,** clear pressed glass, Grape Band patt. ............. **100.00 to 125.00**

**Table lamp,** clear pressed glass, Heart and Stars patt. ........ **100.00 to 200.00**

**Table lamp,** clear pressed glass, Lamax Utah patt. .............. **100.00 to 125.00**

**Table lamp,** clear pressed glass, Palmette patt. ................... **100.00 to 125.00**

**Table lamp,** clear pressed glass, Ring Punty patt. (one of the earliest known kerosene lamp patterns), bulbous ovoid font w/brass standard on square marble base (ILLUS. bottom previous column).. **100.00 to 125.00**

**Table lamp,** clear pressed glass, Rochelle patt. ................... **200.00 to 250.00**

**Table lamp,** clear pressed glass, roughed pattern font w/iron base ................................. **100.00 to 200.00**

*Scroll and Fern Pattern Lamp*

**Table lamp,** clear pressed glass, Scroll and Fern patt., cylindrical font above baluster-shaped standard w/domed foot, Riverside Glass Company (ILLUS.) ........... **100.00 to 125.00**

**Table lamp,** clear pressed glass, Shelley patt., globular font w/screw connector & milk glass base, Atterbury & Co. (ILLUS. top next page) ............................... **150.00 to 200.00**

**Table lamp,** clear pressed glass, Thousand Eye patt., ovoid font above cylindrical standard w/domed & footed base, Adams & Company .......................... **125.00 to 150.00**

*Shelley Pattern Lamp with Milk Glass Base*

*Figural Hand Table Lamp*

*Wheeling Plain Table Lamp*

**Table lamp,** clear pressed glass, Wheeling Plain patt., font has flat top w/raised ridge above angular bottom, brass connector on milk glass standard & base, patented connector dated "May 24th 1870," Hobbs, Brockunier & Co. (ILLUS.) ............................. **125.00 to 175.00**

**Table lamp,** cranberry pressed glass, Coin Dot patt. ........................ **850.00 and up**

**Table lamp,** green opaque pressed glass, Bellevue or Coolidge Drape patt., w/matching chimney ............. **2,500.00**

**Table lamp,** green pressed glass, Empress patt. ................... **200.00 to 225.00**

**Table lamp,** figural, angular glass font w/ribbed bottom, glass connector above a hand grasping the lower portion of standard, all domed base, w/patented drip-through, Hobbs, Brockunier & Co., ca. 1880s (ILLUS.) ............................ **200.00 to 250.00**

**Table lamp,** figural, clear pressed glass font w/iron figure of a milkmaid .......................... **175.00 to 225.00**

**Table lamp,** Ripley Wedding Lamp, blue & clear pressed glass, two matching blue fonts flanking toothpick holder, above white glass base .............................................. **1,400.00**

## PAIRPOINT LAMPS

*Well known as a producer of fine Victorian art glass and silver plate wares, between 1907 and 1929 the Pairpoint Corporation of New Bedford, Massachusetts also produced a wide range of decorative lamps.*

**Boudoir lamp,** 9" d. tapering "Puffy" shade, blown-out rose tree w/two butterflies above pink & yellow roses against blue & white latticework background, black dotted outlines overall, mounted on gilt metal four footed baluster base impressed w/"Pairpoint" marks & "3047½ 8½," minimal flat chip under rim, 16" h. ... **3,105.00**

**Boudoir lamp,** 9" d. domical "Puffy" umbrella-form 'Papillon' closed-top shade w/large blossom clusters molded along the lower scalloped edge w/large butterflies above against a ripple-molded ground reverse painted w/yellow & pink blossoms & two butterflies against a blue & white lattice ground, on a gilt-metal slender paneled baluster-form standard w/a paneled, stepped foot, base impressed "Pairpoint C 3057," 16" h. ............................................. **2,990.00**

*"Puffy" Papillon Pairpoint Lamp*

**Boudoir lamp,** "Puffy" domical flat-topped 'Papillon' closed-top shade w/blown-out design of roses & butterflies, on thin engraved baluster-shaped stem (ILLUS.)...... **5,500.00**

**Table lamp,** 13½" d. domical "Puffy" closed-top 'Rose Bouquet' shade, mold-blown deep maroon red blossoms on a leafy green ground w/yellowish orange accents, mounted on a ring & supports w/pierced arms cast w/iris blossoms joining a silver plate & gilt-metal flaring base w/relief-cast long leaves, impressed "Pairpoint 3055," 21½" h. ...................................... **11,500.00**

**Table lamp,** 14" d. domical "Puffy" closed-top 'Papillon' (butterfly) reverse-painted shade decorated w/blown-out butterflies & red roses, raised on a slender columnar gilt-metal standard cast w/torches above the plinth base cast w/floral swags on a square foot, marked "Pairpoint B3006," 21½" h. (gold worn) .......... **8,050.00**

**Table lamp,** 14" sq. "Puffy" closed-top 'Ravenna' shade w/fanned ribbing

on the sides, reverse-painted w/a Pilgrim scenes, the long sides decorated on one side w/a scene of Priscilla & John Alden walking in a landscape, the other side w/a scene of the Mayflower in high seas, the central panel decorated w/multicolored blown-out blossom wreaths against a red, yellow & white-striped ground, on a gilt-metal slender squared ovoid standard w/wreath-cast oval reserves raised on a shaped squared foot w/cast baskets of flowers & wreaths, marked "Pairpoint B3056," 23½" h... **9,200.00**

**Table lamp,** 15" d. domical "Puffy" closed top 'Grape' patt. shade w/a blown-out design reverse-painted w/dark red grapes & green & amber leaves, mounted on a silvered metal ring support & three arms tapering to a knob-topped standard w/a widely flaring foot decorated w/long undulating leaves, shade & base marked "Pairpoint Corp.," overall 22" h. ............................................. **8,050.00**

**Table lamp,** 15⅛" d. domical reverse painted 'Lansdowne' shade w/stepped top, frosty grey painted w/a harbor scene at dusk, several masted vessels in the foreground & a town in the background, in shades of purple, brown, orange, red, black & yellow, on a turned mahogany urn-form base w/disc foot & brass mounts, shade signed "The Pairpoint Corp.," 20¼" h. (small shade chip) .............. **5,750.00**

**Table lamp,** 16" d. wide conical 'Directoire' shade reverse painted in green, brick red & yellowish amber w/a floral scrolling tapestry design w/decorative spatterwork, mounted on a triple candelabrum base w/a glass sphere w/trapped air bubbles above a short metal pedestal to the octagonal black & green onyx platform base, impressed "Pairpoint D3099," 26" h................................ **2,300.00**

**Table lamp,** 16" sq. domical "Puffy" 'Torino' shade w/closed top & reverse-painted blown-out decoration of roses, daisies, chrysanthemums on two sides & bouquet medallions & millefiori scrolling designs against a rose-colored ground overall, mounted on a unique squared cast-metal base in the Aesthetic taste w/the swelled central portion applied w/a large cluster of leaves & berries against a hammered ground & raised on flaring angular feet, apparently unsigned, 20" h. ............................ **7,475.00**

**Table lamp,** 18" d. flared domical 'Copley' shade w/green, purple & white canopy top bordered by colorful leafy urn & scroll motif on yellow ground topped w/ball finial, mounted on copper colored urn-form metal base stamped w/"Pairpoint" logo, 22" h..................................... **1,610.00**

*Scenic Pairpoint Lamp*

**Table lamp,** 18" d. domical reverse-painted 'Landsdowne' shade decorated w/a continuous rural landscape w/a cottage, farm buildings & cows by a river w/a village beyond, signed "H. Fisher" & stamped "The Pairpoint Corp'n.," on a bronzed metal widely flaring ribbed base w/narrow foot band & bearing Pairpoint marks, 22" h. (ILLUS.) .... **3,335.00**

**Table lamp,** 18" d. domical 'Carlisle' reverse-painted shade decorated w/a Venetian harbor scene w/tall ships & small boats, the city beyond, marked "The Pairpoint Corp'n" & artist-signed "F. Guba," on a vase-form bronzed metal base w/a tall slender standard flanked by long loop handles to the shoulder, squatty base raised on a round foot, base impressed "Pairpoint D3034," 22½" h. ......................................... **3,680.00**

**Table lamp,** 20" d. reverse-painted 'Copley' shade in etched grey painted w/a neoclassical garden w/a pavilion, fountain & balustrade in shades of green, blue, purple, red,

*'Puffy' Apple Tree Lamp*

*Scenic Seascape Lamp*

brown & orange, on an urn-form cast-metal base w/pistol-grip handles & cast floral festoons at the shoulder, shade signed "G. Morley," base signed "Pairpoint" w/company mark & "D6016 - Made in U.S.A.," 24½" h. .............................................. **3,162.00**

**Table lamp,** domical "Puffy" shade in the shape an apple tree in reds, yellows & greens, shows bees flying around fruit, on slender brass base molded to look like a tree trunk (ILLUS. top this column) ............. **25,300.00**

**Table lamp,** domical "Puffy" shade in the shape of a rose bouquet w/metal rim, on thin cylindrical stem flanked by scroll-cut flowers & stems on round base.................................... **14,300.00**

**Table lamp,** conical reverse-painted 'Seascape' scenic shade pictures a sailboat on rough seas against a stormy sky, above three columns surrounding a thin baluster-shaped stem, all on triangular three footed base, shade marked "F.Guba" (ILLUS. bottom previous page)...... **6,600.00**

## TIFFANY LAMPS

*Tiffany Ball Lamp*

**Ball lamp,** "Dogwood," 10" d. spherical leaded glass shade w/a design of dogwood blossoms in shades of opalescent & striated white & beige, some tiles infused w/pink & green confetti glass, w/yellow centers, striated green leafage & brown stems all reserved against a vivid striated blue ground, slender intaglio finish bronze standard w/widely flaring foot, brown patina, base impressed "Tiffany Studios - New York - 1651," 33" h. (ILLUS.) ...................................... **17,250.00**

**Desk lamp,** 18" d. domical shade of green Favrile glass decorated w/intaglio-cut heart-shaped leafage w/trailing stems, suspended from a fixture within a harp above the slender baluster-form bronze standard on a domed, ribbed foot, brown patina,

base stamped "Tiffany Studios - New York - 424," 17½" h. ........................ **3,680.00**

**Floor lamp,** counter-balance-type, "Acorn," 9½" d., domical leaded glass shade composed of graduated rectangular tiles above a medial band of acorn leaves in green mottled & striated w/white, suspended from a counter-balance fixture on a tall slender bronze shaft ending in five tall slender flaring legs w/pad feet, dark brown patina, shade impressed "Tifffany Studios - New York," base impressed "Tiffany Studios - New York - 468," 4' 6" h.. **8,050.00**

**Floor lamp,** counter-balance-type, 10"d. domical white shade decorated w/iridescent amber waves, raised on a tall, slender foliate-cast bronze standard w/dished & fluted round foot, intaglio finish, shade signed "L.C.T. - Favrile - 5," base impressed "Tiffany Studios - New York - 677," 4' 6½" h................................... **7,475.00**

**Lily lamp,** eighteen-light, the long trumpet-form ribbed shades in amber iridescent, issuing from arched clustered bronze stems continuing down to a cluster of lily pad leaves at the base, intaglio finish, four shades signed "L.C.T. Favrile" or "L.C.T.," base impressed "Tiffany Studios - New York - 383," 21" h. (two shades missing, three chipped) ................ **17,250.00**

**Piano lamp,** the ribbed trumpet-form shade in iridescent amber pendent from a curving bronze standard w/a large spherical base & small ball feet, greenish brown patina, shade signed "L.C.T.," base impressed "Tiffany Studios - New York - 11237," 17" l. ................................. **2,300.00**

**Student lamp,** simple dark patina double-posted lamp w/green cased to opal ten-rib damascene shades inscribed "L.C.T.," base manufactured by Manhattan Brass & Co., one minor chip at top edge, 10" h. (ILLUS. top next page) ........ **7,475.00**

**Table lamp,** Favrile glass & bronze, 16" d. shade composed of radiating lozenges & ovals in striated amber & white opalescent ripple glass above four rows of rectangular tiles in striated amber opalescent glass, brown patina, mounted on urn-shaped bottom w/four feet leading to square base, shade impressed "Tiffany Studios New York," base unsigned, 21¼" h. .......................... **7,475.00**

*Tiffany Student Lamp*

*Tiffany Apple Blossom Lamp*

**Table lamp,** "Apple Blossom," 10" d. domical leaded glass shade w/a design of apple blossoms in rose & pink striated w/white & yellow centers, w/stems & leafage in brown & green striated w/white, all reserved against a background of faintly opalescent glass infused w/green & brown confetti glass, the whole within amber ripple glass borders, on a slender, waisted & reeded bronze standard above a domed reeded base w/knob feet, brown patina, w/matching finial, shade impressed "Tiffany Studios - New York - 1443," base impressed "Tiffany Studios - New York - 10648," 22½" h. (ILLUS.)............. **27,600.00**

**Table lamp,** "Bamboo," 16" d. leaded glass shade w/a design of bamboo leaves in striated shades of amber, green & white w/stalks in olive green, reserved against an opalescent white & amber ground, on a bamboo stock bronze base w/flaring roots on a disc foot, brown patina, w/matching finial, shade impressed "Tiffany Studios - New York - 1443," base impressed "Tiffany Studios - New York - 10648," 22½" h. ......................... **32,200.00**

**Table lamp,** "Begonia," 13½" d. domical leaded glass shade in a design of begonia blossoms in striated pink & white w/yellow centers & leafage in shades of green striated w/amber, red & white, reserved against striated shades of blue, yellow & green, on a bronze tree trunk base w/a brown patina, shade impressed "Tiffany Studios - New York - 350-6," shade impressed "Tiffany Studios - New York - 7805," 16½" h. ....................................... **51,750.00**

**Table lamp,** "Bellflower," domical leaded glass shade w/a design of large bellflowers in shades of pink & dusty rose w/leafage in striated shades of deep amber against a mottled green background, raised on a squared bronze framework base inset w/four iridescent red turtleback tiles, the metal w/a rich brownish green patina, base on claw-form knob feet, shade impressed "Tiffany Studios - New York," base impressed "Tiffany Studios - New York - 277," w/Tiffany Glass and Decorating Company hallmark, 17½" h. ......... **20,412.00**

*Tiffany Clematis Lamp*

**Table lamp,** "Clematis," 18¼" d.
domical leaded glass shade
w/clematis blossoms in striated
shades of cobalt blue & violet,
against a mottled & striated green
background streaked & shaded
w/blue, violet & white, green
streaked & shaded w/blue, violet &
white, greenish brown patina
w/small ball finial, mounted on thin
cylindrical neck w/strips & scrolls
above squat bulbous base on four
feet, shade impressed "Tiffany
Studios - New York," base
impressed "Tiffany Studios - New
York - 365," 23" h. (ILLUS. bottom
previous page) ............................ **42,550.00**

*Tiffany Pebble Lamp*

*Tiffany Daffodil Lamp*

**Table lamp,** "Daffodil," 14" d. leaded
glass shade composed of large
naturalistic daffodil blossoms in
mottled & marbleized yellow w/green
spiked leaves & a sky blue
background, rim tag w/"Tiffany
Studios New York," raised on a
slender gilt-bronze standard on a
mushroom pattern round disc foot
impressed "Tiffany Studios New York
337," 18" h. (ILLUS.) ...................... **14,950.00**

**Table lamp,** "Nasturium," 20" d.
leaded glass shade decorated w/a
profusion of nasturium blossoms in
mottled yellow, orange, red & pink &
foliage in mottled green against an
amber ground, raised on a slender
bronze vining scroll-wrapped
standard on a cushion base
w/stylized pods & ribbing, stamped
"Tiffany Studios New York 6004,"
25½" h. ...................................... **26,450.00**

**Table lamp,** "Pebble," 16" d. leaded
glass shade inset w/a floral design of
translucent amberish white pebbles
& glass tiles in shades of white, pink
& green, on a bronze base w/a
bulbous, nearly spherical font
cupped in case rounded leaves
above a slender shaft to the round
dished foot, brownish green patina,
shade impressed "Tiffany Studios -
New York - 1459-1," base impressed
"Tiffany Studios - New York -
29938," 21¾" h. (ILLUS.) ............. **57,500.00**

**Table lamp,** "Pomegranate," domical
lead glass shade w/radiating bands
of rectangular green tiles striated &
mottled w/white, a lower band of
stylized pomegranates in striated pink
& white, raised on a slender ovoid
bronze standard w/four slender open
supports to a short pedestal ending in
a squared foot, brownish green base
patina, w/finial, shade impressed
"Tiffany Studios - New York," base
impressed "Tiffany Studios -
New York - 444," 22½" h. ............... **6,325.00**

**Table lamp,** "Spreading Cherry Tree,"
25" d. domical leaded glass shade,
an overall design of cherry blossoms
in shades of white & pink w/yellow
centers, laden w/red, crimson,
mauve & dusty rose-colored fruit
w/leafage in shades of green
shading from olive to line striated
w/white, all reserved against a clear
glass ground tinged w/opalescence
& infused w/amber, green & pink
confetti inclusions, pierced bronze

branch top & raised on a bronze mangrove tree trunk base w/a greenish brown patina, shade impressed "Tiffany Studios - New York - 351-7," base impressed "Tiffany Studios - New York - 351 - S 168," 29½" h. ............................ **85,000.00**

**Table lamp,** "Tyler," 18" d. domed leaded glass shade w/yellow swirling design against a green shaded ground, set on a spreading metal base w/stylized foliate motif w/stamped marks, mounted on squatty bulbous base w/engraved leaves above ribbed flaring foot, 27" h. .......................................... **11,500.00**

**Table lamp,** "Wisteria," miniature-type, 10" d. domical leaded glass shade w/a network of open bronze branches above a design of pendent clusters of wisteria blossoms in shades of rich purple, puce, striated light blue & cobalt, w/leafage in various shades of striated green shading from line to emerald green to teal, on a bronze tree trunk base w/brownish green patina, base impressed "Tiffany Studios - New York - 554," 17" h. .............. **57,500.00**

## MISCELLANEOUS LAMPS

**Argand lamps,** bronze, Classical-style, each w/urn shaped font w/swan's neck handles & acorn finial above a baluster & foliate standard w/a single arm over a tripartite molded plinth mounted w/three scrolling dolphins, probably American, ca. 1820, 24¼" h., pr. ...................... **3,680.00**

**Art Nouveau table lamp,** bronze, figural half-nude standing maiden holding aloft an arched flowering leafy branch w/light sockets in the blossoms, on a flaring squared plinth, golden brown patina, unsigned, ca. 1900, lower blossom fitting loose, some repairs to leaves, 44½" h. (ILLUS. top next column) ...................................... **4,025.00**

**Arts & Crafts table lamp,** copper & mica, 21" d. four-panel mica shade w/riveted baton dividers, baluster-shaped copper base possibly manufactured by Old Mission Kopper Kraft, ca. 1922, 27½" h. (ILLUS. bottom next column) ......... **4,025.00**

*Figural Art Nouveau Lamp*

*Arts & Crafts Table Lamp*

**Boudoir lamp,** 7½" d. domical reverse-painted shade w/naturalistic landscape decoration, burnished gilt-metal weighted base, 13¾" h. .......... **230.00**

**Bradley & Hubbard table lamp,** 10" d. domical pressed-metal shade w/spread-winged bats in high-relief & glass "jewel" inserts, raised on a spider ring on a slender metal shaft to a domed & dished metal base w/a faux jewel border & flaring ribbed tab feet, base molded "B. & H. 4328," 19" h. (paint wear, inserts loose) ... **1,265.00**

**Bradley & Hubbard table lamp,**
15" d. domical shade w/eight amber
slag glass panels in a floral-cast
metal frame, gilt-metal socket base
w/ribbed shaft & foliate platform
marked "Bradley & Hubbard Mfg.,"
supporting metal surface wear, one
socket replaced, 22" h. .................... **575.00**

**Chicago Mosaic Shade Company
table lamp,** 24" d. domical leaded
glass shade composed of pink &
white lily blossoms & buds among
green leaves against an amber
slag ground w/rippled accents
throughout, raised on a black cast-
metal tree trunk base w/molded
blossoms & grasses, 26½" h. ....... **4,025.00**

*Desk Lamp with Reverse-painted Shade*

**Desk lamp,** 6¾" l. oval reverse
painted shade decorated w/stylized
exotic birds & blossoms, mounted on
a red & gold-painted metal swing
base adjustable in height & angle
w/a wide shaped & ribbed foot,
ca. 1910, 12" h. (ILLUS. top next
column) ........................................... **374.00**

**Duffner & Kimberly table lamp,**
19" d. domical leaded glass shade
w/tuck-under border, intricately
designed w/six repeating orangish
yellow shell forms within deep
green wreaths against bright blue
segments all below six reddish
amber slag shield devices, mounted
on Duffner's trifid base w/cast
foliate designs & a tripartite foot
w/brown & ambergris patina,
23" h. ......................................... **11,500.00**

*Fine Duffner & Kimberly Table Lamp*

**Duffner & Kimberly table lamp,**
"Colonial," 18½" d. domical leaded
glass shade w/ornate quatraform
design w/four raised & four
recessed panels of white, amber &
green segments accents by fiery
amber ripple glass in an intricate
scrolling design, raised on original
dark gilt-bronze slender baluster-
form standard w/swags & ribbing
above the four-lobed foot,
23½" h. (ILLUS. middle next
column) ........................................ **8,050.00**

**Gone With the Wind lamp,** ball
shade & base in pastel blue w/pink
floral decorations, brass can &
footed brass base, electrified,
7½" d., 21½" h. ............................... **295.00**

*Pair of Gone With the Wind Lamps*

**Gone With the Wind lamps,**
decorated on the ball shade & base w/a winter scene of a small house w/mountains in the background, on ornate pierced-metal footed base, pr. (ILLUS. bottom previous page) ... **550.00**

*Millefiori Table Lamp*

*Satin Glass Hall Lamp*

**Hall lamp,** pink satin glass, ovoid paneled shade w/molded high-relief scrolls surrounding white & yellow-centered corelene flowers, w/brass ring at top & brass cap w/knob finial, 17" h. (ILLUS.) ................................... **475.00**

**Jefferson table lamp,** 10" d. shade, greenish black painted metal base below reverse painted domical shade w/naturalistic meadow landscape, artist initialed & numbered 2705, 15" h. .................. **1,495.00**

**Millefiori table lamp,** slender baluster-form base topped by a pierced brass spherical connector & four flat support arms below the wide, domed mushroom-shaped shade, both base & shade decorated in colorful millefiori canes (ILLUS. top next column) ............................... **600.00**

**Moe Bridges boudoir lamp,** 8" d. domical reverse painted shade decorated w/a green, amber & brown landscape under a yellow sky, mounted on a slender baluster-form metal base w/disc foot, base marked "Moe Bridges Milwaukee," 13½" h. ... **575.00**

**Parker table lamp,** 21" d. rounded conical shade of six amber slag bent panels in elaborate foliate frame, copper-bronze base w/repeating raised Art Nouveau designs w/base reads "Charles Parker Co.," 23" h. ... **633.00**

*Green Peg Lamps*

**Parlor lamp,** kerosene-type, large h.p. ball shade decorated w/four jolly monks in the cellar tapping a keg of spirits by candlelight, electrified ..... **3,420.00**

**Peg lamps,** frosted lime green squatty bulbous fonts w/original brass burners, each decorated w/heavy gilt looping scrolls & leaf sprigs, 3⅜" d., 5¾" h., pr. (ILLUS. bottom) .............. **210.00**

**Pittsburgh table lamp,** 14" d. domical glass shade painted w/a border scene of tropical trees & flowering plants under a blue sky, raised on a cast-iron foliate-cast base, 19" h. ..... **633.00**

**Pittsburgh table lamp,** 16" d. domical painted frosted textured shade, decorated on the outside w/stylized large yellow-centered pink & yellow water lilies & leafy vines & pages in green outlined in raised black

*Pittsburgh Table Lamp*

*Satin Glass Table Lamp*

*Slag Glass Table Lamp*

*Fine Student Lamp*

enamel, mounted on an urn-form painted metal base, 20½" h. (ILLUS.) ........................................... **805.00**

**Quezel desk lamp,** 10½" d. domical opal glass-lined shade w/brilliant iridescent gold, the exterior w/five broad pulled feathers in gold, signed "Quezel" inside the top rim, mounted on a three-arm spider support on a slender black metal shaft w/a rounded dished foot w/overlapping radiating leaves, 19" h. .................. **1,725.00**

**Satin glass table lamp,** an inverted tulip-shaped shade w/folded-in sides on a brass burner & connector to the ovoid melon-lobed glass font on a short brass pedestal foot, both shade & font in shaded heavenly blue mother-of-pearl Diamond Quilted patt., white lining, complete w/clear glass chimney, 6⅝" d., 15¾" h. (ILLUS. top next column).. **1,250.00**

**Sewing lamp,** "Massive," kerosene-type, squatty ornately scroll-embossed font w/knobby pedestal on scroll embossed feet, w/old beaded-top chimney, 6½ x 6½", 9½" h. ............................................... **130.00**

**Slag glass table lamp,** 20" d. umbrella-form shade composed of matching blue slag panels in a gilt-metal framework w/pierced metal elaborate repeating urn & bird scenes, raised on a conical base of matching slag glass overlaid w/pierced metal bands & scrolls on the flaring metal foot, base wired for interior lighting, 22" h. (ILLUS. middle next column) ........................ **690.00**

**Student lamp,** double brass ringed fonts on arms joined to a center column w/font at back, raised on domed, ribbed foot, each font w/melon-lobed green-cased domed shade & clear chimney, 10" d. (ILLUS. bottom previous page)...... **1,100.00**

**Table lamp,** 16" d., domical reverse-painted smooth Phoenix-type shade decorated w/a colorful European village scene w/a rocky coastal scene beyond, mounted on a simple baluster-form dark gilt metal base w/an embossed band of crossed scrolls & rectangles around the shoulder & a dished round foot, 23" h. ............................................... **978.00**

*Leaded Glass Table Lamp*

**Table lamp,** 16½" domical leaded glass shade composed of red-centered purplish blue blossoms on an amber slag background, raised on a slender plain gilt-metal standard w/a leaf-cast knob at the bottom above the incised disc foot, 22" h. (ILLUS.) .................................. **690.00**

### OTHER LIGHTING DEVICES

### CHANDELIERS

**Art Deco-style,** five-light, alabaster & bronze, the central tiered wide circular white alabaster inverted shade within a bronze mount supporting four matching small tiered alabaster shades, France, ca. 1925, 33" d., 32" h. ........................ **3,450.00**

*Arts & Crafts Chandelier*

*Early Brass Chandelier*

**Arts & Crafts-style,** six-light, glass & bronze, the six ovoid floriform shades w/ruffled rims in amber w/shading to gold & violet iridescence & decorated w/opalescent white "watered silk" trailings, set into a foliate fixture pendent from a thin spandrel braces hung from a curving arm issuing from a hammered undulating floriform shallow domed ceiling cap, four shades marked "Quezel," two inscribed "Lustre Art," ca. 1920, 15" d., 19½" h. (ILLUS. top)............ **4,025.00**

**Brass,** twelve-light, long ring-turned center shaft issuing two tiers of six S-scroll candlearms above a large ball & ring drop at the bottom, good color & surface, Holland, probably early 19th c., electrified (ILLUS. bottom).. **1,540.00**

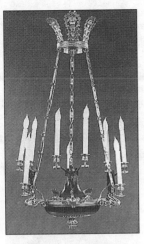

*French Empire Chandelier*

*Unique Quezal Chandelier*

**Empire-style,** ormolu & patinated brass, nine-light, the brass pierced scrolled floral finials above circular brass punch-decorated crown issuing three pierced & decorated chains terminating in brass swan candleholders surmounted by electrified candles flanked by ebonized angles w/extended arms holding candle holders surmounted by electrified candles all over an ebonized circular base w/brass embellishments & a brass acorn drop, French, ca. 1800-1820, 23½" d., 38" h. (ILLUS.)................. **3,450.00**

**Lalique-signed,** "Hirondelles," molded & frosted clear glass in a wide inverted dome form composed of twelve sections, each modeled in low-relief w/three swallows in flight, impressed "R. Lalique," model introduced in 1921, 25" d., w/hanging cords 42" h. (minor chips)............. **10,350.00**

**Leaded glass & bronze,** three-light, Arts & Crafts-style, a large central inverted dome shade & three pendent satellite conical shades each w/a pattern of water lilies, cattails & leafage in striated & mottled shades of pink, green & brown reserved against an amber & white ground, the suspended shades hung from bronze chains attached to the top bronze frame of the center shade, the whole suspended from three heavy chains, ca. 1915, 18¾" d. .......................................... **2,070.00**

**Muller Freres-signed,** the central conical frosted glass shade molded w/panels of stylized foliage & tendrils in pale pink, fitting into a textured wrought-iron circular mount issuing three scrolling arms, foliate caps & matching long conical pink glass shades, all pendent from three wrought-iron terminals w/ceiling cap, shaded molded "Muller Freres - Luneville," France, early 20th c., 19¼" d., 31" h. .............................. **2,185.00**

**Quezal-signed,** eight-light, a foliate-pierced bronze canopy above eight foliate-trimmed down-turned arms each ending in a socket w/a long iridescent gold lily-form shade signed "Quezal," all centering a leaf-form cap suspending slender flaring bars to the bronze circular ring w/pierced palmette-form rim projections & suspending a large domed leaded glass shade composed of brilliant fiery greenish amber segments in a graduated herringbone design, a large acorn-form drop at the bottom center, lower shade 19" d., overall 34" d., 40" h. (ILLUS. above) .................. **12,650.00**

**Rococo-style,** sixteen-light, gilt-bronze, variegated green marble & glass, three slender downswept scrolling arms issuing five lights w/the shades in the form of frosted glass rose blossoms, the other sockets on upswept scrolls all centering a marble disc topped by ormolu-mounted roses, a pierced scroll drop at the base, France, late 19th c., 30" d., 44" h. ..................... **2,200.00**

**Sinumbra-type,** painted tole, a small crown ring w/feathered projections suspending three long delicate chains to the wide font ring w/green paint & gilt reticulated upper & lower borders, the outside edges projecting four feathered arrow tails, original surface, unrestored shade, France, ca. 1820, 20" d., 34½" h. .. **2,640.00**

*Tiffany Peony Chandelier*

**Tiffany-signed,** "Peony," the wide conical leaded glass shade w/lower beaded border, an overall design of red peony blossoms & green leafage in mottled & striated shades of sky blue, white, plum, turquoise, olive green, crimson, teal blue, orange, pink & yellow, reserved against a dark blue ground, pendent from a pierced bronze crown w/geometric designs & scrolling hooks, brown metal patina, shade impressed "Tiffany Studios - New York - 603-17," lacking fittings, 28½" d. (ILLUS.) ... **55,200.00**

*Venetian Crystal Chandelier*

**Venetian crystal,** four-light, the long ornate central standard composed of pink glass balls w/rigaree bands above the four scrolled arms w/deep rolled & fluted socket cups above central tiers of rigaree, the central disc also issuing tall flower stems & blossoms & long serrated scrolling leaves, 24" w., 24" h. (ILLUS. bottom previous column) .............................. **550.00**

## LANTERNS

*Early Candle Lantern*

**Candle lantern,** brass & horn, the pierced conical top w/stamped tulip designs & a metal loop handle above the cylindrical sides w/inset curved horn panels & a hinged door w/horn panel & wire guard above a short pierced cylindrical base, some damage to horn, 9¾" h. (ILLUS.) ...... **165.00**

**Candle lantern,** primitive wood & glass, the rectangular wooden framework holding glass panes, a hinged front w/glass pane, crude wire bail handle & wide strap handle on the top, mortised construction, old patina, 19th c., 10" h. .................. **385.00**

**Candle lantern,** tin & glass, the pyramidal tin top pierced w/stars, large metal loop handle, the tall rectangular frame w/glass sides w/curved wire guards, one side a door, flat base, old black paint, 11¾" h. plus handle ........................ **110.00**

**Candle lantern,** punched tin, so-called "Paul Revere"-type, cylindrical tin sides pierced w/large circle designs w/double circles on the hinged door, the punched conical top w/a small metal loop handle, 13¼" h. plus handle .......................... **204.00**

**Carbide lantern,** nickel plated, "Justrite," pierced domed cap & wire bail handle above clear glass globe w/a bull's-eye lens within wire guards, cylindrical burner on round domed foot, 9¼" h. (spring clip holding font rusted, dent in base) ....... **83.00**

**Carbide lantern,** nickel plated, marked "The Toledo Acetylene Lantern Co., Toledo, O.," 11¾" h. (split in base of font) .......................... **94.00**

**Hall lantern,** brass & Aurene glass, the spherical glass shade in amber iridescence shading to pink encasing a thick layer of white, this shade enclosed within a scrolling filigree brass frame w/a middle band applied w/alternating satyr makes & heraldic crests, pierced crown top & base pendant, hung from four twisted metal bars from a scrolling floral & satyr mask filigree ceiling cap, unsigned, Oscar Bach & Steuben Aurene, ca. 1925, 10½" d., 33" h... **1,610.00**

**Hall lantern,** George III-Style, brass, of hexagonal form headed by ten figures w/urns above a corona mounted with ram's heads, late 19th - early 20th c. (ILLUS. top next column) ......................................... **3,162.00**

**Kerosene lantern,** brass & glass, a tall slender pierced cylindrical cap w/slender chain handle w/end loop above the slightly tapering cylindrical clear glass globe on a tapering brass burners w/wick adjuster on a stepped & domed font, marked "Pat'd Dec. 24, 1867," 9" h. plus chain ................................................ **127.00**

**Kerosene lantern,** tin & glass, a tall cylindrical ridged cone top w/fluted & pointed vent cap & wire bail handle, above the swelling cylindrical clear blown glass globe on a pierced cylindrical base w/flaring foot, brass kerosene burner, brass label marked "J.D. Brown Patent - May 29, 1860," 15" h. (ILLUS. middle next column) .. **220.00**

**Presentation lantern,** silver plate & glass, kerosene-type, the round ringed & pierced cap w/large wire bail handle above a flaring shield mounted w/a presentation plaque inscribed "Evening Record Prize Lantern Number of votes 115537 -

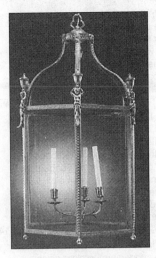

*George III-Style Lantern*

*Early Kerosene Lantern*

*Early Presentation Lantern*

1890," the bulbous ovoid glass globe w/the upper half in dark blue & the lower half in clear engraved w/a leafy wreath enclosing a name, original cylindrical burner on domed font base, ca. 1890, 11¼" h. plus handle (ILLUS. bottom previous page) ............................................ **978.00**

**Ship's lantern,** steel, sheet metal & glass, the cylindrical metal top w/ruffled metal cap & wire bail handle above a squatty bulbous blue glass globe within a wire cage guard, a cylindrical mental font below w/wire bracket, old green paint, marked "Alfred F. Centonl...Birmingham, England," 19th c., 14" h. plus handle (burner missing) ................................ **149.00**

**Ship's lantern,** brass & glass, brass frame supporting the clear glass globe, whale oil burner, marked "Brooklyn Flint Glass Co...Gillands Dioptric Lens - Patented Aug, 10, 1852," 17" h. (minor damage) ............ **330.00**

**Street lantern,** copper, the tapering wide four-sided cap w/a conical top w/scalloped domed cap w/ovoid pointed finial, the tapering rectangular framed lantern section missing its glass panels & mounting bracket, green patina, mid-19th c., 39" h. (finial resoldered) .................... **193.00**

**Whale oil lantern,** tin, glass & cast iron, a cylindrical pierced tin cap w/wire bail handle above the swelled cylindrical clear pressed glass globe on a cylindrical tin font w/a footed cast-iron base, original while oil burner, marked "G.F.J. Colburn, Pat. May 24, 1864," 9½" h. ...................... **193.00**

**Whale oil lantern,** tin, brass & glass, a cylindrical top w/pierced & domed cap & high wire bail handle above a clear blown globe within a wire cage, cylindrical font base w/flaring round foot, original whale oil burner, base marked "Kelly Rochester," 10½" h. plus handle ...................................... **242.00**

**Whale oil lantern,** pierced tin & glass, hexagonal form, the pointed hexagonal cap pierced w/stars & triangular air holes & w/a metal loop handle all above the six sided base w/six glass panels within wire guards, one panel a door, on a round disc foot, tin font w/whale oil burner, font bottom stamped "H & J Sandsters Patent 1851," 12" h. plus handle (soldered repair, some damage) .......................................... **248.00**

**Whale oil lantern,** tin & glass, the pierced cylindrical cap w/large ring handle above a clear blown globe within a wire cage above the pierced cylindrical font base w/a flaring foot, brass collar w/whale oil burner, probably New England Glass Company, old finish w/light rust, 13" h. plus handle (wire cage old addition) ............................................ **248.00**

## SHADES

**Cranberry glass,** tulip-form w/deeply fluted rim, decorated w/small white enameled flowers & gold leaves, 5⅜" d., 4" h. ...................................... **125.00**

*Decorated Cranberry Shade*

**Cranberry glass,** tulip-form frosted decorated w/gold & green leaves, gold vines & small acorn decorations, 5¾" d., 4⅜" h. pr. (ILLUS. of one) ................................ **265.00**

**Daum-signed,** deep bowl-shape w/square edge, mottled amber w/brown, green & red swirls, signed "Daum (cross) Nancy," 12½" w., 6½" h. .............................................. **489.00**

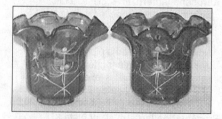

*Lime Green Decorated Shades*

**Lime green glass,** tulip-form w/deeply fluted rim, decorated w/gold leaves & pink buds, 5⅛" d., 4¼" h., pr. (ILLUS.) .............................................. **145.00**

*Unique Newcomb College Shade*

*Tiffany Linenfold Shade*

**Muller Fres.-signed,** wide dished form of frosted mottled earthtones of brown, green, coral & amber, drilled w/three ceiling mounting holes, stamped "Muller Fres. Luneville," France, early 20th c., 16½" d........... **374.00**

**Newcomb College,** pierced brass, conical paneled form w/six panels of stylized leaves & flowers, attributed to Esther Elliot, ca. 1890, 13¼" d., 6" h. (ILLUS. above) ..................... **3,575.00**

**Quezal-signed,** ribbed long trumpet-form w/white satin exterior & gold iridescent interior, each signed, set of 8 (some minor chipping at collet edge) ........................................... **1,380.00**

**Tiffany-signed,** ball-form, case ambergris to opal & decorated w/gold iridescent leaf & vine designs, signed on rim "S9432," 4⅛" d., 12½" h. ............................ **4,140.00**

**Tiffany-signed,** Linenfold-type, conical paneled form w/frosted clear Favrile glass segments w/drapery panels around the center divided by narrow glass bands from smooth top & bottom panels, rim impressed "Tiffany Studios - New York - 1028 Pat. Appl'd for," three smooth panels damaged, 14" w. (ILLUS. above)... **3,220.00**

**Tiffany-signed,** "Lemon Leaf," domical leaded glass open-topped shade w/beaded bronze top collar above the design of graduated rectangular tiles in mottled green w/a wide medial band of scrolling leaf sprigs in orange shading to amber on a mottled green & amber ground within green-tinged orange bands, another green-tinged orange band at the rim, stamped "Tiffany Studios - New York," 15¾" d. (cracked tiles, minor restoration) ........................ **3,162.00**

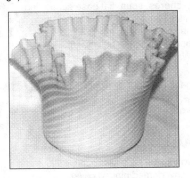

*Satin Glass Shade*

**Satin glass,** tulip-form w/deeply fluted & crimped rim, mother-of-pearl Swirl patt., shaded chartreuse to white exterior, white lining, 8½" d., 6⅜" h. (ILLUS.) ........................................... **350.00**

**Satin glass,** tulip-form, ruffled rainbow mother-of-pearl Diamond Quilted patt., w/pink, blue & yellow rainbow stripes covering three-quarters of shade, white lining, 9½" d., 6" h..... **1,500.00**

**Stevens & Williams,** frosted translucent white stripes alternating w/yellow stripes, 9¼" d., 6" h. ........... **225.00**

# LUNCH BOXES

*Although there were a few character related lunch boxes produced before World War II, it was the arrival of the television age in the 1950s that saw such boxes proliferate. Most of these vintage boxes were rectangular metal and included a matching thermos bottle with both the box exterior and thermos colorfully decorated with a picture relating to the character and their TV series. Beginning in the 1960s lunch boxes in plastic & vinyl became popular and these, as well as the earlier* metal examples, are very collectible today if in top condition. *References on old lunch boxes include* The Illustrated Encyclopedia of Metal Lunch Boxes *by Allen Woodall and Sean Brickell (Schiffer Publishing, 1992) and* Lunch Box: The Fifties and Sixties *by Scott Bruce (Chronicle Books, 1988). Prices are for boxes alone unless otherwise indicated.*

**Alvin,** (The Chipmunks), green vinyl, w/unused thermos, by King Seeley Thermos, 1963, 2 pcs. .................... **$275.00**

**Batman & Robin,** metal, Aladdin Industries, 1966 (shows wear) ............ **50.00**

**Black Hole,** metal, by Aladdin Industries, 1979 ................................ **35.00**

**Curiosity Shop,** plastic, by Thermos, 1966 ................................................ **45.00**

**Fireball XL5,** metal, by King Seeley Thermos, 1964 ................................ **70.00**

**Howdy Doody,** metal, by Adco Liberty, 1950s ............................... **1,000.00**

*Laugh-In Lunch Box*

**Laugh-In,** front w/Arte Johnson riding a tricycle, back w/various cast members' faces w/thermos, by Aladdin Industries, 1970, 2 pcs. (ILLUS.) ............................................. **94.00**

**Lawman,** scene of two lawmen w/guns drawn, w/thermos, by King Seeley Thermos, 1961, 2 pcs. .......... **140.00**

**Tom Corbett,** Space Cadet, steel, red w/full color picture on one side, by Aladdin Industries, 1952 ................. **170.00**

**U.F.O.,** metal, by King Seeley Thermos, 1973 ................................. **35.00**

# MAGAZINES

*All magazines are in excellent, complete condition unless otherwise noted.*

**Fortune Magazine,** 1934, November, eleven page article on Disney Studios, animation, etc. ................... **$25.00**

**Harper's Weekly,** 1898, December 17, Christmas story (in color), all American Football team & Spanish American War articles ...................... **10.00**

**Esquire,** 1940, April ............................. **45.00**

**Farm Mechanics,** 1924, March ............. **8.00**

**Fortune,** 1934, October ....................... **15.00**

**Playboy,** 1954, July ............ **100.00 to 150.00**

**Red Cross Magazine (The),** July 1917 .......................................... **25.00**

# METALS

## ALUMINUM

**Bun warmer,** machine-spun, designed by Russel Wright .............. **$70.00**

**Lamp,** table-type, two-light, the conically tipped cylindrical base supporting a slender standard issuing a domical shade, by Vico Magistretti, 1977, 19½" d., 28" h. ...... **184.00**

**Torcheres,** spun, flat base supporting a tall slender stem w/trumpet-form shade, wrapped trim to top & bottom, wooden ball switch, Russel Wright, 11" d., 65" h., pr. ............ **880.00**

**Tray,** oval, decorated w/tulips w/fancy handles, Rodney Kent, 13" l. ............. **18.00**

**Tray,** square, w/glass insert, marked "EMPC," 13½" sq. .............................. **22.00**

## BRASS

**Bedwarmer,** shallow round brass pan w/low domed hinged cover w/pierced holes & simple punched ringed designs, baluster-, knob- and rod-turned chestnut handle, 42" l. (ILLUS. top next page) .................... **275.00**

**Bedwarmer,** shallow round brass pan w/low domed hinged cover w/small pierced holes & tooled designs, long simply-turned wooden handle, 19th c., 53" l. .................................... **127.00**

**Candlestick,** Arts & Crafts-style, a bulbous socket w/flaring rim raised on a very tall, slender standard above the wide round disc foot, original patina, distorted Jarvie mark, 5½" d., 13½" h. ................................. **413.00**

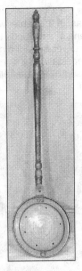

*Brass Bedwarmer*

**Candlesticks,** Neoclassical-style, the
cylindrical flaring candle socket on a
slender stepped cylindrical shaft
above the domed & squared flaring
foot, marked "F. & Co. Patent,"
w/push-ups, 19th c., 8¼" h., pr. ........ **209.00**

**Candlesticks,** a tall cylindrical candle
socket w/flaring rim raised on a
knobbed tall standard w/a squatty
diamond quilted knob above a
ringed knob above an inverted
beehive knob, on a domed &
stepped squared foot, 19th c.,
11¾" h., pr. ..................................... **143.00**

**Desk set:** letter opener, calendar,
inkwell & ink blotter; hand-
hammered, Arts & Crafts-style, each
w/a relief design of orchids, die-
stamped "Made in our craft shop -
Marshall Field & Co.," the set ........... **330.00**

**Fireplace fender,** long low serpentine
design pierced w/Classical scrolled
harps alternating w/bar panels,
looped openwork rim band, on five
small knob feet, supported by iron
bottom plates, 19th c., 55¼" l. (iron
plates loose) .................................... **660.00**

**Flag finial,** model of a spread-winged
eagle, 7" w., 6" h., 19th c. ................... **81.00**

**Lantern,** hall-type, four-light,
cylindrical brass frame w/glass
sides, hung from a ring above
strapwork scrolls w/finials over a
four-light fixture, American-made,
early 19th c., electrified, 12⅛" d.,
26" h. .............................................. **2,760.00**

**Pail w/iron bail handle,** spun, deep
slightly tapering cylindrical form,
marked "Hayden's Patent -
Waterbury Brass Co.," 19th c.,
11" d. ................................................ **50.00**

**Skimmer,** wide shallow rounded brass
bowl w/overall small pierced holes,
w/a long flattened & shaped iron
handle w/ram's-horn tip, 19th c.,
20½" l.............................................. **259.00**

**Smoking set:** cov. cylindrical
humidor, cov. rectangular cigarette
box, round ashtray & upright
matchbox holder; Arts & Crafts-style,
in a Viennese square design w/a
chocolate brown patina, die-stamped
triangular Bradley and Hubbard
mark, early 20th c., humidor 3½" d.,
6½" h., the set ................................... **55.00**

**Tinder box,** cov., short wide
cylindrical form w/small loop handle
at side of base, the flat lift-off cover
centered by a small cylindrical
candle socket, complete w/brass
damper, flint & steel, 19th c., 5" d.
(old resoldering).............................. **330.00**

*Early Brass Trivet*

**Trivet,** sheet-form w/spade-shaped
end pierced w/two small hearts
alternating w/two small diamonds,
rounded tab handle w/hanging hole,
on three turned feet, 19th c., 9" l.
(ILLUS.) ............................................ **94.00**

**Trivet,** sheet-form, long pointed
spade-form blade pierced overall
w/small heards, diamonds & stars, a
turned black wood handle, on three
feet, small stamped flowers &
stamped date "1849," 11¼" l. ............. **165.00**

**Trivet,** sheet-form w/elongated
pointed heart-shaped pierced form
w/rounded discs flanking the long

tip, the long flattened heart-form
handle pierced w/a small diamond &
heart, on three feet, 11⅞" l. ................ **50.00**

**Vase,** hand-hammered, Arts & Crafts-
style, bulbous ovoid form tapering
sharply toward the base & w/a
closed rim, original patina,
impressed script Jarvie mark,
4½" d., 3½" h. .................................. **413.00**

## BRONZE

**Ashtray,** the hemispherical bowl w/a
wide flattened rim decorated in low-
relief w/stylized butterflies & w/four
cigarette rests cast as butterflies in
flight, the entire bowl supported by
four stylized figural cats, by Armand-
Albert Rateau, stamped "A.A.
Rateau INVB 1901 Paris," France,
early 20th c., 8" d., 3¾" h............ **20,700.00**

*Figural Candlestick*

**Candlestick,** figural, a nude female
seated on her calves & holding the
irregular organic candle socket in
one arm, brown patina, signed "E-B-
Barson-Scott" & incised "Roman
Bronze Works N.Y.," first quarter
20th c., 7¼" h. (ILLUS.) ................... **747.00**

**Candlesticks,** a slightly flaring
bobeche above a standard cast as a
bamboo stalk w/a flaring root-form
foot, greenish brown patina,
impressed "Tiffany Studios -
New York - 1205," 10" h., pr. ......... **3,220.00**

**Censor,** figural, model of a *qilin,* the
ferocious beast w/gaping jaw &
bulging eyes beneath the thick
overhanging brow, the stocky body
w/short legs & stylized upright tail,
the head hinged to open to interior
vessel, China, 17th c., 7½" h. ........ **2,300.00**

**Compote,** open, a wide shallow
dished top cast in the center w/a
classical scene of a capped nude
male chariot driver & rearing horses,
on a short pedestal base, signed
"Alph. Dubois - 1871," late 19th c.,
12¾" d., 5" h. ................................... **138.00**

*Jugendstil Jardiniere*

**Jardiniere,** Jugendstil, the deep wide-
mouthed ovoid copper container
mounted w/three bronze side
handles on a pierced curving tripod
bronze base w/a domed scroll-
pierced stretcher, Europe, ca. 1900,
37¼" h. (ILLUS.) ........................... **4,255.00**

**Mortar,** cylindrical w/flaring rim
inscribed "1593 ANNO SALVTIS
NOSTER," above bands of
spearheads, beadwork & figural
decoration, the lower section flanked
by beast-form handles, 16th c.,
4⅛" h. (details worn) ........................ **517.00**

**Vase,** Art Nouveau-style, figural,
bulbous ovoid body w/a wide
shoulder tapering to a short, flaring
neck, the shoulder cast in full-relief
w/two nude maidens sitting &
leaning over the top opening,
inscribed "Ledru - SUSSE Frs Paris
Edt.," impressed "COPYRIGHT - BY
- SUSSE FRERES - 1894 - g,"
August Ledru, France, ca. 1900,
brown patina, 11½" h. ................... **4,600.00**

**Vase,** archaic *hu-*form, the wide
baluster-form body cast w/a pair of
zoomorphic loop handles rising from

a key-fret gold & silver inlaid rim & above a band of lead-form pendants, the body segmented into twelve relief-cast panels, each enclosing stylized dragons or birds within modified fey-fret borders, on tapered foot w/taotie mask & archaizing zoomorphic designs, China, 18th-19th c., 30" h............................. **11,500.00**

*Cobra Watch Holder*

**Watch holder,** figural, cast as a model of a striking cobra, its tongue forming hook for hanging watch, coiled tail forms the base, impressed "E. Brandt," Edgar Brandt, black patina, ca. 1925, 5⅛" h. (ILLUS.) .. **2,587.00**

## CHROME

**Cocktail shaker,** cov., "Dumbbell" patt., Chase, impressed marks, ca. 1935,11½" l................................. **173.00**

**Cocktail service,** traveling-type, 'Zeppelin' design, comprised of a cocktail shaker w/a bullet-shaped body & tail fins, three jiggers, a flask, a strainer, a cover, a spoon & a corkscrew & cap, the shaker stamped "24 D.R.G.M. Germany," ca. 1930, 12¼" h., the set................. **978.00**

**Lamp,** table-type, Art Deco-style, long narrow rectangular chrome shade w/stepped top raised on columnar end standards trimmed w/three thin rings near the base, on a narrow rectangular foot, shade & base w/brass trim, ca. 1930, 16" h., 12½" h. (ILLUS. top next column)...................................... **1,380.00**

*Art Deco Chrome Lamp*

*Art Deco Chrome Vase*

**Vases,** widely flaring bell-form bowl resting on a wide medial band composed of three rings of beading above the tall bell-form bases, impressed "MADE EXCLUSIVELY FOR carole stupell," ca. 1940, 13¾" h., pr. (ILLUS. of one)........... **1,380.00**

## COPPER

**Ashtray,** hand-hammered, Arts & Crafts-style, roughly hammered shallow oblong footed dish w/an upright chunk of walrus tusk at one side of the flanged rim (patina wear), attributed to Albert Berry, unmarked, 4½" w., 2½" h...................................... **55.00**

**Ashtray,** hand-hammered, Arts & Crafts-style, round dished form w/flanged rim, a thin cut-out stylized figure of a stepping man from the rim to the center, raised initials "HJ," impressed Harry L Dixon," original patina, 8" d., 6" h. ............................. **132.00**

**Bed warmer,** the round shallow copper dish w/a hinged slightly domed cover pierced & tooled w/a worn floral design, long ring- and baluster-turned wooden handle, 19th c., 44" l. ........................................ **88.00**

**Book ends,** hand-hammered, Arts & Crafts-style, rounded form w/embossed & pierced design of a tree w/a broad trunk & billowing leaves, original dark brown patina, impressed "NEK," 4½" w., 4½" h., pr. ..................................................... **330.00**

**Book ends,** hand-hammered, Arts & Crafts-style, flat upright sides w/a double-arch top above delicate pierced cut-outs, original patina, impressed mark of Dirk Van Erp, 6" w., 4½" h., pr. .............................. **770.00**

**Bowl,** hand-hammered, Arts & Crafts-style, widely flaring sides w/a four-lobed rim, raised on a low flaring foot, the interior overlaid in silver, the exterior w/a lightly cleaned copper patina, impressed logo of Gebelein, Boston, 6" d., 2½" h. ......................... **209.00**

*Covered Copper Bowl*

**Bowls,** cov., squatty bulbous form w/a closely fitting domed cover, raised on a low footring, plain rounded sides align w/the domed cover centered by a cupped marbleized ivory finial w/a scalloped band around its base, by Marie Zimmermann, one stamped "M. Zimmermann Maker No. 1487-1916," the other stamped "M. Zimmermann Maker No. 1488-1916," early 20th c., ivory partially replaced, 6¾" & 7" h., pr. (ILLUS. of one) .............................................. **5,175.00**

**Box,** cov., hand-hammered, Arts & Crafts-style, short round form w/overhanging fitted cover & rolled footring, stylized initials "HAP" on the

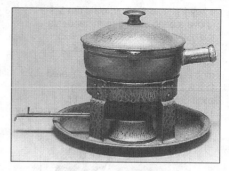

*Copper Chafing Dish*

cover, original dark brown patina, impressed "30 - 4," attributed to Stickley Brothers, 4" d., 1½" h., ........ **220.00**

**Box,** cov., hand-hammered, Arts & Crafts-style, rectangular w/a flat riveted cover w/pierced strap hinges above the slightly canted sides & wide riveted corner legs, the sides w/embossed square medallions of stylized flowers, cedar-lined, original dark patina, England, early 20th c., unmarked, 6½ x 10", 4" h. ................ **990.00**

**Candlestick,** Arts & Crafts-style, a flattened disc-form new bobeche above the swelled neck tapering to a slender waisted shaft on a thin disc foot, original patina, incised "Jarvie," 5¾" d., 13½" h. ............................. **2,970.00**

**Candlesticks,** hand-hammered, Arts & Crafts-style, a cylindrical candle socket w/a widely dished rim above a wide, flaring dished drip pan on a cylindrical shaft applied w/two loop handles above the domed round foot, fine original patina, die-stamped "Benedict Studios" mark w/anvil, 5" d., 8¼" h., pr. ................... **275.00**

**Chafing dish,** cov., Arts & Crafts-style, the deep round brown-glazed pottery dish w/a hammered copper cover & wooden knob finial, raised on a wide hammered copper frame w/four wide strap legs, on a dished circular hammered copper tray centered by a fuel canister, impressed mark of Gustav Stickley, tray 13¼" d., overall 10" h. (ILLUS. above) ......... **1,150.00**

**Chamberstick,** hand-hammered, Arts & Crafts-style, elongated shallow oval form w/a high inwardly curved handle at one end opposite the candle socket at the other, riveted handle, lightly cleaned patina, Craftsman Studios, 3 x 6", 3" h. .......... **66.00**

**Dish,** hand-hammered, Arts & Crafts-style, round w/small round center indentation & a wide flat rim embossed w/four wide hearts, original patina, impressed circle mark of Gustav Stickley, 5½" d......... **770.00**

**Humidor,** cov., hand-hammered, Arts & Crafts-style, rectangular w/a domed cover w/ring handle overhanging the plain sides above the riveted flaring base, original interior cedar box & cover, most of the original patina long removed, die-stamped mark of Gustav Stickley, 5½ x 7½", 5½" h. ............. **1,045.00**

**Humidor,** cov., waisted cylindrical form w/lobed sides applied w/silver strapwork & rivets, the cushion-form cover similarly decorated & surmounted by a loin's-mask handle, gilt interior, mark of Theodore B. Starr, New York, ca. 1905, 9¾" h. (cover hinge detached) .................. **1,840.00**

**Jardiniere,** hand-hammered, Arts & Crafts-style, wide bulbous ovoid form w/a rolled rim, original dark brown patina, die-stamped windmill mark of Dirk Van Erp w/a trace of "D'Arcy Gaw," 14" d., 10" h............ **4,125.00**

*Copper Jardiniere*

**Jardiniere,** Renaissance-style, repoussé & gadrooned jardiniere on later wrought-iron stand w/four scrolled legs topped w/animal heads holding rings, 36" h. (ILLUS.)......... **4,312.00**

**Lamp base,** hand-hammered, Arts & Crafts-style, the tall baluster-form hammered copper body w/a band of pierced holes above the flaring wide

*Arts & Crafts Lamp Base*

foot, applied w/twisted wrought-iron loop handles from flared rim to lower body, attributed to Gustav Stickley, early 20th c., 13⅛" h. (ILLUS.) ...... **3,220.00**

**Measures,** cast, graduated baluster-form bodies on flaring bases, D-form handles, England, 19th c., graduated from half pint to half gill, 6" to 10" h., set of 4 (minor damage, one w/soldered repairs) ........................... **165.00**

**Picture frame,** table model, hand-hammered, Arts & Crafts-style, a flat arched pate w/the tooled decoration of a bare-branched tree along one sides & a tree stump at the bottom w/a large oval picture opening to one side, original dark brown patina, unmarked, 5½" w., 8" h. .................. **231.00**

**Teakettle,** cov., dovetailed construction, wide bulbous slightly tapering body w/a wide shoulder & small domed cover w/brass button finial, high swing strap handle, goose-neck spout, indistinct maker's mark on handle, perhaps "J.H.—T," 19th c., 6¾" h. plus handle (spout w/old reattachment repair) ............... **523.00**

**Teakettle,** cov., dovetailed construction, wide bulbous slightly tapering body w/a wide shoulder & small domed cover w/brass finial knob, high swing strap handle at top, long goose-neck spout, handle stamped "John Seger N.Y.M.K.," 19th c., 7" h. plus handle (minor dents, old soldered repair to bottom edge) ................................................ **798.00**

**Teakettle,** cov., dovetailed construction, wide bulbous body w/a wide shoulder to a small domed

cover w/a loop finial, high swing
strap overhead handle, goose-neck
spout, handle stamped "I. Dunn" &
w/two tulips & six circle designs,
John Dunn, New York, 19th c.,
7¾" h. (dents, soldered repair) ......... **248.00**

**Tray,** hand-hammered, Arts & Crafts-
style, rectangular dished form
w/slightly upturned rounded ends,
radial hammering, impressed "Hand
Wrot by Fred Brosi - Ye Olde
Copper Shoppe - San Francisco -
c. 1900," 4 x 11", 1" h. ...................... **209.00**

**Tray,** hand-hammered, Arts & Crafts-
style, elongated dished rectangular
form w/wide flanged rim, cut-out
heart end handles & broad stylized
corner cut-outs, original dark brown
patina, impressed mark of Benedict
Studios, 8 x 15".................................. **121.00**

**Tray,** hand-hammered, Art & Crafts-
style, wide round dished form
w/small riveted side loop handles,
original reddish brown patina,
circular die-stamped mark of Gustav
Stickley, 17" d. .............................. **1,870.00**

**Tray,** hand-hammered, Arts & Crafts-
style, wide round dished form w/a
wide flanged rim divided into panels
by narrow ribs, impressed open box
mark of Dirk Van Erp, recent patina,
18" d. .............................................. **880.00**

**Vase,** hand-hammered, Arts & Crafts-
style, slender cylindrical form
w/slightly flaring rim, the sides tooled
w/slender pointed leaves & tooled
flowers w/an enameled green
ground, original patina, early orb &
cross of the Roycrofters, w/artist's
mark, 2¾" d., 8" h. .......................... **2,090.00**

**Vase,** hand-hammered, Arts & Crafts-
style, bulbous ovoid body w/a rolled
rim, original dark brown patina,
impressed mark of Dirk Van Erp,
8½" h. (small dents)...................... **1,760.00**

**Vase,** hand-hammered, Arts & Crafts-
style, slender ovoid body tapering to
a short cylindrical neck w/a rolled
rim, new patina, die-stamped
windmill mark of Dirk Van Erp,
5¼" d., 11¾" h. .............................. **2,090.00**

**Vase,** hand-hammered, Arts & Crafts-
style, gently flaring cylindrical form
w/a wide flaring foot, the rim
decorated w/a wide collar of rivets &
elongated embossed ovals between
raised bands, applied loop handles

*Stickley Copper Vase*

at the sides, good recent patina,
attributed to Gustav Stickley, 12" h.
(ILLUS.) ......................................... **2,200.00**

**Vase,** Arts & Crafts-style, tall slender
ovoid form w/a hand-hammered
surface & rolled rim, lightly cleaned
patina, unmarked, attributed to the
San Francisco school, early 20th c.,
13½" h. ............................................ **825.00**

**Wall sconces,** Aesthetic Movement
substyle, each w/a pierced & incised
floral crest above a circular beveled
mirror within an incised frame over a
floral piercework pendant mounted
w/a two-light candlearm, ca. 1880,
11½" w., 18¼" h., pr. ...................... **805.00**

**Weed holder,** a vase form w/a very
long & slender shaft of four slightly
indented sides supported by a
square knob, each side w/recessed
panel stepping down to an oval
protrusion turned an eighth of a turn
from the shaft, the pyramidal four-
sided base repeating the plane of
the shaft, designed by Frank Lloyd
Wright, made by James A. Miller and
Brother, ca. 1895, 29" h. .............. **12,650.00**

## IRON

**Birdhouse,** cast, model of a Victorian
cottage w/pointed arch gables, bay
windows & latticework porches, the
roof w/chimneys & fretwork, painted
white, attributed to the Miller
Ironworks, Providence, Rhode
Island, late 19th c., 10 x 15", 11½" h.
(ILLUS. top next page) .................. **1,610.00**

**Boot scraper,** hand-wrought, upright
"H" form w/wide crossbar, the side
uprights w/spiraling curled tips, set in

*Cast-iron Birdhouse*

a deep square marble block base, 19th c., 11 x 12", overall 13½" h. (rust damage) .................................... **385.00**

**Bread pan,** cast, Vienna-type, two loaf, "Griswold No. 2" ........................ **600.00**

**Cake pan,** cast, bundt-type, "Griswold No. 965" ........................................ **1,000.00**

**Camp stove,** hand-wrought, square form w/wide plate sides w/pierced holes supporting a hinged top plate, framed by bar corner posts w/flattened penny tops, a lower iron open shelf above crossbar supports, a short iron bar w/large turned wood handle at one corner, 19th c., 8½" sq. w/6" l. handle ...................... **468.00**

**Candlestand,** hand-wrought, the short swiveling top crossbar w/a candle socket at one end & a hooked handle at the other raised on a tall slender rod standard w/an upward curved bar to slip into the top bar handle, raised on an arched tripod base, 19th c., 28½" h. ....................... **605.00**

**Cookie mold,** cast, thin oval plate cast on one side w/an indented design of a bird on a leafy branch framed w/a dotted border band, 19th c., 5" l. ...................................... **138.00**

**Door knocker,** cast, modeled as a hinged hand holding a ball, 19th c., 9" l. ................................................... **105.00**

**Figure of a farmer,** the free-standing full-length figure of a farmer cast in the round wearing a straw hat & carrying a wrought-iron scythe in his arms, retains traces of old white paint, American, 19th c., 16¼" h. .... **1,610.00**

**Fireback,** cast, of rectangular form w/molded edge & arched shouldered crest, the center emblazoned w/the Great Seal of The United States, a spread-winged eagle clutching arrows & an olive branch in its talons & w/a fluted shield over its breast, Pleasant Furnace, Monogehela County, West Virginia, 1799-1811, 31¼" w., 29¾" h. .......................... **31,050.00**

**Ice shaver,** cast, "Griswold No. 4" ...... **135.00**

*Model of a Dove*

**Model of a dove,** cast, the stylized figure of a flying dove w/raised wings suspended from a wrought-iron ring covered in old white polychrome, 19th c., restorations to tail & right wing tip, 17" l., 6½" h. (ILLUS.) ...... **7,762.00**

**Model of a letter "F,"** hollow cast in the half-round, the upper case letter retaining much of its original gilding, American, 19th c., 24½" w., 19¾" h.. **345.00**

**Model of a peafowl,** cast in the full round standing in tall grass, w/incised feather & wing detail, American, late 19th c., overall 14" h. .............................................. **1,380.00**

**Model of a sheaf of wheat,** cast in the half-round, the sheaf bound w/a rope, retains traces of old white polychrome, American, 19th c., 14" w., 18½" h............................... **2,875.00**

**Model of the letter "H,"** hollow cast in the half-round, covered w/gilding, American, late 19th c., 32¼" w., 24" h. ........................................... **2,185.00**

*Early Oven Peel*

**Oven peel,** hand-wrought, the shaped handle w/loop end & heart devices attached to the wide flat blade w/rounded top corners, early, 20½" l. (ILLUS.) ........................................... **546.00**

**Pan,** cast, in the shape of a Turk's head, 11 cups, "Griswold No. 20" ..... **150.00**

**Pipe tongs,** long hinged form w/flattened tips, the hinged two-part handle w/hook on one side, simple tooling, 19th c., 16½" l. ..................... **220.00**

**Plant stand,** cast, the central standard supporting eleven movable branches & circular top, stamped "Groll Bolinder, Stockholm (?)," 59" h. (ILLUS. top next column)..... **1,610.00**

**Plant stand,** hand-wrought, six scrolling arms each fitted to hold a plant pot emanating from a central shaft on a tripod strapwork base, painted black, 5' 2¼" h........................ **58.00**

**Plaque,** cast, wall-mounted, rectangular w/a molded narrow frame on the top & sides, the center cast w/a large spread-winged American eagle in high-relief above a slightly arched & scroll-cast bottom edge, old gold repaint, four mounting holes, 19th c., 12½ x 13⅓" (old repair in back plate) .......................... **248.00**

*Ornate Plant Stand*

**Press,** cast, 4 qt., "Griswold No. 4" ....... **70.00**

**Spatula,** hand-wrought, small shaped flattened tip w/a heart cut-out, long flat narrow handle w/a loop end, handle stamped "H. Hantz," 19th c., 17⅝" l. (minor damage to tip) .......... **440.00**

**Stove,** cast, Federal-style, the trapezoidal shaped top w/outset corners surmounted by an acorn-shaped globe w/brass ball finial flanked by a pair of brass ball finials above a brass-mounted, reeded & ropetwist frieze over cast pineapple & ropetwist pilasters, the interior w/cast paterae decoration centering to figures in classical dress w/demilune tray fitted w/an iron & brass fire fender, ca. 1830, 28 x 41½", 5' 1½" h....................... **1,150.00**

**Teakettle,** cov., cast, wide bulbous body w/low domed cover, goose-neck spout, on three short peg legs, w/wrought bail swing handle, brass finial on cover, 19th c., 8" h. ............. **240.00**

**Toaster,** hand-wrought, fireplace-type, a swiveling crossbar supporting a pair of rectangular frames enclosing heart-shaped scroll-trimmed racks, on a long-handled base on angular tripod legs w/penny feet, good detail, 16" l................................................. **413.00**

**Trivet,** cast, round, signed "Midget," 4" d ..................................................... **55.00**

**Trivet,** cast, spade-shaped w/an indented cast bust portrait of George Washington, long flattened handle w/crossbar end, 9⅝" l. ........................ **83.00**

*Iron Stag Trophy*

**Trivet,** hand-wrought, fireplace-type, a round open flat bar end w/a pair of inward scrolling bars from the sides & a central medial bar continuing to form the long twisted handle w/a hinged long spit rest w/three small angled cross bars w/scroll tips, 19th c., 17½" l. (one center scroll w/loose rivet) .................................. **248.00**

**Trophy,** cast, the head of a stag mounted within a roundel, 36" h. (ILLUS. above) .............................. **2,587.00**

*Art Nouveau Iron Vase*

**Vase,** cast, Art Nouveau-style, tall tapering ovoid squared form, the upper rim section cast w/stylized whiplash designs, the body flanked by tapering buttresses forming short legs at the base, brown patina, by Hector Guimard, France, ca. 1900, 13" h. (ILLUS.) .............................. **4,600.00**

## PEWTER

**Basin,** Humphrey Evans, England, ca. 1730-80, stamped "MF," 11" d. (minor dents, pitting scratches) ........ **230.00**

**Basin,** Samuel Danforth, Hartford, Connecticut, ca. 1795-1816, 8¼" d. (minor dents, pitting, minor gouges).. **316.00**

**Basin,** Samuel or Samuel E. Hamlin, Providence, Rhode Island, ca. 1771-1856, 9¼" d. (minor dents, pitting & scratches) ........................................ **690.00**

**Basin,** Thomas Danforth III, Middletown, Connecticut, ca. 1777-1818, 9" d. (minor dents, pitting, scratches) ........................................ **747.00**

**Basins,** William Calder, Providence, Rhode Island, ca. 1817-56, 8" d. (wear, minor dents & pitting)............. **632.00**

**Beaker,** Boardman & Hart, Harord, Connecticut, ca. 1830-50, 5¼" h. (minor dents) .................................... **374.00**

**Beakers,** Oliver Trask, Bevery, Massachusetts, ca. 1832-47, 5¼" h., the pair (minor dents & nicks)........ **1,150.00**

**Cann,** Thomas D. & Sherman Boardman, Hartford Connecticut, ca. 1810-30, 4⅝" d. (dents, minor pitting & scratches) .......................... **805.00**

**Coffeepot,** cov., triple-belly, Boardman & Co., Hartford, Connecticut, ca. 1830, 11½" h.......... **862.00**

**Communion set:** ewer, two plates & two chalices; Leonard, Reed & Barton, Taunton Massachusetts, ca. 1835-40, ewer 10" h. (imperfections) .. **805.00**

**Communion set:** two flagons, footed baptismal bowl, four chalices & plate; cov. flagons w/scrolling handles, William Calder, Providence, Rhode Island, 1817-56, dents & scratches, flagons 10⅝" h., bowl 8⅞" d. (ILLUS. top next page) ....... **3,450.00**

**Deep dish,** Gersham Jones, Providence, Rhode Island, ca. 1774-1809, 15" d. ............................. **575.00**

**Deep dish,** Samuel or Samuel E. Hamlin, Providence, Rhode Island, ca. 1771-1856, 13½" d. (minor pitting, scratches) ............................. **489.00**

**Deep dish,** Samuel Pierce, Greenfield, Massachusetts, ca. 1792-1830 13⅜" d. (minor pitting)....................... **747.00**

**Flagon,** cov., Boardman & Co., Hartford, Connecticut, ca. 1825-27, 8½" h. (minor dents & pitting) ........ **1,955.00**

**Flagon,** cov., stamped w/"BX" quality mark & marked Laughlin, Thomas D. & Sherman Boardman, Hartford, Connecticut, ca. 1810-30, 13¾" h. ... **747.00**

*Fine Pewter Communion Set*

**Plate,** Frederick Bassett, New York City, ca. 1761-1800, 12" d. (minor gouges, scratches, knife marks) ....... **920.00**

**Plates,** Thomas Badger, Boston, Massachusetts, ca. 1787-1815, 8½" d., the pair (scratches).............. **805.00**

**Porringer,** Gershom Jones, Providence, Rhode Island, ca. 1774-1809, 4⅜" d. (minor dents & pitting)........................................... **1,955.00**

**Porringer,** marked "WN," New England, late 18th - early 19th c., 4¾" d. (minor dents, pitting, scratches)...................... **230.00**

**Porringer,** Samuel E. Hamlin, Providence, Rhode Island, ca. 1801-56, 5⅜" d. (dents, minor pitting & scratching) ...................................... **747.00**

**Porringer,** Thomas D. & Sherman Boardman, Hartford, Connecticut, ca. 1810-1830, 5⅜" d. (minor dents & pitting) ......................................... **690.00**

**Porringer,** w/Lee-type handle, early 19th c., 5½" h.................................... **345.00**

## SHEFFIELD PLATE

**Hot water urn,** cov., wide swelled cylindrical body w/a stepped cover & knob finial, rams' heads at sides w/loose ring handles, raised on four slightly incurved fluted legs w/paw feet resting on a dished base centering a copper heating element & set on small ball feet, the body w/a ivory-handled spigot at the lower rim, ca. 1820, 7½" d., 11½" h. ................. **193.00**

**Pepper casters & matching salt cellars,** the casters of baluster-form on stepped circular bases w/gadrooned necks & perforated locking caps w/covered urn finials, the salt cellars circular on stepped circular bases w/spiral gadrooned borders & gilt interiors, each chased w/crest of a rampant lion grasping an arrow, Matthew Boulton & Co., ca. 1800, cellars, 3Ⅿ₆" d., 2" d., casters 5¾" h., 8 prs. ...................... **2,300.00**

**Vegetable dishes,** octagonal, flat bases rising in fluted paneled sides w/applied tongue border on everted sides, the faces chased w/full armorial of rampant stags flanking a crowned shield w/motto "tien ta foy" below "R. Sutcliffe & Co.," late 18th c., 10¼" d., 2⅜" h., pr. (covers missing) .......................................... **518.00**

**Wine coolers,** campana-form, partly chased w/foliage, loop handles rising from Bacchus masks, short ringed pedestal on domed chased foot, detachable rims & liners, ca. 1825, 9¾" h., pr. ...................................... **3,162.00**

## SILVER, AMERICAN (Sterling & Coin)

**Basket,** coin, a deep oval flaring bowl w/a beaded rim & upswept beaded loop end handles, raised on a short flaring pedestal base w/beaded rim, Eoff & Shepherd, Albany, New York, for Ball, Black & Company, New York, mid-19th c., 8¾ x 13⅞", 6¾" h............ **770.00**

*Sterling Silver Bottles*

*Early Silver Butter Dish*

**Bottles,** w/stoppers, each baluster shape on spreading circular base, elaborately repoussé w/floral decoration, the part-fluted neck w/flaking rim, the baluster stoppers chased w/water leaves, marked under base w/maker's mark of Black, Starr & Frost, New York, ca. 1880, 8" h., pr. (ILLUS. top) ..... **1,035.00**

**Butter dish,** cov., circular on pad feet, the fluted cover chased w/acanthus & centering a pheasant, the interior w/a pierced liner, maker's mark of Jones, Ball & Poor, also marked "W&G," Boston, Massachusetts, 1849, 5¾" d. (ILLUS. bottom) ........... **920.00**

**Butter dish,** cover & pierced liner, domed oval form on a spreading oval foot, the base w/two strapwork handles w/stiff leaf & matted scroll joins & cast w/pendent game, the rim applied w/multi-beaded band, the cover finial formed as a cap of maintenance w/a lion passant crest w/a beaded band, marked by Gorham Mfg. Co., Providence, Rhode Island, 1871, overall 7¾" l.. **1,265.00**

**Cake basket,** shaped oblong form, the wide undulating rim elaborately chased & repoussé w/scrolls & beading, the overhead swing handle w/beaded bands, scroll & shaped oblong cartouches, engraved w/a monogram, Tiffany & Company, New York, No. 16677-4066, ca. 1910, 12¼" l. ........................... **2,530.00**

**Cake plates,** plain round & slightly dished form, the rims lightly chased & applied w/a narrow band of shells & waves, each w/two leaping dolphins in relief & each applied w/a gold initial "F," short pedestal bases w/four dolphin-head feet, Barbour Silver Co., division of International Silver Co., 1929, 11⅛" d., pr. ......... **2,300.00**

**Candlesticks,** Art Deco-style, thin molded rectangular base, the knobbed openwork cluster columns each composed of four square-section tubes within five double rings & rising to a rectangular drip pan & cylindrical socket, Reed & Barton, Taunton, Massachusetts, numbered "1020," marked, 1928, 10¼" h., pr. .. **5,750.00**

**Cann,** coin, baluster-form, engraved w/contemporary arms in a baroque cartouche, w/molded rim, cast molded foot, hollow scroll handle w/shaped tip & waved thumbpiece, engraved w/contemporary initials "H*P," marked on each side of the handle "SAMUEL" above "BURT" in cartouche, Samuel Burt, Boston, ca. 1740, 5⅜" h............................. **4,887.00**

**Centerpiece bowl,** deep lobed & flaring bowl w/everted scalloped rim, on a spreading lobed circular pedestal base, James T. Wooley, Boston, ca. 1910, 8½" h. .............. **2,990.00**

**Centerpiece bowl,** large oblong form w/a deep rolled undulating rim applied w/scrolling foliage, the scalloped foot applied w/shells & scrolls, J.E. Caldwell & Co., Philadelphia, late 19th c., 21" l. ..... **4,600.00**

**Compote,** open, hand-hammered, Arts & Crafts-style, wide shallow rounded bowl w/graceful upswept loop side handles, raised on a slender pedestal w/widely flaring round foot, marked "Sterling - 600W," 5½" d., 3½" h...................... **231.00**

*Silver Demitasse Set*

**Compote,** open, Scandinavian-style, a deep round bowl w/a flattened flaring rim fluted into six panels & raised on three stylized heron legs, each atop a ball above w/a carnelian disc screwed to a flat ring base, designed by Eric Magnussen, Gorham Mfg. Co., Providence, Rhode Island, ca. 1930, 6¼" d. ..... **1,795.00**

*Silver Wirework Compote*

**Compote,** open, oval on spreading oval base w/a band of water leaves & beads on a matted ground, the wirework basket w/similar rim, the sides applied w/vacant shields & two pendant ring handles, maker's mark of William Gale & Son, New York, 1862, 10½" h. (ILLUS.) ..................... **633.00**

**Compote,** open, wide round shallow dish w/an upright narrow rim band of strapwork & flowerheads on a matted ground, rising on a knobbed tapering stem w/a round foot w/strapwork & flower band, the bowl rim w/upright tubular loop handles cast w/pendent anthemion, Tiffany & Co., New York, marked "4139 - 2389 UNION SQUARE," overall 12½" d. ......................................... **2,530.00**

**Condiment set:** pair rectangular open salt dishes, pair of baluster-form pepper shakers & a pair of salt spoons; Chrysanthemum patt., monogrammed "AAG," Tiffany & Co., New York, New York, 20th c., the set .......................................... **5,175.00**

**Creamer,** coin, tall classical form w/swelled belted middle band w/beading, the rim w/a high arched wide spout trimmed w/beading, raised on a flaring pedestal base w/beaded band, ornate C-scroll handle, engraved monogram, faint "J.D." mark, early 19th c., 5¼" h. ...... **220.00**

**Cup,** coin, cylindrical w/molded rim & gadrooned foot, monogrammed, William Homes, Jr., Boston, ca. 1800, 3¼" h. ...................................... **431.00**

**Demitasse set:** 9¾" h. tall footed cov. pot, open sugar bowl & creamer & a round tray; each hollowware piece w/a fluted trumpet-form body w/a rounded shoulder to a short neck & domed cover on the coffeepot, each on a short pedestal foot, the tray w/a deeply fluted rim, Webster, early 20th c., tray 10" d., the set (ILLUS. top)..................................................... **413.00**

**Dish,** oval, w/overall spot-hammered surface, on a spreading oval base, the everted rim w/a cast wide band of shells & seaweed w/a gilt field, by Tiffany & Co., New York, No. 7382-859, ca. 1883-91, 7¼" l.................. **1,150.00**

**Ewer,** tall slender classical urn-form, the spreading circular foot chased w/a narrow band of acanthus & gadrooning rising to a stem chased

w/waves & berries, the body applied
w/tall stylized laurel branches, the
upswept leaf-clad tubular handle
w/scrolls & comedy & tragedy mask
body joins & applied w/flowerheads,
the cylindrical neck w/amid-band, a
tall arched undulating spout, the side
engraved w/an "S," marked under
base "14346-5715," marked by
Tiffany & Co., New York, 1902-07,
23" h. ............................................. **8,625.00**

**Goblets,** coin, bell-form bowl w/plain
flaring upper half & a swelled &
gadrooned lower half, raised on a
short flaring pedestal foot, marked
"J. Lownes," Joseph Lownes,
Philadelphia, 19th c., 5¼" h., pr.
(minor dents on foot edges).......... **1,210.00**

**Goblets,** tall flaring bell-form bowl on
a slender short stem & round flaring
foot, marked "Sterling," early 20th c.,
set of 12.......................................... **495.00**

**Gorget,** coin, of crescent shape
w/feather-edge borders, engraved
w/crossed sabers a ribbon engraved
"ULTIMA RATIO," the back
engraved "W. CATTELL," unmarked,
American-made, ca. 1775,
4⅝" w............................................. **6,900.00**

**Julep cup,** coin, tapering cylindrical
form w/molded rim band, engraved
"A.D.," marked "Garner &
Winchester, Lex, Ky.," 19th c.,
3⅜" h. ............................................. **495.00**

**Julep cup,** coin, tapering cylindrical
form w/molded rim band, marked
"Blanchard, 19th c., 3⅜" h. .............. **798.00**

**Julep cup,** coin, slightly tapering
cylindrical form w/molded bands at
the rim & foot, engraved "W.A.C.,"
marked "John B. Akin, Danville, Ky.
P.L.K. Standard," 19th c., 3⅝" h.
(dents) ............................................ **495.00**

**Loving cup,** *Martelé,* three-handled,
wide bulbous baluster-form body
embossed & chased w/ogee panels
of flowers on grounds of concave &
convex hammering, the base
monogrammed, marked by Gorham
Mfg. Co., Providence Rhode Island,
retailed by Spaulding & Co.,
Chicago, w/special order number
"9422," 7½" h. ................................ **3,737.00**

**Mote spoons,** typical form w/pierced
bowl & dark terminals, marked by
Samuel Kirk & Son, Baltimore, 1846-
61, 6" l., pr. .................................... **230.00**

*Victorian Silver Mug*

**Mug,** cylindrical, the sides chased
overall w/hand-hammering, desert
landscape & insects, w/molded rim &
tubular handle, engraved "Sarah
Davis Mercur from Grand Ma
Mercur, Sept 2nd 1886," w/maker's
mark of W.K. Vanderslice & Co.,
San Francisco, California, 1886,
3⅛" h. (ILLUS.) ............................... **805.00**

**Picture frame,** Arts & Crafts-style,
hand-hammered, plain rectangular
flat sides w/a tooled monogram
"ABC" at the bottom, original green
velvet backing & rear support,
marked "Friedell Pasadena -
Sterling," 9½" w., 12" h. ................... **330.00**

**Pitcher,** cov., coin, baluster-form w/a
foliate knob, the spout molded w/a
mask, the body repoussé & chased
w/a Rococo cartouche, Jones, Low
& Ball, Boston, ca. 1840, 10¼" h. ... **1,725.00**

**Pitcher,** water, bulbous nearly
spherical body below a wide tall
cylindrical neck w/pinched spout,
hollow strap handle from rim to
shoulder, the lower body deeply
embossed overall w/overlapping
shells & seaweed, Whiting Mfg. Co.,
ca. 1885, 5¾" h.............................. **1,725.00**

**Pitcher,** large spherical body below a
wide cylindrical neck, ribbed C-form
handle, the lower body chased w/a
band of upright leaves below overall
chased blossoms & leaves, chased
& repoussé bands of leaves &
blossoms around the neck, marked
by Bigelow, Kennard Co., Boston,
ca. 1880, 8¼" h.............................. **2,185.00**

**Pitcher,** hand-hammered, Arts &
Crafts-style, hexagonal ovoid body
tapering to a deep widely arching
spout & hollow long D-form handle,
stamped "Sterling - Hand Beaten at
Kalo Shops - Park Ridge - Ills.," 9" w.,
9¼" h. (ILLUS. top next page) .......... **1,970.00**

*Kalo Sterling Pitcher*

**Pitcher,** coin, wide rounded baluster-form body on a domed foot, tapering to a wide tall arched spout, beaded borders & applied bands of trailing foliage around the shoulder & foot, high arched leaf-clad scroll handle, marked by Samuel Kirk & Sons, Baltimore w/assay marks, 1824-29, 10⅜" h. ......................................... **4,600.00**

**Platter,** coin, rectangular w/rounded corners, on four shell & scroll feet, a wide gadrooned rim band, the center later engraved w/a monogram "ALB," marked by Hayden & Greeg, Charlston, South Carolina, 1838-43, 10¼" l............................................. **3,680.00**

**Porringer,** coin, squatty bulbous round form w/keyhole pierced handle engraved w/contemporary initials "P" above "IM," marked in center of bowl "P.Revere" in script in cartouche, Paul Revere, Sr., Boston, Massachusetts, ca. 1740-50, 4¾" d. .......................................... **4,887.00**

**Punch bowl,** wide deep sides w/a slightly flaring rim, raised on a flaring pedestal base, the sides applied w/a repeating trophy of a spread-winged eagle above a cannon barrel flanked by drums & centered by crossed sabres, also applied w/crossed antique rifles, the pedestal foot engraved w/scenes of a sailing ship, the "Monitor" & a steam yacht in oval cartouches connected by etched anchors & seaweed, the foot rim w/a band of cannonballs & cartridges, marked & numbered "1320," stamped "58 PINTS," Tiffany & Co., New York, New York, ca. 1920, 18¾" d. ......... **20,700.00**

**Punch ladle,** Strasbourg patt., scrolled shaft ending in a shell-form bowl, monogrammed "CD," Gorham Mfg. Company, Providence, Rhode Island, 13" l. ..................................... **275.00**

**Punch strainer,** coin, wide shallow squatty rounded bowl pierced in a concentric flowerhead design, an open cartouche-shaped handle centered by an elongated clip engraved w/the script initial "D," marked on the back of the handle "PS" in rounded rectangle flanked by leaf marks, Philip Syng, Jr., Philadelphia, ca. 1760, 4" d. .......... **3,450.00**

**Salad serving set,** Burgundy patt., pierced fork & spoon, Reed & Barton, 9½" l., pr. ............................. **193.00**

**Serving plate,** Arts & Crafts-style, hand-hammered, round shallow form w/five wide lobes at the rim, marked "Sterling - Hand Wrought at the Kalo Shops - Chicago and New York - 320F," 9½" d. ................................... **286.00**

**Soup ladle,** coin, long down-turned fiddle handle, flat handle engraved w/a monogram, E. J. Johnston, Macon, Georgia, ca. 1840, 12⅛" l............................................ **4,830.00**

*Whiting Soup Tureen*

**Soup tureen,** cov., in the Regency-Style, oval, on four paw feet w/acanthus & foliate joins, the sides fluted & waisted rim, the open tubular handles w/acanthus joins, the shaped rectangular cover chased w/swirling flutes, surmounting a leaf-clad tubular handle, marked under base w/maker's mark of Whiting Mfg. Co., Providence, Rhode Island, ca. 1885, 11¾" l. (ILLUS.) ............................ **2,990.00**

**Soup tureen,** cov., deep & wide rounded body raised on a stepped, domed foot, the sides bright-cut w/bands of foliage & ribbonwork, stag head handles & the stepped & domed cover also w/bright cutting & a full-figure standing stag, engraved w/initials & the date "1860," William Forbes for Ball, Black & Co., New York, 950 standard, overall 16" l.... **1,495.00**

**Soup tureen,** cov., shallow oval body on a spreading oval pedestal base, the body & base rims w/bands of stylized laurels, the shaped tubular loop end handles w/scroll joins & surmounted by figural cherubs, one side w/an applied heart-shaped cartouche, the domed cover engraved w/anthemion scrolls & foliage, applied w/a beaded band & w/disk & cone finial, Wood & Hughes, New York, ca. 1870, overall 18" l. ................................. **4,025.00**

**Sugar bowl,** cov., coin, Classical boat-form body w/stepped, domed cover w/urn finial, angular end strap handles, raised on four small paw feet, John & Peter Targee, New York, New York, ca. 1811, 8" l., 6½" h. ................................. **385.00**

**Sugar bowl,** cov., flower bud finial on bulbous body, applied w/bands of acanthus leaves on pedestal base, marked three times "J.B. Jones," John B. Jones, Boston, Massachusetts, ca. 1820-30, 8" h. (minor dents) ......... **230.00**

**Sugar tongs,** coin, engraved w/bright-cut borders & contemporary script initial "F," the shaped & riveted terminals ending in shell terminals, marked "REVERE" in rectangle, Paul Revere, Jr., Boston, Massachusetts, ca. 1790, 6⅛" l..... **7,475.00**

**Tankard,** cov., coin, plain tapered cylindrical form, molded borders, stepped domed cover w/bell-shaped finial, the S-scroll handle initialed "C/WH" & w/convex oval disc terminal, marked on body & cover "IE" crowned below a shaped shield, John Edwards, Boston, Massachusetts, ca. 1720-30, 8¼" h. (finial repair)........................ **6,900.00**

**Tazza,** *Martelé,* shaped circular dish on a serpentine base, the everted brim chased w/a wide border of stylized florals & scrolls, Gorham Mfg. Co., Providence, Rhode Island, 1899, 9½" d. ................................. **2,300.00**

**Tea caddy,** cov., coin, rectangular upright form w/incurved corners & a cylindrical lift-off cap, w/an octagonally faceted domed cover w/octagonally faceted finial, front engraved "OSWALD AND LYDIA PEEL," the shoulder engraved "Green Tea," mark of Joseph Richardson, Sr., Philadelphia, ca. 1740, 5⅝" h. ....... **81,700.00**

**Teapot,** cov., of inverted pear-shape, the domed cover w/a floriform knob, the body repoussé overall w/an elaborate chinoiserie scene, S. Kirk, Baltimore, Maryland, mid-19th c., 7¾" h. ................................. **920.00**

**Tea & coffee service:** cov. hot water kettle on stand w/lamp, cov. coffeepot, cov. teapot, cov. sugar bowl, creamer & waste bowl; each bulbous spherical body highly repoussé & chased overall w/foliage, raised on paw feet, w/serrated, leaf-clad handles, domed covers w/floral bouquet finials, bases inscribed "F.W.B. to M.P.T. Nov. 2nd 1896," by Samuel Kirk & Son, Baltimore, ca. 1896, kettle on stand 14" h., the set ................................. **9,775.00**

*Tiffany Tea & Coffee Set*

**Tea & coffee set:** cov. coffeepot, cov. teapot, cov. sugar urn & creamer; Federal-style w/tall fluted urn-form bodies w/stepped shoulders & conical covers w/urn finials, the pots w/carved wood C-scroll handles, copied from a set by John McMullin of Philadelphia, Tiffany & Co., New York, New York, 20th c., monogrammed, coffeepot 14¾" h., the set (ILLUS.) ............................ **4,600.00**

**Tea & coffee set:** cov. coffeepot, cov. teapot, cov. sugar bowl, creamer & waste bowl; classical urn-form bodies w/notched corners, domed covers w/urn finials, raised on rectangular flaring base, angled handles, w/engraved monograms, marked "Sterling," early 20th c., 5 pcs. ............................................... **605.00**

**Tea set:** cov. teapot, cov. sugar bowl & creamer; Art Deco-style, the plain faceted upright bodies w/angular handles, flat hinged & detachable lids to the teapot & sugar bowl, marked, Peter Muller-Munk, New York, New York, ca. 1927, teapot 6⅞" h., the set.............................. **10,350.00**

**Teakettle on lamp stand,** the kettle of compressed circular form decorated w/bands of scrolling flowers & leaves, the stand w/four curved supports above the detachable lamp w/three spouts on a square plinth w/four winged paw feet, Tiffany & Co., New York, New York, 1891-1902, 12" h. .................................. **1,840.00**

**Tray,** round, Chrysanthemum patt., the rim band molded w/chrysanthemum blossoms & leaves, Silver, American, Tiffany & Co., New York, 1907-47, 14" d. ..... **2,530.00**

**Tray,** round, fluted rayed border, Reed & Barton, ca. 1948, 15¼" d............... **385.00**

**Tray,** round w/a wide applied scroll & flower rim & curved border embossed w/different birds including a peacock & game birds surrounded by daffodils, narcissus & other flowers, delicate ornate inner engraved scrolling around the center monogram on four paw feet, S. Kirk & Son Co., Baltimore, Maryland, ca. 1900, 21½" d........................... **2,587.00**

**Trophy,** hand-hammered, Arts & Crafts-style, the deep widely flaring bowl raised on a slightly swelling cylindrical standard on a dished disc foot, the side of the bowl engraved "Presented by - The Live Stock World - Chicago - For Best Percheron Foal - Either Sex - Bushnell Horse Show - 1914," impressed "Jarvie - 502," 9" d., 10¾" h............................................... **1,870.00**

**Vase,** *Martelé,* shaped baluster-form on four short feet, wide flattened undulating rim, the surface spot-hammered & repoussé w/flowers & leaves, marked under rim w/Birmingham, England import

marks for 1908, Gorham Mfg. Co., Providence, Rhode Island, ca. 1908, 10¼" h. .......................................... **6,900.00**

*Victorian Vegetable Dish*

**Vegetable dishes,** cov., square, elaborately chased & repoussé w/foliage, the crenellated rims applied w/shells & foliage, the domed covers w/conforming decoration, the removable finial w/calyx of swirling flutes on a square base surmounting leaf-clad bulb & a bead, engraved on interior of cover w/monogram, marked under base w/makers mark of Gorham & of Howard & Co., New York, 1886, 7⅝" l., pr. (ILLUS. of one) ................. **4,025.00**

**Wine coolers,** round w/slightly swelled cylindrical sides pierced & applied w/grapevine swags & bacchic masks, w/scrolling molded rims, on wooden bases, marked by Theodore B. Starr, New York, 1900-24, 6½" d., pr. .............................. **2,645.00**

## SILVER, ENGLISH & OTHERS

*Early German Beaker*

**Beaker,** cylindrical body raised on three ball feet headed by trefoils, gilt rim band, the base inset w/a Charles II English Garter medal dated "1671" & inscribed in French, initialed & dated "1719," marker's mark "CP" in oval, town mark unclear, possibly Christian Poppe, Munster, Germany, 3¾" h. (ILLUS.) .............................. **2,587.00**

**Bowl,** a deep flaring bell-form bowl raised on stylized leaf & bead openwork stems on a circular round flaring, molded foot, marked "17B" on base, designed by Johan Rohde, made by Georg Jensen Silversmithy, Denmark, post-1945, 5⅛" h. .......... **1,955.00**

**Cake basket,** oval lobed & fluted boat-form w/applied rim of reversed shells & foliage, center swing handle decorated w/graduated guilloche rising from stiff leaves, the center engraved w/contemporary arms, pedestal foot w/a cast band of running foliage, Paul Storr, London, England, ca. 1820, 14⅛" l. ............. **9,775.00**

**Candelabra,** Art Deco-style, a circular stepped base w/rosewood mounts, the tubular candlearms upswept w/circular drip pans, the fluted candle sockets w/plain circular rims, a central ring handle, marked on the sides, Tetard Freres, Paris, France, ca. 1930, 10¾" w., pr. .................... **3,450.00**

**Card holders,** each realistically formed as a different fruit w/stem, each marked, Mario Buccellatti, Milan, Italy, 20th c., largest 2¾" l., set of 7 ......................................... **1,955.00**

**Centerpiece,** shaped oval form, the upright sides pierced & applied w/swags of flowers on a trellis ground between herms hung w/trophies, metal liner, Germany, late 19th c., overall 18½" l. ............ **4,312.00**

**Compotes,** open, the bowls of shallow oval form, part-fluted & hung w/long swags from ram's head handles, the tall pedestal bases cast to match w/egg-and-dart rim, engraved w/a monogram & crest, John S. Hunt, London, England, 1864, 12⅝" l., pr. ......................... **8,050.00**

**Ewer,** lobed & fluted baluster-form body w/high arched spout & harp-shaped handle, on screw-on ringed pedestal base w/fluted rim, maker's mark "ZP" separated by a bird, Venice, Italy, ca. 1740, 9" h. .......... **3,162.00**

**Ewer,** cov., tall inverted pear-form w/a tall neck & wide arched spout, domed cover w/finial & openwork handle centered by a demi-faun blowing pipes, the sides applied w/a flying putto above a chased spray of flowers on which perch a bird & butterfly, gilt interior, Germany, ca. 1890, 16¼" h. ........................... **3,737.00**

**Grape shears,** silver-gilt, handles modeled on both sides w/grape clusters, leaves & canes, William, Charles & Henry Eley, London, England, 1824, 7" l. ......................... **431.00**

**Pitcher,** beer, jug-form, the baluster-form body w/gadrooned top & base borders, a short spout & leaf-capped double-scroll handle, engraved w/slightly later arms, the base inscribed, Charles Wright, London, England, 1765, 7" h. ...................... **3,450.00**

**Punch bowl,** Armada patt., wide squatty bulbous body raised on a domed foot, w/lion mask & ring handles, a scalloped flaring gadrooned rim, crested, one side later applied w/a vacant plaque, gilt interior, the foot engraved "Elkington & Co. Ltd., Silversmiths to the Queen, 22 Regent Street," London, England, 1894, 13¾" d. ................. **7,475.00**

**Salt cellars & spoons,** Acorn patt., each cellar of simple shallow round form w/a pierced acorn design handle & matching spoon, blue glass lining, design by Johan Rohde, made by Georg Jensen Silversmithy, Denmark, post-1945, set of 12 ...... **2,070.00**

**Salver,** silver-gilt, ornate oval form, the center engraved w/contemporary arms in an embossed oval of fruit surrounded by four vignettes of hounds pursuing a deer & hare, the shaped rim chased w/more hounds, a boar, two rabbits & a stag, the rim decorated w/buds, the oval reel-shaped foot chased w/flutes & w/a die-stamped border of leaves, apparently unmarked, Spain, early 17th c., 12¼" l. (ILLUS. top next page) .......................................... **17,250.00**

**Sauceboat & ladle,** each in leaf & berry pattern, Georg Jensen Silversmithy, Copenhagen, Denmark, numbered 177 & 141, 1925-32, sauceboat 8" l., 2 pcs. .... **1,725.00**

**Sauceboats,** oval form w/scalloped rims & multiple-scroll handles, raised on three shell feet headed by female masks flanked by applied shellwork, engraved w/contemporary arms in rococo cartouches, marked on base, John Moore, Dublin, Ireland, ca. 1750-60, 9½" l., pr. ................. **6,900.00**

**Soup tureen,** cov., deep bulbous bombé body w/cross celery spray handles, raised on scroll feet

*Early Spanish Salver*

headed by berried foliage, the domed cover w/a large artichoke spray finial, detachable liner, Puiforcat, Paris, France, early 20th c., overall 11¾" l. ................ **6,325.00**

**Soup tureen,** cov., deep oval bombé body on acanthus-headed paw feet, shaped gadrooned rim, reeded & foliate ring finial on the stepped, domed cover & similar end handles on the body, one side w/a contemporary inscription partially erased, marked on body & cover, Kirkby, Waterhouse & Co., Sheffield, England, 1814, overall 15¾" l. ....... **6,900.00**

**Taperstick,** on a shaped octagonal base w/alternating recessed & rising panels forming a Maltese cross w/a baluster body above & a knob at center, w/a cylindrical sconce w/applied horizontal rib, Joseph Bird, London, England, 1728, 4" h. (lacking nozzle) ............................ **1,725.00**

**Tankard,** cov., the barrel form embossed w/sporting tritons & mermaids, the domed foot embossed w/large flowerheads, winged grotesque mask thumbpiece, Germany, in the late 17th c. style, 8" h. ............................................. **4,600.00**

**Tea caddy,** cov., oval upright form w/flush-hinged cover, engraved w/bright-cut borders & w/a vacant urn-topped frame, flower spray finial, marked, Benjamin Stephenson, London, England, 1776, 4" h. ........ **2,300.00**

**Tea & coffee service:** cov. coffeepot, cov. teapot, cov. sugar bowl & creamer; Art Deco-style, each of globular form w/flattened tubular spouts & handles & ring finials, the handles & finials mounted w/rosewood, marked on bases & covers, also French export mark, Tetard Freres, Paris, France, ca. 1935, coffeepot 7¼" h., the set ............................................. **5,175.00**

**Teakettle on lamp stand,** plain spherical kettle w/swan's-neck spout, overhead swing detachable handle, detachable cover w/wood finial rising from cut-card leaves, the brazier-form stand w/detachable lamp & pendent bail handles, marked on kettle, lamp & stand, Jan van Gendt, Maastricht, Holland, 1732-36, overall 14¾" h., the set ... **13,800.00**

**Teapot,** cov., Directoire-style, wide half-round body w/a wide slightly rounded shoulder centered by a low, pierced cover gallery centered by a figural swan finial, a high arched black wooden handle from gallery to shoulder rim, a figural eagle head spout, raised on a wide domed oval foot, Marc Jacquart, Paris, France, 1798-1809, 8⅝" h. ........................ **2,300.00**

**Tea tray,** oval, the pierced low gallery chased w/ribbon-tied festoons, the inner surface engraved w/an inner band of cherub heads & anthemia & an outer band of ribbon-tied running oak leaves & acorns, the loop end handles cast to match as ribbon-tied oak wreaths, on four panel feet, Martin Hall & Co., London, England, 1872, overall 29⅝" l. ..................... **6,037.00**

**Tureen,** cover & undertray, wide bulbous bombé body on a short pedestal above a domed foot, scrolling loop side handles & domed cover w/grape cluster finial, the sides & cover all chased w/rococo ornament, matching round undertray, by Wurbel & Czokelly, Vienna, Austria, ca. 1890, overall 15½" h., the set ................... **5,750.00**

**Wine bottle coasters,** cylindrical w/flared rim & swelled gadrooned base band, the sides pierced in the Grapevine patt., Georg Jensen Silversmithy, Copenhagen, Denmark, dated under base "1941," marked, 3⅞" h., pr. ..................... **11,500.00**

*French Wine Cooler*

**Wine cooler,** urn-form w/a tall lobed & fluted body on a fluted domed foot, a short cylindrical neck w/a flattened chased rim, upright looped scroll shoulder handles, shell & scroll borders, handles linked by applied grapevine, also applied on both sides w/a monogrammed shield below a crowned ermine mantle, Odiot, Paris, France, ca. 1840, 10½" h. (ILLUS.) ........................... **5,980.00**

**Wine coolers,** deep cylindrical form on cast-flower & scroll bases, the lower bodies chased to match & applied w/flowers, grapevine handles at the center sides & leaf-and-flower embossed scalloped rims, crested, marked, detachable liners w/fixed collars, Edward Barnard & Sons, London, England, 1840, 9¾" h., pr. ........................ **25,300.00**

## SILVER PLATE (Hollowware)

*Golfing Ashtray*

**Ashtray,** in the shape of large golf ball w/large opening in side w/one cigarette rest, supported by three golf clubs on circular base, England, 2⅞" d., 6" h. (ILLUS. bottom previous column) ............................. **135.00**

**Butter dish,** cov., the domed, finely pierced cover w/a figural standing cow finial, on a base w/low pierced sides & animal head handles w/loose rings, raised on four paw feet, late 19th c., 6½ x 8½", 6" h. ....... **358.00**

**Cake basket,** low oval boldly fluted base w/a lightly scalloped & beaded rim, swing bail handle, low base, Redfield & Rich, New York, New York, ca. 1850, 12" l., 3" h. ................ **77.00**

**Cake basket,** rounded fluted & scalloped form w/overhead pierced bail handle, floral-embossed border, on a low foot, ca. 1880 .................... **110.00**

**Candlesticks,** Classical-style, a tall tulip-form candle socket w/ribbing on the lower half & an inset bobeche above a stepped band above the slender tall square tapering shaft cast w/classical designs, on a stepped, flaring base cast w/a classical drapery design, weighted base, late 19th - early 20th c., 9½" h., pr. (mismatched bobeches) .. **303.00**

**Candy dish,** decorated w/three applied branches, a 3" cast-iron model of a sparrow & leaf-shaped feet, interior hammered w/Pinwheel patt., 6½" d. ..................................... **385.00**

**Coach lantern,** of hexagonal form w/blue & red glass inserts, inscribed "Merry Christmas and Happy New Year," 8½" h..................................... **575.00**

**Cocktail shaker,** cov., modeled as a stylized figural penguin w/beak-form pouring spout, impressed Napier marks, ca. 1930s, 13" h. ................... **605.00**

**Compote,** open, Aesthetic Movement-style, a small dished pierced leaf-design bowl raised on a forked tree pedestal on a round base, a full-figural standing whippet dog behind the tree, ca. 1880, 7" h. .................... **193.00**

**Epergne,** four-lily, a tall central slender trumpet-form lily w/pierced gallery rim flanked by three arched & pierced scroll arms each supporting a smaller lily, on a domed foot, England, early 20th c., 13¾" h.......... **165.00**

*Gorham Silver Plate Tea & Coffee Service*

**Ice water pitcher on stand,** footed tapering cylindrical body w/a flaring rim, short integral spout, hinged domed cover w/knob finial & long angled handle suspended & swinging in a high arched frame w/pairs of pierced floral scroll panels at the bottom sides supported on a round, stepped disc base, the pitcher w/engraved florals on the sides & on a wide rim band, engraved band around rim of the base, porcelain liner, quadruple plate, ca. 1875, 21" h. ........................ **905.00**

**Mirror plateau,** round w/a deep scroll & floral-embossed border on tab feet, holds a beveled mirror, late 19th c., 13¼" d. ............................... **275.00**

**Mirror plateau,** elongated oval Rococo-style, w/deep flaring gadrooned border w/applied w/center crossed sprigs, forked looped end handles from base rim to top rim, on short block feet, 19th c., 11" w., 21½" l. .................................. **495.00**

**Plateau,** a square beveled silver plate frame w/leaf-cast corners & small ball feet framing a granite insert, marked "Jamieson," 19th c., 11" sq. . **193.00**

**Snuff box,** cov., commemorative, oval, engraved w/a view entitled "Tomb of Washington," dated 1860, 3¼" l. ................................................... **86.00**

**Tea & coffee service:** cov. coffeepot, cov. teapot, water pot, cov. sugar, creamer & waste bowl; Medallion patt., each footed w/globular body, coffeepot has long cylindrical neck, coffeepot engraved "Presented to Mrs. J.B. Booth. By a Few of her

Friends. Boston. May 6th 1871," other pieces monogrammed w/"B," Gorham MFG. Co., Providence, Rhode Island, ca. 1870, minor dents, coffeepot 10⅞" h. (ILLUS. above) ................... **1,380.00**

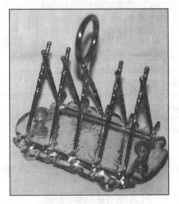

*English Toast Rack*

**Toast rack,** ten golf clubs forming separations w/a single golf ball at each end, all above a rectangular plate w/scalloped edge, English, resilvered, 3½ x 5¼", 5" h. (ILLUS.) .... **295.00**

**Tureen,** cov., oval body w/beaded & Greek fret borders, American-made, 19th c., 13½" h. ................................. **517.00**

**Vase,** a frosted clear glass cylindrical insert molded w/pelicans & palm trees, set in a silver plate Aesthetic Movement-style holder w/upright sunflower-cast handles & a support ring w/cast stylized designs all raised on a slender knobbed pedestal & round disc foot, silver by Webster, New York, overall 9¼" h. ...... **88.00**

## SILVER PLATE (Flatware)

### GRAPE (Rogers)

| | |
|---|---|
| Berry spoon | 55.00 |
| Butter knife, master | 40.00 |
| Child's fork | 30.00 |
| Cream soup spoon | 35.00 |
| Demitasse spoon | 30.00 |
| Iced tea spoon | 40.00 |
| Knife, hollow-handled | 45.00 |
| Meat fork | 45.00 |
| Salad fork | 50.00 |
| Sugar shell | 35.00 |
| Tablespoon, large | 30.00 |
| Teaspoon | 15.00 |

### GRENOBLE (Rogers Prestige Heirloom Plate)

| | |
|---|---|
| Butter knife, master size | 19.00 |
| Butter spreader, individual | 9.00 |
| Cold meat fork | 30.00 |
| Dinner fork | 15.00 |
| Dinner knife | 15.00 |
| Gravy ladle | 35.00 to 40.00 |
| Iced tea spoon | 12.00 |
| Mustard ladle | 75.00 |
| Pastry fork "Gloria" | 35.00 |
| Pie server | 50.00 |
| Salad fork | 55.00 |
| Soup spoon | 22.00 |
| Sugar spoon | 22.00 |
| Salad fork | 12.00 |
| Sugar spoon | 8.00 |
| Teaspoon | 8.00 |
| Vegetable serving spoon | 15.00 |

### HANOVER (Rogers)

| | |
|---|---|
| Bouillon spoon | 7.00 |
| Butter knife, individual | 10.00 |
| Dinner fork | 10.00 |
| Dinner knife | 12.00 |
| Olive spoon, open bowl | 30.00 |
| Salad fork | 30.00 |
| Soup ladle | 85.00 |

### HERITAGE (Rogers)

| | |
|---|---|
| Cold meat fork | 20.00 |
| Stuffing spoon | 85.00 |
| Tomato server | 20.00 |

### LOUIS XV (Rogers)

| | |
|---|---|
| Berry spoon | 150.00 |
| Salad fork | 40.00 |

### LYONNAISE/EASTLAKE (Rogers)

| | |
|---|---|
| Dinner fork | 45.00 |
| Soup ladle | 75.00 |

### MELROSE (Rogers)

| | |
|---|---|
| Cream ladle | 38.00 |
| Cream ladle, pierced, gold-washed bowl | 50.00 |

### MOSELLE (American Silver Co.)

| | |
|---|---|
| Berry spoon | 165.00 |
| Jelly spoon | 95.00 |
| Soup spoon, oval bowl | 25.00 |

### MOSELLE (1847 Rogers)

| | |
|---|---|
| Butter knife, twist handle | 33.00 |
| Cold Meat fork | 50.00 |
| Gravy ladle | 55.00 |

### PEARL (Reed & Barton 1878)

| | |
|---|---|
| Dinner fork | 20.00 |
| Luncheon fork | 15.00 |

### SAVOY (Pearl)

| | |
|---|---|
| Seafood fork | 8.00 |
| Soup ladle, long | 35.00 |

### SOUTH SEAS (Onieda Community)

| | |
|---|---|
| Baby spoon, curved | 9.00 |
| Demitasse spoon | 7.00 |
| Seafood fork | 12.00 |

### VINTAGE (Rogers)

| | |
|---|---|
| Baby spoon, bent-handled | 55.00 |
| Carving set | 135.00 |
| Cheese scoop, hollow-handled | 285.00 |
| Chocolate muddler | 150.00 |
| Citrus spoon | 25.00 |
| Cream soup spoon | 25.00 |
| Demitasse spoon | 15.00 |
| Dinner fork | 14.00 |
| Dinner fork, hollow-handled | 18.00 |
| Dinner knife | 15.00 |
| Dessert spoon | 38.00 |
| Fruit knife | 50.00 |
| Fruit knives | 200.00 |
| Gravy ladle | 20.00 to 30.00 |
| Olive spoon, open bowl | 41.00 |
| Pickle fork, long-handled | 38.00 |
| Ice spoon | 150.00 |
| Salad fork | 28.00 |
| Seafood fork | 6.00 |

Soup spoon............................................... 14.00
Sugar tongs ............................................. 95.00
Tablespoon ............................................... 16.00
Teaspoon .................................................... 8.00

## STERLING SILVER (Flatware)

### ANTIQUE LILY ENGRAVED (Whiting Mfg. Co.)

Berry spoon, 9"................................. 120.00
Cake saw ...................................................... 195.00
Oyster ladle, 11½".............................. 235.00
Soup spoon, oval.............................. 30.00
Tablespoon ...................................... 45.00

### ARABESQUE (Whiting Mfg. Co.)

Berry spoon ...................................... 150.00
Berry spoon, oval, large, bright-cut,
  matte finish, fluted bowl.................... 195.00
Cheese scoop, bright-cut, gold
  washed ............................................. 350.00
Cream ladle...................................... 225.00
Demitasse spoon............................... 20.00
Dessert spoon ................................... 25.00
Dinner fork ....................................... 45.00
Gravy ladle........................................ 125.00
Ice cream set: ice cream slice &
  twelve ice cream spoons; bright-cut,
  13 pcs. ............................................. 750.00
Luncheon fork ................................... 29.00
Pastry fork.......................................... 85.00
Pie server........................... 350.00 to 375.00
Serving spoon w/gold-washed bowl.... 95.00
Soup ladle.......................... 400.00 to 450.00
Soup spoon, oval .............................. 35.00
Tablespoon ....................................... 50.00
Teaspoon .......................................... 18.00

### BEEKMAN (Tiffany & Co)

Butter.................................................. 47.00
Butter, master size .............................. 72.00
Dessert spoon .................................... 38.00
Ice cream fork .................................... 32.00
Ice cream spoon ................................ 48.00
Salad spoon....................................... 150.00
Salt spoon, master size....................... 45.00
Tablespoon ......................................... 60.00

### BERRY (Whiting Mfg. Co.)

Berry spoon ....................................... 178.00
Demitasse spoon................................ 25.00
Dinner fork ......................................... 45.00
Gravy ladle, gold-washed.................... 125.00

Olive fork............................................. 60.00
Preserve spoon .................................. 75.00
Sugar shell.......................................... 40.00
Tea caddy spoon................................ 75.00

### CACTUS (Georg Jensen)

Berry spoon ...................................... 275.00
Bouillon spoon ................................... 58.00
Carving set, roast............................... 300.00
Cheese plane, stainless blade ........... 195.00
Citrus spoon ...................................... 65.00
Cocktail fork....................................... 95.00
Dinner fork ........................................ 98.00
Fish fork ............................................. 75.00
Fruit knife .......................................... 85.00
Gravy ladle......................................... 200.00
Jam spoon .......................................... 95.00
Lemon fork, two-tine .......................... 65.00
Luncheon fork .................................... 95.00
Salad fork ........................................... 95.00
Server, flat .......................................... 95.00
Sugar scoop........................................ 75.00
Tablespoon ........................................ 35.00
Teaspoon ........................................... 65.00

### CANTERBURY (Towle Mfg. Co.)

Almond scoop .................................... 85.00
Almond scoop, gold-washed............. 185.00
Citrus spoon ...................................... 14.00
Confection server.............................. 125.00
Cream ladle........................................ 45.00
Dessert spoon .................................... 19.00
Ice tongs............................................. 395.00
Luncheon fork, 7" l. ............................ 21.00
Olive fork............................................. 55.00
Punch ladle ........................................ 375.00
Sardine fork ....................................... 85.00
Serving spoon .................................... 37.00
Soup ladle .......................................... 250.00
Strawberry fork................................... 35.00
Teaspoon ............................................. 8.00

### CHARLES II (Dominick & Haff)

Cocktail .............................................. 20.00
Cold meat fork ................................... 100.00
Cream ladle......................................... 75.00
Demitasse spoon................................ 18.00
Dessert spoon .................................... 30.00
Luncheon fork .................................... 23.00
Soup ladle, gold-washed bowl ........... 250.00
Strawberry fork.................................... 35.00
Sugar shell ......................................... 35.00
Tablespoon ........................................ 38.00
Teaspoon ............................................ 20.00

## DRESDEN (Whiting Mfg. Co.)

Berry spoon ..................................... 118.00
Cheese scoop, 8⅜" ........................... 155.00
Cucumber server ............................... 125.00
Dinner service: six each luncheon
  forks, tablespoons, salad forks,
  teaspoons, twelve demitasse
  spoons, one sugar spoon, two
  dinner spoon, 39 pcs. .................... 1,010.00
Fish set ............................................ 325.00
Ice spoon .......................................... 325.00
Meat fork (beef) ................................. 95.00
Salad serving set, long-handled ........ 650.00
Sugar shell ........................................ 43.00
Sugar sifter, gold-washed ................... 95.00
Sugar tongs ....................................... 40.00

## EATON (R. Wallace & Sons)

Baked potato serving fork ................. 38.00
Breakfast knife, 3¼" ........................... 33.00
Carving fork, roast, 5" ........................ 32.00
Carving fork, steak, 3⅞" ..................... 26.00
Citrus spoon ...................................... 22.00
Cocktail fork ...................................... 18.00
Cold meat fork, 8¼" ............................ 67.00
Cream ladle ....................................... 50.00
Demitasse spoon ............................... 14.00
English server .................................... 36.00
Fish fork ............................................ 50.00
Fish knife, 7⅛" ................................... 75.00
Fork, 6⅞" l ......................................... 28.00
Fork, 7" l ........................................... 14.00
Fruit knife, 3¼" ................................... 30.00
Grapefruit spoon ................................ 35.00
Gravy ladle ........................................ 150.00
Gumbo spoon, 7" ............................... 47.00
Ice cream fork .................................... 26.00
Serving spoon .................................... 53.00
Serving spoon, pierced ....................... 59.00
Sugar tongs, small ............................. 38.00
Teaspoon ........................................... 20.00

## EMPIRE (Whiting Mfg. Co.)

Berry spoon ....................................... 110.00
Cracker scoop .................................... 225.00
Cream ladle ....................................... 75.00
Dinner knife ....................................... 60.00
Gravy ladle ........................................ 80.00
Ice spoon .......................................... 225.00
Lettuce fork ....................................... 95.00
Pickle fork ......................................... 28.00
Pie server .......................................... 158.00
Sardine tongs .................................... 75.00
Seafood fork ...................................... 13.00

Sugar shell ........................................ 35.00
Sugar sifter ........................................ 75.00
Tablespoon ........................................ 48.00
Teaspoon ........................................... 12.00

## GRECIAN (Whiting Mfg. Co.)

Berry spoon ....................................... 188.00
Gravy ladle ........................................ 125.00
Ice cream server & twelve spoons ... 295.00
Ice tongs ........................................... 150.00
Mustard ladle ..................................... 65.00

## HERALDIC (Whiting Mfg. & Co.)

Asparagus fork ................................... 350.00
Cheese scoop ..................................... 175.00
Cold meat fork .................................... 135.00
Demitasse spoon ................................ 18.00
Dessert spoon .................................... 28.00
Fish fork ............................................ 150.00
Fish server ........................................ 195.00
Fish serving set, 2 pcs. ...................... 195.00
Fruit spoon ........................................ 35.00
Ice cream spoon ................................. 40.00
Jelly spoon ........................................ 40.00
Lettuce fork ....................................... 55.00
Luncheon fork .................................... 22.00
Mustard ladle ..................................... 80.00
Olive fork ........................................... 70.00
Pastry fork, three-tine ........................ 45.00
Pickle fork, two-tine ........................... 12.00
Pickle fork, three-tine ........................ 42.00
Sugar shell ........................................ 40.00
Sugar sifter ........................................ 110.00
Teaspoon ........................................... 18.00

## HYPERION (Whiting Mfg. Co.)

Berry spoon ....................................... 125.00
Bonbon spoon .................................... 35.00
Demitasse spoon ................................ 20.00
Ice cream server ................................ 135.00
Mustard ladle ..................................... 85.00
Salad set, large ................................. 325.00
Sauce ladle, 6" l ................................ 75.00
Strawberry fork .................................. 35.00
Sugar sifter ........................................ 75.00
Sugar spoon ....................................... 25.00
Sugar tongs ....................................... 55.00
Teaspoon ........................................... 31.00

## IMPERIAL (Whiting Mfg. Co.)

Beef fork ............................................ 60.00
Bonbon spoon .................................... 47.00
Butter spreader .................................. 20.00

Chocolate spoon ................................ 18.00
Cold meat fork.................... 75.00 to 100.00
Demitasse spoon................................ 20.00
Dinner fork ........................................ 41.00
Egg spoon .......................................... 43.00
Fish serving set ................................ 395.00
Fish slice ......................................... 195.00
Gravy ladle ....................................... 135.00
Ice cream spoon ............................... 195.00
Pastry fork, 6½" l. ............................. 65.00
Pie server, silver blade ..................... 160.00
Punch ladle ...................................... 450.00
Salad serving set............................... 295.00
Salad spoon ...................................... 135.00
Salt spoon, individual size................. 26.00
Sauce ladle........................................ 68.00
Soup ladle ........................................ 325.00
Sugar shell ........................................ 75.00
Sugar tongs ....................................... 55.00
Teaspoon ........................................... 18.00

### IRIAN (R. Wallace & Sons)

Berry spoon ...................................... 200.00
Bonbon spoon ..................................... 95.00
Bouillon spoon .................................... 95.00
Butter pick......................................... 168.00
Butter serving knife........................... 85.00
Butter spreader.................................. 110.00
Cold meat fork ................................... 150.00
Cream ladle ....................................... 110.00
Dessert spoon ..................................... 45.00
Fish fork ............................................. 75.00
Fish serving fork ............... 250.00 to 275.00
Gravy ladle ....................................... 200.00
Luncheon fork ..................................... 42.00
Meat fork, large ................................ 200.00
Sugar spoon ........................................ 95.00
Teaspoon ............................................ 30.00

### JAPANESE or Audubon (Tiffany & Co.)

Coffee spoon ....................................... 55.00
Demitasse spoon.................................. 50.00
Luncheon fork ..................................... 95.00
Tablespoon ........................................ 135.00

### JAPANESE (Whiting Mfg. Co.)

Berry spoon ...................................... 295.00
Cream ladle ....................................... 195.00
Gravy ladle ....................................... 250.00
Mustard ladle .................................... 125.00
Oyster ladle....................................... 675.00
Punch ladle, small bowl .................... 350.00
Salad serving set, 12" l...................... 695.00
Salt spoon .......................................... 40.00

Serving spoon ................................... 190.00
Sugar shell ....................................... 115.00
Sugar tongs ........................................ 95.00
Vegetable spoon................................ 275.00
Youth set, 3 pcs. .............................. 150.00

### KING ALBERT (Whiting Mfg. Co.)

Baby fork............................................ 16.00
Berry spoon, large ............................ 120.00
Bonbon spoon ..................................... 31.00
Butter spreader, flat-handled.............. 15.00
Citrus spoon ....................................... 18.00
Cocktail fork....................................... 18.00
Cold meat fork ................................... 51.00
Cream ladle ........................................ 31.00
Gravy ladle ......................................... 51.00
Lemon fork ......................................... 20.00
Luncheon fork ..................................... 23.00
Salad fork ........................................... 26.00
Sauce ladle......................................... 20.00
Sugar spoon ........................................ 21.00
Tablespoon ......................................... 41.00
Teaspoon ............................................ 16.00

### LA REINE (Reed & Barton)

Butter spreader, master...................... 65.00
Crumber ............................................. 95.00
Gravy ladle ......................................... 50.00
Ice cream fork .................................... 15.00
Jelly server........................................ 140.00
Pea spoon .......................................... 195.00
Salad fork ........................................... 20.00
Salad set............................................ 300.00
Strawberry forks, set of 6 ................. 195.00
Tablespoon ......................................... 48.00
Teaspoon ............................................ 23.00

### MARIE ANTOINETTE (Dominick & Haff)

Butter spreader, flat-handled.............. 25.00
Cold meat fork, 7½" l. ........................ 55.00
Cucumber server................................ 45.00
Gravy ladle ......................................... 50.00
Salad fork ........................................... 24.00
Sugar spoon ........................................ 35.00

### MAZARIN (Dominick & Haff)

Asparagus fork................................... 235.00
Asparagus server.............................. 350.00
Bouillon spoon .................................... 17.00
Butter spreader.................................. 25.00
Cheese scoop .................................... 125.00
Dessert spoon ..................................... 32.00
Dinner fork ......................................... 28.00

| | |
|---|---|
| Gravy ladle | 90.00 |
| Luncheon fork | 30.00 |
| Luncheon knife | 20.00 |
| Mustard ladle | 95.00 |
| Seafood fork | 20.00 |
| Soup ladle | 350.00 |
| Soup spoon, oval | 25.00 |
| Sugar tongs | 95.00 |
| Teaspoon | 15.00 |

## NEW KINGS (Dominick & Haff)

| | |
|---|---|
| Cocktail fork | 29.00 |
| Dinner fork | 40.00 |
| Dinner knife | 30.00 |
| Fruit knife | 45.00 |
| Luncheon fork | 35.00 |
| Luncheon knife | 25.00 |
| Pea spoon | 495.00 |

## No. 10 (Dominick & Haff)

| | |
|---|---|
| Berry spoon | 100.00 |
| Berry spoon, gold-washed bowl | 125.00 |
| Butter serving knife | 55.00 |
| Butter spreader, flat-handled | 45.00 |
| Butter spreader, master, gold-washed | 55.00 |
| Claret spoon, 15½" | 175.00 |
| Fish slice | 225.00 |
| Ice cream spoon | 30.00 |
| Jelly spoon | 110.00 |
| Lettuce fork | 75.00 |
| Luncheon fork | 30.00 |
| Meat fork, large | 100.00 |
| Muddler & six chocolate spoons | 218.00 |
| Pie server, gold-washed | 173.00 |
| Pie server, pierced | 375.00 |
| Preserve spoon, gold-washed | 75.00 |
| Salad fork | 50.00 |
| Soup ladle, large | 406.00 |
| Sugar shifter | 80.00 |
| Sugar spoon | 50.00 |
| Sugar tongs | 50.00 |
| Tablespoon | 50.00 |
| Tomato server | 95.00 |

## OLYMPIAN (Tiffany & Co.)

| | |
|---|---|
| Asparagus fork | 695.00 |
| Berry spoon, conch | 895.00 |
| Berry spoon | 795.00 |
| Berry spoon, plated | 450.00 |
| Butter spreader, flat-handled | 77.00 |
| Cheese knife | 275.00 |
| Coffee spoon, large | 50.00 |
| Cream ladle, long-handled | 395.00 |

| | |
|---|---|
| Cream ladle, shell bowl | 295.00 |
| Fish knife | 125.00 |
| Fish set | 895.00 |
| Fried egg server | 595.00 |
| Gravy ladle | 250.00 |
| Ice cream server | 715.00 |
| Luncheon knife | 62.00 |
| Olive fork | 125.00 |
| Oyster ladle | 950.00 |
| Pie server | 800.00 |
| Punch ladle | 1,200.00 |
| Sandwich tongs | 750.00 |
| Soup ladle, large | 813.00 |
| Spooner | 47.00 |
| Sugar shell | 95.00 |
| Sugar sifter | 250.00 |
| Sugar spoon | 158.00 |
| Sugar tongs | 95.00 |
| Sugar tongs, shell ends | 150.00 |
| Tomato server | 450.00 |
| Waffle server | 795.00 |

## PERSIAN (Tiffany & Co.)

| | |
|---|---|
| Butter spreader | 65.00 |
| Crumb knife, large | 650.00 |
| Demitasse spoon | 30.00 |
| Gravy ladle | 183.00 |
| Ice cream server, pink gold blade | 550.00 |
| Jelly spoon | 130.00 |
| Soup ladle, bowl/spiral fluted sides | 823.00 |
| Tablespoon | 83.00 |
| Teaspoon | 34.00 |

## PLYMOUTH (Gorham Mfg.)

| | |
|---|---|
| Asparagus fork | 230.00 |
| Berry spoon, small | 70.00 |
| Bouillon spoon | 8.00 |
| Butter serving knife | 30.00 |
| Cocktail fork | 11.00 |
| Dinner fork | 15.00 |
| Dinner knife | 23.00 |
| Ice cream spoon, pierced | 25.00 |
| Lettuce fork | 28.00 |
| Soup spoon, oval bowl | 16.00 |
| Sugar tongs | 30.00 |

## POMPADOUR (Whiting Mfg. Co.)

| | |
|---|---|
| Berry fork | 43.00 |
| Berry spoon, large | 150.00 |
| Bouillon ladle | 80.00 |
| Cake fork, three-tine, 6¼" l | 50.00 |
| Cheese scoop, small | 85.00 |
| Cocktail fork | 22.00 |
| Cold meat fork | 100.00 |

Cream soup spoon ............................. 35.00
Citrus spoons, set of 12 ................... 423.00
Dessert spoon .................................. 22.00
Dinner fork ....................................... 40.00
Gravy ladle ....................................... 95.00
Jelly spoon....................................... 18.00
Luncheon fork .................................. 25.00
Salad fork......................................... 36.00
Sauce ladle...................................... 45.00
Soup ladle ...................................... 225.00
Soup spoon...................................... 30.00
Stuffing spoon ................................ 300.00
Sugar shell ...................................... 25.00
Sugar tongs ..................................... 40.00
Teaspoon .......................................... 15.00

### RENAISSANCE (Dominick & Haff)

Berry spoon, 7⅜" .............................. 235.00
Citrus spoons, set of 6 ..................... 255.00
Claret ladle...................................... 185.00
Cocktail fork...................................... 40.00
Ice cream fork .................................. 45.00
Jelly cake knife ............................... 400.00
Lettuce fork...................................... 145.00
Salad fork, three-tine, 6⅛".................. 60.00
Sardine fork ...................................... 65.00
Sauce ladle...................................... 450.00
Strawberry fork.................................. 38.00

### ROCOCO (Dominick & Haff)

Bouillon spoon .................................. 25.00
Chocolate spoon ............................... 45.00
Grapefruit spoon ............................... 30.00
Ice cream spoon ............................... 35.00
Orange knife ..................................... 45.00
Parfait spoon .................................... 25.00
Pie server, silver blade ...................... 150.00
Sardine fork ...................................... 22.00
Stuffing spoon ................................. 350.00

### VERSAILLES (Gorham Mfg. Co.)

Asparagus........................................ 618.00
Berry fork .......................................... 55.00
Berry spoon, shell shaped bowl,
    gold-washed ................................ 395.00
Bonbob spoon .................................. 76.00
Bonbon spoon, gold-washed bowl .... 225.00
Cheese scoop, small.......................... 95.00
Coffee spoon .................................... 17.00
Cold meat fork ................................. 115.00
Cream soup...................................... 65.00
Dessert fork ...................................... 56.00
Dinner fork ........................................ 55.00
Fish slice, gold-washed...................... 335.00
Fruit knife.......................................... 35.00

Orange knife ..................................... 60.00
Pickle fork ........................................ 65.00
Stuffing spoon ................................. 433.00
Tablespoon ....................................... 62.00
Teaspoon .......................................... 23.00

### WAVE EDGE (Tiffany & Co.)

Asparagus tongs ............................. 775.00
Berry spoon, kidney shaped bowl...... 350.00
Breakfast knife................................... 55.00
Butter knife, flat-handled.................... 40.00
Cheese knife w/picks ....................... 150.00
Cheese scoop .................................. 250.00
Citrus spoon ..................................... 60.00
Dinner fork ........................................ 80.00
Dinner knife....................................... 80.00
Fish knife.......................................... 70.00
Grapefruit spoon, gold-washed bowl .. 55.00
Ice cream spoon, ruffled edge ............. 60.00
Luncheon fork ................................... 53.00
Pancake lifter ................................... 395.00
Pickle fork ........................................ 75.00
Pie server, serrated silver blade......... 455.00
Salad fork ......................................... 45.00
Sauce ladle, double pour.................... 135.00
Sorbet spoon, ruffled ........................ 48.00
Sugar shell ....................................... 65.00
Sugar sifter ...................................... 195.00
Tablespoon ....................................... 78.00
Teaspoon .......................................... 46.00

### WAVERLY (R. Wallace & Sons)

Berry spoon ...................................... 60.00
Butter knife, master size ..................... 35.00
Butter pick........................................ 63.00
Butter spreader, flat-handled.............. 19.00
Cake saw.......................................... 75.00
Cold meat fork, 8¼" ........................... 67.00
Demitasse spoon............................... 15.00
Dinner fork ........................................ 22.00
Dinner knife....................................... 26.00
Fish fork ........................................... 45.00
Honey spoon...................................... 75.00
Horseradish spoon............................. 47.00
Ice cream knife ................................ 165.00
Lettuce fork....................................... 85.00
Mustard laddle .................................. 45.00
Pie server ........................................ 175.00
Sardine fork ...................................... 50.00
Sherbet spoon ................................... 15.00
Spoon, oval bowl ............................... 18.00
Strawberry fork.................................. 25.00
Sugar sifter ...................................... 250.00
Tablespoon ....................................... 20.00
Teaspoon .......................................... 15.00

## TIN & TOLE

**Box,** cov., tole, small rectangular form w/a low domed hinged cover, original dark brown japanning w/white band & decoration & stripes in red & yellow, 19th c., 4¼" l. (some wear) .............................................. **116.00**

**Bread tray,** tole, oval w/deep flaring reticulated sides & half-round open end handles, original red ground w/stylized floral decoration in yellow, white, red & black, 19th c., 7¼ x 13¼", 3½" h. (minor wear) ............. **1,210.00**

**Butter churn,** tin, tall slightly tapering cylindrical form w/hand-grip side handles, the closed top centered by a flaring narrow neck for the wooden dasher handle, w/dasher, late 19th c., 21½" h. ......................... **193.00**

**Candle box,** tin, hanging-type, a long cylindrical container w/a hinged lid & narrow straps w/hanging holes at the back, worn old black paint, 19th c., 14" l. (old repairs, lid hinges old replacements) ................................. **138.00**

**Candleholder,** miniature, tin, saucer base, scalloped cup, blue, ca. 1850, 1¼" h., ⁷⁄₁₆" d. ..................................... **95.00**

**Candle mold,** tin, twelve-tube, flared top & base frame, ear handles at sides, 19th c., 5¾" h. ........................ **165.00**

**Candle sconces,** wall-type, tin, large flat rectangular wall plaque w/deeply cut-out corners, a small half-round bordered base shelf centering a candle socket, minor resoldering, 19th c., 12½" h., pr. ......................... **770.00**

**Canisters,** cov., tole, tall cylindrical form w/wide rounded shoulder to a fitted, slightly domed cap on a short cylindrical neck, black & gold decoration w/large Chinese characters on the front panels & cartouches on the shoulders numbered "20" & "21," China, 19th c., 17" h., pr. (wear, old dents, some soldered repair) ...................... **440.00**

**Chocolate mold,** tin, two-part, boldly embossed scene of a seated bear by a tree stump, w/tin clips, 9" h. ...... **220.00**

**Coffeepot,** cov., tole, tapering cylindrical body w/angled spout & strap handle, low domed cover w/replaced ring finial, original very worn brown japaning w/floral decoration in yellow, red, green & black, 19th c., 8¼" h. ........................ **385.00**

**Coffeepot,** cov., tole, tall tapering cylindrical body w/flared base, domed cover w/tiny finial, angled goose-neck spout, D-form strap handle, worn original dark brown japanning w/large stylized flowers & leaves in red, yellow, white & dark green, 10¾" h. (some old touch-up repair) .............................................. **715.00**

**Compotes,** cov., tole, classical oblong urn-form w/a deep boat-form bowl w/pointed upturned ends w/loop handles curling under to the sides, raised on a flaring rectangular short pedestal base, the high domed cover w/a pineapple finial, worn original cream ground w/black striping, decoupage oval landscapes on the sides of the base, gilded brass fittings, probably Europe, 19th c., 8¼" h., pr. ........................ **1,540.00**

*Rare Tole Cookie Box*

**Cookie box,** cov., tole, deep oval body w/a hinged cover w/wire handle, overall red ground, the front painted in yellow & green w/paired "love birds" flanked by fruit, flowers & leaves, Pennsylvania, ca. 1825, 10" l., 8¾" h. (ILLUS.) .................. **23,000.00**

**Deed box,** cov., tole, rectangular w/low domed cover w/wire handle, original dark brown japanning w/a white band & stylized floral decoration & stripes in red, green & yellow, wear & one hinge loose, 19th c., 6¾" l. (ILLUS. center, top next page) ...................... **116.00**

**Deed box,** cov., tole, rectangular w/low domed hinged cover w/wire handle, original dark brown japanning w/white band & floral decoration in yellow, red, green & black, 19th c., 7" l. (some wear, end of hasp broken, needs reattachment) ........................... **121.00**

*Tole Tea Caddy, Deed Box & Teapot*

*Tin Top Hat*

**Deed box,** cov., tole, rectangular w/low domed cover w/small wire handle, original dark brown japanning w/a white band & yellow striping, decorated w/strawberries in red, green & black, 19th c., 8" l. (wear) .............................................. **330.00**

**Deed box,** cov., tole, deep rectangular sides w/a high domed, hinged cover, original dark brown japanning w/polychrome delicate floral decoration & yellow striping, 19th c., 12¾" l. (damage, loose seams, some splits) ...................................... **165.00**

**Food warmer,** cov., tole, a tall cylindrical two-part container, the lower section w/angled air vents & large D-form strap handles, the smaller upper section w/a low stepped & domed cover w/a small loop handle, very worn black paint w/yellow striping & gold stenciling, tin font w/brass single spout burner, 19th c., 9" h...................................... **176.00**

**Lamp,** tin, whale oil, an inverted cone font w/central wick supports, on a slender cylindrical standard w/a loop strap handle, on a weighted saucer base, adjustable combustion air holes in the stem, 19th c., 9¾" h. (some resoldering)............................ **193.00**

**Model of top hat,** tin, the black-painted top hat w/band rim w/bow over down-turned rim, late 19th - early 20th c., 8¾ x 10⅜", 6¾" h. (ILLUS. top previous column) ........... **978.00**

**Model of an umbrella,** composed of pie-shaped sheets of tin painted alternating red & white w/brown trim, American, 19th c., 9" h. ................. **2,875.00**

**Rain downspout collection boxes,** tin, wall-mounted flattened gradiated containers w/a wide rectangular mouth above narrowing panels, one panel w/embossed spread-winged eagle & shield w/stars, green & gold repaint over pitted & weathered paint, 19th c., 18" h., pr. (some rust damage, hanging braces added) ...... **550.00**

**Sugar bowl,** cov., tole, slightly tapering cylindrical body w/a low domed cover w/a small double loop handle, worn original dark brown japanning w/stylized floral decoration in red & yellow, 19th c., 3¾" h. ......... **275.00**

**Tea caddy,** cov., tole, upright oval cylindrical w/a narrow shoulder to the small fitted cap, worn original dark brown japanning w/floral decoration around the upper half in yellow, red & dark green, 19th c., top & collar a bit battered, 5¼" h. (ILLUS. top left) .................................. **61.00**

**Tea caddy,** cov., tole, low oval box, the flat cover decorated w/a gilded Oriental design w/two figures all against the original red ground, probably China, 19th c., 6¼" l........... **358.00**

**Teapot,** cov., tole, slender tapering cylindrical body w/a long angled spout & strap handle, low domed cover w/small loop handle, worn original red paint w/large stylized floral decoration in yellow, white & dark green, handle resoldered, 19th c., 8¼" h. (ILLUS. right, top previous page)................................. **330.00**

**Tinder box,** cov., tin, low cylindrical form w/a fitted cover centered by a cylindrical candle socket, a small loop handle on the base, w/steel, a piece of marble, a stub of an old candle & a tin damper, 19th c., 4" d. .................... **275.00**

**Tinder box,** cov., tin, low cylindrical form w/fitted flat cover & small loop handle at side of base, traces of old green paint, w/flint, steel & old fiber tinder, 4½" d. .................................. **242.00**

**Torch,** hand-type, tin, a large dished circular reflector w/two long projecting wick tubes in front of the cylindrical font, on a wire frame w/wooden handle, old dark patina, 19th c., 17½" d. (small rust holes & attempted repairs to font) ................ **193.00**

**Tray,** tole, rectangular w/gilt-decorated border of flowers & beadings & w/a pierced & gilt-decorated gallery, beaded edge & two carrying handles, Scotland, ca. 1800, 19 x 27½" (scratches) .... **1,265.00**

**Tray,** tole, wide rectangular form w/a dished border & rounded corners, overall gilt chinoiserie decoration on a Chinese red ground, 19th c., 21⅜ x 26⅞" ..................................... **770.00**

**Urn,** cov., wide tapering paneled body w/a shoulder tapering to a domed & paneled cover, on a flaring molded base w/tab feet, black ground decorated around the shoulder w/a wide scalloped polychrome geometric & floral band, Europe, 19th c., 25" h. (some damage & repair)..................... **660.00**

# MINIATURES (Paintings)

**Bust portrait of a gentleman,** three-quarters sinister, w/reddish hair, blue jacket & yellow waist coat, w/initials "J.T.M." & dated, attributed to John

Thomas Mitchell, 1799, in gold pendant frame w/woven lock of hair on reverse, 2½" h. .................. **$920.00**

*Miniature of a Gentleman*

**Bust portrait of a gentleman,** watercolor on ivory, shows a man w/blue eyes wearing a navy great coat & frilled white stock, in a rose gold colored locket frame w/plaited blond hair & the initial "P" in cut gold on the reverse, mounted within a blue glass border, 2½ x 2⅛" (ILLUS.) ........................................... **920.00**

**Full-length portrait of child,** pencil & wash, child w/blond hair seated in a landscape holding a basket of cherries, in steel & gold trim oval frame mounted on reverse w/another miniature of a gentleman in profile, attributed to David Bouton, ca. 1805, 2¾" h.............................. **1,610.00**

**Half-length portrait of a child,** watercolor on ivory, dark-haired rosey-cheeked child wearing a grey empire gown w/blue ribbons posed against a mottled blue ground, in rectangular ebonized wood frame w/gilt filet, ca. 1800, 1⅝ x 2" ......... **1,150.00**

**Half-length portraits of a Franklin & Jane Pierce,** three quarter sinister, she in blue dress, white fichu set w/a brooch & brown curly hair, he w/dark coat & white shirt, both on blue background, in gilt metal frames set in fitted leatherette cases, attributed to Moses B. Russell, ca. 1835, 3½" h., pr. (cracks) ....................... **2,300.00**

**Profile bust portrait of a young gentleman,** watercolor, pen & ink on paper, shown w/dark tousled hair, wearing a navy blue coat & white vest & tie, attributed to Rufus Porter, in wide giltwood frame, 4 x 5" ........ **2,300.00**

**Profile bust portrait of a young
woman,** watercolor on paper, she is
wearing a blue-ribboned white lace
cap & wide white Bertha collar, in
the original giltwood & gesso frame
inscribed in black ink "Mother,"
American school, 19th c.,
3½ x 4½"...................................... **1,150.00**

*Miniature of a Little Girl*

**Three-quarter length portrait of a
little girl,** watercolor on ivory,
depicts young girl w/dark hair
wearing a flowered dress holding a
bunch of cherries, 2¾ x 2⅜"
(ILLUS.) ........................................ **6,325.00**

**Three-quarter length portraits of
young lady & a gentleman,** she in
a blue striped short-sleeved dress,
he in brown jacket & black cravat, in
gold frames w/locket of hair reverse,
signed "Dresden" & "93" on latter,
right edge, Otto Eckhardt, 1893,
2½" h., pr. ....................................... **546.00**

# MOVIE MEMORABILIA

*Also see: AUTOGRAPHS and PAPER
DOLLS.*

## BOOKS

**"Birthday Book,"** Shirley Temple,
1936, Dell Publishing Co., unused ... **$98.00**

**"Five Books About Me,"** Shirley
Temple, 1936, w/original box............ **125.00**

**"Gone with the Wind Illustrated
Motion Picture Edition,"** 1939......... **35.00**

**"Marilyn,"** Marilyn Monroe biography
by Norman Mailer ............................. **125.00**

**"Strange Death of Marilyn Monroe,"**
ca. 1964, photos & reports, 75 pp.
booklet ............................................... **39.00**

## LOBBY CARDS

**"All About Eve,"** starring Bette Davis
& Anne Baxter, George Sanders &
Celeste Holm, one title card w/heads
of stars over the title & four scenes
depicted below, scene card showing
the four stars conversing, each
11 x 14", set of 2.............................. **460.00**

*"Arsenic and Old Lace" Lobby Cards*

**"Arsenic and Old Lace,"** starring
Cary Grant, one title card, six scene
cards, Warner Brothers, 1944, each
11 x 14", set of 7 (ILLUS.) ............... **345.00**

**"Escape,"** starring Rex Harrison,
matted & framed, 1948, 11 x 14"........ **25.00**

**"King Creole,"** starring Elvis Presley,
matted & framed, 1958, 11 x 14"........ **25.00**

**"Lady from Shanghai,"** starring Rita
Hayworth & Orson Welles, matted &
framed, 1948, 11 x 14" ...................... **25.00**

**"Letter from an Unknown Woman,"**
starring Joan Fontaine, matted &
framed, 1948, 11 x 14" ...................... **25.00**

**"The Man Who Knew Too Much,"**
original 1956 issue, set of 8 (one
damaged at corner) ......................... **195.00**

**"Mutiny on the Bounty,"** starring
Marlon Brando, matted & framed,
1962, 11 x 14".................................... **25.00**

*"Psycho" Lobby Card*

**"Psycho,"** starring Anthony Perkins & Vera Miles, scene depicting Anthony Perkins standing outside the Bates house, single card, Paramount, 1960, 11 x 14" (ILLUS.) .................... **249.00**

**"State of the Union,"** starring Katharine Hepburn & Spencer Tracy, matted & framed, 1948, 11 x 14" ............................................. **25.00**

**"Svengali,"** starring John Barrymore, Marian Marsh & Trilby, one title card w/scene of the three stars, one scene card of Tribly standing in doorway & Marsh reclining on sofa, Warner Brothers, 1931, each 11 x 14", set of 2 ............................ **1,035.00**

**"Union Pacific,"** starring Douglas Fairbanks, one title card, scene of star sitting on rock, holding gun in right hand, seven cards w/various scenes depicted, Paramount, 1943R, each 11 x 14", set of 8 ......... **115.00**

**"Winter Meeting,"** starring Bette Davis, matted & framed, 1948, 11 x 14" .......... **25.00**

## POSTERS

**"At The Circus,"** starring the Marx Bros., colorful animated depiction of Groucho, Chico & Harpo at top, title near bottom above girl lifting weights in one hand, one-sheet, framed, MGM, 1939, 27 x 41" ..................... **1,380.00**

**"Breakfast At Tiffany's,"** starring Audrey Hepburn, colored w/small vignette scene of couple kissing below right of title, Hepburn depicted in center scene, upswept hairdo, large diamond necklace & earrings, long cigarette holder in mouth, cat on shoulder (ILLUS. top next column)... **1,380.00**

**"Chinatown,"** starring Jack Nicholson & Faye Dunaway, depicts Dunaway's facial features, hair

*"Breakfast At Tiffany's" Poster*

formed by curling smoke from cigarette in mouth of man shown to the left, title appears beneath Dunaway, the lower half containing other movie information, three-sheet, Paramount, 1974, 40½ x 76½" ......... **460.00**

**"Citizen Kane,"** starring Orson Welles, depicts Welles face at top w/title & small vignette below, three-sheet, RKO, 1956R, 41 x 81" ........... **374.00**

*"Devil's Double" Poster*

**"Devil's Double,"** starring William S. Hart, colorful scene of Hart wearing fancy vest & tie, playing cards, one-sheet, linen-backed, Triangle, 1916, minor restoration, 27 x 41" (ILLUS. bottom previous page)...... **3,738.00**

**"Dial M for Murder,"** starring Ray Milland, Grace Kelly & Robert Cummings, depicts man & woman struggling, the woman reaching for a dangling phone, one-sheet, Warner Brothers, 1954, 27 x 41".................. **805.00**

*"Father of the Bride" Poster*

**"Father of the Bride,"** starring Spencer Tracy, Joan Bennett & Elizabeth Taylor, depicting Taylor in bridal attire & Tracy, dressed in a tuxedo holding out his empty pants pockets, three-sheet, MGM, 1950, 41 x 81" (ILLUS.) ............................. **403.00**

**"Guns and Guitars,"** starring Gene Autry, depicts scene of stagecoach & horses across top, small vignette of Gene playing guitar, one-sheet, linen-backed, Republic, 1936, 27 x 41"............................................. **489.00**

**"House on Haunted Hill,"** starring Vincent Price, depicting various scenes w/house in background, half-sheet, Allied Artists, 1958, 22 x 28" (rolled) ............................................. **489.00**

**"Indiscreet,"** starring Cary Grant & Ingrid Bergman, depicts Bergman against wall w/Grant leaning toward her, his right hand on the wall, one-sheet, Warner Brothers, 1958, 27 x 41"............................................. **144.00**

*"It's A Wonderful Life" Poster*

**"It's A Wonderful Life,"** starring James Stewart & Donna Reed, depicting scene w/Stewart lifting Reed up in the air, one-sheet, linen-backed, Liberty Films, 1946, medium restoration, 27 x 41" (ILLUS.) ........ **3,450.00**

**"The Little Shop of Horrors,"** starring Jonathan Haze, Jackie Joseph & Mel Welles, depicts man in shabby suit & derby hat, holding an umbrella & a potted plant w/a vine twining around his legs & large open-mouthed flower near his head, three-sheet, Filmgroup, 1960, 41 x 81"................. **115.00**

**"The Mole People,"** starring John Agar & Cynthia Patrick, depicts a woman held by one of the Moles, vignette scene below & above, six-sheet, Universal, 1956, 81 x 81".... **1,380.00**

**"The Outlaw,"** starring Jane Russell, depicting man pulling Russell through doorway, three-sheet, Howard Hughes Production, 1943, 41 x 81"......................................... **1,265.00**

**"Pat and Mike,"** starring Spencer Tracy & Katharine Hepburn, depiction of the two main characters across the top w/the title in

*"The Postman Always Rings Twice" Poster*

oversized letters below, six-sheet, MGM, 1952, 81 x 81"....................... **201.00**

**"Phantom of the Rue Morgue,"** starring Karl Malden, Claude Dauphin, Patricia Medina & Steve Forrest, depicting woman struggling w/the phantom in the window of a tall building w/people on the street below, three-sheet, Warner Brothers, 1954, 41 x 81"................... **115.00**

**"The Postman Always Rings Twice,"** starring Lana Turner & John Garfield, depicts the stars in an embrace, one-sheet, Australian, MGM, 1946, 27 x 41" (ILLUS. above)................................ **403.00**

**"Rear Window,"** starring James Stewart & Grace Kelly, depicts two window scenes, Stewart, holding binoculars & Kelly shown at bottom, one-sheet, Paramount, 1954, 27 x 41"........................................ **1,093.00**

**"Royal Wedding,"** starring Fred Astaire & Jane Powell, depicts background of people dancing w/Astaire dancing in foreground & Powell near right side, w/title surrounding small vignette of kissing couple, three-sheet, MGM, 1951, 41 x 81"............................................ **748.00**

**"The Spiral Staircase,"** starring Dorothy McGuire, George Brent & Ethel Barrymore, depicting McGuire near the staircase, holding a lit candle, bust portraits of Brent & Barrymore in lower left corner, one-sheet, RKO, 1946, 27 x 41".................................. **316.00**

*"Singin' in the Rain" Poster*

**"Singin' in the Rain,"** starring Gene Kelly, Donald O'Connor & Debbie Reynolds, color scene depicting the three stars wearing yellow raincoats, carrying open umbrellas, one-sheet, Australian, linen-backed, MGM, 1952, 27 x 41" (ILLUS.)................................ **633.00**

*"Some Like It Hot" Poster*

**"Some Like It Hot,"** starring Marilyn Monroe, Tony Curtis & Jack Lemmon, depicts Monroe crouched on floor, strumming ukulele, Curtis & Lemmon, wearing dresses & reclining & sitting on lounge, six-sheet, linen-backed, United Artists, 1959, 81 x 81" (ILLUS.) ................ **2,185.00**

**"Stalag 17,"** starring William Holden, depicting bust portrait of Holden on upper left, title in center & line of soldiers & women at lower edge, one-sheet, Paramount, 1953, 27 x 41".............................................. **184.00**

**"A Star is Born,"** starring Judy Garland & James Mason, depicting several vignette scenes & Judy w/hands raised near bottom, three-sheet, Warner Brothers, 1954, 41 x 81"............................................. **690.00**

**"Stranger On The Third Floor,"** starring Peter Lorre, depicting bust portrait of Lorre & the other actors across top, title across center in large type, a hand in the left bottom corner, one-sheet, linen backed, RKO, 1940, 27 X 41" ........................ **345.00**

**"The Time Machine,"** starring Rod Taylor, Alan Young, Yvette Mimieux, Sebastian Cabot & Tom Helmore, depicts two of the actors fighting off pre-historic creatures, three-sheet, MGM, 1960, 41 x 81 " ........................ **230.00**

**"Vertigo,"** starring James Stewart & Kim Novak, center depicts man & woman within swirls w/title at bottom, one-sheet, Paramount, 1958, 27 x 41".................................. **633.00**

**"West Side Story,"** starring Natalie Wood, center depicts star & others dancing, Italian, United Artists, 1961, 39½ x 55"......................................... **633.00**

**"Winner Takes All,"** starring Joe Palooka, movie based on comic strip by Ham Fisher, marked in lower right corner "48/1138," oak frame ..... **450.00**

## MISCELLANEOUS

*Vivien Leigh Cigarette Case*

**Calendar,** Jayne Mansfield, 1957 ........ **35.00**

**Cigarette case,** Vivien Leigh, the sterling silver case stamped "Asprey London" w/hallmarks, engraved in Leigh's hand, "Curley from Vivien Leigh," 1936, 3½ x 4½" (ILLUS. bottom previous column) .............. **2,300.00**

**Coloring book,** "Charlie Chaplin in the Movies," 1917, M. A. Donahue & Co. ...................................................... **75.00**

**Coloring book,** Shirley Temple, 1958 .. **35.00**

**Coloring & paper doll book,** Deanna Durbin, 1941 ...................................... **35.00**

**Creamer,** Shirley Temple, cobalt blue w/transfer of Shirley Temple w/signature below, Wheaties premium made by Hazel Atlas Glass Co., 1936 ......... **30.00 to 50.00**

**Doll,** "Wizard of Oz," cloth, Scarecrow, Wheat Chex premium ........................ **60.00**

*Shirley Temple Doll*

**Doll,** Shirley Temple, wearing white dress w/small red polka-dots, white shoes w/white socks & has red ribbon in hair, w/original box (ILLUS.) ........................................ **1,600.00**

**Fan club button,** Marilyn Monroe, 1980s, 3" d............................................. **8.00**

**Figures,** Laurel & Hardy, clothed w/rubber faces, Knickerbocker, 10" h. .................................................. **95.00**

**Glass,** "Wizard of Oz," enameled, reads "The Wizard of Oz" above image of lion above "The Cowardly Lion," 1939 (ILLUS. top next page) .. **175.00**

*"Wizard of Oz" Glass*

**Glass,** The Creature, Universal Monsters............................................. **33.00**

**Magazine,** "Hollywood," March 1938, Shirley Temple on cover..................... **45.00**

**Magazine,** "Modern Screen," November 1940, Marlene Dietrich on cover............................................. **25.00**

**Magazine,** "Modern Screen," June 1955, Marilyn Monroe on cover.......... **25.00**

**Magazine,** "Movie Life," December 1941, Abbott & Costello wearing cowboy outfits on cover...................... **65.00**

**Magazine,** "Movie Mirror," February 1940, Jeanette MacDonald on cover.. **18.00**

**Magazine,** "Photoplay," February 1947, Ingrid Bergman......................... **45.00**

**Magazine,** "Screenland," August 1936, Shirley Temple on cover........... **45.00**

**Magazine,** "Silver Screen," October 1950, Linda Darnell on cover.............. **15.00**

*Lauren Bacall Magazine Clipping*

**Magazine clipping,** photograph of Lauren Bacall, scene from "To Have and Have Not," autographed "Lauren Bacall" & also autographed "Humphrey Bogart's" (ILLUS. bottom previous column) ............................. **805.00**

**Movie book,** "Lady of the Lake," illustrated, 1943, hard bound w/dust jacket ................................................. **35.00**

**Movie book,** "Phantom of the Opera," Lon Chaney, illustrated, 1911, hard bound w/dust jacket........................... **38.00**

**Movie book,** "Trader Horn," illustrated, 1927, hard bound w/bust jacket ................................................. **24.00**

**Movie flip book,** Shirley Temple, 1930-40s, theater premium ............... **28.00**

**Movie slide,** "The Coconuts," The Marx Brothers, glass slide in cardboard mount, 4" w., 3½" h. (minor soiling) .................................... **44.00**

**Movie slide,** "Pack Up Your Troubles," Laurel & Hardy, glass slide in cardboard mount, marked "April 22" at bottom of slide, 4" w., 3½" h. (minor soiling)...................... **121.00**

*Shirley Temple Mug*

**Mug,** Shirley Temple, cobalt blue glass w/decal portrait of Shirley w/signature below, 4" h. (ILLUS.) ....... **30.00**

**Paint book,** "Gone With the Wind," 1940, expansive cover w/Scarlett, Merrill ................................................. **275.00**

**Phonograph record set,** "Shirley Temple Reads Disney's Bambi," 78 rpm records, set of 3..................... **45.00**

**Photograph of Ann Sheridan,** black & white, autographed.......................... **40.00**

**Photograph of Bette Davis,** black & white, Davis wears a pin-striped dress, leaning on her elbows looking down, stamped on verso "Bette Davis Warner Bros. Pictures" & "Please Credit Photograph by Hurrell," matted 7½ x 9½" ................ **173.00**

**Photograph of Betty Grable,** black & white photograph, inscribed in red pen, "Sincere best wishes, Betty Grable," matted 8 x 10" .................... **345.00**

**Photograph of Billie Burke** .............. **125.00**

**Photograph of Buster Keaton,** black & white photograph of Buster Keaton ashing his cigarette in a tall vase, stamped on lower right "HURRELL" & "Please Credit Hurrell M.G.M." on verso, matted 10¼ x 13¼" (pin holes on borders of photograph) ............... **690.00**

**Photograph of Douglas Fairbanks,** Jr., black & white, signed in black ink, "D. Fairbanks, Jr.," 5 x 7" ............ **95.00**

**Photograph of Jean Harlow,** black & white, shows smiling Jean Harlow in a white fur, stamped on verson "Kindly credit M-G-M Photo By Hurrell" & "874x38" written in pencil, matted, 8½ x 10" .............................. **173.00**

*Leslie Howard Photograph*

**Photograph of Leslie Howard,** black & white portrait of Howard wearing a suit & tie, stamped on lower right "HURRELL" & "Please credit Hurrell M.G.M." stamped on verso, matted, 10 x 13" (ILLUS.) ............................. **230.00**

**Photograph of Dolores Costello** .......... **30.00**

**Photograph of Dorothy Gish** ................ **60.00**

**Photograph of Joan Crawford,** 1926 .. **125.00**

**Photograph of Lillian Gish** ................... **50.00**

*Marilyn Monroe Photograph*

**Photograph of Marilyn Monroe,** "Marilyn in White," one vintage print signed on mat, gelatin silver print, matted & framed, ca. 1954, 11 x 14" (ILLUS.) ........................................ **4,025.00**

**Photograph of Marilyn Monroe,** black & white portrait of Monroe w/her head slightly tipped downward, inscribed on lower left "To Sylvia your realle (sic) wonderful Thanks Marilyn Monroe" in blue ink, ca. 1948, matted, 15½ x 18" (signature in faded from hair salon staining) ........................ **2,300.00**

**Photograph of Marilyn Monroe,** black & white, shows Marilyn posing against white deco-style arch in a black & white bathing suit in coral platform shoes, ca. 1947, matted, 15½ x 18" ......................................... **115.00**

**Photograph of Marion Davies** ............ **50.00**

**Photograph of Rudolph Valentino,** h.p. & lettered poster advertising "Legendary Scenes" w/Vilma Banky & Louise Dresser, mounted on cardboard, 20 x 31" ......................... **403.00**

**Photograph of Tallulah Bankhead,** black & white, depicts Tallulah Bankhead smoking in mirror, stamped on verso "Please Credit Hurrell Hollywood," matted, 8½ x 10" (edges show wear) .......................... **575.00**

**Photograph of Theda Bara** ............... **100.00**

**Postcard of Nelson Eddy,** unused ...... **15.00**

**Program,** "Birth of a Nation," official souvenir w/photos, 32 pp. ................... **65.00**

**Program,** "Gone With the Wind," 1939, original, editor Howard Deitz .... **75.00**

**Program,** "Gone With the Wind,"
1939, souvenir ................................... **50.00**

**Program,** "Morocco," starring Marlene
Dietrich, Grauman's Chinese
Theatre, 1930 ................................. **155.00**

**Program,** "Son of Zorro," 1923, starring
Douglas Fairbanks, souvenir ................ **85.00**

**Program,** "Tarzan & the Amazons,"
starring Johnny Weissmuller, four
pp., 7 x 10¼"..................................... **20.00**

**Script,** unbound, from "Gone With the
Wind," pink & yellow paper in three-
ring canvased binder, 211 pp.,
MGM, ca. 1939, 10½ x 11½" ......... **2,300.00**

*Marilyn Monroe Shadow Box Image*

**Shadow Box color image,** for "The
Seven Year Itch," depicting Marilyn
Monroe & Tom Ewell, ca. 1955,
framed, 16 x 20" (ILLUS.) ................. **345.00**

**Tip tray,** Marilyn Monroe, round
w/nude image of Monroe, 4" d.
(minor scratches to edges) ................. **83.00**

---

# MUSIC BOXES

**Bremond (Swiss) cylinder music
box,** burl walnut case, ratchet-
wound at the side, original tune
sheet inside lid, w/a 13" l. eight-tune
cylinder, late 19th c., 22½" l......... **$1,380.00**

**Polyphon 24⅝ disc music box,**
periphery drive, playing on two
combs, motor in glazed housing at
bottom of case, restored light oak
case, arched glazed door flanked by
columns, pierced spandrels, storage

*Swiss Cylinder Orchestral Box*

*Symphonion Music Box*

base w/tilt front giving access to disc
storage slots, w/winding handle &
complete w/thirty-five metal discs,
German, ca. 1900 (start-stop levers
inoperative) .................................... **3,737.00**

**Regina disc music box,** center drive
on double combs, one w/'banjo'
sound enhancement, side w/winding
handle, tune selector dial & lever,
start/stop/repeat lever, in walnut
case, upper portion w/opening doors
w/cutwork spandrels flanked by half-
columns, complete w/thirty-six metal
discs, No. 65838, German, ca. 1910,
64½" h. (winding wheel ratchet & not
engaging spring) ........................... **8,625.00**

**Swiss cylinder music box,** table
model, rectangular walnut case
w/fruitwood banding, the 19" cylinder
playing twelve tunes as indicated on
original tune sheet, accompanied by
drum, castinet & six bells w/butterfly
strikers, zither attachable at will, late
19th c., 14 x 32", 10" h. (ILLUS. top
this column) ................................... **3,220.00**

**Swiss cylinder music box,**
mahogany case w/fruitwood inlay,
ratchet-wound, original tune sheet
inside lid, w/a 7" l. six-tune cylinder,
late 19th c., 17" l. ............................ **403.00**

**Symphonion music box,** case
w/elaborate scroll decoration &
inside of cover w/image of young
nude children w/instruments & reads
"Symphonion" below, w/over twenty
discs & original stand, 15" h.
(ILLUS. bottom previous page)...... **4,250.00**

# MUSICAL INSTRUMENTS

*Lowden Acoustic Guitar*

**Guitar,** acoustic-type, Lowden,
rosewood body, spruce top, twenty
fret ebony fingerboard w/abalone
inlays, wooden bridge, serial No.
2951, w/hard-shell case, once owned
by Andy Summers (ILLUS.).......... **$3,450.00**

**Guitar,** acoustic-type, Martin 0-28,
rosewood body, spruce top
w/herringbone purfling, mahogany
neck, nineteen fret ebony fingerboard,
solid headstock w/ivory tuning pegs,
ebony pyramid bridge, "C.F. Martin
New York" stamped into the wood, ca.
1870s, w/hard-shell case, once
owned by Steve Howe...................... **1,955.00**

*Gibson Mandolin-guitar*

**Guitar,** electric-type, the back of
strong irregular curl, the sides & top
of light curl, maple neck, bound
rosewood fingerboard w/split block
pearl inlay, labeled "Style ES-350 n,
Gibson Guitar, Number A 5323 Is
Hereby Guaranteed Against Faulty
Workmanship And Materials Gibson,
Inc. Kalamazoo Mich. USA," ca.
1950, w/original case, back 21 1/16" l.,
lower bout 16 15/16" w...................... **2,645.00**

**Guitar,** solid body, the maple body
w/sunburst finish, the maple neck
w/rosewood fingerboard, Fender,
serial No. 96632, ca. 1963,
w/original case................................. **748.00**

**Mandolin,** the two-piece back of
broad curl, the sides of medium curl,
the top of fine to medium grain, the
ebony fingerboard w/pearl eyes,
pearl inlay at the pegboard & the
varnish of a red sunburst, labeled
"Gibson Mandolin, Style F4, Number
24309, Is Hereby Guaranteed" etc.,
w/original case, Gibson Mandolin-
Guitar Co., Kalamazoo, Michigan,
ca. 1915, back 12 13/16" l................. **2,530.00**

**Mandolin-guitar,** acoustic-type, 1918
Gibson archtop model, red sunburst
finish, the two-piece back & sides
plain, the top of fine to wide grain,
mahogany neck, bound ebony
fingerboard w/pearl eyes, labeled
"Gibson Guitar Style 'O' Number
40177 is Hereby Guaranteed" etc.,
w/original case, 17 5/8" h.
(ILLUS. above) ............................ **3,105.00**

*Steinway Grand Piano*

*Pine & Leather Minstrel Tambourine*

**Piano,** grand, "Steinway," w/ebony finish, ca. 1931 (ILLUS. top) .......... **9,000.00**

**Squeeze box,** rectangular, plays chords, signed Hohner, 6 x 11 x 9½" ................. **195.00**

**Tambourine,** carved & painted pine w/leather, minstrel-type, the circular frame painted blue & holding a taughtly stretched leather playing surface painted w/a steam engine paddlewheeler, has red painted turned pine handle, the frame fitted w/cymbals, American, late 19th c., 25½" h. (ILLUS. bottom) ................ **5,175.00**

**Ukulele,** the body & neck made of mahogany, rosewood fingerboard, labeled at the peg head "Martin & Co., est 1833," style "O," ca. 1930, back 9⁷⁄₁₆" l. ....................................... **138.00**

**Violin,** the two-piece back of medium curl, the ribs similar to the scroll of faint curl, the top of wide grain, the varnish of red color, labeled "Paul Malignaggi, Providence, R.I. 1946," American, back 13¾" l. .................... **633.00**

**Violin,** the two-piece back of narrow curl, ribs & scroll similar, the top of medium grain, the varnish of reddish brown color, labeled "Antonius Stradivarius Cremonensis, Facibat Anno 1723," ca. 1920, back 29⁹⁄₁₆" l. ........................................ **3,737.00**

---

# OFFICE EQUIPMENT

*By the late 19th century business offices around the country were becoming increasingly mechanized as inventions such as the typewriter, adding machine, mimeograph and Dictaphone became more widely common. Miracles of efficiency when introduced, in today's computerized offices these machines would be cumbersome and archaic. Although difficult to display and store, many of these relics are becoming increasingly collectible today.*

*"The Chicago" Typewriter*

**Pencil sharpener,** "Futurmatic," desktop-type ..................................... **$26.00**

**Typewriter,** "The Chicago," three-row keyboard, type sleeve, unnumbered model, patent dates, 1889, 1891 & 1892 (ILLUS.) ..................................... **125.00**

**Typewriter,** Crandall, two-row curved keyboard, type sleeve, black metal case w/gilt scroll trim ....................... **750.00**

**Typewriter,** "Ford," three-row, thrust action, ornate scroll-pierced silvered metal case (ILLUS. top next page) ............................................. **1,000.00**

**Typewriter,** "The Fox" four-row keyboard, up-strike mechanism, black metal case ................................. **75.00**

*"Ford" Typewriter*

**Typewriter,** International Model No. 5, index-type, black metal case w/gilt decoration, oval tag metal tag w/name & manufacturer, "New American Mfg. Co., Chicago, Il. U.S.A." .............................................. **175.00**

**Typewriter,** "Mignon," index-type, black metal case ................................. **75.00**

**Typewriter,** Munson Model No. 1, three-row keyboard, type sleeve mechanism, open framework on shaped wooden platform base ......... **350.00**

**Typewriter,** "Remington No. 2," complete .......................................... **250.00**

# OLYMPIC GAMES MEMORABILIA

*First begun in Ancient Greece as a Pan-Hellenic festival of athletic games, as well as choral poetry and dance contests, the Games were held every four years until the 5th century A.D. Not until 1896 were the Olympics revived under the leadership of Baron de Coubertin of France. The first modern Games were held in Athens, Greece and have continued throughout this century with lapses during the two World Wars. It was in 1924 that the first Winter Olympics were initiated so the numbering of the Summer and Winter Olympics does not coincide. Posters, pins and other items from past Olympiads are today highly collectible.*

**Bicycle card,** 1932 ............................ **$15.00**
**Book,** "Helsinki, Finland," 1952 ............. **35.00**

**Book,** "Olympics Committee Report," 1976, in original box .......................... **25.00**
**Book,** Sports Illustrated, "The Olympic Games," soft cover ............................. **20.00**
**Button,** 1936, enameled ...................... **60.00**
**Program,** 1936 German games............ **45.00**
**Stationery,** 1932, three sheets w/envelopes...................................... **24.00**
**Tobacco card,** 1932 Los Angeles, Duke Kahanamoku, Hawaiian swimmer ....................................... **26.00**

# PAPER COLLECTIBLES

**Advertisement,** "Yellow Kid and The Man Hunter," orange w/black lettering, "Globe Museum 10¢ - Monday 12, 1897...," 19½" h., 7" w. (tears & minor touch-up).................. **$33.00**

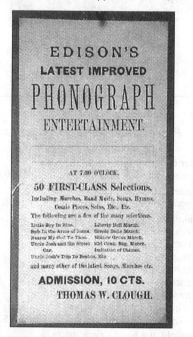

*Edison Phonograph Advertisement*

**Advertisement,** "Edison's Phonograph Entertainment," orange, black lettering reads "Edison's - Latest Improved - Phonograph - Entertainment - at 7:30 O'Clock - 50 First-Class Selections - Admissions, 10 cts. - Thomas W. Clough," minor soiling, 11¾" h., 6" w. (ILLUS.) ........... **11.00**

**Ballot,** sample-type, for woman's
suffrage, 1917 (edges chipped) .......... **20.00**

**Family register,** pen & ink & watercolor
on paper, a green, yellow & pink-tinted
table inscribed "Norton Register"
above floral decoration issuing from a
heart-decorated planter, flanked by
heart & floral decoration, over a
quadripartite register w/names of the
Norton family, birth, marriage & death
dates, all flanked by floral-decorated
columns above a red, yellow, blue &
green painted house, flanked by urn-
shaped planters issuing flowers over
the inscription "JEREMIAH. &
HANNAH.NORTONS.FAMILY," mid-
19th c., 11 x 14" ................................. **2,070.00**

**Travel brochure,** "The Amazing
America," 1938, Greyhound Bus
Lines, 24 pp. ...................................... **28.00**

**Travel brochure,** "California & All the
West," 1950s, Greyhound Bus Lines .. **17.00**

# PAPER DOLLS

*Also see: MOVIE MEMORABILIA*

**"Hollywood Dollies,"** Douglas Mac
Lean, uncut, 1925 ........................... **$115.00**

**"Hollywood Dollies,"** Norma Shearer,
1st series, uncut in original sleeve
w/listings of others in series, 1925 ..... **135.00**

**"Hollywood Dollies,"** Reginald
Denny, uncut, 1925 ......................... **115.00**

**"Baby Sparkle Plenty,"** from Dick
Tracy comic strip, Saalfield,
No. 1510, uncut, 1948 ...................... **58.00**

**"Betty Bonnet,"** by Sheila Young,
Christmas Party, full page, uncut,
"Ladies Home Journal" 1916-17,
11 x 16" ............................................. **50.00**

**"Brother & Sister,"** die cut book
w/statuette dolls glued to cover,
Whitman Publishing Co., No. 1182-
15, uncut, 1950 ................................. **47.00**

**"Brother & Sister,"** heavy board
stand-ups, Whitman Publishing Co.,
No. 4105, w/original box .................... **28.00**

**"Cecelia My Kissin' Cousin,"** 30" h.
w/six outfits, 1960s ........................... **55.00**

**"Children in the Shoe,"** six dolls,
designed by Charlot Bvi, Merrill
Publishing Co., No. 1562-15, uncut,
1949 .................................................. **65.00**

**"Cradle Baby,"** heavy board book is
cradle-shaped, designed by Edith
Reichman, Saalfield Publishing Co.,
No. 5214, 1948 ................................. **32.00**

**"Dress Me Cut-out Dolls,"** by Queen
Holden, Whitman Publishing Co.,
No. 1177, uncut, 1943 ...................... **60.00**

**"Four Sleeping Dolls,"** by Queen
Holden, (eyes open & close),
Whitman Publishing Co., No. 2060,
uncut, 1945 ....................................... **70.00**

**"Judy/Jim Paperdoll Storybook,"**
designed by Miloche & Kane, Simon
& Schuster Publishing Co., uncut,
1948 .................................................. **58.00**

**"Let's Play With Baby,"** four dolls,
Merrill Publishing Co., No. 1550,
uncut, 1948 ....................................... **35.00**

**"Outdoor Pals,"** four stand-ups on
Tekwood, Whitman Publishing Co.,
No. 5347, uncut ................................ **58.00**

**"Sisters,"** large set, two dolls, Samuel
Gabriel & Sons, No. D135, uncut ....... **56.00**

**"Three Cute Girls,"** cloth-like clothes,
Whitman Publishing Co., No. 1178-
15, uncut, 1949 ................................. **32.00**

**"Three Little Girls Who Grew,"** six
dolls, three girls & three grown-up,
w/cloth-like clothes, Whitman
Publishing Co., No. 1176, uncut,
1945 .................................................. **58.00**

**"Trim Dotty's Dresses,"** single
stand-up on Tekwood, Whitman
Publishing Co., No. 5336, w/original
box .................................................... **25.00**

**Betty Grable,** Whitman Publishing
Co., No. 989 ..................................... **75.00**

**Elizabeth Taylor,** Whitman Publishing
Co., No. 2112, 1954, uncut ............... **80.00**

**Girl Scout,** w/real hair, uniforms from
thirty countries, w/original box ........... **58.00**

**Judy Garland,** Whitman Publishing
Co., No. 980 ..................................... **75.00**

**June Allyson,** Whitman Publishing
Co., No. 1956, 1955, uncut ............... **65.00**

**Marilyn Monroe,** Saalfield Artcraft,
No. 1338, uncut ................................ **115.00**

**Princess Paper Doll Book,** Princess
Elizabeth & Margaret, Saalfield,
No. 2216, 1939 ................................. **80.00**

**Raggedy Ann/Andy,** w/coloring book,
Johnny Gruelle, Saalfield, No. 4409,
uncut, 1944 ....................................... **95.00**

**Shirley Temple,** Saalfield Artcraft,
No. 1789, Canadian edition, uncut ..... **75.00**

# PAPERWEIGHTS

*Baccarat "Primrose" Weight*

**Baccarat "Concentric Mushroom" weight,** surrounded by a blue & white twisted torsade, starcut base, salmon, white & green center shamrocks cane surrounded by a ring of blue & white canes, then a ring of white & red starburst canes followed by salmon & green canes & a ring of white starbursts are pulled down to form the stem (minute bubble over center & two tiny spalls on side) .................. **$1,430.00**

**Baccarat "Degrees" weight,** five soft red petals cased in white surround a starburst center w/seven green leaves & curving stem, on clear star cut ground (few dings on base, small spall on top & side & few minute bubbles in glass) ............................ **1,100.00**

**Baccarat "Faceted Running Deer" weight,** acid etched through an amber flash w/one top facet & five side facets, on amber ground, 2⅝" d. (some wear to the edge of amber flash, tiny spall on bottom & few minute bubbles in the glass) ............. **248.00**

**Baccarat "Garlanded" weight,** central white & red & blue & green arrowhead center cane surrounded by red & white canes then two intertwining garlands of green & white starburst canes & red & white canes, over clear ground, 2⅞" d ....... **660.00**

**Baccarat "Macedoine" weight,** tightly placed latticinio bits of white, red, green, yellow, blue & pink, 2⅝" d. (tiny nicks on sides & some striations in glass) ............................ **275.00**

**Baccarat "Primrose" weight,** red & white flower w/white starburst center w/eleven leaves & stem, on clear starcut ground, small bubble at tip of one leaf & minute bubbles in glass, 2⅞" d. (ILLUS. above) .................. **1,320.00**

**Baccarat "Spaced Concentric" weight,** central pink Clichy-type rose surrounded by white & green florets then three rings of red, white & green canes, over clear ground, 2¼" d. (off center w/slightly flat profile & minute bubbles in ground) ......................................... **385.00**

**Bohemian "Deer" weight,** engraved deer on hill w/trees & foliage, on red flash base, 2⅝"d. (tiny bubble in glass) ................................................ **303.00**

**Bohemian "Patterned Millefiori" weight,** central white/blue cane surrounded by pink & white & blue canes then outer garland of green & pink canes alternating w/white starburst canes, over clear ground, 2½" d. (few minute bubbles) ............. **198.00**

**Bohemian "Running Stag" weight,** engraved stag w/large tree & foiliage, on blue flash base, footed, 3⅜" d. (two small chips on foot & nick on top) ...................................... **330.00**

**Clichy "Miniature" weight,** single white & blue cane flower w/five green leaves & stem over clear ground, 1¾" d. ................................. **770.00**

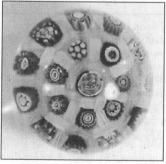

*Clichy "Patterned Millefiori" Weight*

**Clichy "Patterned Millefiori" weight,** large central pink & green Clichy rose surrounded by eighteen complex canes among perfectly placed latticinio, slightly off center, on white latticinio chequer board ground, minute bubbles in ground, small chip on foot, small piece of cullet over canes, 2½" d. (ILLUS.).. **1,760.00**

**Clichy "Spaced Concentric" weight,** large central green pastry mold cane surrounded by six large white canes w/blue crosses & an outer ring of white florets alternating w/purple & green & white complex canes, on translucent cranberry ground, 2⅝" d. (two faint bubbles in ground, tiny scratches on top & one on side) .... **1,100.00**

**Clichy "Sulphide of Benjamin Franklin" weight,** on a clear ground, 2⅝" d. (tiny bubble over sulphide) ........................................ **330.00**

**Kazium (Charles) "Pansy" weight,** two upper petals & three white & blue lower petals surround yellow star center w/three green leaves & stem, gold bee rests on one petal, gold "K" on back, on opaque pink ground, 2¼" d. (area of bubbles over cane center)..................................... **660.00**

**Millville "Crimpled Umbrella" weight,** blue & red pebbles cased in white w/straight stem & tiny bubble in center, one top facet & clear applied foot, 3" d. (faint cloudy area over part of umbrella) ........................ **77.00**

**New England "Fruit" weight,** pink & yellow fruit w/four red cherries & eight green leaves, over white swirling latticinio ground, 2½" d. (three small nicks on foot, several scratches, spall & nick on surface)... **330.00**

**New England "Garlanded Corn-flower" weight,** five blue petals surround white cane center w/two green leaves, curving stem & large, partially opened dark blue bud, flower is surrounded by a garland of green & white canes, over white swirling latticinio ground, 2½" d. (line separation across leaf, four bubbles in latticinio, separation shows white across bud)...................................... **330.00**

**New England "Red Poinsettia" weight,** ten petals surround a blue & white cane center w/three green leaves & a curving stem, on blue & white jasper ground, 2¾" d. (small bubble on petal & leaf, slightly off center, small spalls on side & small chip near foot)................................ **550.00**

**New England "Scramble with Twisted Ribbons & Latticinio Pieces" weight,** white, blue, red, green & yellow colors, over clear ground, large bubble in center & several small bubbles throughout ground, 2½" d. (several dings & scratches to surface & base) ............. **88.00**

**North Bohemian "Scattered Millefiori" weight,** pink, yellow, white & blue on green & silver mica ground, flat base, 3" d. (small bubbles in glass)............................. **303.00**

*St. Louis "Fruit" Weight*

**St. Louis "Faceted Upright Bouquet" weight,** large soft red flower w/yellow matchhead center, white & blue flowers w/bubble centers on either side among a yellow cane flower & a blue cane flower among green leaves, surrounded by white torsade, six side facets, 2¾" d. (bouquet is off center w/few small bubbles) .......... **2,750.00**

**St. Louis "Fruit" weight,** two orange & one yellow fruit w/orange stem, pears among four red cherries & eight green leaves over white swirling latticinio ground, fruit is off center & slightly separated w/light scratches & tiny nicks on surface, 2⅝" d. (ILLUS.) ................................ **550.00**

**St. Louis "Miniature Patterned Millefiori" weight,** central salmon & white cane surrounded by five yellow & salmon canes, over a blue & white jasper ground, 1⅝" d. ...................... **248.00**

**St. Louis "Pink Striped Clematis" weight,** fourteen petals surround yellow & orange matchhead center set on four green leaves & stem, over white swirling latticinio ground, 2½" d. (small piece of cullet & striation in glass, one leaf cracked) .. **770.00**

**St. Louis "Spaced Millefiori" weight,** large central green/white cane surrounded by five blue & white canes & an outer garland of white & red & white alternating canes, over clear ground, 3" d. (slightly irregular blue & white canes, striations & minute bubbles in glass)................... **248.00**

**Sandwich "Cut Decanter" weight,** blue poinsettia in stopper, twelve blue petals surround white cane center, on six green leaves & stem pointing downward into stopper, bulbous-shaped w/rows of cut ovals, thin diamond cut neck & star cut base, 4½" d., 9¼" h. (some wear to cutting, tiny nick on oval) .................. **990.00**

**Sandwich "Red Flower" weight,** ten petals surround a swirl center w/red bud, three green leaves & curving stems, on white swirling latticinio ground, bubble next to stem & on tip of one petal, 2⅞" d. (several spalls & light scratches on surface & sides, small ding on foot) ............. **385.00**

*Sandwich "Red Poinsettia" Weight*

**Sandwich "Red Poinsettia" weight,** twelve soft red petals surround a blue & red & white center cane w/five green serrated leaves & straight stem, on a clear ground, tiny bubble over stem & several nicks & light scratches on surface, 3⅛" d. (ILLUS.) ........................................ **523.00**

**Stankard (Paul) "Botonical Cube" weight,** morning glory, two raspberries above yellow centered amethyst & blue blossoms, one bumblebee, one spirit included, 2 x 2¼" ........................................ **2,657.00**

**Tarsitano (Debbie) "Primrose" weight,** early yellow centered red & white striped blossoms & bud on leafy stem, DT cane, 2½" d. ............. **411.00**

**Whitefriars "Concentric Millefiori" weight,** central white & red cane surrounded by four ring of white, red & blue canes including two rings w/heart centers, ten side facets, on clear ground, 2¼" d. (several small bubbles in glass & around canes) ................................ **176.00**

# PARRISH (Maxfield) ARTWORK

*During the 1920s and 1930s, Maxfield Parrish (1870-1966) was considered the most popular artist-illustrator in the United States. His Illustrations graced the covers of the most noted magazines of the day Scribner's, Century, Life, Harper's, Ladies' Home Journal and others. High quality art prints, copies of his original paintings usually in a range of sizes, graced the walls of homes and offices across the country. Today all Maxfield Parrish artwork, including magazine covers, advertisements and calendar art, is considered collectible but it is the fine art prints that command most attention.*

**Book,** "Arabian Nights," illustrated by Maxfield Parrish, 1909 ................... **$100.00**

**Book,** "Maxfield Parrish—The Early Years," by Skeeters, published by Nash, fine dust jacket, 1975 (jacket tattered) ........................................... **155.00**

**Calendar,** 1930, for Edison-Mazda, entitled "Ecstasy," small, cropped..... **225.00**

**Magazine cover,** Collier's, 1913, May 17, cover showing Comic Policeman.. **60.00**

**Print,** "Daybreak," original frame, print 6 x 10", overall 8 x 12" ...................... **95.00**

**Print,** "The Dinkey-Bird," from "Poems of Childhood," 1905, 11 x 16" .......... **125.00**

# PERFUME, SCENT & COLOGNE BOTTLES

*Decorative accessories from milady's boudoir have always been highly collectible and in recent years there has been an especially strong surge of interest in perfume bottles. Our listings also include related containers such as pocket bottles and vials, tabletop containers & atomizers. Most readily common are examples from the 19th through the mid-20th century, but earlier examples do surface occasionally. The myriad varieties have now been documented in several recent reference books which should further popularize this collecting specialty.*

## BOTTLES & FLASKS

**Amethyst glass,** pressed irregular octagonal corseted-form, tooled mouth, smooth base, 1860-88, probably Boston & Sandwich Glass Company, Sandwich, Massachusetts, 4" h. ........................ **$66.00**

**Amethyst glass,** twelve-sided form, outward rolled collared mouth, smooth base, 1860-88, probably Boston & Sandwich Glass Company, Sandwich, Massachusetts, 6" h. ........ **330.00**

**Cobalt blue glass w/beads & flutes patt.,** tooled lip, smooth base, America, ca. 1870-80, 9¼" h. ......... **1,210.00**

**Cobalt blue glass,** mold-blown twenty-four ribs swirled to left, flattened globular form, sheared mouth, pontil scar, 1820-40, 2⅛" h. ............................................. **110.00**

**Cobalt blue glass,** mold-blown twenty-four ribs swirled to right, flattened ovoid form tapering to base w/applied rigaree on either side, sheared mouth, pontil scar, 1820-40, 2½" h. ............................................. **209.00**

**Cobalt blue glass,** pressed, tall twelve-sided, tooled collared mouth, smooth base, 1860-88, probably Boston & Sandwich Glass Company, Sandwich, Massachusetts, 8¾" h. ..... **330.00**

**Cranberry glass cylindrical body** w/rounded shoulders, w/lacy gold designs in wide bands around middle of bottle, lip trimmed in gold, clear-cut faceted stopper, 1¾" d., 4½" h. ............................................. **165.00**

**Cranberry glass ovoid body** w/lacy gold foliage garlands w/cream color flowers trimmed in gold, top & bottom trimmed in gold, clear-cut faceted stopper, 2½" d., 5" h. ........... **175.00**

**Emerald green glass,** barrel-form w/cut design, ground mouth, smooth base, 1820-40, 2⅛" h. (¼" shallow flake on side of mouth probably in manufacturing).................................... **99.00**

**Emerald green,** pressed cylindrical w/vertical beaded flutes, tooled collared mouth, smooth base w/small oval "Eau de Cologne" label, 1860-88, possibly Boston & Sandwich Glass Company, Sandwich, Massachusetts, 10½" h... **605.00**

**English rose cameo glass** w/white flowers & leaves on rose ground, silver metal screw top, 2" h. .............. **850.00**

*Green Cut to Clear Cologne Bottle*

**Golden amber glass** w/white enameled flowers & light blue enamel trim, ruffled lips, w/amber bubble stoppers, 3" d., 8½" h., pr. ... **295.00**

**Green cut to clear overlay glass,** petticoat design, matching original stopper, attributed to Boston & Sandwich Glass Company, Sandwich, Massachusetts, 7¼" h. (ILLUS. above) ................................. **403.00**

**Opalescent light green glass,** pressed irregular octagonal corseted form, tooled mouth, smooth base, 1860-88, probably Boston & Sandwich Glass Company, Sandwich, Massachusetts, 4¾" h. (some interior stain)........................ **440.00**

**Pink blush glass** w/colorless & frosted glass stopper w/molded nude amid blossoms, Czechoslovakia, 6¾" h. (ILLUS. top next page) .......... **460.00**

**Puce amethyst glass,** pressed tall square form w/beveled corners, wide vertical rib down center on three sides, applied double collared mouth, smooth base, 1860-88, possibly Boston & Sandwich Glass Company, Sandwich, Massachusetts, 11" h. ..................... **193.00**

**Purple amethyst glass,** pressed eight-sided corset waisted body w/rolled lip & smooth base, probably Sandwich, Massachusetts, ca. 1860-70, 6½" h. ................................. **826.00**

*Pink Blush Czechoslovakian Cologne Bottle*

**Teal green glass,** mold-blown tall twelve sided, tooled collared mouth, smooth base, 1860-88, 11" h. (light interior stain spots) ........................... **715.00**

# PEZ DISPENSERS

PEZ, an abbreviation for the German word pfefferminz, meaning peppermint, was 'discovered' by Eduard Haas as he experimented with peppermint oil in 1927. Haas developed a small brick-shaped candy and marketed in towards adults as an alternative to smoking. Although PEZ became quite fashionable, production ceased with the onset of World War II. The first PEZ dispensers were not produced until its reintroduction in 1949. These dispensers were not like the cartoon head dispensers produced today, but resembled cigarette lighters and are known today as 'headless regulars.' Unfortunately, PEZ did not regain its popularity following World War II and quickly failed.

In 1952, Haas introduced a new and improved PEZ to America. He altered the shape of the dispenser, changed the formula of the candy and marketed his new product towards children. PEZ's popularity soared. Over the years, more than 200 PEZ dispensers have been produced.

**Bozo the clown,** die cut ................... $125.00
**Casper the ghost,** die cut ................. 150.00
**Donald Duck,** die cut ......................... 125.00
**Easter bunny,** die cut ....................... 500.00
**Mickey Mouse,** die cut ..................... 140.00
**Dalmatian Pup,** Disney ......... 20.00 to 25.00
**Santa Claus,** full-figure....... 100.00 to 120.00

# PHONOGRAPHS

*Brunswick Model 127*

**Brunswick Model 127,** japanned upright cabinet (ILLUS.)................. **$900.00**
**Columbia front mount disc Graphaphone,** late HJ .................... 825.00
**Columbia Model Q Graphaphone** .... 375.00
**Columbia Type AS coin-operated,** reads "Graphophone" on front w/advertising on back, horn replaced (ILLUS. top left, next page)........... 5,700.00
**Edison Opera,** table model, oak case w/horn, no lid ............................... 3,500.00

*Columbia Type AS*

*Phonolamp Model B*

*Fairy Phonograph*

**Fairy phonograph,** horn-shaped copper & brass footed base, below octagonal phonograph w/black fringe & gold tassels, marked "Burns & Pollack Elec. Mfg. Co. (ILLUS. left).................................................. **3,000.00**

**Phonolamp Model B,** circular base opens to reveal phonograph, below fabric covered shade (ILLUS. above) .......................... **1,600.00**

**Victor Model O,** table model, w/horn (ILLUS. bottom left) ...................... **1,600.00**

**Victor Model P1,** table model (ILLUS. bottom right) ...................... **950.00**

**Victor Type IV** w/mahogany spear tip horn .............................................. **4,750.00**

**Victor Type E,** pre-dog front mount phonograph .................................... **1,050.00**

**Victor Type R Talking Machine** ..... **1,300.00**

*Two Victor Phonographs*

# PHOTOGRAPHIC ITEMS

**Cabinet card,** chess players, ca. 1880s.................................................. **$28.00**

**Cabinet card,** man posed w/violin, ca. 1880s.................................................... **18.00**

**Cabinet card,** man wearing top hat posed w/two dogs, ca. 1880s ............. **18.00**

**Cabinet card,** Salvation Army couple, man w/trumpet, ca. 1880s ................. **18.00**

**Cabinet card,** young girls w/two dolls in elaborate Victorian setting, ca. 1880s .................................................. **25.00**

*Contax Camera*

**Camera,** Contax I 35 mm (ILLUS.) ..... **880.00**

**Camera,** Kodak Bantam, near mint condition, in original box ..................... **75.00**

**Camera,** pen-shaped, Duo Fold Jr., Parker Pen, orange & black.............. **265.00**

**Carte de viste,** Union soldier................ **49.00**

**Daguerreotype case,** brown thermoplastic, Lady Liberty, locomotive & sidewheeler on each side, Civil War era............................... **245.00**

**Daguerreotype case,** brown thermoplastic, oval central design surrounded by a wreath of oak leaves & acorns, Civil War era .......... **95.00**

**Daguerreotype,** quarter-plate, three quarter portrait of two bearded gentlemen sitting close together on cloth draped stools, each wearing suit & broad sash, ca. 1849 (some mold on surface, case has replaced hinge)................................................ **875.00**

**Daguerreotype,** sixth-plate, close-up of spaniel, w/brown thermoplastic case w/"Faithful Hound" design ........ **195.00**

**Daguerreotype,** sixth-plate, three quarter portrait of seated young gentleman, probably a carpenter, holding a hammer & leaning one elbow on draped stool .................. **1,100.00**

*Daguerreotype of Two Gentleman*

**Daguerreotype,** sixth-plate, three quarter portrait of two seated gentleman w/beards, each holding knives, Zanesville, Ohio, ca. 1851 (ILLUS.) ........................................ **1,100.00**

**Daguerreotype,** sixth-plate, outdoor image of at least twenty men & women w/portion of two houses in the background (image weak) .......... **275.00**

**Daguerreotype,** sixth-plate, half portrait of a sheriff, case slightly damaged....................................... **1,200.00**

**Tintype,** cased, four men, one standing & three sitting w/musical instruments, 3½" h., 3" w. (minor wear to case) ...................................... **50.00**

**Tintype,** cased, half-plate, half-length portrait of young Union infantry officer, his rank between Lieutenant & Lieutenant Colonial, in thermoplastic case w/"The Wedding Procession" design on front, Civil War era.............................. **850.00**

# PIN-UP ART

**Calendar,** 1938, "Leading Lady," nude, Earl Moran .............................. **$65.00**

**Calendar,** 1938, titled "Gentlemen Prefer," Earl Moran ............................ **45.00**

**Calendar,** 1940, Alberto Vargas artwork, features different girl every month, for "Esquire," minor tears to cover................................................. **143.00**

*1946 Vargas Calendar*

*Playboy Playmate Calendar*

**Calendar,** 1946, Alberto Vargas illustration, featuring Vargas girls, for "Esquire," copyright Esquire Inc. Chicago, 12" h., 8½" w. (ILLUS.) ........ **33.00**

**Calendar,** 1947, Alberto Vargas ........... **35.00**

**Calendar,** 1947, desk-type, Alberto Vargas ............................................... **45.00**

**Calendar,** 1948, Ben-Hurbax, Fritz Willis & Joe Demera artwork, for "Esquire," each work shows different girl, copyright 1947, w/original envelope (tears to envelope) ............. **72.00**

**Calendar,** 1959, Playboy Playmate calendar, featuring Jane Mansfield for Miss July, w/original envelope (ILLUS.) ........................................... **232.00**

**Illustration,** George Petty (American, 1894-1975), for Jax Brewery, gouache, watercolor & pencil on Whatman illustration board, shows scantily dressed man kissing a scantily clad woman, signed, ca. 1934, 25 x 35" (ILLUS. below) ........................................ **11,000.00**

*George Petty Illustration*

# POLITICAL, CAMPAIGN & PRESIDENTIAL ITEMS

## CAMPAIGN

**Book,** "An American Melodrama, The Presidential Campaign of 1968" ....... **$20.00**

**Flyer,** advertising for the upcoming 1884 campaign biography, 11 x 14" ... **75.00**

**Guest ticket,** 1896 campaign, Republican National Convention, St. Louis .......................................... **35.00**

**Medalet,** copper, 1868 campaign, reads "For President General US Grant 1868," ¾" d. ............................ **75.00**

**Pamphlet,** 1956 campaign, color cartoon drawings of Dwight D. Eisenhower & Richard Nixon w/"Vote for Ike in '56," large................ **15.00**

**Paper,** 1888 campaign, printed on flag ground in faded red, blue & black on white, bust portraits of Benjamin Harrison facing Levi Morton & printed below "Compliments, E.F. Dieker...St Mary's Ohio," framed, 15 x 15½"........................................... **72.00**

**Pin,** 1900 campaign, black & white images of William McKinley & Theodore Roosevelt on blue, white & gold background, celluloid, original backpaper, ⅞" d................................ **45.00**

**Pin,** 1924 campaign, Coolidge (Calvin) & Dawes (Charles), pictures Coolidge & Dawes ............................ **45.00**

**Pin,** 1924 campaign, Coolidge (Calvin), reads "Keep Coolidge" ......... **10.00**

**Pin,** 1928 campaign, Al Smith, model of a brass donkey ............................ **30.00**

**Portrait,** 1844 campaign, Clay (Henry) & Frelinghuysen (Theodore), double sided tinted lithograph of Clay & Frelinghuysen w/pewter bezel, 8½" d. .......................................... **3,105.00**

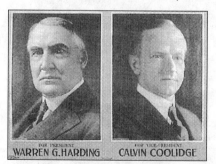

*Harding & Coolidge Poster*

**Poster,** 1920 campaign, close-up portraits of Harding (Warren G.) & Coolidge (Calvin), minor wrinkles & 6" tear on Harding's tie, 21 x 28" (ILLUS. bottom previous column) ....... **77.00**

**Ribbon,** 1864 campaign, green silk w/black screened campaign portrait of beardless Lincoln w/an attached tiny tintype of bearded Lincoln, 7" (some wear).................................. **1,623.00**

*Harrison & Morton Textile*

**Textile,** 1888 campaign, Harrison (Benjamin) & Morton (Levi), printed cotton in red, blue & brown on white w/central scene of flags shown beneath bust portraits in round medallions of Benjamin Harrison facing Levi Morton, American eagle shown in upper center w/"Harrison/Morton 1888, Protect Home Industry" shown below, border of stripes w/stars in corners & outer border, framed, faded & wear w/some color bleeding, 24¾" w., 11¼" h. (ILLUS.) .............................. **165.00**

**Textile,** 1896 campaign, McKinley (William) & Hobart (Garret), printed cotton in black on white, central scene depicts bust portraits in oval medallions of William McKinley facing Garret Hobart, flanked by scrolling flags, eagle, shield & waving flags above & "McKinley/Hobart 1896, Protection" below, framed, minor stains, 22¼" w., 21¾" h. .................... **385.00**

**Transcript,** 1858 campaign, debates between Lincoln & Douglas, second printing 1860 by Follett, Foster & Company, Columbus, Ohio (slightly worn original boards, slight page foxing)............................................... **138.00**

## NON-CAMPAIGN

**Book,** "The Death of A President," by William Manchester, 1st edition .......... **25.00**

**Book,** "Theodore Roosevelt," by McCaleb, 1931, autographed ............ **75.00**

**Books,** depicting thirty-six presidential art medals, Washington to Nixon, Whitman Publishing Company, set of 2 ...................................................... **40.00**

**Book set,** "Memoirs" by Harry Truman, in original dust jackets, inside inscribed to "Miss Nora Kay Nolan, Kind Regards, Harry Truman, 8/17/56," First Edition, Doubleday & Co., Inc. (dust jackets soiled) ........... **154.00**

**Card,** signature of Roosevelt (Theodore) while Gov. of New York, w/State of New York Executive envelope, 2½ x 3" ............................ **275.00**

**Clock,** animated, "FDR Man of the Hour" ................................................ **150.00**

**Cuff links,** presidential set given by Bill Clinton, w/original box .................. **65.00**

**Game,** "Who Can Beat Nixon?" ........... **35.00**

**Newspaper,** over half of broadside devoted to dispatch of hourly accounts of President Taylor's illness beginning July 9th to ultimate death by "bilious cholera Morbus," remaining accounts include Philadelphia's July 9th fire, inked period name of former owner written at top, published by Miami Visitor, Waynesville, Ohio, July 10, 1850, 7 x 14½" .......................................... **193.00**

**Photograph,** Nixon (Richard), inscribed w/"To Delvin S. Allison with best wishes from Richard Nixon," probably signed as Vice President, black & white, 8 x 10" (minor creases & staple mark at top in margin of print) .................................. **55.00**

**Pinback button,** Socialist Party, "Down with the Capitalist Teapot Dome" ................................................ **75.00**

**Portrait,** advertising portrait Abraham Lincoln, oil on canvas, signed & dated, w/advertising stamp "The Lincoln Watch, Illinois Watch Co., Springfield," 7 x 9¾" (scattered losses) ........................................... **144.00**

**Poster,** large black & white lithograph of Taft (William Howard) w/facsimile signature "Sincerely yours, William H. Taft," in period frame, by Enquirer Printing Company, Cincinnati, Ohio, ca. 1907, overall 24½ x 30" (some waterstaining on left side & bottom) .. **110.00**

**Program,** souvenir of 1889 anniversary celebration of Washington's inauguration in 1789 ........................... **35.00**

**Reverse painting on glass,** oval portrait of "Washington," mahogany veneer frame, 10¼" w., 12¼" h. (white border is flaked & blue sky behind Washington's head has touch-up repair) ............................... **220.00**

**Spoons,** each w/presidential portrait up to Franklin D. Roosevelt, w/original envelopes, 1930s, Rogers Silver Plate, 31 pcs. ......................... **140.00**

**Textile,** printed cotton in red, blue & brown on white, striped ground w/central oval medallion w/"Washington" printed over figure leaning against horse w/shield above & below medallion, framed, 22½" w., 30" h. (fading, minor stains, color bleeding, some edge damage & a pinpoint hole) ............................. **908.00**

*Abraham Lincoln Tin*

**Tin,** metal w/portrait of Lincoln in center w/"Exemplar" at top & banner "With Malice Toward None and Charity for All" at bottom, black lettering w/gold background, by C.J. Johnson Cigar Co., Grand Rapids, Michigan, ca. 1900, some rust & pitting, 20 x 24" (ILLUS.) .................. **660.00**

# POP CULTURE COLLECTIBLES

*The collecting of pop culture memorabilia is not a new phenomenon; fans have been collecting music-related items since the emergence of rock and roll in the 1950s. But it was not until the 'coming of age' of the post-war generation that the collecting of popular culture memorabilia became a recognized movement.*

*The most sought after items are from the 1960s, when music, art and society were at their most experimental. This time period is dominated by artists such as The Beatles, The Rolling Stones and Bob Dylan, to name a few. From the 1950s, Elvis Presley is the most popular.*

*Below we offer a cross-section of popular culture collectibles ranging from the 1950s to the present day. Also see: RECORDS & RECORD JACKETS.*

*Beatles Bobbing Head Dolls*

**Beach Boys (The) "gold" album award,** presented by the RIAA to commemorate the sale of more than one million dollars worth of the Capitol Records long-playing album "The Beach Boys Today," matted in original linen & framed, 17½ x 21½" ........... **$1,092.00**

**Beatles (The) air bed,** bright yellow blow-up-type, made in England by Li-Lo., 24 x 57" ............................... **1,150.00**

**Beatles (The) autographed pictorial program,** the "Beatles (U.S.A.) Ltd. Program," signed in blue pen & ink by all four members on the inside cover, each name above the full body pose likeness of the member .................... **1,610.00**

**Beatles (The) autographs,** early signatures of all four in black ink on a large lined sheet of paper, "All the best from The Beatles, Paul McCartney" & "John Lennon, Ringo Starr, George Harrison," matted & framed w/a black & white picture, ca. 1963, 12 x 18" ........................... **2,990.00**

**Beatles (The) autographs,** hardbound copy of the Associated British Cinemas 1964 Annual

w/jacket cover image of Cliff Richards in summer attire, inside first page signed in blue ink "Paul McCartney, Ringo Starr, George Harrison" & "John Lennon," ca. 1964, 8¼ x 11¼" (jacket of book is torn & worn) ................................. **2,070.00**

**Beatles (The) "bed linen" collection,** comprising a selection of four cut fragments of bed linens removed from beds which were used by The Beatles, each fragment attached to letter on The Whittier Hotel stationery dated "September 6, 1964" & facsimile signed "Jimmie Hawkins," matted & framed w/color picture of The Beatles, 14 x 39", set of 4 ............................................. **920.00**

**Beatles (The) "Bobbing Heads" dolls,** h.p., wearing grey collarless suits, each playing the appropriate instrument, on gold colored bases w/facsimile signatures, ca. 1964, Car Mascots Inc., unused, in original box, 8" h., set of 4 (ILLUS. top previous column) ..................... **1,300.00 to 2,000.00**

**Beatles (The) buttons,** circular white & red tin buttons w/deep blue letters reading "I LOVE the 'Beatles'," ca. 1960s, 3½" d., set of 2 .................. **23.00**

**Beatles (The) concert flyer,** features The Beatles & their pictures w/intact "booking" form, reads "Oden-Leeds" for "Sunday, 3rd November," ca. 1963, 5½ x 12" ........................... **747.00**

*Early Beatles Concert Poster*

**Beatles (The) concert poster,** h.p. advertising sign from The Cavern, in blue, yellow, purple, green & white on black poster board, lists the "Friday Lunchtime Special Double Bill on Stage" schedule which included two Beatles shows at 12:20 p.m. & 1:40 p.m., glazed & framed, some creasing, 24 x 34" (ILLUS.) .. **6,325.00**

**Beatles (The) concert tickets,** unused, dated August 29, 1966 at Candlestick Park in San Francisco, California, each ticket is in the lower Stand Gate E, section 44, seats 147 & 148, tickets have image of each Beatle printed on the back, (this was their last concert), each 2½ x 6", pr... **575.00**

**Beatles (The) concert tickets,** Shea Stadium, for August 23, 1966, unused, pr ...................................... **977.00**

**Beatles (The) fan card,** the classic fan card of The Beatles' face shots accompanied by their single first name signature below their faces ..... **575.00**

**Beatles (The) "gold" single record award,** presented by the RIAA to commemorate the sale of more than one million copies of the Capitol Records, Inc. single record "Penny Lane," mounted, framed & glazed 13 x 17" ........................................ **2,415.00**

*Beatles Gumball Machine*

**Beatles (The) gumball machine,** red, contains gumballs mixed w/little charms, top portion labeled "The Beatles In This Machine 'I Saw Her Standing There'," 14" h. (ILLUS.) .. **1,380.00**

**Beatles (The) kerchief,** silk ............... **125.00**

**Beatles (The) lobby poster,** for "A Hard Days Night," shades of yellow & green unusually small lobby theatre poster w/black lettering & depiction of The Beatles playing their instruments, ca. 1964, 13¾ x 22" ........................................ **115.00**

**Beatles (The) poster,** promotional poster for "The Beatles Yesterday and Today," w/the 'Butcher Cover,' 18 x 24" ........................................... **460.00**

**Beatles (The) 'New Sound' toy guitar,** original strings & sticker, manufactured by Selcol, United Kingdom, rare, 23" l .......... **400.00 to 480.00**

**Beatles (The) record player,** blue cased, four speed w/pictures of The Beatles on the front & on the inside, rare, 10 x 18" .............. **3,700.00 to 4,700.00**

**Beatles (The) rug,** colorful rug w/images of the four Beatles, a guitar, musical note & drum, Belgium, 21½ x 33½" ...................... **800.00**

**Beatles (The) store display,** "Beatle flicker-picture rings," cardboard, w/four original rings, 8 x 12" ............ **400.00**

**Beatles (The) shirt,** label reads "The Only Authentic Beatle Shirt," never before worn, w/original store tag, ca. 1960s ......................................... **345.00**

**Beatles (The) talc container,** lithographed tin container w/pictures of The Beatles on the front & back, by Margo of Mayfair, manufactured in Great Britain, 1960s, full .............. **770.00**

**Beatles (The) wallpaper,** the vintage roll of Beatles color wallpaper stamped "33300" on verso, has repeating motif of the Beatles playing & posed along w/their names ............................................... **345.00**

**Beatles (The) Yellow Submarine toy,** metal, brightly colored, by Corgi, in original box, 5¼" l. .............. **747.00**

**Bee Gees signed photograph,** black & white promotional photograph from RSO Records, Inc., signed "Maurice Gibb, Robin Gibb, Barry Gibb," double matted in blue & magenta, 13 x 15½" ......................... **115.00**

**Blues Brothers (The) signed photograph,** black & white still from "The Blue Brothers," signed in red felt-tip pen by John Belushi & Dan Aykroyd, matted & framed, 11 x 14" ........................................... **747.00**

*Bob Dylan Handbill*

*Bruce Springsteen Signed Photograph*

**Bob Dylan handbill & envelope,** black ink on pink toned paper, from gerde's Folk City, advertising April 24-May 6, 1962 show featuring a young Bob Dylan, w/postmarked envelope from gerde's, postmarked April 10 '62, 2 pcs. (ILLUS. of handbill) .......................... **1,150.00**

**Bob Dylan program,** black & white, reads "1966, Tito Burns Presents Dylan '66" ......................................... **201.00**

**Brian Epstein autobiography,** "A Cellarful of Noise," signed on the first flyleaf in dark blue "To Joanna, with kind regards, Brian Epstein - January 22, 1967," British hardcover, 1st edition, Souvenir Press .............................................. **747.00**

**Bruce Springsteen shirt,** concert-worn, extensively worn light blue shirt, w/"Penny's Towncraft" label in the neck, worn throughout his "Darkness" tour, four front pockets, accompanied by two color photographs, signed by John Comerford III, of Springsteen wearing shirt in concert, ca. 1978, the group ............................................... **3,162.00**

**Bruce Springsteen signed photograph,** black & white studio photograph shows Springsteen wearing jeans & leather in front of a billowing canvas backdrop, he is wearing an earring in left ear & is holding a guitar w/his right hand & his nose w/his left, signed "Bruce Springsteen" in gold felt-tip marker, double matted & framed, 17½ x 21½" (ILLUS.) ................................... **460.00**

**Buddy Holly signed record,** for the single "Heartbeat" on the Coral label w/black pen & ink signature of Buddy Holly, matted & framed w/a photo of Buddy Holly & the Crickets, 13 x 17" ......................................... **1,035.00**

**Concert Poster,** Festival '69, the yellow & black poster featuring Fleetwood Mac & The Herd, includes a dance marathon contest "Monday 26th May at Pennycross Stadium Plymouth," 20 x 29" ........... **575.00**

**David Lee Roth gold jacket,** double breasted gold-lamé jacket w/gold fabric trim, an elaborate drawing by Roth of a dragon on the inside lining, worn in his "Just a Gigolo" video, signed twice & dated by Roth, tagged on inside right "Cotroneo Costumes" & "Mr. David Lee Roth" typed on lower portion of tag ........... **920.00**

**Diana Ross & the Supremes concert poster,** in yellow, orange & blue w/photo of the Supremes, reads "Dianne Ross - & the - Supremes - Sun. Aug. 17 - 8:30 p.m. - Sport Arena" etc., 14 x 22" (ILLUS. top next page)......................................... **747.00**

**Elvis Presley concert tickets,** four unused tickets dated August 19, 1977 at Utica Memorial Auditorium in Utica New York, all tickets are in

*Diana Ross & the Supremes Poster*

the Mezzanine, Section 203, Row D,
seats 1,10,11 & 12, each ticket
encased in lucite, each 3½ x 5¾",
set of 4 ............................................. **259.00**

**Elvis Presley handkerchief,** black
silk, worn by Presley in 1962-63
movie "It Happened at the World's
Fair," w/a photo of Elvis w/the
handkerchief in his breast pocket &
a letter of authenticity, the group ...... **575.00**

**Elvis Presley sunglasses,**
rectangular aviator sunglasses w/a
dark brownish rose tint & gold metal
frames, made in Germany w/the
style "Nautic - Neostyle" inscribed on
the inside of the frames, w/case &
letter of authenticity, the group ...... **1,495.00**

**Elvis Presley scarf,** light blue nylon
souvenir scarf w/"Elvis Presley"
screened on one corner in dark blue,
Elvis wore these signature scarves &
gave them away to fans during
performances .................................... **489.00**

**Elvis Presley toy guitar,** brown
plastic guitar w/Elvis' face circularly
framed at top w/an Elvis facsimile
signature in raised plastic on the
body, w/"Elvis Presley Guitar" label
on original box, 33" .......................... **460.00**

**Eric Clapton & Stevie Ray Vaughan
concert poster,** photographic image
of Eric Clapton in grey suit w/yellow
shirt & sunglasses, concert was
billed as "An Evening with Eric
Clapton and his Band with Special
Guest Stevie Ray Vaughan &

Double Trouble" at the Alpine Valley
Music Theatre (this was to be Stevie
Ray Vaughan's last concert
appearance, he was killed the
following day in a helicopter crash),
August 25 & 26, 1990, 14 x 22" ........ **259.00**

**Fats Domino autographed lyrics for
"Blueberry Hill,"** bold black
inscription reading "Luck Always
Fats Domino," matted & framed
w/two black ink handwritten verses
on two white index cards from the
song, signed by Domino & a black &
white photo of Domino, 15 x 28½",
the group ......................................... **977.00**

**George Harrison signed check,**
black ball point pen signature on
Harrisongs Ltd. Check from National
Westminster Check, made out to
Lovely Enterprises Ltd. in the
amount of 43£, dated "25/9/72,"
stamped "Paid 28 Sep.1972" ............ **345.00**

**Jim Morrison autograph,** white
paper inscribed "Jim Morrison" in
blue ink, together w/photocopied
photograph depicting a bare chested
Morrison wearing a string of beads,
matted & framed, matted & framed,
13 x 17" ............................................. **748.00**

**Jimi Hendrix "American Flag"
stage-worn shirt,** long sleeved shirt
composed of red, white & blue stars
& stripes in polyester & polynosic,
label inside collar reading "Robert
Vartin Paris, size 3," purchased in
Paris & worn by Hendrix in 1970 at
the Isle of Wright Festival, w/letter of
authenticity ................................... **2,300.00**

*Jimi Hendrix Poster*

**Jimi Hendrix concert poster,** for concerts at the Filmore Auditorium & Witherland in San Francisco, February 1-4, 1968, features Rick Griffin's flying eyeball, Bill Graham, No. 105, first printing, 14 x 21½" (ILLUS. bottom previous page)...... **1,035.00**

**Jimi Hendrix concert poster,** a series of bars in the design w/the heads of Hendrix & band members on one line & concert information on the other lines, for a concert at the Waikiki Shell for May 30-31, 1969, sponsored by radio station K-POI FM, framed 16 x 22" ..................... **2,415.00**

**Jimi Hendrix handbill,** black & white, for Dallas concert, reads "KFCZ & Concerts West Present - Jimi Hendrix - Ft Worth Will Rogers Coliseum-Sat., May 9 at 8 P.M. - Tickets $3, $4, $5, $6," ca. 1969 ..... **402.00**

**Jimi Hendrix "gold" record award,** presented by the RIAA to Jimi Hendrix Experience to commemorate the sale of more than one 500,000 copies of Reprise/Warner Bros. Album & cassette "Are You Experienced," matted & framed, 17 x 21"............. **1,265.00**

**Jimi Hendrix jacket,** mohair, double breasted, olive green khaki, tagged "Lord Jim Carnaby St.," ca. 1968 ........................... **4,600.00**

**Jimi Hendrix poster,** psychedelic image in pink, orange, purple, blue & green depicting a portrait image of Jimi Hendrix, matted & framed, 32 x 40"............................................ **144.00**

**Jimi Hendrix red sash,** long red sash worn by Hendrix at the Santa Clara County Fairgrounds Pop Festival, May 25, 1969, w/a poster of Hendrix wearing the sash & a letter of authenticity, the group .................. **3,737.00**

**Jimi Hendrix Experience (The) autographs,** pen & ink on green paper, signed in black "Love Love Love Love Love Love Love Love Love Love? Jimi Hendrix," also signed "Noel Redding" & "Love You Too! Mitch xxx" in red ink, mounted under plastic, 4½ x 7" .................... **1,955.00**

**John Lennon "How I Won the War" promotional poster,** close-up shot of Lennon from the United Artists movie, Ballantine Books, ca. 1967, 24 x 38" (ILLUS. top next column).... **400.00**

*John Lennon Poster*

**John Lennon self-portrait,** pen & ink caricature drawing, depicts Lennon w/enlarged nose, trademark glasses & stating within a cartoon speech bubble "enjoyed the trip Tom," signed & dated lower right "love John Lennon 74," matted & framed, image 10⅝ x 13½"......................... **2,415.00**

**Keith Richards inscribed electric guitar,** Squire Stratocaster by Fender, serial No. CN210259, inscribed in blue Sharpie, "Love Keith Richards I Need Love To Keep Me Happy" .................................... **2,070.00**

**Led Zeppelin concert flyer,** reads "Tarrant County Convention Center, August 22nd," ca. 1969 ................... **172.00**

**Madonna signed picture,** large printed picture from tourbook, signed in blue felt-tip pen "Love Madonna," framed, 12 x 16" (ILLUS. top next page) .............................................. **287.00**

**Mick Jagger signed electric guitar,** black Squire Stractocaster by Fender, serial No. VN202202, signed in gold ............................... **1,150.00**

**Monkees playing cards,** full deck........ **35.00**

**Paul McCartney handwritten note,** blue pen & ink note on "The Official Beatles Fan Club" card, matted & framed w/a picture of McCartney, 13 x 17".............................................. **747.00**

*Madonna Signed Picture*

**Petula Clark "gold" record,** presented to Harry Rosen & staff for superior performance on the million selling recording of "Downtown," Warner Bros. Records, 1965, mounted & framed, 11 x 11" ............. **800.00**

**Pink Floyd Concert Poster,** color, for May 9 & 10, 1977 concert at the Oakland Coliseum depicting a giant pig flying over a fog submerged Golden Gate Bridge, designed by Randy Tuten, 19½ x 28" (tear on upper left of poster) ........................... **92.00**

**Queen concert program,** "Jazz" tour, signed on back in black ink by all four members "Freddie Mercury, John Deacon, Brian May, Roger Taylor," ca. 1978 .............................. **460.00**

**R.E.M. electric guitar,** the fender Squier stratocaster, white finish, signed on the body in black "Mike Mills, Bill Berry, Peter Buck" & on the pickboard in blue "Michael Stipe 1995" .......................................... **1,265.00**

**Ringo Starr cap,** black leather, marked "The Ringo Cap" w/original clothing tag ...................................... **230.00**

**Robby Krieger electric guitar,** the Rockwood by Hohner, serial No. LX250G, signed by Krieger in silver ........................................... **1,265.00**

**Rolling Stones (The) autographs,** small white album page signed "To Jean with love from the Rolling Stones, Bill Wyman, Brian Jones, Keith Richard, Mick Jagger & Charlie Boy (sic)" blue ink, ca. 1964, 4 x 4½" ............................................ **978.00**

**Rolling Stones (The) handbill,** yellow & red, from Boston, ca. 1966 ............. **200.00**

**Rolling Stones (The) promotional movie poster,** black & red circus genre poster printed on newsprint for a Rolling Stones concert film billed as the "Stones World Famous Traveling Movie" premiere, 10½ x 34½" (fold creases present) ............................... **115.00**

**Rolling Stones (The) signed magazine picture,** large print color picture from mid-1960s magazine, signed in blue ink by all five members "Mick Jagger, Keith Richards, Bill Wyman, Brian Jones," ca. 1966, framed, 14 x 18" ............. **2,070.00**

**Rolling Stones (The) signed monthly,** color cover featuring the Stones, bottom reads "The Rolling Stones—long hair and leather plus rhythm-and-blues…it all adds up to a rave," w/pen & ink signatures of Brian Jones, Mick Jagger, Keith Richards, Charlie Watts & Bill Wyman, ca. 1964, matted & framed, 19½ x 22" ...................................... **1,265.00**

**Rolling Stones (The) signed photograph,** color group portrait signed by all members of the band in bold felt-tip pen, ca. 1990, matted & framed, 11 x 14" ........................... **1,150.00**

**Rolling Stones (The) signed poster,** stylized color picture of a flying jet above "The Rolling Stones American Tour 1972," felt tip pen signatures w/"Many Thanks to Keeva from all The Stones," w/individual signatures, framed, 24 x 35" ............................... **747.00**

**Roy Orbison signed picture,** the blue pen & ink signed photo of Orbison from a fan magazine/program, matted & framed, 17 x 20½" ........... **1,035.00**

**Sid Vicious photograph,** black & white, shows Sid at Chelsea Art College, pre-Sex Pistols, ca. 1974, matted, 20 x 24" .............................. **345.00**

**Stuart Sutcliffe drawing,** pen & ink on paper, figures of a man from five different angles, sketch was done on a sheet from one of Sutcliffe's notebooks submitted for admission to the Royal College of Art, w/letter of authenticity, ca. 1967, 7 x 9" ........ **747.00**

**Stuart Sutcliffe handwritten song-poem,** blue ink on two pieces of blue-lined paper, composed when he was w/"The Silver Beatles," provocative lyrics typical of his early writing, mounted w/four pictures indicating Stuart & John Lennon, Stuart alone in his studio & w/Astrid Kirchner, his girlfriend, ca. 1960, 13½ x 17½", the group .................. **1,265.00**

**U2 signed album sleeve,** inner sleeve of "The Joshua Tree," w/black & white photograph of the band standing in foreground of desert, signed on the middle right "Bono '94" & "All the Best Edge '94" in black marker, matted in blue & beige felt w/brown & black marbleized frame, 16⅞ x 20¾"...................................... **374.00**

**Velvet Underground electric guitar,** the red Squier Fender Stratocaster "Bullet Series" serial No. NC405026, signed by Lou Reed, John Gale, Moe Tucker & Sterling Morris in blue Sharpie ............................................ **920.00**

**Woodstock "crew" jacket,** blue nylon w/the purple & white Woodstock logo on the back, worn by all working members of the stage crew during the Woodstock Festival, August, 1969 ................................ **1,380.00**

**Woodstock movie jacket,** the navy blue wool jacket w/two front pockets & button front, accented w/matching belt, the Woodstock logo adorns the front right breast & is screened on the entire back of jacket & marked "Warner Bros. Inc." along bottom of design, size medium, probably promotional item, ca. 1970 ............... **345.00**

# PURSES & BAGS

*Alligator Pocketbook*

**Alligator,** black, satchel-style, marked "Herse Florida 964 Buenos Aires," ca. 1950s ........................................ **$172.00**

**Alligator,** black, pocketbook-style, Saks Fifth Avenue label, ca. 1950s ... **230.00**

**Alligator,** brown, pocketbook-style, signed, "Judith Leiber," unused, ca. 1960s (ILLUS. bottom previous column) ............................................. **862.00**

**Basket,** royal blue lacquered straw, Koret, ca. 1950s .............................. **80.00**

**Basket,** w/ivory whale carvings, handle buttons & peg, signed in ink on base "Made in Nantucket Jose Reyes 1963," 7" h. ........................ **1,495.00**

**Beaded,** aqua velvet embroidered w/textured gold sequins, faceted steel beads & faux pearls, gilt metal mount, marked, "Made in France," early 19th c. ....................................... **51.00**

**Beaded,** envelope-style, worked w/a Persian rug design in tiny multicolored beads, lined in green moiré, ca. 1920s ............................... **63.00**

**Beaded,** faceted steel, worked w/gold, silver, black & blue beads in a Near Eastern scrolling design, early 20th c. (losses) ................................. **34.00**

**Beaded,** faceted steel, worked in a Persian design in shades of gold, silver, lilac, red & aquamarine, ca. 1920s (wear) .............................. **103.00**

**Beaded,** faceted steel, 18th century-style figures in a frame in shades of grey, silver, gold, rose & blue, the frame set w/further beads & w/enameled metal & painted porcelain plaques, marked, "Made in France," ca. 1950s, ......................... **201.00**

**Beaded,** fan-shaped, minute beads sewn in arcs of gold, pale yellow & silver grey, gilt metal spherical thumbpiece & chain link shoulder strap, marked "Pierre Cardin Paris," ca. 1960s ...................................... **230.00**

**Beaded,** flapper-style, peacock motif, deep fringe........................................ **240.00**

**Beaded,** floral basket design in center of black beads, beaded design on both sides of bag, fringe, tortoiseshell frame, lined, Czechoslovakia, 6 x 10"................. **295.00**

**Beaded,** stylized palmetto design worked w/dark yellow, green, orange, blue, purple & black beads, the frame of faux tortoise, ca. 1920s.................. **69.00**

**Beaded w/drawstring,** decorated w/morning glories & roses in tiny multicolored beads against an aubergine ground, 19th c.................. **51.00**

**Beaded w/drawstring,** crocheted dark green thread & multicolored beads worked in a design of stars against a cobalt ground w/roses & other flowers against pale grey ground, late 19th c............................ **51.00**

**Brocade,** chartreuse, gold & bright pink brocade, ca. 1933, signed, "Made of Imperial Russian Brocade from the Hammer Collection," accompanied by a typewritten parchment paper document describing the bag as having been made from a collection of Romanoff Imperial Palace chapel brocades assembled by Dr. Armand Hammer.. **402.00**

**Brocade,** puce, pink & silver brocade, gilt metal frame set w/red cabochons, signed, "Bags by Josef," ca. 1930s (except for wear to brocade)............... **51.00**

*Crocodile Pocketbook*

**Crocodile,** pocketbook-style, green w/18k gold chain shoulder strap, lapis ornament & toggle catch (ILLUS.) ......................................... **3,450.00**

**Enameled mesh,** floral design in green, rust, gold & black w/extraordinary enameled frame & enameled drops on bottom of bag, lined, Mandalain Mfg. Co., ca. 1930, 4½ x 8"............................................. **275.00**

**Gold mesh,** 14k yellow gold frame set w/cushion shape citrine within an applied scroll & beaded border, suspended tassel finials, hallmark (ILLUS. top next column)............... **1,840.00**

**Gold mesh,** 14k tri-color gold, foliate frame set w/six diamonds & seven graduated cushion-cut sapphires .. **1,840.00**

*Gold Mesh Purse*

**Leather,** tan calf w/bamboo catch & handle, marked "Made in Italy by Gucci," ca. 1960s (scuffs) .... **258.00**

**Leather,** gentleman's, front embossed "Grafton," interior embossed "Money.4" & flap embossed "1750 B W," interior flap indistinctly inscribed "John C...his money book bought March ye 20 1750," 6½" w............... **517.00**

**Lizard,** black, envelope-style w/self handle flap, gilt metal twisted rope catch, marked "Bonwit Teller Hermes Paris," ca. 1970s ................. **747.00**

**Moiré,** black, embroidered in slate blue w/a dense field of French knots scattered w/celluloid rosettes & a vase of flowers, other French knots sewn w/bronze braid, ca. 1920s ........ **34.00**

**Ostrich,** tan, pocketbook-style w/envelope side pocket, signed "Lucille De Paris," ca. 1950s .............. **74.00**

**Petit point,** garden scene on each side, one w/a cupid on a pedestal, the other w/a courting couple, both viewed through a window w/a balcony, the molded gilt metal frame enameled in red, orange & yellow, the chain link handle w/lapis glass beads, ca. 1920s ............................ **230.00**

**Petit point,** 18th century pastoral scenes, the silver frame pierced & molded w/winged lions & putti harvesting grapes, marked "800 Made in Italy," early 20th c. .............. **143.00**

**Petit point,** scene of a parrot on either side against a stylized floral

needlepoint ground, the gilt metal
frame molded w/harvest goddesses
& faceted cabochons, late 19th c. ...... **63.00**

**Satin,** black, chased silver frame set
on one side w/green beryl, quartz &
garnets in silver (missing one stone).. **374.00**

**Silk faille,** Napoleonic-style, pale
dusty sky blue, embroidered w/small
gold sequins w/a bee & ribbon
entwined vines, the gilt metal frame
molded w/a crowned eagle & sprays
of laurel, 19th c. (fraying) ................... **34.00**

**Silver mesh,** Art Nouveau-style
design, gold frame w/floral design &
drop fringe, Germany ....................... **125.00**

*Silver Mesh Purse*

**Silver mesh,** the silver frame inset
w/black onyx, stenciled design in
black w/Art Deco flowers, chain
handle, marked "800," Vienna,
Austria, accompanying box labeled
"Michael Goldschmidt Soehne Wien I
Palais Equitable," ca. 1925 (ILLUS.) ... **920.00**

**Suede,** cinnamon, envelope-style,
signed "Hermes," ca. 1970s ............. **316.00**

**Velvet,** printed w/poppies in shades of
red & green against a cinnamon
brown, the silver metal frame
molded w/putti & floral scrolls, early
20th c. ................................................ **74.00**

**Tapestry,** worked w/an abstract floral
pattern in shades of green, yellow,
red, blue, taupe & white, the gilt
metal frame set w/pale green

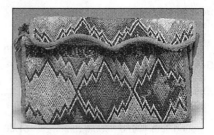

*Rectangular Wool Purse*

cabochons & curved enameled
Persian miniature plaques,
ca. 1940s ........................................... **97.00**

**Wool,** rectangular shape, flame
stitched in various colors
w/scalloped flap, the edges bound in
green wool, opening to a three fold
pocket lined w/magenta silk,
inscribed under flap "John Golden,"
4⅜ x 7⅛" (ILLUS. above) .............. **1,610.00**

---

# RADIO & TELEVISION
# MEMORABILIA

*Not long after the dawning of the radio age
in the 1920s, new programs were being aired
for the entertainment of the national listening
audience. Many of these programs issued
premiums and advertising promotional pieces
which are highly collectible today.*

*With the arrival of the TV age in the late
1940s, the tradition of promotional items
continued and in addition to advertising
materials, many toys and novelty items have
been produced which tie-in to popular shows.*

*Below we list alphabetically a wide range of
items relating to classic radio and television.
Some of the characters originated in the comics
or on the radio and then found new and wider
exposure through television. We include them
here because they are the best known to today's
collectors because of television exposure.*

**Amos & Andy toy,** cast iron, Amos,
Andy & dog seated in orange-
painted taxicab, 6" l. ...................... **$523.00**

**Barnabas Collins - Dark Shadows
game,** board-type, w/contents,
Milton Bradley, 1968 (minor shelf
wear) .................................................. **42.00**

*Charlie McCarthy Radio*

**Batman & Robin clock,** "Talking Alarm," tall plastic case w/the Bat Signal in center of face, 1974, 2½ x 6½", 7" h. ............................... **130.00**

**Batman photograph,** four black & white photographs & one color photo of the cast member from "Batman," signatures include "Adam West" as Batman, "Cesar Romero" as The Joker, "Lee Merriwether" as Catwoman, "Burgess Meredith" as The Penguin, "Yvonne De Carlo" as Batgirl, 8 x 10", set of five .................. **58.00**

**Ben Casey M.D. game,** board-type, complete, Transogram, dated 1961.... **28.00**

**Beverly Hillbillies puzzle,** jigsaw-type, full-color photograph of family sitting in their 1921 truck, Jaymar No. 6572, 100 pieces, 17 x 22".......... **32.00**

**Bewitched "Samantha & Endora" game,** board-type, complete w/box, Gems, 1965, box 10 x 20" (paper tear in corner box) .......................... **220.00**

**Captain Kangaroo's Treasure House game,** die-cut thin vinyl stick-on characters w/insert background board, Colorforms, 1961, box 12 x 18"............................................. **49.00**

**Captain Midnight Decoder Manual,** 1942.................................................... **65.00**

**Captain Midnight decoder,** 1949, "Key-O-Matic Code-O-Graph," complete w/key in original mailer........ **65.00**

**Charlie McCarthy book,** "Speaking for Myself," 1939............................. **100.00**

**Charlie McCarthy dancer toy,** jointed wood figure attached to stick, figure "dances" on board, manufactured by Marks Brothers, Boston, Massachusetts, ca. 1930s, w/original box.................................. **295.00**

**Charlie McCarthy marionette,** composition, 18" h. .......................... **135.00**

**Charlie McCarthy radio,** white plastic case w/figure of Charlie, marked "Majestic" (ILLUS. previous column) ... **900.00**

**Cheers cast photograph,** color photo of some of the cast members & signed "Ted Danson," & "Rhea Perlman" in black ink & "Love, Shelly Long," in purple ink, 8 x 10" .............. **230.00**

**Daniel Boone (Fess Parker) figure,** jointed, complete in box w/accesories, Loius Marx Co.............. **59.00**

**Dragnet "Badge 714" game,** puzzle-type, green plastic tray puzzle w/playing pieces of Sergeant Friday & a fugitive, TransOgram, 1955, 5 x 7"................................................... **29.00**

**Flub-a-Dub (Howdy Doody) marionette,** cardboard w/base insets, ca. 1950-54 .......................... **75.00**

**Fred Flinstone costume,** vinyl costume & plastic mask, in original box w/cellophane window, Ben Cooper, dated 1973 (box slightly crushed on one side) ......................... **55.00**

**Howdy Doody bandana,** 1960s, 20" sq.................................................. **35.00**

**Howdy Doody billfold,** w/assorted pictures on front, ca. 1950-54........... **125.00**

**Howdy Doody book,** activity-type, "Fun Book," w/stickers & follow the dots, copyright 1951 by Kagran Corporation, by Whitman Publishing .. **75.00**

**Howdy Doody bowl,** cereal, ceramic w/character transfers ......................... **38.00**

**Howdy Doody cards,** Christmas, colorful cards w/envelopes, Mars Co., ca. 1950-54, w/original mailer, set of 7............................................. **195.00**

**Howdy Doody doll,** inflatable, 18" h. ... **75.00**

**Howdy Doody key chain,** take-apart-type, plastic, w/instructions, ca. 1950s, 2" h......................................... **60.00**

**Howdy Doody night light,** figural, plastic, manufactured by Nor' east Nauticals, 7" h................................... **325.00**

**Howdy Doody pencil case,** Howdy face is snap-front, copyright Kagran Corporation, 3½ x 8¾"....................... **75.00**

**Howdy Doody pin,** flip-up-type, Wonder Bread premium ................... **20.00**

**Howdy Doody sweatshirt,** cowboy type, w/tag ....................................... **150.00**

**Howdy Doody tin,** shows TV figures riding carousel horses ..................... **250.00**

*J.R. Ewing Beer*

**Howdy Doody tool box,** metal ranch house tool box w/handle, Adco Liberty, ca. 1950-54 .......................... **145.00**

**Howdy Doody toy,** push-up, jointed figure of Howdy w/NBC microphone... **95.00**

**Howdy Doody wrist watch,** w/movable eyes, Patent Watch Co., ca. 1954, w/original box ................... **235.00**

**Huckleberry Hound tie bar & cuff links,** on original card, the set ............ **25.00**

**I Spy photograph,** color photograph of Bill Cosby & Robert Culp as they appeared in the series, signed "To The Olison Family, All the best-Bill Cosby" in black ink on left & "Thanks for the Memory! Robert Culp" in black ink on right, 8 x 10"................. **144.00**

**Jack Armstrong toy,** "Squadron NC 38" cardboard & aluminum airplane, Wheaties premium, ca. 1940, 8½" l.... **95.00**

**Jack Webb (Dragnet) whistle** ............. **12.00**

**James Arness (Gunsmoke)TV Guide,** May 11-17, 1957 ................... **25.00**

**Jetsons toy,** "Planets," Denny's Restaurant premium ........................... **7.00**

**J.R. Ewing beer,** six unopened cans each w/depiction of gold belt buckle against a blue star background, label reads "If you have to ask how much my beer costs, you probably can't afford it." in black lettering w/"J.R. Ewing" screened signature, bottom of can reads "Imported from Texas" (ILLUS. above) .............................. **259.00**

**Laverne & Shirley cast photograph,** black & white, including Lenny, Squiggy & Carmine Ragusa, signed "Penny Marshall 'L'," "Phil Foster," "David L. Lander 'Squiggy'," "Eddie Mekka" & "Betty Garrett" in blue ink & "Cindy Williams" in blue ink .......... **316.00**

**Laverne & Shirley game,** board-type, Parker Bros., 1977, mint & sealed in box ....................................................... **34.00**

**Leave it to Beaver game,** board-type .. **85.00**

**Magazine,** "TV Fan," August 1955, Jackie Gleason, Audrey Meadows, Sid Ceasor & Nanette Fabray on cover .................................................. **100.00**

**Magazine,** "TV Star Parade," Fall 1951, volume I, No. I, Martin & Lewis, Dagmar, Faye Emerson & Dorothy Collins on cover ................. **100.00**

**Milton Berle toy,** windup tin, "Milton Berle Crazy Car," Loius Marx Co., late 1940s, mint in box ...................... **173.00**

**My Little Margie coloring book,** Gale Storm .................................................. **18.00**

**Mr. Magoo toy,** automobile, tin, "Crazy Car," battery-operated, Hubley, mint condition ..................... **275.00**

**Outer Limits game,** board-type, interesting monsters on the cover, Milton Bradley, 1960s, complete in original box ....................................... **222.00**

**Princess Summerfallwinterspring (Howdy Doody) toy,** push-up, jointed figure of Princess w/hands on drum, copyright by Bob Smith, manufactured by Kohner Products...... **145.00**

**Red Skelton coloring book,** 16 x 22".. **18.00**

**Robin Hood game,** target hook board w/rubber rings, Robert Greene on front ..................................................... **75.00**

**Wonder Woman photograph,** color photo of Lynda Carter as Wonder Woman holding up a log against a desert background, signed on lower right "Love, Lynda Carter" in purple ink, 8 x 9⅞" ...................................... **201.00**

# RADIOS & ACCESSORIES

**Radio,** Dalberg pillow radio model 4130, w/pillow speaker, green ........ **$395.00**

**Radio,** Dedold model B402, plastic, brown w/white swirls .......................... **70.00**

**Radio,** Fada model 652, butterscotch Catalin case w/red knobs & red accented trim around dial, ca. 1940s, 5½ x 11", 6¾" h. (ILLUS. top next page) .................................................. **990.00**

*Fada Model 652*

**Radio,** General Electric model 515, plastic, marbelized maroon ................ **60.00**

**Radio,** Nippon Electric model NT61, transistor, 1960, w/original box .......... **75.00**

# RAILROADIANA

*Original Pennsylvania Railroad Bell*

**Bell,** "Pennsylvania Railroad," cast iron & brass, from #K4 engine, 16 x 24", 21½" h. (ILLUS.) .............. **$605.00**

**Book,** "Dining on Rails," by Richard Lukin, 1st edition, autographed, numbered, 320 pp. ........................... **255.00**

**Book,** "Official Guide of Railways, Steam Naval Lines of United States, Puerto Rico, Central America, Mexico and Cuba," May, 1931, history & art, 1,300 pp. ........................................ **100.00**

**Booklet,** "Presidents of the United States," by Union Pacific Railroad, 1946 .................................................... **8.00**

**Brochure,** "California," "Santa Fe Railroad," 1932 ...................................... **7.00**

**Brochure,** London, "Northeastern Railway," 1920s .................................. **12.00**

**Brochure,** "Rock Island Lines," 1913, "Colorado Under the Turquoise Sky" .. **50.00**

**Caboose key,** "UP" (Union Pacific Railroad) ............................................ **20.00**

**Coffeepot,** cov., individual, china, Santa Fe Railroad, Poppy patt., Syracuse China ............................... **195.00**

**Cup & saucer,** china, Minneapolis, St. Paul & Sault Ste. Marie Railroad, Logan patt., marked "Soo Line" ........ **195.00**

**Cuspidor,** "Union Pacific Railroad," brass, 10 x 10" .................................... **95.00**

**Fuel can,** 'Lamptenders,' "B&O RR" (Baltimore & Ohio Railway), tin w/spout/handle .................................. **95.00**

**Glass,** "Pennsylvania Railroad," w/logo & diesel locomotive, 3½ x 4½" ............. **35.00**

**Guide,** "Official Railway Guide," February 1943 ................................... **20.00**

**Lantern,** "AT&SF RY" (Atchison Topeka & Santa Fe Railway), clear embossed globe .............................. **150.00**

**Lantern,** "B&O" (Baltimore & Ohio Railroad), blue globe, Adams & Westlake, No. 250 ............................ **75.00**

**Lantern,** "CP RY" (Canadian Pacific Railway), wire bottom, green cast globe, tall ......................................... **700.00**

**Lantern,** "C&NWRR" (Chicago & Northwestern Railway), bell-bottom, green cast globe, tall ..................... **1,100.00**

**Lantern,** "GNRY" (Great Northern Railway), clear globe, "Safety Always" ................................................ **95.00**

**Lantern,** "LS&MS RY" (Lake Shore & Michigan Southern Railway), wire bottom, amber cast globe, tall ....... **1,000.00**

**Lantern,** "NYC" (New York Central Railroad), bell-bottom, amber cast globe, tall ......................................... **600.00**

**Lantern,** "NYC" tubular, "Vesta" model, Dietz, tall ................................. **65.00**

**Lantern,** "PC" (Penn Central Railroad), blue glass globe, Adlake ...................... **75.00**

**Lantern,** "PRR" (Pennsylvania Rail Road), wire bottom, amber cast globe, tall ......................................... **900.00**

**Lantern,** "PRR" caboose marker, early yellow embossed Pennsylvania Rail Road seal .................................. **150.00**

**Lock,** "L&N" (Louisville & Nashville Railroad) ............................................ **33.00**

**Luggage cart,** wood w/iron wheels & removable handle, 50" l. handle, 17 x 24" cart...................................... **231.00**

**Map,** "A.T. & S.F." (Atchison Topeka & Santa Fe Railroad), 1904, engraved by Ambco, 18 x 36" ............................ **89.00**

**Map,** "Canadian Pacific, Milwaukee & St. Paul Railway" & "S.S.M," etc., 1911, 20 x 44" ................................... **89.00**

**Map,** "Mexican Central Railway," 1903, 22 x 27" ................................. **69.00**

**Map,** "N.P. w/C.B. & Q." (Northern Pacific Railway w/Chicago Burlington & Quincy Railroad, Colorado & Southern Railway, etc.), 1910, 27 x 33" ................................. **89.00**

**Map,** "S.P. & U.P." (Southern Pacific Co. & Union Pacific Railroad), 45" sq. ............................................. **89.00**

**Map of Switzerland,** Swiss Federal, beautifully detailed, 1925 ................... **12.00**

**Map,** Union Pacific System, 1920, 24 x 42" ........................................... **150.00**

**Menu,** "Union Pacific Railroad" 1939, Challenger ..................................... **12.00**

**Menu,** "Union Pacific Railroad," 1954, Hoover Dam ..................................... **11.00**

**Pass,** "ATSF" (Atchison Topeka & Santa Fe Railway), early 1900s .......... **10.00**

**Pass,** "Chicago, Milwaukee & St. Paul Railway," 1914 ................................... **17.00**

**Pass,** "Chicago & Northwestern Railway," 1914 ................................... **18.00**

**Pass,** "Pullman Palace Car Company," 1914 ............................................... **18.00**

**Print of W.H. Jackson** on the west slope of Marshall Pass along the Denver & Rio Grande Railway, photo No. 37, 18 x 25" ...................... **30.00**

**Receipt book,** Fred Harvey Restaurant, 1966 ............................... **15.00**

**Route map,** "Illinois Central Railroad," color, ca. 1870s, framed .................... **65.00**

**Schedule,** "Philadelphia & Reading Railway & Central Railroad of New Jersey," Philadelphia & New York, 1903 ................................................. **30.00**

**Sherbet,** stemmed, china, "Pennsylvania Railroad," Buffalo China, 1930s ..................................... **60.00**

**Sign,** "Seaboard Coast Line Railroad," round, metal, diesel nosepiece ......... **200.00**

**Switch key,** "C.R.I. & P.R.R." (Chicago Rock Island & Pacific Railroad), brass ................................. **35.00**

**Timetable,** "Soo Line," 1929, North Pacific Coast Canada ........................ **28.00**

**Watch fob,** enamel, Brotherhood of Railroad Carmen of America .............. **45.00**

**Wrench,** "Southern Railway," adjustable, large .............................. **150.00**

---

# RECORDS & RECORD JACKETS

*Since the late 1870s when Thomas Edison invented the first phonograph machine, literally millions of records have been produced. Early wax cylinders were soon followed by 78 rpm wax disc records, which became the industry standard. Later 33⅓ rpm and then 45 rpm records evolved and today these have nearly been superseded by CDs. Since there are so many old records still around, collectors need to understand that even very early cylinder and disc records may have only a minimal collector value— especially if they are in poor playing condition.*

**Beatles (The),** "Help," tan label, United Artists 6366 .......................... **$20.00**

**Beatles (The),** "Magical Mystery Tour," Apple label, German ............... **56.00**

**Beatles (The),** "Please Please Me," mono pressing, autographed by all four on back cover in blue ink, also inscribed "To Jan, love from, Ringo Starr," British Parlophone PMC1202, matted & framed w/a reproduction of the front cover, 16 x 28" ................. **3,162.00**

**Beatles (The),** "Rubber Soul," purple label, Capitol Records 46440, digital mastered, w/original wrapper ............ **22.00**

**Beatles (The),** "With The Beatles," blue label, German, w/original wrapper ................................................. **55.00**

**Beatles (The),** "Yesterday and Today," trunk cover, shows the 'Fab Four' sitting in & around an open trunk, St-2553 ................................... **24.00**

**Beatles (The),** "Yesterday and Today," depicts John, George, Paul & Ringo dressed in smocks w/the heads & decapitated torsos of dolls & pieces of meat strewn across their laps & shoulders, this was the original cover for this album, also known as the 'Butcher Cover,' w/letter of authenticity, matted, ca. 1966 (ILLUS. top next page).... **7,763.00**

*"Yesterday and Today" 'Butcher Cover'*

*Blues Brothers Album*

**Blues Brothers,** "Briefcase Full of Blues," depicts Joliet Jake (John Belushi) & Elwood (Dan Aykroyd) in their signature dark sunglasses & ties, signed on middle "Dan Ayckroyd" in blue marker & "John Belushi" on upper right in blue marker, contains original album, ca. 1978 (ILLUS.) ......................... **3,163.00**

**Bob Dylan,** "Nashville Skyline," signed on the cover in black pen & ink ..................................................... **690.00**

**Buddy Holly,** "Raining in My Heart," single, signed in black ink on Coral label, matted & framed w/a photograph of Buddy Holly & the Crickets, 13 x 17"........................... **2,645.00**

**Crosby, Stills, Nash & Young,** "Deja Vu," shows the band members in frontier clothing w/a dog, signed in middle "Neil Young" in gold metallic marker, contains original album, ca. 1970.......................................... **173.00**

**Elvis Presley,** "February 1970, on Stage" signed in blue felt tip pen, RCA 4362, matted & framed, 14" sq. ........... **977.00**

**Elvis Presley,** "Girl Happy," mono, LPM-3338 .......................................... **20.00**

**Elvis Presley,** "Kissin' Cousins," orange label, stereo, LSP-2894 .......... **18.00**

**Frank Zappa,** "I Don't Wanna Get Drafted," sleeve for his 12" single autographed in gold marker Frank Zappa & band member Ray White, early 1980s ....................................... **575.00**

**Frank Zappa,** "Joe's Garage/Act I," signed "F Zappa" in blue sharpie, framed, 13 x 13" ............................... **575.00**

**John Lennon,** "Starting Over" single sleeve, signed, the black felt tip pen autograph on the front cover ......... **1,840.00**

**John Lennon & Yoko Ono,** "Double Fantasy" album cover, signed, blue ball point pen signatures on the front cover, matted & framed, 18½" sq. ...................................... **1,265.00**

**Michael Jackson & Paul McCartney,** "Say, Say, Say," signed on cover middle "Michael Jackson" in gold metallic marker, contains original 12" single, 12⅜" sq. .......................... **288.00**

**Queen,** "The Works," depicting a lone Freddie Mercury on front & a collage of images of the band on back, signed on front cover "Freddie Mercury, Brian May, Deacon John & Robert Taylor," in black marker, ca. 1984........................................... **400.00**

**Rolling Stones (The),** "Black & Blue," signed in blue Sharpie by all five members, "Mick Jagger, Keith Richards, Bill Wyman, Charlie Watts, Ronnie Woods," ca. 1989, framed, 14" sq............................................. **1,035.00**

**Rolling Stones (The),** "Out of Our Heads" album cover, signed by all five original band members in black marker pen (edges of album cover taper together, record in poor condition) ........................................ **805.00**

**Rolling Stones,** "Love Your Love," w/black marker signatures of all current band members, matted & framed .......................................... **1,380.00**

# REVERSE PAINTINGS ON GLASS

**Family group,** in the style of Auguste Edouart, the figures of a family posed in silhouette in a parlor, the original dates to ca. 1830, typed provenance label on the back, framed, 7⅛ x 9" ............................. **$747.00**

**Portrait of 18th c. nobleman on horseback,** Europe, late 19th c., framed 8⅛ x 10¾" (some separation & repainting) ..................................... **546.00**

**Scenes from Shakespeare's "The Tempest" & "Hamlet,"** black liner band & giltwood frame, 19th c., paint separation on each, 15 x 26", pr.. **10,925.00**

**Silhouette bust portrait of Benjamin Franklin wearing a fur cap,** black, within an oval opening in the dark greyish blue border w/gilt banding & four gold stars, a small space below titled in gold "BeNJN FRANKLIN," original narrow frame, American-made, ca. 1800-25 (some edge flakes on frame).............................. **314.00**

---

# RUGS - HOOKED & OTHER

## HOOKED

**Animals,** the rectangular rug worked in red, orange, green, black & yellow cottons centering a red & orange rectangle enclosed by black & green border enclosed by red & orange

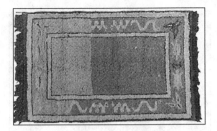

*Animals Hooked Rug*

border w/green turtles, worms & owls enclosed by a green & black border w/fringe, African-American, late 19th c. - early 20th c., 38½ x 62¾" (ILLUS.) ..................... **$230.00**

**Cow,** worked in beige & tan on two tone blue & grey ground w/red border & leaf designs in blue & black, black & pink border, on stretcher, 23 x 37" (very worn w/holes & small repairs) .................. **385.00**

**Farm,** rectangular w/cows, sheep, barn, road, etc. in red, white, black, grey, shades of blue & green, rebacked on stretcher, 19½ x 35½" (some damage & repair).................. **413.00**

**Horse,** worked in brown, beige, cream & peach w/a running horse on a beige- and cream-striped ground, the sides w/scrolled leafage, 19th c., framed, 29 x 58" ........................... **4,600.00**

**Hunter,** horse & hound, the hunter dressed in his riding pinks straddling a dappled horse surrounded by running hounds, worked in tones of red, blue, brown, black, beige & white fabric, late 19th c., 45½ x 84" ......... **3,450.00**

*Rooster Hooked Rug*

**Peacock w/spread tail,** round, shades of blue, black, orange, green, yellow & purple, 35" d. framed, 40½ x 40½" ........................ **770.00**

**Pictorial scene,** rectangular, worked in multicolored cotton & wool threads w/a scene depicting two men at a table raising their glasses in a detailed interior, late 19th c., framed 19 x 30½" ........................................ **173.00**

**Rooster,** worked in pale yellow, cream, lavender, red, grey & black fabric w/a rooster, the corners w/stars on a black ground, late 19th c., framed, some wear & minor repairs, 24¾ x 43¾" (ILLUS. bottom previous page) .............................. **1,265.00**

**Roosters,** worked in olive green brown, blue, red & black fabrics w/two roosters centering an inverted heart, the tops & sides bordered w/a band of blocks, dated "1896," framed, 16¾ x 30¼" (some wear) ................. **2,185.00**

---

# SALESMAN'S SAMPLES

*The traveling salesman or "drummer" has all but disappeared from the American scene. In the latter part of the 19th century and up to the late 1930s, they traveled the country calling on potential customers to show them small replicas of their products. Today these small versions of kitchenwares, farm equipment and even bathtubs, are of interest to collectors and are common in a wide price range.*

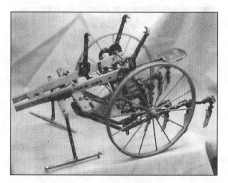

*Iron Age Cultivator*

**Cultivator,** brass & wood, "Iron Age," seat flanked by large spoked wheels, w/wood cultivator at front, 16" l. (ILLUS.) ........................... **$2,000.00 and up**

*Holland Furnace*

**Decoys,** papier-mâché ducks, pr. ......... **95.00**

**Furnace,** cast iron, "Holland Furnace," cylindrical shaped w/heat pipes at top, all flanked by return air pipes, fan under top to force air through hot air pipes, comes w/several different cases (ILLUS.) ................. **150.00 to 400.00**

**Furnace,** coal, disassembles to show all working parts, original paint, w/original hard carrying case, manufactured by Michigan Stove Co., 14" ............................................. **295.00**

**Harnesses,** leather & aluminum, w/all straps & buckles like full-size harnesses, ca. 1905-18, aluminum horses approximately 18", rare ................................. **400.00 to 800.00**

**Hydraulic jack,** cast iron, w/handle, red silver & black coloring, embossed "World's Largest Mfgr. of Lever Screw & Hydrolic Jacks" 3¼" h. (minor paint chips, one handle missing) ............................................. **66.00**

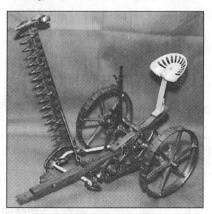

*Salesman's Sample Mower*

**Mower,** brass, raised seat above mechanism flanked by spoke wheels, ca. 1900s, 16" w. (ILLUS. bottom previous page)................................. **2,000.00 and up**

**Pickles,** Heinz, leather case containing six painted zinc graduated pickles, early 20th c. ...... **1,840.00**

**Silo filler,** brass & wood, "Blizzard Silo Filler," engine at end of wood chute, mounted on wood base, approximately 7" h......... **800.00 to 1,200.00**

**Spring butt,** pull down lever, door will swing & when lever is up door is locked, marked "Chicago Spring Butt Company, Chicago, New York, Type No. 6001," 11" h., 8½" w. (minor soiling) ................................................ **11.00**

*Enterprise Windmill*

**Windmill,** wood, "Enterprise Windmill," triangular base below platform, all below wood veins, ca. 1880-1920, 20" h. (ILLUS.)............. **3,000.00 to 4,000.00**

# SCIENTIFIC INSTRUMENTS

**Draftsman instruments,** nickel plated instruments, ebony & ivory rules & watercolor set, rosewood case w/silvered plaque on lid engraved "Presented to R.N. Bowers by the Employees of the Water Department at Fairmont as a token of regard and esteem, June 1873," 10 x 15", 3" h. ................................................ **$977.00**

*Brass Sundial*

**Magnifying glass,** whalebone & figured wood, sailor-made, 19th c., 3½" h., 3½" w...................... **402.00**

**Microscope,** brass, cased, 19th c., 10" h. ................................................ **431.00**

**Pantograph,** brass, cased, signed "Schmalacalder 82 Strand, London," 19th c., 28" l...................................... **172.00**

**Pantograph,** brass, cased, signed "Troughton and Simms London," 19th c., 31" l...................................... **345.00**

**Sundial,** brass, the square plaque w/a surface engraved w/a circular dial inscribed "Isaac Johnson Fecit 1731 - Begon' about - your business - New York" w/Roman numerals, spandrels engraved w/scrolling vine decoration, gnomon missing, 7 x 7" (ILLUS. above) ............................. **5,520.00**

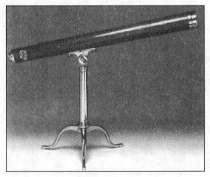

*Victorian Telescope*

**Telescope,** mahogany barrel of brass stand, 19th c., barrel 29" l. (ILLUS.) ...................................... **1,380.00**

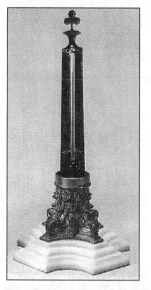

*Brass & Marble Thermometer*

**Telescope,** celestial, brass, two draw, rack & pinion focus, mount & base, 19th c., boxed, barrel 44¾"............... **690.00**

**Transit,** brass, cased, Charles W. Helfricht, Philadelphia, w/maker's label, 19th c. .................................... **172.00**

**Thermometer,** brass, marble & glass, the clover & urn-shaped finial above an inscribed "1848" above two thermometers attached to a sheet inscribed w/measuring numbers on both sides over a brass acanthus carved base above a molded quadripartite stepped base, 10" h. (ILLUS. above) ............................... **1,955.00**

# SCOUTING ITEMS

*Scout rules and regulations, handbooks and accouterments have changed with the times. Early items associated with the Scouting movements are now being collected. A sample follows.*

## BOY SCOUT

**Hatchet,** genuine plumb w/Boy Scout emblem........................................... **$125.00**

**Magazine,** "Boys' Life," August, 1936, cover showing very busy colorful camping scene by Harrison Cady, Coca-Cola advertisement on back cover, complete .................................. **45.00**

**Scarf,** Jamboree-type, 1953 ................ **10.00**

**Tile,** decorated w/Boy Scout in full dress "flagging," tents & trees in background, Mosaic Tile Company, Zanesville, Ohio, 6" sq........................ **95.00**

## BROWNIE

**Jacket,** Girl Scouts, ca. 1920............. **135.00**

**Uniform,** Girl Scouts, 1938 .................. **40.00**

# SCRIMSHAW

*Scrimshaw is a folk art by-product of the 19th century American whaling industry. Intricately carved and engraved pieces of whalebone, whale's teeth and walrus tusks were produced by whalers during their spare time at sea. In recent years numerous fine grade hard plastic reproductions have appeared on the market so the novice collector must use caution to distinguish these from the rare originals.*

**Alphabet & case,** the reeded & domed circular top threaded to a conforming straight-sided cylindrical case w/scrimshawed inscription reading "Spelling Alphabet of M. Palmer," opening to reveal twenty-six separate disks, each scrimshawed w/a letter of the alphabet, 19th c., 3" h., 2" d........... **$863.00**

**Etui,** whalebone, formed as a fish w/shaped tail, scaled body & applied balancing pectoral fins, the pinned articulated head opening to a hollow case, 7¾" l. ...................................... **748.00**

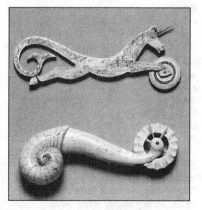

*Scrimshaw Jagging Wheels*

**Jagging wheel,** ivory, of serpentine form shaped to resemble a chambered nautilus, w/inscribed & sectioned shell, the tapering body terminating in an antennaed head fitted w/a carved & decorated coggled wheel, two antennae missing, 6¾" l. (ILLUS. bottom, bottom previous page) .............................................. 1,610.00

**Jagging wheel,** whalebone, the silhouette form carved in the shape of a unicorn w/serpentine forked tail, spiral decorated horn & inscribed decoration depicting on one side a ship & longboat in pursuit of sperm whale, the front hooves fitted w/double circle-inscribed & tapering wheel, 6½" l. (ILLUS. top, bottom previous page) ................................... 518.00

**Knitting needles,** whalebone, each w/pointed ends & circular shafts ending a rounded head w/incised concentric circle decoration, 19th c., 13¼" l.............................................. 173.00

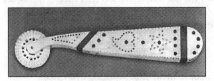

*Scrimshaw Pie Crimper*

**Pie crimper,** the crenellated wheel w/pierced decoration jointed to a tab handled form w/inlaid mother-of-pearl triangled heart & star decoration punctuated by ebonized line & dot decoration, 19th c., 7¼" l. (ILLUS.) ........................................... 805.00

**Spoon,** whalebone & tortoiseshell, the pointed ovoid tortoiseshell bowl joined to a bulging cylindrical handle w/incised reeded decoration ending in turned reeded & pointed terminus, 19th c., 8¾" l................................... 115.00

**Walking stick,** the tapering staff elaborately carved in relief w/words & symbols recalling Thomas Jefferson including a spread wing eagle, Jefferson's tomb, the University of Virginia & the inscription "I resign my spirit to God, my daughter, to my country," dated 1900, 36¾" l..................................... 978.00

**Wantage stick,** whalebone, engraved "Timothy Fitzgerald x June the 16th 1819...wine gallons," 47½" (knob cracked)......................................... 1,495.00

*Engraved Whale Tooth*

**Whale's tooth,** the obverse engraved w/a stylized figure of a lady standing beside an anchor holding the American flag all above "Carolina," the reverse signed & dated "R. Sherman, Whilmington, 1850," 6" h. (ILLUS.) ..................................... 2,300.00

**Wine opener,** whalebone, turned, 19th c., 5¾" h..................................... 86.00

---

# SEWING ADJUNCTS

## PINCUSHIONS

*Sailor's Valentine Pincushion*

**Advertising pin cube,** cardboard w/black glass pins, 1½" sq. (some pins missing)..................................... $14.00

**Conch shell-shaped pincushion,** on cast iron base ..................................... 55.00

**Chinese 'dolls' pincushion,** silk, round, the dolls w/pigtails around edge of cushion ................................. 20.00

**Pincushion,** shell-covered base, marked "Sailor's Valentine," made by Caribbean Island natives & sold to sailors (ILLUS. bottom previous page) ............................................... **25.00**

## SEWING KITS & BOXES

**Bullet shaped sewing kit,** Bakelite ...... **20.00**
**Canvas Army mending kit,** wrap around-type, marked "Soldiers Housewife," ca. 1918 .......................... **20.00**
**Goldtone mending kit w/tassel,** oval, needle thread & thimble inside ........... **10.00**

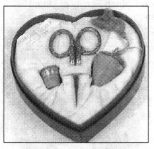

*Sears Embroidery Kit*

**Heart-shaped embroidery kit,** includes thimble, scissors & silk covered emery, ribbon in upper left corner reads "Sterling Silver 925-1000 Fine," offered in Sears, Roebuck 1900 catalog, w/original box (ILLUS.) ..................................... **175.00**
**Hosiery mending kit,** paper matchbook-style, ca. 1942 .................... **3.00**
**Lydia Pinkham sewing kit,** metal tube .................................................. **20.00**
**Mending kit,** egg-shaped, spatter painted ............................................. **12.00**
**Shaker sewing box,** marked "Sabbathday Lake" .......................... **200.00**
**Sterling tube,** including spools & thimble, 1¾" l. ................................. **125.00**

## SOCK DARNERS

*Blue & Ivory Darner*

*Decorated Sock Darner*

*Fabric Holder Sock Darner*

**Celluloid,** blue & ivory egg, no handle, ca. 1905, 2½" (ILLUS. bottom previous column) ............................... **17.00**
**Celluloid,** white (Ivorene) egg on handle, decorated w/garlands of flowers & ribbon bows, ca. 1875, 6⅛" (ILLUS. top) ............................... **30.00**
**Darner w/fabric holder,** plasticized black, door knob shape on handle w/spiral spring to hold fabric, ca. 1890, 4¾" (ILLUS. bottom) .......... **25.00**
**Ebony & sterling silver,** ebony egg on sterling silver filigree handle, hallmark from Unger Brothers of Philadelphia, ca. 1890, 5" (ILLUS. top next page) .................................... **150.00**
**Ebony & horn,** ebony egg on stag horn handle, also known as "stag finished," ca. 1870, 7" l. ...................... **90.00**
**Glass,** free-blown cased glass, spattering of blue, pink & green, large ball on handle, attributed to the Boston & Sandwich Glass Co., ca. 1870, 7½" l. (ILLUS. middle next page) ................................................. **250.00**

*Ebony Darner with Filigree Handle*

*Blown Glass Darner*

*Large Shaker Ball & Block Darner*

**Hollow,** wood, handle contains paper of needles, marked "Patented July 17, 1888," by Herbert G. Armitage, 5⅞" .................................... **55.00**

**Primitive,** wood, beehive on needle holder handle, South Carolina, ca. 1872, 4½" ...................................... **25.00**

**Primitive,** wood, large & small balls at handle (for large & small socks), turned from single block of soft wood, ca. 1850, 5½" .......................... **22.00**

**Primitive,** bird's-eye maple, large egg on handle w/knob at end, turned from single piece of wood, ca. 1865, 6½" ...................................................... **25.00**

**Primitive,** egg on handle w/angular knob near egg & annulated knob at end, turned from single piece of wood, ca. 1850, 7" .............................. **25.00**

**Shaker,** ball & block, large, from Shaker Church Family of Mount Lebanon, New York, ca. 1905 (ILLUS. bottom previous column) ..... **125.00**

*Two Views of Sock & Glove Darner*

**Wood,** concave egg on glove darner handle, egg opens to accommodate thread which pulled through hole in egg, handle holds needles, patented by Elizabeth G. Harley on November 10, 1874, labeled "Harley's Complete Darner for Darning Embroidering and Glove Mending," 5¾" (ILLUS.) ...................... **40.00**

**Wood & sterling silver,** olive wood egg on sterling handle, in strap work-style of 14th century Standard patt., laminated in four sections w/ebony separations & inlaid mother of pearl discat top of egg, made by Shreve & Company of San Francisco, ca. 1900, 6⅜" ..................................... **150.00**

**TAPE MEASURES**
**Apple,** red, celluloid .............................. **25.00**

**Cat face,** embossed brass .................... **50.00**

**Clock,** celluloid w/gold face, ca. 1920,
1½" h. ............................................. **140.00**

**Dog,** sitting, pink & white celluloid
w/big eyes, 2" .................................... **60.00**

**Indian boy's head,** celluloid ................. **60.00**

**Owl,** tin w/brass insert & glass eyes,
ca. 1930, 1⅜" d. ............................... **100.00**

*Philco Radio Tape Measure*

**Radio,** 1930s Philco-style, Bakelite
(ILLUS.) ............................................ **55.00**

**Shoe,** brass, marked floral design,
metal, design over celluloid, 1⅛" d. ..... **95.00**

**Shoe,** brass, marked "Three Feet in
One," 2¼" l. ....................................... **99.00**

**Teakettle,** nickel-plated brass
w/stone handle, ca. 1920 ................. **700.00**

**Turtle,** brass, marked "Pull My Head
and Not My Leg" ................................. **88.00**

## THIMBLES

**Advertising,** aluminum, painted band,
raised letters "Lightens The Burden
Of The Housewife," for Delco Light ...... **3.00**

**Advertising,** aluminum, raised letters
on painted band "Holland Furnaces
make Warm Friends" ................ **2.00 to 4.00**

**Advertising,** aluminum, painted band,
raised letters read "Use H-I Flour" ........ **3.00**

**Advertising,** celluloid, decorated
w/red checkerboard logo for Ralston
Purina chicken feed ............................. **2.00**

**Advertising,** nickel-plated brass,
"Prudential Insurance Company" .......... **5.00**

**Brass,** plain band .................................... **5.00**

**Gold,** semi-precious stone set on
band, by Simons ............................. **150.00**

**Metal,** cast pot metal, marked "FOR A
GOOD GIRL," from a gumball
machine or early Monopoly game ........ **5.00**

**Porcelain,** h.p. w/fruit or flower,
signed, by Royal Worcester ............... **50.00**

**Porcelain,** modern, decaled transfer
print ................................................ **15.00**

**Silver,** decorated w/Louis XV pattern
in high relief, by Ketchum &
McDougall (ILLUS. below) ................ **75.00**

*Louis XV Design Thimble*

*Simons Thimble*

**Silver,** decorated w/raised letters on
band "STITCH IN TIME SAVES
NINE," by Simons (ILLUS.) ............... **500.00**

**Silver,** raised grape pattern, by
Simons ........................................... **165.00**

## POLITICAL

**Political,** Aluminum, painted band,
raised letters read "HOOVER*
HOME*HAPPINESS," from the
Herbert Hoover presidential
campaign ......................................... **15.00**

## SOUVENIR & COMMEMORATIVE

**Silver,** decorated w/alligator in high
relief & "FLORIDA" in raised letters
on band ........................................... **300.00**

**Silver,** marked "New York World's," decorated w/Trylon & Perisphere, by Simons, ca. 1939-40 ........................ **600.00**

**Silver,** Simons-100th Anniversary, decorated w/a transportation theme, including an airplane, boat & truck, by Simons, ca. 1939 ........................ **400.00**

---

# SHAKER ITEMS

*The Shakers, a religious sect founded by Ann Lee, first settled in this country at Watervliet, New York, near Albany, in 1774. By 1880 there were nine settlements in America. Workmanship in Shaker crafts is an extension of their religious beliefs and features plain and simple designs reflecting a chaste elegance that is now much in demand though relatively few early items are common.*

**Basket,** square bottom, round top, bonnet-shaped handle single notched, single wrap over shaped rims, wide uprights, wide weavers w/three rows of narrow weavers at bottom & below rim, bluish green stencil or painted design on weavers, "J.S." impressed twice at top of handle, 7½" d., 10½" h. ........ **$173.00**

**Basket,** ash bottom, iron nails, channel routed out in circular wooden bottom to receive cross members of a spider which is nailed in place, swing handle attached through double notched ear handles, 11" d., 7½" h. .................................. **316.00**

**Box,** cov., pine & maple, oval, original orange stain, shellac finish, two fingers, copper points & tacks, acquired at Canterbury, New Hampshire, 3¼ x 5⅛", 2⅛" .......... **3,738,00**

**Box,** cov., pine & maple, oval, original chrome yellow paint, four extremely delicate fingers, copper points & tacks, Canterbury or Enfield, New Hampshire, 4¼ x 7¾", 11⅛" d. ..... **10,925.00**

**Box,** cov., pine & maple, oval, old red painted surface, two fingers on box point right, the single finger on cover points left, 7¾" l., 2⅞" h. ................... **345.00**

**Carrier,** tin, rectangular shaped w/handle set at midpoint, acquired at Canterbury, New Hampshire, 8 x 11¼", 3" h. ................................ **345.00**

**Chest of drawers,** the molded cornice above five graduated molded drawers, the molded base continuing to bracket feet, Harvard Community, Massachusetts, ca. 1840, 20⅛ x 42", 5' h. ............................................... **2,300.00**

**Chest of drawers,** the molded cornice above eight thumb-molded long drawers, each fitted w/a turned wood knob above a molded base, on bracket feet, 18½ x 39¾", 6' 2½" h. ........................................ **31,625.00**

**Collapsible swift,** pine & maple, yellow wash, w/wooden thumbscrew, dated on blade 1852, in ink on base "Laundry No. 12," 25½" h. ............. **1,840.00**

**Cupboard,** pine, original bright yellow stain, replacement iron latch, single door w/two flat panels, two interior shelves set in dadoes in ends, purchased at Centerbury, New Hampshire, ca. 1870, 17⅜ x 25½", 27½" h. ........................................ **1,955.00**

*Butternut & Pine Shaker Cupboard*

**Cupboard,** butternut & pine, wooden pulls, iron hinges, shellac or varnish finish, two large symmetrical doors over two small doors, feet formed by sides of case, slight overhang at top, upper interior compartment has three shelves, paneled sides, damage to lower right case & door, ca. 1860, 19½ x 49", 60¼" (ILLUS.) .............. **2,760.00**

**Dust pan,** birch, small size, folded corners, rolled top rim, finely turned handle w/scribe lines & small knob at end painted red, inscribed on bottom "Harriet Johns 1880," acquired at Canterbury, New Hampshire, 5 x 13" (small split in side) .............................................. **3,680.00**

**Dust pan,** small, commercially produced, shellac finish, hollow flared handle, gold/bronze stenciled decoration in center of pan, acquired at Canterbury, New Hampshire, 6¼ x 9" .............................................. **86.00**

**Field basket,** ash, rectangular bottom & top, single notch fastened w/front rivet, single wrap over shaped rims, uprights are beveled & tapered slightly at transition from bottom to sides, shaped handle inscribed "Office," 16½ x 22¾", 10" l. ............... **747.00**

**Handkerchief box,** poplarware, kidskin trim, yellow ribbons, yellow satin lining, in original cardboard box inscribed "Manufactured by the Canterbury Shakers, East Canterbury, New Hampshire," written in pencil on outside of box "1.00" & "yellow," mid-20th century .................................. **632.00**

**Lithograph,** "SHAKERS near LEBANON," John Pendleton, hand-colored, shows line dance in Mount Lebanon Meeting House, trees visible through windows, arched line depicting the barrel vaulted ceiling, ca. 1829-1834, 8¾ x 12¾" (minor mat burn) ...................................... **1,035.00**

**Mirror,** diminutive, the rectangular mirror plate within a frame surround, late 19 - early 20th c., 4 x 6" ............. **403.00**

**Pail,** pine staves & bottom, original chrome yellow paint, interior painted white, diamond shaped bail plates, iron hoops w/ends clipped to a V, hardwood handle w/three scribe lines, staves joined w/V-shaped tongue- and-groove joints, painted in black on bottom "E H/5" (East House), "8" impressed into bottom, 7" d., 5⅝" h. .................................... **1,035.00**

**Rocking chair w/arms,** maple, black paint, stamped "#6," on back top slat, Mount Lebanon, New York, ca. 1880, 41¾" h. (replaced seat) ....... **1,380.00**

**Rocking chair without arms,** maple, three-slat back, scribe lines visible on pommels, graduated slats, multicolored tape seat, Canterbury, New Hampshire, 39½" h. (ILLUS. top next column) .............................. **920.00**

*Shaker Rocker without Arms*

**Side chair,** maple, dark reddish brown stain, tilters, three arched slats & boldly turned acorn finials, rush seat, Mount Lebanon, New York, 41¼" ..................................... **1,035.00**

**Table,** "harvest," pine, ash & birch, retains traces of red paint, boldly turned legs, acquired at Canterbury, New Hampshire, height has been modified, 41½ x 71½", 27½" h. (ILLUS. top next page) ................. **2,070.00**

**Tool cupboard,** pine, walnut drawer fronts, grey paint, later iron hardware, wooden pull, large single door w/six panels, dovetailed case, top secured by screws & nails, finished w/quarter-round molded edge, shield shaped escutcheon, interior contains two rows of dovetailed drawers, dovetailed shelf bracket on inside of door for storage of files & shelves, incised "E.W.," above drawer fronts, Harvard, Massachusetts, ca. 1875, 12⅝ x 38¾", 44⅝" h. (escutcheon replaced) ........................................ **1,955.00**

**Wood box,** pine, old greyish green paint over red, iron hinges & hooks, chest w/hinged lid & one drawer, front & back are rabbeted & nailed to sides, ends have half-round cut-outs, thumbnail lipped drawer beneath box w/nailed construction, finely shaped pull, top overhang half-round, evidence for hanger for stove

*Shaker "Harvest" Table*

tools on right side, two cast-iron hooks on left side, purchased at Canterbury, New Hampshire, 16¼ x 23¾", 30¾" h. (left front corner of lid & box are broken away, top left corner of drawer is split) ............... **3,220.00**

---

# SIGNS & SIGNBOARDS

*Also see: ADVERTISING ITEMS, BREWERIANA, COCA-COLA COLLECTIBLES, DRUGSTORE & PHARMACY ITEMS and TOBACCIANA.*

**Apothecary shop,** molded & gilded copper, modeled as a large mortar & pestle molded in the round, retaining much of its original gilding, American, late 19th c., 17" h.......................... **$1,955.00**

**Baking powder,** "BT Babbits," posterboard, green, red, brown, cream & blue image of young girl sitting on box of Babbitts Soap Powder holding up fishing net, marked "Copyright 1894 by the H.E. Knapp Co. NY," framed, 20" h., 15" w. (repaired tears at bottom) ........ **88.00**

**Bank,** "United States Fidelity & Guaranty Co., Baltimore, Maryland," cardboard, pictures young boy wearing colonial-style clothing draped in American flag, advertising shown as company emblem on smaller flag, copyright 1897 Gray Litho Co., 9 x 14" .............................. **150.00**

**Batteries,** "Exide Battery," painted metal, done in the shape of an orange, black & white car battery, 14½" w., 12¾" (minor soiling) ........... **198.00**

**Beer,** "Buckeye Pilsener Beer," painted wood, side mounted w/scalloped edge & applied wooden scrollwork, old grey paint & black letters read "J. Golt Weissenberger - Buckeye Pilsener Beer. - Green Seal.," centered w/deer head, w/original iron mounting hardware, 24½" w., 57" h. (wear & age cracks w/minor damage to scrolls) ............ **1,210.00**

**Bitters,** "Griffith's Opera Bitters," paper, shows a scene of an opera w/a woman performer holding a bottle of bitters, all above "Steam Manufacturing, Oil City, Pa.," printed by Forst & Averell Co., mounted on maroon board, framed, 23 x 28¾"... **1,980.00**

**Bitters,** "Hostetter's Stomach Bitters," reverse painted glass, shows St. George on horseback slaying a dragon, done in black, gold & blue on a white ground, ca. 1870-80, 23 x 29¼" (some discoloration) ........ **605.00**

**Boot maker,** pine, full-bodied, carved in the form of high heeled boot, painted gold w/black trim, suspended from wrought-iron ring, 19th c., 20" h................................. **2,875.00**

**Bourbon,** "Old Crow," wood, round, done in yellow, red, orange & black on cream ground, shows crow dressed in tuxedo flanked by "Old" & "Crow," to the left of "Those in the Know Ask For Crow".......................... **55.00**

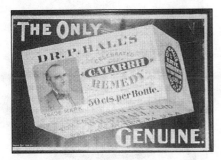

*Dr. P. Hall's Catarrh Remedy Sign*

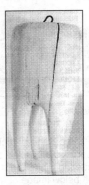

*Wood Dentist's Sign*

**Catarrh remedy,** "Dr. P. Hall's Celebrated Catarrh Remedy," paper w/cloth back, blue, black & white image of box w/picture of Dr. P. Hall that reads "Dr. P. Hall's Celebrated Catarrh Remedy 50 cts. per Bottle" w/"The Only" above & "Genuine" below, ca. 1890-1900, minor stain, 29½ x 43¾" (ILLUS.) ........................ **310.00**

**Cigar store,** carved & painted pine, carved in the form of a brown painted cigar inscribed "Gold Tip 2 for 5 C" in white lettering on a brown ground, American, late 19th - early 20th c., 26" l .................................... **920.00**

*Crack-a-Jack Clothes Sign*

**Clothes,** "Crack-a-Jack Clothes," tin flange, shows a top-hatted man w/box of tailored clothes under his arm & reads "I've Got My - Crack-a-Jack Clothes - Brand - 'A Fit or No Sale' - Measures Taken Here" (ILLUS.) ........................................ **2,145.00**

**Clothiers,** "Groshire Clothes," foam formed hand marked w/symbols on fingers & "Hand Tailored - Hand Basted - Hand Finished - Hand Pressed," surrounded by wood frame marked "For a well-tailored future - Groshire - Hand-Shaped Clothes" on base, 15" w., 17¼" h. ...... **77.00**

**Dentist,** wood, full-bodied, carved & painted molar w/four root sections made from single piece of pine, rusted iron hook in center for hanging, possibly New York State, 20th c., overall weathering (ILLUS.) ................ **578.00**

**Farm equipment,** "New Idea Farm Equipment," neon, lime green, 36" w., 14" h. (no transformer) ........... **99.00**

**Feed,** "Carnation," painted metal, square, painted white w/red & blue circle reading "Carnation - Milling Division Feed," 29½" h., 29½" w. (scratches & rust) ............................... **28.00**

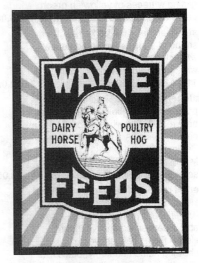

*Porcelain Feed Sign*

**Feed,** "Wayne Feeds," porcelain, rectangular, red, white & blue, "Wayne Feeds" & "Dairy Horse - Poultry Hog" flanking a man on a horse, self framed, minor chips to edges, 12" h., 12" w. (ILLUS.) .......... **275.00**

*Utica Fishing Reel Sign*

**Fishing reel,** "Utica Fishing Reel," die cut posterboard, gold, black & silver, debossed lettering reads "Auto Fishing Reel" below image of reel, 5" h., 10¼" w. (ILLUS.) ...................... **77.00**

**Footwear,** "Goodrich Rubber Footwear," porcelain flange sign, blue background, green border w/white lettering, surface scratches, touch-up, 19" h., 22" w. (ILLUS. top next column) ...................................... **132.00**

**Gasoline,** "Gulf," flange-type, porcelain, done in blue, white & orange, reads "That Good - Gulf - Gasoline - Gulf Refining Company," 22½ w., 18¼" h. (chipping & cracking) ........................................ **110.00**

**Gunmaker,** carved, painted & gilded pine, model of a long rifle, realistically carved & covered in gilding w/traces of yellowish green paint, American, 19th c., 76" l........ **4,025.00**

**Hat,** sheet metal full-bodied, in the shape of a top hat, painted yellow w/black strip, suspended from wrought-iron ring hanger, 19th c., 11" h. ........................................... **2,012.00**

**Hatchery,** "Amstutz Hatcheries," porcelain w/iron holder, rectangular, brown, yellow & white, two images of chicks, reads "Amstutz - Hatcheries - Pedigreed Sired Chicks - St. Johns, Mich," 28" h., 30" w. (soiling & scratches to border)............................ **83.00**

**Herbal remedy,** "Dr. Kilmer's Standard Herbal Remedy," paper, reads "Dr. Kilmer's" above image of dispensary above banner reading "Standard Herbal Remedies" above bottle showing human anatomy, bottle lists what it will cure including: "Indian Cough Cure - Ocean Weed Heart Remedy - Swamp-Root Liver - Complete Female Remedy - They Purify the Blood & Tones the Nerves," marked "Dr. Kilmer & Co., Binghamton, N.Y.," ca. 1880-1900, framed, minor creases, 16 x 32" (ILLUS. middle next column) ......... **7,700.00**

*Goodrich Footwear Sign*

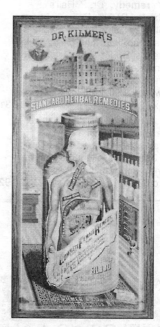

*Dr. Kilmer's Standard Herbal Remedy Sign*

*Deep-Rock Kerosene Sign*

**Kerosene,** "Deep-Rock," painted & embossed tin, red & blue lettering on cream ground, reads "Deep-Rock - Kerosene" w/dark border, scratches, minor rust & waterstains, 23" w., 14" h. (ILLUS.) .................................. **33.00**

**Lager,** "Barclay's," painted tin, done in orange, yellow, blue, brown, cream & black, shows a gentleman standing next to a bottle of Barclay's Lagar holding a pilsner glass aloft, all above "Barclay's," signed "F. Tock May" at bottom, 18" w., 25" h. (scratches & soiling) ........................ **127.00**

**Law office,** "Jas. W. Miller Law Office & Notary Public," gold leaf lettering on black sand paint background ........ **295.00**

**Lumber yard,** "Murphy & Diebold," reverse paint on glass, overall gold & silver paint w/multicolor illustration of lumber yard at center, reads "Murphy & Diebold - 36th Ward Pittsburgh - Planing Mill & Lumber Yard. - Take West End Street Cars - Special attention given to estimating Millwork.," early 20th c., framed, 30 x 46".............................................. **595.00**

**Oil,** "Penn Drake Lubricant," painted metal, rectangular, done in red, white, black & cream, marked "the original drake well, 1859" above image of early well above "Penn Drake - Lubricants," 14" w., 20" h. (minor scratches) ............................ **165.00**

**Paint,** "BPS Lumber Paint," porcelain, two-sided, rectangular, blue, white, orange & black, 24" h., 48" h. (two small holes, some scratches & chips) .................................................. **60.00**

**Paint,** "Dupont Paints," light-up-type, done in blue, white ripple glass front reads "Dupont Paints - Duco Dulux" in blue, red & black, gold plastic frame & metal box, lens 24" l., case 9 x 9" (minor scratches)...................... **88.00**

**Paint,** "Pierce's Fine Paints," flange-type, porcelain, red, white & blue on white ground, shows can of paint marked "Prepared House Paints - Ready for Use," to the left of "Pierce's - Fine - Paints - For Sale Here," 18¼" w., 12" h....................... **495.00**

**Patent Medicine,** "Dr. W.B. Calwell's Syrup Pepsin," flange-type, die-cut metal sign of bearded man holding a box of Syrup Pepsin & pointing w/the other, reads "The Perfect Laxative" below, done in red, gold, white, blue, grey, yellow & black, rare, restored, 16" w., 23½" h. (ILLUS. top next column) ........................................ **4,400.00**

**Patent Medicine,** "Dr. Pierce's Golden Medical Discovery," paper, multicolor image of a cavalry man, w/drawn saber reads "For Blood,

*Medicine Flange Sign*

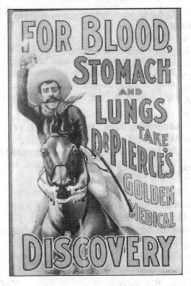

*Patent Medicine Sign*

Stomach and Lungs - Take Dr. Pierce's Golden Medical Discovery," ca. 1880-1900, framed, rough edges & some wrinkles, 21½ x 29½" (ILLUS.) ............................................ **935.00**

**Patent medicine,** "Harter's The Only True Iron Tonic," color lithographed paper, showing a young Victorian girl wearing a large straw hat & standing & leaning on a long fence w/a large rose-covered crescent to the left reading "Harter's," ca. 1890-1900, framed, 22 x 29½" (few minor tears) ................................................ **935.00**

*Perry Davis Painkiller Sign*

**Patent medicine,** "Johnson's American Anodyne Liniment," color lithographed cardboard showing a half-length portrait of a pretty young woman holding up a bottle of the product, ca. 1880-90, framed, 19 x 24" (minor water stains) ............ **935.00**

**Patent Medicine,** "Perry Davis Painkiller," tin, multicolor image of man w/a horse drawn wagon carrying boxes of painkiller, w/farm scene in the background, reads "Painkiller" at top & "Perry Davis Vegetable Painkiller" on fence behind horses, ca. 1880-90, w/oak frame, overall pitting, some stain & overall restoration to paint, 27½ x 32" (ILLUS. above) ................................. **880.00**

**Rest rooms,** porcelain, three joined octagonal blue signs, top reads "Clean," center reads "Rest," bottom reads "Rooms" in white, 18" w., 54" h. (minor chipping & edge wear) ............................................... **225.00**

**Rest rooms,** porcelain, rectangular, two white signs, one reading "Ladies" & the other "Men" in blue, 17" w., 6½" h., pr. ............................. **77.00**

**Rye,** "Quaker Maid Rye," tin, rectangular, done in blue, white, grey, gold & green, shows woman wearing bonnet holding tray w/bottle of rye, to the right of "Quaker Maid - Rye," all above "S. Hirsch & Co., Kansas City, MO.," in wood frame, 31½" w., 46" h. (ILLUS. top next column) ......................................... **1,045.00**

**School bell,** painted wood, relief-carved in the shape of a school bell being held upright by a white-gloved hand, old repaint in black, white & brown, 19½" h. (old repair at base) .. **330.00**

*Quaker Maid Rye Sign*

*Smoking Sign*

**Shoes,** "Niagara Shoes Sign," tin over cardboard, rectangular, red, green & blue, shows Niagara Falls above "Niagara Falls - for youthful feet - Watch the Way they wear," 19" h., 9" w. (minor scratches, piece of paper stuck to bottom) ..................... **165.00**

**Smoking,** "Humble," porcelain, white w/image of gas station attendant, green lettering reads "For Your Safety - We Don't Smoke on Drive Way," edge touched-up, 10½" h., 14" w. (ILLUS. bottom) .................... **440.00**

**Soap,** "Star Soap," paper, reads "Star Soap - Schultz & Co. Zanesville O. - Best For the Family" above multi-color image of mother & child & "'Good Night Prayer' - Send 25 Wrappers to Schultz & Co. - and get this Picture (Panel No. 39) without lettering.," ca. 1890-1900, framed, tear in corner & creases, 19½ x 26" ... **275.00**

*7Up Corner Sign*

**Soft drink,** "7Up," corner-type, painted & embossed tin, done in orange, black & cream, marked "7Up - Take Some Home" amid painted scrolls, marked "Made in U.S.A. Stout Sign Co. St. Louis, Mo." at bottom, early 1940s, minor scratches & paint chips, 10" w., 8" h. (ILLUS.) .....................................**209.00**

**Soft drink,** "Chero-Cola," painted tin, rectangular, done in red, yellow, blue, green & cream, elongated octagon outline surrounding oval marked "Drink - Chero-Cola - There's None So Good," 19½" w., 14" h. (minor scratches & denting)..............**121.00**

**Soft drink,** "Orange Blossoms," painted & embossed tin, done in yellow, orange, blue & white, shows image of soft drink bottle to the left of "Drink - Orange - Blossoms - In Bottles Only," 29½" w., 11½" h. (warped) ...........................................**94.00**

**Soft drink,** "Pepsi-Cola," porcelain, embossed, in the shape bottle cap, done in red, white & blue w/red lettering, 19" d. (soiling & minor chipping) ........................................**358.00**

**Soft drink,** "Smile," flange-type, painted metal, done in orange, blue & cream, reads "Drink - Smile" above an orange head w/bow-tie that reads "Smile," 10" w., 12¼" h. (minor scratches & paint chips) ........**468.00**

**Street,** "One Way," porcelain, in the shape of an arrow, yellow ground w/black letters reading "One Way," two-sided, 36" w., 12" h. (chipping, rust & scratches)...............................**176.00**

**Tackle shop,** in the form of a Northern Pike, carved & painted wood, the large fish clutching a Perch in its mouth, w/carved scale detail, applied fins & painted green, made as sign for tackle shop, probably Upper Peninsula Michigan (wear to paint) ...................**3,795.00**

*Bell System Sign*

**Telephone,** "Bell System," porcelain flange-type, dark blue w/white circle reading "New England Telephone & Telegraph Co. - American Telephone & Telegraph Co." surrounds blue bell marked "Bell System," chipping, water stains on both sides, 16" sq. (ILLUS.) .............. **138.00**

**Telephone,** "Public Telephone," porcelain, white w/blue lettering, image of bell marked "Bell Telephone" in center, 7" d. ...................................... **83.00**

**Throat lozenges,** "Sucrets," color lithographed cardboard, a cartoon fireman standing pouring Sucrets down the flaming throat of a large man's face, reads across the top "For Speedy Throat Relief," ca. 1950, framed 33¼ x 43½" ............... **220.00**

**U.S. Mail,** carved, painted & gilded wood, the United States shield w/chamfered edge, painted red, white & blue & inscribed "U.S. Mail" in gilt lettering, late 19th c., 10" w., 10" h. ............................................. **2,012.00**

*Southeastern Utilities Sign*

**Utilities,** "Southeastern Utilities," porcelain, oval, green, yellow & black, reads around border "Southeastern Utilities - Service Company," surrounds image of power line & the countryside, 11" h., 16¼" w. (ILLUS.)... **258.00**

**Whiskey,** "Green River Whiskey,"
shows old black man w/mule &
reads "Green River Whiskey With
Out Regrets," numbered, 1919,
22 x 28".......................................... **425.00**

# SILHOUETTES

*These cut-out paper portraits in profile
were named after Etinne de Silhouette, Louis
XV's unpopular minister of finance and an
amateur profile cutter. As originally applied,
the term was synonymous with cheapness, or
anything reduced to its simplest state. These
substitutes for the more expensive oil
paintings or miniatures were popular from
about 1770 until 1850 when daguerreotype
images replaced the vogue. Silhouettes may be
either hollow-cut, with the head cut away
leaving the white paper frame for mounting
against a dark background, or the profile itself
may be cut from black paper and pasted to a
light background.*

**Bust Profile portrait of young boy,**
hollow-cut, has tousled hair & wear
frilled white stock, cut paper
mounted over black fabric, ca. 1810,
framed, oval 3 x 3¾".................... **$1,950.00**

**Bust Profile portrait of young boy,**
hollow-cut, wearing top hat, cut
paper over black stock, in brass die-
stamp frame, oval 3 x 3½"................ **575.00**

*Bust Profile Portrait of Two Girls*

**Bust profile portraits of two young
girls,** double hollow-cut, each
wearing a lace-like collar, in pierced
paper frame, framed, 19th c.
(ILLUS.) ............................................ **575.00**

*Full-length Portrait of Child*

**Full-length portrait of child,** hollow-
cut, penciled hair & in a pressed
brass frame, 19th c., 2⅝ x 3⅜"
(ILLUS.) ............................................ **460.00**

# SNUFF BOTTLES & BOXES

*The habit of taking snuff (powdered tobacco
meant for inhaling) began in 17th century
France and reached its peak during the 18th
century, spreading to England, elsewhere on
the Continent, and even to China, probably
introduced there by Spanish or Portuguese
traders. In Europe, tightly hinged porcelain or
metal boxes were considered desirable
containers to house the aromatic snuff.
Orientals favored bottles of porcelain or glass,
or carved of agate, ivory or jade. By the mid-
19th century the popularity of snuff declined.*

## BOTTLES

**Agate,** squatty rounded & flattened
form on a small footring, even tan
color w/a circular inclusion on one
side, China, ca. 1800-80, 2¼" h... **$1,150.00**

**Amber,** realistic piece of fruit w/furled
fingertip, of a deep translucent color,
19th c. (ILLUS. top next page)........ **1,207.00**

**Coral,** well carved w/a pair of *chilong*
scampering up the bottle on both
sides, color of rich tones w/streaks
of white, 2⅜" (ILLUS. bottom next
page) ............................................ **2,300.00**

*Amber Snuff Bottle*

*Overlay Glass Snuff Bottle*

*Coral Snuff Bottle*

**Gold-inlaid white jade,** squatty bulbous round form, decorated w/a wide band of Indian lotus blooms each issuing two smaller blooms, between simple lotus collars at the shoulder & base, the underside w/a four-character *Yongzheng* seal mark within a double square, all incised & infilled w/gold, fitted double square, fitted domed lapis lazuli cover, Moghul-style, China, 2¼" h............ **5,750.00**

**Inside-painted glass,** flattened rectangular form w/rounded corners, one side painted w/boys at play, a dedication on the reverse to Zi Shu & signed by Zhou Shang Young & w/a Shang seal, decorated by a Ma Shao Xuan, China ........................ **2,300.00**

**Overlay glass,** five-layer, flattened rectangular form w/rounded corners & tapering to a short neck, carved through the green, yellow, pink, blue & brown overlay to the clear ground, on one side w/a cat gazing up at two butterflies (*maodie*), a crane & chrysanthemum, the reverse w/a camellia in a bronze vessel, a flowering begonia & Mandarin oranges beneath a bat, one side w/a seal jixiang 'good fortune,' the other w/a crane, Yangzhou School, China, 1800-50 ........................................ **1,610.00**

**Overlay glass,** of elongated form, well-carved w/aquatic plants, bats & a fish in shades of blues, peaches, reds, on ovoid ring foot, ca. 1750-1820, 2¾" h. (ILLUS. above) ........ **2,300.00**

**Overlay glass,** elongated teardrop-form, white overlaid in dark blue & cut on one side w/a torrent of water rushing from the entrance of a fortified tower, the reverse w/a pearl floating on waves w/bats & clouds in the sky, ovoid foot, China, 3⅛" h. ... **1,495.00**

**Overlay glass,** ovoid form, amber body overlaid in dark red & carved in high-relief w/branching prunus spreading over the entire surface & rising from the base, roots forming the foot, China, ca. 1780-1850, 2⅜" ................................................ **1,380.00**

**Rock crystal,** flattened rounded form, the shoulders carved w/mock loose ring mask handles, w/an oblong

beaded foot & short cylindrical neck,
China, 2⅛" h. ............................... **1,285.00**

**Soapstone,** flattened spade shade,
the even brown ground well-carved
in fine relief w/a blossoming flower &
pair of butterflies, slightly concave
base, China, 1⅞" h. .......................... **690.00**

**White glass,** flattened round form,
carved on the edges w/mock mask &
ring handles, China, 19th c. ........... **1,092.00**

**Yellow carved glass,** large ovoid
form, boldly carved w/a frieze of
dragons, an upper border of tendrils
& lower border of lappets, China,
19th c., 3" h.................................... **1,610.00**

## BOXES

**Gold & enamel,** flattened & rounded
rectangular form, the top w/an oval
reserve decorated w/ships sailing in
a river, the sides & base decorated
w/a trellis design trimmed w/green
enamel, Bautte & Mynier, Geneva,
Switzerland, ca. 1825, 3⅛" ............ **3,450.00**

**Gold & enamel,** rectangular w/cut
corners, the top w/a fan-shaped
reserve painted w/a biblical scene
"The Women at the Well," signed
"Richter" & inscribed in French
"Village de Cana en Galilee," the
border of the cover enameled w/a
geometric leaftip design, the base
engine-turned, Geneva, Switzerland,
1810, 3½" l.................................... **8,280.00**

**Painted crystal,** decorated in color on
one side w/a portrait of the Empress
Dowager Cixi, on the other side w/a
brief account of her life, signed by
Wang Quan Guang, China 20th c. ... **920.00**

**Papier-mâché,** round, the cover w/a
transfer-printed allegorical scene of
two classical figures representing
Liberty & America flanking a
grouping of martial implements &
armor w/an oval shield inscribed
"Glory to the American Arms,"
inscribed along the bottom "America
Shows the World the Trophy of Her
Victories," early 19th c., 3½" d.
(small pit in center top) .................... **468.00**

# SODA FOUNTAIN COLLECTIBLES

*The neighborhood ice cream parlor and
drugstore fountain are pretty much a thing of*

the past as fast-food chains have sprung up
across the country. Memories of the slower-
paced lifestyle represented by the rapidly
disappearing local soda fountain have spurred
the interest of many collectors today.
Anything relating to the soda fountains of old
and the delicious concoctions they dispensed
are much sought-after.

## ICE CREAM SCOOPS

**"Clipper,"** size 20 ............................. **$95.00**
**"Gem,"** size 6, w/external spring ........ **160.00**
**"Gem,"** size 8, w/external spring ........ **110.00**
**"Hamilton Beach model 68,"** size
70, squeeze handle, stainless steel.... **65.00**
**"Indestructo model 3,"** size 10 ......... **145.00**
**"Q&E,"** size 10, cone-shaped............. **135.00**
**"Q&E,"** size 20, round ........................ **135.00**

# STATUARY

*Bronzes and other statuary, are
increasingly popular with today's collectors.
Particularly appealing are works by "Les
Animaliers," the 19th century French school of
sculptors who turned to animals for their
subject matter. These, together with figures in
the Art Deco and Art Nouveau taste, are
common in a wide price range.*

## BRONZES

*Bronze Bull*

**Chiparus, Demetre H.,** "The Secret,"
two kneeling figures in an intimate
conversational pose, one wearing a
long-sleeved belted garment
w/flowing skirt & ruffle at the neck,
the other w/a long-sleeved shirt
w/ruffled collar & diamond patterned
pants, their hands & faces carved in

ivory, the clothing painted in shades
of silver, copper, red & gold, on
shaped onyx base, inscribed
"Chiparus," ca. 1925 ................ **$28,750.00**

**Bonheur, Isidore,** "Bull," model of a
walking bull w/tail raised, top of base
signed "I Bonheur," Tiffany & Co.,
ca. 1900, 23" l., 15¼" h. (ILLUS.
bottom previous page) .................. **5,500.00**

## MARBLE

*Marble Bust of Woman*

**Bust of a woman,** shows a woman
w/a single long braid looking to the
side wearing a low-cut ruffled blouse,
on a scrolled base, signed "Moses
Ezekiel," damages (ILLUS.) ............ **2,760.00**

## OTHER

**Terra cotta,** allegorical figures
depicting the seasons, each partially
draped youth w/corresponding
attributes, integral circular bases,
late 19th c., weathered, some
cracking, 43" h., set of 4 (ILLUS.
of two, top next column) .............. **14,950.00**

**Terra cotta,** Bozzeto of Two River
Gods, a figure group w/an aged
river god w/a long beard & laurel
leaves woven through his hair
seated among water reeds, the
other younger bearded god grasping
at the naturalistic rock face as he
emerges from the water w/a dolphin
beneath him, the tail of the dolphin
curls up & around his back, in the

*Terra Cotta Figures*

manner of Lucas Faydherbe,
Flemish, late 17th c., 4' h.
(restorations) ............................ **23,000.00**

# STEIFF TOYS & DOLLS

*From a felt pincushion in the shape of an
elephant, a world-famous toy company
emerged. Margarete Steiff (1847-1909), a
polio victim as a child and confined to a
wheelchair, planned a career as a seamstress
and opened a shop in the family home.
However, her plans were dramatically
changed when she made the first stuffed
elephant in 1880. By 1886 she was producing
stuffed felt monkeys, donkeys, horses and
other animal forms. In 1893 an agent sold her
toys at the Leipzig Fair. This venture was so
successful that a catalog was printed and a
salesman hired, Margarete's nephews and
nieces became involved in the business,
assisting in its management and the design of
new items.*

*Through the years, the Steiff Company has
produced a varied line including felt or plush
animals, Teddy Bears, gnomes, elves, felt dolls
with celluloid heads, Kewpie dolls and even
radiator caps with animals or dolls attached as
decoration. Descendants of the original family
members continue to be active in the
management of the company still adhering to
Margarete's motto "For our children, the best
is just good enough."*

*Gypsy Steiff Doll*

**Doll,** gypsy man, wearing black hat blue jacket, red shirt w/sixteen Steiff buttons, a Steiff button in each ear, black pants & boots, 1908, 12" h. (ILLUS.) ...................................... **$2,300.00**

**Doll,** boy, felt w/black button eyes, blond mohair hair, wearing traditional German costume including black lederhosen, white shirt, beige jacket w/brown leather buttons, green button knapsack on his back w/souvenir lettering "Grus Aus Berchtesgarden," w/miniature shovel & hoe, early 1930s, 27" (metal button missing) ................... **1,035.00**

**Donkey:** "Grissy," dralon plush, black eyes & button in ear, ca. 1950s 20" h. ................................................ **253.00**

**Goat,** U.S. Navy mascot, plush, cream & blue coat....................................... **325.00**

**Llama,** button in ear, 6" h...................... **95.00**

**Snail:** "Nelly," green spotted snail w/black eyes & button, ca. 1950s, 6" l................................................... **253.00**

## TEDDY BEARS

**Teddy bear,** blond plush w/black boot button eyes, black stitched nose & mouth, swivel limbs, excelsior stuffed, wearing beige cotton overall, button in left ear, ca. 1910, 11½" (pads recovered, snout & mouth stitching very worn)........................... **345.00**

**Teddy bear,** blond plush w/black boot button eyes, stitched nose & mouth, swivel limbs, excelsior stuffed, felt pads, ca. 1906, 12" (lacks button, eyes slightly loose) ....................... **1,495.00**

**Teddy bear,** black boot button eyes, clipped elongated nose, brown horizontal stitched nose & claws, swivel head, jointed elongated limbs & cream pads, blank button, ca 1907, 13" ..................................... **1,840.00**

**Teddy bear,** gold mohair, black boot button eyes, brown stitched nose & mouth, swivel limbs, straw filled w/felt pads, blank metal button in left ear, ca. 1904, 13¼" (stuffing slipped in places, face & chest worn, small repair at left ankle)........................ **1,955.00**

**Teddy bear,** blond plush w/button eyes, stitched nose & mouth, swivel limbs, excelsior filled, felt pads, button in left ear, 18½" h. (pads repaired, muzzle worn) ................. **6,900.00**

**Teddy bear,** golden plush, large black button eyes, black vertically stitched nose w/four threads extending to mouth, swivel limbs w/felt pads, stitched claws, straw filled, button in left ear, ca. 1910-20, 19" h. (small hole in chest seam, small hole in pads)............................................. **6,900.00**

*White Steiff Bear*

**Teddy bear,** white mohair, black boot button eyes, brown stitched nose & claws, swivel head, elongated jointed limbs, humped back & cream pads, ca. 1907, 20" h. (ILLUS.) ..... **5,570.00**

**Teddy bear,** short blond plush, black boot button eyes, black stitched nose & mouth, excelsior stuffed body w/growler & back hump, jointed limbs, button in left ear, 28" h.

(original pads covered w/chamois leather, holes in hand pads, wear on nose stitching, old repair on left ankle) ............................................. **2,585.00**

**Teddy bear,** curly cinnamon mohair, black boot button eyes, elongated snout, jointed & elongated limbs, humped back & button in ear w/small portion of white tag remaining, ca. 1910, 30" h. (growler broken, pads recovered) ............................ **7,475.00**

# STEINS

*Anheuser Busch, Diesinger & Mettlach Steins*

**Anheuser Busch (Ceramarte) 'Senior Grande,'** early version 1½ liter (ILLUS. center) ............................. **$1,053.00**

**Character,** "Unhappy Radish," marked "Musterschutz" ..................... **425.00**

**Diesinger,** Model 810, dwarfs decoration (ILLUS. right) ................. **555.00**

**Enameled stein** w/silver base & four tapered enamel bands depicting classical scenes, Austria, 19th c. (ILLUS. top next column) ............. **18,000.00**

**Hauber & Reuther,** pottery, engraved dwarfs & frog party scene, domed pewter lid, ½ liter (ILLUS. right, bottom next page) ............................ **504.00**

**Mettlach,** No. 228, panels of figures in off white relief, two line German verse on each panel, light grey body, silver grapes & leaves in relief around base, 3¾" d., 7½" h. (ILLUS. bottom next column) ............................................. **335.00**

*Viennese Enameled Stein*

*Mettlach Stein*

**Mettlach,** No. 1725, etched scene w/lovers & man holding a stein, signed "Warth," inlaid lid, ¼ liter ....... **395.00**

**Mettlach,** No. 2093, etched panels of playing cards, inlaid pewter lid, ½ liter (ILLUS. center, top next page) ................................................ **847.00**

*Three Mettlach Steins*

**Mettlach,** No. 2103, man on barrel etched design, 1½ liter (ILLUS. left, w/Anheuser Busch stein) ................. **903.00**

**Mettlach,** No. 2582, etched scene of a jester performing on a table in front of a tavern, sized "Quidenus," inlaid pewter lid, ½ liter ............................ **633.00**

**Mettlach,** No. 3043, scene of knight in armor w/decorative shields including one w/the Munchen Child, inlaid pewter lid, ½ liter (ILLUS. above left).................................................. **1,980.00**

**Mettlach,** No. 3089, engraved scene of Diogenes, inlaid pewter lid, ½ liter (ILLUS. above right) ........................ **869.00**

*Regimental and Hauber & Reuther Steins*

**Regimental,** No. 3, Foot Artillary, scenes of Mainz, full-figure canon finial on domed pewter lid, 1908-10, 1½ liter (ILLUS. left)........................ **1,108.00**

**Regimental,** No. 11, Ulan, Saarburg, armed soldiers on horses, domed pewter lid w/figural finial, 1906-09, ½ liter .............................................. **847.00**

# STEREOSCOPES & STEREO VIEWS

*Hand stereoscope viewers with an adjustable slide may be found at $30.00 to $50.00 each in good condition. Elaborate table models are priced much higher. Prices of view cards depend on the subject material and range from less than $1.00 to $10.00 or more.*

## STEREO VIEWS
**Alaska,** shows gold miners & dog team................................................. **$15.00**

**Colorado,** views of Ute Indian & family ................................................. **25.00**

**Fall River,** Massachusetts business views.................................................. **10.00**

**Niagara Falls,** various scenes, ca. 1870, group of 6............................ **23.00**

**Passion Play,** hand-colored photos, ca. 1900, group of 11......................... **45.00**

**Sears, Roebuck and Co.,** scenes of the store interior, original box, as in 1908 catalog, set of 50 ..................... **125.00**

**Teddy Roosevelt at Noblesville** ......... **50.00**

## STEREOSCOPES
**Stereo viewer,** aluminum, 1900, hand held, ca. 1900 ................................... **48.00**

Stereo viewer, Keystone, w/400 photographic cards in original "book bindings" holders, ca. 1895-1910 ..... 950.00

Stereoscope, Underwood & Underwood, metal, folding-type .......... 95.00

# STOVES

*The thought of a family gathered companionably around the parlor stove on a cold winter's evening, or of an apple pie baking in the wood-burning cookstove, brings to some a longing for the "good old days." On a more practical note, many people turned to wood-burning stoves during the 1970s eneregy crisis when they discovered wood was plentiful and by far cheaper than commercial fuels. Aside from the primary function, a handsome old parlor stove adds a distinctive touch with its ornate design and an old cookstove can turn a kitchen into a real family room. Whatever the reason, there has been a renewed interest in old stoves of all types.*

## PARLOR STOVES

Base burner, Victor Base Burner by Rathbone, Sard & Co., Albany, New York, 1892, complete, unrestored rusty condition ............................... $350.00

Complete, fully restored................ 2,500.00

*Bodie 1910 Cannon Stove*

Cannon stove, 1910 Bodie, James Graham Mfg. Co., Newark, California, commonly known as "potbelly" stove, intended for offices, small workshops & other non-domestic installations, complete, fully restored (ILLUS. bottom previous column).... 100.00 to 500.00

*Clematis Cottage Stove*

*Worthy Stewart Stove*

Cottage stove, 1886 Clematis Cottage Parlor Stove, Fuller & Warren Co., Troy, New York, all cast iron w/decorations & mica windows complete, unrestored (ILLUS. top) ... 200.00

Complete, restored..... 2,000.00 to 3,500.00

Cylinder stove, 1915 Worthy Stewart Cylinder Stove, Fuller & Warren Co., Troy, New York, plain-style, complete, unrestored (ILLUS. bottom) .............. 100.00

Complete, restored..... 1,200.00 to 3,000.00

**Gas heater,** 1905 Estate Triple Effect, Estate Stove Co., Hamilton, Ohio, mica windows in bottom section in front, complete, unrestored rusty condition .......................................... **100.00**

Complete, restored .......................... **750.00**

*Estate Oak Stove*

**Oak stove,** 1905 Estate Oak K, Estate Stove Co., Hamilton Stove Co., Hamilton, Ohio, cast-iron jacket & rich decorations, optional mica door makes it more valuable & desirable, complete, undamaged original condition (ILLUS.)............................. **450.00**

Complete, fully restored................ **4,000.00**

*Sterling Oval Airtight*

**Oval Airtight,** 1934 Sterling, The Huenefeld Co., Cincinnati, Ohio, sheet metal (ILLUS.)........................... **35.00**

## KITCHEN RANGES

**Box stove,** 1861 The Shield, John F. Rathbone, Albany, New York, undesirable, complete, good original condition.......................... **225.00 to 700.00**

**Cook stove,** 1956 Success Model 7, Southern Steel & Stove Co., Richmond, Virginia, complete, good original condition.............................. **100.00**

**Gas range,** 1925 Clark Jewel, George M. Clark Co. (division of American Stove Co.), Chicago, Illinois, four-burner, single oven, standard family size, demand has increased lately, excellent condition ......................... **425.00 to 800.00**

**Wood burning range,** 1888 Dockash Range, "Z" series, Scranton Stove Works, Scranton, Pennsylvania, highly decorative, piano base, reservoir & combination high closet, complete, unrestored rusty condition .......................... **500.00 to 1,500.00**

Complete, fully restored................ **5,000.00**

## LAUNDRY STOVES

*Magnet Model 18 Laundry Stove*

**Magnet stove,** Model 18, 1939 Hardwick Stove Co., Cleveland, Tennessee, complete, original condition (ILLUS.) ............. **25.00 to 100.00**

# TEXTILES

## COVERLETS

**Jacquard,** single weave, one-piece, rows of large leaf & blossom medallions alternating w/rows of small round floral medallions within a leafy tree border, corners marked "Made by R. Peter in Heidelberg for _____ AD 1843," red & white, applied fringe, 68 x 79" (minor overall wear) .................................. **$330.00**

**Jacquard,** single weave, one-piece, rows of four-rose medallions alternating w/a band of four-point pine tree devices all within a continuous vintage border, corners marked "Manufactured expressly for _____ 1858" & an eagle w/"Chesterfield, Ohio, 1858," navy blue & natural white, 70 x 90" (minor stains) ............................................. **495.00**

*Coverlet with Eagles*

**Jacquard,** single weave, one-piece, a large central floral ring medallion w/star within a wide floral & scroll cartouche framed by spread-winged eagles in the spandrels all within a running rose & leaf border w/swirled leaf cluster corners, signed on edge "Philip Allabach," red & white, minor stains & soiling, 72 x 79" (ILLUS.) .... **330.00**

**Jacquard,** single weave, one-piece, a large round central floral medallion within a rectangular cross-form reserve filled w/flowers, vines & flowerpots all within a forming border of small light & dark triangles w/American eagle blocks at each corner, column & urn & long cartouche side borders & leafy scrolls & flowers end borders, edge signed "Henry Gabriel, Allentown," navy blue, green, red & natural white, 74 x 90" (overall wear, no fringe) ............................................. **358.00**

**Jacquard,** single weave, one-piece, a large central starburst design framed by circular stylized leafy scroll & blossom bands, triangular corner blocks w/pairs of cornucopia, leaf sprig & urns & columns on three borders, w/fringe, red, blue, green & natural white, 77 x 84" (some stains, minor wear)...................................... **165.00**

**Jacquard,** single weave, one-piece, a large central star medallion framed by four large spread-winged eagles w/shields & a tight leafy scroll border & thick blossom outer border, red, gold, olive green & natural white, w/fringe, 80 x 84" ............................. **330.00**

**Jacquard,** single weave, one-piece, a center star within a ring of small diamonds within a large starburst medallion framed by tiny stars & a continuous rose vine border w/spread-winged American eagles in each corner, side borders of leafy scrolls & harps & end borders of urns & cornucopias, signed along edge "Made by Wm Ney, Myerstown, N. Lebanon Co Pa.," green, red, gold & natural white, 82" sq...................... **770.00**

*Starburst & Eagles Coverlet*

**Jacquard,** single weave, one-piece, a double star in the center within a ring of leaves & small harps all within a large starburst medallion surrounded by a band of small stars & w/large spread-winged American eagles in each corner, the side borders w/leafy scrolls & harps, the end borders w/urns & cornucopias, signed along edge "Made by Wm Ney, Myerstown,

N. Lebanon Co Pa," green, red, gold & natural white alternating stripes, 82" sq. (ILLUS. bottom previous page) ................................................ **1,045.00**

**Jacquard,** single weave, one-piece, rows of large four-leaf cross-form cluster medallions alternating w/small scrolled leaf cross-form clusters, wide border of tiered leaf clusters & blooming trees, corner blocks labeled "Made by C. Fehr for _____ 1842," black, tomato red, deep gold & natural white, 92 x 98" (stains, fringe wear) ......................... **303.00**

**Jacquard,** single weave, two-piece, rows of starbursts in round medallions all within a continuos rooster border, corners labeled "J. Heeter, Scipio township, Seneca County, Ohio," navy blue & white, 64 x 90" (one border spot of moth damage, minor fringe loss) .............. **495.00**

*Dated 1846 Coverlet*

**Jacquard,** single weave, two-piece, rows of scalloped medallions around floral rings centering stars alternating w/four-leaf clusters, pairs of birds & blossoms border, corners signed "William Fasig, Richland County, Ohio 1846," navy blue & white, seams resewn, end turned & stitched, minor fringe loss, 66 x 88" (ILLUS.).............. **660.00**

**Jacquard,** single weave, two-piece, rows of star medallions alternating w/four-lobed medallions all within a continuous vintage border, corners labeled "W. in Mt. Vernon, Knox County, Ohio by Jacob and Michael Ardner 1852," navy blue & white, 70 x 79"........................................... **578.00**

**Jacquard,** single weave, two-piece, rows of scalloped medallions w/floral rings around a central star alternating w/four-leaf clusters, rooster & bird in tree borders, corners w/eagles & signed "F. Yearous, Loudonville, Ohio 1850," navy blue, teal blue, red & white, minor edge & fringe wear, 71 x 85" ........................................... **550.00**

**Jacquard,** single weave, two-piece, rows of four-rose clusters alternating w/rows of small scalloped blossomheads, vintage border, corner blocks signed "Emanuel Ettinger Aronsburg, 1840," navy blue, teal blue, tomato red & natural white, 73 x 86" (some overall wear & stains) ............................................... **358.00**

**Jacquard,** single weave, two-piece, rows of four-rose clusters alternating w/large scalloped flowerheads & small pairs of stars, pairs of birds & flowering tree borders, corner blocks signed "Gabriel Rauser, Delaware County, Ohio 1843," alternating stripes of blue, red & natural white, 76 x 93" (overall wear & stains, minor fringe loss) ............................ **385.00**

**Jacquard,** single weave, two-piece, rows of large round floral medallions alternating w/scrolling leaf & blossom medallions, large roses in border, turkey in tree corner blocks signed "Manufactured by Henry Oberly, Womelsdorf, Penna.," navy blue, sage green, deep red & natural white, 76 x 94" (some minor stains, wear w/fringe loss in some spots) .. **1,100.00**

**Jacquard,** single weave, two-piece, rows of four-lobed stylized thistle & tulip clusters alternating w/rows of leafy scroll medallions, undulating leafy band border & narrow star outer border band, corners labeled "Jacob Daron, 1853, Mary," red, navy blue, olive green & natural white, 82 x 88" (end fringe wear) ...... **303.00**

**Jacquard,** single weave, two-piece, rows of starbursts alternating w/four-blossom & star medallions, pairs of birds & flowering tree borders, corner blocks labeled "Made by C. Yordy, Lampeter Square for Fanny Barr 1838," royal blue, tomato red, salmon red, sage green & natural white, 83 x 92" (small stains at edge, worn chintz binding)......................... **440.00**

**Jacquard,** double woven, two-piece, large floral medallions within octagons alternating w/smaller flowerheads within a continuous trumpet flower & vine border, corners dated "1853," navy blue & white, 76 x 85" (minor wear & stains, top edge turned & stitched) ............. **275.00**

**Lindsey-woolsey,** composed of several narrow navy blue panels quilted w/floral sprays within diamond latticework, the reverse in a bluish brown worsted fabric, probably New England, late 18th - early 19th c., 89 x 96" (some fabric loss, repairs) ................................. **1,380.00**

**Lindsey-woolsey,** composed of narrow panels sewn together of pink fabric elaborately quilted w/baskets of flowers & scrolling vines, the reverse in a moss green worsted fabric, retains most of the original glazing, probably New England, late 18th - early 19th c., 96 x 100" (some fabric loss, staining) ...................... **1,725.00**

**Overshot,** one-piece, all wool, Snowflake & Pine Tree patt., navy blue, red & white, 86 x 103" ............. **248.00**

**Overshot,** two-piece, optic blocks of small circles alternating w/geometric squares, navy blue, tomato red & natural white, 66 x 97" (minor wear)... **165.00**

## LINENS & NEEDLEWORK

**Bed cover,** trapunto & crewel embroidery, the center panel finely trapunto-stitched w/scrolling leafage w/pendent blossoms on a diagonal ground, surrounded by a crewel-embroidered border worked in tones of blue, green, red, yellow & grey w/scrolling flowers, fruit leaves & birds, the outer border cut for a tester bedstead, composed of pieced cotton calico patches arranged in a 'star' pattern on a creamy white ground, probably New England, late 18th c., 93 x 100" (staining, wear, some fabric loss) .. **3,450.00**

**Berlin work,** motto reads "The Lord Will Provide," rich brown tones w/sheaves of wheat, Victorian ......... **135.00**

**Coverlet,** lindsey-woolsey, two-piece, red & black overall plaid w/red & blue edge panel, solid tomato red backing, unlined, 19th c., 74 x 92" (some wear & moth damage, fringe incomplete) ................................... **440.00**

**Coverlet,** crewel-embroidered cotton flax, composed of several long

panels w/seven wide bands of scrolling, blossoming & fruiting vines embroidered in blue on natural white, attributed to Elizabeth Hallack, Matticut, Long Island, New York, ca. 1749, 87 x 95" (some staining & loss, one panel very discolored) ..................................... **1,955.00**

**Handkerchief,** commemorative, copper-printed, printed in tones of red, white & black, the center w/various naval engagements including the "Brilliant Naval Victory On Lake Erie, Sept. 10, 1813" & the "Glorious Victory on lake Champlain, Sept. 15, 1814," interspersed w/the portraits of Perry & Mac Donnough & other patriotic symbols, within a border of American flags, compasses, anchors & seashells, American-made, early 19th c., 28½ x 34¾" (some discoloration) .. **2,300.00**

**Horse blankets,** needlework, the first depicting a standing white horse w/a gold saddle & reins on a deep red ground, within a square panel surrounded by diamonds, the border w/a blossoming vine on a black ground & a red fringed edge, lined, signed "Jacob Weber - 1871," the second depicting a prancing brown horse wearing a maroon saddle & reins on a cream ground, within a square panel of alternating peach & black bands, the border w/a band of geometric decoration on a red ground & a beige & white fringed edge, Victorian, 68" sq. & 76 x 80", 2 pcs. ............................................. **2,070.00**

**Mattress cover,** homespun linen, overall tiny blue, red & white plaid design w/a white backing, machine- and hand-sewn, 56 x 60" (wear, repair, some fading)......................... **138.00**

**Mattress cover,** homespun linen, overall blue & white check design, machine-sewn, 19th c., 56 x 75"....... **220.00**

**Pillow tops,** Crazy quilt-style, composed of odd-shaped patches of velvet, silk, etc., w/intricate embroidery, one w/a Stevengraph-type woven silk ribbon from the Cincinnati Industrial Exposition of 1880, one w/pillow backing, one without backing, late 19th c., 18½ x 19¼", pr. ............................. **121.00**

**Sewing pocket,** crewel-embroidered linen, the long pocket made up of six slitted compartments, embroidered

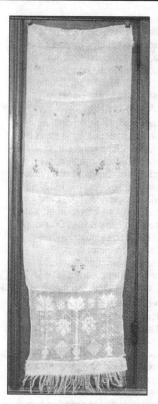

*Early Show Towel*

w/brightly colored figures of perched birds, paired birds & flowering trees, the figure of a young woman holding an umbrella in one hand & a reticule in the other & an angle beneath the inscription "Fear God," the edges trimmed in purple silk, probably Pennsylvania, dated 1812, 4" w., 24" l............................................. **1,380.00**

**Show towel,** homespun linen, embroidered w/clusters of stylized flowers & signed "A.F. 1832," fringe end bands & a cut-work band at one end, 17 x 53" (wear, fading, small holes) ................................................ **110.00**

**Show towel,** homespun linen, a cut-work wide lace panel w/stylized flowers at one end, red & blue embroidery of scattered stylized birds & flowers, signed "Lidia Stumb 1821," wear, some embroidery incomplete, 17 x 54" (ILLUS. top previous column) .............................. **110.00**

**Show towel,** homespun cotton, panels of silk & wool embroidery w/birds, flowers & the signature "Ann Hess 1841," in good colors of red, olive green, brown & gold, knitted fringe, Pennsylvania, mounted on cloth-covered board, 17½ x 67" (wear, repairs, minor stains, some damage to wool thread).................... **160.00**

**Tablecloth,** homespun linen, overall tiny gold & white check pattern, hand-hemmed, 19th c., 40 x 68"....... **220.00**

**Tablecloths,** damask linen, floral designs in white & natural grey, 60 x 76", pr. (minor stains)................. **99.00**

**Table runner,** Arts & Crafts-style, embroidered w/two little girls sitting at a table across from a bouquet of sunflowers & drinking large bowls of coffee, w/a motto at the bottom extolling the virtues of coffee drinking, Sweden, early 20th c., 26 x 56" ........ **468.00**

**Valance,** worked polychrome yarns on linen, shows birds, animals & flowering trees in a hilly landscape, probably Boston area, last half of 18th c., areas of loss (ILLUS. below) .................... **6,900.00**

*Early Crewel Valance*

*Italian Wall Hanging*

**Wall hanging,** rectangular panel w/deeply scalloped bottom w/a central point, three large tassels at the bottom, decorated w/gold & silver thread couchwork & multicolored crewelwork in a central design of a large bouquet of flowers & leaves within a scrolled cartouche & latticework border, fine fringe edging, Italy, 18th c., losses, 26 x 32" (ILLUS.) .............................. **690.00**

**Wall hangings,** crewelwork, each worked in multicolored fabric & depicting an ornate flowering tree w/insects & animals filling the panel, minor staining, Europe, 19th c., 5' 10" x 8", set of 4 ......................... **3,335.00**

## NEEDLEWORK PICTURES

**Needlework embroidery,** all-wool, a large bouquet of stylized varied flowers & leaves w/a bird perched in the center, worked in deep colors of red, pink, green, gold, white & blue on a deep charcoal black ground, w/a presentation letter dated 1888 claiming the piece to be 18th c., in a beveled grained wood frame, 14½ x 18½" (wear, stains, some damage) ...................................... **2,310.00**

**Needlework embroidery & watercolor memorial picture,** depicts a young woman leaning against a large urn-topped monument & mourning beneath a large weeping willow tree, water &

other trees in the background, worked in silk threads, the monument inscribed "Simeon Spalding Obt. April 6, 1785 Philip Spalding Obt. Oct. 5 1799, AE 37," within an eglomisé black & gold mat signed along the bottom "Wrought by Rebecca Warren..." & w/gilt points around the oval center opening & gilt leaf sprigs in the corners, in a wooden frame, early 19th c., 14 x 16½" (minor losses to ground) ......................... **2,185.00**

*Memorial Needlework Picture*

**Needlework embroidery & watercolor memorial picture,** depicts woman standing on island in front of monument below a weeping willow, monument inscribed "sacred to the memory of Mrs. Catherine Sayer who died April 17th 1873, aged 33 and her infant son...," on silk ground, areas of retouch, 20 x 22" (ILLUS.) ........................... **1,035.00**

**Needlework embroidery on black ground,** worked in red, green, blue, yellow & ivory wool threads depicting a variety of flowers centering a floral & foliage ring, American-made, 19th c., 17" sq. .............................. **1,093.00**

**Needlework embroidery on blue wool,** depicting a fully-rigged three-masted sailing vessel, worked in white & gold & rose silk, signed "A. Tucker" on port side of vessel, probably New England, 19th c., some fading & fabric loss, 17⅝" w., 13¾" h. (ILLUS. top next page) ........ **862.00**

*Ship Needlework Picture*

**Needlework embroidery on homespun linen,** a vining floral border framing floral sprigs & a central tree in urn w/two facing perched birds, signed "Leetitia Dubre 1811," worked in silk threads in pastel blues, greens, yellows, brown, tan & black, framed, 19¼" w., 16" h. (stains) .................................. **495.00**

**Needlework embroidery on silk,** depicting a river scene w/cows grazing in the foreground, a sailboat in the middle ground & red, yellow & blue-painted buildings in the background, all enclosed in meandering floral border, worked in brown, beige, green, blue, yellow & red threads, possibly by Louisa Gladding, Newport, Rhode Island, ca. 1812, 18 x 20½" (ILLUS. bottom) ........................................... **10,925.00**

**Needlework embroidery on silk,** a scene depicting the Annunciation of the Virgin worked in ivory, green, blue & red silk threads in a variety of stitches on a painted silk ground, black & gilt eglomisé border, American or English, ca. 1820, 20⅓ x 25" ......................................... **403.00**

## QUILTS

*Eagle & Flowers Quilt*

**Appliquéd Eagle & Flowers patt.,** a spread-winged eagle facing left in the center within an almond-shaped

*Rare Needlework Picture*

reserve framed w/curving flower & leaf sprigs, a wide running floral vine border, in teal blue, yellow calico & solid red, red backing, minor stains, 80 x 94" (ILLUS. right column previous page) .................................. **550.00**

**Appliquéd Friendly Cow patt.,** composed of red, brown, green, ochre & beige patches w/a scene of a cow beside an apple tree & scattered blossoms between two fence borders all on a white cotton ground, sewn inscription under the cow from Robert Louis Stevenson's poem "The Friendly Cow," the reverse composed of red, ochre, green, purple & blue flannel & cotton printed & solid patches, ca. 1928, 64 x 76½" ...................................... **1,610.00**

**Appliquéd Oak Leaf & Floral Spray patt.,** composed of navy blue, orange & terra cotta patched arranged as nine blocks of oak leaves & flowers, white cotton ground w/feather & cube quilting, Nancy Ogden Clearfield, Ferguson Township, Pennsylvania, June 1878, 92" sq. ............................................ **1,840.00**

**Appliquéd Oak Leaf variation patt.,** composed of four squares, each square w/four yellow oak leaves on a white ground within a yellow inner border & white outer border, central field w/diamond & rope quilting, by Laura Bertha Newman Troutman, Freeburg, Pennsylvania, ca. 1930, 81 x 81½" ......................................... **345.00**

**Appliquéd Primitive Garden patt.,** composed of thirty-six blocks each framing a different stylized flower, fruit or leaf sprig, surrounded by a border of single leaves & a running vine, in bluish green, brown, lime yellow, rose & peach, probably New Jersey, 19th c., 89 x 94½" (fading, staining, some discoloration) ........... **460.00**

**Appliquéd Rose of Sharon patt.,** composed of nine large wreath blocks alternating w/plain quilted blocks, the design composed of red, green & yellow printed & solid calico patches, the white cotton background w/diamond point, feather & flowerhead quilting, patches sewn to the backing w/buttonhole stitching, probably Pennsylvania, mid-19th c., 80" sq. (some discoloration & stain) ............ **690.00**

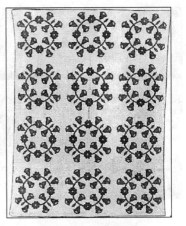

*Rose Wreath Quilt*

**Appliquéd Rose Wreath patt.,** composed of red, green & yellow cotton in twelve blocks w/scalloped & princess feather quilting, the whole bound in green & red cotton, inscribed "A" in corner, probably Pennsylvania, mid-19th c., 97 x 98" (ILLUS.) ......................................... **1,150.00**

**Appliquéd Tulip patt.,** four large tulip clusters pointing inward from a square frame within an undulating ribbon border w/a small tulip in each outer corner, deep yellows, goldenrod & green on a finely quilted white ground, 79" sq. (very minor stains) .................. **935.00**

*Tulip & Vine Quilt*

**Appliquéd Tulip & Vine patt.,** composed of green, yellow & red patches, the white cotton field heightened w/diagonal line quilting, 19th c., some fading & staining, 84 x 88" (ILLUS.) ............................... **575.00**

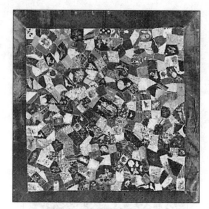

*Victorian Crazy Quilt*

**Crazy quilt,** composed of brightly colored silk, velvet & satin patches w/embroidered, printed & painted decoration, including figures, flowers, birds, animals & trains within a wide royal blue velvet border, some staining, late 19th c., 68" sq. (ILLUS.) ............................... **977.00**

**Crazy quilt,** appliquéd & embroidered, worked in various green, red, black, yellow, plum, taupe, brown & grey fabrics, several blocks w/floral embroidery, the whole bound in pink cotton, late 19th c., 95" sq. ............... **403.00**

**Crib-size,** appliquéd Album quilt., composed of lavender, green, red, yellow, blue & pink-printed & solid patches arranged in forty-five squares each w/a different design including flowers, an American flag, a Union Jack, pinwheels, crosses & other geometric designs, against a white cotton ground w/diagonal line quilting, 20th c., 49 x 83½" (very minor staining) ................................. **805.00**

**Crib-size,** pieced Irish Chain patt., composed of navy blue & white patches, blue narrow binding, 34 x 47" (some wear & edge damage) .......................................... **303.00**

**Crib-size,** pieced Irish Chain variation patt., composed of plain cotton patches in blue, lavender & green on a blue ground w/blue cotton border & binding, the central field w/tulip, heart & channel quilting & the border w/rope quilting, probably Pennsylvania, early 20th c., 33½ x 50¾" ............................. **403.00**

**Pieced Album quilt,** composed of yellow, red & green solid & printed calico patches arranged in twelve stars alternating w/solid white squares, most w/signatures in ink, the field heightened w/shell, floral, concentric circles & heart quilting, Pennsylvania or Virginia, ca. 1850, 79 x 102" ...................................... **1,265.00**

*Rare Baltimore Album Quilt*

**Pieced Baltimore Album quilt,** composed of red, green, yellow & blue calico & solid fabrics arranged in twenty-five blocks, the center w/a spread winged American eagle & flag, several squares signed & dated in ink, the whole heightened w/feather & diagonal line quilting, dated "March 4, 1841," 96 x 97" (ILLUS.) ......................................... **5,462.00**

**Pieced Bird-in-Flight patt.,** composed of pink, blue, green, brown, yellow, purple & brown-printed patches within a wide green calico border w/rope quilting, ca. 1900, 76" sq. ............... **1,035.00**

**Pieced Blazing Star patt.,** composed of brightly colored red, ochre, green & white printed & solid calico patches, the large central star surrounded by clusters of buds, the border w/trailing vines, overall shell quilting, Ohio, late 19th - early 20th c., 90 x 96" (some staining) ......................................... **1,610.00**

**Pieced Bow Tie patt.,** composed of dotted navy blue & white blocks, machine-sewn blue binding, 70 x 88" ............................................. **275.00**

**Pieced Diamond-in-Square patt.,** the red diamond w/eight-point star quilting surrounded by a feathered wreath & tea cup stitching w/indigo blue spandrels w/diamond stitching surrounded by a thin inner border w/pumpkin seed & diamond stitching & red corner blocks, the indigo blue outer border w/feather stitching & red corner blocks, Amish, Lancaster County, Pennsylvania, 1910-30, 77¾ x 78½"................................... **2,185.00**

**Pieced Double Irish Chain patt.,** composed of dotted blue & white blocks, hand-quilted feather wreaths & floral scroll borders, penciled pattern intact, some machine work in piecing, 72 x 84" ............................. **220.00**

*Drunkard's Path Quilt*

**Pieced Drunkard's Path patt.,** composed of red & white calico blocks creating a pinwheel design, minor staining, 75½ x 79½" (ILLUS.) ............. **517.00**

**Pieced Drunkard's Path patt.,** composed of navy blue dotted print & white patches, within a wide blue border band, 76" sq. (minor overall & edge wear, some light stains) ........... **330.00**

**Pieced Flower Basket patt.,** composed of navy blue & white printed & solid calico patches mounted on a white cotton background w/diagonal line & feathered wreath quilting, probably Pennsylvania, mid-19th c., 76 x 78" (some minor fading) ......................... **920.00**

**Pieced Flower Basket with Blossom patt.,** composed of red, white & green cotton patches, in a white cotton field w/feather wreath & diagonal line quilting, initialed "M.E.S." in cross stitching on the backing, probably Pennsylvania, mid-19th c., 92" sq. .......................... **805.00**

**Pieced historical quilt,** composed of red, white & blue fabric, at center the Colonies flag, the United States flag & the Confederate flag surrounded by twenty-eight embroidered historical vignettes, inscribed on the verso "Made 1931 By Mrs. Alice Mahoney, Salmon, Idaho," the field heightened w/diamond & flowerhead quilting, 76 x 90" (some minor discoloration) ............................... **3,450.00**

**Pieced Irish Chain patt.,** composed of slate blue, red & white cotton patches, the background w/cube & diagonal quilting, ca. 1890, 72 x 84" (some fading & discoloration) ........... **575.00**

*Joseph's Coat Quilt*

**Pieced Joseph's Coat patt.,** composed of orange, yellow, green, blue, brown, black, red & pink cotton strips enclosed by a similar striped border, Pennsylvania, late 19th - 20th c., 74½ x 77½" (ILLUS.) ........ **1,725.00**

**Pieced Lone Star patt.,** composed of lavender, orange, salmon, pink, purple, teal, green, plum, navy & yellow plain & satin woven cottons a multicolor star on a navy ground enclosed by a yellow inner border & navy outer border w/slate blue binding, the central field worked in diamond & princess feather quilting, w/tulip quilted inner border & ocean waves quilted outer border, Amish, Indiana, ca. 1931, 84" sq. .............. **1,380.00**

**Pieced Mariner's Compass patt.,** composed of blue, yellow, green, red & pink-printed calico patches, the borders w/scrolling & blossoming vines, 19th c., 83 x 99" (some discoloration, patches on reverse) .. **1,495.00**

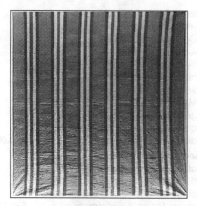

*Split Bar Quilt*

**Pieced Ocean Waves patt.,** composed of navy blue print & white small triangular blocks forming the design, within a wavy band border, well quilted ground, 70 x 80" (some fading, minor wear) ........................... **275.00**

**Pieced Ohio Star patt.,** composed of star blocks of multicolored fabrics w/appliquéd stylized flowers on five of the stars, navy blue ground w/gold floral print, initials & date "1856" worked in the quilting, Pennsylvania, 75 x 76" (stains, some color bleeding) .......................................... **715.00**

**Pieced Rainbow patt.,** composed of brightly colored green, blue, orange & brown patches forming long stripes of color, background diagonal line & cable quilting, probably Pennsylvania, ca. 1859, 70 x 84" ..... **747.00**

**Pieced Rob Peter, Pay Paul patt.,** composed of red & white patches, white ground w/cube quilting, embroidered labels "Bea 1909, 13," & "Alice 61, 1909," 72 x 82" .............. **242.00**

**Pieced Split Bar patt.,** composed of brightly colored red, yellow, green & pink strips, the field heightened w/cable & line stitching, probably Mennonite, Pennsylvania, ca. 1880, 80 x 93" (ILLUS. above) ................... **805.00**

**Pieced Star patt.,** calico & cotton composed of blue, brown, pink, orange & white printed & solid calico patches arranged in a Star patt., mounted on a white cotton ground heightened w/wreath feather & line quilting, probably Pennsylvania, mid-19th c., 80 x 88" (some stains & minor discoloration) ......................... **632.00**

**Pieced Star of Bethlehem patt.,** worked in reds, pinks, yellows & various prints radiating out from a red eight-point star, on a white & pink-printed calico ground w/small yellow & red eight-point stars arranged between points of the large star, the central field w/diamond & rope quilting, Pennsylvania, early 20th c., 81½ x 83¾" .......................... **403.00**

*Star of Bethlehem Quilt*

**Pieced Star of Bethlehem patt.,** composed of red, orange & green cotton patched in star pattern w/appliquéd flowers along border, 20th c., 90 x 91" (ILLUS.) ................ **690.00**

**Pieced Sunshine & Shadow patt.,** composed of pink, beige, red, black, blue, green, yellow & lavender patches w/a wide purple border decorated w/meandering floral vine quilting, Amish, probably Pennsylvania, 20th c., 73 x 80" ......... **1,035.00**

## SAMPLERS

**Alphabets & numerals** above a band of scrolling stylized rose vines over enclosed alphabet banding, above wrought identification "Jane Oliver - Mar 23 1848," over wrought verse "At all times he loved us - T'was for us he died - Yet still hes (sic) determined - That grace shall be tried," surrounded by stylized blossoming trees, urn & flower motifs, birds & a house, the whole enclosed by a meandering flowers & foliage, worked in green, red, blue, dark & light brown silk threads in a variety of stitches, American or English, 1848, 10¼" w. ..................... **805.00**

**Alphabets & numerals** in the upper half above a rectangular floral framed surrounding a basket of fruit flanked by stylized borders & above three arrow devices, inscribed "Pheby Ann Bush, Aged 8 years 1843," wool on homespun linen in shades of red, blue, green, brown & white, in bird's-eye maple ogee frame w/gilded liner, 19¼ x 20" (some wear, missing floss) .............. **358.00**

**Alphabets & numerals w/inscription,** meandering berried border enclosing three alphabetical registers above the wrought verse "This work I did let you see - What care my parents took of me - Aurelia Emeline Jones samplar (sic) - age 8 august 17 1826," over numeric register above large house flanked by birds & baskets of fruit, possibly mid-Atlantic, framed, 14¼ x 18½" .......... **805.00**

*Sampler with Inscription & Basket*

**Alphabets above inscription,** above three hearts & basket of flowers to the left of inscription & "wrought by Lucy Fletcher Aged 8 years" surrounded by leaves, the whole surrounded by meandering leaves & grapes, minor ground discoloration, 17 x 17" (ILLUS.) ........................... **3,100.00**

**Alphabets above inscription,** stylized flowers between alphabets above verse "Elizabeth Horton born February 1779 this sampler wrought the year 1784 Let Virtue be guide to thee," lower panel w/birds flanking a tree, framed 10½ x 13¾" (losses to edges, fading to verse) .................. **2,185.00**

**Alphabets above needlework bands,** all above a large central basket of flowers flanked by a pair of small weeping willow trees, one tree above the word "Weeping," the other above "Willow," all above the inscription "Boston, Mass 1816 Angeline Pratt, born Boston, Nov 26, 1804," all within a scalloped floral vine border, silk on homespun linen in shades of green, blue, red, yellow, black & white, excellent condition, in narrow old gilt frame, 19" w., 18¼" h. ............................ **4,620.00**

**Alphabets, numerals & pious verse** above further alphabets centering a two-story house, all within a meandering berried border, worked in colored silk threads on linen, inscribed by Prudence Spicer, Groton, Connecticut, dated 1829, framed, 14½ x 20" ........................ **1,495.00**

**Alphabets, numerals & pious verse** above crowns, birds & flowers, within geometric borders, inscribed "M.A. Watkins in her 9th years 1856," silk on homespun linen in blue, black, greens & white, new ogee bird's-eye maple frame, 12¼ x 21" (some thread fading) ....... **358.00**

*Rare Ornate Sampler*

**Pious verse & building in landscape,** floral border surrounds church flanked by two trees w/flowers & animals in front above "Mary Ann Boyer Feb 2th 1840 - Then should i fli (sic) far hence away - and leave this world sit - then should my lord put forth his and kindly take me in" flanked by two potted plants worked in shades of pink, blue, green & brown, framed, some needlework loss, small hole & light staining (ILLUS.) .................. **31,500.00**

**Vine & rose border surrounding birds & floral bouquets** above a pious verse flanked by potted flowers & mice above inscribed identification, above a brick house surrounded by trees, birds & deer, worked in green, brown, beige & pink threads in a variety of stitches including cross, inscribed "Remember thy Creator God - For him thy powers employ - Make him thy fear thy love thy hope - Thy confidence and joy" & "Hannah Chaoman - In the 12th year - of her age - 1827," American or English, 1827, 12¾ x 16½"............................ **1,265.00**

## TAPESTRIES

**Aubusson,** depicting wild birds & flowers in a wooded glade w/a castle in the background, France, mid-19th c., 41½ x 62½" (some fiber loss) ............................................ **2,300.00**

**Aubusson,** depicting a castle framed by two trees in the foreground, France, late 19th c., 5' 9" x 6' 9" .... **6,325.00**

**Aubusson,** panels depicting medieval warriors & slogans in Latin, France, 19th c., 5 x 8', pr. ........................... **3,575.00**

**Flemish,** depicting a couple sitting on a bench w/a cherub at their feet, surrounded by trees w/a castle in the background, 18th c., repairs, 5' 8" x 7' 3" (reduced).................... **4,125.00**

**Flemish,** depicting gardeners surrounded by trees, 18th c., 5' 2½" x 10' 2" (reduced)............... **8,050.00**

**Flemish,** a mythological scene w/a lush wooded landscape w/a man working at a baking oven in the background & ladies setting food on a table in the front left, children & a small dog in the center & a village in the distance, scrolling flowers & birds border, fabric losses & some fading, 17th - 18th c. .................... **9,775.00**

**Flemish pastoral tapestry,** a large woodland scene w/figures in the 18th century dress, a lady being pulled in a rope swing by two gentleman, 18th c., 7' x 8' 4" (possibly reduced, repairs) .......... **14,950.00**

**Flemish Renaissance-style tapestry,** a square center landscape scene w/figures in classical garb, a wide fruiting vine & figural border, 18th c., 9' 1" x 9' 3" (fiber loss, fading)............................................ **9,200.00**

*Flemish "Verdure" Tapestry*

**Flemish "verdure"-style,** in two parts, depicting a landscape w/large leafy trees in the foreground w/rabbits, a cockatoo & other birds, in primary tones of green & yellow, losses, 17th c., 5' 9" x 11' 3" (ILLUS.) ........................................ **4,888.00**

*French or Flemish Tapestry*

**French or Flemish "verdure"-style,** a chinoiserie landscape w/a large Chinese temple atop a craggy outcropping above an exotic lake scene w/a large wading bird & a long-tailed parrot in the tree above, mountains in the distance, minor losses, 18th c., 5' 11" x 6' 9" (ILLUS. bottom previous page)...... **7,475.00**

# THEOREMS

*During the 19th century, a popular pastime for some ladies was theorem painting, or stencil painting. Paint was allowed to penetrate through hollow-cut patterns placed on paper or cotton velvet. Still life compositions, such as bowls of fruit or vases of flowers were the favorite themes, but landscapes and religious scenes found favor among amateur artists who were limited in their ability and unable to do freehand painting. Today these colorful pictures, with their charming arrangements, are highly regarded by collectors*

**Basket of flowers,** watercolor & pen & ink on paper, a reticulated basket overflowing w/tulips, roses, irises & morning glories w/hummingbird & butterfly, original giltwood & gesso frame, American school, ca. 1830, 16½ x 19½".................................... **$575.00**

**Basket of fruit,** watercolor & stencils on white velvet, a blue & yellow basket filled w/pears, peaches & bananas w/a blue & green parrot perched on a grapevine above, basket sits on blue-frayed-type mat, appears to be original molded giltwood frame, American school, ca. 1830, 16½ x 18½".................... **3,450.00**

**Basket of fruit,** watercolor & stencils on white velvet, a woven basket w/eared handles filled w/orange & yellow peaches, pears, grapes & melons, in what appears to be the original ogee molded bird's-eye maple frame, American school, ca. 1830, 11½ x 15"...................... **2,530.00**

**Basket of fruit,** watercolor & tempera on paper, lattice work yellow & blue handled basket filled w/apples, peaches, pears, grapes, other fruit & leaves, matted & framed, American school, 19th c., 14½ x 17" .............. **2,645.00**

**Basket of fruit,** watercolor, stencils & pen & ink on white velvet, woven yellow double handled basket filled

w/grapes, peaches, red currants & melon, contemporary giltwood & gesso frame, American school, ca. 1830, 10½ x 14"....................... **2,300.00**

**Bouquet of flowers,** watercolor & pen & ink on paper, a bronze vase w/steer head finials filled w/a bouquet of summer blossoms & greens, stands on platform, original gilded gesso frame, American school, ca. 1840, 15½ x 22" ............ **862.00**

*Bowl of Fruit Theorem*

**Bowl of fruit,** oil on velvet, blue & white bowl on tray filled w/yellow fruit, framed, American school, 1820-30, 11¾ x 14½" (ILLUS.)...... **5,750.00**

**Bowl of fruit,** watercolor & tempera on paper, glass bowl filled w/melon, grapes, strawberries, pears & leaves, initialed in ornamental calligraphy, matted & framed, American school, 19th c., 10⅞ x 13⅞"....................... **2,070.00**

**Bowl of fruit,** watercolor on velvet, a footed blue compote filled w/yellow peaches, red cherries, blue grapes & greens, in what appears to be the original molded giltwood frame, American school, ca. 1830, 17 x 20"........................................ **2,875.00**

*Compote of fruit*

**Compote of fruit,** watercolor on
paper, a white footed compote
w/plums, pears, peaches & grapes,
American school, 19th c.,
13¼ x 17¼" (ILLUS. bottom
previous page) .............................. **2,530.00**

**Goddess of Liberty** offering
sustenance to the American Eagle,
watercolor & pen & ink on white
velvet, appears to be the original
giltwood & gesso frame, American
school, ca. 1830, 16½ x 20" .......... **1,035.00**

**Pineapple,** melons, pears & grapes &
leaves, a still life watercolor & pen &
ink on white velvet, pineapple,
grapes & melon slanted sideways on
top of other fruit, original black &
gold painted corner block frame,
American school, ca. 1830,
18½ x 23".......................................... **805.00**

**Tray of fruit,** watercolor, stencils & pen
& ink on white velvet, watermelons,
grapes, pears & berries on
rectangular tray, framed, American
school, ca. 1830, 18 x 23½" ............ **3,105.00**

*Village of Dreams Theorem*

**Village of dreams,** watercolor,
pencil & stencils on paper, village
scene w/buildings & trees, a horse
& a rooster under a large tree,
American school, 19th c., 7¾ x 9⅝"
(ILLUS.) ...................................... **1,265.00**

**Young lady,** watercolor on white
velvet, lady wearing a white gown &
seated under a tree in a landscape,
black & gold painted frame w/split-
banister sides & corner blocks,
American school, ca. 1825,
8½ x 10⅝" (ILLUS. top next
column) ............................................ **747.00**

*Young Lady Theorem*

# TOBACCIANA

*Although the smoking of cigarettes, cigars
& pipes is controversial today, the artifacts of
smoking related items—pipes, cigar & tobacco
humidors, cigar & cigarette lighters and, of
course, the huge range of advertising
materials—are much sought after. Unusual
examples, especially fine Victorian pieces, can
bring high prices. Below we list a cross section of
Tobacciana pieces. Also see: ADVERTISING &
CANS & CONTAINERS*

### ADVERTISING ITEMS

*Bull Dog Tobacco Sign*

**Advertising figure,** "El Principe de
Gales cigars," pot metal, complete
figure w/plume on hat & matching

strike wand, comes in various paints, including all-green, all-black, gold or multicolored, 10" h......... **$125.00 to 300.00**

**Advertising Sign,** "Bugler Cigarettes," cardboard, red, blue & yellow on cream ground, reads "Bugler 5¢ and 10¢ - Cigarette Tobacco - For Rolling Your Own! - Union Made" w/picture of cigarette pack, 18" h., 12" w. (corner tips are bent) ................................................. **17.00**

**Advertising sign,** "Bull Dog," lithographed tin, printed on top edge of frame, "Cut Plug" above the picture of a bulldog & "Lovell & Buffington Tobacco Co., Covington, KY" below, self-framed, ca. 1900-20, 14" sq. (ILLUS. bottom previous page) ................................ **400.00 to 600.00**

**Advertising Sign,** "Horseshoe Tobacco," flange-type, porcelain, orange, blue & white, marked "We Sell Horseshoe Tobacco" ................. **385.00**

**Advertising Sign,** "J. P. Alley's Hambone 5¢ Cigar," round, cardboard, gold, red, yellow & green, shows black pilot flying a bi-plane smoking a cigar, reads "Above All Five Cent Cigars - Finest Quality," 7" d. ................................................. **170.00**

**Advertising Sign,** "Lucky Strike," tin, done in red, yellow & white, reads "Buy Them Here," 16½ x 25½" ......... **110.00**

**Advertising Sign,** "Nodel Smoking Tobacco," porcelain, has image of a man w/white handlebar mustache smoking on orange background, black letters read "Yes, I said 10¢ Model Smoking Tobacco," 11¼" h., 34" w. (chipping to mounting holes, two chips to face) ................................ **77.00**

**Ashtray/change bowl,** "Smokey Mischief Cigars," glass, roulette game w/ashtray center, minor soiling, 8" d. (ILLUS. top next column) ............................................. **225.00**

**Chair,** "Duke's Cameo Cigarette Tobacco," wood w/lithographed back & seat, shows image of ornately dressed young woman, seat & back replaced, soiled, 14½ x 20½", 30" h. (ILLUS. bottom next column) ............. **44.00**

**Counter display sign,** "Lavenga Havana Cigars," easel-type, depicts factory, National Easel Pat. 1913, 7½ x 10".............................................. **45.00**

*Smokey Mischief Ashtray/Change Bowl*

*Duke's Cameo Cigarettes Chair*

**Counter top display,** cigar store Indian, composition Indian maiden holding a bunch of cigars, simulated wood, early 20th c., approximately 12" h. ................................. **125.00 to 175.00**

**Counter top display,** "Velvet Tobacco," die cut cardboard, red, yellow, black, green & blue, shaped like an old roadster driven by two men, reads "Joy Ride" behind & the words "Velvet Tobacco" surrounding a pipe, easel back, 8¾" h., 6¾" w. (creases & tear to top, minor soiling) ......................... **193.00**

**Dominos,** "Wills Cigarettes," in tin box... **35.00**

*Store Lighter & Clock*

*Chew Mail Pouch Tobacco Thermometer*

**Door push,** "Chesterfield Cigarettes," porcelain, blue ground w/white lettering reads "Chesterfield Cigarettes-and the blend can't be copied," shows Chesterfield cigarette pack, 9" h., 4" w. ............... **259.00**

**Lighter & clock,** store display model, pot metal, colored glass globe on top, ca. 1870-1900, rare, approximately 18" h. (ILLUS. above)... **1,500.00 to 3,000.00**

**Match book dispenser,** book-type, cylindrical, various colors, Diamond Match Company, ca. 1920s-40s ................................. **175.00 to 400.00**

**Match holder,** "Yellowstone Whiskey, J. J. Williams Distributors, Jacksonville, Florida," table model, ceramic, red printing covers three sides of cream colored base, ca. early 1900s ................................... **95.00**

**Thermometer,** "Chew Mail Pouch Tobacco," porcelain, white blue & yellow, reads "Treat yourself to the Best," Cashocton, Ohio, chipping around edges & mounting holes, 38½" h., 8" w. (ILLUS. top next column) ............................................... **77.00**

**Thermometer,** "Pollack Wheeling Stogies," cream, yellow & blue, reads "Smoke Melo-Crowns," 38½" h., 8" w. (minor scratches overall) ............................................ **132.00**

**Trade card,** "Bagleys Mayflower Chewing Tobacco" .............................. **20.00**

## CAN & CANISTERS
**Cigar tin,** "5¢ Bank Roll Cigars," red, gold & green on cream, marked "Factory No. 309/50/12th dist. Pa" & "Besslar Cigar Mfg. Co. Freeland Pa." on bottom, 5½" h., 6" d. (scratches, denting & soiling) ............. **44.00**

**Cigar tin,** "Popper's Ace Cigar 10¢," metal & glass, light green & red w/cream, yellow & black lettering, bi-planes pictured on three sides, marked "Made by E. Popper & Co. Inc. New York," minor paint chip, 5¾ x 6¾", 9" h. ............................... **550.00**

**Cigarette tin,** "Camel Cigarettes," holds 100, 3½" sq. ............................. **90.00**

**Tobacco canister,** "Central Union," black, red & gold, 4" h., 7" w., 4¾" deep (soiled, scratches & rust) ........... **33.00**

**Tobacco canister,** "Blue Boar Inn," silver plated, 1 lb. ................................. **75.00**

**Tobacco canister,** George Washington Cut Plug, 6½" h. (minor painting & paint loss) .......................... **66.00**

**Tobacco canister,** marked "Sweet Cuba Fine Cut" on inside lid, package of Sweet Cuba on sides in cream w/black lettering, minor paint loss & fading, crazing & minor rusting, 8 x 10", 8" h. .......................... **95.00**

**Tobacco lunch box,** Mayo's .............. **75.00**

**Tobacco pail,** Miners & Puddlers, 5½" d., 6½" h. ..................................... **225.00**

Tobacco tin, pocket-type, Bowl of Roses, short ..................................... **125.00**

Tobacco tin, pocket-type, Bagdad ....... **65.00**

Tobacco tin, pocket-type, Central Union ................................................. **80.00**

Tobacco tin, pocket-type, "Florida State Prison Farm" .......................... **450.00**

Tobacco tin, pocket-type, Holiday........ **43.00**

Tobacco tin, pocket-type, Pinkusshohn's Potpourri .................... **60.00**

Tobacco tin, pocket-type, Red Belt (Bagley's)............................................ **60.00**

Tobacco tin, pocket-type, Stag, short .. **75.00**

Tobacco tin, pocket-type, Taxi, driver in taxi w/top hatted gentleman ....... **3,500.00**

Tobacco tin, pocket-type, Union Leader, w/Uncle Sam ........................ **45.00**

Tobacco tin, round, "Genuine 'Bull' Durham Smoking Tobacco," depicts brown & white bull, a girl dressed in pink, tobacco packages are black & gold on label, pack is white & blue, white farm house in background w/blue, green & yellow highlights, lettering is blue outlined in orange, w/original wood frame, 36 x 38" (minor scratches & flaking) ............ **2,200.00**

## CIGAR BOXES

Black Hawk, various sizes & shapes of wooden boxes of twenty-five or fifty cigars, label brightly colored w/a depiction of an Indian Chief & vignette of a teepee & river scene, Andy Dehner Cigar Company, Burlington, Iowa, 1920s & 30s, common ............................... **30.00 to 60.00**

Certified Bond, nailed wood box of fifty cigars packed four deep, label in the form of a bond certificate, unknown Pennsylvania makers, 1930s, inside liner missing, revenue stamp, heavily scratched.................... **15.00 to 25.00**

Chrome box, pillowed design, the top frame inset w/various color pictures, held 100 cigars, original hinges, clasp & inside mirror, unknown maker, factory 408, Philadelphia, 1930s .................................. **30.00 to 40.00**

Daily Double, nailed wood box designed to hold twenty-five cigars in two rows, label printed predominately in red & yellow, depicts race horses, made in Canada, 1940s (ILLUS. top next page) ...................................... **15.00 to 30.00**

*Daily Double Wood Box*

House of Windsor Palmas, boite nature all wood box w/hinges & clasp, routed decorated edge on box designed to hold fifty cigars four rows deep, 1960s & 1970s, near mint ......................................... **3.00 to 5.00**

Humidor, metal box of twenty-five or fifty cigars, Mazer Cigar Co., Detroit, factory 241, 11th tax district of Ohio, 1920s & 1930s, common ......... **5.00 to 8.00**

*Inside Cover of Liver Regulator Box*

Liver Regulator, nailed wood box of 100 cigars, sepia, blue & black Heppenheimer label depicts double vignettes of "Before Smoking" & "After Smoking," displaying the benefits to be had from smoking cigars, made for Kerbs & Speiss by Cousens & Tomlinson, factory 13, New York City, 1880s, excellent condition (ILLUS.) ............ **200.00 to 300.00**

Lucky Lindy Invincibles, nailed wood/cardboard box of fifty cigars in four rows, color inside & end labels depict Lindbergh's Spirit of St. Louis airplane flying above the clouds, unknown maker, factory 1053, Pennsylvania, cigars prices at three for 10 cents, 1934 ............ **100.00 to 200.00**

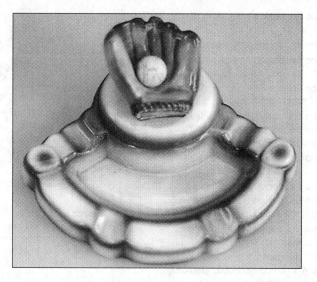

*Baseball Glove
& Diamond
Ashtray*

**"Pirate's chest" box,** cedar w/hinges, clasps & miscellaneous metal decorative strips & buttons nailed on, held fifty cigars in most instances, mirror on inside lid, made by various factories, most frequently Pennsylvania & New Jersey, often marked on bottom as having been made by members of the Boxmaker's Union, 1930s, mint .............................. **25.00**

**Scottie Cigars,** tin can w/slip-top cover, designed to hold fifty cigars upright, depicts dog in yellow circle on red background, P. Lorillard, New York & Virginia, 1920s, 4½" sq., approximately 5½" h......... **125.00 to 200.00**

**Wedding Bells Conchas Especial,** nailed wood box of fifty cigars, colorful label depicts Frances Folsom, bride of then-President Grover Cleveland in 1886, along w/vignette of the White House & Cleveland's country home, Powell & Goldstein, factory 370, Oneida, New York, 1886, near mint ........ **75.00 to 100.00**

## CIGARETTE DISPENSERS & ASHTRAYS

**Ashtray,** advertising, smoked glass w/"Imperial Palace/IP" (Las Vegas) molded into the bottom, 3½" sq. .................................... **2.00 to 4.00**

**Ashtray,** advertising, clear glass w/black imprint "Betty's Hoot'n Holler Cafe, Okmulgee, OK" & cartoon of a pin-up girl in short skirt, 1940s, 3½" h. ..................................... **3.00 to 5.00**

**Ashtray,** advertising, round stacking-style, black glass w/white printing "Flamingo Capri Hotel & Casino, Las Vegas, 3535 Las Vegas Blvd. So. (In the Heart of the Strip) Las Vegas, Nevada, 702-735-4333, featuring Shangri-La the most beautiful pool in Las Vegas," pre-1973, 3½" d. ........................... **5.00 to 10.00**

**Ashtray,** blue & white Italian art glass in the shape of a leaping swordfish over a round base, 1950s, 8½" l., 5" h. ..................................... **40.00 to 60.00**

**Ashtray,** ceramic, three-dimensional figure of a fish w/mouth wide open to hold cigarette, reddish orange glaze ..................................... **8.00 to 12.00**

**Ashtray,** ceramic, in the shape of the state of Maryland, 1950s, approximately 5" l ................. **5.00 to 15.00**

**Ashtray,** ceramic, in the shape of a three-dimensional baseball diamond w/a brown baseball glove & a white ball at the side of the grey diamond, 1950s, 2½ x 6½" (ILLUS. above) ................................. **15.00 to 25.00**

**Dispenser,** red & gold metal, a bird bends to pick a cigarette out of a drawer, 1950s, approximately 6" l. ...................................... **35.00 to 75.00**

## LIGHTERS

**Ronson,** black enamel strike lighter mounted between two chrome-plated holders, indented stepped black gunmetal base, 7" w., 5" h. ................................. **150.00 to 400.00**

*Pal Black Lighter & Case*

**Ronson,** table model, Crown model, 1936-1960s .......................... **10.00 to 20.00**

**Ronson,** table model, Spartan model, 1950s .................................. **20.00 to 40.00**

**Ronson,** lighter & cigarette case combination, Pal model, black finish pink & green florals & silver inset, 1940s-60s (ILLUS. above) .............................. **30.00 to 50.00**

## MATCH BOXES & COVERS

**Advertising box,** Tums on the front & pictures of fishing flies on the back ........................................ **1.00 to 3.00**

**Goldwater for President match cover,** photo of Goldwater & Liberty Bell, 1964 ............................... **1.00 to 2.00**

**Marine barracks match cover,** marked "Subic Bay, Philippines, Semper Fidelis" ....................... **1.00 to 2.00**

**Matchbox,** tin w/hinged cover, gold color w/black lithograph of hunter & dog, Bryant & May, 1878-80s, excellent condition............... **25.00 to 40.00**

**USS Franklin D. Roosevelt match cover (CVA 42),** picturing cartoon of FDR & a Navy man ............... **8.00 to 15.00**

## PIPES & CHEROOT HOLDERS

**Cheroot holder,** Meerschaum, w/carving of two horses & amber bit, bowl at 45 degree angle to stem, original fitted wooden case lined w/satin, covered w/split leather, Europe, 1890-1910, 4" l. ...... **40.00 to 50.00**

**Cheroot holder,** Meerschaum, amber stem in the form of a three-dimensional carving of a box sick from smoking, expertly carved & detailed, made by Hiess & Sohne, late 19th c., 2¼ x 4¾" in original case, mint ........................ **200.00 to 300.00**

**Cheroot holder,** Meerschaum, amber stem, three-dimensional carving of a small skull & cross bones in crook of holder, turn-of-the-century, 1¾ x 4" in original case .................... **40.00 to 60.00**

**Cheroot holder,** Meerschaum, amber bit, straight shape, w/intricate carvings of interwoven ribbons, fitted wooden case covered in split leather, Europe, 1890-1910, 3½" l. .................................... **30.00 to 40.00**

**Pipe,** Meerschaum, carved w/a pastoral or hunting scene w/carved or repoussé metal cap w/14k gold fittings, frequently found w/false early dates inscribed, Austro-Hungaria, ca. 1850, bowl approximately 6" (stem missing) ........................... **200.00 to 400.00**

*Meerschaum Pipe with Turquoise*

**Pipe,** Meerschaum, w/light carvings on bottom, inlaid w/small pieces of turquoise, metal cap & replaced cherry stem w/amber mouthpiece, made in central Europe, mid-19th c., common (ILLUS.) ............. **100.00 to 150.00**

**Pipe,** Meerschaum, carved w/the face of a handsome unidentified black man dressed in ragged clothing, factory colored reddish brown, approximately 5" l.............. **85.00 to 135.00**

**Pipe,** opium, bamboo, China, 1860-1900, approximately 20" l... **75.00 to 200.00**

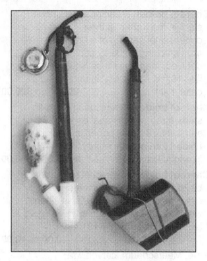

*Porcelain & Cherry Pipes*

**Pipe,** German porcelain bowl w/tin cap on string, plastic molded bit, decal of a deer on 'hand-painted' bowl, cherry stem 5" l. (ILLUS. left) ...................................... **15.00 to 30.00**

**Pipe,** raw cherry wood w/bark & plastic bit, pipe stands upright, smokable, marked "Made in France" on bottom (ILLUS. right) ........... **3.00 to 6.00**

## TOBACCO JARS

*Bagdad Humidor*

**Ceramic,** cylindrical, blue & sea green w/black lettering, shows elaborately dressed middle eastern man wearing a fez, below "Bagdad," minor crazing, 6½" h., 5" d. (ILLUS.) ........................................... **143.00**

## MISCELLANEOUS ITEMS

**Cigar case,** leather & papier-mâché, two-piece slide case, h.p. image of an unidentified 18th c. noble, many variations, most from Europe, 1825-60, 2¾ x 5½" .......... **100.00 to 200.00**

**Cigar clipper,** 14k gold, shaped like scissors, made in Europe, 1890s-1920 ..................... **100.00 to 200.00**

**Cigar cutter,** counter-type, cast iron w/gold highlights, embossed "Empire Tobacco Co., Granby Quebec. No. 2," 6½" h., 17½" l. (soiling & paint loss) ......................................... **55.00**

**Cigar cutter,** counter-type, cast iron, embossed "The Champion Knife Improved Tobaco Cutter - Enterprise Mfg. Co. Philadelphia Patd. April 13, 1875," 6½" h., 17" w. (minor rust) ....... **66.00**

*Eagle & Owl Cigar Cutters*

**Cigar cutter,** pocket or desk-type, bronze, in the shape of a perched eagle, unmarked, Europe, 1880-1910, 4" l. (ILLUS. left) ..... **300.00 to 750.00**

**Cigar cutter,** pocket or desk-type, bronze, in the shape of a perched owl, marked "Austria," 1880-1910, 4½" l. (ILLUS. right).. **300.00 to 750.00**

**Matchbox grip,** bronze, three-sided, h.p. inset earthenware decoration of fashionably dressed woman w/fan, marked "Austria - Steinbock," ca. 1900-20, rare ........................ **40.00 to 75.00**

**Match safe,** brass, three-dimensional eagle head, Europe, 1880-1900, 2½" l. ............................... **125.00 to 400.00**

# TOOLS

**Adze,** "Keen Kutter," carpenters-type .. **$38.00**

**Anvil,** stump-mount-type, w/spike-end base, double horn, 9" head................. 75.00

**Auger,** bung, enterprise-style, 3 x 6" .... 30.00

**Ax,** broad-type, Pennsylvania pattern, unmarked, head only .......................... 25.00

**Ax,** Cooper's side ax w/rectangular blade, 5 x 10" blade (pitted & weld repair) ................................................. 50.00

**Ax,** "Keen Kutter," Western Pattern, double-bit, flat-top............................... 20.00

**Ax,** "Keen Kutter," Yankee-pattern, boys single-bit, hollow beveled head, fine condition ..................................... 35.00

**Ax,** Pennsylvania-style, wortise-type, hammer head on poll, 1¾" bit, 8½" l. head............................................... 95.00

**Blacksmith's bolt header,** double-ended for square or round heads, 12" l....................................................... 20.00

**Blacksmith's forge,** hand-cranked blower connected to bottom of steel dish charcoal pan .............. **75.00 to 125.00**

**Boring machine,** wood-frame upright auger w/bit, egg-shaped hardwood crank handles, deluxe "Millers Falls" model................................................ 150.00

**Brace,** barber-style, modern bit-brace, cocobolo wood head ............ **10.00 to 20.00**

**Brace,** "Millers Falls," No. 502B, corner-type ........................................ 50.00

**Brace,** "Wm. Marples & Sons," ultimatum-style, ebony filled brass frame ............................................... 495.00

**Calipers,** blacksmith-made, double, 16" l...................................................... 65.00

**Calipers,** friction-top by Starrett or Brown & Sharpe, 6" .............................. 12.00

**Chisel,** "Diamond-Edge," socket firmer, 1" bevel edge, no handle........... 5.00

**Chisel,** "Keen Kutter," socket firmer, 1" bevel edge, new handle ................. 11.00

**Chisel,** slick w/knob handle, marked "PS&W," 3" ....................................... 68.00

**Chisel,** "Stanley," ½" socket chisel, hickory handle ..................................... 12.00

**Cobbler's lasting pliers w/hammer jaw,** ¾" w................................ **8.00 to 12.00**

**Compass,** wheelwright's steel wing compass, 14" l. ................................... 35.00

**Cooper's adze,** "D.R. Barton," 9½" head, without handle .......................... 75.00

**Cooper's bung auger,** enterprise-style, unmarked, 3½" d. at top of taper, 16" l. ..................................... 35.00

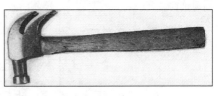

*Double Claw Hammer*

**Cooper's heading knife,** hardwood handles, 12" blade ............................ 30.00

**Corn-husking pins,** palm-held w/strap.................................... **5.00 to 10.00**

**Corn planters,** wood frame, w/seed box attached........................ **15.00 to 40.00**

**Corn sheller,** "Burrall's," cast-iron floor stand ....................................... 150.00

**Draw knife,** "Keen Kutter," ebony finished handles, 10" blade .. **15.00 to 25.00**

**Draw knife,** "Pexto," blond maple handles, 8" blade ............................. 16.00

**Drill,** archimedean-type, brass trim, beechwood, unmarked, 14" l. ............. 75.00

**Drill,** egg beater-style, "Miller Falls," No. 655, w/spoked gear wheel, ................................................. 18.00

**Drill,** hand-type, "Goodell Pratt," open crank wheel w/wood handle, pat. 1896 (side handle missing) .. **16.00 to 20.00**

**Drill,** push-type, "Goodell Pratt," all metal w/seven bits in handle, pat. 1915...................................................... 12.00

**Gauge,** leather-cutting, brass-framed, pistol-shaped w/sliding gauge & blade, ca. 1880.................... **35.00 to 50.00**

**Gauge,** "Stanley," No. 85½, rosewood panel gauge, pat. Aug. 5, 1873 .......... 75.00

**Grinder,** bench-mounted, three-geared, hand-crank grinding stone for household or shop use .................. 25.00

**Hammer,** coachmaker's, fruitwood handle, double-faced, ½" d. head, 9" l., 14" l. handle .............................. 40.00

**Hammer,** "Double Claw," pat. 1903 (ILLUS. above) ................ **150.00 to 295.00**

**Hammer,** "E.C. Simmons," bill poster's-style, magnetized, square face, 4" head ...................................... 22.00

**Hammer,** "Estwing," cowboy leather-washed handled claw-type ................. 12.00

**Hammer,** "Shapleigh's," nail-type, adze eye, bell face, Keen Kutter, 16 oz.................................................... 18.00

**Hammer,** "Snow Knocker," iron, used for cleaning snow from horse's hooves, 4" head ................... **15.00 to 30.00**

**Hatchet,** half-type, flat-top........ **8.00 to 10.00**

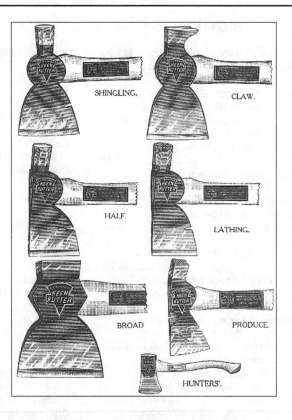

*Keen Kutter Hatchets -
1900-35*

*L. L. Davis Lacy Iron Level*

**Hatchet,** "Keen Kutter," broad-ax shape, w/original handle, single bevel, 5" blade (ILLUS. top)........................................ **30.00 to 50.00**

**Hatchet,** "Keen Kutter," half-type, flat-top w/nail slot (ILLUS. top) ... **14.00 to 20.00**

**Hay knife,** "Lightning," straight pattern, two wood handles ... **20.00 to 35.00**

**Hub boring machine,** "Doles Patent," pat. July 1854, Salem, Ohio ............. **245.00**

**Knife,** "E.C. Simmons," bone-handled farrier's hoof-type, rare ...................... **45.00**

**Level,** "L.L. Davis," filigree or lacy-type iron, w/inclinometer, 12" to 24" (ILLUS. bottom)................ **100.00 to 225.00**

**Level,** "Stratton," No. 1, brass bound plum-type, 24" l .................................. **55.00**

**Lock,** "Simmons," six-lever steel or iron padlock, round body ................... **30.00**

**Lock,** wrought-iron tumbler-type, round or heart shape, without brass trim ......................................... **8.00 to 10.00**

**Mallet,** carpenter's wood-type, 3" to 6" l. head ........................ **5.00 to 10.00**

**Ox yoke,** wooden double yoke w/bentwood necks & iron fitting .................................... **75.00 to 195.00**

**Pitch fork,** manure-type, four metal tines w/wood handle............. **15.00 to 24.00**

**Plane,** "Barry & Way," side bead moulding-type, ⅜" ............................... **20.00**

**Plane,** "Chapin & Co.," screw-arm boxwood plow-type w/ivory tips on worn screw arms, ca. 1840............ **1,250.00**

**Plane,** coach or carriage maker's moulding-type, beechwood, squirrel-tailed ................................... 35.00 to 50.00

**Plane,** "Israel White, Philadelphia," crew-arm plow-type, beechwood, boxed fence, ca. 1835 (rough condition) .......................................... 245.00

**Plane,** "Keen Kutter," No. K35, transitional smoothing-type, wooden handle & bottom, iron top, 2" cutter, 9" l. (90% of original finish) ................. 40.00

**Plane,** "Keen Kutter," iron smoothing-type, 1¾" cutter, 8" l. (50% of original finish) ...................... 35.00 to 45.00

*Keen Kutter Plane No. KK5*

**Plane,** "Keen Kutter," No. KK5, iron fore-type, rosewood handle, 18" l. (ILLUS.) ............................... 48.00 to 70.00

**Plane,** "Greenfield Tool Co.," ogee moulding-type, ca. 1880, 1½" w. ........ 40.00

**Plane,** "Millers Falls," No. 9, iron smoothing-type, ................................. 32.00

**Plane,** "Millers Falls," No. 14, iron jack type.................................................... 40.00

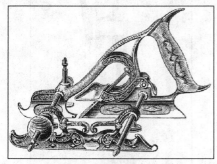

*Miller's Patent 1872 Plane*

**Plane,** "Miller's Patent," combination-type, made by Stanley for one year only, ca. 1872 (ILLUS.) ................. 5,500.00

**Plane,** "Ohio Tool Co.," wooden-screw adjustable sash-type.......................... 48.00

**Plane,** "Rumbold," butt mortise, metal w/two hardwood knobs 1½ x 9¾".......... 65.00

**Plane,** "Sargent," jack-type ..... 18.00 to 28.00

**Plane,** "Siegley's," combination-type w/seventeen cutters & two depth stops ................................................. 295.00

**Plane,** "Stanley," No. 4, metal smoothing-type, ca. 1905..... 35.00 to 45.00

**Plane,** "Stanley," No. 5½, metal jack type w/tall front knob........................... 35.00

**Plane,** "Stanley," No. 7, iron jointer-type, tall rosewood knob & handle w/owner's initials carved in ................ 40.00

**Plane,** "Stanley," No. 37, Jenny-style smoothing-type, w/razee-style wood body (90% of finish remains) ............ 165.00

**Plane,** "Stanley," No. 46, combination type ................................... 75.00 to 175.00

**Plane,** "Stanley," No. 75, tiny bullnose metal-type ........................... 15.00 to 20.00

**Plane,** "Stanley," No. 101, household block-type, black metal cap ................ 12.00

**Plane,** "Stanley," No. 607C, Bedrock pat. April 2, 1895 (dirty w/broken handle)................................................. 58.00

**Plane,** "Stanley," No. H1204, handyman, red & grey finish............... 16.00

**Plane,** unmarked jointer-type, beechwood body & handle, 26" l. ...................................... 24.00 to 35.00

**Pliers/wrench,** "J. Casper," water-pump design, marked "Wiscon, 1918"...................................... 25.00 to 45.00

**Pliers/wrench,** "Plierench," w/set of five jaws............................................. 25.00

**Plum bob,** "Diamond-edge," hexagon steel w/brass top screw, 8 oz. ..................................... 15.00 to 20.00

**Plum bob,** "European," brass turnip-shaped, very ornate 3½" l., 1 lb. ....... 125.00

**Plum bob,** "Goodell-Pratt," wood reel, 5" l...................................................... 18.00

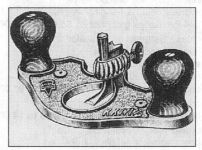

*Keen Kutter 171½ Router*

**Router,** "Keen Kutter, metal frame, wood handles, No. 171½, ca. 1900 (ILLUS.) ............................. 65.00 to 100.00

**Router,** "Stanley," No. 71, nickel-plated closed throat-type w/two wood knobs .......................... **20.00 to 35.00**

**Rule,** "Acme Rule Co.," ivory one-foot, four-fold caliper-style ........ **200.00 to 300.00**

**Rule,** Keen Kutter, boxwood, two-foot, four-fold, fully brass-bound ................ **49.00**

**Rule,** "Stanley," No. 38, ivory, six foot, two-fold caliper-style (tiny cracks) .... **200.00**

**Rule,** "Stanley," No. 64, folding boxwood carpenter's-type, ca. 1875.. **150.00**

**Rule,** "Stanley," No. 82, brass-bound four-fold, two foot, lumber scales...... **175.00**

**Saw,** "Atkins," No. 54, cross-cut handsaw, silversteel .......................... **15.00**

**Saw,** crosscut, two-man-style, nearly 6' l. ...................................... **50.00 to 75.00**

**Saw,** "Diamond Edge," logo, skew back hand saw, 26" l. ........... **15.00 to 20.00**

**Saw,** "E.C. Atkins," straight handled adjustable hacksaw .............................. **8.00**

**Saw,** "E.C. Simmons, Keen Kutter," blued steel back saw w/applewood handle, ca. 1904 ................................. **40.00**

**Saw,** "Henry Disston & Sons, American Boy," hand saw, carved applewood handle, 20" l., boy's name etched on handle ..................... **40.00**

**Saw,** "Henry Disston & Sons," No. D115 hand saw 'Victory' Liberty & eagle mark w/rosewood handle, 26" l. ..................................... **75.00 to 95.00**

**Saw,** ice saw, tiller handle, 54" l. ........... **75.00**

**Saw set,** "E.C. Simmons," pliers-style, dial pattern, pat. 1908, 7" ..... **15.00 to 20.00**

**Scales,** "Fairbanks," grocer's 10 to 36 lb. counter-top scales, cast-iron balance-style w/set of weights & tin scoop................................. **95.00 to 150.00**

**Scales,** cast-iron platform-style w/brass beam & hanging weights, 244 lbs. hanging capacity... **95.00 to 195.00**

**Scales,** "Sargent" or "Chatillions," hanging spring-balance w/rectangular body & brass circular dial, 10 lb. & 20 lb. size (missing chains & pan) ...................... **75.00 to 95.00**

**Scrapers,** box-label & furniture-type, hoe-shape, factory made ....... **8.00 to 14.00**

**Screwdriver,** "Decatur Coffin Co.," brass barrel, steel blade (replaced handle)............................................ **18.00**

**Scythe,** small grass-hook, one-handed-style........................... **8.00 to 15.00**

**Sheep shears,** one-piece spring-handle sheet metal.................. **5.00 to 7.00**

**Shovel,** potato scoop, scoop shovel w/wire bottom ...................... **35.00 to 70.00**

**Spoke shave,** "Cin. Tool Co.," unbent shape w/red stained handles, hollow blade 2" wide, 11" overall .................. **50.00**

**Spoke shave,** "Millers Falls," No. 1, rosewood handled ............................. **38.00**

**Square,** "Oak Leaf," sliding T-bevel, rosewood handle, blue blade, brass trim....................................................... **25.00**

**Square,** sliding T-bevel, rosewood handle, sliding slotted-steel blade ................................... **10.00 to 20.00**

**Square,** "Stanley," trisquare, rosewood stock, 4½' blade ................. **15.00**

**Tin snips,** "Diamond-edge," forged steel, 10½" overall ................................. **9.00**

**Tool holder,** "Keen Kutter," hollow rosewood handle holds nine different awls, drills & gouges.......................... **85.00**

**Traps,** "Victor," small single-spring animal trap, on chain................ **5.00 to 8.00**

**Traps,** double spring .......................... **10.00**

**Traveler,** "Wiley & Russell," five-spoke, open-handle-style .................. **32.00**

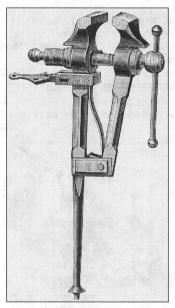

*Typical Blacksmith's Leg Vise*

**Vise,** blacksmith's leg-type, w/iron bar extending to floor, made in same design for 300 years, also called a solid box or staple vise, 40" overall height (ILLUS.) .................. **75.00 to 125.00**

**Vise,** harness maker's oak knee-held type.................................................... **48.00**

**Vise,** miniature, iron, jointer's-style, 4½" l. w/1½" jaws.............................. **32.00**

**Vise,** hand-type, hinged at bottom, thumbscrew adjustable, small ............ **10.00**

**Well hook,** spoked iron wheel w/fender & ring ..................... **15.00 to 30.00**

**Wheelbarrow,** wood, garden-style w/original paint, ca. 1880-1910 ................................ **200.00 to 400.00**

**Wheelwright's tenoning machine,** "Everready," No. 1, pat. Oct. 1911.... **195.00**

**Wrench,** "Bemis & Call," combination pipe & monkey wrench, wood handle, double-jaw ............... **10.00 to 20.00**

**Wrench,** "Deere and Mansure," open-end malleable iron ............................... **9.00**

**Wrench,** "Mc Cormick," No. R197, S-wrench ............................................. **5.00**

**Wrench,** "Merricks Patent," screw adjust nut wrench, dated 1835, rare .................................................. **325.00**

**Wrench,** "Moline," No. A1037, iron imp., 8½".............................................. **7.00**

**Wrench,** "Starr," quick adjust buggy type...................................................... **95.00**

**Wrench,** "Studebaker," iron buggy type w/logo .......................................... **10.00**

**Wrench,** "Susquehanna Fertilizer Co.," buggy-type, 8½" ......................... **40.00**

---

# TOOTHPICK HOLDERS

*Reference numbers listed after the holders refer to the late William Heacock's books,* Encyclopedia of Victorian Colored Pattern Glass, Book 1 *(1974) or* 1000 Toothpick Holders *(Antique Publications, 1977) and* Toothpick Holders: China, Glass and Metal, *prepared by members of the National Toothpick Holder Collector's Society (Antique Publications, 1992)*

**Amber glass,** pressed figural kitten on pillow (ILLUS. top next column) ... **$40.00**

**Amberina glass,** pressed Daisy & Button patt. ...................................... **70.00**

**Amethyst glass,** pressed Croesus patt. w/gold trim ................................. **40.00**

**Amethyst glass,** pressed Swag with Brackets patt.................................... **25.00**

**Bisque porcelain,** figural baby by cup holder.................................................. **25.00**

**Bisque porcelain,** figural owl w/glass eyes on log ...................................... **20.00**

**Blue glass,** footed, pressed Daisy & Button patt. ........................................ **20.00**

*Kitten on Pillow Toothpick Holder*

**Blue glass,** pressed Horse with Cart patt. (1000, No. 326)........................... **50.00**

**Blue glass,** pressed Peek-A-Boo patt. (1000, No. 327) ......................... **20.00**

**Burmese glass,** footed, egg-shaped w/eight-crimp rim ............................. **200.00**

**Burmese glass,** squatty bulbous Swirl Patt. w/piecrust rim, glossy finish .. **1,600.00**

**Burmese glass,** cylindrical w/ruffled rim & enameled floral decoration, Webb (1000, No. 44) ...................... **150.00**

**Burmese glass,** mold-blown Simple Scroll patt., bulbous w/crimped rim w/enameled floral decoration, Mt. Washington Glass Co. (1000, No. 3)................................................ **700.00**

**Burmese glass,** mold-blown Fig Mold, bulbous w/square-shaped fluted rim, enamel overlay decoration on satin finish................. **700.00**

**Carnival glass,** pressed Flute patt., amethyst............................................ **45.00**

**Carnival glass,** pressed Kittens patt., blue .................................................. **175.00**

**Canary glass,** pressed Vermont patt.... **35.00**

**Chocolate glass,** pressed Geneva patt. (1000, No. 127)....................... **550.00**

**Clear glass,** pressed figural crocodile .. **60.00**

**Clear glass,** pressed figural dog w/hat (1000, No. 333) ...................... **20.00**

**Clear glass,** pressed figural Indian maiden w/basket holder, square base .................................................. **20.00**

**Clear glass,** pressed figural kitten on pillow.................................................. **30.00**

**Clear glass,** pressed figural monkey head, "Darwin" .................................... **25.00**

**Clear glass,** pressed figural pig &
barrel on flat cart................................. **90.00**

**Clear glass,** pressed figural rabbit
carrying basket holder ........................ **40.00**

**Clear glass,** pressed Flora patt.,
w/gold trim (1000, No. 98) .................. **80.00**

**Clear glass w/amber stain,** pressed
Esther patt. ....................................... **100.00**

**Coralene glass,** square-top, glossy,
Peach Blow ground w/Coralene
seaweed beading .......................... **1,700.00**

**Cranberry glass,** blown, decorated
w/applied flowers ............................... **40.00**

**Custard glass,** pressed
Chrysanthemum Sprig patt. .............. **220.00**

**Custard glass,** pressed Inverted Fan
& Feather patt., Northwood .............. **475.00**

**Custard glass,** pressed Three Bands
patt....................................................... **20.00**

**Daum Nancy glass,** "Summer
Season decoration," artist-signed ..... **800.00**

**Green glass,** pressed Colorado patt.,
souvenir .............................................. **25.00**

**Green glass,** pressed Vermont w/gold
trim....................................................... **30.00**

**Milk glass,** pressed Maize patt.,
Libbey (1000, No. 95) ...................... **400.00**

**Nippon porcelain,** two-handled,
footed, decorated w/h.p. house scene .. **40.00**

**Pomona glass,** amber top, applied
rigaree, first patent............................ **175.00**

**Pomona glass,** fan-shaped, first
patent................................................. **175.00**

**Royal Bayreuth porcelain,** scene of
woman feeding chicks (NTHCS,
No. 399) ............................................ **130.00**

**Royal Doulton china,** butterfly &
floral decoration on blue ..................... **75.00**

**R.S. Prussia porcelain,** Stippled
Floral mold, violet decoration.............. **50.00**

**R.S. Prussia porcelain,** decorated
w/yellow & pink flowers....................... **35.00**

**Silver over copper,** pedestal urn
w/figural lion heads ............................ **30.00**

**Silver plate,** figural Boston terrier
lying next to holder, souvenir .............. **55.00**

**Silver plate,** figural cherub w/holder
on wings, engraved "Spokane,
Washington" ........................................ **75.00**

**Silver plate,** figural dog at open
basket holder .................................... **140.00**

**Silver plate,** figural elephant w/holder,
No. 3415 ............................................ **170.00**

**Silver plate,** figural girl (Kate
Greenaway-type), holding rope,
Roger Bros. ...................................... **240.00**

**Silver plate,** figural rabbit sitting by
open basket holder (NTHCS Book,
No. 824)............................................. **110.00**

**Silver plate,** figural frog pulling shell
holder................................................... **90.00**

**Silver plate,** figural porcupine............ **100.00**

**Silver plate,** small bird w/bullet-shaped
holder four ball feet on tray ................. **30.00**

**Steuben glass,** Aurene, iridescent
blue, signed & numbered................. **650.00**

**Tiffany glass,** thorn design,
silvery blue iridescence ................... **175.00**

**Tortoiseshell glass,** tricornered........... **30.00**

**Vaseline opalescent glass,** three-
footed, mold-blown Hobb's Hobnail
patt. (1000, No. 109)........................... **55.00**

**Venetian glass,** blue specks over
gold spray, Murano ............................ **20.00**

**White opaque glass,** figural
cornucopia, pressed Scrolled Shell
patt. (1000, No. 394)........................... **25.00**

**White opalescent glass,** pressed
Beatty Rib patt., in silver plated
holder................................................... **70.00**

---

# TOYS

*Hubley Cast-iron Airplane*

**Airplane,** cast iron, finished in yellow,
marked "Friendship" in blue across
top of wings, w/turning propellers,
black rubber tires on wooden
wheels, Hubley Mfg. Co. (Lancaster,
Pennsylvania), two front wheels
broken, 11½" l. (ILLUS.) ............. **$3,737.00**

**Automobile,** "Delux Sedan," cast iron,
rubber wheels, red w/silver striping,
driver & passenger, original clicker &
decal, Arcade Mfg. Co. (Freeport,
Illinois), ca. 1940, 8¼" l.................. **1,840.00**

**Automobile,** Doodlebug, die-cast
metal, painted green, Tootsietoy
(Dowst Bros., Chicago, Illinois),
1930s, 4" l.......................................... **80.00**

**Automobile,** Ford Model A coupe, cast iron, red rumble & rubber wheels, Arcade Mfg. Co., ca. 1928, 5" l. ................................................. **359.00**

**Automobile,** Ford Model T coupe, steel plate, finished in black w/turning front wheels painted w/red spokes, Buddy-L (Moline Pressed Steel Co., E. Moline Illinois), ca. 1925, 10¾" l. ............................. **633.00**

**Automobile,** Ford Model T sedan, cast iron, the four door vehicle painted black w/nickled driver & white painted tires, Arcade Mfg. Co., 6½" l. .................................................. **460.00**

**Automobile,** Graham Roadster, die-cast metal, painted red w/black fenders, dual side mounted tires, Tootsietoy, 1930s, 3¾" l. ......... **144.00**

**Automobile,** LaSalle coupe, die-cast metal, painted orange body, tan top, Tootsietoy, 1930s ............................. **403.00**

**Automobile,** Mercedes Benz 300 SE, tin friction, red, Ichiko (Japan), 1970s, 24" l. ....................................... **87.00**

**Automobile,** roadster w/rumble seat, cast iron, blue w/nickel plated steel wheels, A. C. Williams Co. (Ravenna, Ohio), ca. 1930s, 6" l. (paint loss to roof) ............................. **150.00**

**Automobile,** roadster, cast iron, green w/gold trim w/Arcade decals on door, rumble seat, marked "106" in raised numbers on the inside, Arcade Mfg. Co., 6½" l. (missing driver, some paint chips) .................. **715.00**

**Automobile,** sedan, cast iron, w/rubber wheels, red, Arcade Mfg. Co., ca. 1940, 5½" l. ......................... **200.00**

**Battery-operated,** airplane, "Pan American World Airways," grey & cream, marked "PAA" on tail, four propellers, 20" wingspan, 15" l. (some touch-up) ............................. **440.00**

*Cragston Control Tower*

**Battery-operated,** control tower, remote control, tower w/helicopter & airplane attached to the ends of a metal bar, Cragston (Japan), w/original box, 36" w., 12" h. (ILLUS. bottom previous column) ..... **232.00**

**Battery-operated,** "Crapshooter," figure of crapshooter standing behind podium, No. 71575, Cragston, w/original box, 9" h. ............ **60.00**

**Battery-operated,** police car, Cadillac, lithographed tin, Yonezowa (Japan), 1960, 18" l. (battery door & antenna missing) ............................. **115.00**

**Battery-operated,** "Police Patrol" airplane, remote control, automatic steering & blinking light, marked "Police Patrol" on wings, Cragston, w/original box, 21" wingspan, 15" l. (minor damage to box) ..................... **165.00**

**Battery-operated,** "X-80 Planet Explorer," No 3150, Modern Toys (Japan), w/original box, 8" d. ............ **110.00**

**Bell ringer toy,** airplane, painted pressed steel, maroon painted upper wing, two large wheel & two bells acting as propeller, Watrous Mfg. Co. (East Hampton, Connecticut), 9½" l. .................................................. **230.00**

**Bell ringer toy,** "Boy & Girl on Seesaw," h.p. tin, boy & girl on cast wheeled base teeter-totter, ringing a large center bell, Gong Bell Mfg. Co. (East Hampton, Connecticut), ca. 1900, 7½" l. ............................. **1,150.00**

**Bell ringer toy,** cast iron, elephant on platform w/silvered & webbed wheels, bell attached to elephant's trunk rings when it is pulled along, N. N. Hill Brass Co. (New Jersey), ca. 1905, 7" l. .................................. **575.00**

**Bell ringer toy,** "Jonah in the Whale," cast iron, a blue whale atop blue water swallowing Jonah, all on a four wheel base w/bell underneath, N. N. Hill Brass Co., 6" l. ........................ **1,725.00**

**Bell ringer toy,** pony & cart, boy driver, painted cast iron, young boy in red jacket & blue trousers, seated in two wheel carriage w/bell underneath, driving small trotting pony, Gong Bell Mfg. Co., 6½" l. ...... **345.00**

**Bell ringer toy,** "Teddy Roosevelt & the Rough Riders," three nickel plated cast-iron figures on electroplated steel platform, w/pressed steel heart shaped spoked wheels, ca. 1900, 9¾" l. ....... **575.00**

*"Speed Bike"*

**Bicycle,** "Speed Bike," motorcycle-type, pressed steel, leather seat, pneumatic tires, Metal Specialties Co., decal worn, missing one handgrip, 1930s (ILLUS.) ................. **316.00**

**Blocks,** building-type, wooden interlocking pieces & finials, lithographed paper label, Crandall's, late 19th c., in original box, 6 x 10", 3½" l. (some damage & losses) ........ **115.00**

**Boat,** tug-type, pressed steel, type II, Buddy-L, No. 3000, 1930, restored, 28" l. (ILLUS. top next column) ...... **2,415.00**

**Bus,** Greyhound "Century of Progress Tour Bus," painted cast iron, Arcade Mfg. Co., ca. 1933, 10½" .................. **230.00**

**Bus,** Greyhound GMC bus, cast iron, painted red w/gold stripe, rubber wheels, Arcade, ca. 1937, 7½" l. ...... **460.00**

**Bus,** "Yellow Coach Bus," cast iron, double decker bus finished in green w/gold piping, side mounted chrome wheels, driver, front & rear doors indicated in casting, Arcade Mfg. Co., 13" l. ...................................... **1,035.00**

**Cap pistol,** "Federal," cast iron, No. 1, Kilgore Mfg. Co. (Westerville, Ohio), 5¼" l.................................................. **44.00**

**Circus performer,** Hobo, wooden, Schoenhut, regular size.................... **230.00**

**Circus set,** includes big top tent, two cowboys w/two horses & boxed set of accessories including chairs, stands, flags, weights & poles, Schoenhut & Co., w/original instructions, the set........................... **920.00**

**Circus wagon,** cast iron, w/driver, polar bear in wagon, drawn by two white horses w/two out riders, Kenton Hardware Co. (Kenton, Ohio), No. 231, late 1940s, in original box, 14" l. ............................ **575.00**

*Buddy-L Tug Boat*

**Clockwork mechanism,** cabin cruiser, steel hull & cabin, wooden deck, die-cast deck fittings & anchors, w/display stand, Orkin-Craft (Calwis Industries Ltd., Beverly Hills, California), 1930s, 32" l. (missing three plastic windows) ..... **1,265.00**

**Clockwork mechanism,** coupe, tin, the green vehicle features front headlights, rear brake lever & tinplate wheels, Andre Citreon (Paris, France), 14½" l. .................. **2,070.00**

**Clockwork mechanism,** figures of dancing couple w/painted faces, man w/red felt jacket, black felt pants, woman in yellow cotton dress, Martin, Fernand (Paris, France), early 20th c., 7½" .......................... **1,035.00**

*Clockwork Jockey*

**Clockwork mechanism,** jockey w/two horses, painted tin, a red two-wheeled vehicle features jockey & clockwork mechanism being led by two white horses on a single wheel base, Brown (George W.) & Co. (Forestville, Connecticut), ca. 1860s, 14" l. (ILLUS.) .............................. **12,650.00**

**Clockwork mechanism,** ocean liner, tinplate, hull finished cream w/blue stripe, brown deck, single stack w/key arbor, Fleischman (Germany), post-war, 20" l. (lacking lifeboats) ..... **920.00**

**Clockwork mechanism,** paddle wheel boat, painted tin, the red, white & blue boat has two smoke stacks, stenciling throughout, two wheels, flag & clockwork mechanism w/key, stenciled "Electra" on side, Brown (George W.) & Co., ca. 1860s, 14" l. ............................................. **12,650.00**

**Clockwork mechanism,** parlor oarsman, painted maroon hull w/red & gold stripe, green deck w/red & gold stripes, Ives Corp. (Bridgeport, Connecticut), 11" l. (several missing parts, mechanism separated from hull) ................................................ **1,380.00**

**Clockwork mechanism,** passenger boat, painted wood, Keystone Mfg. Co. (Boston, Massachusetts), w/original box (box tapped at one end) ................................................. **288.00**

**Clockwork mechanism,** sedan, lithographed tin, features four tinplated passengers & rubber wheels, No. 50, Carette, Georges (Nuremburg, Germany), 8" l. ......... **1,150.00**

**Clockwork mechanism,** sedan, painted tin, features headlights, adjustable windshield, dual handbrakes, tinplated driver, Carette, Georges, 13½" l. (replaced rubber wheels & a clockwork mechanism) ....................................... **920.00**

**Clockwork mechanism,** speed boat, painted tin, composition driver, Lionel Mfg. Co. (New York, New York), No. 43, 1930s, w/original box, 17½" l. (missing rudder, steering knob & flag) ..................................... **260.00**

**Clockwork mechanism,** tinplate bird w/paper wings, h.p. bird finished in dark yellow & orange, w/printed paper wings bearing Lehmann trademark, Lehmann (Ernest) Co. (Brandenberg, Germany), early 20th c., 7" (rust on wings & staining on one wing) ..................................... **805.00**

**Clockwork mechanism,** walking bear, fur covered bear holding wire muzzle w/leash, Ives Corp., ca. 1882, 8" h............................... **1,380.00**

**Fire pumper truck,** painted cast iron, w/driver, nickel plated boiler, Kenton Hardware (Kenton, Ohio), ca. 1930 (scratches, surface rust) ................... **575.00**

**Friction-type,** lithographed tin, "Starfire" fighter plane, done in red, white & blue, has removable wings, w/original box, 8½" l. (faded colors, minor scratches & rust)...................... **83.00**

**G.I. Joe action figure,** "Black Adventurer," flocked black hair, scar, wearing two-piece green fatigues w/jacket, black boots, near mint ......... **80.00**

**G.I. Joe action figure,** "Japanese Imperial Soldier," painted brown hair, wearing original outfit including jacket, pants & black boots (many small hair rubs, outfit slightly worn & frayed, one button missing & one seam separated)............................... **400.00**

**G.I. Joe action figure,** "Land Adventurer," flocked hair & beard, scar, wearing one-piece yellow suit (small spot of flocking missing on chin, small eyebrow rub).................... **80.00**

**Gasoline pump,** plastic, "Texaco," covered w/silver, red & black decals, 3" w., 4" h. (soiling) ............................ **72.00**

**Hansom cab,** cast iron, w/driver & lady passenger, Kenton Hardware Co., No. 162, late 1940s, in original box, 14½" l....................................... **575.00**

**Hansom cab,** painted cast iron, black horse w/red blanket, yellow & black body, driver w/blue jacket, black pants & top hat, Pratt & Letchworth (Buffalo, New York), ca. 1890, 12" l. .................................................. **1,495.00**

**Holster set,** "Shootin' Shell Fanner Plainsman Holster Set," die-cast gun, leather holster, Mattel Inc. (Hawthorne, California), ca. 1958..... **184.00**

**Jack-in-the-box,** grain decorated lunch pail w/painted composition woman's head, paper label reads "American Corned Beef, Free of Trichiness," Germany, late 19th c., 3¾" h. (missing handle) ................... **345.00**

**Jack-in-the-box,** papier-mâché & cloth leprechaun in paper covered wooden box, Germany, early 20th c., 3½" sq. (some damage) .................. **115.00**

**Log cart,** cast iron, two black & white oxen pull a four-wheeled cart w/large log, driver sits sideways to drive the team, Kenton Hardware Co., ca. 1910, 15½".............................. **1,210.00**

**Mill,** painted tin, water-driven, Germany, early 20th c., 8 x 13½", 11" h. (missing crank)...................... **403.00**

**Motorcycle,** "Crash Car," cast iron, painted orange, nickel plated wheels, Hubley Mfg. Co. (Lancaster, Pennsylvania), 4½"........................... **230.00**

**Motorcycle,** "Indian," four cylinder, cast iron, painted red, nickel plated

motor & handle bars, Hubley Mfg.
Co., ca. 1930, 9" l. (crack in frame,
missing side wheels) ........................ **805.00**

**Motorcycle w/sidecar,** cast iron, red
& silver, rubber wheels, Hubley Mfg.
Co., ca. 1930, 8½" (replaced handle
bars) ................................................ **374.00**

**Motorcycle w/sidecar,** lithographed
tin, driver wearing an orange uniform
& white cap, woman passenger
holds a parasol, Greppert-Kelch
(Germany), ca. 1925, 6½" l ............ **1,725.00**

**Ox cart,** painted cast iron, a black &
red two-wheeled cart drawn by two
maroon painted yoked oxen, Weler
& Crosby (Brooklyn, New York),
11¼" l .............................................. **920.00**

**Pull toy,** duck, "Quacky Family,"
Fisher-Price (East Aurora, New
York), ca. 1940s ................................ **40.00**

**Pull toy,** elephant on wheels, "Yes-
No" elephant, mohair w/tusks, glass
eyes, bell on end of trunk, on a
metal base w/wooden wheels,
manipulating tail causes elephant to
indicate yes or no, Schuco Toy Co.
(Nuremberg, Germany), original
paper tag, 19 x 22" ...................... **1,380.00**

**Pull toy,** "Hot Dog Wagon," Fisher-
Price, No. 445, ca. 1940, 10" l ......... **115.00**

**Pull toy,** "Space Blazer," Fisher-Price,
No. 750, ca. 1953, 14" l. ................... **110.00**

**Pull toy,** telephone, "Chatter
Telephone," Fisher-Price, No. 747,
1962-87 ............................................. **45.00**

**Pull toy,** train engine, "Looky Chug-
Chug," No. 161, Fisher-Price, 1949,
w/original box .................................. **325.00**

**Pull toy,** train engine, "Toot-Toot,"
Fisher-Price, No. 643, ca. 1964,
w/original box .................................. **150.00**

**Puzzle,** jigsaw-type, Robert E. Lee,
1,000 pieces, ca. 1972 ..................... **25.00**

**Riding toy,** train engine, wooden
construction & cast wheels, pull
handle attached to smoke stack,
42" l ................................................. **483.00**

**Robot,** "Action Planet Robot," windup
tin, black body, plastic head &
hands, chrome details, sparking
mechanism, K. O. (Japan),
w/original box, 8⅞" .......................... **805.00**

**Robot,** "Blue Zoomer," battery-
operated tin, w/wrench, Japan, 9¼" .. **230.00**

**Robot,** "Driving Robot," Y. S. Toys ..... **450.00**

**Robot,** "Flashy Jim," windup, silver,
red, black & blue, early 1950s,
3¼" w., 7½" h. (minor scratches) ...... **330.00**

**Robot,** "Mr. Mercury," battery-
operated tin, lithographed, Louis
Marx & Co. (New York, New York),
13" h. ................................................ **345.00**

**Robot,** "Robbie the Robot," battery-
operated tin, w/red feet, hands &
battery box, chrome details, Japan,
9" h. .................................................. **288.00**

**Robot,** windup lithographed tin, bluish
grey w/red & black striping, Line Mar
(Japan), 1950s, 6" h. (antenna
missing) ............................................ **200.00**

**Robot,** "Zoomer," windup, black &
blue, has original key, early 1950s ... **232.00**

**Service station,** lithographed tin,
"Day and Night Service," garage
marked "Car Washed - Blue Bird -
Cars Greased" single gas pump &
air pump in front, marked "Day and
Night Service," 6½ x 12", 3" h. (bulb
missing from gas pump, soiling) ....... **154.00**

*Arcade "Yellow Cab"*

**Taxi cab,** "Yellow Cab," cast iron,
w/yellow sides & wheels & black top
& hood, w/driver, Arcade Mfg. Co.,
7¾" l. (ILLUS.) ............................. **1,843.00**

**Taxi cab,** "Yellow cab," cast iron,
black roof, rubber tires, nickel plated
grill & license plate, Arcade Mfg.
Co., ca. 1936, 8" l. ........................ **4,025.00**

**Train engine,** electric standard
gauge, No. 8, olive green, Lionel
Mfg. Corp. ........................................ **115.00**

**Train engine,** electric standard
gauge, 0-4-0 No. 9U locomotive
finished in orange, Lionel Mfg. Corp.,
ca. 1928 ......................................... **1,265.00**

**Train engine & tender,** electric
standard gauge, 2-4-2 No. 390E
locomotive w/orange stripe & brass

*Lionel Girl's Train Set*

details & eight-wheeled No. 390T tender, Lionel Mfg. Corp., ca. 1929, 2 pcs. ............................................. **400.00**

**Train engine & tender,** 'O' gauge, 4-6-4 No. 773 Hudson black locomotive w/twelve-wheeled No. 2426W tender, Lionel Mfg. Corp., ca. 1950, 2 pcs. ............................ **1,265.00**

**Train set,** cast-iron engine, tinplate tender, two passenger cars & track, Bing, Gebruder (Nuremberg, Germany), in original box, 13 x 14" .. **460.00**

**Train set,** girl's, 'O' gauge, comprising 2-6-4 No. 2037 pink locomotive, No. 6427-500 shell blue caboose, No. 6436-500 lilac hopper car, No. 6462-500 pink gondola, No. 1130T tender, No. 6464-515 M-K-T yellow box car, No. 6464-510 shell blue box car, Lionel Mfg. Corp., ca. 1957, in original boxes except locomotive, the set (ILLUS. above).................................. **1,610.00**

**Train set,** keywind engine, tender, two passenger cars, a house, three crossing signals & original track, pigmy metal & tinplate, in original box w/lithographed lid, box 10½ x 11", the set............................ **633.00**

**Train set,** painted cast iron, electric locomotive No. 6 marked "PRR," w/three orange "America," passenger cars, Hubley Mfg. Co., ca. 1921, locomotive 8¼" l., passenger cars 6½" l., the set ......... **547.00**

**Train set,** passenger-type, "Flying Yankee," No. 1616 locomotive, No. 1617 & 1618 passenger cars, silver & chrome, Lionel Mfg. Corp., the set.............................................. **200.00**

**Train set,** standard gauge, No. 402 electric locomotive, Nos. 418, 419 & 490 passenger cars, Lionel Mfg. Corp., the set (some rust, missing some wheels) .................................. **400.00**

**Train set,** standard gauge, No. 4670 steam locomotive & No. 4693, four No. 4017 green gondola cars, No. 4021 caboose, American Flyer, Chicago, Illinois (slight surface rust), the set................................................ **489.00**

**Train station,** standard gauge, No. 115 cream w/red roof, base & trim, Lionel Mfg. Corp. ............................. **200.00**

**Train station,** tinplate, marked "Gare Centrale," large h.p. station w/a central arched opening interior, exterior finished as creamy pink masonry, the central section w/arched doorways flanked by two-story side sections w/arched winders, one section marked "Sale d'attende," the other "Telegaphe," each section w/wood-grained opening doors, glass canopy at front, onion domed central tower, on green rectangular base, Marklin (Germany), 21½" w. (largely repaired & restored)..................... **5,462.00**

**Train turntable,** tinplate, features hand crank that activates the center portion, rotating the track to change directions, Marklin, 11" d. .................. **23.00**

**Trolley,** horse-drawn, cast iron, the six window trolley is painted in red & yellow, marked "World's Fair" & "712," drawn by one white & one dark horse, Harris Toy Co. (Toledo, Ohio), 18½" l. ................................. **2,070.00**

**Trolley car,** electric, tinplate, features lift-up roof w/guiding pole, 8" l........... **863.00**

**Trolley car,** electric standard gauge, "Electric Rapid Transit," finished w/cream body, light orange band & black roof, w/embossed framed windows, open celestory & straight short couplers, No. 3, Lionel Mfg. Corp., ca. 1908-09 (some paint loss)............................................... **2,300.00**

*Hubley Dump Truck*

**Truck,** baggage-type, pressed steel, painted, w/hand truck, barrel, skid & three square paint cans, Buddy-L, No. 203B, 1927-29, 26" l. .............. **3,737.00**

**Truck,** contractor's-type, painted cast iron, maroon & yellow & consisting of a driver & three tipping boys in truck bed, Kenton Hardware Co., ca 1918, 8" l. ..................................... **575.00**

**Truck,** dairy-type, pressed steel, black cab, green body, w/six milk cans, w/"Buddy 'L' Milk Delivery" decal, Buddy-L, No. 2002, 1930 (rear chains missing) ............................. **2,185.00**

**Truck,** delivery-type, cast iron, painted white w/rubber wheels, marked "Milk Cream" on sides, Hubley Mfg. Co., ca. 1930, 3¾" l. ................................. **316.00**

**Truck,** dump-type, "Mack," cast iron, painted blue rubber wheels, Arcade Mfg. Co., ca. 1925 (missing front wheel & axle) ................................... **547.00**

**Truck,** dump-type, "Mack," cast iron, green chassis & cab w/driver, red dump box, six rubber tires, Hubley Mfg. Co., ca. 1928, two replaced tires, two replaced hubs, replaced driver, 11" l. (ILLUS. above) ............. **715.00**

**Truck,** dump-type, cast iron, cab painted blue, orange dump bed, Kilgore Mfg. Co. (Westerville, Ohio), ca. 1930 (some surface rust) ............ **144.00**

**Truck,** dump-type, Ford Model T, steel plate, finished in jet black, w/turning front wheels & maroon painted spokes, ca. 1924, Buddy-L, 12" l. (repainted, one fender damaged) ....... **575.00**

**Truck,** dump-type, painted cast iron, International Harvester, red w/chromed driver & dumping apparatus, Arcade Mfg. Co., ca. 1928, 10½" l. (new tires) ............. **552.00**

**Truck,** gasoline-type, "Mack," cast iron, finished in red w/cab driver, gold piping & white rubber tires, marked "American Oil Co.," Dent Hardware Co. (Fullerton, Pennsylvania), 10½" l. . **345.00**

**Truck,** gasoline-type, cast iron, red w/rubber wheels, 5" l. ..................... **144.00**

**Truck,** ice cream-type, cast iron, red, nickel plated grill, rubber wheels, marked "White" on side, Arcade Mfg. Co., ca. 1941, 6¾" l. ........................ **374.00**

**Truck,** pickup, cast iron, nickel plated grill, orange body, tan roof, black fenders, rubber wheels, Hubley Mfg. Co., 6¼" ............................................ **431.00**

*Green Giant Semi Truck & Trailer*

**Truck,** semi & trailer, pressed metal, side of trailer reads "Green Giant Brands" to the left of an image of the Jolly Green Giant, Tonka Toys, 24" l., 9" h. (ILLUS.) ......................... **242.00**

**Truck,** telephone-type, cast iron, red w/rubber wheels, pole carrier, two ladders & three nickel plated tolls, marked "Bell Telephone" on side, Hubley Mfg. Co., 9¾" (broken wrench handle, repaired boom) ........ **978.00**

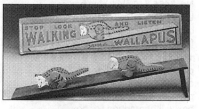

*Schoenhut Walking Wallapus*

**Walking Wallapus,** hand-carved & painted wood, features pair of Wallapus animals that, when placed at the top of an incline, slowly progress down, Schoenhut & Co. (Philadelphia, Pennsylvania), in original box (ILLUS.) ........................ **483.00**

**Windup bear,** glass eyes, brown fur, wooden feet, when wound his jaw opens as bear moves, Decamps (Paris, France), 10" l. ........................ **403.00**

**Windup fabric Charlie Chaplin,** dressed in black jacket, grey pants & red tie, he twirls his cane & shuffles, Shuco Toy Co. (Nuremberg, Germany), 7" h. (ILLUS. top next page) ............................................... **1,093.00**

*Windup Charlie Chaplin*

*Schuco Windup Three Little Pigs*

**Windup felt Three Little Pigs,**
features one pig playing the flute,
one playing the drums & one playing
the violin, Schuco Toy Co.,
w/original key, 5" h. (ILLUS.) ......... **1,495.00**

**Windup mohair bear,** features glass
eyes, brown mohair & red felt scarf
on a pair of rollerskates, Schuco Toy
Co., w/original box & key .............. **1,035.00**

**Windup suede elephant,** features
glass eyes & tusks, once wound it
walks & waves its ears, 14" l. ........... **690.00**

**Windup tin "Sunny No. 2005,"** a
grey felt mouse holding a balloon
driving a red coupe, Schuco Toy
Co., 6" l. ............................................. **403.00**

**Windup tin Army truck,** lithographed,
cloth cover, Louis Marx & Co.,
1920s, 10½" l. .................................... **259.00**

**Windup tin automobile,** "Panne,"
green touring car w/driver, w/original
insignia, Lehmann (Ernest) Co.
(Brandenberg, Germany), 7" l. ........ **1,035.00**

**Windup tin cathedral organ,** plays
organ music, J. Chein & Co. (New
York, New York), w/original box ....... **275.00**

**Windup tin clown,** picks up weight
w/teeth, German, 1926 ................. **1,300.00**

**Windup tin "Dare Devil Rick" rocket
car,** loops the loop & races forward,
w/original decals, J. Chein & Co.,
w/original box .................................... **275.00**

**Windup tin ferris wheel,** colorful
lithograph mainly red, yellow & blue,
bottom shows ticket stand & two
food booths, w/ringing bell in center,
J. Chein & Co., ca. 1930s ................. **375.00**

**Windup tin Ito sedan,** lithographed,
red w/black roof, blue driver,
Lehman (Ernest) Co., No. 679,
ca. 1920, 7" l. ................................. **1,265.00**

**Windup tin merry-go-round,** painted,
w/four horses & riders, Germany,
early 20th c., 14" h. (paint loss to
roof) .................................................. **633.00**

**Windup tin milkwagon,** horsedrawn,
"Toyland Farm Products," Louis
Marx & Co., 1930s, 10½" l. ............... **395.00**

**Windup tin motorcycle,** green
w/brown rider, Lehman (Ernest) Co.,
No. 725, 8½" (some scratches) ..... **1,840.00**

**Windup tin "Musical Aero Swing,"**
lithographed merry-go-round,
J. Chein & Co., ca. 1940s ................. **475.00**

**Windup tin paddle wheel boat,**
features puff-of-smoke key, paddle
wheel & rudder, Carette, Georges
(Nuremberg, Germany), 8" l. ........... **575.00**

**Windup tin rocket ride,** colorful
lithograph in red, yellow & blue, four
rockets connected to top & 'fly'
around central post, J. Chein & Co.,
1940s, 18" ........................................ **650.00**

**Windup tin roller coaster,**
lithographed, includes two cars, J.
Chein & Co., 1950s, in original
color engraved box .......................... **475.00**

**Windup tin "Sam the City
Gardener,"** tin & plastic, jointed
figure walking & pushing wheel
barrel w/two original garden tools,
Louis Marx & Co., ca. 1950,
w/original box ................................... **350.00**

**Windup tin Santa Claus,** celluloid &
tin Santa on bicycle, Japan ................ **65.00**

**Windup tin submarine,** the grey sub
w/rear propeller w/movable rudder &
logo stamped on surface, Bing
(Gebruder), 9" l. ............................... **460.00**

**Windup tin tank,** lithographed tin
camouflage tank marked "E12" in
white on back half of tank,
unknown maker, 10½" l. (soiling &
scratches) ...................................... **2,750.00**

**Windup tin Terra towing car,** lithographed, red w/black roof, blue driver, Lehman (Ernest) Co., No. 720, 10" l. (discoloration, slight surface rust)...................................... **633.00**

**Windup "Turn Monkey,"** monkey has long straight arms & stand, Schuco Toy Co., w/original key & instructions, 4" h. ...................................................... **173.00**

**Wrecker,** cast iron, open cab, green, nickel plated hook, rubber wheels, Hubley Mfg. Co., 1930s, 5" l. .............. **86.00**

**Zeppelin,** pressed steel, w/cradle, instructions, Metalcraft Corp. (St. Louis, Missouri), No. 962, ca. 1928, w/original box (box worn)................. **317.00**

# TRADE CARDS

*The Victorian trade card evolved from informal calling cards and hand-decorated notes. From the 1850s through the 1890s, the American home was saturated with these black and white and chromolithographed advertising cards given away with various products.*

**Clothing,** Celluloid Collars & Cuffs, color, shows boy wearing cuffs sailing enormous waterproof cuff through waves like a boat, marked "Celluloid Waterproof Collars, Cuffs & Shirt Bosoms"............................... **$10.00**

*Ausable Horse Nail Co. Card*

**Farm,** Ausable Horse Nail Co., color, depicts two mules kicking, crowd watches, black man in ring, marked "Ausable Horse Nail Co. - Hot Forged & Hammered Pointed Nails - from - best Norway Iron" (ILLUS. bottom previous column) ................... **20.00**

**Farm,** Central City Road Cart, color, depicts horse standing in harness in front of horse cart w/driver, reads "Buy Central City Road Cart - Cheapest and Best"............................ **55.00**

**Farm,** Deering Binder, greenish tint & white, depicts two scenes, one showing happy farmers on upper half of card & reads "After Harvest With Deering Binder" w/sad farmers below & reads "Oh! Why didn't I get a Deering Binder." .............................. **20.00**

**Farm,** Favorite Hay Rake, color, shows farmer in straw hat riding bright red hay rake pulled by horse, w/distant house in the background, reads, "The Favorite Hay Rake. - Manufactured by - J.W. Stoddard & Co. Dayton, O." ................................... **25.00**

**Farm,** Star Wind Mill, shows aerial view of windmill w/farm scene below, rudder of windmill reads "Flint & Walling MFG Co. - Kendallville, Ind.," card also marked "21 years in constant use - Manufactured in all sizes - 21 Years - In Constant Use." in upper right corner (ILLUS. top next page)............................................ **30.00**

**Farm,** Victor Clover Huller, Victorian couple reclines in field of clover, reads "Ain't we in clover" below, inset of machine below, marked "The Victor The Best Clover Huller in the World - Manufactured by The Newark Machine Co. Columbus, O." .. **25.00**

**Food,** Alden Fruit Vinegar, color, shows a mule bucking a black man as dog barks & apple basket spills apples, lower left corner reads "The Alden Fruit Vinegar"............................ **20.00**

**Food,** Blair's Wheat Food, depicts girl in straw hat & green dress holding puppy, "If you want strong, healthy children - Use Blair's Wheat Food," stock card .............................................. **6.00**

**Food,** Lactart Acid of Milk, color, shows milkmaid holding milk pail on her head while stepping over fence onto stones that read "With Water And Sugar Only," w/cows in the background, top of card reads "Lactart Acid of Milk Makes a Delicious Beverage" .......................... **18.00**

*Windmill Trade Card*

**Glue,** Chase's Liquid Glue, color, shows children pasting trade cards into parlor scrapbook while dad mends chair & mom looks from behind, large glue bottle in front of table, reads "Chase's Liquid Glue - Mends Everything - For Sale Everywhere" ...................................... **15.00**

**Kitchen,** Impervious Safety Oil Can, color, shows mother filling oil lamp from red oil can marked "Kerosene Oil" while young girl holds tiny lamp in one hand & a toy on a string in other, top of card marked "Impervious Safety Oil Can - The Only Safe, Neat & Convenient Oil Can For Family Use - Made in 2,3- 5,6 Gallon Sizes" & "Manufactured By The Impervious Package Co. - For Sale By All First-Class Dealers" ........................................... **24.00**

**Lawn Mower,** Excelsior Side Wheel, color, depicts woman dressed in blue dress & frilly hat mowing lawn while man relaxes on a bench in the distance, reads "Excelsior Side Wheel Mower" across top of card & "Manufactured by - Chadborn & Coldwell Mfg. Co., - Newburgh, N.Y." .................................... **20.00**

**Medicine,** Ayer's Sarsaparilla, color, depicts older man showing bottle to well-dressed man in rocker, top of card reads "Ayer's Sarsaparilla Makes the Weak Strong" ................... **18.00**

**Medicine,** Burdock Blood Bitters, color, shows laughing boy in blue with large ruffled white collar holding up "Burdock Blood Bitters" bottle ........ **10.00**

*Perfume Trade Card*

**Medicine,** Schenck's Seaweed Tonic, color, depicts, black boy in straw hat leaning against fence that reads "Take - Schenck's Seaweed Tonic - for - Dyspepsia - and - Debility." ......... **15.00**

**Perfume,** Hoyt's German Cologne, color, shows blond girl, holding flowers in a basket w/one white bird on the basket & another resting on her shoulder, marked, "Ladies Perfumed Calendar, 1894" & "Hoyt's German Cologne, Rubiform for the Teeth" (ILLUS. above) ....................... **20.00**

**Sewing Machine,** Singer, color, shows boy stands on sewing machine kissing a young girl over a wall, card reads "Romeo and Juliet" across bottom .................................... **15.00**

**Sewing Machine,** Standard, color, soldiers holding large U.S. flag, fife & drum, surrounded by rows of soldiers, reads "Nation's Pride - The Standard Rotary Shuttle Sewing Machine." across top of card & "1848, 1812, 1776" underneath soldiers feet & "Compliments of The 'Standard' Sewing Machine Co. - Cleveland, Ohio"................................. **18.00**

**Soap,** Ivorine, color, depicts young girl wearing pink dress & straw bonnet washing clothes w/a washboard & washtub, w/Ivorine soap box in front of table.............................................. **14.00**

**Sweeper,** Goshen Carpet Sweepers, color, depicts young girl pushing carpet sweeper in the parlor as a young child w/pull toy & doll watches, card reads "The Goshen Sweeper Co. of Grand Rapids, Mich." across top & "Easiest Operated - Carpet Sweepers Made."................................. **25.00**

**Thread,** Brook's Spool Cotton, color, shows men playing tug-of-war while goat dances on huge spool, card reads "Brooks Prize Medal Spool Cotton" across top & "Hand & Machine Sewing" across button ......... **15.00**

**Thread,** J. & P. Coats Six Cord, color, depicts young boy waving his hat as he rides on steam locomotive engine w/spool as engine which reads "J&P Coats - Best Six Cord - 200 Yards - 8," & "We Beat Them All." in the lower right corner (ILLUS. bottom previous column) ............................... **10.00**

**Thread,** J. & P. Coats, shows black woman pulling mule w/thread coming from the spool as man scratching his head watches, card reads "J. & P. Coats' Thread" in upper right corner & "Ef Dis Don't Fetch You Nothing Will" in lower right corner ......................................... **15.00**

**Thread,** Kerr's Spool Cotton, color, shows woman sitting on big spool conducting a six-goose choir w/her violin bow, end of spool marked "Kerr's Spool Cotton - Six Cord" ......... **10.00**

**Vegetable People-style,** woman w/apple shaped body shakes fist, reads "Apple Sauce" in upper right corner, reads " 'I'll fight anybody who says Metropolitan T Co.'s Baking Powder is not the best,' " stock card (ILLUS. below) .................................... **16.00**

**Washing, Bixby's French Blue,** color, shows maid & woman at wash tub sorting wet clothes into basket, card reads "Bixby's French Laundry Blue" .................................................. **16.00**

*Boy on Train Thread Trade Card*

*"Apple Sauce" Trade Card*

*Parker Bros. Catalog*

# TRADE CATALOGS

**10,000 Auto Supply Bargains,** 1921, auto parts ......................................... **$25.00**

**Abercrombe & Fitch,** camping, 1934-35, 94 pp. .......................................... **20.00**

**Abercrombe & Fitch,** guns, 1934, 200 pp. ................................................ **65.00**

**Abercrombe, David,** 1938, 64 pp. ....... **19.00**

**Clow Co.,** Chicago, 1929, plumbing fixtures catalog, 412 pp. ..................... **35.00**

**Colt Revolver Co.,** 1928, dealer's catalog, in brown wrap w/Colt & crossed revolver & pistol in black & green, in original mailer, 45 pp., 6¾ x 7¾" ............................................ **44.00**

**FAO Schwartz,** 1940, Christmas .......... **85.00**

**Hamilton Brown Shoe Co.,** 1918, shoes for men, Women & Children, 104 pp., 10 x 12½" ............................. **50.00**

**Hartman's,** Chicago, Illinois, Christmas, 1920, household goods & toys, 23 pp. ...................................... **10.00**

**L.L. Bean,** 1934, Spring ....................... **49.00**

**L.L. Bean,** 1935, Spring, 34 pp. ............ **55.00**

**L.L. Bean,** 1937, Fall, 64 pp. ................ **65.00**

**MOE Bridges,** lighting equipment, No. 27, mostly colored ..................... **130.00**

**Montgomery Wards,** 1955, Spring & Summer ................................................ **20.00**

**Montgomery Wards,** 1959, Spring & Summer ................................................ **25.00**

**Montgomery Wards,** 1967, Christmas .. **42.00**

**P. Derby Co.,** 1915, furniture, including mission, rush, go-carts, etc., 256 pp. ...................................... **125.00**

**Parker Brothers Co.,** 1913 "The Old Reliable," cover features a clown balancing a shotgun on his nose, reads "Perfect Balance - The Parker Gun," in green, red & black, 25 pp., tiny tear on front cover, 3½ x 5½" (ILLUS. above) ................................. **660.00**

**Sear, Roebuck and Co.,** 1931-32, Fall & Winter ...................................... **40.00**

**Sear, Roebuck and Co.,** 1969, Christmas ........................................... **42.00**

**Sear, Roebuck and Co.,** 1971, Christmas ........................................... **42.00**

**Sears, Roebuck and Co.,** 1933, Spring & Summer ............................. **25.00**

**Sears, Roebuck and Co.,** 1937, Fall & Winter, w/original wrapper .............. **65.00**

**Steiff,** toys & dolls, cover pictures police dog stuffed animals & reads "Steiff kus57 Margarete Steiff's Realistic Toy Animals Button in Ear Brand," 15 color pp. ............................ **60.00**

**Stevens Firearms Co.,** 1914, general catalog in blue wraps w/white lettering, 88 pp., 6 x 9" (wear on spine, browning on rear cover) .......... **55.00**

**Winchester Repeating Arms Co.,** 1933, dealer's catalog No. 88, blue wrap w/red & white lettering, 144 pp. (minor bend in cover) ............. **50.00**

# TRAMP ART

*Tramp art flourished in the United States from about 1875 into the 1930s. These chip-carved woodenwares, mostly in the form of boxes or other useful items, were made mainly from old cigar boxes although fruit and vegetable crates were also used. The wood is predominately edge-carved and subsequently layered to create a unique effect. Completed items were given an overall stained finish which was sometimes further enhanced with painted highlights. Though there seems to be no written record of the artists, many of whom were itinerants, there is a growing interest in collecting this ware.*

*Common Pedestal Box*

**Armchair,** chip-carved, the arched back comprised of crosshatched diamond pointed tabs over a similar open double crosshatch seat flanked by similar arms & arm supports, on double straight legs joined by similar box stretchers, early 20th c., 13" w., 26" h. ......................................... **$230.00**

**Bank,** pine, w/edge layering, notched lozenge-shaped opening for coin slot, initials "J" & "A" on sides, all on stacked feet, sans finish, natural oxidized wood color, ca. 1920-30, 5 x 6", 6" h. (bottom split from prying open) .............................................. **150.00**

**Box,** contemporary, pedestal base, circular pyramids alternate beveled & noted layers, large knob is hollow & tiny tip lifts off to reveal secret ring compartment, made by Boston-area craftsman, ca. 1995, 5¼ x 5¼", 8¼" h. ............................................... **300.00**

**Box,** pedestal base, common form w/twin spade finials on top, drawer w/brass pull, wide layered base, cigar brand pictorial chromolithographs inside, ca. 1880-1900, 5½ x 9", 8" h. (ILLUS. previous column) ................... **250.00**

**Box,** two-tier, cigar box wood, small & large lift-top compartment, one above the other, w/four-layer pentagonal pendant decorations all around lower compartment, all on reverse stacked legs, signed w/address in three places of bottom, ca. 1905-1915, 6¼ x 10½", 6" h. ...... **400.00**

**Box,** pedestal base, very desirable form, highly layered w/hexagonal shapes & pendant pyramids, all wood from cigar box base, original varnish finish, ca. 1875-1895, 10 x 10¼", 7½" h. (top broken off hinges)............................................ **425.00**

*Two-tier Tramp Art Box*

**Box,** two-tier, large & small compartments w/drawers, pyramiding enlivened by many purposeless whittled 'knobs,' on whittled ball feet, found in Nova Scotia, ca. 1915-35, 11 x 14", 12" h. (ILLUS.) .......................................... **550.00**

**Cabinet,** elaborate & varied layered shapes used in design, including hearts, Maltese crosses, 'arrowheads' & circular medallions, w/locking mirrored door, newly refurbished interior w/shelves & drawers, made to hang or stand, German origin, ca. 1880-1900, 6 x 11½", 20" h. (ILLUS. top next page)....................................**600.00**

**Candle box,** canted lid has unique rough-hewn quality, simple but effective design, deeply oxidized patina, hand-made brass hinges, late 19th century, 6 x 7", 10" h. (old repaired split through top)................ **300.00**

*German Tramp Art Cabinet*

*Mantel Clock Case*

**Chest,** edges & panel areas filled w/intricate geometric pyramiding, hinged lid, pad feet, unfinished interior, ca. 1875-1895, 6¼ x 10½", 6" h. (minor losses) ............................ **425.00**

**Clock case,** mantel-type, architectural design w/pilastered & corniced upper section, tiny winding key drawer under round clock opening & two larger drawers in wide lower section, all w/lion's head pulls, sans finish, ca. 1885-1905, some warping, 5½ x 10½", 12½" h. (ILLUS. top next column) ............................................. **375.00**

**Dresser,** doll-size, four drawers w/porcelain pulls, mirror tilts between unusual whittled posts, original varnish finish, ca. 1905-1925, 4½ x 9½", 19" h. ..................... **550.00**

**Frame,** diminutive, crossed corner design made more interesting by transverse crosses at intersections, old varnish w/gold highlighting, ca. 1880-1900, one piece missing, one piece replaced, sight size 2½ x 3½", 6 x 7" overall (ILLUS. bottom next column) ............................................. **125.00**

**Frame,** charming & fanciful design w/lobed corners, deteriorated velvet panels around opening, old worn copper paint over original finish, ca. 1890-1910, sight size 2 x 3½", 8 x 9½" overall ................................. **175.00**

**Frame,** seven-opening, original gold-painted finish, complete w/glass & backing, pictures removed, Danish origin, ca. 1895-1915, 8 x 12" ........... **240.00**

*Diminutive Picture Frame*

**Frame,** half-cylindrical segmented top layer & atypical 90 degree notching, commercial gesso-and-gold liner, original backing board w/cigar labels, square nail construction, ca. 1880-1900, 9 x 11" (one corner missing two layers) ........................... **250.00**

**Frame,** four-layer rosettes on a crossed-corner armature in old, but not original, green, white & salmon paint, frames a good regionalist wood engraving of Paul Bunyan, ca. 1890-1900, repaint ca. 1920-30, sight size 5¼ x 7", 9½ x 11" .............. **400.00**

**Frame,** variation of block-corner design w/large dart-shaped extensions, old darkened varnish w/gold highlighting, ca. 1890-1910, sight size 5½ x 8", 10 x 12½" overall (some repairs) ................................. **225.00**

*Early 20th Century Frame*

**Frame,** cigar box wood & pine, reminiscent of a shield w/wedge-shaped pyramids comprised of smooth & notched layers filling its symmetrical irregular shape, varnished cigar box wood on a heavy one-piece pine base, outside edge & opening painted gold, ca. 1905-1925, sight size 3½ x 5½", 10 x 13" overall ............................... **275.00**

**Frame,** profusion of layered & chamfered symbolic shapes: hearts, stars, horseshoes, pilasters, geometric designs, etc., sans finish, cigar brand imprints visible, several losses & breaks, early 20th c., 12 x 16" (ILLUS. above) .................. **625.00**

**Frame,** designed w/many different shapes of pyramiding, painted silver which has darkened w/age, holds George Washington print, ca. 1920s, sight size 13¼ x 17¼", 20¼ x 26½" overall .............................................. **650.00**

**Frame,** wide rectangular form w/rounded corners, the outer border w/a finely cut notched arrow band w/fan carved corner blocks, a wide inner band w/diamond devices, holds a portrait of a young couple, old finish, 26 x 30" (some edge damage) ......................................... **220.00**

**Lamp,** floor-style, Art Deco, on an armature of thick lumber, the heavy tiered base & tall, thin shaft are covered w/rectangular pyramids

having beveled steps, uniform light brown opaque finish, ca. 1920-40, scratches & minor losses, 14 x 14", 54" h. ...................................... **550.00**

**Lamp,** table-type, crate wood, slightly tapered column constructed from wood of varying thickness, on a wide, heavy platform base, shade printed w/African animals, ca. 1930s, 9 x 9", 16" h. .................................... **550.00**

*Church-form Match Safe*

**Match-safe,** church-form, open-top, tiny mirror on front, crested by three crosses, arched opening w/retaining lip shaped for easy retrieval of matches, emery-covered sides for striking them, dark heavily oxidized, gold finish, ca. 1890-1910, 3¼ x 4½", 10" h. (ILLUS.) ................. **400.00**

**Medicine cabinet,** made from crate wood finished in alternating colors, fine undulant crest, mirrored door over three drawers, towel bar, ca. 1930s, resilvered mirror, carving broken over one hinge, 9 x 15", 35" h. (ILLUS. top next page) ........ **3,200.00**

**Pedestal box,** contemporary, opaque, distressed finish, look for monogram or paper label on bottom, made by Hermitage des Artistes, Troy, NY, 4 x 6½", 6" h. .................................... **100.00**

*Crate Wood Medicine Cabinet*

*Mahogany Cigar Box Wall Pocket*

# VENDING & GAMBLING DEVICES

*Columbus Gumball Machine*

**Planter,** flared sides decorated w/trapezoidal pyramids, on short legs, made by unidentified craftsman responsible for many boxes of similar design, ca. 1910-30, 7¼ x 7¼", 6½" h. (several tips missing) .... **225.00**

**Sewing box of drawers,** multipedestal, five drawers of diminishing size w/spool handles, on spool feet, candlestick form celluloid-thread spindles atop smallest compartments, one of several known by same maker, ca. 1890-1910, 7 x 10", 17" h.. **875.00**

**Storage box,** Eastlake influence, ebonized panels w/incised gilded linear & stippled patterns, angular pyramiding & rounded whittled elements, hinged top, ca. 1885-1905, 7¼ x 10½", 5¼" h. .................. **325.00**

**Urn,** cinerary, tall pedestal-form container w/elaborately stepped base & lid spanned by delicate diagonal strips, excellent condition w/no breaks & original varnish shine, ca. 1880-1900, 10 x 10¼", 7½" h. .... **425.00**

**Urns,** crate wood, sans finish, ca. 1930-1940, 4 x 4", 4½" h., pr. ..... **140.00**

**Wall pocket,** varnished mahogany cigar box wood on a heavy pine base, thirteen-layer crest, early 20th c., 5½ x 10", 11" h. (ILLUS. top next column) .................... **425.00**

**Gambling,** Bally's "Reliance" dice countertop slot machine, 5 cent play, ca. 1936 ..................................... **$4,650.00**

**Gambling,** Jennings' "Sun Chief" countertop slot machine, 25 cent play, 1949 ..................................... **1,250.00**

**Gambling,** Jennings' "Victoria Silent Vendor" ("Peacock Vendor") countertop slot machine w/front vender, 5 cent play, 1932-34 ......... **1,995.00**

**Gumball machine,** "Columbus Gumball Machine," red cast-iron base w/glass globe w/paper label, minor rust & scratching & wear to label, globe 9" d., 16½" h. (ILLUS. above)................................. **440.00**

*Postage Stamp Machine*

**Gumball machine,** Five Star baby grand, oak cabinet w/keys ................ **100.00**

**Postage stamp,** porcelain, domed top, red, white & blue, reads "STAMPS" vertically down sides, 5½ x 12", 21" h. (minor wear) ............. **44.00**

**Postage stamp,** upright, black metal w/red, white & blue porcelain face w/star border, reads "Victory - Insert Coin Here - U.S. Postage Stamps - In Sanitary Folders," above image of Uncle Sam, pull knobs on bottom, minor paint chipping, 4½ x 8", 21" h. (ILLUS. above) ............................... **110.00**

# VICTORIAN WHIMSIES

*Hats, boots and slippers are just a few of the knickknacks turned out in the Victorian era, in both glass and ceramics. Dishes were made in the shape of stoves; bowls were shaped as wide-brimmed hats; toothpick holders as coal scuttles. We list only a few of the wide assortment of Victorian whimsies that abounded in the 19th century.*

*Nailsea Pipe*

**Baton,** free-blown w/squatty bulbous handle tapering to a long cylindrical body, clear w/blue, yellow & shades of green swirls in an alternating pattern, American, ca. 1910-30, 77" l ................................................. **$605.00**

**Boot,** jockey-type, pressed amber glass, marked "M. Dawson, Trainer, J. Watts, Jockey" around top & front marked "Lord Rosenberry's Ladas Winner of Derby - 1894" .................. **110.00**

**Pipe,** blown glass pink & white Nailsea loopings, long slender neck tapering to ovoid bowl, probably American, 19th c., 21" l. (ILLUS. bottom previous column) ..................... **495.00**

**Shoe,** lady's high heel-style, porcelain w/pale yellow lustre ground & embossed decorated w/dark pink lustre & gold trim, Germany, early 20th c., 2 x 6½", 2½" h ........................ **35.00**

**Shoe,** lady's high heel-style, white porcelain w/large molded blossom at the front, gold trim & band around top, Germany, early 20th c., 1¼ x 4", 2½" h. ................................................ **18.00**

**Shoe,** man's, bisque, white w/tan & brown trim, real shoelaces, early 20th c., 1¾ x 5", 2" h. .......................... **75.00**

# WARTIME MEMORABILIA

*Since the early 19th century, every war that America has fought has been commemorated with a variety of war-related memorabilia. Often in the form of propaganda items produced during the conflict or as memorial pieces made after the war ended, these materials are today quite collectible and increasingly important for the historic insights they provide. Most common are items dating from World War I and II. Because 1995 marked the fiftieth anniversary of the end of World War II, there should be added interest in this collecting field.*

### CIVIL WAR (1861-65)

**Certificate,** membership as Private, New York National Guard, September 10, 1862 (slight tearing at folds) .......... **$50.00**

**Engraving of First Kentucky Regiment chaplain,** 1862, framed .... **45.00**

**Roster of Iowa soldiers,** Infantry & Light Artillery regiments ..................... **52.00**

## WORLD WAR I (1914-18)

**Health product,** "Dough-Boy Prophylactic...For The Prevention of Syphilis & Gonorrhea," original cardboard carton w/a picture of a World War I Dough-boy on the front & listings of ingredients, The Reese Chemical Co., Cleveland, Ohio, w/original contents, minor soiling ..... **110.00**

**Magazines,** "The Illustrated War News," pictorial, 1915-16, twenty issues ........ **115.00**

**Paperweight,** cast iron, model of campaign hat, Disabled American Veterans ............................................. **55.00**

**Pillowcase,** souvenir, fringed w/"Sister," colorful scene of soldier in uniform & beautiful Art Nouveau woman w/sword, 17 x 17".................... **65.00**

**Pin,** lapel, United States flag on card from President Wilson ........................ **15.00**

**Poster,** depicts black soldiers marching down street as soldier bids his lady farewell, "Colored Men are no Slackers," framed, 14 x 18" ......... **375.00**

## WORLD WAR II (1939-45)

**Album cover,** leather, red & blue lettering on silver banners read "U.S. Air Force Album Santa Ana Army Air Base Santa Anna, Calif." flanking image of World War II fighter plane, ca. 1940s, minor creases & wear, 8½" h., 11½" w..................................... **72.00**

**Pin,** mechanical, metal, pull the string & Uncle Sam hangs Hitler, reads "Let's Pull Together," 1½" d. ............... **88.00**

**Poster,** "Just Be Sure You Put 10% In War Bonds," sleeping man catches wife going through his pants pockets, 1942 ..................................... **69.00**

**Poster,** depicts Uncle Sam as organ grinder & Hitler as Monkey ................. **55.00**

**Poster,** "Five Sullivan Brothers," w/original envelope........................... **200.00**

## WATCHES

**Open face,** man's, B. Poitevin, Paris, France, minute repeating chronograph-type, 18k gold case, gold lever movement, precision regulator, bi-metalic compensation balance, highly jeweled, slide repeat, white enameled dial w/Arabic numerals & subsidiary seconds dial, gold monogrammed cuvette, polished case, applied monogram, cuvette signed, ca. 1880............ **$31,050.00**

**Open face,** man's, Lepine Horologer, Paris, France, 18k gold case, gilt cylinder movement, jeweled plain three-arm balance, gilt-metal dust cover, repeater activated from the crown, silvered engine-turned dial w/Roman numerals & subsidiary second dial, engine-turned case centered by a small monogrammed cartouche, singed cuvette, No. 800, ca. 1830........................................ **1,380.00**

**Open face,** man's, Touchon & Co., Geneva, Switzerland, minute repeating-type, 18k gold case, highly jeweled nickel lever movement, bi-metalic compensation balance, micrometer regulator, gold cuvette, white enamel dial w/Arabic numerals, subsidiary seconds dial, polished case, ca. 1900................. **2,530.00**

**Open face,** man's, Vacheron & Constantin, 14k gold case, seventeen jewel nickel movement, five adjustments, Arabic numerals & subsidiary seconds dial, serial No. 407459 (stained)............................... **633.00**

## WATCH FOBS

**Advertising,** "Caterpillar Diesel Engines," brass.................................. **$70.00**

**Advertising,** "Columbia Tool Steel," porcelain ............................................. **20.00**

**Advertising,** "Conti Equipment Corp.," cast metal, oval w/three cog wheels w/initials "C - E - C," steam shovel & road grader in background, w/leather strap (minor wear on band) ............... **28.00**

**Advertising,** "De Laval Cream Separators," enameled metal ............. **85.00**

**Advertising,** "Modern Life Insurance Company" w/hunting scene depicted ................................................ **95.00**

**Advertising,** "South Bend Watch," celluloid, shows a watch in a ice cube .................................................... **30.00**

**Advertising,** John Deere company logo, ivory shield mounted w/a metal leaping stag & plow, faded leather band, minor soiling (ILLUS. top next page) .................................................... **77.00**

*John Deere Watch Fob*

**Fraternal,** "Fraternal Order of Eagles," enamel & bronze .............................. 45.00

**Fraternal,** Masonic, enameled metal w/Masonic logo & dated Atlanta 1914 ................................................. 40.00

**Souvenir,** World War I era, sterling silver, for the 57th Infantry .................. 75.00

**Sterling silver,** engraved, w/cigar cutter ................................................. 85.00

# WEATHERVANES

**Angel Gabriel,** pine, the flattened form carved from single pine plank of the winged angel blowing his trumpet, retains traces of original white polychrome, probably New England, 19th c., 47" l., 13" h. (ILLUS. below) .......................... $12,075.00

**Angel Gabriel,** sheet metal, the silhouetted figure of the angel fashioned from sheet metal w/flowing hair & robes blowing her trumpet, mounted on a rod & retaining old gilding & white polychrome, 19th c., 23" w., 29" h. ......................................... 44,850.00

**Banner,** copper, w/cut-out "W," verdigris surface, America, late 19th c. ............................................... 316.00

**Bannerette,** sheet metal, the silhouetted banner cut w/various geometric & scroll designs, now w/an acorn finial, retaining much of the old creamy gold paint, third quarter 19th c., 18" l, 10" h. .............. 977.00

**Bannerette,** sheet iron, the silhouetted bannerette pierced w/C-scrolls & stylized scrolling foliage, some chips to gilding, third quarter 19th c., 75" l., 15¼" h. ......................................... 3,450.00

*Copper Bull Weathervane*

**Bull,** gilt copper, full-bodied figure of animal w/gilded & verdigris surface, America, ca. 19th c., repaired bullet holes, 24" l. (ILLUS.) ...................... 2,070.00

**Cow,** cast iron, molded as a swell-bodied figure of a standing cow w/zinc horns & applied tail retaining old yellow polychrome, mounted on

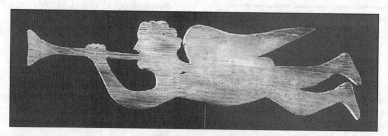

*Angel Gabriel Weathervane*

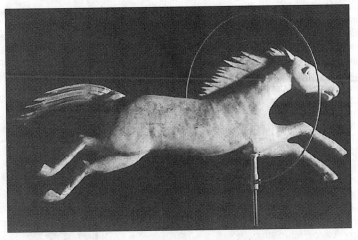

*Horse Jumping Through Hoop Vane*

a black metal base, probably L. W. Cushing & Co., Waltham, Massachusetts, third quarter 19th c., 13" h., 24½" l. ............................... **1,840.00**

**Cow,** painted & molded copper & zinc, the swell-bodied animal w/horns, cast-zinc head & cut sheet-copper tail, retains traces of old yellow & green polychrome, third quarter 19th c., 28" l., 15½" h. (some wear, bullet holes) .................................. **2,300.00**

**Eagle,** molded copper & zinc, the full-bodied bird in flight w/raised copper wings, the body in cast-zinc w/incised feather detail, on a rod in a black metal base, some losses, third quarter 19th c., 10" l., overall 14⅝" h. ......... **2,875.00**

**Eagle,** molded & gilded copper & zinc, the swell-bodied bird w/outspread sheet-copper wings & a sheet-copper tail perched on an orb, beak open on finely detailed head, fine feather detailing, retains some original gilding, mounted on a later rod & black rectangular metal base, some tears & repairs, attributed to A. L. Jewell & Co., Waltham, Massachusetts, third quarter 19th c., 44" l., overall 29" h. ..................... **12,650.00**

**Fish,** painted & molded copper, swell-bodied long narrow fish w/sheet-copper fins, painted yellow, mounted on a rod, now on a pine base w/sheet-metal directionals, third quarter 19th c., 36" l., overall 4' 11" h. ............................................ **2,875.00**

**Flying goose,** molded copper, the body w/molded wing detail perched on an orb & mounted on a rod w/directionals, 20th c., 40½" h., 37" l. ................................................ **1,495.00**

**Fox hound,** molded copper, swell-bodied animal in a running pose w/repoussé fur & ears, covered in old orangish red polychrome, mounted on a rod continuing to a white-painted turned wood finial, probably L. W. Cushing & Co., Waltham, Massachusetts, third quarter 19th c., 27½" l., 22½" h. .... **6,325.00**

**Gamecock,** molded copper, the swell-bodied bird standing on cast-iron legs, perched on an orb & fitted w/a sheet-copper tail, probably New England, third quarter 19th c., 14" l., 20" h. ............................................. **2,012.00**

**Gamecock,** molded copper, the swell-bodied form w/molded wing detail & cast-zinc legs & head perched on an orb mounted on a rod w/directionals, third quarter 19th c., 73" h. ............ **3,565.00**

**Grasshopper,** molded & gilded copper, full-bodied model of a long grasshopper w/head down & wings folded & legs bent, retains original gilding, some old repairs, 19th c., 44½" l. 11" h. ............................... **24,150.00**

**Horse,** jumping, molded & gilded copper, full-bodied figure of a horse w/cast-zinc head jumping through wrought-iron hoop, retains yellow polychrome & gilding, mounted on black metal base, stamped "A.L. Jewel & Co.," Waltham, Massachusetts, third quarter 19th c., 29½" l., 19¼" h. (ILLUS. above) .... **6,900.00**

**Horse,** running, copper, silhouetted running animal, attributed to A. L. Jewell & Co., Waltham, Massachusetts, 26" l. (bullet holes).. **2,760.00**

**Horse,** running, molded copper, the swell-bodied model of the horse "Black Hawk" running w/upright neck & flowing tail, mounted on a rod, retains some original gilding, probably New England, third quarter 19th c., 27" l., 19" h. (some losses & bullet holes) ................................. **5,750.00**

**Horse,** running, copper, swell-bodied running animal, verdigris surface, America, late 19th c., 31½" l. (imperfections).............................. **1,380.00**

**Horse,** running, gilt copper, full-bodied, America, ca. late 19th c., 42" l. (regilt, tail detached) ............. **1,610.00**

**Horse & jockey,** molded & gilded copper, full-bodied, stylized figure of jockey astride galloping horse, both the jockey & horse's head fashioned from cast zinc, retains much of its original gilding, mounted on rod in black metal base, attributed to J.W. Fiske & Co., New York, third quarter 19th c., 31" l., 20" h. ......................................... **8,912.00**

*Horse & Rider Weathervane*

**Horse & rider,** molded & gilded copper, the swell-bodied figure of a gentleman wearing a top hat holding sheet-copper reins astride a prancing horse w/a ridged sheet-copper tail, retains some original gilding, repair to back leg, third quarter 19th c., found in Vermont, 33" l., 21½" h. (ILLUS.)................. **9,200.00**

**Horse & sulky,** molded copper, the swell-bodied model of a running horse w/cast-zinc ears pulling the full-bodied figure of a driver in a sulky, the driver w/a cast-zinc head & holding a whip & sheet-copper reins, weathered to an overall verdigris, stamped "Harris & Co.," Boston, third quarter 19th c., mounted on a later rod & a black metal base, 34" l., 17" h................ **6,900.00**

*American Indian Silhouette Vane*

**Indian,** pine, stylized silhouette of American Indian w/headdress & quiver of arrows, bears traces of original paint, mounted on rod & rectangular wood base, 19th c., cracks & losses, 42" h. (ILLUS.) .... **920.00**

**Locomotive,** molded & gilded copper, full-bodied, detailed model of steam-driven locomotive engine & first car, retaining much of its original gilding & old polychrome, molded on rod in black metal base, Cuching & White, Waltham, Massachusetts, third quarter 19th c., 40½" l., 16½" h. (ILLUS. top next page) ........................... **31,050.00**

**Ram,** molded copper & zinc, the swell-bodied animal standing w/scrolled horns & a zinc head, weathered to an overall verdigris, mounted on a later rod & supports & a black metal base, third quarter 19th c., 30" l., 21¼" h. (ILLUS. bottom next page) ......................................... **10,925.00**

*Fine Locomotive Weathervane*

*Copper Ram Weathervane*

**Rooster,** carved & painted pine, full-bodied stylized model of a rooster w/a sawtooth tail, retains traces of old reddish brown polychrome paint, mid-19th c., 17" l., 10½" h.............. **1,610.00**

**Rooster,** molded copper, the swell-bodied bird w/repoussé feathers & sheet-copper comb & tail, retains some gilding & old polychrome, probably New England, third quarter 19th c., 12" l., 12" h...................... **1,955.00**

**Rooster,** molded copper & zinc, the swell-bodied bird w/a cast-zinc head & feet & repoussé feather, wing & tail detail, weathered to an overall verdigris, mounted on a rod & a later black metal base, L. W. Cushing & Son, Waltham, Massachusetts, third quarter 19th c., 26½" l., 30" h. ....... **5,462.00**

**Rooster,** painted sheet metal, the silhouetted bird retaining much of its original cream colored body paint & red cockscomb, third quarter 19th c., 14" l., 15½" h. ................................... **402.00**

**Stag,** leaping, molded copper & zinc, the swell-bodied animal w/a molded cast-zinc head & antlers, weathered to an overall verdigris, mounted on a rod & a later black metal base, third quarter 19th c., 28½" l., 25½" h. .... **6,325.00**

**Stag,** running, sheet iron, 40" l., 49½" h. (imperfections).................. **1,610.00**

# WESTERN CHARACTER COLLECTIBLES

*Since the closing of the Western frontier in the late 19th century the myth of the American cowboy has loomed large in popular fiction. With the growth of the motion picture industry early in this century, cowboy heroes became a mainstay of the entertainment industry. By the 1920s major Western heroes were a big draw at the box office and this popularity continued with the dawning of the TV age in the 1950s. We list here a variety of collectibles relating to all American Western personalities popular this century.*

**Annie Oakley belt,** mint on card ........ **$75.00**

**Cisco Kid gun,** paper, clicker-type, premium for Tip Top Bread, "Cisco Kid" printed on the handle, 1950s, 8" l....................................................... **25.00**

**Dale Evans & Buttermilk lamp,** composition, Dale riding a rearing Buttermilk........................................... **275.00**

**Gabby Hayes ring,** Cannon premium.. **195.00**

**Gene Autry .44 cap gun pistol,** die-cast, nickel finish, swing-out side

loading action, revolving cylinder
chambers, black horsehead grips,
w/six metal bullets, 1950s 11" l......... **150.00**

**Gene Autry advertisement,**
cardboard, snap gun advertising
rodeo show ........................................ **45.00**

**Gene Autry book,** "Stencil Book,"
cardboard spiral bound, decorated
w/spiral designs, ca. 1959s, never
used.................................................. **75.00**

**Gene Autry briefcase,** flap over top
w/straps, w/image of Autry on a
racing Champion w/three other
horses in background, w/handle ...... **250.00**

**Gene Autry guitar,** plastic, w/original
guitar-shaped box ............................ **165.00**

**Gene Autry phonograph records,**
"Western Classics," 78 rpm, 1947,
the set................................................ **50.00**

**Gunsmoke badge,** Marshall, 1959,
on original card ................................. **35.00**

**Hopalong Cassidy alarm clock,**
black wind up w/black, red & white
image of Hoppy & Topper on the
face w/logo along base, U.S. Time,
in original box w/instruction sheet,
price tag & premium color photo
print, 6" h. ..................................... **1,035.00**

**Hopalong Cassidy badge,** "Sheriff,"
six-pointed star, brass ....................... **65.00**

**Hopalong Cassidy bedspread,** light
wool, light green trimmed w/white,
brown, red & black, features Hoppy
& Topper, corral scenes & Bar 20
Ranch logos, ca. 1950, Belcraft,
72 x 84"............................................ **253.00**

**Hopalong Cassidy binoculars,** black
metal w/two graphic decals .............. **125.00**

**Hopalong Cassidy briefcase,**
canvas, large top flap w/two straps,
small pouch on front w/flap showing
Hoppy on Topper, w/handle,
ca. 1950.......................................... **275.00**

**Hopalong Cassidy coloring book,**
Doubleday, ca. 1950........................... **21.00**

**Hopalong Cassidy counter display,**
Timex, painted cast rubber, features
Hoppy in full cowboy gear, hat,
classic pose w/hands on his belt,
painted, trademark is black & silver,
stands on green base w/silver
lettering "Timex - Fully Guaranteed;
Hopalong Cassidy Shock Resistant -
Wrist Watches," official Timex label
on back reads "These aids must be
used in the display of Timex watches
only," some paint flaking, 15½" h.
(ILLUS. top next column).............. **3,450.00**

*Hopalong Cassidy Counter Display*

**Hopalong Cassidy chair,** "Official
Bar 20 TV Chair," folding-type,
wooden frame w/red, black & white
canvas seat & back, image on cloth
seat depicts Hoppy on Topper,
adjustable, 16 x 16", 2' h.................. **900.00**

**Hopalong Cassidy game,** "Pony
Express Toss Game," masonite
target board has graphic of Hoppy
on a leaping Topper, has three holes
for points, three bean bags & two
long pegs to hold board to floor, by
Transogram, ca. 1950, w/original
box .................................................... **350.00**

**Hopalong Cassidy game,** "Ring Toss
Lasso," figural Hopalong on Topper,
two posts & rings, w/box .................. **225.00**

**Hopalong Cassidy game,** "Target,"
lithographed tin, Louis Marx & Co.,
mint condition, 16 x 27" ................... **275.00**

**Hopalong Cassidy lamp,** heat-type,
center cylinder rotates, image of
Hoppy & Indian around campfire on
one side & Hoppy & Topper on
other, campfire & waterfall in
background, bronze top & base........ **750.00**

**Hopalong Cassidy mask & canasta
set,** boxed latex face in original
lithographed box featuring photos &
Hopalong Cassidy logo, contains
Hopalong Cassidy Official Canasta
Set w/black plastic saddle & base,
plus complete card set, unused
score pad & instructional booklet,
ca. 1950, Pacific Playing Card Co. .. **368.00**

**Hopalong Cassidy pencil case,** cardboard, black & white image w/inscription, two drawers w/top compartment, 5 x 8½"...... **175.00**

**Hopalong Cassidy pin,** Chicago Tribune .......... **25.00**

**Hopalong Cassidy pocketknife,** three blade, black, Imperial Knife Co., ca. 1950s .......... **120.00**

**Hopalong Cassidy puzzles,** Hoppy & Topper, Milton Bradley, No. 4025, in original box, set of 3 .......... **120.00**

*Hopalong Cassidy Radio*

**Hopalong Cassidy radio,** red enamel radio w/silver foil design on front, image of Hoppy on Topper across the speaker, original cords & dials, radio shows aging, 5 x 8" (ILLUS.) ... **518.00**

**Hopalong Cassidy scrapbook,** brown vinyl, embossed color image of Hoppy & Topper, ca. 1950, 10 x 14".......... **165.00**

**Hopalong Cassidy sign,** lithographed pressboard sign w/Hoppy's face, "Hoppy's Favorite" & Bond Bread logo, on sky blue background, 20 x 26½".......... **230.00**

**Hopalong Cassidy toy,** rocking horse, "Topper," plastic & wooden version, 22 x 30".......... **345.00**

**Hopalong Cassidy toy,** Shooting Gallery, wind up, Automatic Toy Co., in original box .......... **423.00**

**Hopalong Cassidy toy,** windup rocking figure, lariat-swirling Hoppy on his horse w/quarter disc-form lithographed base which rocks back & forth, Marx, 11¼" l. .......... **690.00**

**Hopalong Cassidy tumbler,** "Lunch," milk white glass .......... **37.00**

**Hopalong Cassidy wrist watch,** U.S. Time, watch sits on three dimensional Saddle display box, base reads "Hopalong Cassidy Shock Resistant Watch," comes

w/original cardboard sleeve stamped "Hopalong Cassidy - Waterproof strap," includes product identification numbers, original price tag, U.S. Time, w/instructions, official Hoppy Guarantee card, box 4 x 5".......... **437.00**

**Hopalong Cassidy writing paper,** w/color picture of Hoppy & Topper, signed "Best Wishes - William Boyd".. **95.00**

**Hopalong Cassidy & Topper figures,** plastic, figure of Hoppy on Topper, removable hat & movable arm, Ideal Toy Co., ca. 1950, 2 pcs.. **168.00**

**Lone Ranger flashlight,** "Signal Siren," w/silver bullet code, original box.......... **200.00**

**"Lone Ranger Game (The),"** board-type, folding game board, five game pieces, twelve silver discs & two tee-to-tums, box reads "Hi-Yo-o-o-o-o - Silver!," Parker Brothers Inc., ca. 1938.......... **100.00**

*Lone Ranger Hairbrush*

**Lone Ranger hairbrush,** wood w/color decal of the Lone Ranger on Silver, 1939, in original box (ILLUS.).. **95.00**

**Lone Ranger ring,** six-shooter, premium from Kix cereal, 1940s....... **110.00**

**Lone Ranger soaps,** figural, each in original box w/name, dated 1939, set of 3.......... **295.00**

**Lone Ranger toy,** windup tin, the masked man seated on a rearing Silver, when wound the lariat swirls & Silver circles, Marx, 7½" h............ **300.00**

**Red Ryder BB gun,** Daisy Mfg., 1950s, mint on card.......... **225.00**

**Roy Rogers advertisement,** "Crackin Good Snap" cardboard gun, for Roy Rogers cookies.......... **45.00**

**Roy Rogers binoculars,** in original box.......... **175.00**

**Roy Rogers countertop display,** stand-up display for harmonicas, holds twelve, w/six original harmonicas, includes instructions..... **485.00**

**Roy Rogers mug,** hard plastic, modeled in the form of Roy wearing a cowboy hat, Quaker Oats premium, ca. 1950, 4½" h ................... **42.00**

**Roy Rogers on Trigger lamp,** figural plastic w/plaster base, very good original shade, base 12½" h. ........... **175.00**

**Roy Rogers paper dolls,** "Roy Rogers Corral," 1953, uncut .............. **65.00**

**Roy Rogers rifle,** "Big Game Rifle," cap firing replica of a .348 caliber game rifle, Marx, mid-1950s, 34" l. ... **175.00**

**Roy Rogers ring,** sterling silver, w/saddle, signed ............................. **250.00**

**Roy Rogers yo-yo,** "Roundup King," in original cellophane package, ca. 1950s, Western Plastics Inc. ........ **15.00**

**Roy Rogers & Dale Evans book,** "Roy Rogers and Dale Evans Punch-out Book," Whitman, ca. 1952 .......... **295.00**

**Roy Rogers & Trigger gloves,** fabric w/vinyl gauntlets & fringe, marked "Roy Rogers - Trigger," early 1950s, in original packaging ............ **145.00**

**Sky King ring,** Navajo Treasure Ring, ca. 1950 ............................................. **95.00**

**Tom Mix badge,** "Straight Shooter" ...... **90.00**

**Tom Mix compass,** "Glow-In-Dark" ...... **70.00**

**Tom Mix cowboy boots,** w/original box ......................................................... **250.00**

**Tom Mix makeup tin,** "Straight Shooters," black & white, Ralston premium ............................................... **15.00**

**Tom Mix ring,** signature-type, rectangular top w/a copy of his signature engraved .......................... **125.00**

**Tom Mix ring,** sliding whistle-type, Ralston premium, 1949 ................... **120.00**

**Tom Mix wrist band,** "Lucky," no strap ...................................................... **40.00**

**Wyatt Earp cap gun,** Leslie-Henry "44", 9" l. ............................................. **95.00**

# WINDMILL WEIGHTS

*A common adjunct on the American farm between about 1875 and 1925, windmill weights were practically unheard of in urban areas until recent years. The cast-iron weights were used to counterbalance, govern or regulate the windmills commonly used for pumping water in the late 19th and early 20th centuries, before rural electricity was widely*

*common. Since many of the old weights were figural, made in the form of farm animals such as horses, roosters and bulls as well as other objects, they are considered interesting decorative items today. Rare examples in top condition with original paint can bring very high prices today.*

*Arrow Windmill Weight*

*Breyer Bros. Bell*

*"BOSS" Bull*

**Arrow,** 46 lbs., maker unknown, rare, 1½ x 29¾", 7⅝" h. (ILLUS. top) ............. **$2,501.00 to 3,500.00**

**Bell,** marked "Bell MFG By Breyer Bros Whiting Co Waupun Wis Pat'd Nov 17 1908," 13 lbs., rare, 1½ x 8½", 14½" h., 2 pcs. (ILLUS. middle) .......... **1,501.00 to 2,000.00**

**Bull,** original red paint, marked "BOSS," 25 lbs., Dempster Manufacturing Company, Des Moines, Iowa, paint worn, 3½ x 14", 12⅝" h. (ILLUS. bottom previous page) ......................... **1,501.00 to 2,000.00**

**Bull,** thin w/separated tail, original white paint, unmarked, 52 lbs., Fairbury Windmill Company, Fairbury, Nebraska, rare, bull ⅜ x 24¼", 17¾" h.; base ⅜ x 17⅝", 9¾" h. ......................... **1,501.00 to 2,000.00**

**Buffalo,** original white paint, 15 lbs., maker unknown, buffalo ½ x 16", 11" h. (without base), base 5¼ x 15⅝", 1" h. ......................... **2,501.00 to 3,500.00**

*Eclipse Crescent Moon Weight*

**Crescent moon,** points up, marked "A13 - ECLIPSE," 20½ lbs., Fairbanks, Morse & Company, Chicago, Illinois, 2½ x 10⅜", 3¼" h. (ILLUS.) ......................... **100.00 to 250.00**

**Disc,** 40½ lbs., Baker Manufacturing Company, Evansville, Wisconsin, 3 x 10¼" ......................... **Under 100.00**

**Double wheel,** w/original red paint, 56½ lbs., Twin Wheel Windmill Manufacturing Company, Hutchinson, Kansas, rare, wheel 1 x 22", 11" h.; base 9¾ x 17½", ½" h. (some rust) ......................... **5,000.00 and up**

**Football,** 47 lbs., Baker Manufacturing Company, Evansville, Wisconsin, 9" d., 17¾" l ......................... **Under 100.00**

**Governor weight,** (B26), 19½ lbs., Yale & Hopewell Company, Lincoln, Nebraska, rare, 1½ x 11½", 5⅞" h. ......................... **251.00 to 500.00**

**Governor weight,** (B26), marked "CS Co.," 19½ lbs., Cornell-Searl Company, Lincoln, Nebraska, rare, 1¾ x 11¾", 5¾" h. ......................... **251.00 to 500.00**

**Governor weight,** (B75), 27½ lbs., Plattner-Yale Manufacturing Company, 2¼ x 11¼", 6" h. ......................... **250.00 to 500.00**

*Short-tail Horse Windmill Weight*

**Horse,** short-tail, w/galvanized weight box, 13 lbs., Dempster Mill Manufacturing Company, Beatrice, Nebraska, horse ¾ x 17¼", 16⅝" h.; box 6 x 17⅝", 5⁵⁄₁₆" h. (ILLUS.) ......................... **100.00 to 250.00**

**Horseshoe,** w/original white paint, 18 lbs. (excluding base), maker unknown, rare, paint very worn, 1⅝ x 8¾", 10½" h. (without base) ......................... **2,501.00 to 3,500.00**

**Letter - W,** smallest of five sizes, 23 lbs., Althouse, Wheeler Company, Waupun, Wisconsin, 2⁵⁄₁₆ x 16½", 9" h. ......................... **100.00 to 250.00**

**Letter - W,** fourth largest of five sizes, 73 lbs. (including base), Althouse-Wheeler Company, Waupun, Wisconsin, rare, 4¾ x 19⅝", 9¼" h. ......................... **2,501.00 to 3,500.00**

*"C & O" Windmill Weight*

**Letters - C & O,** 34 lbs., Crane & Ordway Company, St Paul, Minnesota, rare, 1⅜ x 25½" (including bracket), 4¾" h. (ILLUS.) ......................... **3,501.00 to 5,000.00**

**Regulator weight,** Star C-24, 24½ lbs., Flint & Walling Manufacturing Company, Kendallville, Indiana, 7" d. ......................... **100.00 to 250.00**

*Short stem Rooster on Ball*

**Rooster,** short stem Hummer, 8½ lbs., Elgin Wind Power & Pump Company, Elgin, Illinois, 1½ x 9⅞", 9" h. .................................. **501.00 to 750.00**

**Rooster,** long stem on cast-iron box, marked "Hummer E 184" on tail, 9¾ lbs., Elgin Wind Power & Pump Company, Elgin, Illinois, rare, 1½ x 9¾", 13½" h. (including stem) ....................... **1,501.00 to 2,000.00**

**Rooster,** short stem on ball, original white paint, marked "Hummer E 184" on tail, 25 lbs., Elgin Wind Power & Pump Company, Elgin, Illinois, 14 x 9½", 11¼" h. (ILLUS. above) .............. **751.00 to 1000.00**

**Rooster,** Woodmanse, small, original paint, 41 lbs., Elgin Wind Power & Pump Company, Elgin, Illinois, paint worn, 3⅝ (at base) x 16¾", 15½" h. (ILLUS. top next column) ..................... **1,001.00 to 1,500.00**

**Rooster,** rainbow-shaped tail, original paint, Elgin Wind Power & Pump Company, 51½ lbs., Elgin, Illinois, paint worn, 51½ lbs., 3 x 16¼", 18" h. .......................... **1,501.00 to 2,000.00**

**Rooster,** hawk-like, 60½ lbs., maker unknown, rare, 3½ x 19¼", 18" h. .......................... **3,501.00 to 5,000.00**

**Rooster,** no-eye, 77 lbs., Elgin Wind Power & Pump Company, Elgin, Illinois, 3¼ x 19", 18¾" h., rare ............................. **3,501.00 to 5,000.00**

*Small Woodmanse Rooster*

*Dempster Shield*

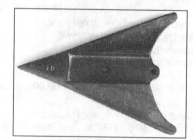

*Leach Spear*

**Shield,** 33 lbs., Dempster, 3⅞ x 8½", 10⅜" h. (ILLUS. middle) ..................... **1,501.00 to 2,000.00**

**Spear,** 22½ lbs. (including base), Leach Windmill Company, Joliet, Illinois, rare, 1½ x 15¼", 11" h. (ILLUS. bottom) .......... **2,001.00 to 2,500.00**

**Spear,** 10 ft., smaller of two sizes, marked "Challenge Co. Batavia Ill.,"

*Carved Cookie Board*

**Candle box,** cov., hanging-type, two storage compartments, crudely-carved pine w/old red repaint, 14" w., 20" h. (wear & some damage, bottom compartment may have had a lid at one time) .............. **605.00**

**Candle box,** cov., table-type, walnut, rectangular w/a sliding lid w/deeply beveled edges & molded top edges, old worn finish, 15¾" l. (some edge damage) .......................................... **303.00**

**Candy mold,** rectangular, crudely-carved wood w/heart & rectangle designs, carved initials on back, old patina, 3½ x 8¾" (age cracks secured by wrought-iron pin) ............ **138.00**

**Coffee bin,** hinged cover, pine w/worn original red paint w/black stenciled labels for Capital Coffee on sides, front & top, 32¾" h. ........................... **550.00**

**Container,** cov., tall tapering cylindrical shape, stave construction, old light patina, 8" h. (stain on lid) ..... **116.00**

**Cookie board,** rectangular, crudely carved Indian within an oval on one side & camel on reverse, edge incised "John Kelly Dec. 29th 1826," black finish, 4⅜ x 5½" ...................... **303.00**

**Cookie board,** rectangular w/rounded ends, horse design on one side w/bird, tree & carved date "1767" on reverse, 5 x 7¼" ................................. **550.00**

**Cookie board,** round, poplar w/old dark patina, inlay in center of back &

at hanging hole in handle, 16¾" d., plus handle (wear on cutting surface) ............................................ **165.00**

**Cookie board,** rectangular, carved chestnut w/old patina, crudely carved design of a couple & of a large cat, slight age crack, 5 x 17¼" (ILLUS. top previous column) .......... **220.00**

**Corner shelf,** hole for hanging, walnut w/old finish, cut-out sides have been ended out at curves where shelf joins, 25" w, 36" h. ............................. **385.00**

**Corset busk,** chip-carved maple, long flat board, heart-shaped base & top, carved floral & heart designs & initials "A. T." within top heart shape, 13½" l ................................................ **165.00**

**Display steps,** carved walnut, architectural stepped platform above three arched recesses, late 18th - early 19 c., Continental, 4½ x 24", 9¾" h. ............................................. **1,035.00**

**Dough box,** cov., wide single board, dovetailed construction, poplar w/old cream-colored paint, good detail & very clean, 30½" l. (two corner chips) ................................................. **248.00**

*Pine Dummy Board*

**Dummy board,** pine, carved & painted, depicting a young girl seated in a/chair wearing a long white dress, a white lace bonnet & holding a rattle, late 17 c., England, cracks & loss to bottom area, 14" w., 25½" h. (ILLUS.) ............................. **9,200.00**

**Firkin (tab-handled bucket),** cylindrical, stave constructed w/laced wooden bands & shaped

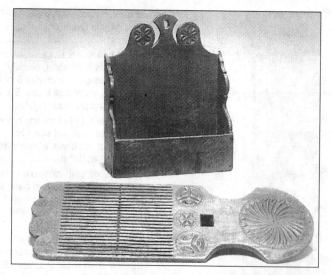

*Pine Tape Loom & Wall Box*

stave handle, traces of old red w/some splashes of black, attributed to Mount Lebanon, New York Shakers, 8½" d. ............................... **715.00**

**Jar,** cov., wide cylindrical body w/carved ring at base, slightly domed lid w/button finial, poplar w/worn original red sponged fans on a yellow ground, 4¼" h. (age crack in side) ............................................ **523.00**

**Jar,** cov., bulbous body w/a wide ring below the flat mouth, low domed cover w/knob finial, attributed to Pease of Ohio, old finish, 8" h. ......... **468.00**

**Knife box,** cov., rectangular, poplar w/worn old green paint, double lid & handle edged in red & two carved starflowers on each lid, 10 x 11" ....... **578.00**

**Kraut kutter,** pine, a rectangular board w/an inset angled metal blade & slot, the top w/a heart-shaped crest w/a heart-shaped hanging hole, old patina, 19th c., 22" l. .......... **121.00**

**Match holder,** hanging-type, walnut, chip-carved leaf shape, old alligatored finish, one point of leaf repaired, 9½" h. ................................. **66.00**

**Planter,** hexagonal, pine w/old worn black paint, yellow striping, red & gold foliage designs, wire corner fasteners & wire nail construction w/drainage hole in bottom, 6¼" h. ...... **83.00**

**Plate rack,** pine, dovetailed construction w/scalloped ends, Europe, 6¾ x 42", 36" h. (traces of old brown paint) ............................. **479.00**

**Salt box,** cov., hanging-type, pine w/old dark reddish brown finish, wire nail construction, a high pierced & scroll-cut crest w/stylized parrots & a relief-carved center diamonds & initials "B.L." above the rectangular box w/a lift-lid & molded base, 10½" w., 15" h. (damage to back of lid at wire hinges)............................. **248.00**

**Salt box,** cov., hanging-type, pine w/old worn red paint & wrought-iron nail construction, 10½" w., 16¾" h. (wear & age cracks from much use).................................................. **413.00**

**Sharpening stone,** wooden block w/carved designs & "James N. Rosser, 1826" & mounted w/sharpening stone, 13¾" l ............. **385.00**

**Spice box,** hanging-type, refinished ash w/shelf above eight drawers, late wire nail constructed, 9¾" w., 16" h. ................................................. **330.00**

**Sugar bucket,** cov., stave construction, slightly tapering cylindrical sides w/two bands, flat fitted cover, worn paper label, "Manufactured by _____Cincinnati," 8" h. .................... **204.00**

**Sugar bucket,** cov., stave construction, slightly tapering cylindrical sides w/two bands, flat fitted cover, traces of old red paint, 9¼" h. ................................................ **165.00**

**Tape loom,** crudely-carved hardwood w/old dark patina, punch-engraved name, initials & date "1741" on crest, 18½" l. (old chip on crest) ................. **275.00**

**Tape loom,** chip-carved pine, arched rectangular form w/tapered neck pierced w/a square, carved w/pinwheels & stellate devices, late 18th - early 19th c., New England, minor cracks, 8½" w, 26⅛" l. (ILLUS. bottom, previous page) .................. 5,750.00

**Wall box,** hole for hanging, rectangular, pine, backplate chip-carved w/two stylized flowerheads, the front panel carved w/stars & pinwheels, mid - late 18th c., New England, probably Connecticut, 4⅝ x 15¾", 12½" h. (ILLUS. top, previous page) .............................. 1,035.00

**Washboard,** wooden frame w/a yellowware pottery insert w/a blue glaze, 13 x 34" (insert wear & chips, framed w/wear & age cracks) ........... 550.00

**Yarn reel,** on mortised base, poplar & other woods w/old worn dark brown paint, 26" h. ........................................ 61.00

---

# WOOD SCULPTURES

*American folk sculpture is an important part of the American art scene today. Skilled wood carvers turned out ship's figureheads, cigar store figures, plaques and carousel animals of stylized beauty and great appeal. The wooden shipbuilding industry, which had originally nourished this folk art, declined after the Civil War and the talented carvers then turned to producing figures for tobacconist's shops, carousel animals and show figures for circuses. These figures and other early ornamental carvings that have survived the elements and years are eagerly sought.*

**Cigar store figure of a Turk,** carved & painted pine, the standing figure of a Turk wearing a turban & cloak continuing to a square base, retains traces of red, yellow & blue polychrome, third quarter 19th c., 62¼" h. (ILLUS. top next column) ...................................... $16,100.00

**Cigar store figure of an Indian scout,** carved & painted, the standing figure wearing a feathered headdress, holding his right hand to his brow, holding small barrel-shaped object in his left hand, standing w/right foot raised on rock-like object, mounted on a

*Cigar Store Figure of a Turk*

rectangular painted wood base, possibly from the shop of Samuel A. Robb, late 19th c., 74" h. not including base (old repaint, minor repairs) ........................................ 19,550.00

**Cigar store figure of an Indian squaw,** carved & painted, the standing figure wears a feather headdress & is pointing into the air, she is standing w/one foot in front of the other atop a painted wood pedestal, America, late 19th c., 43" h. not including base (old repaint, minor repairs) ................. 14,950.00

**Cigar store figure of an Indian,** carved & painted pine, the full length free-standing stylized figure of an Indian w/feathered headdress, cloth & feathered costume painted in tones of red, green, blue, yellow & brown standing on a stylized circular base, now mounted on pine pedestal, late 19th - early 20th c., 60½" h. .......................................... 5,060.00

**Cigar store figure of Punch,** carved & painted pine, the standing figure of Punch wearing a green peaked hat w/gold ball & painted yellow scallops, white collar & two-toned red & green costume w/yellow embellishments, the figure w/a bunch of cigars in one hand standing on rectangular pine base, late 19th c., right arm replaced, 53½" h. (ILLUS. top next page) ............... 46,000.00

*Cigar Store Figure of Punch*

*Figure of an Indian Head*

**Figure of a woman carrying rolling pin,** the heavy set woman w/her hair pulled back, articulated at the shoulders, right hand holding a rolling pin, on a rectangular plinth base, base 3⅜ x 4⅞" h., overall 16" h. (toe of one foot gone) ............. **345.00**

**Figure of Indian head,** carved & painted pine, the intense face of an American Indian chief wearing an American eagle headdress, painted brown, mounted on square base, attributed to Samuel Robb, New York, third quarter 19th c., some abrasion to paint, 19½" h. (ILLUS.) ...................................... **11,500.00**

**Model of an eagle,** the spread winged figure of a perched eagle, the body carved w/cross-hatches & articulated feathered wings, Aaron Mountz, Cumberland Valley, Pennsylvania, late 19th c., 4½ x 19", 9½" h......... **8,625.00**

**Model of an eagle,** the spread-winged bird perched atop a sphere on a shoulder cylinder above a flaring column atop an octagonal pedestal base, painted details, America or Europe, early 19th c., 32" h. (areas of repair).................. **3,162.00**

**Model of a horse,** carved pine, the free standing life-size figure of a horse w/deeply carved mane & tail & stipple carved hide, late 19th - early 20th c., 70" h., 69" l........................ **2,875.00**

**Model of a rooster,** carved & painted pine, the standing figure of as full-bodied rooster w/incised & layered feathers, painted a mottled red, yellow & brown, attributed to John Reber, Germansville, Pennsylvania, early 20th c., 11½" h. .................... **4,312.00**

**Model of a pigeon,** carved & painted pine, the standing bird carved in the round w/incised & layered feather & wing detail, retains old polychrome, now one black metal base, 19th c., loss to bill & wing, 11½" l., 10" h....... **460.00**

**Model of the letter "W,"** painted & gilded pine, carved in the half round, painted w/gilding over red polychrome, American, late 19th c., 39½" w., 26½" h........................... **1,840.00**

*Ship's Figurehead*

**Ship's figurehead,** carved & painted pine, full-length figure of an elegant lady wearing an elaborate flounced dress w/jewels, covered in old cream white polychrome, probably New England, mid-19th c., 49" h. (ILLUS. bottom previous page).... **12,650.00**

**Wall plaque,** model of an eagle, carved & painted pine, carved in high-relief w/eagle's head facing right w/incised feathering & wing detail covered in old white paint w/red details, inscribed in black ink on the reverse "J.W. Pridham, New Castle," Pennsylvania, third quarter 19th c., 41" w., 9" h........................ **2,875.00**

*Two Whirligigs*

**Whirligig,** carved & painted wood, figure of Union soldier w/articulated carved face, blue painted hat & body, w/bladed arms, on rectangular base, 19th c., 13" h. (ILLUS. right) ... **633.00**

**Whirligig,** carved & painted wood, figure of Hessian soldier w/articulated nose & belt, black painted hat & blue, yellow, white & black painted uniform, w/bladed black & yellow arms, on a rectangular base w/canted corners, 19th c., 21½" h. (ILLUS. left) ......... **2,825.00**

# WORLD'S FAIR COLLECTIBLES

*There has been great interest in collecting items produced for the great fairs and expositions held through the years. During the 1970s, there was particular interest in items produced for the 1876 Centennial Exhibition and now interest is focusing on those items associated with the 1893 Columbian Exposition and later fairs. Listed below is a random sampling of prices asked for items produced for the various fairs.*

### 1876 PHILADEPHIA CENTENNIAL
**Bandanna,** 19½ x 24"....................... **$115.00**
**Paperweight,** frosted glass, model of a reclining lion, Gillinder & Sons....... **110.00**

### 1893 COLUMBIAN EXPOSITION
**Booklet,** fold-out views, of the fair, 3¾ x 7"................................................ **40.00**
**Handbook,** Rand McNally Company, 1893................................................... **35.00**
**Sign,** glass, "Van Houten's Cocoa House," shows building, people, ship in background, girl w/cocoa on tray, framed ........................................... **2,750.00**

### 1904 ST. LOUIS WORLD'S FAIR
**Handkerchiefs,** embroidered fair logo, 1904, set of 3 .......................... **100.00**
**Jewelry box,** glass & brass .................. **95.00**
**Tumbler,** clear glass, embossed fair views, 5" h. ......................... **25.00 to 35.00**
**Tumbler,** milk glass embossed fair views, 5" h. (paint worn) ....... **20.00 to 25.00**

### 1907 JAMESTOWN EXPOSITION
**Postcard,** heart-shaped w/fold-out mini-view book.................................... **12.00**
**Vienna Tin Art plate,** center scene of Pocahontus preventing killing of John Smith, w/"Jamestown" over scene, round medallions w/bust portraits of John Smith & Pocahontus on border flanking scene & "1607" & "1907" on pages of book at bottom border, light & dark green, gold & yellow border, 1907, H. D. Beach Company, back of plate indicates design is copyrighted by W. H. Owens & Co., 10⅛" d. ............................................. **120.00**

### 1933-34 CHICAGO "CENTURY OF PROGRESS"
**Bank,** "American Can Company," tin .... **40.00**
**Booklet,** "The Wonder Book of Good Meals," 1934...................................... **20.00**
**Bowl,** 8" d., ruby glass, 1934 ............... **85.00**
**Cigarette case,** metal, 1933................. **45.00**

**Compact,** black w/fair logo on cover,
Elgin-American Company ................. **150.00**
**Cup,** metal, fair views .......................... **25.00**
**Envelope,** depicts Graf Zeppelin .......... **20.00**

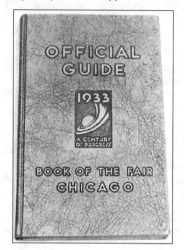

*Chicago World's Fair Official Guide*

**Guide,** authorized edition, Art Deco
cover, hardbound, illustrated,
175 pp., 6 x 9½" (ILLUS.) ................... **24.00**
**Gyroscope,** zeppelin, steamship &
plane depicted on box, w/string &
instructions, 1933, in original box ....... **85.00**
**Key,** brass ............................................. **15.00**
**Map of Chicago,** illustrated &
including World's Fair, 1933, in
original envelope ................................. **9.00**

*Chicago World's Fair Playing Cards*

**Playing cards,** fifty-three photos of
the fair, single deck (ILLUS. bottom
previous column) ................................. **19.00**
**Poster,** photo mechanically produced
poster advertising products of the
International Time Recording Co., a
division of IBM, illustrates many of the
time clocks, phones & switchboards,
19 x 24" (fold lines) .............................. **44.00**
**Poster,** stone lithograph destination
poster, in bright colors & striking
design, by Norman Anderson,
issued by the Rock Island Railroad,
19 x 24" (fold lines) ......................... **330.00**

*Chicago World's Fair Poster*

**Poster,** stone lithograph destination
poster, in striking colors & design, by
Weimer Pursell, printed by Neely
Printing Company, fold lines & three
tiny holes in fold corners, 14 x 20"
(ILLUS.) ............................................ **330.00**
**Token,** metal, A & P stores .................. **10.00**
**Vase,** carved reddish color soapstone,
decorated w/birds & flowers & three
openings, incised "Chicago," 1933,
4 x 8", 9" h. ....................................... **150.00**

## 1936 TEXAS CENTENNIAL
**Ashtray,** "Firestone," rubber tire
w/amber glass insert .......................... **45.00**
**Cowboy hat,** child's ............................. **75.00**

*Homer Laughlin World's Fair Plate*

## 1939 GOLDEN GATE EXPOSITION
**Ticket stubs,** book of twelve ............... **20.00**
**Compact,** metal, Treasure Island
    scene & fair logo on cover ............... **125.00**

## 1939-40 NEW YORK WORLD'S FAIR
**Advertisement,** paper, Billy Rose's
    Aquacade ad for Arco Skates, 1940,
    8½ x 11"............................................. **12.00**
**Bank,** glass, depicts Trylon &
    Perisphere ......................................... **45.00**
**Banner,** felt, fair scene.......................... **95.00**
**Cake plate,** Art Deco design of Trylon
    & Perisphere, Cronin Pottery ............. **60.00**
**Compact,** camera-style, glitter front
    w/fair logo on cover, Girey ................ **150.00**
**Guide book,** 256 pp............................. **35.00**
**Hat,** female employee's blue felt
    w/ribbon trim, ..................................... **75.00**
**Matchbook,** giant size w/Trylon &
    Perisphere graphics, two different
    designs ............................................... **25.00**
**Pin,** brass, three-dimensional .............. **65.00**
**Plate,** china, Art Deco design
    w/stylized scenes around border &
    Trylon & Perisphere in the center,
    designed by Charles Murphy,
    produced by The Homer Laughlin
    China Company (ILLUS. top) ........... **225.00**
**Poster,** Manhattan & the World's Fair
    featured, 25 x 36" .............................. **250.00**

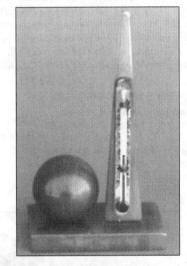

*Figural Thermometer*

**Thermometer,** Bakelite, figural Trylon
    & Perisphere (ILLUS.) ........................ **24.00**
**Thermometer,** desk top-type, red
    swirl Bakelite, figural Trylon &
    Perisphere, base 1⅛ x 2³⁄₁₆", 3¼" h. .... **70.00**
**Tie rack,** wood composition, fifteen
    space, Multi-Products, Chicago,
    1939 ................................................... **95.00**
**Uniform jacket,** man's, gabardine,
    marked "Operations"......................... **250.00**

**Vase,** 4" h., cranberry & clear glass
w/gold lettering ................................. **85.00**

### 1962 SEATTLE WORLD'S FAIR
**Ashtray,** glass, black, 3 x 5" ................ **18.00**
**Medal,** metal, fair scene........................ **20.00**

### 1964-65 NEW YORK WORLD'S FAIR
**Ashtray,** glass, black, painted
decoration, 4 x 7"................................ **22.00**
**License plate,** depicts Unisphere,
6 x 12"................................................ **25.00**

---

# WRITING ACCESSORIES

*Early writing accessories are popular
collectibles and offer a wide variety to select
from. A collection may be formed around any
one segment—pens, letter openers, lap desks or
inkwells—or the collection may revolve
around choice specimens of all types. Material,
design and age usually determine the value.
Pen collectors like the large fountain pens
developed in the 1920s but also look for pens
and mechanical pencils that are solid gold or
gold-plated. Also see: BOTTLES & FLASKS*

### INKWELLS & STANDS
**Blown-three mold glass well,**
geometric, cylindrical, olive amber,
2¾" d., GII-18 ................................. **$116.00**
**Brass stand,** Art Nouveau-style, a
narrow elongated form w/a detailed
design of swirling peacock feather

surrounding the hinged well cover at
one end, a delicately carved
woman's face in ivory peers from the
center of the feather at the other
end, impressed "Made in Austria,"
4 x 7", 3" h. (glass insert missing)..... **440.00**

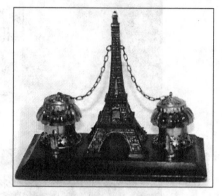

*Eiffel Tower Inkstand*

**Brass & glass stand,** brass Eiffel
Tower in center flanked by a brass
holder w/ribbed sapphire blue
pressed glass insert w/brass lid,
holder for pen in front, all on
rectangular wooden base, 3½ x 7",
6¼" h. (ILLUS.) ................................. **195.00**
**Bronze stand,** a long, narrow
rectangular tray w/a raised rear
section fitted at one end w/a lift-lid
opening to the inkwell & cast at the
other end w/a ground of three long-
tailed pheasants, impressed "F.
Cornik" w/conjoined "AR," fine brown
patina, late 19th - early 20th c.,
15" l., 5¼" h. (ILLUS. below)............. **374.00**

*Bronze Inkstand with Birds*

*Early German Inkstand*

**Bronze well,** Arts & Crafts-style, round w/flaring sides & a dished base rim, the top w/a hinged domed cover, original dark patina, marked "E.T. Hurley - 1920," 5" d., 3" h......... **198.00**

**Bronze well,** Chinese patt., large tapering squared form w/chamfered corners & narrow angled shoulders to the squared, stepped well cover, cast stylized Oriental designs, original bronze patina, original glass insert, marked "Tiffany Studios 1753," 6½" sq., 4" h. (chip to glass insert)................................................ **550.00**

**Bronze & glass well,** "Flying Fish," well cast w/four flying fish at the corners, their outspread tails forming the inkwell rim, each side enclosing multicolored mosaic glass tiles, rich brownish green patina, clear glass well liner & stopper, impressed "Tiffany Studios," liner impressed "THE DAVIS - Pat. Mar. 19, Oct. 22, 89, Feb. 14, 93," 7" l., 3½" h. ......................................... **57,500.00**

**Copper well,** hand-hammered, Arts & Crafts-style, domed round body w/a fitted low domed cover w/an elongated knob finial, original glass insert, original dark brown patina, impressed mark of the Roycrofters, early 20th c., 3½" d., 2½" h.............. **121.00**

**Pottery stand,** Art Nouveau-style, rectangular shaped block w/a stylized aquatic design & an overall organic shaped in rich red, blue & green flambé glaze, the raised back section enclosing two cov. inkwells above a flaring dished front pen tray, die-stamped mark of Dalpayrat, France, ca. 1900, 5¾ x 6½", 3" h. (damage to one well liner, lines to the body, one lid glued) ................... **248.00**

**Pottery stand,** Arts & Crafts-style, a rectangular block w/the raised back section fitted w/two cov. inkwells above the tapering front w/three notched ridges above two dished wells, blue & mustard yellow crystalline glaze, A.E.T. Co., raised stamp mark, early 20th c., 5¾" l., 2" h. ................................................. **248.00**

**Silver stand,** rectangular w/rounded ends, the center chased w/fruits & scrolling foliage, on a stippled ground, w/three circular compartments, two fitted w/a cylindrical well & a cov. caster & chased w/foliate & fruiting garlands, each cover chased w/a flower, one pierced, the base w/a gadrooned rim, the well w/molded glass interior, on four flattened ball feet, marked on base & both pots, Samuel Frey, Augsburg, Germany, ca. 1670-80, 12" l. (ILLUS. above) .................... **3,220.00**

**Silver plate stand,** the faceted glass well w/a stag-form hinged cover, the quatrefoil stand modeled w/a quail, a hare, ducks & deer all on a stylized foliate scroll ground, late 19th - early 20th c., 12¾" l. (chips to base of well) ................................................. **575.00**

**Sterling silver stand,** a rectangular tray w/rounded corners & gadroon, shell & foliate decorated rim raised on four palmette feet, applied w/three circular frames for clear cut glass pounce pot, inkwell & wafer pot each w/a silver rim & hinged cover, engraved w/a presentation inscription, marked on bases, frames & covers, Rebecca Emes & Edward Barnard, London, England, 1809, 11" l. .............................................. **4,025.00**

**Stoneware pottery well,** short cylindrical form w/the flat top pierced w/a large central hole flanked by two smaller holes, cobalt blue slip-quilled curved bands & a central stripe on the top, 3⅝" d. .................................. **495.00**

## LAP DESKS & WRITING BOXES

**Mahogany,** a rectangular box w/a lid lifting to a fitted interior & writing surface, ivory-inlaid diamond-form keyhole escutcheon, inlaid banding, Georgian period, England, ca. 1780, 19" l. .................................................. **358.00**

*Early Lap Desk*

**Mahogany w/brass mounts,** the rectangular box hinged in the center & opening to a fitted interior & slanted baise-lined writing surface, upper section w/quill holder & divided well fitted w/a clear glass inkwell, first half 19th c., purportedly once owned by the Marquis de Lafayette, some repair where hinges broke out, 19½" l., 7½" h. (ILLUS. bottom previous column) ............................**1,495.00**

*Bugatti Secretary-Desk*

**Mahogany,** pewter & brass, secretary-style, in two sections, the floating top w/center drawer inlaid in a geometric pattern w/pewter & brass, continuing to side panels, raised above a lower section w/fall front & side panels inlaid w/stylized blossoms & foliage, opening to reveal a velvet lined fitted interior, has gilt bronze dragonfly pull, signed "Bugatti," ca. 1900, 9 x 15½", 15½" h. (ILLUS.) ............................ **8,625.00**

## PENS & PENCILS

**Auto point pencil,** from Bell Telephone ......................................... **35.00**

**Duro Lite pencil,** w/spinner for dial telephone, from Bell Telephone .......... **30.00**

**Esterbrook ink pen,** from Bell Telephone ......................................... **35.00**

**Eversharp ink pen,** Skyline, 14k point, gold & blue ............................. **65.00**

# INDEX

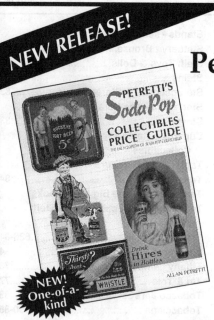